MARY CHESNUT'S CIVIL WAR

Mary Boykin Chesnut

Portrait by Samuel Stillman Osgood, c. 1856, in the possession of Mrs. Hendrik B. van Rensselaer, Basking Ridge, New Jersey. On loan to Smithsonian Institution.

Mary Chesnut's Civil War

Edited by C. VANN WOODWARD

NEW HAVEN AND LONDON / YALE UNIVERSITY PRESS

Designed by Sally Harris
and set in VIP Baskerville type.
Printed in the United States of America by
Vail-Ballou Press, Binghamton, N.Y.

Library of Congress Cataloging in Publication Data

Chesnut, Mary Boykin Miller, 1823–1886.
Mary's Chesnut's Civil War.

Selections from this work were previously published
under title: A diary from Dixie.
Includes bibliographical references and index.
1. Chesnut, Mary Boykin Miller, 1823–1886.
2. United States—History—Civil War, 1861–1865—
Personal narratives—Confederate side.
3. Confederate States of America—History—Sources.
4. Southern States—Biography.
I. Woodward, Comer Vann, 1908–   II. Title.
E487.C5   973.7'82   80-36661
ISBN 0-300-02459-2

10   9   8   7   6   5   4   3   2   1

*To my students
at Johns Hopkins and at Yale*

Contents

Illustrations

Acknowledgments

The first acknowledgment is an indebtedness to a man who knew nothing of the debt. It was nearly twenty years ago that a first look at the manuscripts of Mary Chesnut at the South Caroliniana Library revealed something of their exciting possibilities and suggested the idea of a new and full edition of her book on the Civil War. That impulse might never have been acted upon, had it not been for Edmund Wilson, who in 1962 published an eloquent tribute to Mary Chesnut in his *Patriotic Gore: Studies in the Literature of the American Civil War.* Without ever seeing the manuscript versions of what he knew as her *Diary*—and therefore without quite understanding its nature, the shortcomings of previous editions, or the possibilities his suggestion opened up—Wilson urged that a full edition of this "extraordinary document," which he pronounced "a work of art," be undertaken. In the long run that was the challenge this effort attempted to meet.

When the heirs to the Chesnut manuscripts were approached, they cordially approved of the undertaking, but being preoccupied with other commitments at the time, the editor had to withdraw. Then in 1974 the heirs reopened the question, and within a year the project was under way. Since then the editor has enjoyed the full confidence and cooperation of the family, including the heirs, Mrs. Sally Bland Metts, Mrs. Barbara G. Carpenter, Mrs. Katherine W. Herbert, and Mrs. Sally Bland Johnson and her husband, Charles F. Johnson. Also of great help and encouragement have been Mrs. McCoy M. Hill and Mrs. John H. Daniels. Members of the family have made numerous private documents available and have refrained from any interference whatsoever with editorial decisions. Without their help and confidence the work could not have been done.

Another source of strength, support, and encouragement was Prof. James B. Meriwether of the University of South Carolina, who took keen interest in the project from the start. On his kind invitation the editor spent a semester as visiting fellow of the Southern Studies Program with no duties to speak of save work on the Chesnut Papers with the help of his able students. At the South Caroliniana Library, Mr. E. L. Inabinett, the librarian, and his assistant, Allen H. Stokes, proved extremely helpful.

In the part of the work carried on at the University of South Carolina, Dr. Elisabeth S. Muhlenfeld was indispensable in supervising transcription and collation of the manuscript versions of the diary and in helping with annotation. She developed a miraculous skill at deciphering the Chesnut handwriting. Her own edition of Mrs. Chesnut's novels, cited elsewhere, and her forthcoming biography of the author, were of enormous help. The editor's introduction to this volume profited greatly from her critical reading.

Prof. Stephen W. Meats took a lead in part of the work on annotation in South Carolina, and Dr. David Carlton helped. Prof. Thomas Dasher played a leading part in the collation of the transcript, and Prof. Noel Polk generously assisted. Also assisting in the transcription were Dianne Anderson Cox, Edwin T. Arnold, Karen Endres, George Hayhoe, Beverly Scafidel, Herbert Shippy, and Allie Patricia Wall. Taking part in the collation of transcripts with manuscripts were Elizabeth Adams, Bernard Bydalek III, Kay Bydalek, Steven S. Matthews, John Alexander Moore, Gail Morrison, David Sabrio, and Josephine Shumake.

At the Yale end of the enterprise Michael McGerr worked tirelessly at annotation, spotting errors and inconsistencies and keeping the editor alert to the observance of his own rules, not to mention his own duties. He also prepared the index. So large and indispensable was the part that Michael McGerr took in the work that he deserves to be singled out for special gratitude, and the editor wishes to acknowledge his indebtedness.

Also at Yale, but working in Alabama as well, Carol Wasserloos assisted mightily with annotation. Steven Hahn helped in checking notes and sources, and Robert Sean Wilentz, Rachel Klein, Sarah Blank, and Peter Blodgett in annotation. Yale librarians deserve special thanks for their helpfulness.

Prof. Ludwell H. Johnson of the College of William and Mary kindly read the entire manuscript. The editor is most grateful to him for spotting flaws that only a Civil War specialist such as himself could have caught.

Thanks are due Florence B. Thomas for doing the major part of the huge typing work and to Laura Boucher for the part she did.

At the Yale University Press the undertaking has enjoyed dedicated and expert support and assistance, especially on the part of Ellen H. Graham.

As always, very special gratitude goes to a wife who shared this and all earlier labors in the field in years gone by.

The principal financial support for this work has come from a grant by the National Historical Publications and Record Commission. The University of South Carolina also helped, as did Yale.

Introduction

Diary in Fact—Diary in Form

Literary critics who have written most thoughtfully about the work of Mary Boykin Chesnut have expressed some puzzlement and perplexity. They are generally as much disposed as historians have been to place high value on her book. "This diary," writes Edmund Wilson, "is an extraordinary document—in its informal department, a masterpiece." But he goes on to pronounce it "a work of art"—informal department or not. The puzzlement arises in assessing and understanding the character of the art involved. Mrs. Chesnut, in Wilson's opinion, evidently began the writing with "a decided sense of the literary possibilities of her subject." He goes further to say that he finds "the diarist's own instinct is uncanny" in anticipating such possibilities. "The very rhythm of her opening pages," he writes, "at once puts us under the spell of a writer who is not merely jotting down her days but establishing, as a novelist does, an atmosphere, an emotional tone. . . . Starting out with situations or relationships of which she cannot know the outcome, she takes advantage of the actual turn of events to develop them and round them out as if she were molding a novel." In general he finds "the brilliant journal of Mary Chesnut" to be "much more imaginative and revealing than most of the fiction inspired by the war."[1]

Why the Civil War never inspired a literary treatment worthy of the subject is the question Daniel Aaron pursues in *The Unwritten War*. "The great War novel or epic everyone was calling for or predicting during the War and thereafter," in his opinion, "ought to have been written by a Southerner." Yet most of the Southern writing on the subject "was shot through with sentiment, moonshine, and special pleading." Of the three Southerners of the war generation whom he singles out as writing with detachment and insight, one was the poet Timrod, one the novelist Cable, and the third a diarist, Chesnut. Of these it was neither the novelist nor the poet but the diarist who was "the most likely candidate to write the unwritten Confederate novel." She it was who "had the eye and ear of a novelist as well as the temperament," even though she chose a form other than fiction. "Yet the *Diary*," he agrees with Edmund Wilson, "is more genuinely literary than most Civil War fiction."[2]

What the critics had before them was, of course, clearly entitled a diary and was presented as such by its several editors.[3] Moreover, it bore all the familiar

---

1. Edmund Wilson, *Patriotic Gore: Studies in the Literature of the American Civil War* (New York, 1962), pp. ix, 279–80.

2. Daniel Aaron, *The Unwritten War: American Writers and the Civil War* (New York, 1973), pp. 227–28, 251, 259.

3. Isabella D. Martin and Myrta Lockett Avary, eds., *A Diary from Dixie, as Written by Mary Boykin Chesnut, Wife of James Chesnut, Jr., United States Senator from South Carolina, 1859–1861, and Afterward Aide to Jefferson Davis and a Brigadier General in the Confederate Army* (New York, 1905); Ben Ames Williams, ed., *A Diary from Dixie by Mary Boykin Chesnut* (Boston, 1949).

characteristics of the genre. It proceeded from the start under dated entries beginning in February 1861 and continuing into July 1865. One break of nearly fifteen months occurs between August 1862 and October 1863, in which the diary form is abandoned and the author undertakes, she says, "to fill up the gap from memory." Apart from this section of about two hundred manuscript pages, the diary form is consistently maintained. Through forty-eight copybooks of more than twenty-five hundred pages, the diarist is narrator of her own experiences, and they are "real-life" experiences—flesh-and-blood people, real events and crises, private and public, domestic as well as historic. Recording them in her dated entries, Mary Chesnut adheres faithfully to the style, tone, and circumstantial limitations of the diarist and conveys fully the sense of chaotic daily life. To all appearances she respects the Latin meaning of *diarium* and its denial of knowledge of the future. Unforeseen events crowd in, unexpected guests arrive, messengers come and go. Each day brings its surprises. Illness, accident, violence, crime, death, and tragedy strike randomly and overwhelm. Ambitions, love affairs, conspiracies, and intrigues intimately traced in their day-to-day course, hang fire unfulfilled and await unforeseeable developments. Close friends pictured in the flush of triumph or the gaiety of the social whirl return next day from the front, as corpses. Over all hangs endless speculation, suspense, and anxiety about the fortunes of the war and the outcome of the struggle for Southern independence. The diarist agonizes over these uncertainties. She frets over interruption of her diary writing, weeps over the disappointments of her hopes and the tragedies of her friends, and rages over the beastliness of men, the unfairness of life, and the cruelties of fortune.

The Chesnut *Diary* in its published forms therefore appears to embody the cherished characteristics peculiar to the true diary—the freshness and shock of experience immediately recorded, the "real-life" actuality of subject matter, the spontaneity of perceptions denied knowledge of the future—all this in addition to its author's "uncanny" anticipation and exploitation of "the literary possibilities of her subject."

However that may be, we now know that the version of this work known to the public as "diary" was written between 1881 and 1884, twenty years after the events presumed to have been recorded as they happened. This information will be cause for concern among the many who feel indebted to Mary Boykin Chesnut for her vivid account of the Civil War and who have come to admire the author. The dating of the manuscript will inevitably raise questions among historians about the use of her writings and the way historians have used them extensively in the past. The bare fact of date of composition certainly changes the prevalent conception of the work and removes it from the conventional category of "diary." Much more than that, however, is to be learned from the surviving papers of Mary Chesnut about the sources of her work, the genuine diary she did keep, the subsequent drafts, abandoned experiments she tried, and the self-schooled apprenticeship she served before the writing of her book. The purpose here is certainly not to disparage her work, nor to extol it, but rather to understand and explain its true character and to remove some of the misapprehension and perplexity about it.

Mary Chesnut did keep an extensive diary intermittently during the years of the Confederacy, though she preferred to call it her "journal" or "notes." To distinguish it from her book posthumously entitled *A Diary*, it will be identified here as her "Journal" and the so-called diary, even prior to its publication, as her "book." It is clear for reasons to be explained that the Journal was never intended for publication and equally clear that from its inception the book was. She began her Journal while she was in Alabama with her husband, James Chesnut, Jr., who was at Montgomery, helping found the new Confederate government. Her first entry, dated February 18, 1861, deals mainly with the past instead of the present and serves as an informal introduction. It may have been written as an afterthought, but not long after the date given. It is in large part a look back over her activities during the three months following Lincoln's election and her husband's immediate resignation from the United States Senate on November 10, 1860. Untypical in some ways, the first entry nevertheless sounds notes that echo throughout the Journal: a keen awareness of history in the making, a resolute identification with a cause, ominous forebodings about the outcome, and a wry skepticism and amusement at the participants. She regrets that she has not kept a journal in the past and resolves to do so in the future.

How persistent she was in the resolution we have no sure means of knowing. Among her surviving papers[4] are seven numbers of the Journal, in volumes of varied size containing in all a little more than a thousand pages, large and small. The first five volumes run consecutively from the first entry, in February 1861, through December 8, 1861. Of the two others, one begins in January and covers most of February 1865 and the other runs from May 7 to July 26, 1865. There are none for 1862, 1863, or 1864, and these seven are all that appear to survive, though we do know that more once existed. What we do not know is how much more was ever written, what periods were covered, how much that was written survived the Civil War and was available to Mary Chesnut when she wrote her book in the eighties, and how much that survived Mary still survives.[5]

In her book Mrs. Chesnut makes two references to burning parts of her Journal in 1863, once in connection with a threat on Richmond in May[6] and

4. All at the South Caroliniana Library, Columbia, S.C., unless otherwise indicated. The various manuscript journal versions are available on microfilm by interlibrary loan. Transcriptions of the drafts of the journals in typescript are at the library of the Southern Studies Program, Univ. of South Carolina.

5. Some light on the last question is provided by one of the first editors, Isabella D. Martin, who, in returning the manuscript volumes of both Journal and book to their owner in 1905, remarked quite casually: "Unaccountably two or three numbers have got mislaid. I think considering all their journeyings and handlings it is well there are not more." Isabella D. Martin to David Williams, March 27, 1905, in possession of Catherine Hill, Columbia, S.C. Since the volumes for the book are all accounted for, the "mislaid" numbers appear to have been from the Journal, though they may have turned up later.

6. 1880s Version, XXIV, p. 46, undated (roman numeral indicates copybook number).

once in a more general reference.[7] Whatever she destroyed, she could still write in her original Journal on February 23, 1865, "I have been busily engaged, reading *10* volumes of memoirs of the times I have written," and "still I write on." A refugee from Sherman's path at the time, she adds that "if I have to burn . . . , here lie my treasures ready for the blazing hearth." She says she was "burning papers all day—expecting a Yankee raid,"[8] but she was more likely to have been burning her husband's correspondence on military matters than her Journals. At least she obviously did not burn the volume quoted, and a subsequent one begun two months later also survives.[9] It seems very likely, therefore, that she had at least twelve volumes of the 1860s Journal (five more than now exist) before her when she wrote the revision in the 1880s, and there are indications that more were then at hand.

The probability is that she did not keep a journal with much regularity during 1863 and 1864. Time and circumstance were against it. Mary was very busy with her husband's correspondence and her hospital work; was distracted by houseguests, entertaining, and moving her household between Richmond, Columbia, and Camden; and was frequently laid low by illness. She nevertheless appeared to be consciously accumulating material and impressions for a later work. It is notable that during the periods for which she says no diary existed, other documents and records tend to bulk larger in her papers— newspaper clippings, official papers, and personal letters—all presumably collected to help "fill the gap" created by the missing Journal.[10]

The Journal volumes that remain testify to the trying circumstances in which they were often written—haste, cramped quarters, lack of privacy. As an army wife, even with a husband of high rank, Mary had to make do with one hotel room or boardinghouse after another, living out of her trunk for some periods. She pronounced one of the hotels "a den of abominations." Even when the Chesnuts had a rented house in Columbia or part of one in Richmond, the quarters were small and frequently crowded with guests. Distractions and demands on her time were innumerable. Ill a great deal, Mary did some of her writing in bed. Illness and depression made her dependent at times on opium, and its use possibly affected her writing as well as her mood. When she took pains to do so, she could write good crisp prose, especially in reflective passages. For the most part the writing in the Journal is punctuated by little but dashes of varied length, eccentrically inserted. It is filled with quoted remarks without marks to close them, with unidentified speakers, obscure abbreviations, confused identities, and notes from her reading. Grammar and syntax get scant attention, and sometimes pages go by without a completed sentence, some entries being little more than names, phrases, scraps of information, and

---

7. 1880s Version, XXIII, p. 35, undated.
8. 1860s Journal, Feb. 23, 1865.
9. 1860s Journal, May 7 to July 26, 1865, the final volume of the Journal.
10. Especially in 1880s Version, XI, XII, and XIII, where the verso pages of these volumes become virtual scrapbooks for clippings.

notes. Important names and historic events share entries indiscriminately with nonentities and trivialities. "It is hard, in such a hurry as things are in," she wrote, "to separate wheat from chaff."[11] That was in the simulated diary of her book, but the statement more accurately describes the writing in her Journal.

The Journal, unlike the book, was kept in tight security, under lock and key, and was clearly intended for no eyes but her own, not even those of her husband. In her book she says more than once that "everybody reads my journal," speaks casually of it lying available on her table, and tells of reading or showing passages to friends.[12] No such suggestion appears in the Journal, but instead utmost concern that no one see it but herself.[13] Its contents go far to explaining her concern. While her book later became noted for its candor in many respects, her Journal often goes much further. Here Mary Chesnut permitted herself great frankness and freedom in expressing her feelings about friends, neighbors, in-laws, relatives, and immediate family, including her husband and his parents. It is here we learn, for example, that she believed her father-in-law, for whom she had mixed feelings, had sired children by one of his slaves. "Merciful God! forgive me if I fail," she cries. "Can I *honor* what is dishonorable? *Rachel* and her brood make this place a horrid nightmare to me."[14] She is quite as free with her views of political allies, opponents, and popular heroes, and the morals, manners, and scandals of her own circle. Her scorn does not spare the foundations of the social order—the patriarchy, slavery, even marriage.

Perhaps most closely guarded of all, however, were those secrets of Mary Chesnut's Journal that concerned herself, particularly revelations of her vanity or evidence of conceit, arrogance, and ambition. She recorded with evident pleasure compliments and attentions that men showered upon her—one, for example, telling Mary "how stiff it was at the reception yesterday until I got there—and I went in like a ray of warmth and sunshine—pretty good for a woman of my years."[15] Again, she notes with disarming candor, "I know my dress is the prettiest in the room."[16] Mary was not regarded as a beauty, and she knew that. "I never was handsome," she wrote, and then she added, "I wonder what my attraction was, for men did fall in love with me wherever I went."[17] She was speaking at the time of her youth, but old admirers lingered and new ones gathered around in her late thirties. Flowers, presents, and invitations poured in, and she took some pleasure in the annoyance and occasional explosions of her husband and recorded the displeasure of Mrs. Davis at her capturing the

11. 1880s Version, XIV, p. 23, March 10, 1862.
12. For example, 1880s Version, X, no p., Nov. 12, 1861; XI, no p., Dec. 13, 1861; XXXIX, p. 8, Nov. 25, 1864.
13. She tells that her husband once inadvertently went off with her keys; as a result, she had no way "to open my lock and so could not write in my journal" (1860s Journal, June 29, 1861).
14. 1860s Journal, June 11–12, 1861.
15. 1860s Journal, March 7, 1861.
16. 1860s Journal, March 15, 1861.
17. 1860s Journal, Feb. 28, 1861.

center of attention. After one evening of triumphs she went so far as to write, "I can make anybody love me if I choose."[18]

That last sentence, along with several of the sort she must have found embarrassing, she later erased. It is, in fact, misleading and unfair to quote her in this vein, out of context. Mary was not without her armor of skepticism. "I wonder," she wrote after recording some flattery, "if in the thousand compliments I hear there is one *grain* of truth."[19] While she did not underestimate her appeal, and the evidence of its power is persuasive, she knew very well that her husband was in a position to dispense favors and promotions, and so were her daily associates, from the president and cabinet members on down. She was therefore quite apt to ask herself about a flatterer what office or promotion he was seeking at the moment. Looking back over what she had written, she recorded the date: "1875. Reading this Journal I find I was a vain and foolish old woman to record silly flattery to myself—in short—an old idiot."[20] It was then that she may have seized her eraser and gone to work.

The Journal no doubt gave her other bad moments on rereading. Mary Chesnut did not suffer fools gladly, and she encountered them on all sides. "When you are bored by people," her husband admonished, "you are absent minded, sad and weary of aspect, sometimes you groan and often frown and fidget. I wonder that you can do so."[21] She was likely to mince no words in recording the quantity of human folly, pomposity, and charlatanry she encountered. She also registered her worry about her husband's admonitions and her uncontrollable scorn. "I sometimes fear I am so vain," she admitted, "so conceited, think myself so *clever* and my neighbors such geese that pride comes before a fall. I pray I may be spared."[22] Still other indiscretions glared up at her from the pages of the old Journal in later years. There in page after page were the details of the rather flagrant flirtation with handsome ex-Governor John Manning. Some of this she preserved in her book, but not the details, nor the perverse pleasure she took in her husband's jealousy. "Is it not too funny, and he is so *prosy*."[23] There it was, in black and white. There also she found the painful evidence of the temporary breach in the summer of 1861 of her relations with Varina Davis, later her beloved friend. "What a fool I was," she noted, with the date 1866, the year following her last entry.

If she found entries to be deplored, erased, suppressed, or forgotten in the old Journals, she also found much that justified her in calling them "my treasure." Among the qualifications of the good diarist that Mary Chesnut enjoyed was a generous endowment of luck. "It was a way I had, always," as she herself put it, "to stumble in on the *real show*."[24] The year of crisis, 1859–60, she

18. 1860s Journal, March 15, 1861.
19. 1860s Journal, March 5, 1861.
20. After the entry in 1860s Journal, March 6, 1861.
21. Rough draft of 1880s Version, Sept. 8, 1864.
22. 1860s Journal, Sept. 17, 1861.
23. 1860s Journal, March 30, 1861.
24. 1880s Version, Jan. 9, 1864.

spent in Washington. She was in Montgomery for the founding and early months of the Confederacy, in Charleston for the attack on Fort Sumter, and in Richmond and Columbia at critical periods. Even while she was compelled against her will to rusticate down on Mulberry plantation, things seemed to happen when she was around: the murder of her cousin Elizabeth Witherspoon by her slaves, for example. It was not merely the places she had been but the people she knew and knew intimately. What she often called "my world" comprised a large part of the political, military, social, and economic elite of the Confederacy, from South Carolina and Virginia to Louisiana and Texas. The riches of the crude Journal, however, owe less to all this than to the qualities of intelligence and understanding she brought to the task. Left in its original state, however, the Journal probably would never have been known to the public. It contained too many indiscretions, gaps, trivialities, and incoherencies. If we may judge from the surviving parts, we doubt that Mary would ever have exposed it to the public eye, and even if she had, it would have not been publishable. Knowing this, she was nevertheless resolved to mine it for something that *was* publishable. It was sixteen years before she arrived at a solution.

Her first efforts toward this end were experiments in fiction writing, to which we shall return later. In the meantime she had been rereading the Journal, making notes and collecting material to supplement what she had written. In 1875 she put aside the novels in progress and settled down to the task of rewriting and putting the Journal in shape. Only four sections of this 1875 Version survive; numbered 10, 11, 21, and 22, amounting to nearly four hundred long pages in all and covering periods in 1861 and 1864.[25] On this scale the completed manuscript, if indeed it was completed, would have run well over two thousand pages. The surviving part of the version of the seventies differs in several respects from the version of the sixties and the version of the eighties but more closely resembles the former than the latter. Like both of the others it sustains the diary form consistently. The effort of 1875–76 seems largely limited to weeding out irrelevant, trivial, and indiscreet parts, rounding out incomplete or fragmentary notes, and producing cleaner, though by no means finished, copy. Where comparison with the original versions is possible, events and experiences that are retained are much the same, but new episodes are added and dates are often shifted. The version of the eighties differs mainly in the realization of those "literary possibilities" that Edmund Wilson mentioned and we will explore later.

It seems very likely that Mary Chesnut herself realized that her efforts were falling short of the possibilities she envisioned for the Journal. Whether for this reason or another, she put the project aside about the middle of 1876. She may have been influenced in her decision also by the advice of R. M. T. Hunter, whom she once called "the sanest if not the wisest man in our newborn Confederacy" and for whose literary judgment she had the highest regard.[26] Evidently

25. The four sections of the 1870s Version, numbered as indicated and two of them marked in the upper lefthand corner of the title page "x75."

26. 1880s Version, III, pp. 32–33, May 19, 1861.

at her request, James Chesnut had sounded out Hunter about reading her revised manuscript. He responded cordially that he was "very anxious to see her history of her own times" but added that "if published just now by a So Ca lady, such a work might make the world a little too hot to hold her. . . ."[27] He repeated the advice against publication in a later letter, quoting Chesnut as saying, "It is a little too spicy."[28] At any rate, Mary does not appear to have begun her next and final experiment with the Journal for another five years.

The long suspension of work on the Journal by no means stopped Mary Chesnut's writing activities. Nor did these appear to be slowed very much by the ordeals of misfortune and tragedy that beset her in those years—deaths, family troubles, severe financial stress, and almost constant ill health. She turned to writing for relief. Her projects included translations of French fiction, a biographical essay on her husband, memoirs of her sister, and family history.[29] Of most importance to her development as a writer were her efforts in writing fiction. These began in the late sixties, when she worked on two novels at about the same time, and eventually resulted in three full novels. She made note of her ambitions in her Journal once in 1861 when she said, "The scribbling mania is strong in me—have an insane idea in my brain to write a tale" for publication.[30] Later in the version of the eighties she tells of a sleepless night: "Then came a happy thought. I mapped out a story of the war. The plot came to hand, for it was true. Johnny is the hero. . . ."[31] John Chesnut, James's nephew, twenty-four at the outbreak of war, was a special favorite of his aunt and figured in her Journal and even more prominently in its elaborations.

"The Captain and the Colonel," the novel that was the apparent fruit of this conception, did have a leading character who suggests some aspects of Johnny Chesnut, "the cool Captain" of the Journal and the book. Other figures, situations, and relationships reflect Mrs. Chesnut's wartime experiences, but apart from a few historic figures in the background, this is unmistakably a work of fiction—a serious, ambitious, and unsuccessful novel. It pictures a wealthy planter family of South Carolina headed by a widow of New York origins, unsympathetically portrayed, and her domineering manipulation of the lives and marriages of her three very different daughters. The war is offstage, but its impact is felt. Ill-starred courtships complicate frustrated love affairs, rival suitors and best friends face each other in bloody duel, sister plots against sister, and a Machiavellian mother almost has her way. The novel sags with a limp plot and suffers from improbable coincidence and inadequate characterization and identification. It is the first effort of a beginner who started late, and its author

27. R. M. T. Hunter to James Chesnut, Jr., July 12, 1876, Williams, Manning, Chesnut Collection, South Caroliniana Library (hereafter referred to as WMC Collection).

28. Hunter to Chesnut, Aug. 14, 1876, WMC Collection.

29. The untitled memoir on her sister Kate (referred to hereafter as "Autobiographical memoir") and the untitled essay on James Chesnut, Jr. in WMC Collection; both are included as appendices in Elisabeth Showalter Muhlenfeld, "Mary Boykin Chesnut: The Writer and Her Work" (Ph.D. diss., Univ. of South Carolina, 1978).

30. 1860s Journal, Oct. 3, 1861.

31. 1880s Version, XXXIX, p. 46, Jan. 1, 1864.

must have been pained to see how far she fell short of her literary hero, William Makepeace Thackeray. For the purpose of understanding her development as writer, however, much is to be learned from the surviving manuscripts of her drafts, revisions, and rewritings of "The Captain and the Colonel." In her endless tinkering she is struggling to shape her style, master dialogue, and come to terms with her subject matter. Though she returned to revision half-heartedly and briefly later, she did nearly all this work by 1875 and appears to have given up the idea of publication.[32]

After her abortive revision of the Journal, Mary undertook the rewriting of a second novel, "Two Years of My Life,"[33] a draft of which she had done at about the same time as "The Captain and the Colonel." Parts of two subsequent drafts of the manuscript survive, all but five chapters of one and only three chapters and part of a fourth in another. Different from "The Captain" in several ways, "Two Years" is also clearly fiction, but it is autobiographical in substance, written in the first person, and parallels events in Mary Chesnut's own life between 1836 and 1840. In 1836 her parents had removed her from an elite boarding school in the heart of old Charleston and had taken her to her father's plantation on the Mississippi frontier. In "The Captain" she had contrasted the stable antebellum South with the chaotic instability of wartime, and in "Two Years" she compares the elegance of old Charleston with the crudity, violence, and harshness of the frontier. A romance that recalls her own with James Chesnut is part of the story, and she invents a fictional frontier feud in addition. This novel must also be pronounced a failure, but a rather more interesting failure than the first. Again it is possible to compare successive versions to see what she was working toward with hundreds of revised passages and to estimate her development as a writer. Changes were apparent, changes that for the most part indicated growth of confidence and improvement of style.[34]

Other literary ventures kept Mrs. Chesnut hard at work at the turn of the 1880s. She appears to have offered to the editor of the Charleston *News and Courier* a translation of what he describes as a "novelette" by Pushkin. He agreed to publish it, but no evidence of her writing it remains.[35] Of greater significance is a fragment of a third novel written in this period, a novel she thought of calling "Manassas." Only a few pages survive, but since these are numbered in the 400s they indicate a longer work than either of the two preceding novels. The title suggests that she had returned to the war in her third work of fiction, and the few characters that appear in the surviving pages indicate that she was combining the war theme of the first novel with the autobiographical tendencies of the second. If so, she was moving in both respects back to the deferred

32. MS drafts in WMC Collection; edited text and notes on "The Captain and the Colonel," in Muhlenfeld, "Mary Boykin Chesnut," pp. 280–480 and see also chapter 5.

33. Drafts in WMC Collection.

34. Edited text and notes of "Two Years—Or the Way We Lived Then" (title of later draft of "Two Years of My Life") in Muhlenfeld, "Mary Boykin Chesnut," pp. 482–639 and see also chapter 6.

35. F. W. Dawson to "Madam," July 2, 1880, WMC Collection.

challenge of the Journal. She had been diverted by her fiction experiments, but properly viewed, they had been preparing her all along for the same move. Elisabeth Muhlenfeld, the editor and critic of this fiction, is the first to perceive that it was in these failed experiments that Mary Chesnut developed much of the style and technique of the only work for which she is remembered, her famous book on the Civil War. "Whether or not she realized it," writes Professor Muhlenfeld, "she had completed her apprenticeship."[36]

When Mary Boykin Chesnut finally faced up to the task presented by her Journal, in 1881, she was fifty-eight and in wretched health, plagued by a heart condition, lung trouble, and minor ailments. Among her daily responsibilities were running a dairy farm and a household full of aging, ailing, and often demanding relatives. She probably had these present circumstances in mind rather than the past she was writing about when she broke into an entry for May 1862 with the exclamation: "Oh! Peace—and a literary leisure for my old age—unbroken by care and anxiety!!"[37] Yet in spite of the care and anxiety and the lack of anything that could be called leisure, she managed to write more in the next three and a half years than all of her literary products of previous years combined: two full drafts of the book she now was determined to make of her Journal and her Civil War experience. Most of the first draft and all of the second except what has been torn or cut out—more than forty-two hundred pages in all—still survive. The first is a very rough working draft in purple pencil, apparently written in tandem with the second, from day to day rather than completed in advance of it. Her second and last draft is in ink and fills forty-eight copybooks.

It is a mistake, however, to assume that Mary Chesnut regarded her last draft as in any sense final and finished copy. She obviously intended to do much more work on it. "How I wish you could read over my journal," she wrote Varina Davis in June 1883. "I have been two years overlooking it—copying—leaving myself out. You must see it—before it goes to print—but that may not be just now. I mean the printing—for I must overhaul it again—and again."[38] She did not intend to die in less than three years, nor did she realize that her last two years of life would be filled with misfortunes that forced her to leave her work unfinished. If the rigorous substantive revisions to which she had subjected the drafts of her earlier literary work are any indication, then it is quite clear that this huge manuscript was destined for a great deal of hard labor. Instead, she left it comparatively untouched. She did not even decide how to begin her book but left her editor confronted with four alternative beginnings, three of them incomplete or mutilated drafts, which treat events in the three months before she actually began to keep her Journal, and a fourth, a retrospective introduc-

---

36. Muhlenfeld, "Mary Boykin Chesnut," p. 179.
37. 1880s Version, XVI, pp. 35–36, May 6, 1862.
38. Mary Boykin Chesnut to Varina Davis, June 18, 1883, Museum of the Confederacy, Richmond, Va. Transcription in Allie Patricia Wall, "The Letters of Mary Boykin Chesnut," M.A. thesis, Univ. of South Carolina, 1977, p. 83.

tion, probably written at the time she began the Journal. Which draft to use is but one of hundreds of decisions she bequeathed her editors.

It soon becomes evident that for the revision of the eighties Mary Chesnut had in mind a good deal more than her limited objectives in the revision of the seventies. The new version also eliminates trivialities, irrelevancies, and indiscretions, as had the one of the seventies. But before long it is clear that the techniques that she had in the meantime developed in her "apprenticeship" are being brought into play. Techniques of characterization and dialogue, methods of using dialogue for both narration and characterization—all the arts and skills she had managed to teach herself she now put to service in rewriting diary instead of revising fiction. Sometimes third-person or first-person narrative or speculations and reflections are condensed in dialogues. Sometimes a brief factual entry is expanded into a revealing story. For example, two sentences of an entry in the Journal tell briefly of being awakened by night at Sandy Hill plantation by a commotion old Mrs. Chesnut caused when she smelled something burning. In the new version this incident is expanded into four pages that vividly picture life in the plantation big house and yard, with sixty or seventy slaves looking for the fire, and present characterizations of old Colonel and Mrs. Chesnut, both quite deaf and the latter completely oblivious of the needless commotion she has roused.[39] Similarly, the Journal account of the murder of Mrs. Witherspoon by her own slaves is followed in essentials in the new version, but here whole new dimensions are added. For this time we view the horror that the murder strikes in the heart of the community not only through Mary Chesnut's eyes but through those of others as well, including slaves. Mistress looks on maid, and slave on master, with new eyes. The foundations of society tremble under their feet by day and their beds by night. Old stories are recalled that alter their view of the past, and the future takes on an ominous aspect.[40]

In exploiting material from her Journal of the sixties for her simulated diary of the eighties, Mary Chesnut took many liberties. She omitted much but usually added more than the amount omitted or condensed. The expansions were sometimes elaborations of brief original entries, sometimes new matter entirely, including new episodes and letters or quotations and condensations of letters. More often the expansions took the form of characterizations or conversations of people in the Journal or reflections on events and issues reported there. In the process, sometimes dates get shifted around, entries telescoped, speakers switched, and words and ideas originally attributed to the writer herself are put in the mouths of others. The integrity of the author's experience and perception is maintained in this transformation, but not the literal record of events expected of the diarist.

39. 1860s Journal, one entry under collective dates, June 21, 22, 23, 1861; and 1880s Version, IV, pp. 24-27, June 10, 1861.
40. 1860s Journal, Sept. 21–Oct. 26, 1861; 1880s Version, Sept. 21–Oct. 25, 1861.

One of Mary Chesnut's avowed purposes in her revision of the eighties, as she expressed it to Mrs. Davis, was "leaving myself out." This is not to be taken literally, for she obviously left a great deal of herself in. What she took out were some—but by no means all—of the embarrassing self-revelations mentioned earlier: unflattering confessions of vanity; records of flattery, admirers, suitors, and conquests; early disaffection with the Davises; quarrels with friends, family, and husband. Many of these omissions are natural, but some deprive the reader of needed or revealing information. For example, she bluntly declares in her last version that she prefers public life to private life. "I mean the life of a politician or statesman. Peace, comfort, quiet, happiness, I have found away from home. Only your own family, those nearest and dearest can hurt you." She is thinking specifically about village and plantation life around Camden, where, she says, "everybody knows exactly where to put the knife." That alone would rank her high for candor among diarists. But only in suppressed passages of the Journal do we discover the disappointed ambitions that caused her gloomy reflections. James Chesnut has just told her that John Slidell got the coveted mission to France. Hopes of Paris have collapsed, and so have those for London. "All my pretty chickens at one fell swoop!" she exclaims—quoting Macduff, but in a mood more reminiscent of Lady Macbeth. "Now," she reflects, as if in the cadence of some Elizabethan soliloquy, "if we are not reelected to the Senate! . . . now as James Chesnut's genius does not lie in the military, I suppose Camden is my dark fate . . . but I will harbor so dark a thought against my own peace of mind. Pride must have a fall—perhaps I have not bourne my honors meekly."[41]

We may forgive Mary Chesnut for depriving us of that dramatic monologue for a century, but we could hardly excuse a responsible editor for perpetuating the suppression. Where such omitted passages are relevant and significant, it would seem to be the duty of an editor to share them with the reader, whether the passages are derived from the original or from some other version. The whole corpus of the author's journal manuscripts and other works as well will, in fact, be made subject to editorial use. The existence of extensive parts of the original Journal that paralleled her version of twenty years later opens other exciting intellectual opportunities. At times it speaks directly to that perennial question of the historian puzzling over the written word: "What were they really thinking when they wrote this?" Before the editor sometimes lie both the inner dialogue and the one addressed to the public, the private life and the projected image. The experience sometimes recalls Eugene O'Neill's *Strange Interlude* (1928), in which he alternated outer dialogue with inner, what was spoken with what was actually thought and felt.

The historian will be fascinated by the lapse of time between first and last versions—not merely the passing of two decades, but the most traumatic years in the history of the South. How did they distort the diarist's original impressions? The question evokes the classic historical problems of hindsight and

41. See facsimiles of both versions, each dated Aug. 29, 1861, below, pp. 174–75.

relativism. (To anticipate the answer, she comes off very well.) And finally, comparison of original and late versions provides invaluable sample tests of the author's integrity—some evidence of how far we can trust her, how far she bent to the winds of doctrine and storms of passion—whether, for example, her abolitionist leanings and her militant feminism were afterthoughts. These are but a few of the questions and opportunities that enhance the intellectual rewards of this undertaking.

The editor has kept before him all the questions raised in the preceding paragraph and more of similar character as he worked his way through the maze of the various versions, comparing and assessing the revisions of the Journal. He began in a spirit of skepticism, with misgivings that it would become his duty to expose inconsistencies, anachronisms, distortions, hindsights, and special pleadings that would raise doubts about the worth and integrity of a famous book and its author. Well before the completion of the long task, however, a growing respect for the author and the integrity of her work began to replace the original misgivings. Given the kinds of liberties she took in revising and expanding the original Journal, liberties that have been enumerated and illustrated above, Mary Chesnut can be said to have shown an unusual sense of responsibility toward the history she records and a reassuring faithfulness to perceptions of her experience of the period as revealed in her original Journal. It would be a regrettable and most ironic outcome of this effort to reveal the true nature of her work and an accurate text of what she wrote if it all resulted in lowering the esteem in which her work is held.

The importance of Mary Chesnut's work, of course, lies not in autobiography, fortuitous self-revelations, or opportunities for editorial detective work. She is remembered only for the vivid picture she left of a society in the throes of its life-and-death struggle, its moment of high drama in world history. A common error in assessment of the worth of her work is to value it for the information it contains. That is to miss its real significance. It does provide information, but most of that is obtainable elsewhere, often more reliably. The enduring value of the work, crude and unfinished as it is, lies in the life and reality with which it endows people and events and with which it evokes the chaos and complexity of a society at war. Her cast of characters includes slaves and brown half brothers, poor whites and sandhillers, overseers and drivers, common soldiers and solid yeomen, as well as the very top elite of state, military, and society that thronged her drawing room and saw her daily. She brings to life the historic crisis of her age with the literary techniques she had developed in the meantime, and again it is the rare fortune of the editor to have so much of the manuscript evidence of these experiments before him. The romance of Buck Preston and General Hood that so captivated the imagination of Edmund Wilson as a metaphor for the rise and fall of the Confederate hopes is one of several metaphors Mary Chesnut employed. Here hindsight *was* employed, but the facts bear her out. She did not make them up. She seems to have seen experience as metaphor from the start. Where art starts is hard to say, but it is undoubtedly there.

The two previous editions of Mary Chesnut's book cited earlier[42] require brief critical assessments and the addition of some information about their origins. Both the edition of 1905 and that of 1949 derive from the 1880s Version, and both were published under the same title, *A Diary from Dixie*. There is no evidence that Mary Chesnut ever used or authorized this title, nor was it selected by the editors or the publishers of either edition. It was, in fact, the title chosen without authorization by *The Saturday Evening Post* for the five installments of the first edition which that journal, by agreement with D. Appleton and Company, published in successive issues beginning on January 28, 1905. Appleton persuaded the nominal editors of its volume to adopt the title used by the *Post*.[43] That the term "Dixie" should have been posthumously inflicted on Mary Chesnut's book was an irony she would not have cherished. She consciously avoided use of the word herself, pronounced the sentiment of the song of that name "prosaic," and declared that it "never moved me a jot." Rather than perpetuate the anomalies involved in the term "Dixie," as well as in the term "Diary," the editor has abandoned the *Post* title for the present edition.

Of the two women whose names appeared on the title page of the Appleton edition, Isabella D. Martin, a schoolmistress of Columbia, South Carolina, had possession of the manuscript and believed that her friend Mary Chesnut had given her complete authority over it. She agreed to collaborate with Myrta Lockett Avary, who had recently edited a volume of Civil War memoirs published by Appleton, and with that firm the two women made a contract.[44] The publisher only wanted to use about 130,000 words of a manuscript more than three times that length. Correspondence between publisher and editors reveals that the firm not only took the lead in selecting the parts of the manuscript to be published, but that Francis W. Halsey, an editor within the house, wrote the footnotes, divided the entries into twenty-one chapters, supplied titles and running heads for the chapters, rewrote and reorganized the introduction, and prepared the index.[45] The work was done in considerable haste. Miss Martin was intensely concerned that Chesnut passages out of line with the current Southern version of Confederate legend be deleted. Mrs. Witherspoon's death

---

42. See n. 3 above, p. xv.

43. Robert Adger Bowen, D. Appleton and Company, to Isabella D. Martin, Jan. 16, 1905, in Papers of Myrta Lockett Avary, Atlanta Historical Society. This and other xeroxes of typed copies from the Avary Papers have kindly been supplied to me by Elisabeth Muhlenfeld.

44. Francis W. Halsey, D. Appleton and Company, to Myrta Lockett Avary, Sept. 30, 1904; Martin to Avary, Oct. 22, 1904. The volume Avary edited for Appleton was *A Virginia Girl in the Civil War, 1861–1865; Being a Record of the Actual Experiences of the Wife of a Confederate Officer* (New York, 1903).

45. Halsey to Martin, Nov. 4, 1904, and Nov. 11, 1904; Martin to Halsey, Nov. 16, 1904; Avary to Halsey, Jan. 16, 1905, Avary Papers. It is the conclusion of Professor James B. Meriwether, in an unpublished paper, that Halsey should be considered "editor of the book; Mrs. Avary and Miss Martin were merely its sponsors."

46. On Martin's concern for Southern sensibilities and Confederate legend, see Martin to Halsey, Dec. 12, 1904; and Martin to Bowen, Jan. 20, 1905, Avary Papers.

is mentioned, for example, but with no hint that her slaves had anything to do with it.[46]

The novelist Ben Ames Williams, editor of the 1949 edition, was also swayed by romance in his work on Mary Chesnut. By his own admission, in fact, she figured prominently under a fictional name in a Civil War romance he wrote, entitled *House Divided.* His knowledge of her there was derived from the Appleton edition.[47] Excited by his discovery of her manuscript version of the 1880s and some fragments of the original Journal, he employed a typist to make a transcript and based his edition on the copy. His purpose appears to have been to let nothing stand in the way of readability, and he took great liberties with the text to achieve this end. Both the opening and the concluding passages of the book are his inventions—the opening sentence containing three errors. He published a larger proportion of the manuscript than did the previous editors, but like them he gave no indication of his deletions or omissions, nor of his extensive alterations, or of passages or pages previously mutilated, torn, or cut out. Silently omitted are parts presenting some difficulty of interpretation, unfamiliar personages and relationships, and passages in French. Dates are sometimes altered, and dialogue is occasionally converted into narrative, or vice versa. Williams incorporated two or three passages from the 1860s Journal in his text, but without identifying their origin or indicating their character. The rich texture of Mary Chesnut's literary references is largely missed by the omission of, or failure to identify, quotations. On the whole the editor enjoyed considerable success in attaining his goal of readability, but at heavy cost to the reliability and quality of his editorial contribution.[48]

47. Introduction to Williams, *A Diary from Dixie,* pp. vi–viii.
48. The Harvard University Press reissued this work in 1980, leaving the Williams text unchanged but adding an essay on Chesnut, described as a "Foreword," that Edmund Wilson published in 1962.

Mary Boykin Chesnut, 1823–1886

She loved city life and lived most of her life in the country—mainly on plantations within a few miles of the old town of Camden, South Carolina, about thirty miles northeast of Columbia.[1] She was born on March 31, 1823, at Mount Pleasant, the home of her mother's family, headed by the wealthy planter Burwell Boykin until his death in 1817. Her parents, Mary Boykin and Stephen Decatur Miller, soon moved to their more modest establishment of Plane Hill a mile down the road, near the village of Statesburg. Her father was a busy politician on the way up and could spend little time with his family. He had been a widower with a small son in 1821 when he married Mary Boykin, who was then seventeen. Sixteen years his junior, she was barely nineteen when she bore her first child, Mary. Three more babies, Stephen, Catherine, and Sarah Amelia, were to follow in the next eight years.

Young Mary grew up among her numerous well-to-do Boykin relatives. They were an "old family" tribe, first established in Virginia in the 1680s and present in South Carolina two decades before the Revolution. Mary's mother was one of thirteen children, with brothers and sisters not much older than her firstborn, so that aunts and uncles and cousins and nieces and nephews and in-laws proliferated, to the confusion of generational distinction. Mary remained particularly close to her uncles Burwell and Alexander Hamilton Boykin, who were more contemporaries than elders. She was named for her grandmother, Mary Whitaker Boykin, and as the first granddaughter of the Boykins, she gained special favor and place in the family. Grandmother Boykin became her constant mentor in plantation management and the mysteries of loom room, sewing room, smokehouse, pantry, dairy, storeroom. In an affectionate tribute written years later, Mary describes herself as "her shadow."[2]

Her father Stephen was a more remote, though fascinating, figure in her childhood. Of less distinguished forebears than the Boykins, he described the relatives of his father, whose parents were the first of the Miller family in South Carolina, as "honest respectable & unambitious," with an "exception or two," including a cousin who was "a drunkard & a vagabond." His mother's parents, named White, were Presbyterians who emigrated from Ireland. They appear to have achieved somewhat higher status, one of his aunts on that side having married a cousin of Gen. Andrew Jackson.[3] Stephen and two brothers some-

1. For a full and well-informed biography see Muhlenfeld, "Mary Boykin Chesnut," a revision of which is soon to be published. This sketch owes much to that work.
2. Autobiographical memoir, pp. 3–6, WMC Collection; a transcription of this manuscript under the title "We called her Kitty" is to be found in Muhlenfeld, "Mary Boykin Chesnut," appendix; Edward M. Boykin, *A Record of the Boykins* (Camden, 1876).
3. Stephen D. Miller to "My dear daughter," July 23, 1835, MS copy in M. B. C.'s hand in WMC Collection.

how managed to get an education, and Stephen was graduated from the new South Carolina College in 1808. He then read and practiced law and served a term in Congress (1817–19). His political fortunes continued to advance after a resolution of his, adopted by the state senate in 1824, served to launch the States Rights party in South Carolina. On the strength of that movement, he was elected governor in 1828 and United States senator in 1830. Governor Miller's legislative message in 1829 has been described by the leading historian of the proslavery movement as probably the first significant statement of the "positive-good" position on slavery. Miller became a central figure in the nullification controversy that followed.[4]

At home daughter Mary had learned to read and write and at age nine was writing her father "every saturday when I come home" from school. In one letter she promised to read her father's speech in the Senate on the tariff.[5] It was from the days of the nullification struggle that she later dated her first stirrings of political awareness and "the faith I had imbibed before I understood anything about it. If I do yet."[6] She was to continue her schooling in Camden until she was twelve, staying with her Aunt Elizabeth and Uncle Thomas J. Withers in town and returning home on weekends.

In the meantime her father had resigned from the Senate in 1833, officially for reasons of ill health, but probably for more complicated political and personal reasons. In politics Senator Miller was soon overshadowed in the states rights movement by John C. Calhoun, and on the personal side he longed to be with his growing family and grieved over the death of his first son, which occurred in his absence. He took up the law again at home, but in little more than a year he decided on an even more drastic change. Abandoning his law practice and the political honors gained in his native state, he sold his home and moved his family to Mississippi. There, in the remote and rugged frontier state, he owned three plantations and hundreds of slaves, of which he proposed to take personal charge.

Before the Millers left for Mississippi, they enrolled twelve-year-old Mary in Madame Talvande's French School for Young Ladies, a handsome, high-walled boarding school on Legare Street, Charleston, which she entered in the fall of 1835. Ann Marsan Talvande, a refugee from Santo Domingo, was a headmistress with high standards and stern discipline, evidently a superior teacher. Mary soon learned to read and speak French fluently and to read German, among other accomplishments. She quickly became a favorite of Madame, who seated Mary at her right in the dining room. The taste for Gallic culture that she retained through life she formed as Madame Talvande's pupil and admirer. She also formed lasting social ties and friendships among the daughters of the great planters of Carolina tidewater and up-country who were

---

4. William S. Jenkins, *Pro-Slavery Thought in the Old South* (Chapel Hill, 1937), p. 66; see also William W. Freehling, *Prelude to Civil War: The Nullification Controversy in South Carolina, 1816–1836* (New York, 1966).

5. Mary B. Miller to "My dear Father," March 3, 1832, WMC Collection.

6. M. B. C., 1860s Journal, Feb. 18, 1861.

her classmates. Intimate ties with two school servants and friendship with a young mulatto ward of Madame Talvande appear to have planted new attitudes toward the lot of their people in Mary's mind.[7]

Her closest friend was Mary Serena Chesnut Williams, who was a niece of young James Chesnut, Jr., a recent graduate of Princeton. He occasionally called on his niece, and before long James was seen walking on the Battery with her friend Mary Miller. When word of this friendship, perhaps in exaggerated form, reached her father, he decided to withdraw her from school in the fall of 1836 and take her back to Mississippi with her family on their return from a summer in Camden. The change was much against Mary's will at the time, but the overland trip of four weeks or more through strange country, among real Indians, by carriage and horseback, became high adventure. Life in Mississippi, life in "a double log house"—where the nearest neighbor was the great Choctaw chief Greenwood LeFlore—opened her eyes to a world undreamed of in Charleston. Or dreamed of in terms of Chateaubriand's *Atala,* which she was comparing with realities. She saw Indians and slaves and whites all in a new light. "I received there my first ideas," she later wrote, "that negroes were not a divine institution for our benefit—or we for theirs."[8] In her fictional account of her western experience she wrote: "I learned many things not in my school books, while I was away from innocent slumbrous old Charleston, where like other inhabitants I saw no wrong, and am sure I would never have questioned any existing institutions to my dying day."[9]

The Mississippi adventure was cut short for Mary by the consequences of her attendance at a country ball. New suitors appeared and wrote her letters, suitors her parents found more objectionable than those to be risked in Charleston. In the spring of 1837 her father took her back and placed her once more in Madame Talvande's care. The family remained in Mississippi through the summer this time, and all were plagued with illness. In the fall Stephen Miller brought them to Charleston, installed his wife in a hotel, placed Kitty in school with Mary, and enrolled Sally as a day student. The new arrangement, with weekend escapes from school and a mother to intercede with the headmistress for indulgences, delighted Mary. James Chesnut was still persistent, and there were other young men in attendance as well, though young Chesnut maintained an advantage and Mary responded as seriously as her fifteen years permitted and a watchful mother allowed. In a setting of concerts, theater parties, and balls, the courtship thrived.[10]

The winter's revels in Charleston came to a sad end with word in March that Stephen Miller had died in Mississippi. The family moved to Camden to put the younger children in school, and in October Mrs. Miller took Mary with her to Mississippi to settle the debt-burdened estate of her husband. On the way they

---

7. Life at Madame Talvande's school is fully described in chapters 9–12 of "Two Years—Or the Way We Lived Then."

8. Autobiographical memoir, pp. 7–9.

9. Fragment of "Two Years," pp. 139 and 168.

10. Autobiographical memoir, pp. 10–11.

visited in Mobile and New Orleans and then traveled by steamboat up the river to the plantation log house. "We were there—only my mother & myself in a Mississippi swamp alone—with several hundred negroes. We were never frightened except by gangs of wolves who would go howling round the house at night." She described herself as "a bright happy girl then of fifteen" to whom the world seemed "a place where one could be very jolly." Little escaped her on the journey out: how New Orleans Creoles spoke a French different from that of Creoles from Santo Domingo at Madame Talvande's, how much people of the West lived in terror of violence, how different everything was from "slumbrous Charleston." With nothing else at hand in the swamp, she "read & reread" a borrowed copy of Josephus's *History of the Jews* and a chemistry textbook "over & over again." With the help of Uncles Burwell and Alexander Hamilton Boykin, who later joined them, the estate was finally settled, and they were back in Carolina by March.[11]

Letters had followed Mary from Charleston, proposals of marriage from more than one. Before she left for Mississippi, she received "a most elaborate composition" from James Chesnut, Jr. At fifteen, "not caring to marry—not even thinking of it," she had allowed her elders to reply, or she had more or less followed their instructions in writing rejections. At sixteen, however, things looked different, and young Chesnut had persisted for two years and still pressed his case. She was moved enough to transcribe a verse of his dedicated to her in her copybook and to write one there of her own.[12] On returning home she saw him and promised to marry him.

James was then, however, about to sail for Europe with his older brother John, to consult specialists in France about John's failing health. He wrote her a long and fervent love letter on the eve of sailing in May from Charleston, "this City of arrogance and gloom," to which her presence alone had "lent a charm." He sent the letter, together with a diamond ring, by his sister Sally, from whom he kept secret the contents of the package.[13] The brothers were abroad for nearly five months, part of which James spent in England. The French specialists could not find a cure for John's ailments, nor could the doctors he consulted in New York and Philadelphia on their return. He died near the end of December 1839, leaving a wife and six children. Heavy responsibilities fell on the shoulders of James. Fifteen years older than James, John had been heir apparent of their father, Col. James Chesnut of Mulberry, and had assisted him as manager of the family plantation. He had a reputation for political leadership already established.[14]

Probably because of John's death and his family's grief, the marriage of

11. Ibid., 12-22.

12. "To Miss M on leaving for Mississippi," signed "C," Oct. 8, 1858, in copybook dated 1838, in possession of Katherine Herbert, Columbia, S.C. On the flyleaf the signature "Mary B. Miller" appears three times, but over and under these, in her hand, are the initials "M.M.C." once and "M.C." three times.

13. James Chesnut, Charleston, to Mary B. Miller, Camden, May 9, 1839, WMC Collection.

14. John Chesnut, Philadelphia, to Col. James Chesnut, Camden, Oct. 24 and Nov. 6, 1839, WMC Collection.

James and Mary did not take place for nearly four months. Her fiancé was now the only surviving son of Col. James Chesnut, Sr., one of the wealthiest planters of the state, and with prospects for a brilliant future, he was a more desirable match than ever. Born on January 18, 1815, James, Jr., was prepared for college in local schools and was sent to Princeton, where his father and brother had also gone. He finished with honors in 1835 and delivered an "honorary oration" at his graduation. After declining at his father's insistence an appointment as aide to Gov. Pierce Mason Butler, James read law in Charleston under James Louis Petigru, a leader of the national bar, and began practice of his profession at Camden in 1838.[15] He was well launched on his career when his long romance with Mary Miller finally resulted in their marriage on April 23, 1840, at Mount Pleasant, the old Boykin home, where she was born. She had just turned seventeen, the same age at which her mother married. After a round of parties James took his bride to live with his parents and two unmarried older sisters at Mulberry, the chief country seat of the Chesnuts, three miles out of Camden.

For the young bride, Mulberry meant many adjustments—adjustments she never fully made or accepted. Her life till then had been a succession of small triumphs: oldest of her mother's brood, favorite granddaughter of the Boykins, favorite pupil of Madame Talvande, budding belle of the ball in Charleston, adventurous traveler whisking back and forth from the Wild West, bearing tales of New Orleans, steamboat races on the Mississippi, wild Indians, and wolfpacks. Then Mulberry. Mulberry was magnificent, elegant, luxurious—"with everything that a hundred years or more of unlimited wealth could accumulate"—large, airy living quarters with deep window seats; saddle horses, barouches, carriages, coaches for everybody, anytime; servants to do everything and more than were ever needed. In full bloom the place could be lovely, "old oaks, green lawn, and all."[16] Even Mary could at times admit its charm and grace. More often, however, at the thought of Mulberry, she vented her boredom, frustration, and vexation. There were first of all her elders, including sisters-in-law Sarah and Emma (only eleven and ten years her seniors) to cope with, but especially the senior Chesnuts, James père and Mary mère.

Her unforgettable portrait of the old Colonel pictures him in his nineties, but he must have seemed even more formidable to Mary when she was seventeen and he was sixty-seven. "Partly patriarch, partly grand seigneur, this old man is of a species that we will see no more. The last of the lordly planters who ruled this Southern world. He is a splendid wreck. His manners are unequalled still, and underneath this smooth exterior—the grip of a tyrant whose will has never been crossed. . . . He came of a race that would brook no interference with their own sweet will by man, woman, or devil. But then such manners would clear any

15. John Chesnut to James Chesnut, Jr., Dec. 26, 1836, WMC Collection; J. H. Easterly on James Chesnut in *Dictionary of American Biography*, 4:57.
16. 1880s Version of Journal, Nov. 30, 1861, Dec. 25, 1861; Dec. 27, 1864.

man's character—*if it needed it.*" And in Mary's opinion it *did.* She was revolted by what she took to be his brood of colored children and was enraged at his tight-fisted grip on his vast estates, "his gods," and at the way he sometimes baited his impecunious heir. She called him "as absolute a tyrant as the Czar of Russia, the Kahn of Tartary, or the Sultan of Turkey." In spite of all that, a mutual affection and respect of sorts grew and flourished between the old man and his brash daughter-in-law.[17]

If Colonel Chesnut dominated by his impeccable Old World manners, Mary Cox Chesnut used her angelic *goodness,* sweetness, and charity to much the same end—as she did her efficiency, deafness, and composure. She was exasperating, and she was irreproachable. Mary admired her inordinately and choked with impatience. Mrs. Chesnut refused to see evil in anyone or anything, and Mary saw plenty—in herself as well. Mary Cox came of a distinguished Philadelphia family, and after sixty years in the South she refused to eat hominy for breakfast, rice without a relish, or watermelon, sweet potatoes, hot cornbread, or hot buttered biscuits. Yet she denied herself nothing she wanted (including an incredible number of books) and usually had her own sweet way. Every summer in the old days she took off to visit home in Philadelphia "with coaches and four, baggage wagons—children, nurses, outriders, &c &c." She bore fourteen children and lived to bury eleven. She told Mary that when she met her husband as a Princeton student in the 1790s, "they called him there the Young Prince." It was Mary's view that the Prince had met his match. "Somehow I find her the genius of the place," she wrote.[18]

Speaking of the Chesnut family as Mary pictures it at Mulberry, Edmund Wilson writes, "This household of the old-world Chesnuts reminds one of the Bolkonskys of *War and Peace,*" and he goes on to compare Chesnut père with Bolkonsky père, James, Jr., with Prince André, and so on, with the reflection that "comparisons with Russia seem inevitable when one is writing about the old South."[19] Whether Tolstoy's Bolkonskys measured up to Chesnut standards of hospitality is a question. Rarely were many of the six chambers on the second floor or the six on the third vacant, such was the constant stream of guests, mainly relatives, and their servants. Carriages were always pulling up at the house. Endless activity, but it was not to Mary's taste. She glanced around the Christmas dinner table, across the silver, china, and damask, where "the others sat stiff and lifeless as pins stuck in rows—showing only their heads." Their "one absorbing interest" was "Mrs. Chesnut's health—what he eats—what she says—and nothing more." No, no! "These people have grown accustomed to dullness. They were born and bred to it. They like it as well anything else." But not for Mary.[20]

Yet Mary took a perverse pride in Chesnut family history and legend. She cherished and recorded stories of how the old Colonel's grandfather, a Virginia

17. 1880s Version, May 25, 1865; cf. 1860s Journal, May 25, 1865; 1880s Version, Dec. 8, 1861.
18. 1880s Version, May 29, 1862; Nov. 30, 1861; May 25, 1865.
19. Wilson, *Patriotic Gore,* p. 288.
20. 1880s Version, Nov. 30, 1861; Dec. 25, 1861; June 8, 1861.

landowner, under Washington's command was killed in Braddock's defeat in 1755, how his widow fled with her young sons James and John to South Carolina and James began as planter with title to the Mulberry land signed by George II, how John started as a merchant's clerk, took over Mulberry after James's death and expanded his holdings greatly before the Revolution. John suffered serious property losses in the Revolution and for the rest of his life bore scars on his ankles, left by chains while he was prisoner of Lord Rawdon in Charleston.[21]

The Washington-Chesnut legend on both sides of the family fascinated Mary, who half-seriously regarded a Washington connection as the nearest thing to "a patent of nobility in this country." Mary Cox, whose father had served on the general's staff, was a neighbor and close friend of Nelly Custis, a daughter of Martha Washington, "and a great deal thrown with the Washington household" as a girl in Philadelphia.[22] During his tour of the South in his first term, President Washington was entertained by John Chesnut, and in the family archives was a letter from the president to his host, in which he describes the uses of "one of my drill plows," which he was sending Chesnut, as he had promised.[23] On the walls of the hall at Mulberry hung a portrait of Washington by Gilbert Stuart, along with portraits of John and his son James and wife, by the same painter.[24]

John left Mulberry and another plantation to James and divided four more among other descendants, but James eventually purchased and reunited all the divided lands under his ownership. At their maximum his holdings were said to have run to five square miles. In addition to the usual plantation equipment, Colonel Chesnut daily inspected his sawmills, gristmills, tanyards, and brick-yards, and at the landing on the Wateree River lay his boat that, before the railroad came, took his cotton to Charleston.[25] His cellar was famous for its wines. The maximum number of his slaves is unknown, but in 1849 they numbered "about five hundred, all raised on his plantations," and they multiplied rapidly and were not sold. The family legend about their treatment, condition, and contentment was not unusual save in adherents gained outside. A visitor to the slave quarters of two of the plantations in 1849 wrote to her brother in Massachusetts that at "four o'clock we passed many negroes returning from labours, all were clothed in . . . homespun gray, good shoes, and stockings, walking leisurely, the females knitting." She also remarked on the comfort of

21. "Let Sleeping Dogs Lie," MSS in several versions in M. B. C.'s hand, WMC Collection; "The Chesnut Family Chronicle (Compiled by Miss Sally Chesnut at the Dictation of Her Father James Chesnut)," typescript copy by Stephen Miller Williams, in WMC Collection.

22. 1880s Version, Sept. 21, 1861.

23. G. Washington, Mount Vernon, to John Chesnut, Camden, June 26, 1791, photostat of original in WMC Collection.

24. The Stuart paintings of the family are still in family hands, but the one of Washington had to be sold in the 1870s.

25. Sally Chesnut, "The Chesnut Family Chronicles"; Esther S. Davis, *Memories of Mulberry* (n.p., n.d.), pp. 6–10.

their quarters, the attention to religious services, and the "asylum" for slave mothers and children in the summer months.[26]

Mary chafed under the tedium of plantation life but did not escape from it for any length of time until the summer of 1845, when James, Jr., took her, then twenty-two, to Saratoga and Newport to recover from an illness. James's sister Emma went along as far as New York and from there reported a remarkable recovery in Mary. Although the other ladies took seasick out of Charleston harbor, "she was not at all sea sick, went to every meal, & laughed & talked with any body that was well enough to join her."[27] It was a characteristic response of hers on escaping Mulberry. After a month at the resorts the couple impulsively took ship to England for a brief sojourn. Other Northern trips followed in the next few years, visits with prominent relatives of old Mrs. Chesnut in New York, New Jersey, and Philadelphia. One of these trips was prompted by a more serious illness and depression. The latter trouble may have been partly relieved by moving into their own home, built in Camden in 1848, for her spirits picked up the next year.[28] But part of her troubled spirits came of her failure to have a child, for which there proved to be no remedy. Instead, she began a practice she continued through life of borrowing children, beginning with her "little sweet Williams," children of her sister Kate Williams. A new and grander house built in Camden in 1854 and named Kamchatka made that and other entertainment more feasible.

Meanwhile James's political career gained momentum. The year of his marriage he was elected to represent his district in the state legislature, where he served six years, then six in the state senate, of which he was elected president in 1856. Something of an orator in the rotund style of the time, James was no fire-eater but a moderate. Mary, daughter of a nullification leader, was conscious of casting her lot with the opposition in her union with the Chesnuts, for the old Colonel had opposed nullification and remained a unionist all his life. In temperament and personality as well as in politics, James, Jr., was cool and reserved, traits that proved a frequent source of friction with his more volatile and passionate wife. She followed his political course closely and helped with his correspondence and speeches but retained her right to disagree.[29] People turned to James Chesnut not for inspiration and excitement but when steadiness was required. On such occasions, however—and they were increasingly numerous—he had to be asked, sought out. His code precluded self-serving—

26. Lucy Carpenter, Camden, to Dr. William Blanding, Rehoboth, Mass., Jan. 23, 1849, William Blanding Papers, South Caroliniana Library.

27. Emma Chesnut, New York, to James Chesnut, Sr., Camden, July 20, 1845, WMC Collection.

28. Evidence of depression is in exhortations from St. Augustine, Jeremy Taylor, and others, copied in a daybook she kept in 1848–49, now in the hands of Mrs. Katherine Herbert, Columbia, S.C.

29. While James was a delegate to the Nashville Convention of Southerners in 1850, Mary wrote him she was "in danger of turning a regular somerset in *my* politics. . . . particularly I am not the *hearty* lover of slavery that this latitude requires." M. B. C. to James Chesnut, Jr., May 28, 1850, WMC Collection.

another source of Mary's exasperations. His unanimous election to the United States Senate in 1858 was regarded as a victory for the moderates.[30]

Preparations for life in Washington included the selling of Kamchatka, the purchase of one of the old Colonel's plantations for which James gave his bond, and the assembling of an appropriate wardrobe for Mary. On the latter she had advice from her Philadelphia dressmaker, who knew "just what a Senators wife ought to have," particularly "now at the height of balls and parties and every thing in Lace is bought up."[31] After her long rustication, Mrs. Senator Chesnut must have relished the prospects. Her life in the capital in the crisis years of 1859 and 1860 was a lively and exciting experience that she later recalled as "happy days." She was long enough settled in her house on H Street to absorb the full flavor of Washington society and get to know many of its leaders well. Naturally thrown much with the Southern delegation, she formed close ties with the wife of Sen. Louis Wigfall of Texas and the wife of Sen. Clement Clay of Alabama. She also began her attachment to Varina Davis, wife of Jefferson Davis of Mississippi, which deepened considerably later on. The Washington years were interrupted by summer vacations at White Sulphur Springs and visits with her family in North Carolina, Alabama, and Florida. She was returning from a visit to her sister Kate Williams in Florida when she heard the news of Lincoln's election and soon after that of Senator Chesnut's resignation. Characteristically the senator had reserved judgment on secession, but on November 10 he "burned his bridges" and returned home immediately to help draft the ordinance of secession, urge the cause, and then attend the first Confederate Congress in Montgomery.[32]

In the great war that followed, Mary Boykin Chesnut was for the first time to find fulfillment for some of the yearnings that life with her cool and aristocratic husband had somehow denied her. She feared and dreaded the war, but she embraced its demands with all the fierce passion of her nature. It meant outlet for many frustrated impulses and energies dammed up within her. It meant being involved, challenged, needed, wholly committed, and totally absorbed. It also opened doors of escape from dullness and boredom and self-absorption. "My subjective days are over," she wrote in an early entry of her Civil War diary, "no more *silent* eating into my own heart—making my own miseries. . . ."[33] The diary, she vowed, would be "objective," and into it she poured her wartime experiences. As rewritten later for eventual publication, it gives a vivid picture of the life she led during the war and the distraught society around her. In the original diary, however, despite her vow, much that she would have called "subjective" appears that is omitted from the later version—along with new frustrations.

Watching the political and military affairs of the Confederacy with a keen

30. Charles E. Cauthen, *South Carolina Goes to War, 1860–1865* (Chapel Hill, 1950), p. 11.
31. Mary M. Wharton, Philadelphia, to "Dear Madam," Jan. 7, 1859, WMC Collection.
32. Cauthen, *South Carolina Goes to War,* pp. 60–61.
33. 1860s Journal, March 11, 1861.

and critical eye, from an inside and informed point of view, she often exploded with impatience and disgust at the incompetence, stupidity, and inertia she witnessed at high levels. Again and again she would exclaim, "Oh that I were a man!"[34] or "If I had been a man in this great revolution...."[35] The unmistakable implication was that she (or he!) could have managed things better. "Oh if I could put some of my reckless spirit into these discreet cautious lazy men!" she exclaimed.[36] Once, while she was still hoping that James might get the ministry to France, she burst out, "I wish Mr. Davis would send *me* to Paris."[37] Yet when she compared the "meek humble little thing" she had been with "the self-sufficient thing" she had become, she was startled. "I had grown insufferable with my arrogance," she feared.[38] "Why was I born so frightfully ambitious," she wondered.[39]

Her ambitions, in the nature of things, had to find realization through her husband, and James's aristocratic code proved an obstacle. As Mrs. Davis observed to Mary, James was "too high South Carolina" to lift a hand in his own behalf. After his conspicuous service at Sumter and Manassas, military glory seemed open to him. "I feel so deeply mortified that Mr. C will not accept a commission in the army—everybody says he could get whatever he wanted," confessed Mary to her diary. But he would not ask, and Mary would not insist, "because if anything happened what would I feel then?"[40] Her high hopes for the London or the Paris mission then went aglimmering, again because of James's pride, she felt; and to top that, South Carolina failed to return him to the Confederate Senate, largely because of his refusal to turn a hand to get reelected.[41] Instead he accepted the difficult and thankless post in charge of military affairs on the executive council of five that virtually took over the government of South Carolina from the ineffective Gov. Francis W. Pickens. Toward the end of 1862 he returned to Richmond as aide to Jefferson Davis and settled down with his wife across the street from the White House for over a year. Early in 1864, however, he was commissioned brigadier general and sent back to South Carolina to take charge of conscripting very reluctant troops.[42] "Varied as were his duties," says the historian Douglas Southall Freeman, "James Chesnut was, in reality, liaison officer between the Confederacy and South Carolina."[43] As such he bore the brunt of mounting anti-Davis animus in his state.

Mary Chesnut took her disappointments with what composure she could

34. 1860s Journal, Oct. 25, 1861.
35. 1860s Journal, Oct. 17, 1861.
36. 1860s Journal, April 27, 1861.
37. 1860s Journal, Aug. 12, 1861.
38. 1860s Journal, Dec. 7, 1861.
39. 1860s Journal, Aug. 19, 1861; in the revised version this becomes "Why am I so frightfully ambitious?" 1880s Version, Aug. 18, 1861.
40. 1860s Journal, Aug. 19, 1861.
41. 1860s Journal, Aug. 13, 1861; 1880s Version, Nov. 30, Dec. 6, Dec. 16, 1861.
42. Cauthen, *South Carolina Goes to War*, pp. 143-47, 153, 176-77.
43. Douglas Southall Freeman, *The South to Posterity* (New York, 1939), p. 124.

muster. "I am trying to look *defeat* of my personal ambition in the face," she wrote of one. "So if it does come I can bear it better!"[44] And come it did— regularly. The most dreaded consequence was rustication in Camden. Facing one such exile from Richmond, she exclaimed, "I am having such a busy, happy life—so many friends. And my friends are so clever, so charming. And the change to that weary dreary Camden!"[45] Back and forth on jerky trains she traveled from Richmond to "my country," as she called her native state—two long stays and shorter ones at Mulberry, two extended ones in Columbia (much better), and one at Flat Rock, North Carolina, with her sister Kate—these in addition to the earlier shuttles between Montgomery and Charleston. Most of the time, when not ill, she managed to keep quite busy, to some extent in hospital work—rising at 5:00 A.M. for a time—but mainly helping with her husband's work. So pressing were her duties that she seems to have abandoned diary-keeping between August 1862 and October 1863, but otherwise she put in long hours over the multiplying volumes.

The best of times, from Mary's account, were those in Richmond—first in 1861 at the Spotswood, then at the Arlington Hotel, where life was one extended house party and gossip-fest in cramped quarters with the domestic affairs of great and near-great under close scrutiny. The next round at the capital was the year and a half beginning in November 1862, across the street from the Davises. After a few weeks of strained relations with Varina Davis in 1861 that were recorded in her diary but suppressed in the version she intended for publication, Mary swore eternal loyalty to the Davises and remained for life the devoted friend of Varina and champion of Jefferson Davis.[46] In and out of each other's homes constantly in this period, the Chesnuts and Davises were political allies as well as social intimates. Dragging an often reluctant James along, Mary cut a conspicuous role in Richmond high society, especially in political and military circles. With Buck, Mamie, and Tudy, the beautiful daughters of John S. Preston, as houseguests (more borrowed children), Mary was in great demand. She delighted in amateur theatricals, lavish dinners, good wines, and late parties. Freeman, the historian, finds her an "oddly Gallic" figure, difficult to fit into "hungry Richmond" and his "Anglo-Saxon South."[47]

In the background, however, Mary was always hearing strains of the "Dead March," forever burying her lost relatives and friends, and consoling their survivors. Her story is predominantly one of grief, anguish, pessimism, and anxiety, and her role increasingly Cassandra-like rather than one of Gallic gaiety. She knew she was watching "our world, the only world we cared for, literally kicked to pieces," and she told her story "with horror and amazement."[48] The last three months of the war, while Confederate defenses collapsed and Sherman completed his march, Mary spent as a refugee without any

44. 1860s Journal, Aug. 13, 1861.
45. 1880s Version, April 27, 1864.
46. 1860s Journal, July 1861 entries and Aug. 12, 1861.
47. Freeman, *South to Posterity*, p. 128.
48. 1880s Version, March 13, 1862.

negotiable currency, in makeshift quarters first at Lincolnton, North Carolina, then at Chester, South Carolina. When the fighting finally ended, James joined her there, and together they returned through a ruined countryside to Chesnut's Ferry, where they "had not a cent to pay the ferry man—silver being required."[49]

They found Mulberry heavily damaged and pillaged, the mills and gins and all the cotton burned, 100 bales they had counted on for a new start. Old Mrs. Chesnut had died the year before, and the old Colonel, ninety-three, blind and nearly deaf, had lost everything but his land, and it was encumbered by large debts. The former slaves professed to be "more humble & affectionate & anxious" to stay than ever, but Mary expected them to leave when "they can better their condition."[50] The only cash the Chesnuts saw for months was brought in by Molly, Mary's maid, who peddled butter and eggs on shares. Food enough came from the gardens, but there was no money to operate the plantations—not even enough for postage. The death of his father on February 17, 1866, left James in nominal possession of Mulberry and Sandy Hill plantations and eighty-three "slaves" by name, but he was an empty-handed heir more deeply in debt than ever. As executor of the estate, he was required by the Colonel's will made in 1864 to discharge all debts before dividing the property—which proved to be impossible. He was also made responsible for support of the Colonel's numerous female dependents, to be supplied out of money James owed the estate for the plantation he had given bond for before the war.[51]

Mary Chesnut's personal code prohibited whimpering but permitted an occasional shriek. As she wrote her friend Virginia Clay, "there are nights here with the moonlight, cold & ghastly & the whippoorwills, & the screech owls alone disturbing the silence when I could tear my hair & cry aloud for all that is past & gone."[52] In her diary she described herself as "sick at heart" and "ill and miserable," and in moments of hysteria she more than once wished for death.[53] Her illness seemed tied in with spells of depression. Mulberry and Camden had never been good for that, and now they were worse than ever. Gradually her spirits lifted, however, improved no doubt by her sister Kate's son Miller Williams, and later his brother David, coming to live with their aunt in the familiar role of borrowed children. Early in 1867 Mary visited Varina Davis in Charleston and kept up an ongoing correspondence with her and other old friends.[54]

For more than a year after the war, James was adrift about his own plans, but by 1868 he was deeply involved in politics and public affairs and was thus kept

49. Undated entry on flyleaf of the last volume of the 1860s Journal.
50. 1860s Journal, June 1, 1865.
51. Dated Feb. 16, 1864, the will assigned to heirs some four hundred slaves by name. James, Jr., was given Mulberry and Sandy Hill, but he was involved in administering the will the rest of his life. "A True Copy" of the will was attested by the probate judge of Kershaw District, S.C.
52. M. B. C. to Virginia Clay (ca. April 1866), in Wall, ed., "Letters of M. B. C.," p. 73.
53. 1860s Journal, May 15 and 16, 1861.
54. Margaret G. Howell, Fortress Monroe, to M. B. C., Feb. 25, 1867, copy in M. B. C.'s hand. WMC Collection.

away from home much of the time. Mary took over home affairs and shared management of plantation and business in his absence. From her account books it is evident that the family lived on a tight budget at first and cash was sparse indeed.[55] But under the new management the outlook improved enough for the Chesnuts to build a new house in Camden and move into it in 1873. Mary took special delight in her library with a bay window on the first floor of Sarsfield, as they named the new house. She moved all her books, papers, and Confederate mementos into it from the old quarters on the third floor of Mulberry.[56] It was there that at the age of fifty she began the most productive period of her life and in the next ten or eleven years wrote the numerous works discussed above, including the revisions of her diary.[57]

Literary labors in the Sarsfield library were never long uninterrupted. Hard times came knocking at the door in 1875. Debts of the old Colonel's estate, plus debts for the new house, went unpaid, and to raise money the Chesnuts sold the Gilbert Stuart portrait of Washington to a dealer[58] and scrounged for loans. An indigent aunt and her jobless son were added to the Sarsfield household for a time, and more family dependents were to follow. Mary lost one of the dearest of her kin in the death of Johnny Chesnut in 1868 and, most crippling of all, her sister Kate in April and a favorite niece, Kate's daughter Serena, in September 1876. Mary's decline thereafter alarmed the family, and though she pulled out of the depression eventually, she continued to be troubled with old heart and lung ailments and was never completely well the last ten years of her life.[59]

In spite of poor health, she continued to write voluminously when she could get time from her dairy business and the demands of her ever-growing household. Her nephew Miller Williams, who helped manage plantation affairs, married, and his wife and, before long, two babies added much delight to the family at Sarsfield. When Miller and his family moved to Kentucky in 1882, his younger brother David came to replace him. In the meantime Mary's aging mother had also moved in with the Chesnuts, and for a time her sister Sally. All these people made demands on the distracted writer's work time. On the back of a page from the rough draft of her journal revision she once wrote, "One must have solitude at will—for intellectual work," and added, "I have been interrupted three times in trying to *accomplish* this sentence."[60] Nevertheless the manuscript kept piling up at a remarkable rate.

Also, hard times kept knocking. Crop failures and the old debts probably combined with the needs of the extending family to account for extremely

55. "Annual Expense Book," two of them in WMC Collection.

56. M. B. C. to Varina Davis, June 18, 1883, in Wall, ed., "Letters of M. B. C.," p. 84.

57. See above, pp. xxiv–xxv.

58. Correspondence with W. W. Corcoran of Washington in WMC Collection. The portrait wound up in the Library of Congress.

59. On these years Muhlenfeld, "Mary Boykin Chesnut," is indispensable, and the following account is much indebted to it. A correspondent of James refers to Mary as "a patient sufferer of several long years." Thomas F. Drayton to James Chesnut, Nov. 10, 1879, WMC Collection.

60. A loose page not with the bound scratch pads, WMC Collection.

pinched conditions in the early 1880s. Mary wrote of "scraping and saving" to afford small purchases and pay debts of a few dollars.[61] In these circumstances she tried her hand at earning money by her pen: a short piece called "The Arrest of a Spy" expanded from her current revision of the war diary for the Charleston *Weekly News and Courier* series entitled "Our Women in the War." It was accepted and published, and she was paid ten dollars, the only money she received for the only writing she published, so far as is known, during her entire life.[62] It may have meant some encouragement to her, but by that time, at any rate, what she intended as a preliminary draft of the huge revised manuscript of her war journal was nearly finished. The extensive additional work she intended to do in order to put the manuscript in shape for publication was soon cut short by events beyond her control.

For several years things had not gone well for James Chesnut, as one disappointment followed another. Having taken an active role in the conservative opposition to Republican rule and in the campaign that eventually led to the election of Wade Hampton as governor in 1876, he had reasonable expectation of public office. He succeeded in having his franchise restored in 1878, but an office was not forthcoming.[63] His next disappointment came when President Arthur did not offer him an appointment to the new Federal Tariff Commission that he was expected to get in 1882.[64] Late the following year he fell seriously ill and in January 1885 suffered a stroke. While James was in this condition, Mary's mother began to hemorrhage and appeared to be near her end. On February 1 her husband died, and five days later, her mother. The sudden loss of both those nearest her caught Mary in very poor health herself and in desperate circumstances.

Immediately confronting her was a struggle with lawyers to salvage anything whatever from her husband's estate. He had left her everything he owned, but there proved to be extremely little to which she was legally entitled. The will of his father, the old Colonel, had bequeathed him Mulberry and Sandy Hill plantations during his lifetime only. They then went to a male descendant of the Chesnut name, and Mary was denied any income from them. Furthermore she learned that because of James's "failures as a business man (as connected with this estate)," as executor his debts amounted to several times the property he owned.[65] Mary evidently unburdened her accumulated resentments of the

61. M. B. C. to Jane Williams, undated, ca. 1882, in S. Miller Williams papers, privately owned.

62. F. W. Dawson to M. B. C., Jan. 21 and April 8, 1884, WMC Collection; her piece was reprinted with others in F. W. Dawson, ed., *Our Women in the War* (Charleston, 1885). The same story in shorter form is found in the present volume, pp. 459-61.

63. Wade Hampton to James Chesnut, Sept. 21, 1876, WMC Collection; M. C. Butler to James Chesnut, Jan. 14, 1879, WMC Collection.

64. M. C. Butler to James Chesnut, May 10, 1882, WMC Collection; an undated clipping in box 10, WMC Collection, says Chesnut was offered but declined the appointment. No other evidence of an offer has been found.

65. G. N. DeSaussure to M. B. C., Jan. 31, 1886; Edward McCrady, Jr., to David R. Williams, March 15, 1886. Both letters in possession of Mrs. Sally Bland Metts, Camden, S.C.

old Colonel to her trusted friend Varina Davis, who replied: "The miseries that old men entail by their unbridled wills would be understood by mankind if the sex were reversed and women did it."[66] According to Mary, "one by one the things my husband thought he left me have been taken away from me by these Camden lawyers. . . ."[67]

In the end she was left with Sarsfield and an income of a little more than one hundred dollars a year. She never mentioned the antebellum years of wealth and plenty—though they must have crossed her mind often—but she repeatedly mentioned the paltry income to which she was reduced. To supplement that there was only what she could make by her small butter-and-egg enterprise, "about twelve dollars a month," she estimated, "by strict attention to my dairy." With that, she bravely declared, she could still "laugh & gird at the world as of Yore."[68] But the "strict attention" to the dairy she meant quite literally, including concern for the death of a fine bull named Rex, the dropping of a calf that was his last progeny, and the sickness of a cow named Virginia Dare.[69]

As soon as she could find time for writing again, her first thought was of a suitable memorial for her husband, perhaps a biography, and she sought help in filing his papers and advice about the whole enterprise. Varina Davis wrote, "I think your diaries would sell better than any Confederate history of a grave character."[70] After similar advice from another friend, she must have recalled that she *had* earned money that way, and more was certainly needed. There is no evidence that she ever seriously returned to the enormous task of putting the last draft of her revised Journal in final shape. She did, however, write three revised drafts of one section of the manuscript, dealing with the first two weeks of 1864, that she entitled "The Bright Side of Richmond. Winter of 1864—Scraps from a Diary." Describing a series of charades and amateur theatricals, it is in effect an ironic metaphor of a society on the brink of ruin.[71] Perhaps her last effort at writing, the piece was never published.

The spring and summer of 1886 were cheered by the approaching marriage of her nephew David Williams, who continued living at Sarsfield, to Ellen, the daughter of her old admirer ex-Governor John L. Manning, with whom she had flirted at Charleston on the eve of the firing on Fort Sumter. Mary declared the bride to be "as splendidly handsome & clever" as the groom and took genuine pleasure in the wedding, pleased to find that the "young delight to talk to the old woman yet." In the course of her spirited account of the festivities to Virginia Clay in September, she mentioned her "poor weak heart" twice. "Earthquakes for all & Angina Pectoris for me," she put it.[72] The first reference

66. Varina Davis, Beauvoir, Miss., to M. B. C., March 25, 1885, WMC Collection.
67. M. B. C. to Jane Williams, June 21, 1885, S. Miller Williams Papers, in private hands.
68. Ibid.
69. M. B. C. to Jane Williams, Aug. 16, 1885, S. Miller Williams Papers.
70. Varina Davis to M. B. C., March 25, 1885, WMC Collection.
71. All three drafts in WMC Collection.
72. M. B. C. to Virginia Clay, Sept. 12, 1886, in Wall, ed., "Letters of M. B. C."

was to the terrible quake that had recently shattered Charleston, and the angina was an old story with Mary. She had lived with it a long time. An unexpected attack struck her in November. She died the next day, November 22, 1886, at the age of sixty-three, and was buried at Knights Hill, by the side of James.

Of Heresy and Paradox

The bare facts of Mary Chesnut's biography lend themselves more to deepening the paradox than to advancing the explanation of her heresies. Here was the daughter of the man credited with launching the "positive good" defense of slavery and anticipating Calhoun in nullification and states' rights. More than that, she was the wife of the heir to one of the great slave estates of her time, a product and an elite member of a slave society, an intimate of its chief defenders and champions, and a close friend of President and Mrs. Jefferson Davis. And yet she repeatedly declared her hatred for slavery, a loathing she thought exceeded that of its Northern opponents; she called herself an abolitionist, predicted the end of the institution from the beginning of the Civil War, no matter which side won, and rejoiced at the collapse of slavery at the end of the war.

She combined this heresy with a second that was closely associated in her mind with the first—the heresy of militant feminism and defense of oppressed womanhood. This was less paradoxical than the antislavery heresy, since she thought of herself as a victim rather than a beneficiary of the oppression. The element of paradox lay in the thoroughness with which her life was environed by the patriarchal society into which she was born and the unquestioned male dominance and female subordination that it bred. If anything, this institution was more deeply entrenched than slavery, and Mary's reaction to it was, if anything, more vehement.

Overriding these and minor paradoxes was the greater one that enabled her to combine the provinciality of her life with a cosmopolitanism of outlook that often transcended it. Apart from her school days in Charleston and a few months in Mississippi, her one trip abroad, a few antebellum vacations in the North, her two years in Washington, and travels during the war, Mary Chesnut lived her whole life in one community of her native state—the plantation and village life of Camden. Since this is the most easily resolved of the paradoxes, it may be disposed of at once: she overcame the provinciality by her reading. She was a constant, voracious, and passionate reader. One story will suggest the place of books in her life. It was the eve of Columbia's fall to Sherman and she had to leave on the last train from the city, in a hurry, with light baggage. Seeing her off, her husband even persuaded her to leave behind food that proved to be much needed in her flight. But she *did* find room for the works of Shakespeare, Molière, Sir Thomas Browne, *The Arabian Nights* in French, and the letters of Pascal.[1]

---

1. 1880s Version, March 12, 1865 (see p. 761 below).

Her devotion to literature started early and was encouraged by circumstances. At Mulberry the young bride found a library of more than fifteen hundred calf-bound volumes started in the eighteenth century (many of them there now).[2] Her tastes included French literature, classic and contemporary, and she read German critically. But her deepest roots were always in British letters, lore, and history. As she once wrote, "I was always up to my ears in English novels, English reviews, English tall talk."[3] She often bristled at British arrogance, but English opinion and standards claimed her special attention, if not her deference. Mary Chesnut was an Anglophile chastened by French skepticism and American and Southern nationalism. Writing a cousin after "faithfully" reading Taine's *Histoire de la littérature anglaise,* she said she had "read everything he criticizes" and was "as familiar with his Frenchmen that he kept at his elbow as never failing reference in all cases—La Bruyère, Montaigne, Molière, Balzac, &c&c—as I am with his English." She was not impressed. She found Taine "untrue to our ideas as to men and things, *morals and taste,*" and was appalled at his "preferring Alfred de Musset to Shakespeare," and his "finding Addison commonplace & vulgar, Milton as faulty as any &c&c."[4]

A constant inflow of current books and periodicals, American, British, and French, continued until slowed by war and blockade. Few of her English or French contemporaries of stature appear to have escaped her attention. She read as they were published, usually, or as soon as she could get hold of them, the books of Dickens, Carlyle, Trollope, Thackeray, Disraeli, Tennyson, the Brownings, George Eliot, Charlotte Brontë, Charles Kingsley, Charles Reade, and George Meredith. A contemporary book by Balzac, Sand, Dumas, Scribe, Sue, Hugo, or more ephemeral authors was regularly at hand, often borrowed from the Francophile Preston family.

If American letters were a comparable part of her mental furniture, it is not evident from the record. She continued to read and quote Emerson and mentioned a few Northern novels, but their New England origins evidently put her off. With the Southern literary and intellectual community, on the other hand, she was much at home and knew personally many of its members. William Gilmore Simms was a guest in her home and a political supporter of her husband,[5] and she counted the poets Henry Timrod and Paul Hamilton Hayne among her friends. John Reuben Thompson, poet and editor of the *Southern Literary Messenger,* was another member of her intimate circle, as were numerous authors, editors, and aspiring writers of Charleston and Richmond. Scientists such as the LeConte brothers and scholars of several colleges were among

2. A bound volume listing some fifteen hundred books by short title was prepared in the 1890s, but is not assumed to be complete. WMC Collection.

3. 1870s Version, Jan. 1, 1864.

4. M. B. C. to Mary Kirkland, March 3 [1873], "My fiftieth birthday," in possession of the Chesnut estate.

5. William Gilmore Simms to James Chesnut, Jr., Feb. 5, 1852, WMC Collection; Simms to Chesnut, Jan. 12, 1854, Simms Papers, South Caroliniana Library.

her associates. She was on close terms with William Henry Trescot, historian and diplomat, and with L. Q. C. Lamar, through whom she met Lamar's father-in-law, Augustus Baldwin Longstreet, author of *Georgia Scenes*. The school of southwestern humorists to which he belonged appealed to her, and she referred to their stories often. She was never overly impressed with the Southern literati, but she knew them and kept up with their work.

Another intellectual interest of Mary Chesnut, mainly inspired by the Civil War and her efforts to come to terms with it, was history. She began with a keen sense of participating in historical drama of world significance. Early in the war she manifested a playful impulse toward comparative history and soon developed an interest in other rebellions (slave rebellions included), revolutions, struggles for independence, invasions, defenses, and wars generally—all with a view to gaining perspective on the struggle in which her own people were involved. "Having lived on the battlefield," the Revolutionary battlefields near Camden, she had read a surprising number of revolutionary memoirs, English and American. Clarendon on the English Civil War, Motley on the Dutch Republic, and Carlyle on the French Revolution were at hand, and she reached out for more. A list of "books wanted" in October 1861 included four histories of England. Having hit on Creasy's *Decisive Battles* with relish, Mary was soon spicing her references to daily news with learned references to "Anabasis business" and "Thermopylae business" and to more recent "Moscow business." To keep abreast of the news, she read several local papers in addition to Richmond and Charleston newspapers every day as well as a surprising number of New York newspapers, even in wartime.

Mary Boykin Chesnut was a provincial in a residential sense only. Her mind roved widely over the world of her time and reached out to the past as well. She carried on an eighteenth-century Southern tradition of the plantation intellectual, which was not without worthy precedent. It is interesting to speculate about what figure she might have cut (had her ambition for one of the foreign missions for her husband been realized) in the salons of Paris or London. She could probably have held her own quite well.

The antislavery paradox is rather more complicated. To resolve one question right off, however, there is no reason to suspect that her position on slavery was the consequence of arrière-pensée or the result of hindsight. She had made her views known quite early. In 1842, when she was nineteen, she put them in a letter to her husband. Of this letter she writes: "It is the most fervid abolition document I have ever read. I came across it burning letters the other day. That letter I did not burn. I kept it—as showing how we were not as much of heathens down here as our enlightened enemies think."[6] In her autobiographical novel she suggests that she held such views even earlier, at the age of fourteen. There she quotes the father of her fictional counterpart as calling her "a rabid

6. 1880s Version, Nov. 27, 1861 (p. 246). The 1842 letter has not been found, but see also p. 730.

abolitionist" who was "seized with horror of me as a slave owner."[7] That, of course, is questionable evidence. More to the point is the declaration in her original Journal, a month before the war began, that "Sumner said not one word of this hated institution that is not true. . . . God forgive us but ours is a *monstrous* system, and wrong and iniquity."[8] No Southerner and few Americans went further than that. Charles Sumner said a great many words about slavery, and one of the most noted replies and rebukes to him was delivered by Sen. James Chesnut, Jr., of South Carolina.

Mary Chesnut appears to have made no secret of her heretical opinions, and her outspokenness was probably one cause of the chill of which she complained around Camden. James Team, a Chesnut overseer who shared her view that most white women of the South were "abolitionists in their hearts, and hot ones too," went on to say: "Mrs. Chesnut is the worst. They have known that on her here for years."[9] Mary was given to exaggeration in her insistence on the amount of antislavery sentiment among Southern women. "And they hate slavery worse than Mrs. Stowe," she declared.[10] She was more specific in her discernment of generational and class distinctions in attitudes toward slavery. Among the young in the very wealthiest planter families of her circle (and that circle included virtually all those with a hundred or more slaves) she encountered outspoken unorthodoxy during the war. "Those Preston and Hampton boys loathe slavery—and all its commitments," she wrote. And so did their sisters, even more vocally. She thought it worth adding that the Hampton estate in Mississippi had more than fifteen hundred slaves. Her nephew Johnny Chesnut was "not sound on the goose either, but then it takes four negroes to wait on him—satisfactorily." Asked why they fought, they would likely answer, " 'Southern rights—whatever that is.' "[11]

Her heresies on slavery did not inspire unorthodoxy on race. Moved as she was by their plight and affectionate and close as her relations could be with personal slaves, she never seriously challenged orthodox assumptions about the innate inferiority of the enslaved people. She was indeed capable of casually dropping such stereotypes as "dirty, slatternly, idle, ill smelling by nature" in reference to them in the mass.[12] Referring to slaves of her own family, she fell into the conventional pattern of making an exception. "When I hear everybody complaining of their negroes," she wrote in 1861, "I feel we are blessed, ours are so well behaved and affectionate—a little lazy but that is no crime."[13] The explanation, implied or explicit, was the familiar one that good treatment bred contentment. She was proud to boast that her husband never bought but one slave, and that at the slave's own request, to keep a family intact. But she was

7. Fragment of "Two Years of My Life," p. 163.
8. 1860s Journal, March 18, 1861 (quoted below, p. 29; reproduced p. 30).
9. 1880s Version, Dec. 6, 1861 (p. 255).
10. 1880s Version, Nov. 27, 1861 (p. 245).
11. 1880s Version, March 5, 1862 (p. 298), May 6, 1862 (p. 334).
12. 1880s Version, Nov. 27, 1861 (p. 245).
13. 1860s Journal, Nov. 12, 1861 (p. 235).

candid to admit she relished the attentions of skilled servants who anticipated every wish.[14]

From the outset of the war Mary Chesnut watched the black faces around her for any sign of change. For the most part she marveled at seeing none whatever. They seemed as quiet and respectful as ever. She called them "sphinxes" and wondered what went on behind "their black masks." Laurence, James's man, took charge of their cash and did all their shopping; Ellen, her maid, returned her jewels as if they were so many garden peas; Isaac McLaughlin took care of the family silver. "Why don't they all march over the border?" she wondered.[15] Minor, personal mutinies she noted, and she was disturbed at the defection of some of Jefferson Davis's hired slaves. The great shock, the murder of her cousin Betsey Witherspoon by her slaves, came early in the war and had no apparent relation to it. From the start of the war Mary Chesnut assumed that "slavery has to go of course—and joy go with it." A year later she professed amazement that "there are people who still believe negroes to be property."[16] She thought that if anything could reconcile her to a failure of the South to gain its independence "it is Lincoln's proclamation freeing the negroes." And when it was over she shared "an unholy joy" with her husband at the end of slavery.[17]

Abhorrence of slavery and welcome of its abolition did not prevent Mary Chesnut from embracing many aspects of the romantic Southern legend. She could tell stories of cruelty, brutality, and sadism that matched any the abolitionist agitators had to tell, but they were the acts of "bad" masters. She was not unaware of the unconscious callousness and heedless injustice of "good" masters nor of the blind hypocrisy and self-righteousness of some of them. Little of that escaped her, and she was unsparing of illustrations. On the other hand she told many stories that suggested the loyalty, affection, and content-ment of slaves, their response to paternalistic benevolence, and their devoted service under stress. She did cite instances of treachery, violence, and rebellion among slaves, but on the whole the balance tipped the other way.

The underlying motive in her attention to paternalistic benevolence seems to have been defense of her own people against Northern propaganda rather than defense of slavery itself. What did they know of the evils of slavery, and what did they suffer as compared with Southern white women trapped in the midst of it? They sat in their quiet New England libraries and relieved their consciences by writing outrageous indictments of the South when they did not know the half of it. Mary was frankly intent (as quoted above) upon "showing how we were not as much of heathens down here as our enlightened enemies think." Part of her strategy was to divert attention from the South by appeal to comparative history. "Virtue in a nation is a matter of latitude and longitude," she wrote. "Look at the English in India, or even in Ireland, the French in

14. 1880s Version, Nov. 28, 1863 (pp. 488 and 490).
15. 1880s Version, July 24, 1861 (pp. 113–14).
16. 1880s Version, June 29, 1861 (p. 88); April 29, 1862 (p. 331).
17. 1880s Version, July 3, 1862 (p. 407).

Algiers—both in Turkey." She thought that "Russia ought to sympathize with us. We are not as bad as this even if Mrs. Stowe's word be taken. Brutal men with unlimited power are the same all over the world."[18]

Men and their unlimited power are the thesis of her feminist heresy. But it is interwoven with the antislavery heresy, and neither is completely intelligible without reference to the other. In fact they do much to explain each other.

The plight of the slaves—mistreatment, injustice, oppression—was part of Mary Chesnut's case against slavery, but only a part and not the main part. Her bitterest indictment was what slavery did to the wives, children, and families of the masters, as well as to the masters themselves. Like the slaves, women were all subject to the absolute authority of the patriarchal system. The feature that most offended her was the sexual abuse of the slave women—"we live surrounded by prostitutes"—and their offspring. The men were probably "no worse than men everywhere—but the lower the mistresses the more degraded they must be." And yet "they seem to think themselves patterns—models of husbands and fathers."[19] What outraged her beyond endurance was the hypocrisy of the stern puritanical code these libertarian patriarchs imposed on their womenfolk and children.

In a dozen ways she equated the plight of women with that of slaves, not only in a slave society but elsewhere as well. They were bought and sold, deprived of their liberty, their property, their civil rights, and the equal protection of the law, humiliated and reduced to abject dependency. "There is no slave after all like a wife," she declared. Sufficiently provoked, she could go further: "All married women, all children and girls who live in their father's houses are slaves."[20] It was no wonder that "our women of the planters' wives caste—if they were not *notable* &c, took to patent medicine & hypochondria."[21] To her mind it was their abject plight that accounted for the celebrated personality of Southern womanhood. "So we whimper and whine do we? Always, we speak in a deprecatory voice do we? And sigh gently at the end of every sentence," and "they say our voices are the softest, sweetest in the world." If so, it could be because "we are afraid to raise our voices above a mendicant moan."[22]

Any search for possible sources of inspiration for these heretical ideas in South Carolina could hardly overlook the rebellion of another South Carolina woman of the previous generation. Sarah M. Grimké of Charleston, sister of Angelina Grimké, published her *Letters on the Equality of the Sexes and the Condition of Women*[23] in 1838, while Mary was a schoolgirl at Madame Talvande's. No reference to this work has been found in any writings of Mary Chesnut. In spite

---

18. 1880s Version, Sept. 1, 1864 (p. 642); April 23, 1865 (p. 793).
19. 1860s Journal, March 18, 1861 (pp. 29–31).
20. 1880s Version, May 9, 1861 (p. 59), Feb. 25, 1865 (p. 729).
21. Autobiographical fragment, "We called her Kitty," p. 19.
22. 1880s Version, Feb. 26, 1865 (p. 735).
23. Published in Boston.

of similarities between the ideas the two South Carolina women held of slavery and feminism, there is no evidence of a direct influence of Grimké on Chesnut.

Mary Chesnut was a shrewd and original observer of the human comedy on her own, particularly the man-woman parts of it. Flirtations, philanderings, fornications, courtships, and marriages passed under review, and marriage came off little better than the patriarchy and slavery as an institution. "What a blessed humbug domestic felicity is," she observed. Its fortunes did not depend on what the partners "felt or thought about each other before they had any possible way of acquiring accurate information as to character, habits, &c. Love makes it worse." It raises impossible expectations. At best, marriage is a compromise—"if they have common sense they make believe and get on—so so." "It is only in books that people fall in love with their wives." Men were the main offenders, "blustering around . . . to show that they are the masters." For all men's blunders and mistakes, wives were somehow to blame. "Dogmatic man rarely speaks at home but to find fault or ask the reason why. Why did you go? or why, for God sake, did you come?"[24]

Given the contrast of temperaments and the conflicts of interests between Mary Chesnut and her husband, it is natural to look to their domestic relations for clues to her rebellious feminism. Need for caution on this matter, however, is indicated. It is true that they had their difficulties. Both partners to the union took an obvious interest in the attentions of other members of the opposite sex, and each gave signs of resenting such interests on the part of the other. Since Mary recorded at least some of her experiences and James did not, the evidence is one-sided. It is clear, however, that Mary at times took pleasure in James's jealousy and that she suspected him of carrying some of his adventures further than she did her own. After an improbable plea of mistaken identity that James offered to explain the effusive greetings he received on the street from a handsome woman she did not know, Mary exclaimed, "What a credulous fool you must take me to be!"[25] How much of his coolness and reserve on which she often commented entered into their personal relations is not clear. But it is clear that they shared intervals of warm companionship and could talk at length of war and politics and art and the preposterous human condition on terms of relative equality. She certainly did not think of James as a typical patriarch. None of the charges of dalliance in the slave quarters was aimed at him. Insofar as they were personal, they were directed rather at his father.

Whatever her personal experience, it is evident that Mary Boykin Chesnut was not one of the craven white domestic "slaves" she wrote about. She was no whimperer or whiner, and her voice was not the sweetest or the softest. Something of a Cassandra she turned out to be, but the fortunes of war determined that role. More characteristic of her was her laughter, and all the repressive provinciality of Mulberry and Camden could not smother that. "Thank God it

24. 1880s Version, Aug. 29, 1861 (p. 173); July 3, 1862 (p. 407); Jan. 1, 1864 (p. 523).
25. 1880s Version, May 8, 1864 (pp. 605–06).

is *irrepressible*," she declared, "and I will laugh at the laughable while I breathe."[26] Nor could the weight of patriarchal authority mold her into any of its conventional patterns or crush her indomitable individuality. So long as there was a Mary Chesnut, there would be heresy and paradox of some sort in South Carolina.

26. 1870s Version, Sept. 22, 1864 (p. 645).

Editorial Problems and Policies

Among the reasons for undertaking this edition of Mary Chesnut's book are the excessive liberties taken by previous editors. To replace their work with a more elaborate and complete edition claiming license for erratic and unacknowledged editorial interventions, changes, and deletions would be to invite an ironic outcome of the enterprise. Some liberties will have to be claimed, but they will be taken with full notice and explanation. The general purpose will be to publish *what* the author wrote and, insofar as appears practicable within the rules adopted, *how* she wrote it. Both the *what* and the *how* present difficulties.

What she wrote included a great many quotations from her reading. The original 1860 Journal contains a large number of them, and she retained numerous passages of the sort and occasionally added some in the 1880s Version. When they are of apparent relevance they are preserved, but otherwise they are deleted. Also frequently deleted are characterizations or descriptions of persons whom she refrains from identifying. Deletions are indicated and explained in footnotes.

The problems presented by *how* she wrote are more numerous and complicated. It should be remembered that Mary Chesnut left the last draft of her manuscript unfinished. Her proclaimed intention to "overhaul it again—and again" remained unfulfilled at the time of her death. The manuscript was left virtually devoid of the extensive interlinear revision characteristic of other manuscripts she worked over and polished—works that proved her capable of astute self-criticism. (Editorial tinkering with the manuscript done in handwriting other than her own, if so identified, has been ignored.) Lacking the correction and polish the author might have given it, the manuscript is also encumbered with numerous eccentricities and idiosyncrasies of her own, many of which she probably would not, even with ample opportunity, have removed. These include some quite erratic capitalization, punctuation, and spelling. Capitalization is often rather random, and in any event the distinction in her handwriting between capital and lowercase letters for almost half the alphabet is often arbitrary. Punctuation is largely a matter of dashes of varied length, and quotation marks are employed with high disregard for consistency. Her writing suggests an aristocratic scorn of detail that could be left to others. In spelling, she frequently made two words out of one: "bed side," "stair case," "any thing," "any how," "every body," "friend ship," "break fast," "inter view," "to day," "my self," "with in," and "with out." She sometimes preferred English spelling but often used the American equivalent. A few words—"dispair," "dispite," and "discribe," for example—followed an orthography all her own. Spelling at times seems to have approximated her pronunciation, as in "tobacca," and unfamiliar proper names regularly came off the way they sounded. She spelled McLean three different ways. Overseer Team became Teams if the cadence of the sentence required, and Mr. Chesnut's valet was Laurence or Lawrence, depending apparently on whim.

Some of Mrs. Chesnut's mannerisms were those of her time, such as the superscription and underlining in M̲ᵣ and M̲ʳˢ. Some were of her own making, such as the French use of the dash in dialogue to introduce each speaker—though she often combined the dash with quotation marks. She was lavish in the use of abbreviations and ampersands and the substitution of initials for names. These eccentricities were as characteristic of her original Journal as of the 1880s Version, and in the Journal, syntax received even less attention. In the later version, however, the number of eccentricities, idiosyncrasies, and spelling errors averages about thirty-four to the typewritten page of literal transcription and can run to twice that number or more on some pages.

To preserve tens of thousands of oddities and errors in a formal edition out of literal regard for some standard of textual scholarship seems misguided. Such an editorial policy would be of doubtful fairness to the author and a distraction rather than a service to the reader. Care has been taken not to "improve" her writing or change its substance, but her spelling, capitalization, and punctuation have been regularized, though the edited text still preserves rather more dashes than usual. American spellings are adopted as the norm, instead of English alternatives. Some eccentric spellings are retained (Mrs. Chesnut probably said "Texian" or "Texican" instead of "Texan"), as is her abbreviation "&c" for "et cetera." Initials in place of names are left unchanged when the reference is clear. She very likely called her husband "Mr. C" or "J. C." With these and some other exceptions, abbreviations and contractions, including ampersands, have been silently expanded. Military and political titles are given standard abbreviations when used with the full name, but spelled out with the last name only—for example, Gen. Robert E. Lee but General Lee. All titles of books, periodicals, and newspapers and names of ships have been italicized.

The original paragraphing has been retained insofar as Mrs. Chesnut's divisions are intelligible or recognizable. Some liberties have been taken in quotations from the 1860s Journal, which often has no paragraphing. Indentations, which on the manuscript page vary widely, have been made uniform, as have the lines often used to separate paragraphs and sections of an entry. The manner of dating entries has been made uniform save for an occasional "Christmas Day" or "New Year's"; where errors in dating, such as the wrong month or year, are corrected, the change is noted and explained. Obvious slips of the pen or unintentional repetitions, however, are silently corrected. Conjectural words or passages supplied by the editor are placed in square brackets, save where the missing element is small and obvious. Explanatory insertions by the editor to indicate, for example, a missing or torn page are similarly bracketed but are italicized. All ellipses are the editor's, not the author's, and are not bracketed. Effaced or erased passages that are restored by the editor are printed in angle brackets < >. The author indicates omissions by x x x x.

Other editorial interventions remain to be accounted for and explained. Mary Chesnut made no divisions in her thousands of pages save those of the dated entries and mid-page rules within or between entries. For the sake of readability, the editor has divided the book into chapters and has given them titles. Where feasible, the title is a phrase quoted from the chapter and was selected to suggest its predominant subject matter. The author's treatment of her experiences and impressions lends itself to such divisions, but she left no overt clue of this intention. She also left no title for her book, so far as is known, and the one used for this edition is the choice of the editor.

The selection and use of texts presented unusual problems and exceptional opportunities. As pointed out above, for almost all parts of the book there is more than one version, and for some parts, several. There could be little hesitation in choosing the "final" version of the 1880s as the basic copy text. The real question was what use to make of other versions available to the editor, especially the surviving parts of the original 1860s Journal, which parallel about one-third of the 1880s Version. In this decision conflicting obligations and values make their demands. Insofar as her writing is a conscious work of art, the author's final judgment deserves utmost respect. But whatever art is brought to bear, the subject matter purports to be factual, not fictional. As "diary" it partakes of both autobiography and history and is offered as a faithful account of real people and events and the writer's perception of them. Is it the primary obligation of the editor to confine what he includes strictly to the final (though unfinished) copy text? If so, he will in effect find himself at times silently concurring with the author's decision to withhold from the reader information, incidents, views, and motives that are significant, relevant, important, and sometimes essential to a full understanding of the author and the events of which she is writing. To withhold such information runs very much against the grain of the historian's instincts and values. On the other hand, if the editor intervenes with information from other texts (however scrupulously identified), will he not violate the author's intent and the integrity of a work of art? Perhaps there is no entirely satisfactory way in this instance of reconciling the obligation to history with the obligation to art.

Although full commitment to the final 1880s Version as copy text is retained, excerpts from the other versions and especially from the original 1860s Journal are occasionally used to complement and supplement the 1880s Version. Instead of being relegated to appendices or footnotes, however, such excerpts are inserted directly into the text as near as possible to the place from which they were omitted (if from the 1860s Journal) or where they are most relevant (if from another version). They are always placed within double angle brackets 《   》 and, unless they are identified in footnotes as being from some other version, they are from the 1860s Journal. Unless a different date is indicated in a footnote, the excerpt is from an entry of the same date in the quoted version as the one in which it is inserted. In her 1880s Version, Mrs. Chesnut frequently telescoped or combined under one date entries from more than one date in an earlier version. While deletions from the copy text are both indicated and explained, those in inserted excerpts from other versions are only indicated by ellipses but are not explained. No effort will be made to point out all differences between the 1880s Version and earlier ones, but departures that appear to the editor to be of significance and relevance will be noted or inserted in the text in the manner indicated. The editor is quite aware that the insertion of excerpts does some violence to the integrity of the final version and that this will not please some scholars. It is hoped, however, that the enrichments and new dimensions such excerpts add to the book and the convenience and illumination they provide the reader will more than compensate for the losses.

In rare instances (only three in the entire book) and for exceptional reasons, parts of other versions are substituted for parts of the 1880s Version. The first instance is the very opening pages of the book. Mrs. Chesnut drafted at least three alternative openings and appears never to have decided which to use. All three surviving draft fragments are mutilated or incomplete, or the pages are misnumbered. All are evidently based on an original version in which she summarized the three months before she began keeping her Journal regularly. It is this original version that is substituted for the others. The remaining substitutions are taken from one of the various drafts of the sketches she called "The Bright Side of Richmond. Winter of 1864—Scraps from a Diary." Written near the end of her life with a view to separate publication, this is a polished revision and expansion of a segment of the 1880s Version, which she apparently scratched up in the process of preparing the new revision.

In the annotation all persons mentioned, with a few exceptions, are identified upon first reference if it has proved possible to identify them. With a few exceptions, the facts are only brought up to the time the person is introduced in the text. In addition to those who could not be found are a number considered too well known to require identification. Specific literary references and quotations are identified when possible, but not all literary allusions. No attempt has been made to keep the reader posted in footnotes on the progress of the Civil War, nor was it thought necessary to correct all the false rumors of war news Mary Chesnut records. Some she herself corrects and some seem unnecessary to correct.

The scholar who wishes to compare the original 1860s Journal with any of the later versions, in all their complexities and all their eccentricities, will find the surviving parts of all manuscripts at the South Caroliniana Library at the University of South Carolina. A copy flow reproduction of them is available at the Sterling Memorial Library, Yale University, and literal typescript transcriptions, carefully collated, are to be found at the Southern Studies Program, Lieber College, University of South Carolina.

Editorial Symbols

[   ]   Used for two purposes: (1) to enclose conjectural words or passages supplied by the editor and (2) to enclose in italics explanatory insertions.

< >   To enclose effaced or erased passages restored by the editor.

《 》   To enclose excerpts from other versions inserted in the text. Unless identified in footnotes as being from some other version, they are from the 1860s Journal.

. . .   To indicate deletions by the editor, which are explained when occurring in the 1880s Version but are not explained in other versions.

Mary Chesnut's Civil War

I

Road to Montgomery

《**February 18, 1861.**[1] Conecuh. Ems. I do not allow myself vain regrets or sad foreboding. This Southern Confederacy must be supported now by calm determination and cool brains. We have risked all, and we must play our best, for the stake is life or death. I shall always regret that I had not kept a journal during the two past delightful and eventful years. The delights having exhausted themselves in the latter part of 1860 and the events crowding in so that it takes away one's breath to think about it all. I daresay I might have recorded with some distinctness the daily shocks—"Earthquakes as usual" (Lady Sale).[2] But now it is to me one nightmare from the time I left Charleston for Florida, where I remained two anxious weeks amid hammocks and everglades, oppressed and miserable, and heard on the cars returning to the world that Lincoln was elected and our fate sealed. Saw at Fernandina a few men running up a wan Palmetto flag and crying, South Carolina has seceded.[3] Overjoyed at the tribute to South Carolina, I said, "So Florida sympathizes." I inquired the names of our *few* but undismayed supporters in Florida. Heard Gadsden, Holmes, Porcher, &c&c—names as inevitably South Carolina's as Moses or Lazarus are Jews'. When we arrived in Charleston, my room was immediately over a supper given by the city to a delegation from Savannah, and Colonel Bartow, the mayor of Savannah,[4] was speaking in the hot, fervid, after-supper Southern style. They contrived to speak all night and to cheer &c. I remember liking one speech so much—*voice,* tone, temper, sentiments, and all. I sent to ask the name of the orator, and the answer came: "Mr. Alfred Huger."[5] He may not have been the wisest or wittiest man there—but certainly when on his legs he had the best of it that night. After such a night of impassioned Southern eloquence I traveled next day with (in the first place, a

---

1. The opening pages of the original 1860s Journal are substituted for subsequent revisions, all three of which are either incomplete or mutilated. Clearly derived from the original, all these versions summarize experiences of M. B. C. during the three months before she began keeping her diary. "Conecuh" is the southern Ala. county where her younger brother, Stephen Decatur Miller, Jr., had his plantation. "Ems" seems to be her nickname for her mother, Mary (Boykin) Miller, who then lived with Stephen.
2. Lady Florentia (Wynch) Sale accompanied her husband, Maj. Gen. Robert Sale, during the ill-fated British attempt to conquer Afghanistan. This line from Lady Sale's *A Journal of the Disaster in Affghanistan, 1841–1842* (1843) epitomizes her stoical acceptance of hardship.
3. Somewhat prematurely, since S.C. did not secede until Dec. 20, 1860.
4. Francis Stebbins Bartow was a delegate to the Ga. secession convention, a member of the Provisional Confederate Congress, and colonel of the C.S.A., but never mayor of Savannah.
5. A planter and prominent Unionist serving as postmaster of Charleston.

racking nervous headache and a morphine bottle, and also) Colonel Colcock,[6] formerly member of Congress, and U.S. Judge Magrath,[7] of whom likenesses were suspended, in the frightfullest signpost style of painting, across various thoroughfares in Charleston. The happy moment seized by the painter to depict him, while Magrath was in the act, most dramatically, of tearing off his robes of office in rage and disgust at Lincoln's election.

《 My father was a South Carolina nullifier, governor of the state at the time of the nullification row, and then U.S. senator. So I was of necessity a rebel born. My husband's family being equally pledged to the Union party rather exasperated my zeal, as I heard taunts and sneers so constantly thrown out against the faith I had imbibed before I understood anything at all about it. If I do yet.

《 I remember feeling a nervous dread and horror of this break with so great a power as U.S.A., but I was ready and willing. South Carolina had been so rampant for years. She was the torment of herself and everybody else. Nobody could live in this state unless he were a fire-eater. Come what would, I wanted them to fight and stop talking. South Carolina—Bluffton, Rhetts, &c[8] had exasperated and heated themselves into a fever that only bloodletting could ever cure—it was the inevitable remedy.

《 So I was a seceder, *but* I dreaded the future. I bore in mind Pugh's letter, his description of what he saw in Mexico when he accompanied an invading army.[9] My companions had their own thoughts and misgivings, doubtless, but they breathed fire and defiance.

> Their bosoms they bared to the glorious strife
> And their oaths were recorded on high
> To prevail in the cause that was dearer than life
> Or crushed in its ruins to die.[1]

Consequently they were a deputation from Charleston, risen against tyrants to her representatives in Columbia, telling them they were too slow, to hurry up, dissolve the Union, or it would be worse for them. There was a fire in the rear of the hottest.

《 At Kingsville I met my husband. He had resigned his seat in the Senate U.S. and was on his way home.[2] Had burned the ships behind him. No hope now—he was in bitter earnest.

6. William Ferguson Colcock, collector of the Port of Charleston.

7. Andrew Gordon Magrath, former judge of the U.S. District Court for S.C., was a delegate to the state secession convention from St. Michael's and St. Philip's parishes, Charleston.

8. The Bluffton Movement of 1844 was a short-lived attempt to nullify the tariff of 1842. The movement's leader, Robert Barnwell Rhett, Sr., then a congressman representing Beaufort and Colleton districts, went on to become the state's most prominent secessionist agitator and a member of the S.C. delegation to the Montgomery convention. His son, Robert Barnwell Rhett, Jr., had edited the influential Charleston *Mercury* since 1857.

9. U.S. Senator George Ellis Pugh of Ohio, a pro-Southern Democrat who had been a member of the Chesnuts' "mess" at Brown's Hotel in Washington.

1. Paraphrased from the first four lines of "Stanzas on the Threatened Invasion, 1803," by Scottish poet Thomas Campbell (1777–1844).

2. James Chesnut, Jr. (J. C.), resigned on Nov. 10, 1860.

⟪I thought him right—but going back to Mulberry to live was indeed offering up my life on the altar of country. Secession was delayed—was very near destroyed. The members were rushing away from Columbia. That band of invincibles certainly feared smallpox. But they adjourned to Charleston, and the decree was rendered there. Camden was in unprecedented excitement. Minutemen arming, with immense blue cockades and red sashes, some with sword and gun, marching and drilling.

⟪I spent Christmas at Combahee[3]—a most beautiful country seat. Live oaks in all their glory, camellias as plentiful on the lawn as the hawthorn in an English hedge.

⟪Mrs. Charles Lowndes was with us when the secession ordinance came. We sat staring in each other's faces. She spoke first. "As our days, so shall our strength be."[4] I am truly glad I have seen those lovely Combahee places—they are so exposed, they will doubtless suffer from invasion.

⟪We soon returned to Charleston. At Mrs. Gidiere's[5] we had a set of very pleasant people. Our rage for news was unappeasable—and we had enough. One morning Mrs. Gidiere, coming home from market, announced Fort Sumter seized by the Yankee garrison. Pickens, our governor,[6] sleeping serenely.

⟪One of the first things which depressed me was the kind of men put in office at this crisis, invariably some sleeping deadhead long forgotten or passed over. Young and active spirits ignored, places for worn-out politicians seemed the rule—when our only hope is to use *all* the talents God has given us. This thing continues. In every state, as each election comes on, they resolutely put aside everything but the inefficient. To go back to Pickens the 1st and South Carolina. Very few understood the consequences of that quiet move of Major Anderson.[7] At first it was looked on as a misfortune. Then, as we saw that it induced the seizure of U.S. forts in other states—we thought it a blessing in disguise. So far we were out in the cold alone. And our wise men say if the president had left us there to fret and fume awhile with a little wholesome neglect, we would have come *back* in time. Certainly nobody would have joined us. But Fort Sumter in Anderson's hands united the cotton states—and we are here in Montgomery to make a new Confederacy—a new government, constitution, &c&c.

⟪I left them hard at it and came on a visit to my mother.⟫

3. The Combahee River rice plantation of William Lennox Kirkland, who married M. B. C.'s first cousin, Mary Miles Withers.

4. Sabina Elliott (Huger) Lowndes, wife of Combahee River planter Charles Tidyman Lowndes. The passage alludes to Deuteronomy 33:25.

5. Mrs. P. R. Gidiere ran a Charleston boardinghouse.

6. Francis Wilkinson Pickens, former congressman and U.S. minister to Russia, was elected governor three days before S.C. seceded, as part of a last-minute compromise between radical and moderate secessionists in the state legislature.

7. Maj. Robert Anderson's decision to move the Federal garrison from Fort Moultrie to less vulnerable Fort Sumter. Governor Pickens, like other Southern governors, viewed the action as a violation of Federal assurances that the status of Southern forts would remain unchanged.

II

Nation in the Making

February 19, 1861. I left the brand-new Confederacy making—or remodeling—its Constitution. Everybody wanted Mr. Davis to be general in chief or president.

Keitt and Boyce[1] and a party preferred Howell Cobb[2] for president. And the fire-eaters per se wanted Barnwell Rhett.

Today at dinner, Stephen brought in the officers of the Montgomery Blues. "Very soiled Blues," they said, apologizing for their rough condition.

Poor fellows! they had been a month before Fort Pickens and not allowed to attack it. They said Colonel Chase[3] built it and he was sure it was impregnable.

Colonel Lomax[4] telegraphed to Governor Moore[5] "if he might try, Chase or no Chase," and got for his answer no.

"And now," say the Blues, "we have worked like niggers—and when the fun and the fighting begins, they send us home and put regulars there."

They have an immense amount of powder along. The wheel of the car in which it was took fire. There was an escape for you!

We are packing a hamper of eatables for them. If they fight as they eat, they are Trojans indeed. Just now they are enjoying a quiet game of billiards.

Colonel Chase insulted them by blazing out a road behind them, in case of a sudden necessity for retreat.

It was not needed, for Stephen took one of his men with him to whom cannon was new. A double-barreled gun was his only experience in firearms. He saw the huge mouth of the cannon, and at the firing of the evening gun he dashed for home, straight as the crow flies, and was there by breakfast, cured forever of all weakness for soldiering. Fifty miles or more!

I am despondent once more. If I thought them in earnest because they put their best in front, *at first*—what now? We have to meet tremendous odds by pluck, activity, zeal, dash, endurance of the toughest, military instinct. We had

1. Lawrence Massillon Keitt of Orangeburg and William Waters Boyce of Edgefield, S.C. Both men were former U.S. congressmen and delegates to the Montgomery convention.
2. Howell Cobb, a former congressman, governor of Ga., and secretary of the treasury in the Buchanan administration, was chairman of the Montgomery convention and president of the Provisional Confederate Congress.
3. William H. Chase, a retired U.S. Army Corps of Engineers officer who held a military commission from the state of Fla.
4. Col. Tennent Lomax, commander of the Montgomery Blues, was a lawyer and newspaper editor born in S.C.
5. Andrew Barry Moore, governor of Ala.

to choose the born leaders of men, people who could attract love and trust. Everywhere political intrigue is as rife as in Washington.

Somebody likened it to the boys who could not catch up with the carriage, calling out to the coachman, "cut behind," to dislodge the luckier ones.< At any rate, I hear it said, "Surely if they believed a war inevitable, very different would be their choice"—and that gives us some hope.> Cecil's saying of Sir Walter Raleigh "I know he can labor terribly" is an electric touch.[6]

Clarendon's portraits. These are idlers—they only talk. "Hampden, who was of an industry and vigilance not to be tired out or wearied by the most laborious, and of parts not to be imposed on by the most subtle and sharp, and of a personal courage equal to his best parts. Falkland, who was so severe an adorer of truth that he could as easily have given himself leave to steal as to dissemble."

Above all, let the men to save South Carolina be young and vigorous. While I was cudgeling my brain to say what kind of men we ought to choose, I fell on Clarendon, and it was easy to construct my man out of this material. What has been may be again. So it need not be a purely ideal type.

We keep each other in countenance and exasperate by emulation the frenzy of the time. The shield against the stinging of conscience is the universal practice of our contemporaries.[7]

—Emerson

Aye—aye—sir—

Mr. Toombs[8] told us a story of General Scott[9] and himself a few days before I left Montgomery. He said he was dining in Washington with General Scott, who seasoned every dish and every glass of wine with the eternal refrain "Save the Union"—"The Union must be preserved."

Toombs remarked that he knew why the Union was so dear to the general and illustrated by a steamboat anecdote. An explosion, of course; and while the passengers were struggling in the water, a woman ran up and down the bank, crying, "Oh, save the redheaded man!" The redhead man was saved, and his preserver, after landing him, noticed with surprise how little interest in him the woman who had made such moving appeals seemed to feel. He asked her, "Why did you make that pathetic outcry?" "Oh, he owes me ten thousand

6. M. B. C. took this line and the following paragraph from Ralph Waldo Emerson, "The Uses of Great Men," *Representative Men* (1850). Emerson himself had paraphrased the descriptions of Hampden and Falkland from Edward Hyde, Earl of Clarendon, *History of the Rebellion and Civil Wars in England* (1702–04), book 7, sections 84 and 224.

7. Also quoted from "The Uses of Great Men."

8. Robert Augustus Toombs of Ga., a disappointed aspirant for the Confederate presidency, resigned his seat in the U.S. Senate early in Feb. and became Confederate secretary of state at the end of the month.

9. Winfield Scott, a native of Va. and an unsuccessful Whig presidential candidate in 1852, was general in chief of the U.S. Army.

dollars." "Now, general, the U.S.A. or the Union owes you seventeen thousand a year."

I can imagine the scorn of old Scott's face.

My husband writes in fine spirits, but the daily bulletins are very contradictory.

Down here they did not like the president's message.[1]

February 25, 1861. Montgomery. Found them working very hard here. The cars were so overheated and disagreeable yesterday. As I dozed on the sofa last night could hear scratch, scratch of my husband's pen as he wrote at the table until midnight. After church today Captain Ingraham[2] called. He left me so uncomfortable. He dared to express his regret that he had to leave the U.S. Navy. He was stationed in the Mediterranean, where he likes to be; expected to be there two years. He expected to take those lovely daughters of his to Florence. Then came that ogre Lincoln and rampant Black Republicanism—and he must lay down his life for South Carolina. He, however, does not make any moan. He says we lack everything necessary of naval gear to retake Fort Sumter. Of course he only expects the navy to take it. He is a fish out of water here. He is one of the finest sea captains, so I suppose they will soon give him a ship and send him back to his own element.

At dinner Judge Withers[3] was loudly abusive of the [Provisional] Congress (already?). He said: "They had trampled the Constitution underfoot. They have provided President Davis with a house." It is hardly worth while wasting time in quarrels about nonessentials. He was disgusted with the folly of parading the president at the inauguration in a coach drawn by four white horses. (I thought that all right.) Then someone said Mrs. Fitzpatrick[4] was the only lady who sat with the Congress—and after the inaugural poked Jeff Davis in the back with her parasol, that he might turn and speak to her. "I am sure that was democratic enough," said someone.

Governor Moore came in with the latest news. A telegram from Governor Pickens to the president. "That a war steamer is lying off the bar, laden with reinforcements for Fort Sumter—What must we do?" Answer: "Use your own discretion."

There is faith for you. After all said and done, it is believed there is some discretion still left in South Carolina, fit for use.

Everybody who comes here wants an office. And the many who of course are disappointed raise the cry, against the few who are successful, of corruption. And I thought we had left all that in Washington. Nobody is willing to be out of

1. Jefferson Davis's address at his inauguration as Provisional Confederate president on Feb. 18.

2. Duncan Nathaniel Ingraham of Charleston resigned as a U.S. Navy commander in Jan. 1861 and was commissioned captain in the Confederate States Navy (C.S.N.) in March.

3. Common-law judge Thomas Jefferson Withers of Camden, a delegate to the S.C. secession convention and a member of the Provisional Congress, was M. B. C.'s uncle and former guardian.

4. A friend of the Chesnuts from their days in Washington, Aurelia (Blassingame) Fitzpatrick was the second wife of former Ala. governor and U.S. senator Benjamin Fitzpatrick.

sight. And they take any office. Ex-Governor Manning[5] said he was an ambassador to Louisiana and quite pleased with his position, but Slidell[6] welcomed him coolly, as one of those "itinerant commissioners," and he felt himself held in contempt. Bonham[7] declared he did not mean to be fobbed off with any trashy commission of that sort. They were making merry over their woes, when Governor Moore gravely inquired of Mr. McQueen[8] if they were a party of disappointed office seekers.

Judge Withers denounced the people of South Carolina as fools and knaves—especially the people of Kershaw District. Mr. Chesnut said, "You represent those people. If I thought as you do, I would not stay here a day. I would not represent such a people."

Angry words ensued, and I was awfully frightened. Why will the man be so harsh and abusive of everybody?

Constitution Browne[9] says he is going to Washington for twenty-four hours.

I mean to send by him to Mary Garnett[1] for a bonnet ribbon. If they take him up as a traitor, he may cause a civil war. War is now our dread. Mr. C told him not to make himself a bone of contention.

Tom Taylor[2] and Malley Howell[3] called. Asked me when I was going home. "When this thing breaks up." "But you are not respectful to our Congress! Treason!" cried Alabama Tom Taylor.

"I am from South Carolina. That answers all. The more tenderfooted of you rebels must be more cautious in your speech."

Trescot[4] writes, "That clever, learned creature, naturalist, mathematician,

5. John Laurence Manning of Clarendon District, governor of S.C. from 1852 to 1854, was one of the wealthiest men in the South. The owner of 648 slaves on plantations in S.C. and La., he valued his holdings at more than two million dollars in 1860. Manning served in the S.C. state legislature and secession convention and went to La. to urge that state to join the Confederacy.

6. John Slidell, former U.S. senator from La. and a leading secessionist.

7. Milledge Luke Bonham of Edgefield District, S.C., had resigned his seat in the U.S. Congress in Dec. 1860.

8. John McQueen of Marlboro District, S.C., resigned from the U.S. Congress in Dec. 1860 and served as a commissioner to Tex. to secure that state's secession.

9. William Montague Browne of Washington, D.C., was the Irish-born editor of the Buchanan administration newspaper, the Washington *Constitution*. His commission as colonel in the C.S.A. and his title, assistant secretary of state, were the result of his friendship with Howell Cobb and Jefferson Davis.

1. Mary (Stevens) Garnett, daughter of J. C.'s cousin, Edwin Stevens of N.J. She had lived with the Chesnuts in Washington the year before her marriage to Congressman Muscoe Garnett of Va. in 1860.

2. Thomas B. Taylor, a physician who moved from Richland District, S.C., to Ala. in the 1830s. Taylor's uncle, John Taylor, governor of S.C. from 1826 to 1828, married J. C.'s aunt Sarah Cantey (Chesnut) Taylor. One of Taylor's first cousins, James Madison Taylor, was the husband of M. B. C.'s aunt Charlotte (Boykin) Taylor. M. B. C. probably calls Taylor "Alabama Tom" to distinguish him from his cousin, Thomas Taylor of Richland District, whom she later encounters. Compounded kinship in S.C. often transcends terminology!

3. Jesse Malachi Howell, a planter with interests in Richland District and Miss., was Thomas B. Taylor's second cousin.

4. William Henry Trescot of Beaufort District, S.C., a slaveholder, historian, and author of *The Position and Course of the South* (1850), had resigned as U.S. assistant secretary of state but remained in Washington as an unofficial adviser to the S.C. commissioners negotiating the fate of the Federal forts at Charleston.

&c&c, John McCrady[5] wants to be made a captain of regulars." So everybody means to go in the army.

If Sumter is attacked, then Jeff Davis's trouble begins.

The Judge says a military despotism would be best for us, anything to prevent a triumph of the Yankees.

All right, but every man objects to any despot but himself.

Read *Framley Parsonage* in *Cornhill.*[6] Don't care for elderly loves, so found Miss Dunstable and Dr. Thorne dull because I wanted to see how the young lovers were getting on.

How much I owe of the pleasure of my life to these much reviled writers of fiction.

Mr. Chesnut, in high spirits, dines today with the Louisiana delegation.

Stephen in higher spirits. The Montgomery Blues have presented him with a silver dipper in grateful remembrance of his hospitality.

Breakfasted with Constitution Browne, who is appointed assistant secretary of state. And so does not go to Washington.

Also there was at table the man who advertised for a wife—with the wife so obtained. She was not pretty. ⟨⟨She was ugly as sin.⟩⟩

We dine at Mr. Pollard's[7] and go to a ball afterward at Judge Bibb's.[8]

The *Herald*[9] says Lincoln stood before Washington's picture at his inauguration. Taken by the country as a good sign. Always frantic for a sign.

Let us pray that a Caesar or a Napoleon may be sent us. That would be our best sign of success.

But they still say no war. Peace let it be, kind Heaven!

Mr. Barnwell[1] brought a letter from Wigfall.[2] It was enclosed to him, though addressed to Jeff Davis. Before handing it to the president, Mr. Barnwell was to read it to Mr. C and Robert Barnwell Rhett. It accused the *Mercury*[3] of doing

5. John McCrady, professor of mathematics and zoology at the College of Charleston, served as an engineer in the C.S.A.

6. Anthony Trollope's *Framley Parsonage* (1861) appeared as a serial in the English *Cornhill Magazine* in 1860–61.

7. The home of Charles T. Pollard, a prominent Montgomery merchant and railroad owner, and his wife, Emily Virginia (Scott) Pollard.

8. The home of Montgomery County Court judge Benajah Bibb and his wife, Sophia (Gilmer) Bibb.

9. The New York *Herald.*

1. Robert Woodward Barnwell, senior member of the S.C. delegation to the Provisional Congress, was a moderate rather than a fire-eater like his cousin, Robert Barnwell Rhett, Sr. In his long public career, he had served as a U.S. congressman, a U.S. senator, president of S.C. College, and member of the S.C. secession convention from St. Helena's Parish, Charleston.

2. Louis Trezevant Wigfall, a South Carolinian, moved to Tex. after a duel and became an important secessionist agitator and a U.S. senator from 1859 to 1861. With the approval of Jefferson Davis, Wigfall remained in Washington after the secession of Tex. to buy arms and recruit men for the Confederacy.

3. The Charleston *Mercury* had opposed the Provisional Confederate government from the beginning, fearing that it would promote sectional reconciliation. When the Confederate Congress voted to prohibit the slave trade and retain a protective tariff—measures designed to attract support in still undecided border states—the *Mercury* charged, "South Carolina is about to be saddled with every grievance except abolition for which she has long struggled [*sic*] and just withdrawn from the United States government."

incalculable mischief—insulting and irritating the border states, who held back, saying, "South Carolina apparently was going to secede from the new Confederacy."

———————

"Charitably take him aside and whisper in his ear that little comes of real knowledge but modesty—and doubt of self."

Camden DeLeon, M.D.,[4] called, fresh from Washington. Says General Scott is using all of his power and influence to prevent officers from the South from resigning their commissions.

Among other things, promising that they should never be sent against us in case of war.

Captain Ingraham, in his short, curt way, said: "That will never do. If they take their government pay, they must do its fighting."

A brilliant dinner at the Pollards'. Mr. Barnwell took me down to dinner.

Came home and found Judge Withers and Governor Moore waiting to go with me to the Bibbs'.

And they say it is dull in Montgomery!!

Clayton,[5] fresh from Washington, was at the party—told us, "There was to be peace."

February 28, 1861.   In the drawing room a literary lady began a violent attack upon this mischief-making South Carolina. She told me she was a successful writer in the magazines of the day. But when I found she used "incredible" for "incredulous," I said not a word in defense of my native land. I left her "incredible." Another person came in while she was pouring upon me home truths and asked her if she did not know I was a Carolinian. Then she gracefully reversed her engine and took the other tack—sounded our praises. But I left her incredible—and I remained incredulous, too.

Brewster[6] says the war specs are growing in size. Nobody at the North nor in Virginia believes we are in earnest. They think we are sulking and that Jeff Davis and Stephens[7] are getting up a very pretty little comedy.

The Virginia delegates were insulted at the peace conference. Brewster said "kicked out."[8]

4. David Camden DeLeon, a native of Camden, resigned as a U.S. Army surgeon on Feb. 19 and soon became the first surgeon general of the Confederacy.

5. Phillip Clayton of Ga. had resigned as assistant secretary of the U.S. Treasury. He held the same post in the Confederate government.

6. Born in S.C., Henry Percy Brewster became secretary of war of the Texas Republic and a prominent lawyer in Tex. and Washington, D.C.

7. Former congressman Alexander Hamilton Stephens of Ga. was elected vice-president of the Confederacy on Feb. 6.

8. On Feb. 4, a peace conference requested by the Va. legislature brought representatives from twenty-one of the thirty-three states to Washington in a last attempt to find a solution to the sectional crisis. The "insult" to the Virginians was apparently the selection as second temporary chairman of Christopher Walcott, Ohio's attorney general, who had allegedly moved to adjourn a state court in honor of John Brown. The Va. delegation had not been expelled from the convention, however.

The *Herald* said today, "Hon. James Chesnut was the only son of one of the wealthiest men in Carolina, his father owning a thousand slaves, and found it impossible to ride across his estate in a day."[9]

There is accurate information for you!

I asked Brewster how his friend Wigfall liked being left alone with the Black Republicans.

He replied: "Wigfall chafes at the restraints of civil life. He likes to be where he can be as rude as he pleases, and he is indulging himself now to the fullest extent, apparently."

Mr. Keitt called. He complained of the *Mercury*. It calls everybody a submissionist but R. B. Rhett.

Mr. Mallory[1] then called. ⟨⟨Seemed to have so high an opinion of me, but Captain Ingraham told Mr. Chesnut that he was so notoriously dissolute that a woman was compromised to be much seen with him.⟩⟩ Fortunately the Judge likes him better than anyone here—thinks him so pleasant and witty. The Senate has not yet confirmed him as secretary of the navy.

Found a capital bookstore here. Got from there *Evan Harrington—Or He Would Be a Tailor.*[2] Rather a discouraging name, but it turns out to be an extremely clever book.

The Judge thought Jeff Davis rude to him when the latter was secretary of war. Mr. C persuaded the Judge to forego his private wrong for the public good, so he voted for him. Now his old grudge has come back with an increased venomousness.

What a pity to bring the spites of the old Union into this new one. It seems to me already men are willing to risk an injury to our cause if they may in so doing hurt Jeff Davis.

March 1, 1861.   Dined today with Mr. Hill from Georgia and his wife. After he left us she told me he was the celebrated individual who for Christian scruples refused to fight a duel with Stephens.[3] She seemed very proud of him for his conduct in the affair.

Ignoramus that I am, I had not heard of it.

I am having all kinds of experiences. Drove today with a lady who fervently wished her husband would go down to Pensacola and be shot. I was dumb with amazement, of course.

---

9. This sketch of James Chesnut, Jr., and his father appeared in a column entitled "The Members of the Southern Congress" in the New York *Herald*, Feb. 23, 1861. The owner of 448 slaves in 1860, old Mr. Chesnut was indeed one of the wealthiest men in S.C. and the South. But J. C. shared little of this wealth in his own name.

1. Stephen Russell Mallory of Fla. had resigned from the U.S. Senate in Jan.

2. George Meredith's *Evan Harrington; or, He Would Be a Gentleman* (1860) describes the career of a socially ambitious tailor.

3. During a debate in 1856, Benjamin Harvey Hill called Alexander Stephens "Judas Iscariot." Challenged, Hill declined to face "a man who has neither conscience nor family." Hill, who was married to Caroline (Holt) Hill, served as a delegate to the Montgomery convention, even though he opposed secession.

Telling my story to one who knew the parties, was informed, "Don't you know he beats her?"

So I have seen a man "who lifts his hand against a woman in aught save kindness."

Brewster says Lincoln passed through Baltimore, disguised and at night—and that he did well—for just now Baltimore is dangerous ground. He says he hears from all quarters that the vulgarity of Lincoln, his wife, and his son is beyond credence—a thing you must see before you can believe it. Sen. Stephen Douglas[4] told Mr. C that Lincoln was awfully clever and that he had found him a heavy handful.

Went to pay my respects to Mrs. Jefferson Davis.[5]

She met me with open arms. We did not allude to anything by which we are surrounded. We eschewed politics and our changed relations. ⟨⟨What a chat that was—*two* hours. She told me all Washington news.⟩⟩

She described the Prince of Wales's visit.[6] The various pieces of information she had derived from the noblemen who accompanied the Prince.

Lord St. Germans[7] told her who Sydney Smith was and also Sir Henry Holland,[8] and informed her furthermore that as a statesman they did not think highly of Mr. Calhoun[9] in England.

A girl inquired of a Sir Somebody Elliott[1] if he were a relative of the Carolina Elliotts.

The marchioness of Chandos[2] condemned Mrs. Gwin's[3] extravagance. Her velvet dress was cut up and pinked so it could never be used again for anything else.

And that "Oh, uncommon fine!" was king's English, for the Prince said so at every turn.

Dr. Manly,[4] the celebrated Baptist minister, was very much interested in me as soon as he found out I was the granddaughter of that famous good sister (Baptist) Mrs. Burwell Boykin.[5]

---

4. Stephen Arnold Douglas of Ill.
5. Varina Anne (Howell) Davis of Miss., granddaughter of a Revolutionary War governor of N.J., became Davis's second wife in 1845. A socially accomplished woman of the planter class, she was an ambitious supporter of her husband. Her friendship with M. B. C. began in Washington when their husbands were in the U.S. Senate.
6. In 1860, Queen Victoria sent her son, Edward Albert, on a tour of Canada and the U.S. Mrs. Davis probably saw the Prince in Washington, where he stayed three days at the White House.
7. Edward Granville Eliot, third earl of St. Germans and lord steward of the royal household.
8. Sydney Smith was a founder of the *Edinburgh Review* and canon of St. Paul's until his death in 1845. Sir Henry Holland, a fashionable London doctor and physician to Queen Victoria, was Smith's son-in-law.
9. John Caldwell Calhoun of S.C.
1. Lord St. Germans.
2. Caroline Harvey, wife of the keeper of the privy seal to the Prince of Wales.
3. Mary (Bell) Gwin was the second wife of William McKendree Gwin, U.S. senator from Calif.
4. Basil Manly, Sr., a native of S.C., was pastor of the First Baptist Church in Montgomery and chaplain at the inauguration of Jefferson Davis.
5. Mary (Whitaker) Boykin, second wife of Burwell Boykin.

March 3, 1861.   Montgomery. Everybody in fine spirits—of my world. They have one and all spoken in the Congress to their own perfect satisfaction.

To my amazement the Judge took me aside, and after delivering a panegyric upon himself (and here comes in the amazement), he praised my husband to the skies and said he was the fittest man of all for a foreign mission.

Aye—and the farther away they send us from this Congress, the better I will like it.

The Montgomery Blues were drilling in front of this house. We were in the piazza—second story. Commodore Ingraham, Constitution Browne, Mr. Mallory not yet confirmed secretary of the navy.

The Judge found Mr. Mallory wanted his vote. That is the reason of his frequent presence with us—a desire to propitiate the Judge. ⟨⟨ . . . as if he were not half as attentive to me as he used to be in Washington—for the best reason, I will not let him be since I heard of his character.⟩⟩

Mr. Browne whispered, "Designs upon a man—that is not in his way?"

Mrs. Fitzpatrick, the jolly old girl, handsome as ever, was here with her stepson. Who is none the less interesting that he has jilted—well, never mind who.

Saw Jere Clemens and Nick Davis, social curiosities.[6] They are antisecession leaders. Then George Sanders[7] and George Deas.[8] The Georges are of "the opinion that it is folly to try" and take back Fort Sumter from Anderson and the U.S. That is, before we are ready. They saw in Charleston the devoted band prepared for the sacrifice—I mean, ready to run their heads against a stone wall. Daredevils they were. They had dash and courage enough—but science only could take that fort. And they shake their heads.

March 4, 1861.   The Washington Congress has passed peace measures.[9]

Glory be to God! (as my Irish Margaret prefaced every remark, both great and small).

At last, according to his wish, I was able to introduce Mr. Hill of Georgia to Mr. Mallory—also Governor Moore and Brewster, the latter the only man without a title of some sort that I know—in this democratic subdivided republic.

Then the man who seemed more like a gentleman than any, something of the air and manner of one. Certainly his stories are the nicest—all are jolly, I admit.

6. As up-country allies in the Ala. secession convention, Jeremiah Clemens and Nicholas Davis, Jr., opposed withdrawal from the Union without a popular referendum and simultaneous secession by other slave states, but vowed to defend Ala. in any event. Clemens, a distant cousin of Mark Twain, was a former U.S. senator; Davis, a planter and former state legislator.

7. George Nicholas Sanders of Ky. mingled idealism and fraud as a promoter, supporter of the European revolutionaries of 1848, and founder of the nationalistic, expansionist "Young America" movement of the 1850s. He became a Confederate agent in Canada and Europe.

8. Former U.S. Army officer George Allen Deas, a distant relative by marriage of the Chesnuts, was acting adjutant general of the Confederacy.

9. On March 2, the Thirty-sixth Congress ended with a futile gesture toward sectional reconciliation as the Senate adopted a House resolution calling for a constitutional amendment that would prohibit congressional interference with slavery in the states.

They whisper, "His mother was a washerwoman."[1] "Why not?" sneered the Judge. "She taught him not to go with the great unwashed—cleanliness next to godliness, you know."

So I have seen a negro woman sold—up on the block—at auction. I was walking. The woman on the block overtopped the crowd. I felt faint—seasick. The creature looked so like my good little Nancy. She was a bright mulatto with a pleasant face. She was magnificently gotten up in silks and satins. She seemed delighted with it all—sometimes ogling the bidders, sometimes looking quite coy and modest, but her mouth never relaxed from its expanded grin of excitement. I daresay the poor thing knew who would buy her.

I sat down on a stool in a shop. I disciplined my wild thoughts. I tried it Sterne fashion.[2]

You know how women sell themselves and are sold in marriage, from queens downward, eh?

You know what the Bible says about slavery—and marriage. Poor women. Poor slaves. Sterne with his starling. What did he know? He only thought—he did not feel.

Evan Harrington: "Like a true English female she believed in her own inflexible virtue but never trusted her husband out of sight."[3]

New York *Herald* says, "Lincoln's carriage is not bombproof, so he does not drive out."

Two flags and a bundle of sticks have been sent him as a gentle reminder. The sticks are to break our heads.

The English are gushingly unhappy as to our family quarrel.

Magnanimous of them—for it is their opportunity.

Brewster called Madame Bodisco, who married the English captain last winter, a Leviathan of Loveliness.[4]

March 5, 1861.   We stood on the balcony to see our Confederate flag go up. Roars of cannon, &c&c.

Miss Sanders[5] complained—so said Captain Ingraham—of the deadness of

1. A reference to Stephen Mallory.

2. In Laurence Sterne's "The Passport. The Hotel at Paris," *A Sentimental Journey through France and Italy* (1768), Mr. Yorick, reasoning away the evils of captivity in the Bastille, hears a caged starling say, "I can't get out—I can't get out." Yorick struggles unsuccessfully to free the bird and concludes, "Disguise thyself as thou wilt, still slavery!"

3. A paraphrase from chapter 22.

4. Harriet Beall (Williams) Bodisco, the American-born widow of a Russian envoy to the U.S., had married Capt. Douglas Gordon Scott. Brewster's comment was a common one: Madame Bodisco was well known in social circles, both for her beauty and her size.

5. Identified in the 1860s Journal as a sister or daughter of George Nicholas Sanders.

the mob. "It was utterly spiritless," she said. "No cheering—or so little—no enthusiasm."

Captain Ingraham suggested, "Gentlemen are apt to be quiet—this was a thoughtful crowd. The true mob element with us just now is hoeing corn."

And yet! It is uncomfortable that the idea has gone abroad that we have no joy, no pride in this thing.

The band was playing "Massa in the Cold, Cold Ground." Major Deas was busy telling us why he came south. "The New York clubs were so unpleasant now for Southern men." Although he has always lived at the North, respect for his Deas and Izard blood had been so dinned in his ears by his relatives, he could not fail to feel altogether Southern.

Mr. Chesnut told Mr. Mallory that the Senate had confirmed his nomination as secretary of the navy.

They were standing at my back. I was leaning over the balustrade, watching the flag. Mr. Mallory did not interrupt what he was saying to me but continued in the same placid voice. I did not find this very civil to Mr. Chesnut. So I turned.

"Had you heard that important fact before?"

"No."

"And yet you took no notice of Mr. C's making himself the bearer of good news to you?"

"It was a thing to see, not hear. The secretary of the navy smiled and thanked me with a profound bow," said Mr. C.

Afterward Mr. C told me that Florida, Mr. Mallory's own state, went against him.

Captain Ingraham pulled out of his pocket some verses sent him by a Boston girl.

It amounted to this—well rhymed in—that she held a rope ready to hang him. Still, she shed tears when she remembered his heroic rescue of Koszta.[6]

Koszta—the rebel!—and she calls us rebels, too. Depends upon who one rebels against—whether it is heroic to save or not.

Miss Tyler, daughter of an ex–U.S. president,[7] ran up our flag.

Read Lincoln's inaugural. Oh, comes he in peace—or comes he in war—or to tread but one measure as Young Lochinvar.[8]

---

6. Martin Koszta took part in the Hungarian revolution against Austria in 1848 and fled to the U.S. in 1850. Traveling to Turkey three years later, he was kidnapped and held prisoner aboard an Austrian man-of-war off Smyrna. Duncan Ingraham, commander of the U.S.S. *St. Louis*, forced Koszta's release with an ultimatum on July 2, 1853. This exploit, occurring at a high point of American sympathy for the revolutionaries of 1848 and dislike for Austria, made Ingraham a national hero.

7. Letitia Christian Tyler was the daughter, not of former president John Tyler, but of his son, Robert Tyler of Philadelphia.

8. A combination of two passages, slightly misquoted, from "Lochinvar. Lady Heron's Song," a ballad in Sir Walter Scott, *Marmion: A Tale of Flodden Field* (1808), canto 5.

At Mrs. Davis's reception today. It was crowded. Commodore Tattnall[9]—and too many men of note to attempt to name them.

We laughed at the hospitable, noncommittal Governor Fitzpatrick.[1] In Washington he was always urging us to come down here and see him at his own home. Now in Montgomery, when he is so near at hand, he says, "The roads are so bad, &c&c&c." Hence our small joke.

———————

《Mr. Davis said I ought to be ashamed to fly always at his footsteps. I am afraid of him, a little.》

———————

Lincoln's aim is to seduce the border states.

Trescot at a dinner given to the Prince of Wales. Mistook a question asked him [as being]: What is the meaning of the word "caryatides"?

"Oh, you see them there—gilty women."

"I asked you what kind of a woman was Carry, &c&c."

"Oh, only a caryatid. I thought you pointed to that candlestick."[2]

———————

Mr. Barnwell and Mr. Miles[3] called. They showed me some lines comic enough. Conrad of Louisiana[4] and Barnwell Rhett of South Carolina are always at words, everlasting speakers and wranglers.

The parson being absent, someone suggested in this wise. In case the Lord did not answer Barnwell Rhett, Conrad certainly would.

This helped to pass an evening call merrily. Also they cited Simon Suggs to the Judge, who is always vaunting his own probity and sneering at the venality of everybody else. Simon was always saying—"Integrity is the post I ties to."[5]

When his wife mentioned the fact that there was no bacon in the barrel, Simon said solemnly, "Then somebody must suffer." At camp meeting that day he got religion, handed round the hat, took the offering to the Lord down into the swamp to pray over it, untied his horse, and fled with it—&c&c—hat, contribution, all.

The Judge laughed loudest of any and said for a while he would keep all

———

9. Josiah Tattnall of Ga., a career U.S. naval officer who resigned his commission in Feb. and became a captain and senior flag officer of the C.S.N.

1. Benjamin Fitzpatrick was governor of Ala. in the 1840s and a U.S. senator from 1848 to 1849 and from 1853 until his resignation in Jan. 1861.

2. The 1860s Journal suggests a pun on "gilty" that is not spelled out here.

3. William Porcher Miles, a member of both the S.C. secession convention and the Provisional Confederate Congress, had been a mathematics professor at the College of Charleston, mayor of Charleston, and a U.S. congressman from 1857 until his resignation in Dec. 1860.

4. Charles Magill Conrad, secretary of war during the Fillmore administration, was a member of the Provisional Confederate Congress.

5. In chapter 3 of Alabama humorist Johnson Jones Hooper's *Some Adventures of Captain Simon Suggs* (1845), Simon fleeces a fellow land speculator and observes: "But Honesty's the best policy. . . . Ah yes *honesty*, HONESTY's the stake that Simon Suggs ALLERS ties to! What's a man without his inteegerty." For Simon's remark to his wife and his camp-meeting adventure, see chapter 10.

hints of his transcendental honesty to himself. Political honesty, of course, was only in question. It seems there is a great difference, but I do not seem to see it.

These people—the natives, I mean—are astounded that I calmly affirm, in all truth and candor, that if there were awful things in society in Washington, I did not see or hear of them. One must have been hard to please who did not like the people I knew in Washington.

Mr. Chesnut has gone with a list of names to the president. De Treville,[6] Kershaw,[7] Baker,[8] Robert Rutledge.[9] They are taking a walk, I see. I hope there will be good places in the army for our list.

An adventure today. A devout lady. One who holds Washington and worldly dissipation in holy horror. She dreaded the effect of these congressmen here. They might make Montgomery a second Washington.

When she asked, as they all do, "How do you like Montgomery?"

"Charming—I find it charming."

General Bonham stared. He has been made commander in chief of South Carolina Army. Again, he "will not be fobbed off with that rubbish," he says. "The governor can do all that." He laughs at such a position. He knows his rights—and dares maintain them—to a good place.

"Where is the South Carolina Army that I am to be general of?" he asks. Echo answers, "Where?" General Bonham has been offered no place at all, he said.

The devout lady saw Mrs. Le Vert's book[1] in my hand.

"Oh—the affliction God has sent down upon Mrs. Le Vert. I hope it will be sanctified to her."

Then she asked me to go with her to make a few visits.

A plain-spoken old lady took my arm as we left her drawing room, and then, lagging behind, she inquired, "Why are you in such company?"

"Why not?"

"She is lovely and pious and so clever. Yes, all that—but talked about, you know."

"No, indeed—I did not know."

"It is her pastor, you know." "He prays with her." "Stays with her." By this

---

6. Probably Richard De Treville, a Charleston lawyer and former lieutenant governor of S.C. who became colonel of the Seventeenth S.C. Volunteers.

7. Joseph Brevard Kershaw of Camden, a lawyer, former state legislator, and delegate to the S.C. secession convention, shortly became colonel of the Second S.C. Volunteers.

8. Probably Thomas McDonald Baker, a former state legislator from Claremont, S.C., serving as a captain of the First S.C. Regiment.

9. Robert Smith Rutledge of Charleston, the son of planter John Rutledge, had enlisted as a private in Thomas Baker's company the day before.

1. Granddaughter of a signer of the Declaration of Independence, Octavia (Walton) Le Vert maintained a fashionable salon in Mobile and had written a popular account of her experiences in Europe, *Souvenirs of Travel* (1857). Her "affliction" was the recent death of her mother and the illness of her father and husband.

time the culprit Fay was safely in her carriage, and the chorus around me was in full blast. I put my hands up to my ears and flew out of it all. They screamed after me, "A word to the wise is sufficient," &c&c&c.

A man came in. Some one said in an undertone, "The age of chivalry is not past—oh, ye Americans!"

"What do you mean?"

"That man was nominated by President Buchanan for a foreign mission. Some senator stood up in his place and read a very abusive paper printed by this office seeker, abusive of a woman, and signed by his name in full. So—we would have none of him. His chance was gone forever...."[2]

《Mr. Josselyn,[3] the poet, says I look younger and better than I did in Washington. I wonder if in the thousand compliments I hear there is one *grain* of truth.》

《**March 7, 1861** ... Dr. Tom Taylor was saying how stiff it was at the reception yesterday until I got there—and I went in like a ray of warmth and sunshine. Pretty good for a woman of my years. Saw a flag with stars and stripes, floating in the breeze, and told Miss Tyler, as she seemed head of the flag committee, to have it taken down.》

March 8, 1861. Judge Campbell of the Supreme Court has resigned.[4] Lord! how they must have hated to do it. Above all—Colonel Lay, General Scott's favorite A.D.C.[5]

Now we may be sure the bridge is broken.

And yet, in the Alabama convention they say reconstructionists[6] abound and are busy.

Met a distinguished gentleman that I knew when he was in more affluent circumstances. I was willing enough to speak to him, but when he saw me advancing for that purpose, to avoid me he suddenly dodged around a corner—William, Mrs. DeS's[7] ci-devant coachman. I remember him on his box, driving a pair of handsome bays, dressed sumptuously in broadcloth, brass buttons, &c&c, a stout, respectable, fine looking, middle-aged mulatto.

Then, night after night, we used to meet him as fiddler in chief at all our

---

2. Deleted are four stanzas of an old ballad that a friend gave her.

3. Robert Josselyn of Miss., author of *The Faded Flower, and Other Songs* (1849), was Jefferson Davis's private secretary.

4. The resignation of John Archibald Campbell of Ala., an associate justice of the U.S. Supreme Court since 1853, was falsely reported in early March; he did not resign until April.

5. George William Lay of Va., son-in-law of John Archibald Campbell, soon became a captain in the C.S.A.

6. Those who hoped that secession, by showing the North the necessity of compromise with the South, would bring sectional reconciliation.

7. Eliza Hester (Champion) DeSaussure, wife of wealthy Camden planter John McPherson DeSaussure.

parties. He sat in solemn dignity, making faces over his bow and patting his foot with an emphasis that shook the floor. We gave him five dollars a night—that was his price. His mistress never refused to let him play for any party. He had stable boys in abundance. What was his grievance? He was far above any physical fear for his sleek and well-fed person. How majestically he scraped his foot—as a sign that he was tuned up and ready to begin.

Now he is a shabby creature indeed. He must have felt his fallen fortunes when he met me, one who knew him in his prosperity. He ran away, this stately yellow gentleman, from wife and children, home and comfort.

My Polly asked him: "Why? Miss Liza was good to you, I know."

"Yes, but Marster was so mean. He was not bad. He was mean. In the twenty years I lived in his yard he never gave me a fourpence—that is, in money."

I wonder who owns him now. He looked forlorn. He had not bettered himself!

Wanted to stop and ask Governor Cobb who that beautiful Juliet was, to whom he seemed playing Romeo on the balcony. Mr. C was shocked at my levity, but Governor Cobb was vastly amused at my question.

Mrs. Fitzpatrick wanted the postmaster generalship for the governor. It was offered to Wirt Adams,[8] who declined to accept it. And now Reagan of Texas[9] has it.

March 9, 1861.   La carrière ouverte aux talents.[1] This blessed American freedom to go straight to the top of the tree if you are built for climbing.

Governor Moore brought in, to be presented to me, the president of the Alabama convention.[2] It seems I knew him before. Said he danced with me at a dancing-school ball when I was in short frocks—sash, flounces, and wreath of roses. He was one of those clever boys of our neighbors, in whom my father saw promise of better things, and so helped him in every way to rise, with books, counsel, &c&c.

I was enjoying his conversation immensely, for he was praising my father without stint, when the Judge came in, breathing fire and fury. Congress has incurred his displeasure. We are abusing one another as fiercely as ever we abused Yankees. It is disheartening.

8. William Wirt Adams, a former Miss. legislator who had been commissioner to La. to encourage that state's secession.

9. John Henninger Reagan was a Democratic congressman from 1857 to March 3, 1861, a delegate to the Tex. secession convention, and a member of the Provisional Confederate Congress. He had twice refused the postmaster generality before accepting it.

1. A maxim of Napoleon Bonaparte, cited in Thomas Carlyle, "Memoirs of the Life of Scott," *Critical and Miscellaneous Essays* (1839).

2. Born in the Sumter District of S.C., William McLin Brooks moved to Ala. in the 1830s, where he became a prominent attorney and judge.

Mrs. Childs[3] was here tonight (Mary Anderson from Statesburg) with several children. She is lovely. Her hair is piled up on the top of her head oddly. Fashions from France still creep into Texas across Mexican borders. Mrs. Childs is fresh from Texas. Her husband is an artillery officer, or was. They will be glad to promote him here.

These people were so amusing—so full of western stories. Dr. Boykin[4] behaved strangely. All day he had been gaily driving about with us. Never was man in finer spirits. Tonight in this brilliant company he sat dead still, as if in a trance. Once he waked somewhat. A high public functionary came in with a present for me, a miniature gondola—a perfect Venetian specimen, he said—and said, again and again.

In an undertone Dr. B muttered, "That fellow has been drinking."

"Why do you think so?" I replied, quite shocked at his rude speech.

"Because he has told you exactly the same thing four times."

Wonderful! Some of these great statesmen always tell me the same thing—and have been telling me the same thing ever since we came here.

Mrs. Childs has the sweetest Southern voice—absolute music. But then, she has all of the high spirit of those sweet-voiced Carolina women, too.

Then Mr. Browne came in, with his fine English accent, so pleasant to the ear. He tells us that Washington is not reconciled to the Yankee regime. Mrs. Lincoln means to economize. She at once informed the major domo that they were poor and hoped to save twelve thousand dollars every year from their salary of twenty thousand.

Mrs. Browne said Mr. Buchanan's farewell was far more imposing than Lincoln's inauguration.

Mrs. Gwin sheds many tears, but she will not come South (small blame to her).

So many of these congressmen have been and are Methodist or Baptist preachers. A bad mixture of trades. Tom Cobb,[5] the best of men, in his capacity of preacher is a furious Sabbatarian, tries to have the RR cars stopped on Sunday. In his capacity of Georgia politician, he went off today, Sunday, to attend a Georgia political convention.

March 11, 1861.   In full conclave tonight—the drawing room was full of judges, governors, senators, generals, congressmen.

They were exalting John C. Calhoun's hospitality. He allowed everybody to stay all night who chose to stop at his house. One ill-mannered person refused to attend family prayers. Mr. Calhoun said to the servant, "Saddle that man's horse and let him go."

From the traveler he would take no excuse for the "deity offended."

Then I took up my parable. In the first place, I believed in Mr. Calhoun's

---

3. Mary Hooper (Anderson) Childs, sister of Confederate Gen. Richard Heron Anderson, was the wife of Northern-born Frederick Lynn Childs, who shortly became a captain in the C.S.A.

4. Edward Mortimer Boykin, a Camden physician, was M. B. C.'s second cousin. His wife, Mary Chesnut (Lang) Boykin, was a first cousin once removed of James Chesnut, Jr.

5. Thomas Reade Rootes Cobb, brother of Howell Cobb, was a lawyer and Presbyterian.

profuse hospitality, and I did not in his family prayers. Mr. Calhoun's deity was of the most philosophical type, from all accounts.

Then I told a story which I picked up in a life of Franklin. He stole it from Jeremy Taylor,[6] who filched it from heaven knows where.

Abraham hounded out an eastern traveler because he blasphemed the living God.

At night an angel came in quest of the aforesaid guest.

"I sent him forth in the wilderness for taking the Lord's name in vain."

The affable archangel answered, "Thus saith the Lord, your God: Have I borne with this man lo! this many years—could you not bear with him one night?"

Toleration—and sacred hospitality. The Judge commended me for a quotation aptly made. His good words being like the angel's visits, few and far between, are highly esteemed.

The latest news is counted good news. That is, the last man who left Washington tells us that Seward[7] is in the ascendancy. He is thought to be the friend of peace. He did say, however, "That serpent Seward is in the ascendancy just now."

Miss Lane[8] has eleven suitors. One is described as likely to win—or would be likely to win, but he is too heavily weighted. He has been married before and goes about with children and two mothers. There are limits beyond which! Two mothers-in-law!

Mr. Ledyard[9] spoke to Mrs. Lincoln for the doorkeeper, who almost felt he had a vested right, having been there since Jackson's time, but met with the same answer: she had brought her own girl. She must economize.

Mr. Ledyard thought the twenty thousand (and little enough it is) was given to the president of these U.S. to enable him to live in a proper style and to maintain an establishment of such dignity as befits the head of that great nation.

It is an infamy to economize the public money, to put it in one's private purse. To put the nation to an open shame. One would suppose this money was given them as a reward of merit for getting a plurality of votes.

Mrs. Browne was walking with me when we were airing our indignation against Mrs. Lincoln and her shabby economy. The *Herald* says three only of the Washington families attended the inauguration ball. "The Elite," so-called by the *Herald*. Parkers, Greens, and I forget who.

Mr. Buchanan and his secretary of the interior had a controversy on a point of personal veracity. Mr. Browne of the *Constitution* was cut by President Buchanan for supporting Jake Thompson.[1] The night before the Jake T's left

6. Seventeenth-century English bishop and theological and devotional writer.

7. William Henry Seward of N.Y., Lincoln's secretary of state.

8. Orphaned in 1841, Harriet Lane was raised by her uncle, James Buchanan. When he became secretary of state and then president, she presided over his household and reigned as a Washington fashion setter.

9. Possibly Henry Ledyard, a Washington attorney and former chargé d'affaires in Paris.

1. In Jan., after Buchanan ordered the *Star of the West* to supply Fort Sumter, former Miss. congressman Jacob Thompson resigned from the cabinet, claiming that the president had led him

Washington, they dined at the White House and took an affectionate farewell. Mrs. Browne said: "When Mrs. Thompson told me that, I could not believe my ears. Why, they have cut our acquaintance because Browne denies that Mr. T told a _____. Oh, what fools we do feel!"

Mr. Browne told a funny story of American awkwardness in handling titles.

A raw statesman inquired of him, "Shall I call Lord Morpeth[2] 'My Lord,' 'The Lord,' or 'Oh, Lord'?"

That was going down the Potomac to Mount Vernon. Coming back the American had been made so easy in his mind by mint juleps—he slapped the noble stranger on the back and called him "Moppy."

Mrs. Browne was telling of her English friends last summer: they derided her. "Oh, you are a Yankee girl." And she answered, "The Southern people hate Yankees worse than you do. They are my friends across the water."

Just then our walk led by that sale of negroes. The same place that I saw it before.

"If you can stand that, no other Southern thing need choke you."

She said not a word. After all, it was my country and she was an English-woman.

There are ugly sights all over the world. I could see she was sorry for me in her heart.

The Judge has just come in. He says, "Last night, after Dr. Boykin left in the cars, came a telegram—his little daughter Amanda had died suddenly."

Queer! In some way he must have known it. He changed so suddenly. And seemed so careworn and unhappy. He believes in clairvoyance—in magnetism and all that. Certainly there was some terrible foreboding on his part.

《Mr. Chesnut hurt because Mr. Hill said he kept his own counsel. Mr. C, thinking himself an open, frank, confiding person, asked me if he *was not.* Truth required me to say that I knew no more what Mr. C thought or felt on any subject now than I did twenty years ago. Sometimes I *feel* that we understand each other a little—then up goes the iron wall once more. Not that for a moment he ever gives you the impression of an *insincere,* or even a cold, person. Reticent—like the Indian too proud to let the world know how he feels. ... What nonsense I write here. However, this journal is intended to be entirely *objective.* My subjective days are over. No more *silent* eating into my own heart, making my own misery, when without these morbid fantasies I could be so happy. . . .

《I think this journal will be disadvantageous for me, for I spend the time now like a spider, spinning my own entrails instead of reading, as my habit was at all spare moments.》

---

to believe that no such action would be taken. Buchanan, though he promptly accepted the resignation, insisted that the plan to supply Sumter had been made at an open cabinet meeting and that Thompson had been fully informed.

2. George William Frederick Howard, who was known by the courtesy title of Lord Morpeth before becoming seventh earl of Carlisle in 1848, traveled in the U.S. and Canada in 1842.

March [no day] 1861.   "Now this is positive," they say. "Fort Sumter is to be relieved,[3] and we are to have no war." Poor Sumter—not half as much as we would be!

After all, far too good to be true.

《If there be no war, how triumphant Mr. Chesnut will be. He is the only man who has persisted from the first, that his would be a *peaceful* revolution. Heaven grant it may prove so.》

Mr. Browne told us that in one of the peace intervals—I mean, in the interest of peace—Lincoln flew through Baltimore, locked up in an express car. He wore a Scotch cap.

Baltimore plug uglies have a bad name.

The women here crowd on all sail. They are covered with jewelry—diamonds especially—from breakfast on to midnight. "Lord Southerk, my sister's fiancé, says [*four lines cut out of page*].[4] Now, I was so taken aback by the fact that he was to be "brother-in-law to a three-tailed bashaw,"[5] that his sister was engaged to a live lord, that I forgot to ask what the Lord said unto her regarding jewelry in the morning.

Mrs. Davis said to a lady here of her own age who was hinting at what she would do if she were a widow: "What—when we see all that you could do in your youth and beauty. If _____ is the best you could do when you were fresh and young, what better chance could you hope for, old?"

And Madame Flibbertigibbet deserved every word of it.

We went to the Congress today. Governor Cobb, who presides over that august body, put Mr. Chesnut in the chair and came down to talk to us, jolly old soul that he is.

He thought that Romeo and Juliet scene from the balcony that we interrupted needed an explanation.

He told us why the pay of congressmen was enacted in secret session and why the amount of it was never divulged. To prevent the lodging house and hotel people from making their bills of a size to cover it all. "The bill was sure to correspond with the pay," he said.

In the hotel parlor we had a scene.

---

3. M. B. C. must have meant that the fort would be evacuated.
4. The speaker is identified as Mrs. Browne in the 1860s Journal.
5. A play on George Colman, the younger, *Blue Beard; or, Female Curiosity! A Dramatick Romance* (1798), act 3, scene 4: "'Tis a very fine thing to be father-in-law / To a very magnificent three-tailed bashaw."

Mrs. Scott[6] was describing Lincoln, who is of the cleverest Yankee type, she said. "Awfully ugly—even grotesque in appearance, the kind who are always at corner stores, sitting on boxes, whittling sticks. And telling stories as funny as they are vulgar."

Here I interposed to sigh, "But Douglas said one day to Mr. Chesnut, 'Lincoln is the hardest fellow to handle I have ever encountered yet.'" Mr. Scott is from California. He said: "Lincoln is an utterly American specimen, coarse, tough, and strong. A good-natured, kindly creature.

"As pleasant-tempered as he is clever. And if this country can be joked and laughed out of its rights, he is the kind-hearted fellow to do it. Now, if there be a war and it pinches the Yankee pocket instead of filling it—"

Here a shrill voice came from the next room (which opened upon the one we were in by folding doors, thrown wide open):

"Yankees are no more mean and stingy than you are. People at the North are as good as people at the South."

The speaker advanced upon us in great wrath. Mrs. Scott apologized and made some smooth, polite remarks, though evidently much embarrassed. But the vinegar face and curly pate refused to receive any concession. She said, "That comes with a very bad grace after what you were saying." And she harangued us loudly for several minutes. Someone in the other room giggled outright. We were quiet as mice.

Nobody wanted to hurt her feelings. She was one against so many. If I were at the North I should expect them to belabor us—and should hold my tongue. We separated because of incompatibility of temper. We are divorced, North from South, because we hated each other so. If we could only separate—a "séparation à l'agréable," as the French say it, and not a horrid fight for divorce.

This poor exile had already been insulted, she said. She was playing "Yankee Doodle" on the piano before breakfast to soothe her wounded spirits. The Judge came in and calmly requested her to leave out the Yankee while she played the Doodle. The Yankee end of it did not suit our climate. Was totally out of place. Had got out of its latitude, &c&c.

Mrs. Davis does not like her husband being made president. People are hard to please. She says general of all the armies would have suited his temperament better.

And then Mrs. Watson[7] came in to deplore her husband's having been made adjutant general of the Alabama contingent.

A man[8] said aloud today, "This is nothing—it will soon blow over—only a fuss gotten up by that Charleston clique."

6. Anne (Vivian) Scott of Ala. was the wife of Charles Lewis Scott, a Virginia-born congressman from Calif. Early in March, Scott left Congress, went to Ala. with his wife, and enlisted as a private in the C.S.A.

7. Hugh P. Watson, adjutant general of Ala. militia throughout the war.

8. Identified as George Nicholas Sanders in the 1860s Journal.

Toombs asked him to show his passports, for a man who uses such language is a suspicious character—ought not to travel without passports.

Captain Smith Lee[9] wishes "South Carolina could be blown out of [the] water." He does hate so the disrupting of his dearly beloved (navy?) country.

Mr. Browne quite prides himself at having caught Sumner[1] in the surprising act of extracting so voluminously from Macaulay—and forgetting quotation marks.

There they were. Madame—old, ugly, rich, clever, red hair and blue blood. An heiress she was. He—young, worthless, handsome, good name, good office, small pay.

Now she hangs on his arms. He is not allowed to dance with anyone but his wife! She never loses sight of him. He looks dogged and desperate.

"Look at them. After all, he earns his money—as the Bible says it shall be done—by the sweat of his brow. Any man who married *her* money would have to do that."

"Remember, besides, that in the world we live in, they who wreck character are not as calumnious as they are simply idle. The men and the women who, having nothing to do, do mischief."[2]

Frightful scene. At our first call found the household quarreling. They did not pay us the compliment to suspend the little unpleasantness for our benefit—on the contrary, seemed to welcome us as witnesses.

One called aloud, "By your coming you have averted a tragedy."

The other, bowing to God, with arms extended. That she was a lone woman (here her voice became a scream). She had no husband to defend *her*. But she hoped God might strike her dead, if—&c&c. Here, as she attempted to leave the room, she gave such a lurch I thought God had taken her at her word.

But she turned to us, all tears and smiles, and said, "It is only I am so rickety in my legs."

We waited for many days before we had strength to attack our list of "calls to be returned" again.

The bride, my cousin—"we met, 'twas in a crowd."[3] So very large and handsome and strong. So calm. So covered with a frivle fravle of finery. Silent and grave, she found it all she could do, to take care of her cloud of drapery in that

9. Sydney Smith Lee, elder brother of Robert E. Lee, was in Washington, D.C., as chief of the U.S. Navy's Bureau of Coast Survey. When the Va. convention voted to secede in April, Lee resigned his commission, sold all his possessions, and began an undistinguished career in the Confederate navy.

1. Charles Sumner, U.S. senator from Mass.

2. Misquoted from Charles James Lever, *One of Them* (1861).

3. The first line of the popular song "We Met," by Thomas Haynes Bayly (1797–1839), an English poet and novelist.

crowd. She guarded her dress with her hands. And as it caught the passersby, with quiet dignity she unhooked herself—as on every side the tag end of her costume required to be detached from man or woman.

Her occupation being to take care of her clothes—like the unkind Jew in the parable[4]—I passed on the other side.

The grave Englishman explained to us who Beau Brummell was—illustrated with an anecdote—to enlighten our supposed ignorance. Beau Brummell was asked to dine in the city. He asked, "Where am I to change horses?"

We said nothing. Never explain a farce. Fun thrown back into the system poisons the blood.

So we suffer many things—of many people.

⟨⟨**March 15, 1861.**   Walked to see Mrs. Bethea[5] with Mr. Chesnut, who, however, rushed home and left me at the door.... Went to the party with the Brownes. At first we stood alone and were gazed at.... I know my dress is the prettiest in the room. Then we saw Mr. Clayton, and the remark was made: what a party when we are glad to see Mr. Clayton! Then Mr. Curry[6] walked off with Mrs. Browne. Mr. B and I had a good time. All sorts of stupid people came to interrupt us.... I want to tell Mrs. Browne that the effect upon me last night was not unlike the impression made by my first visit to Washington. The people I thought one mass of vulgarity and finery and horror. How differently I felt when I had been there long enough to separate the wheat from the tares.... I think old Governor Moore was jealous. He said quite peevishly that he must take lessons in the art of pleasing from Mr. M[allory].

⟨⟨Poor Mrs. Browne. How she hated my coming. Actually shed tears. <I can make anybody love me if I choose. I would get tired of it. Mr. B, too—how excessively complimentary he was that night at the party,>[7] and so nicely done. Any woman might have been proud of my three attendants that night....

⟨⟨**March 17, 1861.**   <My poor heart [*two illegible words*]. The seventeenth I got up, nearly frantic with all my own thoughts after that one glimpse of certain misery, hoping nothing, believing nothing that *this world* can now bring, fearing all.... >⟩⟩

March 18, 1861.   Augusta, Georgia. The day before we left Montgomery, in the midst of a red-hot patriotic denunciation of a great many people South and everybody North, someone suggested "yesterday's catastrophe" and threw open the folding doors suddenly, to be sure that the next room contained no spies nor eavesdroppers.

---

4. Luke 10:31.
5. Eugenia (Bethea) Bethea, wife of Montgomery planter and politician Tristram B. Bethea.
6. Jabez Lamar Monroe Curry of Ala., a member of the Provisional Confederate Congress, had belonged to the Chesnuts' Washington mess while serving in the U.S. Congress.
7. Here and below, the brackets < > indicate erasures recovered.

An unexpected tableau. A girl resting in a man's arms, he kissing her lips at his leisure or pleasure.

They were on their feet in an instant. She cried: "Oh! he is my cousin. He is married. He is taking me home from school." In the might of her innocence she seemed quite cool about it. He knew better and was terribly embarrassed. He might well be ashamed of himself.

Governor Moore grew disgusted at modern ways of pleasing ladies—a man reciting *Ingoldsby's Legends*.[8] That was bad enough—I mean selections, of course. He did not give us quite all. Then we had the "Address to a Mummy" and some rejected addresses.[9]

Governor Moore said, "He was no actor, thank God." As grateful as Mrs. Squeers[1] was as to innocence of grammar.

The play upon the word *Sparks* was the last drop—as Mr. Mallory quoted Dr. Syntax:

> Sparks are prone to upwards fly
> So man is born to misery.[2]

I did Mrs. Browne a kindness. I told those women that she was childless now, but that she had lost three children. I hated to leave her all alone. Women have such a contempt for a childless wife. Now they will be all sympathy and kindness. I took away "her reproach among women."[3]

We came along (Sunday) with a Methodist parson—also a member of the Congress. Someone said he was using his political legs—his pulpit feet would not move on a Sabbath day.

A man claimed acquaintance with me because he has married an old schoolgirl friend of mine.

"At least, she is my present wife."

Whispered the Light Brigade, "Has he had them before or means he to have them hereafter?" We had no time to learn. But one parson friend gravely informed us, "If he is the man I take him to be, he has buried two."

One of our party ⟨⟨Mr. C⟩⟩ so far forgot his democratic position toward the public as to wish aloud, "Oh, that we had separate coaches, as they have in England. That we could get away from these whiskey-drinking, tobacco-chewing rascals and rabble." All with votes!! Worse, all armed. A truculent crowd, truly, to offend. But each supposed he was one of the gentlemen to be separated from the other thing.

The day we left Montgomery, a man was shot in the street for some trifle. Mr.

8. *The Ingoldsby Legends; or, Mirth and Marvels,* a popular collection of comic tales by Anglican priest Richard Harris Barham, appeared in three different versions, in 1840, 1842, and 1847.

9. Horace (or Horatio) Smith, "Address to a Mummy," *The Poetical Works of Horace Smith* (1846). Smith, a London businessman, collaborated with his brother, James Smith, on *Rejected Addresses; or, the New Theatrum Poetarum* (1812), parodies of such poets as Wordsworth and Coleridge.

1. The ignorant wife of the schoolmaster in Charles Dickens's *Nicholas Nickleby* (1839).

2. Using Job 5:7 as his text, Dr. Syntax preaches a sermon in English satirist William Combe's *The Tour of Dr. Syntax in Search of the Picturesque* (1812), canto 21.

3. A play on Luke 1:25: ". . . take away my reproach among men."

Browne was open-mouthed in his horror of such ruffianlike conduct. They answered him, "It is the war fever. Soldiers must be fierce. It is the right temper for the times cropping out."

There was tragedy, too, on the way here. A mad woman, taken from her husband and children. Of course she was mad—or she would not have given "her grief words" in that public place. Her keepers were along. What she said was rational enough—pathetic, at times heartrending.

Then a highly intoxicated parson was trying to save the soul of "a bereaved widow." So he addressed her always as "my bereaved friend and widow."

The devil himself could not have quoted Scripture more fluently.

《It excited me so—I quickly took opium, and *that* I kept up. It enables me to retain every particle of mind or sense or brains I ever have and so quiets my nerves that I can calmly reason and take rational views of things otherwise maddening. . . . <and have refused to accept overtures for peace and forgiveness. After my stormy youth I did so hope for peace and tranquil domestic happiness. There is none for me in this world.> "The peace this world cannot give, which passeth all understanding." Today the papers say peace again. Yesterday the *Telegraph* and the *Herald* were warlike to a frightful degree. I have just read that Pugh is coming down south—another woman who loved me, and I treated her so badly at first. I have written to Kate[4] that I will go to her if she wants me—dear, dear sister. I wonder if other women shed as bitter tears as I. They scald my cheeks and blister my heart. Yet Edward Boykin wondered and marveled at my elasticity—was I always so bright and happy, did ever woman possess such a disposition, life was one continued festival, &c&c—and Bonham last winter shortly said it was a *bore* to see anyone always in a good humor. Much they know of me—or my power to hide trouble—much trouble.

《This [life?] is full of strange vicissitudes, and in nothing more remarkable than the way people are reconciled, ignore the past, and start afresh in life, here to incur more disagreements and set to bickering again—one of them. . . .

《I wonder if it be a sin to think slavery a curse to any land. Sumner said not one word of this hated institution which is not true. Men and women are punished when their masters and mistresses are brutes and not when they do wrong—and then we live surrounded by prostitutes. An abandoned woman is sent out of any decent house elsewhere. Who thinks any worse of a negro or mulatto woman for being a thing we can't name? God forgive us, but ours is a *monstrous* system and wrong and iniquity. Perhaps the rest of the world is as bad—this *only* I see. Like the patriarchs of old our men live all in one house with their wives and their concubines, and the mulattoes one sees in every family exactly resemble the white children—and every lady tells you who is the father of all the mulatto children in everybody's household, but those in her own she seems to think drop from the clouds, or pretends so to think. Good women we

---

4. M. B. C.'s younger sister, Catherine Boykin (Miller) Williams of Alachua County, Fla., and Society Hill, Darlington District, S.C. Kate's husband, planter David Rogerson Williams, Jr., was a nephew of James Chesnut, Jr.

men & women are punished
when their masters & mistresses
are brutes & not when they
do wrong — & then we live
surrounded by prostitutes —
an abandoned woman
is sent out of any decent
house — what thinks any
woman of a Negro or Mulatto
woman for being a thing we
can't name. God forgive us.
But ours is a Monstrous
System & wrong & iniquity —
perhaps the rest of it
the world is as bad —
this only I see — like
the patriarchs of old
our men live all in
one house with their
wives & their concubines.
& the Mulattoes one sees
in every family partly
resemble the white
children — & any lady
tells you who is the
father of all the Mulatto
children in everybody's household,
but those in her own, she seems
to think drop from the clouds
or pretends so to think —

"A *monstrous* system," from the 1860s Journal, March 18, 1861

have, *but* they talk of all *nastiness*—tho' they never do wrong, they talk day and night of [*erasures illegible save for the words* "all unconsciousness"] my disgust sometimes is boiling over—but they are, I believe, in conduct the purest women God ever made. Thank God for my countrywomen—alas for the men! No worse than men everywhere, but the lower their mistresses, the more degraded they must be.

《My mother-in-law told me when I was first married not to send my female servants in the street on errands. They were then tempted, led astray—and then she said placidly, so they told *me* when I came here, and I was very particular, *but you see with what result.*

《Mr. Harris said it was so patriarchal. So it is—flocks and herds and slaves—and wife Leah does not suffice. Rachel must be *added,* if not *married.*[5] And all the time they seem to think themselves patterns—models of husbands and fathers.

《Mrs. Davis told me everybody described my husband's father as an odd character—"a millionaire who did nothing for his son whatever, left him to struggle with poverty, &c." I replied—"Mr. Chesnut Senior thinks himself the best of fathers—and his son thinks likewise. I have nothing to say—but it is true. He has no money but what he makes as a lawyer." And again I say, my countrywomen are as pure as angels, tho' surrounded by another race who are the social evil!》

March 19, 1861. Mulberry, South Carolina. Snow a foot deep. Winter at last—after months of apparently May or June weather. Even the climate, like everything else, upside down.

After that den of dirt and horror, Montgomery Hall, how white the sheets look—luxurious bed linen once more, delicious fresh cream with my coffee.

I breakfast in bed.

Dueling is rife in Camden. William M. Shannon[6] challenges Leitner.[7] Rochelle Blair[8] is Shannon's second. Artemas Goodwyn[9] is Leitner's.

My husband has been riding hard all day to stop the foolish people.

More cropping out of the war spirit—the western man would say.

Mr. Chesnut did arrange the difficulty. There was a court of honor—and no duel. Mr. Leitner had struck Mr. Shannon at a negro trial.[1] 《Wm. Shannon

---

5. In Genesis 29–30, Jacob, unhappy with his wife Leah, also marries her sister Rachel. He has children by both women and by their handmaidens as well. M. B. C. apparently believed old Mr. Chesnut had children by a slave whom she calls "Rachel" (p. 72). She confesses no such suspicions of her husband.

6. William McCreight Shannon, a member of the S.C. house. Saved from this duel, Shannon died July 5, 1880, in a much publicized duel, reputedly the last fought in S.C.

7. William Zachariah Leitner, first lieutenant in the Second S.C. Volunteers.

8. L. W. Rochelle Blair, a captain in the C.S.A., had been defended by James Chesnut, Jr., against a murder charge in 1853.

9. Artemas Darby Goodwyn of Richland District, adjutant of the Second S.C. Regiment.

1. Washington, a slave charged with attempting to raise a slave insurrection, was sentenced to hang. Given her usual candor, it is curious that M. B. C. does not mention the nature of the trial, either here or in her original journal.

defending the poor negro, he prosecuting.⟩⟩ That's the way the row begins. Everybody knows of it. We suggested that Judge Withers should arrest the belligerents.

Dr. Boykin and Joe Kershaw were aiding Mr. Chesnut to put an end to this useless risk of life.

John Chesnut[2] is a pretty softhearted slave-owner.

He had two negroes arrested for selling whiskey to his people on his plantation and buying stolen corn from them.

The culprits in jail sent for him. He found them (this snowy weather) lying in the cold on a bare floor. And he thought that punishment enough, they having had weeks of it. But they were not satisfied to be allowed to evade justice and slip away. They begged him (and got it) for five dollars to buy shoes to run away in. I said, "Why, that is flat compounding a felony!"

And Johnny put his hands in the armholes of his waistcoat and stalked majestically before me.

"Woman, what do you know about law?"

Mrs. Reynolds[3] stopped the carriage today to tell me Kitty Boykin[4] is to be married to Savage Heyward. He has only ten children already.

⟨⟨I do not believe it—talked all night—exhausted, and nervous and miserable today—raked up and dilated and harrowed up the bitterness of twenty long years—all to no purpose. This bitter world.⟩⟩[5]

These people take the old Hebrew pride in the number of children they have. True colonizing spirit. No danger of crowding here—inhabitants are wanted.

Old Mr. C said today, "Wife, you must feel that you have not been useless in your day and generation. You have now twenty-seven great-grandchildren. . . ."[6]

⟨⟨Me a childless wretch. . . . Colonel Chesnut, a man who rarely wounds me . . . And what of me! God help me—no good have I done myself or anyone else, with this I boast so of, the power to make myself loved. Where am I now,

---

2. John Chesnut IV, an 1858 graduate of S.C. College, was the son of J. C.'s elder brother, John Chesnut III. This fourth John Chesnut was the favorite in-law of M. B. C., who usually calls him "Johnny," "John C," "the Captain," or "the cool Captain."

3. Mary Cox (Chesnut) Reynolds, widow of Dr. George Reynolds, was the sister of James Chesnut, Jr.

4. Katherine Lang Boykin, M. B. C.'s second cousin and the sister of Dr. Edward M. Boykin, shortly married Thomas Savage Heyward, a Charleston commission merchant and grandson of a signer of the Declaration of Independence. At the time, eight of Heyward's twelve children by his first wife were alive.

5. Under March 21, 1861, in the 1860s Journal.

6. Deleted is an irrelevant quotation from John Lothrop Motley on Maurice of Saxony.

where are my friends? I am allowed to have none. (*He did not count his children!!*)⟩⟩[7]

March 22, 1861.   Trying to forget my country, woes, I read the *Life of Lord Dundonald*[8] today.

The man is so charming till the cold wave comes, the shock! A hero must be like Caesar's wife! His hands must be clean from money—or the suspicion of it. A hero who cheats? On money matters!!!

At my aunt's,[9] heard her coachman give her a message.

"The ladies say I must tell you their father is behaving shameful. He is disgracing hisself. He had not tasted whiskey for 15 years. He took some as physic a month ago, and he ain't drawed a sober breath since."

"Do they not read the Ten Commandments in your church? There is one with a promise 'that thy days may be long.' These people do not heed it, it seems."

"Don't laugh. He does those poor girls dreadfully (his wife and daughters)."

"What does he do?"

"I don't know—now—but when I went to school with them, he seized one of them and dropped her in the molasses hogshead—bonnet, cloak, satchel, and all."

March 25, 1861.   ⟨⟨Today, forlorn and weak and miserable, I am slowly packing to be off to town. . . .⟩⟩

I was mobbed yesterday by my own house servants. Some of them are at the plantation, some hired out at the Camden hotel. Some here at Mulberry.[1]

They agreed to come in a body and beg me to stay at home—to keep my own house once more, as I ought not to have them scattered and distributed every which away.

I have not been a month in Camden since 1858. So a house here would be for their benefit solely, not mine. I asked my cook if she lacked anything on the plantation at the Hermitage.

"Lack anything?" said she. "I lack everything. What is cornmeal and bacon, milk and molasses? Would that be all you wanted? Ain't I bin living and eating

7. Entered under the date March 21, 1861, in the 1860s Journal, but the remark relates to the same comment of old Colonel Chesnut.

8. Thomas Cochrane, tenth earl of Dundonald, *The Autobiography of a Seaman* (1860–61). Dundonald was a British naval hero accused of involvement in a stock exchange fraud in 1814.

9. Identified in the 1860s Journal under March 23, 1861, as M. B. C.'s aunt Elizabeth (Boykin) Withers, the wife of Thomas Jefferson Withers. The "ladies" below were Dinah "Denie" McEwen and Susan (McEwen) Tweed, two sisters who ran a Camden millinery shop. Their father was James McEwen, an eighty-three-year-old Scots-born merchant.

1. James Chesnut's house slaves were distributed in this manner when he sold his house and went to Washington in 1858.

exactly as you does all these years? When I cook for you, didn't I have some of all? Dere now."

So she doubled herself up laughing.

They all shouted, "Missis, we is crazy for you to stay home."

Armsted, my butler, said he hated the hotel. Besides, he heard a man there abusing "Marster," but Mr. Clyburn[2] took it up and made him stop short. Armsted said he wanted Marster to know Mr. Clyburn was his friend and would let nobody say a word behind his back against him, &c&c.

Stay here? Not if I can help it.

"Festers in provincial sloth." That's Tennyson's way of putting it.[3]

---

2. William Craig Clyburn, a planter of Kershaw District.
3. M. B. C. is probably misquoting a line from Tennyson's *In Memoriam* (1850), part 27, stanza 3: "The heart that never plighted troth / But stagnates in the weeds of sloth."

III

"Into the Black Cloud"

March 26, 1861. Charleston. Yesterday we came down here by rail, as the English say. Such a crowd of convention men[1] on board. John Manning flew in to beg me to reserve the seat by me for a young lady under his charge.

"Place aux dames," said my husband politely and went off to seek a seat somewhere else.

As soon as we were fairly under way, Governor Manning came back and threw himself cheerfully down in the vacant place. After arranging his umbrella, overcoat, &c to his satisfaction, he coolly remarked, "I am the young lady."

He is always the handsomest man alive[2] (now that poor William Taber has been killed in a Rhett duel),[3] and he can be very agreeable. That is, when he pleases. He does not always please.

He seemed to have made his little maneuver principally to warn me of impending danger to my husband's political career.

"Every election now will be a surprise. New cliques are not formed yet. The old ones are principally bent upon displacing each other, &c&c."

"But the Yankees, those dreadful Yankees."

"Oh, never mind—we are going to take care of home folks first. How will you like to rusticate? Go back and mind your own business?"

"If I only knew what that was—my business."

Our round table consists of the Judge, Langdon Cheves,[4] Trescot, and ourselves.

Here are four of the cleverest men that we have. Such very different people, as opposite in every characteristic as the four points of the compass. Langdon Cheves and my husband have more ideas and feelings in common.

1. Members of the S.C. secession convention.

2. William Howard Russell, the English journalist, wrote of John Manning, "Who that has ever met him can be indifferent to the charms of manner and of personal appearance, which render the ex-Governor of the state so attractive?" *My Diary North and South* (1863), p. 155.

3. In 1856, William Robinson Taber, editor of the Charleston *Mercury*, died in a duel with Edward Magrath, whose brother had been attacked in a *Mercury* article by Taber's first cousin, Edmund Rhett, Jr. The duel, prompted by one Rhett, enabled another—Edmund's brother, Robert Barnwell Rhett, Jr.—to become editor of the *Mercury*.

4. Langdon Cheves, Jr., son of the former Speaker of the House and president of the U.S. Bank, was a planter and delegate to the S.C. secession convention from St. Peter's Parish.

Mr. Petigru[5] said of that brilliant Trescot, "He is a man without indignation." He and I laugh at everything.

The Judge from his life as a solicitor, and then on the bench, has learned to look for the darkest motives for every action. His judgment on men and things is always so harsh it shocks and repels even his best friends.

Today he said, "Your conversation reminds me of a flashy second-rate novel."

"How?"

"By the quantity of French you sprinkle over it. Do you wish to prevent us from understanding you?"

"No," said Trescot. "We are using French against Africa. We know the black waiters are all ears now, and we want to keep what we have to say dark. We can't afford to take them in our confidence, you know."

This explanation Trescot gave with great rapidity and many gestures toward the men standing behind us. Still speaking the French language, his apology was exasperating. So the Judge glared at him and, in unabated rage, turned to talk with Mr. Cheves, who found it hard to keep a calm countenance.

On the Battery with the Rutledges,[6] Captain Hartstene[7] was introduced to me.

He has done some heroic thing—brought home some ship. Is a man of mark. Afterward he sent me a beautiful bouquet—not half so beautiful, however, as Mr. Robert Gourdin's,[8] which already occupied the place of honor on my center table.

What a dear, delightful place is Charleston.

A lady (who shall be nameless because of her story) came to see me today. Her husband has been on the island with the troops for months. She has just been down to see him. She meant only to call on him, but he persuaded her to stay two days. She carried him some clothes—made by his old pattern. Now they are a mile too wide. "So much for a hard life!" I said.

"No, no. They are jolly down there. He has trained down—says it is good for him. He likes the life." Then she became confidential—and it was her first visit to me, a perfect stranger. She had no clothes down there, pushed in that

5. James Louis Petigru, a noted Charleston lawyer and Unionist. James Chesnut, Jr., read law in his office after graduating from Princeton, and Mary Chesnut was a childhood friend of his daughter Susan.

6. Identified in the 1860s Journal as Robert Smith Rutledge and his sister, Susan Rose Rutledge.

7. Henry Julius Hartstene, a commander of the Confederate navy, charged with guarding the defenses to Charleston Harbor. As an officer of the U.S. Navy, Hartstene had been honored by Queen Victoria in 1856 for delivering the lost Arctic discovery ship *Resolute* to England. Above a clipping about Hartstene's reception, M. B. C. wrote: "My friend Capt. Hartstene. He brings me a bunch of violets every morning. Meets me on my way to breakfast." She spelled his name "Hartstein," as it was spelled in the clipping.

8. Robert Newman Gourdin of Charleston was a lawyer, merchant, and delegate to the S.C. secession convention.

manner under Achilles' tent. But she managed. She tied her petticoat around her neck for a nightgown.

Yesterday is gone! Yes. But well remembered. We think the more of it *now*. We know tomorrow is not going to bring us much.

⟨⟨—Thackeray⟩⟩

March 28, 1861.   Governor Manning came to breakfast at our table—the others had breakfasted hours ago. I looked at him in amazement, as he was in full dress, ready for a ball. Swallowtail and all, at that hour!

"What is the matter with you?"

"Nothing. I am not mad, most noble Madame, I am only going to the photographer. My wife wants me taken *thus*."

He insisted on my going, too, and we captured Mr. Chesnut and Governor Means.[9] The latter presented me with a book—a photo book—in which I am to pillory all celebrities.

Dr. Gibbes[1] says the convention is in a snarl.

It was called as a secession convention—a secession of places seems to be what it calls for first of all. It has not stretched its eyes out to the Yankees yet. It has them turned inward still. Introspection is its occupation still.

Last night, as I turned down the gas, I said to myself, "Certainly this has been one of the pleasantest days of my life."

I can only give the skeleton of it. So many pleasant people, so much good talk—for after all, it was talk, talk, talk, à la Caroline du Sud.

And yet the day began rather dismally. Mrs. Capers[2] and Mrs. Tom Middleton[3] came for me, and we drove to Magnolia Cemetery. There to see the VanderHorst[4] way of burying their dead. One, at least, is embalmed or kept lifelike by some process, dressed as usual—can be seen through a glass case. I did not look. How can anyone?

---

9. John Hugh Means, a prosperous Fairfield District planter and governor of S.C. from 1850 to 1852, was a delegate to the S.C. secession convention and colonel of the Seventeenth S.C. Regiment.

1. Robert Wilson Gibbes of Columbia, a physician of national reputation, was also a writer, former mayor of Columbia, owner of the Columbia *Daily South Carolinian* and the *Weekly Banner,* and an ornithologist. During the war, he served as surgeon general of S.C.

2. Charlotte Rebecca (Palmer) Capers was the wife of Ellison Capers of Charleston, a professor at the Citadel, serving as major of light artillery.

3. Eweretta (Barnewall) Middleton, second wife of Charleston merchant Thomas Middleton. For nearly two centuries, members of the Middleton family had been wealthy planters and prominent figures in S.C. and American politics.

4. The VanderHorsts were an old S.C. family that included Arnoldus VanderHorst, governor of the state from 1792 to 1794.

I did see William Taber's broken column. It was hard to shake off the blues after this graveyard business.

The others were off at a dinner party. I dined tête-à-tête with Langdon Cheves. So quiet. So intelligent. So very sensible withal. There never was a pleasanter person or a better man than he. While we were at table Judge Whitner,[5] Tom Frost,[6] and Isaac Hayne[7] came. They broke up our deeply interesting conversation—for I was hearing what an honest and a brave man feared for his country. And then the Rutledges dislodged the newcomers and bore me off to drive on the Battery. On the staircase met Mrs. Izard,[8] who came for the same purpose. On the Battery, Governor Adams[9] stopped us. He had heard of my saying he looked like Marshal Pelissier[1]—and he came to say at least I had made a personal remark which pleased him, &c&c, for once in my life. ⟨⟨... received orders that I was not to walk any more with men on the Battery. Is not all this too ridiculous at my time of life... ?⟩⟩

When we came home Mr. Isaac Hayne and Chancellor Carroll[2] called to ask us to join their excursion to the island forts tomorrow. With them was William Haskell.[3] Last summer at the White Sulphurs[4] he was a pale, slim student from the university. Today he is a soldier, stout and robust. A few months in camp, soldiering in the open air, has worked this wonder. This camping out proves a wholesome life, after all.

Then those nice, sweet, fresh, pure-looking Pringle girls.[5] We had a charming topic in common—their clever brother Edward.... ⟨⟨Mr. Chesnut made himself eminently absurd by accusing me of flirting with John Manning, and I could only laugh....⟩⟩[6]

March 31, 1861. My 38th birthday. But I am too old now to dwell in public on that unimportant circumstance.

5. Joseph Newton Whitner of Anderson District, a former solicitor of the Western Judicial Circuit of S.C., was a delegate to the S.C. secession convention.

6. Thomas Frost, a Charleston clerk related to the Chesnuts by marriage.

7. Isaac William Hayne, grandson of Revolutionary War hero Isaac Hayne, was attorney general of S.C. and a member of the state secession convention from Charleston District. In Jan., Governor Pickens sent Hayne to Washington to demand the surrender of Fort Sumter.

8. Probably Rosetta Ella (Pinckney) Izard, the widow of wealthy Georgetown District, S.C., planter Ralph Stead Izard.

9. James Hopkins Adams, a Richland District planter who owned 500 slaves in 1860, was governor of S.C. from 1854 to 1856, a member of the secession convention, and one of three commissioners who negotiated with President Buchanan in Dec. 1860, for the transfer of Federal property in S.C.

1. Aimable Jean Jacques Pelissier, duc de Malakoff, was a French general known for his exploits in the Algerian and Crimean wars.

2. James Parsons Carroll of Edgefield District, chancellor of the S.C. Court of Equity, was a delegate to the secession convention.

3. Son of Sophia (Cheves) and Charles Thomson Haskell of Abbeville, S.C.

4. The fashionable western Va. (now W. Va.) resort.

5. Rebecca, Susan, and Edward Jenkins Pringle were the children of planter William Bull Pringle of Charleston and Georgetown District. Edward, a San Francisco lawyer, had stayed with the Chesnuts in Washington during the winter of 1859-60. Omitted is a letter from a friend in Montgomery.

6. From an entry in the 1860s Journal dated March 29 that mentions "Today the 30th."

A long dusty day ahead on those windy islands. Never for me. So I was up early to write a note of excuse to Chancellor Carroll. My husband went. ⟨⟨ Mr. C gave me his cheek for farewell. . . .⟩⟩ I hope Anderson will not pay them the compliment of a salute with shotted guns as they pass Fort Sumter, as pass they must.

Here I am interrupted by an exquisite bouquet from the Rutledges. Are there such roses anywhere else in the world?

Now a loud banging at my door. I get up in a pet and throw it wide open.

"Oh," said John Manning, standing there, smiling radiantly. "Pray excuse the noise I made. I mistook the number. I thought it was Rice's room. That is my excuse. Now that I am here, come go with us to Quinby's. Everybody will be there—who are not on the island. To be photographed is the rage just now."

We had a nice open carriage, and we made a number of calls—Mrs. Izard's, the Pringles', Tradd Street Rutledges'[7]—the[8] handsome ex-governor doing the honors gallantly.

He had ordered dinner at six—and we dined tête-à-tête. If he should prove as great a captain in ordering his line of battle as he is in ordering a dinner, it will be as well for the country as it was for me today.

Fortunately for the men, the beautiful Mrs. Joe Heyward[9] sits at the next table, so they take her beauty as one of the goods the gods provide. And it helps to make life pleasant—with English grouse—&c&c—and venison from the west. Not to speak of salmon from the Lakes, which began the feast. They have me to listen—appreciative audience—while they talk, and Mrs. Joe Heyward to look at.

⟨⟨ <Mr. C came home so enraged with my staying at home he decides [?] to glare [?] until John's leaving. Thus I went to bed in disgust. . . .>⟩⟩[1]

Beauregard[2] called. He is the hero of the hour. That is, he is believed to be capable of great things. A hero-worshiper was struck dumb because I said, "So far he has only been a captain of artillery or engineers or something." I did not see him—Mrs. Wigfall did.[3] And reproached my laziness in not coming out.

7. The family of Frederick Rutledge, a physician and planter of Charleston.
8. The word "the" was originally written "my," then the definite article was superimposed by M. B. C.
9. Maria Henrietta (Magruder) Heyward was the Virginia-born wife of Joseph Heyward, the son of a Colleton District, S.C., rice planter.
1. Recovery of this erased passage leaves the reading of two words, "decides" and "glare," still questionable. The entry in the 1860s Journal is dated April 1, 1861.
2. Pierre Gustave Toutant Beauregard of La., a career officer in the U.S. Army, was appointed a brigadier general of the C.S.A. on March 1, 1861, and given command of the Confederate forces at Charleston.
3. Charlotte Maria (Cross) Wigfall, the daughter of a wealthy Providence, R.I., family, had married her second cousin, Louis T. Wigfall, in 1841.

At church today, saw one of the peculiar local traits—old Negro maumeys going up to the communion in their white turbans.

Being the Lord's table—so-called. Even there—black, white, and brown, separate according to caste.

The morning papers say Mr. Chesnut made the best shot on the island yesterday—target practice.

No war yet, thank God. Likewise they tell me he has made a capital speech in the convention.

————————

Not one word of what is going on now. "Of the fullness of the heart the mouth speaketh," says the Psalmist.[4] Not so here. Our hearts are in doleful dumps. And we are as gay, as madly jolly, as the sailors who break into the strong room when the ship is going down.

First our great agony—we are out alone. We longed for some of our big brothers to come out and help us. Well they are out, too. Now it is Fort Sumter—and that ill-advised Anderson.

There stands Fort Sumter—en évidence—and thereby hangs peace or war.

Wigfall says before he left Washington, Pickens, our governor, and Trescot were openly against secession. Trescot does not pretend to like it now. He grumbles all the time. But Governor Pickens is fire-eater down to the ground.

"At the White House Mrs. Davis wore a badge—'Jeff Davis no seceder,'" says Mrs. Wigfall.

Captain Ingraham comments in his rapid way, words tumbling over each other out of his mouth: "Now, Charlotte Wigfall meant that as a fling at those people. I think better of men who stop to think. It is too rash, to rush on as some do."

"And so," adds Mrs. Wigfall, "the eleventh-hour men are rewarded. The halfhearted are traitors in this row." &c&c&c.

《<I wonder when Mr. C will [*one or two words unrecoverable*] this John Manning. Is it not too funny—and he is so *prosy.*>》[5]

April 3, 1861.   Met the lovely Lucy Holcombe,[6] now Mrs. Governor Pickens, last night at the Isaac Haynes'. I see Miles now begging in dumb show for three violets she had in her breastpin. She is a consummate actress and he well up in the part of male flirt. So it was well done.

"And you who are laughing in your sleeve at the scene—where did you get that huge bunch?"

4. From Matthew 12:34 rather than Psalms.

5. Entry in the 1860s Journal dated March 29 but mentioning "Today the 30th."

6. Lucy Petway (Holcombe) Pickens of Tex. became Francis Pickens's third wife in 1858. Her beauty inspired a S.C. regiment to call itself the "Holcombe Legion" and the Confederate government to engrave her portrait on its currency; her extravagance helped drive her husband far into debt.

"Oh, there is no sentiment when there is a pile like that of anything."

"Oh! Oh!"

Today at the breakfast table—a tragic bestowal of heartsease. Well-known Inquirer, once more, in austere tones: "Who is the flirt now?"

And so we fool on, into the black cloud ahead of us.

⟨⟨<Breakfasted today with John Manning. Mr. C restive because I said I did not tell him everything. Then John Manning brought me a bunch of violets>⟩⟩[7]

April 4, 1861.   Mr. Hayne said his wife moaned over the hardness of the chaperon's seats at St. Andrews Hall. At a St. Cecilia ball she was hopelessly deposited there for hours.

"And the walls are harder, my dear. What are your feelings to those of the poor old fellows leaning there, with their beautiful young wives waltzing as if they could never tire, in every man's arms in the room? Watch their haggard, weary faces—the old boys, you know.

"At church I had to move my pew. The lovely Laura was too much for my boys. They all made eyes at her and nudged each other and quarreled so. For she gave them glance for glance—wink, blink, and snigger as they would. She liked it. I say, my dear, the old husbands have not exactly a bed of roses. Their wives twirling in the arms of young men, they hugging the walls."

While we were at supper at the Haynes', Wigfall was sent for to address a crowd before the Mills House piazza. Like James Fitz James—when he visits Clan Alpine again—it is to be in the saddle, &c&c.[8] So let Washington beware.

We were sad that we could not hear the speaking. But the supper was a consolation—pâté de foie gras, salad, biscuit glacé, and champagne frappé.

A ship was fired into yesterday and went back to sea.[9]

Is that the first shot?

How can one settle down to anything? One's heart is in one's mouth all the time. Any minute this cannon may open on us, the fleet come in, &c&c.

April 6, 1861.   The plot thickens. The air is red-hot with rumors. The mystery is to find out where these utterly groundless tales originate.

7. The erased passage is under the date April 2, 1861, in the 1860s Journal.

8. Wigfall told his audience on the night of April 3 that war with the North was inevitable. Vowing to return to Washington "in the saddle" the next year, the former U.S. senator quoted Fitz James, the Lowland king of Scotland who subdues the rebellious Clan Alpine in Sir Walter Scott's *The Lady of the Lake* (1810), canto 5: "Twice have I sought Clan-Alpine's glen / In peace; but when I come agen, / I come with banner, brand and bow, / As leader seeks his mortal foe."

9. On April 3, the master of the *Rhoda H. Shannon*, an ice schooner from Boston, mistook Charleston Harbor for Savannah and began to sail into port. The Confederate battery on Morris Island fired several warning shots before the ship sailed out of range.

In spite of all, Tom Huger[1] came for us, and we went on the *Planter* to take a look at Morris Island and its present inhabitants.

Mrs. Wigfall and the Cheves girls,[2] Maxcy Gregg,[3] and Colonel Whiting[4]—also John Rutledge[5] of the navy, Dan Hamilton,[6] and William Haskell.

John Rutledge was a figurehead to be proud of. He did not speak to us. But he stood with a Scotch shawl draped about him, as handsome and stately a creature as ever Queen Elizabeth loved to look upon.

Then came up such a wind we could not land. I was not too sorry, though it blew so hard (I am never seasick). Colonel Whiting explained everything about the forts—what they lacked, &c&c—in the most interesting way, and Maxcy Gregg supplemented his report by stating all of deficiencies and shortcomings by land.

Beauregard is a demigod here to most of the natives, but there are always seers who see—and say. They give you to understand that Whiting has all the brains now in use for our defense. He does the work—Beauregard reaps the glory.

Things seem to draw near a crisis. And one must think Colonel Whiting is clever enough for anything. So we made up our minds today—Maxcy Gregg and I—as judges.

The Gregg told me that my husband was in a minority in the convention. So much for cool sense, when the atmosphere is phosphorescent.

Mrs. Wigfall says we are mismatched. She should pair with my cool, quiet, self-poised colonel—and her stormy petrel is but a male reflection of me.

April 7, 1861.   Yesterday Mrs. Wigfall and I made a few visits. At the first house they wanted Mrs. Wigfall to settle a dispute. "Was she indeed fifty-five?" Fancy her face—more than ten years bestowed upon her so freely.

Then Mrs. Gibbes[7] asked me if I had ever been in Charleston before.

Says Charlotte Wigfall (to pay me for my snigger when that false fifty was flung in her teeth), "And she thinks this is her native heath and her name is MacGregor."[8]

1. Thomas Bee Huger of S.C., nephew of Alfred Huger, resigned from the U.S. Navy in Jan. and became a Confederate navy lieutenant. He commanded a battery on Morris Island, which protected the entrance to Charleston Harbor on the south.

2. Mary and Emma Cheves, daughters of Langdon Cheves, Jr.

3. A Charleston lawyer and veteran of the Mexican War, Gregg was commissioned colonel of the First S.C. Volunteers.

4. William Henry Chase Whiting of Miss., a former U.S. Army officer, was a major (not a colonel) in charge of laying out the artillery on Morris Island.

5. A U.S. Navy lieutenant the month before, Rutledge was serving as a lieutenant of the S.C. navy and acting inspector general of the batteries at Charleston.

6. Daniel Heyward Hamilton, U.S. marshal for the District of S.C. before the war, was lieutenant colonel of Maxcy Gregg's regiment.

7. Caroline Elizabeth (Guignard) Gibbes, wife of Surgeon General Robert Wilson Gibbes of S.C.

8. Though his name is proscribed by the crown, Rob Roy refuses to be called by anything else when in the Highlands: "Do not Maister or Campbell me—my foot is on my native heath, and my name is MacGregor." Sir Walter Scott, *Rob Roy* (1817), chapter 35.

She said it all came upon us for breaking the Sabbath, for indeed it was Sunday.

Allen Green[9] came up to speak to me at dinner in all of his soldier's toggery. It sent a shiver through me.

Tried to read Margaret Fuller Ossoli.[1] But could not.

The air is too full of war news. And we are all so restless. ⟨⟨News so warlike I quake. My husband speaks of joining the artillery.... <[*first line and a half of four and a half erased lines unrecoverable*] last night I find he is my all, and I would go mad without him. > Mr. Manning read me a letter from his wife last night—very complimentary."⟩⟩[2]

Went to see Miss Pinckney—one of the last of the 18th century Pinckneys. She inquired particularly about a portrait of her father, Charles Cotesworth Pinckney[3]—which she said had been sent by him to my husband's grandfather. I gave a good account of it. It hangs in the place of honor in the drawing room at Mulberry. She wanted to see my husband, for "his grandfather, my father's friend, was one of the handsomest men of his day."

We came home, and soon Mr. Robert Gourdin and Mr. Miles called.

Governor Manning walked in, bowed gravely, and seated himself by me.

Again he bowed low, in mock heroic style and, with a grand wave of his hand, said, "Madame, your country is invaded."

When I had breath to speak, I asked, "What does he mean?"

"He means this. There are six men-of-war outside of the bar. Talbot and Chew have come to say that hostilities are to begin.[4] Governor Pickens and Beauregard are holding a council of war."

Mr. Chesnut then came in. He confirmed the story.

Wigfall next entered in boisterous spirits. He said, "There was a sound of revelry by night, &c&c&c."[5]

In any stir or confusion, my heart is apt to beat so painfully. Now the agony was so stifling—I could hardly see or hear. The men went off almost immediately. And I crept silently to my room, where I sat down to a good cry.

Mrs. Wigfall came in, and we had it out on the subject of civil war. We solaced

9. Allen Jones Green, Jr., a physician, planter, state legislator, and former mayor of Columbia, was captain of the Columbia Flying Artillery, stationed on Morris Island.

1. The 1860s Journal indicates that M. B. C. was reading a short essay on this feminist and Transcendentalist in Samuel Smiles, *Brief Biographies* (1860).

2. It is less than certain which of the two men mentioned is the antecedent of the pronouns "he" and "him." Manning had written his wife about the flirtation, however, and she had responded lightly with a request for Chesnut's picture and a declaration that she proposed to have a flirtation with him. That only leaves the question why M. B. C. erased the passage (which appears under April 8) in the first place.

3. Harriott Pinckney's father had been a Revolutionary soldier, a delegate to the Federal Constitutional Convention, minister to France, and the unsuccessful Federalist presidential candidate in 1804 and 1808.

4. The corresponding passage of the 1860s Journal is dated April 9. The night before, Robert S. Chew, a State Department clerk, and Capt. Theodore Talbot, an officer who had served at Fort Sumter, notified Governor Pickens that "an attempt will be made to supply Ft. Sumter with provisions only." That is, Lincoln would not yield to the Confederate demands to give up the fort.

5. From canto 3, stanza 21, of Lord Byron's *Childe Harold's Pilgrimage* (1812–18).

ourselves with dwelling on all its known horrors, and then we added what we had a right to expect, with Yankees in front and negroes in the rear.

"The slave-owners must expect a servile insurrection, of course," said Mrs. Wigfall, to make sure that we were unhappy enough.

Suddenly loud shouting was heard. We ran out. Cannon after cannon roared. We met Mrs. Allen Green in the passageway, with blanched cheeks and streaming eyes.

Governor Means rushed out of his room in his dressing gown and begged us to be calm.

"Governor Pickens has ordered, in the plenitude of his wisdom, seven cannon to be fired as a signal to the Seventh Regiment. Anderson will hear as well as the Seventh Regiment. Now you go back and be quiet: fighting in the streets has not begun yet."

So we retired. Dr. Gibbes calls Mrs. Allen Green "Dame Placid."[6] There was no placidity today. Cannons bursting and Allen on the island.

No sleep for anybody last night. The streets were alive with soldiers, men shouting, marching, singing.

Wigfall, the Stormy Petrel, in his glory. The only thoroughly happy person I see.

Today things seem to have settled down a little.

One can but hope still. Lincoln or Seward have made such silly advances and then far sillier drawings back. There may be a chance for peace, after all.

Things are happening so fast.

My husband has been made an aide-de-camp of General Beauregard.

Three hours ago we were quietly packing to go home. The convention has adjourned.

Now he tells me the attack upon Fort Sumter may begin tonight. Depends upon Anderson and the fleet outside. The *Herald* says that this show of war outside of the bar is intended for Texas.

John Manning came in with his sword and red sash. Pleased as a boy to be on Beauregard's staff while the row goes on. He has gone with Wigfall to Captain Hartstene with instructions.

Mr. Chesnut is finishing a report he had to make to the convention.

Mrs. Hayne[7] called. She had, she said, "but one feeling, pity for those who are not here."

Jack Preston,[8] Willie Alston[9]—"the take-life-easys," as they are called—with John Green,[1] "the big brave," have gone down to the island—volunteered as privates.

6. A rather insulting reference to the domineering wife in Elizabeth (Simpson) Inchbald's play *Everyone Has His Fault* (1793).

7. Alicia Paulina (Trapier) Hayne, wife of Isaac William Hayne.

8. John Preston, Jr., a law student, was the eldest son of the Chesnuts' close friends John Smith Preston and Caroline (Hampton) Preston of Columbia (see p. 49, n. 6).

9. Probably William Algernon Alston, Jr., a wealthy Georgetown District rice planter.

1. Probably John Sitgraves Green, a Columbia attorney who was the brother of Allen Jones Green, Jr.

Seven hundred men were sent over. Ammunition wagons rumbling along the streets all night. Anderson burning blue lights—signs and signals for the fleet outside, I suppose.

Today[2] at dinner there was no allusion to things as they stand in Charleston Harbor. There was an undercurrent of intense excitement. There could not have been a more brilliant circle. In addition to our usual quartet (Judge Withers, Langdon Cheves, and Trescot) our two governors dined with us, Means and Manning.

These men all talked so delightfully. For once in my life I listened.

That over, business began. In earnest, Governor Means rummaged a sword and red sash from somewhere and brought it for Colonel Chesnut, who has gone to demand the surrender of Fort Sumter.[3]

———————

And now, patience—we must wait.

———————

Why did that green goose Anderson go into Fort Sumter? Then everything began to go wrong.

Now they have intercepted a letter from him, urging them to let him surrender. He paints the horrors likely to ensue if they will not.[4]

He ought to have thought of all that before he put his head in the hole.

April 12, 1861.   Anderson will not capitulate.

———————

Yesterday was the merriest, maddest dinner we have had yet. Men were more audaciously wise and witty. We had an unspoken foreboding it was to be our last pleasant meeting. Mr. Miles dined with us today. Mrs. Henry King[5] rushed in: "The news, I come for the latest news—all of the men of the King family are on the island"—of which fact she seemed proud.

While she was here, our peace negotiator—or envoy—came in. That is, Mr. Chesnut returned—his interview with Colonel Anderson had been deeply interesting—but was not inclined to be communicative, wanted his dinner. Felt for Anderson. Had telegraphed to President Davis for instructions.

2. The corresponding section of the 1860s Journal is dated April 11.

3. On the afternoon of the eleventh, Chesnut and Capt. Stephen D. Lee, representing Beauregard, and Lt. Col. Alexander Robert Chisolm, representing Governor Pickens, rowed to Sumter with the demand for the fort's evacuation.

4. Angered by Lincoln's decision to provision Sumter, the Confederate authorities stopped Anderson's mail on the eighth. A captured letter from Anderson did not request permission to surrender but questioned the strategic importance of Sumter and protested the decision to supply the fort. "We shall strive to do our duty," Anderson concluded, "though . . . my heart is not in the war which I see is to be thus commenced."

5. Susan (Petigru) King, daughter of James L. Petigru and a classmate of M. B. C. at Madame Talvande's school, was the author of *Busy Moments of an Idle Woman* (1854) and *Sylvia's World and Crimes Which the Law Does Not Reach* (1859). Her husband was a lawyer.

What answer to give Anderson, &c&c. He has gone back to Fort Sumter, with additional instructions.[6]

When they were about to leave the wharf, A. H. Boykin[7] sprang into the boat, in great excitement; thought himself ill-used. A likelihood of fighting—and he to be left behind!

I do not pretend to go to sleep. How can I? If Anderson does not accept terms—at four—the orders are—he shall be fired upon.

I count four—St. Michael chimes. I begin to hope. At half-past four, the heavy booming of a cannon.

I sprang out of bed. And on my knees—prostrate—I prayed as I never prayed before.

There was a sound of stir all over the house—pattering of feet in the corridor—all seemed hurrying one way. I put on my double gown and a shawl and went, too. It was to the housetop.

The shells were bursting. In the dark I heard a man say "waste of ammunition."

I knew my husband was rowing about in a boat somewhere in that dark bay. And that the shells were roofing it over—bursting toward the fort. If Anderson was obstinate—he was to order the forts on our side to open fire. Certainly fire had begun. The regular roar of the cannon—there it was. And who could tell what each volley accomplished of death and destruction.

The women were wild, there on the housetop. Prayers from the women and imprecations from the men, and then a shell would light up the scene. Tonight, they say, the forces are to attempt to land.

The *Harriet Lane* had her wheelhouse smashed and put back to sea.[8]

We watched up there—everybody wondered. Fort Sumter did not fire a shot.

Today Miles and Manning, colonels now—aides to Beauregard—dined with us. The latter hoped I would keep the peace. I give him only good words, for he was to be under fire all day and night, in the bay carrying orders, &c.

---

6. Chesnut, Lee, Chisolm, and Roger A. Pryor (see p. 47, n. 3) left for Sumter at eleven o'clock on the night of the eleventh to give Anderson a final opportunity to surrender before the attack on the fort.

7. Alexander Hamilton Boykin of Kershaw District was M. B. C.'s "Uncle Hamilton," even though he was only eight years older than she. A member of the S.C. senate, Boykin owned 193 slaves and other property valued at 296,000 dollars in 1860.

8. The *Harriet Lane,* one of the Federal steamers sent to provision Fort Sumter, remained outside Charleston Harbor and was unharmed in the bombardment.

Last night—or this morning truly—up on the housetop I was so weak and weary I sat down on something that looked like a black stool.

"Get up, you foolish woman—your dress is on fire," cried a man. And he put me out. It was a chimney, and the sparks caught my clothes. Susan Preston[9] and Mr. Venable[1] then came up. But my fire had been extinguished before it broke out into a regular blaze.

Do you know, after all that noise and our tears and prayers, nobody has been hurt. Sound and fury, signifying nothing. A delusion and a snare.

Louisa Hamilton comes here now. This is a sort of news center. Jack Hamilton, her handsome young husband, has all the credit of a famous battery which is made of RR iron.[2] Mr. Petigru calls it the boomerang because it throws the balls back the way they came—so Lou Hamilton tells us. She had no children during her first marriage. Hence the value of this lately achieved baby. To divert Louisa from the glories of "the battery," of which she raves, we asked if the baby could talk yet.

"No—not exactly—but he imitates the big gun. When he hears that, he claps his hands and cries 'Boom boom.'" Her mind is distinctly occupied by three things—Lieutenant Hamilton, whom she calls Randolph, the baby, and "the big gun"—and it refuses to hold more.

Pryor of Virginia[3] spoke from the piazza of the Charleston Hotel.

I asked what he said, irreverent woman. "Oh, they all say the same thing, but he made great play with that long hair of his, which he is always tossing aside."

Somebody came in just now and reported Colonel Chesnut asleep on the sofa in General Beauregard's room. After two such nights he must be so tired as to be able to sleep anywhere.

Just bade farewell to Langdon Cheves. He is forced to go home, to leave this interesting place. Says he feels like the man who was not killed at Thermopylae. I think he said that unfortunate had to hang himself when he got home for very shame. Maybe fell on his sword, which was a strictly classic way of ending matters.

9. Susan Frances Hampton Preston, a daughter of John Smith Preston.

1. Charles Scott Venable, married to a niece of John S. Preston, was professor of mathematics at S.C. College. He took part in the attack on Fort Sumter as a second lieutenant with the Congaree Rifles.

2. Louisa Hamilton was the wife of John Randolph Hamilton, a former U.S.N. lieutenant. After accepting a commission from the Confederate navy, Hamilton presented plans for a floating ironclad battery, which could be towed into position to attack Fort Sumter's weakest wall. Because the S.C. militia refused to serve on "The Slaughter Pen," the completed battery shelled Sumter safely anchored to a wharf at Moultrieville.

3. Roger Atkinson Pryor, an ardent secessionist who had resigned from the U.S. Congress in March, was one of Beauregard's volunteer aides.

I do not wonder at Louisa Hamilton's baby. We hear nothing, can listen to nothing. Boom, boom, goes the cannon—all the time. The nervous strain is awful, alone in this darkened room.

"Richmond and Washington ablaze," say the papers. Blazing with excitement. Why not? To us these last days' events seem frightfully great.

We were all in that iron balcony. Women—men we only see at a distance now. Stark Means,[4] marching under the piazza at the head of his regiment, held his cap in his hand all the time he was in sight.

Mrs. Means leaning over, looking with tearful eyes.

"Why did he take his hat off?" said an unknown creature. Mrs. Means stood straight up.

"He did that in honor of his mother—he saw me." She is a proud mother—and at the same time most unhappy. Her lovely daughter Emma is dying in there, before her eyes—consumption. At that moment I am sure Mrs. Means had a spasm of the heart. At least, she looked as I feel sometimes. She took my arm, and we came in.

April 13, 1861.   Nobody hurt, after all. How gay we were last night.

Reaction after the dread of all the slaughter we thought those dreadful cannons were making such a noise in doing.

Not even a battery the worse for wear.

Fort Sumter has been on fire. He has not yet silenced any of our guns. So the aides—still with swords and red sashes by way of uniform—tell us.

But the sound of those guns makes regular meals impossible. None of us go to table. But tea trays pervade the corridors, going everywhere.

Some of the anxious hearts lie on their beds and moan in solitary misery. Mrs. Wigfall and I solace ourselves with tea in my room.

These women have all a satisfying faith. "God is on our side," they cry. When we are shut in, we (Mrs. Wigfall and I) ask, "Why?" We are told: "Of course He hates the Yankees."

"You'll think that well of Him."

Not by one word or look can we detect any change in the demeanor of these negro servants. Laurence sits at our door, as sleepy and as respectful and as profoundly indifferent. So are they all. They carry it too far. You could not tell that they hear even the awful row that is going on in the bay, though it is dinning in their ears night and day. And people talk before them as if they were chairs and tables. And they make no sign. Are they stolidly stupid or wiser than we are, silent and strong, biding their time?

So tea and toast come. Also came Colonel Manning, A.D.C.—red sash and sword—to announce that he has been under fire and didn't mind. He said gaily,

---

4. Maj. Robert Stark Means of the Seventeenth S.C. Volunteers was the son of John Hugh Means and Sarah Rebecca (Stark) Means.

"It is one of those things—a fellow never knows how he will come out of it until he is tried. Now I know. I am a worthy descendant of my old Irish hero of an ancestor who held the British officer before him as a shield in the Revolution. And backed out of danger gracefully." ⟨⟨Everybody laughs at John Manning's brag.⟩⟩ We talked of *St. Valentine's Eve; or, The Maid of Perth* and the drop of the white doe's blood that sometimes spoiled all.[5]

The war steamers are still there, outside the bar. And there were people who thought the Charleston bar "no good" to Charleston. The bar is our silent partner, sleeping partner, and yet in this fray he is doing us yeoman service.

April 15, 1861.   I did not know that one could live such days of excitement.

They called, "Come out—there is a crowd coming."

A mob indeed, but it was headed by Colonels Chesnut and Manning.

The crowd was shouting and showing these two as messengers of good news. They were escorted to Beauregard's headquarters. Fort Sumter had surrendered.

Those up on the housetop shouted to us, "The fort is on fire." That had been the story once or twice before.

When we had calmed down, Colonel Chesnut, who had taken it all quietly enough—if anything, more unruffled than usual in his serenity—told us how the surrender came about.

Wigfall was with them on Morris Island when he saw the fire in the fort, jumped in a little boat and, with his handkerchief as a white flag, rowed over to Fort Sumter. Wigfall went in through a porthole.

When Colonel Chesnut arrived shortly after and was received by the regular entrance, Colonel Anderson told him he had need to pick his way warily, for it was all mined.

As far as I can make out, the fort surrendered to Wigfall.

But it is all confusion. Our flag is flying there. Fire engines have been sent to put out the fire.

Everybody tells you half of something and then rushes off to tell something else or to hear the last news. ⟨⟨Manning, Wigfall, John Preston,[6] &c, men without limit, beset us at night.⟩⟩

In the afternoon, Mrs. Preston, Mrs. Joe Heyward, and I drove round the

5. Eachin MacIan, the Highland chief in Sir Walter Scott's *St. Valentine's Day; or, The Fair Maid of Perth* (1828), was nursed as an infant "with the milk of a white doe." His failure of nerve on the battlefield fulfilled an ancient prophecy.

6. John Smith Preston of Columbia, a lawyer, former state legislator, and art collector, made a fortune from his great La. sugar plantations. Living in Europe before the secession crisis, Preston returned to serve, first as a commissioner to urge Virginia's withdrawal from the Union and then as one of Beauregard's aides. He and his wife, Caroline Martha (Hampton) Preston, were old friends of the Chesnuts.

Battery. We were in an open carriage. What a changed scene. The very liveliest crowd I think I ever saw. Everybody talking at once. All glasses still turned on the grim old fort.

⟨⟨Saw William Gilmore Simms,[7] did not know him, although he spent several weeks with us once at our house—he is so changed by his white beard.⟩⟩

Russell, the English reporter for the *Times,* was there.[8] They took him everywhere. One man got up Thackeray, to converse with him on equal terms. Poor Russell was awfully bored, they say. He only wanted to see the forts, &c&c, and news that was suitable to make an interesting article. Thackeray was stale news over the water.

Mrs. Frank Hampton[9] and I went to see the camp of the Richland troops. South Carolina had volunteered to a boy. Professor Venable (The Mathematical) intends to raise a company from among them for the war, a permanent company. This is a grand frolic. No more. For the students, at least.

Even the staid and severe-of-aspect Clingman[1] is here. He says Virginia and North Carolina are arming to come to our rescue—for now U.S.A. will swoop down on us. Of that we may be sure.

We have burned our ships—we are obliged to go on now. He calls us a poor little hot-blooded, headlong, rash, and troublesome sister state.

General McQueen is in a rage because we are to send troops to Virginia.

There is a frightful yellow flag story. A distinguished potentate and militia power looked out upon the bloody field of battle, happening to stand always under the waving of the hospital flag. To his numerous other titles they now add Y.F.

Preston Hampton[2] in all the flush of his youth and beauty, his six feet in stature—and after all, only in his teens—appeared in lemon-colored kid gloves to grace the scene. The camp, in a fit of horseplay, seized him and rubbed them in the mud. He fought manfully but took it all naturally as a good joke.

Mrs. Frank Hampton knows already what civil war means. Her brother was in the New York Seventh Regiment, so roughly received in Baltimore. Frank will be in the opposite camp.

7. The S.C. novelist, biographer, historian, essayist, and orator whose fiction includes *The Yemassee* (1835), *The Partisan* (1835), and *The Kinsman* (1841). This entry in the 1860s Journal is dated April 13, 1861.

8. Already famous for his front-line coverage of the Crimean War, London *Times* correspondent William Howard Russell arrived in the U.S. in March 1861. He recounted his American experiences in *Pictures of Southern Life, Social, Political, and Military* (1861) and *My Diary North and South* (1863).

9. Sally (Baxter) Hampton, a native of N.Y., refused William Thackeray in order to marry Frank Hampton, a Richland District planter.

1. Thomas Lanier Clingman of N.C. had resigned from the U.S. Senate on March 28.

2. Thomas Preston Hampton, a nephew of Frank Hampton and son of Wade Hampton III (see p. 55, n. 5), had left S.C. College to join the C.S.A. at the age of nineteen.

[No date.]³   Home again. In those last days of my stay in Charleston I did not find time to write a line.

And so we took Fort Sumter. Nous autres. We—Mrs. Frank Hampton &c, in the passageway of the Mills House between the reception room and the drawing room. There we held a sofa against all comers. And indeed, all the agreeable people South seemed to have flocked to Charleston at the first gun. That was after we found out that bombarding did not kill anybody. Before that we wept and prayed—and took our tea in groups, in our rooms, away from the haunts of men.

Captain Ingraham and his kind took it (Fort Sumter) from the battery with field glasses and figures made with three sticks in the sand to show what ought to be done.

Wigfall, Chesnut, Miles, Manning, &c took it, rowing about in the harbor in small boats, from fort to fort, under the enemies' guns, bombs bursting in air, &c&c.

And then the boys and men who worked those guns so faithfully at the forts. They took it, too—their way.

Old Col. Beaufort Watts told me this story and many more of the jeunesse dorée under fire. They took it easily as they do most things. They had cotton-bag bombproofs at Fort Moultrie, and when Anderson's shot knocked them about, someone called out, "Cotton is falling." Down went the kitchen chimney, and loaves of bread flew out. They cheered gaily, "Breadstuffs are rising."

Willie Preston⁴ fired the shot which broke Anderson's flagstaff.

Mrs. Hampton, from Columbia, telegraphed him, "Well done, Willie!"

She is his grandmother, the wife or widow of General Hampton of the Revolution,⁵ and the mildest, sweetest, gentlest of old ladies.

It shows how the war spirit is waking us all up.

Colonel Miles (who won his spurs in a boat, so William Gilmore Simms said) gave us this characteristic anecdote.

They met a negro out in the bay, rowing toward the city with some plantation supplies, &c.

"Are you not afraid of Colonel Anderson's cannon?"

"No, Sar. Mars Anderson ain't daresn't hit me. He know Marster wouldn't 'low it."

I have been sitting idly today, looking out upon this beautiful lawn, wondering if this can be the same world I was in a few days ago.

3. Remaining in Charleston for a week after the last entry, M. B. C. returned to Mulberry on April 23. This is a roundup of the events of that week.

4. William Campbell Preston, Jr., a lieutenant of the First S.C. Artillery at Fort Moultrie, was the son of John Smith Preston and Caroline (Hampton) Preston.

5. Mary (Cantey) Hampton was the third wife of Wade Hampton I, a Continental Army officer, U.S. Congressman, and reputedly the wealthiest planter in S.C. at his death in 1835.

Arranging my photograph book. First page—Colonel Watts. Here goes a sketch of his life.

Romantic enough, surely. Beaufort Watts—bluest blood. Gentleman to the tips of his fingers. Chivalry incarnate—and yet such was his fate.

He was given in charge a large amount of money in bank notes. The money belonged to the state, and he was only to deposit it in the bank. On the way he was obliged to stay one night. He put the roll on a table at his bedside, locked himself in, and slept the sleep of the righteous. Lo—next day when he awakened, the money was gone.

Well! All who knew him believed him, of course. He searched and they searched, high and low.

To no purpose—the money had vanished.

Damaging story, in spite of previous character, &c—a cloud rested on him.

Many years after, the house where he had taken that disastrous sleep was pulled down. In the wall, behind the wainscot, was his pile of money. How the rats got it through so narrow a crack it seemed hard to realize.

Like the hole in Mercutio,[6] it was not as deep as a well or as wide as the barn door, but it did for Beaufort Watts—until it was found.

Suppose that house had been burned—or the rats had gnawed up the bills past recognition?

The people in power understood how this proud man had suffered these many years in silence—while men looked askance at him.

They tried to repair the small blunder of blasting a man's character.

They sent him [as] secretary of legation to Russia. He was afterward made consul at Santa Fe de Bogotá. And then, when he said he was too old to wander so far afield, they made him secretary to all the governors of South Carolina—in regular succession.

I knew him more than twenty years ago as secretary to the governor and a made-up old battered dandy. He was the soul of honor. And his eccentricities were all humored. His misfortune had made him sacred.

He stood hat in hand before the ladies and bowed as I suppose Sir Charles Grandison[7] might have done. It was hard not to laugh at the purple and green shades of his overblack hair.

He came at that time to show me the sword presented to Colonel Shelton for killing the only Indian killed in the Seminole War.

We bagged Osceola and Micanopy under a flag of truce. That is, they were snared—not shot on the wing.

To go back to my knight errant.

He knelt, handed me the sword, and then kissed my hand.

I was barely sixteen and did not know how to behave under the circumstances. He said, leaning on the sword, "My dear child, learn that it is a much

---

6. *Romeo and Juliet*, act 3, scene 1.
7. The perfect gentleman of Samuel Richardson's *The History of Sir Charles Grandison* (1753–54).

greater liberty to shake hands with a lady than to kiss her hand. I have kissed the empress of Russia's hand, and she did not make faces at me."

He looks now just as he did then. He is always in uniform covered with epaulettes, aiguillettes, &c&c. Shining in the sun—and with his plumed hat, reins up his war steed and bows low as ever.

Now I will bid farewell for a while, as Othello did, to all the pomp and circumstance of glorious war.[8] And come down to my domestic strifes—and troubles.

I have a sort of volunteer maid. The daughter of my husband's nurse, dear old Betsey. She waits on me because she so pleases—besides, I pay her. She belongs to my father-in-law, who has too many slaves to care very much about their way of life.

So Maria Whitaker came, all in tears. She brushes hair delightfully, and as she stood at my back, I could see her face in the glass.

"Maria—are you crying because all this war talk scares you?"

"No, ma'am."

"What is the matter with you?"

"Nothing more than common."

"Now listen. Let the war end either way, and you will be free. We will have to free you before we get out of this thing. Won't you be glad?"

"Everybody knows Mars Jeems wants us free, and it is only old Marster holds hard. He ain't going to free anybody anyway. You see."

And then came the story of her troubles.

"Now, Miss Mary, you see me married to Jeems Whitaker yourself. I was a good and faithful wife to him, and we were comfortable every way. Good house, everything. He had no cause of complaint. But he has left me."

"For heaven sake! Why?"

"Because I had twins. He says they are not his, because nobody named Whitaker ever had twins."

Maria is proud in her way. And the behavior of this bad husband has nearly mortified her to death. She has had three children in two years. No wonder the man was frightened. But then, Maria does not depend on him for anything. She was inconsolable.

And I could find nothing better to say than: "Come now, Maria! Never mind. Your old Missis and Marster are so good to you. Now let us look up something for the twins." The twins are named John and Jeems, the latter for her false loon of a husband. And Maria is one of the good colored women. She deserved a better fate in her honest matrimonial attempt. They do say she has a trying temper. Jeems was tried, and he failed to stand the trial.

---

8. *Othello*, act 3, scene 3.

Among the glaring inconsistencies of life. Our châtelaine locked up Eugène Sue[9] and returned even Washington Allston's novel,[1] with thanks and a decided hint that it should be burned. At least it should not remain in her house. Bad books are not allowed house room except in the library and under lock and key, key in the master's pocket. But bad women, if they are not white or only in a menial capacity, may swarm the house unmolested. The ostrich game is thought a Christian act. These women are no more regarded as a dangerous contingent than canary birds would be.

If you show by a chance remark that you see that some particular creature more shameless than the rest has no end of children and no beginning of a husband, you are frowned down. You are talking on improper subjects: there are certain subjects pure-minded ladies never touch upon, even in their thoughts. It does not do to be so hard and cruel. Poor things. It is best to let them alone, if they are good servants. Otherwise, do not dismiss them. All that will come straight as they grow older.

And it does!

They are frantic, one and all, to be members of the church. The Methodist church is not so pure-minded as to shut its eyes. And it has them up and turns them out with a high hand if they are found out, going astray as to any of the Ten Commandments.

April 27, 1861.[2] Montgomery. Here we are. Hon. Robert Barnwell came with us. His benevolent spectacles give him a most Pickwickian expression. The Carolinians revere his goodness above all things.

Everywhere the cars stopped. The people wanted a speech. There was one stream of fervid oratory.

We came along with a man whose wife lived in Washington, and he was bringing her to Georgia as the safest place—⟨⟨ *quite tranquilizing, that idea.*⟩⟩

The Alabama crowd are not as confident of taking Fort Pickens as we were of taking Fort Sumter.

Baltimore in a blaze. They say Col. Ben Huger is in command there—son of the Olmütz Huger.[3] General Lee, son of Light Horse Harry Lee,[4] has been

9. Eugène Sue was the nom de plume of Marie-Joseph Eugène, French novelist and supporter of the Revolution of 1848. His best-known work was *Le Juif Errant* (1844–45).

1. Allston was a South-Carolina-born artist, poet, lecturer, and author of *Monaldi: A Tale* (1841).

2. Under this date are treated matters covered under eight entries dated from April 27 to May 7, 1861, in the 1860s Journal.

3. Benjamin Huger of Charleston, a cousin of Thomas Bee Huger, had resigned as a major (not a colonel) from the U.S. Army on April 22 and soon became a brigadier general of the C.S.A. Huger's father, Francis Kinloch Huger, was a twenty-one-year-old medical student traveling in Europe in 1794 when he joined a plot to free Lafayette from the Austrian fortress of Olmütz. Lafayette was quickly recaptured; Huger received six months of hard labor and became a hero in the U.S.

4. Robert E. Lee's father, Henry Lee, fought with Washington's army in Va. and commanded an irregular company of cavalry and infantry in S.C. during the Revolutionary War.

made general in chief of Virginia. With such men to the fore, we have hope.

The *Herald* says, "Slavery must be extinguished, if in blood."

Mr. Chesnut has gone with Wade Hampton[5] to see President Davis about the legion Wade wants to get up.

The *Herald* thinks we are shaking in our shoes at their great mass meeting.[6] We are jolly as larks all the same.

The president came across the aisle to speak to me at church today. He was very cordial, and I appreciated the honor.

Mr. Mallory has a daughter here. Indeed he has a granddaughter. Miss Mallory married a nice Connecticut Yankee. Poor man, he is a fish out of water here.

Wigfall is black with rage at Colonel Anderson's account of the fall of Sumter. Wigfall did behave so magnanimously, and Anderson does not seem to see it in that light.

"Catch me risking my life to save him again," says Wigfall. "He might have been man enough to tell the truth to those New Yorkers, however unpalatable to them a good word for us might have been. We did behave well to him. The only men of his killed: he killed himself or they killed themselves, firing a salute to their old striped rag."

Mr. Chesnut was delighted with the way Anderson spoke to him when he went to demand the surrender. They parted quite tenderly. Anderson: "If we do not meet again on Earth, I hope we may meet in heaven."

How Wigfall laughed at Anderson. "Giving Chesnut a rendez in the other world."

What a kind welcome these old gentlemen gave me. One, more affectionate and homely than the other, slapped me on the back. Several bouquets were brought me. And I put them in water around my plate. Then General Owens[7] gave me some violets, which I put in my breastpin.

"Oh," said my gutta-percha Hemphill,[8] "if I had known how those were to be honored, I would have been up by daylight, seeking the sweetest flowers."

Governor Moore came in, and of course seats were offered him.

5. The inheritor of a great name, vast Miss. plantations, and vast debts, Wade Hampton III of Richland District, S.C., shortly became colonel of "Hampton's Legion," a special regiment combining infantry, cavalry, and artillery. He was the grandson of Mary (Cantey) Hampton, the brother of Frank Hampton, and the father of Thomas Preston Hampton. His first wife (who died in 1852) was a sister of John S. Preston, and his aunt was Preston's wife.

6. On April 21, the New York *Herald* published an extensive story of a demonstration to welcome Maj. Robert Anderson to New York.

7. Probably James Byeram Owens, a S.C. native who became a cotton planter in Fla. and represented his adopted state at the Provisional Confederate Congress. His brother, William A. Owens, also a Fla. planter, was known locally as "General Owens," and M. B. C. may have confused the two men.

8. John Hemphill, former chief justice of the Tex. Supreme Court and U.S. senator, was a member of the Provisional Confederate Congress. The 1860s Journal indicates that "gutta-percha" refers to Hemphill's physiognomy.

"This is the most comfortable chair," cried an overly polite person.

"The most comfortable chair is beside Mrs. Chesnut," said the governor, facing the music gallantly—and he sank into it gracefully. Well done, old fogies!

Browne said, "These Southern men have an awfully flattering way with women."

"Oh—so many are descendants of Irishmen, and some blarney remains yet even— and in spite of their gray hairs."

For it was a group of silver-gray flatterers.

"Yes—blarney as well as bravery comes in with the Irish."

At Mrs. Davis's reception, dismal news, for civil war seems certain.

At Mrs. Toombs's[9] reception Mr. Stephens came by me. Twice before we have had it out on the subject of this Confederacy. Once on the cars, coming from Georgia here. Once at a supper, where he sat next to me. Today he was not cheerful in his views. I called him halfhearted—accused him of looking back. Man after man came and interrupted the conversation with some frivle fravle, but we held on. He was deeply interesting, and he gave me some new ideas as to our dangerous situation. Fears for the future, and not exultation at our successes, pervade his discourse.

Dined at the president's. Never had a pleasanter day. She is as witty as he is wise. He was very agreeable; he took me in to dinner.

The talk was of Washington. Nothing of our present difficulties.

《Mr. C never speaks—lets me talk all—and people encourage me so to talk.》[1]

A General Anderson from Alexandria [or?] D.C., I think, was in doleful dumps. He says they are so much better prepared than we are. They are organized, or will be, by General Scott. We are in wild confusion.

Their arms are the best in the world. We are wretchedly armed, &c&c.

L. Q. Washington[2] was quite as much of a Job's comforter.

Mr. Mallory complained of the Judge to me—as if I am responsible for what he says. Mr. Mallory thinks "it ill-bred, to say the least, to come to one of Mr. Davis's cabinet and abuse him." Who doubts it? "Ill-bred" is a mild word.

Mrs. Walker,[3] resplendently dressed—one of those gorgeously arrayed persons who fairly shine in the sun—tells me she mistook the inevitable Morrow[4]

---

9. Julia (DuBose) Toombs, wife of Robert Augustus Toombs.

1. Under April 29, 1861, in the 1860s Journal. Other excerpts from the original journal below are dated May 4 and 6.

2. L. Quentin Washington, a Washington, D.C., journalist who served as chief clerk of the Confederate State Department.

3. Eliza (Pickett) Walker, the daughter of a Montgomery judge, was the wife of Confederate Secretary of War Leroy Pope Walker.

4. Probably James Morrow of Charleston, a physician who was medical officer on Matthew Perry's expedition to Japan.

for Mr. Chesnut. "Pass over the affront to my power of selection." I told her it was an insult to the Palmetto flag. "Think of a South Carolina senator like that." ⟨⟨Do I look like a woman to marry *old* Morrow?⟩⟩

They come rushing in from Washington with white lips, crying "danger! danger!" It is very tiresome to have these people always harping on this.

"The enemy's troops are the finest body of men we ever saw."

Why did you not make friends of them, I feel disposed to say.

We would have war. And now we seem to be letting our golden opportunity pass. We are not preparing for war.

Talk—talk—in that Congress. Lazy legislators—rash, reckless, headlong, devil-may-care, proud, passionate, unruly raw material for soldiers.

They say we have among us a regiment of spies, men and women sent here by the wily Seward. Why? Our newspapers tell every word that there is to be told—by friend or foe. ⟨⟨Mrs. Lincoln's mother and sisters are here.[5] I should watch them!⟩⟩

Had a two-hour call from the Hon. Robert Barnwell Rhett. His theory is—all would have been right if we had taken Fort Sumter six months ago. He made it very plain to me. He is clever, if erratic. I forget why it ought to have been attacked before.

At another reception:

Mrs. Davis was in fine spirits. Captain Decie here, came over in his own yacht.[6]

Russell of the *Times* wondered how we had the heart to enjoy life so thoroughly, when all the Northern papers said we were to be exterminated in such a short time. ⟨⟨Russell's manner I did not like. He was, I thought, snobbish. Sam Ward[7] was as oily as ever.⟩⟩

May 9, 1861. Virginia commissioners here.[8] Mr. Staples[9] and Mr. Edmonstone came to see me. They say Virginia had no grievance. She comes out

---

5. Mary (Todd) Lincoln's stepmother, Elizabeth (Humphries) Todd of Ky., was a Confederate sympathizer, and three of Mrs. Lincoln's four half sisters had husbands in the C.S.A.

6. Henry E. Decie, the Englishman whose racing yacht *America* was rechristened the *Camilla* and used as a Confederate blockade-runner.

7. Samuel Ward of N.Y., the elder brother of Julia (Ward) Howe, was a writer, adventurer, and society figure who became a well-known Washington lobbyist during the war.

8. Probably a reference to the arrival of the first Va. delegates to the Confederate Congress and to the final approval of a "Treaty of Alliance" under which Va. and the Confederate government coordinated their military activities prior to ratification of the Va. ordinance of secession on May 23.

9. Va. lawyer Waller Redd Staples was a member of the Confederate Congress throughout the war.

on a point of honor. Could she stand by and see her sovereign sister states invaded?

Sumter Anderson has been offered a Kentucky regiment. Can they raise a regiment in Kentucky against us?

Suddenly General Beauregard and his aide (the last left him, of the galaxy who surrounded him in Charleston) John Manning have gone. Heaven knows where—but out on a warpath, certainly.

Governor Manning called himself "the last rose of summer, left blooming alone"[1]—of that fancy staff. A new fight will gather them again.

Ben McCulloch, the Texas Ranger,[2] is here—and Mr. Ward,[3] my gutta-percha friend's colleague from Texas. Mr. Senator Ward in appearance is the exact opposite of Mr. Senator Hemphill. The latter has a face as old and dried as a mummy and the color of tanned leather, with a thousand wrinkles, but with the hair (or wig) of a boy of twenty.

Mr. Ward is fresh and fair, with blue eyes and a boyish face, but his head is white as snow. Whether he turned it white in a single night or by slower process, I do not know. But it is strangely out of keeping with his clear young eye. He is thin and has a queer stooping figure.

This story he told me. On a western steamer there was a great crowd and no unoccupied berth or sleeping place of any sort whatsoever in the gentleman's cabin. Saloon, I think they called it. He had taken a stateroom, 110; but he could not eject the people who had seized it and were asleep in it. Neither could the captain. It would have been a case of revolver or 'leven-inch bowie knife.

Near the ladies' saloon the steward pitied him. "This man, he is 110, and I cannot find a place for him. Poor fellow."

A peep out—of bright eyes.

"I say, steward, have you an old man 110 years old out there? Let us see him. He must be a natural curiosity."

"We are overflowing. Poor old 110! And we can't find a place for him to sleep."

"Poor old soul—bring him in here. We will take care of him."

"Stoop and totter," sniggered the steward, "and go in."

"Ah," said Mr. Ward. "How those houries patted and pitied me and hustled me about and gave me the best berth. I tried not to look. I knew it was wrong, but I did." He saw them doing their back hair. He was lost in amazement at the collapse when the huge hoopskirts fell off, unheeded on the cabin floor, &c&c. One beauty who was disporting herself near his curtain suddenly caught his eye.

---

1. From the first lines of Thomas Moore's "The Last Rose of Summer," in *Irish Melodies* (1807–34).

2. A U.S. marshal and colonel of Tex. state troops, McCulloch was shortly commissioned a brigadier general in the C.S.A. and was given command of Confederate forces in Ark.

3. Matthias Ward, U.S. senator from Tex., 1858–59.

She stooped and gathered up her belongings.

"I say, stewardess, your old a-hundred-and-ten is a humbug. His eyes are too blue for anything." And she fled as he shut himself in, nearly frightened to death.

I forget how it ended. There was so much laughing at his story I did not hear it all. So much for hoary locks and their reverence-inspiring power.

Read *Friends in Council* all day. Awfully clever fellow—this Helps.[4] Wonder I never knew of him before. What he says is so delightful. And so true—one is all the time saying, "Yes—who denies it?"

Have made the acquaintance of a clever woman, too—Mrs. McLean, née Sumner, daughter of the general,[5] not the senator. They say *he* avoids matrimony.

"Slavery the sum of all evil," he says. So he will not reduce a woman to slavery. There is no slave, after all, like a wife.

Mrs. Ellis, Mr. King's niece—minister to France and all that.[6] Mr. Sumner asked her to marry him. I wish he had, only to know what he would have done with her plantation and hundreds of negroes. She is a rich widow and charming.

Russell, the wandering Englishman, was telling how very odd some of our plantation habits were. He was staying at the house of an ex-cabinet minister. Madame would stand on the back piazza and send her voice three fields off, calling a servant.

Now, that is not a Southern peculiarity. Our women are soft and sweet—low-toned, indolent, graceful, quiescent, quand même.

I daresay there are bawling, squalling, vulgar people everywhere.

May 13, 1861.   Dallas County. Came down on the boat to that God-forsaken landing, Portland. Found everybody drunk—that is, the three men who were there.

At last secured a carriage to carry us to my brother-in-law's house.[7]

Mr. C had to drive seven miles—pitch-dark, unknown road. My heart was in my mouth. Which last I did not open. Suddenly, at our elbow, it seemed—"Who's there?"

"Where is my carpetbag?" said Mr. C to me, as quickly.

---

4. Sir Arthur Helps, historian and author, was an adviser to Queen Victoria and clerk of the Privy Council. His *Friends in Council,* earnest dialogues on political questions, first appeared in 1847.

5. Margaret (Sumner) McLean, daughter of U.S. Maj. Gen. Edwin Vose Sumner and the wife of Lt. Eugene McLean of Md. Though his father-in-law was chosen to escort Lincoln to Washington, McLean resigned his commission and joined the C.S.A. Excerpts from Mrs. McLean's diary, "When the States Seceded" and "A Northern Woman in the Confederacy," were published in *Harper's Magazine* 127 (1913–14).

6. Catharine (Kornegay) Ellis, widow of Tuscaloosa lawyer Harvey W. Ellis, became William Rufus King's hostess while he was ambassador to France, 1844–46.

7. Thomas Edward Boykin, a physician and planter, was M. B. C.'s first cousin and the husband of her youngest sister, Sarah Amelia (Miller) Boykin.

"Under your feet."

"Law now! Is that Mars Jeems Chesnut?" called out a negro in joyful manner.

"Yes."

"Law, Mars Jeems, I knowed your voice, the first word you said. Don't you know me? I'm Jonas. I drove Mr. William Lang's carriage out there in Camden.[8] Why, I 'member you jist as well."

So it was all smooth again. Jonas showed us the right road—asking thousands of questions of old Camden people.

Mr. C carefully moved the carpetbag from under our feet.

"There is scarcely any danger greater than trampling on two revolvers." Not to speak of the jolts and bangs of this rough road. He solemnly requested me never again to meddle with his pistols.

"I thought you would want them at hand."

But I was utterly subdued by darkness and fright, and I promised hereafter to leave his carpetbag where he put it himself.

Next day a patriotic person informed us that so great was the war fever, only six men could be found in Dallas, and I whispered to Mr. C, "We found three of the lone ones hors de combat at Portland." So much for the corps of reserves—alcoholized patriots.

Saw for the first time the demoralization produced by hopes of freedom. My mother's butler (whom I taught to read, sitting on his knife board) continued to keep from speaking to us. He was as efficient as ever in his proper place, but he did not come behind scenes as usual and have a friendly chat. He held himself aloof, so grand and stately we had to send him a "tip" through his wife, Hetty, mother's maid. She showed no signs of disaffection—came to my bedside next morning with everything that was nice for breakfast. She had let me sleep till midday. She embraced me over and over again.

I remarked, "What a capital cook they have here."

She curtsied to the ground. "I cooked every mouthful on that tray. As if I did not know what you liked to eat since you was a baby."

Mrs. Fitzpatrick says Mr. Davis is too gloomy for her. He says we must prepare for a long war and unmerciful reverses at first because they are readier for war and so much stronger numerically. Men and money count so in war. "As they do everywhere else," said I, doubting her accurate account of Mr. Davis's spoken words, though she tried to give it faithfully.

We need patience and persistence. There is enough and to spare of pluck and dash among us. The do-and-dare style.

I drove out with Mrs. Davis. She finds playing Mrs. President of this small Confederacy slow work after leaving friends such as Mrs. Emory,[9] Mrs. Joe

8. William Wyly Lang, a wealthy planter, moved to Dallas County in 1845. Lang's first wife was an aunt of M. B. C.; his second was a first cousin of J. C.

9. Matilda (Bache) Emory of Md., wife of U.S. Lt. Col. William Hemsley Emory.

Johnston,[1] &c&c in Washington. I do not blame her. The wrench has been awful with us all.

But we don't mean to be turned into pillars of salt.

Mr. Mallory came for us to go to Mrs. Toombs's reception. Mr. Chesnut would not go, and I decided to remain with him. And it proved a wise decision. First Mr. Hunter[2] came. In college they called him from his initials—R. M. T. —Run Mad Tom Hunter. Just now I think he is the sanest, if not the wisest, man in our newborn Confederacy. I remember when I first met him. He sat next to me at some state dinner in Washington. Mr. Clay[3] had taken me in to dinner, but he seemed quite satisfied that my other side should take me off his hands.

Mr. Hunter did not know me, nor I him. I suppose he inquired or looked at my card lying on the table—as I did his. At any rate we began a conversation which lasted steadily through the whole thing—from soup to dessert.

Mr. Hunter, though in evening dress, presented a rather tumbled-up appearance—his waistcoat wanted pulling down and his hair wanted brushing. He delivered unconsciously that day a lecture on English literature which if printed I still think would be a valuable addition to that literature. Since then I have always looked forward to a talk with the senator from Virginia with undisguised pleasure. Next came Mr. Miles and Mr. Jamison[4] of South Carolina. The latter is president of our secession convention—also he has written a life of Du Guesclin—not so bad.

So my unexpected reception was of the most charming, as the French say. Judge Frost[5] came a little later. They all remained until the return of the crowd from Mrs. Toombs's.

These men are not sanguine. I can't say without hope, exactly. They are agreed in one thing. It is worthwhile to try awhile—if only to get away from New England. Captain Ingraham was here, too. He is South Carolina to the tips of his fingers, but he has it dyed in the wool—part of his nature—to believe the U.S.N. can whip anything in the world. All of these little inconsistencies and contrarieties make it very exciting. One never knows what tack anyone of them will make at the next word.

---

1. Lydia (McLane) Johnston, wife of Confederate Brig. Gen. Joseph E. Johnston of Va. Her father was Louis McLane, secretary of the treasury in the Jackson administration.

2. Robert Mercer Taliaferro Hunter of Va., Speaker of the House, 1839–41; U.S. senator, 1847–March, 1861; and a member of the Provisional Confederate Congress.

3. The Chesnuts and Clement Claiborne Clay, Jr., then U.S. senator from Ala., had been members of the mess at Brown's Hotel during J. C.'s senate term.

4. David Flavel Jamison, a Barnwell District planter, had resigned his post as secretary of war in the S.C. Executive Council earlier in the month. Mrs. Chesnut probably read his *Life and Times of Bertrand Du Guesclin* in manuscript; the biography of this great fourteenth-century French soldier was not published until 1864.

5. Edward Frost of Charleston, father of Tom Frost, was a former circuit court judge, president of the Blue Ridge Railroad, and secretary of the treasury in the S.C. Executive Council.

May 20, 1861. Lunched at Mrs. Davis's—everything nice to eat, and I was ravenous. (For a fortnight I have not gone to the dinner table, even. Yesterday I was forced to dine on cold asparagus and blackberries, so repulsive in aspect was the other food they sent me.) And she was as nice as the luncheon. When she is in the mood, I do not know so pleasant a person. She is awfully clever—always.

We talked of this move from Montgomery. Mr. Chesnut opposes it violently because this is so central a position for our government. Then he wants our troops sent into Maryland to make our fight on the border—and to encompass Washington.

I see these uncomfortable hotels will move the Congress. Our statesmen love their ease. And it will be so hot here in the summer. "I do hope they will go," she said.

"The Yankees will make it hot for us, go where we will. And if war comes—"

"And it has come?" said I.

"Yes—I fancy these dainty folks may live to regret the fare of the Montgomery hotels, even."

"Never."

Mr. Chesnut has three distinct manias. The Maryland scheme is one. He rushes off to Jeff Davis—who I daresay has fifty men every day come to him with infallible plans to save the country. And if he can keep his temper—Mrs. Davis says he answers all in softly modulated, dulcet accents.

What a rough menagerie we have here—and if nice people come to see you, up walks an irate Judge—engrosses the conversation—abuses the friends of the company generally. That is, abuses everybody and prophesies every possible evil to the country, if he finds denouncing your friends does not sufficiently depress you.

Oh, Mr. Chesnut's three crazes: Maryland to be made seat of the war, old Morrow's idea of buying up steamers abroad for our coast defenses, and last of all, but far from the least, make as much cotton and send it to England as a bank to draw on. The very cotton we have now, if sent across the water, could be a gold mine to us.

IV

The Home Front

May 22, 1861. Mulberry. We came with R. M. T. Hunter, Hon. Mr. Barnwell—who has excellent reasons for keeping the cotton at home, but I forget what they are. Generally we take what he says—also Mr. Hunter's wisdom—as unanswerable. Not so Mr. Chesnut. He growls at both, much as he likes them. Also we had Tom Lang[1] and his wife and Dr. Boykin. Surely there was never a more congenial party. The younger men had been in the South Carolina College while Mr. Barnwell was president. Their love and respect for him was unmeasurable. And he benignly received it, smiling behind those spectacles. ⟨⟨Two days never in my life have passed so rapidly and pleasantly— everybody *well* bred, nobody disagreeable, nobody unkind, all clever, some remarkably so. Mr. C was more brilliant than I ever knew him, Mr. Hunter more genial, Mr. Barnwell chatty, clever, *appreciative!* Came home. Were joyfully greeted but overcome with fatigue and the remains of indigestion brought from that den of horrors, Montgomery Hall.⟩⟩

Met John Darby[2] at Atlanta. Told him he was surgeon of the Hampton Legion, which delighted him. He had had adventures. He had remained a little too long in the medical college in Philadelphia, where he was some kind of a professor, and they were in an ace of hanging him as a Southern spy. "Rope was ready," he sniggered. We had only a few moments on the platform to interchange confidences.

At Atlanta when he unguardedly told that he was fresh from Philadelphia, he had barely escaped lynching. Here he was taken up as a Northern spy.

"Lively life among you—both sides," he said, hurrying away.

And I moaned, "There was John Darby—like to have been killed by both sides, and no time to tell me the curious coincidences."

What marvelous experiences a little war begins to make.

Hunted today for these lines, quoted on the way here by a literary creature:

> Nay rather steal thine aching heart
> To act the martyrs' sterner part—

1. Thomas Lang, Jr., and Elizabeth (Rives) Lang lived on a Dallas County plantation. Tom was a nephew of William W. Lang and a brother-in-law of Dr. Edward Boykin. Tom's mother was a first cousin of J. C.

2. Dr. John Thomson Darby, twenty-four, was the son of a noted physician, planter, and member of the S.C. secession convention from Orangeburg District. The passages from the 1860s Journal in the previous paragraph are dated May 20, 1861.

And watch with calm unshrinking eye
The darling visions as they die,
Till all bright hopes and hues of day
Have faded into twilight grey.

—Byron*ish*[3]

Read "Siege of Ishmael" in *Don Juan*. They had alluded to the war picture in that as we came along.

《**May 23, 1861.**   Mulberry. Last night old Mr. Chesnut begged my husband never to leave him again until he died.》

May 27, 1861.   They look for a fight at Norfolk. Beauregard is there. I think if I were a man I'd be there, too.

Also, Harpers Ferry is to be attacked.

The Confederate flag was cut down by a man named Ellsworth, who was in command of Zouaves. Jackson was the name of the person who shot Ellsworth in the act.[4]

Sixty of our cavalry taken by Sherman's brigade.[5]

Deeper and deeper we go in.

Thirty of Tom Boykin's[6] company came home from Richmond. They went as a rifle company and were then armed with muskets. They were sandhill tackies, those fastidious ones. Not very anxious to fight with anything—or in any way, I fancy. Richmond ladies had come for them in carriages, fêted them, waved handkerchiefs to them, brought them dainties with their own hands—in faith that every Carolinian was a gentleman, and every man south of Mason and Dixon's line a hero.

Not exactly descendants of the Scotch Hay who fought the Danes with his ploughshare—or the oxen's yoke—or something that could hit hard and came handy.

Johnny has gone as a private in Gregg's regiment. He could not stand it at home any longer. Mr. Chesnut was willing for him to go, because the sandhill

3. As M. B. C. suspected, these lines were not written by Lord Byron. Six stanzas of another poem that followed are omitted here. "Siege of Ishmael" is cantos 7 and 8 of Lord Byron's *Don Juan* (1819–24).

4. On May 24, the day after the secession of Va., U.S. troops seized Alexandria, Va. One of the invaders, Col. Elmer Ephraim Ellsworth, took down a Confederate flag flying from the roof of a hotel. He was killed coming downstairs by the hotel keeper, James W. Jackson, who was then shot by a Federal private.

5. Only about half this number were captured by Maj. Thomas West Sherman during the seizure of Alexandria.

6. Thomas Lang Boykin of Kershaw, a planter and captain of the DeKalb Rifle Guards of Gregg's regiment, was the son of M. B. C.'s uncle Burwell Boykin.

men said "this was a rich man's war—and the rich men would be officers and have an easy time and the poor ones be privates." So he said, "Let the gentlemen set the example. Let them go in the ranks." So John C is a gentleman private. He took his servant with him, all the same.

Read *Say and Seal*[7] today. Interesting. Piety and pie-making—equally so. As George Herbert says, housemaid's duties made divine—when a beautiful girl does broom work—sweeping, dusting, kneading dough.[8] The hero is a Christian, armed cap-à-pie with texts. He kisses close and often—calls down a blessing from heaven on every embrace—and every caress is chronicled and sanctified by scriptural reference. The hero stands by the heroine lovingly and watches her get breakfast, dinner, and supper. He admires her butter-making, scrubbing, making up beds, and all the honest work she glories in. Strange to say, he stops her from dressmaking. Why? One must draw the line somewhere. It has human interest, and one reads on. Still, why should her dressmaking outrage him so?

Another style of book—*Guesses at Truth*. Not Yankee's guesses—genuine English Hare's.[9]

Johnny reproved me for saying, "If I were a man, I would not sit here and doze and drink and drivel—and forget the fight going on in Virginia."

Said it was my duty not to talk so rashly and make enemies.

He says he had the money in his pocket to raise a company last fall, but it has slipped through his fingers. And now he is a common soldier.

"You wasted it or spent it foolishly."

"I do not know where it has gone. There was too much consulting over me—too much good counsel was given to me, and everybody gave me different advice."

"Don't you even know your own mind?"

"We will do very well in the ranks. Men and officers, all alike—we know everybody, &c&c."

So I repeated Mrs. Lowndes's solemn words when she heard that South Carolina had seceded alone: "As thy days, so shall thy strength be."

Don't know exactly what I meant, but thought I must be impressive, as he was going away. Saw him off at the train. Forgot to say anything there, but cried my eyes out.

---

7. *Say and Seal* (1860) published under the pseudonyms "Elizabeth Wetherell" and "Amy Lothrop" by two sisters from New York, Anna Bartlett Warner and Susan Bogert Warner.

8. A reference to stanza 5 of "The Elixir," in *The Temple* (1633), by the metaphysical poet George Herbert.

9. Julius C. and Augustus W. Hare frequently revised their popular work *Guesses at Truth* (1827). M. B. C. probably had the 1861 edition.

《Poor John! He has been so affectionate—so kind—so respectful to me, I part with him with a pang—the only one of my *kin-in-law* for whom I care one particle.》[1]

Sent Mrs. Wigfall a telegram:

"Where shrieks the Wild Sea Mew?"

Answer:

"Sea Mew at the Spotswood Hotel. Will shriek soon. I will remain here. —C. M. Wigfall."

《**May 30 & 31, 1861.**   Alone at Sandy Hill,[2] where everything good was first emptied out of me. This is the end of the farce and sentimental talk of Mr. Chesnut's family—"They could never bear him out of sight." "He must never leave them." "Just recovering [from] the shock of his joining Beauregard." And *now*, three days after his return for so short a rest at home, go to spend a week with Mrs. Reynolds—who is always here and who never since she was *made* sacrificed one instant or one wish to their pleasure—and leave us *alone* at Sandy Hill. I am happier far without *them* but for the life of me cannot help wondering at such bare-face *cant*, &c.》

《**June 3 and 4, 1861.**   Sunday evening Uncle John and Uncle Burwell came to see us.[3] Such nice good old country gentlemen—so simpleminded . . . 》

June 4, 1861.   Davin! Have had a talk concerning him today with two opposite extremes of people. Mrs. Chesnut praises everybody, good and bad. "Judge not," she says. She is a philosopher. She would not give herself the pain to find fault.

The Judge abuses everybody—and he does it so well. Short, sharp, and incisive are his sentences, and he revels in condemning the world en bloc, as the French say. So nobody is the better for her good word—or the worst for his bad one.

In Camden I found myself in a flurry of women. "Traitor," they cried. "Spies." "They ought to be hanged." "Davin is taken up. Dean and Davis, they are his accomplices."[4]

"What has Davin done?"

"He'll be hung, never you mind."

"For what?"

"They caught him walking in the trestle work in the swamp—after no good, you may be sure."

1. Under an entry dated June 1 and 2, 1861, in the 1860s Journal.

2. A plantation three miles east of Mulberry, used as a summer retreat by the Chesnuts.

3. John Boykin, a Kershaw District planter worth 44,000 dollars in 1860, was an elder brother of M. B. C.'s mother, Mary (Boykin) Miller. Burwell Boykin, Mary Miller's younger brother, was a Kershaw planter whose 163 slaves and other holdings were valued at 250,000 dollars.

4. Contemporary newspaper accounts indicate that J. C., William Shannon, and T. J. Withers were involved in the arrest and trial of a Camden "music teacher named Devine" on charges of treason. No accomplices were mentioned.

"They won't hang him for that."

"Hanging is too good for him."

"You wait till Colonel Chesnut comes."

"He is a lawyer," I said gravely. "Ladies, he will disappoint you. There will be no lynching if he goes to that meeting today. He will not move a step—except by habeas corpus and trial by jury—and a quantity of bench and bar, to speak long speeches."

Mr. C did come and gave a more definite account of poor Davin's precarious situation. They had intercepted treasonable letters of his at the post office. I believe it was not a very black treason after all. At any rate Colonel Chesnut spoke for him with might and main at the meeting. It was composed (the meeting) of intelligent men with cool heads.

And they banished Davin to Fort Sumter. The poor music master can't do much harm in the casemates there.

He may thank his stars that Mr. C gave him a helping hand.

In the red-hot state our public mind is in, short shrift for spies.

Judge Withers said that Mr. Chesnut never made a more telling speech in his life than he did to save this poor Frenchman for whom Judge Lynch was ready.

I had never heard of Davin in my life until I heard he was to be hung.

Judge Douglas,[5] the Little Giant, is dead. One of those killed by the war, no doubt; trouble of mind.

The beautiful Mrs. D is free!

Twenty-eight hundred men have been taken from Bragg at Pensacola,[6] so trouble is looked for at Richmond.

Charleston people are thin-skinned. They shrink from Russell's touches.

I find his criticisms mild. He has a light touch. I expected so much worse. Those Englishmen come, somebody says, with their three p's: pen—paper—prejudices.

I dreaded some of those after-dinner stories. And that day in the harbor he let us off easily.

He says our men are so fine-looking. Who denies it? Not one of us.

Also that it is a silly impression which has gone abroad that men cannot work in this climate. We live in the open air and work like Trojans at all manly sports. Riding hard, hunting, playing at being soldiers.

These fine manly specimens have been in the habit of leaving the coast when

---

5. Stephen A. Douglas.

6. Confederate Brig. Gen. Braxton Bragg of N.C. commanded the coast between Pensacola and Mobile.

it became too hot there. And also fighting a duel or two if kept too long swelter-
ing in a Charleston sun.

The handsome youths whose size and muscle he admired so much as they
prowled around the Mills House would not relish hard work in the fields
between May and December. "Gifts are various," and we give it up. Negroes
stand a tropical or semitropical sun at noonday better than white men. Fighting
is different. They will not mind sun or rain or wind, then.

Major Emory, when he was ordered West, placed his resignation in the hands
of his Maryland brothers. After the Baltimore row the brothers sent it in. After
all, Maryland declined to secede.

Mrs. Emory, who at least is two-thirds of that copartnership—old Franklin's
granddaughter and true to her blood—tried to get it back. The president
refused point-blank, though she went on her knees. That I do not believe. The
Franklin race are stiff-necked and stiff-kneed. Not much given to kneeling to
God or man, from all accounts.

If Major Emory comes to us, won't he have a good time?[7] Mrs. Davis adores
Mrs. Emory. No wonder. I fell in love with her myself.

I heard of her before I saw her, in this wise—little Banks[8] told me the story.
She was dancing at a ball when some bad accident-maker for the *Evening News*
rushed up and informed her that Major Emory had been massacred by the
Indians somewhere out West. She coolly answered him that she had later intelligence; *it was not so.* Turning a deaf ear then, she went on dancing. Next night
the same officious fool met her with this congratulation: "Oh, Mrs. Emory. It
was all a hoax—the major is alive." She cried, "You are always running about
with your bad news," and turned her back on him. Or I think it was "You delight
in spiteful stories" or "You are a harbinger of evil."

Banks is a newspaper man and knows how to arrange an anecdote for effect.
But then, I forget the exact words.

Mrs. Mallory[9] was with her husband in Montgomery. She is a Spanish
Creole, and one can see she has been a beauty. Now she is a grandmother pure
and simple. Her name is Angela, and we gave it angelically—à l'anglaise. Mr.
Mallory, who is very proud of her, gave the Spanish pronunciation—Anhla. We
failed to reproduce the sound in his fashion, and Mr. Browne said it was because
Mallory did it principally with his nose. Anhla.

Polly, my old South Carolina maid, was inclined to give me all of the hotel
scandal—and black enough it was. Her kitchen stories took away the last iota of
my appetite.

One day she came, with eyes and mouth wide open.

7. After resigning on May 9, William Hemsley Emory accepted another commission as a lieutenant
colonel of Union cavalry on May 14.

8. A. D. Banks, then serving as a major on the staff of Gen. Joseph E. Johnston, had been the Washington correspondent for the Cincinnati *Enquirer*, 1859–61.

9. Angela (Moreno) Mallory, wife of Confederate Secretary of the Navy Stephen R. Mallory.

"Well—I believe now—things is upside down. I see a yallar gal slap a white child she was nursing."

"What did you say to her, Polly?"

"I said—Lord gal—if Miss Sally Hamilton was to see you—"

I laughed aloud. I am afraid the girl—who is half-Indian—did not understand the extent of that threat.

Then said Polly: "They got no sense here, niggers ain't. When you got in that open carriage with that lady—what does that impident man do when he sees me up at the window but begin to holler and bawl at me—and ladies in the carriage! His Missis didn't say a word. I was that 'stonished and outdone—if I could er found a rock handy I'd 'a like to chunked him off that box. Talk—on his box—and his Missis in de carriage!"

I had shared Polly's "'stonishment." Wealth—without civilization, I thought.

June 10, 1861.   Have been looking at Mrs. O'Dowd as she burnished the "Meejor's arrms"—before Waterlooo.[1]

And I have been busy too. My husband has gone to join Beauregard. Somewhere beyond Richmond.

I feel blue-black with melancholy. But I hope to be in Richmond before long myself. That is some comfort.

Privateering mad in Charleston. The *Savannah* taken as a prize of war.[2] The *Mercury* newspaper assures the enemy that its vengeance will be fearful if a hair of their head is hurt—poor boys.

Carried a packet of papers to William E. Johnson, president of the bank. He was quite confidential. His wife, all the world knows, is a thousand times too good for him. She is good—he is clever. He told me in his queer plaintive voice: "My wife is a good creature. There is nothing in her. She is honest and simpleminded—that's all. Simple-hearted, too."

The war is making us all tenderly sentimental. No casualties yet, no real mourning, nobody hurt. So it is all parade, fife, and fine feathers. Posing we are en grande tenue. There is no imagination here to forestall woe, and only the excitement and wild awakening from everyday stagnant life are felt. That is, when one gets away from the two or three sensible men who are still left in the world.

Miss McEwen tells me of a pretty picture. Mrs. Kershaw[3] has had her Joe's

---

1. William Thackeray, *Vanity Fair* (1848), chapter 30.

2. The *Savannah*, a Charleston privateer, was captured by the U.S.S. *Perry* on June 3. Since President Lincoln had already declared his intention to treat such captives not as prisoners of war but as pirates, the fate of the captain and his thirteen-man crew was highly uncertain.

3. Lucretia (Douglas) Kershaw, wife of Joseph Brevard Kershaw.

———————

hair made into bracelets and necklace. She sits with bare neck and sleeveless arms, with one hand resting on a beloved offspring, caressingly. Lovely arms and neck, doubtless. I remember she had a thoroughly graceful figure.

When Beauregard's report of the capture of Fort Sumter was printed, Willie Ancrum[4] said:

"How is this? Tom Ancrum and Ham Boykin's names are not here. We thought from what they told us that they did most of the fighting."

⟨⟨Judge Withers has resigned his seat in Congress. What a man.⟩⟩[5]

———————

Colonel Magruder has done something splendid on the Peninsula. Bethel is the name of the battle. Three hundred of the enemy killed—they say.[6]

Our great Republic. After all—"Slow to grow—long to last. Quick to grow, quick to pass."

Maybe the model republic will be like its grand maternal Great Britain. Regularly mined every now and then. But what an immense amount of mining it takes to hurt her at all. For there she stands.

Frightened partridge—half-cooked.

———————

In every day's journey there are three leagues of heartbreaking.
                                                            —Spanish proverb

———————

Our people—Southerners, I mean—continue to drop in from the outside world. And what a contempt those who have seceded a few days sooner feel for those who have just come.

———————

A Camden notable called Jim Villepigue[7] said in the street today, "At heart Robert E. Lee is against us—that I know."

What will not people say in wartimes. Also he said that Colonel Kershaw wanted General Beauregard to change the name of the stream near Manassas Station. Bulls Run is so unrefined.

Beauregard answered, "Let us try to make it as great a name as your South Carolina Cowpens."[8]

---

4. William Alexander Ancrum and his brother Thomas James Ancrum, Camden planters and close friends of the Chesnuts.

5. Under June 12, 1861, in the 1860s Journal.

6. Only eighteen Union troops fell June 10 in the first land battle of the war, fought on the peninsula southeast of Richmond. Confederate commander John Bankhead Magruder of Va. claimed a major victory, however, and won promotion to brigadier general a week later.

7. James Irwin Villepigue, a prosperous Camden merchant who was commissary of Kershaw's regiment.

8. The site of Brig. Gen. Daniel Morgan's decisive victory over British troops in Jan. 1781.

Mrs. Chesnut, born in Philadelphia, cannot see what right we have to take Mount Vernon from our Northern sisters. She thinks that ought to be common to each party. We think they will get their share of this world's goods, do what we may, and we will keep Mount Vernon, if we can.

At Bethel, a poor young soldier, found with a bullet through his heart and a Bible in his pocket, marked: "From the Bible Society to the defender of his country." When love who sent forgot to save. If the Bible can't prevent war, how is it to stop a bullet?

Johnny, the gentleman private, has sent for his man William and a baggage wagon. And he shall have both.

Mr. Kirkland[9] trumped Jim Villepigue's trick. He says, "General Lee will surely be tried for a traitor." "Why, in heaven's name?" "He is blazing out a path behind them, in case of a retreat. To talk of retreat is treason—disheartens soldiers."

No comfort in Mr. Chesnut's letter from Richmond. Unutterable confusion prevails—and discord—already.

In Charleston a butcher has been clandestinely supplying the Yankee fleet, outside of the bar, with beef. They say he gave the information which led to the capture of the *Savannah*. They will hang him.

Mr. Petigru alone in South Carolina has not seceded. When they pray for our president, he gets up from his knees. He might risk a prayer for Mr. Davis. I doubt if it would seriously do Mr. Davis any good. Mr. Petigru is too clever to think himself one of the righteous whose prayers avail so overly much. Mr. Petigru's disciple, Mr. Bryan,[1] followed his example.

Mr. Petigru has such a keen sense of the ridiculous, he must be laughing in his sleeve at the hubbub this untimely trait of independence has raised.

Harpers Ferry evacuated.

Looking out for a battle at Manassas Station.

I am always ill. The name of my disease is a longing to get away from here and to go to Richmond.

Good Lord, forgive me. Your commandment I cannot keep. How can I honor what is so dishonorable or respect what is so little respectable, so

---

9. William Lennox Kirkland, owner of the rice plantation "Combahee."
1. George S. Bryan, a Charleston lawyer and a leader of the Unionist faction in S.C.

disreputable—or love what is so utterly unlovely. Then—I must go—indeed. Go away from here. ⟨⟨ *Rachel* and her brood make this place a horrid nightmare to me—I believe in nothing, with this before me.⟩⟩[2]

Read Cooper's naval history[3] all day. A good book to give one a proper estimate of one's foes.

In England Mr. Gregory and Mr. Lyndsay rise to say a good word for us.[4] Heaven reward them. Shower down His choicest blessings on their devoted heads—as the fiction folks say.

Barnwell Heyward[5] telegraphed me to meet him at Kingsville, but I was at Cool Spring and all my clothes at Sandy Hill. So I lost that good opportunity of the very nicest escort to Richmond.

Kate's German tutor today asked me if, when I did not appear, my time was given up to la lecture et l'écriture.

"No, far from it. While out of sight today I made a pudding and put the finishing touches to a jar of pickles."

Then Molly's baby is ill. Nancy's died last week. So we have a kind of baby epidemic. I had to see the cows fed in Molly's place. She milks, and the cow boy is very trifling and inefficient.

Busy enough.

The German announced the fact that he was careless what he ate.

Quoted in an undertone the solemn belief of a low country gentleman. "Any man who pretends that he does not care for a good dinner is either a d——d liar or a d——d fool."

Tried to rise above the agonies of everyday life—read Emerson. Too restless—Manassas on the brain.

Saw today Napoleon's experience. Two armies always frighten one another. The best general is he who knows how to take advantage of the first panic.

Napoleon ought to know.

Russell's letters filled with rubbish about our wanting an English prince to reign over us.

2. Entry dated June 14 and 15 in the 1860s Journal. See reference to "Rachel" p. 31. The "commandment" referred to is "Honor thy father and mother. . . ." She has in mind her father-in-law.

3. James Fenimore Cooper, *The History of the Navy of the United States of America* (1839).

4. Sir William Henry Gregory and William Schaw Lindsay were the leaders of the small group in Parliament who urged their government to give full diplomatic recognition to the Confederacy.

5. Edward Barnwell Heyward, brother-in-law of Maria (Magruder) Heyward, was a Richland District cotton and rice planter with a taste for art and literature.

He actually intimates that the noisy arming, drumming, marching, proclaiming, at the North scares us. Yes—as the making of faces and turning somersaults of the Chinese scared the English.

Mr. Binney[6] has written a letter. It is in the *Intelligencer*. He offers Lincoln life and fortune; all that he has is put at Lincoln's disposal to conquer us.

Queer. We only want to separate from them, and they put such an inordinate value on us, they are willing to risk all—life and limb and all their money—to keep us, they love us so.

Mr. Chesnut is accused of firing the first shot. And his cousin, the Reverend ex–West Pointer, writes in a martial fury.

They confounded the *best* shot made on the island the day of the picnic, with the first shot at Fort Sumter.

That is claimed by Captain James.[7] Others say it was one of the Gibbeses.

Anderson fired the train which blew up the Union when he slipped into Fort Sumter that night when we expected to talk it all over.

Mrs. Bradford's[8] letter:

> Talladega, Alabama
> June 13, 1861

My dear Madam,

This being the day set apart by our noble President, for prayer for our Southern Confederacy, the interest of our section has come up before my mind in all its bearings, and although I am utterly opposed to *women* taking *any* part in affairs publicly, I am a great advocate for their influence, in the right time and right *direction*.

Some time ago, I took the liberty of sending you a paper from Talladega, containing an article I had written on this subject, but when I met you in Montgomery since, our intercourse seemed so *incidental* that I did not mention it to you.

I however feel such an abiding interest in the part women are to take in this glorious New Republic, that I cannot refrain from saying a few words to you on the subject.

Occupying the position you do—you and the other ladies of the Congress, and of the Cabinet have it in your power to give tone to society for all *time to come.* I trust in God, you will exert it in the right way—and *I believe you will.*

The ladies of your state, I have always admired. There is a well assured

---

6. Horace Binney, noted Philadelphia jurist and brother-in-law of Mrs. James Chesnut, Sr., supported Lincoln's suspension of the writ of habeas corpus and helped give the measure the legitimacy it so badly needed.

7. Capt. George S. James, commanding a mortar battery on James Island, did indeed fire the signal shot at 4:30 A.M. that opened the bombardment.

8. Louisiana (Taul) Bradford was the wife of Jacob Tipton Bradford, the Confederate commissioner of public lands for Ala.

confidence of position about them, that renders any little efforts as to *Etiquette* or *Assumption* on their part unnecessary to convince other people of the fact—And therefore, they are plain and unassuming. This elegant simplicity is so desirable, that I trust it will be kept up in our higher fashionable circles. There are so many *weak minded* women, who attach great importance to the mere *Forms* of *Society* that it will require great effort to counteract their influence.

There has been so much of Christian spirit infused by the *Noble Men* who have formed our Government I do trust it will be felt in all streams which flow from so pure a source—or Fountain!

I presume there were but few women and not many *men* who took a more lively interest in its proceedings than I did. I was present many weeks, all the time Ladies were permitted to remain, and enjoyed it with a degree of admiration and Patriotism bordering on *Idolatry*.

You may consider yourself *fortunate* in being the wife of one of that *Noble Body*, The first *Southern Congress*.

My husband was not a member. But he was a Delegate to Charleston—to Richmond, to Baltimore and claimed his share in bringing about the glorious results.

I am a plain, *old fashioned* woman, and do not go into fashionable company.—But I cannot help feeling a deep interest in you *My Sisters* who are placed there—in the *young*, our sons and daughters who are to come under your influence.

I do trust that good sense and *christian* simplicity will long be the standards in our "Southern Courts and firesides," and that our women may be as *good* as *our men are brave!*

I hope *your husband* and the other members of Congress will not so *fall in love* with *Richmond* as to want to make it the permanent seat of Government.

By all means, let it be established in the Cotton States—*they* fought the first battle—established the Government and deserve it.

If South Carolina were not too far on *one side* it should be there. I think Huntsville Alabama the most eligible point—every way desireable—very accessible—beautiful and wealthy Country—Society elegant and refined. I wish you could see it before your husband casts his vote on that question—I have no personal interest there, but greatly admire that part of the State.

I was much pleased with Judge Withers, 'tho' our acquaintance with him also seemed rather *cramped* I would say; as persons at our hotel appeared not to know much of each other.

Now that *War* is actually going on and its *stern realities* are upon us, there is no danger of *little* things engrossing our attention. Stern duties require our attention. When it is over and *Prosperity* reigns then will come the *danger*.

"May we" as *Patrick Henry* said "profit by the Example," and learn wisdom from our *old* and now broken down Washington Society.

Hoping you will pardon the *great* liberty I have taken I subscribe myself—

Yours respectfully,

Louisiana Bradford

No comment needed. ⟨⟨A preposterous letter . . . answered it as absurdly. . . .⟩⟩

Headquarters, Manassas Junction
June 16, 1861

My dear Mary,

I wrote you a short letter from Richmond last Wednesday and came here next day—found the camp all busy and preparing for a vigorous defense. We have here at this camp seven regiments, and in the same command, at posts in the neighborhood, six others—say ten thousand good men.

The general and the men feel confident that they can whip twice that number of the enemy at least.

I have not yet been able to get to Gregg's camp and have not seen John but hope to see him tomorrow.

I have been in the saddle for two days—all day—with the general to become familiar with the topography of the country and the posts he intends to assume and the communications between them.

We learn General Johnston[9] has evacuated Harpers Ferry and taken up his position at Winchester, to meet the advancing column of McClellan[1] and to avoid being cut off by the three columns which were advancing upon him. Neither Johnston nor Beauregard consider Harpers Ferry as very important in strategic point of view.

I think it most probable that the next battle you will hear of will be between the forces of Johnston and McClellan.

I discover that our generals have not a very high opinion of the efficiency of the administration—especially the War Department.

I think what we particularly need is a head in the field—a major general to combine and conduct all the forces as well as plan a general and energetic campaign. Still, we have all confidence that we will defeat the enemy whenever and wherever we meet in general engagement.

Although the majority of the people just around here are with us, still there are many who are against us.

Send me, by who ever may come this way first, my large sponge—and my gun with the strap on it, with some buckshot and a box of caps to fit it.

I have been to Kershaw's camp. Tell Mr. Team[2] I saw his son. They are all well—except a few cases of measles.

9. Brig. Gen. Joseph Eggleston Johnston of Va., who had resigned from the U.S. Army after the fall of Fort Sumter, was commander of the Army of the Shenandoah.

1. Maj. Gen. George Brinton McClellan, commander of the Union forces that had moved into western Va. from Ohio.

2. James Team, fifty-six, was the chief overseer for old Mr. Chesnut's plantations and also a planter worth 13,500 dollars in 1860.

His son is quite well—and satisfied.

When you write, direct to me at headquarters of General Beauregard, Va.

God bless you—

Yours—&c&c.

James Chesnut, Jr.

My mare is lame. I am riding a horse captured from U.S. dragoons—Fairfax. He is a fine charger.

Just now I called to mind that last delightful luncheon at Mrs. Davis's.

She said I was like Cuddie Headrigg in Scott's novel—I "remembered her always at brose time."[3] In Montgomery, that was. If my lady correspondent who writes with such a craze for republican simplicity could have seen her that day! Maggie Howell[4] and herself were hemming kitchen towels. I am afraid it was a sporadic effort.

In that presidential mansion outside of the Constitution—which has broken the Judge's heart and blighted his faith in any political honesty whatever—one always found, brose time, a charming hostess—kind, clever, and hospitable—and then, she had so good a cook. I had taken into my inmost being a perfect loathing for everything in those hot and unsavory hotels.

Mary Hammy[5] and myself—we are off for Richmond. Rev. Mr. Meynardie[6] of the Methodist persuasion goes with us. We are to be under his care.

War cloud lowering.

Isaac Hayne, the man who fought a duel with Ben Allston,[7] across the dinner table—and yet lives. He is the bravest of the brave. He attacks Russell, the London *Times* correspondent, in the *Mercury*. In the public prints! For saying we wanted an English prince to the fore. Not we, indeed! Every man wants to be at the head of affairs himself—if he cannot be king himself—Then a republic, of course. It was hardly necessary to do more than laugh at Russell's absurd idea.

There was a great deal of the wildest kind of talk at the Mills House. Russell

---

3. Reference to a flirtatious remark addressed to Headrigg, a servant in Sir Walter Scott's *Old Mortality* (1816), chapter 21. "Brose time" means "meal time."

4. Margaret Graham Howell, Varina Davis's younger sister, was known in Confederate society for her keen conversation and caustic wit.

5. Mary Whitaker Boykin, the daughter of Alexander Hamilton Boykin and Sarah (DeSaussure) Boykin, was Mrs. Chesnut's first cousin. M. B. C. probably attached "Hammy" to Mary's name to distinguish her from similarly named members of the Chesnut and Boykin families.

6. E. J. Meynardie of Camden was going to Richmond as the chaplain of Kershaw's regiment.

7. Probably Benjamin George Allston, a lawyer and former state legislator from Beaufort District.

writes candidly enough of the British in India.[8] We can hardly expect him to suppress what is to our detriment.

———————

Down at Sandy Hill again—making ready for Richmond.

Last night I was awakened by loud talking and candles flashing everywhere—tramping of feet—growls dying away in the distance, loud calls from point to point in the yard.

Up I started—my heart in my mouth. Some dreadful thing had happened—a battle—a death—a horrible accident. Miss Sally Chesnut[9] was screaming aloft—that is, from the top of the stairway—hoarsely, like a boatswain in a storm.

Colonel C was storming at the sleepy negroes looking for fire, with lighted candles in closets—&c&c.

I dressed and came upon the scene of action.

"What is it? Any news?"

"No, no—only, mama smells a smell. She thinks something is burning somewhere."

The whole yard was alive—literally swarming. There are sixty or seventy people kept here to wait upon this household—two-thirds of them too old or too young to be of any use. But families remain intact. Mr. C has a magnificent voice. I am sure it can be heard for miles. Literally he was roaring from the piazza—giving orders to the busy crowd who were hunting the smell of fire.

Mrs. C is deaf, so she did not know what a commotion she was creating. She is very sensitive on the subject of bad odors. Candles have to be taken out of the room to be snuffed. Lamps are extinguished only in the porticoes—or further afield. She finds violets oppressive. Can only tolerate a single kind of rose. Tea rose she will not have in her room.

She was totally innocent of the storm she had raised and in a mild sweet voice was suggesting places to be searched.

I was weak enough to laugh hysterically. The bombardment of Fort Sumter was nothing to this.

As I said, this yard is a negro village—for whom taxes are paid—and doctors' bills. They earn their daily bread and their large families' food and clothes and house rent by "waiting in the house."

They rapidly increase and never diminish in numbers. Maria's three children in two years bear witness to their powers that way and is a suggestive fact.

And her free husband—"as good as white, but not quite," as Rachel says. "No wonder Jeems Whitaker deserted her—and lef' ole Missis to support her."

Now this village is just outside of the palings. After this alarum—enough to wake the dead—the smell was found. A family had been boiling soap. Around

8. William Howard Russell, *My Diary in India in the Year 1858-1859* (1860), describes the sometimes savage repression of the Indian Mutiny, a native uprising against the British in 1857-58.
9. Sarah Chesnut, forty-seven, was an older sister of J. C. Mrs. Chesnut sometimes calls her "Miss S. C."

the soap pot they had swept up some woolen rags. Raking up the fire to make all safe before going to bed, this was heaped up with ashes, and its faint smoldering tainted the air—at least, to Mrs. Chesnut's nose, two hundred yards away or more.

Even then, to my inquiry, as I came out of my room, "Any news?" the old gentleman answered sharply.

"We don't send to the office in the afternoon. Good news can keep. Bad news comes fast enough."

So after much mumbling-grumbling, things settled down, and the deadly quiet of Sandy Hill reigned once more.

Yesterday some of the negro men on the plantation were found with pistols.

I have never seen aught about any negro to show that they knew we had a war on hand in which they have any interest.

Mrs. John DeSaussure bade me goodbye—and God bless me. I was touched. Camden people never show any more feeling or sympathy than red Indians. Except at a funeral—it is expected of all to howl there. If you don't "show feeling," indignation awaits the delinquent.

V

Waiting for the Real War

June 27, 1861. Richmond. Mr. Meynardie was perfect in the part of traveling companion. He had his pleasures, too. The most pious and eloquent of parsons is human, and he enjoyed the converse of the "eminent persons" who turned up on every hand and gave their views freely on all matters of state.

Mr. Lawrence Keitt joined us en route. With him were his wife and baby. We don't think alike, but Mr. Keitt is always original and entertaining. Already he pronounces Jeff Davis a failure—and his cabinet a farce.

"Prophetic," I suggested, as he gave his opinion before the administration had fairly got under way—foregone conclusion.

He was fierce in his faultfinding as to Mr. Chesnut's vote for Jeff Davis. He says Mr. C overpersuaded the Judge, and those two turned the tide, at least with the South Carolina delegation. We wrangled—as we always do. He says Howell Cobb's common sense might have saved us. He was a Cobb man. And I averred that Jeff Davis would save us.

Two quiet unobtrusive Yankee schoolteachers were on the train. I had spoken to them, and they had told me all about themselves. So I wrote on a scrap of paper: "Do not abuse our home and house so before these Yankee strangers going North. *Those* girls are schoolmistresses returning from whence they came."

Mr. Ashmore[1] was along, too, but he was silent, humbled, and miserable.

Soldiers everywhere. They seem to be in the air—certainly filled all space. Keitt quoted a funny Georgia man who says we try our soldiers if they are hot enough before we enlist them. If when water is thrown on them, they do not sizz—they won't do—their patriotism is too cool.

It had a lively effect. To show they were wide awake and sympathizing enthusiastically, every woman from every window of every house we passed waved a handkerchief, if she had one. This fluttering of white flags from every side never ceased, from Camden to Richmond. Another new symptom— parties of girls came to every station simply to look at the troops passing. They always stood (the girls, I mean) in solid phalanx, and as the sun was generally in their eyes, they made faces. Mary Hammy never tired of laughing at this peculiarity of her sister patriots.

And then, it was so fearfully hot and dusty.

---

1. John Durant Ashmore of Anderson District, S.C., a U.S. congressman from 1859 to 1860, was elected colonel of the Fourth S.C. Regiment but resigned before his unit was called into service.

At the depot in Richmond Mr. Mallory, with Wigfall and Garnett,[2] met us. We had no cause to complain of the warmth of our reception. They had a carriage for us and our rooms taken at the Spotswood.

But then, the people who were in the rooms engaged for us had not departed at the time they said they were going.

They lingered among the delights of Richmond. And we knew of no law to make them keep their words and go.

Mrs. Preston had gone for a few days to Manassas. So we took her room.

Mrs. Davis kind as ever. Met us in one of the corridors, accidentally. She asked us to join her party and to take our meals at her table.

Mrs. Preston came, and we moved into a room so small there was only space for a bed, washstand, and glass over it. My things were hung up out of the way, on nails behind the door.

As soon as my husband heard we had arrived, he came, too. After dinner he sat smoking. The solitary chair of the apartment tilted against that door. As he smoked—and my poor dresses were fumigated à merci et à miséricorde—I remonstrated feebly.

"Wartimes—nobody is fussy now. When I go back to Manassas tomorrow, you will be awfully sorry you snubbed me about those trumpery things up there."

So he smoked the pipe of peace, for I knew that his remarks were painfully true. As soon as he was once more under the enemies' guns, I would repent in sackcloth and ashes.

He came by order of the general for more ammunition.

The president said at table, "Whoever is too fine—that is, so fine that we do not know what to do with him—we send him to Beauregard's staff." It is truly a wonderful collection of ex-governors—generals—U.S. senators. ⟪The president ridiculed Beauregard's staff—and both Mr. C and I answered. . . . Mr. C told him they had not enough red tape in his shop to measure Beauregard's staff. Wigfall has lost caste here by being a [*one effaced word underlined*] of the president's. Poor Mrs. Wigfall—she feels her position. Mr. Chesnut eats at his *own* table. . . . ⟫

Mrs. McLean is here. Mrs. Davis always has clever women around her. They gravitate to her.

Gen. Joe Johnston says he has not ammunition sufficient to enable him to attack Generals Cadwalader[3] and McClellan.

Captain Ingraham came with Colonel Lamar.[4] The latter said he could only

2. Muscoe Russell Hunter Garnett, the husband of Mary (Stevens) Garnett, was a former U.S. congressman and a delegate to the Va. secession convention.

3. George Cadwalader, major general of Pa. Volunteers, was second in command of the Union troops in the lower Shenandoah Valley.

4. Former U.S. congressman Lucius Quintus Cincinnatus Lamar was the author of the Miss. ordinance of secession and lieutenant colonel of the Nineteenth Miss. Regiment.

stay five minutes. He was obliged to go back at once to his camp, a little before eight o'clock. However, at twelve he was still talking to us on that sofa.

We taunted him with his fine words to the F.F.[5] crowd before the Spotswood—"Virginia has no grievance—she raises her strong arm to catch the blow aimed at her weaker sisters." He liked it well, however, that we knew his speech by heart.

Letter from Mr. Chesnut, sent here from Camden, where it arrived after we left that hot hole.

Richmond
June 12, 1861

My dear Mary,

I got here last night very much worried by heat, dust, &c and found the greatest difficulty to get a place to sleep. This city is crowded, and the hotels are overflowing. I have to remain here today because my horse could not be transported yesterday from Petersburg.

I left her there last night with Laurence, to come this morning—and they have arrived safely. My hands were so full with the four negroes, all green except Laurence, that I had no time to take a meal from the time I left Kingsville until I got here. The negroes had to lie on the trunks all night in the hall of the hotel; and I sent them to the camp this morning by a private soldier, Hinson, of Kennedy's company.[6] I will leave in the morning myself.

I have just seen Mrs. Davis and Mrs. Wigfall and delivered your message to the latter. She will write in a day or so. She does not know at this time where she will go. I have had no time to inform myself of the real condition of affairs, but to a casual observation, things seem still in confusion.

Yesterday we heard that Magruder's command at Bethel Church on the York had several engagements with the enemy and repulsed them each time, with loss on the Federal side; but we do not know the exact truth yet. Reinforcements were sent from here last night, the New Orleans Zouaves. Cash and Bacon's regiments[7] are still here and will move to Manassas tomorrow. Fine bodies of men, both. You must not be surprised if you hear of an advance into Maryland or by flank movement in the rear of McClellan's command. Beauregard's command will be the advancing column.

We have just heard of the landing of Federal forces at Hilton Head.[8] If true, it is only as I predicted.

5. Short for F.F.V., First Families of Virginia.

6. Probably John E. Hinson, a Camden harness maker serving in a company of Kershaw's regiment. His commander, Capt. John Doby Kennedy, was a twenty-one-year-old Camden attorney who owned 269 slaves.

7. Col. Ellerbe Bogan Crawford Cash of Chesterfield District commanded the Eighth Regiment of S.C. Volunteers; Col. Thomas G. Bacon of Edgefield District commanded the Seventh.

8. A false rumor.

Henry Marshall of Louisiana[9] and myself are sleeping in the same bed, and others in the same room. Richmond is hot and comfortless. I will prefer the camp, where I will be tomorrow night.

Love to all—as ever, your &c&c—

James Chesnut, Jr.

This Spotswood is a miniature world. The war topic is not so much avoided as that everybody has some personal dignity to take care of—and everybody else is indifferent to it. I mean the "personal dignity" of *autrui*.

A Richmond lady told me under her breath that Mrs. Davis had sent a baby's dress to her friend Mrs. Montgomery Blair.[1] And Mrs. Blair had responded, "Even if the men kill one another, they (Mrs. D and Mrs. B) would abide friends to the bitter end—the grave—&c&c." "Why not?"

I said nothing because I will be taken aside and told by somebody else, "That Blair story is all false, made up by these malicious, gossipy women, &c&c."

In this wild confusion everything likely and unlikely is told you—and then everything is as flatly contradicted.

At any rate, it is safest not to talk of the war.

Trescot was telling us how they laughed at little South Carolina in Washington. Said it was almost as large as Long Island, which is hardly more than a tailfeather of New York. Always there is a child who sulks and won't play; that was our role.

And we were posing as San Marino—and all model-spirited, "the" small republics.

He tells us that Lincoln is a humorist. He sees the fun of things; he thinks if they had left us in a corner or out in the cold awhile, panting, with our fingers in our mouth, by hook or crook they would have got us back—but Anderson spoiled all.

The Russian minister called us the subjects of Pickens the 1st.[2]

And we were stalking, heads aloft—San Mariners of the West!!!

Somebody asked, What is San Marino? A sort of toy republic which escapes by its insignificance. But where is it? Somewhere near the Mediterranean Sea. Among mountains—vague.

June 28, 1861.   Louis Wigfall kept Mr. C a day longer. Also, Mr. Henry Marshall had him busy getting guns, tents, &c for Gregg's regiment. If Pickens will

---

9. A member of the Confederate Congress.

1. Mary Elizabeth (Woodbury) Blair, the wife of Lincoln's postmaster general. The Davises and the Blairs had been close friends in Washington.

2. Late in May, en route to his new position as U.S. minister at St. Petersburg, Ky. abolitionist Cassius Marcellus Clay delivered speeches in London and Paris which reminded the European powers that their interests lay with the Federal government, not with the "treason" and "despotism" of the Southern Confederacy. The Richmond *Examiner* published Clay's London speech on June 11.

let them keep what they have, Mr. Marshall, because of his love and faith in Maxcy Gregg, will be security for them. Well [that] he is so rich.

<I have worked like a beaver—or rather a mole—for my friends, and this is the first one who has thanked me—seeing shrewdly my fingers in the pie.>

Waco, Texas
June 21, 1861

Hon. James Chesnut

Dear Sir,

I have just received notice of my appointment as district attorney for the western district of Texas. Knowing that you have been instrumental in my favor in this matter and learning from the Hon. John Hemphill that Mrs. Chesnut also expressed much interest in my appointment, I write this note to acknowledge my obligation to you both and promise you that zeal and inclination shall not be wanting in the discharge of the duties which the office may impose upon me.

Mrs. West and little Stark and Mary Lamar join me in thanks. And send greeting to yourself and Mrs. C.

Your friend, respectfully,

John C. West[3]

《Yesterday, for fear of giving offense, had to take tea a second time with Mrs. Davis. She was not civil enough—kept me bandied about for a seat—but I would not tell Mr. C. He was annoyed enough before. . . . 》

In Mrs. Davis's drawing room last night, the president took a seat beside me on the sofa where I sat. He talked for nearly an hour. He laughed at our faith in our own powers. We are like the British. We think every Southerner equal to three Yankees at least. We will have to be equivalent to a dozen now. After his experience of the fighting qualities of Southerners in Mexico, he believes that we will do all that can be done by pluck and muscle, endurance, and dogged courage—dash and red-hot patriotism, &c. And yet his tone was not sanguine. There was a sad refrain running through it all. For one thing, either way, he thinks it will be a long war. That floored me at once. It has been too long for me already. Then said: before the end came, we would have many a bitter experience. He said only fools doubted the courage of the Yankees or their willingness to fight when they saw fit. And now we have stung their pride—we have roused them till they will fight like devils.

He said Mr. Chesnut's going as A.D.C. to Beauregard was a mistake. He ought to raise a regiment of his own. 《《(So he ought!)》》

3. John Camden West, a Waco, Tex., lawyer and insurance man whose father had been mayor of Camden.

Mrs. Bradley Johnson[4] is here, a regular heroine. She out-generaled the governor of North Carolina in some way and has got arms and clothes and ammunition for her husband's regiment.

There was some joke. The regimental breeches were all wrong, but a tailor righted that—hind part before, or something odd.

Captain Hartstene came today with Mrs. Bartow.[5] Colonel Bartow is a colonel of a Georgia regiment now in Virginia. He was the mayor of Savannah who helped to wake the patriotic echoes the livelong night, under my sleepless head into the small hours—Charleston in November last. His wife is a charming person. Witty and wise daughter of Judge Berrien. She had on a white muslin apron with pink bows on the pockets. It gave her a gay and girlish air. And yet she must be as old as I am.

Mr. Lamar, who does not love slavery more than Sumner does—nor than I do, say—laughs at the compliment New England pays us. We want to separate from them—to be rid of Yankees forever at any price. And they hate us so and would clasp us—or hook us, as Polonius has it—to their bosoms with hooks of steel. We are an unwilling bride. I think incompatibility of temper began when it was made plain to us that we get all the opprobrium of slavery and they all the money there was in it—with their tariff.

Mr. Lamar says the young men are lighthearted because there is a fight on hand. But those few who look ahead, the clear heads, they see all the risk—the loss of land, limb, and life, home, children, and wife. As in the brave days of old, they take it for their country's sake. I wish I could remember Macaulay's ballad.[6] It was that way he put it. At any rate, they are ready and willing, come what may. But not so lighthearted as the jeunesse dorée, however.

June 29, 1861.   Saturday—Mrs. Preston, Mrs. Wigfall, Mary Hammy, and I drove in a fine open carriage to see the "champ-de-Mars."

It was a grand tableau out there. Mr. Davis rode a beautiful gray horse. His worse enemy will allow that he is a consummate rider, graceful and easy in the saddle—and Mr. Chesnut, who has talked horse with his father ever since he was born, owns that Mr. Davis knows more about horses than any man he met yet. General Lee was there with him—also Joe Davis[7] and Wigfall, acting as his aides.

---

4. Jane Claudia (Saunders) Johnson was the wife of Bradley Tyler Johnson, organizer and major of the First Md. Regiment.

5. Louisa (Berrien) Bartow, wife of Francis S. Bartow. Her father, John MacPherson Berrien of Ga., was U.S. attorney general, 1829–31.

6. Thomas Babington Macaulay's "Horatius," in *Lays of Ancient Rome* (1842), repeats the phrase "in the brave days of old."

7. Joseph Robert Davis, nephew of the Confederate president.

Poor Mr. Lamar has been brought from his camp. Paralysis—or some sort of stroke. Every woman in the house is ready to rush into the Florence Nightingale business.

I think I will wait for a wounded man, to make my first effort at sister of charity.

He sent for me. As everybody went—Mrs. Davis setting the example—so did I. He will not die this time, or will men flatter and make eyes until their eyes close in death at the ministering angels? Except that he was in bed—with some learned professor at his bedside—and that his wife has been telegraphed for, he was the same old Lamar of the drawing room. ⟨⟨Florence Nightingale would not do with *our* men. They are too excitable. He could scarcely speak—did not know that he would live the night through, and yet he said such things. I asked if he felt better, and he answered: "*Already*. Your being in here would *cure* anyone," and then apologized for being *ill*. . . . He told Mrs. Johnston that my presence made the room feel delicious and that the aroma remained there still—so that I am glad I am going away, for I think his *brain* is affected. He was desperately ill again last night. I think it provokes Mrs. <Davis> that such men praise me so. . . . Mrs. Davis and Jeff Davis proved themselves anything but <well-bred by their talk>. I am so sorry Mr. Chesnut told those men of the fling Jeff Davis made at them—I mean Beauregard's staff.⟩⟩

It is pleasant at the president's table. My seat is next to Joe Davis—with Mr. Browne on the other side and Mr. Mallory opposite. There is a great constraint, however. As soon as I repeated what the North Carolina man said on the cars—that North Carolina had 20,000 men ready and they were kept back by Mr. Walker[8]—&c&c—

The president caught something of what I was saying and asked me to repeat it, which I did, although I was scared to death.

"Madame, when you see that person, tell him his statement is false. We are too anxious here for troops to refuse a man who offers himself—not to speak of twenty thousand men."

Silence ensued, of the most profound. When I take my seat my grace is a prayer to God that I may not put my mouth in at the wrong place—or time.

⟨⟨I continue to dine at Mr. Davis's table, but it is not pleasant. . . . These men call Mrs. Davis the Empress—Eugénie,[9] &c&c—and do not like her. The notorious A. D. Banks abuses her worst of all—says she is so killingly patronizing.⟩⟩

Uncle Hamilton gave me three hundred dollars for his daughter Mary's expenses—making four in all that I have of hers. He would pay me one hundred, which he said he owed my husband for a horse. I thought it an excuse

---

8. Though he had no military experience, Ala. lawyer Leroy Pope Walker was appointed Confederate secretary of war on Feb. 16, 1861.

9. An allusion to Eugénie de Montijo, the wife of Napoleon III.

to lend me money, though I told him I had enough and to spare for all my needs until my colonel came home from the wars.

Ben Allston,[1] the governor's son, is here. Came to see me—does not show much of the wit of the Pettigrews. Pleasant person, however. Mr. Brewster and Wigfall came at the same time. The former, chafing at Wigfall's anomalous position here, gave him fiery advice. Mr. Wigfall was calm and full of common sense. A brave man, and without thought of any necessity for displaying his temper. He said: "Brewster, at this time, before the country is strong and settled in her new career, it would be disastrous for us—the headmen—to engage in a row among ourselves."

Brewster begged him to remember what Governor Houston[2] had said when he heard that Wigfall was elected senator from Texas. "Thank God this country is so great and strong, it can bear even that." Now Mr. Brewster declared he thought this country already strong enough to bear a rupture between Mr. Davis and Mr. Wigfall. He did not think it would be too much for the country.

Mr. Wigfall took it all in high good humor.

I thought I had two new books. *The Crossed Path,* Wilkie Collins.[3] It is only the best of his *Basil,* its old name too good to be forgotten. As *Basil* I think I read it twenty years ago. Frank Sumter[4] brought it to me, and I had the benefit of his brilliant criticism.

As I was brushing flies, fanning the prostrate Lamar, I repeated Mr. Davis's conversation of the night before.

"He is all right," said Mr. Lamar. "The fight had to come. We are men, not women. The quarrel had lasted long enough. We hate each other so—the fight had to come. Even Homer's heroes, after they had stormed and scolded enough, fought like brave men, long and well."

He said if the athlete Sumner had stood on his manhood and training and struck back when Preston Brooks assailed him, Preston Brooks's blow need not have been the opening skirmish of the war.[5] Sumner's country took up the fight because he did not. Sumner chose his own battlefield, and it was the worse for us. What an awful blunder that Preston Brooks business was!

1. Benjamin Allston, a Georgetown District planter, was the son of former governor Robert Francis Withers Allston and Adele Pettigrew (Petigru) Allston.
2. Sam Houston, the former president of the Republic of Tex., had been deposed as governor of Tex. in March because of his opposition to secession.
3. William Wilkie Collins, *Basil: A Story of Modern Life* (London, 1852; New York, 1853) was reprinted under the title *The Crossed Path; or, Basil: A Story of Modern Life* (Philadelphia, 1860).
4. Francis Brasilimo Sumter, a lawyer from Sumter District, was the grandson of the Revolutionary War hero, Thomas Sumter.
5. During the Senate debates on Kansas in 1856, Mass. Senator Charles Sumner called his colleague Andrew P. Butler, of S.C., a "Don Quixote who had chosen a mistress . . . : the harlot, slavery." Butler's nephew, Congressman Preston Brooks of S.C., sought out Sumner on the Senate floor and beat him into unconsciousness with a cane. Sumner was not to return to the Senate for two and a half years. Brooks resigned his House seat but won an easy campaign for reelection.

Told Lamar how Mr. Chesnut laughed when he remembered town and gown fights (students and snobs, so-called there) at Princeton and heard these people say that Northern men would not fight.

Mr. Hunter more placidly philosophical than all—but just as ready to stake all and risk all and let them have it.

Lamar said Yankees did not fight for the fun of it. They always made it pay or let it alone. Wigfall said to the Pennsylvania Cameron[6] in the Senate, who announced himself as furiously out on a warpath: "Then profit will accrue."

All dissatisfied with Walker, secretary of war. Rhymes they make: "W——, W——, I will trouble you"—

A comic coincidence. We were in the aforesaid landau. Today I paid for it—five dollars an hour (yesterday Mrs. Preston had it), but that is the tragic side. Mrs. Wigfall, as we neared home, was giving us a bit of Spotswood gossip. Wife ill, also jealous, husband's room with no outlet but through hers. There he was incarcerated at times. So ladies said who nursed her. We declined to believe the tale. Just then one of the windows above us was cautiously opened, and the military man in question put himself halfway out of the window and silently and energetically kissed his hand to us.

Mr. Wigfall was triumphant at this circumstantial evidence of the truth of his story. Louis Wigfall said: "If they gave him a looking glass and a bottle of hair dye, he will be content. He will not find he is locked in till dinner time."

"Shall we kiss hands back to him?" said polite little Mamie Hammy. "No need—he is only thinking of himself."

"Besides, they would see us and so find him out too. You see, he is behind backs."

Met Keitt and Boyce in the corridor with muskets, or rifles—something murderous in aspect. They were en route to Manassas.

Met Mr. Lyons[7] with news indeed. A man here in the midst of us, taken with Lincoln's passports &c&c in his pocket. A palpable spy. Mr. Lyons said he would be hanged. In all human probability, that is.

---

6. Simon Cameron, the Pa. capitalist and former U.S. senator who was Lincoln's first secretary of war.

7. James Lyons, a prominent Richmond attorney.

Letter from my husband:

Camp Pickens
June 30, 1861

If you and Mrs. Preston can make up your minds to leave Richmond and can come up to a nice little country house near Orange Court House, we could come to see you frequently while the army is stationed here. It would be a safe place for the present, near the scene of action and directly in the line of news from all sides—&c&c&c.

James Chesnut, Jr.

So we go to Orange Court House.

The other old friend with a new name is *Westward Ho!* The well-remembered "Sir Amyas Leigh"—of Kingsley.[8]

Read Soulouque, the Haitian man.[9] It has a wonderful interest just now. Slavery has to go, of course—and joy go with it. These Yankees may kill us and lay waste the land for a while, but conquer us? Never!

July 4, 1861.   Russell abuses us in his letters from New Orleans. People here care a great deal for what Russell says because he represents the *Times*, and the London *Times* reflects the sentiment of the English people. How we do cling to the idea of an alliance with England or France. Without France, even Washington could not have done it.

Somebody said today: "Is not the South as much ours—our country—to declare its independence—as the colonies owned their own country? We were not even colonies from New England."

"Might makes right" was the answer.

Prince Polignac[1] dined with the president today. He was triste and silent—his English not being too ready and the French of the table being more difficult to produce by those on each side of him. Then, when he was here before, they said he mistook Mrs. Browne for Mrs. Davis—after which gaucherie, doubtless, he feels it necessary to be cautious in his approaches.

8. No available evidence indicates that Charles Kingsley's *Westward Ho!* (1855) ever had a different title; nor did Sir Amyas Leigh appear as a character in any other books written by him.

9. Faustin Elie Soulouque took part as a slave in the Haitian revolt against the French in 1803. He became president of Haiti in 1847 and crowned himself emperor two years later. M. B. C. probably read one of several biographies of Soulouque published in Paris in the 1850s.

1. Camille Armand Jules Marie, prince de Polignac, a French veteran of the Crimean War, volunteered his services to the Confederacy and was commissioned a lieutenant colonel two weeks later.

We drove to the camp to see the president present a flag to the Maryland regiment. Having lived on the battlefield (Kirkwood) near Camden, we have an immense respect for the Maryland line. When our militia ran away, Colonel Howard and the Marylanders held their own against Rawdon—Cornwallis, &c. And everywhere near there is named for some doughty captain killed in our defense—Kirkwood, Hobkirk, DeKalb—the last, however, was a Prussian count.[2]

Near our carriage there stood the very handsomest man I ever saw. He seemed madly excited and hurrahed himself hoarse.

Some cool citizen asked, "Where are you from?"

"Baltimore." So the men there are as handsome as the women—if this is a specimen.

We brought home a spy—a spy on our side—just from the other side. A very good-looking creature, too. He is on General Johnston's staff.

[I] copy a letter from my husband, written June 22nd. Easier to do than telling the same story—as they tell it to me here.

My heart was made glad by the sight of your handwriting in the letter brought to me yesterday by James Villepigue.

It was the first time I had heard from home, and it lifted me out of the despond to which I was fast falling.

Until day before yesterday I had been actively in the field, but so many persons were daily brought into camp that the general thought it expedient to bring into requisition my services as judge advocate. So I have been confined to the court tent for two days. I do not like the duty. We are very strongly posted—entrenched—and have now at our command about 15,000 of the best troops in the world. We have, besides two batteries of artillery, a regiment of cavalry, and daily expect a battalion of flying artillery from Richmond. We have sent forward seven regiments of infantry and rifles toward Alexandria. Our outposts have felt the enemy several times. And in every instance the enemy recoils—or runs. General Johnston has had several encounters—the advancing columns of the two armies, and

2. M. B. C. is recalling, somewhat inaccurately, two Revolutionary War battles fought in Kershaw District. At Camden on Aug. 16, 1780, Southern militia fled before the town's British occupiers led by Gen. Charles Cornwallis and Lt. Col. Francis Rawdon. Continental regulars from Md. and Del. under Maj. Gen. Johann DeKalb and Lt. Col. John Eager Howard held the line for a time but were finally forced to retreat. DeKalb, not a Prussian count but the son of Bavarian peasants, was mortally wounded in the battle. The battlefield itself was named for Capt. Robert Kirkwood of Del., who lived to participate in the second major battle around Camden, the battle of Hobkirk's Hill. On April 25, 1781, the British again defeated an American attack in fighting around this ridge, named not for "some doughty captain" but for an old landowner.

with him, too, the enemy, although always superior in numbers, are invariably driven back.

There is great deficiency in the matter of ammunition. General Johnston's command, in the face of overwhelming numbers, have only 30 round each. If they had been well provided in this respect they could and would have defeated Cadwalader and Patterson[3] with great ease. I find the opinion prevails throughout the army that there is great imbecility and shameful neglect in the War Department.

Unless the Republicans fall back, we must soon come together on both lines and have a decided engagement. But the opinion prevails here that Lincoln's army will not meet us if they can avoid it. They have already fallen back before a slight check from 400 of Johnston's men. They had 700 and were badly beaten.

You have no idea how dirty and irksome the camp life is. You would hardly know your best friend in camp guise. The weather is exceedingly hot—and dusty. We send three miles for water. With most of them, ablution is limited to face and hands, which rarely show the proper application of water. I write upon my knee, at present, as our table is otherwise employed.

&c&c&c&c—

James Chesnut, Jr.

Noise of drums, tramp of marching regiments all day long, rattling of artillery wagons, bands of music, friends from every quarter coming in.

We ought to be miserable and anxious, and yet these are pleasant days. Perhaps we are unnaturally exhilarated and excited.

Just now Major George Deas made Mrs. Joe Johnston very unhappy. He said, "A battle was looked for at every minute between Patterson and General Johnston—and Johnston lacked ammunition."

A young Carolinian with queer ideas of a joke rode his horse through the barroom of this hotel. How he scattered people and things right and left!

Captain Ingraham was so incensed at this bad conduct of his young countryman. "He was intoxicated of course," said Captain Ingraham, "but he was a splendid rider."

Mrs. Joe Johnston said, "If my Joseph is defeated I will die."

Mrs. Davis said, "Lydia, beware of ambition. By that, &c&c&c—"[4]

Today some Virginia women called Maxcy Gregg's regiment cowards because they enlisted for two months, and when the two months were out, they disbanded—and a battle looked-for daily.

It was hard to bear. Only a little patience. Maxcy Gregg won't stay long in any

---

3. Maj. Gen. Robert Patterson, commander of Union forces in the lower Shenandoah Valley.
4. "Cromwell, I charge thee, fling away ambition: / By that sin fell the angels." *Henry VIII*, act 3, scene 2.

situation where he can be called a coward. John Chesnut was a private in that regiment. He goes back at once as a private in a cavalry company—Boykin's Rangers.[5]

_____

Today we drove out to the camp of the Hampton Legion.

How very nice our Carolina gentry are. Today I found them charming—indeed, I felt so proud of them.

Heard some people in the drawing room say, "Mrs. Davis's ladies are not young, are not pretty"—and I am one. The truthfulness of the remark did not tend to alleviate its bitterness. We must put Maggie Howell and Mary Hammy in the foreground, as youth and beauty are in request.

At least they are young things, bright spots in a somber-tinted picture.

_____

The president does not forbid our going, but he is very much averse to it. We are consequently frightened by our own audacity, but we are willful women, and so we go.

《《**July 5, 1861.** What a day I have passed—not one moment's peace. After breakfast went into Mr. Lamar's room—found Mrs. Davis there, and she talked two hours [*two lines effaced*] than ever. He begged her to stay when she left. I sat down, and he began to tell me what she had said of me. Until that day had confined himself to praising my beauty! Heaven save the mark. As if I had any, even when I was young—and Mr. Lamar seemed to think there was something better about me than that. However, dans le royaume des aveugles, un borgne est roi—and an uglier set I never saw. He said what she disliked about me was that wherever I sat was the center of a South Carolina group. He told me of his mother, Mrs. Troutman, having heard that Mr. Chesnut and I praised him and how it gratified him.... At dinner Browne and Mallory talked to me, Mrs. Davis trying to listen from the foot of the table.... Went to tell Mr. Lamar goodbye. Saw his wife—so grateful to me, and I had done nothing. Sat by him a moment, queer man. Held my hand to his heart for a moment and then covered his eyes—made them light the gas for two professors to see me, poor old me.... Mrs. Wigfall at twelve o'clock packed my trunks—what a good woman—》》

July 6, 1861.   Fauquier White Sulphur. Mr. Brewster came with us. Mr. Mallory sent for our luncheon the very largest box of crystallized fruit ever seen out of a confectionery shop. Enough and to spare for us all for weeks.

Keitt and Boyce came armed for the slaughter of birds. Also Hon. Mr. Clingman of North Carolina. And the cars were jammed with soldiers to the

_____

5. Company A of the Second S.C. Cavalry, a unit of Kershaw District troops organized and led by M. B. C.'s uncle, Capt. Alexander Hamilton Boykin.

muzzle. They were very polite and considerate, and we had an agreeable journey in spite of heat, dust, and crowd.

Rev. Robert Barnwell[6] was with us. He means to organize a hospital for sick and wounded.

There was not an inch of standing room, even. So sultry, so close, and everybody in tip-top spirits.

Mr. Preston and Mr. Chesnut met us at Warrenton. Saw across the lawn—but not to speak to them—some of Judge Campbell's family. There they wander disconsolate, just outside of the gates of their paradise. A resigned judge of the Supreme Court of the United States!! Resigned—and for a cause that he is hardly more than half in sympathy with. His is one of the hardest cases.

A woman at table said triumphantly, "So they are starving in Charleston."

Mary Hammy meekly responded, "No, they have the whole rice crop of last year yet."

"They have plenty to eat on hand, then?"

"Yes, thank you."

July 7, 1861. This water is making us young again. How these men enjoy the baths.

They say Beauregard can stop the way for sixty thousand—that many are coming.

Women from Washington came riding into their camp—beautiful women. Where will they not go? They bring letters done up in their back hair—in their tournures, &c&c. "They are our spies," spitefully we suggested. "They are for sale. Maybe they are fooling you. Seward can outbid you."

"Never. These are patriotic creatures—risking everything for their country."

"Men," I added.

Mr. Ould here. We were so delighted to meet again. He was made district attorney after Barton Key's fiasco.[7]

An antique female with every hair curled and frizzed is said to be a Yankee spy. She sits opposite to us.

Brewster solemnly wondered: "With eternity and the judgment to come so near at hand, how could she waste her few remaining minutes curling her hair?" He bade me be very polite—for she would ask me questions.

When we were walking away from table, I asked for his approval of my

6. Robert Woodward Barnwell, nephew of the Confederate senator of the same name, was a professor and chaplain at S.C. College. M. B. C. refers to him as "Robert Barnwell" and "Rev. Robert" to distinguish him from the senator, whom she calls "Mr. Barnwell" and "Hon. Robert."

7. At Washington in 1859, Robert Ould had prosecuted Congressman Daniel Edgar Sickles for the murder of Francis Scott Key's son, Philip Barton Key. Sickles, who had suspected the younger Key of an affair with Mrs. Sickles, won acquittal by pleading temporary insanity and went on to become a Union major general in the Civil War. Ould served as Confederate assistant secretary of war and commissioner for exchange of prisoners.

self-control under such trying circumstances. It seems I was not as calm and forbearing as I thought myself.

Brewster answered with emphasis: "Do you always carry brickbats like that, ready in your pocket, for the first word that offends you? You must not do so when you are with spies from the other side."

"I do not feel at all afraid of their hearing anything through me, for I do not know anything."

Brewster relented: "I did like your discourse, however—last brickbat, 'specially."

Girls here are enthusiastic—all wore palmetto cockades.

But our men could not tarry with us in these cool shades and comfortable quarters—water unlimited, excellent table, &c&c. They have gone back to Manassas, and the faithful Brewster with them, to bring us the latest news. They left us in excellent spirits, which we shared until they were out of sight. We went with them to Warrenton and there heard that General Johnston was in full retreat and that a column was advancing upon Beauregard.

So we came back, all forlorn. If our husbands are taken prisoners, what will they do with them? Are they soldiers or traitors?

Mr. Ould read us a letter from Richmond—how horrified they are there at Joe Johnston retreating. And the enemies of the War Department accuse Walker of not sending General Johnston ammunition in sufficient quantities.

Say that is the real cause of his retreat. Now, will they not make the ears of that slow coach—the secretary of war—buzz!

Read *Rutledge*.[8] Excellent. Quand même—that is pretty hard to fix one's attention. Mrs. Preston's maid Maria has a way of rushing in: "Don't you hear the cannon?"

We fly to the windows, lean out to our waist, pull all the hair away from our ears—but cannot hear it.

Lincoln wants four hundred millions of money—and men in proportion.

Can he get them?

He will find us a heavy handful.

Midnight. I hear Maria's guns.

We are always picking up some good thing of the rough Illinoisian's saying.

Lincoln objects to some man.

"Oh, he is too *interruptious.*"

That is a horrid style of man or woman. The "interruptious"—I know the thing but had no name for it before.

July 9, 1861.   Our battle summer. May it be our first and our last. So-called.

After all, we have not had any of the horrors of war. Could there have been a gayer or pleasanter life than we led in Charleston? And Montgomery, how exciting it all was there. So many clever men and women congregated from every part of the South.

8. Miriam (Coles) Harris, *Rutledge* (1860).

Flies and mosquitoes and a want of neatness and a want of good things to eat did drive us away.

In Richmond the girls say it is perfectly delightful. We find it so, too, but the bickering and quarreling has begun there.

At table today we heard Mrs. Davis's ladies described. They were said to wear red frocks and flats on their heads. We sat mute as mice.

One woman said she found that drawing room of the Spotswood was so warm—so stuffy and stifling.

"Poor soul," murmured the inevitable Brewster. "And no man came to air her in the moonlight. Stroll, you know. Why didn't somebody ask her out on the piazza to see the comet?[9] Heavens above, what philandering there was, done in the name of the comet. When you stumbled on a couple in the piazza they lifted their eyes—and 'comet' was the only word you heard."

Said Mary Hammy severely—no doubt she had seen the comet repeatedly— "You are like Cousin Mary. She laughs at everything. She laughs at General Washington."[1]

"Never."

"Then at his statue prancing on that monument!"

"The horse may prance—he is bowing."

"What, does she say, amuses her?"

"Oh, he looks like the top of the castor, and the great Virginians around him on their pedestals, like the cruets—vinegar cruet, pepper pot, &c&c—"

"That is only when you go too near. At a distance it is sublime."

"Worthy of the first—the last—the only one. The Cincinnatus of the West, &c&c."[2]

"She is worse about Henry Clay."

"What? In his bower in the corner of the park?"

"Yes! That small summer house of his. In his swallowtail white marble coat with the collar halfway up the back of his head—and his marble trousers fit so badly. Oh! What a shame to make a great man so absurd. And oh, that mouth! Surely they had no right to do him so."

Brewster came back with a paper from Washington with terrific threats of what they will do to us.

Threatened men live long.

There was a soft and sweet and low and slow young lady opposite to us. She seemed so gentle and refined and so uncertain of anything. Mr. Brewster called

9. Probably Thatcher's comet, first sighted early in April and visible to the naked eye in early July.

1. The discussion is about statues in Richmond's Capitol Square.

2. An allusion to Lord Byron's "Ode to Napoleon Bonaparte" (1814): "The Cincinnatus of the West, / Whom envy dared not hate, / Bequeathed the name of Washington / To make man blush there was but one!"

her Miss Albina McLush—who always asked her maid, when a new book was mentioned:

"Seraphina, have I perused that volume?"[3]

Van Dorn[4] had come, and the men said Earl Van Dorn will fight. We don't like retreaters.

The Prestons are Joe Johnston's cousins. And they were indignant because he only retreats for want of army and ammunition.

Mr. Brewster and Mrs. Preston, accompanied by Mary Hammy, went to Warrenton for news. They came back without any.

Mary Hammy, having a fiancé in the wars, is inclined at times to be sad and tearful. Mrs. Preston quoted her negro nurse to her:

"Never take any more trouble in your heart than you can kick off at the end of your toes."

July 11, 1861.   We did hear cannon today.

The woman who slandered Mrs. Davis's republican court, of which we are honorable members, by saying they, well, were not young, that they wore gaudy colors and dressed badly—I took an inventory of her charms today. She is darkly, deeply, beautifully freckled. She wears a wig which is kept in place by a tiara of mock jewels. She has the fattest of arms and wears black bead bracelets.

The one who is under a cloud, shadowed as a Yankee spy, today confirmed our worst suspicions. She exhibited unholy joy as she reported seven hundred sick soldiers in the hospital at Culpeper—and that Beauregard has sent a flag of truce to Washington.

"Ladies," said Mr. Brewster to us, "do you know you are only thirty miles from Washington?"

What a night we had. Maria had seen suspicious persons hovering about all day, and Mrs. Preston a ladder which could easily be placed so as to reach our rooms. Mary Hammy saw lights glancing about among the trees—and we all heard guns. So we sat up.

Consequently I am writing in bed today.

> The wail of regret, the rude clashing of strife,
> The soul's harmony often may mar;

---

3. From "Miss Albina McLush," a sketch by Nathaniel Parker Willis in *Fun-Jottings; or, Laughs I Have Taken a Pen To* (1853).

4. Brig. Gen. Earl Van Dorn of Miss. was in Tex., not Richmond.

But I think we must own in the discord of life,
'Tis ourselves that often waken the jar.[5]

Audley
July 2, 1861

To James Chesnut, Esq.

Dear Sir,

Though we are nearly related, I have not seen you since you were a boy. Then I was Esther Maria Coxe, now Lewis.[6] I take the liberty of asking you if you can do anything for my son Edward Parke Custis Lewis? He is now on our border, as a ranger with Colonel Edmondson. But his health is not good—his heart is weak, and I fear the exposure to night duty may be too severe.

He has written to his uncle, C. M. Conrad of Louisiana. If in Richmond I would be much obliged to you to ask him for me if he will try to get him a situation more suited to his health.

My four sons are all out in defense of their country.

I hope your mother is well. My best love to her when you write, and kind regards to your father. Also to your wife and all my cousins. I will be much pleased to see you in Clarke, at Audley, my home, if you have time and the enemy leave me a home. We are rather in an exposed place, but at present I do not feel alarmed.

My son Washington is with General Johnston—quartermaster's duty he is performing.

Dangerfield—a cadet—drilling. John Redman Coxe at Jamestown Island Battery; he will be down in a few days and will call on you. He came home to recruit a little after severe duty.

Hoping to hear from you a few lines, I remain, your affecte. cousin,

Esther Maria Lewis

My address is Mrs. Lorenzo Lewis, Audley—near Berryville—Clarke County, Virginia.

Well done for the Lewises—Mrs. George Washington's great-grandsons— every man of them already in the field—man or boy, I should say. Some of them must be very young.

---

5. From Eliza Cook, "The World," in *Melaia, and Other Poems* (1844).
6. Esther was the daughter of J. C.'s uncle John Redman Coxe. Her late husband, Lorenzo Lewis, was the son of George Washington's nephew Lawrence Lewis and Martha Washington's granddaughter Eleanor "Nelly" Parke (Custis) Lewis.

(Our orders to move on:)

July 10th, 1861

My dear Mary,

Here we are still, and no more prospect of movement now than when I last wrote to you. It is true, however, that the enemy is advancing slowly in our front, and we are preparing to receive him. He comes in great force, being more than three times our number. The camp is greatly revived by the fine rain which fell yesterday. Everything looks fresh and clean, and we will be free from dust for a few days.

When do you go down? Don't stay longer than Saturday. The enemy might make a flank movement and cut you off by taking the RR.

When you go to Richmond, inquire of the tailors, called Shaffer and Co., just below the Exchange, for my coat and pants which I ordered to be made. Keep them for me. Drop us a line daily.

Yours, &c&c&c

J. Chesnut, Jr.

Our clothes are at the washerwoman's, but we won't let a trifle like that keep us. To tell the truth, we are terrified women and children, and that touch about the flank movement will send us flying to Richmond.

Is Richmond safe?

Spy—so-called—gave us a parting shot. Said Beauregard arrested her brother that he might take a fine horse [that the] aforesaid brother was riding. Why? Beauregard could have at a moment's notice any horse in South Carolina—or Louisiana, for that matter—at a word. This man was arrested and sent to Richmond. And "will be acquitted as they always are," said Brewster. "They send them first to Richmond to see and hear everything there, then they acquit them and send them out of the country by way of Norfolk, to see everything there. But after all, what does it matter. They have no use for spies. Our newspapers keep no secrets hid. The thoughts of our hearts are all revealed. Everything with us is open and aboveboard. At Bethel the Yankees fired too high. Every daily is jeering them about it yet. They'll fire low enough next time."

"But no newspaper man will be there to get the benefit of their improved practice, alas!"

Brewster continued to beguile the way with stories from Texas before it was annexed. He has managed to secrete a few grains of religion, and it is Roman Catholic, that modicum. His daughters are in a convent somewhere, being educated. How he came to be a vestryman, heaven knows, of an Episcopal

Texas church. A pious Philadelphian sent them a silver communion service, but they could not take it out of the customhouse for want of funds to pay duty on it.

So a judge and some lawyers played cards all night. The man who won the money dedicated it to good works—and delivered the communion service from its durance vile and gave it to the church.

After all, before it was used, "the church was struck by lightning—and knocked into flinders. That's the way in Texas—no fooling with a thing, good or bad."

Furthermore, he took out a letter addressed to Wigfall—which Brewster carefully preserved because it was from a high public functionary. And "fire" was spelt "fiar"—like "liar," indeed—and "drum," "drumb," like "crumb."

VI

"First Sprightly Running"

July 13, 1861.   Richmond. Now we feel safe and comfortable. We cannot be flanked.

Mr. Preston met us at Warrenton. Mr. C doubtless had too many spies to receive from Washington, galloping in with the exact numbers of the enemy done up in their hair.

Wade Hampton is here. Dr. Nott, also—Nott and Gliddon,[1] known to fame. Everybody is here—en route for the army or staying for the meeting of Congress.

Lamar is out on crutches. His father-in-law, once known only as the humorist Longstreet,[2] author of *Georgia Scenes,* now a staid Methodist—outgrown the follies of his youth. He bore Lamar off today. They say Judge Longstreet has lost the keen sense of fun that illuminated his life in days of yore. Mrs. Lamar and her daughter were here.

The president met us so cordially. But he laughed at our sudden retreat, baggage lost, &c&c. He tried to keep us from going, said it was a dangerous experiment. Daresay he knows more about the situation of things than he chooses to tell us.

Today, in the drawing room, saw a vivandière[3]—in the flesh. She was in the uniform of her regiment but wore Turkish pantaloons. She frisked about in her hat and feathers—did not uncover as a man would have done—played the piano, sang war songs. She had no drum, but she gave us "rat-a-plan." She was followed at every step by a mob of admiring soldiers and boys.

Yesterday, as we left the cars, we had a glimpse of war. It was the saddest sight. The memory of it is hard to shake off.

Sick soldiers—not wounded. There were quite two hundred (they said) lying

1. Josiah Clark Nott of Mobile was a prominent surgeon and ethnologist whose wife, Sarah Cantey (Deas) Nott, was a first cousin of James Chesnut, Jr. With English archaeologist George Robins Gliddon, Nott wrote *Types of Mankind* (1854) and *Indigenous Races of the Earth* (1857)—works which argued that whites and blacks were separately created species.

2. Augustus Baldwin Longstreet, author of *Georgia Scenes* (1835), was also a judge, a Methodist minister, and president, successively, of Georgia's Emory College, Louisiana's Centenary College, the University of Miss., and S.C. College.

3. A female attendant of a regiment who served as a nurse and sutler.

about as best they might on the platform. Robert Barnwell was there, doing all he could. These pale, ghastly faces. So here is one of the horrors of war we had not reckoned on. There were many good men and women with Robert Barnwell, doing all the service possible in the circumstances.

When I was writing just now of the sick soldiers, a card was brought me from Mr. Ould. Then they said Hugh Rose[4] had called.

In the drawing room I saw no Hugh Rose, but General Waul[5] and Mr. Ould joined me. We sat opposite the door. I happened to look up and saw Mr. Chesnut with a smile on his face, watching us from the passageway. I flew across the room, and as I got halfway saw Mrs. Davis touch him on the shoulder. She said he was to go at once into Mr. Davis's room, where General Lee and General Cooper[6] were. After he left us, Mrs. Davis told me General Beauregard had sent Mr. C here on some army business.

July 14, 1861.   Mr. C remained closeted with them—the president and General Lee &c&c—all the afternoon. The news does not seem pleasant. At least, he is not inclined to tell me any of it. Satisfied himself with telling me how sensible and soldierly this handsome General Lee is. General Lee's military sagacity was his theme. Of course, the president dominated the party—as well by his weight of brain as by his position.

I did not care a fig for a description of the war council. I wanted to know what is in the wind now.

July 16, 1861.   Dined today at the president's table. Joe Davis, the nephew, asked me if I liked white port wine. I said I did not know—all that I had ever known had been dark red. So he poured me out a glass. I drank it. It nearly burnt up my mouth and throat. It was horrid, but I did not let him see how it annoyed me. I pretended to be glad that anyone found me still young enough to play off a practical joke upon me. It was thirty years since I had thought of such a thing.

Met Colonel Baldwin[7] in the drawing room. Pointed significantly to his Confederate colonel's buttons and gray coat. At the White Sulphur last summer, he was "Union man" to the last point. "How much have you changed beside your coat?" "I was always true to our country. She leaves me no choice now."

---

4. The son of James Rose, a planter of Christ Church Parish, S.C., and Julia (Rutledge) Rose.
5. Thomas Neville Waul, member of the Provisional Confederate Congress from Tex. It is not clear why M. B. C. calls Waul "General"; his commission as a brigadier general of the C.S.A. did not come until 1863.
6. A native of N.J. married to a Virginian, Samuel Cooper resigned as U.S. adjutant general in March and became adjutant and inspector general of the Confederacy. He was a friend and intimate adviser of Jefferson Davis.
7. John Brown Baldwin of Va. voted against secession in his state's convention but became inspector general of state volunteers and later a representative in the Confederate Congress.

Mrs. McLean pitched into Juliet—said she was "free of her love" because of her Southern blood. She was answered, "*Free love* is a Northern persuasion. There is no free love sect out of New England." We are always ready for combat here on any subject—if only North and South and the points of the compass touched upon.

As far as I can make out, Beauregard sent Mr. Chesnut to the president to gain permission for the forces of Joe Johnston and Beauregard to join and, united, to push the enemy if possible over the Potomac.

Now every day we grow weaker and they stronger, so we had better give a telling blow at once.

Already they begin to cry out for more ammunition, and already the blockade is beginning to shut it all out.

A young Emory[8] here. His mother writes to him to go back. Her Franklin blood certainly calls him with no uncertain sound to the Northern side, while his Mary[land] fatherland is wavering and undecided. Split in half by factions. Mrs. Wigfall says he is half-inclined to go. She wondered that he did not. With a father in the enemy's army he will always be "suspect" here—let the president and Mrs. Davis do for him what they will.

I did not know there was such a "bitter cry" left in me. But I wept my heart away today when my husband went off. Things do look so black.

When he comes up here he rarely brings his body servant, a negro man. Laurence has charge of all Mr. Chesnut's things—watch, clothes, two or three hundred gold pieces lie in the tray of his trunk. All these papers &c he tells Laurence to bring to me if anything happens to him. But I said, "Maybe he will pack off to Yankees—and freedom—with all that."

"Fiddlesticks! He is not going to leave me for anybody else. After all, what can he ever be better than he is now—a gentleman's *gentleman?*"

"He is within sound of the enemies' guns, and when he gets to the other army he *is free.*"

Maria said of Mr. Preston's man: "What he want with anything more—ef he was free? Don't he live jest as well as Mars' John do now?"

Mary Stevens calls her son, James Mercer, for some bright particular Garnett of old. Of the ladies here—Mrs. McLean, Mrs. Joe Johnston, Mrs. Bartow,

8. Thomas Emory, a son of Matilda and William Hemsley Emory, was visiting the Davises when the war began. The Confederate president urged him to return to his parents in the North, but he joined the Confederate navy instead.

myself, Mrs. Joe Davis the elder, and Mrs. Joe the younger[9]—six without children. Mrs. Wigfall has three. Mrs. Preston has five—two sons in the army and three daughters grown. These people call us Mrs. Davis's ladies because we dine at her table and our husbands are off with the army.

Mr. Davis is in wretched health. That is a great misfortune to us. He has trouble enough. Care, anxiety, responsibility—and then, his unlucky nervous irritation doubles the trouble.

Today I was ill. Mrs. Auzé[1] kindly insisted on my taking something to ease my pain. She seized upon a small laudanum bottle: "The very thing!" She dropped ten drops, and I drank it with a grave face. I had filled that vial with Stoughton bitters just before leaving home.

I have no intention of drugging myself now. My head is addled enough as it stands, and my heart beats to jump out of my body at every sound.

Mrs. Davis came in and sat for some time. She has so preoccupied an air in spite of her pleasant stories, I am sure something is going on wrong.

《Mrs. Wigfall came and lodged her complaints against Mrs. Davis. I said nothing, because when I was angry I could not get her sympathy. . . . Mrs. Davis sat with me ever so long—abused Mrs. Wigfall[2]》

Mrs. McLean, Mrs. Joe Johnston, Mrs. Wigfall, all came. I am sure so many clever women could divert a soul in extremis.

The Hampton Legion all in a snarl about I forget what—standing on their dignity, I suppose. I have come to detest a man who says, "My own personal dignity—self-respect requires—"

I long to cry, "No need to respect yourself until you can make other people do it."

A quiet moment—a knock—only a basket of delicious peaches. My misery took the form of no appetite at breakfast. It failed to quench my taste for peaches, so I enjoyed them thoroughly.

July 19, 1861. Beauregard telegraphed yesterday, they say, to Gen. Joe Johnston, "Come down and help us or we will be crushed by numbers." The president telegraphed General Johnston to move down to Beauregard's aid.

---

9. Eliza (Van Benthuysen) Davis was the wife of Jefferson Davis's elder brother, Joseph Emory Davis, a wealthy Miss. planter who had been a substitute father for the Confederate president. "Mrs. Joe the younger" was Frances (Peyton) Davis, the wife of the president's nephew Joseph Robert Davis.

1. Margaret (Deas) Auzé, the wife of Charles Auzé of Camden, was J. C.'s first cousin.

2. Under a single entry in the 1860s Journal dated July 17 and 18, 1861.

At Bulls Run Bonham's brigade—Ewell's—Longstreet's—encounter the foe and repulsed him.[3] Six hundred prisoners sent here. Yesterday afternoon, thanks to the fact that it was bitters in that vial and not laudanum—and a light dinner of peaches—I arose, as the Scripture says, and washed my face and anointed my head and went downstairs.[4] At the foot of them stood General Cooper, radiant, one finger nervously arranging his shirt collar, or adjusting his neck to it, after his fashion. He called out:

"Your South Carolina man bonhomme has done a capital thing at Bulls Run—driven back the enemy if not defeated him, killed, and prisoners—&c&c&c."

Clingman came to tell the particulars, and Colonel Sumter (one of the trio [of] Garnett, McClellan, &c sent to Europe to inspect and report on military matters).[5]

Poor Garnett is killed. Cowardice or treachery on the part of natives up there or some of Governor Letcher's appointments to military posts—I hear all these things said. I do not understand, but it was a fatal business.[6]

Mrs. McLean says she finds we do not believe a word of any news unless it comes in this guise: "A great battle fought. Not one Confederate killed. Enemy's loss in killed, wounded, and prisoners taken by us—immense."

Today we were to go with Mr. Mallory to see the new ship *Patrick Henry*. But wild horses could not drag us an inch from here now. To this spot all telegrams tend, the president being here.

I was in hopes there would be no battle until Mr. Chesnut was forced to give up his amateur aideship to come and attend to his regular duties in the Congress.

Keitt has come in. He says Bonham's great battle was a skirmish of outposts.

Joe Davis, Jr., said, "Would heaven only send us a Napoleon!"

"Not one bit of use if heaven did. Walker would not give him a commission."

Congress has been opened. Dr. Gibbes said he sat in Hon. James Chesnut's chair.

3. The battle of Blackburn's Ford, fought a few miles northeast of Manassas Junction on the eighteenth, was a minor victory that encouraged the Confederates on the eve of Bull Run. Milledge Luke Bonham, by then a brigadier general of the C.S.A., commanded the First Brigade of Beauregard's army. Brig. Gen. Richard Stoddert Ewell of the District of Columbia headed the Second Brigade, and Brig. Gen. James "Pete" Longstreet of S.C., nephew of Augustus Baldwin Longstreet, led the Fourth.
4. 2 Samuel 12:20, describing the end of David's mourning for his dead child.
5. Paul Thomas Delage Sumter, former U.S. congressman and brother of Frank Sumter; Union Maj. Gen. George B. McClellan; and Confederate Brig. Gen. Robert Selden Garnett of Va. had separately visited Europe as U.S. Army officers before the war.
6. The first general of either side to die in the war, Garnett was killed on July 13 in western Va. by Union troops rather than by the treachery of Va. Gov. John Letcher's appointees.

We get the very latest news from Mrs. Davis. She was in Mrs. Preston's room last night until 10 o'clock.

Mrs. Davis and Mrs. Joe Johnston—"her dear Lydia"—were in fine spirits. The effect upon nous autres was evident—we rallied visibly.

South Carolina troops pass every day. They go by with a gay step. Tom Taylor[7] and John Rhett[8] bowed to us from their horses as we leaned out of the windows—such shaking of handkerchiefs. We are forever at the windows.

Mrs. McLean harping on the perfect right every man had to be true to his own side.

"Who denies it?" says Brewster. "And I think the president makes a blunder when he puts place and power in the hands of Northern men. Men will feel that they are true to their own, not to us."

"They are true to us—as true as Dalgettys are—but they all, always '*suspect.*'"[9]

Last night the Tuckers[1] were here—John Randolph's half-nephews. Randolph Tucker is a humorist of the first class. Beverley Tucker told us how he passed himself off for Trevellyan Bentinck, Bart, England—and so old Giddings was taken in by him.

It was not such a mere skirmish. We took three rifled cannon and six hundred stands of arms.

Mr. Davis has gone to Manassas. He did not let Wigfall know he was going. That ends the decision of Wigfall's ADCship.

No mistake today. I was too ill to move out of my bed. So they all sat in my room.

Mrs. McLean came in with a splendid baby, her sister's. Mrs. Long,[2] her

7. A Richland District planter serving in Hampton's Legion, Thomas Taylor was the husband of a cousin of J. C.

8. A soldier in Hampton's Legion, John Taylor Rhett was a nephew of Robert Barnwell Rhett, Sr., and the grandson of J. C.'s aunt Sarah Cantey (Chesnut) Taylor.

9. Dugald Dalgetty, in Scott's *The Legend of Montrose* (1819), is a mercenary cynically indifferent to political principle yet loyal to those he serves.

1. John Randolph Tucker and Nathaniel Beverley Tucker of Va. were the sons of Henry St. George Tucker, the half brother of John Randolph of Roanoke. John Tucker was attorney general of Va.; Nathaniel had resigned as American consul at Liverpool to return home and join the Confederate army.

2. Mary Heron (Sumner) Long, daughter of U.S. Gen. Edwin Vose Sumner, married Armistead Lindsay Long in 1860. Although Long was aide-de-camp to his father-in-law, he resigned his commission on June 10, 1861, and was appointed a major of artillery in the C.S.A.

sister, married a Virginian of that name. Miles says she is a fascinating woman, a new beauty. An expression I did not think her capable of was in Mrs. McLean's face—her tenderness and love and pride in that baby. Women need maternity to bring out their best and true loveliness.

July 22, 1861.   Mrs. Davis came in so softly that I did not know she was here until she leaned over me ⟨⟨kissed me⟩⟩ and said—

"A great battle has been fought—Jeff Davis led the center, Joe Johnston the right wing, Beauregard the left wing of the army. Your husband is all right. Wade Hampton is wounded. Colonel Johnson[3] of the Legion killed—so are Colonel Bee[4] and Colonel Bartow. Kirby Smith is wounded or killed."[5]

I had no heart to speak. She went on in that desperate calm way to which people betake themselves when under greatest excitement. "Bartow was rallying his men, leading them into the hottest of the fight—died gallantly, at the head of his regiment.

"The president telegraphs me only that 'it is a great victory.' General Cooper has all the other telegrams." Still I said nothing. I was stunned. Then I was so grateful. Those nearest and dearest to me were safe still.

Then she began in the same concentrated voice to read from a paper she held in her hand.

"Dead and dying cover the field. Sherman's battery taken,[6] Lynchburg regiment cut to pieces. Three hundred of the Legion wounded."

They got me up. Times were too wild with excitement to stay in bed. We went into Mrs. Preston's room.

She made me lie down on her bed. Men, women, and children streamed in. Every living soul had a story to tell. "Complete victory" you heard everywhere.

We had been such anxious wretches! The revulsion of feeling was almost too much to bear.

Today I met my friend Mr. Hunter. I was on my way to Mrs. Bartow's room—begged him to call at some other time. I was too tearful just then for a morning visit from even the most sympathetic person.

A woman from Mrs. Bartow's country was in a fury because they stopped her as she rushed to be the first to tell Mrs. Bartow that her husband was killed. It had been decided that Mrs. Davis was to tell her. Poor thing! She was lying on her bed. Mrs. Davis knocked. "Come in." When she saw it was Mrs. Davis, she

---

3. Lt. Col. Benjamin Jenkins Johnson, second in command of the Hampton Legion, was a prominent Christ Church Parish, S.C., planter and a state legislator.

4. Brig. Gen. Barnard Elliott Bee of Tex., commander of the Third Brigade of Joseph Johnston's Army of the Shenandoah.

5. Brig. Gen. Edmund Kirby Smith of Fla. was wounded, not killed.

6. Probably U.S. Capt. James Brewerton Ricketts's company of artillery, which was not, however, a part of the brigade commanded by Col. William Tecumseh Sherman.

sat up, ready to spring to her feet—but then there was something in Mrs. Davis's pale face that took the life out of her. She stared at Mrs. Davis—and then sunk back. She covered her face.

"Is it bad news for me?" Mrs. Davis did not speak. "Is he killed?"

Today she said [that] as soon as she saw Mrs. Davis's face—and then she could not say one word—she knew it all in an instant—she knew it before she wrapped the shawl round her head.

Maria, Mrs. Preston's maid, is furiously patriotic. She came into my room.

"These colored people say it is printed in the papers here that the Virginia people done it all. Now Mars Wade has so many of his men killed—and he wounded—it stands to reason that South Callina was no ways backward. If there was ever anything plain, that's plain."

Mrs. *Blank* ⟨⟨Mrs. Wigfall⟩⟩ was making her moan.

"*Blank* ⟨⟨Louis Wigfall⟩⟩ ordered off with his regiment—and I can't even see him."

"Indeed you can," said Mary Hammy briskly and then suddenly subsided, all in confusion. Someone had made her a sign to hold her tongue.

The Spotswood is built round a hollow square, and our rooms overlooked the billiard room &c&c on the opposite side of the inner yard. These public rooms were all on the lower story, and we looked into them—in this hot weather all windows wide open—well—freely.

This much lamented husband had been there—in evidence—for several days, in a condition ⟨⟨*drunk*⟩⟩! But he respected Madame too much to make his appearance above. She still continued to bewail her ignorance of where he was or what were his orders, &c&c&c.

When she left us Mary Hammy inquired naively, "Why did you not let me relieve her mind?"

"Because she would a thousand times rather think him under the enemy's guns than under her here, in the basement, *and as he is.*"

"Ah," said Mr. Mallory. "Women like men with winning ways—but not at the card table to exercise them."

"Oh! Oh!" said Mary Hammy. Everybody seemed [to be] giving her new ideas on the mysteries of matrimonial life. "I thought first of all she wanted to know he was safe."

Judge Nisbet[7] and the Hills were grieving over Georgia's loss in Bartow. They said everything that was good of him.

---

7. Eugenius Aristides Nisbet, a former U.S. congressman and judge of the Georgia Supreme Court, was a member of the Provisional Confederate Congress.

Today for the first time came a military funeral. As that march came wailing up, they say, Mrs. Bartow fainted. The empty saddle—and the led war horse—we saw and heard it all. And now it seems we are never out of the sound of the Dead March in *Saul*.[8] It comes and it comes until I feel inclined to close my ears and scream.

Today "the notorious A. D. Banks," whom I have ever found clever and amusing, began to ridicule Mr. Hunter, so I got up and left him.

Dr. Nott said Congressmen Ely and John Cochrane came down to see the fun—come out for wool and got shorn. They were taken prisoners.[9]

Dr. Nott said he slept under the same tree with Joe Johnston. Cried out a shrill female voice, "Mrs. Johnston, don't you wish it had been you—out there?"

Dr. Nott said Mr. Davis got there too late. The foe began to fly just as he arrived.

Mrs. S⸺ with a magnificent solitaire in each ear and tears as large and as clear in her eyes, mad with anxiety—no word can she hear of her husband.

"He's alive—if he were dead, she would be beat up by the Dead March under her windows soon enough. She knows it for all those wet eyes of hers. Her claret cup is—perfection. She is having some now."

It is true. Yesterday Mrs. Singleton[1] and ourselves sat on a bedside and mingled our tears for those noble spirits—John Darby, Toady Barker,[2] James Lowndes.[3] Today, we find we wasted our grief. They are not so much as wounded. I daresay all the rest is true about them—in the face of the enemy with flags in their hands, leading their men.

"But Dr. Darby is a surgeon." "He is as likely to forget that as I am. He is grandson of Colonel Thomson of the Revolution—called, by way of pet name by his soldiers, 'Old Danger.'"[4]

8. The music from act 3, scene 5 of George Frederick Handel's oratorio *Saul* (1739), often used for military funerals.

9. N.Y. Republican Alfred Ely was captured, but not his former Democratic colleague from N.Y., Col. John Cochrane. Ely recounted his experience in Charles Lanman, ed., *Journal of Alfred Ely, a Prisoner of War in Richmond* (1862).

1. Mary Lewis (Carter) Singleton of Richland District, S.C., was the widow of planter John Coles Singleton and the mother-in-law of Rev. Robert Woodward Barnwell.

2. Theodore Gaillard Barker, a Charleston lawyer, was lieutenant and adjutant of Hampton's Legion.

3. Another Charleston lawyer in Hampton's Legion.

4. William Thomson of Orangeburg, S.C., a planter, politician, and soldier best known for his role in the defeat of the British expedition to Charleston in June 1776. John Thomson Darby was actually his great-great-grandson.

Thank heaven, they are all quite alive. And we will not cry next time until officially notified.

⟨⟨Mrs. Davis has been so devoted to me since my trouble. . . . Mrs. Johnston told me President Davis said he liked best to have me sit opposite him. He liked my style of chat. . . .⟩⟩

July 24, 1861.   Here Mr. Chesnut opened my door—and walked in. Of the fullness of the heart the mouth speaketh. I had to ask no questions. He gave me an account of the battle as he saw it (walking up and down my room, occasionally seating himself on a window sill, but too restless to remain still many moments). Told what regiments he was sent to bring up. He took orders to Colonel Jackson—whose regiment stood so stock-still under fire they were called a stone wall.[5] Also, they call Beauregard "Engine" and Johnston "Marlboro" (s'en va—en guerre). Mr. C rode with Lay's cavalry after the retreating enemy, in the pursuit, they following them until midnight. There then came such a rain—rain such as is only known in semitropical lands.

In the drawing room Colonel Chesnut was the "belle of the ball"—they crowded him so for news. He was the first arrival that they could get at, from the field of battle—handle, so to speak. But the women had to give way to the dignitaries of the land, who were as filled with curiosity as themselves—Mr. Barnwell, Mr. Hunter, the Cobbs, Captain Ingraham, &c&c.

Wilmot DeSaussure[6] says Wilson of Massachusetts,[7] senator U.S.A., came to Manassas en route to Richmond, with his dancing shoes ready for the festive scene which was to celebrate a triumph.

The *Tribune*[8] said: "In a few days" they would have Richmond, Memphis, New Orleans. "They must be taken and at once." For "a few days" maybe now they will modestly substitute "in a few years."

They brought me a Yankee soldier's portfolio from the battlefield. The letters were franked by Senator Harlan.[9] One might shed a few tears over some of his letters. Women—wives and mothers—are the same everywhere.

What a comfort the spelling was. We were willing to admit their universal free school education put their rank and file ahead of us *literarily*. Now, these letters do not attest that fact. The spelling is comically bad.

Not so bad as Wigfall's man, however, who spelt "fi-ar" à la mode de "li-ar."

---

5. For this stand, Thomas Jonathan Jackson, a former West Pointer and instructor at Va. Military Institute, received a promotion to brigadier general as well as an enduring nickname.

6. Wilmot Gibbes DeSaussure, nephew of John McPherson DeSaussure, was a Charleston lawyer and state legislator who commanded artillery at Fort Sumter.

7. Antislavery leader Henry Wilson.

8. The New York *Tribune*.

9. James Harlan, Republican from Iowa.

Mrs. Davis's drawing room last night was brilliant, and she was in great force. Outside a mob collected and called for the president. He did speak. He is an old war-horse—and scents the battlefields from afar. His enthusiasm was contagious. ⟨⟨The president took all the credit to himself for the victory—said the wounded roused and shouted for Jeff Davis and the men rallied at the sight of him and rushed on and routed the enemy. The truth is, Jeff Davis was not two miles from the battlefield, but he is greedy for military fame.⟩⟩ They called for Colonel Chesnut, and he gave them a capital speech, too. As the public speakers say sometimes, "It was the proudest moment of my life." My life—the woman who writes here, now. I did not hear a great deal of it, for always when anything happens of any moment, my heart beats up in my ears. But the distinguished Carolinians that crowded round me told me how good a speech he made. I was dazed. ⟨⟨He gave the glory of the victory to Beauregard and said if the president had not said so much for himself, he would have praised him.⟩⟩

Mrs. McLean was very angry with Joe Davis: he forgot her presence and wished all Yankees were dead.

Somebody said he did remember ladies' presence, for the habit of our men was to call them "Damn Yankees." Mrs. Davis was at her wits' end what to do with Joe Davis, for she is devoted to Mrs. McLean. And when she consults anyone, they only grin, the sentiment being one which meets with almost universal sympathy just now.

There goes the Dead March for some poor soul.

Mrs. Wigfall said when her children were small, she broke them of ever using bad words by washing their mouths with soap and water to cleanse them. Joe Davis is not small, alas! And then somebody told a story—a little girl came running to tell on her brother: "Oh, mama, Charlie is using bad language—curse words."

"What is it?"

"He says 'Damn Yankees' are here prisoners."

"Well, mama, is not that their name? I never hear them called anything else."

Today the president told us at dinner that Mr. Chesnut's eulogy of Bartow in the Congress was highly praised. Men liked it. Two eminently satisfactory speeches in twenty-four hours is doing pretty well. And now I would be happy, but this cabinet of ours are in such bitter quarrels among themselves. Everybody abusing everybody.

Last night, while those splendid descriptions of the battles were being given to the crowd below, from our windows I said, "Then why do we not go on to Washington?"

"You mean, why did they not. The time has passed—the opportunity is lost." Mr. Barnwell said to me: "Silence. We want to listen to the speaker." And Mr. Hunter smiled compassionately: "Don't ask awkward questions."

Mr. C said: "They were lapping round Hampton, and I saw they would flank us. Then that fine fellow Elzey[1] came in view—when I saw it was our flag! At first we thought it was the enemy! And we had our hands full before. They were pushing us hard. Almost at the moment that joyful sight of our flag had relieved my mind. I saw confusion in the enemy's wagon train. Then their panic began."

Kirby Smith came down on the turnpike at the very nick of time. Still, the heroes who fought all day and held the Yankees in check deserve credit beyond words. *Or* it would all have been over before the Joe Johnston contingent came. It is another case of the *eleventh-hour* scrape. The eleventh-hour men claim all the credit, and they who bore the heat and brunt and burden of the day do not like that.

Mrs. Wigfall busy as a bee, making a flag for her Texians. Louis is colonel of the regiment.

Everybody said at first: "Pshaw! There will be no war." Those who foresaw evil were called "Ravens"—ill foreboders. Now the same sanguine people all cry "the war is over"—the very same who were packing to leave Richmond a few days ago. Many were ready to move on at a moment's warning, when the good news came.

There are such owls everywhere. But to revert to the other kind—the sage and circumspect, those who say very little, but that little shows they think the war barely begun. Mr. Rives and Mr. Seddon[2] have just called. Arnoldus VanderHorst[3] came to see me at the same time. He said there was no great show of victory on our side until two o'clock, but when we began to win, we did it in double-quick time. I mean, of course, the battle last Saturday.

---

1. Col. Arnold Elzey (Jones) of Md. had taken over the Fourth Brigade from his wounded commander, Edmund Kirby Smith. Elzey's role in routing the Union army won him promotion to brigadier general.

2. William Cabell Rives of Va., a former U.S. senator and minister to France, had been elected in April to the Confederate Congress by a margin of one vote over James Alexander Seddon, a former U.S. congressman, who then won a congressional appointment in June. Seddon became secretary of war the following year.

3. Arnoldus VanderHorst, a Christ Church Parish planter who became a C.S.A. major, was the grandson and namesake of an eighteenth-century S.C. governor.

I was talking with Hon. Mr. Clingman and the friendly Brewster—when a U.S. surgeon on parole came to see Mrs. McLean. A terrible Confederate female of ardent patriotism and a very large damp mouth said, "How I would like to scalp that creature."

"A descendant of Pocahontas, evidently," said Brewster, with a faint snigger. "She must mean Mrs. McLean, who has a beautiful head of hair. The man is shorn to the quick—no hair to get a purchase, to tear his scalp off."

Mr. Clingman could not look more disgusted than he always does.

———

Arnold Harris told Mr. Wigfall the news from Washington last Saturday.[4] For hours the telegrams reported at rapid intervals: "great victory," "defeating them at all points."

About three o'clock the telegrams began to come in on horseback—at least, after two or three o'clock there was a sudden cessation of all news. About nine, bulletins came on foot or on horseback, wounded, weary, draggled, footsore, panic-stricken, spreading in their path on every hand terror and dismay.

That was our opportunity. Wigfall can see nothing to stop us. And when they explain why we did not go, I understand it all less than ever.

———

Yes, here we will dillydally and Congress orate and generals parade, until they get up an army three times as large as McDowell's[5] that we have just defeated.

———

Trescot says this victory will be our ruin. It lulls us into a fool's paradise of conceit at our superior valor.

And the shameful farce of their flight will wake every inch of their manhood. It was the very fillip they needed.

There are a quieter sort here who know their Yankees well. They say if the thing begins to pay—government contracts and all that—we will never hear the end of it. At least, until they get their pay out of us. They will not lose money by us. Of that we may be sure. Trust Yankee shrewdness and vim for that.

———

There seems to be a battle raging at Bethel,[6] but no mortal here can be got to think of anything but Manassas.

———

4. Sent from Washington to recover the body of a N.Y. colonel killed at Bull Run, former U.S. Army officer Arnold Harris had been taken prisoner by Confederate troops and brought to Richmond.

5. Brig. Gen. Irvin McDowell, the Union commander at Bull Run.

6. A false rumor, probably arising from Brigadier General Magruder's attempts to keep slaves from fleeing toward Federal garrisons at Fort Monroe, Hampton Roads, and Newport News.

Mrs. McLean says she does not see that it was such a great victory, and if it be so great, how can one defeat hurt a nation like the North. ⟨⟨What a villain that woman is.⟩⟩

John Waties[7] fought the whole battle over for me. Now I understand it. Before this, nobody could take time to tell the thing consecutively, rationally, and in order.

Again the crowd came, to get Mr. Davis to speak to them. They wanted to hear all about it again.

Afterward they called for Chesnut of South Carolina—who could not be found. He had retired into Mrs. Preston's room.

Mr. Venable said he did not see a braver thing done than the cool performance of a Columbia negro. He brought his master a bucket of ham and rice which he had cooked for him, and he cried, "You must be so tired and hungry, Marster—make haste and eat." This was in the thickest of the fight, under the heaviest of the enemies' guns.

The Federal congressmen were making a picnic of it. Their luggage was all ticketed to Richmond.

"It is a far cry to Lochow"—as the clansmen say.[8]

Cameron has issued a proclamation.[9] They are making ready to come after us on a magnificent scale. They acknowledge us at last—foemen worthy of their steel.

The Lord help us, since England and France won't—or don't. If we could only get a friend outside and open a port.

Mr. Mason[1] came and would march me in state on his arm into Mrs. Davis's drawing room (Maxcy Gregg and Mr. Miles were with me when Mr. Mason and Mr. Seddon called. Mr. Miles and Co. meekly followed). I looked back and wished I was with the unobserved rear guard.

Mr. Mason is a high and mighty Virginian. He brooks no opposition to his will.

They say it is Douglas Ramsey who was killed, and not our friend Wadsworth.[2]

One of these men told me he had seen a Yankee prisoner who asked him what sort of a diggins Richmond was for trade. He was tired of the old concern and would like to take the oath and settle here.

---

7. A Charleston lawyer and clerk of the court of appeals serving in Hampton's Legion.

8. In chapter 12 of Scott's *The Legend of Montrose:* "This menace was received with a scornful laugh, while one of the Campbells replied, 'It is a far cry to Lochow'; a proverbial expression of the tribe, meaning that their ancient hereditary domains lay beyond the reach of an invading army."

9. A false rumor, perhaps arising from Lincoln's approval on July 22 of a bill authorizing the acceptance of 500,000 volunteers.

1. James Murray Mason of Va., brother-in-law of Confederate Adj. Gen. Samuel Cooper, was a U.S. senator from 1847 until March 1861 and a member of the Provisional Confederate Congress.

2. Neither U.S. Maj. George Douglas Ramsey of Va. nor Union volunteer aide James Samuel Wadsworth of the great N.Y. land-owning family had been killed at Bull Run.

They brought us handcuffs found in the debacle of the Yankee army.

For whom were they? Jeff Davis, no doubt. And the ringleaders.

Tell that to the Marines. We have outgrown the handcuff business on this side of the water.

Russell, the Englishman, was in Alexandria. Why did we not follow them there? That's the question.

After the little unpleasantness &c&c between Mrs. Davis and Mrs. Wigfall, there was a complete reconciliation, and Mrs. Wigfall in all amity presented Mrs. Davis with the most hideous Chinese monster I ever saw. A Mandarin, I meant to say.

《All day I was in bed. The night before, sat up too late hearing Mrs. Davis abuse and disabuse Mrs. McLean. Mrs. Joe Johnston and Mrs. McLean have gone to Orange Court House. I am truly glad they did not get to Manassas. Mrs. Davis, Wigfall, &c&c sat with me and told me unutterable stories of the war, but I forget after so much opium. Mr. Chesnut would not go to bed but sat up and gave me such a scolding. . . . Jeff Davis offers Mr. Chesnut anything he wants—and is going to give Mr. Preston a commission. . . .》[3]

Dr. Gibbes says he was at a country house near Manassas when a Federal soldier who had lost his way came in, exhausted. He asked for brandy, which the lady of the house gave him. Upon second thought he declined it. She brought it to him so promptly, he said he thought it might be poisoned. His mind was.

She was enraged.

"Sir, I am a Virginia woman. Do you think I could be as base as that? Here— Bill, Tom, disarm this man. He is our prisoner." The negroes came running, and the man surrendered without more ado. Another Federal was drinking at the well. A negro girl said, "You go in and see Missis." The man went in, and she followed crying triumphantly, "Look here—Missis, I got a prisoner too!"

They were not ripe for John Brown, you see.

This lady sent in her two prisoners, and Beauregard complimented her on her pluck and patriotism and presence of mind.

These negroes were rewarded by their owners. Now if slavery is as disagreeable as we think it, why don't they all march over the border, where they would

3. This entry from the 1860s Journal is dated July 26 but falls between entries dated July 24 and 28, 1861, in the 1880s Version.

be received with open arms? It amazes me. I am always studying these creatures. They are to me inscrutable in their ways and past finding out.

Dr. Gibbes says the faces of the dead grow as black as charcoal on the battlefield, and they shine in the sun.

Now this horrible vision of the dead on the battlefield haunts me.

Old Ruffin has promised me a John Brown pike[4]—and Dr. Gibbes a handcuff—for my very own, trophies for future generations—more especially, as they see I do not believe any stories of pikes or handcuffs or a cage for Jeff Davis.

Hon. Mr. Hammond[5] is here. Our world collects here—gravitates to Richmond, as it did to Charleston and Montgomery.

These young men say the war is doing them good. Hugh Rose, who has a room in this hotel, offered to share it with his father. It was that or the street for the old gentleman—so great is the crowd. They seem to think it an act of superhuman virtue "to have your father in your room." At least they know it was on Hugh Rose's part.

Camden DeLeon is sure to lose his place as surgeon general. Dr. Gibbes wants it. Dr. Nott is looked upon by many as a fit person for it. ⟨⟨DeLeon is always drunk.⟩⟩[6]

Somebody sent me a caricature of Jeff Davis trying to throw sand in John Bull's eyes and stuff wool in his ears.

There are so many wonderful tales here about everybody. That strange-looking man Clingman—I thought the first story funny enough. Dancing is a

4. Sixty-seven-year-old Edmund Ruffin, the Va. agricultural reformer, had served as a "temporary" C.S.A. private at Bull Run. To stir up antiabolitionist sentiment after John Brown's raid, Ruffin had given each Southern governor one of the pikes with which Brown had intended to arm Va. slaves.

5. James Henry Hammond of Edgefield District, a former U.S. congressman, S.C. governor, and U.S. senator, was in Richmond to argue for the establishment of cotton as a basis of Confederate credit.

6. Under July 26, 1861, in the 1860s Journal.

serious business with him. Some young lady spoke to him while he was dancing with her. "Pray withhold all remarks. It puts me out. I cannot do two things at once. If you will talk, I shall have to stop dancing."

Then, when he was presented to Miss Lane, he bowed low and immediately held his nose. Holding it firmly, he said: "Pardon me. I will retire now. I may come back and make a few remarks." He had bowed so low his nose began to bleed, and he had to hold it with all his might.

Fancy Miss Lane's face. The very queen of the proprieties. I cannot imagine her laughing in the wrong place or at the wrong time.

And yet she must have laughed then. Stories of Clingman abound. He cut his throat because he was not as clever as Mr. Calhoun. Made a failure then, too, for it was sewed up—and he lives still.

One of Mr. Chesnut's anecdotes of Manassas:

He had in his pocket a small paper of morphine. He put it there to alleviate pain. Ever since Tom Withers's frightful fractured leg,[7] when the doctors would not give him anodyne enough to put him to sleep and quiet his agony for a time, at least, Mr. C always carried morphine powders in his pocket. These he gave Tom in the night, in spite of the faculty, and the soothing of that poor boy's anguish he considered one of the good deeds of his life.

Now a man was howling with pain on the outskirts of the battlefield—by the way, the only one that made any outcry, at least, that he heard that day, be their wounds as grievous as they might. This man proved to be only a case of pain in the stomach. Him he relieved with the opiate and passed on rapidly where he was sent. Later in the day he saw a man lying under a tree who begged for water. He wore the Federal uniform.

As Mr. C carried him the water, he asked him where he was from. The man refused to answer.

"Poor fellow—you have no cause to care about all that now—you can't hurt me. And God knows I would not harm you. What else do you want?"

"Straighten my legs—they are doubled up under me." The legs were smashed. He gave him some morphine to let him at least know a few moments of peace. He says: "This is my first battle. I hope my heart will not grow harder."

Clingman said he credited the statement that they wanted water, for he remembered the avidity with which he drank water himself from dirty pools.

Captain Ingraham told Captain Smith Lee: "Don't be so conceited about your looks. Mrs. Chesnut thinks your brother Robert a handsomer man than you."

I did not contradict the statement, as Clingman would say, and yet it was false.

---

7. Judge Withers's son, Thomas Jefferson Withers, Jr., died of injuries received in a race with a friend in 1858.

This is how I saw Robert E. Lee for the first time. I had heard of him, strange to say, in this wise. Though his family, who then lived at Arlington, called to see me in Washington (I thought because of Mrs. Chesnut's intimacy with Nelly Custis[8] in the old Philadelphia days—and Mrs. Lee was Nelly Custis's niece), I had not known the head of the Lee family. He was somewhere with the army then.

Last summer at the White Sulphur, Roony Lee[9] and his wife, that sweet little Charlotte Wickham, was there, and I spoke of Roony with great praise.

Mrs. Izard said: "Don't waste your admiration on him. Wait till you see his father. He is the nearest to a perfect man I ever saw." "How?" "Every way—handsome, clever, agreeable, highbred, &c&c."

Mrs. Stanard[1] came for Mrs. Preston and me, to drive to the camp. She was in an open carriage. A man riding a beautiful horse joined us. He wore a hat with somehow a military look to it. He sat his horse gracefully, and he was so distinguished at all points that I very much regretted not catching the name as Mrs. Stanard gave it to us. He, however, heard ours and bowed as gracefully as he rode, and the few remarks he made to each of us showed he knew all about us.

But Mrs. Stanard was in ecstasies of pleasurable excitement. I felt she had bagged a big fish. Just then they abounded in Richmond. Mrs. Stanard accused him of being ambitious &c. He remonstrated—said his tastes were of the simplest. He "only wanted a Virginia farm—no end of cream and fresh butter—and fried chicken. Not one fried chicken or two—but unlimited fried chicken."

To all this light chat did we seriously incline because the man and horse and everything about him was so fine looking. Perfection—no fault to be found if you hunted for one. As he left us, I said, "Who is it?" eagerly.

"You did not know! Why, it is Robert E. Lee, son of Light Horse Harry Lee, the first man in Virginia"—raising her voice as she enumerated his glories.

All the same, I like Smith Lee better, and I like his looks, too. I know Smith Lee well. Can anybody say they know his brother? I doubt it. He looks so cold and quiet and grand.

And so Dr. Moore was made surgeon general.[2] Dr. Gibbes has the sulks.

Reading the *Herald*—filled with excuses for their disaster. Excuses don't count. We must accept facts.

It is wonderful. Kirby Smith, our Blücher, who came on the field in the nick

----

8. Eleanor (Parke) Custis Lewis, granddaughter of Martha Washington, was the mother-in-law of James Chesnut, Sr.'s niece, Esther Maria (Coxe) Lewis.

9. William Henry Fitzhugh Lee, colonel of the Ninth Va. Cavalry, was Robert E. Lee's second son.

1. Martha (Pierce) Stanard was a Richmond widow whose home became a center of Confederate high society.

2. Samuel Preston Moore of Ark., a former U.S. Army surgeon born in Charleston.

of time—as at Waterloo.[3] And now we are as the British, who do not remember Blücher. It is all Wellington. So every individual man I see fought and won the battle. From Kershaw up and down—all the eleventh-hour men won the battle, turned the tide—the Marylanders. Elzey & Co. one never hears of—as little as one hears of Blücher in the English Waterloo stories.

Had a painful adventure, in a small way. The poor soul who was debarred the pleasure of rushing to Mrs. Bartow with the news of her husband's death—they call her "bad accident maker to the evening news"—today she came into my room. Adèle Auzé[4] said, "That woman Cousin Mary calls 'bad accident'"—and there was a look of consternation—for she was among us. Mrs. Davis applauded my adroitness: "Is it true your son has met with a bad accident? We are so sorry to hear it."

"Oh, yes—it is a dreadful wound. He was punched in the side by the butt end of a musket."

The deep and absorbing interest I evinced in that wound and the frowns that I gave Adèle when I could turn my head and Adèle's reckless making of comic faces over her blunder—it was overheating, at this state of the thermometer.

Letter from Columbia, S.C.[5]

Home
July 28, 1861

Many thanks to you, my dear Mrs. C, for your kind letter, which I have vainly hoped would have been followed by many more.

Letters from Virginia are like water to the thirsty, fainting body. We look for tidings with that aching of the heart that seems almost beyond endurance. Such tidings as we have had! Exultingly singing and praising God with one voice and the next moment finding us low at His footstool in weeping and prayer and deep humility. His mercies abound and we will not sully the bright glories of the 21st by more than *natural* tears, in grieving over our brave soldiers. I think every man on that battlefield *on our side* was a hero. And we must admit that a *portion* of the "bad cause" fought as bravely as *ours,* but the heart and principle were wanting, and so God gave us the victory. Our brave and noble men! May the merciful God of battles shield them every moment. I feel that they may be again in conflict—this very hour! When Beauregard puts the seal of secrecy upon his doings and prohibits all intercourse, I look for some great achievement to follow.

That was a *dear-bought,* but such a grand, victory. It seems incredible.

I think Havelock's great movement in the East[6] the only recorded event

3. Prussian field marshal Gebhard Leberecht von Blücher.

4. A Camden resident who later married J. C.'s first cousin John Chesnut Deas.

5. M. B. C.'s correspondent was Mary Sophia Stark, sister-in-law of former S.C. governor John Hugh Means. Theodore, below, was Mary's brother, the keeper of the State House in Columbia.

6. British general Sir Henry Havelock had won fame at the head of a relief expedition that helped subdue the Indian Mutiny of 1857-58.

that outstrips it. God help and keep our brave soldiers! This opens the way to a request from John Means to you. He begs you will oblige him by discovering the whereabouts of a young soldier, John Means Thompson (a nephew of Gen. Waddy Thompson),[7] who was wounded slightly. He belongs to the Washington Light Infantry, Captain Conner,[8] from Charleston. His friends apprehend increased dangers in his case from a delicate constitution with pulmonary tendencies. If not in Richmond, would you get a line to Mrs. Singleton at her post, or Mrs. Carrington in Charlottesville? The arrangements for our soldiers we do not exactly take in—are they scattered in the different hospitals or principally in Richmond and Charlottesville? Stark Means, belonging to the Sixth Regiment S.C.V. Colonel Winder[9] is in Virginia. His mother is here and says I must beg you and Mrs. Singleton or any and all of our friends to remember *her,* if anything happens to her son. She is here now with her daughter Emma—very, very ill, and we fear her case will end in consumption, if not already that. John is down today just to see his child and will return tomorrow. Their hearts are torn between these only darling ones—God help them. How little all these things make me feel.

Old Scott! I only wish every disaster on that battlefield could be photographed on his heart and brain—stereotyped on his *vision*—that mortification, remorse, and shame might balance in some degree the horrors he has brought on our country.

Please say to Mrs. Preston, too, to bear in mind our boys. Oh! If you could realize all we dread and yet long to hear, I am sure you ladies would write. There is no detail that is not precious to us—nothing from the seat of war that has not its value to our anxious hearts, worn with suspense, and taking "*all*" our brave ones into the circle of love and care.

Tell Mrs. Preston her dear old mother turned out today for the national thanksgiving. But our ministers were all absent, and she had to go back home without joining in the *public* praise, but God has heard her hosannas and prayers.

Tell Mrs. Preston I am glad to hear "she is such a charming old lady." Mrs. Taylor[1] says the next thing, you will be calling her an old lady! She joins me, as well as my sisters, in much love to you—to Mrs. P—and *any* and *all* of our dear Columbia friends. You do not know how grieved and mortified I feel that South Carolina and Virginia should feel their "identities" at such a time as this. I cannot realize *individual feeling, personal* sensitiveness. Each man is a modicum of his *country,* and must aim to be the

---

7. A nullifier, former U.S. congressman, and former brigadier general of S.C. militia from Greenville District.

8. James Conner of Charleston, former U.S. attorney for the S.C. District and a delegate to the S.C. secession convention.

9. John Henry Winder of Md.

1. Probably Thomas Taylor's mother, Sally Webb (Coles) Taylor of Richland District. The widow of planter Benjamin Franklin Taylor, she was one of the wealthiest women in S.C.

best portion without reference to his neighbors. It is a grand and glorious cause and should not be sullied by petty envyings and jealousies and strife.

All friends here are quite well, or as well as we can be. John Means begs to be most 'specially remembered to you.

If Theo was here he would send you a message of thanks for your successful effort in John West's behalf. Tell me of our ladies, their whereabouts and doings. Let us know what we can do for the hospitals.

I was delighted at the appropriation from Congress, consecrated as it was by prayer, fasting, and tears. God bless you all.

Most truly yours,

Mary Stark

Copy of a letter I wrote to Harriet [Grant]—[2]

July 25

Dear H,

Mrs. Carrington from Charlottesville writes that there is a great deal needed there for the South Carolina wounded. Today Mrs. George Randolph,[3] who is president of the Ladies' Association here, tells me she wants arrowroot and tamarinds, and there are none to be found. Tomorrow I am going the rounds of the hospitals with her.

Whatever you have to send, direct to Mrs. G. Randolph, Franklin St., Richmond. Always send by express. She is the head and distributes to Winchester, Culpeper, &c&c, and every other place where things are needed.

Ask Kate Williams to get us arrowroot from Florida.

I feel somewhat easy in mind, now Mr. C is once more with the Congress here. But they will try again. It is not all over. We will have a death struggle.

Everyone who comes from Manassas brings a fresh budget of news. We are still finding batteries—at any rate, rifles and muskets. We had eighteen cannons on our side and we captured 63 (pretty good for beginners), mostly rifled cannon.

The negroes come in loaded like mules.

One man brought four overcoats and, when they cheered him, said, "You never mind—I done give the best one to Marster."

There is no end to the stories and talk. Write to Mary Witherspoon[4] to send her things to Mrs. Randolph's care.

Yours, etc.

M. B. C.

2. The orphaned daughter of J. C.'s sister Harriet Serena (Chesnut) Grant and Camden attorney William Joshua Grant.

3. Mary Elizabeth (Adams) Pope Randolph maintained a fashionable Richmond salon with her second husband, attorney George Wythe Randolph, who was a grandson of Thomas Jefferson.

4. J. C.'s niece Mary Serena Chesnut (Williams) Witherspoon of Society Hill, Darlington District, S.C., was the closest schoolgirl friend of M. B. C. in the 1830s. Her husband, John Witherspoon, was Mrs. Chesnut's second cousin.

Kept a copy, in case anything goes wrong. Camden is cranky.

A note from Mrs. Randolph:

My dear Mrs. C,

I am much obliged to you for the money sent by the Camden ladies and will hand it to the treasure on Monday. We have received two boxes from South Carolina and sent them to Charlottesville, with other articles purchased here. I am in doubt what it is best to do at this time but will call upon the ladies, if they can be of service at any time. I am as yet sending nothing to Culpeper, expecting orders from the ladies and surgeons there, having told them to call on us when they have need.

I think many comforts were captured. I know 52 barrels of white sugar were taken.

I will see you in a few days and tell you what we are about.

Yours truly,

M. G. Randolph

Franklin St.
July 27

Mr. Venable was praising Hugh Garden[5] and Kershaw's regiment generally. This was delightful. They are my friends and neighbors from home. Showed him Miss Mary Stark's letter—and we agreed with her. At the bottom of our hearts we believe every Confederate soldier to be a hero. Sans peur, sans reproche.

Hope for the best today. Things must be on a pleasanter footing all over the world. Why? Met the president in the corridor. He took me by both hands. "Have you breakfasted? Come in and breakfast with me?"

Alas, I had had my breakfast. And he said, laughing at his own French, "J'en suis fâché—de tout mon coeur."

When he jokes it is a good sign. "Moi! malheureux! Or is it 'que je suis malheureux?'" he said.

At the public dining room, where I had taken my breakfast with Mr. Chesnut, Mrs. Davis came to him while we were at table. She said she had been to our

---

5. Hugh Richardson Garden of Sumter District, a private and color-bearer in Kershaw's regiment, graduated in 1860 from S.C. College, where Charles Venable was professor of mathematics.

rooms. She wanted Wigfall hunted up. Mr. Davis thought Chesnut would be apt to know his whereabouts. I ran to Mrs. Wigfall's room, who tells me she was sure he could be found with his regiment in camp. But Mr. C had not to go to the camp, for Wigfall came to his wife's room while I was there. Mr. Davis and Wigfall would be friends, if—if—

We have sent the captured white sugar to Charlottesville hospital.

The Northern papers say we hung and quartered a Zouave—cut him in 4 pieces—and that we tie prisoners to a tree and bayonet them. In other words, we are savages. It ought to teach us not to credit what our papers say of them. It is so absurd an imagination of evil.

We are absolutely treating their prisoners as well as our own men. It is complained of here. I am going to the hospitals here for the enemy's sick and wounded to see for myself.

Mr. C is devoted to Mrs. Long and Mrs. McLean. They do not seem to take his compliments to Sumner l'oncle, or cousin—I do not know which he is—in bad part.

Trescot says Keitt, Boyce, Hammond, and many others hate Jeff Davis. He says disintegration has already begun. ⟨⟨Sat up until twelve—he abusing Davis and Mrs. Davis. . . .⟩⟩

Like Martin Luther, he had a right to protest and free himself from the thralldom of Roman Catholic church, but when everybody began to protest against Luther—as it seemed good to them—freely exercising their right of private interpretation—!

Seceding can go on indefinitely with the dissatisfied seceders.

Why did we not follow the flying foe across the Potomac? That is the question of the hour in the drawing room—those of us who are not contending as to "who took Ricketts's Battery?" Allen Green—for one—took it. Allen told us that finding a portmanteau with nice clean shirts, he was so hot and dusty he stepped behind a tree and put on a clean Yankee shirt. And was more comfortable.

I was made to do an awfully rude thing. Trescot wanted to see Mr. C on particular business. I left him on the stairs, telling him to wait for me there, I would be back in an instant.

Mr. C listened until I had finished my story—then locked the door and put the key in his pocket. Said I should not be running up and down stairs on Trescot's errands. Today saw Trescot. He waited on the stairs an hour, he said. He was very angry, you may be sure.

The *Tribune* soothes the Yankee self-conceit, which has received a shock—the national vanity, you know—by saying we had 100,000 men on the field at Manassas. We had about 15,000 effective men in all.

And then the *Tribune* tries to inflame and envenom them against us by telling lies as to our treatment of prisoners.

They say when they come against us next, it will be in overwhelming force.

———————

Lord Lyons, who is not our friend, says to them gravely, "Now, perhaps we may be allowed to call them belligerents."[6]

I long to see Russell's letter to the *Times* about Bulls Run and Manassas. It will be rich and rare.

In Washington it is crimination and recrimination. Well—let them abuse one another to their hearts' content.

⟨⟨Mr. Chesnut met his old flame Miss Lizzie Dallas,[7] now Mrs. Tucker. Found her, he *said, old* but very agreeable. Did not mention it to me for several days.⟩⟩

July 31, 1861.   Dined at the president's table and for the last time. Tomorrow we move to the Arlington. We had tea with Mr. Mason, Mr. Miles, and Eustis.[8] Mr. C accounted for his turning his back on us, and talking to Mrs. Long with such earnestness, by saying: "I had to do it to keep her from hearing Mr. Mason. He was wishing all the Yankees dead. And all of you were forgetting that sort of thing must be unpleasant to her."

Men or women from the North who are here, married to Southern people, must have a trying time. And ours in the same scrape at the North, ditto. Bad words for the enemy in everybody's mouth, and people do not like to hear their native land vilified, come what will.

———

6. Rumored remark of the British minister at Washington, Richard Bickerton Pemell Lyons, the second baron Lyons, to U.S. Secretary of State Seward as they watched Union troops returning in disarray from Bull Run. Lyons was alluding to Northern outrage at the British recognition of the Confederates as "belligerents" (but not a nation) in May.

7. Elizabeth (Dallas) Tucker, daughter of former vice president George M. Dallas of Pa., was the wife of Dr. David Hunter Tucker of Richmond.

8. Former U.S. congressman George Eustis, Jr., of La.

VII

"Who Killed Cock Robin?"

August 1, 1861. Arlington House.
Everybody abusing the Spotswood, where I had no end of a good time.

Captain Boykin—Boykin's Rangers—has appointed John Chesnut 1st lieut., Thurston 2nd lieut., Guerard 3rd.

Mrs. Wigfall, with the "Lone Star" flag in the carriage, called for me. We drove to the fairgrounds. Mrs. Davis's landau with her spanking bays rolled along in front of us. Fairgrounds as covered with tents, soldiers, &c&c as ever. As one regiment moves off to the army, a fresh one from home comes to be mustered in and takes its place.

The president with his aides dashed by. My husband was riding with him. The president presented the flag to the Texians. Mr. Chesnut came to us for the flag and bore it aloft to the president. We seemed to come in for part of the glory. We were too far off to hear the speech. But Jeff Davis is very good at that sort of thing, and we were satisfied that it was well done.

Heavens! How that redoubtable Wigfall did rush those poor Texans about. He maneuvered and marched them until I was weary for their sakes. Poor fellows, it was a hot afternoon. August—and the thermometer in the nineties. Mr. Davis uncovered to speak. Wigfall replied with his hat on—military, is that?

I read somewhere that a high and mighty nobleman would not take his hat off in the king's presence. He maintained he had a right to wear it. The king acknowledged the ancestral right, but—pointing right and left—"No one has a right to keep his hat on in a room where there were ladies." The king had him there, you see.

At the fairgrounds today—such music and mustering and marching—such cheering and flying of flags. Such firing of guns and all that sort of thing. A gala day: double distilled 4th of July feeling.

In the midst of it all a messenger came to tell Mrs. Wigfall that a telegram had been received, saying her children were safe across the lines in Gordonsville. That was something to thank God for, without any doubt.

These two little girls[1] come from somewhere in Connecticut—with Mrs. Wigfall's good sister, the one who gave me my Bogatzky,[2] the only person in the

---

1. Louis Wigfall's teenaged daughters, Louise Sophie "Louly" Wigfall and Frances "Fanny" Wigfall. Fanny published her recollections as Mrs. D. Giraud Wright, *A Southern Girl in '61* (1905).
2. *A Golden Treasury for the Children of God* (1718), a daily devotional by Silesian religious writer Carl Heinrich von Bogatzky, had gone through many editions in English before the Civil War.

world except Susan Rutledge who ever seemed to think I had a soul to be saved. Now, suppose Seward had held Louise and Fanny as hostages for Louis Wigfall's good behavior. Eh?

Excitement number two—that bold brigadier, the Georgia General Toombs,[3] charging about too recklessly, got thrown. His horse dragged him up to the wheels of our carriage. For a moment it was frightful. Down there among the horse's hooves was his face turned up toward us, purple with rage. His foot was still in the stirrup, and he had not let go the bridle. The horse was prancing over him, rearing and plunging and everybody hemming him in, and they seemed so slow and awkward about it. We felt it an eternity, looking down at him and expecting him to be killed before our very faces, down there. However, he soon got it all straight, and though awfully tousled and tumbled, dusty, rumpled, and flushed, with redder face and wilder hair than ever, he rode off gallantly, having to our admiration bravely remounted the recalcitrant charger.

Now, if I were to pick out the best abused, where all catch it so bountifully, I should say Mr. Commissary General Northrop[4] was the most cussed and vilified man in the Confederacy. He is held accountable for everything that goes wrong in the army. He may not be efficient, but his having been a classmate and crony of Jeff Davis at West Point points the moral and adorns the tale.[5] I hear that alluded to oftenest of his many crimes. They say Beauregard writes ⟨⟨to Mr. Chesnut⟩⟩ that his army is upon the verge of starvation, ⟨⟨thirty-six hours without food⟩⟩. Here every man, woman, and child is ready to hang to the very first lamppost anybody of whom that army complains. Every Manassas soldier is a hero dear to our patriotic heart. Put up with any neglect of the heroes of the 21st July—never!

And now they say we did not move on right after the flying foe because we had no provisions—no wagons, no ammunition, &c&c. Rain, mud, and Northrop. Where were the enemy's supplies that we brag so of bagging? Echo answers, where?

Where there is a will, there is a way. No, we stopped to plunder that rich convoy, and somehow for a day or so everybody thought the war was over and stopped to rejoice. So it appeared here.

All this was our dinner-table talk today. Mr. Mason dined with us, and Mr. Barnwell sits by me always. The latter reproved me sharply, but Mr. Mason laughed at "this headlong, unreasonable women's harangue." "Female tactics and their war ways."

Commodore Barron[6] and his family are here. He has lost his wife.

---

3. Robert Toombs had resigned as secretary of state on July 24, five days after his appointment as a brigadier general.
4. Col. Lucius Bellinger Northrop of Charleston.
5. References to Samuel Johnson's *Vanity of Human Wishes* (1749), line 222.
6. Samuel Barron of Va. had been a captain in the U.S. Navy when he resigned in April 1861 to become a captain of the Confederate navy.

Forty-two members of the U.S. Congress voted for a peace proposition.[7]

Two South Carolinians hung.[8] A Virginia woman said, "The president is crazy to threaten to hang four Yankees for two Carolinians."

Table talk. There is no longer any complaint from the army as to food. But this month's mismanagement cannot be remedied. Maybe not for years—and it may be forever, as the song says.[9] A freshet in the autumn does not compensate for a drought in the spring. Time and tide wait for no man, and there was a tide in our affairs which might have led to Washington, and we did not take it and so lost our fortune, this round. Things which nobody could deny!

Carolinians are beginning to brag. "Little dogs begin to bark and bite, for 'tis their nature to," says the hymn.[1]

Mr. Barnwell says the "Gamecock" would have been a good name for the whole state—not for Sumter alone.[2] We are game—we fight to the bitter end, and we are too ready to begin a fight—but then, we flap our wings and crow so.

So we go in for claiming the credit of turning the tide of battle on the 21st. We were being pressed back by the might of heavier columns.

Old Mr. Chesnut never tires of telling us Napoleon said, "Providence was always on the side of the heaviest battalions." To go back to Manassas—suddenly there was a panic, and we raced them back across the Potomac.

Now, who killed cock robin? "I, said the sparrow, with my bow and arrow."

Cock robin has flown. He went at "two forty" speed. If only he had been killed! Requiescat in pace—on a heavy tombstone—with no fear of resurgam.

Dr. Gibbes's story—sad enough. He was seated with a friend of his from Columbia. She could hear nothing of her husband. So she came to find out what

7. On July 29, the House voted 41–85 not to take up Ohio Democrat Samuel S. Cox's resolution proposing a committee of Northerners and Southerners to draw up a constitutional amendment as the basis for sectional reconciliation.

8. A false rumor, probably arising from the continuing controversy over the fate of the crew of the *Savannah.* In late July, the crew was formally charged with piracy in a New York court. The same week, President Davis made public a July 6 letter to Lincoln. Prisoners held by the Confederate government, Davis asserted, would receive "the same treatment and the same fate" as the crewmen.

9. From "Kathleen Mavourneen," first popular in the 1830s.

1. Slightly misquoted from Isaac Watts, "Against Quarreling and Fighting," in *Divine Songs* (1715).

2. Thomas Sumter, for whom the Charleston fort was named, became known as the "Carolina Gamecock" for his exploits as a partisan leader during the Revolutionary War.

she could for herself. She had grown so anxious down there. They were occupying chairs placed in the corridor. The rooms were all crowded at the Spotswood. The lady could not get in there at all, only stopped to beg Dr. Gibbes to help her in her search for some news of her husband.

Some Columbia men came strolling by. Dr. Gibbes went to speak to them.

"What brought you down from the army? I thought furloughs were not so easy to get."

"Oh, we came to bring poor Smith's body." So Dr. Gibbes had to hurry back and get the unhappy woman into a room—or she would have met these men and heard of the death of her husband there—out in that thronged passageway.

Saw a complimentary letter from Mr. Horace Binney to General Scott, who certainly needs the consolation of his friends.

⟨⟨I came in my room by ten, and Mr. C sat in the window and talked until midnight. I do not believe he will join the army again. They want him in Congress.⟩⟩

August 3, 1861.   Went to the Library of the Capitol with Mr. Brewster. The librarian said I must have a separate order from some senator for every two books that I wanted. Mr. Boyce was there, and Messrs. Hunter and Hemphill, so I got four books.

Little Fanny Wigfall, a mere mite of a thing, but Wigfall's offspring. She heard someone say on the cars as she came from Connecticut, "We are now in Virginia." She sprang to her feet. "And now I may be permitted to express my political sentiments," she cried.

Mr. Brewster told me also that a man called Kit Suber[3] had informed him that the northwest of South Carolina had been without a showing for so long a time they were restive. Mr. Chesnut, being from the east, made it a bad lookout for him at the next election.

"It is very hard to be beaten for anything by anybody or in any way," I sighed.

"Yes," added the plain-spoken Brewster, "we might bear the disappointment of our friends, but the exultation of one's enemies—who can bear it?"

McClellan virtually supersedes the titan Scott. Physically, General Scott is the largest man I ever saw.[4] Mrs. Scott said, "Nobody but his wife could ever know

---

3. Christian Henry Suber, member of the S.C. house from Newberry District and a quartermaster in the C.S.A.

4. After Bull Run, Lincoln called McClellan from western Va. to head the defeated Union army at Washington. Three-hundred-pound, six-foot-five Winfield Scott remained general in chief, but the man known as "Little Mac" had emerged as Lincoln's foremost commander.

how little he was." And yet they said old Winfield Scott would have organized an army for them if they had had patience. They would not give him time.

The president and family have gone to their own house—⟨⟨really a handsome establishment⟩⟩ Brockenbrough Mansion—Dr. Brockenbrough, John Randolph's "A No. 1" man. And his wife—hardly number two to anyone—she built the house.[5] And the unmannerly papers call Mrs. President Davis "portly and middle-aged."[6]

Ben McCulloch—the Texian Ranger, we called him before the war—how he hated Indians! Well, he has won a victory somewhere in Missouri.

Miss Garnett, Mrs. Singleton's governess—no relation to our Garnetts, an Irish woman—she met Dick Manning.[7] "I did not think you would kiss me now. I am such a big boy."

"Yes, indeed. I would not mind if you were twice as big."

Governor Manning began to pay himself some of the highest compliments.

Miss Garnett: "Oh! I see your trumpeter is dead."

"What do you mean?"

"Have you not to blow your own trumpet?"

Someone said, "My mother even wears a pistol now."

"What for?"

"Runaway negroes, so many disorderly soldiers, men—nobody knows where."

"No. Why should I wear a pistol? I [am] awfully afraid of a pistol—not the least in the world afraid of a man."

Nor need *she* have been.

[On] July 27th, 1861, Burwell Boykin, son of Burwell Boykin of Mt. Pleasant, died of typhoid fever.[8]

My sister writes, "So we have lost our best man—the very best man I ever knew, the kindest."

One of the largest slave-owners—and in attending to his plantation negroes, among whom this fever raged, he caught it and died.

So many escape in spite of the dangers and perils of the battlefield.

And they die in their peaceful homes. This one could ill be spared. We need

5. The mansion, built in 1818 by Dr. John Brockenbrough and his wife Gabriella, was bought by the city of Richmond and rented to the Confederate government. It became known as the "White House of the Confederacy." John Randolph's description of his intimate friend appeared in Hugh A. Garland, *The Life of John Randolph of Roanoke* (1850), volume 2, chapter 44.

6. Mrs. Davis, then thirty-five, was three years younger than M. B. C.

7. Richard Manning, the son of John L. Manning and his first wife, Susan (Hampton) Manning.

8. M. B. C.'s uncle had died. Mt. Pleasant was her grandfather's plantation in Kershaw District.

just such a well-balanced character, just such a fearless, good man at home, where there are now so few left—and so many women and children and ne-groes.

Dr. Boykin wants the Kirkwood Rangers,[9] of which he is the 1st lieutenant, mustered into service. Also, he says in a letter that Colonel Chesnut must raise a cavalry regiment. There are companions ready to join for that purpose. The aforesaid colonel has gone to see what he can do to pacify Toombs and Maxcy Gregg.

South Carolina troops and Georgians—fighting &c&c on the cars over watermelons Captain Axson was bringing here for Mrs. Davis—a present—&c&c.

Read *Hermsprong; or, Man As He Is Not.*[1] There are ideas in it, after all.

Prince Jérôme has gone to Washington.[2] Now Yankees so far are as little trained as we are—raw troops yet. Suppose France takes the other side and we have to meet disciplined and armed men—soldiers who understand war, French-men, with all the élan we boast of, &c&c&c.

Odd letter from Uncle H. "I acknowledge that usually I am cold to my friends. I do not care much about them. But I did love my brother Burwell."

Ransom Calhoun, Willie Preston, and Dr. Nott's boys are here.[3] These foolish, rash, harebrained Southern lads have been within an ace of a fight for their camping ground with a Maryland company. That is too Irish, to be so ready to fight anybody, friend or foe. They are thrilling with fiery ardor. The red-hot Southern martial spirit is in the air. These young men, however, were all educated abroad. And it is French or German ideas, rather, that they are filled with.

Marylanders were as rash and reckless as themselves and had their coattails ready for anybody to tread on, Donnybrook Fair fashion.

---

9. A company of the Seventh S.C. Cavalry organized by William M. Shannon of Camden.

1. English free-thinker Robert Bage's novel, published in 1796, about a "natural man" raised by North American savages.

2. Not Jérôme Bonaparte, but his half brother, Napoleon Joseph Charles Paul Bonaparte, prince Napoleon, who was the nephew of Napoleon Bonaparte. The prince had landed in New York several days earlier for an American pleasure trip.

3. Capt. William Ransom Calhoun of the First S.C. Artillery, a distant relative of John C. Calhoun, had been a U.S. Army officer and U.S. chargé d'affaires in Paris before the war. His cousin and lieutenant was William Campbell Preston, the youngest son of John Smith Preston. Willie had been at S.C. College in the mid-1850s with Josiah Clark Nott's sons, James Deas Nott of the Twenty-second Ala. and Henry Junius Nott, surgeon's assistant of the Second S.C. Volunteers.

One would think there were Yankees enough and to spare for any killing to be done. It began about picketing their horses. These quarrelsome young soldiers have lovely manners. They are so sweet-tempered here among us at the Arlington.

After twelve o'clock last night Mr. Barnwell sent for Mr. Chesnut.

He told me to go to the door and say he was in bed and asleep, and he made his words good in a few seconds. I had a new novel, so they saw a light in my dressing room.

August 4, 1861.   A heavy, heavy heart.

"Souvent de tous nos maux, la raison est le père."

Another missive from Jordan[4]—querulous, faultfinding. Things are all wrong. Beauregard's Jordan who has been crossed—not the stream "in Canaan's fair and happy land, where our possessions *lie*."[5]

They seem to feel that the war is over here—except the president and Mr. Barnwell—above all, the foreboding friend of mine, Captain Ingraham. He thinks it hardly begun. He is awaiting a crash from the navy. Not heard from yet.

The trouble last night was the Maxcy Gregg-Toombs imbroglio.

Davis, a Georgian, killed Axson, a Carolinian, on the cars, in a quarrel which grew out of watermelons. Two Carolinians mixed up in the row—Gregg will not surrender to Toombs and Georgia reprisals.

Another outburst from Jordan. Beauregard is not seconded properly.

Hélas! To think that any mortal general (even though he had sprung up in a month or so from captain of artillery to general) could be so puffed up with vanity, so blinded by any false idea of his own consequence as to write, to intimate, that man, or men, would sacrifice their country, injure themselves, ruin their families to spite aforesaid general. Conceit and self-assertion can never reach a higher point than that.

And yet they give you to understand Mr. Davis does not like Beauregard. In point of fact they fancy he is jealous of him, and rather than Beauregard shall

---

4. Lt. Col. Thomas Jordan of Va. was Beauregard's adjutant general.
5. The quotation is from the hymn "On Jordan's Stormy Bank I Stand," by Baptist minister Samuel Stennett (1728–95).

have a showing, Mr. President—who would be hanged at least if things go wrong—will cripple the army to spite Beauregard.

Mr. Mallory says, "How we would laugh, but you see it is no laughing matter to have our fate in the hands of such self-sufficient, vain, army idiots." Beauregard called Joe Kershaw a militia idiot. So the amenities of life are spreading.

In the meantime we seem to be lying on our oars, debating in Congress, and the enterprising Yankees are doubling, quadrupling their army at their leisure. A knack of hoping is a great blessing in private life, but a too-hopeful Congress is a positive misfortune.

"They that govern make the least noise. You see, when they row in a barge, they that do the drudgery work, slash, puff, and sweat (swear), but he that governs sits quietly at the stern and is scarce seen to stir."[6]

Hope it is so with us. Who knows what is going on at the executive office?

There is a lull of the winds, but the waves are still running high.

Every day regiments march by. The town is crowded with soldiers.

These new ones are running in, fairly. They fear the war will be over before they get a sight of the fun.

Every man from every little country precinct wants a place in the picture.

August 5, 1861.   Was introduced to a fine-looking young Baltimorean.[7] They say he wrote a comic operetta called "Corcorani," a burlesque founded on the Spaniard's defense of himself by the piano at Mr. C——'s house, where the Spaniard intended an elopement &c&c.

They require 600,000 to invade us. Truly we are a formidable power!

The *Herald* says it is useless to move with a man less than that.

England has made it all up with them—or rather, she will not break with them. Jérôme Napoleon also is in Washington—and not our friend. ⟨⟨Mr. Chesnut is for a second Moscow—burning the cotton. . . . ⟩⟩[8]

---

6. A slight misquotation from chapter 108 of *The Table Talk of John Selden* (1689), a posthumous collection of the opinions of this English legal scholar.

7. Probably Richard Snowden Andrews, a Baltimore architect who was organizing the First Md. Artillery in Richmond. M. B. C. later calls him "Mr. Snowden" and "Dick Snowden."

8. When Napoleon occupied Moscow in 1812, much of the city was destroyed by fires apparently set accidentally by French looters but fanned intentionally by Russians to deprive the invaders of their prize. In Nov. and Dec. of 1861, many planters on the coast of Ga. and S.C. would take up Chesnut's idea.

Dan Murray Lee[9] called us to the window to see a most unwanted sight, two men with *U.S.* buttons—paroled no doubt.

At the Spotswood the want of state in government officials would entrance Mrs. Bradford. Madame has children, mostly babies—a little black Topsy to "mind them." Topsy sleeps with them and "rides the buffets of an outrageous" mistress's hand—but all on an equality with the other children. Topsy is clad as Topsy always is on the stage—one straight homespun garment. She is, however, not maltreated except she shares the general spanking which besets the olive branches. So Trescot tells us. He has no philanthropy, but objects to the chastisement of the infantry because he cannot sleep for the howling. Topsy seems happy as the day is long. So are the objects of her ward and guard. One is ill just now. Madame mère says, with a whimper, "They will play in the dreen." No affectation of high life in all that.

Dr. Gibbes is a bird of ill omen. Today he tells me eight of our men have died at the Charlottesville hospital. It seems sickness is more redoubtable in an army than the enemy's guns. There are 1,100 there hors de combat, and virulent typhoid fever along with them. They want money, clothes, nurses.

So I am writing—right and left the letters fly, calling for help from the sister societies at home. The good and patriotic women at home are easily stirred to this work.

Mary Hammy has many strings to her bow—a fiancé in the army, Dr. Berrien[1] in town. Today she drove out with Major Smith and Colonel Hood.[2] Yesterday Custis Lee was here.[3] She is a prudent little puss. Needs no good advice—if I were one to give it.

Qui se ressemble—s'assemble.

Today had a passage of arms with Mrs. Smith Lee, née Mason.[4] She assaulted Mr. Miles for saying that it was no new thing for him to hate the star-spangled banner. He had always looked on it as it floated over the customhouse at Charleston or the forts—"as a symbol of oppression."

She does not take to the new order of things kindly. Says she was dragged away from Washington and across the long bridge, kicking.

9. Daniel Murray Lee, eighteen-year-old son of Sidney Smith Lee, soon became a midshipman in the C.S.N.

1. James H. Berrien, a Ga. surgeon in the C.S.A., was the son of former U.S. attorney general John McPherson Berrien and the brother of Mrs. Francis Bartow.

2. John Bell Hood of Ky. had resigned his U.S. Army commission in April and had been swiftly promoted by the Confederacy from lieutenant to colonel of the Fourth Tex. Regiment.

3. George Washington Custis Lee, eldest son of Robert E. Lee, had been a career officer in the U.S. Army and then a Confederate major of engineers before becoming a colonel and aide to Jefferson Davis.

4. Anna Maria (Mason) Lee, sister of James Murray Mason.

Toombs and Maxcy Gregg snarl hot as ever over Axson dead and Davis threatened. We got the worst of it. Our man Axson was killed. All the protocols in the world will not bring him to life. But Maxcy Gregg is showing his teeth savagely.

Mr. Preston's body servant Isaac died of typhoid fever. He was faithfully nursed. Mr. Preston was grieved about it. Maria gave me the points of difference between this poor Isaac who died of camp fever and the magnificent Hal, Mr. P's other man. Of course, Isaac, as he is dead and gone, had all the good traits.

Laurence does all our shopping. All of his master's money was in his hands until now. I thought it injudicious when gold is at such a premium to leave it lying loose in the tray of a trunk. So I have sewed it up in a belt which I can wear upon an emergency. The cloth is wadded, and my diamonds there, too. "Ticklish times," I say. "But then are you not late about it? Now there seems no need. Before Manassas we could see the sense of it." It has strong strings—can be tied under my hoops about my waist if the worst come to the worst, as the saying is. Laurence wears the same bronze mask. No sign of anything he may feel or think of my latest fancy. Only I know he asks for twice as much money now when he goes to buy things—at least twice as much as he used to take when it was lying in the tray, for him to do as he pleased with it.

> Naught can make us rue
> If England to herself do rest but true.[5]

—and to us, too.

Shaftsbury on panics: "Panic comes from the god Pan. He went about with Bacchus in India and made such a noise in a wood that the imagination and frantic fears were excited—and they imagined ten thousand where there were none."[6]

See panic of the 21st July.

Read *Hajji Baba*.[7]

"Honesty sometimes keeps a man from growing rich—as civility keeps him often from being witty."

5. The final lines, slightly misquoted, of *King John*.
6. Paraphrase from Anthony Ashley Cooper, third earl of Shaftsbury, *Characteristicks of Men, Manners, Opinions, Times* (1711), volume 1, treatise 1, section 2.
7. Either James Justinian Morier, *The Adventures of Hajji Baba of Ispahan* (1824), or *The Adventures of Hajji Baba of Ispahan in England* (1828).

Many a good laugh has to be suppressed for fear of hurting peoples' feelings. Wit is a rare article, after all said and done.

Such a nice Lieutenant Cooper, [8] son of the adjutant general, nephew of Mr. Mason. He was on Sullivan's Island with us a few years ago. Reminded him of that Silvey[9] affair—how we arrived so silently at the scene of embarkation that we saw Lieutenant Silvey knock a man head-foremost into deep water, where he had to be fished out, and tie another to the main mast, where he howled like a wild Indian. Lieutenant Silvey, who had been so soft and silvery with us—as if butter could not melt in his mouth. Lieutenant Cooper had vivid recollections of Mary W's[1] beauty and the ravings of Vogdes & Co.[2] when that lovely apparition suddenly arose on that lonely island and its lonelier garrison.

Went to Miss Sally Tompkins's hospital.[3] There I was rebuked. I deserved it.
Me: "Are there any Carolinians here?"
Miss T: "I never ask where the sick and wounded come from."
Wade Hampton told me today that Colonel Chesnut led his Legion (Hampton's) in the last charge.

Jeff Davis says he met him at the head of an artillery company.

J. C. himself said he led the last cavalry charge and did not get back to the camp until long after midnight. He says he got off his horse, which was restive, to look at the flag of the unexpected arrival on the turnpike, and he saw, as the wind caught it, that it was Confederate, the Maryland contingent &c. He does not magnify his exploits to the point designated either by the president or Hampton.

It was the first battle of all but the president. I daresay they were excited and do not remember details. ⟨⟨Mrs. Johnston says the generals speak of Mr. C in the highest terms. She says John Manning asks her: does Mrs. C really speak well of me? The deceitful wretch! He suspects everybody! I really wonder what Mr. C means to do. John Manning knows I never believed in him or trusted him—snake in the grass—*beautiful* as he is.⟩⟩[4]

8. Samuel Cooper's son, Samuel Mason Cooper, had been a U.S. Army second lieutenant at Fort Moultrie on Sullivan's Island before the war.
9. William Silvey of Ohio, then a first lieutenant at Fort Moultrie.
1. Identified as Mary (Withers) Kirkland in the 1860s Journal under Aug. 7, 1861.
2. Israel Vogdes of Pa., an artillery officer stationed at Fort Moultrie. He became a Union brigadier general during the war.
3. After Bull Run, Sally Louisa Tompkins had outfitted an old Richmond house as a hospital at her own expense. When the government took over private hospitals, she was allowed to maintain hers, and Jefferson Davis commissioned her a captain, the only woman to hold military rank in the Confederacy.
4. Under Aug. 7, 1861, in the 1860s Journal.

August 8, 1861. Wilmot DeSaussure makes an admirable salad dressing for our tomatoes, and I am so hot, so tired, so feverish I care for nothing else. Today he showed me a sword captured at Manassas. The man who brought the sword in the early part of the fray was taken prisoner by the Yankees. They stripped him, took his sleeve buttons, and were in the act of despoiling him of his boots when the rout began and the play was reversed. Proceedings took the opposite tack.

Afterward Wade Hampton took up his parable. He denounced those men taken prisoner so early in the day—called them cowards, liars, &c&c.

Wilmot DeSaussure is made brigadier general of South Carolina home troops.

Commodore Barron came with glad tidings. We had taken three prizes at sea and brought them in safely—one laden with molasses, one with sugar, one with salt and fruit.

Miss Barron[5] has a letter from Washington. It says Tilly Emory reads them the most amusing letters from our little stockade—as she calls the begirt and shut-in and well-guarded Confederacy.

Mrs. Smith Lee says indignantly, "Who writes those letters?"

Mr. C dined at the MacFarlands'.[6] Mrs. Preston and I drove out to the Lyonses.[7] It was very rural, picturesque and pleasant—found them at tea on the lawn. Quite a party of people.

Mr. Lyons told us Lord Dundas pronounced the blockade incomplete, which Mr. Lyons hailed as good news.[8] Commodore Barron said, "Such a speech would only make the Yankees stricter and cause them to double the ships on guard duty."

No other result would come of it, he thought.

Captain Ingraham did not see how they could keep up a stricter watch. His heart is torn in twain. The U.S. Navy has been his supreme affection, his first thought and duty. Patriotism now calls him to turn and fight his true love—I mean, his first love. Doña Sol, after the Cid had killed her father,[9] could scarcely be more pathetic than some of his moans.

5. Imogene Barron, daughter of Samuel Barron.

6. The home of Richmond banker and member of the Provisional Confederate Congress William Hamilton MacFarland, his wife Nancy, and their daughter, Turner, was a center of Confederate society.

7. James Lyons and his wife Imogene lived a mile from Richmond in their home "Laburnum."

8. Lyons was repeating a false rumor that the commander of a British fleet off Charleston believed the Union blockade of the harbor ineffective and intended to sail into port. Dundas was not even in command of ships outside the harbor.

9. M. B. C. is mistaken here, of course. Doña Sol was the Cid's daughter.

When I tell him he ought to have brought his ships in with him, he is amazed. "That would have been treason," he cries. "No, not more than coming yourself. The ships were ours as much as you were ours. Half of everything was ours. We paid our taxes and cotton and protected factories of it—kept up the revenues, &c&c."

He smiles in pity at a woman pretending to understand things.

I say, "We were a copartnership. When we dissolved it, we had a right to divide assets. Our money helped to build ships, &c&c. And the tariff in some inscrutable way took all our money. We had a right to share and share alike profits and public property."

———————

Mr. Toombs told us that the president complimented Colonel Chesnut when he described the battle scene to his cabinet—&c&c. And so Mr. Toombs is certain Colonel C will be made one of the new batch of brigadiers.

———————

Next came Mr. Clayton, who calmly informed us Jeff Davis would not get the vote of this Congress for president, so we might count him out.

———————

Mr. Meynardie first told us how pious a Christian soldier was Kershaw—how he prayed, got up, dusted his knees, and led his men on to victory with a dash and courage equal to any Old Testament mighty man of war.

Then came John Green, and he reversed the picture. "When Kershaw saw the Legion give way: 'Damn you, you shameful cowards. Turn back or I'll fire on you' &c, with some highly fanciful profanity got up in the fury of the moment—but the classic English 'damn' covered all the ground."

"Impossible. Mr. Meynardie &c&c has just told us, &c&c."

"But whan a fellow's blood is up and good whiskey is abroad—&c&c."

"Never."

"But Butler[1] and the men of the Legion are no ways pious," says one of us. "There will be blood shed truly if they hear you say they fled at Manassas. It will be Greek meet Greek, this last fight."

———————

"Beside—who kept the enemy at bay until Kirby Smith, Elzey, Kershaw and Co. came up at three o'clock? They had been fighting since daylight, you know."

"It was two o'clock."

"An hour or so don't alter the main fact."

"For pity sake—be magnanimous. You are all brave enough. Don't backbite so."

1. Matthew Calbraith Butler of Edgefield District, son-in-law of Gov. Francis Pickens, was captain of the Edgefield Hussars of Hampton's Legion.

From this small rill in the mountain flowed the mighty stream which has made, *at last,* Louis Wigfall the worst enemy the president has in the Congress—a fact which complicates our affairs no little.

Mr. Davis's hands ought to be strengthened. He ought to be upheld. A divided house must fall, &c&c, we all say!

Mrs. Sam Jones, called Becky by her friends and cronies, male and female, said ⟨⟨told Mrs. Davis⟩⟩ that Mrs. Pickens had confided to the aforesaid Jones (née Taylor, and so of the President Taylor family and cousin of Mr. Davis's first wife)[2] that Mrs. Wigfall described Mrs. Davis as a coarse western woman to Mrs. Pickens. Now, the fair Lucy Holcombe[3] and Mrs. Wigfall had a quarrel of their own, out in Texas—and though reconciled, there was bitterness underneath.

At first Mrs. Joe Johnston called Mrs. Davis "a western belle," but when the quarrel between General Johnston and the president broke out, Mrs. Johnston took back the "belle" and substituted "woman" in the narrative derived from the Jones.[4]

Mrs. Johnston was on her way to see Mrs. Ricketts, who is sharing her husband's prison.[5] Ricketts's battery is principally famous for the number of heroes who took it. I know of twenty or more—captains, colonels, majors, even privates—who captured Ricketts's battery.

We went after Dr. Gibbes, who is at Dr. Gibson's.[6] He was furious. Said, "Walker's slowness would cost thousands of lives."

"Slowness in promoting Dr. Gibbes," we whispered to each other. Mrs. Preston and myself were together.

Governor Manning's account of Prince Jérôme Napoleon—
"He is stout, and he is not handsome. Neither is he young, and as he reviewed

2. Sarah Rebecca (Taylor) Jones, niece of Zachary Taylor, was the wife of Brig. Gen. David Rumph Jones of S.C., not of Brig. Gen. Samuel Jones of Va.

3. Mrs. Pickens.

4. This sentence, which has no counterpart in the 1860s Journal, is apparently anachronistic. The ill feeling between Davis and Johnston did not really begin until after Aug. 31, when the president designated Samuel Cooper, Albert Sidney Johnston, and Robert E. Lee ahead of Joe Johnston in seniority as full generals of the C.S.A. Rightly believing himself legally entitled to the first place by virtue of longer service in the U.S. Army, Johnston complained to Davis in mid-Sept. in a letter the president dismissed as "one-sided . . . unfounded . . . and unbecoming."

5. When Fanny (Lawrence) Ricketts learned of the wounding and capture of her husband, U.S. Army Capt. James Brewerton Ricketts, at Bull Run, she crossed the Confederate lines and gained permission from Joseph E. Johnston to tend Captain Ricketts on the battlefield and then in Richmond. Mrs. Ricketts's devotion captured the fancy of Confederate leaders, who sent her gifts of food until Captain Ricketts's exchange in Dec.

6. Charles Bell Gibson, a Richmond surgeon and professor of surgery at Hampden-Sidney College, had served briefly as surgeon general of Va. in 1861 before becoming the head of the Officer's Hospital.

our troops he was terribly overheated." He heard him say "en avant"—of that he could testify of his own knowledge. And he was told he had been heard to say—with unction—"Allons" more than once.

The sight of the battlefield had made the prince seasick, and he received gratefully a draft of fiery whiskey.

Arago[7] seemed deeply interested in Confederate statistics, and praised our doughty deeds to the skies.

It was but soldiers' fare at last—though they did their best. It was hard sleeping and worse eating in camp. Beauregard is half Frenchman and speaks French like a native. So one awkwardness was done away with. And it was a comfort to see Beauregard speak without the agony of finding words in a foreign language and forming them with damp brow into sentences, a fate which befell others who spoke "a little French." The prince said one more battle could end the conflict. May he prove a prophet.

Scott's favorite aide,[8] to us bequeathed so unwillingly, distinguished himself—the aforesaid fiery whiskey being to blame. He sat on the dinner table after dinner, kicking his heels against the table legs—with his *back* to the prince. And nobody hauled him out!!! But his fate overtook him in this wise. In riding around he got into everybody's way. General Beauregard said to Joe Heyward,[9] "Get him off—somehow."

Joe Heyward made short work of it. He seized the A.D.C.'s horse by the bit and roughly backed the horse down in a ditch. Called to some soldiers: "Come here and carry off this fellow." Then Captain Heyward rode back. No word was said, and Captain Heyward was too well-bred to be ruffled by any such trifle. His face betrayed no emotion. But Governor Manning said: "In our hearts we were crying, 'Well done, Joe. You did your work well and thoroughly, in double-quick time.'"

Mrs. Johnston and Mrs. Ricketts have fraternized and wept together. One heartless being asked Mrs. Johnston if she found the prisoner in irons. And being answered in the negative with indignation, the lady added, "I only hope he was tied to the bedpost by a light chain." But such chaffing was voted in bad taste. It continued, however.

Mrs. Ricketts was offered a private apartment. But she sought a martyr's crown. She said she came to nurse her husband and to be with him. She wished to look after the wounded and to share the privations of the prisoners.

And she has had a fine opportunity of testing her zeal, they say, occupying a room with half a dozen men besides Ricketts, &c&c. I tell the tale as it is told to me.

7. A French naval officer accompanying Prince Napoleon.
8. Identified in 1860s Journal as George William Lay (see p. 19).
9. Joseph Heyward, husband of Maria Henrietta (Magruder) Heyward and younger brother of Edward Barnwell Heyward.

General and Mrs. Cooper came to see us. She is Mrs. Smith Lee's sister, Senator Mason's sister.

"Sidney's sister, Pembroke's mother"—&c.[1] They were talking of old George Mason,[2] in Virginia a name to conjure with.

George Mason violently opposed the extension of slavery. He was a thorough aristocrat and gave as his reason for refusing the blessing of slaves to the new states—southwest and northwest—that vulgar new people were unworthy of so sacred a right as that of holding slaves. It was not an institution intended for such people as they were.

Mrs. Lee said, "After all—what good does it do my sons? They are Light Horse Harry Lee's grandsons—and George Mason's. I do not see that it helps them at all."

When Mrs. Lee and the Coopers had gone, what a rolling of eyes and uplifting of hands. Fitzhugh Lee[3] and Rooney were being promoted—hand over fist! Up they go. Custis Lee is A.D.C. to the president—they say because his father wishes it. If he prefers to be in active service, that matters not. He must stay where he can do most good.

That was the drawing room hum at the Arlington.

Saw what Russell the *Times* man wrote to the English consul at Charleston, Mr. Bunch.

Russell gives a ludicrous account of Senator Wilson's flight on the battlefield the 21st of July.

A friend in Washington writes me that we might have walked into Washington any day for a week after Manassas, such was the consternation and confusion there.

The god Pan was still blowing his horn in the woods. Now she says troops are literally pouring in from all quarters. The horses cover acres of grounds. And she thinks we have lost our chance forever.

We have as a prisoner Elder Nelson,[4] the man who gave Pryor such an overhauling in the House of Representatives last year.

Mrs. Wigfall said triumphantly [that] Cobb, Hammond, Keitt, Boyce, and Banks were in the coalition against Jeff Davis. Clay of Alabama was still his

1. An allusion to the epitaph for Mary Herbert, countess of Pembroke, first published with the poems of her son William Herbert and Sir Benjamin Rudyerd in 1660 but of uncertain authorship. M.B.C. discusses the epitaph and quotes it more fully on p. 195.
2. Grandfather of James Murray Mason; author of the Va. Declaration of Rights of 1776; and one of three delegates to the Constitutional Convention of 1787 who would not sign the final draft.
3. A son of Sydney Smith Lee serving as a lieutenant colonel in the cavalry.
4. U.S. Congressman Thomas Amos Rogers Nelson, a Tennessean who opposed his state's secession, had been arrested by Confederate scouts on his way to Washington. On Aug. 13, Jefferson Davis ordered his release.

personal friend. ⟨⟨She says—unless it be Clay of Alabama—that Davis has not a personal friend.⟩⟩

Wigfall, fresh from the army and "bearded like the pard,"[5] stroked his beard and said nothing. He has too much common sense not to see how quarreling among ourselves must end.

Brewster's description of the notorious A. D. Banks: "He looks like a man all the time hunting for something that he ought not to have."

The man named Grey (the same gentleman whom Mr. Secretary of War Walker astounded so by his greeting, "Well, sir—and what is your business?") described the battle of the 21st as one succession of blunders redeemed by the indomitable courage of the two-thirds who did not run away on our side.

Dr. Mason[6] said a fugitive of the other side informed him: "A million of men with the devil at their back would not have whipped the rebels at Bulls Run."

That's nice.

Alex Haskell—Gregg's aide-de-camp, Judge Cheves's grandson, William Haskell, *my* friend's brother, who has all human perfections except that he stammers fearfully in speech but fights without let or hindrance—he is engaged to be married to Rebecca Singleton.[7]

We are all glad of it.

We only know Alex as pious and brave and good-looking, but they say he is ambitious most of all.

Shannons are coming to the surface. Capt. William M. Shannon wishes to flesh his maiden sword[8] on the red battlefields of Virginia.

His father is or was a Union man in our nullification row and that brought himself and old Mr. Chesnut together. He or Charles James Shannon is the original Shannon,[9] the Rudolph of Hapsburg. And he is a fine-looking, well-mannered, presentable man—far more so than his mass of pretentious descendants.

He began life as an apprentice to a gin maker. Then he was a carpenter, then a schoolmaster who taught that he might learn himself. Then tax collector, then little shopkeeper—till he grew to be a rich merchant. That is, rich for Camden—some ten thousand or so a year.

He is one of our most respectable citizens. He married the daughter of old Tommy English, a dreadful old drunkard who lived at English's Mile, about two miles from my grandfather's.

5. The fourth of the seven ages of man: "a soldier, full of strange oaths and bearded like the pard," in *As You Like It,* act 2, scene 7.

6. Probably Asst. Surg. Alexander S. Mason, C.S.A., son of James Murray Mason.

7. Alexander Cheves Haskell was the nephew of Langdon Cheves, Jr., and the grandson of former Speaker of the House Langdon Cheves, Sr. His fiancée, Rebecca Coles "Decca" Singleton, was the daughter of Mary Lewis (Carter) Singleton.

8. *Henry IV, Part I,* act 5, scene 4, and Alexander Pope, trans., *Homer's Odyssey* (1725–26), book 20.

9. Charles Shannon was in fact William Shannon's father and the first of this Scots family in Camden. His middle name was John, not James.

There are Englishes and Englishes—great choice among them. Old Tommy was not a good kind. We met him often on the road to Camden—drunk, with a bundle of cow hides under his arm, in his stick gig.

Of the nice Englishes, John married a niece of Governor Means, and James Doby married an heiress, Sarah English.

Capt. William M. Shannon married Miss Henrietta McWillie, said to be an excellent person in every possible relation in life, but mad on the pedigree question (*wife!*).

The last time we met Abram McWillie, he told Mr. Burwell Boykin and Mr. Chesnut of a hoax that he had enjoyed vastly. He hated his sister-in-law, Mrs. William McWillie, and amused himself making her absurd in this wise. In England he went to the Herald's Office and got from "Lyon King at Arms"[1] a McWillie coat of arms and a pedigree. To make the farce more laughable he caused his ancestor to be called Gillies—McGillies (sons of horse boys). Then they were descended from the Lord of the Isles, then Stuarts—really, some suggested, from the pretender branch of the Stuart family.

Abram McWillie's vengeance was ample and complete. Mrs. Kate McWillie bit eagerly at this painted fly. She was like the Ancient Mariner. She held by her glittering eye every man, woman, and child at the Springs that summer and recounted the wondrous tale. She is awfully clever, and few could evade the dreadful story. She had the Springs in one universal titter while she shed tears over the pathetic adventures of her children's forefathers, the unlucky Stuarts.

Hitherto these Shannons, sturdy self-made people like most Americans, stood firmly on their own feet—relied upon their pluck, energy, brains, and manliness. They had businesslike, getting-along-in-the-world ways.

This sudden overwhelming tide of in-law ancestral greatness has turned the captain's head. He is clean daft, a clear case of genealogical, aristocratic mania.

The Confederacy may benefit, however. He may aim to sustain the high family position they have assumed—and he may do dauntless deeds to match the prowess of his wife's high and mighty ancestors.

To come up to sample he must do tall fighting.

The paternal Shannon ancestor, for he is in the singular number, has no nonsense about him. He has made his own fortune and is proud of the fact.

Maternal Englishes were Tories in our revolutionary war, and Quakers originally—wet Quakers, for they drank like fish. And I do not know what they call a fighting Quaker, but courage has been always deemed one of their inheritances.

1. The administrator of Scots heraldry.

All this came to me through Mary Hammy. I did not know anything more than that there was a very good-looking son and daughter of this ilk that we met sometimes.

The young man, handsome and spending in a dashing way all of his father's income, was immeasurably popular and became engaged to Heywards, Haynes, and haute volée generally, always when the damsels were away from home—and always had his hopes quenched by inexorable parents when they heard the story. So he lost his head, too, and said of the McDowalls here, "We won't know them—we must draw the line somewhere."

Now William Douglas McDowall, whose mother was from Castle Douglas, Scotland, had been in copartnership with the elder Shannon in his shopkeeping days. And Mr. Shannon had often beguiled the time, giving his junior partner his early history. Likewise Mr. William D. McDowall had married the granddaughter of *two* signers of the Declaration—our patent of nobility—old President Witherspoon of Princeton College one of them.[2] I forget which is the other, but he was a North Carolina man. So the McDowall blood rose in arms. And these Shannon "pedigree pour rire" stories were made the town topic—and Shannons a laughing stock. I was ill in bed, and Mary Hammy sat by my bedside and recounted this amazing instance of the sudden forgetfulness of their origin which seizes us on this side of the water sooner or later.

Pride of birth must be deep-seated, must be unalienable. Proud people true in everything else will beg, borrow, buy or steal the semblance of it.

———————

Talking all this over at table, I sat between Mr. Barnwell and Wilmot DeSaussure (of excellent-salad memory)—the last named says he has seen entered on the magistrate's book in Charleston—A row between Jesus Christ—who had been assaulted by Judas Iscariot and bailed out of jail by Barabbas.[3]

———————

Mary Hammy has gone to stay at the president's for a few days with Maggie Howell. Mr. Davis paid Mary a compliment—praise from Sir Hubert, &c&c[4]— "She is a girl any mother might be proud to have brought up."

As the French say, "bien élevée."

Mrs. Davis is being utterly upset. She is beginning to hear the carping and faultfinding to which the president is subjected. There must be an opposition in a free country, but it is very uncomfortable. United we stand, divided we fall. She showed us in the New York *Tribune* an extract from an Augusta, Georgia, paper—"Cobb is our man. Davis is at heart a reconstructionist."

2. M. B. C. has inflated the claims of the McDowall family. Susan Kollock (Witherspoon) McDowall was the great-granddaughter of only one signer—John Witherspoon (1723–94), president of Princeton.

3. The 1860s Journal explains that "Christ," "Iscariot," and "Barabbas" were names given by Charleston Jews before the court.

4. English playwright Thomas Morton's *A Cure for the Heartache* (1797), act 2, scene 5.

We may be flies on the wheel. We know our insignificance. But Mrs. Preston and myself have entered into an agreement—our oath is recorded on high. We mean to stand by our president and to stop all faultfinding with the powers that be—if we can, where we can—be they generals or cabinet ministers.

Above all, the head of our government—there!!

Magnanimous, if we are feeble!

《**August 12, 1861.**   . . . I wish Mr. Davis would send *me* to Paris—and so I should not need a South Carolina legislature for anything else.》

August 13, 1861.   《I am trying to look *defeat* of my personal ambition in the face, so if it does come I can better bear it! And if it does not come, the rebound will be so much more delightful.》[5]

Mr. Robert Barnwell says the *Mercury* influence began this opposition to Jeff Davis before he had time to do wrong. They were offended—not with him so much as with the man who was put in what they considered Barnwell Rhett's rightful place. The latter had howled nullification, secession, &c so long, when he found his ideas taken up by all the Confederate world, he felt he had a vested right to the leadership. He says, "If this influence combine with Orr's country, the northwest of South Carolina,[6] Mr. C will not be sent back to the Senate. He, Mr. C, is now the breakwater between those two extremes."

If so, think of being [*illegible word*] to Camden—those long, long, weary days. Outside friendship with only a handful of people. And no intercourse with those who up to this time have been my world—the Judge's family. God's will be done. "If I had served my God"—as old Wolsey said in his wrath—"as I served that family!"[7]

But it will be if vox populi wills it in this instance—I mean my stay-at-*home-ativeness*.

* * *

Johnston Pettigrew came last night to thank Mr. Chesnut for his trouble in arranging the matter of his regiment.[8] This clever man has studied his profession and prepared himself to take command when the time came. He has been in the field, too. He went to Italy and trained himself in those wars.

5. Anticipating more than one "defeat," M. B. C. has in mind J. C.'s approaching contest in the S.C. legislature for election to the Confederate Senate, as well as her hopes for the Paris or London appointments.

6. James Lawrence Orr of Anderson District was a U.S. congressman from 1848 to 1859, Speaker of the House from 1857 to 1859, and a member of the S.C. secession convention. He had just been named to fill the vacancy left by Judge Withers's resignation from the Provisional Confederate Congress.

7. A play on *Henry VIII*, act 3, scene 2.

8. After fighting in the Italian wars of unification in 1858–59, Charleston lawyer James Johnston Pettigrew had trained S.C. militia. Chesnut helped secure his election as colonel of the Twelfth N.C. Regiment.

He gave us a laughable account of Bonham's difficulties with raw troops and his tough faculty of surmounting them. They have a world of things to learn—all of them—before they can be accomplished soldiers. They are ready enough to risk life and limb, but that is a small part of it.

He said, "No general ever had more to learn than Bonham," when he first saw him in command, and truly he believed no one had ever learned more in a given time.

A handsome Spaniard—Cuban—leader of rebellion there, too. So like Beauregard as to be mistaken for him—and yet Beauregard is not handsome, they say. I have only seen his counterfeit presentment—photographs—which are called, wittily, "Justice without mercy." So happened in Charleston I did not meet him.

This Gonzales, beside his fine person, has a fine voice. He sings divinely. He married a Miss Elliott of South Carolina.[9]

Tonight he told me that Gen. Robert E. Lee was fencing with Rosecrans in the western mountains of Virginia.[1] Miss Lee[2] is staying with Mrs. Stanard. Mrs. Smith Lee has rooms here at the Arlington.

Went to Miss Sally Tompkins's hospital today. Mrs. James Alfred Jones[3] and Mrs. Carter[4] were assisting Miss Tompkins.

Jordan, Beauregard's A.D.C., still writes to Mr. C that the mortality among the raw troops in that camp is fearful. And everybody seems to be doing all they can. Think of the British sick and wounded, away off in the Crimea. These people are only a half-day's journey by rail from Richmond.

With a grateful heart [I] record a fact. Reconciliation of the Wigfalls. They dined at the president's yesterday, and the little Wigfall girls stayed all night. ⟨⟨*Hypocrisy.* I can no longer respect Mrs. Wigfall.⟩⟩

Seward is fêting the outsiders—Napoleon, cousin of the emperor, and Russell, of the omnipotent London *Times.* There is no outside to our Confederate stockade.

Mr. Clayton reports to us a speech of Vice President Stephens. "That the revolution had only begun—and that if we were wise in our conduct we should soon have Washington, and some of the Northern states would join us."

9. Fleeing Cuba after an abortive uprising against Spain in 1848, Ambrosio José Gonzales settled in Beaufort, S.C., and married Harriet Rutledge Elliott. He was in Richmond, overseeing the manufacture of cannon at the Tredegar Iron Works as colonel and chief of artillery for the Department of S.C.
1. Lee had been sent from Richmond at the end of July to coordinate (but not command) the Confederate forces confronting the Union army in western Va. now led by McClellan's replacement, Brig. Gen. William Starke Rosecrans of Ohio.
2. One of Lee's four daughters.
3. Mary (Henry) Jones, wife of a Richmond attorney.
4. Martha Milledge (Flournoy) Carter, widow of Dr. John Carter of Augusta, Ga.

Certainly we undervalued ourselves—we had no idea they would consider it such ruin to lose us. They abused us and called us so worthless—indeed, seemed to find us a disgrace they would be glad to shake off—we had every reason to think!

It is the old story of the Atlantic and Pacific republic, Mississippi being the line now, and not Rocky Mountain watershed.

August 14, 1861. Boykin's Rangers in tantrums because Joe Kershaw says he won the battle. The Rangers came too late. They were on the ground only after the turn of the tide. They left Richmond that morning.

Last night there was a crowd of men to see us, and they were so clever, so markedly critical, &c. I made a futile effort to record their sayings, but sleep and heat overcame me. Today I cannot remember a word. Captain Hartstene, Mr. Seddon, Mr. Mason, &c. ⟨⟨Mr. Seddon was very agreeable and the cleverest man I saw last night, but I do not remember anything he said.⟩⟩

One of Mr. Mason's stories—a thing he heard on the cars—one of our sources of reliable information:

A man entered, of very respectable appearance, and standing in the gangway announced, "I am just from the seat of the war."

Out came pencil and paper—newspaper men on the qui vive.

"Is Fairfax Court House burned?" they asked.

"Yes, burnt yesterday."

"I am just from there—left it standing all right an hour or so ago," said another individual.

"Oh," explained "just-from-the-seat-of-war," "I must do them justice to say they burned only the tavern. They did not want to tear up and burn anything but the railroad."

"There is no railroad at Fairfax Court House," objected the man just from Fairfax.

"Oh! Indeed!" said the seat of the war. "I did not know that. Is that so?" And he coolly seated himself and began talking of something else.

We had a more reliable style of witness last night who described Cash's interview with Ely. Cash was for short work—Black Flag entirely.

"Take him back and shoot him."

This was by no means Ely's idea of war. Of course Cash was stopped in time.[5]

One prisoner had his own way of making himself disagreeable. He was confined in a stable, where he howled at intervals the livelong night. Next day a negro and this parson (maybe what these daredevils called howling was psalm singing or praying aloud) were put in an ambulance to be sent to Richmond.

---

5. Ely wrote in his diary that Cash put a pistol "directly to my head" and said, "G___d d___n your white-livered soul! I'll blow your brains out on the spot." After two Confederates kept their colonel from fulfilling his threat, one explained to the frightened congressman that Cash was drunk. Charles Lanman, ed., *Journal of Alfred Ely, A Prisoner of War in Richmond* (1862), pp. 15–16.

Some hardhearted soldier shouted, "Shoot that congressman—hang that parson—give the negro a good thrashing and a good master."

So much for the amenities of camp life.

Nothing worse than this chaffing befell them, however. Mauvaise plaisanterie only was fired at them.

Mr. Snowden adds another word to Prince Napoleon's already reported speeches. In compliment, no doubt, to his English-speaking hosts, he said "damn" more than once. Credible witnesses so testify.

Read Motley's *Dutch Republic* today—and whenever I can find a quiet moment.

He is consul in the Netherlands[6] now—or minister, if they have one from U.S.A. there. And he ought to be. The oft spoken of, rarely found—the right man in the right place.

―――――

Our people are lashing themselves into a fury against the prisoners. Only the mob in any country would do that. But I am told to be quiet. Decency and propriety will not be forgotten. And the prisoners will be treated as prisoners of war ought to be in a civilized country.

―――――

This was all told me at the DeLeons. They are people of the world, though they began as my dear Columbia DeLeons, who were so good to me when I ran some risks of smallpox as a schoolgirl at Mrs. Faust's school.

―――――

It was suggested that this was not to be our very last battle and that Joe Kershaw and A. H. Boykin and his Rangers may figure in the *Gazette* yet, to their hearts' content.[7]

When Beauregard saw our Joseph's report to the *Mercury*,[8] he stormed— "that militia idiot!"

―――――

These people want to gather a crop of fame when they have hardly begun to sow the seed.

Hold on—wait. In patience possess your souls.[9]

August 15, 1861.   Mrs. Randolph came. With her were the Freelands—Rose and Maria.[1] These men raved over Mrs. Randolph's beauty—called her a mag-

―――――

6. John Lothrop Motley of Mass., author of *The Rise of the Dutch Republic* (1856), had been appointed minister to Austria, not the Netherlands.

7. An allusion to Thackeray: for his characters, the London *Gazette* was the newspaper of record.

8. Kershaw had written several pieces for the Charleston *Mercury* glorifying the role of his troops at Bull Run.

9. Slightly misquoted from Luke 21:19.

1. Rosalie and Maria, popular belles of Confederate society, were the daughters of Richmond tobacco-factory owner Jonathan Freeland.

nificent specimen of the finest type of dark-eyed, rich, and glowing Southern womankind. Clear brunette she is, with the reddest lips, the whitest teeth, and glorious eyes—there is no other word for them.

Having given Mrs. Randolph the prize among Southern beauties, Mr. Clayton said Prentiss[2] was the finest Southern orator. Mr. Marshall and Mr. Barnwell dissented. They preferred William C. Preston.[3]

Mr. Chesnut had found Colquitt[4] the best or most effective stump orator.

Saw Henry Deas Nott.[5] He is just from Paris via New York. Says New York is ablaze with martial fire. At no time during the Crimean War was there ever in Paris the show of soldiers preparing for the war such as he saw at New York. The face of the earth seemed covered with marching regiments.

"Oh—the Crimea. That was playing at war, you know. It was so far away from Paris or London or St. Petersburg. Here it comes home to you."

"Play! That's all you know about it. 'Fight like a Turk'—and it was Turkey clear through—you know the proverb."

"Yes, and I know another. When Greek meets Greek—and the tug-of-war is on one's doorsteps. Was not Spartacus the man who headed the slaves in their outburst for freedom? Well, we have to fight in front, with one eye behind for Spartacus."

How glad Mr. Preston is of his commission—says he is too large for an errand boy, even Beauregard's.[6]

Heard from Captain Buchanan[7] of Maryland the reverse of Deas Nott's appalling picture of New York as armed camp.

Captain B saw the disbanded regiments going home and rejoicing on their way.

---

2. Seargent Smith Prentiss of Miss., Whig congressman from 1838 to 1839, won his reputation as an orator with a three-day speech before the House in 1837, arguing unsuccessfully that he had won a contested congressional election.

3. William Campbell Preston (1794–1860), brother of John Smith Preston, was U.S. senator from S.C. from 1833 to 1842.

4. Alfred Holt Colquitt was a former congressman, a member of the Ga. secession convention, and an officer in the C.S.A.

5. Henry Junius Nott, whose mother was a Deas (see p. 99, n. 1).

6. Preston had been named assistant adjutant general with the rank of lieutenant colonel on Beauregard's staff.

7. Franklin Buchanan, organizer and first superintendent of the U.S. Naval Academy from 1845 to 1847, resigned from the U.S. Navy in April 1861, and was commissioned a captain of the C.S.N. in Sept.

Evans has a fight on hand at Leesburg.
Lee and Loring are face-to-face with Rosecrans.[8]

"All the blood of all the Howards" could not save its possessor from one of Seward's dungeons.[9] John Eager Howard is our Carolina Howard—the commander of the Maryland line in South Carolina during our first war for independence. The Maryland line saved us always when the local militia gave way.

Marion[1] and Sumter may not have had gigantic armies at their command. But so much more genius to work with small means.

Without the checks and hindrances and defeats in detail by Marion and Sumter, Cornwallis would have had safe and comfortable haven in South Carolina. He would not have been driven into Washington's trap at Yorktown. Our guerillas made it too hot for him in the South. *So* I have no patience with these people who deride the persistent effective action of the Swamp Fox because, say,

"Why, at Cowpens there were not a dozen men killed."

They tell me not to feel so disheartened at the way South Carolina men brag—because we are thrown with them so much. If I were with Georgians or Mississippians, the local color would come out as strong.

"Not more than five hundred effective men in Hampton's Legion kept the whole Yankee army at bay until half past two. Then just as Hampton was wounded and half his colonels shot, Cash and Kershaw" (from Mrs. Smith Lee, audibly: "How about Kirby Smith?") "dashed in and not only turned the tide but would have driven the fugitives into Washington, but Beauregard recalled them."

Mr. C finds all this very amusing, as he posted many of the regiments and all the time was carrying orders over the field. The discrepancies of all these private memories amuse him. But he smiles pleasantly and lets every man tell the tale his own way.

Mr. Barnwell says: "How we do crow—gamecocks indeed. Fighting we love and the glorification afterward."

Too much modesty does not oppress us.

The Howard who is incarcerated married one of Star-Spangled Key's daughters. "Even that Key could not unlock Seward's hard heart," said somebody.... [2]

---

8. At Leesburg, in northern Va., Confederates under Brig. Gen. Nathan George "Shanks" Evans of S.C. were watching for a Federal advance across the Potomac. Brig. Gen. William Wing Loring of N.C. was the titular commander of the Confederate army in western Va.

9. Alexander Pope, *An Essay on Man* (1733–34), epistle 4, lines 211–16. M. B. C. is referring to the arrest of Charles Howard, president of the Baltimore Board of Police, on July 1. Howard was a member of one of Md.'s most prominent families: his father, Col. John Eager Howard (see p. 89, n. 2), was a Revolutionary War hero, a member of Washington's cabinet, and a U.S. senator; his wife was a daughter of Francis Scott Key.

1. S.C. partisan leader Francis Marion, the Swamp Fox of the Revolution.

2. References to her reading and quotations are deleted here.

August 16, 1861.   Shanks Evans, they say, has partly captured Banks's army.

And the Federals have taken Aquia Creek.[3]

Mr. Barnwell says fame is an article usually homemade. "You must write your own puffs or superintend their manufacture, and you must see the newspapers print your own military reports. No one else will give you half the credit you take to yourself. No one will look after your fine name before the world, with the loving interest and faith you have in yourself."

This thing of telling a lie until you believe it. They say George the 4th actually believed he had been at Waterloo, disguised as a major. ⟨⟨Then came Mr. and Mrs. Preston, and Mr. Chesnut made the visit detestable by grumbling and complaining and talking *at me,* all the time abusing everybody. He has even got me in a scrape by repeating what Allen Green said to me. I feel miserably today.⟩⟩

Kentucky to the rescue! Crittenden says we began the war—and it must be pushed on us vigorously.[4]

Russell's letters are becoming utterly abominable—not half so bad, however, as his accounts of the British in India. Those Indian letters show up British philanthropy when their own blood is up!

An inferior race to rise against them!

They do not take John Brown views of the sacred rights of insurrection. According to the admirers of Brown, the East Indians treated the English women and children just as they had cause to do.

August 17, 1861.   The victory is in Missouri this time.[5] Far enough off for us to believe anything we choose.

After all, Johnston Pettigrew has been given a crack regiment from North Carolina. He will give a good account of himself—anywhere.

3. False rumors. Maj. Gen. Nathaniel Prentiss Banks of Mass., former Speaker of the House, was commander of Union forces in the Shenandoah Valley.

4. On July 22, the U.S. House of Representatives had adopted resolutions introduced by John Jordan Crittenden of Ky. that blamed the outbreak of the war on the South. But the resolutions, accepted by the Senate three days later, were less hostile than M. B. C. allowed: they declared that the North sought to preserve the Union and not to interfere with the "established institutions" of the South.

5. At Wilson's Creek, Mo., on Aug. 10, Confederate troops led by Ben McCulloch and Sterling Price stopped a Union advance with more than one thousand casualties on each side.

I was ill. Mary Hammy says Shot-Pouch Walker[6] has the handsomest A.D.C. she ever saw and that Gonzales is splendid in gray uniform—or in blue, I forget which, but the uniform he wore today.

No further war news from her. Report of table talk.

Captain Shannon of the Kirkwoods called—stayed three hours. Has not been under fire yet—but keen to hear or to see the flashing of the guns. Proud of himself, proud of his company, but proudest of all that he has no end of the bluest blood of the low country in his troop—F.F.C.'s,[7] he says, of the first water.

He seemed to find my knitting a pair of socks a day for the soldiers droll in some way. The yarn is coarse. He has been so short a time from home he does not know how the poor soldier needs them.

He was so overpoweringly flattering to my husband that I found him very pleasant company.

Read *Oliver Twist* again. ⟨⟨Had forgotten how good it is.⟩⟩

August 18, 1861.   Found it quite exciting to have a spy[8] drinking his tea with us. Perhaps because I knew his profession, I did not like his face. He is said to have a scheme by which Washington will fall into our hands like an overripe peach.

Gonzales after tea told me the story of the Lopez expedition.[9] "Magna pars fui"—at least he was wounded in it. And a wound makes any part great. His way of telling it all was modest and so interesting that the evening slipped away very pleasantly. *Cubans* must be very nice if Señor Gonzales is a sample.

Miss Sally Tompkins laughed at Mrs. Carter—whose face is so strikingly handsome the wounded men could not help looking at her, and one was not so bad off but he burst into flowery compliment. Mrs. Carter turned scarlet with surprise and indignation. Miss Sallie Tompkins said, "If you could only leave your beauty at the door and bring in your goodness and *faculty*."

6. Brig. Gen. William Henry Talbot Walker of Ga. received extensive gunshot wounds in both the Seminole and Mexican wars. Each time, doctors held out no hope of recovery.

7. First Families of Carolina.

8. Identified in the 1860s Journal as George Donellen, a member of the Confederate spy ring in Washington that had sent information on Union troop movements to Beauregard before Bull Run.

9. In 1850, Gonzales served as adjutant general in the filibustering expedition of Cuban revolutionaries and American annexationists led by Narciso Lopez, a vain attempt to free Cuba from Spain. Because of illness, Gonzales remained behind the next year when a second sortie ended with the capture of the expedition and the execution of Lopez and fifty Southerners.

Found that Mary Hammy is competent to pronounce on a man's comeliness. Walker's A.D.C. is all she said he was. A picture of manly beauty. Captain Hartstene, who breakfasted with me, thought women attached too much importance to mere outside show—&c&c.

Harvey and Magrath—in the Fort Sumter business—squally![1]

Governor Means means to be a brigadier. Governor Manning has gone home, with similar intentions, I fancy.

The day for high and mighty A.D.C.'s is over. War means business now, and a young and trained staff is desirable.

Boteler, another of Mr. Chesnut's Princeton College friends, has been taken prisoner.[2] Last year he was distracting us with his Union prônes. A Yankee stockade will convert him effectually.

Mrs. Wynne said, "England and France recognized us yesterday." She had it from a sure hand.

Prophet he must be, too, as it takes some little time to get the news.

Some suggested the spirits had brought the news—up the table legs, no doubt. They annihilate time and space—if they don't make two lovers happy.

The newspapers contain news from over the water that is encouraging.

Some of the Yankee prisoners of a better sort are publishing letters in the *Herald,* denying the stories of their ill treatment here.

I doubt if they are (or that our prisoners in their hands) on a bed of roses, all the same.

《Mr. Chesnut has decided against the military. Hope it may be for the best, but I do not feel that to be the case—far from it! . . . I feel so deeply mortified that Mr. C will not accept a commission in the army—everybody says he could get whatever he wanted.》[3]

1. A native South Carolinian, James E. Harvey was a columnist for the Philadelphia *North American* and a moderate Republican anxious to avert war during the spring of 1861. Working with William Seward, Harvey sent a series of telegrams about Lincoln's plans for reinforcing Fort Sumter to a boyhood friend, S.C. secretary of state Andrew Gordon Magrath. Discovery of the telegrams after the war began led many Northerners to demand Harvey's recall from his new position as U.S. minister to Portugal.

2. Alexander Robinson Boteler, American party congressman from 1859 to 1861 and a member of the Provisional Confederate Congress, had been taken from his home in Jefferson County, Va., by Union troops on Aug. 13 but was released the same day.

3. Aug. 19 entry in the 1860s Journal.

Mr. Barnwell urges Mr. Chesnut to remain in the Senate. So many generals—and men anxious to be. He says Mr. C can do his country more good by wise counsels where they are most needed. I do not say to the contrary. I dare not throw my influence on the army side. For if anything happened!!

Why am I so frightfully ambitious?[4]

Now I will set out from henceforth to care only for my country's salvation.

Johnston Pettigrew has been again disappointed. His regiment is ordered to Yorktown. He wanted to go to Beauregard, as the hottest fire lies in that direction.

Wigfalls gone—all of them.

Mr. Miles told us last night that he had another letter from General Beauregard. The general wants to know if Mr. Miles has delivered his message to Colonel Kershaw. Mr. Miles says he has not done so—neither does he mean to do it. They must settle these matters of veracity according to their own military etiquette. He is a civilian once more. It is foolish wrangle. Colonel Kershaw ought to have reported to his commander in chief and not made an independent report and published it.

Yesterday in the Congress Mr. Chesnut spoke against confiscation of the enemy's things. He says confiscation conflicts with states rights. I know he is right. Can't say I understand it all. Then there is sequestration. That I will give the go-by. I understand it less than the other thing. I hate all bankruptcy and cheating creditors—on all sides and from every quarter, at home and abroad.

Today he is ill in bed, the confiscation effort too much for him, maybe.

Mary Hammy too is ill in the next room, which serves as my dressing room. When not downstairs, I take a chair and seat myself near a window in the corridor—regularly turned out.

While he has fever he gives me all the reasons why the Confiscation Act conflicts with the laws of nations.

Today at dinner an awkward scene. How I wished Mr. Chesnut had been there. He has so much tact as a *pacificator*.

If these men, General Walker and Hon. Robert Barnwell, were but as common folk, I should say "words had passed." And ugly ones.

Two Yankee officers who fought or figured at Manassas have since deserted and come over to us.

I can understand how deserters should be detestable, come they from East or West, North or South.

4. In the 1860s Journal, Aug. 18, 1861, this is: "Why was I born so frightfully ambitious?"

They, the deserters, are going into our army. General Walker said, "If I had had a brother killed at Manassas, I could shoot down these men at sight."

Mr. Barnwell gave that little twittering, nervous laugh of his.

"And then you'd be hanged."

"Never. Twenty thousand Georgians are here. They would create a counter-revolution before they would permit a hair of my head to be touched."

Mr. Barnwell repeated his offensive little laugh.

"Then you would be hanged. You ought to be hanged if you commit murder."

This he fired off at regular intervals, and Shot-Pouch Walker literally raved.

"No, no. My Georgians would know the reason why, &c&c."

Mr. Barnwell grew very quiet but continued his fatuous smile and to the last stuck to his original proposition.

"You'd be hanged."

This made me wretched. Mr. Barnwell was right, but why would he say it anymore?

I was so uncomfortable—as soon as silence prevailed, I left the table. I made a good deal of commotion in leaving the table, on purpose—dropped things to be picked up: fan, handkerchief—all to divert them from their madness or folly. And a man is always in such a faze about his dignity—what is due his own self-respect, &c&c&c, and so contemptuous of feminine folly!

Mr. Snowden thought it funny to say he left Governor Manning all in tears at Manassas Junction—deserted by his pals, Preston, Wigfall, Chesnut, Miles & Co.

Mr. Snowden was deeply offended with our president, who asked him significantly, "Are there no double-barreled shotguns in Maryland?"

And someone else ⟨⟨Maggie Howell⟩⟩ said, with girlish insouciance, "Now I don't like Maryland."

"Poor Maryland," cried Mr. Snowden, with double-barreled scorn. Then he told of some Baltimore belle in the old time, saying to a Frenchman, "Oh, I disapprove of Napoleon highly."

"Poor Napoleon," sighed the Frenchman. "I hope he will never hear it. It would crush him if he did."

Then said the redoubtable Dick Snowden: "Fortunately, with all her troubles Maryland does not know who dislikes *her*. I don't wonder. These bowie-knife six-shooter western people find civilized Maryland rather tame and flat for their amusement."

Someone suggested he did not do Baltimore justice—"plug uglies," "blood tubs," and the everlasting street rows there would satisfy the most sensational in the way of bludgeon sport—and murder as a fine art.

Our government declines to trust the Washington spy's plot, and the spy's scheme to blow up the Capitol by inside and social influence has fallen through.

The New York *Tribune* is so unfair. It began howling to get rid of us. We were so wicked. Now that we are so willing to leave them to their overrighteous self-consciousness, they cry, "Crush our enemy—or they will subjugate us."

The idea that we want to invade or subjugate! We would only be too grateful to be left alone. Only let us alone—we ask no more of gods or men.

Today Mr. C sent to Clyburn twenty-five dollars in gold—said Clyburn being in a strait for cash. And he did it cheerfully, this small loan, because our man Armsted told us that at a hotel table once he saw the aforesaid Clyburn "take up a chair to knock down a man who was abusing Marster."

Mr. C has given his riding horse to General Toombs, I am sure for not half so good a reason.

And Clayton says, "If our bold Brigadier Toombs does only half the mischief he threatens, we will soon have no enemy for Toombs to try and scare."

A General Wool says, "This war is an attempt to extend the area of slavery."[5]

Can that be, when not one-third of our volunteer army are slave-owners—and not one-third of that third who does not dislike slavery as much as Mrs. Stowe[6] or Greeley?[7] And few have found their hatred or love of it as remunerative an investment.

At any rate, they have found they cannot trust to help from the black brother. He will not rise and cut our throats in the rear. They are not really enemies of their masters—and yet I believe they are all spies for the other side. Inconsistent?

There is woman's logical, lucid talk for you—and yet it is all true, if a little confused.

States Rights Gist, who is a real personage—and not an odd name merely—gallantly led the Fourth Alabama when all their officers were killed.[8]

Charles Scott, whilom representative in [the] Washington Congress, from California, was born in Virginia—and his wife is an Alabama woman. He is in our army—entered as a private, for gallantry in action has already been promoted. He is now a major.

The *Mercury*, who cannot make out the whereabouts of all those gunboats, seems to fear they will forget Port Royal. Its noble harbor and its weak defenses it harps upon!

The heat and the excitement—and a sort of slow fever that subdues me quite and takes away all appetite, leaving me to live on tomatoes alone—and Wilmot DeSaussure's salad dressing.

5. U.S. Brig. Gen. John Ellis Wool, a veteran of the War of 1812, in a speech in New York on Aug. 15.

6. Harriet (Beecher) Stowe, author of *Uncle Tom's Cabin* (1852).

7. Horace Greeley, editor of the New York *Tribune*.

8. Brig. Gen. States Rights Gist, a lawyer from Union District, S.C., had performed this feat at Bull Run.

Today he had so much politics to whisper to me I forget even the tomatoes raw. It was all about the rapid growth of the party forming against Mr. Davis. The old cry—dissatisfied Georgians. Cobbs, Keitt, Boyce, Hammond.

Telegrams say Commodore Porter in irons for secession sentiment.[9]

Not true. He held very [different] opinions when I saw him last. Twice last year was I well scolded for South Carolina—by proxy, I may say. Captain Porter blew me up at Mrs. Slidell's[1] garden party, where we had a long talk. The street was bridged over with a tent &c&c—and so Mr. Corcoran's[2] grounds were used for the fête. It was there we were walking. At Hoboken, where Mary Stevens was married, General Scott took a shot at me. He thundered and threatened, and I did not heed his warning. I knew it was coming, and I dreaded it. But I answered as best I might for my side.

Ben McCulloch has, they say, swept away all Yankees from Missouri. Too good to be true.

The soldiers visit all their disasters upon Commissary General Northrop's head. They say the army at Manassas is paralyzed by illness.

From the New York *Herald* we see that at Washington they are calling for all sorts of regiments—from anywhere and anybody—anything. That foolish god Pan is still tooting in their woods, at least round about Washington.

To think! The irrepressible—the notorious—A. D. Banks indulged in a private street fight yesterday. Have not heard who his antagonist was.

Clayton, who is always taunting us, he has an old pamphlet history of Oglethorpe. This account says the British never cared for Georgia, did not value it at all except as a barrier between South Carolina and the savage native beyond.

"Now," he says, "Georgia will still protect you from harm—you poor hotheaded creatures! Leap before you look, little Carolina—you are still 'sayings'; Georgia is 'doings.'"

That beast Nat Willis[3] still peeping around the world. This time he saw Lincoln changing his shirt, and he describes it, of course—and is our Nat's small way of singing and stinging. The great Illinoisian took exactly 22 minutes to dress, by Willis's watch, all at an open window—Franklin's air bath thrown in.

9. A false report about Cdre. William David Porter of the U.S. Navy, whom M. B. C. describes as "my friend" in the 1860s Journal.

1. Mathilde (Deslondes) Slidell, wife of John Slidell.

2. William Wilson Corcoran, a Washington banker and philanthropist sympathetic to the Confederacy.

3. Popular journalist Nathaniel Parker Willis, then Washington correspondent of the New York *Home Journal.*

Picture Lincoln adonizing. They say Lincoln is frightfully uncouth and ugly—with the keenest sense of coarse humor.

Gen. Tom Drayton[4] asks Mr. C how many scalps he took at Manassas. Mr. C says, "I saved my own, you see, but then at Falls Church we took forty prisoners—whom we did not scalp."

It is General Lee's army now who are abusing Northrop. They can't move, either, for want of commissary stores. That terrible Northrop.

Went to the hospital with a carriageload of peaches and grapes. Made glad the hearts of some men thereby. When my supply gave out, those who had none looked so wistfully as I passed out that I made a second raid on the market. Those eyes sunk in cavernous depths haunted me as they followed me from bed to bed.

Met Anthony Kennedy from Camden.[5] He coolly helped himself and ate my soldiers' peaches—as if peaches grew as trees here, free to all.

Mr. Chesnut angry with Mr. Barnwell because the latter defeated a private bill for Edward Stockton's relief.[6]

Edward Cantey Stockton, our cousin, is always in trouble.

Mr. C rode with the president today—and now he has fever again. It is almost a tertian, it is so regular in its coming.

《In a bad humor—I do not know yet if it is because Mr. Barnwell defeated Edward Stockton or that the president offended him.》[7]

Wilmot DeSaussure harrowed my soul by an account of a recent death by drowning on the beach at Sullivan's Island. A Mr. Porcher who was trying to save his sister's life lost his own and his child's.

People seem to die out of the army quite as much as in it.

Mrs. Randolph presided in all her beautiful majesty at an aid association.

The ladies were old ones and all wanted their own way. They were cross-grained and contradictory, and the blood would mount rebelliously into Mrs.

---

4. Thomas Fenwick Drayton, a Beaufort District planter and former U.S. Army officer, was not named a brigadier general until Sept. 28.

5. John Doby Kennedy's father, a wealthy Scots merchant.

6. Edward Cantey Stockton of Camden, a second lieutenant in the Confederate marines, had been dismissed from the U.S. Navy in 1858. He was a cousin of both J. C. and M. B. C.

7. Under Aug. 22 in the 1860s Journal.

Randolph's clear-cut cheek, but she held her own with dignity and grace—quand même.

One of the causes of disturbance: Mrs. Randolph proposed to divide everything sent us equally with the Yankee wounded and sick prisoners. Some were enthusiastic from a Christian point of view. Some shrieked in wrath at the bare idea of putting our noble soldiers on a par with Yankees—living, dying, or dead. Shrill and long and loud it was. Fierce dames some of them—august, severe matrons—who evidently had not been accustomed to hear the other side of any argument from anybody, just old enough to find the last pleasure in life in power—and the power to make their claws felt.

Russell is evenhanded. He scores the Yankees for cowardice after all their vaunting and trumpeting of their prowess. And now—how will we feel if we are ever defeated? We vaunt ourselves, too. It is rather painful, the extent of boasting we do now.

Souvent de tous nos maux, la raison est le père.

Those old ladies had all philanthropic schemes, but they held to their own and would listen to no other. They had sharp tempers—and Mrs. Randolph was willful and masterful. Maybe such warmth will hurry on the good work.

General Walker (Shot-Pouch) fears McClellan will take advantage of our army being prostrated by disease to attack us. One good of Bulls Run: it has made them make haste cautiously.

In Whiting's command 400 out of 1,700 are unfit for service.

A most pathetic account of Lyon's death in Missouri[8]—no doubt with a view to rouse Northern hearts to action.

8. Brig. Gen. Nathaniel Lyon died commanding the U.S. forces at the battle of Wilson's Creek on Aug. 10.

James Chesnut, Sr., as a student at Princeton. Watercolor on ivory by James Peale. Yale University Art Gallery. Gift of Mrs. John Hill Morgan.

James Chesnut, Sr., as master of Mulberry Plantation. Portrait by Gilbert Stuart. Privately owned.

Mary Cox Chesnut. Portrait by Gilbert Stuart. Privately owned.

Stephen Decatur Miller, father of Mary Boykin (Miller) Chesnut. Artist unknown. Privately owned.

James Chesnut, Jr., husband of Mary Boykin Chesnut. Portrait by William Harrison Scarborough. Privately owned.

Mulberry Plantation big house. The Kershaw County Historical Society.

rance hall at Mulberry. The Kershaw County Historical Society.

Mulberry Plantation. An aerial photograph of the Wateree River winding through much of the proper
with the big house at the top.

Mulberry Plantation. An aerial view of the house and grounds.

Stairwell at Mulberry. Mary's quarters and library were on the top floor. The Kershaw County Historical Society.

John Bell ("Sam") Hood. Photograph by Matthew B. Brady. Library of Congress.

Sally Buchanan Campbell ("Buck") Preston. The portrait bust, by Hiram Powers, has suffered mutilation. The Columbia Historical Foundation.

Catherine Miller Williams, Mary Chesnut's favorite sister, Kate. Portrait by Samuel Stillman Osgood, 1856. In the possession of Mrs. Hendrik B. van Rensselaer, Basking Ridge, New Jersey.

VIII

"I Am Always on the Women's Side"

August 23, 1861. A brother of Dr. Garnett[1] has come fresh and straight from Cambridge, Massachusetts—says (or is said to have said—and all the difference there is between the two) that recruiting up there is dead. He came by Cincinnati and Petersburg. Says all the way through it was so sad and mournful and quiet—looked like Sunday.

Meantime the camp is a hospital. That terrible sickness continues there—and with it the abuse of the person in power. They seem to hold the War Department responsible, as if they could help it.

I asked Mr. Brewster if it were true Senator Toombs had turned brigadier.

"Yes. Soldiering is in the air. Everyone will have a touch of it. Toombs could not stay in the cabinet."

"Why?"

"Incompatibility of temper. He rides too high a horse—that is, for so despotic a person as Jeff Davis. I have tried to find out the row but can't. Mrs. Toombs has been out with them all for months."

It will leak out. Everything does. But it takes a little time.

There is a perfect magazine of discord and discontent in that cabinet—only wants a hand to apply the torch and up they go. Toombs says old Memminger[2] has his back up as high as any!

Gonzales 〈〈 he likes so much to hear of his likeness to General Beauregard 〉〉 lit my candle for me—and at the foot of the stairs gave me a bag of quinine pills for my husband, whose fever lingers still.

These foreigners have a way of doing things—gracious and graceful—no native [of the] U.S.A. can approach.

---

1. Dr. Alexander Yelverton Peyton Garnett left his private practice in Washington, D.C., to become director of two Richmond military hospitals and private physician to Jefferson Davis and his family.

2. Christopher Gustavus Memminger, a fifty-eight-year-old Charleston lawyer, was secretary of the Confederate treasury.

But oh, such a day! since I wrote this morning.

Have been with Mrs. Randolph to all the hospitals.

I can never again shut out of view the sights I saw of human misery. I sit thinking, shut my eyes, and see it all. Thinking—yes, and there is enough to think about now, God knows. Gillands was the worst. Long rows of ill men on cots. Ill of typhoid fever, of every human ailment—dinner tables, eating, drinking, wounds being dressed—all horrors, to be taken in at one glance. That long tobacco house!

At the almshouse, Dr. Gibson in charge. He married a Miss Ayer of Philadelphia. He is fine looking and has charming manners. The very beau idéal of a family physician—so suave and gentle and pleasant. The Sisters of Charity are his nurses. That makes all the difference in the world. The sisters! They told us Mrs. Ricketts was there. Mrs. Randolph did not ask for her. One elderly sister—withered and wrinkled and yet with the face of an angel—spoke severely to a young surgeon. "Stop that skylarking," she said. And he answered, "Where have you sent that pretty sister you had here yesterday? We all fell in love with her."

The venerable Sister of Charity was ministering to a Yankee with his arm cut off.

Everything was so clean—and in perfect order.

Dr. Gibson approached this presiding genius and asked her some questions. I did not hear her answer, but he said: "No. No, I have no time now—but it will be all right. Tomorrow we two will lay our heads together and arrange a new plan."

"Stop, doctor. We can't wait until tomorrow. It must be done tonight."

"All right," laughed the doctor—and he gravely turned to us. We had the joke all to ourselves, however. She did not see it.

After a while she said, "Honi soit qui mal y pense."

I said, "We did not know you angels of mercy made merry sometimes over your work." The wounded soldiers enjoyed every word that was said.

Occasionally one looked sulky, for were we not the hated Southerners? But I think as a general rule all that was forgotten in the hospital.

Then we went to the St. Charles. Horrors upon horrors again—want of organization. Long rows of them dead, dying. Awful smells, awful sights.

A boy from home had sent for me. He was lying in a cot, ill of fever. Next him a man died in convulsions while we stood there.

I was making arrangements with a nurse, hiring him to take care of this lad. I do not remember any more, for I fainted. Next that I knew of, the doctor and Mrs. Randolph were having me, a limp rag, put into the carriage at the door of the hospital.

Fresh air, I daresay, brought me to. First of all we had given our provisions to our Carolinians at Miss Sally Tompkins's. There they were, nice and clean and merry as grigs.

As we drove home, we brought the doctor with us, I was so upset.

He said: "Look at that Georgia regiment marching there. Look at their servants on the sidewalk. I have been counting them—making an estimate. There is $16,000—sixteen thousand dollars worth of negro property which can go off on its own legs to the Yankees whenever it pleases."

We saw among the wounded at the Federal hospital a negro soldier. He was with the others, on equal terms—and a sister was nursing him.

Russell, I think, in his capacity of Englishman despises both sides.

He derides us equally, North and South. He prefers to attribute Bulls Run to Yankee cowardice rather than to Southern courage. He gives no credit to either side for good qualities. After all, we are mere Americans!

August 24, 1861.   Today the wife of the kind surgeon of yesterday called.

Whenever I see much of a man and he immediately sends his wife to make my acquaintance, I know it is a compliment.

It is the pleasantest kind of flattery.

Mr. Miles and Mr. Mason came to go with us to the president's reception. I was hors de combat. Mr. Miles is going home with Mr. Mason, who lives near Winchester. There revels the Yankee Banks.

Should he capture William Porcher Miles—what fun for them! Think of the scorn our friend Miles heaped upon Congressman Ely. The same cup to his own lip would be bitter.

Mrs. Davis asks me to luncheon on Monday ⟨⟨she was affability itself⟩⟩. And the president ⟨⟨kinder than ever⟩⟩ said I must make Chesnut ride with him every evening. For it is evening more than afternoon when they go.

Such extraordinary-dressing ⟨⟨comical people there⟩⟩—a grass green dress with a gold belt and gold wheat in the fair one's hair.

You see, I did go to the reception.

Daniel[3] of the *Examiner* was at the president's! Wilmot DeSaussure wondered if a fellow did not feel a little queer, paying his respects in person at the house of a man whom he abused daily as Daniel abuses Jeff Davis in his newspaper.

Also De Bow of the *Review*[4]—so-called—was there. He is no myth—our men

---

3. John Moncure Daniel, editor of the Richmond *Examiner*.
4. James Dunwoody Brownson De Bow, the South Carolinian who edited *De Bow's Review* in New Orleans before the war, became chief Confederate agent for the purchase and sale of cotton.

knew him. Now, Mrs. Lee says there is no Mrs. Daniel—so I begin to suspect I did not see any Mr. Daniel in the lion's den, either.

A fiasco—A.D.C. engaged to two young ladies in the same house. They were quarreling. They made friends unexpectedly, and his treachery was revealed among many other secrets under that august roof; fancy the row when it all came out.

When we left the reception we found our coach but no coachman. We searched for him long and diligently. When he was found he was not in a condition to drive, so one of the gentlemen of our party took his place and drove us home. At home we found James Lowndes awaiting us. He said General Beauregard said to Col. Joseph Kershaw, "Is this the report of a colonel or a major general?"

The report of the battle they hurried off for their own glory to the *Mercury*.

Colonel Kershaw answered pleasantly that he would soon learn military etiquette on such matters.

Hampton's Legion says the report business is more easily disposed of than his assuming to himself the capture of Ricketts's battery—or worse still, presuming to claim the credit of hounding back to the battlefield deserters from the Legion.

Caesar's *Commentaries* would have been mere gasconade if Caesar had not been Caesar, wisely commented one of the party.

Then another told [of] the old Charleston man's horror of a war and its consequent heroes—"crop of damned heroes," to use his very words. Said it would take forty years for the truth to put them down.

Mr. Lowndes said that we had already reaped one good result from the war. The orators, the spouters, the furious patriots that could hardly be held, who were so unduly anxious to do or die for their country—they had been the pest of our life. Now they either had not tried the battlefield at all or had precipitantly left it at their earliest convenience. For very shame—we were rid of them for a while.

I doubt it.

Last night an irrepressible Carolinian knocked down four men before he could be smashed by a club. They say the club gave him a cruel blow, but he soon was up again and went off singing, apparently in fine spirits after his fight.

Today B. F. Perry[5] came—the Union Man per se, the one man left among us bold against popular clamor as Mr. Petigru—and as fervent a defender of free speech. He will not, however, take sides against his country.

---

5. Benjamin Franklin Perry, lawyer and former state legislator from Pendleton District, S.C.

Bright's speech—so dead against us.[6] Reading this does not brighten one.

August 25, 1861.   Mr. Barnwell says democracies lead to untruthfulness. To be always electioneering is to be always false. So both we and the Yankees are unreliable as regards our own exploits. How about empires? Were there ever more stupendous lies than the emperor Napoleon's?

He went on. "People dare not tell the truth in a canvass. They must conciliate their constituents. Now, everybody in a democracy always wants an office."

"At least, everybody in Richmond just now seems to want one."

Never heeding interruptions: "As a nation the English are the most truthful in the world."

"And so are our country gentlemen. They own their constituents—at least, in some of the parishes where they are so few white people, only immense estates and negroes."

Thackeray tells of the lies on both sides in the British wars with France— England keeping quite alongside of her rival in that fine art. They lied there as fluently as Russell does now about us.

Went to see Agnes DeLeon,[7] my Columbia school friend. She is fresh from Egypt. And I wished to hear of the Nile and the crocodiles and the mummies and the sphinxes and the pyramids. But her head ran upon Washington life, such as we knew it, and her soul was here. No theme was possible but a discussion of the latest war news.

———————

Hon. Clayton, assistant secretary of state, says we spend two millions a week. Where is all that money to come from? They don't want us to plant cotton but to make provisions. Now, cotton always means money—or did, when there was an outlet for it, anybody to buy it. Where is money to come from?

A rose by any other name—that is, our Florence Nightingale—is Sally Tompkins. Went to her hospital today.

None of our names are high-toned. Dug Springs. Pig Point.[8] Bulls Run.

Mr. Barnwell's joke—daresay it is a Joe Miller,[9] but B laughed till he cried—

A man was fined for contempt of court. And then, his case coming on, the judge talked such arrant nonsense and was so warped in his mind against the poor man, the "fined one" walked up and handed the unjust judge a five-dollar bill.

6. At an election meeting on Aug. 1, English Liberal member of Parliament John Bright had linked British prosperity with the success of the Union.

7. Agnes was the sister of David Camden DeLeon and Edwin DeLeon, who had been U.S. consul general in Egypt when the war began.

8. Early in June 1861, the *Harriet Lane* bombarded the Confederate Pig Point battery on the James River in Va. Skirmishes near Dug Springs, Mo., on July 25 and Aug. 2, 1861, opened the fighting between Union and Confederate forces in that state.

9. That is, a stale joke. The phrase derives from John Mottley, *Joe Miller's Jests* (1739), ostensibly a collection of jokes made by Joseph Miller, a popular but illiterate comedian of the time.

"Why? What for?"

"Oh, I feel such a contempt of this court coming on again."

These men say—Miles, Barnwell, &c—that our judge ⟨⟨Withers⟩⟩ left the Confederate Congress because he thought the five thousand dollars voted by Congress for Mr. Davis's Montgomery house unconstitutional. And he hated Mr. Davis so because when he was secretary of war in Washington he had been rude to the judge.

So I came up, tired to death, took down my hair, had it hanging over me in a crazy Jane fashion. Sat still, hands over my head, half-undressed but too lazy and sleepy to move. I was in a rocking chair by an open window, taking my ease—and the cool night air.

Suddenly the door opened, and Captain _____ walked in. He was in the middle of the room before he saw his mistake.

He stared—transfixed, as the novels say. I daresay I looked an ancient Gorgon.

Then, with a more frantic glare, he turned and fled without a word.

I got up and bolted the door after him. And then I looked in the glass and laughed myself into hysterics. I will never forget to lock the door again.

It does not matter. I looked totally unlike the person bearing my name who, covered with lace caps, &c&c, frequents the drawing room. I doubt if he knows me again.

I have evident symptoms of that hospital slow fever.

Young Stewart brought in prisoners taken on board the merchant vessel they captured. One of these men rabid—he fairly foamed at the mouth. Said he had lost his all; the rest of his life would be devoted to vengeance against us.

And yet they turned him loose.

The others were foreigners who cared not a fig for either side.

August 26, 1861. Evidently I am in for fever. Such headaches—and I am so miserably nervous and depressed.

The handsome A.D.C. felt it necessary as a precautionary measure to say his wife and child were at Fort Hamilton when Doubleday of Fort Sumter fame[1] arrived there.

---

1. The reputed inventor of baseball, Abner Doubleday was a captain stationed in Charleston Harbor in 1860-61.

The child was but thirteen months old but had been taught to "hurrah for Jeff Davis." That is, the poor little atom cried, "Dadis an Boga." But Doubleday shrewdly suspected such a child to be the product of rebel progenitors— stormed at the baby and threatened its father with arrest. A.D.C.'s wife wrote this at once to him—and he came home not by New York at all but by Cincinnati, fearing to be arrested.

A polite little Southerner said to Mrs. Foster—"How do you do, ma'am."

She responded in a voice of thunder: "How dare you speak to me! You rebel!"

The Southerner was meek and easily frightened, and he cowered in silence. Rebel against her majesty!! As he came through North Carolina, a woman came aboard the cars. She surveyed the Yankee prisoners curiously.

She told them solemnly, "If you kill all of our men, remember: here are the women, and they will run you out with broomsticks."

And the virago in her fierceness looked quite equal to the performance of her threat.

Governor Cobb has a body servant, the exact type of our Laurence. Mrs. Stowe has painted him with oiled hair and polished boots. These creatures of ours have not yet been tried by adversity, for all good careless masters do not die. Clayton witnessed this scene today. Or rather, this interview between master and slave.

Governor Cobb, in tones of suppressed emotion: "Come now—let us understand one another. Let there be no mistake about the footing we are on. Am I to wait on you—or do you intend to wait on me? Say now?"

We asked, "What answer did the man make?"

"Oh, never a word. He sniggered as if it was a good joke. But I fancy he intends the governor to continue to wait on him."

We hear the French consul has sent Trescot here on a secret mission.

"The Terror" has full swing at the North now. All papers favorable to us have been suppressed.

How long would one mob stand a Yankee paper here? But newspapers against our government, such as the *Examiner* and the *Mercury,* flourish like green bay trees.

A man up to the elbows in finance said today: "Clayton's story is all nonsense. They did pay out two millions that week, but they paid the soldiers. They don't pay the soldiers every week."

"Not by a long shot," cried a soldier laddie with a gun.

"Why do you write in your diary at all, if, as you say, you have to contradict every day what you wrote yesterday?"

"Because I tell the tale as it is told to me. I write current rumor. I do not vouch for anything."

Mr. Chesnut has gone off to see Jeff Davis: he means to take a colonelcy of cavalry if they will give it to him.

Jeff Davis ill in bed: did not see him, consequently.

Wilmot DeSaussure in ecstasies over a cooking stove invented by the soldiers. It is cut out of the earth on hillsides. Very ingenious indeed—chimney and all perfect. Only it is a fixture. They have not faith to move mountains. So must leave the hillside with its stove cut therein when they change camp.

He thinks I would be a valuable adjunct to Mr. C's cavalry regiment if I went along and superintended the cuisine. It would add so much to the strength of the army if the men were decently, properly fed. ⟨⟨If Mr. C takes a colonelcy I will go as cook.⟩⟩

Mary Hammy presented an emerald and diamond ring to Maggie, who took it, placed it on her finger, and thanked the friendly donor politely. She did not, however, look at it. Not at all. Not once. She looked straight ahead. Afterward she raised her level eyes to the ceiling. But look down at the ring? Never.

We then went to Pizzini's, that very best of Italian confectioners. From there we went to Miss Sally Tompkins's hospital, loaded with good things for the wounded. The men under Miss Sally's kind care looked so clean and comfortable. Cheerful, one might say. They were pleasant and nice to see. One, however, was dismal in tone and aspect, and he repeated at intervals, with no change of words, in a forlorn monotone, "What a hard time we have had since we left home."

But nobody seemed to heed his wailing. And it did not impair his appetite.

At Mrs. Toombs's. She is raging. She is so anti-Davis she will not even admit that the president is ill.

"All humbug."

"But what good could pretending to be ill do him?"

"That reception, now—was not that a humbug? Such a failure. Mrs. Reagan[2] could have done better than that." ⟨⟨Says Mrs. Reagan is the lowest woman she ever saw—little negroes and her children sleep together.⟩⟩

Mrs. Walker—a Montgomery beauty ⟨⟨find her pretty, silly and, I really believe, half-crazy⟩⟩. Such magnificent dressing. She was also an heiress. So dissatisfied with Richmond. Seems to be accustomed to be a belle, but under different conditions. As she is as handsome and well dressed as ever, must be the men who are all wrong.

Mrs. Smith Lee on Southern women: she does not like their languor and easygoing ways, low voices, laziness, &c&c, would have them like the morning that Hamlet saw the ghost: "with an eager and a nipping air."[3]

2. Edwina (Nelms) Reagan was the second wife of John H. Reagan, postmaster of the Confederacy.

3. Slightly misquoted from *Hamlet,* act 1, scene 4.

"Now there was Loulou Corcoran[4]—loud-talking, rough-spoken, like the rest of us about Washington. Her grandmother was loud and hearty and strong. So much the better. Have you seen Loulou Eustis since she has spent a winter with the Eustises in New Orleans? She is as soft and sweet and faint-voiced and languid and fine-lady as any Eustis of them all. Gentle and quiet and aggravating as those Southern women all are. And then she takes it easy. We thought she would worry about her father. Not at all. She is not the least uneasy. Fine ladies don't fret and make any disturbance. A year ago she would have howled or we would have found her unfeeling."

"Did you give Laurence that fifty-dollar bill to go out and change? Suppose he takes himself off to the Yankees."

"And he would leave us with not too many fifty-dollar bills. He is not going anywhere, however. I think his situation suits him."

That wadded belt of mine with the gold pieces quilted in: it has made me ashamed more than once. I leave it under my pillow, and my maid finds it and hangs it over the back of a chair, in evidence as I reenter the room after breakfast. I forget and leave my trunk open, and Laurence brings me the keys and tells me, "You oughten to do so, Miss Mary." And Mr. C leaves all his little money in his pockets, and Laurence says that's why he can't let anyone but himself brush Mars Jeems' clothes.

"You are a fatuous set. No wonder you are always poor."

Arnoldus VanderHorst and Theo Barker here today. The latter [did] Beauregard's French shrug of the shoulders to perfection when Colonel Kershaw calmly told him how he came to send his military report to the *Mercury* before he did to the commander in chief, namely, Burnet Rhett[5] wished him to do it because he wanted the *Mercury* to have it as soon as possible.

Heard the wife of a high public functionary say today (and I repeated it to Mrs. Davis, who moaned, "And we were to leave all vulgarity behind us in Washington?"): "No use to talk to me," ⟨⟨Mrs. Toombs says.⟩⟩ "If one of them Yankees kills my husband, I'll kill one of them, certain and sure." ⟨⟨All the time ridiculing Mrs. Reagan's want of polish and education.⟩⟩

Here comes the London *Post*. Said to be the mouthpiece of the men in power there.

In it I read: "The Southern States of America have achieved their independence."

And a Scotch paper which has the very best account of us yet published across the water.

---

4. Louise (Corcoran) Eustis, daughter of William Wilson Corcoran and wife of George Eustis.
5. Andrew Burnet Rhett, the son of Robert Barnwell Rhett, Sr., was an artillery major in the C.S.A.

August 27, 1861.   Toady Barker and James Lowndes. The latter has been wretchedly treated.

A man said ⟨⟨Mr. C . . . said to my amazement⟩⟩, "All that I wish on earth is to be at peace—and on my own plantation."

Mr. Lowndes said quickly: "I wish I had a plantation to be on. But just now I can't see how anyone would feel justified in leaving the army."

Toady Barker was bitter against this spirit of braggadocio so rampant among us.

The gentleman who had been answered so completely by James Lowndes said, with spitefulness, "Those women who are so frantic for their husbands to join the army would like them killed, no doubt."

Things were growing rather uncomfortable, but an interruption came in the shape of a card. An old classmate of Mr. Chesnut's—Captain Archer,[6] just now fresh from California, followed his card so quickly that Mr. C had hardly time to tell us that in Princeton College they called him Sally Archer, he was so pretty when he entered. He is good-looking still. But the service and consequent rough life have destroyed all softness and girlishness. He will never be so pretty again.

Today I saw a letter from a girl crossed in love. It was shown to me and my advice asked. Her parents object to the social position of her fiancé, in point of fact forbid the banns.

She writes, "I am *missereablle.*" Her sister she calls a "mean retch."

For such a speller I said a man of any social status would do. They ought not to expect so much for her. If she wrote her "pah" a note, I am sure that "stern parient" would give in.

I am miserable, too, today—with one *s* and one *l*.

The North consolidated. They move as one man—no states, army organized by the central power.

Russell in the Northern camp is cussed of Yankees for that Bulls Run letter. Everything not "national" arrested. It looks like business of Seward's part.

And we see people here everywhere. I wonder why they let them stay. They are not true to us.

Mr. Chesnut says I am like the man in the French convention who howled by the hour for "l'arrestation de tous les scélérats et de tous les coquins."[7]

> Friend after friend departs
> Who has not lost a friend.
> There is no union here of hearts
> That has not here an end.[8]

6. James Jay Archer of Md. resigned his captain's commission in the U.S. Army to become a colonel and eventually a brigadier general in the C.S.A.

7. Carlyle describes the invasion of the convention in *The French Revolution* (1837), book 7, chapter 5. A single episode symbolizes the degeneration of republicanism into mob rule: "One man we discern bawling 'for the space of an hour at all intervals' . . . 'I also demand the arrest of the knaves and dastards. . . .'" Carlyle has it in French somewhat different from M. B. C.'s version.

8. From "Friends," in *The Poetical Works of James Montgomery, Collected by Himself* (1841).

Governor Letcher said, "Through the treachery of the guides, General Lee's plan for surprising Rosecrans had miscarried."

"Oh, I hope they hanged the guides." ⟨⟨I said.⟩⟩

"Oh, you hardhearted, bloodthirsty woman!"

Custis Lee was present. He said simply, in answer to all this, "I have heard nothing from my father."

I do not know when I have seen a woman without knitting in her hand. Socks for the soldiers is the cry. One poor man said he had dozens of socks and but one shirt. He preferred more shirts and less stockings. It gives a quaint look, the twinkling of needles, and the everlasting sock dangling.

A jury of matrons, so to speak, sat here on Mrs. Greenhow. They say Mrs. Phillips and Mrs. Gwin have been arrested also.[9]

No doubt Mrs. Greenhow furnished Beauregard with the latest news of the Federal movements—and so made the Manassas fiasco a possibility. She sent us the enemy's plans. Everything she said proved true, numbers, route, &c&c.

⟨⟨Mr. Davis—no fever, but so weak that even talking in the room with him makes him flushed and feverish.⟩⟩

It is a despotism over there now, with Seward's little bell.[1] But our men say it enhances their chances three to one. We are a frantic, dissatisfied, leveling republic. They say here a one-man power is required in war.

David Porter cleared from the aspersions. Wish they had outraged him to the point of driving him in to us.

They have arrested William B. Reed[2] and Miss Windle.[3] She boldly proclaiming herself a secessionist. Why should she seek a martyr's crown? Writing people love notoriety. It is so delightful to be of enough consequence to be arrested. I have often wondered if such incense was ever offered as Napoleon's so-called persecution—and *alleged* jealousy of Madame de Staël.[4]

Now today we were talking of the Caesar talents—writing, speaking, fighting. It was suggested that [the style was] according to the genius of the two peoples, even. Did ever Napoleon—with his "Sun of Austerlitz" or his "generations looking down from the pyramids" &c, "Soldats" &c&c, "Mes enfants"—touch

9. Rose O'Neal Greenhow led the Washington spy ring that passed Union secrets to the Confederates before Bull Run. On Aug. 23, Pinkerton agents searched Mrs. Greenhow's home, placed her under house arrest, and detained several of her associates, including Eugenia (Levy) Phillips, the wife of a former Ala. congressman. The news of Mary (Bell) Gwin's arrest was false.

1. Rumor had it that Secretary of State Seward had told Lord Lyons, " I can touch a bell on my right hand, and order the arrest of a citizen of Ohio; I can touch a bell again, and order the arrest of a citizen of New York; and no power on earth, except that of the president, can release them."

2. William Bradford Reed, a Philadelphia-born pro-Southern Democrat. Reports of his arrest were subsequently retracted.

3. Mary Jane Windle, the Delaware-born author of *Life in Sulphur Springs* (1857) and *Life in Washington and Life Here and There* (1859), had been a correspondent for the Southern press before she was arrested leaving Alexandria, Va., on Aug. 22.

4. Anne Louise Germaine, baronne de Staël-Holstein (1766–1817), author of *De l'influence des passions sur le bonheur des individus et des nations* (1796), *De l'Allemagne* (1813) and other works, introduced the ideas of German Romanticism to France. Political disputes with Napoleon led to her exile from France between 1803 and 1814, and her intemperate pursuit of Benjamin Constant made her a favorite subject of literary gossip.

the French as Wellington's "Hold on, my lads, for a while longer"? Or that absurd answer to the French general in a tight place in the peninsula who sent an envoy to treat of an armistice. Wellington's answer to his interpreter—"Tell him he be d____d, but be sure and put it in polite French."

That tickled the English sense of fun and fighting. It does mine.

Now, this assemblage of army women or Confederate matrons talked pretty freely today. Let us record, after that digression.

"You people who have been everywhere, stationed all over the U.S.—states, frontiers—been to Europe and all that, tell us homebiding ones: are our men worse than the others? Does Mrs. Stowe know? You know?"

"No, Lady Mary Montagu did. After all, only men and women— everywhere.[5] But Mrs. Stowe's exceptional cases may be true. You can pick out horrors from any criminal court record or newspaper in any country."

"You see, irresponsible men, county magnates, city millionaires, princes, &c do pretty much as they please. They are above law and morals."

Russell once more, to whom London and Paris and India have been an everyday sight—and every night, too, streets and all—for him to go on in indignation because there are women on negro plantations who were not vestal virgins! Negro women are married and after marriage behave as well as other people. Marrying is the amusement of their life. They take life easily. So do their class everywhere. Bad men are hated here as elsewhere.

"I hate slavery. I hate a man who — You say there are no more fallen women on a plantation than in London, in proportion to numbers. What do you say to this? A magnate who runs a hideous black harem and its consequences under the same roof with his lovely white wife and his beautiful and accomplished daughters? He holds his head as high and poses as the model of all human virtues to these poor women whom God and the laws have given him. From the height of his awful majesty he scolds and thunders at them, as if he never did wrong in his life.

"Fancy such a man finding his daughter reading *Don Juan*.[6] 'You with that unmoral book!' And he orders her out of his sight.

"You see, Mrs. Stowe did not hit the sorest spot. She makes Legree[7] a bachelor. Remember George II and his like."[8]

"Oh, I knew half a Legree, a man said to be as cruel as Legree—but the other half of him did not correspond. He was a man of polished manners. And the best husband and father and member of the church in the world."

5. "This world consists of men, women, and Herveys." Lady Mary (Wortley) Montagu, *Letters* (1763), volume 1. Lady Montagu, the wife of an adviser to George I, chronicled the scandals of London society.

6. Lord Byron, *Don Juan* (1824).

7. Simon Legree of *Uncle Tom's Cabin*. M. B. C. spells the name "Legare," like the S.C. family of that name, though it is pronounced the way Mrs. Stowe spelled it.

8. The ten-year relationship of George II with Mrs. Henrietta Howard was an open secret, as were several more casual liaisons.

"Can that be so?"

"Yes, I know it. Exceptional case, that sort of thing, always."

"And I knew the dissolute half of Legree well. He was high and mighty. But the kindest creature to his slaves—and the unfortunate results of his bad ways were not sold, had not to jump over ice blocks. They were kept in full view and provided for handsomely in his will.

"His wife and daughters in the might of their purity and innocence are supposed never to dream of what is as plain before their eyes as the sunlight, and they play their parts of unsuspecting angels to the letter. They prefer to adore their father as model of all earthly goodness."

"Well, yes. If he is rich, he is the fountain from whence all blessings flow."

"The one I have in my eye—my half of Legree, the dissolute half—was so furious in his temper and thundered his wrath so at the poor women they were glad to let him do as he pleased in peace, if they could only escape his everlasting faultfinding and noisy bluster. Making everybody so uncomfortable."

"*Now.* Now, do you know any woman of this generation who would stand that sort of thing?"

"No, never—not for one moment. The make-believe angels were of the last century. We know—and we won't have it."

"Condition of women is improving, it seems. These are old-world stories."

"Women were brought up not to judge their fathers or their husbands. They took them as the Lord provided—and were thankful."

"If they should not go to heaven, after all—think of what lives most women lead."

"No heaven, no purgatory, no _____, the other thing—never. I believe in future rewards and punishments."

"How about the wives of drunkards? I heard a woman say once to a friend of her husband, tell it as a cruel matter of fact, without bitterness, without comment: 'Oh, you have not seen him. He is changed. He has not gone to bed sober in thirty years.' She has had her purgatory—if not what Mrs. _____ calls 'the other thing'—here in this world. We all know what a drunken man is. To think, *for no crime* a person may be condemned to live with one thirty years."

"You wander from the question I asked. Are Southern men worse because of the slave system and the—facile black women?"

"Not a bit. They see too much of them. The barroom people don't drink. The confectionary people loathe candy. They are sick of the black sight of them."

"You think a nice man from the South is the nicest thing in the world."

"I know it. Put him by any other man and see!"

"And you say no saints and martyrs now—those good women who stand by bad husbands? Eh?"

"No use to mince matters—no use to pick words—everybody knows the life of a woman whose husband drinks."

"Some men have a hard time, too. I know women who are—well, the very devil and all his imps."

"And have you not seen girls cower and shrink away from a fierce brute of a father? Men are dreadful animals."

•

"Seems to me those of you who are hardest on men here are soft enough with them when they are present. Now, everybody knows I am 'the friend of man,' and I defend them behind their backs, as I take pleasure in their society—well—before their faces."

"That was old Mirabeau—'L 'Ami des hommes'—&c&c."[9]

"Mr. Mason's going to be sent to England."[1]

"Do you hear? There goes your bread and butter—and on the buttered side. In your heart you have been dillydallying, hoping your husband and you would be sent there."

《J. C. would have suited that place better than any man in the Confederate States, says M. B. C.》[2]

"I never loved a dear Gazelle"[3]—&c&c—said she who explained the Mirabeau-friend-of-man allusion.

"Have you seen any Yankee letters taken at Manassas? The spelling is often atrocious. And we thought they had all gone through a course of blue-covered Noah Webster spelling books. *Our* soldiers do spell astonishingly."

"There is Horace Greeley. They say he can't read his own handwriting. He is candid enough and disregards all time serving. He says in this paper that in our army *they* have a hard nut to crack!"

"Bully for our boys!"

"Here he says the rank and file of our army is superior in education and general intelligence to theirs. Our gentlemen go *in* there, you see. Theirs do not. If they can't get a commission, they get an Irishman or German in their place."

"My wildest imagination will not picture Mr. Mason as a diplomat. He will say 'chaw' for 'chew,' and he will call himself 'Jeems,' and he will wear a dress coat to breakfast. Over here, whatever a Mason does is right in his own eyes. He is above law. Somebody asked him how he pronounced his wife's maiden name. She was a Miss Chew from Philadelphia."

"The finest and best of women they say. I don't care how he pronounces the nasty thing—but he will do it, chew tobacco. In England a man must expectorate like a gentleman—if he expectorates at all."

"If he would only take Mr. Miles with him?"

"They say the English will like Mr. Mason. He is so manly, so straightforward, so truthful and bold. A fine old English gentleman—but for tobacco. So said Russell to me."

---

9. Victor Riqueti, comte de Mirabeau, the father of the French revolutionary orator and the author of *L'Ami des hommes* (1757). Mirabeau was finally able to end his unhappy marriage when he obtained evidence of his wife's adultery.

1. Davis designated James Murray Mason as Confederate commissioner to Great Britain on Aug. 24.

2. Under Aug. 29, 1861, in the 1860s Journal.

3. Thomas Moore, "The Fireworshippers," in *Lalla Rookh: An Oriental Romance* (1817): "I never nurs'd a dear gazelle / To glad me with its soft black eye, / But when it came to know me well, / And love me, it was sure to die." The passage was parodied by Charles Dickens in *The Old Curiosity Shop* (1841).

"I like Mr. Mason and Mr. Hunter better than anybody else."

"And yet they are wonderfully unlike."

"Now, you just listen to me. Is Mrs. Davis in hearing? No? Well, this sending Mr. Mason to London is the maddest thing yet. Worse in some points of view than Yancey—and that was a catastrophe."[4]

"Silence—What do you know about war, woman?"

And so on for hours.

《I am getting well—and bear losing the English mission nobly.》

"I did not see Clayton today. He is my man for the latest news."

"Whom the gods wish to destroy they first make mad."

Said Explainer General,[5] "How is that apropos of Mr. Mason?"

"You have made us all mad enough."

"You mean 'angry.'"

"Never. I mean 'mad'—mad as March hares. We fall down and worship the great Virginians."

"You army people are cosmopolitan. You don't care for *states*."

"Slidell is splendid.[6] Mrs. S suits exactly. And they say Eustis is to be secretary of legation."

August 29, 1861.   No more feminine gossip, but the licensed slanderer, mighty Russell of the *Times*—he says the battle of the 21st was fought at long range: 500 yards apart were the combatants. The Confederates were steadily retreating when some commotion in their wagon train frightened the Yanks, and they made tracks. In good English, they fled amain. And on our side we were too frightened to follow them. In high-flown English, to pursue the flying foe.

In spite of all this, there are glimpses of the truth sometimes. And the story reads to our credit, with all its sneers and jeers.

When he speaks of the Yankees, cowardice and falsehood, dishonesty, braggadocio—the best words in his mouth.

He repeats the thrice-told tale, so oft repeated and denied, that we were harsh to wounded prisoners.

Dr. Gibson told me that their surgeon general has written to thank our surgeons. The Yankee officers write very differently from Russell, Dr. Gibson says. I know in that hospital with the Sisters of Charity they were better off than our men at the other hospitals. That I saw with my own eyes.

Our party of matrons had their shot at those saints and martyrs and patriots, the imprisoned Greenhow and Phillips.

4. In March, radical secessionist William Lowndes Yancey, a former U.S. senator and member of the Ala. secession convention, had been appointed chairman of a committee sent to England and France to secure recognition of the Confederacy.

5. One of M. B. C.'s several pseudonyms for herself.

6. He had been named commissioner to France on the twenty-fourth.

These poor souls are jealously guarded night and day. It is a hideous tale, what they tell of their suffering.

Mrs. Lee punned upon the odd expression "Ladies of their age being confined."

These old Washington habituées say Mrs. Greenhow had herself confined and persecuted, that we might trust her the more. She sees we distrust her after all. The Manassas men swear she was our good angel.

And the Washington women say: up to the highest bidder, always. And they have the money on us.

Women who come before the public are in a bad box now. False hair is taken off and searched for papers. Pistols are sought for [under] "cotillons renversés." Bustles are "suspect." All manner of things, they say, come over the border under the huge hoops now worn. So they are ruthlessly torn off. Not legs but arms are looked for under hoops. And sad to say, found. Then women are used as detectives and searchers to see that no men come over in petticoats.

So the poor creatures coming this way are humiliated to the deepest degree. ⟨⟨I think *these* times make all women feel their humiliation in the affairs of the world.... Women can only stay at home, and every paper reminds us that women are to be violated, ravished, and all manner of humiliation.⟩⟩

To men—glory, honor, praise, and power—if they are patriots.

To women—daughters of Eve—punishment comes still in some shape, do what they will.

Mary Hammy's eyes were starting from her head with amazement. And the very large and very handsome South Carolinian talked rapidly.

"What is it?" after he had gone.

"Oh, what a year can bring forth—one year. Last summer you remember how he swore he was in love with me. He told you, he told me, he told everybody. And if I did refuse to marry him, I believed him.

"Now he says he has seen—fallen in love with, courted, married—another person. And he raves of his little daughter's beauty. And they say time goes slowly," said Mary Hammy, with a sigh of wonder at the wonderful cure.

"Time works wonders," said the Explainer General. "What conclusion did you come to as to Southern men? The grand powwow, you know."

"They are nicer than the nicest. The gentlemen, you know. There are not too many of that kind anywhere. Ours are generous, truthful, brave, and—and—devoted to us, you know. A Southern husband is not a bad thing to have about the house."

"Mrs. Frank Hampton said, for one thing, you could not flirt with those South Carolinians. They would not stay at the tepid degree of flirtation. They grow so horridly in earnest before you know where you are."

A hospital nurse from North Carolina says she likes everything Confederate but the "assisting surgeons." She does not "like their ways." They take the white sugar and give the patients moist brown. They take the lemons and give the sick men citric acid. And as for the whiskey, brandy, &c, many a man has died because the surgeon did not leave from his own toddy whiskey enough to keep a typhoid case alive. . . .[7]

"Do you think two married people ever lived together without finding each other out? I mean knowing exactly how good or how shabby—how weak or how strong—above all, how selfish each was?"

"Yes—unless they are dolts—they know to a tittle. But you see—if they have common sense, they make believe and get on—so so—like the marchioness's[8] orange peel wine—in *Old Curiosity Shop,* you know—&c&c."

Mr. Barnwell was ill today. When Laurence brought me the milk and rice which I had prepared my way, I made him take part of it to Mr. Barnwell. Laurence came back delighted.

"Miss Mary, he eat it like he was famished. Nothing here is like home cooking."

A violent attack upon the North today in the *Albion.*[9] They mean to let freedom slide awhile until they subjugate us. The *Albion* says they use lettres de cachet, passports, and all the despotic apparatus of regal governments.

Russell hears the tramp of the coming man, the king and kaiser—tyrant that is to rule them. Is is McClellan? Little Mac?

We may tremble when he comes. We have only "the many-headed monster thing," armed democracy.[1] Our chiefs quarrel among themselves.

Those sweet little Slidell girls,[2] so gentle and modest, clinging to "Maman." Johnny said they opened their mouths like mockingbirds. Then they all speak French, and Mrs. Slidell knows something of the world and its ways. Beauregard is her brother-in-law. She is a better general, I fancy.

《Had a row with Mr. C for not wanting to answer John S. Preston's telegram. Accused him of the prevailing *insolence* of office here. Shall tell him what I have heard my father say of Calhoun's attention to Carolinians. I see every state is organizing to take care of its own ilk.

《Mr. Chesnut came home today to say Slidell will be minister to France. So "all my pretty chickens at one fell swoop."

《Now if we are not reelected to the Senate! . . . Now as J. C.'s genius does not lie in the military, I suppose Camden is my dark fate if he is defeated in November. But I will harbor so dark a thought against my own peace of mind—pride must have a fall—perhaps I have not borne my honors meekly.》

7. Four enigmatic puns with unintelligible abbreviations are deleted here.

8. Sophronia Sphynx, the mistreated servant in Charles Dickens's *The Old Curiosity Shop* (1841).

9. A New York newspaper.

1. An allusion to Samuel Daniel, *History of the Civil War* (1595-1609), book 2, stanza 13, and Philip Massinger, *The Unnaturall Combat* (1624?), act 3, scene 2.

2. Matilda and Rosina Slidell, daughters of John and Mathilde Slidell.

the tramp of the man
who ever he may be.
(McClelland?) is already
heard who is to be
then despot — Here
are horrible times —
we can easily fight
the "many headed monster
thing" but pretending
to govern —
Had a row with Mr C.
for not wanting to
answer John L Preston's
telegram — Accused
him of the prevailing
insolence of office
here — Shall tell him
what I have heard
my father say of
Calhoun's attention
to Carolinians —
I see my State is
organizing to take

care of its own [illegible]
Mr Chesnut came
home today to say
Slidell will be
Minister to France —
So "all my pretty
chickens at one
fell swoop"
Now if we are not
reelected to the Senate!
My experience reverses
all others — private
life is wrangles &
rows. & strife & ill
blood & [illegible]
& family scrapes —
public life has been
peace & happiness
quiet & comfort —
now as J C's genius
does not lie in the
military I suppose
Camden is my dark
fate if he is defeated
in November — but I will

those sweet little Slidell girls –
So gentle and modest – clinging to
"Maman". Johnny said they spend their
months like mocking birds. Then
they all speak French – and Mrs Slidell
knows something of the world and its
ways – Beauregard is her brother in
law. She is a better general than I fancy –

My Experience does not coincide
with the general idea of public
life – I mean the life of a politician
or statesman. Peace – comfort –
quiet – happiness, I have found away
from home – Only your own
family – those nearest and dearest
can hurt you. Wrangling –
Jars – heart burnings – bitterness
envy – hatred and malice – unbrotherly
love family snarls neighbourhood
strife and ill blood – A lonely
word I have conjured up – But
they were all there – and for
these many years I have almost
forgotten them – I find them
always alive and rampant when
I go back to some village life.

"Peace away from home," from the 1880s Version, August 29, 1861

My experience does not coincide with the general idea of public life. I mean the life of a politician or statesman. Peace, comfort, quiet, happiness, I have found away from home. Only your own family, those nearest and dearest, can hurt you. Wrangling, rows, heart burnings, bitterness, envy, hatred and malice, unbrotherly love, family snarls, neighborhood strife, and ill blood—a lovely brood I have conjured up. But they were all there, and for these many years I have almost forgotten them. I find them always alive and rampant when I go back to semi–village life. For after all, though we live miles apart—everybody flying round on horses or in carriages—it amounts to a village community. Everybody knows exactly where to put the knife.

Last night—could stand it no longer. In spite of fever, went down to hear what Mr. Clayton had to say. He always knows everything.

He thinks Mrs. Phillips's nine children ought to have been hostages to fortune. How can a motherly soul with nine children be suspected of mischief? But she is caged up, all the same.

Seward's little bell reigns supreme.

McClellan is of a forgiving spirit. He does not resent Russell's slurs upon Yankees—but with good policy has Russell with him as a guest.

The Adonis of an A.D.C. avers, as one who knows, that Sumter Anderson's heart is with us, that he will not fight the South.

After all [is] said and done, that sounds like nonsense. Sumter Anderson's wife was a daughter of Governor Clinch of Georgia.[3] Does that explain it?

Also he told me something of that Garnett who was killed at Cheat Mountain.

He has been an unlucky man clear through.

In the army before the war, the A.D.C. had found him proud, reserved, and morose. Cold as an icicle to all.

But for his wife and child, he was a different creature. He adored them and cared for nothing else.

One day he went off on an expedition. They were gone six weeks. It was out in the Northwest, and the Indians were troublesome. When he came back, his wife and child were underground. He said not one word. But they found him more frozen and stern and isolated than ever—that was all.

The night before he left Richmond, he said, in his quiet way: "They have not given me an adequate force. I can do nothing. They have sent me to my death."

It is acknowledged that he threw away his life. "A dreary-hearted man," said the A.D.C. "And the unluckiest."

---

3. Duncan Lamont Clinch (1787–1849), whose daughter Elizabeth married Maj. Robert Anderson, was not the governor of Ga. but only an unsuccessful candidate for the office in 1847.

Captain Ingraham says Butler and his fleet and 40,000 men will give Charleston the go-by.[4] Ripley[5] is ready for them there. They are off Cape Hatteras now.

Gonzales has telegraphed Port Royal he thinks the fleet means to make for that magnificent door to South Carolina—too big to be properly barred.

If Butler lands in North Carolina! Won't old Rip rouse and give herself a shake! She can pour out more men if she pleases. Already she is sending them swiftly to the front. And with so little noise.

On the front steps every evening we take our seats and discourse at our pleasure. A nicer or more agreeable set of people were never assembled than our present Arlington crowd.

Tonight it was Yancey who occupied our tongues.

Send a man to England who had killed his father-in-law in a street brawl![6] That was not knowing England or Englishmen, surely. Who wants eloquence? We want somebody who can hold his tongue. People avoid great talkers, men who orate, men given to monologue, as they would fire, famine, or pestilence.

Yancey will have no mobs to harangue. No stump speeches will be possible— superb as are his of that kind. A little quiet conversation with slow, solid, commonsense people who begin to suspect as soon as any flourish of trumpets meets their ear. If he uses fine words, who cares for that over there?

"Now. Do you think they will bear Mr. Mason's tobacco or Yancey's murder best?"

"We will wait and see."

"Could they have found anyone, even if they searched diligently, to send there who was capable of judiciously holding his peace and listening?"

"I don't know. There are people in this country that I have never seen—or heard!!"

Then the navy men came under discussion. One said, "They are like the people St. Paul cited who were sawn asunder."[7]

There is an awful pull in their divided hearts.

Faith in the U.S. Navy was their creed and their religion. And now they must fight it—and worse than all, wish it ill luck.

Commodore Barron has left us. He has hoisted his flag in the good ship *Manassas*. Not half so grand a vessel as his beloved and lost *Wabash*, but he is proud of her. His two launches he calls *Mosquito* and *Firefly*. The navy men seem the pick of the nation.

"A splendid set of fellows—they ought to find something for them to do," said [a] soldier.

4. U.S. Maj. Gen. Benjamin F. Butler commanded the expedition that captured two Confederate forts at Hatteras Inlet, N.C., on Aug. 28. Only 880 Federal troops were involved.

5. Brig. Gen. Roswell Sabine Ripley, an Ohioan who married a South Carolinian and moved to Charleston in the 1850s, was commander of the Department of S.C., Ga., and Fla.

6. In 1839, Yancey shot and wounded his wife's uncle, not her father, in a political argument.

7. Hebrews 11:37.

Commodore Barron when he was a middy accompanied Phil Augustus Stockton to claim his bride. He, the said Stockton, had married an heiress (Sally Cantey) clandestinely.[8] She was married by a magistrate and returned to Mrs. Gréland's boarding school until it was time to go home—that is, to Camden.

Lieutenant Stockton (of the descendants of the signer) was the handsomest man in the navy—and so irresistible. The bride was barely sixteen.

And now he was to go down South among those fire-eaters and claim her. And Commodore Barron, then his intimate friend, went as his backer. They were to announce the marriage and defy the guardians.

Commodore Barron said he expected a rough job of it all. But they were prepared for all risks.

"You expected to find us a horde of savages, no doubt?"

"We did not expect to get off under a half-dozen duels." They looked for insults from every quarter.

They found a polished and refined people who lived en prince, to say the least of it.

They were received with a cold and stately and faultless politeness, which made them feel as if they had been sheep-stealing.

The young lady had confessed to her guardians, and they were for making the best of it. Above all, for saving her name from all scandal or publicity. Col. John Boykin,[9] one of them, took young Lochinvar to stay with him, his friend Barron also a guest. Colonel Deas[1] sent for a parson and made assurance doubly sure by marrying them over again. Their wish was to keep things quiet and not to make a nine-days' wonder of the young lady.

Then there came balls and parties and festivities—no end. He was enchanted with the easygoing life of these people, with dinner parties the finest in the world, hunting—deer and fox hunting—dancing, pretty girls, everything that heart could wish. But then, said Commodore Barron: "The better it was, and the kinder the treatment, the more ashamed I grew of my business down there. After all, it was stealing an heiress, you know."

And I told him how the same fate still haunted that estate. Mrs. Stockton sold it to a gentleman, who sold it again to an old man who had married when near eighty and left it to the daughter born of that marriage late in life.

This child of his old age of course was left an orphan quite young. At fifteen she was runaway with, and married by, a boy of seventeen, a canny Scotchman. The young couple lived to grow up, and it was after all a happy marriage. (This last heiress left six children—so it will be divided and no longer tempt fortune hunters.)

Commodore said, "To think, we two, youngsters in our blue uniforms, went

8. Philip Augustus and Sarah (Cantey) Stockton were the parents of Edward Cantey Stockton. Sarah, a first cousin of old Colonel Chesnut, died in 1835; Philip served as U.S. consul general to Saxony from 1856 to 1862 and then returned to the North. He was not, as M. B. C. claims, a direct descendant of Richard Stockton of N.J., a signer of the Declaration of Independence.

9. The father of Dr. Edward M. Boykin, John Boykin (1790–1840) was M. B. C.'s first cousin once removed.

1. James Sutherland Deas, the brother-in-law of James Chesnut, Sr.

down to bully these people—" He was more at Colonel Chesnut's. Mrs. Chesnut being a Philadelphian, he was at ease with them somewhat, and it was the most thoroughly appointed establishment he had then ever visited.

"Sam Jones has just come from Washington."

"Been tolerably slow in coming. Who is Sam Jones?"

"His brother Roger burnt the Navy Yard. Catesby Jones is his brother, too. And Walter. All are on our side. His wife is Becky Taylor—you know.[2] He says so many people are leaving Washington. They are afraid. Washington is not considered safe."

"From us—or from Seward's little bell?"

"Oh! Mr. Corcoran has been imprisoned.[3] But Mr. Elisha Riggs, his partner in the bank—'Corcoran and Riggs,' you know—he has come back from Europe a red-hot Union man. He says he had just as soon live in South Carolina as go to his brother George Riggs's house. There is so much treason afloat there. It is both spoken and taught there."

"What?"

"Treason, I suppose."

"And Seward makes it lively times among the 'suspect.'"

"We are pretty well up with the Sam Jones news. Mr. Clayton says the State Department pays 30 dollars a month for the New York *Herald* and gets it regularly two days after it is published—and then we have Clayton's edition of it."

Captain Mason[4] said he heard a rumor coming from Charleston that Mr. James M. Mason was to represent us at the Court of St. James.

"Now, did you ever? We knew that a month ago but thought it a profound secret. Only for the elect to be trusted with, because only those in executive session can know it. Several members of the Senate told me—but I dared not breathe it. He wants to get off before the Yankees hear it."

"You pretend the British don't care for eloquence—that they have an apathy in that line. How about Lord Derby?[5] And Bright and Gladstone and all those talking fellows. Plenty of that sort over there, too. What but Bright's gift at public speaking has pushed him up sky-high?"

2. Once again, M. B. C. has the relationships of the Joneses confused. Roger, Catesby, and Walter Jones were indeed brothers, but they were not related to Brig. Gen. Samuel Jones. Nor were they all Confederates. Catesby Jones, a former U.S. Navy officer, was later second officer on the *Merrimack*, and Walter resigned a lieutenant's commission to join the C.S.A. But Lt. Roger Jones, commander of the Federal arsenal at Harpers Ferry, destroyed the armory before the Confederates could capture it in April and remained in the U.S. Army. Finally, Rebecca (Taylor) Jones was not the wife of Samuel Jones (see p. 136, n. 2).

3. A false rumor.

4. The 1860s Journal makes it clear that M. B. C. intended to write "Captain Ingraham."

5. Edward George Stanley, fourteenth earl of Derby, was the leader of the opposition in Parliament.

"Bright—I dined with him in Washington. He was dull as ditch water. He must keep all of his wit to retail when he is on his legs. Seated in a chair, he was downright stupid."

"You could not appreciate him."

"Oh," said the Explainer, "you found his name a misnomer, if Bright was dull company."

Went with our Leviathan of Loveliness[6] to a ladies' meeting. No scandal today. No wrangling. All harmonious. Everybody knitting. Daresay that soothing occupation helped our perturbed spirits to be calm.

Mrs. C____ is lovely. A perfect beauty. And, said Brewster, in Circassia, think what a price would be set upon her. There beauty sells by the pound.

Coming home, the following conversation:

"So Mrs. _____ thinks Purgatory will hold its own—never be abolished while women and children have to live with drunken fathers and brothers."

"She knows."

"She is too bitter. She says worse than that. She says we have an institution worse than the Spanish Inquisition—worse than Torquemada and all that sort of thing."

"What does she mean?"

"You ask her. Her words are sharp arrows. I am a dull creature. I will spoil all, repeating what she says."

"It is your own family she calls the familiars of the Inquisition. She declares they set upon you, fall foul of you, watch and harass you, from morn till dewy eve. They have a perfect right to your life night and day. Unto the fourth and fifth generation. They drop in at breakfast. 'Are you not imprudent to eat that? Take care now, don't overdo it. I think you eat too much so early in the day.' And they help themselves to the only thing you care for on the table. They abuse your friends and tell you it is your duty to praise your enemies. They tell you all of your faults candidly—because they love you so. That gives them a right to speak. The family interest they take in you. You ought to do this, you ought to do that. And then—the everlasting 'You ought to have done.' That comes near making you a murderer—at least in heart."

"Blood's thicker than water," they say. And there is when the longing to spill it comes in.

No locks or bolts or bars can keep them out. Are they not your nearest family? They dine with you, dropping in after you are at soup. They come after you have gone to bed. All the servants have gone away—and the man of the house is in his nightshirt tail, standing sternly at the door with the huge wooden bar in his hand nearly scares them to death. And you are glad of it."

6. Identified in the 1860s Journal under Aug. 30, 1861, as Martha (Flournoy) Carter (see p. 149).

"Private life indeed!" She says her husband entered public life and they went off to live in a faraway city. Then for the first time in her life she knew privacy. She never will forget how she jumped for joy as she told her servant not to admit a soul until after two o'clock in the day. Afterward she took *a* day. Then she was free indeed. She could read and write, stay at home, go out at her own sweet will. No longer sitting for hours with her fingers between the leaves of a frantically interesting book while her kin slowly dribbled nonsense by the yard. Waiting, waiting, yawning—would they never go? Then, for hurting you, who like a relative? They do it from a sense of duty. For stinging you, for cutting you to the quick, who like one of your own household? In point of fact, they only can do it. They know the raw. And how to hit it every time. You are in their power. She says: "Did you ever see a really respectable, responsible, revered, and beloved head of a family? He really thinks that is his business in life. All enjoyment is sinful. He is here to prevent the women from such frivolous things as pleasure, &c&c."

"A woman who talks that way is a dangerous character. It is awfully upsetting—all that stuff."

"Suppose the women and children secede?"

"Knit your stocking. We have had enough for today."

Aside: "She was trying to imitate Thackeray."

"But you know, our women all speak in that low, plaintive way because they are always excusing themselves for something they never did."

"And the Yankee women are loud and shrill because they fight it out—fair field and no favor—and when incompatibility comes in, they go out for divorce. And they talk as if *money only* bought black women in slave countries. Women are bought and sold everywhere."

I sat placidly rocking in my chair by the window, trying to hope all was for the best. Mary Hammy rushed in, literally drowned in tears. I never saw so drenched a face in my life. My heart stopped still.

"Commodore Barron is taken prisoner. The Yankees have captured him and all his lieutenants. Poor Imogene! And there is my father scouting about, the Lord knows where. I only know he is in the advanced guard. The Barrons' time has come. Mine may come any minute. Oh, Cousin Mary—when Mrs. Lee told Imogene, she fainted!"

"Those poor girls. They are nearly dead with trouble and fright. Go straight back to those children. Nobody will touch a hair of their father's head. Tell them I say so. They dare not. They are not savages quite. This is civilized war, you know."

When she came in, throwing her bad news at my head, I nearly suffocated. But as she wept and wailed her long story, my senses came back to me.

Mrs. Eustis knows her world better. Mrs. Lee said to her yesterday, "Have you seen those accounts of arrests in Washington?"

Mrs. Eustis answered calmly: "Yes—I know all about it. I suppose you allude to the fact that my father has been imprisoned."

"No, no," interrupted the Explainer. "She means the incarceration of those mature Washington belles."

Mrs. Eustis continued, "I have no fears for my father's safety."

Mrs. Lee added hastily, "I did not know Mr. Corcoran had been arrested, or I never would have said a word to you on the subject."

"In a casual rencontre with his daughter," explained the chorus.

More trouble—Fort Hatteras has gone up. When Commodore Barron was here three weeks ago, he foretold this disaster—as poor Garnett did his, if adequate measures were not taken to strengthen him. But not the slightest heed did Mr. Mallory pay to his words.

Commodore Barron continued to say day and night while he was here: "This point needs as effective a force to hold it as Fortress Monroe, Fort Pickens, or Charleston. But they leave it to take its chance."

Now—ho! For Port Royal!

August 31, 1861. Fever every day now. Captain Ingraham will not remember all of Commodore Barron's Cassandra talk. No wonder, he was one of those who refused to hear or heed him.

I believe the zeal of individuals is carrying on this war. Men will come with companies—with regiments. They pour in. They will try to have a navy—and above all, they will fight. The good of the heads of departments is to put the brakes down and hold hard. These men accomplish things, and no amount of snubbing will prevent their going ahead.

The poor Barron children came to tea. The pale faces and red eyes of those girls were too much for me. I dare not look again. It was hard work keeping back a good cry myself.

They say we have driven back two regiments at Manassas. Here we have Hatteras on the brain. It is useless to try and interest anyone in anything else.

Congress adjourns today.

Jeff Davis ill ⟨⟨too ill to see J. C., so he cannot get his commission—he seems puzzled⟩⟩. We go home on Monday if I am able to travel. Already feel the dread stillness and torpor of one Sahara of a Sandhills creeping into my veins. It chills the marrow of my bones. Now for good neighborly hate.

"Provincial sloth, festering"—as Tennyson says.

The congressmen's pay, $450.00. ⟨⟨Much is it needed.⟩⟩

Mr. Miles is said to be the secretary of legation, the English embassy.

He would make a good minister plenipotentiary. He is a born diplomat. He has all the points—manners, culture—and can hold his tongue when necessary and listen.

Commodore Barron's little son was in my room. A nice boy. He went out on a shopping expedition for me, bought me some wools for my knitting. He was so pleased—called himself my "confidential agent." Sent him again for a vast amount of confectionary. Some to carry home to Kate's children and some for himself, but he does not know that.

Jenny Barron, Jenny Cooper,[7] and Mary Hammy have gone to have their photographs taken as "tricoteuses," each armed with their knitting. It will be a lovely group.

I am reveling in the noise of city life ⟨⟨that I so dearly love⟩⟩. I know what is before me.

Nothing more cheering than the cry of the poor whippoorwill will break the silence at Sandy Hill. Except, as night draws in, the screech owl will add his moanful note.

The streets here are gay with soldiers. Now they are uniformed. L. Q. Washington says: "Theatrical Joe Kershaw war is over—or the reports of it—and war and fighting in bitter earnest will soon spoil this pretty show and leave no time for columns of sensational stuff in the newspapers."

We have such a knack of hoping. Our government looks for news from Europe by every mail which shall bring us comfortable allies—if not peace.

But the wolf is at the door. In it at North Carolina—and ready to prowl around us.

These coast inroads were our despair from the first.

September 1, 1861.   At the Arlington. With fever still. There has not been an unpleasant person at this house, and not one of those disagreeable small wars that made the Spotswood so hot.

Missed Mr. Mallory. I was too ill to go down. Sent me word he had come to tell me the astounding story of the conspiratoresses in Washington, Mrs. Phillips, Mrs. Greenhow, &c&c. Mrs. Smith Lee saw him. She afterward came up and told me all she could remember—also she added the stirring annals of the Rhett-Mason internecine struggle.[8] I am always on the women's side—and

7. The daughter of Adj. Gen. Samuel Cooper.
8. In the 1840s, two brothers, Thomas Grimké Rhett and Charles Hart Rhett, married, respectively, Florence and Matilda Mason, daughters of Eliza (Price) Mason. The men, later officers in the C.S.A., were nephews of Robert Barnwell Rhett, Sr.; their wives were nieces of James Murray Mason.

Madame Mère was too much for even Rhett son-in-laws ⟨⟨funny tales of a platonic marriage of a Captain Gardiner who did not go in his wife's room⟩⟩.

North Carolina writes for arms for her soldiers. Have we any to send? No.

Brewster, the plain-spoken, says: "The president is ill—and our affairs are in the hands of noodles. All the generals away with the armies—nobody here—General Lee in western Virginia, &c&c."

Rowdy row. What is it?

"Oh, Ransom Calhoun's artillery passing—and a cavalry company just after it—North Carolina."

Reading the Third Psalm.

The devil is sick—the devil a saint would be.[9]

Lord, how are they increased that trouble me? Many are they that rise up against me!

I will not be afraid for the thousand of the people that have set themselves against me round about.

Up, Lord, and help me!

Sunday—and a beautiful night. I looked down from my windows high. And the south wind blows softly.

September 2, 1882 [*sic*].[1] Arlington House. Sam Slick[2] says, "Young people never care for religion unless they are sick or sorry."

Here is an old person who was both yesterday—and, I see by the page before me, very piously inclined.

Answered a letter for Mr. C from Mr. Garlington[3]—direly threatening the administration if they continue to neglect a man named James.

Amenities of Clingman:

He told a Baltimorean that a Georgia negro was now freer than a Maryland legislator.

Then words grew so angry I was utterly in despair. Fortunately Mr. Mallory came in with a paper. In it a note from Mrs. Gwin is published. After all said and done, she is quietly at West Point. She clears her skirts of all prison stories. She has never been molested at all.

---

9. A variant of an old proverb of uncertain origin. The three sentences following come from the first, sixth, and seventh verses of the Third Psalm.

1. Dated 1861 in the 1860s Journal.

2. The Yankee clock peddler and cracker-barrel philosopher who appeared in several books by Canadian humorist Thomas Chandler Haliburton (1796-1865).

3. Either Albert Creswell Garlington, a Newberry District lawyer and major of the C.S.A., or Henry William Garlington, a planter and member of the S.C. secession convention from Laurens District.

Russell says we will never survive the death of Hamptons, Prestons, &c&c in South Carolina.

Explainer General: "I think we can."

And let us try one of Jeremy Taylor's methods for raising one's spirits! Fancy being happier because you know other people are more miserable.[4]

I am far better off than the wives and children of those men in Yankee dungeons or the womenkind of the men who lie sick or wounded in hospitals or in camp.

Now this plan of thinking or thanking God—"it is well with me as wot it is"—fills me with utter despondency.

Mr. Miles says he is not going anywhere at all, not even home. He is to sit here permanently—chairman of a committee to overhaul camps, commissariats, &c&c.

We gave our ideas of Mr. Mason, in which we agreed perfectly.

In the first place, he has a noble presence—really a handsome man—a manly old Virginian—straightforward, brave, truthful, clever, and very beau idéal of an independent, high-spirited F.F.V. If the English value a genuine man, they will have it.

That in every particular he is the exact opposite of Talleyrand, who denies? He has some peculiarities. He had never an ache or a pain himself. His physique is perfect. And he loudly declares that he hates sick people. It seems to him an unpardonable weakness.

Again, he loathes mountains.

"What are they good for? What do you see pretty in rocks and forlorn trees, and how can you care to scramble over rough ground, uphill all the time— nothing but rocks and snakes, &c&c&c." We agreed that we adored Mr. Mason. Everyone does that he deigns to like.

Today when Mr. Mallory came, Imogene Barron entered the room, with her sad face, to get us, she said, all the comfort she could from the secretary of the navy.

"Could he find anyone to exchange prisoners and so release her father?"

He answered, "I would give all Richmond for him!"

《Mr. Mallory says Mrs. Davis don't like me—I wish he had not told me.》

It began to grow late. So many people came to tell me goodbye.

And I had fever as usual today—but in the excitement of this crowd of friends, the invalid forgot fever.

Mr. Chesnut held up his watch to me warningly and intimated, "It was late indeed for one who had to travel tomorrow."

---

4. Jeremy Taylor, *The Rule and Exercises of Holy Living* (1650), chapter 2, section 6: "Of contentedness in all estates and accidents."

So as the Yankees say after every defeat, I "retired in good order."

Not quite, for I forgot handkerchief and fan. Gonzales rushed after and met me at the foot of the stairs. In his foreign, pathetic, polite, highbred way, he bowed low and said he had made an excuse of the fan &c, for he had a present to make me. And "then though startled and amazed—I paused, and on the stranger gazed." Alas, I am a woman approaching forty, and the offering proved to be a bottle of cherry bounce. Nothing could have been more opportune and, with a little ice &c, helped, I am sure, to save my life on that dreadful journey home.

No discouragement now felt at the North. They take our forts and are satisfied for a while.

Then the English are sturdily neutral. Like the woman who saw her husband fight the bear, "it was the first fight she ever saw that she did not care who whipped."

Mrs. Lee gave us an anecdote of one of the incarcerated ladies. She is the wife of a celebrated lawyer—at any rate, a lawyer who was employed to defend Sickles when he killed Phil Barton Key.[5]

This lawyer's wife patted Sickles on the back: "Now we have got you off this time. Now you be a good boy."

⟨⟨Had the most affectionate messages from Mrs. President, but Mr. Davis's illness and the want of her carriage kept her from coming to see me. If we had not been so interrupted, I should like to have had more particulars from Mr. Mallory of what Mrs. Davis said about me. He seemed quite inclined to tell everything. "Incompatibility of temper and manners" could not be the reason. He told the same tales as Mr. Lamar. When I was spoken of, she only said, "Yes, she *is* pretty," but would allow nothing else. Now my friends think—and so do I—that that *pretty* is all humbug—to be able to say something which will do me no good. It seems J. C. saw Jeff Davis last night. As he rushed out of the room frantically when I asked him about it, I suppose it was not a pleasant recollection. He certainly asked him for no commission of any kind whatsoever.... I asked J. C. what Mr. Davis said to him and find it most flattering.⟩⟩

The end of Mr. Chesnut's colonelcy of cavalry. Mr. Davis told him while he was ill ⟨⟨that fool⟩⟩ Mr. Secretary of War Walker took it on himself to order an election for colonels of the two regiments Mr. Davis intended to give Tom Drayton and Mr. Chesnut.

This election was ordered without consulting the president. Mr. Davis, however, urges Mr. Chesnut to remain in the Congress. He will be needed there. If

---

5. Identified in the 1860s Journal as Eugenia Phillips. Her husband Phillip was only briefly involved with the case.

all the men of sense go into the army, what will become of the legislative branch? Brains in the conduct of affairs is a great want now.

Mr. Davis was very kind about it all. He told Mr. Chesnut to go home and have an eye to all the state defenses, &c&c, and that he would give him any position he asked for, if he still wished to continue in the army.

Now, this would be all that heart could wish, but Mr. Chesnut will never ask for anything.

What he asks for? That's the rub.

I am certain of very few things in life now. This is one of them. Mr. C will never ask mortal man for any promotion for *himself* or *for one of his own family.*

Mrs. Joe Johnston told us of the appeal made by General Scott to her husband when he heard our Joseph intended to leave U.S.A. General Scott also spoke to Mrs. Johnston.

"Get him to stay with us. We will never disturb him in any way."

"My husband cannot stay in an army which is about to invade his native country," she answered.

"Then let him leave our army—but do not let him join theirs."

She answered: "This is all very fine—but how is Joe Johnston to live? He has no private fortune. And no profession, or no profession but that of arms."

Mlle. Scudéry:[6] "Whosoever attempts to put down what fifteen or twenty women say when they get together will write one of the worst books in the world." She means the silliest, I think—superadded.

All the same, I am always putting down what they say. They always decry and abuse men. Now the men praise women. But then, when twenty men are together without any women, I am not there. So I can't say they are not even with us.

My mother once accused my father of flattering all women whenever he approached them.

"Not flattery at all. I tell them the truth. That they are clever and good and pretty—and they like to hear it. The simple truth!"

"But all women are not good and pretty, &c&c."

"And I never go near the bad and ugly ones."

At any rate, the men who form my circle of friends have very different topics of conversation from the womenfolk.

With Mary Hammy's swarms of gay and gallant youths, splendid in their martial array and in the highest spirits, it is all love and war.

The sad seniors who prowl around the Arlington:

"'Begin,' Napoleon says. 'God is always on the side of the heaviest battalions.'"

"Parsons are all telling the women God is our side, you know."

"Frederick the Great, now—he fought Europe in arms. But Russia lost her

6. Madeleine de Scudéry, a seventeenth-century French author whose long romances featured frequent conversational digressions on education and politics.

czar at a critical moment, and the new sovereign joined Frederick as opportunely as Blücher came on the field of Waterloo."

"Or Kirby Smith at Manassas?"

"Now, the Netherlands, you forget those,[7] and our own revolution, &c&c."

"The dove, that is, our navy, must find a spot to rest her foot."

"How I wish she could come back to our ark with a French olive branch, or English! We only need a port to refit in; to take our prizes in; to build ships, &c&c&c."

"Fortunately in such stirring times one has not the chance to think too much."

"I think a czarina died, and a foolish young emperor who took Frederick for a model came to the fore."

"It was the coming at the nick of time—not so much who came"—&c&c&c.

---

7. The willingness of Queen Elizabeth I to overlook the fact that Dutch sea captains were using England as a base from which to attack the Spanish fleet was a significant factor in the Netherlands's successful war for independence from Spain.

IX

Witherspoon Murder Case

September 9, 1861. Home again. Left Richmond September 2nd, 1861.

Did not see the armed camp in North Carolina, so-called. At Wilmington met George Deas, fretting and fuming.

We came with the Moses family, mother and son[1]—also a young Hayne with a wounded soldier they were taking care of. They averred we had fifteen thousand such as he (i.e., wounded, sick, and sore) in Virginia.

The patriarch Moses said we had lost eight thousand men on the 21st July. Mr. C answered, "No, nearer five thousand."

"Well, well," said old Moses, nowise inclined to be obstinate about it. Patriarch Moses has cross-eyes. He looks both ways, seeing things from two points of view at once—makes him liberal-minded.

Team and his wife, who went to nurse their son, have brought home his dead body.

Came home with the fever in full possession of me.

Found this beautiful country place, with its placid outlook by no means the abode of innocence and peace. The tales told around my sickbed made me draw up the sheets over my head—absolutely in shame and disgust. No fear I should repeat them. As I heard that frantic woman I recalled what I have seen somewhere: "The most unhappy people are the people who have *bad thoughts.*"

My physician, Dr. Boykin, now lieutenant of cavalry, came to see me once—said it was only a case for nursing. And went his way with his company to Virginia.

And my sister Kate, my ideal woman, the most agreeable person I know in the world, with her soft, low, and sweet voice, her graceful, gracious ways, and her glorious gray eyes that I looked into so often as we confided our very souls to each other.

Well, well! As old Moses said, she nursed me.

The first lieutenancy of Kirkwood Rangers has routed all of the country doctor left in Dr. Boykin. Few and brief were the words he said to Kate as to my case, but he made up for that by the jolly camp stories he told and the joyous atmosphere of certain success that he was taking to the wars.

1. Franklin J. Moses, Sr., a prosperous lawyer, had represented Sumter District in the S.C. senate for twenty years. His wife was Jane (McClelland) Moses; his son, Franklin, Jr., was Governor Pickens's private secretary.

God bless old Betsey's yellow face. She is a nurse in a thousand and would do anything for "Mars Jeems' wife."

My small ailments in all this comfort set me mourning over the dead and dying soldiers I saw in Virginia. Feeble my compassion proves, after all.

Rev. John Johnson[2] presented the Rangers with a flag. Harriet Grant in costume, a veiled prophet, had the management of it and a front place in the picture, veiled because of something the matter with her face just now. She got up tableaux and a concert.

John Lee called—John Boykin Lee,[3] I must say always—came to request Mr. Chesnut to use all of his influence in high places to get John Boykin Lee a commission. Naturally he does not want to stay in the ranks.

I wonder why the Rangers are so daft to go to Virginia. They will be wanted here. The fleet which is to land an immense invading force is looked for daily. Port Royal, they say, will be invaded by an overwhelming army. And our army reached from that quarter.

The *Mercury* explains to them—while it is warning us—that the tides now are high enough to bring in any vessel of their navy.

The mother of that poor lad I went to see die at the tobacco factory in Richmond met me. She says it is the same we sent to Miss Henrietta's school.[4] It is a nice thing when the grateful hearts remember and the idle people who did the kind act forget. At any rate, I had forgotten until she said her son's claim on me was that I had helped him before. It was gratifying; that I will admit. Now they are raising money to bring his body home. Too late. A little of it would have made him comfortable—maybe saved his life. When I think of the filth and squalor in which I found him—his clothes unchanged for weeks, an atmosphere of horror on every side, wounded men packed in rows like sardines in a box—no wonder I fainted. And now we are efficient at last and have money to bring home the body.

In this world—if we could only know in time.

I handed my aged P[5] a letter from his grandson in the army, thinking he would be glad to learn something of one of them. At one time they seemed all in all with him. That is, before they developed exactly what material they were made of, and hope told a flattering tale.[6] We had no children. They were to carry on his line and inherit the estates he loves so well.

2. An Episcopal minister from Camden.

3. A nineteen-year-old from Camden, serving in the Kirkwood Rangers.

4. Henrietta DeLeon, who ran a private school in Camden, was the aunt of Agnes and David Camden DeLeon.

5. Wemmick's term of endearment for his father in Charles Dickens's *Great Expectations* (1861). M. B. C. is referring to old Colonel Chesnut.

6. From William Barnes Rhodes, *Bombastes Furioso* (1790): "Hope told a flattering tale / Much longer than my arm / That love and pots of ale / In peace would keep me warm." M. B. C. could have been referring to an otherwise unmentioned miscarriage—in view of the sentence following.

Now he is under no delusion. He said, as he folded up the missive from the seat of war: "With your husband we die out. He is the last of my family."

Now, this old man of ninety years was born when it was not the fashion for a gentleman to be a saint. And being lord of all he surveyed for so many years— irresponsible—in the center of his huge domain, it is wonderful he was not a greater tyrant. The softening influence of that angel wife, no doubt.

Saint or sinner, he understands the world about him—*au fond*.

———————

There stands Gonzales's big black bottle that saved my life, possibly. How sentimentally he handed it to me—cherry brandy to a woman of forty.

Of all that hot, dusty, stifling journey home I remember little—but this stands out. They were discussing Miles and his interview of Mr. Congressman Ely. Someone cried, "And Miles is the best-mannered man I know."

"Of course," said Mr. C. "And yet, that is not my idea. In fencing as in fighting, one is taught to salute politely one's antagonist. Ravenswood, now. That tragedy impressed my youth wonderfully. That entrance of his in the hall. His quiet pale face: 'I am an armed man—and a desperate man.'"

"You call *The Bride of Lammermoor*[7] a tragedy?"

"Why not? It is one of the deepest. But that is not my point. They had quarrel enough, heaven knows. Still, as Ravenswood rode away he passed his foes on the lawn, the lover who had supplanted him and the brother who had insulted him. He raised his hat in mute salutation as he looked them steadily in the eye. And they returned his bow with grave politeness. That's my idea of behavior to a foeman. I mean behavior worthy of the chivalry, as they call us."

"Rudeness comes easy," said someone, "when you hate people."

Read *César Birotteau*.[8] Remembered Commodore Barron's account of the reception when they faced the chivalry so gallantly in quest of the stolen bride.

"The almost impertinent solemnity of these men of the world, whose grave politeness was hiding incipient epigram."

What a nice way of putting it—formally, patiently polite—but laughing at us in your sleeve.

In Missouri, Ben McCulloch caught a Dutch parson in the act of making some men take the oath of allegiance to the U.S.A. He ordered him to take his Bible again in his hand and unswear them as quick as possible.

It is encouraging when one hears of a piece of fun, however broad. If one can afford to laugh, things are mending.

Kentucky does not mean to come to us. Neither does she mean to free her slaves. And they will let her keep what she will if she keeps the peace.

———

7. Edgar, master of Ravenswood, is one of the principal characters of Sir Walter Scott's *The Bride of Lammermoor* (1819). Despite a feud between the Ashton and Ravenswood families that Edgar is pledged to avenge, he falls in love with Lucy Ashton. At the close of the novel, the chivalrous behavior admired by Chesnut has driven Lucy to madness and death and has led Edgar to death by drowning in a bog. It could be read as M. B. C.'s tacit critique of James's code of "chivalry"— sharpened perhaps by the reference to Balzac immediately following.

8. *Histoire de la grandeur et de la décadence de César Birotteau* (1837), a volume of Balzac's *Comédie humaine*, is an account of the rise and fall of a socially ambitious perfume merchant.

She means to keep her slaves, at any rate, but already they are barking and snapping at McClellan's way of snubbing fugitives from over the border.

In North Carolina they have dropped Bragg and—Clingman!![9] I have been trying to picture Clingman not in senatorial robes but in soldier's clothes. He must be one or the other.

⟨⟨I sometimes fear I am so vain, so conceited—think myself so *clever* and my neighbors such geese that pride comes before a fall. I pray I may be spared.⟩⟩[1]

Have a violent attack of something wrong about my heart. It stopped beating—then took to trembling and creaking and thumping like a Mississippi high-pressure steamboat. And the noise in my ears was more like an ammunition wagon rattling over the stones in Richmond.

That was yesterday—and yet I am alive. That kind of thing makes one feel very mortal.

Russell writes how disappointed Prince Jérôme Napoleon was with the appearance of our troops. And that he did not like Beauregard at all.

Well! I give Bogar up to him. But—how a man can find fault with our soldiers—as I have seen them individually and collectively, in Charleston, Richmond, &c&c—that beats me.

Looks are not everything. Hear what King Harry says of his fine fellows the night before Agincourt:

> Why should they mock poor fellows thus!
> The man that once did sell the lion's skin
> While that beast lived—was
> Killed with hunting him.
> And many of our bodies shall no doubt
> Find native graves—upon the which I trust,
> Shall witness live in brass of this day's work.
> Tell the constable we are warriors of the working day;
> Our gayness and our gilt are all besmirched,
> With rainy marching in the painful field.
> There is not a piece of feather in our host.
> Good argument. I hope that we shall not fly.
> And time has worn us into slavery:[2]
> But by the mass our hearts are in the trim,
> And my poor old soldiers tell me, yet ere night
> They'll be in festive robes.

---

9. Former U.S. congressman Thomas L. Clingman and former governor Thomas Bragg were the U.S. senators from N.C. in 1860, but both failed to secure election to the Confederate Senate in 1861.

1. A week of entries in the 1860s Journal is summarized under this date. This entry is dated there Sept. 17, 1861.

2. Shakespeare had it "slovenry." *Henry V*, act 4, scene 3. Four lines farther down, it was "fresher" instead of "festive robes." There are other misquotations.

Men of Manassas changing their soiled clothes for the enemy's purple and fine linen on the battlefield.

> We are the sons of men
> Who conquer'd on Cressy's plains
> And what our father did
> Their sons can do again.

———————

Now I feel better—Napoleon, Prince, and Russell correspondent to the contrary notwithstanding.

War. "That makes such a waste in brief mortality:"

> For God doth know how many now in health
> Shall drop their blood in approbation,
> Of what your reverence shall incite us to.
> Therefore take heed how you impawn our person.
> How you wake the sleeping sword of war.
> We charge you in the name of God—take heed![3]

———————

About as much too late, these words of wisdom, as the collection of money to send for that poor boy's body, now that he is dead. Which money sent in time might have saved his life. For he died of neglected typhoid fever, not of wounds received in battle.

September 18, 1861.   Yesterday was rather rough on a convalescent. We had actually a reception—six men and a boy.

Two of the interesting creatures came for overseer's places and sat for hours—Jackson Revel, a country sandhill neighbor from his youth upward. The young ladies of this house taught him to read, and his son is named for my husband. The leisure these people have. Some of these stupid, slow, heavy-headed louts sat from twelve o'clock till five—and Mr. C would never have forgiven me if I had shown impatience. The boy came to beg, while his mother and sisters sat at the gate. Mr. C was in imminent danger of going mad, but they sat steadfast. ⟨⟨One, named Love, came to get a pass to return to the wars. He was with J. C. at Manassas.⟩⟩ All remained to dinner, boy included, even though he knew his family did "await like love-lighted watch-fire: all day at the gate."

Then after dinner the two Workmans[4] came. They told us of the family camping out, impatient for their son.

The Yankees in their papers claim every victory that we claim in ours. It is

———

3. *Henry V,* act 1, scene 2.
4. Probably John and William C. Workman, brothers who were Camden merchants. John's son William was J. C.'s law partner after the war.

very tantalizing, puzzling. Only this: if they were fairly victorious, would not they be down upon us, instead of hovering around the coast or dancing along the border line—outside, not in? Like a man who wants to rob a house but prudently stands beyond the fence because there is a bad dog in there.

That poor, abused, badgered Walker, he has resigned.[5] As soon as I heard he took it on himself to order military elections without the president's knowledge, I knew his days were numbered, because beyond Mr. Davis he had no friends.

He was of Mr. Clement Clay's recommending. After all, he had a hard time. Nobody satisfied, and he had to bear the brunt.

The British is the most conceited nation in the world, the most self-sufficient, self-satisfied, and arrogant. But each individual man does not blow his own penny whistle. They brag wholesale. Wellington—he certainly leaves it for others to sound his praises. Though Mr. Binney thought the statue of Napoleon at the entrance of Apsley House[6] was a little like "Who killed Cock Robin." "I, said the sparrow, with my little arrow—I saw him die—" But then, it is so pleasant to hear them when it is a lump sum of praise. No private crowing—Trafalgar—Waterloo—Scotch Greys—[illegible word] fighting this, fighting that—their crack corps. It stirs the blood, and every heart responds. Three times three!—hurrah!

Our people send forth their own reported prowess. I did this—I did that. I know they did it—but I hang my head.

Those Tarleton memoirs, Lee's memoirs, Moultrie's, Lord Rawdon's letters[7]—self is never brought to the front. I have been reading them over and admire their modesty and good taste as much as their courage and cleverness.

That kind of British eloquence takes me. Soldats—marchons—gloire? Not a bit of it.

"Now, my lads, stand firm—and then—"

"Now, up and let them have it."

Enough for British bulldogs, with their fighting blood of generations.

Our name has not gone out of print.

Today the *Examiner* as usual pitches into the president. It thinks "Toombs, Cobb, Slidell, Lamar, or Chesnut would have been far better." Considerable choice, among that lot. Five men more utterly dissimilar were never named in the same paragraph.

5. Plagued by ill health and complaints about administrative inefficiency, Secretary of War Leroy Pope Walker resigned on Sept. 16 and became a brigadier general in command of unarmed Ala. troops. Davis replaced him with Atty. Gen. Judah Philip Benjamin of La.

6. The Piccadilly residence of the Duke of Wellington.

7. Sir Banastre Tarleton, *A History of the Campaigns of 1780 and 1781 in the Southern Provinces of North America* (1787): Henry Lee, *Memoirs of the War in the Southern Department of the United States* (1812); William Moultrie, *Memoirs of the American Revolution* (1802). Lord Francis Rawdon's only account of his experiences in the Revolution was a letter written in 1813 to Henry Lee and published as an appendix to Lee's *Campaign of 1781 in the Carolinas* (1824).

Miss Mitford's idea of appreciation by one's own family—who, however, are eager enough to appropriate any reflected glory.

At Wilton House there was a copy of *Arcadia* in which Sir Philip Sidney had written with his own hand: "The Countess of Pembroke's *Arcadia*." Two centuries after his death a governess in the family, happening to open this volume, found in it, beside the inscription already mentioned, a lock of hair wrapped in paper. And in Sir Philip Sidney's well-known hand, written upon it: "the hair of Her Gracious Majesty Queen Elizabeth."

For two hundred years no Sidney, no Herbert, had felt tempted to take down this prose poem &c&c&c.

> Underneath this sable hearse
> Lies the subject of all verse.
> Sidney's sister, Pembroke's mother.
> Death, ere thou hast slain another
> Learned, fair, and good as she,
> Time shall throw a dart at thee.

Moral: no curiosity in the Sidney family or no parade *over* our Sir Philip or his *Arcadia*.[8]

September 19, 1861.   Sandy Hill. Small war in the Ladies Aid Society. Harriet president, Sue Bonney[9] V.P.—and already secession in the air—a row all the time in full blast.

At first there were nearly a hundred members—eighty or ninety always present at a meeting—now ten or twenty are all that they can show.

The worst is, they have forgotten the hospitals, where they really could do so much good, and gone off to provision and clothe the army. A drop in the bucket—or ocean.

A painful piece of news came to us yesterday—our cousin, Mrs. Witherspoon of Society Hill, found dead in her bed.[1]

She was quite well the night before.

Killed, people say, by family troubles—contentions, wrangling, ill blood, among those nearest and dearest to her. She was a proud and high-strung woman. Nothing shabby in word, thought, or deed ever came nigh her. Of a warm and tender heart, too—truth and uprightness itself. Few persons have

8. Mary Russell Mitford (1787–1855), British poet, playwright, and novelist, related this anecdote in her *Recollections of a Literary Life* (1852). "Wilton House," where Sir Philip Sidney composed his pastoral romance *Arcadia* (1590), was the home of his sister Mary Herbert, Countess of Pembroke.

9. Susan Bonney, the daughter of Camden merchant Eli W. Bonney.

1. Elizabeth (Boykin) Witherspoon was the widow of John Dick Witherspoon, a wealthy planter, lawyer, and state legislator of Darlington District. She was a first cousin of M. B. C.'s mother and the mother-in-law of J. C.'s niece Mary Serena Chesnut (Williams) Witherspoon.

ever been more loved and looked up to. A very handsome old lady of fine presence, dignified and commanding.

"Killed by family troubles." ⟨⟨If so, it is the third of that family the same has been said of.⟩⟩ So they said when Mr. John N. Williams died.[2] So Uncle John said yesterday of his brother Burwell.

"Death deserts the army," said that quaint old soul, "and takes fancy shots of the most eccentric kind nearer home."

The high and disinterested conduct our enemies seem to expect of us is involuntary and unconscious praise.

They pay us the compliment to look for from us—and execrate us for the want of it—a degree of virtue they were never able to practice themselves. A word of our crowning misdemeanor, holding in slavery still those Africans they brought here from Africa or sold to us when they found they did not pay. They gradually slided (or slid?) them off down here. Freed them prospectively, giving themselves years to get rid of them in a remunerative way. We want to spread them, too—west and south—or northwest, where the climate would free them or kill them, improve them out of the world as they do Indians. If they had been forced to keep them in New England, I daresay they would have shared the Indians' fate. For they are wise in their generation, these Yankee children of light. Those pernicious Africans!

Result of the conversation between Mr. C and Uncle John—both ci-devant Union men. Now utterly for states rights.

Queer! how different the same man appears, viewed from different standpoints.

"What a perfect gentleman—so fine-looking, highbred, distinguished. Easy, free and, above all, graceful in his bearing—so high-toned! He is always indignant at any symptom of wrongdoing. He is charming, the man of all others I like to have strangers see—a noble representative of our country."

"Yes. Every word true. He is all that. And then, the other side of the picture is true, too. You can always find him—you know *where* to find him!—wherever there is a looking glass, a bottle, or a woman. There will he be also."

"My God! And you call yourself his friend."

"Yes, I know him—down to the ground."

This conversation I overheard from an upper window—looking down on the piazza below.

---

2. John Nicholas Williams of Darlington District, a planter and cotton mill owner, died in April 1861. His first wife was J. C.'s sister Esther Serena Chesnut; his second was Elizabeth (Boykin) Witherspoon's daughter Sarah Cantey Witherspoon. David Rogerson Williams, Jr., the husband of M. B. C.'s sister Kate, was a child of his first marriage.

A complicated character, beyond La Bruyère[3]—what Mrs. Preston calls "the refinement" spread thin—skin-deep only.

———————

"Do you expect men to be better here than anywhere else in the world?"
"Yes." "Oh! Beast out of thy stall! Look upon high, and thank thy God for all."[4]
Kate came down as fresh—as sweet, as smiling—as a spring morning. She is the proudest and happiest mother.
"Mary, tell Auntie your analysis of character at _____ house.[5]
"Oh," said the loveliest blonde with the blackest *blue* eyes, not ten years old yet, "She likes everybody. She longs for peace with everybody—and she wants her children to go every[where] they are asked. She is happy and she wants her children to be happy. He dislikes every living soul out of that house. He tells something dreadful of everybody. He is perfectly wretched, and he is miserable if he can't make everybody as wretched as he is. And all of his children are exactly like him."

———————

"Mama sent Dr. Boykin a salmon pie while they were in camp near us. It was huge. Thompson said it smelt so good—as he was taking it to the Rangers, he thought he'd have some scraps, coming home with the dish. Never a scrap. The white gentleman handed him the baking dish, scraped as clean as if niggers had licked it in the kitchen."

———————

An iron steamer has run the blockade at Savannah. We raise our wilted heads like flowers after a shower. This drop of good news revives us.
Kate says: "They are so injudicious. Among them up there. They will kill that poor little Callie Perkins.[6] A widow—almost before she is a woman grown."
《Lady Sale's entry in her journal, "Earthquakes as usual," may soon be possible here—tremble as the idea shakes me. We have had two in a month—we hear of death and mortality on every side.
《Men murdering each other wholesale in these great battles—and *sickness* and disease God-sent—laughing their puny efforts to scorn—ten men dying in hospitals where one dies on the battlefield—and our friends who never leave home and are thought safe dying in their beds and found dead, cause un-

3. Jean de La Bruyère, *Les Caractères de Théophraste, traduits de Grec, avec les caractères ou les moeurs de ce siècle* (1688).
4. A modernization of lines from Chaucer's "Balade de Bon Conseyl" (also known as "Truth"), which M. B. C. quotes more fully on p. 214.
5. Identified as the Withers's home in the 1860s Journal under Sept. 20.
6. Caroline Jumelle (Perkins) Perkins, seventeen, was the widow of planter Roger Griswold Perkins of Camden.

known. God shows he can *make trouble* and disregards our puny efforts to make it for ourselves. But this thing of feeling the ground struck from under our feet—a wonderful thing to shake one's nerves.⟩⟩

September 21, 1861.   Last night when the mail came in, I was seated near the lamp. Mr. Chesnut, lying on a sofa at a little distance, called out to me, "Look at my letters and tell me about them."

I began to read one aloud; it was from Mary Witherspoon—and I broke down. Horror and amazement was too much for me. Poor Cousin Betsey Witherspoon was murdered! She did not die peacefully, as we supposed, in her bed. Murdered by her own people. Her negroes.

I remember when Dr. Keitt[7] was murdered by his negroes. Mr. Miles met me and told the dreadful story.

"Very awkward indeed, this sort of thing. There goes Keitt, in the house always declaiming about the 'beneficent institution.' How now?"

Horrible beyond words.

Her household negroes were so insolent, so pampered and insubordinate, that she lived alone and at home. She knew, she said, that none of her children would have the patience she had with these people who had been indulged and spoiled by her until they were like spoiled children. Simply intolerable.

Mr. Chesnut and David Williams[8] have gone over at once.

I went up to see Caroline Perkins. Her mother would not permit me to see her. Priscilla has spent her life in mourning.[9] Gloom hangs over her like a pall. This beautiful *French* young thing. Does she expect to make her as miserable for life as she is? Never. The mother will never understand the daughter. She may, however, shut her up and mope her to death. The child is too young. She can throw off any grief now if they will only let her alone. Live it down, as Schiller's man says.[1]

September 24, 1861.   The party to Society Hill have come home again. Nothing very definite so far. William and Cousin Betsey's old maid Rhody in jail. Strong suspicion, no proof of their guilt yet. The neighborhood in a ferment. Evans and Wallaces[2] say these negroes ought to be burnt. Lynching proposed!

7. Lawrence M. Keitt's brother, Dr. William J. Keitt, had his throat cut by his slaves while he lay sick in bed on his Fla. plantation in Feb. 1860.

8. Kate's husband, David Rogerson Williams, Jr.

9. Priscilla Bryan (Jumelle) Perkins was the widowed daughter of a French refugee from the slave rebellion on Santo Domingo.

1. Probably Friedrich von Schiller, *Wallenstein* (1798–99), act 4, scene 2, in which Wallenstein's daughter has just heard of the death of her beloved. Wallenstein says, "Let her sorrow express itself. Allow her to lament / . . . , for she / Has lived through the experience of great grief . . . ," C. E. Passage, trans. (1958).

2. Members of two prominent Society Hill planting families related to the Witherspoons.

But it is all idle talk. They will be tried as the law directs, and not otherwise. John Witherspoon[3] will not allow anything wrong or violent to be done. He has a detective here from Charleston.

Again I went to see the Perkinses. Miss Ogier met me at the door. No admittance. She said, in solemn tones, shaking her head, the poor old maid: "Not eighteen—and twice widowed, *as it were.*"

"Great comforters are ye all," said Job. The child! And they talk, those old women, as if her life was over. Mrs. Perkins asked Judge Withers if he did not think Caroline should wear widows' caps. "That young thing," I said. "I wonder they don't shave her head and make her rend her garments and sit in sackcloth and ashes."

Hitherto I have never thought of being afraid of negroes. I had never injured any of them. Why should they want to hurt me? Two-thirds of my religion consists in trying to be good to negroes because they are so in my power, and it would be so easy to be the other thing. Somehow today I feel that the ground is cut away from under my feet. Why should they treat me any better than they have done Cousin Betsey Witherspoon?

Kate and I sat up late and talked it all over. Mrs. Witherspoon was a saint on this earth. And this is her reward.

Kate's maid came in—a strong-built mulatto woman. She was dragging in a mattress. "Missis, I have brought my bed to sleep in your room while Mars David is at Society Hill. You ought not to stay in a room by yourself *these times.*" And then she went off for more bed gear.

"For the life of me," said Kate gravely, "I cannot make up my mind. Does she mean to take care of me—or to murder me?" I do not think she heard, but when she came back she said, "Missis, as I have a soul to be saved, I will keep you safe. I will guard you."

We know Betsey well. Has she soul enough to swear by? She is a great stout, jolly, irresponsible, *unreliable,* pleasant-tempered, bad-behaved woman with ever so many good points. Among others, she is so clever she can do anything. And she never loses her temper—but she has no moral sense whatever.

That night Kate came into my room. She could not sleep. Those black hands strangling and smothering Mrs. Witherspoon's gray head under the counterpane haunted her. So we sat up and talked the long night through.

Dined next day with Mary Boykin.[4] She was sad, ill, and miserable. Made no effort to be otherwise—her husband and son under the enemy's guns. Kate Heyward, handsome as ever, absolutely jolly, said, "And can your country find

---

3. Mary Serena Chesnut (Williams) Witherspoon's husband, a resident of Society Hill who owned more than one hundred slaves in Marlborough District.
4. Mary Chesnut (Lang) Boykin was the wife of Dr. Edward M. Boykin and a first cousin once removed of J. C.

nothing better for you to do than knit stockings for soldiers?" A compliment from her is something to boast of.

The Judge thought as Uncle Hamilton had given ten thousand dollars to raise the company called Boykin's Rangers and then subscribed twenty thousand more to the Confederacy, William E. Johnson ought not to be allowed to unseat him as senator.

That is it, then. This is the upshot of all those whispers forever being poured in my ears as to A. H. B.'s unpopularity. The cat is out of the bag. They want his seat in the state senate.

That's the outcome of it all. *She* is fearfully practical.[5] Burwell broke his arm. She left him at the John DeSaussures'. When she did go to see him, she entered the room, shaking her finger at the boy, graceful and beautiful, with her face wreathed in smiles: "So you see now, my son, what comes of disobeying your mother."

Went over just now to have a talk with that optimist my mother-in-law. Blessed are the pure in mind, for they shall see God.[6] Her mind certainly is free from evil thoughts. Someone says the most unhappy person is the one who has bad thoughts. She ought to be happy. She thinks no evil. And yet she is the cleverest woman I know.

She began to ask me something of Charlotte Temple[7] (*so-called* to keep back true name).

"Has she ever had any more children? Is she as beautiful as ever?"

"She has one more. I do not see her now at her window. Can't answer for her beauty."

"Is she married?"

"Not."

"Is she a bad girl—*now, really?*"

"Yes."

"Oh, no! Don't say that. Poor thing! Maybe after all she is not really bad, only to be pitied—&c&c. Remember our Savior &c&c&c."

I gave it up. I felt like a fool. Here was one thing I had made sure of a fixed fact. In this world, an unmarried girl with two children was necessarily not a good woman. If that can be waived aside I gave it up in utter confusion of mind.

Mrs. Chesnut, ever since she came here sixty or seventy years ago as a bride

---

5. Alexander Hamilton Boykin's wife Sarah James (DeSaussure) Boykin, who was the niece of John McPherson DeSaussure and the first cousin of Wilmot Gibbes DeSaussure. Her son Burwell was eleven.

6. Matthew 5:8, slightly misquoted: "Blessed are the pure in heart, for they shall see God." The verse would be inscribed later on Mary (Cox) Chesnut's gravestone.

7. The heroine, a woman of uncertain virtue, in Susanna Rowson's popular novel, *Charlotte: A Tale of Truth* (1794).

from Philadelphia, has been trying to make it up to the negroes for being slaves. 1796 I think was the year of her marriage. Today someone asked her about it when she was describing Mrs. Washington's drawing [room?] to us. Through her friendship for Nelly Custis and living very near, and stiff stern old Martha Washington not liking to have her coach horses taken out for trifles, and Mrs. Cox letting Nelly Custis and Mary Cox[8] have the carriage at their pleasure—she was a great deal thrown with the Washington household. Colonel Cox, too, at one time had been on Washington's staff. And his camp chest is here en évidence. Colonel Cox raised a regiment at his own expense. And likewise, as he owned Valley Forge, was able to assist nobly as quartermaster &c&c, commissary general, or assistant to Greene,[9] &c&c, in keeping that forlorn Valley Forge army alive and unfrostbitten, &c&c. And as she eloquently related for the hundredth time all this:

"How came you to leave that pleasant Philadelphia and all its comforts for half-civilized up-country and all the horrors of slavery?"

"Did you not know that my father owned slaves in Philadelphia? In his will he left me several of them. Also he left them to be freed after a certain time &c."

In the Quaker city, and in the lifetime of a living woman now present, there were slaveholders. It is hard to believe. Time works its wonders of change like enchantment. So quickly we forget.

"Grandma is so awfully clever, and you can't make her think any harm of anybody. Now I have my doubts. She knows more than she seems to see in this wrong world of ours—eh?"

"She is a resolute optimist." [*Remainder of the page cut off here.*]

"It took an angel, didn't it, to entertain M____ with close questioning as to the beauty and goodness and children of Charlotte Temple?"

"Didn't you know the scandal there was—about her—and—?"

"But it was not true."

"That has nothing to do with it. It was said. And she knew what every one of us was thinking."

"A pleasant topic—tact and taste—and a kind heart to suggest it. The sight of _____ seems always to suggest it. Anyhow, *she* faced the music gallantly. She sat there and screamed her answers at the top of her voice. She did not show that she was annoyed. Neither does she show any uneasiness [over] being a childless woman. The glory of <being> the mother of so many children—seems to crop up in the conversation as soon as she comes about."

"_____[1] is scant of patience, and she loves, and she hates, and she thinks evil of her neighbors, and she speaks it out at her leisure. She said, 'It was better for the world to call a fallen woman by her people's name. It might be unchristian and nasty, just as it was better for the world to hang a murderer—however unpleasant for the individual.' She said she did not believe in seduced women.

8. Old Mrs. Chesnut's maiden name.
9. Nathanael Greene, major general and quartermaster general of the Continental Army, and commander of the Southern armies 1780–83.
1. The unsupplied name would seem to be that of M. B. C.

They knew the consequences. Amiably, and with a lovely face and a sweet voice calling evil good—would hardly do for everybody to try, if there was to be any distinction made between right and wrong. So she would call a spade a spade—be the holder of it white, black, or tan color."

Mr. Grant[2] ordered his daughters to put down Tasso's *Jerusalem Delivered*[3] as an accused thing.

Mrs. C said: "Why? I remember when I first read it. My foot was on the rocker of my baby's cradle. I do not recollect anything wrong." Armida.[4]

"Don't you think she hides her head like the ostrich and thinks nobody sees, as she won't see?"

"No—she hides her head in soft, comfortable wraps. She is blind to all but beautiful things, rose-tinted beliefs and pure imagining. And she is happy— quand même. You may depend [on it that] the French woman is right—the unhappiest people are those who have bad thoughts."

Mrs. C has a greediness of books such as I never saw in anyone else. Reading is the real occupation and solace of her life.

In the soft, luxurious life she leads, she denies herself nothing that she wants. In her well-regulated character she could not want anything that she ought not to have.

Economy is one of her cherished virtues. And strange to say, she never buys a book or has been known to take a magazine or periodical. But she has them all. They gravitate toward her. They flow into her room. Everybody is proud to send or lend any book they have compassed by any means, fair or foul. Other members of the family who care nothing whatever for them buy the books, and she reads them.

She spends hours every day cutting out baby clothes for the negro babies. This department is under her supervision. She puts little bundles of things to be made in everybody's workbasket and calls it her sewing society. She is always ready with an ample wardrobe for every newcomer. Then the mothers bring their children for her to prescribe and look after whenever they are ailing. She is not at all nervous. She takes a baby and lances its gums quite coolly and scientifically. She dresses all hurts, bandages all wounds, &c&c. These people are simply devoted to her. Proving they can be grateful enough, when you give them anything to be grateful for.

Two women always sleep in her room in case she should be ill or need attention during the night. And two others sleep in the next room to relieve guard, so to speak. When it is cold, she changes her nightclothes. Everything is dried before these women give her the second dress. They iron every garment to make sure that it is warm and dry enough. For this purpose smoothing irons are always before the fire. And the fire is never allowed to go down while it is

2. Harriet's father, William Joshua Grant, who died in 1855.

3. Torquato Tasso, *La Gerusalemme liberata* (1575), recounts the feats of Godfrey of Boulogne on the First Crusade.

4. In *La Gerusalemme liberata*, Armida is a sorceress employed by Satan to sow discord among the Christians. Her seduction of Rinaldo, an Italian crusader, is a minor theme of the poem.

cool enough for the family to remain at Mulberry. During the summer at Sandy Hill it is exactly the same, but then she gets up and changes everything because it is so warm, &c&c.

It amounts to this, these old people find it hard to invent ways of passing the time, and they have such a quantity of idle negroes about them—some occupation for them must be found.

In the meantime her standing employment is reading. And her husband's is driving out with a pair of spanking thoroughbred bays which have been trained to trot as slowly as a trot can be managed.

《I do not see what Mr. C means.[5] He writes to no one—knows nothing that is going on. If he has *one* active friend in the state I do not know it, unless it be Wilmot DeSaussure and Bob McCaa.[6] In the meantime at these fiery times he is as peaceful here and as *secure!* Making arrangements to spend the winter in Richmond.... Davis has given Tom Drayton a generalcy. If J. C. made Jeff Davis president—has he not been rewarded as usual...?

《A letter from Trescot yesterday, impudent message to me, and says so many new members are to be elected [that] the future senatorship puzzles conjectures. And J. C. dashing aside letters and not answering them, as if he was *heir* apparent to the throne of *the world* and his election certain!...

《I feel so depressed for my country and for *myself* and for my future political hopes.

《God grant I may not be left destitute in my old age....》

October 1, 1861. Went to the Ladies Aid Society. My initiation fee was ten dollars. Someone said they were in debt. Mrs. Lee[7] (Jersey woman) dolorous. Louisa Salmond[8] active and efficient. Everybody knitting. Quantities of things were being packed and baled up to send off. I sat with poor Milly Trimlin and the likes of her, who came for work. So this society does good in more ways than one—gives work and aid to the poor soldiers' wives.

They got into debt making underclothes for Tom Warren's company.[9]

These good people are not gushing. "Ladies in stays—as stiff as stones." Kate came in, bowing and smiling on every side. Dear, graceful sister, you make these wooden pegs stiffer than ever. Someone (a man, of course) said she was like a beautiful deer among stolid cattle—chewing the cud, those cows were.

---

5. From the 1860s Journal (entries dated Sept. 27, 28, and 29, 1861).

6. M. B. C. probably meant to write "McCaw." Robert Gadsden McCaw was a large plantation owner of York District who served in the S.C. legislature before the war.

7. Ann (Cooper) Lee, the wealthy widow of Episcopal minister Francis P. Lee and the mother of John Boykin Lee.

8. Ann Louisa Salmond, daughter of Camden banker Thomas Durham Salmond, was a second cousin once removed of J. C.

9. The editor of the Camden *Journal*, Thomas Warren, organized the Kershaw Guards of the Fifteenth S.C. Regiment.

And then he said he got that figure of speech from Lady Georgiana Fullerton.[1] He could not remember the name of the book.

Dr. Young,[2] just from Richmond, reports the president ill—gone off with his physician to a farm. Things in a distracted state, consequently.

_____[3] in ecstasies over the senseless abuse heaped upon Jeff Davis. I have to swallow a great deal, for with her, at least, I must hold my tongue. It is my duty not to quarrel there.

Keitt is out in a defense of Stephens of Georgia. Who's attacking him? I have not had any of it.

I always find Lawrence Keitt immensely clever and original. Some girl described him as saying "the quintessence of efflorescence." And the name abided by him. What he was really saying he told me, quoting Milton, and fools did not know: "Bright influence of bright essence increate."[4]

I held my tongue when they quoted Keitt against Mr. Davis. How I longed to say, "Oh, please keep your private spites until we are out of the woods." Oh! It is a hopeless business, if one cannot work together for one year in peace.

Republics—everybody jawing, everybody putting their mouths in, nothing sacred, all confusion of babble, crimination, and recrimination—republics can't carry on war. Hurrah for a strong one-man government.

"To keep our army still till the others had time to gird up their loins and come after us again—wretched work, wretched policy," they cry, and the fleet still hovering around Port Royal. We never had a plan. We sit still and wait the chapter of accidents. Circumstances, that unspiritual God and miscreater—him we worship.

Mercury you see doing its worst. . . .[5]

Sam Shannon[6] says he met Governor Manning at Kingsville. He threw his arms around Sam's neck.

"'I am completely cast aside. I never see my name in print now.' And then he goes for Jeff Davis."

"Why do you hate republics?"

"Because the mob rules republics."

"And the mob always prefers Barrabas to Jesus Christ. And yet people do so love to be popular and to have the votes of the mob."

One begins to understand the power which the ability to vote gives the meanest citizen.

---

1. Lady Georgiana Charlotte Fullerton was the author of *Ellen Middleton* (1844) and *Lady Bird* (1852), novels designed to broaden popular understanding of Catholicism.

2. James Andrew Young, a Camden physician and silversmith.

3. Identified in the 1860s Journal as Elizabeth Withers.

4. *Paradise Lost*, book 3, line 6.

5. Deleted is an abortive list of "Synonimes"—"can't find now."

6. Samuel Davis Shannon, a planter, fought with his brother William M. Shannon in the Kirkwood Rangers and became an aide of Gen. Richard Heron Anderson. As such, he was a prominent member of wartime Richmond society.

We had been at one of Uncle Hamilton's splendid dinners—plate glass, Sèvres china, and everything that was nice to eat. In the piazza, when the gentlemen were smoking after dinner, in the midst of them sat Squire Mac-Donald, the well digger. He was officiating in that capacity at Plane Hill then. Apparently he was most at his ease of all. He had his clay pipe in his mouth. He was cooler than the rest, being in his shirtsleeves, and leaned back luxuriously in his chair tilted on its two hind legs, with his naked feet up on the bannister. Said Louisa McCaa,[7] "Look, the mud from the well is sticking through his toes."

"Uncle H is going in for courting the country *strong*."

"No—he is a free white man, and he is a near-relation, descendant, or something, of Jasper MacDonald,[8] who nailed up our colors at Fort Moultrie, &c&c."

"See how solemnly polite and attentive Mr. Chesnut is to him."

"Oh! that's his way. The raggeder and more squalid the creature, the more polite and the softer Mr. Chesnut grows, &c&c."

Enough of foresight sad, too much of retrospect have I;
And well for me that I sometimes can put these feelings by.
From public ills, and thoughts that else,
Might weigh me down to earth,
That I can gain some intervals
Of healthful, hopeful mirth.

October 3, 1861.   The *Mercury*'s correspondent from Richmond grows more audacious. Last night we read of his hopes: "When another battle was won, we would not have to wait half a year for wagons or for Jeff Davis to recover his health or for Beauregard to write a fancy report of the battle."

"When I came to that part of his report—'Oh, mon patrie'—bad taste, I said—horrid!"

"Oh, papa! Beauregard is a Frenchman. Never in this world did he say '*mon patrie*.'"

"He's a Creole, but it is his country. Whose country is it, then?"

"That would be worse than a crime; it would be a blunder."

"What's the row?"

"Papa, *patrie* is feminine."

"Fiddlesticks!" said paterfamilias, unabashed, unashamed. "Frenchmen make worse mistakes than that when they try to speak English."

"In English, one's country is feminine. Webster—the great Daniel! Suppose he had said: "There is my state. There is Massachusetts. Look at *him!*"

7. Ann Louisa (McCaa) Haile, the wife of Kershaw planter Columbus Haile, was M. B. C.'s first cousin.

8. A reference to Sgt. William Jasper, a hero of the defense of Charleston against the British in July 1776.

"You are not more powerful than an act of Parliament. You don't change the sex of your country. Judge Brevard[9] said that was the only thing Parliament could not do. Make a man a woman."

> Lightly is life laid down among us now
> And lightly death is mourned—
> We have no time to mourn.

Dr. Deas brought us confirmation of Price's victory away off somewhere.[1] But then, here is Port Royal under our noses. They can take their revenge there. Yesterday the *Mercury* cited their attention to Wilmington, which it said was totally undefended and crammed with military stores.

Lila Davis, commenting on this, said her Uncle George[2] wrote they would not be ready for the enemy at Wilmington for a fortnight. Let us hope the enemy will have sufficient polite consideration to wait that time at least. I am sure we always do that good part by them—and lay on our oars until they can complete all of their preparations to annihilate us. We let them make their arrangements in peace.

We told Dr. Deas: "Prevention was better than cure. If the Confederacy had chosen to elect Barnwell Rhett president instead of Jefferson Davis—or had Mr. Davis made Hon. B. R. secretary of state—we might have escaped one small war, at least—the war the *Mercury* was now waging with the administration."

Breckinridge, William Preston, and Clay have escaped Seward's little bell and are safe now in the part of Kentucky which is loyal to the South.[3]

"Oh, Breckinridge is too late. He is too slow. How much good he might have done us if he had come in time. What a splendid war minister he would have made, instead of that lame, tame Walker, whose genius lay in exasperating everybody who had anything to do with him."

October 4, 1861. So Mr. Dallas,[4] too, has made a violent speech against us ⟪the ungrateful wretch⟫ pledging their last man and their last dollar. John R.

9. Joseph Brevard, a Camden lawyer and judge of the S.C. Supreme Court, 1801–15.
1. Lynch Horry Deas, a well-to-do Camden physician, was probably reporting the capture of Lexington, Mo., on Sept. 20 by Sterling Price, commander of the state's Confederate militia.
2. Ann Eliza Davis was the daughter of the Episcopal bishop of S.C., Thomas Frederick Davis, Sr., and the niece of George Davis, a member of the Confederate Congress, from N.C.
3. John C. Breckinridge, William Preston, and James Brown Clay were forced to flee toward Albert Sidney Johnston's army near Bowling Green after the Unionist Ky. legislature threatened to arrest them for treason. The former vice-president accepted a brigadier general's commission in the C.S.A.; Preston, a former Ky. congressman, U.S. minister to Spain, and brother-in-law of A. S. Johnston, became a colonel on the general's staff. Clay, also a former Ky. congressman and the son of Henry Clay, was arrested and was later deported to Canada.
4. Vice-president of the U.S. under James K. Polk, George Mifflin Dallas of Pa. was equally opposed to abolitionism and secession.

Thomson,[5] ditto—Moffat of Princeton,[6] educated by Mr. Douglas[7] of this place. The Douglases think he might have spared us his denunciation.

Edward Haile[8] was awfully shocked when Mr. Chesnut said any man who came out of this war without being ruined in his estate would be lucky. "What if we are victorious?" "Even so."

"Why, I went into it meaning to double mine. And so I will—so help me God."

"That's where God's help will come in. It is as God pleases," said Kate.

"Somehow I never associate the name of God with doubling fortunes."

> War is mercy, glory, fame.
> Waged in freedom's holy cause,
> Freedom such as man may claim
> Under God's restraining cause."

All depends upon the venue—whether she means to locate, as we say on this side of the water, in England, *or* in Ireland, *OR* in India.

Edward Haile said that the government at Richmond had given the states notice they must take care of themselves.

Easy enough to say—not so easy to do. How can they? They have stripped themselves of men and money for the armies of the Confederacy.

New York *Herald* prophesies that the North will be too hot for Beecher[9] and Greeley if we succeed. And yet, would either of them be received with open arms here? Never. Also, N.Y. *Herald* is delighted to hear of our internal dissensions and divisions—says it is an omen of good for them. And the *Inquirer*[1] grows sarcastical and advises us to win the spoils before we proceed to divide them.

An appalling list of foreigners in the Yankee army. These newspapers tell of the Hungarians, Russians, Prussians—French dukes de Chartres and Joinville.[2] We have Polignac as a setoff. He took Mrs. Constitution Browne for Mrs. Davis. May he prove of clearer vision on the field of battle.

----

5. John Renshaw Thomson, U.S. senator from N.J. since 1853, had been among the Chesnuts' social circle in Washington.

6. James Clement Moffat, a classmate of J. C. at Princeton, became professor of ecclesiastical history at Princeton Theological Seminary in 1861.

7. A Camden merchant, James Kennedy Douglas.

8. This planter of Alachua County, Fla., was Louisa (McCaa) Haile's brother-in-law. His wife Mary (Chesnut) Haile was a niece of James Chesnut, Jr.

9. Henry Ward Beecher of N.Y., Congregationalist minister, abolitionist, and brother of Harriet (Beecher) Stowe.

1. Probably the Philadelphia *Inquirer*.

2. Prince de Joinville and his nephews Comte de Paris and Duc de Chartes were exiled members of the French royal family. Traveling in America at the start of the war, the three men became aides on George B. McClellan's staff.

Last night my husband was saying his father's twenty thousand acres of unoccupied land might cut up into small farms and make us a much more prosperous country.

The swamplands only are utilized now for the black man—a creature whose mind is as dark and unenlightened as his skin.

《Mr. Chesnut was saying his father's 10 thousand acres cut up into 8 hundred farms would make such a *prosperous* country—and *now*, it is one profitless plantation, where the black man must be kept as dark and unenlightened as his skin.》[3]

This kind of talk is fearfully distasteful to the octogenarian chief. His idea of the whole duty of man is [that] one should keep his estate intact, as he received it from his father, or go on buying out the neighbors and enlarging one's borders.

October 7, 1861. Mrs. Davis and Mrs. Joe Johnston have been upset—the former not exactly in a situation to abide upsets without harm to herself.[4] Mrs. Johnston's arm is broken. I have written to each of the errant ladies.

My whole mind was riveted upon the dangers that encompass our men. Never dreamed our womenfolk were in any danger of life or limb.

Uncle H writes, "All this marching and countermarching—it seems so aimless and futile. We take a place with heavy loss of men and ammunition, then retire. The enemy then takes it from the few we left to guard it, and then we have to go and capture it anew—at the same expense of life, &c—*da capo.*

He adds that the president's visit to the army roused enthusiasm once more to fever heat.

"To those whose God is honor, disgrace alone is sin."

From Hare's *Guesses at Truth:*

To remould and frame a constitution anew are works of the greatest difficulty and hazard. The attempt is likely to fail altogether or not succeed thoroughly under many years. It is the last desperate resource of a desperate people. A striking double or quits with evil. Still, it is a resource. We make use of cataplasm to restore suspended animation. Burke himself might have tried Medea's kettle on a carcass.[5]

---

3. Such changes in substance and tone as occurred between this passage in the 1860s Journal, Oct. 6, 1861, and the two paragraphs above in the 1880s Version are not characteristic of the revision, but they did sometimes appear.

4. Mrs. Davis was soon to have a baby.

5. Both quotations above are paraphrased from Julius and Augustus William Hare, *Guesses at Truth* (1861), pp. 17 and 19.

Thousands of overcoats—think of that. Captain Lynch has captured a steamer with all those overcoats.[6]

Just as I feared. A rush of all Europe *to them* as soon as they raised the cry that this war is for the extirpation of slavery. If our people had read less of Mr. Calhoun's works and only read the signs of the times a little more. If they had known more of what was going on around them in the world.

———————

"Half the failures in life arise from pulling in one's horse just as he is leaping." And here they use whip and spur—and then pull in.

———————

And now comes back on us that bloody story that haunts me night and day, Mrs. Witherspoon's murder.

The man William, who was the master spirit of the gang, once ran away and was brought back from somewhere west. And then his master and himself had a reconciliation, and the master henceforth made a pet of him.

The night preceding the murder, John Witherspoon went over to his mother's to tell her of some of William and Rhody's misdeeds. While their mistress was away from home, they had given a ball fifteen miles away from Society Hill. To that place they had taken their mistress's china, silver, house linen, &c&c. After his conversation with his mother, as he rode out of the gate, he shook his whip at William and said, "Tomorrow I mean to come here and give every one of you a thrashing."

That night Mrs. Witherspoon was talking it all over with her grandson, a half-grown boy who lived with her—slept, indeed, in a room opening into hers.

"I do not intend John to punish these negroes. It is too late to begin discipline now. It is all nonsense. I have indulged them past bearing, they all say. I ought to have tried to control them. It is all my fault. That's the end of it."

Mrs. Edwards,[7] who was a sister of Mrs. Witherspoon, was found dead in her bed. It is thought this suggested their plan of action to the negroes. What more likely than she should die as her sister had done.

They were all in great trouble when John went off. William said, "Listen to me, and there will be no punishment here tomorrow." They made their plan, and then all of them *went to sleep,* William remaining awake to stir up the others at the proper hour.

What first attracted the attention of the family was the appearance of black and blue spots about the face and neck of the body of their mother. Then

6. Capt. William Francis Lynch, famous before the war as an explorer of the Jordan River and the Dead Sea, commanded the Confederate naval defenses of N.C. Mrs. Chesnut is probably referring to the capture of the Federal supply ship *Fanny* in Pamlico Sound on Oct. 1.

7. Probably Elizabeth Boykin (Cantey) Edwards, who was a niece, not a sister, of Elizabeth Witherspoon.

someone in moving the candle from the table at her bedside found blood upon their fingers.

Looking at the candlestick, they saw the print of a bloody hand which had held it. There was an empty bed in the entry, temporarily there for some purpose. As they were preparing to lay her out, someone took up the counterpane from this bed to throw over her. On the underside of it—again, bloody fingers.

Now they were fairly aroused. Rhody was helping Mary Witherspoon a little apart from the rest. Mary cried:

"I wish they would not say such horrid things. Poor soul, she died in peace with all the world. It is bad enough to find her dead. Nobody even touched a hair of her head. To think any mortal could murder her. Never! I will not believe it!"

To Mary's amazement, Rhody drew near her, and looking strangely in her eyes, she said:

"Well done! Miss Mary. You stick to dat, my Missis. You stick to dat."

Mary thrilled all over with suspicion and dread. She said nothing, however.

There was a trunk in Mrs. Witherspoon's closet where she kept money and a complete outfit ready for traveling at any moment—among other things, some new and very fine nightgowns. One of her daughters noticed that her mother must have opened that trunk, contrary to her custom, for she wore then one of the nightgowns above spoken of. They then looked into the closet, found the trunk unlocked and all the gold gone. The daughters knew the number of gold pieces she always kept under lock and key in that trunk.

Now they began to scent mischief and foul play in earnest, and they sent for the detective. Before he came they searched all houses and found bloody rags.

The detective dropped in from the skies quite unexpectedly. He saw that one of the young understrappers of the gang looked frightened and uncomfortable. This one he fastened upon and got up quite an intimacy with him. Finally he told this boy that he knew all about it. William had confessed privately to him to save himself and hang the others. But as the detective had taken a fancy to this boy, if he would confess everything, he would take him as state's evidence instead of William. The young man was utterly confounded at first but fell in the trap laid for him and told every particular from beginning to end.

Then they were all put in jail, the youth who had confessed among them, as he did not wish them to know of his *treachery* to them.

This was his story. "After John went away that night, Rhody and William made a great fuss—were furious at Mars John threatening them after all these years—to talk to them that away."

William said: "Mars John more than apt to do what he say he will do. You-all follow what I say and he'll have something else to think of beside stealing and breaking glass and china and tablecloths. If ole Marster was alive now, what would he say? Talk of whipping us at this time of day, &c&c."

Rhody kept the key of the house to let herself in every morning. So they arranged to go in at twelve. And then William watched, and they slept the sleep of the righteous.

Before that, however, they had a "rale fine supper and a heap of laughing at the way dey's all look tomorrow."

They smothered her with a counterpane from a bed in the entry. He had no trouble the first time because they found her asleep and "done it all 'fore she waked." But after Rhody took her keys and went into the trunk and got a clean nightgown—for they had spoiled the one she had on—and fixed everything, candle, medicine, and all—she came to! Then she begged them hard for life. She asked them what she had ever done that they should want to kill her? She promised them before God never to tell on them. Nobody should ever know. But Rhody stopped her mouth by the counterpane. William held her head and hands down. And the other two sat on her legs. Rhody had a thrifty mind and wished to save the sheets and nightgown. She did not destroy them—they were found behind her mantelpiece. There the money was also, all in a hole made among the bricks behind the wooden mantelpiece.

A grandson of Rhody's slept in her house. Him she locked up in his room. She did not want him to know anything of this fearful night.

That innocent old lady and her gray hairs moved them not a jot.

Fancy how we feel. I am sure I will never sleep again without this nightmare of horror haunting me.

Mrs. Chesnut, who is their good angel, is and has always been afraid of negroes. In her youth the St. Domingo stories were indelibly printed on her mind.

She shows her dread now by treating everyone as if they were a black Prince Albert or Queen Victoria.

We were beginning to forget Mrs. Cunningham, the only other woman we ever heard of murdered by her negroes.

Poor Cousin Betsey was goodness itself. After years of freedom and indulgence and tender kindness, it was an awful mistake to threaten them like children. It was only threats. Everybody knew she would never do anything.

How about Mrs. Cunningham? He was an old bachelor, and the negroes had it all their own way till he married. And then they hated her. They took her from her room, just over one in which her son-in-law and her daughter slept. They smothered her, dressed her, and carried her out—all without the slightest noise—and hung her by the neck to an apple tree, as if she had committed suicide. Waked nobody in the house by all this. If they want to kill us, they can do it when they please—they are noiseless as panthers.

They were discovered—first, because dressing her in the dark, her tippet was put on hind part before. And she was supposed to have walked out and hung herself in a pair of brand-new shoes whose soles evidently had never touched the ground.

We ought to be grateful that any one of us is alive. But nobody is afraid of their own negroes. These are horrid brutes—savages, monsters—but I find everyone like myself, ready to trust their own yard. I would go down on the plantation tomorrow and stay there, if there were no white person in twenty miles. My Molly and half a dozen others that *I know*—and all the rest I believe—would keep me as safe as I should be in the Tower of London.

《 . . . drove today with Betsey to Mulberry, took a look among my goods and chattels. Did not find as much as I expected for the soldiers—found a good deal for myself and for Kate. David says she wants to go to Buncombe for the winter—too cold. Found some capital old books—library in sad disorder—but what a mine of pleasure it will be to me if debarred society. . . .》

《Got to Kate's for dinner. Found as I feared that negroes and overseer and all had tried to make it unpleasant to her and she wishes to go to Buncombe. . . . Mr. Chesnut found a superb crop on John's place, but sulky and dissatisfied negroes.》

《Went to Mulberry and spent the day alone, arranging library and assorting boxes of letters and papers—got about half-through—a melancholy pleasure, reading my French cook Thérèse's bills for the delicious dinners Mary Stevens and I ate so ravenously in Washington, with the appetite our frantic exercise and fatigue in the pursuit of pleasure gave us. . . .》 [8]

Romeo was the negro who first confessed to the detective—then Rhody, after she found they had discovered the money and sheets where she had hidden them. But William and Silvie still deny all complicity in the plot or the execution of it.

John Williams's bride! [9] Has she not married South at a fine time. She is terrified. Who can blame her? She did not come back with the Edward Stocktons and the Smiths. She sent a letter and a present of a piece of worsted work. It will be a miracle if she don't bolt altogether. The very name of Society Hill enough to scare the life out of anyone. The war was sufficient to a Philadelphia woman, one would think. But this! To expect the bride to come back, simply because her husband was here, and with details of that black tragedy ringing in her ears! Indeed, it was too much. I daresay she would as soon take up her abode in Sodom or Gomorrah.

It was Rhody who pointed out the blood on the counterpane. They suppose she saw it, knew they would see it, and did it to avert suspicion from herself.

October 11, 1861. Read a letter from Robert J. Walker[1] aloud—and very loud indeed it had to be, for old Colonel Chesnut is so very deaf. My breath was

---

8. The excerpts from the 1860s Journal in the three preceding paragraphs are dated, in order of appearance, Oct. 7, 10, and 12, 1861.

9. Augusta Rebecca (Howell) Williams married John Witherspoon Williams, who was the half brother of David Rogerson Williams, Jr., the son of John Nicholas Williams, and the grandson of Elizabeth (Boykin) Witherspoon.

1. Robert James Walker, a former senator from Miss., secretary of the treasury, and territorial governor of Kans. who sided with the Union during the war. The letter M. B. C. read aloud to Colonel Chesnut probably reflected Walker's Unionist sentiments.

wasted after all, for he remarked ⟨⟨. . . he thought it was Mr. Secretary of War Walker⟩⟩ "For a secretary of war to the Confederacy, some of those sentiments sounded very odd." The old gentleman is ninety, but he wants to know everything that is going on. He is blind, but he takes interest in the affairs of the world with wonderful tenacity.

James Boykin[2] writes, if the Yankees will delay one month longer, we will be quite ready for them in Mobile. Hope they will be considerate enough to wait. We always wait for them to get ready for us.

Beauregard, Joe Johnston, and Smith, generals all, deny emphatically that this delay or inaction is in any way the fault of the president.

October 13, 1861.   Went to hear Tom Davis[3] preach. It was a political sermon. He ended it by commenting on a remark made by a celebrated person from Washington who said he was bored with politics all the week. And if he could not hear a little pure religion, undefiled, on Sunday, he would not go to church.

Nudged me: "That's you. You are always grumbling at political sermons." "But I am not the least celebrated." However, the whispered dispute was soon settled. Henry Clay was the man who hoped to eschew politics one day in seven.

Our parson cited Lord Nelson as a case of good prayer from a bad man. At the battle of Trafalgar he prayed fervently, and his prayer was answered. And there he died, saying, "Thank God I die doing my duty." Again my whisper: "He prayed, too, for Lady Hamilton, and he left her a legacy to his country— ungrateful country would not accept the bequest."[4]

At Mulberry we went in the afternoon to the negro church on the plantation. Manning Brown,[5] Methodist minister, preached to a very large black congregation. Though glossy black, they were well dressed—some very stylishly gotten up. They were stout, comfortable-looking Christians. The house women in white aprons and white turbans were the nicest looking. How snow-white the turbans on their heads appeared. But the youthful sisters flaunted in pink and sky blue bonnets which tried their complexions. For *the family* they had a cushioned seat near the pulpit, neatly covered with calico.

Manning Brown preached hell fire—so hot I felt singed, if not parboiled, though I could not remember any of my many sins worthy of an eternity in torment. But if all the world's misery, sin, and suffering came from so small a sin as eating that apple, what mighty proportions mine take.

Jim Nelson, the driver—the stateliest darky I ever saw. He is tall and straight as a pine tree, with a fair face—not so very black, but full-blooded African. His forefathers must have been of royal blood over there.

2. A planter who valued his holdings at 285,000 dollars in 1860, James William Boykin of Dallas County, Ala., was M. B. C.'s second cousin once removed.
3. Lila Davis's half brother, Thomas Frederick Davis, Jr., was associate pastor of the Grace Episcopal Church in Camden. His wife was M. B. C.'s first cousin.
4. The night before his death at the battle of Trafalgar, Horatio Nelson added a codicil to his will, leaving his mistress Lady Emma Hamilton and their daughter Horatia "a legacy to my king and country" and asking that they be given a pension. The will was not made public, and no such grant was ever made.
5. A nephew of Old Colonel Chesnut who lived in Sumter District.

This distinguished gentleman was asked to "lead in prayer." He became wildly excited. Though on his knees, facing us, with his eyes shut, he clapped his hands at the end of every sentence, and his voice rose to the pitch of a shrill shriek. Still, his voice was strangely clear and musical, occasionally in a plaintive minor key that went to your heart. Sometimes it rung out like a trumpet. I wept bitterly. It was all sound, however, and emotional pathos. There was literally nothing in what he said. The words had no meaning at all. It was the devotional passion of voice and manner which was so magnetic. The negroes sobbed and shouted and swayed backward and forward, some with aprons to their eyes, most clapping their hands and responding in shrill tones, "Yes, my God! Jesus!" "Aeih! Savior! Bless de Lord, amen—&c."

It was a little too exciting for me. I would very much have liked to shout, too. Jim Nelson, when he rose from his knees, trembled and shook as one in a palsy. And from his eye you could see the ecstasy had not left him yet. He could not stand at all—sunk back on his bench.

Now, all this leaves not a trace behind. Jim Nelson is a good man—honest and true. And so he continues. Those who stole before steal on, in spite of sobs and shouts on Sunday. Those who drink continue to drink when they can get it. Except that for any open, *detected* sin they are turned out of church. A Methodist parson is practical—no mealy-mouth creature. He requires them to keep the commandments. If they are not married and show they ought to be, out of the church they go. If married members are not true to their vows and it is made plain to him by their conduct, he has them up before the church. They are devoted to their church membership. And it is a keen police court.

Suddenly, as I sat wondering what next, they broke out into one of those soul-stirring negro camp-meeting hymns. To me this is the saddest of all earthly music—weird and depressing beyond my powers to describe.

> The wrestling of the world asketh a fall;
> Here is no home: here is a wildernesse.
> Forth Pilgrim! forth! Oh! beast out of thy stall!
> Look up on high—And thank thy God for all.

> —Chaucer

[To James Chesnut, Jr.:]

Charleston
4 October 1861

Mrs. Chesnut far overrates my ability in thinking I am able to give all the news as asked for in her kind note of 2 October. For to use Mrs. Chesnut's phrase, the Father of Lies has not remained wholly with our adversaries but has entered largely into Confederate service, so that the news of today proves on tomorrow wholly untrue. In Charleston little is heard of except the blockading fleet and preparations for war at home and abroad. The fleet has been within the last week . . . increased to four vessels, and it is generally believed the increase has been made to intercept Messrs. Mason and Slidell. These gentlemen are now here and had proposed to take a steamship escape under cover of night and be carried in this Confederate steamer to Europe. The increase to the blockading fleet will probably alter all of their plans. Mr. Mason carries as his secretary Mr. MacFarland of Richmond; Mr. Slidell carries Mr. Eustis of Louisiana.

The preparations for war are seen in the continued drilling of troops, in the foundries where ordinance stores in prodigious quantities are being cast, in all the varied workshops where munitions, implements, and equipments can be made. Vast piles of clothing are being prepared for the troops both in Virginia, and in service along the coast of our own state.

The defenses of the coast of South Carolina are, I believe, much more strong than those of any of the other states. Batteries are erected at all of the inlets of any draft of water, and heavy guns mounted and being mounted. About seven thousand men are placed along the seaboard, some three thousand in camp in the interior. Three thousand are held in Charleston, ready to be used in any direction required. Should an invasion be made, about twelve or thirteen thousand men can be brought into the field with about forty-eight hours' delay. General Gonzales has not yet been able to obtain all of the guns he wished and is still at Richmond. I return there in about a week and would not be at all surprised to find him still at the Arlington House. The unfortunate affair of Hatteras has given rise to very great demand for guns, and doubtless this has detained General Gonzales. It was the Hatteras affair which carried Colonel Gregg's regiment down toward Norfolk. An attack by the way of the canal in rear of Norfolk was apprehended, and all the troops near Richmond which were in condition for prompt removal were sent there.

The continued attacks of the *Mercury* upon Mr. President Davis are making something of a party against him. It will not have strength to do anything but will be heard through the *Mercury*. The policy which prevents forward movements by our army does not meet the approval of this party, and they, far removed from the seat of war and ignorant of what reasons prevent a forward movement, deem themselves far more competent to judge of what is proper to be done than those who, bearing the brunt and seeing everything, are.

I do not hear of any opposition to Mr. W. Porcher Miles for Congress, and do not think any could be successful. Of the senators I have not heard a single person speak. Mr. Barnwell Rhett will certainly be pressed by his friends and will I think be as certainly defeated.

Scandal is dead at present, so that I cannot give you a word. Mrs. DeSaussure says she has some, but as she has not confided it to me I cannot tell it. With her eight children about her and scandal dead, she certainly has been ingenious in finding it. Like a well-trained man and obedient to the better half of the house, your note was shown to her, and it was then that she said if the note had been written to her, she could have told all these things. I privately suspect the assertion was made in a little spite at your writing the note to me.

To obey Mrs. Chesnut's wish is a pleasure, and if in obeying it I have proved tiresome, it has been from faithfully trying to comply with that wish and from the paucity of material out of which to write "a good long letter telling all the news."

Will Mrs. Chesnut be so good as to present me with much respect to Mr. Chesnut.

I have the honor to be Mrs. Chesnut's obt. sert.,

Wilmot G. DeSaussure

October 15, 1861. Kate came. We knitted away at our socks, and she gave various items of news.

First, Mr. Chesnut's favorite fad—the little steamship, the rams he would have from the patent office—has been immensely successful on the coast near New Orleans.

Hatteras is evacuated.

Mason and Slidell have left Charleston in the *Gordon* for Nassau or some British port.

When I told Kate of Jordan's letter, that "from disease and neglect our Army of the Potomac was weakening daily," she turned white as a sheet and then red—ended by weeping hysterically. Now, my sister is the coolest, calmest woman I know. It is the mad excitement of the day. It has caught her, too. She is so quiet, but after this agitation she was so excited and confused—worthy of me.

News yesterday that we had driven back an invading squadron on the Potomac. At what loss we know not yet.

At Annapolis their steamers swarm, armed and manned. And yet when I said I quaked, Kate shamed me.

Where will they land?

Miss Denie McEwen, sister-in-law to the telegraph operator (therefore as good authority as the man on horseback who is always coming in with "reliable news"), says Captain Ingraham and a lot of old seadogs of the first water have gone with Mason and Slidell to take command of a fleet of ironclad steamers.

Name of the port where this imaginary flotilla rides at anchor not given.

An article in the *Courier*[6] sillier and as mischievous as the *Mercury.* It shows how utterly undefended Fort Sumter was last summer and how slim the defenses are now. Somebody suggested it was a ruse to tempt the enemy in to his ruin. We think it sheer stupidity to make this public statement and that it is in all probability perfectly true.

Shocked to hear that dear friends of mine refused to take work for the

6. The Charleston *Daily Courier.*

soldiers because their sempstresses had their winter clothes to make. I told them true patriotesses would be willing to wear the same clothes until our siege was raised. They did not seem to care for the couleur, Isabeau—or Isabel.[7] They have seen no ragged, dirty, sick, and miserable soldiers lying in the hospital, "no lack of women's nursing, no lack of women's tears"[8] but an awful lack of a proper change of clean clothes. They know nothing of the horrors of war. One has to see to believe. They take it easy and are not yet willing to make personal sacrifices. Time is coming when they will not be given a choice in the matter.

The very few stay-at-home men we have are absorbed as before in plantation affairs, cotton picking, negro squabbles, hay-stealing, saving the corn from the freshet, like the old Jews while Noah was building the Ark.

《If I had been a man in this great revolution—I should have either been killed at once or made a name and done some good for my country. Lord Nelson's motto would be mine—Victory or Westminster Abbey.》

He that hangs or beats out brains,
The devil is in him if he feigns.

—Hudibras[9]

Woe to those who began this war—if they were not in bitter earnest.

Lamar (L. Q. C., and the cleverest man I know) said to me in Richmond, in one of those long talks of ours, "Slavery is too heavy a load for us to carry." We agreed to take up David Crockett's slogan, "My country, may she be right—but my country, right or wrong."

Russell does not see why we cannot be subjugated.

Another letter for Kate to cry over.

October 18, 1861.   Mrs. Witherspoon's death has clearly driven us all wild. Mrs. Chesnut this morning I found in great force. She talks admirably well. She is a wonderfully clever woman. She bored me, however, by incessantly dwelling upon the transcendent virtues of her colored household—in full hearing of the innumerable negro women who swarm over this house.

Mrs. Chesnut takes her meals in her own rooms. Today she came in while we were at dinner.

"I warn you. Don't touch that soup. It is bitter. There is something wrong about it."

---

7. "Isabella" is a yellowish gray color. According to a popular but inaccurate legend, the term originated with the refusal of Princess Isabella of Austria to change her linen during her father's three-year siege of the town of Ostend.

8. Slightly misquoted from Caroline Elizabeth Sarah (Sheridan) Norton, "Bingen on the Rhine," in *Poems by the Hon. Caroline Elizabeth Norton* (1857).

9. Lines slightly misquoted from Samuel Butler, *Hudibras* (1663–78), part 2, canto 1, in which a widow maintains that a man can prove his love only by suicide.

The family answered her pleasantly but continued calmly to eat their soup.

"Go back, mama, the soup is very nice—don't worry yourself—&c&c."

The men who waited at table looked on without change of face.

Kate whispered: "It is Cousin Betsey's fate. She is watching every trifle—and terrified."

My husband gave his mother his arm, and she went quietly back to her room.

Afterward Kate said to me: "Poison—she is afraid they will poison us. Did you ever hear the story of Dr. Keitt?

"No? He is the first and only man I have ever heard of poisoned by negroes. I have often wondered they did not, if half the stories are true [that] people tell of bad masters. So I have made up my mind: either they are not so savage—or the masters are not so bad.

"People's imaginations run away with them. Nothing the matter with the soup today. Romeo's soup is perfection. Dr. Keitt was one of the kindest of men and masters. But he was passionate and impulsive, not warranted to act reasonably if he was too much excited about anything. He had some chronic ailment—was always ill. A friend said: 'Keitt, yours is a queer case. I begin to think these villainous negroes are trying to poison you. Come with me at once—and to my house. See if a change will do you any good.' Dr. Keitt refused.

"'Yours is an extraordinary disease. Do not let these people suspect that I have put you on your guard or that you are coming to our house tomorrow.' Dr. Keitt promised to be prudent and to come the next day.

"As soon as his friend left, a negro woman brought him a cup of tea. In stirring it a white powder became evident, settled at the bottom of the cup. In a moment he believed what his friend had suspected.

"He dashed the tea in her face.

"'You ungrateful beast, I believe you are trying to poison me.'

"Next morning he was found with his throat cut from ear to ear.

"Afterward it was discovered that they were putting calomel in his coffee every morning.

"The woman was hung, but two of the men were allowed to escape.

"Lawrence Keitt refused to touch a cent of his brother's money. He said, 'There is blood on it.'

"Mr. Taylor, a plain, strong-minded, hard-sense, clear-headed man—not given to nonsense in any shape. Neither romantic, sentimental, nor superstitious—a truthful character. In a word, an honest gentleman. Mr. Taylor was riding to his plantation. At a certain point of the road Dr. Keitt had been in the habit of waiting for him, as part of their way lay together. He usually found him dismounted and sitting on a log by the roadside.

"And now, there was the murdered man, seated as hitherto. It was all so natural Mr. Taylor was neither startled nor alarmed. He rode up and said: 'Why, old fellow! How are you? Somehow I have got it in my head that you were dead.'

"Then they spoke calmly of neighborhood news. Then the thing he took for

Dr. Keitt said, 'So you hanged the wrong person at last—you let the rascals who cut my throat go,' and instantly vanished.

"For the first time Mr. Taylor felt all the horror and dread which comes with any idea of dealing with the supernatural. He rode back home, pale and trembling. His wife laughed at his story. 'Go to bed—take a good sleep—this nightmare will then vanish.' While they were arguing the matter, a brother of Dr. Keitt rode up. He made a futile attempt at commonplace talk but he gave it up. He was so pale, so agitated, so utterly disordered in mind and manner and he broke out: 'My brother came in last night. We had a long talk. He says I screened the rascals who cut his throat.'

"Mrs. Taylor said she wondered that he could let a dream worry him so. He must not take it to heart.

"'I said nothing about a dream. I was as wide-awake as I am now. He came in. I saw him and talked with him, just as if nothing was the matter. It seemed perfectly natural while he was there.'

"The two negro men accused in this strange way had been sent out of the country—and so this queer story ended."

"A story for Robert Dale Owen—with his *Footprints of Another World*."[1]

The materialists and science have done away with witches and ghosts. I suppose they eliminate our souls next. At any rate, hell and the devil having gone up, we need not now fight for our lives to save our souls. Kate was shocked at such light discourse. I believed every word she said—but then, of course I knew it was not true. How could it be?

October 20, 1861.[2] *Mercury* today says Carolinians were sold in the convention. It was utterly exasperating in its taunts and abuse of the Confederate government. Simply atrocious. Could they not wait one year? There are the Yankees to abuse. If our newspapers would only let loose their vials of wrath on them—or *pour out,* to use the right word—and leave us, until the fight is over, a united people.

It is our only hope. We have *élan* enough and to spare. If we only had patience and circumspection. If we were horses that could stay. The idea is that in pluck and dash our strength lies. The others have the numbers for us to dash our brains against. Now, to think the newspapers are trying to take the heart out of us. We believe we can do it—and so we can—but if they persuade us that everybody in office is fool, knave, or traitor, how can we? It is awfully discouraging. I agree with Carlyle—a few able editors hung might save us yet.

Mr. Miles says, "Ah, Mrs. Chesnut, but it must be so: Her Majesty's government—and Her Majesty's opposition. One is as true and loyal as the other."

"But it won't do here. We cannot spare a single malcontent of them all, and now it seems there is *no* government party. All run into the opposition ranks."

"The wounded men and the sick men, the widows and orphans, must feel

1. *Footfalls on the Boundary of Another World* (1860) reflects the interest of this Northern social reformer in the cult of Spiritualism.

2. M. B. C. misdates this and two subsequent Oct. entries "November." They have been redated according to the 1860s Journal.

pretty flat when they read in the *Examiner* and the *Mercury* that they were done to death by their own inefficient government. Everyone should do all they can to keep up the fire of our enthusiasm."

"And they who play disheartening slander and abuse as if from a hose upon this fire. They ought to be burned alive as traitors," said Kate, the meek and sweet-voiced, coming in with her soft footfalls. I was repeating to Mr. Chesnut what Miles said in Montgomery.

Our friend Senator Wilson has a regiment. In making a speech to it, he scorns long range. "Give them the bayonet!" Come closer in your wrath—give us the awl. Awl! They say here paper-soled shoes enough from his factory the poor negroes have had, and thanks to his sympathetic awl.[3] High-souled as he soars now, with "give them cold steel" the best word in his mouth. He disclaims all idea of vengeance. It is to punish us for our good that he is coming.

Today, read Lamartine's *Geneviève.*[4] He cites the servants of Augustus Caesar's time to prove fidelity among that class, and also, during the French Revolution nine out of ten were faithful unto death. The African slaves certainly were faithful when the British had possession here.[5]

Now we are here at Sandy Hill—half a dozen of the whites or dominant class, sixty or seventy negroes—miles away from the rest of the world.

Old Mr. Chesnut said his wife must know everything: "I want her to know." So my husband had to write several sheets of paper filled with poor Mrs. Witherspoon's tragedy. We thought it could so easily have been kept from Mrs. Chesnut's ears—she is so deaf. But he ordered it otherwise. And now she is simply overwrought on the subject. I have never known her so nearly thrown from her balance—for she is a calm, philosophical personage.

Hume says, "Mighty governments are built up by a great deal of accident with a very little of human foresight and wisdom."[6]

We have seen the building of one lately with no end of Jefferson and a constant sprinkling of Calhoun, &c&c&c. Which is the wisdom—where the accident or foresight? Somebody said Jefferson and Calhoun were the stern lights and did not help us to see what is before us.

One thing Mrs. Browne and I discussed. There were in Richmond and in Montgomery the safe, sober, second thoughts of the cool, wise morning hours. There in that drawing room after dinner—how much more in the smoking congresses where women were not—came what we called ideas—preserved in alcohol. The self-same wild schemes, mad talk, exaggerated statements, inflamed and irrational views—our might and the enemies' weakness, &c&c. If

---

3. Mrs. Chesnut's puns are based on Wilson's self-celebrated origins as a journeyman shoemaker, "the cobbler from Natick."

4. Alphonse de Lamartine, *Geneviève, histoire d'une servante* (1850), part 3.

5. Actually, J. C.'s grandfather lost slaves to the British.

6. David Hume, *History of England* (1754–62), volume 2, chapter 23.

"in vino veritas," God help us. After all it was not, could not be, unadulterated truth—it was truth, alcoholized.

I care no more for alcoholized wisdom than I do for the chattering of blackbirds—[*remainder of page cut off*].

Hard on the poor innocent birds! They were made so. And the great statesmen and soldiers deliberately drink down their high inheritance of reason and with light hearts become mere gabbling geese. *Alcools*—

Hume, after his kind, talks of *accident.* Lamartine says, "Dieu est Dieu—ce que les hommes appellent *rencontre,* les anges l'appellent Providence."[7]

Thank God for pine knots. Gas and candles and oil are all disappearing in the Confederacy. Lamb thinks for social purposes candles so much better than the garish light of the sun.[8] The unsocial nights of our ancestors in their dark caves. They must have laid about and abused one another in the dark. No, they went to sleep. And women then were too much slaves to dream of curtain lectures—which is one form of lying about and abusing one another in the dark. "What repartees could have passed, when you had to feel around for a smile and had to handle your neighbor's cheek to see if he understood you?"

> Fool enough to attempt to advise.
>   Ah, gentle dames! It gars me greet,
> To think how many counsels sweet,
>   How many lengthened sage advices
> The husband from the wife despises.[9]

《poor me—》

> Respect to your great plan!
>   And let the Devil
> Be sometimes honored for his burning throne![1]

> And he that stands upon a slipping place,
> Makes nice of no vile hold to stay him there.[2]

7. A paraphrase from *Geneviève,* part 116.
8. Paraphrased from Charles Lamb, "Popular Fallacies, XV.—That We Should Lie Down with the Lamb," in *The Last Essays of Elia* (1833). The quotation at the end of this paragraph derives from the same essay, although M. B. C. does not reproduce Lamb's wording exactly.
9. Slightly misquoted from Robert Burns, "Tam o' Shanter" (1791).
1. From *Measure for Measure,* act 5, scene 1.
2. Slightly misquoted from *King John,* act 3, scene 4.

⟨⟨ I hope I may not be too conceited and spoil J. Chesnut's affairs by writing in such a hurry letters for him. Today I have written: to the president, Jeff Davis, 1; to Benjamin, secretary of war, 2; to Mallory, secretary of the navy, 1; to Warren Nelson,[3] 1; to Henry Gourdin,[4] 1; all with the best intentions possible. I hope it may prove so—in the end.⟩⟩[5]

October 22, 1861.

> Send danger from the East unto the West,
> So honour cross it from the North to South!
>   And let them grapple!
>
> Ah, the blood more stirs
> To rouse a lion than to start a hare.[6]

> Better be with the dead
>   Whom we to gain our place have sent to peace,
> Than on the torture of the mind to lie.[7]

So the poets say what we feel—do much clearer than we could say it ourselves.

"Would it were bed time, Hal! and all were well."[8]

October 23, 1861.   Magruder is fighting somewhere about Lord Cornwallis's Yorktown.

Lieutenant Warley and Tom Huger engaged in that brush near New Orleans.[9] Tom Huger was my ideal of a dashing, devil-may-care sailor. And I felt certain if any chance came in his way he would do something heroic.

October 24, 1861.   At Bonney's store heard that at Leesburg, Shanks Evans had defeated Yankees,[1] taken three hundred prisoners, and they left five

3. Samuel Warren Nelson, member of the S.C. house, from Clarendon District.
4. The brother and business partner of Robert Gourdin.
5. In the 1860s Journal dated Oct. 21, 1861.
6. Hotspur in *Henry IV, Part I*, act 1, scene 3.
7. Slightly misquoted from *Macbeth*, act 3, scene 2.
8. Falstaff, slightly misquoted, in *Henry IV, Part I*, act 5, scene 1.
9. The Federal blockade at the mouth of the Mississippi had been briefly disrupted after an engagement on Oct. 12 in which South Carolinian Alexander F. Warley commanded the Confederate ironclad *Manassas* and Lt. Thomas B. Huger served aboard the C.S.S. *McRae*.
1. The battle of Ball's Bluff, Va., Oct. 21.

hundred dead on the field. Besides a great number who were drowned. Allowing for all exaggeration, it must be a splendid victory. Among the prisoners ten (10) officers.

Mrs. Ben Lee[2] gave us an account of the last ship which ran the blockade. She represented herself (the ship) as being bound for Bath, Maine. She was entrusted by the blockaders with letters for New York, which, being brought into Charleston, were opened. These letters told that our coast was to be attacked simultaneously at four separate points. Bull Bay, Stono, and Port Royal. I forget the other point. This was to prevent our concentrating to defend any particular place.

Her husband is in the army. She looked so lovely—her dress was exquisite—and her one thought—*clothes.* She discussed what she had and what she intended to get. Neither husband nor baby came in for one word.

I fled—and yet she is beautiful as a picture.

My next visit was hard on the chivalry. Johnny lent Kate his house, fully furnished. She did not know that the furniture was his brother's, which Johnny thought he had bought. He considered the purchase as a matter settled.

The Florida brother ⟨⟨James⟩⟩ in a huff, sent word to have everything of his (list of his furniture sent) taken out of that house if the house was inhabited. So without one word of warning, the wagons came. And one of the fairest ladies of the land and her children—her husband away in the wars—was left on bare boards, and so I found her. Indignant was a faint word to express her state of mind, and we wondered what that pride of cavaliers and gentlemen would say to such boorish conduct.

A case of pure spite—so it must have been women's work. She was principally concerned at the amount of mortification Johnny would feel.

As she was going to North Carolina in a few days, it seemed hardly worthwhile. There was not a stick of anything in the house, only her trunks and her children.

⟨⟨I mentioned these things last night and was insulted both by Harriet Grant and Miss Sally [Chesnut]. The former asked me *insolently* if Kate was quarreling with the McCaa Chesnuts, too.[3] I went off to bed, enraged but trying to keep my temper and not *sin* as I did before. I felt last winter that all the mortification and misery I endured were a fit punishment for my sinful hatred of these people.... They remind me of dogs, with eager eyes watching a man eating,

---

2. Eliza (Lee) Lee, sister-in-law of Ann (Cooper) Lee and the wife of Charleston banker Benjamin Lee.

3. Johnny Chesnut's brother James was married to M. B. C.'s first cousin, Amelia (McCaa) Chesnut.

with mouths open, watching to catch any bone, and snapping and quarreling at every other dog who comes near, for fear he should get anything. The miserable, degraded, money-loving, grasping spirit these poor people have from dogging this poor old man for forty years for his money.⟩⟩

After all! "These dreadful engines of war. At Taunton during the Wars of the Roses, on that battlefield more men were killed, than at Vimiero, Talavera, Albuena [?], Salamanca, Vittorio, *and Waterloo!*"

The Molochs of the human race, who are indebted for the larger part of their meteoric success to their total want of principle and who surpass the generality of their fellow creatures in one act of courage only—that of daring to say, with their whole heart, "Evil be thou, my good."[4]

And yet, we want a hard soldier. A sort of Suwarrow[5] who will lead to victory, come what may. In a long drawn-out rosewater war we will certainly go under from pure exhaustion.

Found Mr. Chesnut reading aloud a speech of Mr. Petigru's [that was] sneering at our weakness. And Isaac Hayne in his audience partly acknowledging it. Lost my temper. ⟨⟨Oh, that I was a man!⟩⟩[6]

Though our bark cannot be lost
Yet it shall be tempest tossed—[7]

October 25, 1861. The Witherspoons here. Mary W repeated what she heard her negroes say ⟨⟨showing they know we are afraid of them⟩⟩:[8] "Let us go to that hanging. It's a warning to us all."

Trescot's letter to Mr. Chesnut a gentle warning. "Many a slip between the cup and the lip," he says, alluding to the senatorship. Adds—Mrs. Joe Johnston's arm is still very weak. In a letter to me he says it is too weak still for her to answer my "delightful letter"—strong enough, apparently, for her to write to him. He does not believe I can write "a delightful letter." I certainly do not write such to him. He wrote a state secret to my husband, and I answered

4. *Paradise Lost,* book 4, line 110.

5. "Suwarrow" was the common nineteenth-century transliteration of the surname of Aleksandr Vasilyevich Suvorov (1729–1800), the great Russian field marshal who never lost a battle. Here and in later references to the general, M. B. C. was probably thinking of his declaration, "I know nothing of defensive warfare; I only know how to attack."

6. Under Oct. 25, 1861, in the 1860s Journal.

7. Slightly altered lines of the First Witch in *Macbeth,* act 1, scene 3.

8. Under Oct. 27, 1861, in the 1860s Journal.

the letter. He wrote a piece of society scandal to me—"strictly confidential"— and so in a business letter's postscript Mr. C alludes to it. He does not know how to deal with such a mixed-up establishment.

At any rate, I acknowledge he is clever and that he writes a very impudent *and* a charming letter.

Laurence, Mr. Chesnut's man, is an excellent tailor, not a bad accomplishment for a valet. He darns stockings beautifully. Mrs. Clay[9] never tired of laughing at the picture he made seated cross-legged on Mr. Chesnut's trunk, darning. He is so stout—a perfect copper-colored Count Forco[?]. His master never trusted to Laurence's tailoring before. Now it will be a great comfort. He is making me a sacque at present.

Yankees' principal spite to South Carolina—fifteen war steamers have sailed, or steamed out against us. Hot work cut out for us whenever they elect to land.

They hate us, but they fear us, too. They do not move now until the force is immense—"overwhelming" is their word. Enormous preparations, cautious approach are the lessons we taught them at Manassas, Bethel, &c&c. McClellan is to come against us, front and rear.

And now we have many little wars beside the great one.

The Judge raging in tantrums. He speaks to me, but he has ceased to look at me. It is months since I have caught his eye. ⟨⟨That means mischief!⟩⟩

The president writes, asking for particulars of that interview 13th July.[1] There were present Col. John S. Preston, General Lee, General Cooper, Mr. Chesnut, and the president. General Beauregard says he sent the president by his aide, Colonel Chesnut, a plan of battle which the president rejected.

Are we going to be like the Jews when Titus was thundering against their gates? Quarreling among ourselves makes me faint with fear.

⟨⟨**October 31, 1861.** . . . J. C.'s election for senator does not come off until December. I hope he is right. I hope he will be senator. If he had gone in the army it would have made matters certain. . . . I must not let myself think of all this. Read yesterday Balzac and *Road to Ruin.*⟩⟩[2]

9. Virginia Caroline (Tunstall) Clay, wife of former U.S. senator Clement Claiborne Clay, Jr., of Ala. Mrs. Clay recounted her wartime experiences in Ada Sterling, ed., *A Belle of the Fifties* (1904).

1. Davis and Beauregard, increasingly at odds after Bull Run over questions of rank, command, and strategy, were disputing Beauregard's rejected plan for an attack on Washington, which J. C. had presented orally from notes to the president on July 14 (not July 13). Amid press charges that Davis sought the destruction of his popular general, the president insisted privately that Beauregard had offered only a general, presumably unofficial, proposal. Beauregard maintained that his was a specific, formal plan and suggested that the president consult Chesnut's report of the July 14 meeting.

2. Probably Thomas Holcroft's melodrama, *The Road to Ruin* (1792), but possibly Edwin F. Roberts, *The Road to Ruin: or, The Dangers of the Town* (1854), or George Thompson [Greenhorn], *Road to Ruin; or, The Felon's Doom* (1851).

November 3, 1861.   ⟨⟨. . . and now if the legislature turns us out, woe is me, for I dare not look plantation and Camden life in the face. I am ruined for that by Washington and Richmond.⟩⟩

Wrote a copy today of Mr. Chesnut's report to Beauregard, written while the guns were firing on the 18th. Surely Beauregard had forecast—to stop a man to write then showed he wanted justification prepared *en cas.* Looked out for his own fame. The eyes of posterity and all that.

Now I remember Mr. C's talk when he came back to our rooms. Lee and the president thought any movement on our part premature. The enemy was still too near his cover. I bear that in mind, and also Mr. C's praise of General Lee's clear, soldierly views—and his disgust because I would interrupt him to say how handsome General Lee was—such a splendid-looking soldier—but that I liked Smith Lee best.

Saw Uncle Hamilton. He tells us they have made it too hot for the reporter of the *Mercury* in their brigade. He has had to leave.

Also he told me that he had heard Toombs and Miles say Mr. Chesnut could never have justice done him until the documents of the secret sessions were published.

Then we interviewed Leb Cureton[3] of Boykin's Rangers. He affirms that the army have enough and to spare of everything. And that the waste and extravagance is awful.

The Mississippi regiment who faced the enemy so gallantly at Leesburg and covered themselves with glory, so to speak, was the same who behaved on the 21st July something like Frederick the Great at his first battle. They asked for a place of danger and difficulty, that they might redeem themselves or the name of their regiment.

The Yankees are finding out that the government organ did not tell the truth about Leesburg.

⟨⟨**November 4, 1861.**   Had a letter from mother. She wants to get rid of her negroes. Scared by the Witherspoon tragedy.⟩⟩

November 6, 1861.   Mr. Chesnut has gone to Charleston—Kate to Columbia, on her way to Flat Rock.

Partings are sorrowful things now.

Read Mrs. Shelley's book, *The Last Man,*[4] written to sell—filthy lucre—not so bad—I mean the book. She used Byron and Shelley. The book stirred me. She wrote of things she knew. Poor Shelley. *He* saw—at all events,

---

3. Everard B. Cureton, a Kershaw District slaveholder.
4. Mary (Wollstonecraft) Shelley, *The Last Man* (1826).

> The light that never was on land or sea
> The consecration and the Poet's dream.[5]

As for the dunderheads here, I can account for their stolidity only in one way. They have no imagination. They cannot conceive what lies before them. They can only see what actually lies under their noses.

I see that Gonzales is offended that the president did not give him an office of adequate importance—I mean something suitable to his dignity—and has gone as an aide to Ripley. He means to do his duty, and as he is so clever, may he be a real aid to Ripley.

The *Mercury* has a faint and feeble defense of its obstreperous correspondent "Kiawah," who was put out of the Palmetto Brigade—and in this defense it insults both the Army of Virginia and the president.

To me it is evident that Russell, the *Times* correspondent, tries to tell the truth, unpalatable as it is to us. Why should we expect a man who recorded so unflinchingly the wrongdoing in India to soften matters for our benefit—sensitive as we are to blame.

He describes slavery in Maryland but says that it has worse features further south. Yet his account of slavery in Maryland might stand as a perfectly accurate picture of it here. God knows, I am not inclined to condone it, come what may. It is very well done for a stranger who comes and in his haste unpacks his three p's—pen, paper, and prejudices—and hurries through his work.

So the mighty Scott has resigned[6]—our six-feet-six general, head and shoulders above the multitude—and little McClellan is to try on his boots. I remember Van Buren in the caricature, swallowed up in Jackson's—"following in his footsteps."

Lincoln seems inclined to throw the blame of their failures on these two men.

5. Lines from William Wordsworth, "Elegiac Stanzas, Suggested by a Picture of Peele Castle, in a Storm, Painted by Sir George Beaumont" (1805), stanza 4.

6. In Oct., Lincoln accepted Winfield Scott's request to retire and named George McClellan as his successor as commander in chief of the U.S. Army.

X

Fall of Port Royal

November 8, 1861.   The Reynoldses[1] came, and with them terrible news. The enemy are effecting their landing at Port Royal.

I ordered the carriage and rushed off to Camden to hear the worst. Again, it could only be traced to that "reliable man" whose blunders are proverbial.

At the marketplace we encountered Major (militia major before the war) John McPherson DeSaussure. He confirmed the bad news. But it did not affect his spirits, which are always light and airy. He held us there, not like the Ancient Mariner—for he lacks the glittering eye—but literally he lay hold of the carriage door and stood between the wheels thereof.

He wanted us to hear what a fine crop Harry[2] was making—gave us all the particulars of Harry's ways of commanding success as a planter. As if all that mattered now. Harry is with his company in Virginia.

Met Aunt S. H.,[3] matching ribbons at Miss McEwen's. She said, "If this is true, Mr. B will go at once to Charleston," and then dismissed the subject from her mind and conversation. Mr. B would settle it. It was his business, not hers. There is faith for you!

I do not know where my husband is. He went to Charleston a week ago, but at his approach the sun and moon do not stand still. Aunt S. H. said she did not feel the least uneasy, and went on matching her ribbons.

Miss McEwen told me they were very unhappy at the Judge's because Mr. Kirkland was down there in the midst of it all, on General Drayton's staff. At any rate, Combahee is so near Beaufort. So I drove there at once.[4] I found them at dinner and in fine spirits. No allusion whatever was made to Port Royal. The Judge opened fire on me by telling me that he had reliable information from Baxter Springs,[5] who had received a letter from Governor Pickens, announcing himself as candidate for the senatorship. And strange to say, at the same time he had five other letters from distinguished gentlemen who each wanted the senator's position.

Then Aunt Betsey took up her parable and added significantly: "I did not inquire the names of other distinguished five, as the senator's election is a

1. Mary Cox (Chesnut) Reynolds and her daughters Emma, Sarah, Ellen, and Esther.
2. John McPherson DeSaussure's son, Lt. Henry William DeSaussure of the Sixth S.C. Regiment. Henry's wife, Mary (Reynolds) DeSaussure, was a daughter of Mary (Chesnut) Reynolds and a niece of J. C.
3. Sarah (DeSaussure) Boykin, the wife of "Mr. B"—Alexander Hamilton Boykin.
4. That is, to Judge Withers's home.
5. Andrew Baxter Springs represented York District in the S.C. secession convention.

matter that does not concern us in the least. We take no interest in it. When the battle at Fort Sumter was raging, I began wringing my hands and running up and down the piazza. Monroe came out. 'My Missis, don't take on so. You ain't got nobody there that you care for.' Then I remembered that indeed, I had not—and in a moment I was as cool and calm as an icicle."

The Judge said, "Betsey is at least beginning to see for herself what I have so often told her—the meanness and dishonesty, the corruption and depravity of all men." [*Rest of page cut off.*]

"I don't believe all men are so bad as you say. We are but average mortals, and God has not miraculously made us different from the others. We know we are not dishonest or depraved, &c&c, and I don't know how anyone dares speak ill of those soldiers down there on the coast or in Virginia. Are they selfish and all that is base? Dying, fighting, lying in the hospitals, suffering a thousand martyrdoms—I've seen it, you know. Here we are, in slippers and dressing gowns—snug fires—good dinners. Do you know what a camp dinner is? General Drayton dined with his son. The solitary dish was served in its own frying pan, burnt to the bottom—literally it was paste, flour and water. At night the soldier lad said to his father: 'Try it again. It will come out now, I borrowed a rind of bacon and greased the pan in honor of you.'

"My idea of our men is that they are as good as they are brave—the soldiers— the army. They are the very flower of Southern life, &c&c."

"Have you heard aught in this house disrespectful in regard to the Confederate army?" said the Judge angrily. "Have you heard one word?"

"You said 'all men' were rogues and rascals, &c. All of our men are in the army! Oh! If you mean to abuse only those who shirk the fighting, I beg your pardon."

Aunt B said amicably—she had fired her shot at Mr. C, and she was satisfied: "Come in and sit down. Why do you stand off there? You make us uncomfortable."

"No. Thank you. I do not wish to take a seat. Under the guns at Port Royal would be pleasant, compared to my warm reception here."

All this because we will not join in the scandalous abuse of Jeff Davis—and indeed of everybody but the Judge's own family.

There was a striking picture upstairs. A perfect beauty[6] is an uncommon sight—and here was one. Nobody denies that. It is in evidence. It is her profession. And yet she can't bear to go out and show herself. She is as beautiful as flesh and blood ever gets to be. And she is always exquisitely dressed. Today it was soft mull muslin. All fluffy and fluted—and covered with Valenciennes lace. And all this—as the Presbyterian catechism says of the Lord's way of doing things—"for his own glory."

Port Royal was not so much as named among us. She said she did not expect to ask anyone into her room, and she did not mean to leave it. She was in a terrible fret. The trimming they had brought her from Camden to finish her

6. Identified as Mary (Withers) Kirkland in the 1860s Journal.

baby's fine frock did not suit her taste at all. We had a few minutes' polite conversation on immaterial subjects—and I left her as I found her, in a rage of disappointment about that trimming.

At the gate, I took the reins that Armsted might open it. When he came again to the carriage, he looked in.

"Why do you come here, my Missis. They make you cry so. Please don't come anymore."

For I was sobbing to break my heart.

The apathy at the telegraph office was worse. Though they told me there that at Port Royal our generals were telegraphing for artillery, infantry, &c&c—reinforcements at once, or they should be cut off.

As I drove down the street I said to myself: "Never mind those people and their inconceivable indifference. They are only civilians. Our men are in the army."

I forgot one thing. As I went upstairs the Judge shouted after me: "I forgot to tell you Orr and Pickens have coalesced against Mr. Chesnut. It is a settled bargain between them." There followed a roar of laughter at my probable discomfiture.

All the way home I was crooning this:

> Hie upon Hielands—and low upon Tay
> Bonnie George Campbell rade out one day
> Saddled and bridled and gallant rade he,
> Hame came the gude horse—but never came he.
>
> Out came his old Mither, greeting full sair
> Out came his bonnie bride riven her hair—
> Saddled and bridled, and booted rade he,
> T'oom came the saddle, but never came he!
>
> My meadow lies green and my corn is unshorn
> And my barn is too big—my baby unborn,
> Saddled and bridled, and gallant rade he—
> Hame came the gude horse—but never came he![7]

Utter defeat at Port Royal. DeSaussure's and Dunovant's regiments cut to pieces.[8]

General Lee sent them, they say. Preux chevalier. Booted and bridled and gallant rade he. So far his bonnie face has only brought us ill luck.

---

7. Fragment of a traditional Scots ballad appearing in varying forms in several collections. See, for example, William Motherwell, *Minstrelsy Ancient and Modern* (1827).

8. Col. William D. DeSaussure, commander of the Fifteenth S.C. Regiment, was the brother of Mrs. Alexander Hamilton Boykin and the nephew of John McPherson DeSaussure. Col. Richard M. G. Dunovant led the Twelfth S.C. Regiment in the unsuccessful defense of Port Royal that cost the Confederates sixty-six men.

Kirkland is an aide to Ripley, not Drayton, as Miss McEwen said yesterday. That explains the want of interest in the Port Royal fight at the Judge's.

Combahee is quite near and open also to the Gulf—body may be safe and mind easy, but estate is in danger. That's plain enough.

Passed Rev. Mr. Hanckel[9] with the old blind bishop,[1] slowly walking up and down before the bishop's door. Mr. Hanckel is from Beaufort. Sure, this is a day for Christians to comfort one another as best they may. Consolations of religion—now or never.

Drayton wounded and one of his aides. All this disaster caused, they say, by want of ammunition. Governor Pickens wrote that he did not want any more troops when Mr. C offered to raise another regiment—"South Carolina is now one armed camp."

> Let rather Roman come again, or Saxon—Norman or the Dane,
> In all the bonds we ever bore, we sighed, we wept
> We never blushed before.

Is there anything in beauty to make a woman hardhearted? They are, the beauties.

> The lovely maid whose form and face
> Nature has decked with every grace
> But in whose breasts no virtues glow—
> Whose heart ne'er felt another woe—
> Whose hand ne'er smoothed the bed of pain—
> *Or eased* the *captive's galling* chain.
> But like the tulip caught the eye
> Born just to be admired and die,
> When gone no one regrets its loss
> Or scarce remembers that it was.

The *Examiner* newspaper published a very silly letter today from Beauregard. The editor hints: "Soldiers should beware of the pen. So far the world has had but one Caesar."

> When the house doth sigh and weep,
> And the world is drowned in sleep

9. Probably James Stewart Hanckel, a professor at the Episcopal Seminary in Camden.
1. Thomas Frederick Davis, Sr., had been pastor of the Grace Episcopal Church of Camden since 1846 and bishop of the diocese of S.C. since 1853.

Yet mine eyes the watch do keep—
Sweet spirit comfort me!
When the passing bell doth toll
And the furies, in a shoal
Come to fright a parting soul
Sweet spirit comfort me.

Sick in heart sick in head—
With doubts discomforted—[2]

Old Mr. Chesnut says coolly: "Raw troops will run. That British fellow, the one who burnt Washington City—he told them he did not care if it rained militia."[3]

Then he said: "For fifty years Bluffton has been spoiling for a fight. And now I think he has got it. That is the center spot of the fire-eaters. Barnwell Rhetts and all that."

When Mr. Hoar and his daughter came to Charleston, envoy extraordinary from Massachusetts, with some message about her colored seamen,[4] Stuart[5]—the witty and brilliant editor of the *Mercury,* a Beaufort man—said, in his speech in the legislature: "Let Mr. Hoar alone—and his sweet little daughter. Go down there to Fort Moultrie and grapple with the old eagle on the flagstaff."

They are trying conclusions with the old eagle in the flagstaff now.

The friends we've tried are by our side—
The foe we hate before us!

At Hoboken last summer, General Scott said to me: "I know your little South Carolina. I lived there once. It is about as big as Long Island, and two-thirds of the population are negroes. Are you mad?"

Bluffton must be satisfied now. It has about as much fighting on its hands as anybody need want—fire-eaters or otherwise.

Camden people do not in the least take in what it means—one's country successfully invaded.

And *I know* now what it means when people say one's heart is like lead in one's bosom.

2. From Robert Herrick, "His Letanie, to the Holy Spirit," in *Noble Numbers: or, His Pious Pieces* (1647).

3. In the War of 1812, British troops under Maj. Gen. Robert Ross and Rear Adm. Sir George Cockburn burned the Capitol after routing American militia on Aug. 24, 1814, in a battle that became known as the "Bladensburg Races."

4. In 1844, the governor of Mass. sent Samuel Hoar, a former congressman, to Charleston to challenge the constitutionality of state laws requiring black sailors on ships in S.C. ports to be imprisoned and, if they were unable to pay their jail fees, to be sold into slavery. When the S.C. legislature demanded Hoar's expulsion from the state and a mob surrounded his hotel, he returned home without fulfilling his mission.

5. John Allan Stuart (1800–52), a brother-in-law of Robert Barnwell Rhett, Sr.

Papers say Pillow has had a victory—away off somewhere. First he lost, then he was being reinforced.[6] Faraway news—I care not for it.

We know now what it means, "Lies like a bulletin."

Those Beaufort men—Captain Cuthbert[7] &c—how do they feel, with their troops in Virginia, their homes invaded, destroyed?

Such a meeting we had—all the churches joined to pray. They sung:

> Dread Jehovah! God of Nations
> From thy Temple in the skies
> Hear thy people's supplication
> Now for their deliverance rise.[8]

Not one doubt is there in our bosoms that we are not the chosen people of God. And that he is fighting for us. Why not? We are no worse than Jews, past or present, nor Yankees.

November 11, 1861.   Yesterday Mr. John DeSaussure came, absolutely a lunatic. His preposterous and ill-timed gaiety all gone. He was in a state of abject fright because the negroes show such exultation at the enemies making good their entrance at Port Royal.

Cannot see any change in them myself. Their faces are as unreadable as the sphinx. Certainly they are unchanged in their good conduct. That is, they are placid, docile, kind, and obedient. Also as lazy and dirty as ever.

So as far as man can destroy, that beautiful Beaufort is gone. Mrs. Elliott and Mrs. Cuthbert—Septima Washington;[9] how those women used to rave to me of that bay—their homes in the very garden spot of the world. An earthly Paradise.

Last night Rochelle Blair came to say there was a dispatch from Governor Pickens for my husband. "They wanted Colonel Chesnut's address." He has a way of happening (although he has no command) at battles. He happened to be at Fort Sumter, and he happened at Manassas, although he ought to have been in his seat in Congress.

6. On Nov. 7, Brig. Gen. Ulysses S. Grant and Union troops sent down the Mississippi River from Cairo, Ill., landed at Belmont, Mo., but Brig. Gen. Gideon Johnson Pillow's Confederate garrison, aided by reinforcements under Maj. Gen. Leonidas Polk, forced the Federals to return upriver.

7. George Barnwell Cuthbert, a St. Helena's Parish planter and first cousin of Joseph and Edward Barnwell Heyward.

8. From a hymn by Catherine Foster, first published in 1804, which appeared in hymnals under the heading "In Time of Trouble—National."

9. Three planters' wives: Mary (Barnwell) Elliott, the wife of George Parsons Elliott; Mrs. William Cuthbert; and Septima Martha (Washington) Strobhart, the wife of James A. Strobhart.

Maybe—for we do not know where he is—he may happen to be at Beaufort. That devoted town they are shelling—already millions of property is destroyed.

Troops from all quarters are hurrying there—too late.

November 12, 1861. That telegram to Mr. Chesnut was a grand secret, surely. Judge Withers knew it. So I heard it in the street. Will not write it, even—for everybody reads my journal as it lies on the table in my room.

Went to the turnout at Mulberry for Mr. C. Met only Minnie Frierson.[1] She says they are hanging negroes in Louisiana and Mississippi, like birds in the trees, for an attempted insurrection. But out there they say the same thing of South Carolina, and we know it is as quiet as the grave here and as peaceful, except that one spot—Beaufort. We have no reason to suppose a negro knows there is a war. I do not speak of the war to them. On that subject they do not believe a word you say.

"How do I know that?"

"Watch the sudden deadening of their faces. The utter want of any possible expression as soon as one of these men has in his mouth a word that comes now so often—'Damn Yankee.'"

East Tennessee going against us—burning RR bridges, &c&c.

A genuine slave-owner born and bred will not be afraid of negroes—quand même. Here we are mild as the moonbeams and as serene. Nothing but negroes around us—white men all gone to the army.

Now Governor Pickens writes to Mr. C to raise that regiment. When it was practicable, he refused it. He wants more troops for state defense. "South Carolina one armed camp" is no longer the watchword and reply.

Beauregard and Pickens were telegraphing all yesterday.

Mary Stevens Garnett calls her son James Mercer for feu Garnett père. That he may not be nicknamed "Jim," he shall be called Mercer, she says.

Mrs. Reynolds and Mrs. Withers, two of the very kindest and most considerate of slave-owners, aver that the joy of their negroes at the fall of Port Royal is loud and open.

There is no change of any kind whatever with ours.

A man named Parker has got home from Beaufort. Two Camden men killed. A Jew, Somers—an Irishman, Wilson.

---

1. Harriet Grant's sister Mary Chesnut (Grant) Frierson was the wife of Sumter District planter James J. Frierson.

Parker says it was all a botch on our side. General Drayton ordered DeSaussure's regiment to an island to draw off attention from Drayton maneuvers around the forts. DeSaussure, finding his men cut to pieces for no earthly good, cried, "Save yourselves." And now they are scattered from Richmond to Montgomery.

The official report says 15 missing. Parker speaks, not I. He may be only a "reliable man on horseback" or he may be good authority—I know not.

For the first time the *Examiner* is on Jeff Davis's side. He condemns the conduct of Shot-Pouch Walker in making a difficulty about which regiment he should take. The president is accused of making a place for his brother-in-law, Dick Taylor. After all, it is only transferring Walker, a Georgian, to a Georgia regiment and giving Walker's regiment, which is from Louisiana, to Dick Taylor *of that ilk*.[2] Walker says he has disciplined and trained this regiment and now Dick Taylor will have all the benefit of his work. Forgetting their country—quarreling for their own glory. For shame!

Mrs. Reynolds's conversation with her jet black butler, Ammon.

"Missis, at Beaufort they are burning the cotton and killing the negroes. They do not mean the Yankees to have cotton or negroes."

She tried to make him understand, in vain.

"Would I kill you or let anybody else kill you? You know nobody kills negroes here. Why will you believe they do it there? Are we any better than other white people?"

"We know you won't own anything against your side. You never tell us anything that you can help."

Ammon has been that nuisance, a pampered menial, for twenty years at least. The summer after we were married and Mr. Chesnut was a candidate for the legislature, he had to risk his election to defend Ammon, who was brought before a magistrate for insulting some gentleman of the town. And Mr. C got him off scatheless—to the regret of most people. His insolence has always been intolerable. The Chesnut negroes are spoiled to a degree, but then, they have such good manners, they are so polite you forget everything else. And they make you so comfortable if you can afford ten to do the work of one servant. 《When I hear everybody complaining of their negroes, I feel we are blessed, ours are so well behaved and affectionate—a little lazy, but that is no crime.... Came home ill from anxiety....》

My husband is at home again. Yesterday at Kingsville, as he was on his way to Richmond—summoned by Beauregard, who continues to snarl at the president—he met Governor Pickens's telegram telling him to seize all salt for the use of the army. So he came home to see about it—not to seize it, I hope. And also Governor Pickens directed him to raise another regiment here immediately.

2. Richard Taylor of La., son of former president Zachary Taylor and brother of Davis's first wife, received a promotion to brigadier general and replaced Walker as commander of a brigade on Oct. 21. Eight days later, Walker resigned temporarily from the army, supposedly because of ill health.

East Tennessee against us makes it as hot for Kate at Flat Rock as she was here.

Charleston is being fortified on the land side. When the enemy overran James Island, the negro men went to the fleet, but the women and children came to us. So many more mouths to feed—a good way to subdue us by starvation.

How they laugh at our calamity. And mock when our fear cometh.[3]

The enemy *grins* at us. We jeered so when they ran at Manassas. It is slow work raising regiments now. The best fighting material went off at the first tap of the drum. But the recruiting goes on, for better or for worse.

Mr. Preston again telegraphs for Mr. C to go back to town about this Davis-Beauregard imbroglio. I do not seem to feel that it is a life-and-death business that Beauregard should be misunderstood. Let him stand to his guns: there is fighting enough to do ahead of him. Bygones can take care of themselves.

Today a newspaper said, "Mr. C in our Senate would not have Sumner to rouse him from his usual close, calm, quiet attention to business." ⟨⟨So today I reread Sumner and J. C. I must confess J. C. was very bitter, and Sumner deserved it.⟩⟩[4]

The men are picked out—those they mean to hang if a hair of the heads of our men captured in the *Savannah* is touched.

Thât looks like business. No rosewater war this. The ways of war are not ways of pleasantness.

The stateliest cavalier of them all:

> Mills House
> Charleston, S.C.
> 14 Nov. 1861

My dear Sir.

I have this moment received your dispatch. Last Sunday I received a telegram from General Beauregard urging me to meet Mr. Miles in Richmond instantly.

At Kingsville yesterday Mr. DeSaussure or Mr. Hanckel from Camden

---

3. An allusion to Proverbs 1:26.

4. Sumner's long speech "The Barbarism of Slavery" was his first since returning to the U.S. Senate, four years after Preston Brooks's physical assault. Chesnut replied immediately, very briefly, but with uncharacteristic violence, that "We are not inclined again to send forth the recipient of punishment howling through the world, yelping fresh cries of slander and malice." Chesnut said he had "quietly listened," but added that the senator from Mass. was "the incarnation of malice, mendacity, and cowardice." *Congressional Globe,* 36th Congr., 1st sess., June 4, 1860, pp. 2590-2603. The excerpt from the 1860s Journal appears there under Nov. 14, 1861.

told me that you had a dispatch of like effect. Knowing the reticent habit of our general and seeing the newspaper rumors, it seemed to me the summons must import something of grave consequence. This morning Mr. Miles explains to me that the general and the president may be at points in the matter which you brought down before the battle of Manassas, and probably General Beauregard desires your statement and mine to corroborate it. If you and Miles think it necessary, I will go with you to Richmond.

I think I have a clear recollection of the matter in all its details and of the attendant circumstances.

I will be at Charleston for some days (Yankees permitting) and would be glad to hear from you.

Great terror prevailing here, and no preparation. Neither troops nor defenses! I regard the [city of Charleston as] in hourly peril. I believe it could be taken in six hours. This war will have to be continued above tidewater, as it was in the Revolution.

Wherever a gunboat can go we must leave, our only chance is to draw them off from their ships or patiently endure the loss of the seacoast.

Wherever they can float and fight, they are our masters. I believe they will have Charleston within thirty days.

General Lee is here, visiting the defenses. He is never hopeful and does not seem in particular good humor concerning things here. It seems to me there is miserable confusion, ignorance, and inefficiency in every department. My only consolation is the consciousness of my own ignorance, in which I may make false estimates.

With cordial and respectful salutations to Mrs. Chesnut.

Yours faithfully,

John S. Preston

November 16, 1861.   We fasted and prayed—and we think our prayers are answered, for lo! good news has come. Another ship with ammunition and arms has slipped into Savannah. If our prayers are to be so effective, let us all spend our days and nights on our knees.

Memorandum—Never lend furniture. When you need it again yourself, the person to whom you lent it shows you how ill-used they feel. You are robbing them of what they feel to be theirs by right of possession.

It has been made cruelly unpleasant to me. But I had strength of mind to claim my things.

Slander says Drayton put his forts in the wrong place. John DeS——— is blatant—DeSaus*sorry*, because of the fatal mistake of putting DeSaussure's regiment in the wrong place, too.

November 17, 1861.   Did not go to church. See what Bishop Hall says:

> Lord what am I? A worm—dust. Vapor—nothing.
> What is my life? A dream—a daily dying.
> What is my flesh? My soul's uneasy clothing.
> What is my time? A minute ever flying.
> My time—my flesh—my life and I?
> What are we, Lord, but vanity.[5]

Our life here would be very pleasant if there were no Yankees.

Old Mr. Chesnut's library is on the first floor. My husband's, a beautiful room in the third story, overlooking this beautiful lawn and grand old oaks up here—all is my very own. Here I sit and make shirts for soldiers, knit, or read or write journal, as I see fit. Under my own vine and fig tree—and none to make me afraid.[6] Out of the way of all callers or intruders—all that goes on downstairs.

John DeSaussure says it is a mistake that he is anxious. He means in case of trouble to take refuge under the Federal flag with his cotton and his negroes. And he is fool enough to think they will let him keep them.

If we could shake off this black incubus! I would almost be willing to allow them the credit of their philanthropy. After all, there is where the shoe pinches.

November 19, 1861.   Oh, for a growl from the British Lion. Look out for hoarse thunder. I have heard a British goddamn swear on St. Catherine docks. I know how thoroughly they can do it.

Slidell and Mason seized under the Meteor Flag of England—and brought back to Fortress Monroe prisoners![7]

Something good obliged to come of such a stupid blunder. Yankees must bow their knee to the British—or fight them.

Also that huge Humphrey Marshall—he has given the Yankees a drubbing somewhere in Kentucky.[8]

Governor Means wants Mr. Chesnut to join him. Colonel Preston says they are going to Richmond, "Yankees permitting." Y.V. instead of D.V.

Wrote sixteen pages in answer to the president's letter anent the Beauregard

---

5. The first stanza of "Anthem I" in Joseph Hall, "Anthems for the Cathedral Exeter," *The Shaking of the Olive Tree* (1660).

6. 1 Kings 4:25.

7. Taken from the British ship *Trent* by the U.S.S. *San Jacinto* near Cuba on Nov. 8, Mason and Slidell arrived at Fortress Monroe, Va., on Nov. 15. Many Northerners and Southerners believed the incident would bring British recognition of the Confederacy and perhaps war between England and the Union.

8. Troops in the command of this brigadier general from Ky. had been in skirmishes at Ivy Mountain and Piketon on Nov. 8 and 9.

ante-Manassas plan of battle. And after all, we outsiders have pretty well settled it that Bulls Run is a battle that fought itself.

Sir Thomas Browne on wives:[9]
> When Orpheus went down to the regions below
> Which men are forbidden to see.
> He tuned up his Lyre as Historians show
> To set his Eurydice free.
>
> All Hell was astonished, a person so wise
> Should rashly endanger his life
> And venture so far—but how vast their surprise
> When they found he came for his wife!
>
> To find out a punishment due for such fault
> Old Pluto long puzzled his brain
> But Hell had no torment sufficient he thought,
> So he gave him his wife back again.
>
> But Pity succeeding soon vanquished his heart,
> And pleased with his playing so well.
> He took her again, as reward of his Art.
> Such power had music in Hell.

Opened Sir Thomas Browne idly—first sentence my eye fell upon. He could never persecute anyone for what he thought. How did he know that he might not think so, too—tomorrow. So I read on, and I have stuck to Sir Thomas Browne, urn, burial, and all, like a leech ever since.

November 20, 1861.   Found Camden in a ferment. The irrepressible Maj. John M. DeSaussure attacked Mr. Cureton[1] for spreading a report that Major DeS said he would take refuge under the Yankee flag.

Mr. Cureton answered promptly—

"I only repeated word for word what I heard you say. It is called the fight of Grannie's quarter."

"Coosawhatchie is safe. The march of the invader is stayed."

"Why?"

"Don't you see who they have sent there?" ⟨⟨I hear Pickens is there.⟩⟩

9. The passage is not by this seventeenth-century English physician and author but is a poem by eighteenth-century Anglican bishop Samuel Lisle that was inserted as a footnote in several editions of Browne's *Pseudodoxica Epidemica; or, Enquiries into . . . Common Errors* (1646). See, for example, Simon Wilkin, ed., *The Works of Sir Thomas Browne* (1846), volume 2, p. 220, n. 8.

1. Probably James Belton Cureton, a Kershaw District planter who was the father of Everard B. Cureton.

As I read the Northern newspapers the blood rushes to my head. In the words of the fine fiction writers, "My cheek is mantling with shame."

Anyhow, down they must go to old England. Knuckle on their marrowbones. To keep her on their side—or barely neutral. Seward is too smart a Yankee to undertake the British Lion with us on his hands.

The England of history cannot let this insult to her flag pass.

So our hope and fear alternate. *Mercury* sees no cause for war on British part. Richmond *Examiner* sees every cause for it.

Somehow—it is borne in on me that it does not so much matter what the *Mercury* or the *Examiner* think. It is what England will think.

Suppose Mr. Mallory had taken up poor old Morrow's idea, so fiercely backed by Mr. Chesnut, and got all of those iron steamers to defend our rivers and our coast. It was spoken of in time. We could have armed and manned them then and sent cotton to pay for them.

Six companies offered Mr. Chesnut for his regiment. Yesterday he heard from Massey of Lancaster.

Mr. Chesnut has offered his over-the-river lands to some gentlemen from the low country who are burnt out and adrift in the world.

Today's *Herald* calls this small South Carolina "The Land of Rhetts, Keitts, Orrs, and Chesnuts." Par nobile fratrum.

A General Thomas[2] reports to Cameron and Lincoln that it will take two hundred thousand men to have and to hold Kentucky for them. All the young blood is for us. This piece of information, the Northern papers say, has been most injudiciously published and acknowledged. Such melancholy stories ought to be suppressed as too disheartening for the million.

Lafayette Seabrook, now Mrs. Hopkinson of Philadelphia, has burnt her cotton gins and all, on Edisto Island.[3] At Madame Talvande's[4] the girls called her Le *Fiat*. She is apparently as positive still. Goes in for a patriotic Moscow business. How well I remember her beautiful black eyes.

Another troop offers itself—Captain MacIlvaine's cavalry.

The Captain came in person—and then Captain Boykin in full uniform.

---

2. Brig. Gen. Lorenzo Thomas, adjutant general of the U.S. Army.

3. Carolina Lafayette (Seabrook) Hopkinson, wife of wealthy Colleton District planter James Hopkinson.

4. The French School for Young Ladies, which M. B. C. attended in Charleston between 1835 and 1838. See introduction, p. xxxi.

Mary DeSaussure was groaning over Colonel DeSaussure's mischance. "He is a lion," she cries. "There never was so brave a man." Then she went for Johnny. He sent a message to "Henry DeSaussure's wife."

"I have a name, I hope," she said, her Irish blood flaming in her face.

Here we agitate ourselves for such trifles.

A man repeating Manassas stories.[5] The men he took prisoners, who had hid in a well. How they marched Jackson's mother, a poor old body, over eighty years old, to Washington. The brother of Jackson and son of this old prisoner said to his captain, "Let me go—I have an account to settle with these devils," and he went off with his rifle.[6]

All this war talk (or ⟨⟨from eating⟩⟩ macaroons unlimited)—nearly died of fright and horror in the night. ⟨⟨Waked J. C., screaming.⟩⟩ Nightmare in its worst shape.

Being told last night that my conversation was like the bluster of Barnwell Rhett, I kept up here. All day I have looked out—from my window high—upon the sky, with a secret chuckle at the inanity that I was escaping. Nobody is saying down there what I am thinking. As I said to Captain MacIlvaine last night, "Our men are heroes all—brave as Marshal Ney—bravest of the brave.[7] We know all that. But they are all in the army now, and in one year we seem at the end of our row. Armies must be recruited—a fool knows that. Men are food for powder and many other things in camp. No new supply possible—unless we put negroes in our army. Can we trust them? Never."

Old Mr. Chesnut tramped about and said: "Without the aid and countenance of the whole United States, we could not have kept slavery. I always knew that the world was against us. That was one reason why I was a Union man. I wanted all the power the United States gave me—to hold my own—&c&c."

As for them, there is no limit to their recruiting. The whole world is open to them. England is patting both sides on the back. She loves to see a Kilkenny cat fight. After all, she is not dying for the want of our cotton. She is prospering and pampering her India cotton and will magnanimously accept any apology for the Mason and Slidell affair that smart Yankee Seward will tender her.

Captain Boykin said: "Noise from below never moved England. She would stand firm if all her manufacturers starved. When her plans and her policy was fixed, millions of discontents might go to the devil for her."

5. Identified as A. H. Boykin in the 1860s Journal under Nov. 22.

6. In *My Imprisonment and the First Year of Abolition Rule in Washington* (1863), Rose O'Neal Greenhow recalled that the elderly mother of James Jackson, the man who killed Col. Elmer Ellsworth, was for a time imprisoned in Mrs. Greenhow's home. Federal records make no mention of such an incident.

7. Napoleon described Michel Ney, one of his marshals, as the "bravest of the brave" after the battle of Friedland in 1807.

Captain MacIlvaine said there were parts of Lancaster without a dozen white men of any age left at home. Fighting Catawba! Children of the stout-hearted old seceders—and by no means a slaveholding district.

Read Dickens's *Pictures from Italy.*[8] Pleasant company in my airy retreat.

Last January I sent for all the English reviews. *Blackwood's,* &c&c—*Atlantic, Harper's, Cornhill,* &c.[9] Threw away my subscription money. Everything stopped with Fort Sumter. How I miss that way of looking out into the world! The war has cost me that. How much more?

Can't for the life of me see how my last night's conversation recalled Barnwell Rhett's bluster. I seemed to whimper. All the same C intended to insult me, and I cannot get over my sulks easily.

November 24, 1861.   Hymn at church:

> Save us, Lord, or we perish
> When through the torn sail the wild tempest is howling;
> When o'er the dark wave the dread lightning is gleaming.[1]

I could have rested my head on that cushion and sobbed and shrieked like a new convert at a revival camp meeting. But not an eyelash moved. So much for civilized self-control.

November 25, 1861.   Mr. Chesnut has gone to Richmond. And now there is nothing but frivle fravle talked in this house. And the earnest interest, deep and abiding [interest] they feel, apparently take in it—and in that only—while outside, "the torn sail, and the tempest is howling." To me this calm, monotonous baby talk is maddening.

Colonel Preston writes from Columbia, "I am here to muster in troops—with an awful lack of material out of which troops are mustered." How bitter he is. "The deep-mouthed vengeance—the oath, the cry, the rush to arms, when the sacred soil of Carolina is invaded—well, *they ain't here.*"

In the army of Virginia—there is where you will find it all—sacred soil of Virginia called all them—first and foremost.

A painful raising of old ghosts—looking over and destroying letters all day.

I see people writing to me as my dearest friends whose very names and existence I have long forgotten.

---

8. Published in 1846.

9. *Blackwood's Edinburgh Magazine* (Edinburgh and London, 1817-); *Cornhill Magazine* (London, 1860-). Though published in New York, *Harper's New Monthly Magazine* (1850-) serialized the work of contemporary English authors. The *Atlantic Monthly* (1857-) was published in Boston and dealt almost exclusively with the work of New England authors.

1. Lines slightly misquoted from a hymn by Reginald Heber appearing in *Hymns Written and Adapted to the Weekly Service of the Year* (1827).

Kingsley's *Two Years Ago*.[2]

Capital work of the imagination. There will never be an interesting book with a negro heroine down here. We know them too well. In fact they are not picturesque—only in fiction do they shine. Those beastly negress beauties. Animals—tout et simple—cordifiamma—no—*corpi*fiamma.[3]

A white heroine who goes two volumes under the stain in her lover's heart, or mind, of being a thief—apparently tough materials, but it is a charming book. There is not much difference, after all, between the hut—where all ages, sizes, sexes sleep promiscuously—and our negro cabins. I mean the things so awfully made plain in "The merry brown hares are leaping."[4]

Now for a story taken down from Maria's lips, she who is left forlorn for the sad and involuntary crime of twins. For "Jeems" Whitaker is unapproachable in his ire still.

———

Martha Adamson is a beautiful mulatress. That is, as good-looking as they ever are to me. I have never seen a mule as handsome as a horse—and I know I never will—no matter how I lament and sympathize with its undeserved mule condition. She is a trained sempstress and "hired her own time," as they call it. That is, the owner pays doctor bill, finds food and clothing, &c. The slave pays his master five dollars a month, more or less, and makes a dollar a day if he pleases.

Martha, to the amazement of everybody, married a coal black negro, son of Dick the barber—that Dick who was set free fifty years ago or more for faithful services rendered Mr. Chesnut's grandfather.

When asked in words such as these: "How could she? She is so nearly white—how could she marry that horrid negro? It is positively shocking!"—answer: "She inherits the taste of her white father—her mother was black."

"How coarse you are."

The son of this marriage, a bright boy called John, is grown—reads and writes—&c&c. The foresaid Martha is now a widow. Her husband was free though black.

Last night there was a row. John beat a white man who was at his mother's. Poor Martha drinks. John had forbidden Mr. T___ to bring whiskey to the house, and he found him seated at table with his mother, both drunk. So he beat him all the way home to his own house. Verdict of the community: "Served him right." Maria's word: "White people say, 'Well done! Go it, John—give it to him!'" Those are my cordifiammas—the only kind anybody will find, in fact. But the fiction is fine, all the same.

2. Published in 1857.

3. In general, meaning "passionate" and "sensual," but stronger connotations are indicated.

4. The opening line, slightly misquoted, of the poem "A Rough Rhyme on a Rough Matter," in Charles Kingsley's novel *Yeast* (1848), chapter 11. Quoted often by M. B. C., the line always evokes her horror at the cruelty laboring people suffer, whether free or enslaved, and the bitterness they harbor toward their oppressors.

After all said and done, Pickens will not muster in Mr. C's mounted companies—says the state has enough of that sort. So they will join the Confederate service.

A writer signing himself Poplius writes, "General Lee says they cannot have—they shall not have—Charleston." Those brave words carry balm to our wounded spirits. The expatriated low-country people are desperate. Susan Rutledge writes that General Lee wants to man the forts with *navy* men, but the Rhetts are of a totally different opinion. To think how I neglected all of Mrs. George Elliott's and Mrs. Cuthbert's invitations. And now—their beautiful homes I will see no more forever. And I was so near, last Christmas at Combahee!

One poor lady of the Stuart family was just out of her confinement—could not move when her house was bombarded, or fired, I forget which. He lifted her into a piano case, which was fortunately there. She and her newborn child were then borne out of the back window—an improvised litter. The lady is still alive.

Mrs. Preston's letter:

Columbia
Nov. 25th, 1861

My dear Mrs. Chesnut,

I was greatly gratified on receiving your kind note, although it evinces that you participate fully in the gloom which hangs over us all. None can resist the dreadful conviction that our cause and our country are in imminent peril. The wretched and merciless savages are driving our friends from their homes and devastating the land. God only knows when they may be still nearer to you and to me.

Yet I trust in His mercy to protect us, for I feel in my heart that our cause is in His hand and He will protect and save us.

One of my sons is in Fort Sumter, the other one at Norfolk, and Mr. Preston is here, under orders for forwarding troops to the seaboard.

He says they come in slowly and languidly.

The town is filled with refugee women and children and is dull beyond measure.

Although you may not thank me for it, I am glad Colonel Chesnut is getting up a command, for I heard Mr. Preston say in a public speech (at a serenade) that Colonel C had as much military talent as any man in the state.

In the two or three months he has to spare, before February, he may render good service to the country.

I fear we lack men of ability both in war and council. We certainly need something to redeem the disgraceful disaster of Port Royal. My dear friend, did you ever imagine _____ would run, leaving flag and sword behind?

Cannot you come over and lighten our gloom? Your genial cheerfulness and devoted patriotism would make me forget our invasion. Be assured it would give us such pleasure to have you with us without ceremony—and in war ways.

Will you say to dear little Mary Boykin, with my love, how delighted I should be if she can come with you.

Believe me, dear Mrs. Chesnut, sincerely and affectionately, your friend,

Caroline Preston

November 27, 1861. "Ye who listen with credulity to the whispers of fancy," pause and look on this picture and that.

On one side Mrs. Stowe, Greeley, Thoreau, Emerson, Sumner, in nice New England homes—clean, clear, sweet-smelling—shut up in libraries, writing books which ease their hearts of their bitterness to us, or editing newspapers—all [of] which pays better than anything else in the world. Even the politician's hobbyhorse—antislavery is the beast to carry him highest.

What self-denial do they practice? It is the cheapest philanthropy trade in the world—easy. Easy as setting John Brown to come down here and cut our throats in Christ's name.

Now, what I have seen of my mother's life, my grandmother's, my mother-in-law's:

These people were educated at Northern schools mostly—read the same books as their Northern contemners, the same daily newspapers, the same Bible—have the same ideas of right and wrong—are highbred, lovely, good, pious—doing their duty as they conceive it. They live in negro villages. They do not preach and teach hate as a gospel and the sacred duty of murder and insurrection, but they strive to ameliorate the condition of these Africans in every particular. They set them the example of a perfect life—life of utter self-abnegation. Think of these holy New Englanders, forced to have a negro village walk through their houses whenever they saw fit—dirty, slatternly, idle, ill-smelling by nature (when otherwise, it is the exception). These women are more troubled by their duty to negroes, have less chance to live their own lives in peace than if they were African missionaries. They have a swarm of blacks about them as children under their care—not as Mrs. Stowe's fancy paints them, but the hard, unpleasant, unromantic, undeveloped savage Africans. And they hate slavery worse than Mrs. Stowe. Bookmaking which leads you to a round of visits among crowned heads is an easier way to be a saint than martyrdom down here, doing unpleasant duty among them—with no reward but John-Browning drawn over your head in this world and threats of what is to come to you from blacker devils in the next. They have the plaudits of crowned heads. We take our chance, doing our duty as best we may among the woolly heads. I do not do anything whatever but get out of their way. When I come home, I see the negroes themselves. They look as comfortable as possible and I hear all they have to say. Then I see the overseer and the Methodist parson. *None* of these complain of each other. And I am satisfied. My husband supported his plantation by his law practice. Now it is running him in debt. We are bad managers. Our people have never earned their own bread.

Take this estate. John C says he could rent it from his grandfather and give him fifty thousand a year—then make twice as much more for himself. What does it do, actually? It all goes back in some shape to what are called slaves here—operatives, tenants &c elsewhere, peasantry &c. I doubt if ten thousand in money ever comes to this old gentleman's hands. When Mrs. Chesnut married South, her husband was as wealthy as her brothers-in-law, Mr. Binney or Mr. Stevens.[5] How is it now? Their money has accumulated for their children. This old man's goes to support a horde of idle dirty Africans—while he is abused and vilified as a cruel slave-owner. I wish his "Uncle Tom"—for he has one who has never tasted calamity in any shape and whose gray hairs are honored, though they frame a black face—could be seen or could be heard as he tells of "me & master"—&c&c&c. I say we are no better than our judges North—and *no worse*. We are human beings of the nineteenth century—and slavery has to go, of course. All that has been gained by it goes to the North and to negroes. The slave-owners, when they are good men and women, are the martyrs. And as far as I have seen, the people here are quite as good as anywhere else. I hate slavery. I even hate the harsh authority I see parents think it their duty to exercise *toward their children*.

There now!! What good does it do to write all that? I have before me a letter I wrote to Mr. C while he was on our plantation in Mississippi in 1842. It is the most fervid abolition document I have ever read. I came across it, burning letters the other day. That letter I did not burn. I kept it—as showing how we were not as much of heathens down here as our enlightened enemies think. Their philanthropy is cheap. There are as noble, pure lives here as there—and a great deal more of self-sacrifice. . . .[6]

《Heard from J. C.—he is still sanguine as to his being senator. So mote it be.》

November 28, 1861.   How disheartened I am. Have just seen Kirkland, with his bad low-country news. Low-country gentlemen curse Lee and Drayton alike. Only Mr. Barnwell stands by Jeff Davis. While they were pitching into the president, I said my say—unfearing consequences. The Rev. Mr. Hay[7] gave me a benignant smile of approbation, but he did not by words fly in the face of his sisters in their presence.

Of course the Judge told for the hundred-thousandth time the story of the

5. Edwin Stevens of N.J., an inventor and entrepreneur.
6. Deleted is a characterization of an unidentified friend of J. C.
7. Samuel Hutson Hay, pastor of the Presbyterian church in Camden.

house in Montgomery rented for Jeff Davis—unconstitutionally. So wasting time killing dead snakes while the live ones are rattling.

⟪Came home disheartened and miserable.... Was so ill I had to take morphine.... I know I talked sad nonsense all the evening. I felt mad with suspense and anxiety and morphine!⟫

XI

"Provincial Sloth"

November 30, 1861. Tobin named his company Chesnut Rangers. Mr. C forgot to answer his letter telling of the compliment for a fortnight. Lo! we saw in the papers that he had changed the name. It now is "Hammond Huzzars"—huzzah.

I will not repine nor be an ill foreboder. That is, if I were 21 and five feet nine, I'd go and be a sodjer.

My Molly came to complain—a black catalogue of crimes urged against Team, the overseer—crimes against *me,* not against "cullud people." She brings me for my butter so much more butter than I expected, but she says Team takes as much as he pleases and he *will not pay her* for it.

She says the poultry business pays splendidly. She has not lost a chicken. "Nobody will steal Missis' chickens." But then she says Team proclaims aloud, if one of Molly's Missis' chickens is stolen—Molly will reach out and seize in the place of it the very first chicken she sees, no matter who it belongs to. That makes it the interest of all "not to tetch Missis' chickens." But he takes my butter and "yo things." His wife has grown so fat she has to go through the big gate—the little one too narrow for her now. No wonder Sundays "they puts two of yo' hams" on their dinner table.

"Bless God! Two hams they eats!"

Molly orating and gesticulating round the room like the orator she was born: "Yourn, Missis. Yourn overseer takes yo' things."

Cum grano salis—I hope that Latin is all right.

Fancy how shocked Mrs. Chesnut was—she who is content to dwell in proprieties forever. A wrathful woman cries: "My idea of Hell is a place where a big black devil dominates and a crowd of little black devils swarm round you. And you are overheated and have not a cent, not even to buy ice to cool your tongue—nor a fan to keep off tiny devils of mosquitoes and gnats. And have we not lived just so all our lives?"

"Yes—how I envy those saintly Yankee women in their clear, cool New England homes. Writing books to make their fortunes and to shame us. And the money they earn goes to them. Here every cent goes to pay the factor who supplies the plantation &c&c."

Mrs. Lee is a Yankee woman who married a Southern clergyman—and has been always harder on negroes than any native. She can't get over the idea that they ought to behave like white people. I mean work. And if they do not, beneficent whip must make them do it, she says. Today in church before the service she offered to sell me a carriage she bought before the war but has not used it. When she found that I did not offer to pay for it until "peace should be proclaimed," she backed out and subsided into her prayer book.

Mr. John Raven Matthewes[1] has burned his cotton, his gin houses, and his negro houses. Moscow complete. The Moscow idea is rampant.

How old Mr. Chesnut sneers whenever he hears of "another such fool as that." He is deaf and blind and ninety years old, but he will hear everything, and his comments are racy indeed. The papers are read to him in a shrieking voice every night. He dozes until you slip—then he wakes and sternly demands why.

"What's the matter?" he shouts. "Who told you to stop?" Sometimes he breaks out in talk of his own.

"I was always a Union man. The world's against us. But for the strong powers of the United States—repressing insurrections and keeping the hands of outsiders off—he would not keep slavery a day. The world will not tolerate a small slave power with our long frontier and freedom the other side of it. The thing is done. March of mind, wife. Modern improvements. We are out-of-date. Fool and his money soon parted. Outside barbarians—that's what they think of us. I told Edwin Stevens so."

Negroes say: "Mars Jeems, he don't care for niggers. He'll git rid of the trouble of 'em soon as they are *hisen*. Not a bit like Ole Marster. He hole 'em tight." And here he chuckles: "Well, Mars Jeems won't be boddered wid niggers maybe, a'ter all."

"Ole Marster, he know what niggers worth. Mars Jeems, never in dis world will he worry his head wid dem." He loves his laugh at his heirs' expense. And he sees his five estates slipping away from him. These are his gods. He worships his own property.

George the II's name is attached to the Mulberry patent. They were granted their lands mostly, so they came cheap. Cheaper came the slaves from Yankee slave ships. Then the big fish ate up all the little ones—so the great estates grew up here. I mean the large plantations. There are only two or three of such in every district: Williams's and Peedee country—Hamptons, Taylors, Adams on the Congaree. Singleton—Richardsons in Sumter. One important feature. No primogeniture law and subdivision of estates. This one has been kept together by three generations of only sons. McRae's[2] estate made six wealthy families.

---

1. Owner of a large plantation in Colleton District.
2. Duncan McRae, a Scots merchant who bought more than thirty-two hundred acres in Kershaw District in the 1790s, was the husband of J. C.'s aunt Mary (Chesnut) McRae.

My grandfather Boykin left enough for six sons. And a provision in his will odd enough—"My land is not to be sold, even for division."

One thing seems to rush out of old Mr. Chesnut's mouth unbidden as he walks up and down this large hall. He stops, throws up his hands, which are usually clasped behind him: "Napoleon said numbers will tell in the end."

When this establishment at Mulberry breaks up, the very pleasantest easygoing life I ever saw will be gone. Mrs. Chesnut, with all her angelic mildness, sweetness, &c, has a talent for organizing, training, making things comfortable, and to move without noise and smoothly. He roars and shouts if a pebble of an obstacle is put in his way. Somehow I find her the genius of the place....[3]

My sleeping apartment is large and airy—has windows opening on the lawn east and south; in those deep window seats, idly looking out, I spend much time. A part of the yard which was a deer park once has the appearance of the primeval forest—the forest trees having been unmolested . . . are now of immense size. In the spring the air is laden with opopanax, violets, jasmine, crab apple blossoms, roses. Araby the blest never was sweeter in perfume.[4] And yet there hangs here as in every Southern landscape the saddest pall. There are browsing on the lawn, when Kentucky bluegrass flourishes, Devon cows and sheep, horses, mares and colts. It helps to enliven it. Then carriages are coming up to the door and driving away incessantly.

I take this somnolent life coolly. I could sleep upon bare boards if I could once more be amidst the stir and excitement of a live world. These people have grown accustomed to dullness. They were born and bred in it. They like it as well as anything else.

Mrs. Chesnut tells us that fifty or sixty years ago she was never satisfied unless she went north every summer. And a tolerably troublesome job that must have been. Four weeks to her home in Philadelphia with coaches and four, baggage wagons, children, nurses, outriders, &c&c.

After all her outspoken praises of negroes, she would never trust her children except to a white head nurse. Fortunately she found a good one, who remained with her until the poor old soul died. From the eldest to the fifteenth—which was my husband, who was left the only son. Mammy Baldwin died a few months before I was married—in the nursery at Mulberry, cared for and loved as one of the family.

The maids here dress in linsey-woolsey gowns and white aprons in the winter—and in summer, blue homespun. These deep blue dresses and white turbans and aprons are picturesque and nice looking. On Sundays their finery is excessive and grotesque. I mean their holiday, church, and outdoor getup. Whenever they come about us they go back to the white apron uniform.

3. Another reference to J. C.'s unidentified friend is deleted.
4. An allusion to William Wordsworth, "Eminent Reformers," in *The Ecclesiastical Sonnets*, part 2, no. 39.

My dear old maid is as good as gold, and pretty much of that color. She has a sour and discontented air, but it is only a way she has. She chooses to wait on us because she "nussed Mars Jeems"—and she likes me. She only attends to me here. She never leaves home. She is Maria Whitaker's mother. She is as noiseless in her ministrations as the white cat. She brings water and builds up a fire. She lets that burn down to warm the room. She then makes a positive bonfire and says sternly, "Ain't you gwine to git up? And fust bell for breakwus done ring."

Which mandate, if I disregard, she lets me sleep as long as I please and brings me—oh! such a nice breakfast to my bedside.

While I loiter over my breakfast she gets my room in what she calls "apple pie." When I am in my dressing room and bath, she sweeps and dusts. It all seems cleaning and getting to rights by magic, no trouble of disorder. Mrs. Chesnut had the art of training servants, and so had Mammy Baldwin!

[*Here a page is torn out.*]

Prolific African fashion! And an immense income is consumed by the young and old unprofitable servants here.

From my window high (I sit here in the library alone a great deal), I see carriages approach. Colonel Chesnut drives a pair of thoroughbreds—beauties, mahogany bays with shining coats and arching necks. It is a pleasure to see Scip drive them up. Tiptop and Princess are their names. They are Monarch colts.

Mrs. Chesnut has her carriage horses and a huge family coach for herself, which she never uses. The young ladies have a barouche and their own riding horses. We have a pair, for my carriage; and my husband has several saddle horses. There are always families of ten children or grandchildren of the house, visiting here—with carriage and horses, nurses, children, &c&c. The house is crammed from garret to cellar, without intermission.

Now, as I sit here writing, I see half a dozen carriages under the shade of the trees—coachmen on their boxes, talking, laughing, &c, some "hookling," they call it. They have a bone and hook, something like a crochet needle, and they hook themselves woolen gloves. Some are reading hymnbooks, or pretending. The small footmen are playing marbles under the trees.

A pleasant, empty, easygoing life. If one's heart is at ease. But people are not like pigs; they cannot be put up and fattened. So here I pine and fret.

Mrs. Chesnut describes to us Colonel Cox's house at Bloomsbury, Trenton, where they received de Grasse and Rochambeau[5]—&c. When anyone here transgresses some plain rule of good breeding, her mild rebuke is, "Ah, you were not brought up at Bloomsbury."

She tells us how she sung sweet old English ballads—and the enthusiastic delight of the Frenchmen—&c&c.

Have been reading and destroying old letters. Love letters from a young girl

---

5. François Joseph Paul, comte de Grasse, and Jean Baptiste Donatien de Vimeur, comte de Rochambeau, commanded, respectively, the French navy and army sent to aid the American colonies in the Revolution.

to an old woman. Mine from Mary Kirkland—and from Caroline Perkins. Like Wolsey, I tear my hair and cry, "If I had served my God, as I have done you." They both bow politely when they pass me.

No wonder that I find no place for the word "gratitude" in this world but in the dictionary.

No sooner is Israel's thirst slaked than God has an Amalekite ready to assault them. The Almighty hath choice of rods to whip us—and will not be satisfied with one trial. They must needs be quarreling with Moses—without a cause—and now God sends Amalekites to quarrel with them.

God is just. They who would be contending with their best friends should have enemies sent them and work enough cut out for them, contending with enemies. So says Bishop Hall[6]—Moses—our president—Amalekites—Yankees.

《**December 1, 1861.** Last night, slept like a top, so am not so miserably ill today.

《Went to church and made this resolution which only with God's help I can keep—not to be so bitter—not to abuse people and not to hate them so. At dinner I found myself afoul of Tom Davis and stopped instantly. Knelt at the communion with Mrs. Kirkland. I do not know who wept most, she or I. I have been so reckless a sinner, and God's mercy has been so manifest. . . . 》

December 2, 1861. Met Louisa Salmond at the gate, going down on a visit of condolence to Aunt Mary L.[7] I had not seen her since Lemuel's death, so was easily persuaded to join the expedition. On the front seat was Old Penny, Mrs. Salmond's[8] maid. Louisa said Penny had elected herself to be their bodyguard. Ever since Dr. Salmond had gone to the wars Penny had deserted her comfortable quarters, left her warm bed to sleep on the floor and take care of them. Little Maggie calls Penny "our Beauregard."

At Aunt Mary's everything was quiet and sad. Once only there was bitter words. Aunt Mary said, with an outburst of grief, "I never see a coffin leave this house but *I* wish I was in it."

Mr. Kirkland's anecdotes of Ripley's staff:

An aide who was recalcitrant—would not go. Bayard Clinch[9] said, "Give me your horse—I will carry the message."

---

6. From Joseph Hall, "The Foil of Amalek; or, The Hand of Moses Lift Up," *Contemplations upon the Principal Passages in the Holy Story* (1612–15).

7. Mary (Hopkins) Boykin, the widow of M. B. C.'s uncle Lemuel, was a planter with holdings in Kershaw District. Her eldest son, Lemuel, Jr., had just died.

8. Probably Isabel (Whitaker) Salmond. Her husband Thomas Whitaker Salmond, a second cousin of J. C. and the brother of Louisa Salmond, was a surgeon with the rank of captain in Kershaw's regiment.

9. Nicholas Bayard Clinch, a son of Duncan L. Clinch.

The man who was loath to venture his precious carcass under fire got down promptly and with smiling grace changed horses, and Bayard Clinch was off at full speed in a second.

"Why change horses?"

"Oh! Bayard was riding one of his finest horses. He did not wish to risk that."

"Was the fire so hot?"

"Into the gates of Hell rode the six hundred—see Tennyson."

"So Bayard is well named."

"Yes—that other fellow is a curious exception. Devil-may-care reckless bravery is the rule down there."

《I *fell* from my high position taken on my knees on Sunday.》

At it again. Once more I have been under grape and chain shot. I stood it until forbearance ceased to be a virtue, and then I gave back shot for shot. I do not think I was ever so angry in my life. My country and everybody in it abused, suspected, assigned such despicable motives. And there sat the Comfortable Cynic,[1] calling himself the only true patriot. In times like these, there he sat, in his warm, soft dressing gown, sleeping sweetly at night and eating of the best, his taste studied in every particular. And must I stay there and hear him malign and vilify the unfortunates who are lying in snow and mud; risking life and limb, deserting home, wife, children, worldly goods, periling all—maybe their very souls—for what they believe their *own* country and no Yankee land? A *Union*, let them call it—empire and kingdom. We in this Union would be an unwilling bride—a Union where one party is tied and dragged in, *if* he can be well dubbed first!

However, my interlocutor hated the Union enough and admired our army en masse, but he gave each individual man the meanest motive for going there, the worst record since he has been there.

December 6, 1861. A heavy fall![2] but no bones broken. Inward bruises and stunned somewhat. Miss Catherine Eccles[3] said whenever she had a craze, wanted anything with all her might—up to the utterly unreasonable point—she always got it, but in a way that made it a punishment not a pleasure, in a way which if she had been a heathen, she would have thought the Fates were laughing at her. All her life she felt so ill-used. Everybody could go to New York—poverty forbade in her case. Then she was sent there with the person she cared most for in life, to consult physicians. They pronounced him dying. The longest, the most miserable, the bleakest, the most hopeless days of her life were spent in New York. The very thing had come that she so coveted—and what was it.

1. Identified in the 1860s Journal as Judge Withers.
2. The news of J. C.'s defeat for election to the first Confederate Congress.
3. The daughter of Jonathan Eccles, a Camden merchant.

That was my way with this senatorship. I wanted that and nothing else—until my husband was sent to Washington. Then—but that is my private howl—words are vain.

Mr. A. H. Boykin refused to allow Mr. Barnwell and Mr. Chesnut's [names] to be placed together. He thought as Mr. C was the incumbent he should be reelected first—&c&c. Mr. Barnwell's friends then coalesced with Orr, and those two are our senators.

To ride a high horse so foolishly at this time! And when Mr. Davis, Mr. Barnwell himself, &c had so urged Mr. Chesnut to remain in the Congress. And so he had let everyone who pleased take the offices he could have had in the army.

This is Governor Manning's account of the fiasco. He said, "It is Ham Boykin's extraordinary handling of his friend's election."

And A. H. B. says, "What troubles me so, I see it was my fault."

How I tormented Mr. C. Do this—do that—do not do the other—you will give offense, make enemies, &c&c. I can't say that he ever heeded my "sage advices" in the least.[4] Still, this election did not turn on the candidates at all—but upon the skillful manipulations of their electioneering friends. Or—and this I do believe—this vote shows how the wind blows. It grows cooler. Orr is and always was a Union man, and so was left out in the first Congress. Then Mr. Barnwell is sent because otherwise he has no way to support his family. He is one of the unhappy ones whose estate and whose home was destroyed at Beaufort. Besides, does it not read as a vote of disapprobation? Mr. C was the first man to resign when Lincoln was made president. These legislators have been in the army for a year, and no doubt they mean to hang on to the bitter end. They seem by an afterthought to prefer the men who were slowest to move off from the old Union! Orr—Pickens, et omne genus.

《Now let us look this thing in the *face*. This is an end of J. C.'s political life. I do not wish him to serve South Carolina again if he could, but he must do what he can for his home and his friends.》

If we are not improved from the face of the earth, as the Yankees clear away the Indians, to military heroes all political high places will be given. There is a soft spot in everybody's heart for a fighting, dashing soldier—bronzed, weather-beaten, the more wounded the better.

Offices of trust and confidence will be their natural heritage. Personal courage and self-devotion—we all understand that.

So the rage for elderly, halfhearted leaders will soon be over. Thank God!

Reaction—swing back of the pendulum—that's all.

---

4. An allusion to Robert Burns, "Tam o' Shanter."

Last night I read the most bravely indelicate letter from Mrs. Greenhow.[5] She wants us to know how her delicacy was shocked and outraged. That could be done only by most plain-spoken revelations. For eight days she was kept in full sight of men—her rooms wide open—and sleepless sentinels watching by day and by night. Soldiers tramping—looking in at her leisurely by way of amusement.

Beautiful as she is, at her time of life few women like all the mysteries of their toilette laid bare to the public eye.

She says she was worse used than Marie Antoinette when they snatched a letter from the poor queen's bosom.

Mr. Team was here today. He is a stalwart creature, a handsome old man. Perhaps the finest black eye I ever saw. He has been an overseer all his life. Most people detest overseers, but Mr. Team is an exception. He has the goodwill and respect of all the world—our small world, I mean.

How those magnificent eyes blazed today. He is disgusted at the way Mr. C has been left out in the cold. His expression would change when he caught my eye—and then he was as gentle and sympathetic as he had been fierce before. Here is a specimen of his talk:

"Our only chance is to be ahead of them—free our negroes and put them in the army. In all my life I have only met one or two womenfolk who were not abolitionists in their hearts—and hot ones, too. Mrs. Chesnut is the worst. They have known that on her here for years. Tom Haile[6] said as soon as he married he found all the ladies of this family hated slavery."

"How did they show it? I am sure they are lazy enough and take more waiting on than a little."

"Oh—they are so sorry for them, so good to them, the fat, idle, good-for-nothing things."

We told him Uncle Tom's story as invented or imagined by Mrs. Stowe. Said he had not seen many of that sort. If there was any, money could not buy 'em.

We said, "Daddy Abram was as good."

"He was not tried in affliction. You don't know. His life was easy as an old shoe. Quash says Ole Abram is a saint. Marster trusts him with the wine cellar key, and he takes a little because the Bible 'lows it, for his stomach's sake."

His old overseer's stories were horrid. Still, he said, "I never knew—murdered or burnt—but if the marsters are bad or drunken, look out. It is a thing too unjust, too unfair to last. Let us take the bull by the horns. Set 'em free, let 'em help us fight, to pay for their freedom."

Old Mr. Chesnut did not hear, and I noticed no voice was raised to enable him to hear. He is like the emperor of Austria. His métier is to be an autocrat, a prince of slaveholders. And he will so die. His forefathers paid their money for them. They are his by that right divine, he thinks.

5. In the 1860s Journal, M. B. C. wrote, "I had a wonderful letter from Mrs. Greenhow."
6. Like his brother Edward, Thomas Haile was an Alachua County, Fla., planter married to a niece of J. C.

Our votes are not counted—women, alas!

Team said, "Slavery don't tend to make Uncle Toms, nary time. It does not make good mothers—teaches them to expect other people to take care of their children." Then told a tale of a woman so lazy she tied her child to her back and jumped in the river. She said she did not mean to work—nor should her child after her.[7]

Mr. Legree was a bachelor, you say.

"Yes. That Miss Stowe don't know nothing. The way a man's wife and chillen stops things or suffers—when men are so bad, that's where the trouble comes in."

Here old Mr. Chesnut, who has not lived ninety years for nothing, asked him: "What do you say, sir, about black regiments? You can't trust them—not on our side. They won't fight for what they think they are going to have anyhow. They have got it in their heads that this war frees them anyway. Bad times, Team, and worse coming."

Team had had us crying over his stories. Now we laughed, that we might not cry.

We are lighthearted by nature, a gay people, and our hopefulness is excessive. Too buoyant to be long kept doleful.

The Southern landscape is always sad. Now the freshet is up on every side. The river comes to our doors. To sit here and see the lower limbs of the trees dip mournfully in the water—so much sheep, cattle, &c&c has been driven up—it is a Noah's Ark. And their lowing and bleating adds to the general despairing effect. We are surrounded now by water on three sides. There is nothing left to be desired, since this water view has walked in. This is not at all like the Sandy Hill house—with all its godforsaken makeshift wretchedness. There hot wind, night and day. Moonlight only brings weird sounds of lonely whippoorwills or screech owls.

Here everything is fresh, bright, cool, sweet-scented, and a mockingbird is singing. And a woodpecker at work, or a yellowhammer, for I cannot see the small bird who is making such a noise. I hear loud laughing among the negroes. And every sound comes up of a jolly contented life. Neither silence nor solitude.

All the same—it is mournful. A dismal swamp feeling hangs round us still. In my youth, none could have been happier or gayer, but that lonely clump of pines on James Island filled me with sad foreboding. They haunted me. Later, as we passed up and down the Mississippi, the gloom set in. I could never shake it off—the Southern swamp depression, call it.

Have seen a copy of Gen. T. W. Sherman's proclamation to the people of Carolina. He says he comes in a friendly spirit and does not desire to interfere with our *local institutions*.

---

7. In the 1860s Journal, under Dec. 7, the slave woman's suicide is given a quite different and wholly sympathetic interpretation by Team, who says she was "driven to despair" and complains that "the man who caused it was not hung."

Things have been and are not, and yet,
Life loiters, keeps a pulse at even measure,
And goes upon its business and its pleasure,
And knows not the depth of its regret.[8]

Team said: "We beat 'em? God knows, I hope we will, fur I hate 'em body an' bones. And we will be a great nation—but you-all take my word. Slavery is done for. Hurray for honest poverty."

Read Émile Souvestre—*Au bord du lac* series—"L'Esclave," "Le Serf," &c&c.[9] He ought to have kept up the chain—come over here—had our slave-Yankee help—last of all, universal equality and help yourself.

Another Russell letter. Yankees satisfied they will get what cotton they want. Almighty dollar always wins its way. That was written before Port Royal. Russell thinks he knows the fervid beating of this strong Southern heart, to credit that. He knows we will destroy everything before their approaching footsteps.

The *Examiner*'s fling. He is easy in his mind about the Mississippi. There will be no Port Royal there. Western men are as brave as Carolinians and so much more practical. They will not give up because two small forts are taken with one hundred artillery men in each. And they will not fire so badly as to upset their own guns. There is a taunt for you—Drayton & Co.!

Russell finds our courage a fact past controversy. We are a brave and dauntless people, after all said and done. In point of fact, if our money was as palpable a fact—as visible to the naked eye as our soldierly qualities—no mortal could doubt the issue of this conflict.

Poetry answers to express my sentiments often better than I can do it myself:

Do you think of the friends that are gone, Jeanne?
As ye sit by your fire at night.
Do ye wish they were around you again once more
By the hearth they made so bright.

---

8. Slightly misquoted lines from part 1 of the "Prologue" of *The Wanderer* (1859), written under the pseudonym Owen Meredith by Edward Robert Bulwer-Lytton, English diplomat and poet.

9. "L'Esclave," "Le Serf," and two other stories appear in *Au bord du lac* (1852).

I think of the friends that are gone, Robin.
They are dear to my heart as then—
But the best and the dearest among them all
I have never wished back again.

⟨⟨**December 7, 1861.** I have been busy all day, reading old letters. What a meek, humble little thing I was. How badly J. C. has played his cards to let me develop into the self-sufficient thing I am now. For I think this last bitter drop was for *me*. He will care very little, but I had grown insufferable with my arrogance.⟩⟩

December 8, 1861. My husband is ill in Richmond, with pneumonia. Mrs. Huger[1] found him in his room, forgotten of all (Laurence was not there) and nearly dead, his dinner of three days before beside his bed, untasted. She and her daughter Meta nursed him through it. He will be home today or tomorrow. He takes the senator business coolly, says he was not looking out for a new deal—but his consolation is [that] he has been put aside by the same wise body which put in Pickens.

⟨⟨Yesterday I did not go down after J. C.'s letter. I was too intensely miserable. . . . He said Miles came in his room and read the senatorial election with *great disgust*. Miles is the only friend he has in the South Carolina delegation. J. C. says it was unexpected, but he accounts for it by the act having been performed by the same legislature which gave the present gubernatorial incubus. He says it is moonshine to him; he is afraid it will annoy me, that it gives him his freedom once more to attend to matters much more important. I would send Laurence on at once if I knew exactly when he would come home. What he says of his motions I do not care for, as he is always decided by accidents and does not object to changing his mind twenty times in an hour.⟩⟩

I do not think anybody would mind the troubles of life if nobody felt bound to talk it over with us. The triumph of one's enemies is a feature of the case to be considered—but it does not approach in annoyance the condolence and sympathy of one's voluble friends.

Mrs. Chesnut attributes her peculiar ideas—we call it her angelic goodness—to her having been trained by a Scotch schoolmistress, a Mrs. Graham. The Graham no doubt was a wonderful woman, but Mrs. Chesnut was born without any bad qualities—so goodness came easy to her.

She reproved me today for saying to Maum Betsey—who after all is no worse than Rachel, George Sand,[2] &c—"Why did you never marry?"

---

1. Elizabeth Allen (Deas) Huger, mother of Margaret "Meta" Deas Huger, the wife of John Middleton Huger, and the sister-in-law of Brig. Gen. Daniel Elliott Huger and Mrs. Charles Lowndes.
2. French tragic actress Elisa Félix (1820–58), known as Rachel on the stage, remained unmarried and had two children. Her contemporary, Amandine Aurore Lucie Dupin, who wrote novels under the pseudonym George Sand, maintained well-publicized romantic relationships after a marriage of convenience ended in divorce.

"'Cause nobody here please me. I could not fall in love because a man lived on our plantation. Old Marster had to go way to Philadelphia' fore he fine one to suit him."

At which the old gentleman chuckles.

"Betsey is now a good Christian and a self-respecting woman," says Mrs. C.

Methodist minister and Mr. DePass[3] dined here. The circuit rider, as they call their parson (I mean the colored church), is a genuine Catholic priest, an infallible pope, meddling, putting everybody to rights. He is afraid of no delicate investigation. He looks into everything, and if palpable commandments are not kept, he turns out church members. They dislike to be up before the church and excommunicated, more than aught else in the world. So it is a wholesome discipline.

Mr. Shuford,[4] the man who has charge here now, was my nearest neighbor in Kirkwood. So I know him, and also Mrs. Shuford and the little Shufords, well.

We went to church in the grove. There was a negro wedding after service.

When Mr. Shuford preached I saw from whence Jim Nelson got his ideas of eloquence, though he improved on his models. Mr. Shuford begins each sentence in a low chaunting voice distinct enough, then he works himself up—shuts his eyes, clenching his fist—and the end of the sentence might be addressed to a congregation over the river, so loud and shrill is the shriek. It is like nothing I have ever heard but calling the ferryman. I did not listen as attentively as I ought—but that shout would bring back the dead from the land of dreams.

"Claiborne a black rascal," old Mr. C says. "James only keeps him as his headman because he once saved his life. I hear he has joined the church. We will see if his Christianity will hold water. By their fruits shall ye know them."

Oh! the bridal party—all as black as the ace of spades. The bride and her bridesmaids in white swiss muslin, the gayest of sashes—and bonnets too wonderful to be described. They had on red blanket shawls, which they removed as they entered the aisle and seemed loath to put on when the time came to go out—so proud were they of their finery. But it grew colder and colder—every window and door wide open, sharp December wind.

Gibbes Carter arose amidst the ceremony and threw a red shawl over the head of the congregation, to a shivering bridesmaid. The shawl fell short and wrapped itself about the head of a sable dame comfortably asleep. She waked with a snort, struggled to get it off her head, with queer little cries. "Lord ha' mussy! What dish er here now." There was for a moment a decided tendency to snigger—but they were too well-bred to misbehave in church, and soon it was unbroken solemnity. I know that I shook with silent laughter long after every dusky face was long and respectable.

The bride's gloves were white, and the bridegroom's shirt bosom was a snowy expanse fearfully like Johnny's Paris garments, which he says disappear by the

---

3. James Perriman DePass of Camden, a Methodist minister who served as a Confederate chaplain during the war.
4. Methodist minister Jacob L. Shuford.

dozen. This one had neat little frills and a mock diamond of great size in the middle. Miss Sally Chesnut said, "Those frills marked it Camden or homemade."

Maria was hard on Mr. Shuford as she combed my hair at night. She likes Manning Brown. "He is old Marster's nephew—a gentleman born—and he preaches to black and to white just the same. There ain't but one Gospel for all. He tells us 'bout keeping the Sabbath holy, honoring our fathers and mothers, and loving our neighbors as ourselves. Mr. Shuford, he goes fer low-life things—hurting people's feelings. Don't you tell lies—don't you steal—and worse things yet, real indecent. Before God we are white as he is. And in the pulpit he has no need to make us feel we are servants, repeating poetry about sweeping brooms to the glory of God."[5] &c&c.

Now, I took up the cudgels for Mr. Shuford. Years ago I went to see some sick negroes. And I left the carriage at the overseer's house and with my basket went down the line on foot.

I passed what I knew to be an unoccupied house and heard coming from it queer sounds. So I softly drew near. It was Mr. Shuford teaching the little negroes. They were answering all together and seemed to know their catechism wonderfully well.

And yet there were those among them who made awful work of it. After the fashion of the boy who answered the question "Who made you?" with "Out of the dust of the ground." "What do you mean by that nonsense?" "Oh, I'm all right. The boy that God made is sick."

I sat there listening more than an hour. I know how hard it is to teach them, for I have tried it, and I soon let my Sunday school all drift into singing hymns—which all parties did well. Lord Monboddo's ideas were always in my head while engaged with my Sunday class—*Vestiges of Creation*, &c&c. I determined to wait until they developed more brains.[6] But Mr. Shuford's patience. was sublime. How he wrestled in prayer for those imps of darkness. And he thought only God saw or heard him. How blithely the whole crowd rushed into their psalm singing. Their heart was in that.

---

5. Allusion to George Herbert's "The Elixir," in *The Temple*.
6. M. B. C. is referring to two pre-Darwinian advocates of evolutionary theory: James Burnet, Lord Monboddo, an eighteenth-century Scottish jurist, anthropologist, and eccentric who wrote *Of the Origin and Progress of Language* (1773-92), and *Antient Metaphysics* (1779-99); and Scottish publisher Robert Chambers, the anonymous author of *Vestiges of the Natural History of Creation* (1844). Chambers's idea of black intellect is indicated by his contention that man started as a Negro and evolved through Malay, Indian, and Mongolian stages to become a Caucasian. While Monboddo suggestively reports that African women copulate with orangutans, M. B. C. may be thinking of his argument that children learn only gradually to form ideas.

Read Hedley Vicars.[7] The best of Christians do strange things—without their special wonder—when they are soldiers, moreover. That English officer could shoot down the princes!!! Prisoners in his hands. British in India—Christianity—&c&c&c. I am puzzled—straight out. I do not believe a genuine follower of Christ can be a soldier. It is a trade which calls for all that he forbids. There! The Christ's religion eliminates war and slavery. Mr. Shuford, unconsciously with a shot at us:

"Go to, you rich men. Weep, howl, for your miseries have come upon ye."

"Behold the hire of the laborer, &c&c&c."

"Ye have lived in pleasure. &c&c."[8]

Hitherto I have felt so poor and have fancied my life devoid of pleasure, inclined to grumble at Providence. Today, under Mr. Shuford's ministrations, I began to tremble—to shiver. Maybe after all we were the rich who were threatened with howling and also about the pleasures of life. I went whimpering to Mr. C. He said coolly: "Let the galled jade wince. My withers are unwrung."[9] He said the saddle was on the other horse and that his negroes owed him about fifty thousand dollars now for food and clothes. "The lazy rascals! They steal all of my hogs, and I have to buy meat for them. They will not make cotton. If they don't choose to make cotton—spin it and weave it—they may go naked for me. Yes—as naked as they went in Africa. There are plenty of sheep. Let them shear the sheep and spin that, too."

That means I must look after the spinners and weavers. And it can be done easily. Everybody else is beginning to do it.

One joke at Mr. Chesnut's expense always made him very angry. At an agricultural dinner Mr. Taylor told: "Chesnut offered his crop to his overseer for his wages. Overseer answered, 'La! Colonel, you don't catch me that way.' Now he sees negroes better begin to learn to support themselves, &c."

He is like his mother in feeling and likes to be thought like his father, whose bark is worse than his bite. How men can go blustering around—making everybody uncomfortable simply to show that they are masters—and we only women and children at their mercy.

She is a sample of "blessed are the pure in heart—they shall see God"—even here on this earth. She reforms everybody. "Her gentleness moves them more than force moves them to gentleness." Her influence over the negroes is wonderful.

The master is kind and amiable when not crossed. Given to hospitality on a

---

7. Either Hedley Shafto Vicars, *Walking with God before Sebastopol: Reminiscences of the Late Captain Vicars, 97th Regiment* (1855), or Catherine M. Marsh, *Memorials of Captain Hedley Vicars, Ninety-seventh Regiment* (1856).

8. Allusion to James 5:1, 4–5.

9. Slightly misquoted from *Hamlet*, act 3, scene 2.

grand scale. Jovial, genial, friendly, courtly in his politeness. As absolute a tyrant as the czar of Russia, the khan of Tartary—or the sultan of Turkey.

Mr. DePass reported the poor soldiers' wives eating dry bread. Colonel C said he gave, the day before, thirty bushels of corn to one of them. Where the bacon was to come from he did not know, with Cincinnati cut off.

Best description of Mrs. C:

"To be liking everything and everybody better than they deserve—*and* praising them beyond what we feel" . . .[1]

Read Émile Souvestre, "Collaboratrice."[2] *The De Lisle; or, The Sensitive Man.*

"All proud persons are much attached to the 'convenances'—without a due respect for which a person meaning to be civil is often very impertinent."[3]

A refugee, Mr. Stephen Robinson,[4] said on the cars as he came up that he chose Camden, as he knew so many people. It would be jolly.

"Who do you know?"

"Old Colonel Chesnut, Mr. Tom Lang, Miss Susan, and Murray Lang, &c."[5]

He was told that the list did not have a jolly sound. Colonel C over ninety—deaf and blind—not very available for social purposes. Mr. Lang has been dead for several years—remaining: Susan and Murray!

December 13, 1861.   Charleston is in flames, one part of the city utterly destroyed. On the night of the 11th we had here a furious windstorm. We rather enjoyed it—in the interest of the fleet outside of the bar. As the blast howled, we said, "How now, blockaders?" Evil thoughts are like chickens come home to roost.

When the telegram came today I was too much shocked to speak. Suffering, death, and destitution on every side. In all this confusion they might attack us. What then!

Old Colonel C said, "Charleston has been twice burned down before in my recollection." He described the other two fires. He seemed greatly relieved that the Yankees had no hand in it. The theater gone—St. Andrew's Hall, sacred to St. Cecilia balls, and St. Finbar's Cathedral.

---

1. An unidentified poem is omitted.

2. A story in Souvestre, *Récits et souvenirs, romans des familles* (1853).

3. Paraphrased from Elizabeth Caroline (Duncan) Grey, *De Lisle; or, The Sensitive Man* (1828), part 2, chapter 13.

4. Probably Stephen D. Robinson, a Charleston cotton factor.

5. Thomas Lang, Sr., a wealthy Kershaw planter whose wife was a first cousin of J. C. Susan and Murray Lang were his spinster nieces living together in Camden.

Suddenly the old gentleman waked up. "Why do the Yankee papers say, 'Now Sumner is avenged'?"

"Oh, Port Royal, you know. They then returned Preston Brooks's blows over our heads."

"And then the South Carolina legislature, when it cut off Mr. Chesnut's head—I mean, took away his seat in the Senate—that avenged Sumner, too."

Everybody reads my journal, but since I have been making sketches of character at Mulberry I keep it under lock and key. Yesterday I handed this book to my new little maid Ellen, who is a sort of apprentice under Betsey, trying to learn her trade. When I gave Ellen the book I pointed to an armoire. She mistook the direction of my finger and took it into Miss Sally Chesnut's room, where she laid it on the table.

Today I looked for it in the armoire. It was gone. "Ellen, where is the book I write in? I gave it to you." She flew into Miss S. C.'s room, which happened to be empty just then, and brought it. Words were useless. And in my plain speaking and candor, what have I not said—intending no eye save mine to rest upon this page.

The things that I cannot tell exactly as they are I do not intend to tell at all.

Most of these servants read. I have taught several myself. They tire of it before I do. In the ABC department they show no stupidity whatever, but they do not care for any more when they can read a little.

Now old Colonel C will lend the Sandy Hill house, because the Charleston catastrophe was a visitation from God. He has no patience with people who run away from their homes and destroy them to spite Yankees—&c&c.

Mrs. Browning's Mrs. C:

> She never found fault with you: never implied
>   Your wrong by her right; and yet men at her side
> Grew nobler—girls purer. As through the whole town
>   The children were gladder that plucked at her gown[6]—

December 14, 1861.   Carolina Institute, where secession was signed, burned down. From East Bay—along Broad St. down to the river—Mr. Petigru's house. So being antisecession does not save. The fire, as the rain, falls on the just and the unjust. Fire appeared simultaneously in several places.

John DeSaussure has sent a hundred bales of cotton to be sold. Says he knows they will slip it into Old England or New England.

---

6. From Elizabeth Barrett Browning's "My Kate," *Last Poems* (1862).

Horace Greeley says in his *Tribune,* "South Carolina is the meanest and the vainest state in the Union (does not count us out of it yet) and nobody will feel any compunction at laying it waste."

———————

Read a Yankee novel today—genuine article: *Chapel of St. Mary.*[7]

———————

Who is it says, "After forty we repent, but we never reform"?[8]
Still I am under that awful age.
Lesson of today, in church as the parson read it. It was a little alarming. Fortunately it was not of the parson's own selection, for he had to read it according to the rubric. It was from Isaiah and applied so clearly to Charleston and its fire and destruction.

———————

"All things are less dreadful than they seem."[9]
Mrs. Roper said, "Not a house left on Logan St. but Tom Frost's."
The Judge gravely replied, "That is a reward for his marrying an up-country girl and for such a pious mother-in-law."
"Oh?" said Mrs. Roper, not understanding the joke at all—but she smiled vacantly and did not pursue the subject.[1]
That so clever a man should not be able to see how such cynical abuse of everybody can have no sense in it. Today it was the South Carolina legislature. He called it the weakest, stupidest, most venal body of men ever assembled. He had not heard that the convention was called.
"I thought one year ago Mr. C was standing up for you against the world. You acknowledged yourself that his influence made you a member of the convention. Since then you have had apparently but one object in life—making enemies for yourself *and for Mr. Chesnut*—out of pure gratitude!"
He said Johnson[2] complained that his family used so many pounds of butter and so many pounds of tea a week. He asked Johnson if they gave tea and butter to his horses.
He quoted Kate Williams, who had said, "Complaining of the foolish extravagance of your family was a vulgar, parvenu way of bragging of your money."

———————

7. [Mrs. Clara M. Thompson], *The Chapel of St. Mary* (1861) is the story of a dutiful, religious woman who spends time in a convent.
8. Probably Edward Young, "Night I," in *The Complaint; or, Night Thoughts on Life, Death, and Immortality* (1742–45), lines 417–22.
9. From Wordsworth, "Recovery," in *The Ecclesiastical Sonnets,* part 1, no. 7.
1. Tom Frost's mother-in-law was Sarah Cantey (Witherspoon) Williams, a cousin of Mrs. Withers. M. B. C.'s guest, Mrs. Roper, was probably the wife of Charleston commission merchant Richard Roper.
2. William Dalrymple Johnson, planter and delegate to the S.C. secession convention from Marlboro District.

December 16, 1861. Mr. A. H. Boykin says he did not know that there was any opposition to Mr. C until the night before the election. Then Mr. Barnwell's friend told him Mr. B's negroes had all gone to the fleet at Port Royal, &c&c, and Mr. C and Mr. B must be placed on the same ticket. It was absolutely necessary for Mr. B's friends to find a place for him. Mr. A. H. Boykin acknowledges he lost his temper and insisted that it was due Mr. C to elect him first. Mr. B's friend then went to Orr with the same proposition, and they coalesced. Governor Means, one of Mr. C's greatest friends, went to see his daughter who was ill. General Gist, for whom Mr. C had done so much, had to go to his ill father. None of them knew the election was coming off or that there was any opposition. At last Mr. Orr had only six more votes than Mr. C. And at least half a dozen of Mr. C's friends were not there because they did not know there was to be any opposition. So much for leaving yourself in your friends' hands in political affairs. Mind your own business there most of all. But it is useless to talk now. Another thing urged against Mr. C—the only night he was in Columbia, he stayed in his own room, did not go to see anybody, thought it unseemly to electioneer for such a place as senator. The legislators thought otherwise—and that he was too grand and that a taking down would do him good. All this says A. H. B.

In Richmond Mr. Barnwell told Mr. Chesnut how much he regretted that he was not his colleague but that it was all for the best. "Some men with brains ought to be left in the state."

Boxes and boxes of provisions and clothes sent to the needy and burnt-out in Charleston.

Northern newspapers gloating over our misfortunes and fiery destruction.

Mrs. Davis's new baby called William Howell.

Met Mary H[3]—she made a long rigmarole—her horse would not stand still—she was on horseback. She seemed to be talking principally of Willie Bull.[4] Thinking it over, sorting out the disjointed parts, I came to see she meant to let me know her engagement to Ned Cantey[5] is ratified and announced.

Letter from Robert McCaw. He is despondent. He finds the blusterers grow tiresome. They are unwilling to suffer anything in a war they of all others brought on.

England demands Mason and Slidell to be replaced under the aegis of her flag.

3. Mary "Hammy" Boykin.
4. William Izard Bull, the son of a rich Beaufort planter, served as a surgeon with the First S.C. Regiment.
5. Capt. Edward Boykin Cantey of Kershaw District was a cousin of both M. B. C. and J. C.

Lord Lyons talks of breaking the blockade &c&c. France is counted good, to do whatever England will. Troops are ordered to Canada—&c&c.[6]

Read *Dr. Thorne*[7] last night. A refuge from so much sentiment, sympathy, and want of feeling. How she ought to thank God that she has none—incapable of it. If she had! Where would she be! As Mr. Petigru said of Trescot, she has no indignation for any wrong—to her or to anyone else.

Letter from Charleston:[8]

Sunday night, 15th Dec. 1861

Thanks for your kind note today, dear Mrs. Chesnut. Comfortable clothing for them will be a great help. For the children, anything that you can spare. Charleston looks like a mutilated body! The first impulse would be to turn away and hide your face!

That fearful night—no human power could stand against that gale. For a little while it seemed as if God had left us to ourselves (of all trials the hardest to struggle with), but his hand was over us still—loss of property is nothing compared to loss of life. That which *makes home* is left. It would have cheered you to see how by next morning people were taken in and cared for. What noble generosity Georgia is showing us.

Today we have good news from western Virginia—so give us your hand! And look up!

The fire began in a negro house next to the blind factory—carelessness—and the wind rose with the flames until it got beyond control. Picture to yourself Mr. Alfred Huger seated on the steps of the poorhouse next morning—with only a blanket around him—his fancy! There was Mr. Wm. Huger's house in Broad St., out of the way of the wind, where he could have been comfortable and private (as he was afterward). He would not allow his furniture &c to be saved *in time;* thought the house was safe. While it was burning he remained opposite in an armchair, with his desk in his lap. I wonder if the Yankees think as Job's friends did? We don't!

Brother was out on guard over the bar but seeing the flames, came to our help, with sixteen of our men—had Miss Pinckney's property moved—valuables, china, wine—everything carried over to the customhouse. Thought he had saved the house—but the roof caught again, and it was so

6. M. B. C. is probably setting down somewhat inaccurate newspaper speculation. The British government had ordered to Canada troops to repulse a possible Union invasion and ships sufficient to break the Union blockade of Southern ports. But Lord Lyons maintained careful silence during the *Trent* affair and did not transmit to Secretary of State Seward the British demand for the return of Mason and Slidell until Dec. 19.

7. Anthony Trollope, *Doctor Thorne* (1858).

8. M. B. C.'s correspondent was Susan Rose Rutledge.

hard to get engines. Aunt Julia[9] says he saved *them*. A bakery at the foot of their lot was burnt, and a quantity of light wood in the yard added to their danger, but she said brother put heart and life in everyone. There he stood, scorched—nearly suffocated at times—giving orders in that calm, clean, resolute way that carries everything before it. Working with a will, too—tearing off the roof, cutting away wood, keeping hay saturated with water &c until they were safe; then he went to others. The Tradd St. Rutledges' house could have been saved if they could have got water enough, but the firemen were exhausted. He got everything out; heavy pieces, Lize[1] said, that had not been moved since this house was built.

John Laurens had fixed his house so prettily. Gardens &c&c for Maggie, just growing up.[2] All gone! The loss falls heavily on some.

Two poor women were sitting in the street, without even a suit of clothes saved. The youngest had a shawl wrapped round her bare arms and neck. They had gone to bed, the people telling them there was no danger. Afterward packed in haste—but the fire falling so thick, were obliged to rush out undressed. Could get no one to assist them in moving—so all their clothes were burnt up in their trunks. They were comfortable off, neat little place—garden, pictures, piano—well-to-do in the world. Now everything is gone. Miss Drayton[3] took them in out of the street.

Some of the Edisto people had moved furniture here—now all is lost. But I must say good night—tomorrow is a busy day.

Yours,

S. R. R.

Tell Fanny Hanckel[4] I will write when I can. She knows how it is—and my best thanks for her letter.

———————

So we are comparatively well off here—without being again senator—eh? . . .[5]

December 22, 1861.   Anniversary of secession. For one thing, the reality is not as dreadful as the anticipation. I have seen not half as much as I dreaded of fire and sword—*bad as it is.*

Lord Lyons demands his passports. That is a ray of sunshine—a patch of blue sky as broad, as the saying is, as a dutchman's breeches—in a clouded heaven. One can hope always for fair weather if that ample pattern of blue comes anywhere aloft.

9. Julia (Rutledge) Rose, mother of Hugh Rose.
1. Susan's second cousin, Eliza Pinckney Rutledge, who lived on Tradd St. with her father, Frederick Rutledge.
2. Former U.S. Customs official John Laurens and his thirteen-year-old daughter, Margaret, descendants of Revolutionary War political leader Henry Laurens.
3. Hester Tidyman Drayton, a cousin of Susan Rutledge.
4. The wife of Rev. James Stewart Hanckel.
5. A page from "Dr. South, *Consolations of Religion*" is deleted.

"Passports or Mason and Slidell"—that is Lord Lyons's word.[6] The *Mercury,* whose first instinct is always to insult, alienate, and drive off friends, says England does this because she wants tobacco and cotton—she does not resent the insult to her flag. Fortunately the queen nor the emperor—neither is, I daresay, a subscriber for the *Daily Mercury,* published by Rhetts & Co., Charleston, South Carolina.

We dined with the friend who thinks he has quite repaired his fault and shortcomings in the senator's election when he says: "Really, James, I think it was all my fault. You see I lost my temper, and I did not ascertain in time that there was to be opposition—and I ought not to have offended Mr. Barnwell's friends, &c&c—and if I had only let your friends know that, they might have been there to vote, &c&c."

It was not an agreeable subject, and we said nothing—literally. On Mr. C's part it was a clear case of not having minded his own business. Let it drop, for pity sake, thought I.

The conversation turned on Joe Johnston. "Now," says Mr. Hamilton Boykin, "we all knew Sid Johnston,[7] the general's brother. Never in his life could he make up his mind that everything was so exactly right, that the time to act had come. There was always something to fit that would not fit. Joe Johnston is that way, too. Wade Hampton brought him here to hunt—he is Mrs. Hampton's cousin.[8] We all liked him—but as to hunting, there he made a dead failure. He was a capital shot, better than Wade or I, and we are not so bad— that you'll allow. But then with Colonel Johnston—I think he was colonel then—the bird flew too high or too low—the dogs were too far or too near— things never did suit exactly. He was too fussy, too hard to please, too cautious, too much afraid to miss and risk his fine reputation for a crack shot. Wade and I bulged through the mud and water briars and bushes and came home with a heavy bag. We shot right and left—happy-go-lucky. Joe Johnston did not shoot at all. The exactly right time and place never came.

"Unless his ways are changed, he'll never fight a battle—you'll see. Oh, yes—he is as brave as Caesar. An accomplished soldier? Yes—who denies it? You'll see. I know Sid, and I've hunted with Joe. He is too particular—things are never all straight. You must go it rash—at a venture to win—&c&c&c."

---

6. Again, this is a speculative but largely accurate report. Had the Union refused to agree to the return of Mason and Slidell within one week from the official presentation of Britain's ultimatum on Dec. 23, the English would have broken off diplomatic relations, and Lyons would have asked for his passports and returned home.

7. Algernon Sidney Johnston (1801–52) was a Columbia, S.C., publisher.

8. That is, a cousin of Wade Hampton III's first wife, Margaret Frances (Preston) Hampton, who died in 1852.

Edward Johnson[9]—he is a cousin to the Prestons, too—spells his name differently. Oh, he is a different part of speech. He has had a rough-and-tumble fight in the west of Virginia.

We knew him, too, in Washington.

Read "Sur la mer."[1] Never tire of Émile Souvestre.

December 25, 1861. Dies Irae—Christmas Day 1861.

We did not exactly achieve a victory at Dranesville.[2] Frank English was killed. His father wrote to Mr. C to get a discharge for him—his health was so feeble. His is discharged now, poor boy, from this earth and its troubles.

The negroes who murdered Mrs. Witherspoon were tried by the law of the land and were hung. A man named Wingate, with a John Brown spirit—namely that negroes were bound to rise and kill women, and his philanthropy taking that turn, he made himself devil's counsel and stood by the negroes clear through. At the hanging he denounced John Witherspoon bitterly. And had high words, too, with George Williams.

Afterward George Williams, having raised a company, was made captain of it. The men were actually on board the train, and Captain Williams was sitting in a chair, near at hand, ready to jump on when the whistle blew. Wingate came behind him, rested his gun on the back of the chair, and shot him dead. There—before the very faces of his soldiers. It was very hard to rescue Wingate from the hands of George's men, who wanted to shoot him instantly—no wonder. (The people who laud and magnify John Brown's philanthropy must adore Wingate.)[3]

But he was taken from them by the law and lodged in jail. George Williams leaves a young wife with two babies, the eldest not two years old. Widows and orphans—it comes easy to be that now.

The servants rush in—"Merry Christmas," &c&c&c—I covered my face and wept.

Mr. C in good spirits, he is trying a new horse. As long as he has a dollar left in the world it will go in horseflesh. If fate will leave him a fine horse to ride, she can never utterly depress him otherwise.

9. Brig. Gen. Edward Johnson of Va. commanded the Confederate troops that fought a sharp but inconclusive battle at Camp Allegheny, near Cheat Mountain, on Dec. 13.

1. Perhaps *Scènes et moeurs des rives et des côtes* (1852).

2. A minor fight in Va. on Dec. 20.

3. The circumstances surrounding the murder of George Frederick Williams, Elizabeth Witherspoon's grandson, remain obscure. It is unlikely that Capt. W. H. Wingate was motivated by abolitionist sentiment, however. The jury that convicted him of the murder recommended leniency, and his only punishment was banishment from S.C.

At our Christmas dinner. The Hugers here. A charming mother and daughter. Meta the clever addressed her whole conversation to Mr. C and myself. She talked incessantly, but was interesting always. The family were all gathered, of course, and the table was very long. The others sat, stiff and lifeless as pins stuck in rows, showing only heads.

Meta affected me as champagne does one lately accustomed to that exciting beverage—and now surrounded by—what shall I say? Well! Something as dull as ditch water.

There was everything nice to eat at that table. Romeo is a capital cook—and the pastry looked as good, with his plum puddings and mince pies. There was everything there that a hundred years or more of unlimited wealth could accumulate as to silver, china, glass, damask—&c&c. But without Meta! Fancy it. She showed us L. Q. C. Lamar's likeness. Clever people gravitate toward one another. And she had helped him—written his letters for him—&c&c.

"Oh. Another of your p's and q's—Mr. L. Q. Washington kissed my hand, but he said, 'Carry that to Mrs. Chesnut. It is for her.'"

Mr. Chesnut called my attention, with a broad grin, to the grimace of disgust made by Mrs. Reynolds aside to her daughters.

I told the reproof given me by Colonel Beaufort Watts: "One kisses the hand of a queen. One shakes other people's."

Mrs. Huger has not been here for twenty years—but wishes to be kind and gracious to all old acquaintances. Mr. Hanckel came in. She advanced to meet him gaily, extending both hands—in hearty welcome, she greeted him as an old familiar friend. He responded in the same spirit. The "don't you remember's" fell fast and thick. Mr. Hanckel, being a clergyman, finally felt some scruples of conscience and ceased to smile assent to all she said. He became utterly dense to her allusions to "old times."

An explanation naturally followed.

"For whom do you take me, madam?"

"Willie Ancrum—of course."

Mr. Stephen Robinson said to me, "Your husband does business with our house?"

"You mean you are his factor. I wonder how you recollect it—he sends so little cotton. I forget it—so little money comes of it all."

Meta said Miss M—who is fearfully aristocratic—asked, with a supercilious air, "Did you know Mr. Miles in Charleston?"

"Certainly. I knew him well."

"I mean before he went to Norfolk or to Congress, before he was anybody in particular—only a pedagogue. His manner is pedagogic now."

"I met him at my grandfather's—where people who are not comme il faut do not go—Judge Huger's, you know?[4] Besides, his grandmother was a Porcher; so was one of mine. I daresay Mr. Miles and I are blood kin."

4. Daniel Elliott Huger of Charleston (1779-1854), a circuit court judge, Unionist, and U.S. senator.

"We are only connections. Your uncle married my aunt."

"Ah, yes—so he did!"

The same girl: "Mrs. Myers[5] is not pretty, after all."

"The men think so—and we are not pretty enough ourselves to be allowed an opinion on other women's beauty."

"Miss Huger, how can you? We are not ugly."

"But the men think so—and that settles it, practically." Miles had neglected the young person—or offended her.

In a revolution shy men are run over. No one stops to pick them up.

Unstable as water, thou shalt not excel.[6]

The enemy within nine miles of the Savannah RR.[7]

Mr. C gone back to Columbia.

Mrs. Huger on matrimony:

"There is not six months' difference between a beauty and an ugly woman. In that time the husband has totally forgotten her looks either way: grown callous from habit or—after the first year no man can tell whether he married for love or money. It is what a woman really is, not what he supposed her to be, that makes it good or bad for her—worse still, in his case."

"Ce n'est que le premier pas qui conte—alors."

"Ah, but mama—that is taking the end of the matrimonial six months for granted. Without beauty it is hard for a woman *to begin* that six months' ordeal."

A letter from Richardson Miles.[8] The very nicest man in the world, be the other who he may:

"My depression of spirits has not been helped by the result of the senatorial election.

"I am pained and mortified. Such an unjust rebuke—as it will be considered.

"I have not heard a single reason given for the slight thus put upon Chesnut—nor a fault of any kind urged against him."

---

5. Marion (Twiggs) Myers, daughter of Confederate Gen. David Emanuel Twiggs and wife of Confederate Quartermaster Gen. Abraham Charles Myers, was a popular figure in wartime Richmond society.

6. Genesis 49:4.

7. Federal forces based at Beaufort, S.C., and Tybee Island, Ga., posed an obvious threat to the coastal railroad but were, for the moment, inactive.

8. Prominent Charleston lawyer Charles Richardson Miles, a brother of William Porcher Miles, became Confederate States attorney for S.C. in 1862.

Letter from my husband. His regiment is there nearly formed. He was then going out to the camp. He says both Mr. Barnwell and R. Barnwell Rhett quite excited still by the condition of things in the low country.

December 30, 1861.   Prince Albert is dead! Comes the selfish thought: will that affect us? No, he has had the absolute wisdom to efface himself—and by so doing he brought no trouble upon his devoted wife. As kings and queens go, what a happy couple. Curiously happy, if it had been love in a cottage. Princess Charlotte's cry: "I have been the happiest wife in England."[9]

That was a rare tribute to a princely husband. Queen Victoria, too, seems to have had a husband *good and true*. Because my democratic husband loves to tell you the gay young girl graciously returned his bows in the park the year before she was married. And maybe because I was married, too—in the spring of 1840. I have watched her with interest—her domestic life and all that looked on from afar.

More gossip of the crowned heads—Mrs. Huger says a Frenchman told her the Prince Royal was an imperial necessity—a supposititious heir—better than none. Eugénie introduced hoopskirts to hide a lack, not an exuberance, of figure.

Went to Kirkwood and gave Captain DePass's company my fifty pairs of drawers and socks and shirts. . . .[1]

9. Probably Queen Charlotte Sophia, wife of George III.

1. The brother of Rev. James P. DePass, William Lambert DePass was a Camden attorney and captain of Company C, Palmetto Battery of Light Artillery. There follows a formal letter of thanks from the captain, omitted here.

XII

The Politics of War

January 1, 1862.

> A happy new year to the distant brave
> Who combat the foemen or battle the wave:
> For each in his home, there is a heart that still burns;
> God send them say I—many happy returns.

Sentiment better than the versification.

Columbia. We came over today on the train. There were Mrs. Huger, Meta, Tanny Withers,[1] and Franklin J. Moses.

Tanny Withers is a boy with the war spirit so prematurely developed that he brickbatted his teacher, Barnwell Stuart.[2] So he is sent to a military academy to try what that discipline will do for him. He regards the fight with Barny Stuart with feelings of great complacency. The difference in ages and sizes—weight, so to speak—was as much against him and in Barny's favor as it is against us in our present combat with the U.S.A. The schoolboys' applause was balm to Tanny's bruises.

I was pleasantly *located* on a trunk (it was a freight train and no seats) surrounded by little negroes, pumpkins, boxes, bags &c.

We found Mr. Chesnut dressed for dinner, on the wing to a dinner at the Prestons. And we, to waste no time after the social desert of Sahara of Camden, went to tea at the Greens'.[3]

We plunged into society at once. Were told our men were losing hope and heart—so many blunders on the coast.

January 2, 1862.   At the Greens last night—a new feature, incident to wartimes. No men—not one.

As we were about to break up, Mr. John Izard Middleton came for his sister Mrs. Henry Middleton.[4] Mr. M lost all of his rare and beautiful pictures in the fire at Charleston. That was a catastrophe for a century.

1. William Randolph Withers, the fifteen-year-old son of Judge Withers.
2. The assistant principal of the Columbia Male Academy and the son of John A. Stuart.
3. The home of Allen J. Green, Jr.
4. The son of a S.C. governor and the nephew of Eweretta Middleton, John Izard Middleton owned large plantations in Beaufort and Georgetown districts and served in the S.C. secession convention. His sister-in-law (not his sister) was English-born Ellen (Goggin) Middleton, wife of writer and traveler Henry Middleton.

On Pinckney Island the negroes have been reinforced by runaways and outlaws. They are laying supplies, getting in provisions, making a king—&c&c.

January 3, 1862. Went to drive with Mrs. Preston. Saw the Yankee prisoners—the jail is opposite Madam Togno's, where I went to see Kate Withers.[5]

Met Colonel Preston in full uniform—a splendid specimen of humanity, certainly. Mrs. Izard[6] calls him "the magnificent John."

It is a little too much that so handsome a man—six feet four—should be clever and charming in like degree.

As Swift defines aristocracy, he has the three essentials—brains, blood, wealth. And he is as lucky in his wife and children. One would think he had nothing to wish for in this world. He is a bitter, a disappointed, man. The popular breath cares for none of these things, and he is ambitious for what the *popular* vote alone can give—political distinction. And he does seem to have so many things which dwarf these poor democratic high stations into nonentity nearly. . . .[7]

January 5, 1862. I saw Mr. Keitt as I came up. We had a long talk. I leaned over the bannister, and he looked up. I like him. Il vous donne la république, as the French say. He is quick as a flash. No one gets the better of him. And though he covers himself with words—the longest and the finest, as a garment—still there is the strongest common sense always at the bottom of it all. Whenever I leave Mr. Keitt I have something to tell as good and as self-evident as a proverb—something original and new that I had never thought of before.

"Mr. Chesnut is to [be] colonel of a regiment and Keitt the lieutenant colonel," he said.

"No," I replied. "Never. Before you leave this convention you will put him in some political role. Smother him with fine words, and you march off with the regiment. See if you don't. Mr. Barnwell urged him not to take a regiment but to stay in Congress. And Mr. Barnwell has his seat in the Senate. Now you want him back in the army—and you mean to put him back in civil life and seize his colonelcy."

"You are awfully spiteful—all women are—your program is too good to be true."

January 7, 1862. And now it is all out. I had a hint when I wrangled with Lieutenant Colonel Keitt over the staircase and he laughed at me so good-naturedly.

5. Katherine Withers, sixteen-year-old daughter of Judge Withers. Ascelie Togno ran the Barhamville Female Institute just outside Columbia.

6. Mary Cadwallader (Green) Izard, the widow of planter Walter Izard, lived with her brother Allen J. Green, Jr.

7. Omitted is a transcribed letter from L. Q. Washington to M. B. C., dated Oct. 10, 1861, with news already related.

There is to be a council of safety—a bundle of sticks and crutches for old Pickens.[8] If I were asked to go into such a council, I would throw the nasty office in their faces.

He is to be chief of the Military Department of South Carolina. If he accepts that place, he goes on the shelf—forever! Today he dined with Governor Pickens. Mrs. Pickens was bitter against the convention for giving Governor Pickens these guardians—or this guard of honor, or this council, call it as you will. It means that Governor Pickens has been felt to need aid and council. I asked if all authority was not absorbed by the Confederate government. "Yes."

January 8, 1862.   Pleasant day at the Prestons—went to dinner with Governor Manning. Those beautiful girls[9] declaimed for us in French early in the evening. Later we went to Mrs. Herbemont's.[1] Two or three things in one day—dinners, parties, &c. After life at Mulberry it is a waking up. There, one absorbing interest for all. That and nothing else: Mrs. Chesnut's health—what he eats, what she says, and nothing more.

January 9, 1862.   Called on Mrs. Pickens. We flattered each other as far as that sort of thing can be done. She is young, lovely, clever—and old Pick's third wife. She cannot fail to hate us. Mr. C put as [a] sort of watch and ward over her husband.

Mrs. Herbemont called attention to Madame Togno, who keeps a girls' school here. One of the refugees from Charleston. Mrs. Herbemont accuses the lady of being a friend of Percival Drayton,[2] an admirer and follower of Mr. Petigru—and as climax of iniquities, she openly rejoiced when the Yankee fleet came into Port Royal. "Just as she always said they would do," she cried exultingly.

A man talked boastfully to me of his three plantations on Combahee—to me, who knows so well how poor people may be with ever so many plantations and negroes.

Mrs. Harry Middleton, who is English, mistook Governor Manning for Mr. Chesnut.

Then she asked me, "Is he as handsome as that?"

8. Expressing a widespread lack of confidence in Governor Pickens, the S.C. secession convention reconvened late in 1861. Although its authority to do so was questionable, the convention placed the executive power of the state in the hands of a five-man council, charged mainly with raising and supplying troops. The council, which met Jan. 9, consisted of Governor Pickens, Lieutenant Governor W. W. Harllee (see p. 277, n. 8), Attorney General Isaac Hayne, former governor W. H. Gist (see p. 285, n. 8), and J. C. Because of its extensive war powers, the council was abolished at the end of Pickens's term in Dec. 1862.

9. John S. Preston's three daughters: Susan "Tudy" Preston, Sally Buchanan "Buck" Preston, and Mary Cantey "Mamie" Preston, whom M. B. C. often calls "Mary C," "Mary Cantey," or "Mary P."

1. Martha Davis (Bay) Herbemont was the wife of Alexander Herbemont, U.S. consul to Italy before the war.

2. Though born in S.C., Drayton remained in the U.S. Navy and commanded the *Pocahontas* during the attack on Port Royal, where his brother Thomas was in charge of Confederate fortifications.

"No," answered Mrs. Manning with emphasis.

"But ever so much cleverer," I replied as emphatically.

"How American women praise their husbands!"

"Life is, I daresay, pretty much the same game everywhere. Whatever one says of one's husband here is always repeated to him by some shabby women present. It is well if they do not lay a trap for you."

January 11, 1862. At Mulberry. Headache. And I had not an ache or a pain in Columbia. It is dullness striking in.

Cromwell's Latin secretary: "When the task of answering the King's defense was given to me by public authority, being both in an ill state of health, and the sight of one eye gone already, the Physician openly predicting the loss of both if I undertook this labour, yet nothing terrified by their premonition, I did not long balance whether *duty* should be preferred to my sight."[3] I stumbled upon this today, when I heard a member of the convention[4] plead some slight indisposition as a reason why he did not go, as his duty called him, to Columbia. Duties of life greater than life itself—a view of things which seems not to have reached that brilliant mind.

The Englishwoman hit the patriarchal system heavy blows. It hardly sounded decent: she scarcely found the patriarchy less degraded than their flocks and their herds, their Leahs and Rachels—and L and R's maidservants and their children, all dwelling under one tent. It was turned off by a remark as to its impossibility in that hot climate.

Colonel C is so quiet and comfortable. He has forgotten the war—he is busy making another will telling each negro to whom he intends to leave him or her—as if there were no Yankees and Yankee proclamations in Beaufort.

Some startling shock will come and wake us up again.

> Yet even this—the cold beneficence
> Seizes my praise, when I reflect on those,
> The sluggards pity—vision weaving tribe,
> Who sigh for wretchedness—yet shun the wretched
> Nursing some in delicious solitude
> Their slothful loves and dainty sympathies.[5]

At the convent in Columbia where I went with Mary Preston, I fancied the mother superior had a hope of Mary's going over to them. Mrs. Buist Lamb[6]

3. A slight misquotation from a translation of John Milton's *Angli, pro populo Anglicano defensio secunda* (1654).

4. Judge Withers.

5. A paraphrase of lines from Samuel Taylor Coleridge, "Reflections on Having Left a Place of Retirement" (1796).

6. M. B. C. has prematurely married off Martha Allston White and confused her husband's name. Miss White did not marry George Lamb Buist, a Charleston lawyer and Confederate officer, until May 1862.

was about to be baptized by Bishop Lynch.[7] Ellen Spann had just been made a nun—and taking the vows at the time, she turned the attention of idle heads and restless hearts to the repose and safety of the cloister.

Mary asked the name in grace of the new nun. When we came away it was commented on that she called the lady superior "mother." "Certainly," said Mary, "as I would call Napoleon 'emperor'—and not 'Mr.,' as the New York shoemaker did when he sent him a specimen of New York shoes."

The nuns told us how their veils cured headaches—that they were cool in summer and warm in winter. One said before she took the veil, she was a martyr to dyspepsia. She had never felt a twinge since she left the world, &c&c. Mary described scenes and ceremonies at Rome which she had witnessed, and they listened with fascinated attention.

Mrs. Preston was not alarmed for Mary's orthodoxy—least of all that she would join a convent. Mary loved the world too well.

Ransom Calhoun is under arrest for writing an insulting letter either to or about General Ripley.

Coming home, General Harllee[8] told us a significant fact. On board were the bodies of two men. These dead men had been bringing negroes from the coast—negroes who did not want to come. They laid down their guns and went to sleep. The negroes took the guns, shot the owners of them, and went back to the fleet.

> Time's dull deadening;
> The world's tiring;
> Life's settled, cloudy afternoon—

The amount of virulent nonsense I have had to hear and to bear today.

Among other things Mr. C called a first consul. The beginning of the Bastille and the guillotine, &c&c.

"But Mr. C is so mild," suggested the daughter. "Not the least likely to do anything horrid."

Answer: "They chose their mildest men for triumvirs in France. You see what came of it." I said nothing—things looked a little mixed. The beginning of the Bastille and the setting up of the guillotine—actions in opposite directions. And those meek triumvirs?

7. Patrick Nieson Lynch, Roman Catholic bishop of Charleston.
8. William Wallace Harllee of Marion District, the lieutenant governor of S.C. and a member of the newly formed Executive Council, was also a delegate to the secession convention and a major general of militia.

Words are vain. I see he has selected his role. He means to denounce Mr. C as a tyrant, do what he will.

This pleasant Sabbath day, read Gideon's battle of Manassas and the rewards thereof. They told the timorous to depart—of the thirty thousand, twenty thousand left silently in the night.

And of the tribe of Ephraim who did not come to fight the Amalekites—but who found it easy and pleasant to fight their brethren of Manassas afterward for the spoils.[9]

Nothing will ever equal that "first sprightly running"[1] of our foes—at our Manassas.

January 13, 1862.   Mr. C gone. I was ill, but I did not say so, as he had to go and had better go with an easy conscience, which might not have been the case if he had left me in bed. And I kept up the game to the last. Sung out to him from the piazza as he drove off:

> All ladies beware of the gay young knight
> Who loves—and who rides away.

Old Fuller says we sell ourselves for earthly distinctions—"Gladly risk our heads to be able to put a feather in our caps."[2]

And Voltaire puts it: "Fasten a feather in his cap and march him away to glory."

Something in the human heart the devil can't satisfy, grumbles Mephistopheles to Faust.

So they do not satisfy me. They have fobbed it off with this trouble-bringing and no-glory-giving office. And Keitt takes his regiment. [That] I told you so does not comfort me—far from it. And his colonel's uniform came home today.

While we were in Columbia our Kershaw general[3] of boundless ambition was told that he was to have a serenade. He gathered together the sleepy ladies at the hotel: "Keep awake, there is to be a serenade tonight *for* me." He made ready his fiery eloquence. Hélas! Alas! None came to serenade.

Read *Castle Richmond*. In this one thing Trollope manages his elderly lady in love better than Thackeray[4] in *Esmond*. Marrying your mother-in-law—as the

---

9. M. B. C. has interpreted the story for her own purposes: see Judges 7 and 8.

1. John Dryden, *Aureng-Zebe* (1676), act 4, scene 1.

2. M. B. C. was probably reading Thomas Fuller, *The History of the Worthies of England* (1662).

3. Joseph Kershaw.

4. The central characters of Anthony Trollope's *Castle Richmond* (1860) are the Countess of Desmond, a thirty-eight-year-old widow, and her daughter Clara. Both women are in love with Owen Fitzgerald, the ward of a neighboring squire. Although Clara eventually marries another man, Owen spurns the attentions of the countess, who remains alone at the end of the novel.

Germans say, heart's mother-in-law—was painfully revolting to me, a discordant note which continued to vibrate throughout *Esmond*—which is the best of Thackeray's, after all.[5]

Then, as I could not compass a new book, tried the very oldest—*Sakúntala*, translated by Sir William Jones.[6] Now, see how those old Hindus were refined—beyond the classic. Their idea of a joke, when they were tired of an old wife: make her bedmaker to the new one. The Hindu says, Treat her like a lady because you are a gentleman—a free translation of this marriage prône.

"Retain thy love for this girl which arose in thy bosom without any interference of her kindred: And look on her among thy wives with the same kindness they experience. *More* cannot be demanded: *since* particular affection must depend on the will of Heaven."

When Esmond was told all of the shortcomings of Trix and her wrongdoings beside, he sighed, "I know—but I want that one." That's love's philosophy—or put it in Hindu: "since particular affection is independent of man's will."

"When Mrs. Middleton pitched into the patriarchs and picked them to pieces and Mrs. W picked at the president, you sat dumb. Why?"

"Answer not a fool according to her folly.[7] What does it matter to them now? Poor old Jews. If the Lord liked them, they can afford to put up with Mrs. M's derision."

She said worse. "While those kind-hearted preachers are doing away with Hell, why don't they abolish this world, too? It is next door to it. What earthly thing escapes the torments of the damned in some shape."

Mrs. M says Mrs. Stanard loves mankind—every man of them—but in such different ways.

The old ones as fathers, middle-aged as brothers, young ones—as sons. P. M. Holt[8]—seasick pelican because he was so good, so pure, so on, to the end of the list of human virtues.

January 15, 1862.   Mrs. Pringle's little grandchild is dead! Lovely little thing, away from her parents—she was a daughter of Donald Mitchell—*Reveries of a Bachelor* and all that.[9]

---

5. William Makepeace Thackeray, *The History of Henry Esmond, Esq.* (1852). For much of the novel, Esmond's affections are divided between Rachel, the wife of his guardian, and Beatrix, her daughter. In the end, he marries the widowed Rachel and begins a new life in Va.

6. Sir William Jones (1746-94), judge of the British High Court at Calcutta, founder of Oriental studies in England, and translator of the fifth-century Hindu poet Kalidása's drama, *Sakúntala; or, The Fatal Ring* (1799). The quotation below is from act 4, scene 1.

7. A play on Proverbs 26:4.

8. Possibly Joseph Holt, a Kentuckian who was Buchanan's postmaster general.

9. Hesse Alston Mitchell, the granddaughter of Mary (Alston) and William Bull Pringle, died in Charleston at the age of seven. Her father was Donald Grant Mitchell of Conn., who wrote *Reveries of a Bachelor* (1850) and other popular works under the pseudonym Ik Marvel.

Mrs. K's new baby—Ethel Newcome. Just as soon call it Morleena Kenwigs. Much prefer Tabitha or Dinah. That is, if Dinah was a family name. Shabby genteel names from novels makes the child a laughingstock.[1]

New York legislature for peace—and the banks tired of paying out money.[2]

There is a ray of sunlight on the horizon's edge—but Burnside is afloat.[3] And like the dog, while Sam Jones was hanging in the meal bag—who knows where he will nip.[4] We have not men enough even to watch Port Royal.

London *Times* abuses the murderous policy of the Union—so-called. . . .[5]

January 16, 1862.   Mrs. Henry DeS hard on men who do not fight and die for their country. Miss Fanny Hay[6] hard on the Ropers, who ate apples or gingerbread on the sacred Camden pump Christmas Day.[7] Thornwell Hay of the Haystock, who brained the Dane with a plowshare—Hays of Clan Marty. This Thornwell hopes to be president of the United States—slip of the pen—Confederate States. For while all the others are in the ranks—and so they (the boys) will be without education—he is at school and studying hard. He is too young, he says, to be in the army. Worthy sentiment, truly!

———

Mrs. D. Huger[8] said repeatedly in her brief remarks that Jackson Pickens—alas. Our Pickens the 1st so soon! And in return friends of the Pickens called her Rough Huger—(refugee?).[9] Also she said Manigault's regiment[1] was the only one armed and at Georgetown. And they are expected to hold their own against the tide of war Burnside can pour in there if he so pleases.

So far the Union estimates it has lost 22,000 men. That is a flea bite for them. They hardly feel it. They can waste life at their own sweet will. . . .[2]

———

1. M. B. C. is referring to Mary (Withers) Kirkland, who finally named her third child Elizabeth. Ethel appears in Thackeray's *The Newcomes: Memoirs of a Most Respectable Family* (1854–55); Morleena Kenwigs is in Dickens's *Nicholas Nickleby* (1839). M. B. C. borrows a phrase from Thackeray, *A Shabby Genteel Story and Other Tales* (1852).

2. On Dec. 28, many Northern banks that had subscribed heavily to Federal war bonds were forced to suspend specie payments. In New York, where the situation was especially critical, the state legislature strongly backed the action of local bankers but passed no peace resolutions.

3. U.S. Brig. Gen. Ambrose Everett Burnside commanded the 100 ships and 15,000 troops that left Hampton Roads, Va., for N.C. on Jan. 11.

4. In William Tappan Thompson's story "The Christmas Present in a Bag," in *Major Jones's Courtship* (1843), Joseph (not Sam) Jones hangs all night in a meal bag to surprise his sweetheart on Christmas morning. When a dog comes sniffing about, the major, afraid of being bitten, doesn't "know whar abouts he'd take hold."

5. Quotations from unidentified writers deleted.

6. Frances Snowden Hay and James Thornwell Hay, below, were the teenaged children of Rev. Samuel Hutson Hay.

7. Probably the daughters of Mrs. Richard Roper.

8. Isabella Johannes (Middleton) Huger, the widow of Judge Daniel Elliott Huger.

9. In S.C. the name Huger rhymes with "refugee."

1. Arthur Middleton Manigault was a Georgetown District rice planter and the colonel of the Tenth S.C. Infantry. His wife Mary was the granddaughter of Isabella Huger.

2. Unidentified quotation on the doing of one's duty is deleted.

They were rating two of Mr. C's nephews for not being in the army.[3]

"His lungs are weak. I heard that when we married—unsound, they said he was then."

"Why did your niece marry him then?"

"Because he was sound on the goose," I placidly explained.

"What does she mean?"

"Oh, mama, don't you know that slang expression? It means he had a plantation and no end of negroes."

"Do you mean"—turning to me savagely—"to insinuate my niece married, from mercenary motives, a poor stick?"

"Did you mean to insult and slander my nephew *in law* when you said he shirked the army?" It was as broad as it was long.

There is no need of fetters. He shall be bound—chained by an idea, says Cecil, speaking of men's tormenting spirit.

Pretty is as pretty does, we say. See how Schiller puts it: "Even the little-beautiful—even the not-beautiful—can have a beautiful behavior."

Mrs. Sumter—née de Lage.[4] When Mr. S could not pay his debts, he refused to live in luxury. Mr. Sumter and his children fared in accord with their altered circumstances. But for Madame—born Natalie de Lage, thrown by a cruel fate on our rough shores—they provided, as her delicate tastes and habits required, separate pantry, separate cuisine. Miss S. C. had been so trained to admire the beautiful and accomplished lady, she could not see in this anything but what was right—no selfishness, no coldheartedness. It was but her due, her just rights.

Heard loud talking below, to the point of exasperation, so threw down my book and flew. Arrived not a second too soon. Old Mr. C was mistaking my guest Mrs. Roper for Mrs. Hocott,[5] the turpentine man's wife—and she was losing her patience in futile explanation. . . .[6]

---

3. The conversation concerns Johnny Chesnut's brothers Thomas and James, who were both planters in Alachua County, Fla. M. B. C. is talking with Mary Kirkland and Mrs. Withers, whose niece Amelia was married to James.

4. A refugee of the French Revolution, Natalie (de DeLage) Sumter was the widow of Thomas Sumter, Jr., and the mother of Francis Brasilimo and Paul Thomas DeLage Sumter. Her husband, the son of the hero of the American Revolution, served as U.S. minister to France and U.S. minister to Brazil.

5. E. S. Hocott, wife of Camden merchant Daniel D. Hocott.

6. Quotations deleted.

Everyone who calls disposes of the Roper case. Poor Roper girls! They did not recognize little Pedlington—or its pump.[7] Hence this flutter. Even Rev. Mr. Hay's soul was filled with horror *not* unspeakable. It was hard to hear such preposterous nonsense as eating apples by a pump in the street solemnly denounced by the clerical gentleman and keep a grave face. Such importance does little Pedlington attach to "trifles—light as air."[8]

Life in the old land yet—
My Maryland. . . .[9]
Passed the awkward squad. They were drilling. The order must have been "Wipe your noses," they were doing so thoroughly well. Every handkerchief in air. It was hopelessly wet underfoot, and a mild soaking drizzle seemed to [be] seeking every pore.

Last night I sat up until one o'clock, reading a very bad book. But enchanting because its portraitures of the absurdities of village life—country life—is so finely illustrated to me daily, to me who suffers under it so.

"Muse du Province"—par exemple.[1] Think of the emptiness of life in wartimes. Mr. Hay, the reverend gentleman, tells a story nearly a month old against the Ropers. They sat by a pump and ate apples Christmas Day in the streets of Camden. Streets as desert as Sahara.

M. W.'s letter.[2] The widow of two weeks, accompanied by her sister, went to a drill of the "Williams Guard"—poor George's company. She had crape on her Garibaldi hat. Sister crape also on her "pork pie," as *Punch* calls that style of headgear.

Little Nancy's baby born today. My maid Nancy. She married Charles, Eben's son. Eben is the butler here, so it was a marriage among the upper ten. She does not like to live on the plantation. Yesterday she sent me some eggs—she knew Missis wanted them fresh for her breakfast.

So Nancy's baby is born 19th January 1862.

---

7. John Poole's satire *Little Pedlington and the Pedlingtonians* (1839) mocked the hypocrisy of a small town.

8. *Othello*, act 3, scene 3.

9. Deleted are lines from three Civil War songs: "Maryland," by James R. Randall, and two different versions of "There's Life in the Old Land Yet." All three appear in Thomas Cooper DeLeon, ed., *South Songs* (1866).

1. Balzac's story "La Muse du département" appeared in *Scènes de la vie de province* (1843), a volume of the *Comédie humaine*.

2. Mary (Williams) Witherspoon, George Williams's half sister. His widow was Frances Virginia (McIver) Williams.

January 20, 1862.   Neuralgia of eyes. Have slept, wept, and prayed—cannot see to read or to work—only tears and despair—feel abandoned of God and man, here in this dismal swamp.

That cry on the cross must have come from the mortal part of our Savior—the cruelest pang a mortal can feel.

"My God, my God—why hast *Thou* forsaken me."

The irate one in Richmond who sneered so at the effacer of Hell—she said: "Oh, you see so little unmerited suffering on earth. You cannot believe a benevolent Providence will permit merited punishment hereafter." Those poor mangled horses in battle—what have they done? Have they bought any slaves from Yankees—or revolted against Yankee rule?

The Reynoldses—Harriet's Pinks of Perfection. They are here. They have enlivened things somewhat. They disapprove of me highly and primly let me see it with that eternal chorus of astonishment: "Why, Aunt Mary!" But they are so quiet and ladylike, so polite and so little interfering.

People who interrupt, people who ask questions, people who interfere perpetually in trifles—they make life difficult.

Lincoln's idea, "I hate an interruptious fellow"—not half a bad description.

Team here. Mr. C lent his Goldbranch plantation to the Trapiers and Jenkinses.[3] "Jenkins," said Team, "is a parson. There now, that took me. I called him a rip-roarer, a reg'lar buster. Two of his niggers run away a'ready. They are from the ocean wave. They call our river the big Wateree—they call it a spring branch. They swim like ducks across the river. They laugh at ferries and bridges an' tollgates. Did you all ever have a runaway?"

"Never—pretty hard work to keep me from running away from them. Have these negroes gone back to the fleet at Beaufort?"

"Straight as the crow flies."

January 24, 1862.   Columbia—at Mrs. Preston's. Mr. C was seized with a new freak today. Drew me out—and Mr. Venable's ready laugh drew me on. I did more than my share of the talking—felt ashamed of myself. Expected a lecture, such as I am accustomed to when it is all wrong. Late at night, when we were seated alone in the upper piazza, which opens out of our rooms, Mr. C said gravely, "This has been a very happy day."

A story at dinner of Mrs. Scott. She did not accept Winfield Scott until after many offers on his part and refusals on hers.

Finally, after her marriage, someone said, "And so you married Captain Scott, after all."

---

3. Probably the families of Rev. Richard S. Trapier and Rev. Paul Gervais Jenkins, Episcopalian ministers from St. John's Parish. Trapier's brother Paul was a professor at the Camden Episcopal Theological Seminary.

"No—I refused Captain Scott to the last. I accepted the general." But she kept the broad Atlantic between them after a brief matrimonial experience. Mrs. Scott could not be accused of the crime of proximity. Which I heard of today for the first time. A post office was closed and its postmaster dismissed. The poor man asked why. Too great proximity to another P.O. rendered that one unnecessary. He expostulated earnestly with the department. Pecuniarily he did not mind. So far it had only brought him in 62½ cents a month, but then to be accused of proximity was more than he could bear, and he would not stand it. Neither would Mrs. Scott.

Ex-President Tyler dead. Zollicoffer dead and defeated. East Tennessee and North Carolina, which borders on E.T., is gone—that is, if they have Cumberland Gap.[4]

How downhearted are we, who were so happy yesterday.

John Frierson[5] has sent his feu beau-père's wooden leg to the hospital. They ought to exorcise it—Dr. Gibbes told us this—with the "by bell and candle" addition, also his comment. "A wonderful machine it is—and a queerer present."

A report has spread which cannot be traced even to the reliable man. That Burnside's fleet has sunk. A wild hope, no doubt without foundation.

I have fallen in love with a whole family.[6] No exception whatever.

Edmund Rhett here all the time. Mary C is very clever; but the charming Edmund has always a motive, as Hood puts it. He is never good for nothing. What is the Something now? He is queer about women and matrimony and money.[7]

Surely women have a right to a maintenance even when they are penniless girls—before the wedding. That is, when they bring no dowry. "With all my worldly goods I thee endow."

We had our share of my father's estate. It came into our possession so long after we were married, and it was spent for debts already contracted. A man with a rich father is offered every facility for plunging in debt head-foremost. That being the case, why feel like a beggar—utterly humiliated and degraded—when I am forced to say I need money? I cannot tell, but I do. And the worst of it is, this thing grows worse as one grows older. Money ought not to be asked for or given to a man's wife as a gift. Something must be due her. And that she should have—not as now, with growling and grumbling, warnings

---

4. Confederate Brig. Gen. Felix Kirk Zollicoffer of Tenn. died in a demoralizing defeat at the battle of Mill Springs, Ky., on Jan. 19. M. B. C. overreacted to the news, however. The loss of the Gap did not mean the loss of east Tenn. or western N.C.

5. John Napoleon Frierson, a wealthy planter and former state legislator from Sumter District.

6. The Prestons.

7. This son of Robert Barnwell Rhett, Sr., was a captain in the C.S.A. who died unmarried in 1871.

against waste and extravagance, hints as to the need of economy. Amazement that the last supply has given out already.

What a proud woman suffers under all this, who can tell. And one thing is sure: nothing but the direst necessity drives her to speak of *deficit*—empty purse—&c&c. What a world of heart burning some regular arrangement of pin money must save.

From this for many a day will I be saved by my belt of gold. Besides, the two Mollys bring me their butter and chicken money. We run that business on shares.

Mr. C thinks I will never be willing to go home again. This is certainly a charming house. The very kindest and most agreeable people I ever knew. And then, everything to tempt an invalid's capricious appetite—and I am ill, there is no denying that—oysters, game—

That soup à la Reine today! I think it had everything nice in the world in it.

January 29, 1862. Still house-hunting. Went to party at Dr. Gibbes's last night.

Such queer dressing—such wonderful singing. Two beautiful girls went with me—Buck and Mary C.

Mr. Venable solemnly made Governor Gist[8] tell over and over again his pun—of which the governor was so proud. A poor woman came to him. "I am forced to drink *Rio* coffee." "Do not bewail your fate, Madame, there are those who drink *rye.*"

It seems people parch rye and drink it for coffee.

The governor's lady was there—she received in state. She did not rise from her chair as we spoke to her—we are only of the governor's council. Young Moses—Franklin, Jr.—is secretary to Governor Pickens. He hung over the lovely Lucy, standing or bending over her from the back of her chair. It suggested the devil whispering in Eve's ear in the primeval days. In the toad state, before Ithureal spear brought him out in his true shape.[9]

Mr. C has taken a senseless aversion to Little Moses—says he is a liar, a sneak, has no moral sense, &c&c. A true son of old Franklin I—Moses, in a word.

February 11, 1862. Congaree House.[1] After an illness. It came to a point while I was dining at Mrs. Ben Taylor. She sent for Dr. Trezevant,[2] and they

8. A member of the Executive Council, William Henry Gist of Union District preceded Francis Pickens as governor of S.C. Gist was the father of States Rights Gist.

9. *Paradise Lost*, book 4, lines 788–821.

1. A Columbia hotel.

2. Daniel Heyward Trezevant, a Columbia physician.

moved me back to Mrs. Preston's, where I was staying. Mrs. Ben Taylor, everybody knows, is the kindest, most hospitable Virginia woman in the world. Lucky for me that I fell into her hands that day. After several weeks' illness—dawdling on, kept alive by Dr. T's opium—once more I was on my feet.

While ill, an amusing thing happened. I have nervous fainting fits. Mrs. Preston had left Mary beside my bed. She had gone down to the very end of that beautiful garden to look after a cow with which something was amiss. All at once Mary came flying to her. "Come, come—Mrs. Chesnut is dying, if not dead."

"Who is with her?"

"Nobody."

"Did you leave her," cried Mrs. Preston, coming back at full speed, "alone?"

"Surely, mama," whimpered Mary, as white as the wall herself. "You would not have me stay there to see her die. I could not—she looked too awful."

Confederate affairs in a blue way. Roanoke taken, Fort Henry on the Tennessee River open to them, and we fear the Mississippi River, too. We have evacuated Romney—wherever that is.[3] New armies, new fleets, swarming and threatening everywhere.

We ought to have as good a conceit of ourselves as they have of us—and to be willing to do as much to save ourselves from a nauseous union with them as they are willing to do by way of revengeful coercion in forcing us back.

You'll never win us back, no never—&c&c.[4]

England's eye is scornful and scoffing as she turns it toward us—and on our miseries. I have nervous chills every day. Bad news is killing me.

Mr. C had a jolly good time in Charleston dining with Gourdins, Yeadons, et cie.[5]

He came here unexpectedly—heard I was ill.

Miss Sally Chesnut writes affectionately—raps me over Mary Brownfield's knuckles.[6] Mary is Mrs. Sumter's daughter, and Mrs. Sumter was a daughter of the old regime—Countess de Lage, &c&c—"But Mary can be happy in their quiet peaceful home at Mulberry." I can't. I give it up.

Besides, to make yourself heard there now, you would have to outroar the steam whistle and to read newspapers aloud at that pitch. Must be done by one's very own children—a daughter-in-law—or any other in-law can't compass it.

---

3. Burnside's expeditionary force captured Roanoke Island, N.C., on Feb. 8. The fall of Fort Henry two days earlier to the force under Brig. Gen. U. S. Grant and Cdre. Andrew Foote opened the Tennessee to Union gunboats as far as Muscle Shoals, Ala., and compelled the Confederacy to abandon central Ky. and middle Tenn.—a grave reverse. Romney, in western Va., was soon occupied by Union troops.

4. An allusion to the popular Southern war song, "You Can Never Win Them Back," which appears in Thomas Cooper DeLeon, ed., South Songs.

5. Like Robert Newman Gourdin, Richard Yeadon, the editor of the Charleston Courier, was a vocal opponent of the Executive Council.

6. Natalie Sumter's daughter, Mrs. John Brownfield, whose Christian name was Pauline and not Mary.

Gloomy enough at the Prestons. Buck ill. Mrs. Preston had a bad fall and was in bed from it. Mrs. Frank Hampton with a child in extremis.

And Mr. C pretends to be as hopeful as ever. I fancy he takes that tone with my wildly excited nerves—something must be done to soothe them. I do not credit anything but his good intention, and so he fails to comfort me.

For the enemy is exultant and bent upon our destruction. We are a rattle-snake Confederacy. We have taught them to think twice before they move. No rash advancing now—followed by the first sprightly running of Bulls Run.

William R. Taylor—the man John Chesnut (black freeman) beat for drinking at his house and at table with his colored mother—now is made a member of the convention, in place of Judge Withers.[7]

What a triumph to the Judge in his scorn of Kershaw District. This man is stupid—dissipated—and all that story implies. The Judge, the very best intellect we have, with a moral standing as pure as ever, sported the ermine—a little bitter of speech, a little hard of judgment.

But, heavens! The difference between this first choice of theirs—and this one!

Governor Pickens is angry because of the council appointed him, and it is evident there will be no concord among them. I think they take too high a hand with him. And he ought to make the best of it or resign. If he is not wise, he is cunning. Someone said today he would outwit them all yet, with the aid of the lovely Lucy, who is a host in herself.

Scandal from the Spotswood. Painted jezebels, as of yore. Men seen in rooms where ought [not?] to be. Folly not to be believed; no mortal does believe any of the nasty nonsense. Generals are called in to settle it all—duels after the war among possibilities, &c&c.

Dr. Gibbes has accused Colonel Preston of being too kind to Yankee prisoners.[8] Too lenient and not half strict enough in his guard. As if anybody ever expected Mr. Preston to be hard on prisoners. However, Columbia is stirred to its depths.

I was surprised. Judge Withers always says, "When Gibbes dies he hopes to go to the Hamptons and Prestons."

7. The Judge had resigned his seat in the S.C. secession convention. Taylor was a Camden lawyer.
8. John S. Preston had been given command of the prison camp at Columbia on Jan. 28.

February 13, 1862.   Read a book, utterly abominable, there is no gainsaying that—Balzac's *Cousine Bette*.[9] And yet a book can be worse. Mr. Venable sent me *Charikles*.[1] But coarseness and brutal morality, indecency, does not strike one so when the performers had not to face an altar or a training as pure and clean as the Christian religion.

At this Congaree House Mrs. Preston still takes charge of my diet. For fever comes as it listeth still, and long nervous depression subsequent—and consequent.

William comes with that appetizing tray. Rice and milk, oysters, partridges, &c&c.

Everything nice and prepared as only they do there. Also Mrs. Ben Taylor sends me the crackers and muffins her cook is so famous for.

Susan Rutledge writes in a queenly way. Hugh Rose seems to have taken their affairs in hand. And a good thing for them. Their father has not been to his plantation in ten years. Emily R[2] describes her life: "buried alive at Flat Rock— that is, buried in the earth with your head out."

As I lie here in bed, I cannot shake off the horrid image.

Mrs. Preston came for me to drive. Then she stopped at her house, where Mr. Preston lifted me out bodily and sent for Mr. C to come to dinner, as they meant to keep me.

William R. Taylor we described to them as a man who was selected by the people left in Kershaw—the best and the bravest are in the army, of course. Well, then—such men as are left in Kershaw have selected this man to represent them. He is the representative of the stay-at-homes.

Judge Withers was acknowledged to be the best judge on the bench—of as high and pure a character as any in America.

An uncomfortable aggravating temper, too much given to endless faultfinding.

"Faultfinding his fault—eh?"

"Yes, useless and uncalled for, mostly—only a bad habit."

It is nearly nineteen years[3] since the mob voted for Barrabas—not Jesus. Still, we believe the mob is the best of all powers to rule by its votes. Salvation we believe is to come to us by the votes of the mob.

At first I did not believe the crowd were in earnest, loud as they cried. I could not think they meant war, when at the head of every important state office they put unearthed fossils, incapables, &c&c.

And when it came to a one-man power, the mob howled. There was Memminger, Mallory, Walker, Toombs, Yancey, Mason, and Benjamin—who is thought by Mr. Chesnut the very cleverest man we had in the Senate—at any rate, the best speaker. The mob only calls him "Mr. Davis's pet Jew," a King

9. *La Cousine Bette* (1846), a volume of the *Comédie humaine,* is a tale of sexual intrigue and jealousy within the family of a French government official.

1. Wilhelm Adolf Becker, *Charikles, Bilder altgriechischer Sitte* (1840).

2. Probably Emma Fredricka Rutledge, a sister of Eliza Pinckney Rutledge.

3. She means "centuries."

Street Jew, cheap, very cheap, &c&c. Old Reagan defies them and holds his own. His department pays.

When Reagan was elected congressman first, Wigfall met a country man.

"I hope you will vote for Reagan."

"No, I won't. I done cast my vote for my old neighbor Riggins."

By which name he was known in the countryside—Texas. And now they sing: "[*Illegible word*] look out for the *riggins* of Billy Barlow."[4]

To hear the discontented talk you would think we had invented Jeff Davis since secession, without a peradventure. He was our leader in the Senate at Washington. So acknowledged then by the Joe Johnston and Barnwell Rhett, who seem to think now that their enemy found him to perplex and annoy them.

Everybody believes that when the time comes the right man to save the country will step forward. Let him step. The time has come for him—if ever.

I see cheerful and comfortable Yankee prisoners every day. They seem to be laughing at us, so sure are they that their time is at hand. The jail is opposite Mrs. Togno's school, where I go so often for Kate Withers. One of the girls (Ida DeSaussure[5] at least acknowledged it—many did it) waved her handkerchief to a prisoner because he looked so sorrowful up there. They knew women were kind to ours, wherever they were. Madame was told of it. And "she raised an awful shindy"—girls' account. "Treason, stratagem, and spoils"—the best word in her mouth—&c&c.

It was so wrong and imprudent—a girls' school! Must be so particular, &c&c.

Young Wade Hampton,[6] a manly young fellow—open, honest, fair, but not handsome like that splendid boy, his brother Preston. You feel that come what may, in any emergency you can rely on Wade the 4th.

Last night Mr. C had a telegram from John Cunningham. It ran thus: "Critical situation—Row in Evans's brigade—come down."[7]

It suited Mr. C to consider this as sensational, or he did not see what good he could do, so he did not go.

Dismal without and within.

The Villalonga[8] from Savannah are here, and firmly believe Savannah will be attacked today because it is the time of their high spring tides.

---

4. "Billy Barlow," a character probably based on a jester who lived in London's East End, figured in many comic songs of the mid-nineteenth century.

5. A daughter of John McPherson and Eliza (Champion) DeSaussure.

6. Wade Hampton III's eldest son, who was serving on the staff of Gen. Joseph E. Johnston.

7. Cunningham, a colonel of militia and member of the S.C. legislature from Charleston, was probably referring to Brig. Gen. Nathan Evans's attempt to court-martial four officers who had refused to obey orders.

8. M. B. C. shortly corrects herself about the surname of John L. Longavilla, a Savannah commission merchant and alderman.

North Carolina papers with a shower of brickbats for Jeff Davis. They taunt him with only remembering North Carolina when he wants more troops.

Now that I am old, I want peace most of all things. And I can only hear of wars and rumors of wars. Mr. C says, "Would you prefer a disgraced country as your home?"

"No. Never."

Read a play of Scribe's.

"Always reverence a scholar, my dear, if not for the scholarship, at least for the suffering and self-denial which he has had to endure to gain a scholar's proficiency."[9]

Alabama cousin, student of the South Carolina College, fine looking, manly young fellow, and clever enough, but he had a trick of tagging every sentence with "Certain and sure." It grew comic beyond endurance, and yet I did not so much as smile.

February 16, 1862.   Awful newspapers today. Fort Donelson a drawn battle. You know that means in our mouths that we have lost it.[1]

That is nothing. They are being reinforced everywhere. Where are ours to come from, unless they wait and let us grow some.

Governor Manning and Gonzales here today.

A pleasant duo—they say Charleston is threatened and the RR from Port Royal at the same time.

Emma Lee[2] and her mother are here—Longavillas said they were staying at "the Shams."[3] "Did not know that family in Columbia?" Governor Manning suggested, "And yet a large family everywhere—like the Smiths, Jones, Robinsons, &c." Mrs. Lee came, however, bringing me fresh butter and a hank or two of knitting cotton my Molly sent me. Fancy her feelings. ⟨⟨It turned out . . . they were at⟩⟩[4] The Rev. Mr. Shand—rector of Trinity Church—his wife, old Mrs. Pinckney's niece—or something or other to the Izards—the "Reverent" &c.

You ought to be ashamed to laugh at such follies.

"How was I to know?" You see Mrs. Lee is the widowed relict of a reverent too—magnifies her ex-position.

The negro girl who brought the note from Madam Togno was in a great state of excitement. She had witnessed a frightful outrage on the street. She was so

---

9. A translation from Augustin Eugène Scribe, *Le Savant* (1835).
1. M. B. C.'s suspicions proved correct. Fort Donelson, ten miles east of Fort Henry on the Cumberland River, fell to U. S. Grant on Feb. 16, after several days' siege.
2. The daughter of Ann (Cooper) Lee of Camden.
3. The family of Dr. Peter J. and Mary (Wright) Shand. Rev. Shand was an Episcopalian minister.
4. From the rough draft of the 1880s Version.

graphic she had to be silenced. A drunken soldier assaulted "a lady, a real lady dressed fine. She fought like a tigress, and two negroes ran to her help, being nearest—but the soldier drew his pistol and held the lady by one pantalette leg—and his pistol in the other hand—but such a crowd was tearing up there and she was yelling like a stuck pig and dancing an' prancing, &c&c—"

Ladies in the drawing room made allowance for the luxuriant black imagination.

The soldier was carried off to the guardhouse—unknown lady in fine clothes went her way with double-quick speed. It is hard to be forced to think ill of a soldier, drunk or sober.

February 17, 1862.   Mrs. Preston says it is expensive, educating a large family abroad. The Mannings were with them, too—making, in all, four girls and five boys. Still, she thought they had better spend their own money that way than any other.

She described Eugénie, the empress. One day she saw her create a street sensation.

A carriage was smashed, the horse ran away, a crowd collected. The inmates of the carriage were picking themselves up and being inspected to see how much or how little they were hurt. When with a great clatter the empress's carriage [came] flashing along, it drew up, and she sent an equerry to inquire if anyone had been hurt. This delighted the mob, and they began shouting, "vive l'emperatrice."

Mrs. Preston said she saw the face of that beautiful woman—sad yet smiling—as she bowed low, right and left. She fell quite in love with that graceful, kindly creature. She wore that day, for the street, a simple dress. Muslin and silk mantilla—English straw bonnet. She saw her very often afterward—once in the spring, with bunches of violets in her bonnet, &c&c. And everybody else seemed to do so, too.

Napoleon the Great when he was about to depart for Elba told them he would be back with the violets. So when he came, they went to meet him with violets in their hands. In Paris they said the Prince Imperial was the emperor's child, and she accepted the cheat to avoid Josephine's fate.

Mrs. Preston delighted to watch this little personage from her window. His behavior was inimitable sometimes. Bowing politely, when he was told, to the crowds on the sidewalks &c&c. Oftener he kicked and fought, being tired of it—clutched his nurses, screaming, "Je ne veux pas," as any spoiled child would most naturally do.

Men depressed today. "Men can find honorable graves—we do not see what is to become of the women and children."

"Has it come to that?"

"Oh, no—we are sure to get through. You never fear that. It will be—all right." So they put on their military cloaks and left me to pleasant thoughts.

Then Mrs. P sent me oysters, toast, and jelly. Almost simultaneously came Mrs. Ben Taylor's tray—biscuits, butter, fruit.

Can one eat with one's heart in one's mouth—as those men left me?

Youth is a blunder, manhood a struggle, old age, one long regret.[5]

A person who is nice and scrupulous, observant of his own claims and merits, misses golden opportunities—especially in wartimes.

I was crushed. Cedar Keys gone, and they have Nashville—with thousands upon thousands of our few and precious soldiers.[6]

John McRa[7] says it is not true, because they have not had time to get to Nashville. But John Manning hates Jeff Davis, so he rejoices in anything which will prove discomfiture to him. Just as the election of William R. Taylor *was nuts* to the Judge, it pleases him so to find the people of Kershaw District as shabby as he had always proclaimed them. "When the district disgraces itself, you see my bad opinion of it is justified."

February 19, 1862.   Fancied I was very ill—Mr. C loitered about the house all day. Better today. John Manning prayed Jeff Davis would go to the front and be taken prisoner.

Saw a letter from De Treville, saying Charleston is unprotected from the Edisto side.

They say Governor Pickens is in an awfully bad humor. Also they say Nashville is not taken, and when he hears that he may recover his spirits.

About Nashville I declined to believe the good news. Mr. C said with dignity, his military cloak thrown over his arm, "My dear wife, do you think I would deceive you?"

I laughed in his face—I was forty years old, my last birthday.[8] "To think of trying the 'mutual confidence' dodge on me!" I cried.

Today I read a French play—*Avant—pendant—après.*[9] But everything is flat after *Mariage de Figaro*—which was yesterday's bonne bouche—and the day before, *Barbier de Séville.*[1] The Prestons have sent me Beaumarchais's works and a pile of Scribe to beguile the slow and solitary hours when I do not leave my bed.

5. A slight misquotation from Benjamin Disraeli, *Coningsby* (1844), book 3, chapter 1.
6. On Jan. 16, Federal forces raided Cedar Keys but made no attempt to hold these small islands off the west coast of Fla. Nashville remained in Confederate hands—but only for a few more days.
7. A Scotsman from Camden who was chief engineer of the S.C. Railroad.
8. In fact she was thirty-eight.
9. Augustin Eugène Scribe, *Avant, pendant et après* (1828).
1. *Le Mariage de Figaro* (1784) and *Le Barbier de Séville* (1775), by French dramatist Pierre-Augustin Caron de Beaumarchais.

February 20, 1862. Had an appetite for my dainty breakfast. Always breakfast in bed now. But then my morning's *Mercury* contradicted so bad news. That is an appetizing style of matutinal newspaper.

Fort Donelson has fallen, but no men fell with it. It is prisoners for them that we cannot spare. Or prisoners for us that we may not be able to feed, that is so much to be "forfended," as Keitt says.

They lost six thousand—we two thousand.[2] I grudge that proposition.

In vain, alas, ye gallant few. Few but are dismayed. Again they make a stand.

They have Buckner, Beauregard, Albert Sidney Johnston.[3] With such leaders—and God's help.

We may be saved from the hated Yankees—who knows.

February 21, 1862. A crowd collected here last night and there was a serenade. I am like Mr. Nickleby—who never saw a horse coming full speed but he thought the Cherryble brothers had sent posthaste to take Nicholas with copartnership.[4] So I got up and dressed, late as it was. I felt sure England has sought our alliance at last. And we would make a Yorktown of it before long.

Who was it? Will you ever guess? Artemas Goodwyn and General Owens of Florida.

Just then Mr. C rushed in, put out the light, locked the door. And sat still as a mouse.

Rap, rap, at the door.

"I say, Chesnut, they are calling for you, &c&c&c."

At last we heard Janney[5] (hotel keeper) loudly proclaiming from piazza that "Colonel Chesnut was not here—at all, at all."

After a while they had all gone from the street. And the very house itself has subsided into perfect quiet. Again the door was roughly shaken.

"I say, Chesnut! Old fellow, come out. I know you are there. Nobody here now wants to hear you make a speech—that crowd has all gone. We want a little quiet talk with you. I am just from Richmond."

That was the open Sesame. And today, I hear, none of the Richmond news is encouraging.

Colonel Shaw blamed for the shameful Roanoke surrender.[6]

Toombs out on a rampage. Swears he will not accept a seat in the Confederate

---

2. In fact, the Union suffered only twenty-eight hundred casualties and the Confederacy around fifteen hundred. But about twelve thousand Confederates surrendered.

3. Three Confederate generals in the West. Brig. Gen. Simon Bolivar Buckner of Ky. had surrendered at Fort Donelson. After his controversies with Jefferson Davis, Gen. P. G. T. Beauregard had been sent to Ky. in Jan. to become second in command to Gen. Albert Sidney Johnston of Ky., the head of the Confederate western armies.

4. In Charles Dickens's *Nicholas Nickleby.*

5. James C. Janney, proprietor of the Congaree House.

6. Actually, Col. Henry M. Shaw and the outnumbered Confederate defenders of Roanoke Island had little choice but to surrender to Burnside. The loss of the island prompted a special congressional investigation and strong criticism of Jefferson Davis's administration.

Senate given in the insulting way his was, by the Georgia legislature.[7] Calls it shabby treatment. And adds that Georgia is not the only place where good men have been so ill-used. That true men should be last and the last shall be first is the new order of the day—&c&c.

The governor and council have fluttered the dovecotes. At least, the tea tables. They talk of making a call for all silver &c&c. I doubt if we have enough to make the sacrifice worthwhile making, but we propose to set the example.

General Ripley says he has 4,000 effective men—Shanks Evans but 1,500.

Wade Hampton claims Cheves McCord's company[8] for his Legion.

So he leaves the state also. We are so weak already that we [look] with longing eyes at any company of soldiers marching away from us.

February 22, 1862.   What a beautiful [day] for our Confederate president to be inaugurated.[9] God speed him. God help him. God save him.

———————

Miss Sally Chesnut knows nothing of man and wife being one. I sent for a carriage blanket, calling it mine. She sent me a shabby old shawl.

"There was a blanket or rug there of James." She saw nothing of mine.

I wrote back. She did not understand marital rights. He would call that dreadful old shawl his, if he wanted it upon a pinch. So whoever she thought it belonged to, send it—or I could get an order from the governor and council for it. I told her to read the marriage ceremony. "Mine is thine. Thine is mine"—which, however, is not in it, but "with all my worldly good" includes carriage rugs.

John Chesnut's letter was just what we needed. The spirit is all that we could ask. He says: "Our late reverses are acting finely with the Army of the Potomac.[1] A few more thrashings and every man will enlist for the war. Victories made us too sanguine and easy. Not to say vainglorious. Now for the tug—and let them have it!"

Drove with my two pretty schoolgirls. They wanted to see everything. Kate Withers and Emma Lee. Also Ida DeSaussure was of the party, recovered from Madame's scolding in regard to Yankee prisoners. Ida is a great pet of mine.

Madame's anecdote while I called there:

A lady wrote to Mrs. Bunch, "Dear Emma, when shall I call for you to go and see Mme de St. Andre?"

Was answered: "Dear Sue, I cannot go with you to see Mme de St. Andre. But

7. Because the legislature took five ballots to elect him senator in Nov. 1861, Toombs turned down the office.

8. Langdon Cheves McCord, captain of the Columbia Zouaves, was the only son of planter and author Louisa (Cheves) McCord (see p. 304, n. 7).

9. But in Richmond there was a heavy rainstorm for Davis's inauguration as president of the permanent Confederate government.

1. That is, the Confederate (not the Union) Army of the Potomac, which had been known officially as the Army of Northern Va. since Oct. 1861.

will always retain the kindest feeling toward you on account of our past relations"—&c&c.

The astounded friend wrote to ask what all this meant. No answer. Then she sent her husband to ask and to demand an explanation.

He was answered: "My dear fellow, there can be no explanation possible. Hereafter there will be no intercourse between my wife and yours. Simply that, nothing more."

So the men meet at the club as before. There is no further trouble between them. The lady upon [whom] the slur is cast says, "And I am a woman—I can't fight!"

These boarding-school girls were to dine at the Gibbes's. I left them there. They were wild with excitement. René Beauregard[2] was to meet them. A young Beauregard. Did I not know? &c&c&c.

A Yankee prisoner escaped and John Preston blamed, as if he could help it. The whole town in a ferment.

Also Magrath has written for Mr. C. General Lee and General Ripley wish to draw in their lines. State authorities are wanted for something.

February 23, 1862.   While Mr. C is in town, I am here at the Prestons. John Cochrane and some other prisoners ask to walk on these grounds, visit the Hampton Gardens and some friends in Columbia.[3] After the dreadful state of the public mind at the escape of one prisoner, Colonel Preston was obliged to refuse. Mrs. P and the rest of us wanted him to say yes—and to find out who were his treacherous friends in Columbia. The persons he wished to call on— pretty bold people they must be, to receive Yankee invaders in the midst of the row over one enemy turned loose amidst us.

Colonel P said, "We were about to sacrifice life and fortune for a fickle multitude who could not stand up to us at last." The harsh comments made in this place as to his lenient conduct to prisoners have embittered him. I told him what I had heard Captain Trenholm[4] say in his speech. He would listen to no criticism but from a man with a musket on his shoulder—and who had beside enlisted for the war. Who had given up all—and had no choice but to succeed or die.

February 24, 1862.   The irrepressible Foote,[5] who once found our name so

---

2. René Toutant Beauregard, the general's eldest son, served as a lieutenant of artillery in the C.S.A.

3. M. B. C. still mistakenly believed that Congressman John Cochrane of N.Y. was captured at Bull Run (see p. 107, n. 9). She doubtless confused him with Col. Michael Corcoran, the flamboyant commander of the Sixty-ninth N.Y. Militia who had been captured at Bull Run and then imprisoned in Columbia.

4. William Lee Trenholm, eldest son of prominent Charleston merchant George A. Trenholm and captain of the Rutledge Mounted Riflemen.

5. Henry Stuart Foote, a former U.S. senator and governor of Miss., was a longtime political foe of Jefferson Davis. Despite his Unionist past, Foote was a member of the Tenn. delegation to the Confederate Congress, where he presented a resolution calling for a more aggressive prosecution of the war after the defeats of early Feb. By 1863, however, he was publicly urging Davis to accept Lincoln's peace terms.

amusing, now has turned his attention to annoying and impeding as much as lies in a Foote—Mr. Davis and his cabinet.

Congress and the newspaper render you desperate—ready to cut your throat. They represent everything in our country as deplorable. Then comes someone from our gay and gallant army. The spirit of our army keeps us up, after all. Letters from the army revive you. They come as welcome as flowers in May. Hopeful and bright, utterly unconscious of our weak despondency.

February 25, 1862.   Got Creasy's *Decisive Battles* from the library. Through Mr. Venable also he brought me Alison's maps, Theodore Hook[6] in extenso, and Mrs. Browning. So I am provisioned for a siege.

Chorus: Given up—Nashville, Charleston, and Savannah RR—given up.

And they have taken at Nashville more men than we had at Manassas.[7] Bad handling of troops—we poor women think, or it could not be. And Mr. Venable adds bitterly: "Giving up our soldiers to the enemy means giving up the cause. We cannot replace them. The up-country men were Union men generally and the low-country, seceders. They now growl they never liked those aristocratic boroughs and parishes: 'We had a good and prosperous country—a good constitution. We were satisfied. But we had to go—to leave all and fight for you who brought all on us. And you do not show too much disposition to fight for yourselves.'"

That is extreme up-country.

Now extreme low country says Jeff Davis is not enough out of the Union yet. His inaugural reads as one of his speeches did four years ago in the U.S.A. Senate.

Met a man whom I knew. He said with emphasis, "I want my wife and children out of this slaughter pen."

Calculated to raise my spirits!

Mrs. Preston says: "There is a resource left, when all is lost. Hoist the flag of England over the Molyneux silver." But when people are bent on being lugubrious, they will not be made to see any joke whatever—not even one taken with British ensign. And comes Mr. Boyce with a regular Toombs explosion. Guillotine and that sort of stuff. It is humiliating. People take us for such fools.

Letter today in the morning paper accusing Mr. C of staying too long in Charleston.

---

6. Sir Edward Sheperd Creasy, *The Fifteen Decisive Battles of the World* (1851), and Sir Archibald Alison, *Atlas to Alison's History of Europe . . . , With Vocabulary of Military and Marine Terms* (1848). Theodore Hook was an English novelist, magazine editor, and satirist.

7. A false rumor. Union troops occupied the city on Feb. 25.

The editor was asked for the writer's name. He gave Little Moses, the governor's secretary. When Little Moses was spoken to, in a great trepidation he told that Mrs. Pickens wrote it and got him to publish it. So it dropped, for Little Moses is such an arrant liar no one believes him. Besides, it [is] that sort of thing amuses Mrs. Pickens. Let her amuse herself. It would kill Mr. C to stay at home, attending to his own business while a war is upon us. I daresay being sufficiently tormented doing his duty here will satisfy him quite as well as any other similar position.

For one thing heaven be thanked.

The Yankee prisoners have been removed from Columbia. Mr. Preston says now he will have some peace of *his* life. He calls governor and council "our herd of governors."

March 5, 1862.   Mary Cantey Preston went with me to Mulberry. She found a man there tall enough to take her into dinner. Tom Boykin—six feet four, the same height of her father. Tom was very handsome in his uniform, and Mary prepared for a nice time, but then he looked as if he had so much rather she did not talk to him. And he set her such a poor example, saying never a word.

Old Colonel Chesnut came for us when the train stopped. Quashie, shiny black, superb on his box, as glossy and perfect in his way as his blood bays—but the old Colonel would stop and pick up the dirtiest little negro I ever saw, who was crying by the roadside. This ragged little black urchin was made to climb up and sit beside Quash. It spoiled the symmetry of the turnout. But it was a character touch, and the old gentleman knows no law but his own will. He had a biscuit in his pocket which he gave this sniffling little negro, who proved to be his man Scip's son.

I was ill at Mulberry—never left my room. Dr. Boykin came, more military than medical. Colonel Chesnut brought him up. Also Team—who said he was down in the mouth: our men were not fighting as they ought—we had only pluck and luck and a dogged spirit of fighting to offset their weight in men and munitions or war. I wish I could remember Team's words. This is only his idea. His language is quaint and striking—no grammar, but no end of sense and good feeling. Old Mr. C, catching a word, began his litany: "Numbers will tell, Napoleon, you know, &c&c&c."

At Mulberry the war has been ever afar off, but the threat to take the silver came very near indeed, silver that he had before the revolution, silver that he brought from Philadelphia. Colonel Cox, first Congress, Madame Bowes,[8] French counts—all off in the dim distance.

---

8. Probably Mary (Cox) Chesnut's grandmother.

Wade Manning came to see his cousin.[9] Without emulating Mrs. Stowe, how can I tell Wade's tales. He is miserable where he is. Those Preston and Hampton boys loathe slavery—and all its concomitants. Zack Cantey[1] and Dr. Boykin came back on the train with us. Wade Hampton is their hero. For one thing he is sober. Wigfall, Whiting—all tarred with the same stick. And the pity of it. They are capable of the greatest things.

《 How he [James Chesnut] does regret his mistake going with this council.》[2]

Letters came to the council, warning them to watch Mrs. Henry Duncan.[3]

The men cannot be made to watch and worry women.

Read *Young Duke.*

Sweet May Dacre. Lord Byron and Disraeli make their rosebuds Catholic. May Dacre is another Aurora Raby.[4] I like Disraeli. I find so many clever things. I like the sparkle and the glitter.

Also *Confidences.*[5] Nice little thing—a new man and a clever one—Hamilton Aïdé—I mean a new novel writer. He may be, as to years and name, old as the hills.

Now for Theo Hook's book. Year 1996. London. Duke of Bedford's family. *Progress of Philanthropy,* the name of it.

Servants, having been long equal, soon grew superior to their masters. Then the upward progress grew so rapid, coach horses found out their rights and their mights and kicked against the traces.

The old gray mare protested—refused to go between the shafts, as conduct amounting to servitude, disguise it as you will.

Lady Bedford begged and implored the duke that she might be allowed to seize the opportunity, while a few unenlightened horses still remained, to fly. They had still some dull horses who could be prevailed upon to drag them off and out of the country.

Carlyle does not hold up his hands in holy horror of us because of African slavery.[6]

Lord Lyons has gone against us. Lord Derby and Louis Napoleon are silent in our hour of direst need.

They call me Cassandra—for I cry, outside hope is quenched.
From outside no help cometh to this beleaguered land.

9. Wade Hampton Manning, a son of John L. Manning, serving as an orderly in the Fourth S.C. Cavalry. Mary Cantey Preston was his first cousin.
1. Zachariah Cantey, a Camden planter and lieutenant of the Kirkwood Rangers, was a second cousin of James Chesnut, Jr.
2. Rough draft of the 1880s Version.
3. A member of a Unionist Miss. planting family friendly with the Hamptons.
4. May Dacre, a character in Benjamin Disraeli's *The Young Duke* (1831), and Aurora Raby, from Lord Byron's *Don Juan.*
5. Published in 1859.
6. See, for example, Carlyle's essay "The Nigger Question," in *Critical and Miscellaneous Essays,* volume 4.

March 7, 1862. David Williams adds not to our encouragement. Bluer, blacker in Florida than here, he says.

He was answered: "As for the particular settlement to which you refer, they are in no danger. They have not taken up arms against U.S.A. They have not aided or abetted us. They can mention all that when Yankees come along." David, though in the army himself, found the saying bitter as applied to his friends and neighbors.

Governor Letcher would not let Virginia take Fortress Monroe at the proper time. When she could, she would not. "Now she shall have nay," as the old song says.

Fifteen sail have again emerged, threatening us from that quarter.

At tea, introduced David to our party. Governor Gist—Judge Glover[7]—and stopped there because I had not warned him, and it was dangerous to say suddenly "Colonel Quattlebaum."[8] He might laugh.

Judge Withers is denouncing governor and council to all his grand juries. He tells them they are living under a despotism. It does not matter, *if* we get out of this scrape. And if we do not, he will perhaps find harder work to do than going round the country, criticizing and abusing his friends.

Edward Boykin bragged—they said he was no saint, but he had made the women and children God had given him happy. There was no happier family than his in the world. There was no skeleton in his closet. John W was ready to be canonized, but—

March 9, 1862.   Can it be possible, said Halcott Green,[9] that Colonel Chesnut is opposed to the aggressive policy?

"'Aggress,' did you say? Why, we have not men to defend."

Then he said, [in] our game of rouge et noir, the run had been upon the black lately. Luck must turn, &c&c. Today he stopped me at the church door.

"The run on the red has begun."

And he told the wonderful *Merrimack* news.[1]

Mrs. Middleton was dolorous indeed. General Lee had warned the planters about Combahee &c&c. "They must take care of themselves now—he could not do it."

---

7. A judge from Orange District, Thomas Worth Glover was also a planter and member of the secession convention.

8. Probably Paul Quattlebaum, a former state legislator and member of the secession convention with extensive landholdings and manufacturing interests in Edgefield and Lexington districts.

9. Halcott Pride Green of Columbia helped his brother Allen J. Green, Jr., run the family plantations. His wife, Virginia (Taylor) Green, was the daughter of Sally Webb (Coles) Taylor and thus a distant relation of J. C.

1. The Confederate ironclad *Virginia,* converted from the captured Yankee frigate *Merrimack* (often spelled *"Merrimac"*), sank the U.S.S. *Cumberland* and burned the U.S.S. *Congress* off Hampton Roads, Va., on March 8. The *Virginia's* famous encounter with the *Monitor* took place the next day.

Confederate soldiers had committed some outrages on the plantations, and their officers had punished them promptly.

She poured contempt upon Yancey's letter to Lord Russell.[2] It was the letter of a shopkeeper—not in the style of a statesman at all.

We called to see Mary McDuffie.[3] She asked Mary what Dr. Boykin had said of her husband as we came along in the train. She heard it was very complimentary. Mary tried to remember—then lightly, "For one thing, he said you could always find Uncle Wade sober."

"That's horrid news. I notice they never promote any but topers to be brigadiers." We said, "Colonel C has just recommended Wilmot DeSaussure as a brigadier. He is sober enough."

Mary was amazed to hear of the list of applicants for promotion. One delicate-minded person accompanied his request for a high lift by asking for a written description of the Manassas battle. He had heard Colonel C give Uncle a brilliant account of it in Governor Cobb's room.

No names were called, of course, but Mary McDuffie coolly repeated, "Do you not think we have fool brigadiers enough already?"

The *Merrimack* business came like a gleam of lightning, illumining a dark scene. The sky is black and lowering.

Commodore Buchanan is only wounded—not killed, as reported. Four men were killed.

Judge Withers saw his daughter Kate at my window and he came up. He was very smooth and kind. It was really a delightful visit. Not a disagreeable word. He abused no one whatever—for he never once spoke of anyone but himself. And himself he praised without stint. He did not look at me once, though he spoke very kindly to me.

2. On March 5, the *Mercury* published a letter William Lowndes Yancey sent British Foreign Secretary John Russell before leaving England in Aug. 1861. Defending the right of secession and vowing the Confederacy would not give up, Yancey intimated that Britain would be responsible for the suffering caused by a long war, should she fail to recognize the South.
3. Mary (McDuffie) Hampton, the second wife of Wade Hampton III.

XIII

"With Horror and Amazement"

March 10, 1862. Congaree House. Second year. Confederate independence. I write daily for my own distractions. These memoirs pour servir may some future day afford dates, facts, and prove useful to more important people than I am. I do not wish to do any harm or to hurt anyone. If any scandalous stories creep in, they are easily burned. It is hard, in such a hurry as things are in, to separate wheat from chaff.

Now I have made my protest and written down my wishes. I can scribble on with a free will and free conscience.

U.S.A. Congress is down on us. The talk largely of hanging slave-owners.[1] They say they hold Port Royal as we did when we took it originally from the aborigines, who fled before us. So we are to be exterminated and improved à l'Indienne—from the face of the earth.

The Columbia paper—Pelham editor[2]—denouncing the governor and council for calling out college boys and mechanics. "That should not be done until the state *is invaded*—reserved for the last," &c&c. Did you ever! Where is Port Royal—where is Beaufort? How soon they forget!

We are so busy fighting each other. The great Pickens fight with the council. We forget everything out of sight. Our fighting powers are engrossed—used up by home consumption. Confederate Congress exhausts itself, vituperating Jeff Davis. To hamper, harass, and thwart him seems their whole duty. Pickens, Gibbes, and Withers go into the same business. Never mind Yankees—until they have exterminated the council.

Reading Creasy's *Decisive Battles*. Did Marathon today. Asked Mr. C if he were an archon. Said I meant to call him a polemarch. He did not see the joke and stared gravely. So I had to laugh for two.[3]

1. A reference to a speech in the U.S. Senate by Lyman Trumbull on Feb. 25. The Ill. senator defended the constitutionality of a bill permitting the confiscation of all property owned by those "in a state of insurrection and rebellion" against the U.S. government.
2. The *Southern Guardian,* a daily published by Charles P. Pelham.
3. Creasy somewhat misleadingly describes archons as generals elected to represent each of the tribes of Athens in a council of war, and the polemarch as a sort of overall commander.

Medea—when asked: "Country, wealth, husband, children—all gone. What remains?" "Medea remains."[4]

Marie Antoinette: "I count upon my own courage—not upon the chapter of accidents."

General Foy: "We advanced to Waterloo as the Greeks to Thermopylae. Most of us without hope. All without fear."[5] I had a sort of recollection of this before, as said by a French[man] on the disastrous retreat from Moscow.

Sir Thomas Browne: "To weep onto stone is a fable. Sorrow destroys us—or itself."[6]

"Why, Albert—you here. Have you run away to escape being drafted into the army?"

"Yes, aunt, and I will tell you why. I cannot live upon eleven Confederate dollars a month."

"There is a time in most men's lives when they resemble Job, sitting among the ashes and drinking in the full bitterness of complicated misfortune."[7]

I paste in Timrod's "Carolina."[8] *He* thinks we are invaded.

"Nothing is more unpartial than the streamlike public. Always the same and never the same; of whom sooner or later each misrepresented character obtains justice—and each calumniated one, honor. He who cannot wait for that is either ignorant of human nature or feels that he was not made for honor."

March 11, 1862. An article in *Blackwood's* singularly inviting—scattering abuse of Yankeedom is to our taste now exactly.

We are in sympathy for once with the Edinburgh high Tory.

Mars Kit[9]—"I told Mr. Venable and the girls how pleasant he was last night. So well preserved &c."

4. Seneca, *Medea,* act 2: "Medea superest."
5. A quotation from *Decisive Battles,* chapter 4. Maximilien Sébastien Foy (1775–1825) was one of Napoleon's commanders.
6. Paraphrased from Browne's *Hydriotaphia. Urn Burial; or, A Discourse on the Sepulchral Urns Lately Found in Norfolk* (1658).
7. Job 2:8.
8. Opposite this page appears a clipping of the seven-stanza poem written in the winter of 1862 by the "poet laureate of the Confederacy," Henry Timrod of S.C.
9. Christopher Fitzsimons Hampton, a younger brother of Wade Hampton III, owned plantations in Richland District and Miss.

"Neither stuck up nor solemn?"

"Not at all."

"She said 'well preserved.' Who by? Mrs. H. D.[1] Preserved in syrup. Done up in sweets. I like things kept that way better than in alcohol. As most of his contemporaries are."

"Fancy Mars Kit bottled up."

And then the McGillie legend came up—descendants of the Stuarts when they were pretenders.

Oh, she was the condensed essence of all pretenders—and to hear her calmly at the Springs. Gillie, a horse boy, of the blood of the Stuarts—wonderful how people will grub, fight, bleed, and die for a genealogical tree in this democratic republic.

"You know, Macaulay says the last pretender—or nearly the last—did not disdain, in search of adventures, to overhaul a dustpan."

"Thackeray said that."

"No, Thackeray went for the Hanoverians."[2]

A freshman came, quite eager to be instructed in all the wiles of society. He wanted to try his hand at a flirtation. Requested minute instructions, as he knew nothing whatever—he was so very fresh.

"Dance with her, and talk, walk with her and flatter, dance until she is warm and tired—then prepare to walk in a cool, shady piazza. It must be a somewhat dark piazza. Begin your promenade slowly. Warm up to your work—draw her arm closer and closer, then break her wing."

"Heavens, what is that?"

"Why, you do not know even that? Put your arm round her waist, and kiss her. After that it is all plain sailing. She comes down when you call, like the coon to Captain Scott—'You need not fire, captain,' &c&c."[3]

The aspirant for fame as a flirt followed these lucid directions literally—but when he seized the poor girl and kissed her, she uplifted her voice in terror and screamed as if the house was on fire. So quick sharp and shrill were her yells for help that the bold flirt sprang over the bannister, upon which grew a strong climbing rose. This he struggled through and ran toward the college, taking a beeline. He was so mangled by the thorns he had to go home and have them picked off by his family. *Her* brother challenged him. There was no mortal combat, however. For the gay young fellow who led his ignorance astray stepped forward and put things straight. Explanation and apology at every turn hushed it all up. Now we all laughed at this foolish story most heartily. But Mr. Venable remained grave and preoccupied.

1. Mrs. Henry Duncan.

2. In chapter 9 of *Henry Esmond*, Thackeray notes that the last of the Jacobite pretenders "was often content to lay the dignity of his birth and grief at the wooden shoes of a French chambermaid and to repent afterwards (for he was very devout) in ashes taken from the dust pan...."

3. U.S. Army Capt. Martin Scott became almost legendary for his excellent marksmanship while stationed in Ark. According to a frequently repeated story which first appeared in the *American Turf Register* (Oct. 1832), a treed raccoon hears he is being hunted by Scott and gives himself up because he knows he has no chance to escape the captain's rifle.

"Why are you so unmoved? It is funny."

"I like more probable fun. I have been in college, and I have kissed many a girl, and never a one *scrome* yet."

Mary Witherspoon has sent a silver teapot and a note with her name signed to it, to be published as her gift to the gunboat.[4]

Foote and Botts—bottle them up together—false-tongued traitors, every one.[5] Foote says he knows no man in Mississippi who will sacrifice their cotton for their country. Already many have done so!

Last Saturday was the bloodiest we have had, in proportion to numbers. The enemy lost 1,500.[6]

The handful left at home are rushing to arms—at last. Bragg has gone to join Beauregard at Columbus, Mississippi.

Old Abe truly took the field in that Scotch cap of his.

No. Will never give in—no never—down to the last verse.

Mrs. McCord, she who wrote *The Mother of the Gracchi*—the eldest daughter of Langdon Cheves—she got up a company for her son, raised it at her own expense.[7] She has the brain and energy of a man. Today she repeated a remark of a low-country gentleman who is dissatisfied:

"This government (Confederate) protects neither person nor property." Fancy the scornful turn of her lip. Someone asked for Langdon Cheves, her brother.

"Oh, Langdon," she replied coolly. "He is a pure patriot, he has no ambition. Tom Drayton is using Langdon's brains. Tom Drayton is muddleheaded. Langdon's head is clear and strong."

He was letting Confederate soldiers ditch through his gardens while I was there and ruin him at their leisure. Cotton five cents a pound. Labor of no value at all. It commands no price whatever. People gladly hire out their negroes to have them fed and clothed. Which latter cannot be done. Cotton osnaburgs at

4. The young women of Columbia's upper class were organizing a fair to raise money to purchase a gunboat for the Confederate navy.

5. When martial law was declared in and around Richmond on March 1, Jefferson Davis ordered the imprisonment of former Va. congressman John Minor Botts, an opponent of the war. Botts was released a few weeks later, however.

6. The battle of Elkhorn Tavern (Pea Ridge), Ark., fought on March 7 and 8.

7. The author of *Caius Gracchus: A Tragedy in Five Acts* (1851), Louisa Susannah (Cheves) McCord of Columbia is best known for her articles popularizing free trade, defending slavery, and arguing that woman's proper sphere lies within the home. Widowed in 1855, Mrs. McCord continued to manage her own plantation in Richland District but ceased writing to devote herself to the education of her son, Langdon Cheves McCord. During the war, she operated a military hospital and made her plantation a model for those who encouraged planters to raise provisions rather than cotton.

37½ cents a yard—leaves no chance to clothe them. He was for martial law—and the bloodsuckers made to disgorge their ill-gotten gains. We poor fools who were patriotically ruining ourselves would see our children in the gutter while treacherous dogs of millionaires went rolling by in their coaches—coaches acquired by taking advantage of our necessities.

This terrible battle of ships. All hands on board the *Cumberland* went down. She fought gallantly and fired a round as she sunk.

The *Congress* ran up a white flag. She fired on our boats as they went up to take off her wounded. She was burned.

The worst of it is, it will rouse them to more furious exertions to destroy us. They hated us so before. How now?

Only ten thousand Athenians at Marathon. So long ago—and the Greeks say so. Very little experience of wartimes makes us so incredulous.

Then, on the other hand, the Roman muster roll in the Punic Wars. Seven hundred thousand foot, seventy thousand horse. They were the sort of U.S. this empire in America is.

I am deep in Creasy.

Let the evil speaker against Alexander the Great bear this in mind. Let him reflect on his own insignificance and the pettiness of his own circumstances and affairs—and the blunders and mistakes he falls in about these, trifling as they are! Then let him ask himself if he be a fit person to censure and revile such a man as Alexander![8]

—Arrian

A course of democratic republicanism has changed all that. Here, now, in Columbia I do not know a half-dozen men who would not gaily step into Jeff Davis's shoes, with a firm conviction they could do better in every respect than he does.

The monstrous conceit, the fatuous ignorance of these critics!

It is pleasant to hear Mrs. McCord on this subject, when they begin to shake their heads and tell us what Jeff Davis ought to do.

March 12, 1862. Today's paper calls enlisting students exhausting "seed corn." All right. How about preserving land wherein to plant your corn?

---

8. This quotation from *The Anabasis of Alexander* by the second-century Greek historian Arrian appears in *Decisive Battles*, chapter 3. The two observations immediately above are also drawn from *Decisive Battles*, chapters 1 and 4.

Your little corn patch seems slipping away from you. You need boys, even women's broomsticks, when the foe is pulling down your snake fences.

In the naval battle the other day we had 25 guns in all. The enemy had 54 in the *Cumberland*—44 in the *St. Lawrence* besides—a fleet of gunboats filled with rifled cannon. Why not? They can have as many as they please. No pent-up Utica contracts their powers. The whole boundless world is theirs to recruit in—only this one little spot of ground. The blockade or stockade which hems us in—only the sky open to us. And for all that, how tenderfooted and cautiously they draw near.

Floyd and Pillow are suspended from command for—Fort Donelson.[9]

And the people of Tennessee demand the like fate for Albert Sidney Johnston! They say he is stupid. Can human folly go further than this Tennessee madness?

An anonymous letter. It purports to answer Colonel Chesnut's address to the South Carolinians in the Army of the Potomac. The man says all that bosh is no good. He knows lots of people whose fathers were notorious Tories in our War for Independence, and they made their fortunes by selling their country. They have the best places. Their sons (of course) and they are cowards and traitors still, names given, of course. The writer seemed a Jew. He was awfully scandalized at an illegitimate Jew being a celebrated person. The bar sinister was a bar indeed to any uprising of Jews, it seems.

Mr. C threw the letter in the fire. I think he was very sorry that I saw it.

March 13, 1862. Halcott Green came with dismal news. Ben McCulloch is dead—and Price, killed in the last great victory.[1]

Victory? Where? So far off. Nobody believes a word.

Mr. C fretting and fuming. From the poor old blind bishop downward, everybody besetting him to get off students—theological and otherwise—from the army. One comfort is, the boys will go.

Mr. C's answer pretty strong. Wait until you have saved your country before you make preachers and scholars. When you have a country, there will be no lack of divines, students, scholars, to adorn and purify it. He says he is a one-idea'd man. That one idea is to fit every possible man in the ranks.

Professor LeConte is an able auxiliary. He has undertaken to supervise and carry another powder-making enterprise.[2]

9. When Grant's army besieged Fort Donelson in Feb., Brig. Gens. John Buchanan Floyd and Gideon Johnson Pillow fled, leaving Brig. Gen. Simon Bolivar Buckner to surrender the fort. Both Floyd and Pillow were removed from command without a court of inquiry. M. B. C. may have taken a special interest in the matter because Floyd, a former governor of Va. and secretary of war in the Buchanan administration, was married to a sister of John S. Preston.

1. McCulloch, dressed in a black velvet suit, was in command of the right wing of Earl Van Dorn's army when he was killed at Elkhorn Tavern on March 7. Sterling Price survived the Confederate defeat and was promoted to major general.

2. Both John LeConte and his brother Joseph, professors of physics and chemistry, respectively, at S.C. College, worked for the Confederate government in the production of niter and other chemicals.

The very first attempted in the Confederacy—and Mr. C is proud of it. It is a brilliant success, thanks to Mr. LeConte.

Mr. Chesnut's second project is to set Captain Ingraham, Jack Hamilton, &c building a gunboat after a fashion of their own. A *Merrimack* for Charleston. Large ideas.

Mr. C receives anonymous letters urging him to arrest the Judge as seditious. They say he is a dangerous and disaffected person. His abuse of Jeff Davis and the council is rabid. Mr. C laughs and throws the letter in the fire. "Disaffected to Jeff Davis—disaffected to the council—that don't count. He knows what he is about. He would not injure his country for the world."

Read *Uncle Tom's Cabin* again.

Keating Simons[3] said: "Putting down distilleries can only be done at the point of a bayonet. By stopping cotton from going out, they mean to try and lower the price of cotton osnaburgs."

These negro women have a chance here women have nowhere else. They can redeem themselves. The "impropers." They can marry decently—and nothing is remembered against them, these colored ladies. It is not a nice topic, but Mrs. Stowe revels in it. How delightfully pharisaic a feeling it must be, to rise superior and fancy we are so degraded as to defend and like to live with such degraded creatures around us. Such men as Legare [Legree] and his women.

The best way to take negroes to your heart is to get as far away from them as possible. As far as I can see, Southern women do all that missionaries could to prevent and alleviate the evils. The social evil has not been suppressed in England or New England, London or Boston. And they expect more virtue from a plantation African than they can practice with all their high moral surroundings—light, education, training, and supports.

Lady Mary Montagu says, "Only men and women at last." "Male and female created He them," says the Bible.

There are cruel, graceful, beautiful mothers of angelic Evas—North as well as South, I daresay. The Northern men and women who came here have always been hardest, for they expect an African to work and to behave as a white man. We do not. I have often thought—from observation, truly—that perfect beauty hardens the heart—and as to grace, what so graceful as a cat, a tigress, a panther.

So much love, admiration, worship hardens the idol's heart. They become utterly callous and selfish. They expect to receive all, to give nothing.

They even like the excitement of seeing people suffer. I speak now of what I have watched with horror and amazement.

Topsys I have known—but none that were beauties—or ill-used. Evas are

---

3. A wealthy planter of Charleston District.

mostly in the heaven of Mrs. Stowe's imagination. People can't love things dirty, ugly, repulsive, simply because they ought, but they can be good to them—at a distance. You see, I cannot rise very high. I can only judge by what I see.

March 14, 1862.   Thank God for a ship. It has run the blockade with arms and ammunition.

There are no negro marital relations, or the want of them, half so shocking as Mormonism. And yet U.S.A. makes no bones of receiving Mormons into her sacred heart.

Mr. Venable said England held her hand over "the malignant and the turbaned Turk" to save and protect him, slaves, seraglio, and all. But she rolls up the whites of her eyes at us. When slavery, bad as it is, is stepping out into freedom every moment through Christian civilization.

They do not grudge the Turk even his bag and Bosporus privileges. To a recalcitrant wife it is: "Here yawns the sack. There rolls the sea"—&c.

And France, the bold, the brave, the ever free—she is not so tenderfooted in Algiers.

But then, "you are another" argument is but a shabby one.

"You see," says Mary P sagaciously. "We are white Christian descendants of Huguenots and Cavaliers, and they expect of us different conduct from mere Turks and infidels and Algerian pirates."

Mr. Venable came with a plan to reduce to some order and consistence this mad rush for commissions. There is a new levy of 5,000 men.

1. Ask every captain who has served for a year, for his best subaltern—promote him first.

2. Take the best of the graduates of the military schools.

3. And last of all give a chance to the kid-gloved, pink-nailed gentry who have leisurely loitered to the eleventh hour and now want to command those they left to do and die or to bear the heats and the burden of a year's fightings.

Mr. C read this paper to the council. Said a lady sent it to him.

They laughed at it but adopted something not so very different.

Went to drive with my boarding-school girls in Mrs. Preston's landau. At my door met J. F., who wanted me then and there to promise to help him with his commission or put him in the way of one. At the carriage steps—was handed in by Gus Smith, who wants his brother made commissary.

The beauty of it all is they think I have some influence. And I have not a particle.

The subject of his military affairs, promotions, &c is never mentioned. If I told him these men wanted my influence with him, I think he could be in a fury. They think he listens to me—he does not.

March 15, 1862.   When we came home, there stood Warren Nelson, propped up against my door, lazily waiting for me. The handsome creature. He said he meant to be heard, so I walked back with him to the drawing room.

They are wasting their time, dancing attendance on me. I cannot help them. Let them shoulder their muskets and go to the war like men.

After tea came "Mars Kit"—he said, for a talk, but that Mr. Preston would not let him, for Mr. P had arrived some time before him. Mr. P said "Mars Kit" thought it "bad form" to laugh. After that, you may be sure, a laugh from "Mars Kit" was secured. Again and again, he was forced to laugh with a will. I reversed Oliver Wendell Holmes's good resolution never to be as funny as he could.[4] I did my very utmost.

Mr. Venable interrupted the fun, which was fast and furious, with the very best of bad news: New Berne shelled and burned, cotton, turpentine, everything. There were 5,000 North Carolinians in the fray, 12,000 Yankees.[5]

Now there stands Goldsboro. One more step and we are cut in two. The RR is our backbone. Like the Blue Ridge and the Alleghenies with which it runs parallel.

So many discomfitures. No wonder we are downhearted.

Mr. Venable thinks as we do. Garnett is our most thorough scholar. Lamar the most original and the cleverest of our men. Muscoe Russell Hunter Garnett. L. Q. C. Lamar—time failed me to write all of his name.

March 17, 1862.   Back to the Congaree House to await my husband, who has made a rapid visit to the Wateree region.

As we drove up Mr. C said: "Did you see the stare of respectful admiration E. R. bestowed upon you? So curiously prolonged. I could hardly keep my countenance."

"Yes, my dear child. I feel the honor of it, though my individual self goes for nothing in it. I am the wife of the man who has the appointing power just now. So many commissions to be filled. I am nearly forty, and they do my understanding the credit to suppose I can be made to believe they admire my mature charms. They think they fool me into thinking that *they* believe me charming. There is hardly any farce in the world more laughable."

Last night a house was set on fire, last week two. "The red cock crows in the barn." Our troubles thicken indeed, if they ever begin to come from that dark quarter.

When the president first offered Johnston Pettigrew a brigadier generalship, his answer was: "Not yet—too many men are ahead of me who have earned their promotion in the field. I will come after them—not before. So far I have

4. From "The Height of the Ridiculous," in *Poems* (1836).
5. Moving inland after securing control of the coast, Federal forces captured New Berne, N.C., on March 14.

done nothing to merit reward &c." He would not take rank when he could get it. I fancy he may cool his heels now, waiting for it. He was too high and mighty.

There was another conscientious man. Burnett of Kentucky.[6] He gave up his regiment to his lieutenant colonel when he found the lieutenant colonel could command the regiment and Burnett could not maneuver it in the field. He went into the fight simply as an aide to Floyd.

Modest merit just now is at a premium.

Gilmore Simms here. Read us his last poetry. Have forgotten already what it was about. It was not tiresome, however—and that is a great thing, when people will persist in reading their own rhymes.

I did not hear what Mr. Preston was saying. "The last piece of Richmond news," Mr. C said, as he went away—and he looked so fagged out. I asked no questions. I knew it was bad.

At daylight there was a loud knocking at my door. I hurried on a dressing gown and flew to open it. "Mrs. Chesnut, Mrs. M says, please don't forget her son. Mr. Chesnut, she hears, has come back. Please get her son a commission. He must have an office."

I shut the door in the servant's face.

If I had the influence these foolish people attribute to me, why should I not help my own? I have a brother—two brothers-in-law. And no end of kin, all gentlemen privates—and privates they would stay to the end of time before they said a word *to me* about commissions.

Mary P was giving Wade Manning's story of his Aunt Camilla's[7] bed of justice. The lady is of the stoutest—with a fiery red face and straggling gray hair. Her room opens on a stairway up and down which all the world goes, is obliged to go, for it is the only staircase in the house. With her door wide open she sat in bed with a bundle of switches, and every Monday morning everybody in the yard was there to give an account of their deeds or misdeeds for the past week. They were mustered in a row and waited. She solemnly rehearsed their misdemeanors. Some were adroit enough to avert their fate. Those whom she condemned stepped up to the bedside and received their punishment, screaming, howling, and yelling to the utmost of their ability to soften her heart. With her nightcap flying—and her gown in horrid disarray from the exercise of her arm. Wade found her dreadful to think of, as he fled from the sound and sight. Peace once restored and everybody once more at the daily avocations—they were as jolly as larks. With perspiration streaming, Wade moaned: "It shocks and makes me miserable—and they don't seem to mind a switching, Cousin

---

6. Henry Cornelius Burnett, a member of the Confederate Congress, fought at Fort Donelson as colonel of the Eighth Ky. Infantry.

7. Wade Hampton Manning's great-aunt Camilla (Richardson) Cantey of Kershaw District was the widow of planter James Willis Cantey, a first cousin of old Colonel Chesnut.

Mary, not ten seconds after it is over. And this is the place my father sends me to be *educated!*"

Mrs. Greenhow is coming. Now not a word of the past history. Washington gossip—so Browne says. She must not come handicapped with her old life. What a list of friends she boasted. British legation were her sponsors—President Buchanan, Seward, Old Joe Lane,[8] Governor Brown,[9] and Ed Pringle!

————————

Sensible old French woman. Madame de Créquy. Just read her ideas on Mesmer's fantastic tricks.[1]

Mary C said to Mr. Venable: "I would like that story of Wade's to be *beStowed.* What would she think of it, or make of it?"

"Mrs. Stowe would feel exactly as we do, but then she would take an extraordinary freak of nature as a specimen of a class—a common type."

"Why," Wade says, "everybody at breakfast was as jolly, as pleasant, as smiling, as if there had been no human tornado raging a few minutes before."

"The beswitched and all?"

"Yes, the howlers and all?"

"Don't take on so," says Mr. Venable. "A fat old thing like her can't hurt much."

"Remnant of barbarism."

"Did you never read Dickens? We are no worse than other people. Sally Brass,[2] now. Do you fancy there are many Sally Brasses in this world?"

They asked me if I had ever heard of this devil's matins before.

"Yes, but I heard it was a daily service."

"Oh no, no," said Wade, "once a week is as much as mortal could bear of a row such as that in any house."

"You were only a passenger—and a pretty rapid one. I generally fled for my life."

It is only on Mondays. One woman has the length of her foot, says she gathers up all the scandals of the town. "Miss too keen to hear the news to trouble me. I brings her plenty 'bout everybody, specially them she don't like."

So we were disgusted and revolted, and the men went off to the bulletin board.

Whatever else it shows, good or bad, there is always woe for some house. The killed and wounded.

8. Joseph Lane of Oreg., the pro-Southern Democratic senator who ran for vice president on the Breckinridge ticket in 1860.

9. Probably Albert Gallatin Brown, former governor and U.S. senator from Miss., and a member of the Confederate Senate.

1. Renée Caroline de Froulay, marquise de Créquy, *Les Souvenirs de la Marquise de Créquy* (1834), volume 6, chapter 6.

2. Sally Brass, a character in *The Old Curiosity Shop*, is a cunning spinster who mistreated and starved her servant.

We have need of stout hearts. I feel a sinking of mine as we drive near the board.

March 18, 1862.   Last night read a French play. *Calomnie et le Ministre*[3]—can understand that plot.

My war archon is beset for commissions. And somebody says for every one given, you make one ingrate and a thousand enemies.

Today, as I entered Miss Mary Stark's, I whispered, "He has promised to vote for Louis." What radiant faces.

To my friend, Miss Mary said: "Your son-in-law. What is he doing for his country?"

"Tax collector."

Then spoke up the stout old girl. "Look at my cheek—it is red with blushing for you—a great hale, hearty young man! fie on him! fie on him, for shame! Tell his wife, run him out of the house with a broomstick. Send him down to the coast, at least."

Fancy my cheeks, I could not raise my eyes to the poor lady so mercilessly assaulted.

My face was as hot with compassion as the outspoken Mary pretended hers to be.

Next to her, sweet and saintly Mrs. Bartow. She read us a letter from Mississippi—not so bad.

"More men there than the enemy suspected. And torpedoes on the river to blow up the wretches when they came."

Next to see Mrs. Izard. She had with her a relative just from the North. This lady had asked Seward for passports, and he told her, "Hold on a while, the road to South Carolina would soon be open to all, open, and safe."

Today Mrs. Arthur Hayne[4] heard from her daughter that Richmond is to be given up. Mrs. Beall is her daughter.

Met Mr. C. New Madrid is given up, do not know any more than the dead where New Madrid is. It is bad, all the same, this giving up—I can't stand it.[5]

"The hemming process is nearly complete. The ring of fire is almost unbroken."

---

3. Probably Augustin Eugène Scribe, *La Calomnie* (1840), a play about Raymond, "le premier ministre."

4. Elizabeth Laura (Alston) Hayne of Charleston, second wife of former U.S. senator Arthur Perroneau Hayne. Their daughter Frances Alston (Hayne) Beall was the wife of Col. Lloyd James Beall, commandant of the Confederate Marine Corps.

5. The Union capture four days earlier of New Madrid, Mo., on the Mississippi River, led to the seizure of Island No. 10 on April 8 and thus opened the river route to Fort Pillow, Tenn.

To all of which Mr. C assented cheerfully. So I know that he has some good news in reserve.

His negroes offered to fight for him if he would arm them. He pretended to believe them. He says one man cannot do it. The whole country must agree to it.

He could trust such as he would select. And he would give so many acres of land and his freedom to each one as he enlisted.

Mr. Preston said—"That man of yours (you pretend Chesnut cares for his country?)—while I was pouring out my budget from Richmond, *metaphorically* he went to sleep and snored. At Manassas, to the last he and Manning would sleep until ten o'clock every morning if nobody waked him. I do not believe in patriotism that can't even rouse a fellow from his nap after dinner."

Mrs. Albert Rhett[6] came for an office for her son John. I told her Mr. C would never propose a kinsman for office, but if anyone else brought his name forward he could vote for him, certainly, as he is so eminently fit for a soldier's place. Now he is a private.

The church was crowded today—only one man, Halcott Green. It is plain why there is no marrying nor giving in marriage to heaven.

The church is the gate to heaven, and the church is apparently filled with women only going up there.

March 19, 1862. He who runs may read. Conscription means that we are in a tight place. This war was a volunteer business—

Tomorrow conscription begins.[7] The dernier resort.

The president has remodeled his cabinet, leaving Bragg from North Carolina. His war minister is Randolph of Virginia. A Union man par excellence, Watts of Alabama is attorney general.[8]

And now, too late by one year, when all the mechanics are in the army &c&c&c, Mallory begins to telegraph Captain Ingraham to build ships—at any expense. We are locked in and cannot get "the requisites for naval architecture," says a magniloquent person.

Henry Frost[9] says all hands wink at cotton going out—why not send it out and

6. The widowed Sarah Cantey (Taylor) Rhett was the sister-in-law of Robert Barnwell Rhett, Sr., and a first cousin of J. C.

7. Called upon to furnish 18,000 troops for the duration of the war, S.C. had filled only a third of its quota by Feb. 1862. The Executive Council sought to remedy the deficiency in early March by approving a conscription bill proposed by J. C. No volunteers were to be accepted after March 20, but the threat of conscription alone provided more than enough men.

8. On March 17, Thomas Hill Watts, an Ala. Whig who had become a secessionist only after Lincoln's election, was named to replace Thomas Bragg as attorney general. At the same time, Davis announced that George Wythe Randolph, who had been a member of the Va. delegation sent to persuade Lincoln to avoid the use of force in 1861, was to become the new secretary of war.

9. A brother of Tom Frost serving as a first lieutenant on the coastal defenses around Charleston.

buy ships? "Every now and then there is a holocaust of cotton burning," says the magniloquent.

Conscription has waked the Rip Van Winkles. The streets of Columbia were never so crowded with men.

Did Varus and Arminius today in my *Decisive Battles*. Am quite encouraged as to invaders.[1]

Alexander the Great, successful invader, had a small number of troops—invading hordes are what we have to dread.

To my small wits: wherever people were persistent, united, and rose in their might, no general, however great, succeeded in subjugating them. Have we not swamps, forests, rivers, mountains, every natural barrier?

The Carthaginians begged for peace because they were a luxurious people and could not endure the hardship of war. Though the enemy suffered as sharply as they did!

"Factions among themselves"[2]—the rock on which we split.

"The very rumor that a fresh consul and a fresh army had come up when heard on a battlefield would settle the business." Bulls Run.

"They would have all credit of the victory and of having dealt the final blow." Kirby Smith &c&c&c.

  Honour is heavy when it comes on the best terms; how should it be otherwise when all men's cares are cast on one—but most in a troubled state. No man can put to sea without danger, but he that launcheth forth in a tempest can expect nothing but the hardest event.

—Bishop Hall

So much for J. C.'s going with this council.

Now for the great soul who is to arise and lead us—why tarry his footsteps?

---

1. From chapter 5 of Creasy's *Decisive Battles*. Arminius, a Germanic general, led Varus's Roman legions far into rebel territory, then surrounded and defeated them. The references to Alexander and the Carthaginians are from chapters 3 and 4 of the same work.
2. From Philip Massinger's play *The Bond-man* (1623), act 1, scene 3.

"When God hath any exploit to perform, he raiseth up the heart of some chosen instrument with heroical notions for the achievement—when all hearts are cold and dead, it is a sign of intended destruction."

Stir up our hearts!

March 20, 1862. The *Merrimack* now called the *Virginia*. I think these changes of names so confusing and so senseless—like the French *Royal Bengal Tiger*, *National* Tiger, &c&c. Rue this, and next day rue that, the very days and months a symbol, and nothing signified.

Well, the rebaptized *Virginia* is to be so prepared that she may board the *Ericsson*.[3] In a few days we will have in New Orleans a similar ship with forty guns. ·

I was lying on the sofa in my room—and two men slowly walking up and down the corridor talked aloud—as if necessarily all rooms were unoccupied at this midday hour. I asked Maum Mary who they were. "Yeadon and Barnwell Rhett, Jr."

They abused the council roundly, and my husband's name arrested my attention. Afterward, when Yeadon attacked Mr. Chesnut, he [C] surprised him [Y] by knowing beforehand all he had to say. Naturally I had repeated the loud interchange of views I had overheard in the corridor.

First Nathan Davis called. Then Gonzales, who presented a fine soldierly appearance in his soldier's clothes—and the likeness to Beauregard greater than ever. Nathan, all the world knows, is by profession a handsome man.

General Gonzales told us what in the bitterness of soul he had written to Jeff Davis. He regretted that he had not been his classmate. Then he might have been as well treated as Northrop. In any case he would not have been refused a brigadiership. Citing General Trapier[4] and Tom Drayton. He had worked for it—had earned it. They had not—&c&c. To his surprise, Mr. Davis answered him—and in a sharp note of four pages. Mr. Davis demanded from whom he quoted. "Not his classmate," General Gonzales responded. "From the public voice only." Now he will fight for us all the same but go on demanding justice from Jeff Davis until he gets his dues. At least, until one of them gets his dues, for he means to go on hitting Jeff Davis over the head whenever he has a chance.

"I am afraid you will find it a hard head to crack."

Reply, in his flowery Spanish way: "Jeff Davis will be the sun—radiating all

---

3. M. B. C. means the ironclad *Monitor*, which was designed and built by John Ericsson.

4. Commissioned a brigadier general in Oct. 1861, James Heyward Trapier of S.C. was later condemned by Braxton Bragg and the Fla. state convention as unfit for command.

light, heat, and patronage. He will not be a moon reflecting public opinion. For he has the soul of a despot. And he delights to spite public opinion. See—people abused him for making Crittenden brigadier; straightway he made him major general, and just after a blundering, besotted defeat, too."[5] Also he told the president in that letter: "Napoleon made his generals after great deeds on their part. And not for having been educated at St. Cyr or Brie or the Polytechnique—&c&c."

Nathan Davis sat as still as a Sioux warrior. Not an eyelash moved.

And yet he said afterward that he was amused while the Spaniard railed at his great namesake.

Gonzales said: "Mrs. Slidell would proudly tell she was a Creole. They were such fools they thought Creole meant—" Here Nathan interrupted pleasantly.

"At the St. Charles, New Orleans, on the bill of fare there was 'creole eggs.' When they were brought to a man who ordered them, with perfect simplicity he held them up: 'Why they are only hens' eggs, after all.' What in heaven's name he expected them to be, who can say?" smiled Nathan the elegant.

After our fiery Spaniard left, Nathan told me how ugly the world was growing. In Greenville a man who was at all good-looking was absolutely followed by women in the streets. "In perfect simplicity" the handsomest man of his day said this.

"He wanted anything. He could take even the place of a private in ranks if it was offered him."

"Then go and take it—they will not give it to you, but I'll answer for it. Nobody will hinder you from enlisting tomorrow—high private."

"You are always laughing at me."

Lady No. 1 (as I sat reading in the drawing room window while Maum Mary put my room to rights): "I clothe my negroes well. I could not bear to see them in dirt and rags. It would be unpleasant to me."

Lady No. 2: "Yes, well, so do I, but not fine clothes—you know, I really—now—feel it one of our sins as a nation, the way we indulged them in sinful finery. We let them dress too much. It led them astray. We will be punished for it."

They are attacking gunboats at Wadmalaw.[6] The enemy entered Charleston Harbor, placed three buoys—and were driven out again.

Last night Mrs. Pickens met General Cooper. Madame knew General Cooper only as our adjutant general—and Mr. Mason's brother-in-law. In her slow, graceful, impressive way, her beautiful eyes eloquent with feeling, she inveighed against Mr. Davis's wickedness in *always* sending men born at the North to command at Charleston. General Cooper is on his way to make a tour of inspection there now.

---

5. Although his father, U.S. Congressman John Jordan Crittenden, remained with the Union, George Bibb Crittenden of Ky. left the U.S. Army in 1861 and joined the C.S.A. He was already a major general when humiliated at the battle of Mills Springs, Ky., in Jan. 1862. Arrested and censured, he resigned his commission in Oct.

6. Probably a false rumor. Wadmalaw is a coastal island south of Charleston.

The dear general settled his head in his cravat with the aid of his forefinger; he tugged rather more nervously with the something that is always wrong inside of his collar. And looked straight up through his spectacles. Someone crossed the room, stood back of Mrs. Pickens, murmured in her ear: "General Cooper was born in New York."

Sudden silence.

Dined with General Cooper at the Prestons. General Hampton and Blanton Duncan[7] were there also. The latter a thoroughly free and easy western man—handsome and clever. More audacious than either, perhaps. He pointed to Buck. "What's that girl laughing at?"

Poor child, how amazed she looked. He bade them not despair. All nice young men would not be killed in the war. There would be a few left. For himself, he could give them no hope. Mrs. Duncan was uncommonly healthy.

She is also lovely. We have seen her.

General Cooper, recovered from that cold blast from the North, was quite genial in that atmosphere. He forgot to snuggle his neck into his cravat. He has been in Carolina before, on a visit to General Sumter. High Hills of Santee. So he has seen the very prettiest part of our country. Also he thinks Statesburg would in case of invasion be a safe place—he found it almost inaccessible, from the necessity of crossing those Santee swamps.

Dr. Berrien repeated something after the same fashion of Blanton Duncan's consolation.

"Sam Cooper says: 'Let us wait awhile, be in no hurry. Those fine fellows down there, see how they are being killed and cut up. Arms and legs flying right and left. Now the young surgeons who have taken care of their well-made bodies—preserved them free from harm—will bring a good price after the war.'"

"And you did not see he was insulting you?"

Mem Cohen[8] dreads the overwhelmingly pious Mrs. Young—the Reverend, she is called. Mrs. Bartow refused her offer of united prayer. Seems Mrs. B prayed on her own hook.

"I am a Jewess, and she will want to convert me. That kind always do. Now, you despise a Jew in your heart. Don't answer—I know you do. You like me, but that is in spite of my being one. We are a stiff-necked race. Let us stick to the father of Abraham and Isaac, for shabby as a Jew is in your eyes, he is a miracle of respectability, compared with a *converted Jew*. That is the very lowest thing out."[9]

A member of the company bragged of a wounded son—a wound was an honor now.

7. A Louisville, Ky., lawyer who was in Columbia as an engraver of bank notes for the Confederacy.

8. Miriam (DeLeon) Cohen was the widow of Dr. Lawrence Cohen and a first cousin of David Camden and Agnes DeLeon.

9. Mem Cohen's aunt, Henrietta DeLeon, had converted to Christianity.

These women never know when to let *well* alone.

"Where and how was your gallant son wounded?"

"As he galloped along, his foot caught in a tree—he was dragged from his horse, &c&c&c."

"A tree cannot inflict an honorable wound."

"Why?"

March 24, 1862.   I was asked to the Tognos' tea, so refused a drive with Mary P as I sat at my solitary casemate, waiting for the time to come for the Tognos'.

Saw Mrs. Preston's landau pass. Mr. Venable making Mary laugh at some of his army stories, as only Mr. Venable can.

Already I felt that I had paid too much for my whistle, that is, the Togno tea.

The Gibbeses and Trenholms,[1] Edmund Rhett, &c there. The latter has very fine eyes. He makes fearful play with them. He sits silent and motionless, with his hands on his knees, his head bent forward, and his eyes fixed upon you. I could think of nothing like it but a setter setting a covey of partridges.

On President Davis he sunk into a lower depth of abuse than even Gonzales. I quoted Yancey to him. "A crew might not like their captain, but if they were mad enough to mutiny while a storm was raging, all hands were bound to go to the bottom."

After that I contented myself with a mild shake of the head when I disagreed with him. And at last I began to shake so persistently it amounted to incipient palsy.

"Jeff Davis is conceited, wrongheaded, wranglesome, obstinate, a traitor—"

"Now I have borne much in silence, but that is pernicious nonsense. Do not let us waste any more time listening to your quotations from the *Mercury*."

He very good-naturedly changed the subject—which was easy just then, for a delicious supper was on the table, ready for us. But Dr. Gibbes began anew fighting and "the old blunderbuss," Madame T called him, he gave me some pâté, not foie gras, said Madame, [but] perdreaux. Dr. Gibbes, however, gave it a flavor of his own. "Eat it, it is good for you, rich and wholesome, healthy as cod-liver oil."

We had charming music—both vocal and instrumental—from Torriani[2] and the young Tognos.[3]

Altogether it was a very agreeable evening. Everybody clever and accomplished—if we did not all think alike. Even the Blunderbuss is more than average clever in his mistakes.

Unlucky Nathan. Engaged, that is, off and on to one beloved object for

---

1. Charleston merchant and banker George Alfred Trenholm and his wife Anna (Holmes) Trenholm. The Liverpool branch of Trenholm's firm acted as a front for the Confederate government in the purchase of English weapons, ships, and ammunition.

2. Eugenio Torriani, an Italian opera singer stranded in the South when the war began.

3. Madame Togno's daughters, Ascelie and Elize.

twenty years or more—&c&c. The Turkey fiasco, &c&c.[4] Today he hobbled up in the corridor, trying to retain upon his feet a [pair] of forlorn old slippers a mile too big for him. He had put his boots out at his door to be blacked. And they were stolen—an irremediable loss in the Confederacy—even when one has money to buy anything.

Of course he treated it as a bad joke.

Edmund Rhett held me responsible for all misunderstandings.

Miles announces a bill for appointing a generalissimo for the army, which bill, Mr. Miles adds, has the president's approbation.

The president vetoes it. Explain that, if you can?

"I know nothing. It is all these horrid newspaper men," I cry in despair.

A queer thing happened. A man saw a small boy open the box of the governor and council at the post office with a key, then take the contents of the box and run for his life. Of course this man called to the urchin to stop, which he did not, but seeing himself pursued and about to be overtaken, he began tearing up the letters and papers. He was caught and the fragments were picked up. Finding himself taken prisoner, he showed them the negro who gave him the key to open the box. The negro was arrested.

How reluctantly J. C. moved to Mrs. McMahon's.[5]

Mr. Preston said, "All lodgers are alike."

Governor Pickens called to see me today. We began with Fort Sumter. For one hour did we hammer at that fortress. We took it gun by gun. He was very pleasant and friendly in his manner.

J. C. has been so nice this winter, so reasonable and considerate—that is, for a man. The night I came from Mme Togno's, instead of making a row about the lateness of the hour, he said he was "so wide awake and so hungry." So I put on my dressing gown and scrambled some eggs &c&c, there on our own fire. And with our feet on the fender and the small supper table between us, we enjoyed the supper and a glorious gossip. Rather a pleasant state of things, when one's own husband is in a good humor and cleverer than all the men outside.

This afternoon the entente cordiale still subsisting. Maum Mary beckoned me out mysteriously. Mr. C said: "Speak out, old woman. Nobody here but myself."

"Mars Nathum Davis wants to speak to her."

---

4. Davis may have been involved in an unsuccessful experiment in growing cotton in Turkey during 1846.

5. A Columbia boardinghouse operated by a widow, Mary McMahon.

So I hurried off to the drawing room, Maum Mary flapping her down-at-the-heels shoes in my wake.

"He's gwine bekase somebody done stole his boots. How could he stay bedout boots?" So Nathan said goodbye. Then we met General Gist. Maum Mary still hovering near, and I congratulated him on being promoted. He is now a brigadier. This he received with modest complaisance.

"I knowed he was a general," said Maum Mary, as he passed on. "He told me as soon as he got in his room befo' his boy put down his trunk!"

As Nathan the unlucky told [*word effaced*] goodbye, he said a Mr. Reid[6] from Montgomery was in the drawing room, who wanted to see me. Mr. Reid had traveled with our foreign envoy Yancey.

I was keen for news from abroad. Mr. Reid settled that summarily.

"Mr. Yancey says we need not have one jot of hope. He can bowstring Mallory for not buying arms in time. That figure of mutiny in a storm he used to a New Orleans crowd. The very best citizens wanted to depose the state government and take things in their own hands, the powers that be being inefficient.

"Western men hurrying to the front. They are bestirring themselves. In two more months we will be ready."

What could I do but laugh. "I do hope the enemy will be considerate and charitable enough to wait on us."

Sherman's roughs that he had at Port Royal??

Mr. Reid's head was turned Yancey-ward. Mr. Yancey was going to stir Richmond as he had stirred New Orleans.

Mr. Reid's calm faith in the power of Mr. Yancey's eloquence was beautiful to see. He asked for Mr. Chesnut. I went back to our rooms swelling with news like a pouter pigeon.

Mr. Chesnut: "Well! Four hours—a call from Nathan Davis of four hours!"

Men are too absurd. So I bear the honors of my forty years gallantly. I can but laugh. Mr. Nathan Davis went by the five o'clock train. It is now about six or seven—maybe eight. "I have had so many visitors. Mr. Reid of Alabama is asking for you out there."

He went forth without a word. I doubt if he went to see Mr. Reid. My laughter made him so angry.

At last Lincolnton [*sic*] has issued a proclamation abolishing slavery—here, in the free Southern Confederacy. And they say McClellan is deposed.[7] They want more fighting, I mean the government, whose skins are safe. They want more fighting—and trust to luck for the skill of the new generals.

We have turned over Pensacola and Mobile to raw troops. Anderson and

6. Probably Samuel Gersham Reid, editor and part owner of the Montgomery *Advertiser*.

7. In a message to Congress on March 6, Lincoln urged the adoption of a resolution offering Federal financial aid to any state which chose to emancipate its slaves. Five days later, Lincoln's War Order No. 3 removed McClellan as general in chief but retained him at the head of the Army of the Potomac. Henceforth, the president assumed overall direction of the Union armies.

Villepigue commanding, both South Carolina men trained at West Point.[8] Governor Shorter[9] thinks they can hold them. Yancey says the Yankees have laid in a supply of powder and shot—arms &c&c for a ten-years' war.

I did leave with regret Maum Mary. She was such a good, well-informed old thing. My Molly, though perfection otherwise, does not receive the confidential communications of new-made generals at the earliest moment. She is of very limited military information. Maum Mary was the comfort of my life. She saved me from all trouble, as far as she could. Seventy, if she is a day. She is spry and active as a cat, of a curiosity that knows no bounds—black and clean. Also, she knows a joke at first sight. Honest—I fancy they are ashamed to see people as careless as J. C. and myself.

One night just before we left the Congaree House, Mr. C forgot to tell some all-important thing to Governor Gist—who left on a public mission next day. So at the dawn of day he put on his dressing gown, and he went to the governor's room. He found the door unlocked and the governor fast asleep. He shook him. Half-asleep, he sprung up and threw his arms around Mr. C's neck.

"Honey, is it you?" The mistake was rapidly set right. The bewildered plenipotentiary was given his instructions. Mr. C came into my room, threw himself on the sofa, and nearly laughed himself to extinction, imitating again and again the particular tone of the governor's greeting.

At Mrs. McMahon's:

Mr. Chesnut calls Laurence "Adolphe"[1] but says he is simply perfect as a servant for him. Mary Stevens said last winter, "I thought Cousin James was the laziest man alive until I knew his man Laurence!" He will not move an inch or lift a finger for anyone but his master. Mrs. Middleton politely sent him on an errand—and he was very polite about it, too. Hours after, she saw him sitting on the fence of the front yard. "Didn't you go after all?"

"No, ma'am, I am waiting for Mars Jeems."

Mrs. Middleton calls him now "Mr. Take-it-easy."

My very last day's experience at the Congaree. I was waiting, too, for Mars Jeems in the drawing room.

A lady there declared herself the wife of an officer in Clingman's regiment.

A gentleman who seemed quite intimate with her told her all Mr. Chesnut said, thought, intended to do, wrote—and *felt*.

---

8. Bragg's transfer to Ky. left Col. John Bordenave Villepigue, a native of Camden, in command of Pensacola. On March 25, however, Villepigue was promoted to brigadier general and sent to Corinth, Miss., where Beauregard was deploying troops after the Fort Donelson disaster. Brig. Gen. Richard Heron Anderson had already joined Longstreet in Va.

9. John Gill Shorter, a member of the Provisional Confederate Congress and governor of Ala., 1861–63.

1. The dandified valet who dominates his owner, Augustine St. Clare, in *Uncle Tom's Cabin.*

I asked, "Are you certain of all these things you say of Colonel Chesnut?"

The man hardly deigned to notice my impertinent interruption—a stranger presuming to speak who had not been introduced!

After he went out, the wife of Clingman's officer suddenly was seized with an intuitive curiosity.

"Madam, will you tell me your name?"

I gave it, adding, "I daresay I showed myself an intelligent listener after my husband's affairs were under discussion."

At first I refused to give my name because it would embarrass her friend if she told him who I was.

The man was Mr. C's secretary, but I had never seen him before.

Letter from Kate. She had been up all night, preparing David's things. He had left them for the army that day. Little Serena sat up and helped her mother. They did not know they would ever see him again. Whereupon I wept—and J. C. cursed the Yankees.

Fourteen new regiments have been raised in Alabama. Mississippi is equally alive.

The pilot of the *Merrimack* No. 2[2] is here with cannon for his ship, at New Orleans. Commodore Tattnall has the command of No. 1. May the cannon and ammunition for No. 2 arrive in time.

The defining of positions laughed at today—Governor Gist mistaking Mr. C for his wife, Mr. C's secretary mistaking Mr. C's wife for an impertinent stranger, &c&c.

March 30, 1862.   Story told of Morgan.[3]

At Nashville he sat at the table d'hôte, just opposite General Buell, a Yankee commander.[4] He nearly bagged Buell and would have done so, but the tollgate keeper warned Buell in time. Next day the tollgate keeper committed suicide. At least, he was found, hanged, near his own gate, and nobody did it.

Our beauty—she is a beauty, in spite of her teeth. And her neck is too long and ever so little scraggy. Now all the harm that can be said of her appearance is over. Her eyes are blue and beautiful, her hair brown and beautiful, her nose straight and perfect, her complexion as exquisite as complexion is ever made. With those violet eyes she looks into the very souls of men. And they come down and surrender as the coon did to Captain Scott. They don't stop to parley—nor need she use firearms. Though she wears a dagger and has been known to stab a man "for scorning her mother," she gathers around her all the men who will

---

2. Probably the *Louisiana,* commanded by Capt. Charles F. McIntosh.

3. Capt. John Hunt Morgan of Ky. led a daring cavalry raid into Nashville to burn a Federal steamer on Feb. 26, the day after the Union army occupied the city.

4. Brig. Gen. Don Carlos Buell was the Union commander in Nashville.

be of use to her—that is, to her husband. She is the most loyal of wives and mothers.

April 1, 1862. Went with Mr. C to Governor Pickens's reception. Few men—but the nicest of suppers—Fair Lucy, lovely and a charming hostess.

I played whist—Judge Carroll my partner—against Mrs. Herbemont and Mr. Henry Middleton. With that card table I actually felt young. Absolutely I was comparatively young.

April 2, 1862. Pâté de fois gras and dindon aux truffes exactly suit this invalid. We dined today at the Prestons with that bill of fare. Now, at McMahon's, everything gives me headache.

Gave the girls a quantity of soldiers' flannel shirts to make. Also a string of pearls to be raffled for the gunboat fair.

Lieutenant Fairfax is here. Mr. C's establishment is preparing to mold guns &c.

A man enrolled himself "one leg short," hoping to be exempt. The next man put down his name with "both legs short."

Mrs. Sue King invited me to Madame Togno's to hear Sue herself read her new book.[5]

What a fool Congress is! Passed a bill: "free trade with everybody but a Yankee!"

Dr. Trezevant, attending Mr. C who was ill, came and found his patient gone. He could not stand the news of that last battle. Got up and dressed, weak as he was, and went forth to hear what he could for himself. The doctor was angry with me for permitting it. More angry with him for such folly. I made him listen to the distinction between feminine folly and virulent vagaries and nonsense.

He said, "He will certainly be salivated, after all that calomel, out in this damp weather."

Today the ladies in their landaus were bitterly attacked in the morning paper. Lolling back in their silks and satins. Tall footmen in livery &c&c—driving up and down the streets—the poor soldier's wives on the sidewalks.

Old story—rich and poor! My little barouche is not here, nor has J. C. any of his horses here. So "our withers are unwrung"—but then, I drive every day with Mrs. McCord and Mrs. Preston, either of whose turnout fits the bill. The governor's carriage, horses, servants, &c are splendid. Just what they ought to be. Why not? As a wealthy citizen he can afford it—even if he were not governor of the state—and a certain state and dignity of equipage required of him.

5. Probably *Gerald Gray's Wife,* published during the war in *Southern Field and Fireside* and afterward in pamphlet form.

April 14, 1862.   Our English woman read her husband's letter at breakfast. "He will be here tonight, and now my American independence has ended."

Our fair is in full blast. We keep a restaurant. Our waitresses are Mary and Sally Preston, Isabella Martin,[6] Grace Elmore.[7] There are also four nice young gentlemen waiters.

April 15, 1862.   Columbia—Mrs. McMahon's.

When our fair Lydia Languish[8] came to our table, in her quality of wife of our governor, I waited on her myself. Honor to whom honor, &c&c.

We have made bushels of money. All the world came. Last night Sue King with an infatuated Gwin ten or twelve years younger than herself—utterly upset by love and consumption. It was pitiful—poor young soldier!

Last night—a beautiful show. Cadets and schoolgirls. We had gone in person and begged a holiday for them from Captain Thomas[9] and Madame Togno.

Trescot is too clever ever to be a bore. That was proved today, for he stayed two hours. As usual Mr. C said "four." He was very surly—calls himself ex-secretary of states of the U.S. America. Now, nothing in particular—of South Carolina Confederate States of America. Then he yawned. "What a bore this war is. I wish it was ended, one way or another."

He speaks of going across the border and taking service in Mexico.

"Rubbish—not much Mexico for you," I answered. "Another patriot cause, then," he said. "I will take my family back to town, that we may all surrender together. I gave it up early in the spring."

Trescot made a face behind backs and said "Lâche!"

The enemy have flanked Beauregard at Nashville.

There is grief enough for Albert Sidney Johnston now. We begin to see what we have lost.

We were pushing them in the river when General Johnston was wounded. Beauregard (Felix?) was lying in his tent at the rear in a green sickness—melancholia—no matter the name of the malady.[1]

He was too slow to move and lost us all the advantage gained by our dead

6. Daughter of William Martin, Methodist minister of Columbia, Isabella was born June 24, 1839. As one of the group of young admirers who surrounded M. B. C. in the war years, she appears infrequently and plays a small role in the 1860s Journal. In the postwar years, however, her friendship with the older woman grew closer, and she was eventually entrusted with editing and publishing the 1880s Version. In the later version, Mary Chesnut often uses "the irrepressible" Isabella as a mouthpiece for her own views and endows her with more prominence than the original account suggests.

7. The daughter of J. C.'s widowed first cousin, Harriet Chesnut (Taylor) Elmore. Grace's father, Franklin Harper Elmore, died in 1850 shortly after replacing John C. Calhoun in the U.S. Senate.

8. A character in Richard Brinsley Sheridan's play The Rivals (1775).

9. John P. Thomas, superintendent of the Arsenal Academy in Columbia.

1. M. B. C.'s account of the battle of Shiloh, Tenn., on April 6–7, is based on an inaccurate rumor. Beauregard, still suffering from a throat operation, was in the fight and not at Nashville, which had been given up to the Union in Feb. When Johnston fell on the sixth, Beauregard took command and led the defeated Confederates south toward Corinth the next day.

hero. Without him, no head to our western army. Pulaski fallen! What more is there to fall?[2]

Trescot gave me rough truths to digest. His brains bristle like bayonets, but what a relief. Of late the sofa pillows have been downy—so pestered were we with fools suave, soft, polite, punctilious. I wonder why he hates Mrs. Davis so. Clever people usually gravitate toward her. He says people do not mind Sue King's being fast. They only talk of her flirtations and keep out of her way because she is quarrelsome.

Judge Wardlaw on his brother Judge.[3] Judge Wardlaw combines two good things: he is perfectly polite and well-bred and as cultivated, educated, and clever as the rudest genius of them all.

Of his brother on the bench he says, "I knew friend ——— always would make a fool of himself to amuse the crowd on RR cars and at tavern dinner tables. But I did not expect him to carry his buffoonery on the bench." This long talk with Judge Wardlaw was a great comfort to me. He thinks my husband is doing great service to his country in his organization of all military matters—his niter bureau, foundry, &c&c.

Mr. Middleton: "How did you settle Molly's little difficulty with Mrs. McMahon—that 'piece of her mind' that Molly gave our landlady?" "Oh, paid our way out of it, of course—and I apologized for Molly, of course."

Gladden, the hero of the Palmettos in Mexico—he is killed.[4] Shiloh has been a dreadful day to us. Last winter Stephen, my brother, had it in his power to do such a nice thing for Colonel Gladden. In the dark he heard his name. Also that he had to walk 25 miles in Alabama mud—or go on an ammunition wagon. So he introduced himself to Colonel Gladden as a South Carolinian—whom he knew only by reputation as colonel of the Palmetto Regiment in the Mexican War. And then drove him in his carriage comfortably to where he wanted to go, a night drive of fifty miles for Stephen, for he had the return trip, too.

I would gladly go to Liberia—worse, to Sahara—than to live in a country surrendered to Yankees!

Today's paper: "Died gloriously on the field of battle—Colonel Deas of Alabama." Is that our Zack?[5]

---

2. The capture of Fort Pulaski, near the entrance to Savannah harbor, on April 11, greatly strengthened the effectiveness of the Federal blockade.

3. David Lewis Wardlaw of Abbeville District, a circuit court judge and member of the secession convention. He was probably talking about Judge Withers.

4. Severely wounded in the Mexican War as a lieutenant colonel of Charleston's Palmetto Regiment, Adley Hogan Gladden moved from Columbia to New Orleans and became a member of the La. secession convention. Commissioned a brigadier general of the C.S.A. in Sept. 1861, Gladden was fatally wounded at Shiloh.

5. J. C.'s first cousin, Col. Zachariah Cantey Deas of the Twenty-second Ala. Regiment, was wounded, not killed, at Shiloh.

The *Carolinian*[6] says the conscription bill passed by Congress is fatal to our liberties as a people.

Let us be a people—"Certain and Sure," as poor Tom Boykin says—and then talk of rebelling against our home government.

Two thousand dollars we made at the fair. It is for the gunboat.

Very touching letter from Colonel C of Mulberry. Says he fails to please anybody now in his own house but his wife. The others think him in his dotage. They are tormenting him to make another will. He makes a heroic resistance. He wants his land to go to his son—but what can a poor old man do? They beset him with the cry they will be paupers: negroes are to be freed, and he has given them only negroes and bank stock. He says they are tired of waiting for dead men's shoes.

Vanity Fair once more. Can always reread Thackeray.

Mrs. Stark[7] came. Says French minister here—on his way to Richmond to recognize us.[8]

Too good to be true. Maybe she meant the French consul. No, says Mr. Middleton—minister plenipotentiary. Just landed from a ship. And his mission means all that is delightful. In regard to this glorious advent I find it pleasanter to take these ladies' word than J. C.'s, who doubts everything systematically.

Sat up all night. Read *Eothen*[9] straight through—our old Wiley and Putnam edition we bought in London, 1845.

How could I sleep? The power they are bringing to bear against our country is tremendous. Its weight may be irresistible—I dare not think of that, however.

April 21, 1862.   Have been ill. One day I dined at Mrs. Preston's—pâté de foie gras and partridges, as I like them prepared for me. I had been awfully depressed for days and could not sleep at night for anxiety, but I did not know that I was bodily ill.

6. Robert Wilson Gibbes's paper, the Columbia *Daily South Carolinian*.
7. Eliza Stark, the wife of Theodore Stark.
8. Baron Henri Mercier de l'Ostende was the French minister to Washington. Hoping to demonstrate that the Confederate government had been badly demoralized by recent Federal victories, Secretary of State Seward allowed Mercier to leave for Richmond on April 14. Mercier evidently tried, and failed, to persuade Southern leaders to allow England and France to negotiate an end to the war on the basis of reunion.
9. *Eothen; or, Traces of Travel, Brought Home from the East* (1841) was the work of English M.P. Alexander William Kinglake.

Mrs. Preston came home with me. She said emphatically, "Molly, if your mistress is worse in the night, send for me instantly." I thought it very odd.

I could not breathe if I attempted to lie down, and very soon I lost my voice. Molly raced out and sent Laurence for Dr. Trezevant. She said I had the croup. The doctor said, "Congestion of the lungs."

So here am I. Stranded—laid by the heels. Battle after battle—disaster after disaster.

Every morning's paper enough to kill a well woman [or] age a strong and hearty one.

Isabella was here. She is nothing if not funny. She says her dismay is caused by this: the man she is ordained by fate to marry (if he lives) may be killed before she knows him or before he knows *it*.

Dr. Trezevant, the kind and sensible physician, sits by my bedside hours. He comes every day and brings the latest budget of "reliable" reports. Everybody comes—and is kind. Most of all Mrs. McCord and Mrs. Preston.

Today the waters of this stagnant pool were wildly stirred.

The president telegraphed for my husband to come to Richmond. Offered him a place on his staff.

I was a joyful woman. It was a way opened by Providence from this slough of despond—this council whose counsel no one takes. To leave Pickens the 1st. It seemed we were to be lifted up anew.

But no, J. C. says, his duty is here. I have no taste for self-abnegation. I do not love to be flayed alive. I do not like endless rows of pins stuck into me in this grand court of the Great Buzzfuzz. And by Little Moses—not even out of the bullrushes yet—an infant Jew.

I wrote to Mrs. Davis "with thanks—and begging your pardon—how I want to go."

Mr. Preston agrees with me—J. C. ought to have gone. Through Mr. Chesnut the president might hear many things to the advantage of our state, &c&c&c.

Letter from Quentin Washington. That was the best tonic yet. He writes so cheerfully. We have fifty thousand men on the Peninsula, and McClellan eighty thousand. We expect that much of disparity of numbers—we can stand that.

So much that we believed is not true—McClellan has not been superseded. Also, another painful fact not so important to the rest of mankind is utterly false.

Zack Deas is ever so much alive! Not killed—not the least bit in the world.

Also Count Mercier—if he came to recognize us—has made no bow to us yet—not even touched his hat. Faites votre révérence, Monsieur. Dépêchez-vous.

XIV

"Nothing to Chronicle but Disasters"

April 22, 1862. Follies of the wise.

From Mrs. McCord today I heard some odd stories. Now Mrs. McCord is the clearest-headed, strongest-minded woman I know, and the best and the truest.

She says Dr. Trezevant believes with all his heart, with all his mind, with all his soul—in spirits. Listens with credulity to their rappings—credits every word a medium conveys to him from the spirits. So does Waddy Thompson, my father's friend.

She repeated with verbal minutia a conversation between Powers, the sculptor in Florence, and herself.[1] The old monks haunt his rooms. He has his quarters—studio, I ought to say, but we are so military now—in a dilapidated old monastery which is still peopled with cloistered ghosts. And they subject Powers to continual annoyance by persistently haunting the place. At one time they were so on a rampage—in their fury they tore off a part of Mrs. Powers's gown. They continued still, though somewhat quieter, to make signs of the cross on everybody.

April 23, 1862. April 23rd 1840 I was married, aged 17—consequently, the 31st of March, 1862, I was 39.

A little touch of the genuine lodger's stamp today.

Mrs. Middleton asked me, sitting here by my bedside, if my husband was annoyed by that newspaper attack—"Dr. Gibbes's paper, you know." Far from it. He traced it at once to the lowest source—Little Moses. And when he spoke to Moses, the miserable little traitor took refuge behind his liege lady's petticoats.

Mrs. Middleton soon departed. In rushed Mrs. McMahon, breathless with haste.

"I do hope you did not say anything to Mrs. Middleton that you did not wish the governor's wife to know, because she hardly took time to put on her bonnet before she was off and away down the street to the Pickenses."

Which is only two doors off.

"All right. If Mrs. Pickens likes that small Moses anecdote as well as I do, things will be established on a more satisfactory basis."

In utter bewilderment Mrs. McMahon left me.

I saw a wedding today from my window, which opens on Trinity Church.

---

1. American sculptor Hiram Powers lived in Italy with the aid of John S. Preston.

Nanna Shand[2] married a Dr. Wilson. Then a beautiful bevy of girls rushed into my room. Such a flutter and a chatter—"bride and bridesmaids"—they talked of nothing else.

Well! Thank heaven for a wedding. It is a charming relief from the dismal litany of our daily song.

A letter today from our octogenarian at Mulberry. His nephew Zack Deas had two horses shot under him. The old man has his growl. "That's enough for glory—and no hurt, after all."

He ends, however, with his never-failing refrain. We can't fight all the world—two and two only make four—it can't make a thousand—numbers will tell, &c—and more personal, the only moral I have ever heard him enforce, "A fool and his money soon parted." Now, as we have no money, we need not accept the insult hung out in that oft-repeated bit of wisdom.

He says he has lost half a million already in RR bonds. Bank stock. Western notes of hand. Not to speak of negroes to be freed, lands to be confiscated—for he takes the gloomiest view of all.

We are fighting Senig's [?] battle over the new gunboat's name.

Dr. Gibbes—Mrs. Pickens's knight errant (knight erran*d*, odd-jobber, says Mrs. McCord) and bodyguard in one—wants to call it Lucy Holcombe. We wanted to call it Caroline, for our old darling Mrs. Preston—but after Mrs. McCord's outburst we were mum.

No Lydia Languish for her. "No Lucy Long-tongue business for me. If we are to have a female name, let it be "she-devil," for it is the devil's own work it is built to do."

Mrs. Nott's two gallant boys unhurt. Deas and Henry. They were in the Shiloh fiasco.

Mr. Preston came. More splendid looking today, I think, than ever. Better than that, he is so very agreeable, so kind, so sensible. He is a great admirer of Mrs. McCord—and I repeated her gunboat fiat and her amazement about "the prisoners'" faultfinding.

"Did he look in Mrs. Preston's face and live—dared he look straight at her? *I* have always treated him as a poodle of the Hamptons—of the family. Whenever I saw him, he was walking on his hind legs for their amusement—or rolling off the rug to get out of the way of their feet. He keeps his poodle nature, but he has changed masters, I see."

April 26, 1862. Doleful dumps—alarm bells ringing. Telegrams say the mortar fleet has passed the forts at New Orleans.

2. A daughter of Rev. Peter J. Shand.

Mrs. Mason Smith (Eliza Huger, of my friends) badly hurt yesterday on the RR—where there was a smash-up. She is lying ill at the Manigaults.[3] The Elmore child is dead.

Down into the very depth of despair are we.

April 27, 1862. New Orleans gone—and with it the Confederacy. Are we not cut in two? That Mississippi ruins us if lost. The Confederacy done to death by the politicians. What wonder we are lost. Those wretched creatures the Congress and the legislature could never rise to the greatness of the occasion. They seem to think they were in a neighborhood squabble about precedence.

The soldiers have done their duty.

All honor to the army. Statesmen busy as bees about their own places or their personal honor—too busy to see the enemy at a distance. With a microscope they were examining their own interest or their own wrongs, forgetting the interest of the people they represent. They were concocting newspaper paragraphs to injure the government. No matter how vital, nothing—nothing—can be kept from the enemy. They must publish themselves night and day and what they are doing, or the omniscient Buncombe will forget them.

This fall of New Orleans means utter ruin to the private fortunes of the Prestons. Mr. P came from New Orleans so satisfied with Mansfield Lovell[4] and the tremendous steam rams he saw there. While in New Orleans, Burnside offered Mr. P five hundred thousand dollars, a debt due from him to Mr. P, and he refused to take it.[5] He said the money was safer in Burnside's hands than in his. And so it may prove—ugly as the outlook is now. Burnside is wide awake. He is not a man to be caught napping.

A son of Hilliard Judge.[6] A little more than twenty years ago we saw Mr. and Mrs. Judge on their bridal tour. A six-foot man has come into existence since then and grown up to this—full length, we would say. His mother married again, is now Mrs. Brooks—wants to come and live in Columbia.

Live! Death, not life, seems to be our fate now.

They have got Beauregard—no longer Felix, but the shiftless—in a cul-de-sac.

Mary Preston was saying she had asked the Hamptons how they relished the idea of being paupers.

"If the country is saved, none of us will care for that sort of thing."

Philosophical and patriotic.

Mr. C came in.

3. Eliza Carolina (Huger) Smith, widow of a rice planter, was the aunt of Mrs. Arthur Manigault.

4. A civil servant in New York City before the war, Lovell was commissioned a major general of the C.S.A. and assigned to command New Orleans in 1861.

5. John S. Preston sold his extensive La. sugar plantations to John Burnside, a New Orleans merchant, in 1857. These holdings helped make Burnside the greatest sugar planter in the state during the 1860s.

6. Hilliard M. Judge, Sr., was a Methodist minister in Camden who died in 1857.

"Conrad has been telegraphed from New Orleans that the great ironclad *Louisiana* went down at the first shot."

J. C. and Mary Preston walked off—first to the bulletin board, then to the Prestons.

April 29, 1862. Grand smash. News from New Orleans fatal to us. Met Weston[7]—he wanted to know where he could find a place of safety for two hundred negroes. I looked in his face to see if he were in earnest—then to see if he were sane.

There were a certain set of two hundred negroes that had grown to be a nuisance. Apparently all the white men of the family had felt bound to stay at home to take care of them. There are people who still believe negroes to be property. Like Noah's neighbors, who insisted that the Deluge would only be a little shower, after all.

These negroes, however, were Plowden Weston's—a totally different part of speech. He gave Enfield rifles to one company and forty thousand dollars to another.[8] He is away with our army at Corinth.

So I said, "You may rely upon [it]. Mr. C will assist you to his uttermost in finding a home for these people."

Nothing belonging to that patriotic gentleman shall come to grief, if we have to take charge of them on our own place.

Mr. C did get a place for them, as I said he would.

Another acquaintance of ours wanted his wife to go back home. They live in Charleston, and while he is in the army she could protect their property.

"Would you subject me to the horror of a captured and a sacked city?"

He answered, vacantly staring at her, "What are they?"

Afterward Mrs. Izard said Byron's "Siege of Ishamael" ought to have been given to him to read. It might have suggested a few new ideas.

Had to go to the governor's—or they would think we had hoisted the black flag.

They said we were going to be beaten—as Cortez did the Mexicans—by superior arms. Mexican bows and arrows made a poor showing in face of powder and shot. Our enemies have such superior weapons of war—we, hardly any but what we capture from them in the fray. The Saxons and the Normans were in the same plight.

War seems a game of chess—but we have an unequal number of pawns to

---

7. Probably Francis Weston, one of the wealthiest of Georgetown District's rice planters.

8. The owner of 350 slaves, Plowden Charles Jennet Weston was indeed lavish in his generosity to his regiment, the Georgetown Rifle Guards, providing not only uniforms and rifles but four slaves to clear brush and four to provide military music. In the summer of 1862, Weston purchased a farm in Fairfield District, safely away from the coast.

begin with. We had knights, kings, queens, bishops, and castles enough. But our skillful generals—whenever they cannot arrange the board to suit them exactly, they burn up everything and march away. We want them to save the *country*. They seem to think their whole duty is to destroy ships and *save* the *army*.

Lovell's dispatch set me crying.

The citizens of New Orleans say they were deserted by the army. Oh, for an hour of brave Jackson that the British turned their backs on.[9]

———————

The citizens sent word to the enemy to shell away—they did not mean to surrender.

Surely this must be that so-often-cited darkest hour before our daylight.

Last night Governor Pickens sent twice for Colonel C. He could not be found. The governor turned.

"Has he run away?"

"No. If he has, the war is over. This council is 'an exigency of the war.' While the war lasts—in spite of all I can do or say, he seems inclined to cleave to you."

Telegram from Mr. Venable, dated Camp Moore, twenty miles from New Orleans.

There is a report abroad that Jeff Davis is expected here.

Not he. He will be the last man to give up heart and hope.

Mr. Robert Barnwell wrote that he had to hang his head for South Carolina. We had not furnished our quota of the new levy—five thousand men.

Today Colonel Chesnut published his statement to show that we have sent thirteen thousand instead of the mere numbers required of us. So Mr. Barnwell can hold up his head again.

[A] pity Mrs. Governor P selected General Cooper for her communication, but facts seem to prove her theory—old Union and born Yankees are awfully unlucky statesmen and commanders for the Confederacy. In high places, they are dangerous indeed. They believe in the North in a way no true Southerner ever will. They see no shame in surrendering to Yankees. They are halfhearted clear through. Stephens as vice president—Lovell—Pemberton—Ripley.[1] A general must command the faith of his soldiers. These never will, be they ever so good and true.

Today the *Courier* pitches in, too, with the native talent which we undoubtedly possess—to think of choosing Mallory and Walker for navy and army! Whom they first make mad—"We can but feel it in this case."

Fancy our carrying the pamphlets and papers twice to Montgomery—fire

9. A play on a Scottish verse that M. B. C. quotes on p. 466.

1. Philadelphia-born John Clifford Pemberton left the U.S. Army in 1861 perhaps because his wife's family was from Va. The commander of the Department of S.C., Ga., and Fla., Pemberton had risen to the rank of major general in the C.S.A. Mansfield Lovell was born in Washington, D.C.; Roswell Ripley in Ohio; Alexander Stephens in Ga.

ships and war steamers. How they laughed at J. C.'s fad! They were never looked at except by himself—their collector.

The Congress was so busy constitution making and all that rubbish— furnishing a house afire—not running for the engine and the fire company to save the building.

Cart before the horse.

April 30, 1862.   The last day of this month of calamities. Lovell left the women and children to be shelled and took the army to a safe place. I do not understand. Why not send the women and children to the safe place and let the army stay where the fighting was to be? Armies are to save, not to be saved—at least, to be saved is not their raison d'être, exactly. If this goes on the spirit of our people will be broken.

Passage of arms:

"The up-country are a new people, it seems—the old blood of the cavaliers, &c&c—near the saltwater."

"Yes, I accept the charge. We are new, fresh, not little, nor ugly, nor dwarfed, nor pretentious, nor purblind. We are new, fresh, handsome, full grown, wealthy, accomplished, agreeable—brave as the bravest."

"Oh! Oh! I meant nobody in particular."

"Neither did I." A grave silence. Suddenly a horse laugh from a listener—in which the interlocutors joined most heartily.

One ray of comfort from Mr. Henry Marshall: "Our army of the Peninsula is fine—so good I do not think McClellan will venture to attack it." So mote it be.

May 6, 1862.   It is a painful, self-imposed task. Why write when I have nothing to chronicle but disasters? So I read instead.

First *Consuelo*, then *Colomba*. Two ends of the pole, certainly. And then a *translated* edition of *Elective Affinities*.[2]

Food enough for thought in every one of this odd assortment of books.

At the Prestons, where I am staying (because J. C. has gone to see the crabbed old father, whom he loves, and who is reported ill), I met Mars Kit. He tells us Wigfall is out on a warpath, wants them to strike for Maryland.

The president's opinion of the move not given.

Also, Mars Kit met the first lieutenant of the Kirkwoods—E. M. Boykin—says he is just the same man he was in the South Carolina College. In whatever company you may meet him, he is the pleasantest man there.

---

2. George Sand, *Consuelo* (1843); Prosper Mérimée, *Colomba* (1841); and Goethe's *Die Wahlverwandtschaften* (1809), which appeared as *Elective Affinities* in R. Dillon Boylan, trans., *Novels and Tales by Goethe* (1854).

Mr. Preston accuses me of degenerating into a boardinghouse gossip. And is answered triumphantly: "But, papa, one you love to gossip with full well."

Hampton estate has fifteen hundred negroes on Lake Washington, Mississippi. These girls talking in the language of James novels:[3]

"Neither Wade nor Preston, that splendid boy, would lay a lance in rest, or couch it—which is the right phrase for fighting?—they hate slavery as we do."

"What are they fighting for?"

"Southern rights—whatever that is—and they do not want to be understrappers forever for those nasty Yankees. They talk well enough about it, but I forget what they say. John Chesnut says: 'No use to give a reason—fellow could not stay away, you know—not well.' Johnny is not sound on the goose, either, but then, it takes four negroes to wait on him satisfactorily."

A beautiful and a deceitful minx has been to talk me over. I found her charming while she was here. Utterly forgot my opinion of her while she was beguiling me. She carried off *Elective Affinities*. Now in cold blood I think it all over. I trust her as little as ever. A mischief-making gadfly, Dr. _____, has stirred to this.

Telegram: "Repulsed the enemy at Williamsburg." Oh, if we could drive them back "to their ain countree."[4] Richmond hard pressed this day.

Mercury of today: "Jeff Davis now treats all men as if they were idiotic insects."

Mary Preston said all sisters quarreled.

No, we never quarrel. I and mine. We keep all our bitter words for our enemies. We are frank heathens. We hate our enemies and love our friends. Some people (our kind) can never make up after a quarrel—hard words once only, and all is over. To us, forgiveness is impossible. Forgiveness means calm indifference—philosophy. While love lasts, forgiveness of love's wrongs are impossible. Those dutiful wives who piously overlook, well, everything, do not care one fig for their husbands—settled that in my own mind years ago. Some people think it magnanimous to praise their enemies and to show them impartiality and justice by acknowledging the faults of their friends. I am for the simple rule, the good old plan—I praise when I love and abuse when I hate.

3. George Payne Rainsford James, a poet, historian, and British consul in Mass. and Va. in the 1850s, wrote many minor social and historical novels.

4. Retreating toward Richmond, the rear guard of Joe Johnston's army stopped McClellan only temporarily on May 5 near Williamsburg, Va. Federal troops occupied Williamsburg the next day. Two nineteenth-century Scottish airs—"Hame, Hame, Hame," by Allan Cunningham, and "Oh, Why Left I My Hame?" by Robert Gilfillan—popularized the phrase "to my ain countree."

Mary Preston translating Schiller—aloud. We are boiled up with Bulwer's translations—Mrs. Austin, Coleridge, and Carlyle—and we show her each renders the passage she is trying to make English.

In *Wallenstein*, at one point of the Max and Thelka scene, I like Carlyle best [of] all—better than Coleridge, though they say Coleridge's *Wallenstein* is the only translation in the world as good as the original.

Mrs. Bartow repeated some beautiful scraps of Uhland's which I had not heard before.[5] She is to write them for us. Oh! Peace—and a literary leisure for my old age, unbroken by care and anxiety!!

Sent to Mrs. Bartow for Uhland.

The only answer—copy of a telegram: No fighting today—armies being engaged burying their dead—Lou Bartow.

Mrs. Middleton has been busy burying her dead. That is, covering up the Herbemont Bay fiasco.

One thing too good to go unrecorded.

"Why did you marry him? Candidly answer that."

"For love." We had leaned forward to catch the answer to this astounding question. And when it came, with innocent softness and simplicity and a clear blue eye facing the enemy unflinchingly, we owned Mrs. Herbemont defeated—routed—horse, foot, and dragoons.

Was Williamsburg a victory? John Chesnut is there. They belong now to Stuart's brigade of cavalry.[6]

Quentin Washington writes that the Clays and Mallorys have taken wing for happier climes than Richmond. Safer, at any rate.

Lady today, weeping and lamenting: "How will we feel if death come or worse?" She dealt especially on the worst.

Was stupidly wanting in comprehension—preferred to be taken for a fool, to indulge her in such horrid talk.

Someone said: "Americans will never trouble women. All the horrors of war will fall on our men. It is for them I fear."

---

5. Johann Ludwig Uhland (1787–1862), German Romantic poet and folklorist.
6. The independent command of J. E. B. Stuart of Va., which had been part of Joe Johnston's rear guard at Williamsburg.

Then could have driven out delightfully—if I could have divided myself in four. The Prestons came for me. Mrs. Singleton came for me, Mrs. Ben Taylor, and finally Mrs. McCord. The same message to all—too ill to leave my bed.

Mrs. McCord came up to see for herself—found Mrs. Bartow. With such agreeable people time flew. And I forgot my aches and pains—

Mrs. Bartow brought me *Peau de chagrin*.[7]

Another sellout to the devil.

It is this giving up that kills me. Norfolk they talk of now. Why not Charleston next?

Read western letter: "Not Beauregard, but the soldiers who stopped to drink the whiskey they had captured from the enemy lost us Shiloh." Cock Robin is as dead as he ever will be now. What matters it who killed him?

May 12, 1862. Drove out with the Togno schoolgirls. Stopped at the bulletin board. John Haskell[8] read the latest news and came to the carriage to tell us. Kate W said, with that bright little smile of hers,

"What a pleasant episode, girls, to see a man so near."

So we let them take another view of mankind that night at the Christy Minstrels.

An awful squeeze.

A mournful miner sung. In song and rhyme his sweetheart Sally sent him to dig for gold in California. And then she would marry him. Returning with the gold, he found her married already. Her new flame had red hair. The refrain: "Enough to make a fellow swear—Sally with a baby—and the baby (whimpering)—with red hair." Here he wrung tears from the very dirtiest pocket handkerchief miner ever pocketed. To watch the faces of my well-brought-up boarding-school girls—no expression whatever, maybe a transient shade of disgust—so slight, scarcely perceptible.

There they sat—prim, demure, stiff. From the pursed-up lips of the one nearest me escaped the words "very improper," although the lips moved not.

My Molly will forget Lige and her babies, too. I asked her who sent me that beautiful bouquet I found on my center table. "I give to you—'twas give to me." And Molly was in a moment all wriggle-giggle blush—golden crown blushes.

A lodger's heroine told her history today a little differently from what she told it yesterday.

In her native wilds she had refused a man because he had nothing. And so had she. He was struggling for life on a miserable stipend. Her sister had tried

---

7. *La Peau de chagrin, roman philosophique* (1830–31), a volume of Balzac's *Comédie humaine.*
8. A major on the staff of Gustavus Woodson Smith, John Cheves Haskell was the brother of Alexander Cheves Haskell.

that sort of thing—married and gone to China as a missionary. She was glad enough to get back from that celestial kingdom to this terrestrial republic.

Today to the same audience she came. She evidently felt she had not pitched her key high enough yesterday. Today the man she had refused owned a splendid house in the country and a handsome one in town—carriages, horses, gold galore. And all this with the palms of her hands turned outward—did I refuse for my dearest—dear.

After her departure:

"Do we look like *marine* animals?"

"You did look, more than you ever dreamed you were looking. Tell that to the marines."

J. C. says he is very glad he went to town. Everything in Charleston so much more satisfactory than it is reported. Troops in good spirits.

It will take a lot of ironclads to take that city.

Yeadon told them he had held off—let the council alone until he found they did not mean to give his man anything. Now to look out; he intended to open his batteries—using all his guns.

Isaac Hayne said at dinner yesterday that both Beauregard and the president had a great opinion of Mr. C's natural ability for strategy and military evolution. Mr. Barnwell concurred—that is, Mr. Barnwell had been told so by the president.

"Then why did not the president offer me something better than an *aideship*."

"I heard he offered to make you a general last year—and you said you would not go over other men's shoulders until you had earned promotion. You are too hard to please."

"No—not exactly that. I was only offered a colonelcy, and Mr. Barnwell persuaded me to stick to the Senate. Then he wanted my place, and between the two stools I fell to the ground."

Mr. Middleton, slowly orating at our dull dinners, said, "Milton laid perdu until Addison unearthed [him]."[9] And then he solemnly quoted pages of Dryden.

I was on pins for an opening to match his speech with one of Mrs. Wise (née Everett): "Oh, how people had forgotten Washington—until papa talked him up so cleverly."[1]

And one of the Washington collaterals going nigh to prove Mrs. Wise's assertion: "Oh, George, that is not the distinguished name of our family. The old

9. In 1712, Joseph Addison published a series of papers on *Paradise Lost* in *The Spectator*.

1. Charlotte Brooks (Everett) Wise was the daughter of Edward Everett, former governor of Mass., U.S. minister to England, president of Harvard, secretary of state, and U.S. senator. During 1856-60, Everett delivered the same lecture on George Washington 129 times to raise money for the preservation of Mount Vernon.

family name for generations has been Lawrence." Lawrence was lying perdu, too—until George with his broad shoulders lifted him up to view.

"Oh," said Miss Matilda Middleton,[2] "old blood and good blood are not synonymous always."

Today our literary lion was on the hunt for plagiarists.

"Nothing new under the sun," said Madame Flippant, "and what are we to do but say the same things about them as they happen. Now, look what I have been reading today. A queer old flirtation—liable to misconstruction &c—Nausicaa and her maidens washing her regal father's clothes." Interruption:

"Kings were so common in those days—anyhow in the Bible. They were as cheap as South Carolina colonels or Georgia majors. Maybe it was their way of saying *squire*."

A look of scorn, and classical driveler continued.

"Nausicaa, as we were saying, washing her father's clothes, found Ulysses without any clothes at all, cast by upon their reedy shore.[3] She lent him some male apparel at his own modest request and drove back into town, with him sitting beside her. When they get near town, she bethinks her of evil tongues. A young unmarried woman cannot be too particular. So she put him out to walk. The lodgers of those days 'would talk, you know.' "

"Nothing new under the sun—you see."

"What are you laughing at, over there?"

"The way they gossiped and flirted in the time of Ulysses."

"Mrs. Pickens says the only comfort left in all this misery is a little good talk now and then," said Mrs. M, with a sigh.

"Take care," said Monsieur austerely, "that you do not talk too much."

"There is a touch of sadness or remorse in your accent."

"No—we were talking of you."

"Then I know you had a good time. How you must have enjoyed the _____
_____ _____. Well, I daresay I deserved all that you said."

Mrs. Bartow quoted, apropos of Regina's gloves:

> Wear seemly gloves: not black nor yet too light.
> And least of all the pair that once was white.
> Let the dead party where you told your loves
> Bury in peace its dead bouquets and gloves.
> Shave like a goat—if so your fancy bids,
> But be a parent—don't neglect your kids.[4]

We played whist—wasn't fair. Two were slightly deaf, and vain old souls would not put on their spectacles. Only two spoke French, and somehow a great

---

2. Susan Matilda Middleton was the niece of Henry Middleton and the daughter of Colleton District planter Oliver Hering Middleton and Susan Matilda (Chisolm) Middleton.
3. *The Odyssey*, book 6.
4. Quoted from Oliver Wendell Holmes, Sr., "A Rhymed Lesson," in *Poems* (1846).

deal of French was spoken. So they who could see and hear and understand each other in many languages won all the games. It was a poor joke—and one player at least was ashamed of it. We did not play for love.

Nor money, however.

Mrs. M, who is English: "You lost the sympathy of England when you sent Yancey, a manslayer, as your representative."

"Louis Napoleon now—the queen lets him kiss her. What is he? England's prudery and her prejudices never interfere when she really wants to do anything."

"What's the matter with the emperor Louis Napoleon?"

"Heavens—she does not know that he is a jailbird, a slayer of men, women, and children. Surely you have read an account of the coup d'état."

At one time Parliament and the London *Times* said all that and worse. Now the wind sets in another quarter. He is the guest of the nation. And the queen lets him kiss her—and more amazing, lets Prince Albert kiss Eugénie.

Mrs. M was in a rage. Her husband said: "Not a word, dear. It is a fair retort. You abused her country, you know."

May 13, 1862.   Read Beverley Tucker's *Partisan*.[5]

Just such a rosewater revolution he imagines as we fancied we were to have—and now the reality is hideous and an agony.

Read *Alton Locke*—and *Yeast*.[6]

"The merry brown hares come leaping."

The color of slaves—that is all—the misery of poverty, alike everywhere, only a person can be beaten with many stripes by his own family—his father or mother—or schoolmaster or superior officer by land or sea, or master, if he is an apprentice, *or* her husband, if she is a woman—everybody who chooses, if she be a child.

Wherever there is a cry of pain, I am on the side of the one who cries.

The Britannia-rules-the-waves joke was in this wise. We are block tin. Britannia—blocked out. Ruling the waves does not aid Britannia to bring her ware in—&c&c.

Norfolk burnt—the *Merrimack* sunk without striking a blow.

5. Nathaniel Beverley Tucker (1784–1851), political economist and professor of law at William and Mary. In 1836, Tucker's fantasy about a war to found a Southern confederacy, *The Partisan Leader; A Tale of the Future*, was published under a pseudonym. In 1861, when fantasy had become reality, the book appeared under Tucker's own name.

6. *Yeast* and *Alton Locke, Tailor and Poet: An Autobiography* (1850), both by Charles Kingsley, were novels designed to dramatize the hardships of the English poor.

Queer episode.

Mr. C had a lovely note asking him to receive the writer at his office—on business. As I write a hand exactly like his when I please, he got me to answer the note. At Mrs. Preston's, found the noble master of the house inclined to brag of some mysterious compliment. Being led on, it turned out he had an exactly similar note. Each of them had an interview, and each of them made love as best they knew how.

"We made all the love possible, as we were in duty bound"—opening his blue eyes widely and waving his carving knife.

"And you not interfering with the vested rights of two others?" said Spiteful.

"Are we not rather de trop in this comparing of notes?"

"No, there is no harm in it all—only, no fool like an old fool—that's for both of you."

Vicarious sacrifice was spoken of. The fellow who jumped into the gulf—&c. Hanging all the state officials was proposed. "Save the country that way—and spare the rank and file."

"Oh, I won't mind," said Mrs. P, radiantly young and beautiful. "Let them hang the governor, if it can save the state."

Whereupon a horselaugh. This was one of the jokes repeated as having occurred down at the state house. Mrs. P calls the governor's other wives gone before her No. 1, No. 2, &c&c.

These men say she is as clever as she is handsome.

"She put it this way: oh, hang an old husband, if that would save the country!" added Mr. P, who is verbally correct always when he repeats.

Regular rebellion against state authority in the eastern part of the state.

The best and the bravest went first. Now the lag lasts do not want to be conscripted. As officers they would gladly face the music. The few that are left are old or middle-aged, and nothing remains for them but the ranks. They hoped to reap where others had sowed—to win where they did not work. Without a murmur they sent their sons. They grumbled when asked for money but gave it. Kill a man's wife (or son), and he may brook it. Keep your hands out of his breeches pocket. Their own sacred skins they respect, but there was not a regular shriek until sacred property was touched.

This never-to-be-too-much-abused council wants to take their negroes and send them to work at the forts—hence these tears. How long before they will lay violent hands on negroes and put them in the army? The only question now: could they be induced to stand fire on our side?

Council are in bitter earnest to fortify the outpost, to prepare for the worst. And the few remaining big braves, the stay-at-homes, thought talk was to do it. At any rate, negroes were to stay and work while they overlooked them. And they are ready to cut the council's throats. For they are forced now into the army.

May 17, 1862.   Fast day—at church. And my husband respectably at my side, seated in a pew.

Then went to see old Mrs. Pinckney. She said Seward asked her, "What do you want to go south for?"

"Don't you see I am as Methuselah. I want to go and lay my bones among my own people."

They traveled with Mr. Julius Pringle.[7] After giving us samples of Mr. P's wisdom and power, she added: "I wonder Jeff Davis does not send for Jane Lynch. She would soon settle it all for him."

Things that *I have been said* to have said. Dr. Gibbes heard me make scoffing remarks derogatory to the dignity of the governor and council—or he thinks he hears me. J. C. wrote him a note that my name was to be kept out of it—indeed, he was never to mention my name again under any possible circumstances.

It was all preposterous nonsense, but it annoyed my husband amazingly. He said it was a scheme to use my chatter to his injury. He was very kind about it. He knew my style so well that he could always tell my real imprudence from what was fabricated for me. He was very kind about it.

Read a letter from Mr. Venable. He does not see how we could have made a worse mess of it than we did at New Orleans.

He could see no reason for burning either the *Louisiana* or the *Mississippi*. And the reckless, wanton waste and destruction of provisions and ammunition &c which could so easily have been saved. Even after the Yankees were in actual possession of the city, Mr. Venable was sent back in citizen's clothes and saved a great deal.

Read Milton.

See the speech of Adam to Eve in a new light. Women will not stay at home—will go out to see and be seen, even it be by the Devil himself.[8]

Very encouraging letters from Hon. Mr. Memminger and from L. Q. Washington.

They tell the same story in very different words. It amounts to this—not one foot of Virginia soil is to be given up without a bitter fight for it. We have one hundred and five thousand men in all, McClellan one hundred and ninety thousand. We can stand that disparity.

At the Prestons, Mr. Daniel Blake and his son.[9] They were all talking, and in another part of the room Mr. C had induced Sally to declaim, in French,

---

7. John Julius Izard Pringle, a Georgetown District rice planter. Jane (Lynch) Pringle, his wife, and their three sons were in Europe when the war began.

8. Probably *Paradise Lost,* book 9, in which Adam blames their trouble on Eve's willfulness and her "strange / Desire of wand'ring. . . ."

9. Born in England, Daniel Blake kept more than five hundred slaves on his plantation in St. Bartholomew's Parish, Colleton District. He had three sons.

something of Joan of Arc which she does in a manner to touch all hearts. Mr. C turned to young Blake, [who] was listening to one of the other girls chatter, and said, with his finger raised in tragic attitude, "Ecoutez." Young Blake stared at him a moment in bewilderment and then gravely got up and began turning down the gas.

Isabella said, "Ecoutez means 'put out the lights,' then." As Othello says:[1] Then put out the lights—da capo.

Footprints on the boundaries of another world—once more.

Willie Taylor, before he left home for the army, fancied one day—day, remember, not night—he saw Albert Rhett standing by his side.[2] He recoiled from the ghost in horror.

"You need not do that, Willie, you will soon be as I am."

Willie rushed into the next room to tell them what had happened and fainted. It had a very depressing effect on him. The other day he died in Virginia.

May 19, 1862.   Mary McDuffie[3] a martyr to truth. Mrs. Pickens said enthusiastically, "I think Wade Hampton the handsomest man in the world except the czar, emperor of Russia."

"Do you?" said Mary McDuffie. "I don't."

"Oh," said Mrs. Pickens, "don't be modest. I own that I think Governor Pickens very handsome."

"Do you?" said Mary, more surprised than ever. "I don't."

Canard? Young Robert Barnwell brings the very latest news from Richmond, which is: "Beauregard and Bragg have notified the authorities that they will obey no further orders of Jeff Davis." Pas vraisemblable.

May 21, 1862.   Mrs. H, being strong-minded, harangued.

She adored intellect in women. She wished to be introduced to Mrs. King, who was maligned. Now Mrs. _____ that we all know full well—she received a Yankee into her room night and day, wrote to him, exchanged photos with him. The very worst was said.

While the row was at its worst, in walks Monsieur le Mari. He takes Madame by the hand and treats her with the profoundest respect and consideration. In a moment every voice is hushed. She is invited everywhere. Every ghost of a

---

1. *Othello,* act 5, scene 2.

2. William Hayne Taylor was the son of wealthy Richland District planter Alexander Ross Taylor and Sarah Martha (Hayne) Taylor. Albert Rhett, a son of Albert Moore Rhett and Sarah Cantey (Taylor) Rhett, was Willam's first cousin. Both men were cousins of J. C.

3. Mrs. Wade Hampton III.

cloud is blown away from her. So if Mrs. King's husband had stood up to her! (Poor Henry.) This man should uphold his wife, too.

Now, I assert, the theory upon which modern society is based is all wrong. A man is supposed to confide his honor to his wife. If she misbehaves herself, his honor is tarnished. How can a man be disgraced by another person's doing what, if he did himself (that is, if he committed the same offense), he would not be hurt at all in public estimation? He would only be "a little gay"—a Sad Dog—a Lothario of a fellow—&c&c&c. If an action did not disgrace him, how could the same action by his wife disgrace her—or him?

To all of which we listened in silence. Then she bade me tell Mr. C she was ready to serve her country in any capacity. She would go in any disguise, male or female—within Yankee lines or across the Atlantic, &c.

Among other theories of hers—"Women are more dangerous to men at thirty or forty years of age than when younger."

There was a sort of dissenting murmur.

"Hear me. If a man's heart is the point upon which the attack is designed, youth is a fatal weapon."

Faint murmur: "The older the men grow, the younger they like their wives."

"That is, widowers who go courting."

"As I was saying when interrupted—if a flirtation, a war of words, is the only design, the older the women, the better."

A sigh of relief.

She complained of not being appreciated. So few persons visited her. Her reception day was Wednesday.

There is said to be an order from Butler, turning over the women of New Orleans to his soldiers![4] Then is the measure of his iniquities filled.

We thought that generals always restrained by shot or sword, if need be, the brutal soldiery.

This hideous cross-eyed beast orders his men to treat the ladies of New Orleans as women of the town. To punish them, he says, for their insolence.

Lent the Middletons *L'Homme de neige*[5] to take to Henderson, North Carolina, where they are bound. I will soon follow—to Flat Rock, which is very near there.

General McQueen came to see us. So great a friend of ours—so sympathetic. Denounces everybody. Legislature—Orr—convention—Pickens—and the rest of mankind.

4. Responding to the hostility his troops encountered from women, Benjamin F. Butler, the Federal military governor of New Orleans, issued his famous Order No. 28: ". . . when any female shall, by word, or gesture, or movement, insult or show contempt for any officer or soldier of the United States, she shall be regarded and held liable to be treated as, a woman of the town plying her vocation." This and other actions led Southerners to dub the general "Beast Butler."

5. A novel by George Sand, published in 1856.

"So Gilmore Simms saved his MSS in the Charleston fire," cried a heartless girl. "I am so sorry." "Why, you need not read his books if you don't like them."

"That is not it. In the great fire, if all his things had been burnt, there was a chance for the Southern literary phoenix rising from Simms's ashes.[6] You see it, don't you?"

We are admirers of William Gilmore Simms. Yesterday he said, "The anticonvention faction is led by an insane man (Yeadon) who is further warped aside by interested motives."

So I found Simms the novelist a sage politician likewise. We being the convention faction.

May 23, 1862.   Mem Cohen missed me. The Jewish angel. She came with healing on her wings. (She found me very ill.) That is, in her hands she bore opium.

Another old school friend, Anna Coffin, now Mrs. Guignard[7]—sent me delicious arrowroot and apricots.

Two victories for us. Mem says, "Now you will get well."

Mr. Middleton: "Grisi[8] is not a singer, merely—she is as good an actress as Rachel."

Up went both of my hands.

"Yes, Rachel is only a declaimer. She was taught by Legouvé.[9] He is an accomplished man."

"Then, for pity sake, why don't he teach somebody else?"

Jere Clemens has gone to the Yankees. How I wish all of that kind would at once take that road. The ultra Union men—the halfhearted, the half-handed, the outspoken abusers of our Confederate government—let it do what it will.

Mr. Frank Hampton asked, "Are you in for the frenzied patriotic style?"

"How?"

6. The joke is particularly apt in light of later events. After the burning of Columbia in 1865, Simms edited a paper called the Columbia Phoenix.

7. Anna Margaret (Coffin) Edwards Guignard was the second wife of James Sanders Guignard, Jr., who owned plantations in Edgefield and Lexington districts and a residence in Columbia.

8. Giulia Grisi, a famous Italian soprano.

9. Ernest-Wilfred Legouvé, French dramatist and sometime collaborator with Augustin Eugène Scribe.

"I mean, do you knit socks and join associations with lots of vulgar people? The ladies of Charleston have voted that sort of thing down. They leave it to the lower orders."

"You are under a delusion in some way—but if it is vulgar to love one's country and to be willing to do all one can for it, I am a vulgar patriot," said Mary Preston.

When those people went today—"the driveler at the dinner table," he was called—Mrs. Bartow gave us a champagne party in her rooms to celebrate our deliverance.

May 24, 1862.   The enemy are landing at Georgetown.[1] With a little more audacity, where could they not land—but we have given them such a scare they are cautious. If it be true, I hope some cool-headed white men will make the negroes save the rice for us. It is so much needed. They say it might have been done at Port Royal, with a little more energy. South Carolinians have pluck enough. But they only work by fits and starts.

There is no continuous effort. They can't be counted on for steady work. They will stop to play—to enjoy life in some shape.

Mr. C has offended Trescot mortally. He has given Wilmot DeSaussure the position Trescot asked for. So they have now Trescot's *pen* against them. And they have not made a friend of Wilmot DeSaussure, for the council is unpopular. It forces men into the ranks, and it sends negroes away from their master's plantation to work on the coast fortification.

J. C. on a high horse with me. If Wilmot DeSaussure was a proper person to make general, why should I be grumbling?

Disheartening. Two-thirds of the time of the council is taken up hearing excuse from men who do not want to go in the ranks.

Without let or hindrance Halleck is being reinforced.

Beauregard unmolested is making some fine speeches and proclamations while we were fatuously looking for him to make a tiger's spring on Huntsville.[2] Why not? Hope springs eternal in the Southern breast.

---

1. On May 22, two Federal ships based near Port Royal sailed up the Sampit River to Georgetown but made no attempt to take the undefended village.
2. Maj. Gen. Henry Wager Halleck commanded the Federal army facing Beauregard near Corinth, Miss. Beauregard, meanwhile, had issued a proclamation urging Southerners to redouble their defense of the Confederacy after the fall of New Orleans.

Mrs. Bartow's sketch [of] a militia captain, painfully in earnest—

Went into battle with his sword belted on and his walking stick in his hand, which he used to shake at and threaten any member of his awkward squad who failed to manage any military maneuver to his liking. When things began to wax hot, he would shout out in his excitement, "I'll give you five dollars for every good shot!" or "I'll break the head of every man jack who makes a bad one."

He ordered an advance, in his zeal—and the frightened little drummer beat a retreat. He flew at him in his fury, boxed his ears, shouting, "Little fool! Rascal—how dare you, coward, &c&c."

My Hebrew friend Mem Cohen has a son in the war—he is in John Chesnut's company. Cohen is a high name among Jews. It means Aaron.

She has long fits of silence and is absent-minded. If she is suddenly roused, she is apt to say, with overflowing eyes and clasped hands, "If it please God to spare his life."

Her daughter is the sweetest little thing—the son is the mother's idol.

Mrs. Cohen was Miriam DeLeon. I have known her intimately all my life.

Mrs. Bartow—the widow of Colonel Bartow who was killed at Manassas—was Miss Berrien, daughter of Judge Berrien of Georgia. She is now in one of the departments here, cutting bonds, Confederate bonds, for five hundred Confederate dollars a year—a penniless woman. Judge Carroll, her brother-in-law, has been urgent with her to come and live with them. He has a large family, and she will not be a further burden to him. In spite of all he can say, she will not forego her resolution. She will be independent. She is a resolute little woman—with the softest, silkiest voice and ways. And clever to the last point.

I think I write a plain hand easy to read. *But* I sent to Team for some things and he sent me 4 sugar-cured (home-cured) hams. Now what word of mine he mistook for hams, I wonder. At lodgers, as I am, I can but give away the hams.

This Columbia is the place for good living—pleasant people, pleasant dinners, pleasant drives.

I feel that I have put the dinners in the wrong place. They are the climax of the good things here. This is the most hospitable place in the world, and the dinners are worthy of it.

Miss Gracia Bay[3]—called "scratcher," not for feminine claws of catlike ferocity nor in derision as a rhyme to her name, but for a flea anecdote unworthy of the dignity of history.

She came yesterday with almond cakes and an invitation to tea at Mrs. Herbemont's. At which house everything is in perfection. Company, music, cake, tea.

In Washington there was an endless succession of state dinners. I was kindly

------

3. A sister of Martha Davis (Bay) Herbemont.

used. I do not remember ever being condemned to two dull neighbors—one side or the other was a clever man. So I liked Washington dinners.

In Montgomery a few dinners—Mrs. Pollard's &c—but the society was not smoothed down or in shape. It was, *such as it was,* given over to balls and suppers.

In Charleston, Mr. Chesnut went to gentlemen dinners all the time. No ladies present. Flowers were sent to me. And I was taken to drive and asked to tea. There could not have been nicer suppers, more perfect of their kind than were to be found at the latter end—the winding up of those so-called teas.

In Richmond there were balls—which I did not attend—very few to which I was asked. The MacFarlands and Lyonses—all I can remember. J. C. dined out nearly every day.

But then, the breakfasts. The Virginia breakfast is a thing comme il y en peu in the world.

Always pleasant people. Indeed, I have had a good time everywhere—always clever people and people I liked. And everybody so good to me.

Here in Columbia the family dinners are the specialty. You call or they pick you up and drive home with you. "Oh, stay to dinner." And you stay gladly. They send for your husband. And he comes willingly. Then comes, apparently, a perfect dinner. You do not see how it could be improved. And they have not had time to alter things or add because of the additional guests. They have everything of the best. Silver, glass, china, table linen—damask—&c&c. And then the planters live "within themselves," as they call it. From the plantations come mutton, beef, poultry, cream, butter, eggs, fruits, and vegetables. It is easy to live here—with a cook who has been sent to the best eating house in Charleston to be trained. Old Mr. Chesnut's Romeo was apprenticed at Jones's in town. I do not know where Mrs. Preston's got his degree, but he deserves a medal.

The Middletons said of Millwood: "I am sorry you were not here when Colonel Hampton was alive. He lived en prince."

"But there is nothing changed," said Mr. Arthur Huger.[4]

And now for a document à la Stowe—

Mrs. Preston's butler William and his sister, her maid Maria. Though they are leading a pleasant life, they have had their rocks to jump over, and they have ended here, their lives in comfortable places.

In Richmond, Mrs. Preston always engaged a room next or opposite hers for

---

4. Arthur Middleton Huger, a Charleston importer, was the brother-in-law of Elizabeth (Deas) Huger and the uncle of Mrs. Arthur Manigault.

Maria. Maggie Howell and Mary Hammy were forced to hunt up a recalcitrant maid late at night. They found the maids sleeping under the roof, where it was almost impossible to stand. They were stretched out in that hot, suffocating place, like sardines in a box.

"Maria, do you know how blest you are," said Mary H, after her return to cleaner and cooler regions. "But I must say, in that stifling, low room, where our damsel was stowed away, with her likes packed as if in a box, we found them hilarious. The din was so great, we could hardly make ourselves heard," said Maggie.

Maria often smoothed a dress for me. She loved to talk—first of her nursling "Buckie." "Oh, she is the sweetest, the best, the prettiest child." Then, the glories of Miss Caroline and Mars John. Of her marital relations she was so sad and mysterious in her dark revelations—I cannot make them very clear. She was married. Her husband ill-used her—he did something very bad—that is, *very wrong*—and he left her. They were separated—then he died. She had no children. She loved Buck more than people loved their own children, and Buck loves her mammy.

Then she would go off to her family history, which indeed I had heard from Mrs. Preston when we were at the Fauquier White Sulphur.

This is not a pretty story—but Maria told it, leaving all ugly words. Her mother died when they were quite young. She belonged to a Scotchman, a doctor. After her mother's death her father married a white lady who did not like Maria and her two brothers, but she was not bad to them while her husband lived. Then the Scotchman died. And the widow found their whitey brown children in her yard a blot on the Scotchman's escutcheon. She sent them to Columbia to be sold, for they belonged to her. That was her way of clearing the horizon of a dark spot or cloud.

They were delighted to be sold, for they hated her worse than she hated them. Somebody told Miss Caroline "the pitiful story," and she told Mars John to buy them for her. William is now her butler and confidential servant. Maria was Buck's nurse, and since Buck no longer needed a nurse, Mrs. Preston's maid—or Buck's, as things chanced. William is a good man, and he could not be in a better place—Maria ditto. John is a drunken good-for-nothing, "the black sheep," says Maria. "He ain't bad when he is sober."

Before I knew the history of the Walkers (William, Maria, John), I remember a scene which took place at a ball given by Mrs. Preston while Mr. Preston was in Louisiana.

Mrs. Preston was resplendent in diamonds, point lace, velvet train, &c. There was a gentle dignity about Mrs. Preston which is very attractive, and her voice is low and sweet. And her will is iron. (I have grown devotedly attached to her.) She is an exceedingly well-informed person, but exceedingly quiet, retiring, and reserved. Indeed, her apparent gentleness almost amounts to timidity. She has a majestic figure, perfectly molded. And chiseled regularity of feature. Governor Manning said to me: "Look at Sister Caroline. Does she look as if she had the pluck of a heroine?" "How?" "A little while ago, William came to tell her that John Walker was drunk in the cellar—mad with drink—that he had a

carving knife which he was brandishing in his drunken fury and keeping
everybody from their business, because he threatened to kill anyone who dared
to go in the basement. They were like a flock of frightened sheep down there.
She did not speak to one of us but followed William down to the basement,
holding up her skirts. She found the servants scurrying everywhere, screaming
and shouting that John was crazy and going to kill them. John was bellowing
like a bull of Bashan,[5] knife in hand, chasing them at his pleasure. Mrs. Preston
walked up to him.

"'Give me that knife.'" He handed it to her. She laid it on a table.

"'And now, come with me,'" she said, putting her hand on his collar. She led
him away to the empty smokehouse. And then she locked him in and put the
key in her pocket. And she returned, without a ripple on her placid face to show
what she had done. She told me of it, smiling and serene, as you see her now."

Before the war shut him in, Mr. Preston sent to the lakes for his salmon, to
Mississippi for his venison, to England for his mutton and grouse. It is good
enough—the best dish at all of these houses what the Spanish call "the hearty
welcome." Thackeray says at every American table he was first served with
"grilled hostess." At the head of the table sat a person, fiery-faced, anxious,
nervous, inwardly murmuring, like Falstaff, "Would it were night, Hal—and all
were well."

At Mulberry the house is always filled to overflowing. And one day is curiously like another. People are coming and going—carriages driving up or
driving off. It has the air of a watering place where one does not pay and where
there are no strangers. At Christmas the china closet gives up its treasures. The
glass, china, silver, fine linen reserved for grand occasions, comes forth. As for
the dinner itself—it is only a matter of greater quantity. More turkey, more
mutton, more partridge, more fish, &c, and more solemn stiffness. Usually a
half-dozen persons unexpectedly dropping in makes no difference. They let
the housekeeper know—that is all.

Miss Mary Stark says she is a Jeff Davis man—she is thorough, she stands by
him. He is one of the institutions of her country. He is an implement of war. He
must never be allowed to fall into the hands of Yankees. If there is no alternative but his destruction or his falling into the hands of Yankees, for the first time
she will be one to blow him up. As we did the *Merrimack,* to save him from our
enemies.

People are beginning to come here from Richmond. One swallow does not
make a summer, but it shows how the wind blows. These straws do. The Sos-
nowskis,[6] Mrs. Constitution Browne, Mrs. Wise. The Gibsons[7] are at Dr.
Gibbes's. It does look squally. We are drifting on the breakers.

Mem Cohen's son writes a stirring account of the cavalry charge at

5. Psalms 22:12-13.
6. Madame Sophie Sosnowski, a widow from Germany, ran a girls' school in Columbia.
7. Dr. Charles Gibson had sent his wife Ellen and daughters Mary and Anne to Columbia,
safely away from the fighting near Richmond.

Williamsburg. Mem's eyes are wonderful to see—she laughs and weeps and reads it all to us.

"Our soldiers, thank God, are men after our own heart," cries Miriam of the house of Aaron. Mrs. Petticola—the black servant called her Caterpillar. How little it takes to make us laugh when we are dying of nervous anxiety and dread.

Mrs. Preston and I have determined. Coûte que coûte—or come what will, survive or perish—we will not go into one of the departments. We will not stand up all day at a table and cut notes apart, ordered round by a department clerk. We will live at home with our families and starve in a body. Any homework we will do. Any menial service—under the shadow of our own rooftree. Department—never!

Annie[8] had a letter from a loiterer in the Hampton garden, who witnessed the parting and exchange of photos between herself and John Haskell.

> Too late I stayed, forgive the crime,
> Unheeded flew the hours—
> For noiseless falls the foot of time
> That only falls on flowers.[9]

> —Signed, Ask all

Mr. Preston said the quotation was apt—in a note dated from a garden.

We put our trust now in Beauregard and Joe Johnston.

Magruder is to supersede Lovell (Berrien, he is on the spindle side), and Mercer takes Ripley's place.[1] On our side Yankees are unlucky, to say the least.

May 29, 1862.   Read Madame de Créquy all day—that is, at intervals.

Betsey, recalcitrant maid of the Williamses, is sold to a telegraph man. She is handsome as a mulatto ever gets to be. And clever in every kind of work. My Molly thinks her mistress very lucky in getting rid of her. She was a dangerous inmate. But she will be a good cook, a good chamber maid, a good dairy maid, a beautiful clear starcher (and the most thoroughly good-for-nothing woman I know) to her new owners, if she chooses. Molly evidently hates her but thinks it her duty to stand *by her color.*

8. Ann Fitzsimons Hampton, the eighteen-year-old daughter of Kit Hampton. M. B. C. calls her "Annie" to distinguish her from her aunt, Ann Hampton.

9. From "To the Lady Anne Hamilton" by William Robert Spencer (1769–1834).

1. Magruder did not replace Lovell as commander of the Confederate forces that had withdrawn from New Orleans to Jackson, Miss. Brig. Gen. Hugh Weedon Mercer of Ga. did replace Roswell Ripley in command of the Second Military District of S.C., but only for a few weeks.

Mrs. Gibson is a Philadelphia woman. She is true to her husband and children, but she does not believe in us—the Confederacy, I mean. She is despondent and hopeless—as wanting in faith of our ultimate success as Sally Baxter.[2]

I make allowances for those people. If I had married North, they would have a heavy handful in me just now.

Mrs. Chesnut, my mother-in-law, has only been sixty years in this country[3]—and has not changed in feeling or in taste one iota. She cannot like hominy for breakfast and rice for dinner without a relish to give it some flavor. She cannot eat watermelon and sweet potatoes sans discretion, as we do. She will not eat hot cornbread avec discrétion—and hot buttered biscuits without any.

"Richmond is obliged to fall," sighed Mrs. Gibson. "You would say so, too, if you had seen our poor soldiers."

"Poor soldiers, are you talking of Stonewall Jackson's men? Poor soldiers indeed!" I flared up.

She said her mind was fixed on one point—had ever been, though she married and came South. She never would own slaves. "Who would, that was not born to it?" I cried, more excited than ever.

She is very handsome, very clever, and has very agreeable manners.

"Dear Madame," she says, with tears in her beautiful eyes, "They have *three* armies."

"But Stonewall has routed one of them already, Heth another."[4] She only answered by an unbelieving moan. "Nothing seemed to suit her," I said, as we went away.

"You did not, certainly. You contradicted every word she said—with [some] sort of indignant protest."

We met Mrs. Hampton Gibbes[5] at the door, another Virginia woman as good as gold. They told us Mrs. Davis was delightfully situated at Raleigh. North Carolinians so loyal, so hospitable—she had not been allowed to eat a meal at the hotel.

"How different from Columbia," said Dr. Gibbes, looking at Mrs. Gibson, who has no doubt been left to take all of her meals at his house.

"Oh, no," cried Mary. "You do Columbia injustice. Mrs. Chesnut used to tell us that she was never once turned over to the tender mercies of the Congaree cuisine. And at McMahon's it is fruit, flowers, invitations to dinner every day."

After we came away: "Why did you not back me up? Why did you let them slander Columbia?"

"It was awfully awkward, but you see, it would have been worse to let Dr. Gibbes and Mrs. Gibson see how different it was—with other people."

---

2. Mrs. Frank Hampton.
3. Meaning South Carolina.
4. Stonewall Jackson defeated N. P. Banks at the battle of Winchester on May 25. Two days earlier, Brig. Gen. Henry Heth of Va. attacked Col. George Crook at Lewisburg, Va., but was repulsed.
5. Jane (Mason) Gibbes, daughter-in-law of Dr. Robert Wilson Gibbes.

Took a moonlight walk after tea. We had tea at the Halcott Greens, and all of the company did honor to the beautiful night by walking home with me.

Uncle Hamilton here—or more correctly, staying at the DeSaussures'.[6] He says, "Manassas was play, [compared] to Williamsburg." He was at both. He led a part of Stuart's cavalry in the charge at Williamsburg—riding a hundred yards ahead of his company!

Words are useless.

Col. Arthur Manigault writes to his family here: "If ever men fought, the New Orleans men will fight now." Beauregard's wife is still in N.O., and he gnashes his teeth. She will not leave a doctor who (only in the world) understands her case.

A Judge Morse told Mem the army have cold confidence but perfect confidence in Joe Johnston—but no enthusiasm. Stonewall Jackson creates a furore.

Toombs is ready for another revolution—curses freely everything Confederate, from a president down to a horse boy.

He thinks there is a conspiracy against him (Toombs) in the army. Why? Heavens and earth—why?

Let us get through with our Yankee fight first. But if you are too impatient to wait, I will waive rank and go out with you tomorrow morning.

A note in the *Courier* from Mr. Barnwell. Yeadon, without being authorized, published a private interview of his with Mr. Barnwell, including the whole conversation. Mr. Barnwell seems to think praise of Jeff Davis an injudicious thing to print now, for there is nothing else in the thing—nothing.

Dr. Berrien shows us how Magruder lisps and swears at the same time. And the combination leads [to] comical results. "Charge—and chawge fuwiously."

Mr. John Izard Middleton lost two hundred barrels of rice. His wife and daughter were nearly taken prisoners. But the negroes fled to the woods, and the overseer saved the ladies.

6. The home of William Ford DeSaussure, a wealthy attorney and brother of John McPherson DeSaussure.

XV

"Fiction Is So Flat, Comparatively"

June 2, 1862. A battle is said to be raging around Richmond.[1] I am at the Prestons'. J. C. has gone to Richmond. [*The rest of this page is cut out.*]

J. C. went off suddenly to Richmond, on business of the military department. It is always his luck to arrive in the nick of time and be present at a great battle.

Molly heard yesterday that one of her children was ill. Her mother, the best woman in the world, is given nothing else to do but take charge of Molly's children. Lige, Molly's husband, does not amount to much as an anxious parent. So Molly went off by the next train. She is to come back or stay as she pleases, for though I cannot well do without her, she would be a nuisance if she were dissatisfied. Everything depends upon the health of that child, I daresay.

Mrs. Bartow and Dr. Berrien—we had a pleasant drive. She was hard on the chivalry.

An old maumer on a plantation—South Carolina side of the Savannah— whining pathetically: "Massa Buckra. Enty, you see! we own Massa gone— obeshee gone. Everyting gone. Ain't lef' we so much as leetle dog to sic on Yankee if he come."

Scene—Dr. Berrien and Mary on the sofa between the windows—Mrs. Bartow and Mrs. Preston near the table.

"Have some Beauregard cakes with your raspberries?"

"There is fame for you—a cake named for a general."

"Can anyone separate the idea of Nesselrode from Nesselrode pudding?"

Wade Hampton shot in the foot and Johnston Pettigrew killed!

Telegraph says Lee and Davis both on the field.[2] Enemy being repulsed.

Telegraph operator: "Madam, our men are fighting."

"Of course they are—what else is there for them to do now but fight?"

---

1. The battle of Seven Pines (Fair Oaks), fought just five miles from Richmond on May 31 and June 1.

2. Pettigrew was wounded and captured, but not killed. On June 1, Robert E. Lee assumed field command of the Army of Northern Va. for the first time.

"But, Madam, the news is encouraging."
Each army burying its dead. That looks like a drawn battle.

We haunt the bulletin board.

In Saturday's *Mercury* there was a vindication of Ripley. And to do plainly, a map of all the coast and its defense were given, as not the very cleverest spy in the world without help from our headquarters could have given them to the enemy. General Ripley has now gone to Richmond. No doubt he has with him his aides Kirkland and Lowndes.[3]

Back to lodgers—Mem is ill. Her daughter Isabel warns me not to mention the battle raging around Richmond—young Cohen is in it.

She tells me her cousin Edwin DeLeon is sent by Mr. Davis on a mission to England.[4]

Mrs. Preston anxious and unhappy about her sons. John is with General Huger at Richmond. Willie in the swamps on our coast with his company.

Robert Barnwell has gone back to the hospital. Oh, that we had given our thousand dollars to the hospital and not to the gunboat.

"Stonewall Jackson's movement," the *Herald* says, "does them no harm North: it is bringing out volunteers there in great numbers." And a Philadelphia paper abused us so fervently—I felt all the blood in me rush to my head with rage.

Allen Green said, "Johnston Pettigrew was rash, I suspect."

"Could you not find a better word to use? You are speaking of a hero dead upon the field of battle."

Then he began to qualify his rash expression and to praise him. He repeated Charles Lee's insult to Washington—"That rascally virtue discretion, of which your excellency possesses so much."[5]

3. Capt. William Lennox Kirkland and Capt. Rawlins Lowndes, the twenty-four-year-old son of Charles Tidyman and Sabina (Huger) Lowndes.

4. Serving as U.S. consul general in Egypt when the war began, David Camden DeLeon's brother Edwin returned home with an Arabian horse, which he gave to Jefferson Davis.

5. Gen. Charles Lee, second in command of the Continental Army, called an unauthorized retreat at the battle of Monmouth in June 1778, and was censured by Washington. Lee demanded

Edwin DeLeon writes, "If we can only hold on till July!"

"Till he gets to England," says Mem significantly. Is that it?

June 3, 1862.   Dr. John Cheves making infernal machines in Charleston to blow the Yankees up. Pretty name they have—those machines.[6]

Yeadon will be worse than ever. The adopted son whom the council would not promote—he has been killed.[7]

My horses, the overseer says, are too poor to send over. There was corn enough on the place for two years, they said in January. Now in June they write that it will not last until the new crop comes in. Somebody is having a good time on the plantation—if it be not my poor horses.

Molly will tell me all when she comes back—and more.

Mr. Venable made an aide to Gen. Robert E. Lee. He is at Vicksburg. He writes, "When the fight is over here, I will be glad to go to Virginia." He writes in capital spirits. I notice army men all do.

Dr. Berrien said he found Fort Sumter like a gun just cleaned and loaded, leaning against the wall, ready for the fall.

At Fort Johnson he could not so much as find out who was in command there.

Miss Bay handed me a *Courier* and said, with an air of surprise, "There is no attack upon the council in it."

This ever-blooming elderly Bay blossom I answered: "Council indeed! And a life-or-death struggle going on at Richmond. Where will your *Courier* be if Richmond falls?"

I gave her a race last night. I am glad it did not kill her. We walked home together. Suddenly I remembered Mrs. Bartow's adventure—and I fled, leaving her to keep up as best she might.

---

an apology in insulting terms and was court-martialed for disobedience and disrespect. Convicted and suspended from command, he attempted to vindicate himself in a newspaper campaign so offensive to Washington that one of the commander in chief's aides fought a duel with him.

6. To protect Charleston Harbor from Union ships, the doctor, a brother of Langdon Cheves, Jr., was supervising construction of "submarine batteries"—underwater torpedo mines that could be detonated from shore.

7. A corporal in Hampton's Legion, Richard Yeadon, Jr., had been adopted by his uncle only a few months before his death at Seven Pines.

Mrs. Bartow and Dr. Berrien met Tradewell[8] dreadfully drunk the night before. They tried to evade him, but he would not let them escape. He was insolent and aggressive. He got in front of them and blocked the way. Dr. Berrien raised his stick, but Tradewell drew a pistol. So did Dr. Berrien. Mrs. Bartow threw her arms around her brother &c&c&c&c.

Telegrams from Richmond, ordering troops from Charleston. Cannot be sent, for they are attacking Charleston, too—doubtless for this very reason, to prevent reinforcements from being sent from there.

Sat down at my window—beautiful moonlight. Tried hard for pleasant thoughts.

A man began to play on the flute, with piano accompaniment. First "Ever of Thee I Am Fondly Dreaming," then "Long, Long, Weary Day." At first I found it but a complement to the beautiful scene, and it was soothing to my wrought-up nerves.

But von Weber's last waltz was too much. Suddenly I broke down. Heavens, what a bitter cry. Such floods of tears. The wonder is, there was any of me left.

I see in Richmond the women go in their carriages for the wounded, carry them home, and nurse them. One was a man too weak to hold his musket. She took it from him, put it on her shoulder, and helped the poor wounded fellow along.

If ever there was a man who could control every expression of his emotion, who can play stoic or an Indian chief, it is Colonel Chesnut. But one day when he came from the council he had to own a breakdown (or nearly). He was awfully ashamed of his weakness. There was a letter from Mrs. Gaillard, asking him to help her, and he tried to read it to the council. She wanted a permit to go on to her son, who was wounded in Virginia. He could not control his voice—and there was not a dry eye there.

Suddenly one man called out, "God bless the woman!"

Lewis Young, Johnston Pettigrew's A.D.C., says he left his chief mortally wounded on the battlefield. Left him?

Just before he went to Italy to take a hand there in their war for freedom and self-government—I met him one day at Mrs. Frank Hampton's.[9] Mr. Pettigrew,

8. Probably James D. Tradewell, a Columbia attorney.
9. The pronouns refer to Pettigrew. "In no other Southerner did romantic ideals show to greater advantage than in James Johnston Pettigrew, a young lawyer of Charleston." Clement Eaton, *Freedom of Thought in the Old South* (1941), p. 54.

Mr. Preston, and myself were the only people who dined there that day. Mr. Preston announced the engagement of the beautiful Miss W[1] to Hugh Rose. I was too annoyed to speak. In his very quick, excited way, Johnston Pettigrew asked, "Why do you say that?"

"Well, it seemed to startle you, but it is so. I have never heard it, but I saw it. In London a month or so ago, I entered Mrs. Williams's[2] drawing room—they were seated on a sofa opposite the door—"

"That amounts to nothing."

"No, not in itself, but they looked so foolish and so happy. I have noticed newly engaged people always look that way."

"But they are not?"

"I am very sorry."

"You? Why?"

"Because when I see a splendid creature like that unmarried, I think what a deal of happiness some fellow is losing."

Johnston Pettigrew was white and red in quick succession during the turn of the conversation. He was in a rage of indignation and disgust.

"I think this kind of talk a liberty with the young lady's name—and an impertinence *in us*."

Mrs. Hampton said to Mrs. Preston afterward, "They say he is in love with Miss W himself."

"Do they? Well! I hope he will stand fire under the enemy's guns better than he did a little *fun* today."

"Fun?"

I met him soon after, in the corridor of the Congaree House. I had just read that first pamphlet of his, against the slave trade.[3] And I stopped and told him how good I thought it was.

He showed his pleasure as frankly as he had shown his displeasure the day before.

I fancy him—left dying! I wonder what they feel—those who are deserted and left to die of their wounds on the battlefield. Hard lines.

----

1. Mary (Withers) Kirkland.
2. M. B. C.'s sister Kate.
3. In an essay published in *De Bow's Review* (Aug.–Sept. 1858), Pettigrew argued that proposals to reopen the slave trade ignored the "vast difference between a system of civilized and a system of barbarian slavery." The essay appeared as a pamphlet the same year.

Once long ago I went with a family in dire distress—grief for the death of a promising eldest son—to Sullivan's Island. In April we expected to find it a desert island. We counted without Fort Moultrie and the U.S. troops stationed there.

As we crossed the bay in the ferryboat, opposite to us sat Captain Vogdes and Lieutenant Silvey, not [that] we knew their names then—we only saw they were U.S. officers. And they evidently recognized the fact that on our side of the deck sat an astonishingly beautiful woman. For Miss W was a beauty. So great as to take one by surprise on first sight. Here was a new comet that the astronomers had not foretold. A beautiful girl had arisen, and there were evident perturbations in the official planetary system.

They came singly—and together. There was boating, bands of music, walks upon the beach. The solitary desert island was a delusion and a snare.

Agreeable men, clever and cultivated men, seem to spring up from the sands of the sea—among them, Johnston Pettigrew we have just accounted for. Captain, now General, Vogdes is repaying our kind hospitality by hammering away like a cooper somewhere on the outside of this poor, damaged, unhooped Confederacy.

Trescot, the very cleverest writer we have, is sulking, not in his tent like Achilles—far from it. I am sure he is in some very comfortable house.

John McCrady—where is he? He was so good-looking, so clever, we predicted a brilliant future for him. They told us he was scientific, and from the depth of our ignorance we appreciated that. Perhaps, like Professor LeConte at the niter bureau, he is doing some great work which makes a tremendous noise in the world of itself but does not mention its creator's name as it fulminates against the enemy. Lieutenant Cooper has risen in rank. Lieutenant Silvey, somebody said, was paralyzed &c&c&c.

Mrs. Pickens said, alluding to that savage attack upon the five ladies lolling in their landaus:

"Why not? General Washington attended the assembly balls and wanted everything done that could be done to amuse his soldiers and comfort and refresh them, give them new strength for the fray, when they came home for a short visit."

Comfort. Free schools are not everything. See this spelling.

Yankee epistles found in camp show how illiterate they can be, with all their boasted schools. Fredericksburg is spelled "Fretrexbug," medicine, "met-son," "to my *sweat* brother," &c&c.

"Well," said Mem, "Lieutenant Chesnut's horse bolts with him, but right into the heart of the enemy. No excuse like that man in the Crimea to make excuses that his horse bolted and took him out of the fight. Remember the sneer, 'We will not do Colonel _____'s (I forgot whose) magnificent horsemanship the injustice to say we believe him.'"

Mem gave me this scrap—one of her Jews is in it.

Isabel says when there is a battle and her brothers come out all right, Mem takes up on her Hebrew Bible and sings that glorious hymn of her namesake Miriam: "Sing ye to the Lord, for He hath triumphed, &c&c&c."

Mem is proud of her high lineage. She tells some great stories. Some man was terribly angry with his son, who had a weakness for some beautiful Jewess, swore at all Jews, and used bad language freely. Being high church and all that, he read the service for them on Sunday.

Son: "I do not want to hear anything from Isaiah or Solomon or Moses and the prophets—or Matthew, Mark, Luke, or John."

"Silence, sir—with your ribaldry."

"But, my father—you know they are only 'damned old Jews' anyhow."

Now, for the first time in my life, no book can interest me. But life is so real, so utterly earnest—fiction is so flat, comparatively. Nothing but what is going on in this distracted world of ours can arrest my attention for ten minutes at a time.

Wigfall's program—that is, *if* he had been president:

"Every afternoon, business hours over, I would walk down and stand on the pavement before the Spotswood. I would talk with all comers. How else is one to keep abreast of public opinion? It is the place to hear what all the world is saying."

It was suggested that the *Examiner* enlightened our president as to what his enemies were saying.

"No, no—that is not my idea at all. No one-sided affair. Every side. What everybody is saying. Vox populi vox dei. One might as well be in a balloon as shut up in that Brockenbrough house. Now, who dares tell the president the truth? Everybody is afraid of him."

Somebody sniggered and said, "The truth is coming in now, like the Yankee Army from Bulls Run—on horseback, on foot, by land, and by water. The very fowls of the air were bringing it."

There is the "reliable man on horseback." The president must encounter him in his rides. He has always the best of bad news in his saddlebags.

June 4, 1862.   Battles near Richmond.

Bombardment of Charleston. Beauregard said to be fighting his way out—or in.[4]

4. Beauregard was retreating south from Corinth toward Tupelo, Miss., while McClellan's army remained only a few miles from Richmond. In S.C., Federal troops sporadically shelled Stono and other islands just below Charleston.

Mrs. Gibson is here at Dr. Gibbes's. Tears are always in her eyes. Her eldest son is Willie Preston's lieutenant. They are down the coast. She owns that she has no hope at all. She was a Miss Ayre of Philadelphia. Says: "We may look for Burnside now—our troops which held him down to his iron flotilla have been withdrawn. They are three to one against us now, and they have hardly begun to put out their strength. In numbers, I mean. We have come to the end of our tether. Except we wait for the yearly crop of boys, as they grow up to the requisite age."

She would make despondent the most sanguine person alive.

They have sent for Captain Ingraham, from Charleston. In this hour of our sorest need, they want him for a court-martial. One would think that could wait. So it was with Captain Hollins.[5] They telegraphed for him. He answered that his presence was absolutely essential at New Orleans. In a few moments a peremptory reply from the secretary of the navy.

"Come on at once."

When he arrived at Richmond, they met him with the news that New Orleans had fallen. In his excitement he rushed into the executive office. And he said outright, without any reserve, "I believe if I had been there in my proper place this might not have happened." Jeff Davis buried his face in his hands.

Now, remember, I write down all that I hear, and the next day, if I hear that it is not so, then I write down the contradiction, too.

Captain Slocum[6] has not been killed. Nor has his wife been "riven her hair." Though no doubt the pearly drops of anxiety are still in her eyes. More beautiful to the *oversoul* than the glistening solitaire in each ear.

"As a general rule," says Mrs. Gibson, "government people are sanguine, but the son of one high functionary whispered to Mary G as he handed her into the cars, 'Richmond is bound to go up.' Do you know, only one doctor in Richmond will take pay from wounded soldiers. Oh, the idea now is that we are to be starved out. Shut us in—prolong the agony. It can then have but one end."

In her rage she says, "The baboon's commissary general."

"Who is the baboon? Lincoln?"

"Oh, yes. One gets very bitter, with one's eldest son under his guns. His best friends say the Yankee president is just the ugliest, most uncouth—the nastiest jokes—&c&c."

---

5. Capt. George Nicholas Hollins, commander of the Confederate Mississippi River fleet.
6. Probably Cuthbert H. Slocum, a New Orleans merchant wounded at Shiloh while serving as a quartermaster.

Governor Pickens has been telegraphed for men for Stonewall. Frémont[7] may flank him. Down here we sleep securely, with the serenest faith that Stonewall is to flank everybody and never to be flanked himself.

Mrs. Preston and I whisper. Mrs. McCord scorns whispers. She speaks out. She says: "There are our soldiers. Since the world began, there were never better, but God does not deign to send us a general worthy of them. I do not mean drill sergeants or military old maids who will not fight until everything is just so. The real ammunition of our war is faith in ourselves and enthusiasm in our cause. West Point sits down on enthusiasm—laughs it to scorn. It wants discipline.

"And now comes a new danger. These blockade-runners. They are filling their pockets, and they gird and sneer at the *fools who fight*. Don't you see? This Stonewall—how he fires the soldiers' hearts! He will be our leader—maybe—after all. They say he does not care how many are killed. His business is to save the country and not the army. He fights to win—God bless him—and he wins. If they do not want to be killed, they can stay at home. They say he leaves sick and wounded to be cared for by those whose business it is to do so. His business is war. They say he wants to hoist the black flag—have a short, sharp, decisive war and end it! Then he is a Christian soldier."

"Let us drop all talk of the merciful Christ just now."

"They say Stonewall comes down upon them like a house afire," said Miss Mary Stark.

Mrs. McCord continued, "The great Napoleon knew all about the *business* of war. He left nothing to chance and worthless understaffers. He knew every regiment, its exact numbers. Its officers, down to the least sergeant and corporal.

"Now, ask a general here for some captain or major in his command—he stares at you. He has lived up in Wigfall's balloon—high up in the air, too high up for his business."

Miriam's Mrs. McCord V.[8] The lady was more Confederate than the Confederation. She railed at that ape Lincoln—to whom she owed her devastated plantations. Lincoln's hordes—his rascals—his traitors &c&c.

And yet "spy" was whispered here and there, under the breath.

"Why?" "You see, one of the party wore green goggles and an enormous

---

7. Maj. Gen. John Charles Frémont, the western explorer and Republican presidential candidate of 1856.

8. Wilhelmina (McCord) Vernon, a journalist and secretary of the Richmond Ladies Defense Association, died in May 1862.

straw flat [hat] flapping over her face. 'Disguised,' they said. She was queer looking. No wonder they had hard thoughts of her. Then, you know—we are all crazy with suspicion, wartimes."

Miriam became acquainted with her in this way: She had a house to rent in town—and Mrs. McC. V. came to rent it. "Your maison garnie," she said, but she was too fluent and pointed out to Mem the duty of every woman to remain at her post to succor the ill and the wounded, to cheer, support, and stimulate the fainting soldier, &c&c. Mem knew she was leaving her house because she was afraid to stay. She suppressed her weakness and began to talk highfalutin back to Mrs. McC. V. That it was her duty to be near her son, who was with the Army of the Potomac &c. Here poor Mem laughed aloud—and then she cried a little.

"Many a true word spoken in jest," she said. As she saw Mem hesitate, Mrs. McC. V. offered to pay—monthly, weekly, in advance. Mem need not look to Mr. McC. V. When Mrs. McC. V. borrowed money from him, she gave him her note as she did any other man, and he dealt with her in like manner. She thought women who left their husbands and sons forfeited them to those who stayed and nursed them.

At this, Dr. Cohen,[9] whose wife had left the city, showed signs of life.

"No, sir. No, this is not for you. I have a splendid husband already and three more, ready to take his place in case of accident." Dr. Cohen leaned back, showing signs of relief.

She then related the only personal conflict she had ever engaged in.

"At my friend Fillmore's (ex-president) we met some Connecticut Yankees. On Mr. Fillmore's account I was civil. One day at Saratoga a bright-eyed Indian child inquired if they knew of her brother who was at the South. The poor ignorant Indian thought the "South" was a village.

The Connecticut Yankee said to the Indian girl: "Don't let that woman touch you. She is a nigger stealer. She whips negroes for the fun of it when she is at home."

"I struck a heroic attitude. 'Back, slanderers!—at your peril.'"

The Connecticutter did not back, however. Not a bit of it. She continued to warn the Indian child to beware of Mrs. McC. V. She even addressed the lady as a "nigger stealer."

Thereupon the much incensed Southron lost all self-control.

"I fell aboard of her and pommelled her soundly. Up rushed the husband of the creature. Coattails pigeoning in the air as he flew and fluttered—'Do you think this lady is a slave, that you beat her?'

"My hand was in, so I boxed his ears soundly. And I can tell you, the pigeon tails flew away faster than they came."

Mem protested that she used Mrs. McC. V.'s very words. Furthermore, the lady combatant averred that Governor Cobb, who was a spectator of the com-

9. Miriam Cohen's brother-in-law, Dr. Phillip Melvin Cohen of Charleston.

bat, pronounced it the neatest little fight and the most complete victory he ever saw.

Here someone said, "Was your acquaintance then put in the guardhouse?" Another interrupted, "Did you rent her your house?"

"I was completely cowed. I dared not refuse to rent her my house. That is, then—face-to-face—so I shilly-shallied—and after she left, one of my sisters-in-law asked me, 'To whom does she refer you?' 'Nobody. I was afraid to ask. I have too great a respect for my ears to rouse this boxer.'"

However, some male member of the family got Mem out of it. Mem said: "I sneaked out as best I might! Then it came out that the vigilance committee had its eyes on her—&c&c&c."

The lady, however, soon procured a house—which was closed hermetically from the time she and her party moved into it. Mrs. McC. V. was seen flitting here and there with a man in uniform. She also wrote innumerable letters of the most extravagantly patriotic type, which were always mailed in the open and aboveboard manner by the person in goggles. Of course, they were instantly pounced upon by the sagacious vigilance committee—opened and read.

The ostensible cause of the sojourn of these people in Charleston was to nurse at the hospitals.

One day the landlord received a note from Mrs. McC. V., saying she had gone for a few days to see her husband, who she heard was in Richmond; she had not seen him for fifteen months. She would be back at once. Indeed, her friend was, as the French would say, "faisant ses couches" in the house at that time and so could not leave it. The lady who was confined could not be told that her husband was killed. This was no time for grieving, so she was made to believe he had been taken prisoner.

The confiding landlord spoke of this letter from the brilliant woman to whom he had rented a house.

"Why! Your house is empty, wide open—deserted!"

So Mem screamed, "No payments—biannually, quarterly, monthly, weekly, daily, or in advance—in point of fact, no pay at all! Forgive me, I am a Jew. When people let themselves be cheated, I laugh."

So the landlord sorrowfully went to see for himself. He found on the front steps a congregation of old oyster women in tears and milkmen in arms, swearing like mad. Bread cart left in the lurch—perfect and impartial—pay-nobody style.

In Richmond again, Mem ran across her quondam would-be tenant. She held her tongue, for the lady was a "lionne." She had embroidered Mrs. Davis a point appliqué collar. ("'Point appliqué' means lace and not embroidery," interrupts one of the company.) "Oh! don't bother about nonessentials. I am not half-through," persisted Mem. "She was seen in the president's carriage. She was the president herself of all western associations—at the head of gunboat fairs, making speeches, instituting bazaars."

Miriam held her peace but watched and waited. Every day she expected to hear the magnificent lady was "over the border and awa'" wi' Jock of Hazeldean[1]—or anybody of the other side.

"When, lo—the poor soul was struck down with fever. And it was death at last with whom she made her flitting."

"Oh, Mem—what a shame! to have made us laugh like that at the poor thing—we feel so ill-used. Who could have expected such an ending? It was a farce—and all at once the tragedy sweeps in."

"I was ready for a catastrophic screaming farce—and you throw death in our faces."

"Well, in these climes and these times, that's the way it all ends. Very unexpected things come about. Now, these Yankees. They were depicted to us—held up to us in all the colors of the rainbow—marked cowards. And now, in their armies, you know, they are not acting so *very* cowardly, you know?"

"Yes, we know."

"Do you know," said a little girl, "that all the people would have it Mrs. McC. V. was a man in disguise—but Uncle H said he knew that was not true."

"Since the poor woman is dead, not another word."

June 5, 1862. Beauregard retreating—and his rear guard cut off. If Beauregard's veterans will not stand, why should we expect our newly levied reserves to do it?

Landing on John's Island and James Island—those awful Yankees![2]

Someone said we had recovered Johnston Pettigrew's body.

The Yankee general who is besieging Savannah announces his orders are to take Savannah in two weeks' time—and then proceed to erase Charleston from the face of the earth.

A man named Albert Luria, whose true name was Moses—I can understand why he changed his name: to Moses and the prophets he means no disrespect. It is the modern Moses that he did not want to be thought the tribe of.

This Luria was killed in the battle of June 1st. *Last* summer a bomb fell in the *very thick* of his company. He picked it up and threw it into the water. A bomb—put your hand on a bomb! Think of that—those of ye who love your life. The company sent the bomb to his father. Inscribed on it was "Albert Luria—bravest where all are brave." Small Isaac Hayne[3] did the same thing at Fort Moultrie.

---

1. A reference to the last two lines of Sir Walter Scott's ballad "Jock o' Hazeldean," which first appeared in Alexander Campbell, *Albyn's Anthology* (1816–18).
2. On June 2, Federal troops moved across John's Island and landed on James Island in preparation for an attack on Charleston, ten miles away.
3. The son of Attorney General Isaac Hayne.

We discussed clever women who help their husbands politically. Some men hate every man who says a good word of or to their wives. They can't be helped. Just as well. These lady politicians—if they are young and pretty—always get themselves a "little bit" talked about. Does anything pay for that? Besides, the most charitable person will think they must be a trifle too kind, to make such devoted adherents.

"I am writing to Mrs. Davis," said Mrs. Gibson.

"Dear mama," cried Mary, "do tell her how funny Columbia people are. How she will laugh!"

Mrs. Gibson frowned her down severely and tried to make an aside sign toward me.

"Oh, you need not fear me—I am only one of the 'exigencies of the war.' This is not my home. I am one of the floating population, like yourselves."

Mrs. Gibson turned upon me and said with grave dignity of manner, "I am sure I have seen nothing to laugh at in Columbia. How could I? I have been out of Dr. Gibbes's house but once, and then only to drive. It seems a charming place."

Mary turned her back to her mother and made a significant grimace to me....[4]

Reading de Créquy—but the slightest noise brings me at a bound to the window.

"There he goes, newly done up—spic and span. New rig, new hat, new alpaca coat. Old India-rubber face. I know one could squeeze it into all manner of expressions."

"How can you?"

"His face resembles the India-rubber dolls that can be done that way."

Wilmot DeSaussure telegraphs for sandbags, cannon powder, and flatboats. Powder sent—the other things not ready.

Those rude Yankees. They will not wait until we are properly prepared to receive them.

We take it easy. We love the dolce far niente. We are the true Lotos Eaters. We cannot get accustomed to be hurried about things.

This race have brains enough, but they are not active-minded. Those old revolutionary characters—Middletons, Lowndes, Rutledges,[5] Marions, Sumters—they came direct from active-minded forefathers, or they would not

---

4. Omitted is an appeal for volunteers by J. C., addressed "To the Soldiers of South Carolina not yet in Confederate Service."

5. Henry Middleton was president of the Continental Congress and his son Arthur signed the Declaration of Independence. Rawlins Lowndes succeeded John Rutledge as president of S.C. in 1778. (Later state executives were known as "governor.") Rutledge and his brother Edward served in the Continental Congress. A signer of the Declaration, Edward also helped draft the Constitution.

have been here. But two or three generations of gentlemen planters—how changed the blood became! Of late all of the active-minded men who spring to the front in our government were the immediate descendants of Scotch, or Scotch Irish. Calhoun, McDuffie,[6] Cheves. Petigru, who Huguenotted his name but could not tie up his Irish.

Our planters are nice fellows but slow to move. No—impulsive but hard to keep moving. They are wonderful for a spurt—put out all their strength and then like to rest.

Hammond's father was a Yankee. And Orr—well, he is the Rudolph Hapsburg of his race.

Last winter, how Mr. Venable worried to have pontoons made for those very rivers—and not gunboats that the Yankees were sure to take.

June 6, 1862.   Paul Hayne, the poet, has taken rooms here.[7]

J. C. came and offered to buy me a pair of horses. He says I need more exercise in the open air.

"Come now, are you providing me with the means to beat a rapid retreat? I am pretty badly equipped for marching."

Our commissary here, being *a man,* telegraphs to General DeSaussure to know of what kind of cloth sandbags ought to be made.

A woman by this time would have had half Columbia sewing night and day with their machines and the other half sending them off.

"The other half filling them with sand."

"But," said J. C., without a smile, "they will not be filled with sand until they get to the coast. There is sand enough there."

After all! Johnston Pettigrew and Lomax are alive and in a Yankee prison.[8] So says the N.Y. *Herald.*

What fun for Johnston Pettigrew to read his own splendid obituary.

"Look out!" I hear from Mem's window. "There goes 'Insensible to Fear.'"

"They called Johnston Pettigrew eccentric, crack-brained, &c&c. Why?"

---

6. The father of Wade Hampton III's second wife, George McDuffie served as a U.S. congressman, governor of S.C., and U.S. senator before his death in 1851.

7. Paul Hamilton Hayne of S.C., one of the most popular Southern poets and critics, was the author of *Poems* (1855) and *Avolio, A Legend of the Island of Cos* (1860).

8. Although Pettigrew was alive, Col. Tennent Lomax, commanding the Third Ala. at Seven Pines, had been killed.

Because he was so much in earnest. He did not waste time haranguing "Kentucky resolutions," "states rights," "cotton is king"—&c&c. That fatuous style left the talkers [looking] imbecile when the time for action came and the time for talk was over.

Someone boldly declared: If we ever have a man who will simply state the business in hand, go direct to the point at issue, and not try to enlighten the universal world by a long speech about everything else, he will be our leader. Can no man be found to spare us Madison, Jefferson, Monroe? Was Wigfall caricaturing all this when he began with Christopher Columbus? He is capable of it. You see, when Gabriel blows his horn, elect Americans will be found on a platform *speaking*.

Glory be to God, as my Irish Margaret said as an opening to all discourse—
Glory be to Him now—because they are washing the windows of Trinity Church.

Hitherto Mr. Shand has used the college chapel. During the communion service he puts the bread and wine, the consecrated body and blood, on the steps of the stage, where the students walked up and down! I am not the high church, but I felt shocked.

"Desecration! He is a good old man. I wish he would not do it! But we are going back to a genuine church."

Mrs. Rose Greenhow is in Richmond. One-half of these ungrateful Confederates say Seward sent her. J. C. says the Confederacy owes her a debt they never can pay. She warned them at Manassas. And so they got Joe Johnston and his paladins to appear upon the stage in the very nick of time. In Washington they said Lord Napier[9] left her a legacy *to* the British legation. And they accepted the gift. Unlike the British nation, who would not accept Emma Hamilton and her daughter Horatio—though they were willed to the nation by Lord Nelson.

Dreadful scene on the cars. Godard Bailey had heard that Mr. C was appointed one of the new brigadiers.

So, calling J. C. by name, he asked to be appointed one of his staff. Somebody asked J. C. who Godard Bailey was. Another man got up and told the story of that Floyd business—bonds &c&c—and denounced Godard Bailey bitterly, using the very ugliest and most exasperating epithets. Mr. Bailey drew his pistol. J. C. put his hand on it and forcibly prevented his shooting the man who

---

9. Lord Francis Napier, career diplomat and later governor of India, was the British envoy to Washington between 1857 and 1859.

had so gratuitously insulted him. Anne Sabb, his wife, said coolly, "Everybody knew Mr. Bailey came into the Confederacy under a cloud."[1]

One of our boarders here at lodgers is a German woman. She has been very ill. Dr. Fair attended her. She is still very feeble. Mem says that Dr. Fair advised her today to try and speak English—German was a very heavy language for one as weak as she was. "A very difficult language to speak," he said, turning to Mem. "She had better try French until she gains some strength—if she does not understand English. And the woman meekly responded, 'My own tongue is lighter for me.'"

Yeadon down on Mr. Barnwell, who said publishing his private conversation upholding Mr. Davis "was ill timed."

Now says Yeadon in his newspaper, "How can you think a vindication of Mr. Davis wrong at any time?"

He has him there.

And now a heavy blow! Joe Johnston, the staff upon [which] we leaned so heavily—his shoulder blade has been broken in battle.[2]

Someone said of Godard Bailey and the Floyd fuss: "Bailey is wonderfully clever and a very pleasant companion. I know, poor fellow, that he is a man to spend money and to waste it. Not one to make it. Or to *take it*."

Mem fresh from the hospital, where she went with a beautiful Jewess friend. Rachel we will call her (be it her name or not) was put to feed a very weak patient. Mem noticed what a handsome fellow he was, and how quiet and clean. She fancied by those tokens that he was a gentleman.

In performance of her duties, the lovely young nurse leaned kindly over him and held the cup to his lips. When that ceremony was over and she had wiped his mouth, to her horror she felt a pair of by no means weak arms around her neck and a kiss upon her lips—which she thought strong indeed. She did not say a word. She made no complaint. She slipped away from the hospital and hereafter she will in her hospital work fire at long range no matter how weak and weary, sick and sore, the patients may be.

---

1. In Dec. 1860, Godard Bailey, then a clerk in the Interior Department, confessed to the theft of 870,000 dollars in Indian bonds held in trust by the U.S. government. Bailey had used the bonds to prop up a firm of military contractors with which his wife's cousin, Secretary of War John B. Floyd, had dealt extensively. Both men were indicted but had their cases dismissed.

2. Johnston was severely wounded on the first day of Seven Pines.

"And," said Mem, "I thought he was a gentleman."

"Well, a gentleman is a man after all—and she ought not to have put those red lips of hers so near &c&c&c."

Joe Johnston has two ribs broken beside the shoulder-blade disaster. And now, pray, what are we do? Who will take command until he gets well?

When the ironclads attack Drewry's Bluff, then Richmond must go—so say Mrs. Gibson's letters.

At Georgetown, Captain Ward commanded a battery which could have riddled with ease the old hulks sent to capture Georgetown, but Major Emanuel forbade him to fire upon them.

June 7, 1862.   Captain Ward was so surprised, so exasperated, so mortified, tears of rage came into his eyes.

Commissary Jones told Mrs. McCord, "Each sandbag cost fifty-five cents." She answered, "You had but to put two lines in the morning paper, and every woman in Columbia would have been there with her needle and scissors—and they would have cost you nothing."

Cheves McCord's battery on the coast has three guns and one hundred men. If this battery should be captured, John's Island and James Island would be open to the enemy—and so Charleston exposed utterly.

Mrs. McCord spent the morning with me. She knew Mrs. Pickens before her marriage. At the White Sulphur several years ago Governor Pickens brought the beautiful belle Lucy Holcombe to see her. Lucy the fair was not slow and low-voiced and languid then. She was bright and fluttering. Unfortunately Mrs. McCord directed her conversation to Mr. Pickens. As they left the room, Miss Lucy Holcombe, who was not accustomed to play second fiddle or to be overlooked, was on her high horse and gave Mrs. McCord a Parthian shot.

"I came here supposing you were my friend, Mrs. Wilhelmina McCord, who is the editress of a New Orleans newspaper."

So a sidelight thrown on Mem's dark problem—Mrs. McC.V. was no man in disguise but a friend of Mrs. Governor Pickens.

Apricots, apricots. I am ill, so my friends shower apricots on me. And I am not too ill to eat them—far from it.

Mercury reduced to a half-sheet. Mrs. McCord stopped her paper when it published a map of the coast defenses in defense of Ripley. By the way, it was a false report. General Ripley is not dead. He has been given a command in Longstreet's division.

Wade Hampton writes to Mary McDuffie that Chickahominy[3] was not as decided a victory as he could have wished.

Fort Pillow and Memphis given up.[4] Next? And next?

Provost marshal in Richmond orders everyone to furnish a bed for a wounded soldier. If they are not given, they will be taken.

June 9, 1862.   Bratton, who married Miss Means, taken prisoner. Beverly Means killed, his mother-in-law a few days ago found *stone dead* in her bed. Misfortunes enough for one family, surely.[5]

When we read of the battles in India, in Italy, in the Crimea—what did we care? Only an interesting topic like any other to look for in the paper.

Now you hear of a battle with a thrill and a shudder. It has come home to us. Half the people that we know in the world are under the enemy's guns.

A telegram comes to you. And you leave it on your lap. You are pale with fright. You handle it, or dread to touch it, as you would a rattlesnake— worse—worse. A snake would only strike you. How many, many, this scrap of paper may tell you, have gone to their death.

When you meet people, sad and sorrowful is the greeting; they press your hand, tears stand in their eyes or roll down their cheeks, as they happen to have more or less self-control. They have brothers, fathers, or sons—as the case may be—in the battle. And this thing now seems never to stop. We have no breathing time given us. It cannot be so at the North, for the papers say gentlemen do not go in the ranks there. They are officers or clerks of departments, &c&c&c. Then, we see so many foreign regiments among our prisoners. Germans— Irish—Scotch. The proportion of trouble is awfully against us. Every company on the field is filled with our nearest and dearest—rank and file, common soldiers.

---

3. Seven Pines.

4. Left indefensible by Beauregard's evacuation of Corinth on May 30, Fort Pillow and Memphis on the Mississippi were surrendered to the Union in the first week of June.

5. Col. John Bratton of the Sixth S.C. Regiment, whose mother and not his wife was a member of the Means family, had been captured at Seven Pines, where his brother-in-law, Sgt. Maj. Beverly William Means of the same unit, was killed.

Miriam's story today:

A woman she knew heard her son was killed—had hardly taken in the horror of it, when they came to say it was all a mistake—mistake of name. She fell on her knees with a shout of joy. "Praise the Lord, oh, my soul!" she cried in her wild delight. The household were totally upset. The swing back of the pendulum from the scene of weeping and wailing of a few moments before was very exciting. In the midst of this hubbub, the hearse drove up with the poor boy in his metallic coffin.

Does anybody wonder so many women die? Grief and constant anxiety kill nearly as many women as men die on the battlefield. Miriam's friend is at the point of death with brain fever; the sudden changes from joy to grief were more than she could bear.

Story from New Orleans:

As some Yankees passed two boys playing in the street, one of the boys threw a handful of burnt cotton at them, saying, "I kept this for you." The other, not to be outdone, spit at the Yankees: "And *I* kept *this* for you." The Yankees marked the house. A corporal's guard came—Madame affably conversing with a friend. In vain the friend, who was a mere morning caller, protested he was not the master of the house. He was marched off to prison.

Now the Mississippi is virtually open to the Yankees. Beauregard has evacuated Corinth.

Henry Nott was killed at Shiloh. Mrs. Auzé wrote to tell us.

She had no hope. To be conquered and ruined was always her fate, strive as she might—and now she knew it would be her country through which she would be made to feel. She had had more than most women to endure—and the battle of life she had tried to fight with courage, endurance, faith. We all knew that—&c. Long years ago, when she was young, her lover died. She was to have been married, but fever came instead. Afterward she married. Then her husband died, then her only son. When New Orleans fell, her only daughter was there, and Mrs. Auzé went for her—Butler to the contrary notwithstanding—and brought her back with her.

Well may she say that she has bravely borne her burden till now.

Stonewall said, in his quaint way, "I like strong drink—so I never touch it."

May heaven, who sent him to help us, save him from all harm!

How Mr. Moise[6] got his money out of New Orleans. He went to a station with

6. Born in Charleston, Edwin Warren Moise abandoned his medical practice and moved to New Orleans where he became a lawyer, state legislator, U.S. district attorney, and, at the beginning of the war, judge of the state supreme court.

his two sons, who are still small boys. When he got there the carriage that he expected was not to be seen. He had no money about him, for he knew he would be searched. Some friend called out, "I will lend you my horse, but then you will be obliged to leave the children." This offer was accepted, and as he rode off one of the boys called out, "Papa, here is your tobacco, which you have forgot." He turned back, and his son handed him a roll of tobacco which he had held openly in his hand all the time. Mr. Moise took it, galloped off, waving his hat to them. In that roll of tobacco was encased twenty-five thousand dollars.

At the church door Mr. Preston joined me. Mary McDuffie was ill, he said. And a child of Mrs. Frank Hampton was dying.

"And now, Madame, go home, and thank God on your knees that you have no children to break your heart. Mrs. Preston and I spent the first ten years of our married life in mortal agony over ill and dying children."

"I won't do anything of the kind. Those lovely girls I see around you now— they make your happiness. They are something to thank God for—far more than anything *I have not*."

"They are nice. I do not see how I could live without them now."

Mrs. McCord has a Frenchman in her hospital so dissatisfied she thinks he is dangerous. She has taken possession of the college buildings for her hospital. "Gifts are various."[7] After my failure, illnesses, and fainting fits in Richmond, I have deemed it wise to do my hospital work from the outside. I felt humiliated at having to make this confession of weakness to Mrs. McCord.

The Paul Haynes are here, but not a member of the family have shown themselves so far. Paul Hayne himself came into the drawing room to speak to me.

J. C. traced Stonewall's triumphal career on the map. He has defeated Frémont and taken all of his cannon. Now he is after Shields.[8] The language of the telegram is vague—"Stonewall has taken *plenty* of prisoners." Plenty, no doubt of it—enough and to spare. We can't feed our own soldiers. How are we to feed prisoners?

A small fray at the Chickahominy. They tried to cross and did not make it out. They lost forty men—we lost two.

---

7. An allusion to Alexander Pope, *An Essay on Man* (1734), epistle 4, lines 67–68.

8. Jackson brought his brilliant Valley campaign to a successful conclusion by defeating Frémont at Cross Keys on June 8 and James Shields at Port Republic on the ninth.

They denounced Toombs in some Georgia paper which I saw today, for planting a full crop of cotton. They say he ought to plant provisions for the soldiers.

And now the *Guardian* must try its hand after the fashion of the *Mercury*. It calls Federal attention to Columbia in denouncing governor and council for not fortifying it. It demonstrates how easily it could be taken and shows what a rich prize it would prove if it fall into Yankee possession. We have all noticed—as soon as our newspapers point out some weak point which needs protection and have gratified their spleen by abusing men in power for not doing their duty in fortifying such a place—the Yankees quietly go there and seize the defenseless spot so indicated to them.

And now every man is in Virginia and the eastern part of South Carolina in revolt because old men and boys are ordered out as a reserve corps—and worst of all, sacred property, that is, negroes, seized and sent to work on the fortifications along the coastline. We are in a fine condition to fortify Columbia.

June 10, 1862.   General Gregg writes that Chickahominy was a victory *manqué* because Joe Johnston received a disabling wound and G. W. Smith[9] was ill. The subordinates in command had not been made acquainted with the plan of battle.

Letter from John Chesnut. He says it must be all a mistake about Hampton's wound, for he saw [him] in the field to the very last—that is, until late that night.

Hampton writes to Mary McDuffie that the ball was extracted from his foot on the field and that he was in the saddle all day. But that when he tried to take his boot off at night, his foot was so inflamed and swollen the boot had to be cut away—and the wound more troublesome than he had expected.

Mrs. Preston sent her carriage to take us to Mrs. Herbemont's. Mary Gibson calls her Mrs. Bergamot. Miss Bay came down—ever blooming, in a cap so formidable I could but laugh. It was covered with a bristling row of white satin spikes. She coyly refused to enter Mrs. Preston's carriage—"put foot into it," to use her own words—but she allowed herself to be overpersuaded.

---

9. Maj. Gen. Gustavus Woodson Smith, a veteran of the U.S. Army, briefly took command from the wounded Johnston at Seven Pines.

Mrs. McCord makes a frightful list of what her hospital needs. She has J. C.'s ear, and he does all he can for her. No wonder she is so devoted to him. Her complaints are never without cause, so he gives heed at once.

And I am so ill. Mr. Ben Taylor said to Dr. Trezevant: "Surely she is too ill to be going about. She ought to be in bed."

"She is very feeble—very nervous, as you say—but then, she is living on nervous excitement. If you shut her up she would die at once."

A prostration of the heart, I have. Sometimes it beats so feebly I am sure it has stopped altogether. Then they say I have fainted, but I never lose consciousness.

Mr. Preston and I were talking of negroes and cows. A negro, no matter how sensible he is on any other subject, can never be convinced that there is any necessity to feed a cow. "Turn 'em out, let 'em grass—grass good 'nouf for cow."

Famous news from Richmond—not so good from the coast.

Mrs. Izard said, quoting I forgot who, "If West Point could give brains as well as training!!"

Smith is under arrest for disobedience of orders—Pemberton's orders. This is the third general Pemberton has displaced within a few weeks. Ripley, Mercer, and Smith.[1]

Another boat escaped to the Yankee fleet. Whatever the Charleston press fails to communicate daily to the Yankees, a boat openly puts out to sea and tells the latest news.

Mrs. McCord again—she is as little afraid of personal responsibility as the Jacksons—Andrew or Stonewall. She wishes to remedy this state of things.

"Routine work—visiting nurses consult head nurse before they dare act. Head nurse must see the steward, and the steward must speak to the doctors. All this complicated machinery takes time. They consult among themselves and waste time. The poor wounded soldier consults nobody and dies, meanwhile."

I see one new light breaking in upon the black question.

Even my Molly speaks scornfully when she alludes to "them white people." She says there is salt enough on the plantation. Master had the [salt] sent to the coast, three days' journey—"but we don't git enough. There is plenty of bread—and all the people has fine fat hogs, but you see our people n'usen to salt as much as they choose—and now they will grumble."

1. Brig. Gen. William Duncan Smith relieved Hugh Weedon Mercer as commander of S.C.'s First Military District on June 6. Although Pemberton repeatedly ordered Smith to move decisively against the Federal forces on James Island, Smith was never placed under arrest.

When I told J. C. that Molly was full of airs since her late trip home, he made answer. "Tell her to go to the devil—she or anybody else on the plantation who is dissatisfied. Let them go. It is bother enough to feed and clothe them now."

It was a blow. When he went over to the plantation, he came back charmed with their loyalty to him—their affection for him &c&c&c.

June 11, 1862. Sixteen more Yankee regiments have landed on James Island. Eason[2] writes, "They have twice the energy and enterprise of our people."

Is answered: "Wait awhile. Let them alone until climate and mosquitoes and sand flies and dealing with negroes take it all out of them."

No doubt this is told of Pemberton because he is a Yankee born.

He has stopped the work of obstructing the harbor—and he has them busy making rat holes in the middle of the city, for men to hide in. Why? No one knows. All the cannon is on the battery—no casemates there for men to retire into.

Crimination and recrimination. Everybody's hand against everybody else. Pemberton said to have no heart in this business, so the city cannot be defended.

Stonewall is a regular brick! going all the time—winning his way wherever he goes.

Governor Pickens called to see me. His wife is in great trouble—anxiety, uncertainty. Her brother and her brothers-in-law are either killed or taken prisoners.

Mrs. Herbemont said last night that Mrs. Pickens calls his former wives No. 1, No. 2.

Parody of the matchmaking mother.

June 4, 6, 9, 11, 1862.[3]

> Have husbands now to each affixed.
> The rest have still to hunt for one,
> Except the second girl alone

---

2. Probably J. M. Eason, a privateer and contractor for the Confederate Ordnance Department.
3. M. B. C. wrote "May" but obviously intended "June."

Who has no earthly chance in five—
Till leap year gives her to counter mine.

Splendid little boy of Paul Hayne's says he is a colonel—pulls out his commission, given him by Governor Pickens, who is his cousin.

"Need not show us that," says Miriam Cohen. "All good Carolinians are entitled to take the rank of colonel if they have property enough. In Alabama, if the boat takes a hundred bales from a man's plantation, he is a colonel. Before the war it required from three hundred to a thousand bales to make him a general."

Miss Mary Stark proudly declares, "I never knew a Yankee in my life."

Molly all in tears because I asked her if she were going to turn against me.

No, she would follow me to the ends of the earth—that is, she would if it warn't for her children. But this is the reason she was out. Jonathan is her father, and he is driver, headman of the colored people (she never says "negroes"—the only "nigger" is the devil—that's her idea). Overseer and Claiborne, head of the plows, connive together to cheat master "outin everything. Marster—the best marster the lord ever send." So much lying, cheating, on a plantation—no wonder she came back outer sorts. "Overseer's wife gitten so fat on yo' substance she can't git through the little gate—have to open the wagon gate for her. Sometimes of Sundays two hams is put on their table—de 'oman sho' to die of fat."

So Molly and I are reconciled, and she is as good and as attentive as ever. All the same, she was awfully stuck up when she first came back.

Tom Taylor says Wade Hampton did not leave the field on account of his wound.

"What heroism!"

"No, what luck. He is the luckiest man alive. He'll never be killed. He was shot in the temple. That did not kill him! His soldiers believe in his luck."

Tom Taylor has a glorious beard still—but so far no commission.

General Scott on Southern soldiers. He says we have élan, courage, woodcraft, consummate horsemanship, endurance of pain equal to the Indians, but that we will not submit to discipline. We will not take care of things or husband our resources. Where we are, there is waste and destruction. If it could all be done by one wild desperate dash, we would do it. But he does not think we can stand the long blank months between the acts—waiting! We can bear pain without a murmur, but we will not submit to be bored, &c&c&c.

Now for the other side. They can wait. They can bear discipline. They can endure forever—losses in battle nothing to them, resources in men and materials of war inexhaustible. And *if they see fit* they will fight to the bitter end.

Nice prospect for us—as comforting as the old man's croak at Mulberry, "Bad times, worse coming."

Old Mr. Chesnut says, "We could not have kept slavery here a day, but the powerful government of the U.S.A. protected it for us."

"They will wear you out," said General Scott. Now Seward says, "We will starve you out."

So nobody is allowed to go out of this huge stockade, and they will not even take their prisoners away—leave them here to help eat us out, says our poetical friend.

"We are like scorpions girt by fire—&c&c&c."[4]

"Not fair play."

"Far from it."

"Everything fair in love and war."

"This is war."

"Well! We must bear the ills—as we brag of the good of our hot Southern blood."

"Misery is everywhere suffered on this terrestrial globe."

"Stop that. Tell us something new. Who denies that?" says John Green snappishly.

Mrs. McCord says, "In the hospital the better born—that is, those born in the purple, the gentry, those who are accustomed to a life of luxury—they are better patients. They endure in silence. They are hardier, stronger, tougher—less liable to break down than the sons of the soil."

"Why is that?"

"The something in man that is more than the body."

The soldier boy for me.

> He who from battle runs away
> May pray and sing, sing and pray.
> Natheless Alcaeus—how so e'er
> Dulcet his song and warm his prayer
> And true his vows of love may be
> He ne'er shall run away with *Me*.

I know how it feels to die—I have felt it again and again.

For instance. Someone calls out, "Albert Sidney Johnston is killed." My heart stands still. I feel no more. I am for so many seconds, so many minutes—I know

---

4. A reference to Byron's *The Giaour: A Fragment of a Turkish Tale* (1813), lines 422–23, 433–34.

not how long—I am utterly without sensation of any kind—dead. And then there is that great throb, that keen agony of physical pain—the works are wound up again, the ticking of the clock begins anew, and I take up the burden of life once more. Someday it will stop too long, or my feeble heart will be too worn out to make that awakening jar, and all will be over. I know not—think when the end comes that there will be any difference except the miracle of the new wind up, throb. And now good news is just as bad—"Hurrah—Stonewall has saved us!" Pleasure that is almost pain—my way of feeling it!

Miriam's Luria—and the coincidences of his life. Luria (born Moses) and the hero of the bombshell.

His mother was at a hotel in Charleston. Kind hearted Anna DeLeon Moses went for her sister-in-law, gave up her own chamber to her, that her child might be born in the comfort and privacy of a home. Only our people are given to such excessive hospitality. So little Luria was born in Anna DeLeon's chamber. After Chickahominy, when this man was mortally wounded—again Anna, who is now living in Richmond, found him, and again she brought him home—her house being crowded to the doorsteps. Again she gave up her chambers to him—and as he was born in her room, so he died.

June 12, 1862.   Yesterday I was reading Madame de Créquy. Someone came in.

"Oh! At old Creaky still. Oh! how can you at such a time!! &c&c&c. A battle raging on James Island."

Willie Preston writes, "Never you fear. We will hold James Island—our men fight so well."

J. C. was not so hopeful. He said we had supinely let them possess themselves of the best places from which to bombard and assail us. Pemberton, Pemberton—alas!

Dr. Trezevant told me something he had just heard from young Thornwell.[5]

Butler of Hampton's Legion found himself unsupported when he saw the others hold back. He said, in his coolest manner, "Then, Palmetto boys, we will do it ourselves." And the Yankees were driven out.

Mr. Preston says we will not fight on equal terms until our press is muzzled—as Seward muzzles theirs.

New England's Butler, best known to us as Beast Butler, is famous or infamous now. His amazing order to his soldier and comments on it are in every-

5. James Henley Thornwell, Jr., whose father was a noted S.C. clergyman (see p. 402, n. 8).

body's mouth. We hardly expected from Massachusetts behavior to shame a Comanche.

One happy moment in Mrs. Preston's life. I watched her face today as she read the morning papers. Willie's battery is lauded to the skies. Every paper gave him a paragraph of praise.

There was a cry of amazement and horror at the breakfast table! Followed by indignant denials of the fact.

The fact announced was this. No noted public character, no highly placed politician, could do anything so wrong as to disgrace him in this state.

"What if he goes contrary to all the prejudices of the people?"

"No. Mr. Petigru, he is as much respected as ever. Maybe his astounding pluck has raised him in the estimation of the people he flouts and contradicts in their tenderest points, but we meant moral turpitude."

"Mr. Calhoun was as pure a man, &c&c, and he was our idol."

"Oh, yes—but we are now talking of a member not quite as clever or as good as Mr. Calhoun."

"We will not call names."

"No necessity for that. State facts—and the names will attach themselves instantly in every mind."

Mr. Preston was indignant and eloquent in defense of the state.

Mrs. Preston's voice was heard in her low, distinct, tones: "Henry Junius Nott[6] said that. I have often heard him say moral obliquity was not an obstacle to a man's rise in public affairs in America."

"Did you ever see a man cut for any offense whatever?"

"Yes—cheating at cards, cowardice."

"No, not cowardice. Somebody always took his part—or the church did."

"I have seen two men only in all my life who were sent to Coventry thoroughly and deliberately—one a fine young officer in all his bravery of naval costume, traveling with a rich old harridan, at her expense, &c&c&c."

I asked why no one spoke to him—and they gave me no answer but a smile or a shrug of the shoulder. That was at Saratoga. In Washington I saw Mr. Sickles sitting alone on the benches of the Congress—House of Representatives, you know. He was as left to himself as if he had smallpox. There he sat—unfriended, melancholy, slow, solitary, sad of visage.

"What had the poor man done?"

"Killed Phil Barton Key."

"No, no. That was all right, they said. It was because he condoned his wife's profligacy and took her back."

---

6. Probably Josiah Clark Nott's brother, a noted lawyer and writer who died in a shipwreck off the N.C. coast in 1837.

They say, according to the Scripture rule, he had no right to cast a stone at her.

Chorus: "He had a perfect right to shoot down Key at sight. And the jury acquitted him."

"Unsavory subject," said Mr. P, with a sniff of disgust. "But there are Crawford,[7] Judge O'Neall,[8] Governor Perry, Mr. Petigru. They openly condemn this war—but no hand is lifted to turn them aside from any public praise or honor."

"We know they are honest. They have a right to their opinion."

"In times of war, few people have been so considerate."

"They think us wrong—they do not take sides against us—&c&c&c."

"We are awfully magnanimous—that's our weak point."

"Now, listen—here it all is in a nutshell. Men may be dishonest, immoral, cruel, black with every crime. Take care how you say so unless you are a crack shot and willing to risk your life in defense of your words. For us, soon as one defamatory word is [uttered], pistols come at once to the fore. That is South Carolina ethics."

"Takes a woman to talk wildly."

"If you have stout hearts and good family connections, you can do pretty much as you please. Old Washington, our George of Mount Vernon, and Alexander Hamilton—the Federalists, pure and simple—they thought democratic republics no great things."

"Surely you know condoning vice in high places is not peculiar to democracies."

"Let the lives of great men alone. Burr was so much worse than Hamilton, whom he killed."

"Hamilton, now—the way he put the blame on that poor woman.[9] He was worse than our father Adam. Eve was his wife—'The woman tempted me.'"

"Surely no man with the instincts of a gentleman would have written that defense of himself."

"And his wife—how she must have hung her proud head for him."

"And yet Hamilton was nearer a gentleman than most men this side of the water."

Listen to Hamlet. This is his opinion of mankind at large and himself in particular, given with much violence to Ophelia:

"I am indifferent honest. And yet I could accuse me of such things—that it

7. The pen name used by George S. Bryan (see p. 71, n. 1), one of S.C.'s leading Unionists, during the nullification debates.

8. As a member of the S.C. Court of Appeals in the 1830s, Judge John Belton O'Neall had opposed nullification. Although he served as chief justice of the state from 1859 until his death in 1863, O'Neall did not participate in the secession controversy and the disputes of the war years.

9. In 1797, a disappointed office seeker published allegations that Secretary of the Treasury Alexander Hamilton had used government money to purchase the silence of his mistress, Mrs. James Reynolds, and her husband. Hamilton countered by publishing his correspondence with the couple, implying that the pair had consciously set out to blackmail him and proving that they had failed.

were better my mother had not borne me: I am very proud, revengeful, ambitious—&c&c—What should such fellows as I do, crawling between earth and heaven. We are arrant knaves all; believe none of us."

"Shut the door on him—that he may play the fool nowhere but in's own house." Eh?

"I'll give this plague for thy dowry." (Politicians?) "Be thou chaste as ice, pure as snow. Thou shall not escape calumny—"[1]

Paul Hayne says the governor has telegraphed the president to remove Pemberton. He added that Colonel Chesnut thought we surrendered when we gave up Cole's Island.[2]

It seems the governor has asked for Beauregard in Pemberton's place.

These governors of states must be a great nuisance to the War Department.

South Carolina was at Beauregard's feet after Fort Sumter. Since Shiloh she has gotten up and looks askance, rather, when his name is mentioned.

And without Price or Beauregard, who takes charge of the western forces? Beauregard has just lost his wife. She was Mrs. Slidell's sister. Beauregard's true name is Toutant. He took this fine one from some place he owned.[3] Just now they say he is horribly depressed. In a sort of green melancholy.

And yet this is [his] second experience of wives who die.

"Can we hold out if England and France hold off?" cries Mem.

"No—our time has come."

"For shame—faint heart." Oratorically: "Our people are brave, our cause just, our spirit and our patient endurance beyond reproach, but—"

"I'll tell you what we wanted was a republic, strong, young, vigorous. What we did was to give [up], and we put in power, whenever we could, effete incapables. Worn-out old *U.S.A.* public servants."

Here came in Mary Cantey's strident voice: "I may not have any logic, any sense—I give it up. My woman's instinct tells me, all the same, slavery's turn has come. If we don't do it, they will."

What an actor Mr. Preston would have made! He has a regular genius that way. Then his wonderful voice. What a Coriolanus he would be!

After all this—tried to read *Uncle Tom*. Could not. Too sickening. A man send his little son to beat a human being tied to a tree? It is bad as Squeers beating Smike in the hack.[4] Flesh and blood revolts. You must skip that—it is too bad—or the pulling out of eyeballs in *Lear*.

---

1. Paraphrased from *Hamlet,* act 3, scene 1.

2. The island, which protected a naval access to Charleston, was abandoned on March 27, over the objections of Governor Pickens.

3. Caroline (Deslonde) Beauregard was ill in New Orleans, as M. B. C. has reported, but she did not die until the spring of 1864. Toutant was added to the Beauregard family name as the result of a seventeenth-century marriage settlement.

4. Dickens, *Nicholas Nickleby,* chapter 13.

Back to lodgers:

An old lady opposite giggled all the time. She was in a muslin print gown and diamonds.

I felt uncomfortable and wondered if there was anything amiss with me. I dressed in the dusk of the evening. Generally I hold Molly responsible that I shall not be a figure of fun. This afternoon she was not at home.

Maybe the old lady is always so. Some women are born with a constitutional titter, and it holds on till they die.

Mr. Preston's story of Joe Johnston as a boy.

A party of boys at Abingdon out on a spree—more boys than horses. So Joe Johnston rode behind John Preston, who is his cousin; while going over the mountains, tried to change horses and get behind a servant who was in charge of them all. Servant's horse kicked up, threw Joe Johnston, and broke his leg—a bone showed itself.

"Hello, boys! Come here and look—the confounded bone has come clear through," called out Joe coolly.

They had to carry him on their shoulders, relieving guard. As one party grew tired, another took him up. They knew he must suffer fearfully, but *he never said so*. He was as cool and quiet after his hurt as before. He was pretty roughly handled, but they could not help it.

His father was in a towering rage because his son's leg was to be set by a country doctor and it might be crooked in the process. At Chickahominy, brave but unlucky Joe had already eleven wounds.

XVI

"In All This Death and Destruction"

June 13, 1862. Decca's wedding—which happened last year. We were all lying on the bed or sofas near it taking it coolly as to undress. Mrs. Singleton had the floor.

They were engaged before they went up to Charlottesville. Alexander the great was on Gregg's staff—and Gregg was not hard on him. She was the worst in-love girl I ever saw.

Letters came while we were at the hospital, from Alex, urging her to let him marry her at once. In wartimes human events, life especially, was very uncertain.

For several days consecutively she cried without ceasing. Then she consented. The rooms were all crowded, so Decca and I slept together in the same room. There were so many lady nurses at the hospital. It was arranged by letter that the marriage should take place. Then a luncheon at her grandfather Minor's, and then she was to depart with Alex for a few days at Richmond. That was to be their brief slice of honeymoon.

The day came. The wedding breakfast was ready. So was the bride, in all her bridal array. No Alex! No bridegroom—alas, such is the uncertainty of a soldier's life.

The bride said nothing, but she wept like a water nymph.

At dinner she plucked up heart, and at my earnest request she was about to join us. And then the cry, "The bridegroom cometh." He brought his best man and other friends. We had a jolly dinner. "Circumstances over which he had no control had kept him away."

His father sat next to Decca and talked to her all the time as if she were married. It was a piece of absent-mindedness on his part, pure and simple, but it was very trying. And the girl had had a good deal to stand that morning—you can well understand.

Chorus: "To be ready to be married—and the man not to come! The most awful thing of *all* we can imagine."

Immediately after dinner the belated bridegroom proposed a walk. So they walked up the mountain—for a very short walk indeed. Decca upon her return said to me: "Send for Robert Barnwell. I mean to be married today."

"Impossible—no spare room in the house. No getting away from here. The trains all gone—&c&c. Don't you know, this hospital place [is] crammed to the ceiling."

"Alex says I promised to marry him today. It is not his fault he could not come before." I shook my head.

"I don't care," said the positive little thing. "I promised Alex to marry him today, and I will. Send for the Rev. Robert Barnwell."

"Jack[1] and John Darby called him the Proud Prelate."

"Oh, don't interrupt—"

We found Robert, after a world of trouble, and the bride, lovely in Swiss muslin, was married.

Then I proposed they should take another walk. Then I went to one of my sister nurses and begged her to take me in for the night, as I wished to resign my room to Mr. and Mrs. Haskell. When the bride came from her walk, she asked, "Where are they going to put me?" That was all. At daylight next day they took the train for Richmond, and the small allowance of honeymoon permitted in wartime.

Beauregard's telegram. He cannot leave the Army of the West. His health is bad. No doubt the sea breezes would restore him, but he cannot come now.

Such a lovely name—Gustave Toutant de Beauregard. But Jackson and Johnson and Smith and Jones will do—and *Lee*—short and sweet.

Ransom Spann,[2] another displaced man, came to see me—stayed several hours. All these wealthy young planters raised companies—often entirely at their own expense. Now the government, to induce the men to reenlist for the [duration?], gives them leave to choose their own captains &c. As a general rule the former captain is thrown out. He will not go down to the ranks of his own company. And he comes home to hunt another place with a commission attached. It is really very hard. These men have worked for more than a year to discipline and drill a company any man might be proud of. Then the strict martinet goes by the board. They elect a captain—a good fellow, one of themselves, one [who] will not be too strict with them.

Ransom Spann says in any case he goes straight back to the army. That sort of rough life in the open air agrees with him. He was never so well and hearty in his life.

And if the worst comes—if we fail! He has selected his vocation. He will be a highway robber—he knows the swamps.

"And there will be no danger of runaway negroes there!"

"No—that terror of swamps will be over. I am too old and too lazy to work. I mean to harry the new inhabitants who will come to replace us."

---

1. John Preston, Jr.
2. A planter from Sumter District.

"Every day," says Miriam, "they come here in shoals—*men*—to say we cannot hold Richmond, we cannot hold Charleston, much longer. Wretched beasts— why do you come here? Why don't you stay there, then, and fight? Don't you see that you own yourselves cowards by coming away in the very face of a battle? If you are not liars as to the danger, you are cowards to run away from it," roars the practical Miriam, growing more furious at each word. These Jeremiahs laugh. They think she means the others—not present company.

While Ransom Spann was here, Franklin J. Moses, father of Governor Pickens's secretary, came to see Miriam Cohen. The elder Moses' eyes are similar to Beast Butler's. They are what are commonly called badly crossed. That is the reason he is mostly neutral—he sees both ends of the way at once. Again, another Moses last night, said to be the fiancé of Isabel Cohen. A fair-haired Jew. Miss Bay, like a venerable bluejay, kept hopping in and out of her room to watch Isabel and her lover. What could they be to Miss Bay? That amused me.

What the Middletons told me of Pemberton:
He goes about, saying his mistakes are now made plain to him. He sees that he ought not to have given up Cole's Island. Our men had the worst of it on James Island. But he told them there was nothing for them to do but fight to the death. He had no way of getting them off, in case of defeat.

Tom Huger resigned his place in the U.S. Navy and come to us. The *Iroquois* was his ship in the old navy. They say as he stood in the rigging, after he was shot in the leg, his ship leading the attack upon the *Iroquois* &c&c, his old crew in the *Iroquois* cheered him. And when his body was borne in, the Federals took off their caps, in respect for his gallant conduct. When he was dying, Meta Huger said to him: "An officer wants to see you. He is one of the enemy."

"Let him come in. I have no enemies now."
But when he heard the man's name:
"No, no. I do not want to see a Southern man who is now in Lincoln's navy."
The officers of the U.S.N. attended his funeral.

Paul Hayne began with Carlyle, which led to Emerson. We were having a good time with Longfellow when Miss Bay interrupted. Whenever we are fairly underway, somebody is sure to come and turn the conversation to ——— rubbish.

Miss Bay, in honor of the presence of Paul Hayne, poet, produced this. . . .[3]

June 14, 1862. Drop a tear for Turner Ashby.[4] The hero of the Valley. They say he is killed!

3. Miss Bay's poem, and comment thereon, deleted.
4. Ashby, the businessman and farmer from Va. who, despite his lack of military experience, became Stonewall Jackson's legendary cavalry commander, died in a minor action on June 6, 1862.

All things are against us. Memphis gone—Mississippi fleet annihilated.

And we hear it all, as stolidly apathetic as if it were a story of the English war against China which happened a year or so ago.

Mrs. McCord gives her whole soul to the hospital. "The saddest confusion prevails still," she says. Insufficient medical aid. Good nurses needed. Those she hires eat and drink the things provided for the sick and wounded.

She is the woman to put it straight, with her good common sense, her great administrative ability, and her indomitable will.

As Mrs. McCord went away, Rev. Mrs. Young came.

She wants rooms here. She laid her hand on my arm and said impressively: "You know I must have a room to myself. No third person must come between me and my God."

"Stupid that I am," said the irrepressible Miriam, after she left, "I thought she wanted to be alone for her bath—until she uttered the unexpected word we Jews fear to take in vain."

Gave the poor German woman the bouquet Mrs. McCord brought me. The German in her gratitude kissed both of my hands—queer sensation, a woman kissing your hand.

The sons of Mrs. John Julius Pringle have come. They were left at school at the North. A young Huger is with them. They seem to have had adventures enough. Walked, waded, rowed in boats, if boats they could find—swam rivers when boats there were none. Brave lads. One can but admire their pluck and energy. Mrs. Fisher of Philadelphia, née Middleton,[5] gave them money to make the attempt to get home.

Matilda Middleton was hard on my friend—"Do not name him, Mrs. C. I have no patience with any man who remains two years in the enemies' country—and his own country invaded.

While the Middletons were here, our venerable Bay blossom flew in and out—popped in, popped out upon the most preposterous errands. We could hear her ask of all passers in the corridor, "Who are they?" Alas, in this house nobody could tell her.

Finally she came for Mr. C and Paul Hayne to be witness to her will.

"I drew it myself. I am a lawyer's daughter."

Mr. C said, "It is all wrong."

"What does it matter?" she said. "There is nobody to contend for my estate. I have no heirs."

"And very few of us will have any estate to contend for, I fear, before long."

---

5. Elizabeth Izard (Middleton) Fisher, an aunt of Susan Matilda Middleton, was the wife of Joshua Francis Fisher, a publicist, historian, and humanitarian reformer.

June 16, 1862. Felt suddenly ill in church. As I tried to slip by Mr. Preston unperceived, he looked up, and in his deepest tragic tones: "Shall I go with you?"

"No," I snapped, in a sharp treble.

After service they came to see why I had forsaken them. The heat was so oppressive I should certainly have fainted.

Now, they say, we are to have fighting on James Island. Pemberton has given Evans command there for five days.

Stuart's cavalry have rushed through McClellan's lines and burned five of his transports.[6]

Jackson has been reinforced by 16,000 men. And they hope the enemy will be drawn from around Richmond, and the Valley be the seat of war.

John Chesnut is in Whiting's brigade, which has been sent to Stonewall. Mem's son is with the Boykin Rangers—company A No. 1, we call it. And she has persistently wept ever since she heard the news. It is no child's play, she says, when you are with Stonewall. He don't play at soldiering. He don't take care of his men at all. He only goes to kill the Yankees.

Somebody rushed in to tell us. Wade Hampton, who came home (wounded) last night, says: "France has recognized us. Now, that is a sure thing."

Louis Napoleon does not stop at trifles. He never botches his work; he is thorough. The coup d'état, par exemple. So we hope [he] will not help us with a half-hand.

And now, not a word of all this true. Wade Hampton is here, shot in the foot, but he knows no more about France than he does of the man in the moon. Wet blanket he is just now. Johnston badly wounded—Lee is king of spades. They are all once more digging for dear life. Unless we can reinforce Stonewall, the game is up. Our chiefs contrive to dampen and destroy the enthusiasm of all who go near them. So much entrenching and falling back destroys the morale of any army.

This everlasting retreating, it kills the hearts of the men. Then we are scant of powder, &c&c&c.

J. C. is awfully proud of LeConte's powder manufacturing here. LeConte knows how to do it. J. C. provides him the means to carry out his plans.

Ripley, Pemberton, &c—why don't they put us in the hands of some Southern man who would rather die than [*page ends with incomplete sentence*]

---

6. Stuart completed his daring three-day reconnaissance operation around McClellan on June 15.

The Hampton girls[7] have asked their father's friends Mr. and Mrs. Rose and Mr. and Mrs. Alfred Huger to stay with them at Millwood. Spend the summer, at any rate.

Anecdote of Mrs. Huger, née Rutledge. She was proud of her exquisite figure. And the fashion of the day enabled them to appear in next to nothing. Pink stockinet and a book muslin classically cut gown—nothing more.

It was by this liberal display of herself as nature made her that put the final stroke to Jérôme Napoleon. But I have wandered off to Miss Patterson.[8]

Mr. Venable don't mince matters. "If we do not [strike] a blow—a blow that will be felt—it will be soon all up with us. The Southwest will be lost to us. We cannot afford to shilly-shally much longer.

"Thousands are enlisting on the other side in New Orleans. Butler holds out inducements. To be sure, they are principally foreigners who want to escape starvation.

"Tennessee we may count as gone, since we abandoned her at Corinth, Fort Pillow, and Memphis. A man must be sent there—or it is all gone."

In my heart I feel "all is gone" now.

"You call a spade by that name, it seems, and not an agricultural instrument."

"They call Mars Robert 'Ole Spade Lee,' he keeps them digging so."

"General Lee is a noble Virginian. Respect something in this world. Caesar—call him Old Spade Caesar. As a soldier he was as much above suspicion as he required his wife to be, as—as Caesar's wife, you know. If I remember Caesar's *Commentaries,* he owns up to a lot of entrenching. You let Mars Robert alone. He knows what he is about."

"Tell us of the Creole way of taking the fall of New Orleans."

"Men, women, children ran around distracted, screaming, chattering, gesticulating. There was no head, no order—all was mere confusion and despair." Then he defended Lovell valiantly, for we charged with all our chivalry.

"Lovell had only 25 hundred regulars to follow him when he left New Orleans. The crack regiments of New Orleans remained. Butler captured twenty thousand men capable of bearing arms. And now they are spading for Butler at Fort Jackson. Many of the wealthiest citizens are there in their shirtsleeves, spade in hand."

"Don't you think they wish they were with Lovell?" cried the girls.

"It is possible they do."

"Tell us of the womenfolk—how did they take it?"

---

7. The unmarried sisters of Wade Hampton III—Mary Fisher, Caroline Louisa, Ann, and Kate—who ranged in age from twenty-nine to thirty-eight.

8. In 1803, while visiting the U.S. on an unauthorized leave from the French navy, Jérôme Bonaparte, Napoleon's youngest brother, married Elizabeth Patterson, daughter of a Baltimore merchant. When he tried to return to France, Bonaparte found that his wife was forbidden to land anywhere on the Continent and that he faced a court-martial for desertion. The charge was dropped when he agreed to renounce his wife and child.

"They are an excitable race. As I was standing on the levee, a daintily dressed lady picked her way, parasol in hand, toward me. She accosted me with great politeness, and her face was as placid and unmoved as in antebellum days. Her first question: 'Will you be so kind as to tell me? What is the last general order?'

"No order that I know of, Madame. General Disorder prevails now."

"'Ah, I see. And why are those persons flying and yelling so noisily, and racing in the streets in that unseemly way?'

"They are looking for a shell to burst over their heads at any moment."

"'Ah!' Then—with a curtsy of dignity and grace—she waved her parasol and departed, but stopped to arrange her parasol at a proper angle to protect her face from the sun. There was no vulgar haste in her movements. She tripped away as gracefully as she came. I had failed to discompose her by my fearful revelations. That was the one self-possessed soul (that I know of) then in New Orleans.

"Another woman drew near to me, so overheated and out of breath she had barely time to say she had run miles of squares in her crazy terror and bewilderment when a sudden shower came up. In a second she was cool and calm. She forgot all the questions she came to ask.

"'My bonnet—I must save it at any sacrifice'—so turned her dress over her head and went off, forgetting her country's troubles and screaming for a cab."

At Secessionville we went to drive the Yankees out, and we were surprised ourselves.

We lost one hundred, the Yankees 400. They lost more men than we had in the engagement.[9]

Fair shooting, that! As they say in the West, "We whipped our weight in wildcats." And some to spare.

Henry King was killed. He died as a brave man would like to die. From all accounts they say he had not found this world (or his life in it) a bed of roses.

Timrod and Paul Hayne were discussing this battle tonight with eager excitement.

"Oh," said Mrs. Bartow, "I hope each of them will give us a poem on it."

Went to see Mrs. Burroughs[1] at the old DeSaussure house. She has such a sweet face, such soft, kind, beautiful dark gray eyes. Such eyes are a poem; no wonder she had a long love story. We sat in the piazza twelve o'clock of a June day, the glorious Southern sun shining his very hottest. But we were in a dense

9. On June 16, an outnumbered force of 500 Confederates stopped the Federal drive up James Island at the hamlet of Secessionville. The Union suffered 683 casualties; the Confederates, 204.
1. Eliza Gibbes (DeSaussure) Burroughs, widow of Henry K. Burroughs.

shade. Magnolias in full bloom—ivy, vines of I know not what. And roses in profusion closed us in. It was a living wall of every[thing] beautiful and sweet. I have been thinking of it ever since. In all this flower garden of a Columbia, this is the most delicious corner I have been in yet.

Isabella awaited me at home. Mrs. McMahon was distinctly giving our old maid to understand that she must go. She could not afford to rent so large a room to a single person.

Whispered Isabella, "The cruelty of it! Don't she see how the spinster is doing her best still? It is not her fault that she is not double. Look at the false hair, the rouge, &c&c. What more can a woman do? And to be taunted with her failure!"

Dr. Tennent proved himself a crack shot at Secessionville. They handed him rifles loaded, in rapid succession. And at the point he aimed were found thirty dead men. Scotchmen—for the regiment of Federals at Secessionville were Scotch. And madly intoxicated. They had poured out whiskey for them like water. "With Tarintosh I fear no evil. With Usquabaugh I'll fan the Devil," says Scotch Burns.[2]

Got from the Prestons' French library *Fanny,* with a brilliant preface by Jules Janin.[3] Now, then, I have come to the worst. There can be no worse book than *Fanny.*

The lover is jealous of the husband. The woman is for polyandry rule of life. She cheats both and refuses to break with either. But to criticize it, one must be as shameless as the book itself. Of course, it is clever to the last degree, or it would be kicked into the gutter. It is not nastier or coarser than Mrs. Stowe, but then, it is not written in the interests of philanthropy.

De Créquy on de Genlis. . . . [4]

Decca Singleton, now Mrs. Haskell of a year's standing, has a daughter. Mary Manning[5]—at the top of her voice:

2. Slightly misquoted from Robert Burns, "Tam o' Shanter": "Inspiring bold John Barleycorn! / What dangers thou canst make us scorn! / Wi' tippenny, we fear nae evil; / Wi' usquebae, we'll face the devil!"

3. Ernest-Aimé Feydeau, *Fanny,* 2nd edition (1858). Jules-Gabriel Janin was a celebrated mid-nineteenth-century literary critic.

4. Translated passages omitted. Stéphanie Félicité du Crest de Saint-Aubin, comtesse de Genlis (1746–1830), wrote popular novels and educational tracts, tutored Louis Philippe, and furnished Napoleon with letters on literature and politics.

5. Probably Mary (Cantey) Manning, a second cousin of J. C. Her husband, Brown Manning of Clarendon District, was John Manning's younger brother.

"*Little* Decca Singleton has a daughter. I don't believe a word of it!"

Mr. Preston said of ——— : "I felt so mortified. It must have been my gray hairs. She came down, she said, as soon as she saw my card. She did not make up for me. I know what that means. It means I am an older man than I thought myself. My dear friend—taken au naturel, she is sallow and freckled. And so careless in her dress. She had a rough, dried yellow gown. Some of the buttons were missing, and she held it together with her hand, but I stayed two hours because, after all, she is so interesting, charming, fascinating."

Mr. Chesnut gave quite otherwise his account of his reception by her. "Her complexion is the loveliest thing I ever saw, quite a dazzling pink and white. Her gown was miraculous—white muslin and pink ribbons in knots all about and a train yards long—her beautiful hair was crepe and done up in the most intricate style. She was stiff as a stone—did 'grande dame' for me. It was an awful bore. I only stayed a few minutes."

"Oh! oh!" said Mr. Preston. "Which of us did she mean to flatter? For me she had her hair à la chinois—with the two tails of plaits hanging down behind. She has a noble brow. I did not [mind?] its being bared. I am humiliated. I am an old man—and she has found it out.'

"Another visit she sat on the goggle board[6] and bounced up and down between every sentence. All that was not goggle was giggle. She does not put on her dignity with me—I don't mind. She is awfully clever."

"You mean her eyes are beautifully blue."

"Why not? To have such eyes is the cleverest thing a woman can do."

I like them like Maintzey's, with the dark charm, you know—"rubbed in with a dirty finger." The perfection of all eyes.

We had an unexpected dinner party today. First Wade Hampton came and Mary McDuffie. Then Mr. and Mrs. Rose. I remember that the late Colonel Hampton[7] once said to me a thing I thought odd at the time. "Mr. James Rose" (and I forget now who was the other) "are the only two people on this side of the water who know how to give a state dinner."

Mr. and Mrs. James Rose. If anybody wishes to describe old Carolina at its best, let them try their hands at painting these two people.

Wade Hampton still limps a little, but he is rapidly recovering. Here is what he said—and he has fought so well that he is listened to:

"If we mean to play at war as we play a game of chess—West Point tactics prevailing—we are sure to lose the game. They have every advantage. They can

---

6. A bouncing board still found sometimes on Charleston piazzas.
7. Wade Hampton II.

lose pawns ad infinitum—to the end of time—and never feel it. We will be throwing away all that we had hoped so much from. Southern hot-headed dash, reckless gallantry, spirit of adventure—readiness to lead forlorn hopes—&c&c."

He says England is sending troops to Canada. And that she has refused to give up the *Emily St. Pierre* and that she has demanded the *Bermuda*. There is a rumor that Lord Lyons has demanded his passports.[8]

Mrs. Rose is Miss Sarah Parker's aunt. Somehow it came out when I was not in the room—but those girls tell me everything. It seems Miss Sarah Parker said, "The reason I cannot bear Mrs. Chesnut is that she laughs at everything and at everybody."

If she saw me now, she would give me credit for some pretty hearty crying as well as laughing.

It was a mortifying thing to hear of oneself, all the same.

Mr. Preston came in and announced that Mr. Chesnut was in town. He had just seen Mr. Alfred Huger, who came up on the Charleston train with him. Then Mrs. McCord came and offered to take me back to Mrs. McMahon's to look him up. I found my room locked up. Laurence said his master had gone to look for me at the Prestons'.

Mrs. McCord proposed we should further hunt up my errant husband.

At the door we met Governor Pickens, who showed us telegrams from the president of the most important nature. The governor added, "And I have one from Jeems Chesnut, but I hear he has followed it so closely, coming on its heels, as it were, that I need not show you that one."

"You don't look interested at the sound of your husband's name?"

"Is that his name?"

"What does she mean?" to Mrs. McCord.

"I suppose she thought it was James."

"My advice to you is to find him, for Mrs. Pickens says he was last seen in the company of two very handsome women. And now you may call him any name you please."

---

8. In early June, Lord Lyons asked for and received permission to return to England for consultation with his government. Though his action caused speculation about a possible change in British policy, none was forthcoming. The number of British troops in Canada remained constant and restrained negotiations proceeded over the fate of the *Emily St. Pierre*, a Confederate blockade-runner whose crew had risen against their Federal captors and escaped to England.

It was not a case of Evangeline[9]—and both on the same errand, we soon met. The two beautiful dames Governor Pickens threw in my teeth were Sanders from Rafton Creek, almost neighbors. They only live fifteen miles from Camden.

Sandy Brown[1] and Grayson (the poet and friend of Mr. Petigru) are at it shovel and tongs. Sandy Brown is the man who stabbed William Izard Bull[2] in a brawl.

At Mrs. Preston's it was a feast of apricots. They break them in half, pile them up on a dish, and eat them as you do peaches, with cream and sugar.

By way of pleasant remark to Wade Hampton:
"Oh, general! The next battle will give you a chance to be major general."
"I was very foolish to give up my Legion," he answered gloomily.
"Promotion don't really annoy many people."
Mary Gibson says her father writes to them that they may go back. He thinks now that the Confederates can hold Richmond.
Gloria in excelsis!

Another personal defeat. Little Kate: "Oh, Cousin Mary, why don't you cultivate heart? They say at Kirkwood that you had better let your brains alone awhile and cultivate heart."
She had evidently caught up a phrase and repeated it again and again for my benefit. So that is the way they talk of me!

The only good of loving anyone with your whole heart is to give that person the power to hurt you. To hear those people complained of my want of heart! How it hurt.
And now, see how I am improving my mind. De Créquy, *Cousine Bette,* and last of all *Fanny.*

---

9. In Henry Wadsworth Longfellow, *Evangeline: A Tale of Acadie* (1847), a young woman searches for her fiancé, who had mysteriously disappeared on their wedding day. When she finds him on his deathbed, the shock of the discovery kills her.
1. Alexander Henry Brown was a member of the secession convention and provost marshal of Charleston who specialized in admiralty law. A former U.S. congressman, William John Grayson combined an ardent defense of slavery with opposition to secession. He wrote *The Hireling and the Slave* (1854) and *James Louis Petigru: A Biographical Sketch* (1866), which appeared posthumously.
2. Like Brown, William Izard Bull, Sr., a wealthy planter and longtime state legislator, lived in St. Andrew's Parish.

The merry brown hares are leaping—&c&c. How that thing seized me by the throat!

Free England—upon whose soil a slave has only to set his foot and the shackles fall off. And yet the rhymes of Kingsley touched a chord which vibrated, because this thing fitted into a slave state of things so well.

———

The possibilities of slavery the same everywhere.

June 24, 1862.   Mr. C, having missed Secessionville fight by half a day, was determined to see the row around Richmond. He went off with General Cooper and Wade Hampton. Blanton Duncan sent them for a luncheon on board the cars—ice, wine, and every manner of good thing.

Mr. Preston came for me—said J. C. had ordered me to report to him. And the carriage with Mrs. Preston would be here in the course of a few minutes.

Mrs. McCord came for me, too. Mrs. Preston heard with dismay her hospital stories. Dismal enough they are.

Dr. ——— a good creature, conscientious to the last degree, does his very best. The Yankee prisoners sent in a round robin begging "for God sake" that he might be called off. He was killing them off so rapidly by his zeal without knowledge.

So they sent him to Mrs. McCord to try his hand there. She says if a "for God sake" appeal relieved the Yankee prisoners of him, she has one of the same sort ready to send in at once. Mr. Preston hoped he would turn traitor and go over and give the Yankees the benefit of his skill. "Anything to get rid of him," said Mrs. McCord. "He is so scientific, too. Our authorities do not know where to send him out of harm's way. He is so obtusely bent upon being of use to his country."

In all this death and destruction, the women are the same—chatter, patter, clatter.

"Oh, the Charleston refugees are so full of airs—there is no sympathy for them here."

"Oh, indeed! That is queer. They are not half as exclusive as these Hamptons, Prestons, &c. The airs these people do give themselves."

"Airs—airs," laughed Mrs. Bartow, parodying Tennyson's "Charge of the Light Brigade." "Airs to the right of them—airs to the left of them—someone had blundered—"

"Volleyed and thundered—rhymes but is out of place."

The worst of all airs—a democratic landlady who was asked by Mrs. President Davis to have a carpet shaken shook herself with rage.

"You know, Madame, you need not stay here if my carpet or anything else does not suit you."

———

John Chesnut gives us a spirited account of their ride around McClellan. I sent the letter to his grandfather.

The women ran out, screaming with joyful welcome as soon as they caught sight of their gray uniform. Ran to them, bringing hands full and arms full of food for them. One gray-headed man, after preparing a hasty meal for them, knelt and prayed for them as they snatched it—as you may say. They were in the saddle from Friday until Sunday. They were used up—so were their horses. He writes for clothes and more horses. Miss Sally Chesnut says, "No need to send any more of his fine horses to be killed or captured by the Yankees." She will wait and see how the siege of Richmond ends. For though on patriotism she is bent, she bears a frugal mind.[3]

The horses will go all the same, as Johnny wants them.

June 25, 1862. I forgot to tell of Mrs. Pickens's reception for General Hampton.

My Miriam dear described it all. "The governess"—("But Mem, that is not the right name for her. She is not a teacher, &c." "Never mind, it is the easier to say than the Governor's wife." "'Madame la Gouvernante' was suggested." "Why? That is worse than the other.")—"met him at the door, took his crutch away, putting his hand upon her shoulder instead. 'That was the way to greet heroes,' she said. Her blue eyes were aflame, and in response poor Wade smiled and smiled, until his face hardened into a fixed grin of embarrassment and annoyance. He is a simple-mannered man, you know, and does not want to be made much of by women.

"The butler was not in plain clothes but wore, as the other servants did, magnificent livery brought from the Court of St. Petersburg. One man of gold embroidery, &c&c. They had Russian tea, champagne, a samovar—thing to make tea in as it is made in Russia. Little Moses was there. Now, for us they have never put their servants into Russian livery nor paraded Little Moses under our noses, but I must confess, the Russian tea and the champagne always set before us left nothing to be desired."

"How did Gen. Wade Hampton bear his honors?"

"Well, to the last he looked as if he wished they would let him alone."

Met Mr. Ashmore fresh from Richmond. He says Stonewall is coming up behind McClellan—and then comes the tug-of-war. He thinks we have so many spies in Richmond. They may have found out our strategic movements and so will circumvent them.

---

3. A slight misquotation from William Cowper, "The Diverting History of John Gilpin" (1785), stanza 8.

Lent the poet Paul Hayne "Love me little, love me long."[4] Mem says he inquires discontentedly, "Where does she flit so often and so unexpectedly?"

Jack Cunningham writes. No use fooling about it any longer. He must have a commission or an office of some sort to support his family. They are burnt out of house and home. So he can no longer fight without pay.

Mrs. Bartow's story of a clever Miss Toombs. So many men were in love with her, and the courtship while [it] lasted, of each one, was as exciting and bewildering as a fox chase. She liked the fun of the run—but she wanted something more than to know a man was in mad pursuit of her. That he should love her, she agreed, but she must love him, too. How was she to tell? Yet she must be certain of it before she said yes. So as they sat by the lamp, she would look at him and inwardly ask herself, "Would I be willing to spend the long winter evenings forever after sitting here, darning your old stockings?" Never, echo answered. No, no, a thousand times, no—so they had to make way for another.

Our girls showed me letter from a gallant soldier boy—who talks well enough, too, but certainly his ideas of spelling are eccentric—"Oh, I am so glad to hear General Hampton's wound is a slit one."

" 'Slit one'—what does he mean?"

"Stupid guesser that you are—a *slight* wound."

"I was thinking the general's foot had been slit."

Little Moses, par exemple—I fear the small enemies J. C. makes—and he despises them. His hatred and contempt for Little Moses amounts to a craze. "Ah! si vous croyez qu'un misérable et faible ennemi ne puisse pas nuire, c'est comme si vous supposiez qu'une étincelle ne saurait produire une incendie."

Captain Shurtz has named his company "Chesnut Light Artillery," and in a very handsome letter says, "and so identifying it with one of the names by which the revolution was inaugurated and indissolubly connected with its famous history."

I confess I found all this very fine and was in a manner bragging of it. Oh, we know him—he is our cousin, too. Let us see his initials. Yes, there it is—F. C. Shurtz. Frilled Cotton Shirts.

Wade Hampton sat with Mr. Chesnut in a pew in church. In front of them was a girl with earrings made in the form of golden ladders.

Wade Hampton perpetrated the following impromptu:

> Lydia swears her prudish ear
> No word of love shall ever reach—

---

4. An English poem, composed anonymously ca. 1570.

> Then—tell, I pray, why doth she wear
> What does another lesson teach?
> A sign that's plain to every eye
> She's not as deaf as any adder,
> And he who hopes to climb so high,
> Has but to use a golden ladder—

Now, did he make that in church *or remember it?*

June 27, 1862.   We went in a body (half-dozen ladies, no man on escort duty, for they are all in the army) to a concert. Mrs. Pickens came in alone, too. She was joined soon by Secretary Moses and Mr. Follen.[5] Dr. Berrien came to our relief. Nothing could be more execrable than the singing. Financially the thing was a great success, for though the audience was altogether feminine, it was a very large one.

Telegram from J. C. "Safe in Richmond." That is, if Richmond be safe—with all the power of the U.S.A. battering her gates.

Strange, not a word from Stonewall Jackson, after all!

Dr. Gibson telegraphs his wife, "Stay where you are—terrible battle looked for here."

Rebecca Haskell is dead—poor little darling! Immediately after her baby was born, she took it into her [head] that Alex was killed. He was wounded, but they had not told her of it.

She surprised them by asking, "Does anyone know how the battle has gone since Alex was killed?"

She could not read for a day or so before she died. Her head was bewildered, but she would not let anyone else touch his letters, so she died with several unopened ones in her bosom.

Mrs. Singleton fainted dead away, but she shed no tears. We went there. We saw Alex's mother, who is a daughter of Langdon Cheves.

Annie was with us. She said, "This is the saddest thing for Alex." "No," said his mother, "death is never the saddest thing. If he were not a good man, that would be a far worse thing." Annie, in utter amazement, whimpered, "But Alex is so good already." "Yes—seven years ago the death of one of his sisters that he dearly loved made him a Christian. That death in our family was worth a thousand lives."

One needs a hard heart now. Even old Mr. Shand shed tears. Mary Barnwell[6] sat as still as a statue—as white and stony. "Grief which can relieve itself by tears is a thing to pray for," said Rev. Mr. Shand.

Then came a telegram from Hampton: "All well—so far we are successful."

5. G. A. Follen, a clerk in the S.C. adjutant general's office.
6. Mary (Singleton) Barnwell, the wife of Rev. Robert Woodward Barnwell, was Rebecca Haskell's sister.

Robert Barnwell had been telegraphed for. His answer came: "Can't leave here—Gregg is fighting across the Chickahominy."

"Then," said Mrs. Haskell, "my son Alex may never hear this sad news." And her lip settled rigidly.

"Go on. What else does he say?"

"Lee has one wing of the army. Stonewall the other."

"Then he is there!!"

Ann Hampton came to tell us the latest news, that we have abandoned James Island and are fortifying Morris Island. And now she says, "If the enemy will be so kind as to wait, we will be ready for them in two months."

Rev. Mr. Shand and that pious Christian woman Mrs. Haskell (who looks into your very soul with those large and lustrous blue eyes of hers) agreed that the Yankees, even if they took Charleston, would not destroy it. I think they will, sinner that I am.

Mr. Shand: "Madame, you have two sons in the army."

Mrs. Haskell: "I have had *six* sons in the army!"

To go down to meaner themes. The Clarendon attack upon the council[7]— because the council wants to organize a reserve corps. And wants to send negroes to relieve the soldiers working on the fortifications. Naturally Clarendon does not wish to do either.

They need not publish that they would like to stay at home. Everybody knows that already. And their saying a thing as a general rule has a tendency to make people doubt it.

But like Dogberry,[8] this fact, even if stated over the signatures of the magnates of Clarendon, "will go far to be believed." Though such a miracle as believing them does not happen in a thousand years. This formidable instrument, a sort of last will and testament, was written, it is said, by Sergeant Buzfuzz—whose alias is Yellow Flag Jimmy. And it is signed, sealed, and delivered by all of the Ex-Gubernatorial Carte of Clarendon.

They gave their sons to their country cheerfully. But when the council calls for men over forty for the reserve corps—and sacred property in the shape of negroes for coast defenses—a howl.

Most classically fine it is. They raise the right hand and swear to protect their

7. On June 20, two dozen citizens of Clarendon District—including M. B. C.'s friend John Manning—joined the increasingly strong public protest against the Executive Council. Their resolutions, first published in the Columbia *Southern Guardian*, avoided the common tactic of challenging the constitutionality of the council and questioned instead the wisdom and fairness of the impressment of slaves to construct coastal defenses.

8. The chief constable in *Much Ado About Nothing*.

lives and property from "a disorderly soldiery" and the council. And it is all in such fine language, too. "Exercitus," "corpus," &c&c.

They swear they will stick at home and see it out. In this case, no doubt they will keep their word. And then the sneer at "helots" and classical flings at our volunteers. How will the soldiers like it?

A letter that I found among Mr. C's papers today:

> I daresay some "damned good-natured friend," as Sheridan has it,[9] will hand you the attack upon you and Hayne in the *Carolinian* today. It is signed "Q." It strikes me "P" would be nearer the mark. At any rate, it behooves you to mind your P's and Q's.
>
> There are people here too small to conceive of any larger business than quarreling in the newspapers. One laughs at squibs in the papers now. In such times are these! with the wolf at our doors. Men safe in their closets, writing fiery articles—denouncing those who are at work—all beneath contempt. Only critics with muskets on their shoulders have the right to speak now, as Trenholm said the other night.
>
> Now when the "herd of governors do again congregate"—issue a thundering proclamation for five more regiments. Arrange it so as to catch every man who has leisure to stay at home and abuse his neighbors. March him off to the war.
>
> Come back to Columbia, and make old Pickwig wish he had left you in peace, to serve your country as your own good sense dictated.
>
> God keep you from harm—
>
> *X X X*

The Clarendon Manifesto is in everybody's mouth. Isabella, who says she is like Shakespeare in one thing only—she knows small Latin and less Greek—undertook to translate its brave words to us. "Corpus" and "exercitus," she said, was a way they had of exercising their bodies by staying at home.

And at the end, the lamentable lame conclusion. They say they stay at home to guard their wives and beeves from our "disorderly soldiers."

June 28, 1862.   In a pouring rain we went to that poor child's funeral, Decca Haskell. They buried her in the little white frock she wore when she engaged herself to Alex Haskell and which she again put on to marry him about a year ago. She lies now in the churchyard—in sight of my window.

Is she still to be pitied? She said she had had months of perfect happiness. How many people can say that? So many of us live their long dreary lives, and then happiness never comes to meet them at all. It seems so near—and yet it eludes them forever.

---

9. Richard Brinsley Sheridan, *The Critic*, act 1, scene 1.

The Clarendon downpour on the council is in the air—one hears of nothing else.... [1]

Tanny said Kirkland sent all of his letters to Charleston. Rawly Lowndes will not write, and Kirkland puts on the outside of his: "Rawly is well." Lowndes père takes them out, reads that, and sends them on their way rejoicing, to their destination in Camden.

Alfred Brevard[2] was taken prisoner at Chickahominy. He and another badly [wounded] Confederate were sent off, guarded by one Yankee. Alfred saw General Anderson and his staff. He seized the Yankee, held him in a close embrace, and called to his wounded comrade to disarm him: which the wounded man did, and they went back to General Anderson. When the general asked, "With your tremendous strength, why did you not take the Yankee prisoner in his turn?" with his usual coolness he replied, "I was only too glad to be rid of the companionship of the disagreeable creature."

Mrs. Haskell is a high-hearted being. She spoke of Alex. "If he were still alive," she said, "his soul is pure and true—such a conscience as he has is a heaven in itself."

June 29, 1862.   Victory! Victory heads every telegram now, one reads on the bulletin board.[3]

It is the anniversary of the battle of Fort Moultrie.[4]

They went off so quickly. I wonder if it is not a trap laid for us, to lead us away from Richmond—to some place where they can manage to do us more harm.

And now comes the list of killed and wounded.

Victory does not seem to soothe the sore hearts. Mrs. Haskell has five sons before the enemy's illimitable cannon. Mrs. Preston two.

A call from that dark-eyed one—Mrs. C. She has adopted a languid and helpless manner. She has taken her belle-mère example to heart, but the latter has been found out. She may talk in as silly a manner as she pleases, she will never deceive anybody into thinking her a fool anymore.

This fair one rejoices that her sons were too young to be soldiers. "Of course, one fretted and worried about one's husband—but then, everyone knew hus-

---

1. Deleted are quotations from de Créquy.
2. Lt. Alfred Brevard, Jr., the son of a Camden physician, was a cousin of J. C.
3. Reports of the Seven Days campaign, the successful Confederate defense of Richmond.
4. On June 28, 1776, William Moultrie helped repel the British invasion of Charleston. The site of Moultrie's heroics, a palmetto-log fort on Sullivan's Island, became known as Fort Moultrie.

bands had a way of taking care of themselves. But, oh—the heartbreak and misery if one's son was there, &c&c&c."

Then she gave us details of the fight. "McClellan is routed. And we have 12,000 prisoners."

"Prisoners! My God! And what are we to do with them? We can't feed our own people." &c&c.

For the first time since Joe Johnston was wounded at Seven Pines, we may breathe freely. We were so afraid of another general, or a new one. Stonewall cannot be everywhere—tho he comes near it.

Magruder did splendidly at Big Bethel—out there. It was a wonderful thing, how he played his ten thousand before McClellan like fireflies and utterly deluded him—keeping down there ever so long.

"It was partly the Manassas scare we gave them. They will never be foolhardy again."

"Now we are throwing up our caps for R. E. Lee."

"We hope from the Lees what the first sprightly running (at Manassas) could not give."

We do hope there will be no "Ifs." "Ifs" have ruined us.

Shiloh was a victory—if Albert Sidney Johnston had not been killed. Seven Pines—if Joe Johnston had not been wounded. At Manassas the "Ifs" bristled like porcupines.

That victory did nothing but send us off into a fool's paradise of conceit. And it roused the manhood of the Northern people—for very shame they had to move up.

Tudy interrupted with a schoolboy's story:

"Don't call yourself Jule—give us your whole name."

"Julius." The next boy, whose name was Bill, called himself "Billious." Then came Tom—"Thomas." That Jack—who knew no other way to give himself a proper name than to follow Thomas—"Jackass."

June 30, 1862.   First came Dr. Trezevant, who announced Burnet Rhett's death. "No. No—I have just seen the bulletin board—it is Julius Grimké Rhett."[5]

When the doctor went out, it was added—"Howell Trezevant's death on the battlefield is there, too. The doctor will see that as soon as he goes down to the board."[6]

---

5. M. B. C. is confusing two brothers who were nephews of Robert Barnwell Rhett, Sr. John Grimké Rhett, not Julius Moore Rhett, died at Cold Harbor on June 27.

6. Corp. Jesse Howell Trezevant, the son of Daniel Heyward and Epps Goodwyn (Howell) Trezevant, was serving as a courier for Brig. Gen. James J. Archer when he was killed during the Seven Days. Lucy, below, was the youngest of the Trezevant children.

The girls went to see Lucy Trezevant. The doctor was lying still as death, on a sofa, with his face covered. They hurried by him to Lucy's room. Mrs. Trezevant is ill in bed.

At church every face was anxious. It is a great deliverance, but the list of killed and wounded is to come.

Mrs. Izard said in her crisp way, "With the Yankees it is reculer pour mieux sauter. Halleck is ordered up with fifty thousand fresh troops."

A French man-of-war lies at the wharf in Charleston, to take off French subjects when the bombardment begins.

William Mazyck[7] writes the enemies' gunboats are shelling and burning, up and down the Santee River. They raise the white flag, and the negroes rush down to them. They might as well have let these negroes be taken by the council to work on the fortifications!

Mrs. McCord in her outspoken way was denouncing a surgeon for some malpractice at her hospital. Mrs. Thornwell (bravo for old Waxhaws!)[8] said promptly: "The man is my nephew. My carriage is at the door. Let us go at once and investigate this matter. If these charges be true, I give him up." Mrs. McCord, nothing daunted, went with Mrs. Thornwell. The charges were true, but the delinquent was not Mrs. Thornwell's nephew but an assistant surgeon.

A doctor spoke roughly to a soldier who wanted a wooden leg.

"You can do without it. They are too expensive to give to everybody."

"Cheer up and be of good heart," said Mrs. McCord. "My fine fellow, order your wooden leg and send the bill to me." Mrs. Thornwell said she forgave her on the spot. Up to that time she had felt a little wrathy as to the reckless arraignment of her nephew.

---

7. A Charleston cotton factor.

8. M. B. C.'s father and Nancy White (Witherspoon) Thornwell, the daughter of a lieutenant governor of S.C., were both born in the Waxhaw settlement in Lancaster District near the N.C. border. Mrs. Thornwell's husband, James Henley Thornwell, was a Presbyterian clergyman, a former president of S.C. College, and a professor at Presbyterian Theological Seminary in Columbia.

Richmond
June 29th, 1862

My dear Mary,

For the last three days I have been witness of the most stirring events of modern times. On my arrival here I found the government so absolutely absorbed in the great pending battle that I found it useless to talk of the special business that brought me to this place. As soon as it is over, which will probably be tomorrow, I think I can easily accomplish all that I was sent for. I have no doubt that we can procure another general and more forces, &c&c.

The president and General Lee are inclined to listen to me and to do all they can for us. General Lee is vindicating the high opinion I have ever expressed of him, and his plans and execution of the last great fight will place him high in the role of really great commanders.

The fight on Friday was the largest and fiercest of the whole war—some 60,000 or 70, with great preponderance on the side of the enemy. Ground, numbers, armament, &c all in favor of the enemy. But our men and generals were superior. The higher officers and men behaved with a resolution and dashing heroism that has never been surpassed in any country or in any age.

Our line, by superior numbers and superior artillery impregnably posted, was three times repulsed when Lee, assembling all the generals to the front, told them that victory depended on carrying the batteries and defeating the army before them, ere night should fall. If night came without victory, all was lost, and that the work must be done by the bayonet. Our men then made a rapid and irresistible charge, without powder, and carried everything. The enemy melted before them and ran with the utmost speed, though of the regulars of the federal government. The fight between the artillery of the opposing forces was terrific and sublime. The field became one dense cloud of smoke, so that nothing could be seen but the incessant flashes of fire through the clouds.

They were within sixteen hundred yards of each other, and it rained storms of grape and cannister.

We took 23 pieces of their artillery, many small arms, and some ammunition. They burnt most of their stores, wagons, &c&c.

The victory of the second day was full and complete. Yesterday there was little or no fighting, but some splendid maneuvering which has placed us completely around them.

I think the end must be decisive in our favor. We have lost many men and many officers. I hear Alex Haskell and young McMahon among them, as well as a son of Dr. Trezevant. Very sad indeed. We are fighting again today, will let you know the result as soon as possible. Will be at home sometime next week. No letter from you yet.

With devotion, yours,

James Chesnut, Jr.

9 o'clock A.M.
Camp near Richmond
June 2nd, 1862

Dear Grandfather,

One year has passed since I left home, a year fraught with events. We have been fighting for the last two days; our loss has been pretty heavy. Twenty-five hundred, I think, from all I can gather, will cover our loss in killed, wounded, and missing. The Yankee loss much heavier; we have driven them back at every point, and taken a great many prisoners. Nearly 500 had reached Richmond yesterday, and they were still pouring in.

They fight well, though not equal to our boys. Gen. J. J. Pettigrew was killed. General Anderson's brigade (of S.C.) behaved beautifully. They were in the engagement Sunday evening from six o'clock P.M. until dark. More execution was done during that part of the day than at any other time.

We have been on picket 36 hours out of every 48 until the fight began, and then were ordered to take our position on the enemy's left wing. So you see we have had very little time to do anything. Our horses have not had anything to eat for two days but grass. And our men one day's rations of hard bread in that time—except some meal I bought. All are in fine spirits and ready for any emergency. They have behaved finely. I had three men on one post—William Ancrum[9] among the number—when eight Yankees charged up, but they found the Boykin Rangers would not give ground, altho' only three to eight, so they had to give ground. William Ancrum killed one of them.

We are waiting every moment for the ball to open again. I suppose the cessation is only to bury the dead. The citizens of Richmond have done all that it is possible for a people to do, going out in their carriages and all kinds of vehicles they could get, removing the wounded and dead. Their houses have been thrown open, and the ladies are ministering to the wants of the wounded and dying in every possible manner. When the fight is again renewed, it will be terrific.

So far all my men have escaped unhurt. I have lost all of my things; if one can get a change of clothes every two weeks, he fares well. General Johnston is reported to be slightly wounded, and General Hatton of Tennessee was killed.[1] General Hampton is reported wounded, but I doubt it. I saw him in the field until late at night.

I saw a New York *Herald* of the 26th. The Yankees are terribly frightened about Jackson taking Washington. Some prisoners were taken

9. William Alexander Ancrum, a private in Johnny's company, was the son of J. C.'s friend Thomas J. Ancrum.

1. Robert Hopkins Hatton, a former congressman promoted to brigadier general of the C.S.A. only eight days before his death at Seven Pines.

who had not fired a shot, declaring they did not care one way or the other, only entered the army for a livelihood.

All of our friends in the different regiments are well, as far as I have ascertained. I received Aunt Sally's letter on the battlefield.

The [fighting] is beginning again. The cannon is now dealing destruction—

Love to all.

John Chesnut

Telegram from my husband:

Richmond
June 29th

Was on the field—saw it all. Things satisfactory so far. Can hear nothing of John Chesnut—he is in Stuart's command. Saw Jack Preston—safe so far. No reason why we should not bag McClellan's army or cut it to pieces. From four to six thousand prisoners already.

J. C.

Dr. Gibbes rushed in like a whirlwind to say we were driving McClellan into the river.

XVII

"The Best and the Bravest"

July 1, 1862.   No more news. It has settled down into this—the great battle, the decisive battle, has to be fought yet.

Conner from Charleston, formerly captain in the Hampton Legion, now colonel and in command of a N.C. regiment, has been badly wounded.

Edward Cheves—only son of John Cheves—killed. His sister kept crying, "Oh, mother, what shall we do—Edward is killed!" But the mother sat dead still, white as a sheet, never uttering a word or shedding a tear.

Are our women losing the capacity to weep? The father came today, Mr. John Cheves. He has been making infernal machines in Charleston to blow up Yankee ships.

While Mrs. McCord was telling me this terrible trouble in her brother's family, someone said, "Alex Haskell died of grief!"

"Stuff and nonsense. Now you come with your silly sentiment. Folly! If he is not wounded, he is alive. Poor John may die of that shattered arm in this hot weather. Alex will never die of a broken heart. Take my word for it."

Mr. Thornwell, who is a cousin of my father's, was telling me how clannish he was. He was walking with someone in Lancaster village and mentioned where he intended to stay while there. It was told her little brother, who ran home and shouted to his mother who was *there* talking with Governor Miller. "Oh, mother, look out! They say in the village that the governor is coming here—*to our house.*" To their great amusement and the child's dismay, when he found out who the stranger was.

July 2, 1862.   Met Governor Pickens and his bodyguard Follen and Moses.

Intimated to him how shabby a trick it was of his, not to send me J. C.'s telegrams—promised to do so hereafter.

July 3, 1862.   Miriam says she feels like sitting down, as an Irish woman does at a wake, and howling night and day—"Why did Huger let McClellan slip through his fingers?"

Arrived at Mrs. McMahon's at the wrong moment. Mrs. Bartow was reading to the stricken mother an account of the death of her son. The letter was written by a man who was standing by him when he was shot through the head. "My God!" That was all—and he fell dead.

James Taylor[1] was color-bearer. He was shot three times before he gave in. Then he said, as he handed the colors to the man next him, "You see, I can't stand it any longer"—and dropped stone dead.

———

If anything can reconcile me to the idea of a horrid failure after all to make good our independence of Yankees, it is Lincoln's proclamation freeing the negroes. Especially yours—Messieurs who write insults to your governor and council dated from Clarendon. Three hundred of Mr. Walter Blake's[2] negroes have gone to the Yankees.

Remember, recalcitrant patriots, property on two legs may walk off without an order from the council to work on fortifications.

———

Have been reading Potiphar's papers.[3] Can this be a picture of New York socially?

———

Somebody suggested a name for a new house just built—Heim Leben. Then they began to pick at names of the high and mighty. First a great warrior Pick[4]—then a little Pickens; a huge Mug—then a little Muggins; &c&c&c. A giant Parental Hug—no end of little Huggins.

"Why do we wait and whimper so in our soft Southern speech—we poor women?"

"Because," said Mrs. Singleton, in quick and emphatic way, "you are always excusing yourselves. Men here are masters, and they find fault and bully you. You are afraid of them and take a meek, timid, defensive style."

———

Mary C dramatically explains: "Dogmatic man rarely speaks at home but to find fault or ask the reason why. Why did you go? or: why, for God sake, did you come? I told you never to do that. Or: I did think you might have done the other. My buttons are off again—and be d——d to them. Coffee cold! Steak as tough as the devil! Ham every day now for a week! What a blessed humbug domestic felicity is—eh? At every word the infatuated fool of a woman recoils as if she had received a slap in the face. And for dear life, she begins to excuse herself for what is no fault of hers. And explains the causes of failure, which he knows beforehand as well as she does. She seems to be expected to put right

———

1. A cousin of J. C. who died during the Seven Days.
2. A British-born planter of Beaufort District.
3. George William Curtis, *The Potiphar Papers* (1853).
4. Brig. Gen. Andrew Pickens (1738–1818), the grandfather of Governor Pickens.

every wrong in the world. Mrs. S fought, she did not apologize; hence her freedom from slavish whining &c&c."

The governor had fifteen guns fired for our victory.

The Yankee prisoners say Mac has only taken shelter under the guns of his fleet until his reinforcements arrive.

Mrs. General Huger,[5] in a letter to Mrs. Preston, asks, "Why are Yankee generals, on parole, walking about the Spotswood while ours are in Yankee cells on bread and water?"

I am reading *Gallus*.[6]

Below, Annie is practicing with a perseverance worthy of any cause "The Girl I Left Behind Me" with *piano fortissimo* accompaniment.

When the six girls troop in I wonder if a handsomer group was ever collected in one room. [*The rest of this page is cut out.*]

If it were not for this horrid war, how nice it would be here. We might lead such a pleasant life. This is the most perfectly appointed establishment—such beautiful grounds, flowers and fruits, indeed, all that heart could wish—such delightful dinners, such pleasant drives, such jolly talks, such charming people. But this horrid war poisons everything.

July 5, 1862.   Frank Ravenel killed.[7] Eheu!

Drove out with Mrs. Constitution Browne, who told us the story of Ben McCulloch's devotion to Lucy Gwin.[8] Poor Ben McCulloch—another dead hero.

J. C. and Hayne away. Another well-timed attack—a meeting denouncing the council. Hard lines! We had to work double tides. Meet our enemies inside of the state, as well as those from without.

Sally Hampton parodies plantation rhymes:

> Lee bake de hoe cake
> Set Huger to mine it—

---

5. Elizabeth Celestine (Pinckney) Huger, the wife of Benjamin Huger.
6. Wilhelm Adolf Becker, *Gallus, oder römische Scenen aus der Zeit Augusts* (1838).
7. Charleston merchant Frank Gualdo Ravenel, who died during the Seven Days.
8. The eldest daughter of former Calif. senator William M. Gwin, who had come south in 1861.

Huger went to sleep
And McClellan came an' stole it.

Read a book called *Wife and Ward*[9]—scene laid at the siege of Cawnpore.[1]
Who knows what similar horrors may lie in wait for us!

When I saw Siege of Lucknow dramatized in that little theater at Washington,
what a thrill of terror ran through me as those black and yellow brutes came
jumping over the parapets! These faces were like so many of the same sort at
home. To be sure, John Brown had failed to fire their hearts, and they saw no
cause to rise and burn and murder us all—like the women and children were
treated in the Indian Mutiny. But how long would they resist the seductive and
irresistible call "only rise, kill, and be free"?

Called at the Tognos'—saw no one—no wonder. They say Ascelie Togno was
to have been married to Grimké Rhett in August—and he lies dead on the
battlefield. I had not heard of the engagement before I went there.

July 8, 9, 1862.   Gunboat captured on the Santee—so much the worse for us.
We do not want any more prisoners—and next time they will send a fleet of
boats if one will not do.

The governor sent me J. C.'s telegram with this note.

Sunday morning

To Mrs. Chesnut

My dear Madam
    I received the enclosed telegram at twelve o'clock last night and would
have sent it, but it was so late.
    You will see that you may have the pleasure of his arrival tomorrow.
    I trust your anxiety will then be over.
    I regret the telegram does not come up to what we had hoped might be,
as to the entire destruction of McClellan's army.
    I think, however, the strength of the war with its ferocity may now be
considered as broken.
    With great respect, I have the honor to be yours very truly,

F. W. Pickens

P.S. Please send back the telegram, as I desire to send it to the council.

---

9. Edward Money, *The Wife and the Ward; or, A Life's Error* (1859).
1. The British were overrun at Cawnpore during the Indian Mutiny of 1857–58. Lucknow,
mentioned below, also fell to the native rebels.

Table talk today:

This war was undertaken by us to shake off the yoke of foreign invaders. So we consider our cause righteous. The Yankees, since the war has begun, have discovered it is to free the slaves they are fighting—so their cause is noble. They also expect to make the war pay. Yankees do not undertake anything that does not pay. They think we belong to them. We have been good milk cows. Milked by the tariff, or skimmed. We let them have all of our hard earnings. We bore the ban of slavery. They got the money. Cotton pays everybody who handles it, sells it, manufactures it, &c&c—rarely pays the men who make it. Secondhand, they received the wages of slavery. They grew rich, we grew poor. Receiver is as bad as the thief. That applies to us, too—we received these savages they stole from Africa and brought to us in their slave ships. Like the Egyptians, if they let us go, it must be across a red sea of blood.

Fair Texian in the governor's piazza. A mermaid, she sat combing her beautiful hair! She is not a beauty like our fleur-de-lys de Texas. She is of another type, too. She does not stop to parley. She says yes and flies—I ought to say "dives," as she is a mermaid.

Miriam says that everybody has his best foot foremost at McMahon's because the stray Englishman there is supposed to be writing a book. They ask him questions, disconnected ones such as: Do you know Bulwer? Do you smoke?

July 10, 1862. J. C. has come. He believes from what he heard in Richmond that we are to be recognized as a nation by the crowned heads across the waters at last.

Mr. Davis was very kind. He asked J. C. to stay at his house, which he did and went every day with General Lee and Mr. Davis to the battlefield, as a sort of amateur aide of the president. Likewise they admitted him to the informal cabinet meetings at the president's house, &c&c.

He is so hopeful now that it is pleasant to hear him, and I had not the heart to stick the small pins of Yeadon and Pickens in him—yet awhile.

Public opinion is hot against Huger and Magruder for McClellan's escape.

Dr. Gibbes gave me some letters picked up on the battlefield.

One, signed "Laura," tells her lover to fight in such a manner that no Southerner could ever taunt them again with cowardice. She speaks of a man at home she knows "*who is still talking* of his intention to seek the bubble reputation at the cannon's mouth." "Miserable coward," she writes, "I will never speak to him again."

Another writes, "If Hell is a thousand times hotter than a Methodist parson paints it, still I hope all Confederates will be sent there."

It was a relief to find one silly young person fill three pages with a description of her new bonnet—and the bonnet still worn by her rival.

Those fiery Joan d'Arc damsels who goad up their sweethearts bode us no good.

Rachel Lyons was, in Richmond, hand-in-glove with Mrs. Greenhow. Why not? "So handsome, so clever, so angelically kind," says Rachel of the Greenhow, "and she offers to matronize me."

Mrs. Phillips, another beautiful and clever Jewess, has been put in prison again by Beast Butler, for laughing as a Yankee funeral procession went by.

Mr. Chesnut brought Henry DeSaussure's watch for his wife.

At Kingsville he met Captain A. H. Boykin, who gave him Lieutenant Boykin's version of Shannon's treachery. Uncle Hamilton is bitter against William Shannon.

Captain B also told of John Chesnut's prank. Johnny was riding a powerful horse captured from the Yankees. The horse dashed with him right into the Yankee ranks. A dozen men galloped after him, shouting "Stuart! Stuart!" Johnny had by that time conquered his horse. The Yankees mistook this mad charge for Stuart's cavalry, broke, and fled. Daredevil Camden boys—who ride like Arabs!

Mr. Chesnut says he was riding with the president—Colonel Browne, his aide, was along, too. General ⟨⟨Lee⟩⟩[2] rode up and, bowing politely, said, "Mr. President, am I in command here?"

"Yes."

"Then I forbid you to stand here under the enemy's guns. Any exposure of a life like yours is wrong. And this is useless exposure. You must go back."

Mr. Davis answered, "Certainly I will set an example of obedience to orders—discipline must be maintained &c—" but he did not go back.

Fighting Dick Anderson, one of the playfellows of my childhood, was ordered to keep his corps in reserve. By some mistake he got in advance, was not supported, and got cut to pieces.

J. C. adds always: "It is dangerous to repeat what you hear. In military circles there is envy, slander, backbiting, jealousy, &c. Military jealousy is the worst form of that bad passion."

This is disheartening, truly.

J. C. met the Haynes. They went on to nurse their wounded son—found him dead. They were standing in the corridor at the Spotswood. Although he was staying at the president's, J. C. retained his room at this hotel. So he gave his room to them. Next day, when he went back to his room, he found that Mrs. Hayne had thrown herself across the foot of the bed—and never moved. No

---

2. According to the rough draft of the 1880s Version.

other part of the bed had been touched. She got up and went back to the cars—or was led. He says these heartbroken mothers are hard to face.

After all, suppose we do all we hoped. Suppose we start up grand and free—a proud young republic. Think of all these young lives sacrificed! If three for one be killed, what comfort is that? What good will that do Mrs. Hayne or Mary DeSaussure? The best and the bravest of one generation swept away! Henry DeSaussure has left four sons to honor their father's memory and emulate his example. But those poor boys of between 18 and 20 years of age—Haynes, Trezevants, Taylors, Rhetts, &c&c—they are washed away, literally, in a tide of blood. There is nothing to show they ever were on earth.

At Kingsville J. C. saw a woman with a basin of water and a sponge and an armful of clean linen, going through the cars, washing and dressing the soldiers' wounds. The governor and council have organized a hospital there. Dr. Gibbes has it in charge; he says he has dressed the wounds of nearly three hundred as they pass along to their homes. What a comfort it must be to them.

Professor Holmes has answered the Clarendon folk. It is an admirable paper. Some say it was written by Isaac Hayne.[3]

Miriam says a Presbyterian pastor is but a man—pious though he be. Some of the busybodies of the house urged him not to tell Mrs. McMahon of her son's death. He waved them back.

"I know my duty." Tell her he would—he would not wait further tidings.

The young sister flew out, tears streaming from her beautiful eyes. He drew her to him and tenderly kissed her. Tough old Mrs. McMahon came slowly forward, bathed, too, in tears. He gave her no kiss, but unfolded his tale of woe, telling her to look to the Lord for help and consolation.

The next mail brought a letter from young McMahon.

Then they sent him a telegram—answered.

"All right. I am quite alive, thank you."

What amused Mem was the tenderness of the shepherd for the lambs of his flock.

July 12, 1862.   McMahon's.

Our small colonel, Paul Hayne's son, came into my room. To amuse the child I gave him a photograph album to look over.

"You have Lincoln in your book! I am astonished at you—I hate him." And he placed the book on the floor and struck old Abe in the face with his fist.

---

3. The Clarendon resolutions attacked Francis Simmons Holmes's authority to act as special agent for the state in the impressment of slaves. Before the war, Holmes was a planter and professor of geology at Charleston College.

Our Englishman told me Lincoln had said, had he known such a war would follow his election, he never would have set foot in Washington nor have been inaugurated. He had never dreamed of this awful fratricidal bloodshed. That does not seem the true John Brown spirit. But I was very glad to hear it—to hear something from the president of the United States which was not merely a vulgar joke, usually a joke so vulgar that you are ashamed to laugh—funny as it is.

I did not go down to dinner, but Mem came into my room and repeated the following conversation.

Mrs. Hayne: "Colonel Chesnut, you ought to be grateful for your narrow escape. We hear while you were there, the president's house was riddled with balls."

Colonel C: "Not so bad as that. Some shells fell—the thing was exaggerated."

"Ah, I see you have not read the paragraph I allude to."

"Of course," said Mem, "Colonel C could not know what had happened to the house he was in, until a paragraph enlightened him. Seeing he was not inclined to enlarge upon his perils and hairbreadth escapes."

"What a charming Englishman we have had here."

"Ah!"

"Have you not seen him? We heard you had."

"Of whom are you speaking?"

"Oh! Mr. _____, who was staying here, you know."

In came another person. Seating herself at the dinner table, she attacked poor J. C. at once.

"Ah, colonel! I was so glad to hear you had that long talk with the Englishman—that he heard at last someone who could make him understand our side."

"What was the name of the person you allude to?"

"Oh! you know him—Mr. _____. He says you gave a brilliant account of the battles around Richmond. That it was the most graphic description. He was charmed."

"Who says all that?"

Mem was dying to laugh. J. C. forgot the wonderful Englishman's name and fame as often as they told it to me.

I have gone back to my books, *Modeste Mignon* and *Eugénie Grandet*[4] [which] I brought home from the Prestons.

July 13, 1862.   Halcott Green came to see us. Bragg is a stern disciplinarian, according to Halcott. He did not in the least understand citizen soldiers. In the retreat from Shiloh, he ordered that not a gun should be fired. A soldier shot a chicken. The soldier was shot. "For a chicken!" said Halcott. "A Confederate soldier for a chicken!"[5]

---

4. Novels by Balzac published in 1844 and 1833, respectively.
5. A false story.

Mrs. McCord's troubles—a nurse who is also a beauty had better leave her beauty with her cloak and hat at the door.

This lovely lady nurse asked a rough old soldier, whose wound could not have been dangerous, "Well, my good soul, what can I do for you?"

"Kiss me!"

Mrs. McCord's fury "at the woman's telling it." It brought her hospital in disrepute. And very properly. She knew there were women who would boast of an insult if it ministered to their vanity of personal appearance. She wanted nurses to come dressed as nurses—as Sisters of Charity—not as fine ladies. Then there would be no trouble. When she saw them coming in angel sleeves, displaying all of their white arms, and in their muslin, showing all of their beautiful white shoulders and throats, she felt disposed to order them off the premises. That was no proper costume for a nurse.

Mrs. Bartow goes in her widow's weeds. That is after Mrs. McCord's own heart. But Mrs. Bartow has her stories, too. A surgeon said to her, "I give you no detailed instructions. A mother necessarily is a nurse."

And she passed on as quietly, "as smilingly acquiescent, my dear, as if I had ever been a mother of anything."

A Savannah paper has been very harsh in its rebuke to Yeadon of the *Courier* for dragging Mrs. Bartow's name into his paper.[6] "The living as well as the dead should be respected," says the Savannah editor.

Mrs. Bartow was bitterly mortified.

Mrs. Greenhow enlightened Rachel Lyons as to Mr. Chesnut's character in Washington. "One of the very few men that there was not a word of scandal about. I do not believe, my dear, that he ever spoke to a woman there. Yes, he did know Mrs. John R. Thomson."[7]

Mrs. Bartow stands up at a desk and cuts bonds apart. Miss Carroll[8] calls them "revenue clippers."

Walked up and down the college campus with Mrs. McCord. The buildings all lit up with gas. Soldiers seated under the elms in every direction, in every stage of convalescence. Could see the nurses flitting about through the open windows. It was a strange, weird scene.

Walked home with Mrs. Bartow—we stopped at Judge Carroll's; Mrs. C gave us a cup of tea. When we got home, found the Prestons had called for me to dine at their house to meet General Magruder.

6. On July 2, Yeadon reported that while visiting Columbia he had found Mrs. Bartow "cutting Treasury notes, to aid in [her] maintenance."

7. Josephine (Ward) Thomson, the wife of the N.J. senator.

8. A daughter of James Parsons Carroll and his wife Eliza Anciaux (Berrien) Carroll.

Last night the Edgefield band serenaded Governor Pickens. Harris and Mrs. Harris[9] (not Mrs. Gamps) stepped on the porch and sang the "Marseillaise" for them. It is more than twenty years since I have heard her voice. It was a very fine one then—but there is nothing which the tooth of time lacerates more cruelly than the singing voice of women. There is an incongruous metaphor for you.

Robert Barnwell writes the active measures of the council have done wonders in redeeming the credit of the state.

The negroes on the coast received the Rutledge Mounted Rifles, apparently with great rejoicings. And the troops were gratified to find the negroes in such a friendly state of mind. One servant whispered to his master, "Don't you mind 'em—don't trust 'em." So the master dressed himself as a Federal officer and went down to a negro quarter that night. The very first greeting: "Ki! Massa, you come for ketch rebels?"

"We can show you whey you can ketch thirty tonight."

So they took him to the Confederate camp—or pointed it out, then added for his edification, "We kin ketch officer for you whenever you want 'em."

Met Dr. Gibbes weeping and wailing. He is afraid his arm will have to be cut off—from some hurt he received in the hospital at Kingsville. If his arm is amputated, I hope it will be buried with all the honors of war, for it was wounded in manful work—saving life, not taking it.

Bad news. Gunboats pass Vicksburg. The Yankees are spreading themselves over our fair Southern land, like red ants. Did you ever see a [*omitted words*] which ants had marked for its own?

July 14, 1862.   Alex Haskell has come. I saw him about dusk ride up and go to the graveyard. I shut my window on that side! Poor fellow!

Yesterday we went to see Mrs. Browne at the Congaree House. She was perfectly happy. "Browne had come." Someone said to her: "You ought to be a proud woman. It is very far for him to come to stay so short a time." She says she told Browne what this lady said to her. She blushed like a girl of sixteen. "Browne says he would go fifty times as far as that to see me."

In the afternoon we drove out with Mr. and Mrs. Browne. He defended Mr. Mallory, whom it is the fashion just now to abuse.

9. William Alexander Harris and Sarah Harris. Mr. Harris, a wealthy Columbia resident, was the author of a defense of Pickens, *The Record of Fort Sumter . . . during the Administration of Governor Pickens* (1862).

The Yankees call for three hundred thousand men—more. That is a compliment to our powers. We have never had that many in the field yet—all put together.

They say Seward has gone to England. And his wily tongue will turn all hearts against us.

Browne told us there was a son of the duke of Somerset in Richmond.[1] And he laughed his fill at our ragged dirty soldiers. But he stopped his laughing when he saw them under fire. Our men strip the Yankees dead of their shoes, but they will not touch the shoes of a comrade. Poor fellows—they are nearly barefoot.

July 18, 21, 1862.   General Huger sent to inspect ordnance. Sent to Coventry?

Jackson gone into the enemy's country. Joe Johnston and Wade Hampton to follow.[2]

Think of Rice—Mr. Senator Rice[3]—who sent us the buffalo robes. I see from his place in the Senate—speaks of us as savages who put powder and whiskey in the soldiers' canteens to make them mad with ferocity in the fight. No—never. We admire coolness here—because we lack it. We do not need to be fired by drink to be brave. My classical lore is small indeed. I faintly remember something of the Spartans who marched to the music of lutes—no drum and fife was needed to fillip their fainting spirits. In that one thing we are Spartans. The powder we cannot spare from one musket. Alas, we have so little of it, and we need so much.

Mrs. Fisher and Mrs. Izard have instituted a wayside hospital at the point where all the RRs meet.[4] The Columbia Junction, in fact. I am ready and thankful to help every way, subscription and otherwise. But too feeble in health to attend in person. All honor to Mrs. Fisher.

Mrs. Bartow's adopted son has had the ball extracted from his arm. She is nursing him faithfully. The doctors fear a sinew has been cut, which may disable him—that is, that he may never regain the use of his hand.

Paul Hayne read Tennyson to Mrs. B and myself.

He began with "Break, Break, O Sea."[5] And I thought of poor Frank in the

---

1. Edward Seymour, earl St. Maur, fought in the Seven Days battles as a volunteer aide, then returned to England.

2. Apparently a false rumor.

3. Henry Mower Rice, a fur trader who negotiated the treaty that opened southwest Minn. to white settlement, served as U.S. senator from Minn. between 1858 and 1863.

4. Opened by the Young Ladies Hospital Association in March 1862, the Wayside Hospital cared for Confederate soldiers stranded by inadequate railroad service. The president of the association was Jane (Coles) Fisher, the wife of a Columbia physician and druggist.

5. Tennyson, "Break, Break, Break," in *Poems* (1842).

next room. "Oh, for the touch of a vanished hand and the sound of a voice that is still."

Mrs. Carrington at Mrs. Preston's, nursing a wounded son: "Have you seen him?"

"No, the girls say there is nothing to see. He is reduced to freckles and whiskers."

"For shame—to laugh at a wounded hero."

What Mrs. Browne heard a man say at the Congaree House: "We are breaking our heads against a stone wall. We are bound to be conquered. We cannot keep it up much longer, against so powerful a nation as the U.S. of America. Crowds of Irish, Dutch, Scotch are pouring in to swell their armies. They are promised our [*word omitted*], and they believe they will get them. Even if we are successful we cannot live without Yankees."

"Now," says Mrs. Browne, "I call that a Yankee spy."

"If he were a spy, he would not dare show his hand so plainly."

"To think," says Mrs. Browne, "that is not taken up. Seward's little bell would tinkle, a guard would come, and the Grand Inquisitor of America would order that man to be put under arrest in the twinkling of an eye, if he had ventured to speak against Yankees in Yankee land."

Mr. Preston said he had the right to take up anyone who was not in his right place—and send him where he belonged.

"Then do take up my husband instantly. He is sadly out of his right place in this little governor's council."

Mr. Preston stared at me and slowly uttered in his most tragic tones, "If I could put him where I think he ought to be!"

This I immediately hailed as a high compliment and was duly ready with my thanks.

Upon reflection, it is borne in upon me—he might have been more explicit. He left too much to the imagination.

Then Mrs. Browne described the Prince of Wales, whose manners, it seems, differ from those of Mrs. Ennery M——.[6] She arraigned us from morn to dewy eve and upbraided us with our ill-bred manners and customs.

The Prince conformed at once to whatever he saw was the way of those in whose house he was and closely imitated President Buchanan's way of doing things. He took off his gloves at once when he saw that the president wore none. By the by, I remember what a beautiful hand Mr. Buchanan has.

The Prince of Wales began by bowing to the people who were presented to him, but when he saw Mr. Buchanan shaking hands, he shook, too.

Smoking affably with Browne in the White House piazza, he expressed his content with the fine "segar" Browne gave him. The president said, "I was keeping some excellent ones for you—but Browne has got ahead of me."

Long after Mr. Buchanan had gone to bed, the Prince ran into his room in a jolly, boyish way.

6. Mrs. Henry Middleton.

"Mr. Buchanan, I have come for the fine segars you have for me."

The British contingent liked Floyd best of our cabinet ministers. Jake Thompson and Howell Cobb were too boisterous. Laughed too loud and too often.

As I walked up to the Prestons', along a beautifully shaded back street, a carriage passed, with Governor Means in it. As soon as he saw me, he threw himself half out of it. And kissed both hands to me—again and again. It was a *whole-souled* greeting, as the saying is. And I returned it with my whole heart, too. "Goodbye," he cried—and I answered, "Goodbye." I may never see him again. I am not sure that I did not shed a few tears. [*Rest of page and top of next page cut off.*]

Mr. Preston and Mr. Chesnut were seated in the piazza of the Hampton house as I walked in. And I opened my batteries upon them in this scornful style.

"You, you cold, formal, solemn, overly polite creatures, weighed down by your own dignity. You will never know the rapture of such a sad farewell as John Means and I have just interchanged. He was in a hack and I was on the sidewalk. He was on his way to the wars, poor fellow. The hackman drove steadily along in the middle of the street. But for our gray hairs I do not know what he might have thought of us. John Means does not suppress feelings at the unexpected meeting with an old friend. And a good cry does me good, too. It is a life of terror and foreboding we lead, my heart is in my mouth half of the time. But *you two*—under no possible circumstances could you forget your manners."

I do not see how the *Herald* or the *Tribune* could do us more injury than the *Examiner* of today.

A bomb from the enemy's camp exploding in the *Examiner*'s office would not have hurt the Confederate cause.

Read Russell's *India* all day. Saintly folks, those English, when their blood is up. Sepoys[7] and blacks we do not expect anything better from. But what an example of Christian patience and humanity the white "Angels" from the West set them!

Mr. Chesnut and Paul Hayne are faithful in their attendance upon Frank Bevel—Paul Hayne was reading aloud there all morning. Mr. C says complacently—Mrs. Bartow is so charming that attention to her wounded boy is not a hard duty.

The beautiful Jewess Rachel Lyons was here today. She flattered Paul Hayne so audaciously. And he threw back the ball. She is daft about J. C., but Miriam

---

7. Indian natives serving in the British army.

Cohen says she has not learned his hours yet. So far she has always called to see me when he is from home. She gave Paul Hayne the benefit of her philosophy. Married or single, all men were alike to her. She could only marry one of her own faith (a Jew). She added: Timrod would never introduce her to Paul Hayne; he dreaded her liking Paul Hayne best. And that thought was more than he could bear.

She asked me what I understood by the word "flirtation" and answered her own question: "A mere pretence of lovemaking, a semblance of love, not the reality. As soon as love itself was waked, it was no longer a flirtation. Is kissing legitimate in a flirtation?" she asked. "Some girls say you cannot keep a man off and on, as it is necessary to do, in a flirtation, unless you let him kiss you—indeed, he will kiss you."

Here Miriam's face assumed such a look of amazement and disgust that Miss Lyons brought herself up shortly.

"I think *those sorts* of freedoms horrid—I never let men kiss me."

Today I saw the Rowena to this Rebecca.[8] Mrs. Robert Barnwell called. She is the purest type of Anglo-Saxon. Exquisitely beautiful, cold, quiet, calm, ladylike, fair as a lily. With the blackest and longest eyelashes—and her eyes so light in color, someone said they were the hue of cologne and water. At any rate, she has the patent right to them. There are no more like them to be had. The effect is startling but lovely beyond words.

If I chronicled all of the good things sent me, I would have time to write of nothing else. Today the tray of peaches and muskmelons which came to me from Mrs. Guignard is really so great a treat that it deserves honorable mention. Frank Bevel, poor wounded boy, has something nice sent him every ten minutes by our patriotic women.

She, the high and lofty one, said she had read *Wilhelm Meister*[9] and *Elective Affinities* in their native German. All the same, she borrowed my translations of them.

Miriam remarked after her departure: "You tried to make her say Goethe. I wonder why she dodged it so adroitly, if she be so good a German scholar. I pronounce it as I do any other Gutter," said Mem dauntlessly. "I know no German whatever—not one word of it—but I am not such a fool as to say Go-e-the."

Another style of beauty came today. She was as handsome as any of them, Jew or Gentile—a brilliant creature, too, in her conversation, but when she thinks she has made a point, she screams with delight and slaps you on the knee.

8. In Sir Walter Scott's *Ivanhoe* (1820), Rowena is the daughter of a Saxon nobleman, and Rebecca, the daughter of a Jew.

9. Goethe, *Wilhelm Meisters Lehrjahre* (1796) and *Wilhelm Meisters Wanderjahre* (1821–29).

Paul Hayne has had another hemorrhage. Make a note of it. It is illness which keeps our poet from the wars.

Blanton Duncan told us a story of Morgan in Kentucky.

He walked into a court where they were trying some secessionists.

The judge was about to pronounce sentence, but Morgan rose and begged that he might be allowed to call some witnesses. The judge asked who were his witnesses.

"My name is John Morgan, and my witnesses are 1,400 Confederate soldiers."

Mrs. Frank Hampton is dead. Her mother could not come South. The war killed Sally Baxter.

Mrs. Izard witnessed two instances of patriotism in the caste called "sandhill tackies." One forlorn, chill-and-fever, freckled creature, yellow, dirty, and dry as a nut, was selling peaches at ten cents a dozen. Soldiers collected around her cart. She took the top off and cried, "Eat away—eat your fill, I never charge our own soldiers anything." They tried to make her take pay, but when she steadily refused it, they cheered her madly and told her, "Sleep in peace—how we will fight for you and keep off the Yankees."

Another poor sandhill man refused to sell his cows but gave them to the hospital.

Camden

July 29th, 1862

My dear Aunt Mary,

I have just left Mrs. Brownfield in a state of the utmost suspense. She begs me to ask of Uncle James if he knows of any possible means by which she might be able to trace her son.[1]

He was seen by several on the field the day after the battle, wounded but perfectly himself and walking about saying he would rather go to a private house than to a hospital. Later in the day John Darby saw him in an ambulance going to Richmond and said he repeated his wish to be taken to a private house but was then delirious.

This *all* they can hear, except a horrible rumor that some ambulance driver says he had an officer who died on the road and was put out and buried by the roadside.

---

1. Lt. Thomas Sumter Brownfield, great-grandson of the Revolutionary War hero Thomas Sumter, was fatally wounded at Malvern Hill on July 1.

It seems very improbable that they would have delayed an ambulance full of wounded men long enough to bury a man, when they were in a few miles of Richmond, and an officer, without keeping anything by which to identify him. And the wound was so slight as to permit him nearly twenty-four hours after to be walking about. It is scarcely probable that it proved fatal before he reached Richmond.

Their only hope is that he may be in some family, unable to give his name. His poor mother is nearly frantic, she asks Uncle James if there is any way of finding a trace of him. His father and brother are both on [their way] there now. I know it troubles Uncle James to read letters and therefore wrote to you instead. Poor Sumter, he was my earliest and warmest friend, and five minutes spent by John Darby in tending to him or asking the destination of the ambulance might have saved him.

Yours affectionately

Harriet C. Grant

They tell me when he was last seen his brains were showing, his head had been so shot away. And this child writes about "slight wound" and that a surgeon with his hands full can be expected to hunt up relatives &c&c.

Mary DeSaussure's letter:

Camden
July 14th, 1862

Dear Aunt Mary,

Your kind letter reached me on Saturday, and I write at once to ask you to send the watch by Dr. William Reynolds[2] if he is coming over. He is expected here shortly. If he is not coming, keep it until you or Uncle James come over, for I cannot risk it by the express.

Say to Uncle James for me that I cannot tell him how much I thank him for all his kindness and attention.

I can never repay it, but deeply have I felt it; it but adds another and more sacred link to the tie which binds me to him. I assure you it has been a great source of comfort to me that he was near and that he would do all that was possible for our loved and lost one, and that he and not a stranger saw the last sad offices performed and the precious body laid where we can as soon as possible secure it and bring him home to rest where he wished to sleep, in our own quiet graveyard.

Thank you for your kind sympathy; it is soothing and gratifying to know that our friends feel for us and with us. Though earth can give no comfort to grief like mine.

I know who sent the crushing blow. He doeth all things well. May He

2. Mary (Reynolds) DeSaussure's uncle, a Columbia physician.

grant me strength to bear it and to bring up my orphan boys as my husband would have done.

Poor mother is utterly crushed. I fear she will never be again what she was, and father, too, looks as though years had been added to his life. Henry was *their* prop and stay as well as my all. May God help us now.

Affectionately yours

Mary R. DeSaussure

The redemption of our native land from the rule of the foreigner! I have shared in such an attempt.

Recalling all the ties it dissolves, all the blood it commands to flow, all the healthy industry it arrests, all the madmen it arms, all the victims that it creates. I question whether one man really honest, pure, and humane who has gone through such an ordeal could ever hazard it again. Unless he is assured victory is secure. Aye! and the object for which he fights not to be wrested from his hands amidst the uproar of the elements that the battle has released.

—Bulwer (Riccabocca)[3]

The 1st August 1862, I left Mrs. McMahon's for Flat Rock, North Carolina. I was ill, and it was very hot and disagreeable for an invalid in a boardinghouse in that climate.

The LaBordes[4] and the McCord girls[5] came part of the way with me.

The cars were crowded, and a lame soldier had to stand, leaning on his crutches in the thoroughfare that runs between the seats. One of us gave him our seat. You may depend there was no trouble in finding a seat for our party after that feat. Dr. LaBorde quoted a classic anecdote. In some Greek assembly an old man was left standing. A Spartan gave him his seat. The Athenians cheered madly, though they had kept their seats. The comment— "Lacedaemonians practice virtue, Athenians know how to admire it."

Nathan Davis happened accidentally to be at the station at Greenville. He took immediate charge of Molly and myself, for my party had dwindled to that. He went with us to the hotel, sent for the landlord, told him who I was, secured good rooms for us, and saw that we were made comfortable in every way.

At dinner I entered that immense dining room alone: but I saw friends and acquaintances on every side.

3. From a speech by Dr. Riccabocca, one of the eccentrics in Edward George Bulwer-Lytton, *My Novel; or, Varieties in English Life* (1852), part 1, chapter 8.
4. Maximilian LaBorde, physician, author, journalist, and professor at S.C. College, served as chairman of the Central Association for the Relief of S.C. Soldiers. His wife, Elizabeth (Carroll) LaBorde, was the sister of James Parsons Carroll.
5. Hannah Cheves and Louisa Rebecca Hayne McCord, teenaged daughters of Louisa (Cheves) McCord.

My first exploit was to repeat to Mrs. Ives,[6] Mrs. Pickens's blunder—in taking a suspicious attitude toward men born at the North and calling upon General Cooper to agree with her. Martha Levy[7] explained the grave faces of my auditors by saying that Colonel Ives was a New Yorker. My distress was dire.

Mrs. Ives's brother, Senator Semmes of Louisiana,[8] danced a "hoedown" for us—a negro corn-shucking "heel and toe" fling—grapevine twist &c. Martha Levy applauded heartily and cried, "The honorable senator from Louisiana has the floor."

Louisa Hamilton was there. She told me that Captain George Cuthbert, with his arm in a sling from a wound by no means healed, was going to risk the shaking of a stagecoach; he was on his way to his Cousin William Cuthbert's at Flat Rock.

Now, George Cuthbert is a type of the very finest kind of Southern soldier. We cannot make them any better than that. Before the war I knew him: he traveled in Europe with my sister Kate and Mary Withers.

At once I offered him a seat in [a] comfortable hack Nathan Davis had engaged for me.

Molly sat opposite to me, and often when I was so tired held my feet in her lap. Captain Cuthbert's man sat with the driver—we had ample room. We were a dilapidated concern. I was so ill I could barely sit up. I had to draw his match, light his segar—&c. He was very quiet, grateful, gentle and, I was going to say, "docile."

He is a fiery soldier, one of those whose whole face becomes transfigured in the battle—so one of his men told me, describing his way with his company. He does not blow his own trumpet—but I made him tell me the story of his duel with the *Mercury*'s reporter.

He seemed awfully ashamed, wasting time in such a scrape. He told me of Sumter Brownfield and that fearful wound in the head—brains exposed.

That night we stopped at a country house, halfway toward our journey's end. There we met Mr. Charles Lowndes. Rawlins Lowndes, his son, is with Hampton. General Ripley in his report tried to put a stigma upon his aides— Rawley Lowndes and Kirkland—but he failed utterly. Everybody knew them, and they knew him—and their behavior since has made his "bad word" more absurd still.

First we drove by mistake into Judge King's yard. Our hackman supposed that was the hotel. Then we made Farmer's Hotel (as the seafaring men say).

Burnet Rhett was at the door, caparisoned, horse and man, with as much red

6. Cora (Semmes) Ives. Her husband, Joseph Christmas Ives, known before the war as the explorer of the Colorado River, was born in New York City, but resigned his U.S. Army commission to serve as a colonel of engineers in the C.S.A. He was soon to become an aide to Jefferson Davis in Richmond.

7. The sister of Eugenia (Levy) Phillips.

8. In 1861, attorney Thomas Jenkins Semmes of New Orleans, first cousin of Confederate Adm. Raphael Semmes, helped draft the La. secession ordinance and served as judge of the Confederate District Court before being elected to the Senate.

and gold artillery uniform as they could bear—sash &c&c. He held his horse. The stirrups were Mexican—I believe they looked like little sidesaddles. Seeing his friend and crony George Cuthbert alight and leave a veiled lady in the carriage, this handsome and undismayed young artillerist walked round and round the carriage, talked with the driver, looked in at the doors, at the front, &c&c. Suddenly I bethought me to raise my veil and satisfy his curiosity.

Our eyes met, and I smiled. It was impossible to resist the comic disappointment of his face—a woman old enough to be George Cuthbert's mother, with the ravages of a year of gastric fever, almost fainting with fatigue then. He instantly mounted his gallant steed and pranced away to his fiancée. He is to marry the greatest heiress in the state, Miss Aiken.[9] Then Captain Cuthbert told me his name &c&c. Albert Elmore[1] says there is great choice in Rhetts—a first-rate Rhett is one thing, but a second-rate Rhett is the devil, &c&c.

Captain Cuthbert said this was a first-rate Rhett.

At Kate's I found Sally Rutledge.[2]

And then for weeks life was a blank. I remember nothing. The illness which had been creeping on for so long a time took me by the throat.

Before he left Flat Rock, Captain Cuthbert dined at Kate's—arm still in a sling. The little girls were so proud that they were allowed to sit by him—cut up his food and do everything that the want of a right arm made him helpless to do for himself. He told us of his first lieutenant Robert Brownfield.[3] The ambulance driver could never be found, nor his body. A terrible grief to his family, who are Roman Catholics and would be so relieved to find his body. They mourn over the fact that he is not buried in consecrated ground.

Captain Cuthbert was wounded at Manassas but got back in time for Seven Pines.

At Greenville I met so many friends. I witnessed the wooing of Barny Heyward—once the husband of the lovely Lucy Izard, now a widower and a bon parti. He is there nursing Joe, his brother. So was the beautiful Henrietta Magruder, now Mrs. Joseph Heyward. Poor Joe died.

There is something magnetic in Tatty Clinch's large and lustrous black eyes.[4] No man has ever resisted their influence. She says her virgin heart has never beat one throb the faster for any mortal here below—until now.

Well, as I said, Joseph Heyward died. And rapidly and with a light heart did the bereaved beauty shake the dust of this poor Confederacy from her feet and plume her wings for flight across the water.

9. Henrietta Aiken was the only child of Harriet (Lowndes) Aiken and former governor William Aiken of Charleston and Colleton District. A rice planter, Aiken owned 700 slaves in 1860.

1. Elmore's wife, Alexina, was a first cousin once removed of James Chesnut, Jr.

2. One of the "Tradd St. Rutledges," Sarah Henrietta Rutledge was a daughter of Frederick Rutledge.

3. M. B. C. means Thomas Sumter Brownfield.

4. Catherine Maria Clinch was a daughter of Duncan Lamont Clinch.

XVIII

"A World Kicked to Pieces"—Memoirs

I destroyed all my notes and journal—from the time I arrived at Flat Rock —during a raid upon Richmond in 1863.[1] Afterward—I tried to fill up the gap from memory.

September 23, 1863. Bloomsbury. So this is no longer a journal but a narrative of all I cannot bear in mind which has occurred since August 1862. So I will tell all I know of that brave spirit, George Cuthbert. During the winter of '63, while I was living at the corner of Clay and 12th St. [Richmond], he came to see me. Never did man enjoy life more. The Preston girls were staying at my house then, and it was very gay for the young soldiers who ran down from the army for a day or so. We had heard of him, as usual gallantly facing odds at Sharpsburg. And he asked, if he should chance to be wounded, would I have him brought to Clay St.

He was shot at Chancellorsville, leading his men. The surgeon did not think him mortally wounded. He sent me a message that he was coming at once to our house. He knew he would soon get well there. Also that I need not be alarmed; those Yankees could not kill him.

He asked one of his friends to write a letter to his mother. Afterward he said he had another letter to write but that he wished to sleep first—he felt so exhausted. At his request they then turned his face away from the light and left him. When they came again to look after him, they found him dead. He had been dead for a long time. It was so bitter cold—and the wounded who had lost so much blood weakened in that way. Lacking warm blankets and all comforts, many died who might have been saved by one good hot drink or a few mouthfuls of nourishing food.

One of his generals said to me: "Fire and reckless courage like Captain Cuthbert's were contagious. Such men in an army were invaluable. Such losses weakened us indeed."

But I must go back to Flat Rock and not linger longer around the memory of the bravest of the brave—a true specimen of our old regime—gallant, gay, unfortunate.

---

1. While the battle of Chancellorsville was fought to the north, detachments of U.S. Maj. Gen. George Stoneman's cavalry rode within several miles of the Confederate capital on May 3–4, 1863, in an effort to cut communication lines.

Mr. Daniel Blake drove down to my sister's in his heavy substantial English phaeton with stout and strong horses to match.

I went back with him and spent two delightful days at his hospitable mansion. I met there, as a sort of chaplain, the Rev. Thomas Davis of Camden. He dealt unfairly by me: we had a long argument, and when we knelt down for evening prayers, he introduced an extemporaneous prayer—and prayed *for me* most palpably. There was I, down on my knees, red-hot with rage and fury. David said it was a clear case of hitting a fellow when [he] was down. Afterward the fun of it all struck me—and I found it difficult to keep from shaking with laughter. It was not an edifying religious exercise, to say the least, as far as I was concerned.

Then came fatal Sharpsburg. My friend Colonel Means—killed on the battlefield, his only son wounded and a prisoner. His wife had not recovered from the death of her other child, Emma, who had died of consumption early in the war. She was lying on a bed when they told her of her husband's death—and then they tried to keep Stark's condition from her. They think now that she misunderstood and believed him dead, too. She threw something over her face. She did not utter one word. She remained quiet so long, someone removed the light shawl which she had drawn over her head. She was dead. Miss Mary Stark said afterward: "No wonder! how was she to face life without her husband and children. That was all she had ever lived for."

These sad, unfortunate memories—let us run away from them.

What Colonel Chesnut did in 1862. All of our South Carolina troops were in Virginia; here we were, without soldiers or arms. He raised an army, so to speak, and imported arms through the Trenholms' house. He had arms to sell to the Confederacy.

He laid the foundation of a niter bed; and the Confederacy sent to Columbia to learn of Professor LeConte how to begin theirs. He brought up all of the old arms and had them altered and repaired. He built ships. He imported clothes and shoes for our soldiers, for which things they had long stood sorely in need. He imported cotton cards and set all idle hands carding and weaving—all the world was spinning cotton. He tried to stop the sale of whiskey, and alas, he called for *reserves*—that is, men over age—and the unforgivable offense he committed of sending the sacred negro property to work on fortifications away from their owners' plantations.

Yeadon sang, "Lay the proud usurper low,"[2] and Dr. Gibbes, in his newspaper, sung paeans to Pickens and devoted the head of the military to the infernal gods.

2. A play on a line from Robert Burns, "Scots Wha Hae" (1794).

So we left Columbia in a blaze because of his tyranny.

———————

In Richmond, when we arrived there, the president said: "When Richmond is threatened, Virginia says, 'If you do not, we will defend the capital.' Charleston is threatened, and *your* legislature disbands eight thousand good troops thoroughly organized and begins to call on us for troops from the Confederate army."

As usual, John Manning tricked John Preston. Bonham was made governor.

So far the world does not seem to think it can have more Edgefield than it can bear![3]

———————

Speaking of that legislature, we must remember the good seed are in the army—only the chaff remains at home now.

———————

Judge Withers denounced the council from the bench. He became angry with Colonel Chesnut during the Montgomery Congress, and as time went on he grew more and more spiteful. With him it was a personal enmity, for his contempt for Governor Pickens was open and avowed.

Sending laggards to the front by conscription, organizing the reserves—above all, taking a part of the negroes from the crops and sending them to the coast fortifications, where they had a chance to run away, raised such a tempest of wrath against the council that although it would die a natural death in December, the convention was called to annihilate it at once.

When the convention met, a committee of twenty-one was appointed to consider the subject. Mr. Barnwell was chairman. There was a subcommittee of which Judge Inglis[4] was chairman.

In plain English, this committee was to try the council for its life.

The committee, composed of the elite of the convention (a convention which was called the ablest body of men ever assembled in South Carolina), pronounced an eulogium on the council and its work.

Like Balaam who was called to curse, it blessed instead.[5] Colonel Chesnut was exonerated from blame and applauded for the amount of good work he had done in so short a time. It is from Mr. Barnwell that I have extracted the summary of what Colonel Chesnut had accomplished in a year. Judge Inglis's report was even stronger in his behalf.

The governorship, or any high office in South Carolina, is like the kingdom

———————

3. Edgefield District had been the home of Governor Pickens, as well as of nullifier George McDuffie, former U.S. senator Andrew P. Butler, Preston Brooks, and Confederate Senator Louis T. Wigfall of Tex.

4. John Auchincloss Inglis of Chesterfield District, chancellor of the S.C. Court of Equity and chairman of the committee that presented the secession ordinance to the convention.

5. Numbers 22–24.

of heaven in one respect: it can be taken by violence—and Edgefield has violence enough to take anything.

Bonham of Edgefield being made governor, we made a brief stay at home and then went on to Richmond, Mr. Davis having appointed Colonel Chesnut on his staff.

Reading Mrs. Stowe or Redpath's *John Brown*,[6] one feels utterly confounded at the atrocity of African slavery. We look upon the miserable black race as crushed to earth, habitually knocked down, as John Brown says, "by an iron shovel or anything that comes handy." At home we see them, the idlest, laziest, fattest, most comfortably contented peasantry that ever cumbered the earth—and we forget there is any wrong in slavery at all.

I daresay the truth lies between the two extremes.

We came to Richmond in company with Mrs. Stanard, one of the leaders of society in that city for twenty years—beautiful and agreeable still.

Molly, who is a capital cook, besides being so good a lady's maid, had looked after one lunch basket, and J. C. had selected his wine and brandy from his father's cellar.

As Mrs. Stanard ate and sipped the old brandy, she smiled in his face, "My dear friend, if one will eat, they must drink."

Mr. Phoenix was along, the man who married Sissy Blake. He drank to some purpose. He disappeared. I did not see him go out. I looked under the seat to see if there was a hole in the floor of that rickety old car and he had dropped through.

At the Ballard House we met Mr. Boteler, one of J. C.'s college friends. From him I had a full account of Stonewall Jackson, the Confederate hero par excellence. Mr. Boteler said he had often slept under the same blanket with Stonewall. Besides, he gave me his photograph—Stonewall's, of course.

While in Columbia we saw Cheves McCord at his mother's. He had been badly wounded at Second Manassas, in both the head and the leg.

Mrs. McCord went at once to Richmond and found he was still at or near Manassas Junction. She went to Mr. Miles to get her a passport to go down for him. He said the thing was impossible. Government had seized all trains, and no passports were given. "I let him talk," said Mrs. McCord, "for he does it beautifully. That very night I chartered a special train. We ran down to Manassas and I brought back Cheves in triumph. You see he is nearly well, with our home nursing."

"Mother of the Gracchi," we cried.[7]

But he grew restless, and they could not keep him from his duties in camp. He was not fit for duty. The ball had never been removed from his head, and it

6. *The Public Life of Capt. John Brown* (1860) by antislavery journalist James Redpath.
7. A reference to Mrs. McCord's play, *Caius Gracchus*.

gave him so much trouble that his servant brought him back to Richmond, taking him to the house of Mrs. Myers, a friend of theirs.

The surgeons thought the ball moved its position. At any rate, he died that night.

We went at once to Mrs. Myers—too late. I think I shed the bitterest tears that ever came into my eyes—for him, cut off so soon—and for his mother!! Not twenty-one yet—his beautiful bride—and baby unborn.

I meant to copy Mrs. McCord's letter, but the cry of a soul like her in agony—I could not do it. Heartbroken, she is.

We took leave of the Ballard House and made our home with some "decayed ladies" forced by trouble, loss of property, &c to receive boarders.

A dreadful refuge of the distressed, it was. The house was comfortable and the table good. But you paid the most extravagant price, and you were forced to assume the patient humility of a poor relation. So fine was the hauteur and utter scorn with which you were treated.

At the gate of this antique mansion met Colonel Ives (the rhyme of the nine wives, cats, and lives was always running in my head at the sound of his name). He came slashing along in his heavy cavalry boots, spurs rattling—quite the picture of a soldier. We stopped and had a regular talk. This handsome creature gave me the clue of many of the Richmond mysteries.

Mr. and Mrs. Davis met us with warmth and cordiality.

Once for all, let me say—Mrs. Davis has been so kind to me—I can never be grateful enough. Without that I should like her. She is so clever, so brilliant indeed, so warmhearted, and considerate toward all who are around her. After becoming accustomed to the spice and spirit of her conversation, away from her things seem flat and tame for awhile.

Then we took a floor at the corner of Clay and 12th Sts.

A few days before I left Columbia, Dr. Thornwell came to see me at Mrs. McMahon's. Dr. Gibbes had called, and I was sitting with him, just opposite the door of the drawing room, when Dr. Thornwell came in. Dr. Gibbes sprang to his feet hurriedly and said: "Oh! I am going, he does not speak to me. No doubt he will tell you all about it."

Dr. Thornwell stayed two hours, but he did not allude to the Gibbes business. I was ill so soon after this, I have no distinct recollection of this long talk—[remainder of page cut out]. Except that evening I amazed some of my friends who thought themselves very clever indeed, by saying, "Dr. Thornwell is the very cleverest man I know."

During the winter of 1863 we lived in the house of a Mrs. Lyons, occupying one floor—drawing room, dining room, chamber, and two servants' rooms for Molly and Laurence. Then the Preston girls came. [Remainder of page cut out.] We changed the dining room into an apartment for them.

The poor drawing room now saw rare sights, in its capacity of room of all work. It was the only parlor we had, the only dining room. There we danced to the music of an old ramshackle piano—and had a good time generally. We received there all that the Confederacy had of good and great, from Mr. President Davis, the Lees, Mr. Hunter, down to the humblest private, who was often our nearest friend or relative.

We had no right to expect any better lodgings, for Richmond was crowded to suffocation—hardly standing room left.

At first Mr. Chesnut was too civil by half. I knew it could not last—going everywhere with us, to parties, to concerts, to private theatricals, even to breakfasts. Then he broke down and denounced us for being so dissipated.

Mr. Davis came to our relief and sent the recalcitrant head of our household to inspect and report [on] Charleston and the Southern armies generally.

We must not forget Morgan's man, Robert Alston.[8] Him Mr. Chesnut brought forward, leading him by the hand quite tenderly—a brilliant creature, truly, and no doubt a fair specimen of the western daredevils who rally around John Morgan.

He declaimed "I am dying Egypt."[9] We had never heard of it before, and he claimed the authorship for a soldier of the western army. Since then, [along] with "All quiet along the Potomac tonight"[1]—it possesses as many fathers as the church.

The night my girls[2] came, they found me dressing for a party at the Semmeses and Iveses. I made them go with me.

There was nothing then or ever in the Confederacy so sweet, so lovely, so stately, so accomplished as these interesting friends of mine.

From the time that they came until they left me, months after, it was one scene of perfect enjoyment.

We had no battle—Fredericksburg was over and the Wilderness not dreamed of.

The town was filled with our friends, and it was our duty to make our soldiers forget the discomforts of camp when they ran down for a few days.

Buck, the very sweetest woman I ever knew, had a knack of being "fallen in love with" at sight and of never being "fallen out of love" with. But then, there seemed a spell upon her lovers—so many were killed or died of the effects of

---

8. A major in John Hunt Morgan's cavalry, Robert A. Alston was a member of the prominent rice-planting family of S.C.

9. A popular wartime song by Williams Haynes Lytle, based on *Antony and Cleopatra*, act 4, scene 15.

1. This song, inspired by George McClellan's reports of "all quiet" before Bull Run, was written by Ethelinda (Elliot) Beers.

2. The Preston girls, Buck, Mamie, but apparently not Tudy.

wounds. Ransom Calhoun, Braddy Warwick,[3] Claude Gibson, the Notts.

In Columbia she came, in her girlish way: "Shall I answer him? See here."

Annie, on hearing the name: "Answer! Did you see the paper today? He is killed." Annie the practical.

Once she came in and sat on the edge of my bed. In those Columbia days, a cloud had come over her bright face. "Buck, what makes you so pale, dear—and why have that black mantle around you this warm day?"

"Why not? I feel so sad—black suits me. Alfred Rhett has killed Cousin Ransom in a duel."[4] Here she drew the mantle close around her face.

"You know, he was so good to me, those years I was left at school in Paris. How can I forget it all?"

She wore the black mantle several days.

But the days were beautiful, and she so young and lighthearted, her grief was but a summer cloud—fleeting and leaving no trace behind for any of them.

"What is the matter with Buck? She has been languishing on that sofa, profoundly indifferent to me and to the rest of mankind," said John Darby.

"Don't you know her yet? She would not listen to that poor fellow while he was alive, and now that he is dead she is brokenhearted. Let her alone, she will soon recover," said Mary C cheerfully.

Johnny was asked if he were not succumbing, too, to Buck's fascinations. It was a road they all traveled.

"No, never." He looked alarmed at the bare suggestion. "I dare not. I would prefer to face a Yankee battery. They say So-and-So is awfully in love with Miss S. P. Then I say, look out! You will see his name next in the list of killed and wounded."

This was very hard on Buck, but our brave young soldiers faced the music gallantly. Let who would die or be killed, there was always a new crop of flourishing dimensions growing vigorously around her. Lovers were never wanting. I think she was loyal to the dead and missing.

The darling! She has her peculiarities. Who can describe her? This I know. I would not have, if I could, anything altered about her mentally, morally, physically. Of how many people can one say that?

That first night—Mrs. Ives's party.

Ruby Mallory recited "Bingen on the Rhine."[5] It was too appropriate. It brought a choking sensation to our throats.

Then we had delightful teas at Mrs. Stanard's and Mrs. Randolph's, where

3. At nineteen, Virginian Bradfute Warwick had joined Garibaldi's army in the battle for the unification of Italy in 1859. Returning home after Va. seceded, he served as lieutenant colonel of John Bell Hood's regiment until his death during the Seven Days.

4. The duel between Maj. Alfred Moore Rhett of the First S.C. Artillery and his former superior, Col. William Ransom Calhoun, occurred outside Charleston on Sept. 5, 1862.

5. Only seven when the war began, Confederate Secretary of the Navy Stephen Mallory's daughter Ruby won a place in Richmond society with elocution displays like this one.

statesmen and warriors were incited to meet us without stint. And what few literate they could bag or scare up—John R. Thompson,[6] &c&c.

Splendid dinners at the MacFarlands' and Lyonses'.

Johnny, now Captain Chesnut of the dragoons, came for three [visits?]. Boykin Rangers, of which he is captain, is now swallowed by the army—Company A &c&c one mounted something-or-other. We heard it all often enough to remember. We managed to get a room for him from Mrs. Lyons. He had two servants. The girls had theirs. Mr. C had left Laurence to cater for us.

Laurence has simple ideas but effective: "You give me the money, I'll find everything you want." There is no such word as "fail" with him. "Starvation—and there ain't nothing to eat in Richmond—not a bit of it. You give me the money." Molly was housekeeper, cook, anything and everything, as the time required.

This was her spirit. One night we came from a ball and found Molly and Anne in the drawing room—huge fire, gas lit, &c.

"Well, we have had our frolic, too—Anne and me are going to do all of our clear starching ironing in here, when you are out of our way. There you go, night after night, with your *sinful* frolicking." Molly and Anne were pious Methodists to whom dancing was a crime against religion.

They were our maids, and we had washerwomen with whom we were satisfied—not so our maids.

They turned up their noses at such washing and ironing. We would never have asked these creatures to wash and iron by day, much less by night.

Anne said, "Marster says to our white people, 'For God sake don't economize in your washerwoman's bill.'"

The Infant Samuel[7] came, spruce, dapper, pleasant as ever—a perfect magazine of news. Knew most people and affected to know everything and everybody. After for a week or two adding very much to our company, suddenly he sunk beneath our horizon—a lost Pleiade.

Afterward we heard that a stormy life in front of the Spotswood had led to friends bodily forcing him back to the army. Then came letters in shoals. One in particular, containing an enthusiastic expression which caused me a laugh and a groan—"I could not present myself before you with the flush of wine upon my brow!" They grew more energetic, these epistles, being unanswered. Then I wrote, "Desist [*remainder of page cut out*]. Stop it—or we will have a drama, or a sensational novel in the *Tribune,* made up of your intercepted letters and entitled the 'Rebel's Remorse.'"

Every night our parlor was crammed to its utmost capacity. John Darby, who appeared simultaneously with the Preston contingent, taught them to play

6. John Reuben Thompson, the Va. poet who edited *The Southern Literary Messenger* before the war, was working for *The Southern Illustrated News*.

7. Probably Samuel Davis Shannon (see p. 204, n. 6). The epithet "Infant" is apparently a humorous tribute to Shannon's large size.

casino. Afterward that was the favorite game. There was an immense amount of taffy made. We were happy.

These were days of unmixed pleasure, snatched from the wrath to come.

At first John Darby came soon after breakfast, but soon the clanking of his cavalry spurs could be heard upon the pavement long before, and Anne awakened the girls with: "Get up, Dr. Darby is here—been here ever so long."

Of course, there were never chairs enough. One night we witnessed the republican independence of the Wigfalls.

Mr. Hunter of Virginia came in with Miles and Garnett. L. Q. Washington made a signal to me. I turned and saw the president of the Confederacy had quietly entered and was standing in front of the Wigfalls. They kept their seats and turned their backs on him! It seems incredible—but Edgefield and Texas combined makes one stouthearted enough for anything. Louis Wigfall was not there—only his daughters.

Somebody whispered, with a snigger as I passed rapidly to that end of the room: "Bully! The Wigfalls are trying to snub Jeff Davis!"

I am sure the president did not notice it, for the rest of us made obeisance before him, as was due to his position. I was proud to receive him in my house—for himself, Jeff Davis. The others stood up to receive the head of the Confederacy as well. So he was met with all the honors due him. He stood, for there were not chairs for half the company. And the Prestons and myself stood, too, of course. It was a remarkable episode.

One day he came by for me, to go to church. I had not intended to go but hurried on a hat and shawl and was down in a twinkling.

By way of apology, as I entered I quoted Louis XIV. "*Almost* you have been kept waiting."[8]

He said, "You are not to blame, for you did not know we were coming."

Once I remember telling the president when he walked home from church with me that I was *wae*, as the Scotch say, that I had no grandchildren. I would like to keep my prayer book which he carried for me and tell them, "This prayer book was carried often to church and from it by Jeff Davis."

The president gave us a breakfast. His aides were all there—the Prestons and myself the only ladies. He was so kind and so amiable and agreeable, we were all charmed, but Buck came away in a very ecstasy of loyalty. As we got into the lonely Clay Street, she hurrahed for Jeff Davis and professed her willingness to fight for him to the death.

When Mrs. Davis came home, she gave us a matinée musicale. Miss Hammersmith sang. And Mrs. Dick Anderson[9]—Mrs. Semmes who played[1]— General (Prince) Polignac was there—and some Germans. Custis Lee and Mr.

---

8. A play on a supposed remark by the Sun King as he watched his coach arrive just in time to pick him up: "J'ai failli attendre" ("I almost had to wait").

9. Sarah (Gibson) Anderson, wife of Maj. Gen. Richard Heron Anderson.

1. Myra Eulalia (Knox) Semmes, wife of Confederate Sen. Thomas Jenkins Semmes of La., was an accomplished harpist and a leading Richmond hostess.

Davis' staff—Browne, Ives, & Co. The Germans played and sang, accompanying themselves in piano and guitar. All the morning I had been reading German with Mary Preston. I asked her now,

"What is Miss Hammersmith singing?"

"Good heavens! Don't you know? It is the ballad we were translating just before we came from home today."

So I found out I did not know as much German as I thought I did.

Buck declaimed "Jeanne d'Arc" and "Dandolo." She has the very sweetest voice, and it is admirably trained. She was so lovely withal that the Frenchmen and German compliments rained upon her. They never left her again. It was such a comfort, apparently, to find a beautiful American girl who spoke their languages with ease and comfort to herself and to them.

Strange stories got out. At Mrs. Davis's breakfast the foreigners all did something—a gathering and exhibition of all the talents. I was asked wherever I turned, "What do you do?" More frequently, "What did Mrs. Davis do?"

"We held our tongues. You know that is what we can do best of all." Finally, out of patience with so much idle curiosity, I cried,

"We danced on the tightrope."

"Have mercy, dear," whispered Mrs. Davis. "Never say that again. They will believe you. You do not know this Richmond.

"They swallow scandal with such wide open mouths, and their easy credulity is such—next winter they will have the exact length of our petticoats, and describe the kind of spangles we were sprinkled with."

Turkeys were thirty dollars apiece, but Laurence kept us plentifully supplied. Molly cooked admirably. We lived well—kept open house indeed. Our friends the soldiers from the army breakfasted, dined, and supped at the corner of Clay and 12th Sts.

We had sent us from home wine, rice, potatoes, hams, eggs, butter, pickles. About once a month a man came on with all that the plantation could furnish us.

Above us lived a family with an unpronounceable Polish name, which they with much worldly wisdom changed for one easily pronounced by American lips.

They had a young lady. And men innumerable scampered up the steps used by us in common. None of whom, however, were known to us!

One day this young person, in the course of a morning call, gave me her heart history briefly.

"I was engaged to such a nice young man, but he lost everything in that Yankee raid around Winchester. Que faire? Would you have me marry and starve? Never. They did not leave him enough to buy me shoestrings! Mamma is perfectly miserable, because I am flirting now with a Frenchman and he not even of our faith." (She is a Jewess.) She is wasting her time fretting. A Confederate soldier with 95 Confederate dollars a month—that would not keep me in hairpins."

The Frenchman sat with her on the piazza, which opened upon the street. In our parlor we could not see them, and we had no choice but to hear.

"Oh! Oh! don't," on her part, and "Ah, you naughty girl!" on his.

I asked what can they be after?

"Not much—they are in an open piazza on a level with the public street," answered Mr. Chesnut shortly, "and I daresay that phrase is the only English the man knows."

Madame Mère was so polite she called both of her servants "aunt"—Aunt Betty and Aunt Maria. The mistress was a little bit of a woman, the maids exceeding tall. One day there was a row in the kitchen, and Molly reported that Madame had stood upon a chair and boxed Aunt Betty's ears soundly. Then she turned to Molly.

"And pray, what are you standing there with your eyes and mouth wide open for? Go out of here, you impudent creature!" But Molly stood her ground and went on with her work. Aunt Maria said she shook in her shoes; she expected her mistress to fly at Molly and box her next.

I begged Molly to be careful and respectful. If this woman assaulted her, what could I do? Certainly I could not undo it, no matter how angry I grew.

Those dear girls made Richmond a happy home to me. Heim leben, as my German book says.

Maria Freeland came with her fiancé John Redman Coxe Lewis, who is a cousin of my husband's through his mother Esther Maria Coxe of Philadelphia. His father Lorenzo Lewis was a grandnephew of Washington, and a grandson of Mrs. Custis, Washington's wife.

Miss Nelly Custis married Washington's sister's son. Is that clear enough? At any rate, the Washington-Lewis part of it is a patent of nobility in this country. And Maria says when she is married she will call General Lee "Cousin Robert," because he, too, married a Miss Custis of the Mount Vernon family.

Mrs. Lewis of Audley was stripped by the Yankees of all her earthly possessions. It began by degrees.

One day a card was brought her—"Mr. John Washington." Now the name of the father of his country opened all doors at Audley, so the gentleman was promptly asked into the drawing room. He proved to be a crow black negro—black beyond the usual darkness allowed them by nature, and glossy withal. He produced a note from Milroy.[2]

Now the wife of Mr. John Washington was one of Mrs. Lewis's women, and the order ran thus: "Mrs. Lewis must send John Washington's family in one of her carriages. She must also send a white driver if she wants her horses re-

2. U.S. Brig. Gen. Robert Huston Milroy.

turned to her, for her slaves are all freed by Lincoln's proclamation—consequently would not return to her."

Mrs. Lewis stood at her window and [watched] the cavalcade file off. Many of the negroes refused to leave her, of course.

Rose Freeland, the other sister, was a beautiful girl, too. A few days after this visit of Maria and John Lewis, the Prestons came flying in, nearly bursting with a secret. They had solemnly promised Rose not to tell—and yet Rose was engaged to Captain Harrison.[3] He was only to be in town three hours. She had been engaged to him ever so long, and now nothing would do him but he must be married and march away. So they hurried off to dress for this sudden and private wedding.

As they went off: "Oh! Mrs. Chesnut, his company has orders to march at three—he has only two hours more here."

"Tell that to the marines! After the ceremony is over, I'll make you a bet—Captain Harrison will invite his superior officer to the wedding. You will see him there. And they will cause his hard heart to relent. See if they don't. And he will grant Captain Harrison two or three weeks' furlough."

They laughed me to scorn. Two weeks after or more, the beautiful bride, lovelier than ever, called with her splendid-looking husband—for there never was a handsomer pair. He was still to leave the next day!

This was February 1863. Today I write—October of the same year—Captain Harrison came home to die of his wounds. Poor Rose and her newborn baby died, too, with him, one might say—for it was so soon after.

All three lie buried at Hollywood cemetery.

When Mr. Preston urged me to begin this journal and keep it regularly—during the year '63 I burned so much, lost so much—that there are few scraps left me—and I find it hard to arrange them.

Soon I made the unpleasant discovery that we had forgotten Yankees and were fighting each other.

In Montgomery I heard the first gun of the stay-at-home brigade. Mr. Miles said to me significantly, "Her Majesty's government and Her Majesty's opposition."

"What does it mean?"

"Only Judge Withers is furious because Jeff Davis has accepted a house at the hands of the Congress. The Confederate Constitution says he shall have a salary and nothing more."

---

3. Randolph Harrison, a physician and direct descendant of the great Va. planter, Benjamin Harrison II.

Mr. Henry Marshall, the Judge's most devoted friend, explained.

"No, he hates Jeff Davis. When Davis was secretary of war, he refused to be introduced to the Judge. Now Withers says Chesnut induced him to vote for Jeff Davis and Stephens, and he will never forgive himself for it—or Chesnut either."

"Stephens does not believe in this thing at all—that is evident."

"Then why did he take a place in our government?"

"Halfhearted people will be our ruin. We want faith that will move mountains."

"And Toombs?"

"I do not know what is the matter there, but Mrs. Toombs takes a tone of bitter dissatisfaction. You know, when it comes to expressing their opinions the Toombses are like old Pick—'insensible to fear.'"

In Columbia it was spite, spite—anything to hurt the council.

Internecine war—and a woman's petticoat, the banner flung to the breeze— or hung on the outer wall.

When I first went back to Richmond in spite of Colonel Ives's hints at the Jones's gate, I thought all things smooth and pleasant once more. The woman's war at the Spotswood was over. The belligerents are dispersed. And Joe Johnston (who planted his horsetails in front of the cave of Adullam like the great bashaw that he is and invited all whose ambition was dissatisfied to come and dwell there) has gone west.[4]

Soon enough I found out my mistake. The Congress of 1863 gave up its time to fighting the battle of Colonel Myers—Mrs. Myers.[5]

Wigfall, as true-hearted a man as ever lived, came to our house again and again.

He did not fail to see where this confusion and quarreling would land us, but—

Once Mr. Chesnut harangued Garnett and Wigfall till after midnight. We were on opposite sides but friends all the same. We asked what was the Toombs difficulty.

"Incompatibility of temper," laughed Wigfall.

---

4. Recovered from his wounding at Seven Pines, Johnston hoped to return to his command in Va. But Davis was not about to take the Army of Northern Va. away from Robert E. Lee. Instead, the president sent Johnston to run the newly created Department of the West in Nov. 1862. I Samuel 22:1–2 tells how David, with the idea of becoming king of Israel in mind, escapes to "the cave of Adullam.... And every one that was in distress,... in debt, and ... discontented, gathered themselves unto him...." The "horsetails" and "great bashaw" are allusions to George Colman, the younger, *Blue Beard*, act 3, scene 4. See p. 24, n. 5.

5. For reasons that are unclear, Jefferson Davis became unhappy with his quartermaster general, Abraham Charles Myers of S.C. After the Congress tried to promote Myers by reclassifying his office as a brigadier general's post early in 1863, the president dismissed him. But that was not the end of the affair because, as M. B. C. notes, Congress was not ready to accept Myers's dismissal. While Mrs. Myers had apparently made offensive remarks about Mrs. Davis, the precise role of the quartermaster general's wife in the controversy is also uncertain.

The Confederate Congress devoted the winter of 1863 to a hand-to-hand fight with Mr. Davis on account of Mr. Quartermaster General Myers. Here again, who pulled the wires? Not Colonel Myers, surely? Who cared a fig for him?

The friends of Mrs. Myers, led by Mr. Miles, and the enemies of Mr. Davis formed a brigade of great strength—formidable indeed for perfect equipment and drill.

Northrop—what a bone of contention he is! Even if the army is mistaken and Northrop is not inefficient—still, if they believe it, something ought to be conceded to their prejudices. We need popular enthusiasm to take men triumphantly through the martyrdom this life in camp surely is to them. Somebody else might have been found to satisfy the army—so Mr. Davis's best friends thought.

One day I saw Mr. Northrop at the president's. He is an eccentric creature. He said newspapers were not without some good uses. He wore several folded across his chest, under his shirt, in lieu of flannel. He said they kept out the cold effectually.

Think of him with those peppery articles in the *Examiner* next his heart. There is abuse of Northrop in some of those papers that would warm up the spirit of the angel Gabriel—if he be the angel of peace.

Apropos of Daniel in the Lyons' den[6]—

Buck was in doleful dumps because of Claude Gibson. She would not go. Mary had a bad cold and headache, but people do not believe in either colds or headaches when one has accepted an invitation to dinner a week in advance. So Mary was amenable to reason, and we drove out to the Lyonses about dusk in the evening.

It was a great affair, that dinner. The magnificent lord of the mansion, for he was truly that, stood on the hearth rug, with his feet wide apart like the Colossus of Rhodes. And he talked admirable, looking three feet over our heads.

There is no hospitality like that of Virginia, and no one knows better than he how to dispense it. That day he bore "all of the expenses" of the conversation, as the French say. His beautiful young wife was ill and did not appear. His shoulders are broad, he could bear it all. He took me down to dinner. On the other side of me sat a clever unknown who apparently knew me and talked straight off, from the very beginning. Foolishly, I thought this gentleman's name a matter of no importance—if only he were agreeable, as indeed he was to the last degree. He said,

"The man opposite, sitting by Miss Preston, is called the best match in Virginia."

Then I looked at Mary, upon whom so high an honor had been conferred—sending her down with "the best match" &c&c.

In this highly critical position, I saw, alas! how the bad headache, though not

6. That is, John Moncure Daniel in the home of James Lyons.

enough for an excuse, was enough to damage her appearance, assisted by the bad cold.

Her face was scarlet all over, including her eyes, which were also half-shut, with an unmistakably sleepy expression shining through. She looked dead sleepy—nothing more. That beautiful mouth of hers, the ideal cupid's bow in perfection, now only a round O—trying to draw a breath into her suffocated lungs. What a cruel thing to have brought her out!

Next day I inquired, "What did 'the best match' have to say to you, after all?"

"Once I caught something like this—'What effect has Raphael's Madonna on you?'—I knew it did not matter what one answered to rubbish like that. So I did not try to rouse. I sunk back into my idiotic state, without a pang of regret. I think we were five hours at table."

Now I do not think it was more than from six to nine.

Now my neighbor, a bold, bad man, was bright and clever beyond my wildest hopes. He knew everybody and everything, and his paragraphs were as cool and ready, as incisive and as decisive as the *Examiner*'s. Epigrammatic—in the most unexpected places. I said, "Don't try that style—that is as bad as the *Examiner*." Which remark caused him a moment's reflection. Someone had the bad taste to arraign the president to his handsome stentor of a secretary, Burton Harrison.[7]

"How rude! I know how angry Mr. Harrison feels. They do that to me, although I am the wife of one of Mr. Davis's A.D.C."

"And you! You hit harder and nearer than an aide-de-camp tonight."

"How? What do you mean?"

"In all innocence, for you do not know who I am, apparently. And we have had an altercation."

"'Conversation,' you ought to say, but that is not too bad a name to give it—for you have abused everybody, friend or foe, and *you* hit so hard I shiver even for my enemies."

He asked, with the unmoved face which he had never changed in all these long hours of bitter disputing and discussion,

"Do you include the *Examiner* among the newspapers you denounce as giving aid and comfort—or doing yeoman service for the Yankees?"

"Yes, they are splitting us into a thousand pieces. I think of the editor of the *Examiner* in his cozy den—warm dressing gown and comfortable slippers, good fire, good cigar! And the president for a tidbit to tear and crunch. You know, we live opposite Mrs. Webb's[8] hospital, and I see wagon loads of those poor fellows come down. They have not a word to say of their hardships. They sleep in the snow and find a fence rail a luxury for a bed. It keeps them out of the mud

---

7. Twenty-four-year-old Burton Norvell Harrison of New Orleans had been an assistant professor of physics at the University of Miss. before replacing Robert Josselyn as Davis's private secretary in 1861.

8. Lucy (Mason) Webb, wife of Richmond wholesale grocer and commission merchant Lewis N. Webb.

and slush. And they are cut and so [*word omitted*] that you can hardly bear to look at them. You make them think that all this is for nothing—that they are wounded and die in vain. It is easy to write an article remorseless as the grave, filled with dull growls of dissatisfaction, but it is striking the feet from under the soldiers. And when you think of them, maimed for life!"

"Did you tell Mrs. Petticola you hoped to see Daniel hanged?"

"I do not know. I say too much—as you may have noticed—but you must own that he deserves it! He is a standing note of dissatisfaction with the administration. We can't change it for a better if we would, and the *Examiner* is fomenting direst division. When the army believes the *Examiner,* they will go home."

"Did you ever meet a man who was satisfied with his own position?"

"Yes, both Jeff Davis and Robert E. Lee think it morbid ambition—that everlasting wish to rise. They think men should serve their country from motives of pure patriotism. And then my friends the gentleman privates, they do not care a snap. You may growl or you may intrigue for power—they mean to fight it out. They go in to win, and they mean to stay until they do—or die. They never question their own position—they feel equal to king or kaiser. If I were a shouting character, I should say three cheers for the gentleman privates—à la lanterne, messieurs, the distracting editors. And as for Congress —would blow them from the guns, as the English did the Sepoys[9]—and the Sepoys only did what they laud and magnify John Brown for trying to get the negroes to do here."

Here I stopped to take breath. The man eyed me oddly. To be sure, I was too much dressed. I wore my sage green velvet and my diamonds—more dressed than other people. I am so often at the other end of the pendulum's swing (worse dressed) that I tried not to feel the discomfort of it.

After we were once more in the drawing room: "What a brilliant conversationist Mr. Daniel is! Mr. Daniel of the *Examiner.*"

"Is Mr. Daniel here?"

"He sat by you at table."

"That was it, then—and I had told him at his own particular request what a black-hearted traitor he was. Hung, drawn and quartered, with his head stuck over the gate—was the best words I had for him"—said, both hands held up in horror!

"Don't fret. Someone on the other side said they had never seen him so much amused."

And now comes a strange story. Today I read a letter from my sister. She wrote to inquire of her old playmate, friend, lover, Boykin McCaa.[1] It is nearly twenty years since they were both married. Each of them has children nearly grown. "To tell the truth," she writes, "in these last dreadful years, David in Florida, where I cannot often hear from him—everything dismal, anxious, and

9. English troops committed this and other atrocities in putting down the Indian Mutiny of 1857–58.
1. Burwell Boykin McCaa, an Ala. planter born in Camden, was M. B. C.'s first cousin.

disquieting, I had almost forgotten Boykin's existence. But he came here last night! He stood by my bedside and spoke to me kindly and affectionately, as if we had just parted. I said, holding out my hand, 'Boykin, you are very pale.' He answered, 'I have come to tell you goodbye.' Then he seized both of my hands. His were as cold and hard as ice. They froze the marrow of my bones. I screamed again and again. My whole household came rushing in—then the negroes from the yard. All had been wakened by my piercing shrieks. This may have been a dream, but it haunts me."

Now, last summer I met a friend of his who said Boykin had something on his mind he wanted to say to Kate.

"I'll never die until I have asked her pardon—&c. I used to pretend I was engaged to her, and I know now that I did wrong, &c&c&c. We were never engaged, but I fancied we might be if &c&c&c." This I told at the breakfast table—then went on with Kate's letter.

"Someone sent me an old paper with an account of his wounds and his recovery. I know he is dead!"

"Stop," said Mr. C. And he read from that day's *Examiner*.

Capt. Burwell Boykin McCaa—found dead upon the battlefield, leading a cavalry charge, at the head of his company. He was shot through the head.

Coincidences are queer sometimes.

Nicknames. Buck asked John Darby scornfully, "Do you think Mamie will marry you?" Striking a majestic attitude, he answers,

"Perseverentia omnia vincit."

So Buck dubbed him P. V., and P. V. he was to us ever after.

The famous colonel of the Fourth Texas—by name John Bell Hood—him we called Sam, because his classmates at West Point did so still—cause unknown.

P. V. asked if he might bring his general—bragged of him extensively, said he had won his three stars &c under Stonewall's eye and that he was promoted by Stonewall's request.

When he came, with his sad Quixote face, the face of an old crusader who believed in his cause, his cross, his crown—we were not prepared for that type exactly as a beau idéal of wild Texans. Tall—thin—shy. Blue eyes and light hair, tawny beard and a vast amount of it covering the lower part of his face—an appearance of awkward strength. Someone said that great reserve of manner he carried only into ladies' society. Mr. Venable added he had often heard of the "light of battle" shining in a man's eyes. He had seen it once. He carried him orders from General Lee and found [him] in the hottest of the fight. "The man was transfigured. The fierce light of his eyes—I can never forget."

Hood came to ask us to a picnic next day at Drewry's Bluff. The naval heroes were to receive us, and then we were to dine at the Texian camp. We accused John Darby of having instigated this unlooked-for festivity. We were to have bands of music, dances, turkeys, chickens, buffalo's tongues.

Next morning, just as my foot was on the carriage step, the girls standing behind, ready to follow me with Johnny and "the Infant Samuel"—up rode P. V. in red-hot haste, threw his bridle to one of the men who was holding the horses, and came toward us, rapidly clanking his cavalry spurs with a despairing sound. "Stop! It's all up. We are ordered back to the Rappahannock. The brigade is marching through Richmond now."

So we unpacked, unloaded, dismissed hacks, and sat down with a sigh.

"Suppose you go and see them pass the turnpike."

The suggestion was hailed with delight, and off we marched. Johnny and the Infant were in citizen's clothes, and the Straggler,[2] as Hood calls John Darby since the Prestons have been in Richmond, was all plaided and plumed in his surgeon's array. He never bated an inch of bullion or a feather. He was courting. He stalked ahead with Mary P, Buck, and Johnny. The Infant and myself, both stout and scant of breath, lagged last. They called back to us, as the Infant came toddling, "Hurry up or we will leave you."

At the turnpike we stood in the sidewalk and saw ten thousand men march by. We had seen nothing like this before. Hitherto, it was only regiments marching, spic and span in their fresh smart clothes, just from home on their way to the army.

Such rags and tags—nothing alike—most garments and arms taken from the enemy—such shoes! "Oh, our brave boys!" moaned Buck. Such tin pans and pots tied to their waists—bread or bacon stuck on the ends of their bayonets. Anything that could be spiked was bayoneted and held aloft.

They did not seem to know their shabby condition. They laughed and shouted and cheered as they marched by. Not a disrespectful or light word. But they went for the men huddled behind us—who at last seemed trying to be as small as possible and to escape observation in our rear.

"Ladies, send those puny conscripts on to their regiments."

"Captain, either take off your shoulder straps or come on to the Rappahannock. Maybe you did not know there was fighting going on there."

Johnny began to grumble.

"This is my first furlough. I have not missed a battle—not one."

"Don't answer. Those rough and ready Texians will make you rue it, if you give them a chance," cried Dr. Darby.

Hood and his staff came galloping up, dismounted, and joined us. Mary P gave him a bouquet. He unwrapped a Bible which he wore in his pocket carefully—he said his mother gave it to him—and he pressed a flower in it. Mary P suggested he had not worn or used it at all. It was fresh and new and beautifully kept.

"Not hurt by daily use—eh?"

Every word of this the Texians heard as they marched by, almost touching us. They laughed and joked and made their own rough comments.

"Ah, general! Is that the matter with you? All right, we know how it is ourselves—&c&c."

Buck stood somewhat apart, rather as a spectator of this scene. She had refused to appear the night Hood came to tea. Now as they passed, P. V.

---

2. John Darby now has two nicknames, "P. V." and "the Straggler." M. B. C. also called him "D" and "the D."

introduced the general. After he had mounted his horse—before he rode away—he looked at her, turning his horse to do so, and he said something to P. V. which caused the latter to smile. The surgeon came back for more adieus, and Buck walked up. She asked eagerly, "What was that he said to you? About me?"

"Only a horse compliment—he is a Kentuckian, you know. He says, 'You stand on your feet like a thoroughbred.'"

Then they marched these poor creatures, these soldiers, four days through the snow and sleet and freeze—and then they marched them back again.

Mrs. Ould[3] had just received in some occult way a cask of whiskey. She had it rolled out on the sidewalk and gave each half-starved soldier a drink. Thirty died on that four days' senseless march (senseless, as far as we could see).

"Ah, general!" said Mrs. Ould, "I wish there was enough for everyone of them!"

Mr. Ould came home to dinner that day and wanted his whiskey.

"Surely you need not grumble that I gave it to those poor frozen soldiers?"

"But my dear, out of a cask you might have saved me a tumbler."

"What, no kindly drop for me?" as Juliet says to Romeo, in the tomb of the Capulets.

That night our little parlor was crammed with soldiers.

We were playing casino. Buck was winning as usual. Mary made her plaint. "Everybody gives her cards—nobody ever gives me anything."

The infatuated P. V. placed that beautiful hand of his on his heart and looked unutterable things. He missed fire because she did not look up from her cards. She did not see the pantomime, but the general did and asked his surgeon, in slow, solemn, practical tones,

"Doctor, what does that signal mean?"

"Oh," replied the doctor, utterly bewildered. "So you caught me. I put two fingers on my heart, as a hint she should play the deuce of hearts."

That small joke was made to go a long way. Certainly never did a game of casino cause so much uproarious mirth. At supper the general explained the fun to me.

They were then ordered to Suffolk. And there, as the balls were falling fast, Hood leaned upon John Darby—who said he was keen to move on. He thought the spot too hot for loitering.

"I say, doctor, this is not as pleasant as the corner of Clay St. *and casino*."

General Hood was wounded at Gettysburg and barely well enough to join his command, which was ordered to Bragg—before Chattanooga.

The surgeon stayed sweethearting a day too long in Richmond, basking in the smiles of love and beauty, said the Infant. For the battle of Chickamauga was won, and Hood had [his leg] cut off before he got there. But the general's life was despaired of. And P. V., the surgeon and the straggler, nursed his chief faithfully.

3. Sarah (Turpin) Ould, the wife of Confederate bureaucrat Robert Ould.

September 1863. Bloomsbury. As for her ladyship at Chelsea—she was now of an age when danger to any second party doth not disturb the rest much.[4]

Maj. Edward Johnson did not get into the Confederacy until after the First Manassas. For some cause, before he could evade that potentate and power, Seward rang his little bell and sent him to a prison in the harbor of New York. I forget whether he was exchanged or escaped of his own motion. The next thing I heard of my antebellum friend, he had defeated Milroy in western Virginia. So many Johnsons. For this victory they named him Allegheny Johnson.

He had an odd habit of falling into a state of incessant winking as soon as he was the least startled or agitated. He seemed persistently winking one eye at you, but he meant nothing by it. In point of fact he did not know it himself. In Mexico he had been wounded in the eye—and the nerve vibrates independently [*illegible word*] of his will.

During the winter of '63 he was on crutches. After a while he hobbled down Franklin Street with us—we proud to accommodate our pace to that of the wounded general.

His ankle continued stiff, so when he sat down, another chair was put before him. And he stretched out his stiff leg on it, straight as a ramrod. At that time he was our only wounded knight. And the girls waited on him and made life pleasant to him. He was devoted, too—to taffy.

One night I listened to two love tales at once—in a distracted state of mind between the two. Mr. William Porcher Miles was in a perfectly modulated voice, in cadenced accents and low tones, narrating the happy end of his affair. He was engaged to sweet little Bettie Bierne![5] And I gave him my congratulations with all my heart. It was a capital match, suitable every way—good for her, good for him—&c&c. I was deeply interested in Mr. Miles's story—but din and discord on the other hand. Old Edward, our pet general, sat diagonally across the room, with the leg straight out, like a poker wrapped in red carpet leggings, as red as a turkey cock in the face. His head is so strangely shaped—like a cone, an old fashioned beehive, or as Buck said: "There is three tiers of it. It is like the pope's tiara."

There he was, with a loud voice and a thousand winks, making love to Mary P. I make no excuse for listening. It was impossible not to hear. I tried not to lose a word of Mr. Miles's idyll as the despair of the veteran was thundered in my other ear. I lent an ear to each.

Mary P cannot altogether control her own voice, and her shrill screams of negation—"No, no, never"—utterly failed to suppress her wounded lover's obstreperous asseverations of his undying affection for her.

---

4. M. B. C. is probably referring to Sally Chesnut.
5. The daughter of Va. planter Oliver Bierne.

Buck said afterward, "We heard every word of it on our side of the room, even when Mamie shrieked to him that he was talking too loud."

"Now, Mamie, do you think it was kind to tell him he was forty if he was a day?"

Strange to say, the venerable Edward rehabilitated his love in a day at least. Two days after, he was heard to say he was paying attention now to his cousin, John Preston's second daughter. "Her name was Sally, but they called her Buck—Sally Buchanan Campbell Preston, a lovely girl, sir."

And with her he now drove, rode, and hobbled on his crutches. Sent her his photograph and in due time cannonaded her from the same spot with proposals to marry him.

Buck was never so decided in her nos as Mary. ("Not so loud at least," amends Buck, who always reads what I have written and makes comments of assent or dissent.) So again he began to thunder in her ears his tender passion for her as they rode down Franklin St. Buck says she knows the people on the sidewalk heard snatches of it, though she rode as rapidly as she could and she begged [him] not to talk so loud. Finally they dashed up to our door, as if they had been running a race, for she only answered at last by an application of her whip to her horse.

Unfortunate in love but fortunate in war, our general is now winning new laurels with Ewell in the Valley or with the Army of the Potomac.

Major Venable, A.D.C. to General Lee, dined with us. He joined Mr. C in ridiculing the weakness of men who tattled to women secrets of state or important army news. Apropos of Dick Anderson, the most silent and discreet of men, his wife showed Mrs. Davis and ourselves a letter from General A. "Remain in Richmond—we may be ordered there at any moment."

"That's nothing! The best of men will tell any lie to keep their wives out of camp. Very few men can bear their wives trailing after them to the army."

Afterward they discussed the last secret dispatch of General Lee to Longstreet.

"Surely," said Mr. Venable, in tones of solemn reproach, "you have not told your wife that."

L. Q. Washington came with some executive office wit—so-called. "Why is C——r a parenthesis?" "Because he can be left out without injury to the sense of the administration."

"Why is Cl——n like the *Merrimack?*" "Because he cannot be boarded."

It seems the poor man eats so much, they will not have him at any price— neither at public houses or private boardinghouses. [*Remainder of this page and the entire page following cut out.*]

In the park where we were walking, Mr. Henry Marshall said everything looked so beautiful, so calm, so peaceful—the contrast so painful between inanimate nature and our distracted country.

Our grief for the dead came back to us so sharply [on] such a day as this. Why? I spoke of George Cuthbert.

L. Q. Washington said, "Now you two are blundering on—and here it is."

> There have been tears and breaking hearts for thee,
> And mine were nothing had I such to give;
> But when I stood beneath the fresh green tree,
> Which living waves where thou didst cease to live,
> And saw around me the wide field revive
> With fruits and fertile promise, and the Spring,
> Come forth, her work of gladness to continue,
> With all her reckless birds upon the wing
> I turned from all she brought, to all she could not bring—
> I turned *to thee!* to thousands of whom, each,
> And one, as all, a ghastly gap did make
> In his own kind, and kindred, whom to teach
> Forgetfulness were mercy for their sake;
> The Archangel's trump, not glory's, must awake
> Those whom they thirst for; though the sound of fame
> May for a moment soothe, it cannot slake
> The fever of vain longing, and the name
> So honored, but assumes a stronger bitterer claim.[6]

Thackeray of Marlborough's wars—our Lee, like Wellington, forbids the ruthless rapine so described:

And now having seen a great military march through a friendly country; the pomps and festivities of more than one German court, the severe struggle of a hotly contested battle, and the triumph of victory—Mr. Esmond beheld another part of military duty: our troops entering the enemies' country, and putting all around them to fire and sword: burning farms, wasted fields, shrieking women. Slaughtered sons and fathers, drunken soldiery carousing in the midst of tears, terror, and murder. Why does the stately Muse of History that delights in describing the valour of heroes and the grandeur of conquest leave out these scenes so brutal, mean, degrading, that yet by far form the greater part of the drama of war?

You gentlemen of England who live at home at ease, and compliment yourselves in the songs of triumph unto which our Chieftains are bepraised! You pretty maidens of England that come trembling down the stairs when fife and drum call you—And huzza for the British Grenadier—Do you take account that these items go to make up the amount of the triumph you admire, and form part of the duties of the heroes you fondle![7]

6. Slightly misquoted from Lord Byron, *Childe Harold's Pilgrimage,* canto 3.
7. Thackeray, *The History of Henry Esmond, Esq.,* book 2, chapter 9.

I think I have told how Miles, still so gently o'er one leaning, told of his successful loves while General Ed Johnson roared with anguish and disappointment over his failures.

Mr. Miles spoke of sweet little Bettie Bierne as if she had been a French girl just from a convent, kept far from the haunts of men, just for him. Now Bettie has a younger sister, married and a widow, and a younger still, who was grown and going into society with her four years ago.[8] One would think to hear him that Bettie had never cast those innocent blue eyes of hers on a man until he came along.

Now since I first knew Miss Bierne in 1857, when Pat Calhoun[9] was to the fore, she has been followed by a tail of men as long as a Highland chief's. Every summer at the Springs old Oliver appeared in the ballroom a little before twelve and chased the three beautiful Biernes home before him, in spite of all entreaties. And he was said to frown away these too numerous admirers at all hours of the day.

This new engagement was confided to me as a profound secret engagement. Of course I did not mention it, even to my own household. Next day little Alston, Morgan's adjutant, and George Deas called. As Colonel Deas removed his gloves, he said

"Oh, the Miles and Biernes imbroglio—have you heard of it?"

"No. What is the row about?"

"They are engaged to be married—that's all!"

"Who told *you?*"

"Miles himself—as we walked down Franklin St. this afternoon."

"And did he not beg you not to mention it? That Bettie did not wish it spoken of?"

"God bless my soul! So he did, and I forgot that part entirely."

Colonel Alston begged the stout Carolinian not to take his inadvertent breach of faith too much to heart. Miss Bettie's engagement had caused him a dreadful night. A young man who was his intimate friend came to his room in the depths of despair and handed him a letter from Miss Bierne, the cause of all his woe.

Not knowing that she was prematurely engaged to Miles, he had proposed to her in an eloquent letter, and in her reply she politely stated that she was positively engaged to Mr. Miles.

And instead of thanking her for putting him at once out of his misery, he considered the reason she gave as aggravating trebly the agony of the love letter and the refusal. "Too late!" he yelled, "by jingo!" So much for the secret.

Miss Bierne and I became fast friends, our friendship based upon our mutual admiration for the honorable member from South Carolina.

Colonel and Mrs. Myers—Colonel and Mrs. Chesnut were the only friends of Mr. Miles who were invited to his wedding. At the church door the sexton demanded your credentials. No one but those whose names he held in his hand

8. Nannie (Bierne) Parkman and Susan Bierne.
9. U.S. Army Capt. Patrick Calhoun (1821–58), son of John C. Calhoun.

were allowed to enter. Not twenty people were present, a mere handful grouped around the altar in that large empty church.

We were among the first. Then a faint flutter, and Mrs. Parkman (the bride's sister, swathed in weeds for her young husband, who had been killed within a year of her marriage) came rapidly up the aisle alone. She dropped upon her knees in the front pew. And there remained, motionless, during the whole ceremony—a mass of black crape and a dead weight on my heart. She has had experience of war. A cannonade around Richmond interrupted *her* marriage service—sinister omen—and in a year her bridgroom was stiff and stark, dead upon the field of battle.

Then, while the wedding march turned our thoughts from her and thrilled us with sympathy, the bride advanced in white satin and point d'Alençon.

Mrs. Myers whispered it was Mrs. Parkman's wedding dress. She remembered the exquisite lace, and she shuddered with superstitious foreboding.

After the beautiful bride on her father's arm came the beauty of old age— surely gray hairs never shaded a sweeter face than Mrs. MacFarland's. A bevy of bright young girls—Frank Miles[1] as best man—and little Wilmer as rear guard.

Bettie advanced and knelt at the altar rail for a moment. Mr. Miles, looking ever so nice, seemed undecided as to the necessity of a similar move on his part, but Bettie arose and the ceremony began.

Mr. Minnegerode[2] told us after supper that night that he was so familiar with the inevitable, scared, foolish hangdog looks of the average bridegroom, the gallant way Miles faced him so took him by surprise he nearly lost his presence of mind. He said Mr. Miles regarded him coolly, calmly, even with a critical air. In spite of his daily drill in the marriage service, the astonished parson nearly blundered.

After it was all over, Mrs. Bride sailed gracefully down the aisle, bowing and speaking to her friends on the right and on the left. Miles put her hand on his arm, whispering as he bent over her. Mrs. Myers cried enthusiastically, "Don't Miles make love beautifully!" On my other side someone muttered, "They say she knows."

All had been going on so delightfully indoors, but a sharp shower had cleared the church porch, which had [been] left crowded by the curious. And as the water splashed, we wondered how we were to assemble ourselves at Mrs. Mac-Farland's. All horses in Richmond had been impressed for some sudden cavalry necessity a few days before. I ran between Mr. MacFarland and Senator Semmes, with my pretty Paris rose-colored silk turned over my head to save it. And when we arrived at the hospitable mansion of the MacFarlands, Mr. McF took me straight into the drawing room—manlike, forgetting that my ruffled plumes needed a good smoothing and preening.

1. Dr. Francis Turquand Miles, younger brother of William Porcher Miles.
2. Charles Minnegerode, rector of the fashionable St. Paul's Episcopal Church and a friend of Jefferson Davis.

Mr. Hunter said Miles will make his home a pleasant one, and his wife will be a happy woman. "We lived in the same house four years in Washington. Bachelors' quarters." He had never known Miles do an inconsiderate; an impolite, or a selfish thing. "Pretty high praise—for after all we were only a parcel of old men"—Garnett and himself the youngsters of the household.

Mr. Miles then informed me that a man's wife had nothing to do with his bachelor scrapes. But for the faith and loyalty due other women, he would not scruple to tell her all of his past life, for it was not her affair at all.

Deluded wretch. Jealousy of the past is most women's hell. It is one of the hopeless irritations, the pest of married life.

Mrs. Myers and Colonel Chesnut led the way. Colonel Myers and myself followed. Mrs. M called out, as she heard us splashing along:

"Follow your leader. And you will keep out of mud puddles."

Colonel Myers gravely remarked to me: "I walk straight. Madame never tracks after me. She rocks around on her own hook and so gets into no end of trouble."

Many an arrow at random sent—finds mark the Archer little meant—and all that. . . .[3]

We were walking on Franklin St. A gay, debonair couple dashed by on horseback.

"By heavens, she has pluck. She was confirmed last Sunday—so was he."

"It is little more than a month since her confinement. She ought not to be on horseback so soon!"

"So soon after which? Confinement—or confirmation?"

"Confirmation strong as holy writ.[4] When I saw him to up to the altar, I thought a new leaf was to be turned."

"Honi soit—mauvaise langue!"

Queer and rapid were our changes of scene in [the] great camp of Richmond. Barracks at last—nothing more.

A wounded friend came on his crutches; his wife lay at the point of death; would I go? "Yes—at once."

I found her unconscious—masses of beautiful black hair thrown back over the pillow. The lame husband crawled to the bedside and knelt. When I touched her hand it was bathed in his tears. And yet he was practical. He had insisted on my bringing my dressing gown and slippers. And now, in spite of that precaution, whenever I moved, a rustling sound.

"Go in the next room; take off whatever makes that noise."

3. Slightly misquoted from Sir Walter Scott, *The Lord of the Isles* (1815), canto 5. Omitted is an account of a pointless parlor game.
4. Slightly misquoted from *Othello,* act 3, scene 3.

I obeyed without a word. Molly had put too much starch in one of my petticoats. I came back. The husband was kneeling at her feet.

The doctor sat by her side. If ever mortal man strove to keep a woman alive, that handsome, red-haired, fervid physician did, that long night through. He gave no rest to the sole of my foot. Before day we had our reward. The fever passed away. She fell into a deep sleep. He pronounced her "saved."

Mrs. Lee sent for me. She was staying at Mrs. Caskie's.[5]

I was taken directly to her room. She was lying in the bed. She said, before I had taken my seat, "You know, there is a fight going on now at Brandy Station."[6]

"Yes. We are anxious. John Chesnut's company is there, too."

She spoke sadly but quickly.

"My son Rooney is wounded. His brother has gone for him. They will soon be here, and we will hear all about it—unless Rooney's wife takes him to her grandfather's.[7] Poor lame mother—I am useless to my children."

Mrs. Caskie said: "You need not be alarmed. The general said in his telegraph that it was not a severe wound. You know, even Yankees believe General Lee."

Mrs. Lee was right in her vaticinations. He was taken by his wife to Mr. Carter's, and there he was captured. Why not? It was within the enemies' lines. He is kept as hostage for some Yankee miscreant—and dear little Charlotte Wickham repents her willfulness in refusing to let him be brought down to Richmond. They say Custis Lee offered himself to the Yankees in place of his brother, as he was a single man with no wife and children to be hurt by his imprisonment or made miserable by his danger. But the Yankees preferred Rooney.

That day Mrs. Lee gave me a likeness of the general, a photograph taken soon after the Mexican War. She likes it so much better than the later ones. He certainly was a handsome man then—handsomer even than now. I shall prize it for Mrs. Lee's sake, too.

She said Mrs. Chesnut and her Aunt Nelly Custis (Mrs. Lewis) were very intimate in the old Washington administration, Philadelphia days. I told her Mrs. Chesnut was the historical member of our family. She had so much to tell of the old Revolutionary times. And then she was one of the "white-robed choir" at Trenton Bridge—which everybody who writes a life of Washington asks her to give an account of.[8]

Mr. C had been sent to see Vallandigham out of the Confederacy at Wilmington. The Federals had no use for him, so they handed him over to us. And

---

5. Ellen Jeal (Gwathmey) Caskie, wife of Richmond tobacco dealer James Kerr Caskie.

6. The major cavalry battle of the war was fought around this Va. town on June 9, 1863.

7. Charlotte (Wickham) Lee's grandfather was William Carter of "Hickory Hill," in Hanover County, Va.

8. En route to his first inauguration as president, George Washington was met at Trenton on April 21, 1789, by what he described as "the white-robed choir": little girls dressed in white who strewed flowers in his path and joined the women of the N.J. town in a song of welcome.

we are speeding the parting guest. He will never help us against his own people—of that we may be sure.[9]

We came near having a compliment today, but a further development of Dr. Rufus's taste deprived it of all value.

"Mrs. Davis, Mrs. Clay, and you—I do declare, you are the cleverest ladies in the Confederacy. Mrs. Clay, now—you know I proclaim her supreme for wit and beauty as well as refinement."

"Now, one of you girls sing 'Lorena.' 'Lorena,' of all the songs I know—it is supreme as to melody and also for beauty of versification."

He quoted "If we may forget." That's touching.

> For if we try we may forget—
> Were words of them long years ago.
> 'Tis just a hundred months, Lorena,
> Since first I held thy hand in mine—
>   'Twas flowery May
> When up the Hills we climbed,
> To watch the dying of the day—
> And hear the church bells chimed.

I quote him from memory, for I have never seen the song.

Maggie Howell says there is a girl in large hoops and a calico frock at every piano between this place and the Mississippi, banging on the out-of-tune thing—and looking up into a man's face who wears [the] Confederate uniform. Very soiled is that uniform and battle-stained, but the man's heart is fresh enough, as he hangs over her, to believe in Lorena. "Is it not lovely?" said our doctor of the ruby and garnet hues.

"It has not had a fair chance. We hear it squalled so—and banged accompaniments—discord itself—and see, the heartbroken lover was constant. Twelve into a hundred—eight times and four over—I mean four months. He had the heart to do that sum."

"No, it was the exigence of the rhyme and meter—else he would have said eight or nine years—you may depend."

Mrs. Ould and Mrs. Davis came home with me. Laurence had a basket of delicious cherries. "If there was only some ice." Respectfully Laurence said—and also firmly, "Give me money and you shall have ice."

By the underground telegraph he had heard of an icehouse over the river, whose fame was suppressed by certain sybarites—as they wanted it all. In a wonderfully short time we had mint juleps and sherry cobblers.

Altogether it had been a pleasant day. And as I sat alone, laughing lightly now

---

9. In May, Union authorities had banished Ohio copperhead leader and former U.S. congressman Clement Laird Vallandigham to the Confederacy as a traitor. But Jefferson Davis did not want this advocate of sectional reconciliation either and ordered him to Wilmington, N.C., to await passage on a blockade-runner bound for Bermuda in mid-June.

and then at the memory of some funny story, suddenly a violent ring—and a regular sheaf of telegrams were handed me.

I could not have drawn away in more consternation if they had been a nest of rattlesnakes.

First—Frank Hampton killed at Brandy Station. Wade telegraphed Mr. C to see Robert Barnwell and make necessary arrangements to receive the body. Mr. C still at Wilmington. I sent for Preston Johnston,[1] and my neighbor Colonel Patton[2] offered to see that everything proper should be done.

That afternoon I walked out alone. Willie Munford[3] had shown me where the body—all that was left of Frank Hampton—was to be laid in the Capitol.

Mrs. Petticola joined me for a while and then Mrs. Singleton. Preston Hampton and Peter Trezevant[4] with myself and Mrs. Singleton formed the sad procession which followed the coffin. There was a company of soldiers drawn up in front of the State House porch.

Mrs. Singleton said we had better go in and look at him before the coffin was finally closed.

How I wish I had not looked! I remember him so well in all the pride of his magnificent manhood. He died of a saber cut across the face and head and was utterly disfigured. Mrs. Singleton seemed convulsed with grief. In all my life I had never seen such bitter weeping. She had her own troubles, but I did not know. We sat for a long time on the front steps of the State House. Everybody had gone. We were utterly alone.

We talked of it all. We had gone to Charleston to see Rachel in *Adrienne Lecouvreur*,[5] and as I stood waiting in the passage near the drawing room, I met Frank Hampton bringing his beautiful bride from the steamer. They had just landed.

Then at Mrs. Singleton's place in the country we had spent a delightful week together.

And now, it is only a few years, but nearly all that pleasant company are dead—and our world, the only world we cared for, literally kicked to pieces. And she cried,

"We are two lone women—stranded here!"

"Robert Barnwell is in a desperate condition. Mary is expecting her confinement every day."

It was not until I got back to Carolina that I heard of Robert Barnwell's death and—scarcely a day's interval—Mary's and her newborn baby. They were brought—husband, wife, and child—and buried at the same time in the same grave in Columbia. And now Mrs. Singleton has three orphans. What a woeful year it has been to her.

1. Col. William Preston Johnston of Ky., son of Gen. Albert Sidney Johnston, was aide-de-camp to Jefferson Davis.
2. Col. John Mercer Patton, Jr., of the Twenty-first Va. Infantry, a lawyer before the war.
3. William Preston Munford of Richmond, secretary of the James River and Kanawha Canal Company.
4. A son of Dr. Daniel Heyward Trezevant serving as a courier to Wade Hampton III.
5. A play by Augustin Eugène Scribe.

Robert Barnwell insisted upon being sent to the insane asylum at Staunton. On account of his wife's situation the doctor also advised it. He was carried off on a mattress. His brave wife tried to prevent it. She said: "It is only fever. He is too weak to be dangerous if it were anything worse." And she nursed him to the last. She tried to say goodbye cheerfully. And she called after him, "As soon as my trouble is over, I will come to you at Staunton." At the asylum they said it was typhoid fever which caused his mental aberration. And he died the second day after he got there.

Poor Mary fainted when she heard the ambulance drive away with him. Then she crept into a low trundle bed kept for the children in her mother's room. That she never left again. When the message came from Staunton that it was *fever* the matter with Robert, nothing more, Mrs. Singleton says she will never forget the triumphant expression of Mary's eye as she turned and looked at her. She cried, "Robert will get well. It is all right." And her face was radiant, blazing with light. That night the baby was born. Mrs. Singleton got a telegram, "Robert is dead." She did not tell Mary. She was standing at the window while she read it, and she was also looking for Robert's body, which she knew might come at any moment. As for Mary's life being in danger—she had never thought of such a thing. She was thinking of Robert. A servant touched her and said, "Look at Mrs. Barnwell." She turned and ran to the bedside. The doctor who had come in said, "It is all over—she is dead."

Not in anger—not in wrath—came the angel of death that day.[6] He came to set her free from a world grown too hard to bear.

In Stoneman's raid I burned my journal proper. It was Molly who constantly told me: "Missis, listen to the guns. Burn up everything. Mrs. Lyons says they are sure to come, and they'll put in their newspapers whatever you write here every day."

The guns did sound very near. And when Mr. C rode up and told me if Mrs. Davis left Richmond I must go with her, I confess I lost my head.

Very much tempted to copy all of my Flat Rock letters, as I have lost all but scraps of my journal. I can pick up a handful of my letters to Mr. Chesnut from every table—or from every coat pocket (linen) that goes to the wash.

Without date

After reading today's papers I am so glad—I truly rejoice in your determination to resign. Those meetings in Lexington and Marlboro—

South Carolinians have a cowardly fear of public opinion. Pickens's

6. Misquoted from Henry Wadsworth Longfellow, "The Reaper and the Flowers," *Voices of the Night* (1839).

jealousy of his miserable little authority and Yeadon's Chinese drums and gongs they take for *public opinion*. And so they fancy the convention all wrong and the council alarmingly unpopular. As soon as you are out of it—*I don't care*. I am truly sorry the state can't have more of its Pickens. Is there no hope he will be made governor next time?

It is a comfort to turn to our grand battles—Lee and Kirby Smith, now—after Pickens and Yeadon.

So Lee has turned out all you said he was when he was so unpopular—and Joe Johnston the great god of war. Keep cool. Take care of yourself &c&c.

No date

I think I. W. Hayne writes better when he signs himself Professor Holmes than he does over his own signature. His letter which Pickens published was very flat.

Who is *K* in the *Guardian*? Somebody from Kershaw, doubtless. He does not defend you half as boldly as I would.

I would contrast the state of So. Ca. now and its condition when Port Royal was captured and Pickens telegraphing the president, "So. Ca. is one armed camp."

Of this I have made up [my] mind. The low-country gentry called a convention to save their negroes—and as the convention failed to do that, they will none of it.

How does your saltpeter manufacture come on?

&c&c—

My letters always come from the P.O. *open*.

No date

How I thanked God on my knees last night for our Second Manassas.[7]

Julia Rutledge and I had a charming walk to the Urquharts.[8] Like all sublunary things, our pleasure has its drawbacks. Red bugs are our bane. They infest the woods here.

Poor distracted So. Ca.! to be torn in fragments by the wounded vanity of Mrs. Pickens—when every thought should be given to preparation to meet the enemy in the fall.

Moses, Yeadon, Buist[9]—I'd hang them all to the first lamppost.

---

7. Fought Aug. 29–30, 1862.

8. Probably the home of Lt. Col. David Urquhart of La., a former aide to Braxton Bragg serving in the adjutant general's office. Julia Rutledge was the sister of Susan Rose Rutledge.

9. Probably George Lamb Buist's brother, Henry, who was a Charleston lawyer and state legislator.

September 18, 1863[1]

I think your friends in the convention would gladly get rid of *you* (Executive Council) if they knew how, without hurting your feelings! Why don't you resign and save them from their embarrassment? Surely they have complimented you enough, at least, as much as they dare.

Is it not rather inglorious work, this great struggle—this fight with John Phillips?[2] And such a different fight going on in Virginia. I see Maxcy Gregg has given Governor Pickens a certificate. Like Trescot, I say, 'Que cela finisse.' The very sound of the word "convention" or "council" is wearisome. Come here first, and then let us try Jeff Davis awhile. Not that I am quite ready for Richmond yet. We must look after home and plantation affairs, which we have sadly neglected.

Heaven help you through the deep waters—

As ever—affectionately—

M. B. C.

At the William Cuthberts (by the way, he says he was at Rice Creek Military School with you—Captain Partridge—Lattamandé and all that) met Mrs. George Elliott—the same 'Bowen,' the witty. She had queer Columbia gossip of Hayne, and Pickens gossip—Madame P's finger in the pie, of course. Then to the Frederick Rutledges. There I gathered many rare French and English books—and now for a week or so I am independent of the world.

We had a fright here. The North Carolina people threatened to burn down Mr. Andrew Johnstone's place because he brought his negroes here.[3]

The gentlemen collected there—but no one came. It has all blown over.

Mrs. Lowndes told us yesterday that Burnet Rhett was to marry Miss Aiken Thursday week. The gay and gallant captain corroborated the story to David at the billiard room. So we are to be waked up by a wedding in the neighborhood.

The Aikens are staying with Mrs. Mat Singleton.[4]

I see they are likely to impeach you for putting distilleries [out of business?]—making arms and ammunition and organizing the military &c&c.

I wonder if they thought you would, like your governor, go buzzing, and banging, fuming, fretting—a noisy old horsefly doing nothing—or only hiring people to write for the newspapers, abusing friend and foe but praising Yeadon and his p's and q's. What a miserable old blunderbuss. But Hayne made an awful blunder, too, when he wrote that letter—

1. She obviously meant to write "1862."
2. A Charleston lawyer who replaced Andrew Gordon Magrath in the secession convention in 1862.
3. The people of Flat Rock believed the presence of about two hundred slaves from Johnstone's Beaufort District, S.C., rice plantation would drive up food prices.
4. Martha Rutledge (Kinloch) Singleton, widow of Richland District planter Richard Singleton.

What were you to do but arm and organize—and make saltpeter &c? Your blunder was making enemies of gnats—one not much, but a host such as Moses, Harris, Buist, rather irritating, buzzing about one's ears. A spark begins a conflagration—so much for a small enemy.

Ah, what a world of sage advises
The husband from the wife despises—
                    Says Tam o' Shanter

So goodbye—

I picked up a scrap: "The Yankees keep their hands off Johnston. They say if all South Carolinians had the sense of William Aiken, there would be no war—consequently none of the horrors of war."

"High praise, if there be no worse thing than war."

Miss Aiken's wedding.

Julia Rutledge was one of the bridesmaids, and we could not for a while imagine what she would do for a dress. Kate remembers some [material?] she had in the house for curtains bought before the war and laid aside as not needed now. The stuff was white and sheer, if a little coarse, but then we covered it with no end of beautiful lace. It made a beautiful dress. And how altogether lovely she looked in it!

The night of the wedding it stormed as if the world was coming to an end. Wind—rain—thunder and lightning. An unlimited supply.

She had a duchesse dressing table—muslin and lace—not one of the shifts of honest poverty war-driven, but a millionaire's attempt at being economical—thinking that style better taste as bringing them more on the same plane as their unlucky compatriots. A candle was left too near this light drapery, and it took fire. Outside, lightning to fire the world—inside, the bridal chamber ablaze. Wind enough to blow the house down the mountainside.

The English maid behaved heroically and, with the aid of Mrs. Aiken's and Mrs. Mat Singleton's servants, put the fire out without disturbing the marriage ceremony which was then being performed below.

Everything in the bridal chamber was burnt up except the bed—and that was a mass of cinders, smut, flakes of charred and blackened wood.

Mrs. Singleton said, "Burnet Rhett has strong nerves. And Etta, the bride, is too good to be superstitious."

To go back to my trip home—I saw men sitting on a row of coffins, smoking, talking, and laughing, with their feet drawn up tailor fashion, to keep them out of the rain. War hardens people's hearts.

Met J. C. at Wilmington. He only crossed the river with me and then went back to Richmond. He was violently opposed to sending our troops into

Pennsylvania[5]—wanted all we could spare sent west to make an end there of our enemies.

He kept dark about Vallandigham. I am sure we could not trust him to do us any good or to do the Yankees any harm. The Coriolanus business is played out.[6]

There must have been hard hitting, the day Frank Hampton was killed—hand to hand. That ghastly cut across his head has haunted me.

As we came home Molly sat by me in the cars. She touched me and, with her nose in the air: "Look, Missis."

There was the inevitable bride and groom, *I thought*. And the irrepressible kissing and lolling against each other I had seen so often before. I was rather astonished at Molly's prudery, but there was a touch which was new. The man required for his peace of mind that she should brush his cheek with those beautiful long eyelashes of hers. Molly became so outraged in her blue-black modesty that she kept her head out of the window not to see! When we were detained at a little wayside station, this woman made an awful row about her room.

She seemed to know me and appealed to me—said her brother-in-law was adjutant to Colonel K—&c&c&c.

Molly said, "You had better go yonder, ma'am, where your husband is calling you."

She drew herself up proudly and with a toss.

"Husband indeed—I'm a widow. That is my cousin. I loved my dear husband too well to marry again ever—ever."

Absolutely, tears came into her eyes.

Molly, loaded as she was with shawls and bundles, stood motionless.

"After all that gwine on in the cars! Oh, Lord—I should a' let it go—'twas my husband and *me!* nigger as I am."

Here I am at home, on a soft bed of every physical comfort.

Life one long catechism.

The curiosity of stay-at-home people in their narrow world.

"Who is that—the man who is passing there?"

"Only a servant."

"Oh, I see he is not white—but whose servant?"

"How do I know? I daresay I would not know his master."

In Richmond Molly and Laurence quarreled so. He declared he could not put up with her tantrums. Unfortunately I asked him, in the interest of peace

---

5. Chesnut was talking about the Gettysburg campaign.
6. In Shakespeare's play, the exiled Roman Coriolanus joins Tullus, an enemy of Rome, in a war against the city.

and a quiet house, to bear with her temper. *I did.* She was so good and useful. And he was shabby enough to tell her that, their next quarrel.

The awful reproaches that she overwhelmed me with then! She said she was mortified that I had humbled her before Laurence. But the day of her revenge came.

At negro balls in Richmond they were required to carry "passes"—and in changing his coat Laurence forgot his.

Next day Laurence was missing, and Molly came to me laughing *to tears.*

"Come and look. Here is the fine gentleman, tied between two black niggers and marched off to jail." She laughed and cheered so, she could not stand without holding onto the window. Laurence disregarded her and called to me at the top of his voice.

"Please, ma'am—ask Mars Jeems to come take me out of this. I ain't done nothing."

As soon as Mr. C came home, I told him of Laurence's sad fall, and he went at once to his rescue. There had been a fight and a disturbance at the ball. Police was called in—every man made to show his "pass"—and so Laurence was taken up as having none.

He was terribly chopfallen when he came home, walking behind Mr. C. He is always so *respectable* and well behaved and stands on his dignity.

At the place Mr. C found Laurence, a good Confederate soldier popped up. Dirty, drunk, miserable, the pride of his family at home—one whose courage and patriotism and every earthly virtue we heard lauded and magnified ad nauseam—this man had been taken up for brawling in the street. Mr. C said he never would forget the shame and despair of the poor fellow's face as he begged to be "gotten out of that." His eyes were bloodshotten, his face haggard and soiled, his clothes worse, and all in disorder.

"Something must be forgiven to the spirit of liberty, as General Hamilton said," quoted Mr. C. As Artemus Ward would say, "He spoke it sarcastical."[7]

In spite of the short time which had elapsed since Mrs. Hampton's death, I went over to Mrs. Preston's.

Camden became simply intolerable to me.

Buck said Mamie has grown P. V.-ish—heart and mind, soul and body.

Then there came the telegram. I must go to my mother, who was ill [*in Alabama*]. Colonel Goodwyn, his wife, and two daughters were going, so I joined the party.[8] I telegraphed Mr. C for Laurence, and he replied by forbidding me to go at all. It was so hot, the cars so disagreeable—fever would be the inevitable result.

---

7. Humorist Charles Farrar Browne in "A Visit to Brigham Young," *Artemus Ward, His Book* (1862), referring to "noble red men of the forest," added, "This is rote Sarcasticul."
8. Probably Thomas Jefferson Goodwyn, a physician and planter who was mayor of Columbia.

Miss Kate Hampton, in her soft voice, said: "The only trouble in life is when one can't decide in which way their duty leads. Once know your duty—then it is all easy."

I do not know whether she thought it my duty to obey my husband. I thought it my duty to go to my mother, as I risked nothing but myself.

Apropos of somebody on board, Colonel Goodwyn asked if I had ever heard of a woman servant who was a Jewess, or a plowman who was a Jew?

No.

And said Mrs. Goodwyn, "They say there has never been known a fallen woman among them."

"Rachel—a shining light to the contrary."

"Colonel M—they say he is a Levite."[9]

"No—don't you know? Levites are all of the priestly caste."

"But all old Jews fought—even the high priest."

"Well, well. He is a soldier—if of the tribe of Levi. Of what tribe is she?"

"Of the 'lost tribe,' unless she is awfully slandered," said the colonel slowly and solemnly.

We had two days of an exciting drama under our very noses—before our eyes—&c&c&c.

A party had come to Columbia who said they had run the blockade—came in by flag of truce &c.

Colonel Goodwyn asked me to look around and see if I could pick out the suspected crew.

It was easily done. We were all in a sadly molting condition. We had come to the end of our good clothes in three years, and now our only resource was to turn them upside down or inside out—mending, darning, patching.

Near me sat a young woman with a traveling dress of bright yellow—a profusion of curls and pink cheeks, delightfully airy and easy in her manners, absorbed in a flirtation with a Confed major. Who in spite of his nice, new gray uniform and two stars had a very Yankee face—fresh, clean-cut, sharp, and utterly unsunburned—florid, wholesome, handsome. What more can one say of one's enemies? Two other women faced this man and woman. We knew them to be newcomers by their good clothes.

One of these last-named women was a German. She it was who had also betrayed them. I found that out afterward.

The handsomest of the three women had a hard Northern face. All in splendid array—feathers, flowers, lace, jewelry.

If they were spies, why were they so foolish as to brag of New York—and compare us unfavorably with the other side all the time—and in loud shrill accents? Surely that was not the way to pass unnoticed in the Confederacy.

A man came in, stood up, and read from a paper—"the surrender of Vicksburg." I felt a hard blow struck on the top of my head, and my heart took

9. Quartermaster Gen. Abraham Myers.

one of its queer turns. I was utterly unconscious—not long, I daresay. The first thing I heard was joy and exultation of Yankee party. My rage—and humiliation.

A man slept through everything, always in earshot of this party. He had a greyhound face—eager and inquisitive when awake—but then he was one of the Seven Sleepers. Colonel Goodwyn wrote on a blank page of my book (one of the De Quincey's—the note is there now)[1] that the sleeper was a Richmond detective. We called him, in memory of *Bleak House,* Mr. Bucket.[2]

How very Yankee that Confederate major was.

And now I must put my finger in the pie. A fair and comely youth joined my two—one I called "Cashmere Shawl," the other "Yellow Gown." He told them in a furtive undertone, "You can trust me. I am from Tennessee—plenty of good Union people there." I wrote this in my book and gave it to Colonel Goodwyn. He took care that Mr. Bucket saw it, too, in one of his brief waking intervals.

"That boy is one of my subalterns," came back to me, written below my foolish evidence.

Bucket was now introduced to the fine dames by his young understaffer and he plied with everything nice—watermelons, fruits of all kinds.

Finally, hot and tired out, we arrived at West Point. The dusty cars were still except for the giggling flirtation of Yellow Gown and her major.

From the door at their backs stalked in two of the tallest and sallowest Confederate officers I ever saw. I felt mischief in the air. One of these was lame and leaned heavily on the other. He sat down on the arm of the seat opposite the unconscious major and touched his shoulder. The major was whispering low to his Dulcinea[3] and bent over her to do so.

He started and turned quickly to meet the cold stare of that grim and sallow pair of Confederate officers.

Instantly every drop of his blood left his face. It became pallid with terror, and a spasm seized his throat. It was a piteous sight, and I was awfully sorry for him at once.

I said to Colonel Goodwyn: "Did you see him? He is guilty. Look at his face."

"He is not half as pale as you were when you heard Vicksburg had fallen into Yankee hands. Maybe he has something wrong about the heart."

He was then asked for his commission.

The Confederates looked over his papers.

"This is an unusual thing. They are filled up and signed by the same hand. And that is not Mr. Seddon's handwriting."

The major said huskily, "I am from Maine, it is true, but I have fought for the Confederacy from the first."

He ought never to have breathed the word Maine in that crowd. It condemned him then and there. He added, "I have been in the commissary department—got my discharge because of a disease of the heart."

1. Probably Thomas De Quincey, *The Confessions of an English Opium-Eater* (1822).
2. Police inspector in Charles Dickens, *Bleak House* (1853).
3. The peasant girl idealized by Don Quixote.

Did he hear Colonel Goodwyn's reproof to me?

He certainly was deadly pale and breathed with difficulty.

The cruel Confederate officer smiled. "In our service officers are allowed to resign from any personal disability. They are not discharged. Tell me where you served as commissary and I will telegraph?"

There was a great deal more of this painful scene—and they marched him out of the car.

Poor Yellow Gown's color was fast. She could not lose it without soap and water, I daresay. But the whites of her eyes were lurid, and her whole face was changed. She wept real tears and wiped them upward to spare those cheeks and their false bloom. Bucket—who had only been made known to Cashmere Shawl and Frau Judas—now was presented formally to Yellow Gown in her dire distress. He went out with the party who led the male spy away captive, but had soon returned, no longer in the least sleepy-headed.

Now he began to make mischief among the deserted females.

He told Yellow Gown that the major was throwing all the blame on her. He heard him. He stayed as long as he could to hear all. He only came back as the train was slowly moving away from the station.

The major was saying she had tried to seduce him from his allegiance to the Confederate States. She had tried to make him a traitor.

How she flamed out in her wrath and vilified the poor major, the wretch, and she had never laid eyes on him till she met him in these cars.

And yet they seemed so intimate from the first!

Mr. Bucket's condolence and sympathy was inexhaustible. We left them all together, for we got off at Montgomery. They went on to Mobile. I heard them say again and again, with fervent gratitude, what would they have done without Mr. Bucket. Of the women we never heard again. They never do anything worse to females, the high-toned Confederates! than send them out of the country—and if they are not patriotic indeed, they are only too glad to shake the dust from their feet and go.

Some time afterward we saw that a spy had been executed. As we did not know the name of ours, we could not [be] certain of his fate.

At Montgomery the boat waited for us—and in my haste I tumbled out of the omnibus and with Dr. Robert Johnson's[4] assistance nearly broke my neck.

The thermometer high up in the nineties—and they gave me a stateroom over the boiler. I paid out my Confederate rags of money freely to the chamber[maid] to get out of that oven. Surely, go where we may hereafter—an Alabama steamer in August, lying under the bluff with the sun looking down, will give one a foretaste, almost an adequate idea, of what's to come, as far as heat goes. The planks of the floor burned one's feet under the bluff at Selma, where we stayed nearly all day. I do not know why.

Met James Boykin, who had lost 1,200 bales of cotton at Vicksburg and charged it all to Jeff Davis in his wrath.

---

4. Robert B. Johnson, a Camden physician.

Which did not seem exactly reasonable to me.

At Portland there was a horse for James Boykin, and he rode away, promising to send a carriage for me at once. But he had to go seven miles on horseback before he reached my sister's—and then they were to send.

On that lonely riverside Molly and I remained—dismal swamps on every side, immense plantations, white people few or none.

In my heart I knew my husband was right when he forbade me to undertake this journey.

There was one living thing at this little riverside inn—a white man who had a store opposite. And oh! how drunk he was! Hot as it was, Molly kept up a fire of pine knots. There was neither lamp nor candles in that deserted house. The drunken man reeled over now and then with his lantern. And he would stand with his idiotic drunken glaze—solemnly staggering round us, always bowing in his politeness until he nearly fell over us.

I sprang out of his way, and he asked, "Well, Madam, what can I do for you?"

Shall I ever forget the headache of that night and the fright? My temples throbbed with dumb misery. I sat upon a chair—Molly on the floor, with her head resting against my chair. She was as near as she could get to me, and I kept my hand on her.

"Missis, now I believe you are scared, scared of that poor drunken thing. If he was sober I could whip him—fair fight—and drunk as he is, I kin throw him over the bannister—ef he so much as teches you. I don't value *him* a button!"

Taking heart from such brave words, I laughed. It seemed an eternity, but the carriage came by ten o'clock. And then with the coachman as our sole protector, we poor women drove eight miles or more—carriage road, through long lanes, swamps of pitchy darkness, plantations on every side.

It had never crossed my brother-in-law's[5] head to come for me.

As we drew near the house it looked like a graveyard in a nightmare—so sad, so weird, so vague and phantomlike in its outlines.

I found my mother ill in bed, feeble still, but better than I hoped to see her.

"I knew you would come" was her greeting, with outstretched hands.

Then I went to bed in that silent house, a house of the dead, it felt. I supposed I was not to see my sister until the next day. But she came in sometime after I had gone to bed. She kissed me quickly, without a tear. She was thin and pale, but her voice was calm and kind.

As she lifted the candle over her head to show me something on the wall, I saw that her pretty brown hair was white. It was awfully hard not to burst out into violent weeping. She looked so sweet—and yet so utterly brokenhearted. But as she was without emotion, apparently, it would not become me to upset her by my tears.

Next day, at midday, I may say, Hetty, mother's old maid, brought my breakfast to my bedside. Such a breakfast! Delmonico could do no better.

5. Dr. Thomas Edward Boykin, husband of Sarah Amelia (Miller) Boykin.

"It is ever so late—I know."

"Yes, we would not let Molly wake you."

"What a splendid cook you have here."

"My daughter Lenah is Miss Sally's cook. She's well enough as times go, but when our Miss Mary comes to see us *I does it* myself." And she curtsied down to the floor.

"Bless your old soul," I cried. And she rushed over and gave me a good hug.

She is my mother's factotum—has been her maid since she was bought from a Virginia speculator (her mother and all her children) at six years old. She is pampered until she is a rare old tyrant at times. She can do everything better than anyone else. And my mother leans on her heavily. Hetty is Dick's wife. Dick is the butler. They have over a dozen children and take life very easily.

Sally came in before I was out of bed.

And she began at once in the same stony way, pale and cold as ice, to tell me of the death of her children. It had happened not two weeks before.

Her eyes were utterly without life—no expression whatever. And in a composed and sad sort of way she told the tale, as if it was something she had read and wanted me to hear.

"My eldest daughter Mary had grown up to be a lovely girl. She was between thirteen and fourteen, you know. Baby Kate had my sister's gray eyes. She was evidently to be the beauty of the family. Strange—that is one of my children who has lived and has gone, and you have never seen her at all. She died first, and I would not go to the funeral. I thought it would kill me to see her put under the ground.

"I was lying down—stupid with grief. Aunt Charlotte[6] came to me after the funeral with this news—'Mary has that awful disease, too.'

"There was nothing to say. I got up and dressed instantly—to Mary. I did not leave her side again in that long struggle between life and death. I did everything for her, with my own hands. I even prepared my darling for the grave. I went to her funeral, and I came home and walked straight to my mother, and I begged her to be comforted. I would bear it all without one word, if God would only spare me the one child left me now."

She has never shed a tear—and twenty years older—cold, hard, careworn. With the same rigidity of manner, she began to go over all the details of Mary's illness. "I had not given up hope—no, not at all—as I sat by her side," she said. "'Mama, put your hand on my knees. They are so cold.' I put my hand on her knee. The cold struck to my heart. I knew it was the coldness of death." She put out her hand—and it seemed to recall the feeling. She fell forward in an agony of weeping, [*remainder of page cut out*] and this lasted for hours. The doctor said this reaction was inevitable. Without [it] she must have died or gone mad.

While her mother was so bitterly weeping, the little girl—the last of them—a bright child of three or four—crawled into my bed.

"Now, auntie," she whispered, "I want to tell you all about Mamie and

6. Charlotte (Boykin) Taylor.

Katie—but they watch me so. They say I must never talk about them. Katie died because she ate blackberries. I know that. And then Aunt Charlotte read Mamie a letter, and that made her die, too. Maum Hetty says they have gone to God, but I know the people saved a place between them in the ground for me."

Once or twice this child missed some member of the family, and she came to me—put her little hand to hide her whisper.

"Don't tell mama. I just know they are dead, too."

Uncle William[7] was in despair at the low ebb of patriotism out there.

"West of the Savannah River it is property first, life next, honor last."

He gave me an excellent pair of shoes. What a gift! For more than a year I have had none but some dreadful things Armsted makes for me—and they hurt my feet so. These do not fit, but that is nothing. They are large enough and do not pinch anywhere. Absolutely a respectable pair of shoes!!

Uncle William [says] the men who went into the war to save their negroes are abjectly wretched. Neither side now cares a fig for their beloved negroes—would send them all to heaven in a hand basket, as Custis Lee says, to win in the fight.

General Lee, Mr. Davis, &c&c—soldiers everywhere—want them [slaves] to be put in the army. Mr. Chesnut and Mr. Venable discussed the subject one night. Would they fight on our side or desert to the enemy? They don't go to them, because they are comfortable where they are and expect to be free anyway.

When we were children our nurses gave us our tea out in the open air, on little pine tables scrubbed white as milk pails.

As he passed us with his slow and consequential step, we called, "Do, Dick—come and wait on us."

"No, little missies, I never wait on pine tables. Wait till you get big enough to put your legs under your pa's mahogany."

I taught him to read as soon as I could read myself—perched on his knife board. He won't look at me now. He looks over my head—he scents freedom in the air. He was always very ambitious. I do not think he ever troubled books much. But then as my father said, Dick, standing in front of his sideboard, had heard all subjects of earth or heaven discussed—and by the best heads in our world.

He is proud, too, in his way. Hetty his wife complained the other menservants were so fine in their livery.

"Nonsense, old woman—a butler never demeans himself to wear livery. He is always in plain clothes." Somewhere he had picked up that.

He is the first negro that I have felt a change in. They go about in their black masks, not a ripple or an emotion showing—and yet on all other subjects except the war they are the most excitable of all races. Now, Dick might make a very respectable Egyptian sphinx, so inscrutably silent is he.

---

7. William Boykin, fifty, was a Dallas County planter worth 150,000 dollars in 1860.

He did deign to inquire about Gen. Richard Anderson. "He was my young Marster once. I always will like him better than anybody else."

When Dick married Hetty, the Anderson house was next door. The two families agreed to sell either Dick or Hetty, whichever consented to be sold. Hetty refused outright, and the Andersons sold Dick, that he might be with his wife. Magnanimous on the Andersons' part, for Hetty was only a lady's maid, and Dick was a trained butler on whom Mrs. Anderson had spent no end of pains in his dining room education. And of course if they had refused to sell Dick, Hetty had to go to them. Mrs. Anderson was very much disgusted with Dick's ingratitude when she found he was willing to leave them. As a butler he is a treasure. He is overwhelmed with dignity, but that does not interfere with his work at all. My father had a body servant who could imitate his master's voice perfectly. And he would call out from the yard after my father had mounted his horse.

"Dick, bring me my overcoat. I see you there, sir—hurry up." And when Dick hastened out, overcoat in hand—and only Simon! Particularly after several obsequious "Yes, Marster—just as Marster pleases," my mother had always to step out and prevent a fight. And Dick never forgave her laughing.

Once in Sumter, when my father was very busy preparing a law case, the mob in the street annoyed him, and he grumbled about as Simon made up his fire. Then he said in all his life he had never laughed so heartily. Suddenly he heard the Hon. S. D. Miller—Lawyer Miller, as the gentleman announced himself in the dark—appeal to the gentlemen to go away and leave a lawyer in peace to prepare his case for the next day—&c&c. My father said he could have sworn to his own voice. The crowd dispersed, and some noisy negroes came along. Upon them Simon rushed with the sulky whip, slashing around in the dark, calling himself Lawyer-Miller-who-was-determined-to-have-peace.

My father heard him come back, complaining, "Them niggers run so he never got in a hundred yards of one of them." [*Remainder of page torn out.*] Simon was not aware that his master knew of his tricks or his personification of him. Simon was a black ape and Dick copper color.

C. Haile[8] was at Portland when we went there on our way back to the outside world. He said: "You will never make me believe Edward Boykin likes a soldier's life. He is too fond of his own ease and comfort. And he never will be reconciled to have his property destroyed. I wish we lived in Florida. Easy times, they say, down there."

"And yet they are obliged to get substitutes there, as you do here. They are making money by blockade-running, cheating the government, and skulking the fight."

"Yes, that is all true," he answered pleasantly, not taking offense. "Substitutes run away. On our army list we have fifty thousand missing. Thirty thousand would have saved Vicksburg. There are folks such as you describe everywhere. They love to make money and have no stomach for the fight."

---

8. Columbus Haile, the husband of Louisa (McCaa) Haile.

He was there, he said (not to me—one of the Hailes repeated it to us) with a thousand dollars in his pocket to buy another substitute for state service. He has one already in the Confederate army. And he has sent all his cotton through McRae & Co. to Liverpool. Busy laying up his treasures where neither Yankees nor Confederate can burn or molest them.

No staterooms for us [aboard riverboat returning]. My mother alone had one. My aunt and I sat, nodding in armchairs, for the floors and sofas were covered with sleepers, too. On the floor that night—so hot and so little covering of clothes or anything could be borne—lay a motley crew—black, white, yellow—disported themselves in promiscuous array—children and their nurses bared to the view. Wrapped only in the profoundest slumber.

"No caste prejudices here. Garrison,[9] John Brown, or Gerrit Smith[1] never dreamed of equality more untrammeled." And a crow black, enormously fat negro man waddled in every now and then to look after the lamps, &c&c&c.

The atmosphere of that cabin was stifling, and the sight of those obscene birds on the floor did not make it more tolerable. So we soon escaped and sat out near the guards.

The next day was the very hottest I have ever known. And our supreme consolation—watermelons, the very finest, and ice.

A very handsome woman—I did not know her—rehearsed our disasters all along the line. And then, as if she held me responsible, she faced me furiously.

"And where are our big men?"

"Who do you mean?"

"I mean our leaders, the men we have a right to look to, to save us. They got us into this scrape. Let them get us out of it. Where are our big men?"

I sympathized with her and understood her, but I answered lightly, "I do not know the exact size you want them."

Stonewall is gone across the river—and Albert Sidney Johnston—and we cried:

Oh, for an hour of Wallace wight
And well-skilled Bruce to rule the fight!

She scorned generalities.

"We are tired of waiting. Our big men ought to come out of that and lead us to victory."

"Those fine fellows in Virginia are pouring out their heart's blood like water," I said. "Virginia will be heroic dust—the army of glorious youth that has been buried there."

In Montgomery we were so hospitably received. Ye gods, how those women talked—and all at the same time.

9. William Lloyd Garrison.
1. The New York abolitionist who helped John Brown plan the Harpers Ferry raid.

"I tried to explain," cried the loudest, "to Montgomery people that they had no bien séance."

"Well, and we don't [have] any. What is 'bring sing,' anyway?" I daresay they thought it a new drink.

They put me under the care of a brother-in-law of General Dick Taylor, a Mr. Gordon who married one of the Bringiers.[2]

A very pleasant arrangement for me. He was kind and attentive and vastly agreeable, with his New Orleans anecdotes.

On the first of last January all of his servants left him but four. To those faithful few he gave free papers at once, in case of Confederates turning up in authority once more.

He paid high wages, and things worked smoothly for some weeks.

One day his wife saw some Yankee officers' cards on a table.

"I did not know any of these people had called!"

Her maid answered: "Oh, Missis, they come to see me. I have been waiting to tell you. It is too hard. I cannot do it. I cannot dance with these nice gentlemen at night at our Union balls and then come here and be your servant next day—I can't."

"So," said Mr. Gordon, "freedom must be followed by fraternity and equality."

One by one the faithful few slipped away, and they were left to their own devices. Why not?

Mr. Gordon, like Laurence, says with money you can live anywhere. And until he had paid away all of his in bribes &c he lived very comfortably in New Orleans.

When Gen. Dick Taylor's place was sacked, his negroes moved down to Algiers, a village near New Orleans. An old woman came to Mr. Gordon to say they wanted him to get word to Mars Dick that they were dying of disease and starvation. Thirty had died that day. Dick Taylor's help being out of the question, Mr. Gordon applied to a Federal officer. He found this one was not a philanthropist. He said:

"All right. It is working as I expected. America for the white race—improve negroes, Indians, &c, off the continent. Their strong men we put in the army. The rest of them will disappear like cotton after a frost."

To save his property a man offered to take the oath of allegiance to the U.S.A.

"Oath be d——d," they said, and took whatever they wanted of his and forced him to be their guide. At least, when he came back he said he had been "forced."

I told Mr. Gordon of a little soliloquy at the president's.

A man telling us how the Yankees had forced him to do something, dragged and kicked him, &c&c. Mrs. Davis said in her sweetest tones,

"I should have died."

---

2. Martin Gordon, a New Orleans merchant, married Louise Françoise Bringier, daughter of a prominent Creole family. Her younger sister, Louise Marie Myrthé (Bringier), married Gen. Richard Taylor, C.S.A.

"Why? Merely because you were kicked?"

"No—not exactly that. But I think I should have kicked and fought them, and then they would have killed me. One can die but once."

Mrs. Johnston in Montgomery. She said, when she came to see me at the T's:

"To keep alive I sit with my Byron open on my lap. This horrid! horrid Confederacy. Hoffman's Anodyne and Valerian at my elbow."

"Madame," said Mrs. T, "Why 'horrid Confederacy'?"

"It is unendurable. My God! This den of thieves. I have lost everything but my virtue. My clothes all gone. This dress—it is an old toilette table cover. Do you not feel inclined to stick pins in me?"

Mrs. Taylor, gravely: "Do you not wish Lincoln was dead and the war over?"

"No. There are worse men—worse presidents on this continent than Lincoln."

"What is Joe Johnston doing now?" asked Mrs. T.

"Increasing his reputation in the way he made it—retreating and saving his army."

"I hope he may save his country," said Mrs. Taylor gravely. We laughed.

"Women forbear," said Mrs. T, spreading out her arms over us. "Your mirth is unseemly. The Lord omnipotent reigneth." She was standing up, drawn up like a sibyl to her full height.

"Don't mix up things, ma. These ladies don't want your solemn mockeries."

Mrs. J. said of Mrs. Wigfall: "She is unlike the French woman. She adores innocent pleasures and the beauties of nature. She is content to abide at Orange Court House."

Cried Mrs. Taylor, "Louis Wigfall called an innocent pleasure—and his company a harmless recreation!"

Then came the history of Mrs. F——, taking away our breath. And then Mrs. J departed to dine with her fair friend.

Said Mrs. T, "When they talk of Mrs. F, I feel that I am reading a translation of one of Balzac's novels." Then, "What have I heard!"

Beauregard sulking in Charleston. By supreme negligence he has lost us Morris Island.[3] He is accused of saying they put him in Charleston because he could make no reputation there. Faith! But he can lose what he has there. He has lost it? He never had much brains—eh? And now he is losing heart. Wife won't come away from New Orleans. But they say she is dead, poor thing—second wife, too.

Johnston can sulk, too. He is sent west, he says, that they may give Lee the army Joe Johnston trained. Lee is reaping where he sowed. But then he was backing straight through Richmond when they stopped his retreating. That was the time the president ought to have sent him back to the Yankees, a free

---

3. Replaced by Braxton Bragg after allowing the evacuation of Corinth, Beauregard had been assigned to the south Atlantic coast. On Sept. 6, 1863, he ordered the evacuation of Morris Island after a fifty-eight-day Federal siege.

gift. And that stupid log of a halfhearted Yankee Pemberton lost us Mississippi.[4]

Bragg—thanks to Longstreet and Hood, he won Chickamauga. So we looked [for] results that would pay for our losses in battles, at least. Certainly they would capture Rosecrans. No! There sits Bragg—a good dog howling on his hind legs before Chattanooga, a fortified town—and some Yankee Holdfast grinning at him from his impregnable heights.[5] Waste of time.

"How?"

"He always stops to quarrel with his generals."

September 20, 1863.[6]   Yesterday I heard the same sentiment expressed by two very different styles of men.

A letter from Jim Frierson, read to us by his wife.

"Eat, drink, and be merry—tomorrow you die. I mean, buy the fifty-dollar shoes, of course. The crash has got to come. Enjoy yourself all you can while you may."

Judge Withers—apropos of my selling cotton and carrying supplies to Richmond: "Yes, buy, sell, do as it suits you for the moment. Enjoy the brief interval which remains to you before your ruin comes—for come it must."

J. C., who refused to hear what my friends wrote from Charleston—"too scandalous." Here is what he says—just from town.

General—on the Battery, utterly intoxicated.

Beauregard had a sore throat and had to keep out of drafts.

"They treated me more as a Yankee spy at General B's headquarters than as an aide-de-camp of the president of the Confederacy."

Now, that is condensed scandal, as my female correspondents write it.

Generals drunk—Beauregard given over to hopeless invalidism—blockade-runners supreme in power.

Male and female made he them—I mean scandalmongers. Eh?

"One lucky woman in the Confederacy made friends with the Mammon of unrighteousness—head, center, blockade, and telegraphs spread like network over the land.

"*Everywhere* meet Mrs. R—— and place everything at her disposal."

At Kingsville I caught a glimpse of our army. Longstreet's corps going west. God bless the gallant fellows. Not one man intoxicated—not one rude word

---

4. Promoted and sent west, Lieutenant General Pemberton was in command at Vicksburg, the last Confederate stronghold on the Mississippi, when it fell to the Union in July 1863.

5. "When I envied the finery of any of my neighbours, [my mother] told me that 'Brag was a good dog, but Holdfast was a better.'" Samuel Johnson, *The Rambler* (1750–52), no. 197.

6. An anachronism, since M. B. C. has discussed immediately above the aftermath of the battle of Chickamauga, fought Sept. 19–20, 1863. She is, however, still using the memoir form.

did I hear. It was a strange sight—miles, *apparently,* of platform cars—soldiers rolled in their blankets, lying in rows, heads and all covered, fast asleep. In their gray blankets, packed in regular order, they looked like swathed mummies.

One man near where I sat was writing on his knee. He used his cap for a desk, and he was seated on a rail. I watched him, wondering to whom that letter was to go. Home, no doubt—sore hearts for him there!

A feeling of awful depression laid hold of me. All these fine fellows going to kill or be killed. Why? And a word got to beating about my head like an old song—"the unreturning brave."

When a knot of boyish, laughing young creatures passed me, a queer thrill of sympathy shook me. Ah, I know how your home folks feel, poor children. The throng was dense. General Kershaw came up to where I was sitting alone and offered to marshal me through, and as I took his arm—Molly at my heels, laden with shawls, bags, bundles—my general remembered his Caesar. They did not open out a path for us soon enough to please him. He called out:

"These must be citizens, not soldiers. They do not make way for ladies." With what alacrity and smiling faces they moved aside.

Mem Cohen said, "Catch me making myself town talk, grieving for any man, be I ever so much married to him. Oh, this war! The liberty men take! There may be another woman across the way with as good a right to moan as the lawful wife—better, for he cares for her. But madame wife is the only one who never knows her hard fate"—&c&c. Rachel[7] says, "Yes, everybody knows—that is, everybody but her." "Who do you mean by *her?*" "Gentleman's wife, ma'am?"

Ellen[8] stood there, handsome as ever—erect, pale, careworn—her face shaded by a black hat and heavy black plume. Moreover, she bore aloft a peacock fly brush as a sort of banner flung to the breeze. A flag of defiance—for her whole attitude was game! I said gaily,

"You here—he there." For he sat on a pile of boxes near at hand.

"I may be a fool, as Captain Calhoun says, but I know there is collusion somewhere."

"There is no collusion. Hush—he will hear you." I saw tears in her eyes.

"And if he does? Is it to be tragedy in five acts—or end as a comedy does, with a happy marriage? And bless ye, my children. You were engaged to the man, they say, before I was married. I have been married over twenty years. And you have been off-and-oning ever since—jilting and making up. No tremendous mischief, I should say, if he does hear!"

He was seated in his nice new uniform, on a box of raw beef. He was the

---

7. Rachel Lyons.
8. Ellen Bradley, member of a Sumter District planting family. Her companion was Ransom Spann (see p. 384, n. 2).

dandy of his day at dancing school with me thirty years ago, and he is young and good-looking now. He was evidently in a reckless mood. She stood off with a hectic flush on her cheek and watched us, brandishing aloft her peacock's brush.

"What's the matter? Why don't you two make it up and marry?"

"Ask her. Barkis is willing!"[9]

Then he began to tell of Harriet Grant's feats—knitting flannel shirts and drawers for the soldiers. Charity covers a multitude of sins, he said, but he did not say whose sins.

Another scandalous letter.

That sweet, sad, demure widow. The man—an Admirable Crichton—lawyer, parson, foreign ambassador, colonel of a Confederate regiment. In his parson character he converted her from her faith to his.

What she enclosed was printed matter from the lawyer's pen—the parson's faith and the soldier's audacity—for it required all of that to publish those three columns. It was six weeks only after the unconsolable husband's wife's death. The wife was spoken of in the letter "as the removal of the sole obstruction."

When the wedding guests assembled, the party to be married appeared—she sweet and modest as ever, leaning on his arm.

In lieu of wedding ceremony he read the long paper elaborately prepared.

He had been married several weeks, privately married to the lovely being at his side. His love for her had been of so long standing he could not tell when it began. It seemed to have grown with his growth and strengthened with his strength, &c&c&c.

This scene took place six weeks after his wife's death. The happy pair at once departed from that place where he was in charge of a church. To his own church he explained that he married this lady so promptly after his wife's death (a few days) because he was in the army and death might come to him any day. And it was the only way to leave her his property. And they did not intend to acknowledge the marriage for a year, but circumstances forced his hand. This was entitled a true—but Braddonish—story.[1]

No—not at all. "Braddon" means bigamy. Not a grain of bigamy here—both parties married and married again and again—death and destruction follow their footsteps—but they wait decorously "till death us do part."

More like Henry the VIII's pious regard for religions and morals. And legal ceremonies—not a suspicion, even, of murder, which is high Braddon, too. They wait until the weaker vessel breaks against the hard metallic one. A pretty sure game—so the fable says.

Queer place, the first time I saw it. We traveled there in a stagecoach with a

9. Barkis, the bashful carter in Charles Dickens's *David Copperfield* (1850), instructs David to tell Clara Peggotty that "Barkis is willing" to marry her.

1. Mary Elizabeth (Braddon) Maxwell, popular English novelist and author of the enormously successful mystery *Lady Audley's Secret* (1862).

beautiful bride and her husband. Three days after we saw, she had hanged herself to the bedpost. That made an impression on me. I was only fourteen then, and I never have seen Montgomery since without remembering it.

Another scandal.

A father forbade his daughter's marriage. There was a party at the house—he saw something which made him consent at once—and joy go with her.

"Oh, what could it be? What?"

Stern parent, dozing in the piazza, which was not lighted, saw the forbidden man sitting by a window, his back turned to the piazza.

Lightly his daughter tiptoed out. She daintily raised the red hair from the back of that stout freckled neck and kissed it.

"Things have gone that far—let her marry," swore the father. Can you blame him? So much for traveling. I might have stayed at home forever and never have known of girls who kissed the back of horrid men's necks—faugh! Or widows who brushed with their eyelashes their cousin's cheeks in the public cars. And they talk of American prudery!

No superstitions now—no witches to bewilder men to their ruin—no devils now cast out of Magdalene![2]

Fables—says science!

Never mind all that. Tell us the end—when the father consented.

Oh—they married without *further demurrer*.

Once last winter persons came to us with such strange stories of Alston, Morgan's man—stories of his father, too. Turf tales, murder—or at least, how he killed people. He had been a tremendous favorite with J. C., who brought him in, leading him by the hand.

Now J. C. said, "With those girls in the house we must be more cautious"—and I agreed to be coldly polite, after what had been told me. "After all," I said, "I barely know him."

Then he called. And I was very glad to see him, utterly forgetting that he was under a ban.

We had a long confidential talk. He told me of his wife and children, of his army career. Told Morgan stories—grew more and more cordial. So did I. He thanked me for the kind reception given him in that house—told me I was a true friend of his and related to me a scrape he was in which if divulged would ruin him, although he was innocent. But time would clear all things.

Begged me not to repeat anything that he had told of his affairs—not even to Colonel Chesnut. Which I promised promptly—and then he went away.

I sat, poking the fire, thinking what a curiously interesting creature he was. This famous Bob Alston!

2. Christ cast seven devils out of Mary Magdalene. Mark 16:9 and Luke 8:2.

The foldings slowly opened, and Colonel C appeared. He came home two hours ago from the War Office with a headache and had been lying on the sofa behind that folding door, listening for mortal hours.

"So—this is your style of being coldly polite," he said. Fancy my feelings.

"Indeed, I forgot all about what they said of him while he was here. The lies they tell on him never once crossed my mind. He is a great deal cleverer and I daresay just as good as those who malign him."

For one thing, he was smart enough to keep out of the penitentiary with striped breeches and cropped hair &c when the Yankees have shut up Morgan and his men. I heard of him paroled in Columbia the other day.[3]

Mattie Ready[4] (I knew her, a handsome girl, in Washington, several years ago) got tired of hearing Federals abuse John Morgan. One day they were worse than ever. She grew restive. By way of putting a mark against the name of so rude a girl, the Yankee officer said,

"What is your name?"

"Write Mattie Ready now—but by the grace of God, one day I hope to call myself the wife of John Morgan."

She did not know him at all. He heard the story. A good joke it was said to be. So he made it a point to find her out. And as she was as pretty as she was patriotic, by the [grace] of God she is now Mrs. Morgan.

These timid Southern women! And under the guns they can be brave enough.

Aunt Charlotte's story of my dear mother. They were up at Shelby, a white man's country where negroes are hated.

These ladies had with them several negroes who belonged to my uncle, at whose house they were staying in its owner's absence. A negro man had married in the neighborhood and for some cause was particularly obnoxious among them.

My aunt and my mother, old-fashioned ladies shrinking from everything outside of their own door, knew nothing of all this. They occupied rooms on opposite sides of an open passageway. Underneath—the house was open and unfinished. Suddenly my aunt heard a terrible noise, apparently a man running for his life, pursued by men and dogs—shouting, halloing, barking. She had only time to lock herself in. Utterly cut off from her sister, she sat down, dumb with terror.

There was a loud knocking at the door—men swearing, dogs tearing round, sniffing, racing in and out of the passage, in and out below, barking underneath like mad, &c&c. Aunt C was sure she heard the panting of the negro as he ran in a few minutes before. What could have become of him? Where could he have hid? The men shook the doors and windows and loudly threatened vengeance.

---

3. Captured after an abortive raid into Ind. and Ohio in July 1863, John Hunt Morgan was treated not as a prisoner of war but as an ordinary convict.

4. Martha Ready, daughter of former congressman Charles Ready of Tenn. and a popular figure in Washington society.

My aunt pitied her sister, so feeble, so cut off in that room. The fright might kill her.

The cursing and shouting continued. A man's voice in harshest accents made itself heard over all.

"Leave my house, you rascals! If you are not gone in two seconds I'll shoot."

There was a dead silence except the noise of the dogs. Quietly the men slipped away. Once out of gunshot, they began to call their dogs.

After it was all over, my aunt crept across. "Sister, what man was it scared them away?"

My mother laughed aloud in her triumph. "*I am the man.*"

"But where is John?"

Out crept John from a pile of rubbish in the corner of the room my mother had thrown over him.

"Lord bless you, Miss Mary opened de door fer me and dey was right behind running me."

Aunt C says mother is awfully proud of her prowess. And she showed some moral courage, too.

At the springs near them she found people unkind to Mrs. Lovell because she was a Northern woman and her husband had lost us New Orleans.[5] ("Newerleens," they called it.) Soon my mother heard, in addition to all this, that Mrs. Lovell had an ailing baby. She drove down to the springs and saw that it was true. Her countrywomen looked askance at Mrs. Lovell. "And I was ashamed [of] them," said my mother. "So before their faces I asked her to drive with me every day. It would do the baby so much good, taking it out in the open air."

Now to beat the Yankees is the old lady's "dream by night and prayer by day," but—

Nearly opposite my house, corner of Clay and 12th Streets, was Mrs. Webb's hospital. Girls have no business at hospitals, so I did not know much about it until the Prestons left me.

It was all so neat, clean, comfortable. When I remember my first visit to that tobacco-house hospital, when I fainted, what a contrast! We have learned how to do it.

Mrs. Webb stands by, closes the eyes of the dead, writes letters to the friends of the dying and, what is better, nurses many a fine fellow shot to pieces back to life again.

The day I went there first she was sitting by the bed of a poor wretch horribly maimed. He had been a stalwart creature over six feet and had that day for the first time attempted to walk out. Some brutes on the lawn, wounded soldiers themselves, laughed at him. And he came back, threw himself on his cot, and was weeping as hysterically as a woman. I must confess she was soothing and consoling him as tenderly as if he had been a baby.

---

5. Emily (Plympton) Lovell, wife of Maj. Gen. Mansfield Lovell. Her Massachusetts-born father had been a career officer in the U.S. Army.

I saw her in a fierce mood, too. It was the day before the fight at Brandy Station. It was a queer scene. An omnibus drove up. Some men got out and came in, rather sneakily, I thought. Her whole face changed.

"You see those men," she cried, with a gesture of contempt and turning her back on them. "I know them well. Do they look like sick soldiers? They always come down just before a battle, say they are sick, and want to take the beds that should be kept for better men."

I slipped away, without looking at them again, hanging my head for the poor devils so insulted. She called out to me, scorn in her voice.

"You'll soon hear of a battle. See if you don't!"

At the president's. General Lee there. Constance and Hetty Cary[6] came in, also Miss Sanders.

Miss Constance Cary was telling some war anecdote. That is an attempt to get up a supper the night before at some high and mighty F.F.V.'s house.

Several of them went into the kitchen to prepare something to eat by the light of one forlorn candle. One of the men of the party, not being of a useful temperament, turned up a tub and sat upon it. Custis Lee, wishing to rest, found nothing upon which to rest but a *gridiron*.

Mrs. Davis inquired softly: "Was he tender on the gridiron? He has never been known to be so anywhere else?"

Major McLean[7] said one miss of strong family affection said it would satisfy her to have it inscribed on her tombstone "Sister Hetty Cary, Cousin of Constance." But, added the Major meekly, "I do not think she would dislike 'Beloved wife of _____' &c&c."

As he went away we could see General Lee holding the beautiful Miss Cary's hands in the passage outside, though we could not hear what she was saying.

Miss Sanders rose to have her part in the picture and asked Mr. Davis to walk with her into the adjoining drawing room. He seemed surprised but rose stiffly and with a scowling brow was led off. As they passed where Mrs. Davis sat, Miss Sanders, all sails set, looked back.

"Don't be jealous, Mrs. Davis. I have an important communication to make to the president."

Mrs. Davis's amusement! and her significant "Now—did you ever?"

Someone asked Hetty Cary if it was true that the Englishman Lawrence

---

6. Constance Cary, whose widowed mother was a volunteer nurse in Richmond, was one of the most popular belles of wartime society. After the war she became the author of more than a dozen books, including a memoir of the war years, *Recollections Grave and Gay* (1911). Her cousin Hetty, the daughter of a Baltimore teacher and notary public, had been forced to flee to Richmond after waving the Confederate flag at Union troops.

7. Maj. Eugene McLean, the husband of Margaret (Sumner) McLean. Removed as chief quartermaster of the Army of Miss. after the evacuation of Corinth, McLean had returned to Richmond, where a court of inquiry absolved him of charges of misconduct.

wanted to come over the lines with her in that open boat.[8] She crossed in a little boat, sitting on her trunk.

"Yes, but I said no, I will not go traveling in that kind of way with the author of *Guy Livingstone*."

She is engaged to General Pegram,[9] who is promoted regularly after every one of his defeats. Shows what faith they have in him, a conspicuous mark of the confidence his superior officers have in his merits.

After one of his catastrophes he was at home, and there was a party at his mother's house. Suddenly, armed at all points in full panoply, that is, a beautiful Baltimore ball dress, the unlooked-for apparition of Hetty Cary dawned upon them. They thought her in Maryland.

General Pegram absolutely fell back, fainting with joyful emotion.

Mr. Venable taunted us.

"The matter with you is no man ever fainted for love of you."

And we could not say that one ever did.

"No," said a belle. "Of all the love that has come my way, no man has fainted under his load of it yet."

"You whimper that spitefully."

Buck and Captain Chesnut rode out, not remembering how cold it is in Richmond. With silk stockings and thin boots, Buck's feet were nearly frostbitten. Buck has the feet and hands of a duchess. She was ill—Anne said, threatened with "brown kretin" [*bronchitis*]. At any rate, it was a bad sore throat. And she lay on the sofa, wrapped in cashmere shawls and muffled in laces &c&c about the face and neck.

Our surgeon dropped on his knees by her side.

"What is that for?" said the Captain, standing up brusquely and placing his hands on the back of a chair.

"I mean to try auscultation, percussion, &c&c, to see if her lungs are affected."

"Come now, that sort of thing won't do."

"Miss Sally," said the surgeon P. V., "this sort of thing is done every day. It is strictly professional. I *must* rest my head against your chest. It is absolutely necessary for a medical diagnosis."

I daresay I am making a muddle of John Darby's technical phrases.

"No, you don't," said the Captain. "If I had a sore throat you would drag me to the window, make me stretch my mouth from ear to ear, put a tablespoon down until I choked, make me stick out my tongue, and then order me a nasty

---

8. In sharp contrast to the aggressive hero of his popular novel, *Guy Livingstone; or, 'Thorough'* (1857), George Alfred Lawrence spent three months in Baltimore vainly trying to arrange to cross the Potomac and join the Confederate army in Va. He was eventually deported by Federal authorities.

9. John Pegram of Va. had been commissioned a brigadier general in Nov. 1862 after taking part in the invasion of Ky.

gargle. Or, more than probable, barely touch my pulse and say, 'Oh, nothing's the matter with you.' That's you fellows' way in camp. Auscultation and listening under shoulder blades you keep for the women."

"Nonsense. Let me put my head where I can hear you breathe."

"This furniture is rented. I believe it does not belong to Aunt Mary. If you don't want to see a chair smashed, take care not to move a peg nearer."

The surgeon got up, dusted his knees, and said, "Everybody knows what a narrow-minded donkey you are."

The Captain received this compliment smilingly.

"You ought to have waited till I went out. The other fellow feels, too, like a fool while that auscultation goes on &c&c."

Stoneman's raid.

It was Sunday, and I was in Mrs. Randolph's pew. The battle of Chancellorsville was raging. And the rattling of the ammunition wagons, the tramp of the soldiers, the everlasting slamming of those iron gates of the Capitol Square just opposite the church, all made it hard to attend to the service.

Then began a scene calculated to make the stoutest heart quail.

The sexton quietly walking up [to] persons members of whose family had been brought down wounded, dying, or dead, and the pale-faced people following the sexton out.

Finally Mr. Minnegerode himself leaned across the chancel rail for a few minutes' whispered talk with the sexton. Then he disappeared, and the assistant clergyman went on with the communion which he was administering.

At the church door stood Mrs. Minnegerode, as tragically wretched and as wild looking as Mrs. Siddons.[1]

She managed to tell her husband.

"Your son is at the station—dead."

When the agonized parents reached the station, it was someone else—a mistake. Somebody's son, all the same. Pale and wan came Mr. Minnegerode back to his place within the altar rails. After the sacred communion was over, someone asked him what it all meant.

"Oh, it was not my son who was killed, but it came so near—it aches me yet."

At home I found L. Q. Washington, who stayed to dinner. I saw J. C. and himself were utterly preoccupied by some event which they did not see fit to communicate to me.

Immediately after dinner Mr. C lent Mr. Washington one of his horses, and they rode off together.

I betook myself to my kind neighbors the Pattons for information. There I

---

1. English actress Sarah (Kemble) Siddons (1755–1831), Fanny Kemble's aunt, was famed for her performance of tragic roles.

found Colonel Patton gone, too. Mrs. Patton, however, knew all about the trouble. She said there was a raiding party within forty miles of us, and no troops in Richmond. They asked me to stay to tea, those kind ladies, and in some way we might learn what was going on. After tea we went out to the Capitol Square, Laurence and three menservants going to protect us.

They seemed mustering in the citizens by the thousands. Companies after companies forming—then battalions, then regiments. It was a wonderful sight to us—looking through the iron railing, seeing them fall into ranks.

Then we went to the president's. They were at supper. We sat on the white marble steps in front, and General Elzey told me exactly how things stood—and our immediate danger. It was nearly as exciting as the park. Pickets were coming in. Men were spurring to and from the door as fast as they could ride—bringing and carrying. Calmly General Elzey discoursed upon our present weakness and our chances for aid.

After a while Mrs. Davis came out and embraced me silently.

"It is dreadful," I said. "The enemy are in forty miles of us—only forty."

"Who told you that tale? They are within three miles of Richmond."

I went down on my knees, like a stone.

"You had better be quiet. The president is ill. Women and children must not add to the trouble."

She asked me to stay all night there, which I was thankful to do.

We sat up—officers coming and going—and we gave them what hasty refreshment we could from a side table kept constantly replenished.

Finally, in the excitement of the scene and the constant state of activity and constant change of persons, we forgot the danger. The officers told us such jolly stories and seemed in such fine spirits—gradually we took heart, too. There was not a moment's rest for anyone. Mrs. Davis said something more amusing than ever.

"We look like frightened women and children, don't we?"

Early next morning the president came down. He was still feeble and pale from his illness. Custis Lee and J. C. loaded his pistols, and he drove off in Dr. Garnett's carriage—J. C. and Custis Lee on horseback, riding alongside.

By eight o'clock the troops from Petersburg came in. And the danger was over. They will never strip Richmond of troops this way again. We had a narrow squeeze for it. But we escaped. It was a terrible night, although we made the best of it.

———

A scrap from the winter of '63. I have already written of the summer of '63, when Vicksburg did fall.

I was walking on Franklin Street, and I met J. C. "Come with [me] for a minute to the War Office, and then I will go home with you."

What could I do but go? He took me up a dark stairway and then down a long dark corridor, and he left me sitting in a window. He would not be gone a second—that he was obliged to go into the secretary of war's room. There I sat mortal hours. The men came to light the gas. From the first I put down my veil so that nobody might know me. Numbers of persons passed that I knew, but I scarcely felt respectable, seated up there in that odd way, so I said not a word but looked out of the window. Judge Campbell slowly walked up and down with his hands behind him. The saddest face I ever saw.

He jumped down, in his patriotism, from judge of the Supreme Court, U.S.A., to undersecretary of something or other, I do not know what, C.S.A.[2]

No wonder he was out of spirits that night!

Finally Mr. Ould came. Him I called. He joined me at once, in no little amazement to find me there, and stayed with me until Colonel Chesnut came. In point of fact, I sent him to look up that stray member of my family.

When J. C. came, he said, "Oh, Mr. Seddon and I got into an argument and time slipped away. The truth is I utterly forgot you were there."

When we were once more out in the streets, he began: "Now, don't scold me, for there is bad news. Pemberton has been fighting the Yankees by brigades, and he has been beaten every time. And now Vicksburg must go!" I suppose that was his side of the argument with Seddon.

Once again I visited the War Office. I went with Mrs. Ould to see her husband at his office. We wanted to arrange a party on the river on the flag-of-truce boat and to visit those beautiful places, Claremont and Brandon.

J. C. got into one of his too-careful fits—said there was risk in it. And so he upset all my plans.

Just then I was to go up to the John Rutherfoords' by the canal boat.[3]

That, too, he vetoes—"too risky." As if anybody was going to trouble us!

One day Gen. Edward Johnson was walking with us in the Capitol Square, and the Robbs[4] hurried up so as not to miss us. The Robbs wanted us to join a party who were going to Drewry's Bluff the next day. Joyfully I acceded to their request. Drewry's was a place I wished to see. Our Gibraltar. At the boat next day we were joined by a very handsome Englishman who had lost a leg in Seven Pines. He proved himself to be as agreeable as he was good-looking. Our party consisted of Captain Robb and his son Phil, Mrs. Lewis[5] and her daughter, Captain Clarke,[6] &c&c. "Such pleasant people," said Mrs. Lewis. "Our chances of having a good time are good indeed."

---

2. Because many Southerners suspected him of treachery in negotiations with U.S. Secretary of State Seward over the fate of Fort Sumter in 1861, John Archibald Campbell held no office in the Confederacy until Oct. 1862, when he was appointed assistant secretary of war with special responsibility for administering the conscription law.

3. "Rock Castle," the home of prominent lawyer John Coles Rutherfoord and his wife Anne Seddon (Roy) Rutherfoord, was about twenty-five miles away on the James River.

4. Robert Gilchrist Robb, a former U.S. Navy officer commanding the Confederate naval works at Richmond Station. His son Phillip probably served on his staff.

5. Ann Ogle (Tayloe) Lewis was the wife of Henry Howell Lewis, captain of the C.S.S. *Rappahannock* at Richmond Station.

6. Capt. Maxwell T. Clarke, a prominent Richmond tobacco merchant.

I was repeatedly told how interesting the scenery was between Richmond and Drewry's. Can't say I remember anything about it.

Captain Smith Lee met us at the bluff. I had seen his wife, but never himself before since the grand smash.

He was awfully glad to see me. Captain Robb called out, "I think Captain Lee is carrying you bodily up the bank."

"Not quite. I am no lightweight, but he is helping me to go up slowly. He remembers how my heart beats when I climb. He used to wonder that I ever went up those long stairs at the Capitol in Washington."

He took us to his quarters—as clean and as neat as a man-of-war's quarter-deck. And then I sat until I got my breath again. How he pitched into my country.

"South Carolina be hanged. She brought us into this snarl. How I did want to stay in the old navy! My side came down on me with Light Horse Harry Lee—and [*illegible word*] with the old Mason. Virginia comes first with us all, you know—so I am here."

He told us he must hurry back to receive a grand party who were expected—Secretary of the Navy Mallory, Attorney General Watts, &c&c, Mr. Senator Orr of So. Ca. "To be—Orr—or not to be?" he laughed [*page torn out*] a South Carolina senator—as Mr. Orr wiped his mouth, drawing one cuff of his coat sleeve and then the other across his mouth from ear to ear after drinking the whiskey punch.

Mr. Mallory offered me his arm, and we set off to visit and inspect the fortifications of this, "our Gibraltar of the River Jeems," of whose deeds they are so proud. It holds its own against all comers. Mr. Butler King[7] joined us and a number of officers. We were marching at the head of quite a procession—and certainly, from the sounds of laughter and loud talking from the rear, a very gay one.

At the officers' quarters the honors were done by a handgun. Some naval hero whose good looks stood out boldly against the formidable ugliness of the political guests. Everywhere we went the troops presented arms—&c. I was fool enough to ask Mr. Mallory why they did that.

With a suppressed titter: "I daresay because I am at the head of the Navy Department."

These navy heads came to try a new gun. After our two luncheons we adjourned to Captain Lewis's ship, and he gave us dinner. I mean, our obscure party who came with Captain Robb. The secretary's party were off somewhere trying their gun, whose boom-boom was the solemn accompaniment of festive repast.

After dinner Captain Smith Lee and I walked the quarterdeck for one good hour—and had what he called a dear, delightful, Washington talk to our hearts' content.

---

7. Thomas Butler King, a former state legislator who represented Ga. in Europe early in the war. King visited Richmond in 1863 to gather the effects of a son killed in battle.

We kissed our hands in return to the secretary of the navy's party as they steamed by us on their way home. They were in the grand boat. We had betaken ourselves to the small affair which brought us down there. Regretfully we turned our faces home, for as Captain Robb said, "This has been a happy day—no drawbacks, everything nice and pleasant everywhere."

So we supposed his navy affairs had been inspected to his perfect satisfaction. Naval men require things flawless.

Arrived at Three Rocketts, we landed. No carriage to meet us. Then they found one. The lame Englishman lost his leg in our cause, so I said I preferred to walk and gave him my seat. Then Phil Robb and I set off for Cary Street. For three long miles I dragged my weary limbs along. When we got home I was utterly worn-out—dead beat. Molly scolded me violently and made me go to bed at once. There I stayed for nearly a week—with fever, headaches, &c&c. Tossing around in dreams, I could see marines falling in line, saluting Mr. Mallory, everywhere great guns firing, marine bands playing, &c&c.

In Columbia. Met Mrs. S grieving over the loss of her clothes—trunk gone astray hopelessly.

"You go on as if you had lost a child."

"No, indeed! No embargo on children down here," answered the heartless creature. "But clothes once gone are gone forever. Then one can make shift to live without children, but how can one do without decent drapery—&c&c."

The fair and fatal Felicia[8] had grown stout though handsome still. She has such an innocent, respectable appearance in her rich black silk and plain linen collar. Good people around her in all the colors of the rainbow—cheap woolen stuffs—fagoter, as the French have it.

Surely they were seen to great disadvantage by her side.

Miss Olivia Middleton[9] said the Darby alliance surprised her. They thought Mary P would marry a general—major general—lieutenant general—not one of the ten thousand brigadiers now so common. Johnny said, "Surely we heard a major general propose to her openly and aboveboard."

Alluding to Gen. Edward Johnson's loud appeals in our very small drawing room.

October 1863.   Bloomsbury. J. C. at home on his way back to Richmond. Has been sent by the president the rounds of the western armies.

---

8. In the fourteenth-century English poem "Guy of Warwick," Felice La Belle compels her suitor Guy to prove he is the greatest knight in the world before she will marry him. Guy weds Felice after many adventures but regrets the battles he fought to win her.

9. The twenty-five-year-old daughter of Oliver Hering and Susan (Chisolm) Middleton.

Says Polk is a splendid old fellow. They accuse him of being asleep in his tent at seven o'clock when he was ordered to attack at daylight.[1]

Too good a conscience, to sleep so sound.

The battle did not begin until eleven at Chickamauga, when Bragg ordered the advance at daylight. No end of [*word omitted*] among them then, Bragg and his generals. I think a general worthless whose subalterns quarrel with him. Something wrong about the man. Good generals are adored by their soldiers. See Napoleon, Caesar, Stonewall, Lee, &c&c.

Old Sam (Hood) received his orders to hold a certain bridge against the enemy—and he had already driven the enemy several miles beyond it while the slow generals were still asleep. So Hood has won a victory—and has only one leg to stand on.

Mrs. McLean writes that it is even worse since Mr. Davis was there. He could not reconcile them. Atlanta is crammed with displaced or dissatisfied generals.

J. C. was with the president when he reviewed our army under the enemy's guns before Chattanooga. He said it was a splendid cavalcade. And the scene altogether so striking—man and nature. He has promised to write a description of it for me.

The officers in Atlanta were so hospitable and friendly (J. C., being the president's aide, was accustomed to the scant civilities of Beauregard and Joe Johnston's camp). We have just sent a box of old brandy, old wine, and good home hams to them, in kind remembrance of his visit there.

He brought a funny story from their campfires—no doubt a Joe Miller, but new to me. And I know the man to whom it is stuck now.

He drank fearfully. Suddenly, to the surprise of friend and foe, he ceased.

And it was a dream which checked his mad career.

In his dream he died and went directly to Hell—or Hades—if the first word is too rough for ears polite.

The Devil opened the door for him with ready politeness (as Byron has it—Said His Darkness to His Brightness—with an air of great politeness), bowed low—was too civil by half.[2] Said he was charmed to see him. Indeed, had been looking for him for some time. Knew his habits and knew how quickly that sort of thing brought people to his hospitable abode. Then His Darkness—after saying in a pleasant way, "Drinking soon brings people to the Devil, you see"—shouted, without turning round to his Imps below:

"Hello! down there. You hear! Fire up Number 9 for Jack Brown."

J. C. said he told Mr. Davis that every honest man he saw out west thought well of Joe Johnston. He knows that the president detests Joe Johnston for all the trouble he has given him. And General Joe returns the compliment with

---

1. On Sept. 29, 1863, Braxton Bragg removed his subordinate, Lt. Gen. Leonidas Polk, for failing to attack promptly during the battle of Chickamauga. Jefferson Davis, however, refused to allow the court-martial of Polk, the Episcopal bishop of La., and shortly sent him to command the Department of Ala., Miss., and East La.

2. Paraphrased from Lord Byron, *The Vision of Judgment* (1822), stanza 35.

compound interest. His hatred of Jeff Davis amounts to a religion. With him it colors all things.

Joe Johnston advancing, or retreating, I may say with more truth, is magnetic. He does draw the goodwill of those by whom he is surrounded. Being such a good hater, it is a pity he had not elected to hate somebody else than the president of our country. He hates not wisely but too well.

Our friend Breckinridge received him with open arms. Nothing narrow, nothing self-seeking about Breckinridge. He has not mounted a pair of green spectacles made of prejudices, so that he sees no good except in his own red-hot partisans.

While he was telling these things, Mrs. General _____ asked with languid interest, "Is Breckinridge on our side—or a Yankee general?"

So much for fame—even at home.

A country gentleman was here who complained. He had taken provisions to the Atlanta hospitals. In attendance upon a wounded friend, he found he lacked sugar for his tea.

When he asked for it, the surgeon answered curtly, "There is none, sir." Afterward he dined with a mess and saw them take the identical bag of white sugar he had carried to Atlanta and mix for their own surgical mouths many a good hot toddy.

They little dreamed that he had brought that bag.

That sort of thing takes the heart out of one. It is human nature at its lowest.

XIX

"In Spite of Blockade"

Dates once more—and not a jumble of scraps and letters.

October 27, 1863. Bloomsbury. Young Wade Hampton has been here for a few days, a guest of our nearest neighbor and cousin, Phil Stockton. Wade, without being the beauty or the athlete that his brother Preston is, is such a nice boy.

We lent him horses, &c&c—ended by giving him a small party. What was lacking in company was made up for by the excellence of Colonel Chesnut's old Madeira—champagne. If everything in the Confederacy was as truly good as old Mr. Chesnut's wine cellars!

Then we had a salad and a jelly cake. Gen. Joe Johnston is so careful of his aides that Wade has never seen a battle—says he has always happened to be sent afar off when the fighting comes.

He does not seem too grateful for this and means to be transferred to his father's command. He says, "No man exposes himself more recklessly to danger than General Johnston, and no one strives harder to keep others out of it. But the business of this war is to save the country. And a commander must risk his men's lives to do it." French saying, can't make an omelet unless you are willing to break the eggs.

November. Then Johnny ran down here for a few days. Extract from one of his Richmond letters: "Her dress was none too high in the neck, and by no means tight-fitting around her lovely high-born F.F. bosom. The oysters were red-hot. One fell—she screamed. B____ dived for it with a fork—fished it up in a thrice. Much confusion of face and an instantaneous drawing up of light shawl."

"With a fork!" commented Johnny. "The muff! I should have risked burning my fingers that time!"

November 5, 1863. For a week we have had such a tranquil, happy time here at home—both my husband and Johnny at home.

J. C. spent his time sauntering around with his father or stretched on the rug before my fire, reading *Vanity Fair* and *Pendennis*.[1] By good luck he had not read them before. We kept *Esmond* for the last—bonne bouche.

He owns that he had a good time. He did not think it was in human nature for

---

1. Thackeray, *The History of Pendennis* (1849-50).

Colonel Esmond to stand that everlasting twitting—bastard, bastard. He could not fancy the maternal mistress—nor Trix—of course. Colonel Esmond has the whole philosophy of love. When they slowly recapitulated Trix's faults—"Ah, I know! but I want that one." Love is the one thing that cannot be bribed or bought.

———

Johnny was happy, too. He does not care for books. He will read a novel now and then if the girls continue to talk of it before him. Nothing else whatever in the way of literature does he touch. He comes, pulling his long blonde moustache irresolutely, as if he hoped to be advised not to read it. "Aunt Mary—will I like this thing?"

He was but a baby when his father died—was a delicate boy—and has never been in robust health in his life. He is fair and frail, tall and thin. His schools were selected with an eye to his health. Finally a private tutor was tried. He took his diploma at the South Carolina College. [*Page torn out.*] He keeps his face so absolutely devoid of expression—except upon rare occasions, one knows nothing of any thoughts or feelings of his. He knows nothing of politics and cares less.

Roughing it in camp, instead of killing him, as we thought it would, has made him comparatively strong and hardy. He rides like an Arab and loves his horses in the same way. He is devoted to what he calls "good eating," and he will have it. Coûte que coûte.

I think he is happiest when he sends one of his fine horses to some girl who is worthy to ride such a horse. She must be beautiful and graceful. Then, superbly mounted, he goes to ride with her. He is sure to go slowly along, where everybody can see them and admire the horses and the girl. Strange to say, he has not one jot of personal vanity. Being so silent, one does not suspect him of being a close observer, but he is. Always taking notes—and he is a keen and merciless, caustic and cruel, critic of men and manners. Above all things he waits and watches for the shortcomings of women.

I do not think he has an idea of what we are fighting about—and he does not want to know.

He says "my company," "my men," with a pride, a faith, and an affection which is sublime.

He came into his inheritance at twenty-one (just as the war began), and it was a goodly one, fine old houses and an estate to match.

Yesterday Johnny went to his plantation for the first time since the war began. John Witherspoon went with him and reports in this way.

"How you do, master! How you come on?" from every side, in the noisiest welcome from the darkies. Johnny silently shaking black hands right and left as he rode into the crowd.

As the noise subsided, to the overseer: "Send down more corn and fodder for my horses." To the driver: "Have you any peas?"

"Plenty, sir."

"Send a wagon load down for the cows at Bloomsbury while I stay there. They have not milk and butter enough there for me. Any eggs? Send down all you can collect. How about my turkeys and ducks? Send them down two at a time. How about the mutton? Fat? That's good. Send down two a week."

As they rode home, John Witherspoon remarked, "I was surprised that you did not go into the fields to see your crops, &c&c."

"What was the use?"

"And the negroes—you had so little talk with them."

"No use to talk to them before the overseer. They are coming down to Bloomsbury day and night by platoons, and they talk me dead. Besides, William and Parish go up there every night, and God knows, they tell me enough plantation scandal—overseer feathering his nest—negroes ditto, at my expense. Between the two fires I mean to get something to eat while I am here."

He keeps up a racket in the house, with his horses, his dogs, and his servants, and the everlasting junketing that he has set afloat never ceases. I forgot—he loves dancing with all his heart. It is a pleasure that he takes slowly, sadly, and in earnest.

For him we got up a charming picnic at Mulberry. Everything was propitious —the most perfect of days. The old place in great beauty—those large rooms delightful for dancing. As good a dinner as mortal appetite could crave—the best of fish, fowl, and game—a cellar that cannot be excelled. In spite of blockade, Mulberry does the honors nobly yet.

Mrs. Edward Stockton drove down with me. She helped me with her taste and tact in arranging things. We had no trouble, however. All of the old servants who have not been moved to Bloomsbury scented the prey from afar off, and they literally flocked in and made themselves useful.

This is a sketch of Captain Chesnut, Company A, Butler's brigade.[2] He enjoys life thoroughly. He loves dancing as well as riding and fighting, swimming, horses, jumping fences, or foxhunting. He sneers at women, being now a few years over twenty, and he has been idiotically in love with one woman all his life. Her presence brings a hectic flush in his pale face, as clear and distinct as a girl's. But that subject is tabooed, for of course she loved another.

"Johnny is always making love to somebody, but he never gets into any trouble he can['t?] take care of himself."

"You see," says the Captain, "I am not a marrying man. My people, now, they say, 'Marster, why don't you marry and leave a n'young Missy here to look after we?' Not she. Stay here and look after you! Never. She'd be trotting after me in the army—bothering everywhere. Lord, what a nuisance they are. Now, just you wait. After this cruel war is over—then, look out."

November 28, 1863.   Richmond. Our pleasant home sojourn was soon broken up. Johnny had to go back to Company A No. 1. And J. C. was ordered by the president to make a second visit to Bragg's army.

2. The unit of Army of Northern Va. cavalry commanded briefly in Sept. and Oct. 1863 by Brig. Gen. Matthew C. Butler (see p. 737, n. 6).

So we came on here, where the Prestons had taken apartments for me. Molly was with me. Adam Team[3] with Isaac McLaughlin's help came with us to take charge of the eight huge boxes of provisions I brought from home. Isaac is a servant of ours, the only one J. C. ever bought in his life. Isaac's wife belonged to Rev. Thomas Davis, and Isaac to somebody else. This owner of Isaac was about to go west, and Isaac was distracted. They asked one thousand dollars for him. He is a huge creature, really a magnificent specimen of a colored gentleman. His occupation had been that of a stage driver. Now he is a carpenter, or he will be some day. He is awfully grateful to us for buying him, is really devoted to his wife and children, though he has a strange way of showing it, for he has a mistress, en titre, as the French say, which fact Molly never failed to grumble about as soon as his back was turned.

"Great big good-for-nothing thing, come a-whimpering to Marster to buy him for his wife's sake. And all the time, he an—"

"Oh, Molly, stop that."

Mr. Chesnut sold one negro—bought one and sold one. Bob's wife wanted him to go with her; her master was moving to Louisiana. Bob elected to go with her and was sold. He has been writing to be bought back ever since.

———

I did not find time to tell J. C. regularly, that is, how much I enjoyed that day at Drewry's Bluff.

Smith Lee and I compared it to a day when he got up a similar party for Mrs. John R. Thomson and ourselves, down the Potomac in a government barge. He had the Japanese embassy in charge, and when we asked how he would get rid of that duty when the time to go was at hand, he said, "You just wait and see."

So he went up and had a solemn parley with the interpreter, came back, and said to our hostess: "The Japanese are very anxious for your permission to' retire. They want to go, and at once, they say." So without further ado they even huddled off home.

Until then I had not thoroughly understood how useful an interpreter might be.

Smith Lee said doggedly he had no doubt the Japanese did want to go, with all their yellow hearts.

———

I was daft with delight to get away from home November 11th.

My last public act before leaving Camden was to matronize a party down at my mother's old home, seven miles from town.

After dinner Uncle John came to me, with tears in his eyes. I had not asked him to say grace before dinner. Such a thing had never happened in that house before. He was cruelly mortified at my heathenism. In vain I said: "But it is only a picnic stand-up meal. Nobody asks grace at a picnic."

———

3. A son of James Team working as an overseer for the Chesnuts.

"Your mother's house, &c&c," over and over—[*remainder of page and part of next page cut out*].

I was too sorry to have hurt his feelings, and it spoiled all my pleasure.

The young people, however, cared for none of these things. They had a jolly good time.

Mr. Davis, our president, visited Charleston and had an enthusiastic reception. Beauregard, Rhetts, Jordan to the contrary notwithstanding.

He described it all to Mr. Preston. Mr. Aiken's perfect old Carolina style of living delighted him.

Those old gray-haired darkies and their automatic noiseless perfection of training—one does miss that sort of thing. Your own servants think for you, they know your ways and your wants; they save you all responsibility, even in matters of your own ease and well-doing. Eben the butler at Mulberry would be miserable and feel himself a ridiculous failure, were I ever forced to ask him for anything.

I had an adventure at Kingsville. Of course, I know nothing of children. In point of fact am awfully afraid of them.

Mrs. Edward Barnwell[4] came with us from Camden. She had a magnificent boy of two years old. Now, don't expect me to reduce that adjective.

For this little creature was a wonder of childlike beauty, health, and strength. Why not? If like produces like, with such a handsome pair to claim as father and mother!

The boy's eyes alone would make any girl's fortune.

At first he made himself very agreeable, repeating nursery rhymes and singing.

Then something went wrong. Suddenly he changed to a little fiend—fought and kicked and scratched like a tiger. He did everything that was naughty. And he did it with a will, as if he liked it.

His lovely mama, with flushed cheeks and streaming eyes, imploring him to be a good boy.

We stopped at Kingsville. I got out first, then Mrs. Barnwell's nurse, who put the little man down by me.

"Look after him a moment. I must help Mrs. Barnwell with the bundles &c." She stepped hastily back, and the cars moved off. They ran down a half-mile to turn. I trembled in my shoes. This child! No man could ever frighten me so. If he should choose to be bad again! It seemed an eternity while I waited for that train to turn and come back again.

My little charge took things quietly. For me he had a perfect contempt. No fear whatever. And I was his abject slave for the nonce.

4. Harriet (Hayne) Barnwell was the wife of Capt. Edward Hazzard Barnwell, a nephew of Sen. Robert Woodward Barnwell.

He stretched himself out lazily at full length. Then he pointed downward. "Those are great legs," said he solemnly, looking at his own. I immediately joined him in admiring them enthusiastically. Near him he spied a bundle.

"Pussycat tied up in that bundle!" He was up in a second and pounced upon it. If we were to [be] taken up as thieves, no matter. I dared not meddle with that child. I had seen what he could do. There were several cooked sweet potatoes tied up in an old handkerchief—of some negro, probably. He squared himself off comfortably, broke one in half, and began to eat. Evidently he had found what he was fond of. In this posture of events Mrs. Barnwell found us. She came with comic dismay in every feature. She did not know what our relations might be when she came back to us—if we had undertaken to fight it out alone as best we might. The old nurse cried, "Lausy me!" With both hands uplifted, without a word, I fled. In another moment the Wilmington train would have left me. She was going to Columbia.

We broke down only once between Kingsville and Wilmington. But between Wilmington and Weldon we contrived to do the thing so effectually as to have to remain twelve hours at that forlorn station.

The one room that I saw was crowded [with] soldiers. Adam Team succeeded in routing out two chairs for me, upon one of which I sat and put my feet on the other. Molly sat flat on the floor, resting her head against my chair. I woke cold and cramped. An officer—he did not give his name but said he was from Louisiana—came up and urged me to go near the fire. He gave me his seat by the fire, where I found an old lady and two young ones with two men in the uniform of common soldiers.

We talked as easily to each other all night as if we had known each other all our lives. We discussed the war, the army, the news of the day. No questions were asked, no names given, no personal discourse whatever. And yet if these men and women were not gentry, and of the best sort, I do not know ladies and gentlemen when I see them.

Being a little surprised at the want of interest Adam Team and Isaac showed in my well-doing, I walked out to see, and I found them working like beavers. They had been at it all night. In the breakdown my boxes were smashed. They had first gathered up the contents and were trying to hammer up the boxes so as to make them once more available.

At Petersburg a smartly dressed female came in, looked around in the crowd, then asked for the seat by me. Now Molly's seat was paid for the same as mine, but she got up at once, gave the lady her seat and stood behind me. I am sure Molly believes herself my bodyguard as well as my servant.

The lady then, having arranged herself comfortably in Molly's seat, began in plaintive accents to tell her melancholy tale. She was a widow. She lost her husband in the battle around Richmond.

Soon, someone going out, a man offered her the vacant seat. And straight as an arrow she went in for a flirtation with the polite gentleman.

Another person said to me, a perfect stranger: "Well, look yonder. As soon as she began whining about her dead beaux I knew she was after another one."

"Beau indeed!" cried another listener. "She said it was her husband."

"Husband or lover, all the same. She won't lose any time. It won't be her fault if she don't have another one soon."

But the grand scene was the night before.

Crowded with soldiers, of course. Not a human being that I knew.

An Irish woman, so announced by her brogue, came in. She marched up and down the car, loudly lamenting the want of gallantry in the men who would not make way for her. Two men got up and gave her their seats, saying it did not matter—they were going to get out at the next stopping place.

She was gifted with the most pronounced brogue I ever heard, and she gave us a taste of it. She continued to say that the men ought all to get out of that; that car was *shuteable* only for ladies. She placed on the vacant seat next to her a large looking glass. She continued to harangue until she fell asleep.

A tired soldier coming, seeing what he supposed to be an empty seat, quickly slipped into it. Crash went the glass. The soldier groaned, the Irish woman shrieked. The man was badly cut by the broken glass which he sat upon, but she did not mind that, she was simply a madwoman. She shook her fist in his face, said she was a lone woman and he had got in that seat for no good. How did he dare &c&c&c. I do not think the man uttered a word. The conductor took him into another car to have pieces of glass picked out of his clothes &c&c. And she continued to rave. Adam Team shouted aloud and laughed as if he were in the Hermitage swamp. The woman's unreasonable wrath and absurd accusations were comic, no doubt. Soon the car was silent, and I fell into a comfortable doze.

I felt Molly give me a gentle shake.

"Listen, Missis, how loud Mars Adam Team is talking. And all about old Marster and our business, and to strangers. It's a shame."

"Is he saying any harm of us?"

"No, ma'am, not that. He is bragging for dear life, how old ole Marster is and how rich he is an' all that. I gwine tell him stop." Up stalked Molly.

"Mars Adam, Missis say please don't talk so loud. When people travel they don't do thataway."

It reminded me of Mrs. Frank Hampton's explanation of why she wanted to know Mr. Chesnut. Bill Dogan has a laugh that nothing rivals in sound but the falls of Niagara. The very noisiest laugh ever known on this continent. He has been laughing &c for twenty years, for he is a good fellow, and people considered him as inevitable as one of the forces of nature. He joined Frank Hampton and Mr. C on the street in Columbia, shouting with glee, running first one side with a story at which he alone laughed, then on the other side, bumping them out of the straight path, stepping in front of them, and walking backings, trampling on their toes, sticking his face in theirs as he roared to force them to listen to them.

Frank Hampton took him as hopelessly as the east wind, which he would try and get out of the way of. Not so Mr. C. He said: "Mr. Dogan, do go and walk on the other side of the street. I never can bear a man to make me conspicuous by noise in a public place."

And with a loud laugh at the funniest of all ideas, Dogan went.

Mr. Frank said, "I do love a cool hand."

After Molly had disposed of Adam Team's home narrative, she politely offered me some luncheon from her basket. Said she had cooked some things she knew I liked. Broiled chicken, and turnovers as light as a feather. Said she could bang out the cooks at Bloomsbury, little as they thought it.

"But Lawd, Missis, where is my basket? There ain't no niggers to steal in this car," she cried, looking round. Then she was as loud and violent as the Irish woman. "Showly white gentlemen ain't stolen a servant's basket of *vittles?*"

She was raging out. "White mens, which of you stole my chicken?"

I touched her.

"Sit down and hold your tongue."

She went down like a shot.

"Who is making a noise now? You are as bad as Adam Team or the Irish woman."

No answer. And a dead silence prevailed. When we got up to leave the car, Molly's empty basket was found beside her. Two men were not awakened by Molly's vociferation when she missed her basket.

Those hungry individuals I suspected but kept my thoughts to myself.

When Molly told Sally Preston, instead of going off in sympathetic abuse of the soldiers who made a raid on her basket, Sally paid Molly this compliment: "And did you worry Mrs. C that way by making a fuss? You know Molly, I have told you over and over. You are a good soul, but your manners are atrocious."

To which Molly responded by the broadest grins of delight. She is absolutely devoted to Sally. And Sally has undertaken to teach her better manners.

I found Mr. Preston's man Hal at the depot with a carriage to take me to my Richmond house. Mary P had rented these apartments for me.

I found my dear girls there with a nice fire, &c&c, everything looked so nice and inviting to the weary traveler. Mrs. Grundy, who occupies the lower floor, sent me such a real Virginia tea—hot cakes, rolls, &c&c. Think of living in the house with Mrs. Grundy, and having no fear "of what Mrs. Grundy will say."[5]

J. C. has come—likes house, Grundys, everything. Already he has bought Grundy's horse for 16 hundred Confederate dollars cash.

He is nearer to being contented and happy than I ever saw him. He has not

5. The surname of M. B. C.'s downstairs neighbors, Thomas Billop Grundy and Clara (Haxall) Grundy, reminded her of a line from Thomas Morton's play, *Speed the Plough* (1798), which had become a proverbial expression about the tyranny of social convention. Dame Ashfield, always afraid to offend her neighbor, Mrs. Grundy, asks, ". . . what will Mrs. Grundy say?"

established a grievance yet. But I am on the lookout daily. He will soon find out whatever there is wrong about Cary Street, &c&c&c.

Ives, the A.D.C., is out of favor. Opens too many of Mrs. Davis's private letters—by mistake.

"By mistake," said Mr. Chesnut. "Of course, can anyone doubt it?"

"Yes, by mistake, as you say. But *they* say you and Custis Lee, John Taylor Wood,[6] nor Browne ever make that mistake."

Hood is here at somebody's house. Mrs. G. W. Smith at the same house. *G. W.* is his cousin, *they say.*

J. C. came on with them. Hood, Mrs. G. W., John Darby, &c&c&c.

Buck saw me sending a nice pudding to the wounded man. It seems he cares for no other dainty.

Whereupon she said, in her sweetest, mildest, sleepiest way: "I never cared particularly about him. Now that he has chosen to go with those people, I would not marry him if he had a thousand legs instead of having just lost one."

Then I gave a party.

Mrs. Davis very witty. Preston girls very handsome. Isabella's fun fast and furious. No party could have gone off more successfully, but J. C. decides we are to have no more festivities. This is not the time or the place for such gaieties.

Maria Freeland is perfectly delightful on the subject of her own wedding. She is ready to the last piece of lace, but her hardhearted father says no. She adores John Lewis—that goes without the saying.

She does not pretend, however, to be as much in love as Mary P. In point of fact, she never saw anyone who was. But she is as much in love as she can be with a man who, though he is not *very* handsome, is as eligible a match as a girl could make. He is all that heart could wish. And he comes of such a handsome family. His mother, Esther Maria Coxe, was the beauty of a century, and his father nephew of General Washington, &c&c.

For all that, he is far better looking than John Darby or Mr. Miles.

She always intended to marry better than Mary P or Bettie Bierne.

Lucy Haxall positively engaged to Captain Coffey, an Englishman.[7] She is positive, says she will marry him. It is her first fancy. And she is over thirty, says Grundy, her brother-in-law.

Browne adds, Captain Coffey belongs to Her Majesty's "Orse H'artillery."

Mr. Venable, of Lee's staff, was at our party. So out of spirits. He knows everything that is going on. His depression bodes us no good.

---

6. Colonel Wood, Davis's nephew and Zachary Taylor's grandson, was naval aide to the president.

7. Miss Haxall, eldest daughter of Richmond flour-mill owner R. Barton Haxall, later married Edward Lees Coffey, who was an Irish veteran of the British army serving the C.S.A. as a drillmaster.

John Darby hilarious, asking conundrums. "Who was the first man to get a free ticket?"

"Joseph, when they put him in the pit."

Colonel Preston amended it by saying,

"I should call Joseph in a bad box, rather, at that time."

Today General Hampton sent J. C. a fine saddle that he had captured from the Yankees in battle array.

Mrs. Scotch Allan (Edgar Allan Poe's patron's wife)[8] sent me cream and Lady Cheek apples from her farm.

If Bragg had only been not only a good dog but a Holdfast, which is better, we might be happy yet—with such friends as Hampton and Mrs. Allan.

John R. Thompson, the sole literary fellow I know in Richmond, sent me *Leisure Hours in Town*—by a Country Parson.[9]

J. C. says he hopes I will be contented because he came here this winter to please me. If I could have been satisfied at home, he would have resigned his ADCship and gone into some service in South Carolina. I am a good excuse, if good for nothing else.

Our old tempestuous Keitt breakfasted with us yesterday. I wish I could remember half of the brilliant things he said. J. C. has now gone with him to the War Office. Colonel Keitt thinks it is time he was promoted. He wants to be a brigadier.

Stephen Elliott is promoted—who deserves it more? J. C. has certainly been a friend to the Elliotts. He found that fine fellow Stephen Elliott's paper pigeonholed, wrapped up in his father's application for a chaplainship. And he lent them Sandy Hill. Would take no rent from a family doing their duty to the country, as were the Elliotts.[1]

Now Charleston is bombarded night and day. It fairly makes me dizzy to think of that everlasting racket they are beating about people's ears down there.

8. Louisa Gabriella (Patterson) Allan was the widow of John Allan, a Richmond merchant whose first wife persuaded him to raise the orphaned infant, Edgar Poe, in 1811. The Scots-born merchant and his family were known as the "Scotch Allans" to distinguish them from another Richmond family Mrs. Chesnut later encountered, the "Irish Allens."

9. Rev. Andrew Kennedy Hutchinson Boyd, *Leisure Hours in Town, by the Author of "The Recreations of a Country Parson"* (1862).

1. Stephen Elliott, Jr., a planter and member of the S.C. House from Beaufort, had been promoted to lieutenant colonel for his work as commander of Fort Sumter. His father, Stephen Elliott, Sr., was Episcopal bishop of Ga. and a founder of the University of the South at Sewanee, Tenn.

Bragg defeated and separated from Longstreet.[2] It is a long street that knows no turning. And Rosecrans not taken, after all!

One begins the day with "What bad news next, I wonder?"

---

2. Bragg, who had weakened the Army of Tenn. by sending troops under Longstreet to lay siege to Knoxville, was driven from his position before Chattanooga in the battles of Orchard Knob, Lookout Mountain, and Missionary Ridge during Nov. 23–25.

XX

Between War and Peace

November 30, 1863. Anxiety pervades. Lee fighting Meade. Misery everywhere.[1]

Bragg falling back before Grant.

Longstreet—the soldiers call him Peter the Slow—sitting down before Knoxville.

Colonel Waring[2] came, wanted J. C.'s help to make Evans a major general.

J. C. says, "Surely you exaggerate my influence oddly."

At Mrs. Huger's, to see Willie Preston. Mrs. Huger said: "Hard measure had General Huger. One man may steal a horse—the other must not look over the hedge. Was General Huger ever behind time, as Bragg and Longstreet are always?"[3]

General Bragg's aides advised Preston Johnston to do as they did—destroy nine out of every ten letters sent the general by noncombatants—women and children, &c&c. P. J. was horrified. Women and children are sacred to him, and their complaints came nearer his heart than any.

"How many of such letters do you show the president?" asked Mrs. Davis gravely.

"Oh, about one in sixty," answered Colonel Johnston, with that contagious giggle of his.

"General Lee requires us to answer every letter," said Mr. Venable, "and to do our best to console the poor creatures whose husbands and sons [are] fighting the battles of this country."

Some women wrote to complain of Stuart, "whose horse the girls bedecked with garlands. And he was in the habit of kissing girls." Answer: "General Stuart was forbidden to kiss one unless he could kiss *all*."

She called her husband—that happy young bride—"Peedee."

1. Maj. Gen. George Gordon Meade and the Army of the Potomac had crossed the Rapidan River on Nov. 26 in hopes of driving Robert E. Lee and the Army of Northern Va. toward Richmond.

2. Lt. Col. Joseph Frederick Waring of the Jefferson Davis Legion of Miss. His family was from S.C.

3. Mrs. Huger was thinking of the criticism leveled at her husband, Benjamin Huger, by Longstreet and others, for supposedly allowing McClellan's troops to escape during the Seven Days battles the year before.

I said, "That is the Indian name of one of our rivers. We have Peedee, Santee, Wateree, Congaree."

This sober remark was received with a burst of derision.

"P.D. means 'precious darling'—as D.C. means 'delicious creature'!"

December 2, 1863.   Bragg begs to be released from his command. The army will be relieved to get rid of him. He has a winning way of earning everybody's detestation. Heavens, how they hate him. The rapid flight of his army terminated at Ringgold.

Hardee declines even a temporary command of the western army.[4]

Preston Johnston has been sent out posthaste, at a moment's warning. Not even allowed time to go home and tell his wife goodbye. Or as Browne the Englishman added, "to put a clean shirt in his traveling bag."

Lee and Meade facing each other gallantly.[5] [*Remainder of page cut out.*]

The 1st of December we went with a party of Mrs. Ould's getting up to see a French frigate which lay at anchor down the river.[6]

The French officers went on board our boat.

At half-past six in that bitter cold Molly had a scalding hot cup of coffee for me and a good fire in the dining room. After all, we had to wait one mortal hour for Maggie Howell and the P. S. [*Prestons?*] Colonel Preston always [says], "While I wait for you my dears, I spend the time in thinking of all your faults." Mrs. Myers joined in, with a black feather flapping over her beautiful eyes. Mrs. Randolph, at that early hour, looking more magnificently handsome than ever. The Lees were along.

The French officers were not in the least attractive, neither in manners nor appearance, but the ladies were most attentive to them and showered bad French upon them with a lavish hand. Always accompanied by queer grimaces to eke out the scanty supply of French words. Sentences ending usually in a nervous shriek.

"Are they deaf?" asked Mrs. Randolph.

The French frigate was a dirty little thing. Dr. Garnett was so buoyed up with hope that the French were coming to our rescue that he would not let me say, "An English man-of-war is the cleanest thing known to the world."

Captain _____ said to Mary Lee,[7] with a foreign leer, "I's bashlor."

Mr. Ould said, as we went to dinner on our own steamer: "They will not drink

4. On Nov. 30, while the Army of Tenn. regrouped at Dalton in northwest Ga. after retreating through nearby Ringgold Gap, Davis accepted Bragg's resignation. Two days later, Gen. William Joseph Hardee did take command on a temporary basis.

5. That day, however, Meade gave up trying to find a weak point in Lee's line and completed his withdrawal across the Rapidan to winter quarters.

6. At the end of Nov., the corvette *Grenade* arrived at Richmond to take the French consul to Washington for negotiations over the fate of Southern tobacco that the French had bought but could not ship through the Federal blockade.

7. Mary Ann Randolph Custis Lee, twenty-nine, was Robert E. Lee's eldest daughter.

our president's health. They do not acknowledge us to be a nation. Mind none of you say 'emperor'—not once."

Dr. Garnett interpreted the laws of national politeness otherwise. He stepped forward, his mouth fairly distended with so much French.

"Vieff l'omperorr!"

Young Gibson[8] seconded him quietly,

"Vive l'empereur."

But silence prevailed.

The lieutenant's name was Rousseau. And on the French frigate, lying on one of the cabin tables, was a volume [of] Jean Jacques's works, side by side, strange to say, with a map of South Carolina. This lieutenant was asked by Mary Lee to select some lady that she might introduce him. He answered, "I choose you," with a look and a bow that was a benediction and a prayer.

Said Mrs. Ould to young Gibson, "You could not do that?"

"Who wants me to do it?"

Mrs. Ould had not witnessed the Garnett fiasco. Mr. Ould stood in the door, the picture of distress. She turned to me.

"Look at Robert! They have not given him any wine, and he is going to cry about it."

Preston Hampton was the handsomest man on board. "The figure of Hercules, the face of Apollo," cried an enthusiastic girl.

Preston was as lazy and as sleepy as ever. He said of the Frenchmen, "They can't help not being good-looking, but with all the world open to them—to wear such shabby clothes!"

After "shoosing," Mary Lee came to where she was talking with Mrs. Myers and ourselves. "'Shurshing' her," he said. "'Churching'?" said one.

"No, a compromise between a French 'chercher' and an English 'search.'"

For one thing, their English was no better than our French, but somehow it does not seem so discreditable.

At dinner Preston Hampton stood behind my chair, a great hungry six-foot-two boy. I asked for everything on the table and passed it over my shoulder to Preston, who stood at ease and ate at his leisure.

Captain Owen[9] said, with a sigh: "How Confederate women pitch into a good dinner. Where I have been? I saw them eat the last oyster." And I retired in dismay. And now I am in fine condition for Hetty Cary's starvation party, where they will give thirty dollars for the music and not a cent for a morsel to eat.

Preston said contentedly: "I hate dancing, and I hate cold water. So I will eschew the festivities tonight."

The Governor Letcher party clung together and sang without ceasing.

---

8. Perhaps a son of Dr. Charles Bell Gibson.

9. M. B. C. probably did not catch the correct rank of Maj. William Miller Owen, a young artillery officer from New Orleans who was a popular figure in Richmond society.

Dr. Garnett in a patronizing way said he played a poor game of whist but quite good enough to play with ladies. The ladies beat the braggart with ease and triumphed as only women can.

Found John R. Thompson at our house when I got home. So tired. He brought me the last number of *Cornhill*. He knew how much I was interested in Trollope's story, *Framley Parsonage*.

Next went to tell Mrs. Davis all about the river expedition. Found her under arms, giving an inquiring Englishman the chief points of Jeff Davis's life.

Mrs. Wigfall asked me with a sneer if the distance between Cary Street and the White House was not disagreeable to me.

Wigfall, without giving me an opportunity to reply, began: "They say Benjamin wrote the president's message. Never. Jeff Davis writes his own messages. Besides, the blame of all our disasters is laid on God the Father in this message. If Benjamin had written it, the Jew would have accused Jesus Christ instead."

Wigfall said all this to give Mrs. Wigfall and myself no time to spar.

Young Hudson was there.[1] He went with me last spring that moonlight night—shall I ever forget the pain and fear of it all?—to see Stonewall Jackson lying in state at the Capitol.

December 4, 1863.   J. C. bought yesterday at the commissary's 1 barrel flour, 1 bushel potatoes, 1 peck of rice, 5 lbs. of salt beef, 1 peck of salt. All for sixty dollars. In the street a barrel of flour sells for one hundred and fifteen dollars.

Met Miles yesterday at the Wigfalls. We fought fiercely over Beauregard. Beauregard à la créole. I took my stand on Folly Island, Beauregard's Folly Island that has cost us so much.[2]

December 5, 1863.   Wigfall was here last night. He began by wanting to hang Jeff Davis. J. C. managed him beautifully, and he soon ceased to talk that virulent nonsense and calmed down to his usual strong common sense. I knew it was quite late, but I had no idea of the hour.

J. C. beckoned me out.

"It is all your fault."

"What?"

"Why will you persist in looking so interested in all Wigfall is saying? Don't let him catch your eye! Look in the fire. Did not you hear it strike two?"

---

1. Probably Edward M. Hudson of Va., a captain on the staff of General Elzey.
2. Federal troops occupied Folly Island, outside Charleston, in April 1863.

This attack was so sudden, so violent, so unlooked for, I could only laugh hysterically.

However, as an obedient wife I went back gravely, took my seat, and looked into the fire. I dared not even raise my eyes to see what J. C. was doing. If he, too, looked in the fire.

Wigfall soon tired of so tame an audience and took his departure. He said of Colonel Lay: "Don't care how much they lay, so they don't hatch. It is a bad breed." Gravely: "There is Captain Hatch. He heard his name!"

"Worse still, the Campbells are coming. Look out."

Personal remarks are hazardous on a crowded riverboat.

General Lawton was here last night. He superseded Colonel Myers last winter in spite of Miles, with the Congress at his heels.[3]

He was one of Stonewall's generals. So I listened with all my ears.

"Stonewall could not sleep. So every two or three nights you were waked up by orders to have your brigade in marching order before daylight and report in person to the commander. Then you were marched a few miles out and then a few miles in again."

"A little different from the western stories—and some generals nearer Richmond asleep several hours after they had been expected to attack *the day of a battle.*"

"The restless, discontented spirits move the world—unsatisfied, I mean."

"All this was to make us always ready, ever on the alert. And the end of it was this, Jackson's men had gone half a day's march before Peter Longstreet waked and breakfasted. I think there is a popular delusion about the amount of praying that he did. He certainly preferred a fight on Sunday to a sermon [*remainder of page cut off*]. Failing to manage a fight, he loved next best a long Presbyterian sermon Calvinistic to the core.

"He had no sympathy with human infirmity. He was a one-idea'd man. He looked upon broken-down men and stragglers as the same thing.

"He classed all who were weak and weary, who fainted by the wayside, as men wanting in patriotism.

"If a man's face was as white as cotton and his pulse so low that you could not feel it, he merely looked upon him impatiently as an inefficient soldier and rode off, out of patience. He was the true type of all great soldiers. The successful warrior of the world, he did not value human life where he had an object to accomplish. He could order men to their death as a matter of course.

"Napoleon's French conscription could not have kept him in awe. He used up his command so rapidly. Hence, *while he was alive,* there was much fudge in the talk of his soldiers' love for him, their sympathy with him, &c&c. They feared

3. Jefferson Davis appointed Brig. Gen. Alexander Robert Lawton, a former state legislator from Ga., to take Col. Abraham Myers's place as quartermaster general in Aug. 1863. The Senate, however, refused to abandon Myers and ordered an investigation into the affair on Dec. 10.

him and obeyed him to the death. Faith they had in him, stronger than death. I doubt if he had their love. Their respect he commanded.

"And now that they begin to see a few years more of Stonewall Jackson would have freed us from the yoke of the hateful Yankees, they deify him. They are so proud to have been one of the famous Stonewall brigade."

"Like to be brick from that wall."

"But be ye sure, it was bitter hard work to keep up with Stonewall Jackson, as all know full well who ever served with him. He gave his orders rapidly and distinctly and rode away. Never allowing answer nor remonstrance.

"'Look there. See that place. Take it.' When you failed, you were apt to be put under arrest. When you reported the place *taken*, he only said 'Good.'"

Again (yesterday) the *Examiner* publishes the account of Mr. Davis's cotton remaining unburned.

This was settled last year. Mr. Davis's cotton was burnt, and all the world knows it, but the *Examiner* knows that the everlasting harping on this sort of thing must annoy Mr. Davis. So it persists.

Spent seventy-five dollars today for a little tea and sugar. Have five hundred left. J. C.'s pay never has paid for the rent of our lodgings since the war began.

John Thompson sent me *Blackwood's Magazine*.

Mrs. Davis gave me a love of a parasol.

A day to be marked in white.

December 7, 1863.   Judge Campbell has come from Alabama, bringing a supply of butter and hams given him by Mrs. Fitzpatrick. Neither Clay nor Fitzpatrick returned to the Senate.

"All very well," said Wigfall. "Sister Clay would have been dangerous if Fitz had got it."

J. C. came in with dreadful news just now.

I have wept so often for things that have never happened, I will withhold my tears now for a dead certainty.

Today a poor woman threw herself on her husband's coffin and kissed it.

She was weeping bitterly. So did I, in sympathy.

J. C. would see me, and everything that he loved, hung, drawn and quartered, without moving a muscle if a crowd was looking on. He could have the same gentle operation performed on himself and make no sign.

To all of which violent insinuation he answered in unmoved tones: "So would any civilized man. Savages, however, Indians, at least, are more dignified in that particular than we are. Noisy, fidgety grief never moves me at all. It annoys me. Self-control you need. You think yourself a miracle of sensibility. Self-control is what you need. That is all that separates you from those you look down upon as unfeeling."

"So you are civilized," I said. "Someday I mean to be."

Wigfall was here yesterday. And I think J. C. amazed him utterly.

He showed him Joe Johnston's letter to the president asking him not to remove Bragg "in spite of the injustice done him by the country."

For once Wigfall succumbed. It was an unexpected blow.

Gloom and unspoken despondency hang like a pall everywhere.

———————

Today I saw an account of the sales of Judge Campbell's and Dr. Garnett's and Colonel Ives's houses in Washington.

Patriotism is a pretty heavy load to carry sometimes.

Someone sent me the Englishman's pamphlet on Gettysburg and the Pennsylvania campaign.[4] He pays a very handsome compliment to General Hood.

———————

Life of Savonarola. I am absorbed in it, up to the ears, body and soul given up to Savonarola.

———————

Not half so much as I am today in *Romola.* John Thompson sent me *Savonarola*—no doubt to tune me up for *Romola.*[5]

———————

Wigfall here. He has to acknowledge the strength and unanswerable logic of Manigault's pamphlet where he arraigns and convicts Beauregard of supine and culpable negligence, when Beauregard failed to guard the islands that [are] the keys to Charleston Harbor.[6]

———————

Christian soldier, &c&c. There cannot be a Christian soldier. Kill or be killed, that is their trade, or they are a failure. Stonewall was a fanatic. The exact character we wanted was willing to raise the "black flag." He knew: to achieve

———

4. "The Battle of Gettysburg and the Campaign in Pennsylvania. Extracts from the Diary of an English Officer Present with the Confederate Army," *Blackwood's Edinburgh Magazine,* Sept. 1863, pp. 365–94. The article's author was Arthur James Lyon Fremantle, a British army officer. Editions of a fuller account of his experiences, *Three Months in the Southern States: April–June, 1863,* soon appeared in London, New York, and Mobile.

5. Pasquale Villari, *The History of Girolamo Savonarola and of His Times,* trans. Leonard Horner (1863). The fifteenth-century Italian religious reformer is a character in George Eliot's historical novel *Romola* (1863).

6. The untitled pamphlet by Gabriel Manigault (1863) begins: "September 12, 1863. To Gov. M. L. Bonham." Manigault, the elder brother of Arthur Manigault, had been a Charleston lawyer, rice planter, novelist, and state legislator before serving as a member of the S.C. secession convention and the state's board of ordnance.

our liberty, to win our battles, men must die. The religion of mercy, love your neighbor before yourself, prefer [*word omitted?*] in every act—why, that eliminates war and the great captains.

December 9, 1863.   Today the girls were to come here before luncheon. Mary arrived first. She is the punctual member of the family. As I was giving Laurence some orders in the dining room, she called out suddenly.

"Come here, Mrs. C. They are lifting Hood out of his carriage, here, at your door."

Everybody had been to see General Hood except the Prestons and myself. So he came here.

Mrs. Grundy promptly had him borne into her drawing room, which was on the first floor.

Mary P and I ran down and greeted him as cheerfully and as cordially as if nothing had happened since we saw him standing before, as a year ago.

He was lying on a sofa with a carriage blanket thrown over him.

Soon the party was all assembled. Had he heard of it? Or was this a casual coincidence?

Mary P assisted me in behaving as if nothing was the matter. The others were hopelessly depressed. They looked as if it would be a luxury to pull out their handkerchiefs and have a good cry.

Our wounded friend Sam watched the door wishfully. To end suspense, we asked, "How is Buck?"

"Better, but she has been ill in bed for several days."

Some Durchheimer still remained in the sideboard, which the general enjoyed with his luncheon. Heavens, how he was waited upon! Some cut-up oranges were brought him.

"How kind people are. Not once since I was wounded have I ever been left without fruit, hard as it is to get now."

"The money value of friendship is easily counted now," said someone. "Oranges are five dollars apiece."

Many persons called—among them, Mrs. Randolph. Sam whispered, "She is handsomer than ever."

Sniggered Brewster, "He knows a pretty woman when he sees one." Until the newcomers were launched upon us, there had been never a sigh nor a word of sympathy. This did not suit our friends. They cultivated heart and were all condolence and tears. It was "leg," "leg," "leg."

Old Sam groaned, "My God, it is hard!" Mary P made a gesture of despair.

Mrs. Mallory came in, who in warm terms hailed him "as a martyr to his country." The Wigfalls were here, too.

"I do not mean to stay at home," said Sam, who by this time had a hectic flush of fever on his face. "This is the first house I have had myself dragged to. I mean to be as happy a fool, well, as a one-legged man can be. Send me off now. So many strangers scare me always. I can't run now as I did before."

December 10, 1863.   At Mrs. Preston's. Met Mrs. Huger, who was miserable because she had heard General Lee was to be sent west.

The restless Hood was there. Buck talking to him, with tears not quite in her eyes but audible in her voice.

The Infant was there. He looked out of sorts, had a really hangdog way with him.

"What you doing here?"

"How is your father? We heard he was ill."

"He is dead. I am on my way home."

"Good heavens! That is dreadful!"

"He died last Saturday."

"This is only Tuesday!"

"Oh! They telegraphed me."

For a moment I felt inclined to cry, but as he did not indulge his grief in that form, there was no call for me to do so.

Mrs. Davis and Mrs. Lyons came. We had luncheon brought in for them.

And then a lucid explanation of the chronique scandaleuse, of which Becky J[7] is the heroine.

We walked home with Mrs. Davis. Met the president riding alone. Surely that is wrong. It must be unsafe for him, when there are so many traitors, not to speak of bribed negroes. Burton Harrison says he prefers to go alone. And there is none to gainsay him.

Mr. Seddon, being a pious Presbyterian, speaks of Stonewall's death as that "accursed mischance." How does that show he is a blue-light Calvinist? He can't say "damn such luck," as the rest of the world does. Or "Stonewall's death was a blow which we feel most damnably."

"The army is always in Flanders, when you come to bad language, eh?"[8]

J. C. laid the law down last night. I felt it to be the last drop in my full cup.

"No more feasting in this house. This is no time for junketing and merrymaking. There is a positive want of proper feeling in the life you lead."

"And you said you brought me here to enjoy one winter before you took me home and turned my face to a dead wall."

He is the master of the house—to hear is to obey.

December 14, 1863.   Mrs. Ould, who lunched with us at Mrs. Davis's, told of Mrs. Stanard's wedding finery, which has come by flag of truce—favor of

---

7. Sarah Rebecca (Taylor) Jones.

8. An allusion to Laurence Sterne, *The Life and Opinions of Tristram Shandy, Gentleman* (1759–67), book 3, chapter 11.

Schenck and Beast Butler.[9] Saw Mrs. T. D. there, asked about her pretty little girl that we knew on Sullivan's Island.

Dead.

Never will I ask again for anyone I do not see. The horror of this wrong-timed question hung around me all day.

Drove out with Mrs. Davis. She had a watch in her hand some poor dead soldier wanted sent to his family. First we went to her mantua maker; then we drove to the fairgrounds, where the band was playing. Suddenly she missed the watch! She remembered having it when we came out of the mantua maker. We drove instantly—and there the watch was lying, near the steps of the little porch in front of the house. No one had passed in—or no one had seen it.

"Blessed chance!" she cried.

She rates Fitzhugh Lee far above Hood—far, as a commander.

Preston Hampton went with me to see Conny Cary. The talk was frantically literary, which Preston thought hard on him. I had just bought "St. Denis" number of *Les Misérables*.[1]

Sunday Mars Kit walked to church with me. Coming out, General Lee was slowly making his way down the aisle, bowing royally right and left. I pointed this out to Christopher Hampton. When General Lee happened to look our way, he bowed low, giving me a charming smile of recognition. I was ashamed of being so pleased. I blushed like a schoolgirl.

We went to the White House. They gave us tea. The president said he had been on the way to our house, coming with all the Davis family to see me. But the children became so troublesome they turned back.

Just then little Joe rushed in and insisted on saying his prayer at his father's knee, then and there.[2] He was in his nightclothes.

Mr. Christopher Hampton came. Mrs. Davis was in the act of telling us that the police had orders to keep a look out for Mrs. H. D.[3] Malapropos, indeed.

A Catholic Mr. London[4] had the floor afterward. He was orating as to the necessity of sending an envoy to the pope.

I was having such a good time, seated between Mr. Preston and Mr. Hunter, two of the most agreeable men I know, and the cleverest. J. C., not having any such pleasant companions, grew restless and routed me out to go home. When on the pavement, from the window Mrs. Davis called to me. She had something to say. J. C. came up, saying, "Are you waiting for Kit Hampton?"

9. Maj. Gen. Robert Cumming Schenck, U.S. congressman from Ohio and, until his resignation on Dec. 5, commander of the Union's Middle Department and Eighth Corps at Baltimore. Ben Butler was in command of the Department of Va. and N.C.

1. Victor Hugo's novel appeared in five parts in 1862. The fourth was "L'Idylle rue Plumet et L'épopée rue Saint-Denis." M. B. C. probably read the Confederate imprint of the book, published in Richmond during 1863–64.

2. Four-year-old Joseph Evan Davis, the president's second son.

3. Mrs. Henry Duncan.

4. Daniel Higginbotham London, a wealthy resident of Richmond.

When he saw how angry I was, he said, "Can't you take a joke?"

J. C. then had a dinner party—our company Howell Cobb, R. M. T. Hunter, Custis Lee, Constitution Browne, and John Taylor Wood.

While I was shelling pinders, Maria F came in—wedding talk. At my busiest time came the ever-welcome Venable.

He says Buck can't help it. She must flirt. He does not think she takes in the situation herself. She does not care for the man. It is sympathy with the wounded soldier. Helpless Hood.

At dinner, one principal topic. Lincoln's proclamation.

After tea Mrs. Huger and Pinckney came in.[5] She said, "I would be ashamed if my husband was not within the ring of Lincoln's hanging threat."[6]

Brewster came. He announced the fact that Hood and himself were to dine up two pairs of stairs, with an Englishman named Lawley.[7]

At dinner Mr. Hunter said: "The parsons tell us every Sunday that the Lord is on our side. I wish, however, he would show his preference for us a little more plainly than he has been doing lately."

December 17, 1863.   A box has come from home for me. Taking advantage of this good fortune and a full larder, have asked Mrs. Davis to dine with me Wednesday next. Garnett dined with us today. He says it is the Senate which cross-hobbles Mr. Davis. The House is not so bad.

The House is 9 to 10 against Memminger. They are lukewarm as to any scheme of financial reform because they know Memminger will spoil it, do what they may.[8]

Miss Street came to ask us to Maria Freeland's wedding. Miller Owen came to tell of the Lawley dinner to Hood which he attended. Then Hood came in person to ask me to give him a casino party. J. C. readily agreed to it. You may

5. Mrs. Benjamin Huger was probably with her son, Thomas Pinckney Huger.

6. In his "Proclamation of Amnesty and Reconstruction" issued on Dec. 8, Lincoln offered pardons to Confederates taking an oath of loyalty to the Union and presented a plan whereby the loyal citizens of a Confederate state could form a government recognized by Washington. The "hanging threat" was the denial of amnesty to high-ranking Confederate military officers, members of the Confederate government, all those who had left the U.S. government, military, or judiciary to join the Confederacy, and those who had mistreated prisoners of war. While these men were presumably considered traitors, the proclamation did not explicitly threaten them with hanging.

7. Francis Charles Lawley, a former member of the House of Commons who had replaced William Howard Russell as American correspondent for the London *Times*. Lawley's dispatches are collected in William Stanley Hoole, *Lawley Covers the Confederacy* (1964).

8. In his report to the Confederate House on Dec. 7, Secretary of the Treasury Memminger had proposed several means of reducing the amount of currency in circulation and securing revenue for the government.

[be sure?] that he was not reminded of our resolution "not to see company." He seems to have forgotten it.

My dinner. Wade Hampton sent me a basket of game. We had Mrs. Davis, Mr. and Mrs. Preston.

After dinner we walked to the church to see the Freeland-Lewis wedding. Mr. Preston and Mrs. Davis on his arm. J. C., Mrs. Preston.

Burton Harrison and myself brought up the rear. Willie Allan[9] joined us. And we had the pleasure of waiting one good hour.

Then the beautiful Maria, loveliest of brides, sailed in on her father's arm. Then Major John Coxe Lewis followed with Mrs. Freeland.

After the ceremony—such a kissing, up and down the aisle.

The happy bridegroom kissed wildly. Several girls complained, but he said, how was he to know Maria's kin that he ought to kiss? Better show too much affection for his new relations than too little.

When we came home found Dr. Garnett and Mrs. Ould, who proposed a game of whist. Sent for Mrs. Grundy to make up our two tables.

My dinner satisfied me, but J. C. found fault. Said it was ill served. And that the kitchen was too far off, things were cold, above all, the dining room was too small. We must give it up—no more dinners.

While Mrs. Davis was here Hon. Robert Barnwell called. He is a devoted friend of the president's.

Mrs. Davis had taken me to drive where we got some beautiful white violets for the bride. Found Mrs. Ould and Mrs. Browne at my door, where J. C. joined us—and effectually quenched us. The Yankees were at Salem and also near Fincastle.[1] Bad news indeed.

Louly Wigfall snubbed Mrs. Preston.

Mary P, lifting her hands to heaven in protest: "Not even to see three stars on John Darby's coat collar could I bear to have mama's feelings hurt."

We could see no connection between the two things, but Mary's heart is always right.

---

9. Mrs. John Allan's son, William G. Allan, was a captain in the C.S.A.
1. U.S. cavalry sent from W.Va. under Brig. Gen. William Woods Averell had feinted toward Fincastle in southwestern Va. before raiding the Va. and Tenn. Railroad at nearby Salem on Dec. 16.

December 18, 1863.   Brewster in all that soaking rain. He ran in to say General Hood was below in a carriage and wanted me to go to a taffy pulling at the Prestons'.

Isabella was declaiming. She had been at the Congress.

> Beyond this vale of tears, sir
> There lies a land above! sir
> And all that land is love, sir.[2]

Came home, slept like a log until night came, and with it, visitors. Joe Johnston made commander in chief of the Army of the West. General Lee had this done.[3]

Mrs. Stanard came. She could not understand why I had not called on her. She was still more amazed that J. C. had not done so.

"While you were gone! It was so different." He went to see her regularly. He lived opposite—put out a fire—at least, it was nearly a fire. When the bells began to ring, he ran over—caught her with only one stocking on. She was trying to huddle on the other, &c&c&c.

Then Miss Agnes Lee and "little Robert" (as they fondly call General Lee's youngest son in this hero-worshiping community) called.[4]

They told us the president, General Lee, and General Elzey had gone out to look at the fortifications around Richmond. J. C. came home, saying he had been with them—lent General Lee his gray horse.

Met Mrs. Lawson Clay, says she is coming here tonight for eggnog and casino.[5] I stopped then at the Prestons'. Isabella wrote a note for me to Shirley Carter[6] and Robert Lee. Then I asked Maggie H and Burton Harrison, as I was driving with Mrs. Davis. And then I told her of what a scrape I was in. J. C. had positively ordered me to give no more tea parties. And he is decidedly master of his own house.

To be sure, I had game, partridges, &c&c, General Hampton had sent me.

---

2. A play on lines from the hymn, "The Issues of Life and Death," by James Montgomery (1771–1854).

3. While Lee did confer with Davis about Bragg's replacement in command of the Army of Tenn. (Army of the West), no source other than M. B. C. indicates that the general urged the selection of Johnston.

4. Twenty-two-year-old Eleanor Agnes Lee was Robert E. Lee's third daughter. Robert E. Lee, Jr., twenty, was a lieutenant on the staff of his brother, Rooney Lee.

5. Harriet Celestia (Comer) Clay of Ala. was the wife of Lt. Col. Hugh Lawson Clay of the Adjutant and Inspector General's Office in Richmond and the sister-in-law of Confederate Senator Clement Claiborne Clay, Jr.

6. Charles Shirley Carter of Va., an assistant surgeon in the Richmond military hospitals, was a distant relative of the Lee family.

No end of eggs and butter from home—brandy from home, for the eggnog and apple toddy, &c&c.

She laughed at my difficulties, said she was to have a grand dinner for the splendid cavalcade which had left her house for [a] ride round the fortifications. She would make it a point to keep J. C. there to dinner as long after as possible. That was the only way she could help me out of trouble of *my own making*.

Mary P and Brewster made the eggnog. Burton Harrison came, after it was all gone.

L. Q. Washington and some men who called at the Prestons' and heard they were here followed them. Maggie H brought Captain Fearn,[7] who gave me a screed of his doctrine on the subject of Carlyle and Thackeray (ill-matched pair!). Daresay he was told I was that way given. A little literature goes a long way in Richmond, and mine is very little indeed, for the name it has.

J. C. escaped from Mrs. Davis. He did not go in the house at all. So she failed to capture him.

He came straight home and found the party in full blast.

He did not know a word about it. How could he? It grew up after he left home. I trembled in my shoes.

He behaved beautifully, however.

If he had refused to dine at the president's because he wished to attend a party at my house, he could not have done better. He seemed to enjoy the whole thing amazingly. Played casino with Mrs. Lawson Clay, looked after Hood, &c&c.

Today he spoke. I was very penitent, subdued, submissive, humble. And I promised not to do so anymore.

"No more parties," he said. "The country is in danger. There is too much levity here."

So he laid down the law.

December 21, 1863.   Mrs. Howell[8] says a year ago on the cars, a man said, "We want a dictator."

She replied, "Jeff Davis will never consent to be a dictator." The man turned sharply toward her.

"And pray who asks him? Joe Johnston will be made dictator by the Army of the West."

7. John Williams Walker Fearn of Ala., a U.S. foreign service officer before the war, had just returned from a Confederate diplomatic mission in Europe and taken a place on the staff of Gen. William Preston.

8. Probably Varina Davis's mother, Margaret Louisa (Kempe) Howell, whose husband, William Burr Howell, had died in March 1863.

"Imperator," it was suggested.

Of late the Army of the West has not been in a condition to dictate to friend or foe.

Certainly Jeff Davis did hate to put Joe Johnston at the head of what is left of it. Detached from General Lee, what a horrible failure. What a slow old humbug is Longstreet. The Manigault pamphlet shows the small caliber of the little Beauregard. For a day of Albert Sidney Johnston, out West! And Stonewall, could he come back to us here!!!

Sam, the wounded knight, came for me to drive. I felt I would soon find myself chaperoning some girl, but I asked no questions. He improved the time between Cary and Franklin St. by saying, "I do like your husband so much."

"So do I," I replied simply.

Buck was ill in bed, so William said at the door, but she recovered her health and came down for the drive in black velvet and ermine, looking queenly. And then with the top of the landau thrown back, wrapped in furs and rugs, we had a long drive that bitter cold day.

In the afternoon Mrs. Davis came for me. We went to see Mrs. Allan. She has suffered. One son killed, the wife of another is being tried now for treason.

Yesterday as we were coming back from the fairgrounds, Sam, the wounded knight, asked Brewster what were the symptoms of a man's being in love. Sam (they call Hood Sam entirely—why, I do not know) said he did not know. At seventeen he had fancied himself in love, but that was "[a] long time ago."

Brewster, on the symptoms of love: "When you see her, your breath is apt to come short. If it amounts to mild strangulation, you have got it bad. You are stupidly jealous, glowering with jealousy, and a gloomy, fixed conviction that she likes every fool you meet better than she does you, especially people that she has a thorough contempt for. That is, you knew it before you lost your head. I mean, before you fell in love. The last stages of unmitigated spooniness I will spare you," said Brewster, with a giggle and a wave of the hand. "They are too much to inflict on a gay young party."

"Well," said Sam, drawing a breath of relief. "I have felt none of these things so far, and yet they say I am engaged to four young ladies—liberal allowance, you will admit, for a man who cannot walk without help."

"To whom do they say you are engaged?" asked Buck, staring at the horses' heads.

"Miss Wigfall is one."

"Who else?"

"Miss Sally Preston." Buck did not move an eyelid. She watched the horses' heads.

"Are you annoyed at such a preposterous report?"

"No."

Brewster aside to me: "God help us! He is going to say everything right out here before our faces."

Buck continued coolly: "Richmond people are liberal, as you say. I never heed their reports. They say I am in engaged to Shirley Carter and to Phil Robb."

"*Or* to Phil Robb," suggested the alert Brewster.

Sam said viciously: "I think I will set a mantrap near your door and break some of those young fellows' legs, too. However, the 'stern parents' will send such light-winged birds flying."

After she had been deposited safely at home, he said, with what seemed a little like one of Brewster's symptomatic strangles: "Well! well! It must be pretty dangerous company for those young soldiers. You see, they are men who dare hope for something in this world."

I said never a word.

Mr. Venable's story, "Let him die, my joke killed him," came uppermost in my mind as an appropriate warning, but it was none of my business.

Next day we called, on our way from church, to see Mrs. Wigfall. She was ill, but Mr. Wigfall insisted upon taking me into the drawing room to rest awhile. He said Louly was there. So she was, and so was Sam, the wounded knight, stretched at full length on a sofa and rug thrown over him.

"Do you know General Hood?"

"Yes."

He laughed with his eyes as I looked at him; but he did not say a word. I felt it a curious commentary upon the reports he had spoken of the day before.

Louly Wigfall is a very handsome girl. Wigfall began to me: "You call Preston the stateliest cavalier of them all. They say you make short work of a civilian who finds fault with a wounded soldier? Eh?" (Here I nodded my head.) "And Brewster says yesterday when you left Hood in the carriage, Preston asked if he should have a doctor for the party when you got back. It was freezing out-of-doors. And the drive was madness. You agreed, and said you would not risk freezing for any two-legged animal in the world."

I felt faint.

"I say, friend Wigfall, you have been too long in Texas. Your jokes are too rough. Where is your American prudery? To talk before ladies of legs, off or on. Never did I dream that people would say such things about a man's horrible mutilation before his face."

This last speech was as Wigfall walked out with me to the front door.

"You intimate I am ill-bred."

"It is the cruelest behavior in the world."

"You don't know how the camp hardens a fellow. The general don't mind it a button. I know what I am about. He was pleased."

I doubted that statement.

Isabella told a story of J. C.'s sangfroid. Brewster is the man who is described in *Blackwood's Magazine* by a traveling Englishman as seated in the piazza reading a Greek play, with his chair tilted and his feet on the bannister.

Colonel Fremantle is the writer, if I am not mistaken. Brewster is the most careless creature. He may have godliness, but he has not the next thing to it. Preface enough to Isabella's joke: "Colonel Chesnut looked at Mr. Brewster's hands at dinner, then he said gravely, 'My dear fellow if you have such an aversion to water, why not grabble in a little clean sand?'"

L. Q. Washington brought me the last number of *Tony Butler,* Lever's book, coming out in *Blackwood's.*[9]

He then piled one foot on the other until, Johnny remarked, they were nearly as high as his head. Mr. Washington was saying, "Byron believed that good blood showed itself in small hands and feet." (His feet are huge—his hands very small and well shaped.) He grew enthusiastic in his description of Mary P's hands. Someone went to the card table to verify his eulogy and came back in amazement.

"John Darby's hands are smaller and whiter and better shaped than hers. Hood's, prettier and smaller than any of them."

"John Chesnut wears six and a half ladies' gloves; it is his only vanity."

"And these are not effeminate men," drawled Washington, "two of them stalwart fellows, and one shot to pieces."

"Captain Chesnut is effeminate in his appearance. Such a pale face. Such light hair, soft and silky, and a Roman nose!"

"Well, that is aristocratic, too."

"Let Johnny alone. General Young[1] says he is as bold and reckless a dragoon as ever sat in saddle."

Buck went across the room after her brave defense of Johnny, with Captain Robb, and they sat down by our wounded general (Sam).

"I was beginning to think you meant me to go away without a word. I cannot run after you now. I depend upon the charity of my friends."

After a while in distinct tones we heard: "Eyes right, look my way awhile. Talk to me. I really have something to tell you."

Then Captain Robb impatiently: "Surely wounded major generals are an intolerable bore. 'Look to the left. I have a word to say to you.'"

Buck was intensely amused. She is lovely at such times, with that mischievous gleam in her soft blue eyes—or are they gray or brown or black as night? I have seen them of every color, raging with the mood of the moment.

Mary Preston reproved her mother and myself sharply. We went to the monumental church. The preacher was so dull, and we sat afar off, very near

9. This novel by Charles James Lever was published in book form in 1865.
1. Brig. Gen. Pierce Manning Butler Young of Ga., who had replaced Matthew C. Butler at the head of Johnny's brigade.

the door indeed. So we bad old women fell to whispering, and even to noiseless laughter, as the conversation grew interesting.

We enjoyed our scolding, too, as we walked home.

"The Captain and I are great friends," said General Young. "We row in the same boat. That is, we often ride 20 miles out and 20 miles in, these cold nights, for a dance with the Gongleses."

"I trump that trick," said the Captain, with his impassive face. "Think of a man so lost as to tell of Gongleses before one's aunt."

"Or before one's sweetheart!" supplemented the irrepressible Brewster.

The Captain made a furious dig at his long yellow moustache.

"Where is this seductive Gongles?"

"Where are they, you mean. There are several of them," answered the Captain.

"Don't you fret, cousin Mary," says Tom Burwell.[2] "They are everywhere. These fellows that like dancing and suppers and all that find Gongleses wherever we camp."

Tom Burwell wished to calm my perturbed spirit.

"No tales out of school, general!" grumbled the Captain, turning a rebuking eye upon his superior officer.

December 24, 1863. Buck and I were out walking today. Brewster joined us. She looked up at the sky.

"I wrote a note to Captain Robb this morning to beg him to excuse me. The weather would not permit me to ride. It has turned out such a beautiful day. If he had any sense he would come, after all."

When we arrived at the Prestons, there stood Captain Robb, impatiently waiting.

"Captain," said Brewster, with an urbane wave of the hand. "You have been tested and you have borne the test nobly."

The Captain looked puzzled, but Brewster belonged to the enemies' camp, so he disdained to ask questions.

As we walked, Brewster reported a row he had with the general.

Brewster had told those six young ladies at the Prestons' that "old Sam" was in the habit of saying he would not marry if he could any silly, sentimental girl who would throw herself away upon a maimed creature such as he was. When he went home, he took pleasure in telling Sam how the ladies complimented his

---

2. Perhaps Thomas Boykin, the son of M. B. C.'s uncle Burwell. M. B. C. probably calls him "Tom Burwell" to distinguish him from the other Tom Boykins in the family.

good sense. The general rose, in his wrath, and threatened to break his crutch over Brewster's head. To think he was such a fool, to go about repeating to everybody his *whimperings.*

J. C. and I dined alone. And in peace. He put a map on the table, which he said General Lee had examined, to see if [*illegible name*] could find his way to Danville.

But General Hampton came for me and I went off with him to Mrs. Preston's. J. C. back to the president's.

Brewster came with what he called a Texican. By the way, Brewster was secretary of war or *something* in the government of Texas while it was a lone state, after it had thrown off the yoke of Mexico and was not yet annexed by U.S.A.

Isabella was still harping on congressional oratory.

The pomp of power, sir:
And all that beauty—all that wealth ever gave, sir—[3]

She said her idea of our representatives in Congress assembled had been so high. Their eloquence consists in this: no matter what commonplace thing they say, and tag it with "sir," bringing their heels down sharply to the floor, that's a speech, but it must begin "Mr. Speaka."

The Texican wore shiny, wrinkly new black broadcloth. "One touch of nature makes the world akin." When I saw him glance with dismay at Brewster's hands, I knew he was a nice fellow. That was when Brewster offered to help beat up the eggnog.

Then somebody declaimed the "Charge of the Light Brigade." It was nearly the death of the Texican.

Mrs. Preston walked with me to Mrs. Davis. She was from home. We went up to Mrs. Howell's room and heard she was over the way, attending a wedding at Judge Campbell's. One of his daughters marries today a son of Mr. Carlson Mason. Pendleton Mason is his name.[4] A lady came in from the wedding. She was excited at a new aspect of bonnets which had pervaded the company. Feathers, flowers, bows of ribbon mounted on top, like barbet guns.

I had a run for it to get home in time for dinner. This is but one certain thing in this distracted world. I never keep J. C. waiting at that hour.

I was taking my seat at the head of the table when the door opened, and Brewster walked in unannounced. He took his stand in front of the open door

---

3. Isabella was making a play on lines from Thomas Gray, "An Elegy Written in a Country Church Yard" (1751).

4. John Archibald Campbell's daughter Mary Ellen married Maj. Arthur Pendleton Mason of Va., who was the son of Thomson F. (not Carlson) Mason and the great-grandson of George Mason.

with his hands in his pockets and his small hat pushed as far back as it could get from his forehead.

"What, you are not ready yet? The generals are below. Did you get my note?"

"No."

I begged J. C. to excuse me and rushed off to put on my bonnet and furs.

Met the girls coming up with a strange man. The flurry of two major generals was too much for me. I forgot to ask his name. They went up to dine with J. C. in my place—who sat eating his dinner, with Laurence's undivided attention given to him, amid this whirling and eddying in and out of the world militant.

Mary P and I went to drive with the generals. The new one proved to be Buckner, who is also a Kentuckian. These men told us they slept together the night before Chickamauga. It is useless to try—*legs* can't be kept out of the conversation now.

General Buckner said, "Once before I slept with a man, and he lost his leg next day." So he had made a vow never to do so again. "When Sam and I parted, that morning we said, 'You or I may be killed, but the cause will be safe all the same.'" Everybody came in to tea. J. C. in a famous good humor, and we had an unusually gay evening. It was very nice of J. C. to take no notice, for my conduct at dinner had been open to criticism. And all the comfort of my life depends upon his being in a good humor.

Met the Prussian, Major von Borcke.[5] He has been shot through the throat.

Johnny has been out in all this freezing weather for fifty-six hours at a time, without food, sleep, &c&c. Poor fellow. If they will only give a furlough at Christmas, won't we feast him!

Mrs. Lawson Clay and Captain Seabrook at tea.[6] She is so bright and so pretty, and J. C. was so devoted to her.

I said, "Your plan for a solitary life in Richmond seems to have failed."

Christmas Day, 1863.   Letters from Camden. Emma Stockton found dead in her bed. Emma Lee married to Barney Stuart.

At Maria's wedding we spoke of poor Rose Freeland. Not one year ago she came to see us. Dr. Harrison and his beautiful bride. Now, husband, wife, child, all gone, wiped out, nothing to show they have ever lived.

Yesterday dined at the Prestons', with one of my handsomest Paris dresses (from Paris before the war). Three magnificent Kentucky generals. Orr, senator from S.C., and Mr. Miles.

5. Heros von Borcke, a soldier on leave from the staff of the prince of Prussia, ran the blockade in 1862 and became J. E. B. Stuart's chief of staff. He wrote *Memoirs of the Confederate War for Independence* (1866).

6. John Lawton Seabrook of S.C. was the son of a Sea Island planter and the nephew of Carolina Lafayette (Seabrook) Hopkinson.

General Buckner repeated a speech of Hood's to him, to show how friendly they were.

"I prefer a ride with you to the company of any woman in the world." Buckner's answer: "I prefer your company to that of any man, certainly."

This was the standing joke of the dinner, it flashed up in every form. Poor Sam got out of it so badly, if he got out of it at all.

General Buckner said patronizingly: "Lame excuses, all. Hood never gets out of any scrape; that is, unless he can fight out."

A man came. I will not give his name, as, sotto voce, Maggie said, "Rich, sentimental, traveled, and a fool."

General Buckner had seen a Yankee pictorial. Angels were sent down from [heaven to] bear up Stonewall's soul. They could not find it, flew back, sorrowing. When they got to the Golden Gates above, found Stonewall by a rapid flank movement had already cut a way in.

As they drove up to the Preston door met a crowd of schoolboys—one cried, "Boys, here's a fellow lost his leg at Chickamauga—cheer with a will."

Somebody confessed they used half corn, half coffee as a beverage—but it was always popcorn, for while they roasted it the popcorn popped out.

Others dropped in after dinner, without arms, without legs. Von Borcke, who cannot speak because of a wound in his throat.

Isabella said, "We have all kinds now but a blind one." Poor fellows, they laugh at wounds and yet can show many a scar.

We had for dinner oyster soup, soup à la reine. It has so many good things in it. Besides boiled mutton, ham, boned turkey, wild ducks, partridges, plum pudding. Sauterne, burgundy, sherry, and Madeira wine.

There is life in the old land yet!

And now for our Christmas dinner. We invited two wounded homeless men who were too ill to come. Alex Haskell, however, who has lost an eye, and Hood came.

That lovely little Charlotte Wickham, Rooney Lee's wife—she is dying. Her husband is in a Yankee prison.

Today my dinner was comparatively a simple affair—oysters, ham, turkey, partridges, and good wine.

Last night I saw from Buck's face that she was having a hard battle to fight. Nobody went to her assistance. I had described to J. C. the behavior of the Texican when he heard of the "Charge of the Light Brigade" for the first time.

So he tried it on Hood. J. C. reads admirably.

Hood was excited beyond anything I ever imagined. He sat straight up. His eyes grew flaming, scintillating. And he made a gesture, which J. C. said was like the motion of a soldier receiving his orders in a battle, at the end of every line.

While Alex Haskell and J. C. sat over their wine, Sam (Hood) gave me an account of his discomfiture last night. Said he could not sleep after it. That it was the hardest battle he had ever fought in his life. "And I was routed, as it were. She told me there was '*no hope*'—that ends it. You know, at Petersburg, on my way to the western army, she half-promised me to think of it. She would not say yes, but she did not say no, that is, not exactly. At any rate, I went off, saying, I am engaged to you, and she said, I am not engaged to you. After I was so fearfully wounded, I gave it up. But then, since I came, &c&c&c."

"Do you mean to say that you had proposed for her before that conversation in the carriage when you asked Brewster the symptoms? I like your audacity."

"Oh, she understood, but it is all up now. She says *no*. I asked her about her engagement to Ransom Calhoun. She explained it all. Then I said he was a classmate of mine, and he had made me his confidant. 'Heavens,' she said, laughing in my face. 'If I had only known that, what a different story I would have told you.' I do not know what this laugh and confession had to [do] with it, but somehow, after that I did not care so much for the no as I did before. Besides, she told me to say South Carolina, to rattle the *r* and not to pronounce it as if it had two *l*'s and no *r*. And she did not like my way of asking for more of that good Burgundy wine at dinner. &c&c&c."

Mrs. Rooney Lee died yesterday. One of her babies died, too. She was not twenty-three. He is a prisoner still.

December 26, 1863.   Last night the girls came here with the Haskells, drew straws which should be allowed to walk home with J. C. After all, I believe he likes this life that he grumbles so much at. At any rate, he likes the company of those girls. No wonder. They are devoted to him.

Called to see the bride, our new cousin Maria Freeland Lewis, found her handsomer than ever, in a scarlet dressing gown, darning an old war-worn uniform of John Lewis's.

J. C. said I was extravagant.

"No, my friend, not that, I had fifteen hundred dollars, and I have spent every cent of it in my housekeeping. Not one sou for myself. Not one sou for dress or any personal want whatever."

He called me "hospitality run mad."

I picked up a letter written by me to Mrs. Davis, dated Sept. 30th, 1863. Extracts:

I am living a thoroughly outdoors life this heavenly weather. Some clever women here have houses and nothing else.

Now you know I am on a visit to my husband's father, so I have a carriage and horses and nothing else. So I visit my friends and drive with them night and day.

And I wish with all my heart that I was once more on foot and so very uncomfortably lodged as I was in Richmond once more. Poor Mrs. Nott, she has lost her other son, her eight children, one left, and he has lost an arm.

Also, we are busy looking after poor soldiers' wives. (I mean the poor wives of good soldiers.) There are no end of them here. And they never have less than nine or ten children.

Sorrowing "for the unreturning brave." Hoping they will return and support their large families once more.

The whole duty here consists in abusing Lincoln and the Yankees. Praising Jeff Davis and the Army of Virginia. And wondering when this horrid war will be over.

There is not one of us who seems to believe for a moment that we will ever again have an ache or a pain or a trouble or a care, if peace were once proclaimed and a triumphant Southern Confederacy waving its flag in defiance of the world. What geese we are! &c&c.

There was yet another party—politicians and men with no stomach for fighting, who found it easier to *cuss* Jeff Davis and laud Joe Johnston and stay at home than to go to the front with a musket.

The kind who came out almost as soon as they went in the war, dissatisfied with the way things were managed. Joe Johnston is the polar star, the Redeemer, the cave of Adullam for all such.

We had enough of them in South Carolina, God knows, but Alabama was worse. And Georgia under Joe Brown does not even cover itself with a Joe Johnston make-believe.[7]

December 28, 1863.   J. C. had a long talk with Seddon, secretary of war, and Wigfall, the very spirit of war. They say Orr and Hill are aiding the Yankees by throwing out the substitute bills.[8]

7. Ga. governor Joseph Emerson Brown had opposed virtually every attempt made by Richmond authorities to centralize the war effort. He challenged Davis's right to assign Ga. troops to other areas, denied the constitutionality of the conscription laws and at times blocked their operation, and tried to prevent the impressment of military supplies within his state.

8. The Confederate government was seeking repeal of the provision in the conscription law that allowed a potential draftee to hire a substitute to serve in his place.

We are always mum when conundrums have the floor, a favorite amusement with the six girls at the Prestons'. I found one and went away with it to Isabella.

What are the points of difference between the Prince of Wales, an orphan, a bald-headed man, and a gorilla? Answer—Prince of Wales, an heir apparent. Orphan, ne'er a parent. Bald-headed man, no hair apparent. Gorilla has a hairy parent.

XXI

"Enjoy the Brief Hour"

January 1st, 1864. God help my country.

Table talk.

"After the battles around Richmond, hope was strong in me. All that has insensibly drifted away."

"I am like David after the child was dead. Get up, wash my face, have my hair cut, &c&c."

"That's too bad. I think we are more like the sailors who break into the spirits closet when they find out the ship must sink. There seems to be for the first time a resolute feeling to enjoy the brief hour and never look beyond the day."

"I now long, pine, pray, and grieve—and—well, I have no hope. Have you any of old Mr. Chesnut's brandy here still?"

"It is a good thing never to look beyond the hour. Laurence, take this key—look in such a place for a decanter marked &c&c&c."

General Hood's an awful flatterer—I mean an awkward flatterer. I told him to praise my husband to someone else—not to me. He ought to praise me to somebody who would tell J. C., and then praise J. C. to another person who would tell me. Man and wife are too much one person to receive a compliment straight in the face that way—that is, gracefully.

"That"—as an American demonstrative adjective pronoun, or adjective pure and simple—we give it illimitable meaning. Mrs. King, now, we were "weeping and commenting over a stricken deer," one who would say yes but was not asked. "Do you mean to say she is looking to marry him?" Mrs. King, with eyes uplifted and hands clasped: "*That* willing!" Again, of a wounded soldier: "Do you mean to say he is willing to leave the army for so slight an excuse?" Again: "Willing indeed! *That* willing!"

A peculiar intonation, however, must be given to *that* to make it bear its mountain of meaning.

Again, Grundy père was said to be a man of "des absences délicieuses."

"That's Madame Deffand's wit.[1] I made a note of it—fits so many households."

---

1. Marquise du Deffand (1697–1780), known for her correspondence with Horace Walpole, Voltaire, d'Alembert, Montesquieu, and de Staël.

"List of the halfhearted ones—at least we all know they never believed in this thing. Stephens—vice president—No. 1. Ashmore, Keitt, Boyce—of the South Carolina delegation. Orr—he was lugged in, awfully against the grain.

"There now, look at our wisdom. Mr. Mason! We grant you all you are going to say. Who denies it? He is a grand old Virginia gentleman. Straightforward, honest-hearted, blunt, high-headed, and unchangeable in his ways as—as the Rock of Gibraltar. Mr. Hunter, you need not shake your wise head. You know it set all the world a-laughing when we sent Mr. Mason abroad as a *diplomat!*"

"About tobacco, now—the English can't stand chewing—&c&c. They say at the lordliest table Mr. Mason will turn round halfway in his chair and spit in the fire!"

Jack Preston says the parting of high Virginia with its sons at the station is a thing to see—tears streaming from each eye, a crystal drop, from the corner of each mouth a yellow stream of tobacco juice.

"You know yourself, General Lee and General Huger's hearts were nearly rent asunder when they had to leave the old army."

"Oh! Did not Mrs. Johnston tell you of how General Scott thought to save the melancholy, reluctant, slow Joe for the Yankees? But he is a genuine F.F., and he came."

"One more year of Stonewall would have saved us."

"Chickamauga is the only battle we have gained since Stonewall went up!"

"And no results—as usual."

"Stonewall was not so much as killed by a Yankee. He was shot by Mahone's brigade.[2] Now, that is hard."

"General Lee can do no more than keep back Meade."

"One of Meade's armies, you mean. They have only to double on him when he whips one of theirs."

"General Edward Johnson says he got Grant a place. Esprit de corps, you know, would not bear to see an old army man driving a wagon. That was when he found him out west. Put out of the army for habitual drunkenness."

"He is their man, a bullheaded Suwarrow. He don't care a snap if they fall like the leaves fall. He fights to win, that chap. He is not distracted by a thousand side issues. He does not see them. He is narrow and sure, sees only in a straight line."

"Like Louis Napoleon—from a bath in the gutters, he goes straight up."

"Yes, like Lincoln, they have ceased to carp at him because he is a rough clown, no gentleman, &c&c. You never hear now of his nasty fun—only of his wisdom. It don't take much soap and water to wash the hands that the rod of empire sways. They talked of Lincoln's drunkenness, too. Now, since Vicksburg they have not a word to say against Grant's habits."

"He has the disagreeable habit of not retreating before irresistible

----

2. Jackson was fatally wounded on May 2, 1863, not by William Mahone's troops but by soldiers of the Eighteenth N.C. Regiment.

veterans—or it is reculer pour mieux sauter—&c&c. You need not be afraid of a little dirt on the hands which wield a field marshal's baton, either."

"General Lee and Albert Sidney Johnston, they show blood and breeding. They are of the Bayard,[3] the Philip Sidney order of soldiers."

"Listen, if General Lee had Grant's resources, he would have bagged the last Yankee or had them all safe back, packed up in Massachusetts."

"You mean, if he had not the weight of the negro question on him?"

"No, I mean, if he had Grant's unlimited allowance of the powers of war—men, money, ammunition, arms—[top of page cut off]."

"His servant had a stray pair of French boots down here, and he was admiring his small feet and moving one so as to bring his high instep in better line of vision. For an excuse to give him a furlough, they sent some Yankee prisoners down here by him. I said, 'What sort of creatures are they?'"

"Damn splay-footed Yankees, every man jack of them."

"As they steadily tramp this way, I must say, I have ceased to admire their feet myself. How beautiful are the feet &c&c, says the Scriptures."[4]

"Eat, drink, and be merry—tomorrow ye die—they say that, too."

"Why do you call General Preston[5] 'Conscript Father'? On account of those girls?"

"No, indeed. He is at the head of the Conscription Bureau."

"General Young says, 'Give me those daredevil dandies I find in Mrs. C's drawing [room]. I like fellows who fight and don't care what all the row's about.'"

"Yes, and he sees the same daredevils often enough, stiff and stark, stripped, stone-dead on the battlefield."

"Oh, how can you bring all that to our eyes here!"

"What? Not compliment your drawing-room friends, the fellows who dance and fight with light hearts—who battle fire and famine, nakedness, mud, snow, frost, gunpowder, and—well, no words about it. Take it all as it comes."

"Talking feet—the bluest-blooded American you know, you call him 'the giant foot.'"

"They found that name for him in Bulwer's last.[6] In the last page. A giant foot comes out of the darkness and kicks over the sort of Medea's cauldron of a big pot they were brewing."

———

Mr. Ould says Mrs. Lincoln found the gardener of the White House so nice she would make him a major general.

3. Pierre Terrail, seigneur de Bayard (ca. 1473–1524), the French Renaissance soldier whose name had become a synonym for the perfect knight.

4. Slightly misquoted from the Song of Solomon 7:1.

5. An anachronism. John S. Preston, who had become the head of the Confederate Conscription Bureau in 1863, was not made a brigadier general until June 1864.

6. Edward Bulwer-Lytton, *A Strange Story* (1862).

Lincoln said to the secretary, "Well! the little woman must have her way—sometimes."

She has the Augean perquisite of cleaning the military stables. She says it pays so well. She need never touch the president's saddle.

"The Roman emperor found all money of good odor."

"We do pitch into our enemies."

"As the English did into the French. And, later, into the Russians."

"They got up in a theater and huzzahed—when they heard the emperor of Russia was dead."

Marriage in high life. Senator Johnson of Arkansas—some[where] out West, I may not "locate" him properly—his friends fondly say "Bob Johnson."[7]

He explained his marriage to Mrs. Davis. He is a devoted friend of the president.

With his foot on the carriage steps, so to speak, he married his deceased wife's sister. He wished to leave her power over his children, to protect them and take care of them while he was away.

Mrs. Davis asked, "Pray, why did you not tell us before?"

"I did not think it a matter worth mentioning. I only proposed it to her the morning I left home, and it was done at once. And now my mind is easy. I can stay here and attend to my business, as a man should. She is quite capable of looking after things at home."

We did not know Mrs. Lawton,[8] and I inquired of Mary P, who did, if she was not unusually clever.

"*That* clever!" said Mary P, imitating the gesture attributed to Mrs. King. "How did you guess it?"

"General Lawton will hear every word I say. No matter how 'superior' the men are who surround us, I knew he was accustomed to hear things worth listening to at home."

Know now why the English, who find out the comfort of life in everything, send off a happy couple to spend the honeymoon out of everybody's way or shut them up at home and leave them. Today the beautiful bride and the happy bridegroom came to see me. They had not one thought to give, except to themselves and their wedding. Or their preliminary love affairs. How it all was, when it was, &c&c&c. She did tell a capital story—if I could write it!

Mrs. Wright of Tennessee[9] came for me to go with her on a calling expedition. Found one cabinet minister's establishment in a state of republican simplicity. Servant who asked us in—out at elbows and knees.

7. Confederate Senator Robert Ward Johnson, whose first wife died in 1862. *A Marriage in High Life* (1828) is a light novel by Lady Charlotte Susan Maria Bury.

8. Sarah (Alexander) Lawton, wife of Brig. Gen. Alexander Lawton.

9. Either Georgia (Hays) Wright, wife of Congressman John Vines Wright, or her half sister and sister-in-law, Pauline (Womack) Wright, wife of Brig. Gen. Marcus Joseph Wright.

The next a widower, whose house is presided over by a relative.

"Bob Johnson?" whispered Mrs. Wright.

"Not quite," answered another visitor. "Splendid plan, though. Like the waiter in Dickens's book—'Here on suiting—and she suits.'"

"Wigfall's speech—'Our husbandless daughters.'" Said Isabella: "No wonder. Here we are, and our possible husbands and lovers killed before we so much as knew them. Oh! the widows and old maids of this cruel war."

Read *Germaine*—About's.[1] It is only in books that people fall in love with their wives. The arsenic story more probable—science, then, and not theory. After all, is it not as with any other copartnership, say, traveling companions? Their future opinion of each other, "the happiness of the association," depends entirely on what they really are, not what they felt or thought about each other before they had any possible way of acquiring accurate information as to character, habits, &c. Love makes it worse. The pendulum swings back further, the harder it was pulled the other way.

Mrs. Malaprop to the rescue—"Better begin with a little aversion."[2] Not of any weight either way, what we think of people before *we know them*. Did two people ever live together so stupid as to be deceived? What they pretend does not count.

The *Examiner* gives this amount of pleasant information to the enemy.

He tells them we are not ready, and we cannot be before spring. And that now is their time.

Our safeguard, our hope, our trust is in beneficent mud, impassable mud. And so feeling, I hail with delight these long, long rainy days and longer nights. Things are deluging, sloppy, and up to the ankles in water and dirt, enough to satisfy the muddiest-minded croaker of us all.

We have taken prisoner some of Averell's raiders.

Somebody in secret session kicked and cuffed Foote, Foote of Mississippi, in the Senate.

So ends the old year.

The last night of the old year. Gloria Mundi[3] sent me a cup of strong, *good* coffee. I drank two cups, and so I did not sleep a wink.

Like a fool I passed my whole life in review—and bitter memories maddened me quite. Then came a happy thought. I mapped out a story of the war. The

---

1. Edmund About, *Germaine, 2ème série des mariages de Paris* (1857).
2. From Richard Brinsley Sheridan, *The Rivals* (1775), act 1, scene 2.
3. Identified in the 1860s Journal as Mrs. Grundy.

plot came to hand, for it was true. Johnny is the hero—light dragoon and heavy swell. I will call it F.F.'s, for it is F.F.'s both of South Carolina and Virginia. It is to be a war story, and the filling out of the skeleton is the pleasantest way to put myself to sleep.[4]

Old Hickory fought for Aunt Rachel of questionable fame. That is, she was married before her other husband died, or before her divorce was settled, or something wrong, but she did not know she was doing wrong. She is said to have been a good woman, but it is all a little confused to my straitlaced ideas. They say when someone asked if old Hickory was a Christian, the answer: "I don't know, but if he wants to go to heaven, the devil can't keep him out of it." And then he stood by Mrs. Eaton in good report and in evil. And now Richmond plays old Hickory with its beautiful Mrs. M.[5]

I can forgive Andrew Jackson the headlong wedding business, but that duel! when he deliberately waited—and after the other man had missed, or failed in some way to shoot at him—slowly and coolly killed him.[6] But the pious North swallowed Andrew Jackson because he put his sword in the balance where we nullifiers were concerned.

England declined Nelson's legacy of Lady Hamilton, but she accepts his glory and his fame as a typical naval hero. English to the core.

There are breaking hearts this beautiful New Year's Day.

Young Frasier, on his way back to Maryland to be married, was shot dead by a Yankee picket.

Read *Volpone*[7] until J. C. emerged for his breakfast. He asked me to make out his list for his New Year's calls.

Mrs. Davis, Mrs. Preston, Mrs. Randolph, Mrs. Elzey,[8] Mrs. Stanard, Mrs. MacFarland, Mrs. Wigfall, Mrs. Miles, Mrs. John Redman Coxe Lewis.

At the president's, J. C. saw L. Q. C. Lamar who, unconfirmed by the Senate, has had to come home from Russia. They must have refused to confirm his nomination simply to annoy [and] anger Jeff Davis. Everybody knows there is not a cleverer man on either side of the water than Mr. Lamar, or a truer

4. By the time M. B. C. set down this passage in the 1880s, she had written such a story—"The Captain and the Colonel." See the introduction, p. xxii.

5. Discovering that they had mistakenly married before Mrs. Jackson's divorce was final, Andrew and Rachel (Donelson) Robards Jackson participated in a second, legal, ceremony. The scandal, however, followed them throughout their lives. Thus in 1829, when Washington society ostracized Secretary of War John Eaton and his new bride, the recent widow of an apparent suicide, President Jackson went out of his way to support the younger couple. "Mrs. M" is Marion (Twiggs) Myers, wife of the quartermaster general.

6. Jackson's duel in 1806 with Charles Dickinson, a Nashville lawyer allied to an opposing political faction. Jackson gave his opponent the first shot, then, severely wounded, shot and killed the lawyer.

7. Ben Jonson, *Volpone; or, The Fox* (1605).

8. Ellen (Irwin) Elzey, wife of Brig. Gen. Arnold Elzey.

patriot. J. C. said Lamar put his arms round him (he has a warm heart) and said, "*You* are glad to see me, eh?" Lamar is changed so much that at first J. C. did not recognize him. Colonels Browne and Ives there, in full fig, swords and sashes, gentlemen ushers. J. C. was in citizen's dress and stood behind Mrs. Davis all the time, out of the fray. So he enjoyed the fun immensely. No responsibility.

The *Examiner* indulges in a horse laugh. "Is that your idea? England come to the help of a slave power?" Turkey! Why not, O Daniel come to judgment? and India?

But slavery was the sore spot on this continent, and England touched up the Yankees *that they so hated* on the raw when they were shouting hurrah for liberty, hurrah for General Jackson, whom the British turned their backs on, but who did not turn his back on the exconquerors of Waterloo! English writers knew where to flick. They set the Yankees on us by incessant nagging, jeering at the inconsistency. Now the Yankees have the bit in their teeth. After a while they will ascend higher and higher in virtue, until maybe they will even attack Mormonism in its den.

"Little Vick[9] is going to do the best she can for her country. The land of our forefathers is not squeamish but looks out for No. 1," said the irreverent Wigfall. And then he laid sacrilegious hands on the father of his country! He always speaks of him as an old granny, or the mother of his country, because he looked after the butter and cheese on Madam Martha's *Mount Vernon* farm.

"There is one thing that always makes my blood rise hot within me—this good slave-owner who *left* his negroes free when he no longer needed them. He rides his fine horse along the rows where the poor African hoes corn. He takes out his beautiful English hunting watch and times Cuffy. Cuffy, under his great master's eyes, works with a will. With his watch still in hand, Farmer George sees what a man can do in a given time. And by that measure he tasks the others— strong, weak, slow, swift, able-bodied, and unable. There is magnanimity for you! George the 1st of America—the founder of the great U.S. America."[1]

"But Wigfall! You exaggerate. He was not a severe disciplinarian. He was the very kindest of men. Everyone knows that. But you only rave in this manner and [say] such stuff to be different from other people."

"I get every word of it from his own letters."

"He was no harder on Cuffy than English, French, German landlords are to their white tenants."

"Do you mean to say a poor man must not work for his living, but his rich neighbor must support him in idleness?" &c&c&c.

---

9. Queen Victoria.
1. Wigfall took these incidents from Jared Sparks, ed., *The Writings of George Washington* (1834– 37), volumes 1, 2, and 12.

After he had gone: "You see, we did not expect Wigfall, who shoots white men with so little ceremony, to be so thoughtful, so tender of the poor and helpless—but it is so, it seems. He was in bitter earnest. Did you notice his eyes?" At this moment Dangerfield Lewis and Maria came—and in another second L. Q. Washington was at their heels. J. C. said,

"If walls could speak, what a tale these would have to tell you!"

"How? what?"

"Oh, Louis Wigfall's perversity. He says Lamar is as model a diplomat as Mr. Mason!" I hastily put in, "I really thought the *Washington Lewis* family ought not to hear—well! how aggravating Louis Wigfall can be—so I stopped you. For one thing, he is the very best husband I know and the kindest father."

January 4, 1864. At Mrs. Davis's.

The president's arm stiff with the New Year's shaking, and Mrs. Davis's hand tender to the touch!

A day of disasters. Laurence drunk! And the kitchen stove fallen in. Molly and Laurence had a grand row. He will have a fire in his room, and as he keeps the key of the coal cellar—that is as *he* pleases. Molly says, "As master dresses without fire to economize—and he taking a cold bath, reg'lar as the day comes—you might."

"Oh," says Laurence. "Have I got anybody to rub me with a coarse towel till I am red-hot?"

"Who's Laurence, I like to know?" cries Molly. "He can't set by the kitchen fire like the rest of us. You watch your coal hole—that's all."

"You told me two minutes ago it was underwater!"

"That's only now something's broke and water fillin' the cellar. An' then across the way, they've lost every mouthful of their provisions for the year. And hit hid away up in the garret!"

"How?"

"Niggers stole it. Nobody else could be that mean but their own niggers. You needn't look that scared. You sleep in your bed—easy. Why should we takes 'em in de bulk? We takes 'em as we wants 'em. Don't *I* make things last better than you ever did? Tell you why. We ain't going to the Yankees, and we keeps your keys, and we is going home to our husband and chillun when you go home. Much Laurence cares for home and wife and chillun, tho' the Lord knows he's got enough of both 'em."

"But why do my things last? You forget to tell me that?"

"Because we only want what we can eat ourselves. At home there's the children. If any woman tells you she won't give her children anything good to eat if they hangs round her and begs for it, don't you believe it. Dey gets a little of all dat's goin'."

Did not go to Mrs. Stanard's party. Maggie wrote to say it was too cold. I need not go by for her. Then J. C. behaved like a trump and offered to take me, but I stayed at home and read *Silas Marner*.

As good as *Adam Bede*.[2] I understand her poor folk—the cobbler and the golden-haired treasure trove, God-given in the bitter moment. And the worthless gentleman and the prim good [woman], with her heart dried up within her for want of proper aliment, the childless wife! She, the writer, is not quite so orthodoxly pious as she was. Of course I took *Silas* at a draught—did not stop until I had swallowed the last word.

Today my Kentucky team came in to tell me of Mrs. Stanard's party. General Preston made up an Indian play for our charades—from Sir William Jones's <translations, doubtless>, but he was very fluent and clever about it all. We did not see his drift at first. It was deeply sensational, this drama—a pariah, then a Brahmin, juggernauts, Bengal lights, Mahratta horse—*suttee*.

The mot d'énigme—*Burn the widows*, he explained.

Mrs. Ives wants us to translate a French play. Genuine French captain came in from his ship on the James River and gave us good advice as [to] how to select a play. General Hampton sent another basket of partridges. And all goes merry as a marriage bell!

J. C. came in and killed us. He brought this piece of "latest news." "North Carolina wants to offer terms of peace."[3] We only need a break of that kind to finish us. I really shivered nervously, as one does when the first handful of earth comes rattling down on the coffin in the grave of one we cared for *more than all* who are left.

January 5, 1864.   At Mrs. Preston's met the Light Brigade in battle array, ready to sally forth, conquering and to conquer. They would stand no nonsense from me about staying at home to translate a French play.

Indeed, those which have been sent us are so indecent, I scarcely know where the play is to be found that would do at all.

While at dinner, the president's carriage drove up with only General Hood. He sent up to ask, in Maggie Howell's name, would I go with them. I tied up two partridges between plates with a serviette for Buckie, who is ill, and then I went down. We picked up Mary P. It was Maggie's drive. As the soldiers say, I was only on escort duty. At the Prestons', Major Venable met us at the door and took

---

2. George Eliot, *Adam Bede* (1859) and *Silas Marner* (1861).

3. J. C. had evidently seen Governor Vance's letter of Dec. 30 to President Davis, which asserted that antiwar sentiment in N.C. could be appeased "only by making some effort at negotiation with the enemy." The letter, together with Davis's response that Lincoln refused to negotiate and demanded unreasonable peace terms, remained unpublished until May 1864.

in the partridges to Buck. As we drove off, Maggie said, "Major Venable is a Carolinian, I see."

"No, Virginian to the core, but then he was a professor in the South Carolina College before the war."

Mary P said, "She is taking a fling at your weakness for all South Carolina."

Came home and found J. C. in a bitter mood. It has all gone wrong with our world. The loss of our private fortunes—the smallest part. He intimates—with so much human misery filling the air—we might stay at home and think.

"And go mad? Catch me at it! A yawning grave—piles of red earth thrown on one side. That is the only future I ever see.

"You remember Emma Stockton. She and I were as blithe as birds, that day at Mulberry. I came here the next day, and when I got here—telegram—'Emma Stockton found dead in her bed.' It is awfully near—that thought of death—always. No, no. I will not stop and think."

"Women are too illogical!"

"Did you say 'irrational'? No matter, it all comes to the same thing."

"Very well, I will wait for the worst before I give up."

January 8, 1864.   《Snow of the deepest.[4] No one can come today. But they did come, braving wind and weather. First my girls. Then Constance Cary, the clever Miss C. Hetty is the beauty—so-called. But Hetty has brains enough and to spare, and Constance has a classically correct outline of face. Her admirers rave of her perfect profile. The four tall Kentucky generals came, followed by Preston Hampton, as tall and strong as they are and ever so much handsomer.

《At night, just as I was ready to go out, J. C. came home. He asked what I paid for that carriage at the door. "Twenty-five dollars an hour" was my cool reply. "Senseless extravagance—stupid charades," he continued to say, working himself up to such a pitch of wrath that he finally swore by all his gods the play was not worth the candle.

《"The carriage, you mean," was my impetuous rejoinder. Then he gradually quieted down. "After all, it is in Confederate money. That sounds so much worse than it really is."

《After this lively overture it never crossed my brain to ask the irate gentleman to accompany me. So he had to break ground himself.

《"I came home, intending to go with you, but I see you do not ask me."

4. Substituted for the parallel account in the copy text because it is clearer and better written, the following version is from one of the three drafts M. B. C. wrote of the charade episodes under the title "The Bright Side of Richmond. Winter of 1864—Scraps from a Diary." Apparently polished in 1885–86 with a view to separate publication, this appears to be the last thing she wrote. M. B. C. seems to be suggesting that by 1864 Confederate defense had become a charade.

《"What else have I done, but ask you in vain, for twenty years?" I cried tragically.

《I was behind time, so I could not stay for him to dress, but I sent that twenty-five-dollar-an-hour carriage back for him when at last I arrived at the Semmeses' door.

《But before that, I had to wait for Conny Cary. Round the corner at the Carys' I found von Borcke, the Prussian, Preston Hampton, and Hetty Cary in the drawing room. I challenge the world to produce nobler specimens of the human species than these three.

《"Did you see that Congress has passed a vote of thanks to Major von Borcke? For his services to the Confederate States."

《"Ah! That is a compliment indeed!"

《And now the immense Prussian, in spite of his huge proportions, was as shy and modest about it as a girl.

《"Yes. It was a proud day for me. As I take my paper at breakfast, I see it. And I try to hide my face with the paper, for I feel that I grow so red. But my friends, they find it, too, and they shout out to me, and they laugh, and I try to read the so kind words of the Congress, and—I cannot."

《His English is broken, and the wound in his throat has not healed. He articulates with difficulty and it is all very touching—and also very hard to understand.

《General Preston of Kentucky has secured a mission to Mexico. He is a diplomat now, who needs no longer be diplomatic. So he chides a lady who laughs at some gurgling blunder that Major von Borcke makes in his throat. He gives his indignation full fling.

《"So you dare to make game of Fun Buck" (as he calls him—but then the Prestons' Charles announces him as Major Bandbox. All names come alike to the Prussian von Borcke).

《"Then never, I swear, will I let Yankee bullet make a hole in my gullet. No—not to save you from &c&c&c." I felt he was right. Then, as he always does, he explained,

《"Quoted Byron, you know, who says of Izaak Walton he wishes he had a 'hook in his gullet—and a small trout to pull it.'"[5]

《In its second trip, the carriage brought J. C., Captain Tucker,[6] and the beautiful Hetty.

《Now, this Semmes party was a charming affair, throughout.

《To begin at the beginning: sweet little Mrs. Lawson Clay had reserved a seat for me among the women. The female part of the congregation were strictly segregated from the male. A gay parterre; we were planted in rows, edged by men in gray uniforms or in black coats. Looking back toward the door, the mass of black and gray grew solid.

5. Paraphrased from Lord Byron, *Don Juan*, canto 13, stanza 106. Sir Izaak Walton was the author of *The Compleat Angler; or, The Contemplative Man's Recreation* (1653).
6. Lee M. Tucker, an assistant paymaster in the Confederate navy.

《Between charades Captain Tucker came aft, to speak nautically, to bewail his fate. Stranded out there in the cold, with only horrid men. When he saw us laugh, he knew the fun along those benches was worth a thousand charades. He preferred a talk with a clever woman to any known way of amusing himself— &c&c.

《"So do I. That is when like 'music the heavenly maid is young.'"[7]

《"And pretty."

《In front of all, on a sofa of state, sat Mr. and Mrs. Davis. They came to see little Maggie, who was one of the children on the stage. They were doubtless proud of her. She acted well, and her splendid black eyes flashed as she gracefully moved in her appointed course.

《As far as I can remember, the charades were as follows:

《1. Scene. Peasants drinking in front of a house. A girl came in with glasses. The inevitable kiss—and the equally certain-to-follow box on the ear ensued. This very attractive barmaid was Conny Cary in one of my caps.   (*Inn.*)

《2. Mistress and maids. A scene of dusting, sweeping, scolding of lifelike vehemence. Hitherto I had only encountered Mrs. Webb, our Florence Nightingale, at her hospital on 12th Street. And there she is the center of sweet charities and a bright sample of all the Christian virtues. She was the mistress (last night), and Conny Cary, with Mrs. Ives, the maids. One of Captain Tucker's stories. Far out in the dim distance, where only men herded together, a voice was audible asking, "Who are those ladies?" And from the crowd, in resigned and melancholy tones, came the answer. "She who scolds so well is my wife."   (*Dust.*)

《3. Judges. Lawyers. A formidable and stern array. Cooper DeLeon[8] gotten up as a first-class felon. He strongly resembled the murderer in that fine picture, "The First Trial by Jury." Mrs. Semmes as his brokenhearted wife, so true to nature she made us all miserable.   (*Trial.*)

《4. Mrs. Webb was the matron of a school. She does all things well—but I forget the details.   (*Industrial.*)

《The next charade.

《1. A Turkish scene. Where all is safe to go well—given beautiful houris. They had secured eminently satisfactory ones. So said the band of capable critics near the door.   (*Harum.*)

《2. Constance the statuesque scared out of her senses. And I have forgotten by what—do you know. At any rate, she fell down stone-dead in magnificent style.   (*Scarum.*)

《The whole word—*harum-scarum*—was very obvious indeed—by a gang of girls bothering an old man. And we prayed for the wild beasts to come out and rend them, as they did for the same kind of thing in the Bible when the children

---

7. The first lines, slightly misquoted, from William Collins, *The Passions* (1747).

8. Thomas Cooper DeLeon, the twenty-five-year-old brother of David Camden and Edwin DeLeon, was always at the center of wartime society and later chronicled it in his *Four Years in Rebel Capitals* (1890) and *Belles, Beaux, and Brains of the 60's* (1907).

cried "go up, old bald head."[9] Everything depends on acting, and this was a failure.

《Again, another charade.

《1. An apothecary compounding his pills. Mr. Dobbin,[1] the pill-taking invalid, was cured by these pills to such a degree that he grew almost before our eyes, from the facsimile of Romeo and Juliet's apothecary, or that lean and hungry Cassius, into a very Falstaff. Or, as someone called out, "Daniel Lambert,"[2] and was corrected. "Say Humphrey Marshall, if you wish Confederates to understand you mean size."

《I forget both *grim* and *age*. I have a vague idea that Mrs. Semmes did some famous acting as an old beggar woman.

《*Pilgrimage* was the word, and as the shrine came in view, a chorus of voices rose up on all sides, "perfectly splendid." This was the climax of the evening's entertainment—and ought to have been the last.

《The shrine was a triumph of art. The Semmeses and Iveses are Roman Catholic, and so they know what they are about in this matter of an altar.

《The first pilgrim, a palmer gray, scallop shell and all. Next, slowly followed, sad and solitary, the loveliest of brokenhearted penitents (Mrs. Ives). Then came a group of Eastern pilgrims. They wore such ravishing clothes, we longed to know how women endowed with Christian piety so fervid came by such odalesque costumes.

《Then Mrs. Ould—bless her heart! She came as a crowned queen. As handsome and as regal, withal, as one could wish. With her walked a suitable king. I must have heard his name, but I forget it now. A resplendent knight of St. John was followed, in contrast, by an American Indian. Burton Harrison, the president's young and good-looking secretary, filled this part of "big brave" from Oonalaska's shore. The dress was presented to Mr. Davis years ago by some Indian tribe, to whom he had it in his power to be kind. A complete red man's outfit. They do not need much—only a fresh coat of paint for full dress. The feathers in the back of this chief's head had a truly comic effect, not to speak of the feathers trailing at his heels. . . .

《Here we ought to have wound up. "No, there is yet another."

《Jane Eyre[3] is responsible for Bridewell—to a much bored society. She originated that charade, and for our sins they continue to give it to us yet.

《1. The Bride. All brides are lovely alike. A bride's veil can hide even ugliness, as it can heighten the charm of beauty, "half-hidden from the light." Our bride, however, was chosen because of her beauty.

《2. Mrs. Semmes did that Jewish maiden Rebecca at the well, on the lookout for Isaac—and also taking a last farewell of earth, sky, and water.[4] Rachel, the

9. 2 Kings 2:23–24.
1. Robert A. Dobbin, a Baltimore publisher and lawyer before the war.
2. The English jail keeper who became famous for his corpulence. At his death in 1809, Lambert weighed nearly seven hundred and fifty pounds.
3. Charlotte Brontë, *Jane Eyre* (1847).
4. Genesis 24.

French Hebrew of classic memory, need not have disowned or been ashamed of acting such as Mrs. Semmes's. She left us tearful and depressed after the prison scene. "Why do they tear our nerves by these painful scenes? It is not up to heroic and tragic tears. It is simply unpleasant. The better they do it, the worse we feel."

《《"They ought to have things to amuse us—so absurd as to create a laugh under *the ribs of death,* where we are," someone grumbled.》》

Mr. and Mrs. Davis had a royal table behind the scenes for them and their party along.

Senator Hill of Georgia took me in to supper—ices, chicken salad, oysters, champagne. The president came in alone, I suppose, for while we were talking after supper, your humble servant was standing between Mrs. Randolph and Mrs. Stanard. The president offered his arm, and we walked off oblivious of Mr. Senator Hill.

Remember, ladies, and forgive me for recording this last act. Mrs. Stanard and Mrs. Randolph are the handsomest women in Richmond. And I am *no older* than they are, or younger, either, sad to say.

Now the president walked with me slowly, up and down that long room, and our conversation was of the saddest. Nobody knows so well as he does the difficulties which beset this hard-driven Confederacy. He has a voice which is perfectly modulated. I think there is a melancholy cadence in it which he is unconscious of as he talks of things as they are now. A comfort in this loud and rough soldier's world.

J. C. was so utterly charmed with Hetty Cary that he declined to accompany his wife home in the 25-dollar-an-hour carriage. He ordered it sent back for him. But his wife, a good manager, packed Carys and J. C. in with her and left the two other men who came with the party—when it was divided into 3 trips—to make their way home in the cold. At our door—near daylight of that bitter cold morning—I had the pleasure to see J. C., like a man, stand and pay for that carriage.

Today he is pleased with himself, with me, and with all the world. Says if there was no such word as "fascinating," you would have to invent one to describe Hetty Cary.

Queer scene today—not a charade. Someone was asking how Captain Fearn's name was pronounced. "Fern"—to rhyme to "her'n"—or "Feearn" to rhyme to "eon."

Mrs. Davis turned to Willie <Munford>. "I hear you are a poet. At least, you write burlesque operas. What do you say? Do you?" The young man turned white and red, green and gray. He has written for private circulation (strictly private) a burlesque poem satirically dealing with Mrs. Myers's quarrel with Mrs. Davis, the notorious ladies' quarrel. And he is Mrs. Myers's champion—*her knight.* So you may imagine how Mrs. Davis is dealt with in that poem. It seems she has seen it.

At this moment—knowingly or unknowingly, who knows—Gen. William Preston rushed into the breach. He faced the music gallantly in the very nick of time. He began shaking hands violently with Willie M. He said, "From your name, my lad, you must be my cousin"—and their Virginia cousinship and all its ramifications raised such a fog around us, everything else disappeared in it.

But Mr. Willie M had his mauvais quart d'heure.

I hear the music. They are bringing in our escaped hero, Morgan, with a triumphal procession.[5]

At the Prestons' someone said, "Colonel Jordan proclaims there is no patriotism in Charleston."

"Does that coward dare to say that?" "Stop, Mary. Not another word!" Mr. Venable interposed, with hands uplifted. "When a woman says 'coward,' she has done her worst."

Took the Carys to rehearse at Mrs. Randolph's. Found there Captain Tucker, Mr. Denègre,[6] and an Englishman—Vizetelly[7] by name—who, as Dick Swiveller,[8] smoked, played cards, and put his feet on the table. He was admirable. He was as free as air—air in free America. Kissed the girls' hands—&c&c.

Hetty Cary was to have a hood conspicuously placed upon her head in some part of the charade. Isabella fancied one Englishman dropped his h's. She repeated a conversation between them as following—"Who is the 'ood, Miss Cary?" "Whenever Lord 'Artington[9] writes to me, he always inquires about Miss Preston."

"No doubt," said Isabella, "he does *whenever* he writes."

Came home, found the doorbell broken, all the gas given out in some inexplicable way, J. C. sitting up, waiting for me by the light of a coal fire. Placidly he received me.

"Fortunately," he said, he had "found solitude, darkness, and quiet delightful."

5. Morgan and some of his officers broke out of the Ohio State Penitentiary on Nov. 27, 1863, and reached the Confederacy with the aid of Southern sympathizers.
6. Joseph Denègre of La., a captain in the Confederate Ordnance Department.
7. Frank Vizetelly, war correspondent and artist for the *Illustrated London News*.
8. The scheming bachelor in Dickens's *The Old Curiosity Shop*.
9. William Cavendish, marquis of Hartington and seventh duke of Devonshire, visited Richmond in the spring of 1863.

January 9, 1864. Met Mrs. Wigfall. She wants me to take Halsey[1] to Mrs. Randolph's theatricals. I am to get him up as Sir Walter Raleigh. She showed me a note from Lamar.

"And now," I said, "what will you do when he hears it was Louis Wigfall who moved heaven and earth to have him recalled from Russia?" She said Gen. William Preston had just sent her his photograph.

"Her Majesty's government and Her Majesty's opposition." Evidently wise ones do not fall out with either the opposition or the court.

Now General Breckinridge has come. I like him better than any of them. Morgan is here. These huge Kentuckians fill the town. Isabella says: "They hold him accountable for the loss of Chattanooga. The follies of the wise, the weakness of the great." And she shakes her head significantly when I begin to tell why I like him so well.

Last night General Buckner came for her to go with him and rehearse at the Carys for Mrs. Randolph's charades.

General Preston making farewell visits—General Morgan's triumphant entry into town. I was marching off to the Preston window to see the military and hear the music of the Morgan show. But I met Mrs. Randolph and Miss Carrie Barton. And we sauntered on slowly to see it all (quite out of harm's way, at the tail end of the procession).

We saw Mayor Mayo introduce General Morgan to the crowd, and as A. P. Hill could not speak,[2] J. [E.] B. Stuart did, with all his voice.

Then Governor Moore took the stand. Mrs. Randolph at once proposed that we should move on.

"We care only for soldiers. They have got down to *governors* and that sort of thing." As we were then ankle-deep in the snow, it was a prudent step. A fine-looking young Kentuckian as tall and strong as any general of them all stood near us. He expressed himself as greatly flattered by our homage (it was so palpably rendered) to Morgan. He pointed out General Morgan. In all that brilliant cortege he seemed to think Morgan the star of greatest magnitude. He had shared the general's imprisonment and described their escape. I do not remember any peculiarly romantic incident.

But never did women—two of whom were not, well, as young as the other one—enjoy a jollier tramp or have a pleasanter chat with a charming, totally unknown young soldier. The gray coat is passport enough to our old hearts.

---

1. Maj. Francis Halsey Wigfall, son of Charlotte and Louis Wigfall. Halsey's mother took an active interest in his career and helped him to secure a place on the staff of John Bell Hood in the fall of 1863.

2. Lt. Gen. Ambrose Powell Hill, General Morgan's brother-in-law. After 1863, Hill, who had a distinguished record with the Army of Northern Va., was frequently the victim of what are now thought to be psychosomatic illnesses.

The Preston girls, who were contented with their window privileges on Franklin St. until they found out all *we* had seen and heard, abused me roundly for not going for them. "It was a way I had, always to stumble in upon the *real show.*"

The *Examiner* today down on us all. He gave the government precedence, of course, in his abuse. Then demolished our Mr. Miles. Then failed to respect even our feminine insignificance. He went for the merrymakers, the partygoers, the promoters and attenders of festivities at such a time.

"Ah, I see," says Isabella. "The president was at Mr. Semmes's. He is hitting at Jeff Davis over our small heads."

Johnny has been down to Essex to see Mary Garnett. He sent us baskets of partridges, and we returned him his baskets filled with books and *hams.*

Colonel Alston met a man in Yankee land, once a clergyman, now a soldier, who said he was our cousin and spoke very patronizingly of us all down South. He would have taken our part, but the infamous conduct of Southern leaders changed his feeling toward us utterly. "Don't be angry with him. He won't do us much more harm," added Colonel Alston. "Poor soul, he is dying of consumption."

The president's man Jim that he believed in, as we all believe in our own servants—"our own people" <as we are apt to call them>—and Betsy, Mrs. Davis's maid, decamped last night. It is miraculous that they had fortitude to resist the temptation so long. At Mrs. Davis's the hired servants are mere birds of passage. First they are seen with gold galore, and then their wings sprout, and they fly to the Yankees. And I am sure they have nothing to tell. The Yankees waste their money.

I do not think it had ever crossed Mrs. D's brain that these two would leave her. She knew that Betsy had ($80) eighty dollars in gold and 2,400 dollars, two thousand four hundred, in Confederate.

"And they followed suit. After all, that Jim and black Betsy!" says my Molly in <amazement>, with her eyes starting out of her head. "I like Mrs. Davis, but Betsy did give herself such airs because she was Mrs. President's maid."

January 11, 1864. ⟪Have been to see Mrs. John Morgan.[3] Knew her before as Mattie Ready, a graceful girl and a Kentucky belle in Washington during the winter of 1859. We were glad to meet once more under altered skies. Colonel Alston, the famous Bob Alston, did the honors. General Morgan was not at home, so we could talk of him. Colonel Alston had the floor, and as he told his

---

3. Substituted for the parallel entry in the copy text for the same reason and from the same version cited above, n. 4, p. 528.

tale, fancy Mattie Ready's eyes. She is now that highly placed woman, Mrs. John Morgan.

⟨⟨ "At Covington the general hardly knew where to turn, or whom to trust. He went to Mrs. Ludlow, however. Such a welcome as he met from her! She was prompt, and in a moment horses were at the door. 'Do not lose time. Off with you! My son, this is Morgan. I hold you responsible for him. Now ride for your lives!' She was not afraid of what Yankees could do unto her if they heard she had aided that arch traitor Morgan in his escape. The women of Kentucky were all alike. Men, money, horses, were offered whenever he needed them &c&c."

⟨⟨ General Preston told us how he felt when he saw the first Confederate soldiers lying stiff and stark, grim in death, with eyes staring wide open, on the battlefield. Frozen they were, too.

⟨⟨ Wigfall was here today. He began: "That is a hard saying. The *Examiner* calls M [William Porcher Miles] Wamba the Witless."[4] Of course we laugh. So did Miles, when Daniel was belittling the government to the best of his ability. It is infamous though, to speak so of our only literary fellow, our learned professor. He knows Latin and Greek. Does anybody else?⟩⟩

L. Q. Washington dined here today. He is going to London to write for a Confederate paper there.

⟨⟨ General Preston is forced to leave for Mexico without being able to see his wife and children.[5] He has left his sword and a sealed package with Mrs. John Preston.

⟨⟨ "In case I am heard of no more."

⟨⟨ "What harm can come to him out of the Confederacy?" inquired Isabella.

⟨⟨ "He may be drowned at sea or assassinated by Mexican guerillas," answered Constitution Browne. Then to me: "By the way, you remember Jake Thompson, who was secretary of the interior during President Buchanan's administration? He is now a captain. His company is a partisan one out in Mississippi. They are called guerillas. A recruit coming in asked for Captain Thompson. 'Don't you know him? He is a parteesian gorilla.'"⟩⟩

January 12, 1864.   ⟨⟨ At the Carys' all in confusion and the rehearsal in full blast. John Saunders makes a perfect Smike.[6] Miss Giles as the "Fair Penitent"[7] is beautiful beyond any words of mine to describe.

---

4. The jester in Sir Walter Scott's *Ivanhoe* (1820).

5. Substitution as in n. 4, p. 528, from same version. M. B. C. is talking about William, not John, Preston.

6. Maj. John S. Saunders, chief of artillery in Gen. Richard H. Anderson's division of the Army of Northern Va. Smike is Ralph Nickleby's lost son in Dickens's *Nicholas Nickleby*.

7. Elizabeth Peyton Giles had slipped through Union lines near St. Louis, and arrived suddenly in Richmond in July 1863 with a full trousseau purchased in Europe. Her engagement to Confederate Gen. William A. Quarles broken off, Giles became one of the "belles" who were a prominent part of the Chesnuts' social circle. She was portraying the central character in Nicholas Rowe's sentimental tragedy *The Fair Penitent* (1703).

⟨⟨"The Fair Penitent, now," said General Breckinridge. "You know, there is a play by that name. I wonder if that girl ever read it."

⟨⟨"No," replied Isabella. "I am sure she has not. Neither has anybody else here ever read it. So it does not matter in the least."

⟨⟨Mr. Hudson came today. . . .

⟨⟨Mr. Hudson's mission is to substitute Halsey Wigfall for himself in the part of Sir Walter Raleigh.

⟨⟨So I am busy making a character ruff for Halsey as Sir Walter.

⟨⟨Mr. Vizetelly and Mrs. Pember[8] were fun enough for one day. His part is to dandle and stifle the cries of a screaming baby while the strong-minded mother writes and dashes aside sheet after sheet of MSS. Three stalwart youths behind the scenes simulated that baby's yells, and they cried well. Next day they were all hoarse. When Mr. Vizetelly had exhausted all known methods of quieting an infant (in vain), his despair was comic. He threw the baby on a chair and sat on it.

⟨⟨Finished Halsey's ruff, then made a cap for the marchioness in the Dick Swiveller scene.⟩⟩

After Halsey, Hetty Cary's radiant face appeared. She was in the act of gathering up an armful of my velvets, feathers, laces, flowers. Then the thump was heard on the stairs, like the sound of the statue coming up in *Don Giovanni*[9]—Hood's crutches—and he appeared on the scene. Soon Buck's sweet face peeped in, followed by Isabella and Simon the Poet, as they call General Buckner. Hood is Sam the Soldier.

Then Mrs. Caskie, who announced herself later on as a cousin of Lucy, the well-beloved wife of Governor Pickens.

The city of Richmond entertains John Morgan. He is at free quarters. To-night there will be a great gathering of the Kentuckians. Morgan gives them a dinner.

The girls dined here. Connie Cary came back for more white feathers. Isabella had appropriated two sets and obstinately refused Constance Cary a single feather from her pile.

She said sternly: "I have never been on the stage before, and I have a presentiment when my father hears of this I will never go again. I am to appear before the footlights as an English dowager duchess, and I mean to rustle in every feather, to wear all the lace and diamonds these two houses can compass." (Mine and Mrs. Preston's.)

8. Phoebe Yates (Levy) Pember, the widowed sister of Mrs. Eugenia Phillips, was the first female administrator appointed at Chimborazo, a military hospital on the outskirts of Richmond. She later recounted her experience in *A Southern Woman's Story* (1879).

9. The statue of the Commendatore killed by Don Giovanni arrives at the impenitent murderer's house to consign him to hell in Mozart's *Don Giovanni* (1787), act 2, scene 5.

She was jolly but firm, and Constance departed without any additional plumage for her Lady Teazle.[1]

J. C. wants to coach Hetty Cary for archidama. No doubt!

January 14, 1864.   Gave Mrs. White twenty-three dollars for a turkey. Came home, wondering all the way why she did not ask for twenty-five. Two more would not have made me back out of the bargain, and twenty-three sounds odd.

Mrs. Randolph's charades.

I have been wearing an old uniform coat of J. C.'s, made into a sacque for me. It is not pretty, but then it is so comfortable. Its great defect is this—it is so awfully thick and warm, when I must dress up a little and I change it for my old velvet sacque to go out at night, I take cold. Well, then! with such a cold as never was before, I still resolved to go. The Prestons sent their carriage for me after it had left one load of passengers at the Randolphs'. So I found there Tudy with a young Louisiana cousin at her feet, making love audibly in the solemn stillness of those nearly empty rooms. Buck from the opposite side of the room sent to stop it. Someone called out, "Miss Preston, that is a cruel move of yours." She answered with distinctness. "No, people ought to control their feelings in a place like this."

Said Sam, moving his crutches nervously: "Suppose they can't."

A bill was handed us, and this program was asked for by those in the rear.

"Oh, I will be so tired of waiting for matrimony," said an unknown girl's voice in the crowd. "Don't you see, it is the last charade on the list." Her second remark was forced out by a titter which followed her first, which sounded like an outbreak of eagerness for matrimony.

To our amazement Hood, who is a fighter and no talker, took up his parable.

"Oh, I do hate to see nice girls so hauled about. They could act without all this clawing, clapper-clawing, pulling, pawing—augh!"

Ruby Mallory made a perfect Marchioness. She is a truly wonderful child. She had us all wiping our eyes the other night at Mrs. Semmes's when she recited "Bingen on the Rhine". . . .[2]

At Mrs. Randolph's Mr. Hudson came for me to congratulate him; his substitute, Halsey Wigfall, had done so well as Sir Walter Raleigh. He was quite satisfied he had made a good thing of changing places.

In the spirit of the men who are so proud of the prowess of their substitutes in the army—actually, they say, put up monuments to them when they are killed! [*Remainder of page cut off.*] Captain Tucker came to be praised for his Sir Peter Teazle. And he deserved all that I could say.

J. C. flirting still with Mrs. Ives and the Carys. As if this was not the second

---

1. The young wife of the elderly nobleman, Sir Peter Teazle, in Richard Brinsley Sheridan's *The School for Scandal* (1777).
2. References to an unidentified person are deleted.

night only that he had vouchsafed us the sanction of his presence at our
frivolities. He goes out so rarely, I was asked several times who he was, as we
were apt to make a laughing remark to each other in passing.

"Who is the man, always with Mrs. Randolph or the Carys? There he is."

I looked, wondering what I should think of him if I saw him for the first time.
I came to a very pleasant conclusion. "There, with the colonel's uniform?" Not
without pride, I answered: "Oh! that is my husband. Have you never met
Colonel Chesnut before?"

Immediately back of us sat Mrs. Stanard. At least, Maggie Howell found it so.
Mrs. Stanard was telling her over my shoulder how great a favorite she was.
Maggie doubtless lacked faith, for she answered sweetly, "I don't like your way
of backing the favorite." Then, sharply, "Your knees are in my back."

What a day the Kentuckians have had. Mrs. Webb gave them a breakfast.
From thence they proceeded en masse to General Lawton's dinner, and then
straight here. It is equal to one of Stonewall's forced marches.

General Lawton took me in to supper. In spite of his dinner, he has misgivings, too. A l'*Examiner.*

"My heart is heavy, even here. This seems too light, too careless for such
terrible times. It is all out of place here in battle-scarred Richmond."

"I have heard something of that kind at home," I replied. "Hope and fear are
both gone. And it is distraction or death with us. I do not see how sadness and
despondency could help us." If it would do any good, we would be sad enough.

We laughed at General Hood. General Lawton thought him better fitted for
gallantry on the battlefield than playing with a lute in my lady's chamber.

When Miss Giles was electrifying the audience as the "Fair Penitent," someone said, "Oh, that is so pretty."

"That is not pretty, it is elegant," Hood cried out, with stern reproachfulness.

Not only had my house been rifled for theatrical properties, but as the play
went on they came for my black velvet cloak.

When it was over I thought I should never get away. My cloak was so hard to
find. But it gave me an opportunity to witness many things behind the scenes,
that cloak hunt did. Behind the scenes!!! I know a little what that means now.

General Stuart was at Mrs. R's in his cavalry jacket and high boots. He was
devoted to Hetty Cary. Constance Cary said to me, pointing to his stars, "Hetty
likes them that way, you know, gilt-edged and with stars."

At supper Isabella said: "Hetty Cary's beauty lit up the scene, 'Coming
through the rye.' There was no rye. Mr. Vizetelly had only painted a sparse
patch of oats on the back of a screen. A group of actors hid that. And Captain
Tucker's kisses were make-believe."

"He came near enough to like it, judging by his face," came from an unknown
voice in the crowd.

Mrs. Randolph's comment: "While that baby cried—and really, the young men behind the scene had perfected themselves in the art of crying—that baby yelled to break any mother's heart. Mr. Vizetelly asked for so many things—first a spoon, then a bottle, then a teakettle. I wondered what would come next."

The voice.

"What babies care for most was there most temptingly exposed."

"Ball dress must tantalize a baby."

"Can storied urn or animated bust, sir."

"But all that rhymes to 'dust, sir' and does not answer to a baby's scream."

"The rhyme is 'fleeting breath provokes this silent dust,'" said our Explainer. But any talk of silence in this din is absurd." Here comes in Isabella's Gray's "Elegy"....[3]

January 15, 1864.   Mrs. Preston decided that we might have our French play at her house, but there should be no audience—sudden death of the French play!

Now that the substitute and conscript bill have both passed, "how it does fetch 'em." Substitute men are hurrying in, all wanting offices.[4] Modest, to say the least of it. That eleventh-hour parable is a hard saying. Who can bear it?

A visit from the president's handsome and accomplished secretary, Burton Harrison. I lent him *Country Clergyman in Town* and *Elective Affinities.* He is to bring me Mrs. Norton, *Lost and Saved.*[5]

Every Sunday Mr. Minnegerode cries aloud in anguish his litany. "From pestilence and famine, battle, murder, and sudden death," and we wailed on our knees, "Good Lord, deliver us." And on Monday and all the week long, we went on as before, hearing of nothing but battle, murder, sudden death. Those are the daily events. Now a new book—that is the unlooked-for thing, the pleasing incident in this life of monotonous misery. We live in a huge barrack. We are shut in, guarded from light without.

At Mrs. Randolph's, J. C. complimented Constance Cary, who had amply earned his praise by her splendid acting. She points to Burton Harrison.

"You see that wretch. He has not said one word to me!" J. C. innocently: "Why should he? And why is he a wretch?"

"Oh! You know!"

Going home I explained this riddle to J. C., who is always a year behind in gossip.

"They said those two were engaged last winter. There seems a screw loose, but that sort of thing always comes right."[6]

3. That is, the references above are to "An Elegy Written in a Country Church Yard." More charades follow.
4. The Confederate Congress had just passed laws that not only made substitutes illegal but also made men who had hired them in the past subject to the draft.
5. A novel by Caroline (Sheridan) Norton, published in 1863.
6. Constance Cary and Burton Harrison were married in 1867.

At breakfast today, a card, and without an instant's interlude, <Barny Heyward>, perhaps the neatest, most particular man in South Carolina. I was uncombed, unkempt, tattered, and torn. In my most comfortable, and soiled, wadded green silk dressing gown and a white woolen shawl over my head to keep off drafts. He has not been in the war yet. And now he wants to be captain of an engineer corps. I wish he may get it. He has always been my friend, so he shall lack no aid that I can give. And if he can stand the shock of my appearance today, we may reasonably expect to continue friends until death. The fastidious Barny, to come in—of all men. He faced the situation gallantly.

Last night Barny Heyward went with us to a reception at the president's.

After our obeisance before the highest in the land, Maggie took me from Mr. Mallory. She had promised a wounded knight to lead me to his sofa, she said. When I found him entrenched, he was holding an unwieldy sofa cushion next to him to keep a vacant seat for me. When I had occupied the reserved place, there was the cushion still left in his arms. And he dandled it by no means so gracefully as Vizetelly did the squalling baby a few nights before. In an agony of awkwardness: "What shall I do with this thing?"

"Throw it behind the sofa."

"Ah!" and a sigh of relief. But the old woman who was at the other end of the sofa?

She was submerged by my flounces and Confederate hoops &c&c—but she was doing battle nobly. Though she was effaced for a while, she soon came to the surface, trying to smile but very red in the face. I was redder and more energetic in hammering away at my hoops and flounces.

《General Lee's eldest brother was there. They have everything in that family. This one, Carter Lee, I found witty and amusing beyond measure.》[7]

"The virgin," as these girls call Virginia Clay, came up with Colonel Ives. She said in an aside, "He always suggested St. Ives of nursery rhymes and his nine wives and cats and lives." "St. Ives is not a man—no man at all! It is a place, where a man can be met with nine &c&c&c," suggested Constitution Browne, who knew something of soldiers' lives &c&c and St. Ives.

Met Mr. Davis, new cabinet minister, brother of Bishop Davis of South Carolina.[8] This man is a North Carolinian, as was the bishop. When he was introduced to me, I said politely:

"I have had the pleasure of meeting Mr. Davis before. I remember seeing him at the bishop's in Camden."

He replied, with ponderous dignity: "I do not recollect you at all. It is possible, though, that you may have seen me somewhere."

Fancy Mr. Mallory's unholy joy at my receiving such a facer. When I told the girls, they dubbed him at once "the lout in high life."

7. From the rough draft of the 1880s Version. Charles Carter Lee, then sixty-six, was a Harvard graduate and lawyer.
8. George Davis had been named attorney general.

January 17, 1864.   Today comes a grand announcement made by the Yankee Congress.

They vote one million of men to be sent down here to free the prisoners they will not exchange. I actually thought they left all these Yankees here in our hands as part of their plan to starve us out. All congressmen under fifty years of age are to leave politics and report for military duty or be conscripted.[9]

"What enthusiasm there is in these councils!"

"Confusion, rather, it seems to me!" Mrs. Ould says the men who frequent her house are more despondent than ever since this thing began.

Isabella snubbed us.

"Civilians, civilians all. We keep company with soldiers only, and they are sanguine. *Their* hearts do not fail them."

Dinner party yesterday at the Prestons'—Kentuckians, with Breckinridge, who is a cousin of the Prestons, Lamar, and General Lawton. The dinner was given to General Morgan, who failed to appear, however. He came at half-past six and was sent off by the just new servant from Columbia.

"Not at home." When we came into the drawing room at ten from the dining room, there were all these cards—besides Barny Heyward, L. Q. Washington, &c&c—eight of whom had been asked to tea.

When the girls were made to understand the blunder of the man who answered the bell, there was a genuine feminine groan of disgust.

January 18, 1864.   Invited to Dr. Haxall's last night to meet the Lawtons. Mr. Benjamin dropped in. He is a friend of the house. Mrs. Haxall is a Richmond leader of society, a ci-devant beauty and a belle, a charming person still, and her hospitality is of the genuine Virginia type.[1]

Everything Mr. Benjamin said we listened to, bore it in mind, gave heed to it diligently. He is a Delphic oracle. He is of the innermost shrine, supposed to enjoy the honor of Mr. Davis's unreserved confidence.

The Carys prefer J. C. to his wife. I don't mind. Indeed, I like it. *I do, too.*

Lamar was asked to dinner here yesterday, so he came today. We had our wild turkey cooked for him yesterday. And I dressed myself in an inch of my life with the best of my four-year-old finery. Two of us—J. C. and I—did not damage the wild turkey seriously. And today Lamar enjoyed the réchauffé, and

9. M. B. C. is referring to a resolution of Jan. 8 calling for a temporary adjournment of Congress and the recruitment of one million volunteers "to carry food and freedom to every captive held in rebel prisons." The measure died in committee. For some time, the demands of both North and South had blocked a prisoner exchange agreement. The Union, holding by far the larger number of prisoners, insisted on a one-for-one exchange, and the Confederacy refused to consider the release of captured black soldiers and their white officers.

1. Dr. Robert William Haxall, a founder of the American Medical Association, and his wife Jane (Higginbotham) Haxall. Lucy Haxall was their niece.

he commended the art with which Molly hid the slight loss we had inflicted upon its mighty breast. She piled fried oysters over the turkey so skillfully— unless we had told it, no one would ever have known the huge bird was making his second appearance upon the table. Lamar was more absent-minded and distrait than ever. J. C. behaved like a trump—a well-bred man with all his wits about him—so things went off smoothly enough.

Lamar had just read *Romola*. Across the water he said it was the rage. I am sure it is not as good as *Adam Bede* or *Silas Marner*. It is not worthy of the woman who was to "rival all but Shakespeare's name below."

"What is the matter with *Romola*?"

"Tito is so mean—and he is mean in such a very mean way. And the end is so repulsive. Petting the husband's illegitimate children and left-handed wives may be magnanimity. But human nature revolts at it in disgust."

"Women's nature?"

"Yes. And now another test. Two weeks ago I read this thing with intense interest. And already her Savonarola has faded from my mind. I have forgotten her way of presenting him as completely as I always forget Bulwer's *Rienzi*."[2]

"Oh, I understand you now. Milton's Devil. He has obliterated all other devils. You can't fix your mind upon any other. The devil must always be of Miltonic proportions, or you do not believe in him. Goethe's Mephistopheles disputes the crown of the causeway with him. Soon you begin to feel Mephistopheles is a lesser devil, an emissary of the Devil only. Is there any Cardinal Wolsey but Shakespeare's? 'If I had served my God as I have served my King, &c&c&c.' Carlyle's Mirabeau—but the list is too long of those stamped into your brain by genius—&c&c."[3]

The saintly preacher. The woman who stands by Hetty and saves her soul— those heavenly minded sermons preached at us by the authoress of *Adam Bede*. Bear them well in mind while I tell you. This writer who so well imagines and depicts female purity and piety. She was a governess, or something of that sort, perhaps wrote for a livelihood. At any rate, she had an elective affinity, which he responded to, for Lewes. So she lives with Lewes.[4] Lamar does not know if she caused the separation between Lewes and his legal wife. They were living in a villa on some Swiss lake, the Mrs. Lewes of the hour—a charitable, estimable, agreeable, sympathetic woman of genius. A fallen woman living in a contented—nay, happy—state of immorality. Such a terrible shock to our pre-conceived ideas of her. Lamar seemed without prejudice on the subject. At least, he expressed neither surprise nor disapprobation.

He said something of "genius being above law," but I was not very clear as to what he said at that point. As for me, I said nothing, for fear of saying too much.

2. Edward George Bulwer-Lytton, *Rienzi, the Last of the Tribunes* (1835).

3. Thomas Carlyle, "Mirabeau," appeared in *Westminster Review* (1837) and in *Collected Works* (1857-58).

4. References are to George Eliot's sympathetic portrayal of Hetty Sorrell, a character in *Adam Bede* who is convicted of murdering her illegitimate child, and to Eliot's involvement with journalist George Henry Lewes.

"My idol was shattered, my daystar fled."

"You know that Lewes is a writer."

"Some people say the man she lives with is a nobleman. Oh, we give it up. You know, they say she is kind and good, if—a fallen woman!" And here the conversation ended.

———————

Met crowds coming away from Mr. Minnegerode's church. No standing room left, even. I knew the old gray-haired sexton would find me a seat. So I persisted in going in. And he did lead me up to the president's pew.

Yesterday's dinner party of men appeared mounted at my door today. They came for J. C. to ride round and look at the entrenchments. They are to lunch at Mr. Lyons's. It was a notable cavalcade.

When J. C. came home, he told me that Mr. Lyons "not wisely but too well" pitched into Breckinridge for his conduct of affairs at Missionary Ridge.

"Well, sir, how came we to lose Chattanooga?"

General Breckinridge coolly responded, "It is a long story," turned away, and began talking to someone else.

Our Congress is so demoralized, so confused, so depressed. They have asked the president, whom they have so hated, so insulted, so crossed and opposed, and *prevented* in every way, to speak to them and advise them what to do.

In the *Examiner* today, an account of Hood on horseback for the first time. "Young Harry with his beaver up."[5] He rode erect, and everybody took off their hats and cheered.

Mrs. Grundy came to say she had been robbed of a barrel of sugar. A calamity, surely, at this juncture. I remembered Molly's saying, "Always, the stealing is from the inside of the house, your own black people," but I held my tongue.

When Laurence ushered Mrs. Grundy in, J. C. and I were both sound asleep on opposite sides of the fireplace, where two sofas are cosily drawn. J. C. waked at a touch and behaved beautifully. But I sat up—and for a moment could not remember where I was. Indeed, I was not wide-awake until several others came in—Muscoe Garnett, Barny Heyward, and such other agreeable people. B. H. said of his great kinsman:

"Cousin Robert is the best of men and a wise man, too. But he will always give the preference to a low churchman, and zealously promote—even up to the post of cabinet minister in a war administration—a man that he esteems because he is a Sunday school teacher. No mortal can tell the injury he has done his country by this little peculiarity."[6]

———————

5. Slightly misquoted from *Henry IV, Part I,* act 4, scene 1. A beaver is the visor of a medieval helmet.

6. Barny Heyward's mother and Sen. Robert Woodward Barnwell were first cousins. The senator was one of Secretary of the Treasury Memminger's strongest supporters.

Speaking of the secretary of the treasury, the *Examiner* says today that the country needs in that place "a man, and not [an] aged spider."

Mr. Heyward was at one of the departments yesterday when a boy rushed in with a telegram.

The man at the desk said to the boy: "Now! You are a devil of a fellow. Where have you been loitering!"

He turned to Barny and said,

"Here is a reprieve at one o'clock for a man who was to be shot at twelve." Barny was horrified. Immediately it was all looked up. Fortunately the man who had charge of the execution was slower even than the telegraph boy, and the poor soldier's execution was one hour behind time, and so he was saved.

"Good to be dilatory in some things."

"I daresay the Confederates are reluctant to do shooting like that."

At the Prestons' door last night, where the invited company was turned away by the new servant, Mr. Heyward says a messenger from the telegraph office was among the number absolutely refused admittance by the inexorable Charley.

"*Go way*—I ain't going to bother Marster at the dinner table with none er yo' notes nur messages."

Barny shrugged his shoulders: "I hope that blunder did not hang some other man. Time means something, I find, in Richmond."

January 19, 1864. Yesterday the Kentuckians came en masse, led by General Breckinridge. They sent their carriage for the girls after I had consented to let them make taffy.

Breckinridge rarely sat down. He walked up and down my small drawing room like a caged lion.

Semmes's bill for restricting the heads of departments to two years service is called today. If it is passed, Mr. Davis will resign his place at once.

The Army of the West desire the negroes freed and put in the ranks. They wonder it has never been done before.[7]

January 21, 1864. Both of us too ill to attend Mrs. Davis's reception. It proved a very sensational one. First a fire in the house, then a robbery said to be an arranged plan of the usual bribed servants there and some escaped Yankee prisoners. Today the *Examiner* is lost in wonder at the stupidity of the fire-and-arson contingent. If they had only waited a few hours until everybody was asleep—*after* a reception the household would be so tired and so sound asleep. Thanks to his kind council, maybe they will wait and do better next time.

---

7. Maj. Gen. Patrick Cleburne, an Irish-born division commander of the Army of Tenn., made this revolutionary proposal in a "memorial" to an officers' meeting on Jan. 2, 1864. Noting the sorry fortunes of the Confederacy, Cleburne put the matter squarely: "As between the loss of independence and the loss of slavery, we assume that every patriot will freely give up the latter—give up the Negro slave rather than be a slave himself." Not yet ready to concede that the South must make that choice, the president quickly ordered the suppression of Cleburne's memorial and prohibited further discussion of freeing and arming the slaves.

Letters from home have carried J. C. off today. Heavens! How glad he was to go. How thankful for a decent excuse to leave us.

Lost and Saved. People tell so much that they do not know they are telling. Mrs. Norton's career has been varied—the Melbourne business, the mean husband, &c&c.[8] Somehow one reads queer things between the lines. It has, however, what all of Mrs. Norton's books have—mortal cleverness and that thing called "interest" so indispensable and yet so often lacking in a novel.

Thackeray is dead.

I stumbled upon *Vanity Fair* for myself. I had never heard of Thackeray before. I think it was in 1850. I know I had been ill at the New York hotel. And when left alone I slipped downstairs and into a bookstore that I had noticed under the hotel for something to read.

They gave me the first half. I can recall now the very kind of paper it was printed on—and the illustrations as they took effect upon me. And yet when I raved of it and was wild for the other half, there were people who said it was slow!! That he was evidently a coarse, dull, sneering writer, that he stripped human nature bare, made it repulsive, &c&c&c.

General Breckinridge said he knew Mrs. S[9] was going to run the blockade. Old C had told him "and then put up his withered old hand and whispered, 'but don't tell that I said so—or she will give me a curtain lecture.' Now come! Don't try to look shocked. You know C is an old bachelor and attaches no technical meaning to 'curtain lecture.' He only thinks of it as behind the curtain, not before the footlights—theatrical slang, you know. However, she is going out to buy her trousseau to marry another just such an old driveler. Come now! All this is under the sacred seal of secrecy."

8. Caroline (Sheridan) Norton, unhappily married to George Chapple Norton, was involved in a scandal with William Lamb, viscount Melbourne, in 1836. After Mr. Norton unsuccessfully brought court action against Melbourne, the Nortons separated.
9. Possibly Martha Stanard.

XXII

Buck and the Wounded Knight

January 22, 1864. At Mrs. Lyons's met another beautiful woman—Mrs. Penn, the wife of Colonel Penn, who is making shoes in a Yankee prison. She had a little son with her, barely two years old, a mere infant. She said to him, "Faites comme Butler." The child crossed his eyes[1] and made himself hideous, then laughed and rioted around as if he enjoyed the joke hugely.

Went to Mrs. Davis's. It was sad enough. Fancy having to be always ready to have your servants set your house on fire—bribed to do it. Such constant robberies—such servants coming and going daily to the Yankees, carrying one's silver &c, does not conduce to make home happy.

Saw Hood on his legs once more. He rode off on a fine horse, though he is disabled in one hand, too.

After all, as the woman said, "He has body enough left to hold his soul."

"How plucky of him to ride a gay horse like that."

"Oh! A Kentuckian prides himself upon being half horse, half man."

"And the girl who rode beside him. Did you ever see more beauty? Three cheers for South Carolina!!"

Barny has no end of scandal, which he derived from his grandfather. It is rough on American aristocracy. He does not allow credit anywhere. Nobody is anybody—so to speak—but Heywards and a few families into which they had intermarried. Mary Preston said I scored one when I adroitly made him tell of the tailor who married into the Heyward family. She absolutely thought I blundered on that tailor, and I had been leading up to him for half an hour. As he let out the skeletons in everybody else's closet, I was carefully stalking tailor—as fitting retribution to his vanity.

Saw a lovely Jew. Elsewhere Jews may be tolerated. Here they are the haute volée. Everybody everywhere has their own Jew exceptions. I have two—Mem Cohen, Agnes DeLeon. Mary Preston has her Rachel Lyons.

---

1. Benjamin "Beast" Butler had a crossed eye.

This Willie Myers,[2] of whom I now write, was so angelically beautiful that at first they thought he must be their still expected messiah.

Mrs. Huger on Butler: "Why make a proclamation against Beast Butler? Is he any worse than the rest of them? By all this nonsense thousands of good Confederates are rotting in Yankee prisons."

She lent me *Martin Chuzzlewit*.[3] "Now that we separate ourselves in thought from the Yankees Dickens laughs at, it will bear a second reading. He would not come South because of slavery. So he does not know we spit as much as the Yankees."

Says Brewster, whose French is not as good, apparently, as his Greek: "People call names so differently. Now Mrs. Grundy says 'Saint Martin.' So do I. I like straight English. The little sinner calls himself *Samartan*."

"Why 'sinner'?"

"Ain't he Benjamin's brother-in-law? &c&c&c."[4]

Tonight we had General Hampton, von Borcke, and the Kentucky generals, for they move as one body. And Brewster as their advanced guard.

"No, skirmisher thrown out in front."

Today Johnny sent me six wild ducks and a perfect monster of a wild turkey.

I imparted a plan of mine to Brewster. I would have a breakfast, a luncheon, a matinee, call it what you please—but I would try and return some of the hospitalities of this most hospitable people. "Just think of the dinners, suppers, breakfasts we have been to. They have no variety, wartimes, but they make up in exquisite cooking for want of that."

"Variety! You are hard to please. Terrapin stew, gumbo, fish, oysters in any shape, game, wine as good as wine ever is. I do not mention juleps, claret cups, and apple toddy, whiskey punches, and all that. I tell you it is good enough for me. Variety would spoil it. Such hams as these Virginia people cure—such homemade bread—there is no such bread in the world—&c&c&c. Call yours 'a cold collation.'"

"Yes, I have eggs, butter, hams, game—everything from home—no stint just now. Even fruit."

"You ought to do your best. They are so generous and hospitable and so unconscious of any merit, or exceptional credit, in the matter of hospitality."

"They are no better than the Columbia people were to us—always."

So I fired up for my country.

By the way, Mr. Heart, former editor of the *Mercury*, writes to J. C. He denounces Colonel Jordan of Beauregard's staff roundly. He says the Charleston people think Colonel Jordan suppresses communications addressed to

---

2. William Barksdale Myers, a major on John C. Breckinridge's staff, was the son of a prominent Jewish family of New York and Richmond.

3. Charles Dickens, *The Life and Adventures of Martin Chuzzlewit* (1843–44).

4. Jules St. Martin, a clerk in the Justice Department, was indeed Benjamin's brother-in-law and close friend.

General Beauregard. Also that the obnoxious colonel openly expresses the hope that he may live to see Charleston once more in flames.

January 24, 1864.   My luncheon was a female affair exclusively.

Mrs. Davis came early and found Annie and Tudy making the chocolate. Laurence went south with J. C., so we had only Molly for cook and parlor maid. After the company assembled we waited—and waited. Those girls were making the final arrangements. I made my way to the door which opened into the dining room, and as I leaned against it, ready to turn the knob, Mrs. Stanard held me like the Ancient Mariner.

How she had been prevented by a violent attack of cramps from running the blockade, how providential it all was—&c&c&c. All this floated by my ear, for I heard Mary P's voice raised in anger on the other side of the door.

"Stop. Do you mean to taste away the whole dish?"

"Buck, if you eat many more of those fried oysters, they will be missed. Heavens! She is running away with a plug, a palpable plug out of that jelly cake!"

I listened to Mrs. Stanard, on thorns. Later in the afternoon when it was over and I was safe—for all had gone well—Molly had not disgraced herself before the mistresses of those wonderful Virginia cooks—Mrs. Davis and I went out for a walk. Barny Heyward and Dr. Garnett joined us, the latter bringing the welcome news that "Muscoe Russell's wife had come."

We had a joyful meeting—Mary Stevens (Muscoe Russell Garnett's wife) brought only number 2—a lovely baby named Mary Barton. The boy she left at home.

January 25, 1864.   The president walked home with me from church. (I dined with Mrs. Davis.) He walked so fast I had no breath to talk. So I was a good listener, for once. The truth is, I am too much afraid of him to say very much in his presence. We had such a nice dinner.

After dinner Hood came for him to ride.

Mr. Hunter of Virginia walked home with me. He made himself utterly agreeable by dwelling on his friendship for, and admiration of, my husband. He said it was high time Mr. Davis should promote him and that he had told Mr. Davis his opinion on that subject today, &c&c.

January 28, 1864.   Gave my newly arrived friend Mrs. Garnett a party Monday night. I must say, now at my house it is *a party*, day and night.

No longer in awe of J. C., who is in Carolina, the girls are here always—and where they are, &c&c&c.

Monday morning the Clays were here rehearsing for Mrs. Ives's private theatricals.[5] Mrs. Clement Clay is to be Mrs. Malaprop, Mrs. Lawson the maid.

---

5. Cora Ives was staging a benefit performance of Richard Brinsley Sheridan's *The Rivals* (1775) and William B. Rhodes's *Bombastes Furioso*. Like other Richmond papers, the *Enquirer* condemned this as "reckless frivolity . . . a mockery of the misery and despoilation that covers the land."

The latter cried, "Sister Virginia, you have only to be perfectly natural—peacock around, frisk your last frisk as an old woman parting with the desperate hope of still being able to catch a lover for her very own."

At night Dr. Garnett and all of the Kentucky contingent—Major von Borcke, Major Latrobe,[6] Barnwell Heyward, &c&c. You do not often find such nice men for a tea party anywhere.

Dr. Garnett tried the supercilious Barny's patience, but he was too well-bred to show the slightest annoyance. We were playing whist.

"Hold on there, major!"

"Don't promote Mr. Heyward too rapidly. 'Mr.' is a distinction in the military mob."   ·

"Oh then, this pseudomajor—whose name always escapes me—&c&c—must not play, &c&c—"

And the Heyward—a signer of the Declaration![7]

Barny was calm and imperturbable. He might have been deaf and dumb, blind indeed—as far as Dr. Garnett was concerned.

Bill of fare for my supper: wild turkey, wild ducks, partridges, oysters, and a bowl of apple toddy made by Mrs. Davis's recipe.

Tuesday Barny Heyward went with me to the president's reception. And from there to a ball at the MacFarlands'.

Breckinridge alone of the generals went with us. The others went to a supper given by Mr. Clay of Alabama. I had a long talk with Mr. Orr, Mr. Benjamin, and Mr. Hunter. These men speak out their thoughts plainly enough. What they said means "we are rattling down hill—and nobody to put on the brakes."

I wore my black velvet and diamonds point lace. They are borrowed for theatricals, and I wear them whenever they are at home.

Mrs. Wigfall said she was afraid Louly would be taken for a young lady.

"So she dressed her as an old woman," commented Isabella. Louly is lovely. And she was not crushed by a red poplin with a train trimmed with shabby black velvet. She wore a huge honiton lace collar high up in the neck—all because she was fifteen and not out. Her black eyes, however, saved the situation.

Johnny here, gravely explaining "Gongles"[8] and his general's stories. It is a cruel injustice to respectable young persons, the way Tom Boykin talked [about "Gongles"]. They live over their father's shop. (They do eat cheese at teatime.) But they give little dances. "The Captain, you know, will go [to] the devil's for a

6. Probably Osmun Latrobe, a lawyer and member of a prominent Baltimore family who served on Longstreet's staff.
7. Thomas Heyward, Jr. (1746–1809), Edward Barnwell Heyward's great-uncle.
8. See above, p. 512.

round dance." The Captain permitted himself an unmistakable scowl. Then came Custis Lee. John Rutherfoord and Major Cox dropped in.

January 29, 1864. Barny Heyward came and reports Myers crushed by the contending powers between the upper and nether millstone, &c&c. And he is ill in bed. The Senate has resolved to confirm anyone whom Mr. Davis appoints in Myers's place, be he who he may.[9]

———————

January 31, 1864.   Mrs. Davis gave her "luncheon to ladies" only on Saturday. Many more persons there than at any of those luncheons which have gone before. Gumbo, ducks and olives, suprême de volaille, chickens in jelly, oysters, lettuce salad, chocolate jelly cake, claret soup, champagne, &c&c&c.

General Hood informed today that he was ordered to the Army of the Tennessee, that he was now a corps commander. Suddenly his eye blazed as he said this.

Said I to myself, "All that ambition still—in spite of those terrible wounds." Did he read my thoughts? He added, "This has been the happiest year of any, in spite of all my wounds."

Again his eye blazed up.

"When I am gone, it is all over. I will not come back." I said quickly, "Are you not threatening the wrong end of the sofa?" He laughed heartily, turned his back to Buck, who was on the other side of the sofa, and said to me eagerly, "Will she care?"

"How do I know?" And I went away. There was a star with a diamond center which looped up Hood's hat. When he was going away, I saw this was missing. I said in a fright, "Where is your diamond star?"

In a moment I saw I had made a blunder somehow. There was mystery and confusion.

Someone sent us up a supper of terrapin stew, oysters, and Rhine wine, and a box of sugarplums. I have not the slightest idea who sent it.

Everybody stayed till late. There was a nice man here whose name I will not write—for Buck murdered him.

"Oh, he wants to be introduced to you—but don't. He is a substitute man!" General Breckinridge said he heard this on the stump out west.

"When this cruel war broke out—gallantly I rushed to the front. I hired a substitute and sent him to bleed and die for my country. And now my martyred substitute's bones bleach the battlefields of my country."

Brewster said, as Hood went off out of hearing: "How I want him to go back to the army. These girls are making a fool of him."

After they were all gone, Buck, the loveliest of them all, advanced with

9. A few days before, the Myers controversy reached a climax when the Senate resolved that the quartermaster general was still entitled to office because the president had not submitted the name of his replacement, Alexander Lawton, for confirmation. Davis then offered Lawton, and the Senate finally confirmed the new quartermaster general in Feb.

gravity and dignity, though we were alone. She began sweetly dignified but broke down. The staid gravity fled and she was all giggle, blush.

"Oh, Mrs. C, you know I have Sam's diamond star. I am to put it on his new hat for him. But you know, how could I explain before all those people?"

Johnny and Tom Burwell went with me to tea at the Prestons'. *Met,* I think, all of the generals in town. Tom Burwell said, "What suits me about these people—they like me, a simple private, as well as any general of them all!"

"Stop there, my dear boy," cried Captain John. "Not exactly! They are as kind and polite to you, maybe—not the other thing—never!"

The Captain grows cynical. He thinks this winter not half so pleasant as the last.

The very air darkened with generals.

"What are they all doing here, anyhow? Why are they not with the army? There is enough for them to do there, God knows," growls the Captain—left in the lurch and spiteful.

Today for a pair of forlorn shoes, I gave 85 dollars. Colonel Ives drew J. C.'s pay for me. I sent Laurence for it. (J. C. ordered him back to us—we needed a manservant here.) Colonel Ives was amazed I should be willing to trust a darky with that great bundle of money. But it came safely. Mr. Pettigrew says you take your money to market in the market basket and bring home what you buy in your pocketbook.

General Breckinridge said la belle fiancée sent for Mrs. Ould to go down to the boat with her. She thought there would be an impropriety in her going alone with old S. "Now," says M, "he must have been going for the impropriety, for when he saw Mrs. Ould he shut the carriage door and said he would walk." General B adds, "There are senseless and uncalled-for panics among old girls as well as among armies."

February 5, 1864.   Old lady: "Have you seen Fitzhugh Lee? Not so handsome as his father—too much em bon point"—"on bom pon," she pronounced it.

When Laurence handed me J. C.'s money, I said (six hundred dollars it was), "Now I am pretty sure you do not mean to go to the Yankees, for with that pile of money in your hands, you must have known that was your chance." He grinned but said nothing.

At the president's reception Hood had a perfect ovation. Mr. Preston navigated him through the crowd, handling him as tenderly on his crutches as if he were the Princess of Wales's newborn baby that I read of today. Bad for the head of any army to be so helpless. But old Blücher went to Waterloo in a carriage and a bonnet on his head to shade his inflamed eyes. A heroic figure truly, an old red-eyed woman, apparently—back in a landau in a bonnet! And yet, Blücher to the rescue—*or*—

Afterward at the Prestons'—for we left the president's at an early hour— Major von Borcke was trying to teach them his way of pronouncing his own name and telling them of the numerous travesties of it in this country. Charles threw open the door.

"A gentleman has called for Major Bandbox."

The Prussian major acknowledged this to be worst he had heard yet.

Once a German who wished to give me to understand his social position at home said, "At one time my sister carried the trail of a dyed queen."

After mature reflection we translated, "Trainbearer of a queen now dead."

Off to to the Ives's theatricals.

General Breckinridge walked with me—Major von Borcke with Mary Preston.

Our party kept together. Buck would take a seat behind us. Mary P after a while turned to Buck angrily.

"Don't you see this man is making you more conspicuous, twisting his neck off looking back, than if you would come (sensibly) alongside." She spoke in French.

"Stop it!" said Buck, in her softest voice. "Do you suppose nobody speaks French but you?"

"And if she scolds you in German I will understand," said von Borcke.

Buck came as she was ordered and sat by the man whose head she was ordered not to turn. However, she was not pleased at the row over her, and she turned her back to him. He amiably remarked: "Plenty of room. Do not be afraid. I do not mind *scrouging*."

The arrangement apparently was satisfactory, however, for we sat there five hours, and in coming away the general said he was never less tired in his life.

Mrs. Clay's Mrs. Malaprop was beyond our wildest hopes. And she was in such utter earnest when she pinched (Connie Cary) Lydia Languish's shoulder and called her "an antricate little huzzy." Lydia showed she felt it, and next day it was black and blue.

The back, even, of Mrs. Clay's head was eloquent as she walked away.

"But," said General Breckinridge, "watch Hood. He has not seen the play before, and Bob Acres amazes him."

When he caught my eye, General Hood nodded to me and said emphatically, "I believe that fellow Acres is a coward."

"That's better than the play," whispered Breckinridge. But [it] is all good, from Sir Anthony down to Fag.

Between acts Mrs. Clay sent us word to applaud—she wanted encouragement—the audience was too cold. To that hint General Breckinridge responded like a man. After that, following his lead, she was fired by thunders of applause.

Those mighty Kentuckians-turned-claquers were a host in themselves. Constance Cary not only acted well but looked perfectly beautiful. Lydia's folly gave her so many opportunities for her favorite trick of posing.

During the farce Mrs. Clay came, in all her feathers, diamonds, and fal-lals and took her seat by me. Said General Breckinridge, "What a splendid head of hair you have!"

"And all my own!" Afterward she said they could not get false hair enough, and they put a pair of black satin boots on top of her head and piled hair over them.

Bombastes Furioso was the farce. Mr. Randolph sang a comic opera. "Hope told a flattering tale." Those were the only words, but he gave us a few bars of every air from nearly all the well-known operas, and the effect was comic indeed—this endless repetition of words and variety of tune.

We went in before the crowd arrived, and the gentlemen who went in with us sat by us. Otherwise the sexes were separated as before—the men banked in a black cloud behind the seats. We were regarded with an evil eye for our presumption in contravening the arrangements. I was punched in the back by a fan, and a solemn old lady told me, "If you laugh so much, you will make yourself conspicuous!"

We adjourned from Mrs. Ives's to Mrs. Ould's—where we had the usual excellent Richmond supper. We did not get home until three. It was a clear moonlight night, as light as day, almost. As we walked along I said, "You have spent a jolly evening."

"I do not know. I have asked myself more than once tonight, 'Are you the same man who stood gazing down on the faces of the dead on that awful battlefield?' The soldiers lying there—they stare at you with their eyes wide open. Is this the same world? Here—and there—&c&c."

Last night the great Kentucky contingent came in a body. Hood brought Buck in his carriage. She said she did not like General Hood, and she spoke with a wild excitement in those soft blue eyes of hers—or are they gray—or brown? She then gave her reason in the lowest voice and loud and distinct enough for him to hear.

"Why?"

"He spoke so harshly to Cy as we got out of the carriage. I saw how he hurt Cy's feelings, and I tried to soothe Cy's mortification."

"You see, Cy nearly caused me to fall by his awkwardness, and I stormed at him," said the general, vastly amused. "But she salved it over. She told Cy how good he was and that I could not do without him."

"I hate a man who speaks roughly to those who dare not resent it."

The general declared himself charmed with her sentiments but seemed to think his wrongdoing all a good joke.

She said she was sorry that she had said if her father and mother did not oppose it she would care for him and all that. She repented it already— [*remainder of page cut off*].

"You foolish child! To whom did you tell that?"

"I told him so as we came here. I told him so himself, and now I am very sorry I said it, for it is not true."

Good heavens, now I wish the man was gone! This poor child!

At Mrs. Ives's play—while she was standing guard, one might say, to prevent the crowd rushing against him as he stood leaning on his crutches in the passageway, General Breckinridge said: "That is a beautiful picture. Will she marry him?"

"Half of it is sympathy. The girls are all wild about him. She has always no end of men in love with her. That is about what it amounts to."

General B growled: "He cares awfully for her. No wonder. She is so sweet. Poor old battered hero—I am enthusiastic myself about him."

Johnny here on his way home says he must have a party tonight, that over and above all the game, &c&c, we had in the house, the cream Mrs. Allan sent me &c&c, it would not cost more than a hundred Confederate dollars. Major Venable here, too.

Another disaster at the president's. Their trusty man Robert broken out with the smallpox. And half Richmond at the reception.

Buck reads my journal.

"What [did] you say when General Breckinridge asked you *plump*—'Will she have him?' More than is written there, I know."

I gave her that frank interview between the general and myself, without reserve. She opened her beautiful eyes in amazement—so little do people know themselves.

"He said most men would think themselves engaged, upon what those girls at Mrs. Preston's say had passed already."

"What?"

"For one thing—in answer to something said by you—they heard him say 'Oh, *you!* You are so childish and sweet.'

"Now, Buck! You know you are not childish, that you have more strong, good common sense than anyone in that house except your mother. Why are you playing with him in that way? I told General Breckinridge that you had been engaged before and probably would be engaged again. You were very kind and sympathetic, and as soon as you found an 'engagement so-called' fastened upon you, you began to reconsider, to reason. Your good sense came to the surface, and you tired of it."

"Oh, how could you be so cruel! so unfair!"

"You are so unhappy about so many of those men who cared for you having been killed. It was odd, you say, that Hood was always lucky till he fell in love with you, that you were ever so sorry for him, and so many farewells nowadays (with the chances never to meet again softening a girl's heart) ended in 'engagements.' Chickamauga is the only real victory we have had since Stonewall Jackson—and this man is the hero of Chickamauga. Our victories are splendid, you know. Then we move back. Women cannot understand that, Breckinridge said. And yet it is very plain. Alps on Alps arise, you know.[1] There is always

---

1. An allusion to Alexander Pope, *An Essay on Criticism* (1711), part 2.

another army of Yankees, fresh and ready for us behind the one we have just defeated." So I wandered away from personalities. Buck said:

"*We* wondered what you two were about. You were so sad and in such dead earnest. Hood said it was the war, but I knew it was *me*." (Regardless of grammar.) "You always look that way when you are talking of me—because you love me, and you love so few people."

"There is nobody in the world like my darling. I told him you had never been in love with anybody, after all. I doubted if you knew what love meant, and that you were not the least in the world in love now."

"How could you say that?"

"Because, my blessed, you tell every word that passes. Those girls come here and tell me about it as if it were a game of chess and each move had to be studied and *recorded*."

"Say 'backgammon,' for this is a chance game. All depends upon the throw, you know—lucky or unlucky. You know how I hated him when he lost his temper because poor Cy stumbled. There are two things certain in this world. One is, I will never love anybody as I do brother Willie. Next, I will never disobey mama and papa. There—are you satisfied?"

"All right. But as soon as another girl takes her seat by Sam, don't go straight there and show you have a right to him."

"An engagement in Richmond means so little."

"What are they engaged for? What does 'engagement' mean?"

Major Venable says, "For one thing, it does not mean a wedding." He pointed out a handsome woman. "She has been married twice, but I am engaged to her still. We became engaged while I was at college, and it was never broken off. I married the loveliest woman in the world—be the other who she may. When I met my fate I had half that enchantress over there."

"But she married before you did. You said so just now."

"That would have made no difference!"

At Mrs. Davis's breakfast there was an ancient dame, bluest blood, even in that assemblage of F.F.'s. If not Pocahontas, some other royal American savage had been her ancestress.

A western girl was under the hands of skillful dissectors. She was about to leave the house of one of the interlocutors.

"Why can't you let the poor thing stay? She is so gay, so attractive."

"My dear, she screams. She is too nervous. She takes fright at night. Twice she has raised the house with her untimely screams."

"A well-brought-up girl never screams," said a lady who would have been hideous without a harelip—which she had. "No young girl should ever be the heroine of an inexplicable affair. She must not be talked of for any affair whatever. Let her hold her tongue. Everything blows over. Scream—and it is all up. Who believes explanations? Nobody.

"Once I was tried, and so I know how it is myself. It was in New York. I saw a man enter my room. He used a false key. Did I scream? No. To pretend horror that one man should see you in déshabille. And then cry out and bring fifty more. Never. *I* kept perfectly still. I saw him searching. My purse was under my head. I saw him approaching my bed. I sat up. It was moonlight, but I struck a match. I lit the gas and glared at him. The creature turned to stone. He turned and shot out of [the] room as if the devil and all his imps were after him. I did not trouble myself to bolt the door. I knew he would lack the nerve to come back after what he had seen."

Mrs. Davis described my behavior. She said I began to laugh early in the story, and it was as good as a play to watch my face change as I perceived that this was not to be taken as a funny story but listened to as a didactic lecture.

Not even this shocked the foundation of solemn, ponderous Richmond society.

"Moral: never scream." And Mrs. Davis, Mrs. Preston, and I were literally *screaming* with laughter.

Then Johnny, the *Captain*, of dragoons only.

"Too many generals here this winter. They have demoralized society. Not half as pleasant as last winter. Then, auntie, you were on the first floor and your apartments were South Carolina barracks. Now you have gone up a flight of stairs, and our men say there are too many stars on the soldiers' collars up there for a private to venture up. Then there is Hood. They have sent him out West. The men say at the head of Fourth Texas he was as sure to bring the coon down as Captain Scott. But buckled up in a carriage, somebody else will have to lead his Texians. And there—there are all the generals whose heads he has stepped over with his one leg. Already every man jack who was a general while he was a colonel grumbles and says he is going up too fast."

"All this amounts to what you begin with. Last winter when Buck had you in hand it was pleasanter." Captain C smiled blandly. He would let you tear his heart out with an unmoved face if he so pleased to conduct himself.

Think of Barny Heyward's composed and impassive face, pale and cold, and the perfect accuracy with which he shuffled the cards he held in his white hands while Dr. Garnett continued his irritating "I forget your name, sir." Self-control, or no civilization possible. At the play the other night, a succession of shrill, modest little screams as Bob Acres took off his dressing gown.

"Heavens, will he undress right here before us!" All this set General B roaring with laughter. He approved of the homely old maid's theory, "Never scream until you are hurt—and not then, if you are wise."

Here L. Q. Washington came in with a treasure trove. He had found at some shop such nice pocket handkerchiefs. He displayed one—strong, white, and large as a tablecloth.

The Captain was in a brown study.

"I say, here are some handkerchiefs just run the blockade. Don't you want to know where they are to be bought?"

"No. I hope the war will end before I need any more."

"Have you any as nice as this?"

"Yes."

"Let me see," said the incredulous Washington.

The Captain took out of his rusty uniform pocket a neatly folded white mesh—fine as gossamer. He shook it out and showed Washington his monogram, beautifully embroidered.

"Nonsense. Some girl gave you that one. That's not fair." The Captain left, as in disgust. I explained:

"You know he was in Paris the year before the war and of course ordered that sort of thing—dozens upon dozens. And well for us he did. A lucky thing for me, as I made a raid upon his supply in times of need."

"That scrap would scarcely cover his Roman nose," said Washington spitefully. "With his dainty ways, I wonder he is not afraid of being called effeminate."

"Ask Butler—or Young or Lipscomb.[2] He is captain of a set of daredevil Camden boys, and he rules them. General Young said he wished there were a million like them."

"Fellows who can fight and ride and dance round dances."

"Suppose they lost their fortunes and there was no need to be soldiers—what would they do?"

"They could die. That seems easy enough nowadays."

Johnny has no unreasonable estimate of his own merits. He says if he should chance to be ruined after the war, he means to establish a chicken farm—that when he was a boy he succeeded wonderfully with his own chickens in his mother's yard.

This was after General Breckinridge came to say goodbye. He was vastly amused at Mrs. S's being afraid to risk herself alone with the infatuated elderly lover, alone in a hack. Said *stage* fright in a hack was queer. He thought them game—the lady, certainly—game chickens never hacked. Oh, they were afraid of what people would say.

"Mrs. Grundy, as it were," said Sam. "Unaccountable panics seize the bravest bodies of men—and women."

A love story:

"How did you enjoy the ride? I saw you from my window." His eye blazed—no smile on his face, but a lazy queer twinkle of inward delight in his eye.

"Oh—the only word for it—a delicious day it has been. I feel bound to tell you—that is, I am dying to tell somebody, and I know for her sake you will be cautious, safe and all that. You see, I asked her if she liked me as well as anybody else. 'Yes.' Better than anyone else—say that's so. 'Yes.'

"Then, will you let me try to make you love me?

"'That's just as you please'—with cool indifference. But you see I did not want any more today."

---

2. T. J. Lipscomb, colonel of Johnny's regiment.

"Will the parents interfere?"

Here General Breckinridge's voice broke in. "They are my cousins, so I determined to kiss them goodbye. Goodbye nowadays is the very devil. It means forever, in all probability, you know, all the odds against us, you know. So I advanced to the charge gravely, soberly, discreetly, and in the fear of the Lord. The girls stood in a row—four of the very prettiest I ever saw. Sam stood with his eyes glued to the floor, but he cried, 'You are afraid—you mean to back out.' But I did nothing of the kind. I kissed every one of them honestly and heartily."

Miss Martin, in an audible whisper: "Old Sam dares not look up—he is bursting with envy."

February 9, 1864.   This party for Johnny was the very nicest I have ever had and I mean it to be my last. I sent word to the Carys to bring their own men. They came alone, saying they did not care for men.

"That means a raid on ours," growled Isabella.

Mr. Lamar was devoted to Constance Cary. He is a free lance, so that created no heart burning.

"Heavens! if we had ships of war whose aim was as sure and as deadly as these!"

"Whose?"

"There!"—pointing first to Mrs. Davis on one side of the room, then to Mrs. Clay on the other.

Buck and Tudy declaimed, as they always do, with brilliant success.

Isabella said: "When the girls act among strangers I am so uneasy. They might say something—these strange people—to make me feel uncomfortable."

"I never do. She never fails. It was delicious. She is the noblest woman God ever made."

"Good gracious!" said Isabella. "Which one?" No answer was designed. "The amount of courting one hears in these small rooms. Men have to go—and they say their say desperately. I am beginning to know all about it. But this style is unique, is it not?"

"Since I saw *you* standing on your feet last year at the corner by the turnpike gate, you know, my battle cry has been 'God, my country, and *you!*'"

Mr. Venable says it is not "the devil on two sticks." The farce is now "Cupid on crutches."

General Hood took Mrs. Davis in to supper, and they remained at a small table prepared for her more than an hour after the rest of us left the supper room.

Mrs. Davis told us afterward she could hear B's clear, ringing, musical, Patrick Henry voice uplifted in amazement.[3] She had gone back to flirting with Johnny and Shirley Carter.

"Absurd—engaged to that man! Never—for what do you take me? &c&c&c."

---

3. Patrick Henry was Buck's great-great-uncle.

Mrs. Davis repeated what General Pendleton[4] said. If he had been so often hit, he would wince and dodge at every ball.

"Why wince—when you would thank God for a ball to go through your heart and be done with it all?"

Now she continued. "I thought, this is high tragedy and not farce, for there was the bitterness of death in his tone *for a moment*—and the silvery voice from the other room came, calm and clear, 'absurd—oh, you foolish creatures—to fancy I would &c&c&c.'"

Afterward, when the whole thing was over—and a succès fou—lights put out, &c&c—here trooped in the four girls, who stayed all night with me. In dressing gowns, they stirred up a hot fire, relit the gas, and went in for their supper—réchauffé was the word—oysters, hot coffee, &c. They kept it up till daylight. Maggie Howell put her feet through her nightgown sleeves and then tied up the skirts of it, leaving a huge bundle at the end to represent a stuck-up bunchy Shanghai fowl's tail. She was a comical bird as she hopped around, and I came near strangling, so long and violent was my laughter. But I could not keep awake even to laugh, so I left them. Of course, we slept very late next day. As they came in to breakfast, I remarked: "The church bells have been going on like mad. I took it as a rebuke to our breaking the Sabbath. You know, Sunday began at twelve last night."

"It sounds to me like fire bells."

About two my young people went home.

Soon the Infant dashed [in]—done up in soldier's clothes.

"The Yankees are upon us. Don't you hear the alarm bells? They have been ringing day and night."

Alex Haskell came then, and he explained matters. John C and himself went off to report to Custis Lee and to be enrolled among his "locals," who are always detailed for defense of the city. They were gone all day. At night Alex Haskell came back for a while to tell me how things were going.

Alexander the Great, as Isabella calls him, is awfully ambitious. He means to go straight up or die trying. He means to earn his honors honestly, but honors he will have. As a rule our boys are inconsequent. They look to no future; they fight whenever the time to fight comes and in the meantime whistle as they go about, "When this cruel war is over"—with that long shake on "over." It is but fair to say Alex H is clever as clever can be and brave as the bravest.

Isabella said to me, "Listen at those reckless creatures—and in a crowded drawing room, too."

"I do not hear anything."

"Johnny does. See how restless he is and how often he changes his base. He

---

4. Brig. Gen. William Nelson Pendleton of Va., chief of artillery for the Army of Northern Va.

hears more than he wants to hear. She is answering aloud to stop it. Can't you see her answers are irrelevant? 'I would not mind his lameness if otherwise I was willing to be his wife.'"

"Isabella! For God sake—don't mistake sympathy, friendship, and the ambition that seems to devour the young women nowadays when you marry. *She* does not love him—one bit."

"She thinks she does, and he is beginning to think so, too."

We sketched her on top of a baggage wagon on the way to Dalton—our idea of a soldier's wife.[5]

"What did she say?"

"Said that was what she wanted to do."

"That was bravado."

"Worse than that—said she was willing to tie up her bundle, swing it on her back, and follow the soldier laddie that she loved."

"Oh! Oh! but who is he, after all?"

"She says this one will not take no, and after she has snubbed him and she sees he is so hurt, she feels &c&c&c&c."

This time the attack upon Richmond has proved a false alarm.

We went to the Webb ball. Such a pleasant time we had. After a while the P.M.G.[6] took his seat in the comfortable chair next to mine and declared his determination to hold that position. Mr. Hunter and Mr. Benjamin essayed to dislodge him. Mrs. Stanard said: "Take him in the flirtation room. There he will soon be captured and led away." But I did not know where that room was situated; besides, my bold Texian made a most unexpected sally. "I will not go —and I will prevent her from going with any of you." Supper was near at hand. Mr. Mallory said: "Ask him if the varioloid[7] is not at his house. I know it is."

I started as if I was shot, but I took Mr. Clay's arm and went in to supper.

Venison, ice, everything nice.

February 12, 1864.   Love story again:[8]

"She treated him shamefully. We can see that. As she came in from riding with him, she yawned in his face, said she was so tired and sleepy."

She turned too calmly as they left the room. "Idiots! It is all over. As we rode, he held out his hand. I said, 'Ah! don't do that. Let it all rest as it is. You know I like you. You want to spoil all.'

"'Say yes or say no. I will not be satisfied with less. Yes—or no, is it?'

"Well, he would *keep* holding out his hand. What could I do?" Cy riding behind them! "So I put mine in his. Heavens, what a change came over his face. I pulled my hand away by main strength.

5. Dalton was the headquarters of the Army of Tenn. in northwest Ga.
6. Probably John H. Reagan, the postmaster general.
7. A. modified form of smallpox then rife in Richmond.
8. Buck and Hood.

"The practical wretch, he said at once: 'Now I will speak to your father. I want his consent to marry you at once.'

"Did you ever know so foolish a fellow?"

So the tragedy has been played out, for I do not think *even now* that she is in earnest. Such a beamingly beautiful, crimson face as she turned to me as she began. Her clear blue eye looked straight in mine.

"Do you believe I like him now?"

"No." She did not notice my answer.

"What fools those girls were when we came in yesterday afternoon. They did not see. They did not understand, and yet it was plain enough in his face."

Parents wept in despair. And yet a month ago they could so easily have stopped it all. They looked to time and the thousand accidents of life to come between—and they so look still.

"I am made nearly as miserable by the discontent at home as if they had refused outright to consent. They say I must not announce my engagement. That is, they expect nothing will come of it.

"There is always such a vague hope when people decide upon a secret engagement.

"Then he is so preposterously sanguine and happy. He is actually alarming. He looks triumphantly contented.

"And then go up to mama, and she so brokenhearted," added the darling child so wistfully.

At the reception, the padre—looking forward to all the dangers which now beset his lovely daughter.

"Why did you wait until now to tell her all this? Three months ago was your turn to warn and forbid it all."

"How did I know? Who tells a girl's father what is going on?"

"But you can see. It was all before your very eyes. Old Mrs. Blair's drawing room is not twenty feet square."

"Then the enemy took possession of me. I am so proud. So grateful. The sun never shone on a happier man! Such a noble girl—a queen among women!" He did not notice that I answered never a word.

John C. had a basket of champagne carried to my house—oysters, partridges, &c&c, for a supper after the reception. He is going back to the army tomorrow.

The Infant came with the girls. He was engaged to be married to an F.F. of the first water. And was so bereft of his senses as not to speak to her at the reception—walking with the president's sister-in-law, with our girls all the time! Next day she, the fiancée, sent him a note breaking off the engagement. Which note he brought M.P. to read. She waved it off indignantly. She is the mirror of truth and constancy, our Mary C. P.

The poor child came today: "Look here! My engagement is announced in the Charleston *Mercury*. Mama blames me. How could I keep it?" I knew their secret engagement was not worth a fig. He is too proud of it. He cannot keep the secret if he tried. "He tells everybody. Did he tell Colonel C?"

"Yes—the first time he met him!"

"There! Now!"

The Chivalry of Our Day

Ah foolish souls, and false! who loudly cried
"True chivalry no longer breathes in time!"
The heroic lives we witness! far and wide,
Stern vows by sterner deeds are justified;
Self abnegation, calmness, courage, power,
Sway with a rule august our stormy hour,
Where'er the loftiest hearts have wrought and died,
Wrought grandly, and died smiling!
                                   Thus Oh God!
From tears and blood and anguish thou hast brought,
The ennobling act, the faith sustaining thought
Till in the marvellous present, one may see
A mighty stage, by knights and patriots trod,
Who had not shamed earth's haughtiest Chivalry.

Stephen Elliott

And high among these chiefs of Iron grain
Large statued natures, souls of Spartan mien,
Superbly brave! inflexibly serene!
Man of the hope the sleepless brain,
Well dost thou guard our fortress by the main
And what tho' inch by inch old Sumter falls
There's not a stone that forms these sacred walls,
But holds a tongue, which shall not speak in vain!
A tongue that tells of such heroic mood,
Such nerved endurance, such immaculate will,
That after times shall hearken and grow still,
With breathless admiration; and on thee
Whose stern resolve our glorious cause made good
Confer an antique immortality.

—Paul Hayne[9]

9. Both sonnets above were written during the war by Paul Hamilton Hayne. M. B. C. alters the text of each and omits the third line of "Chivalry": "Look round us now; how wondrous, how sublime."

J. C. arrived on Wednesday. Buck asked him what he thought of her engagement, and he answered by giving her his opinion of the propriety of one of her performances last night. She came to our house first, and after a while the general's carriage drove up, bringing some of our girls. They told her that he could not come up but begged she would go down there for a moment. She flew down and stood ten minutes in that snow, Cy holding the carriage door open.

"But Colonel C, there was no harm. I was not there ten minutes. I could not get in the carriage because I did not mean to stay one minute. He did not hold my hand—that is, not half the time. Oh, you saw—well, he did kiss my hands. Where is the harm of that?"

"You ought not to have gone down."

"Did you not hear Annie? *He sent for me!*" Then she turned to me. "Now do you believe I care for him? See, I have braved Colonel Chesnut for him—and you know how awfully afraid I am of Colonel C &c."

Laurence has gone back ignominiously to South Carolina. At breakfast already, in some inscrutable way he had become intoxicated. He was told to move a chair, and he raised it high over his head, smashing Mrs. Grundy's chandelier. J. C. said: "Mary—do tell Laurence to go home. I am too angry to speak to him." So Laurence went with[out] another word said. He will soon be back, and when he comes he will say, "Shoo! I knew Mars Jeems could not do without me." And indeed he cannot.

Brewster asked me for a bottle of brandy "to travel on," said I had promised it to him, and I replied, "Whenever you bring that roll of linen cambric you said you had from a blockade-runner for me."

J. C. said gravely, after Brewster left with the brandy bottle, "Surely you did not ask that man for a bolt of linen cambric?"

Surely I had.

And now Burton Harrison at the executive office has given so lively an account of my parties while J. C. was gone that he is riding a very high horse indeed. He would not let me go with Mrs. Ould to the theater last night, and so I missed Mrs. Ould's supper afterward.

Molly came in and reported a queer scene. The husband came back, saying he had forgotten something. Next day Madame Femme gave him a daylight breakfast and sent him off in time for the train. To her amazement, *that night* he came back from the wars once more, and his wife met him in a rage. "Do you expect to stay here until a file of soldiers come and carry you handcuffed away to be shot as a deserter?"

J. C. said: "Women are so cruel. No doubt the poor soldier had his reasons—which Madame did not understand." He knew the man and liked him. What was the matter with him? "A person with or of—des absences délicieuses."

"When did you pick up that? It is *delicious*."

"Here, in Madame Deffand. And now listen—as to matrimony:

> Chez les époux, tout ennuie et tout lasse—
> Chez les amies, tout plaît, tout est parfait
> Chez les amants, tout plaît—tout est parfait."[1]

Isabella says that war leads to lovemaking. She says these soldiers do more courting here in a day than they would do at home, without a war, in ten years.

"Where did that fling at époux come from?"

"Here in La Fontaine. I was looking for this:

> Errant parmi les bois
> Il regarde à ses pieds les favoris des Rois;
> Il lit au front de ceux qu'un vain luxe environne
> Que *la Fortune* vend ce qu'on croit qu'elle donne."[2]

February 13, 1864.   J. C. writing out some resolutions for the Congress. He is very busy, too, trying to get some poor fellows reprieved. He says they are good soldiers but got into a scrape. Buck came. She had on her last winter's English hat with the pheasant's wing. J. C. kissed her tenderly. She asked for congratulations. He said he would go and congratulate the general. Then he said, "You know, if I speak of him at all I must speak handsomely, for he has won his honors like a man and he was promoted at Stonewall's request—&c&c&c." She sat down so overcome I had to hand her a glass of water. Just then the person spoken of entered most unexpectedly. She was very quiet—though so flushed. Said the blunt soldier:

"You look mighty pretty in that hat. You wore it at the turnpike—where I surrendered at first sight."

She nodded and smiled and flew down the steps after J. C., looking back to say she meant to walk with him as far as the executive office.

The general walked to the window and watched until the last flutter of her garments was gone.

He said, "The president was finding fault with some of his officers in command. And I said: 'Mr. President, why don't you come and lead us yourself? I would follow you to the death.'"

"Actually—if you stay here in Richmond much longer, you will grow to be a courtier. You came a rough Texian!"

---

1. Lines from "Belphégor" (1682), a fable by Jean de La Fontaine.
2. Lines from La Fontaine's fable "Philémon et Baucis" (1685).

He said an Englishman named Cavendish had requested a place on his staff.[3]

Then Johnny came to say goodbye, too. He had been to the P's. He met Buck on the front steps. She told him not to whisper to her behind his hat. Two old gray-headed men were watching them from the opposite windows and took them for what they were not—lovers.

"I will never marry now," said Johnny mournfully.

"No, you never will marry. There is one insuperable bar to that. You must first ask some woman to marry you. Nobody is going to ask you. You know you will never muster up courage to ask that question?"

"Now, if I had asked you in time—would you have refused me?"

"No," and a laugh of derision.

"Now, you might have spared me that," he said. "You women are like cats— you never tire of tormenting a rat." He would tell no more.

Details are melancholy.

February 14!!   The president said yesterday: "No wonder men were willing to fight for such a country as ours—and such women. They were enough to make heroes of any material."

Little Jeff[4] rode on his pony by the carriage, and a mob of little boys ran shouting after him, from street to street.

He was very red in the face, but he rode on and did not look back.

Annie came with Major Blanton.[5] It was an innovation—Mrs. P never letting them go out alone with a gentleman. She said, no, they have broken the ice. I suppose we will soon have all of the other girls engaged to his staff.

February 15, 1864.   Said Brewster, "Were you ever able to get it into a girl's head that the love story is a mere episode in a man's life?"

"The love story—I thought their lives abounded in episodes of that description."

As we walked to church, Tudy whispered, "The general wants so much to come to church, but he can't, you know."

"Why not? He stumps up two flights of stairs at my house. He goes to plays—&c&c."

As we took our seats, the thud of crutches behind us, and the sexton marshaled the man in question slowly by us, up to the president's pew. That being empty, the general went to the extreme end to be out of the way. Buck, seated in

---

3. Refused a position by Hood, "Lord Charles Cavendish" persuaded Fitzhugh Lee to make him a staff officer in May. When Cavendish disappeared, leaving bad checks behind him, it turned out that he was a commoner named Short.

4. Six-year-old Jefferson Davis, Jr.

5. B. H. Blanton, Hood's adjutant and inspector general.

the Wynham Robinson pew, was near at hand—indeed, a slight board petition was all that divided them. She never raised her head or her veil. He told Tudy after church, in describing this unexpected and startling propinquity: "I was a little nervous when I saw who it was. It took my breath away, as it were."

After the service the president gave the wounded soldier his arm and slowly helped him down the church steps. The mob of boys said:

"That's jolly of the president. If it wasn't Sunday, we'd cheer."

The president asked why I began to gather up my things to depart as soon as he came in the room. Then he became very jocular as to the open-mouthed lamentations of those girls at Chesnut's return. "Those girls run from Chesnut, I believe, as you do from me."

Brewster, after J. C. came in, ceased to gossip, and a discussion of the currency began at once—then the news from the west. Mr. Davis wants Pemberton in Charleston, Beauregard in Florida. J. C. wanted Bragg to stay west, and I thought that the maddest idea of them all.

Johnny's wisdom: He who will not when she may—&c&c—she would have him fast enough now. She has the prevailing epidemic about his heroism &c&c—and there is something awfully taking about that rough Texan wooing, those girls say.

"Can you tell the witches' charm she has to make fools of men? No? Well, it is the laugh in her big blue eyes—glorious, those eyes are—and the slow way she lifts those long lashes. She is so sympathetic, and her voice is so low and sweet. She never says anything. She is absolutely a silent woman. You don't [know?] any such? Well, she is one—listens and lets the fools do their own talking till they are up to the eyes in a bog, and then all the king's horses and all the king's men can't pull them out again. Take my word—if she don't go with him now, it will blow over. If any girl says to me, 'I will have you,' I would not care a snap for her family—never—not all the family she could pile on. That's my trouble—parents are willing enough. Say I am a safe match. The girls giggle and say, 'Oh, it is only Johnny,' and they won't have me at any price. I'd take her now—Lochinvar fashion—see if I didn't."

The rash subaltern's tactics, however, he kept for our private benefit—not the general's.

"Parents' ways are incomprehensible to me.[6] I can't see through it all. They let me ride with her, drive with her, come and go unmolested. They asked me to dinner, to breakfast, to tea. When I became engaged to their daughter, I expected to have the run of the house. No—far from it. I never see them at all. I am never asked there. When I call, or when I go to spend the evening there, I see her only in the drawing room, where there are always a parcel of giggling girls listening, watching, and that Brewster setting them on. But I'll kill him."

Brewster came in, unaware of his friend's bloodthirsty state of mind.

6. M. B. C. is now quoting Hood.

He told a long story of Mrs. G. W. and Mrs. J. J.,[7] whose high and mighty husbands were to fight a duel after the war because of their quarrels.

"Stop that, Brewster, I never could understand women's rows. I know if any man talks about my wife, I'll kill him."

"Hello! That's regular Fourth Texas logic!" said Brewster.

Mrs. Davis and General McQueen came. He tells me Muscoe Garnett is dead.

Then the best and the cleverest Virginian I know is gone. He was the most scholarly man they had, and his character was higher than his acquirements &c&c.

Today a terrible onslaught upon the president for nepotism. Burton Harrison and John Taylor Wood's letters denying the charge that the president's cotton was unburnt—or that he left it to be bought by the Yankees—has enraged the opposition. How much those people in the president's family have to bear. I have never felt so indignant.

February 16, 1864. Saw in Mrs. Howell's room the little negro Mrs. Davis rescued yesterday from his brutal negro guardian. The child is an orphan. He was dressed up in little Joe's clothes and happy as a lord. He was very anxious to show me his wounds and bruises, but I fled. There are some things in life too sickening, and cruelty is one of them.

Maggie said people who knew General Hood before the war said there was nothing in him. As for losing his property by the war—he never had any. West Point was a pauper's school, after all. It was only military glory—and all that he had gained since the war began.

"Now," said Burton Harrison, "*only* the military glory! I like that! The glory and the fame that he has gained during the war—that is Hood. What was Napoleon the Great before Toulon—&c&c. He has the impassive dignity of an Indian chief. He has always a little court around him of devoted friends. Wigfall himself said he could not get within Hood's lines."

Today in the Senate Wigfall said he believed the president to be an honest and loyal man. The president's neck was in as much danger as Wigfall's, in case things went wrong. Wigfall, however, had no faith in the president's judgment. And he said it that should not [*sic*]. If Jeff Davis's judgment had been as good as Wigfall's, neither Vicksburg nor Missionary Ridge need have fallen.

Had a letter from Sally Tom Taylor.[8] She wants Torriani exempted. She describes him as "a soul-starved man. He requires sunshine and flowers and his beloved Italy." Above all, he requires to get away from our snow and sleet and squalor and fighting Confed fashion.

Found everything in Main Street twenty percent dearer. They say it is the new currency bill.

---

7. Presumably the wives of Gustavus Woodson Smith and Joe Johnston.
8. Sally (Elmore) Taylor, the wife of Thomas Taylor of Richland District.

General Lee told us what a good son Custis was. Last night their house was so crowded Custis gave up his own bed to General Lee and slept upon the floor. Otherwise General Lee would have had to sleep in Mrs. Lee's room. She is a martyr to rheumatism and rolls about in a chair. She can't walk.

Constance Cary says, if it would please God to take poor Cousin Mary Lee—she suffers so—wouldn't these Richmond women *campaign* for Cousin Robert? In the meantime Cousin Robert holds all admiring females at arm's length.

Found Lydia and Captain Absolute[9] at my house—wondered if they had stopped making (theatrical) love yet. Colonel Preston was there with J. C. Firelight only and one tallow candle. Gas stopped all over Richmond.

Told Colonel P of my telegram to Isabella—that Mary P might know the general was on the wing. "Look out"—as it were—"will be in Columbia Saturday." He said, "Will she understand?"

Constance Cary gave me a Parthian shot unconsciously. Her words are often too picturesque for the occasion. She described my parties to J. C. as "little orgies." I shook in my shoes. Such a stupid word. Who enjoyed my parties more than Conny Cary? Mrs. Davis calls J. C. "High South Carolina." When he takes on stiffly, he is terrible. South Carolina as a rule does not think it necessary for women to have any existence out of their pantries or nurseries. If they have none, let them nurse the bare walls. But for men! the pleasures of all the world are reserved! Besides, J. C. takes words literally; he makes no allowance for sensational language. It blew over. After they were all gone he did not refer to it. But about a week after: "I say Mol[?], that was a queer speech of Miss Cary's. I do not like *my house*" ("apartments—second floor—Mrs. Grundy's," said I) "to be so spoken of. Really, I will be afraid to leave home."

I preferred to converse upon the subject of Joe Johnston's movements.

"Is General Johnston ordered to reinforce Polk?"

"They said he did not understand the order. After five days' delay he replied. They say Sherman is marching to Mobile. When they once get inside of our armies, what is to molest them—unless it be women with broomsticks!!"[1]

General Johnston writes that the governor of Georgia refuses him provisions and the use of his roads. The governor of Georgia writes, "The roads are open to him and in capital condition," and that he has furnished him abundantly with provisions from time to time, as he desired them. I suppose both of these letters are placed away side by side in our archives.

9. I.e., Constance Cary and L. M. Tucker, who played these roles in *The Rivals*.
1. U. S. Maj. Gen. William Tecumseh Sherman's expedition east from Vicksburg early in Feb. had precipitated yet another squabble between Jefferson Davis and Joseph E. Johnston. Fearful that Sherman would attack Mobile or Montgomery, Davis telegraphed Johnston at Dalton, Ga., on Feb. 11 to "do what you can to assist" Lt. Gen. Leonidas Polk, whose troops were falling back before Sherman. Johnston, unwilling to weaken his defenses and expose Atlanta to attack, did nothing to help Polk. After Johnston refused to heed several more suggestions to send troops to Miss., Davis bluntly ordered his general to do so on Feb. 17. But Johnston delayed until it became clear on Feb. 23 that Polk no longer required reinforcements: Sherman had turned back from Meridian, Miss., to Vicksburg.

Bless these two Joes. General and governor—a pair of nuisances.

February 20, 1864.   At Mrs. Davis's. Met there Mr. Senator Clay. Heavens! He knows how to quarrel! It was a battle à l'entrance. Mr. Clay still professes to be devoted to "Jeff Davis." It was a miserable hour for me. I was afraid every moment some word might fall—too much—more than could be smoothed away afterward.

On Broad St. I gave 280 dollars for 24 yds. of flannel to make some soldiers' shirts.

At Burton Harrison's office, he gave us some apples and we sent for J. C.

"What does Hood talk to you about? He is only a rude soldier. He can't talk of literature and high art."

"Neither can I—no, nor Shakespeare and the musical glasses."[2]

Maria Lewis came. She can talk of nothing but the little great-grandnephew of George Washington that [she] feels now she has a right to expect. She has no thought, no mind, no heart, no imagination that is not engrossed by this coming event—which casts its shadow before.

Mrs. Preston was offended by the story of Buck's performance at the Iveses'. General Breckinridge told her it was the most beautifully unconscious act he ever saw. The general was leaning against the wall, B standing guard by him— "on her two feet." The crowd surged that way, and she held out her arm to protect him from the rush. After they had all passed she handed him his crutches, and they too moved slowly away. Mrs. Davis said, "Any woman in Richmond would have done the same joyfully—but few could so gracefully." B is made so conspicuous by her beauty. Whatever she does cannot fail to attract attention.

Read *At Odds.*[3] Interesting—to the fascinating point. If impossible. Men never pass self-denying ordinances after they are married—*Marriage in High Life.* And pas vraisemblable—I mean the married-but-in-name business!

---

2. "They would talk of nothing but high life, and high-lived company, with other fashionable topics, such as pictures, taste, Shakespeare, and the musical glasses." Oliver Goldsmith, *The Vicar of Wakefield* (1766), chapter 9.

3. Jemima Montgomery, baroness Tautphoeus, *At Odds: A Novel* (1863).

Johnny only stayed at home one day, went to his plantation, got several thousand Confederate dollars, and in the afternoon drove out with Mrs. K.[4] Well, on revient toujours à ses premiers amours. At the Bee Store he spent a thousand of his money—brought us *cuir*-colored gloves, linen, &c&c. Well, one can do without gloves, but linen is next to life itself.

Yesterday the president walked home from church with me, said he was so glad to see J. C. at church, had never seen him there before, how well he looked, &c. I replied:

"He looked so well because you have never before seen him in the part 'of right man in the right place.' J. C. has no fancy for being planted in pews, but he is utterly Christian in his creed."

Annie had heard so much of the wounded in Richmond hospitals. A few days ago she said to Mrs. Preston: "Auntie, I must go home. I can't stay here. Their cries break my heart. I can't stand it."

"What cries? Whose cries?"

"The poor wounded soldiers. I cannot sleep. It goes to my very heart."

"Nonsense. You cannot hear any such thing. Besides—wounded soldiers are nowhere near us. And they never cry out. When you hear one, call me."

Annie came flying in ten minutes.

"There—there," and she clapped her hands to her ears to keep out the cruel sound.

"Charcoal—charcoal" was being shrieked in tones of agony, like a soul in torment—a sound so familiar to us all in Richmond that we never hear it at all.

T. F., Johnny says, is in the toils. The young lady says he tried playing off and on with her. She means to make him speak out, show his hand, and then she will quietly say, "truly sorry—but I am engaged." Besides, adds Johnny, T. F. is strangely fascinating to girls now—since the story that he is half-married. He was married in fun by a man who happened to be a magistrate. In fun it was, but—the Scotch law prevailing in South Carolina—some say it is in earnest, a bona fide marriage until death us do part. No fun in that.

Mrs. Memminger[5] has never called on Mrs. Davis. There is manners for you, and a knowledge of proper etiquette.

---

4. Probably Mary (Withers) Kirkland.
5. Mary (Wilkinson) Memminger, wife of the secretary of the treasury.

Oh—I have been to see a delicious married beauty! So soft, so silly, so lovely, so kindly! Forbear!

The Captain gave us a luncheon at Pizzini's—Maggie, Buck, and myself. B wore the beautiful gloves he had brought her. Said Maggie,

"Poor creature, do you not know she is for another, she never can be thine?"

"Yes, I know," said the Captain, looking silly beyond words of mine to portray.

"Yes, he knows," says B. "And that makes his behaving so nicely—kind—that is, doubly so."

"Oh," said Maggie, the plain-spoken, "so you are in love with her yet. You are half in love with her *yet,* I see."

"He never was more than that," [said] B softly.

He walked home with Maggie. B and I came home together. He remained four hours with M. Came home at two forty speed but could not stop for dinner because he had an engagement to ride with Tudy. Came home after dark—had only time to brush his hair, freshen up a little, and rush off to the Carys'. It was twelve before he returned. Truly the life of a young captain of dragoons in Richmond—in "active service indeed."

Next day Mr. and Mrs. M called.[6] We were discussing the Captain's fast if pleasant life. Said Mr. M, with a sigh:

"I too once kept late hours. Now Bettie requires me to retire early and to be regular &c&c&c." She said, with a nervous laugh,

"How can you make me so absurd?"

Mr. Miles turned pale when I met him, and he spoke of his friend Garnett's death. He seems to have found time to stop for a while in all this whirl and grieve for poor Garnett, who was worthy indeed of many tears.

The Prussian von Borcke showed the girls a plain gold ring soon after he came here.

"I am betrothed. In Germany a little girl waits for me." We told them it was horrible. The man distinctly felt it necessary to warn them off the premises. They do not seem to mind, however, and he has an "emphatically good time." Johnny, who has transferred his attentions to Tudy, said to her:

"I could raise a company of cavalry from among the men I met every night at your house—for special service—to join the Army of Tennessee—and every man of them would be B's poor, infatuated, deluded, bereft lovers."

"And I would make you captain of them," promptly responded Tudy.

Mrs. Huger says Bragg is to supersede General Cooper. Est-il possible? "No matter," she adds. "It will be several years before that slow coach Cooper finds it out."

6. William Porcher Miles and Bettie (Bierne) Miles.

Lent General Preston *Mrs. Lirriper's Lodgings,* our latest Dickens.[7] He says he holds me responsible for his reading, as Judge Withers did.

February 23, 1864.   At the president's. General Lee breakfasted there. A man named Phelan[8] told him all he ought to do, planned a campaign for him. General Lee smiling blandly the while, though he did permit himself a mild sneer at the wise civilians in Congress who refrained from trying the battlefield in person but from afar dictated the movements of armies.

J. C. said, to his amazement, at the executive office General Lee came into his room, "to pay his respects and have a talk," he said.

"Dear me! goodness gracious!" said I. "That was a compliment from the head of the army—the very first man in the world, we Confederates think!"

February 24, 1864.   They came to boil taffy. I think they kept it from being sufficiently cooked to be pulled on purpose, for they stayed here the livelong day. They played cards. One man, a soldier "of my friends," had only two teeth left in front, and they lapped across each other, on account of the condition of his mouth, no doubt. He had maintained a dignified sobriety of aspect, though he told funny stories. Finally one was too much for him, and he grinned from ear to ear. Maggie gazed, then called out, as the negro fiddlers do dancing figures,

"Forward two and cross over!" Fancy our faces! The hero of the two teeth told us that among the country people cavalry was called "critter companies," and infantry "web-footed"—or ducks to tramp. He said, relapsing into a decorous arrangement of mouth: "Cavalry are the eyes of an army. They bring the news. The artillery are the boys to make a noise. But the infantry do the fighting. And a general or so gets all the glory."

Read Bulwer's play—*Richelieu.* And there are people also deny Bulwer's high place as an author! Then *Cinq-Mars*—another view of the same old cardinal.[9]

February 26, 1864.   We went to see Mrs. Breckinridge,[1] who is here with her husband. Then paid our respects to Mrs. Lee. Her room was like an industrial school—everybody so busy. Her daughters were all there, plying their needles, and several other ladies. Mrs. Lee showed us a beautiful sword recently sent to the general by some Marylanders now in Paris. On the blade was engraved, "Aide-toi! et Dieu t'aidera." When we came out:

7. Charles Dickens contributed chapters 1 and 7 to *Mrs. Lirriper's Lodgings,* the Christmas, 1863, issue of *All the Year Round.*

8. James Phelan, whose term as Confederate senator from Miss. had ended a few days earlier.

9. Edward Bulwer-Lytton, *Richelieu; or, The Conspiracy* (1839) and Alfred Victor, comte de Vigny, *Cinq-Mars; ou, Une Conjuration sous Louis XIII* (1826).

1. Mary Cyrene (Burch) Breckinridge, wife of John Cabell Breckinridge.

"Did you see how the Lees spend their time! What a rebuke to the taffy parties!"

Finegan in Florida and Stephen Lee in Mississippi each claim a victory. On account of the latter success, no fears are now felt for Mobile.[2] Our papers are now jubilant. The mud keeps all armies quiet. Beneficent mud! No killed or killing on hand. No rumbling of wagons laden with dead or dying.

We enjoy this reprieve. We snatch a fearful joy.[3] It is a brief interlude of comparative peace.

February 29, 1864.   Leap Year.

Mrs. Davis and our party did not agree as to the cause of Memminger's appointment as secretary of the treasury. She says the South Carolina delegation recommended him. The South Carolina delegation to a man say they repudiated him, except Mr. Barnwell alone. He is on Mr. Barnwell's sole responsibility. It is one of the *Mercury*'s grounds of complaint against the president that he consulted no one but Mr. Barnwell. Teddy Barnwell[4] says his good uncle chose Mr. Memminger because of his fine low-church proclivities and his high standing in the Sunday school! "That always blinds Uncle Robert."

The annals of the Memminger family are sensational and mythic enough near home, but before they reached Richmond, or since, the stories have attained frightfully exaggerated proportions. They read now like a ballad from Percy's *Reliques*.[5] Will only record one thing belonging more to the realistic than to the romantic anecdotes. One lady of the family was an heiress. Why? When she was young an eccentric rich bachelor uncle looked at her nose. "It is so short—she'll never find a husband." So he left her all his fortune in his will by way of compensation. The better-*nosed* were cut off with a shilling.

Buck's account of the general's visit to "brother Willie" in camp—her blue eyes gleaming and beaming with fun and that smile of hers—which I believe after all does most of the mischief. It is so wonderfully sweet.

Brother Willie says: "As a general rule lieutenant generals[6] don't call on majors of artillery, but this one did and said such nice things, too. The outsiders who did not understand how the 'land lay' must have been amazed."

---

2. At Olustee, Fla., on Feb. 20, Brig. Gen. Joseph Finegan of Fla. halted the westward advance of a Union force that had landed at Jacksonville. Suffering over eighteen hundred casualties, the Federals retreated to Jacksonville and made no further major attempt to overrun the state. On Feb. 24, Maj. Gen. Stephen Dill Lee reported that Maj. Gen. Nathan Bedford Forrest's cavalry had routed U.S. Brig. Gen. William Sooy Smith's larger force of cavalry at Okolona, Miss. Smith, already turning back from an abortive attempt to join William T. Sherman's army at Meridian, Miss., soon returned to his base at Memphis, Tenn.

3. "Still as they run they look behind, / They hear a voice in every wind, / And snatch a fearful joy." Thomas Gray, "On a Distant Prospect of Eton College" (1742), stanza 4.

4. Capt. Edward Hazzard Barnwell, whose uncle was Sen. Robert Woodward Barnwell.

5. Thomas Percy, ed., *Reliques of Ancient English Poetry* (1765).

6. Hood, now a lieutenant general, was in Columbia.

He stayed at Mary McDuffie's (Mrs. Wade Hampton), and Mary Preston gave him a state dinner at the old Hampton house. Out in that fine old garden he made his moan.

"What a splendid place this garden would be for lovers. Love would make itself here—no effort needed. This beautiful shade, such comfortable seats in out-of-the-way nooks and corners. How different from Richmond. Little stuffy drawing rooms twenty feet square—every eye turned on you without blinking—a parcel of giggling girls who knew more of your affairs and how you stood with your lady love than you did yourself. When you began to say anything, the very thing you cared most to say, you know, open flew the door, and Charley announced Major This, Colonel That, or Captain T'other. Then a general move, a confusion, and your girl escaped. If you went to ride, there was the groom at your heels—and when he rode too near, if you lost your temper and cried 'fall back' sharply, Buck would not speak to you the rest of the ride because 'you had hurt Cy's feelings.' Pretty rough on a fellow who had so much to do and so little time to do it in. And then, all the little boys followed as if you were the circus come to town—cheering, running alongside, saying such things! When you got to the door and said goodbye to your sweetheart, with a sly kiss of her hand, as you looked up you could see eyes from every window of every house in Franklin Street peering down on you. Now here you have a whole square to yourselves—such high walls, such close hedges, &c&c."

"Oh, lovemaking—that is what a garden was first used for. Adam and Eve played at that little game until they had the very devil himself bursting with envy. Bible truth, that!"

Annie H was here. She says she knows "her Angel," as she calls Buck. She reports that R. L.[7] has arrived and that she believes R. L. is the only man B really cares for. Le roi est mort—vive le roi. There is hardly a day's interval between the king who goes and the king who comes.

An arrant F.F. came to complain of Mr. Miles.

"What is it?" After an immense amount of laughing and twisting this way, twisting that way.

"Oh! Such indelicacy! and before us."

"But Mr. Miles is the pink of propriety, delicacy itself. What did he say?"

"Oh! When they asked for his sister-in-law or somebody, he said right out, 'she is in her confinement.'"

And I gravely replied, "I do not see the indelicacy, and I do not see the fun."

Another maimed hero engaged to be married. Sally Hampton[8] has accepted John Haskell. There is a story that he reported for duty after his arm was shot off. Suppose in the fury of the battle he did not feel the pain.

---

7. Rawlins Lowndes.
8. Sally Preston Hampton, daughter of Wade Hampton III.

General Breckinridge, "What's the name of the fellow who has gone to Europe for Hood's leg?"

"Dr. Darby."

"Suppose it is shipwrecked?"

"No matter—half a dozen are ordered."

Mrs. Preston raised her hands!

"No wonder the general says they talk of him as if he were a centipede. His leg is in everybody's mouth."

XXIII

"How Hardened We Grow"

March 3, 1864. Mrs. Grundy lent me *Romola*. I had read it before, but I was hurried then. Now I will take time, consider my ways, and not presume to judge George Eliot rashly.

Hetty the Handsome and Constance the Witty came. The former too prudish to read *Lost and Saved* by Mrs. Norton after she had heard the plot.

"Why don't your cousin marry that Pegram man who is so daft about her? They say she is engaged to him."

"Oh! How can you think of such a thing? She is having such a good time. She is so much admired."

"He is in love with her, then, and she is grateful or something sympathetic and kind, or she would not refuse to marry because she was having a good time, because she was so much admired—&c&c&c."

Constance seemed to turn this over in her mind.

"Hetty will be very angry with us if she hears that we doubt her devoted attachment to General Pegram."

Conny was making a bonnet for me. Just as she was leaving the house, her friendly labors over, J. C. entered and quietly ordered his horse.

"It is so near dinner."

"But I am going with the president. I am on duty. He goes to inspect the fortifications. The enemy, once more, are in a few miles of Richmond."[1]

Then we prepared a luncheon for him. C. C. remained with me. She told me her life's history—the Burton Harrison imbroglio, the entanglement of the hour—&c&c&c. As Annie says of Buck, "I believe she only cares for B. H.—let them quarrel as they may."

After they left I sat down to *Romola*—and I was absorbed in it. How hardened we grow "to war and war's alarms." The enemies' cannon or our own are thundering in my ears—and I was dreadfully afraid some infatuated and frightened friend would come in to cheer, to comfort, and interrupt me. Am I

---

1. Chesnut was bringing word of the Kilpatrick-Dahlgren raid. Prompted by reports of poor treatment of Federal prisoners in Richmond, Lincoln ordered Brig. Gen. Hugh Judson Kilpatrick's cavalry to seize the Confederate capital, release the prisoners, and distribute amnesty proclamations. Kilpatrick's operation was foolhardy: the Confederates learned of the raid on Feb. 29, the day after Kilpatrick set out, and established the defenses that Chesnut went to inspect. Kilpatrick, faced with these preparations, turned back on March 1, but units led by Col. Ulric Dahlgren proceeded. After much blundering, Dahlgren's troops were trapped outside Richmond on the night of March 2 and beaten back. The fiasco cost the Union 335 casualties.

the same poor soul who fell on her knees and prayed and wept and fainted as the first guns boomed from Fort Sumter?

Once more we have repulsed the enemy. But it is humiliating indeed that he can come and threaten us at our very gates whenever he so pleases. If a forlorn negro had not led him astray (and they hung him for it) on Tuesday night, unmolested they would have walked into Richmond.

Surely there is horrid neglect or mismanagement somewhere!

Hampton with N.C. troops beat up their quarters in a night attack. There were several thousand troops under Kilpatrick.

Mrs. Randolph saw the mounted prisoners as they were brought in, she told me.

Henley's battalion saved Richmond—that is the cry now.[2] While J. C. was riding with Jeff Davis, an ambulance of wounded men passed. One asked, "Is that the president?"

Then they cheered. Pretty plucky for wounded men. It is not the army but civilians only who hate Jeff Davis.

March 4, 1864.   Enemy reinforced and on us again.[3] Met Wade Hampton, who told me J. C. was to join him with some volunteer troops, so I hurried home. Such a cavalcade rode up to luncheon—Captain Smith Lee and Preston Hampton: the handsomest, the oldest and the youngest of the party.

This was at the Prestons'. Smith Lee walked home with me. Alarm bells ringing—horsemen galloping—wagons rattling. Dr. H stopped us to say Beast Butler was on us with 15 thousand men. How scared the doctor looked. And after all, it was only a notice to the militia to turn out and drill.

Custis Lee said, "It would not do for me to take a general's commission now, over the heads of men who have been in active service from the beginning while I was doing office work." J. C. says the same, and yet they chafe so at the aideships. Some way will have to be found—new commands, new regiments—not over other people's heads.

March 5, 1864.   Tom Ferguson[4] walked home with me. He told me of Colonel Dahlgren's death and the horrid tablets found in his pocket. He came with secret orders to destroy this devoted city, hang the president and his cabinet, and burn the town.[5]

2. Although a troop of government clerks hastily raised by Maj. John A. Henley of Ala. participated in the defense of Richmond, Confederate cavalry played the crucial role in the fighting with Dahlgren.

3. On March 4, General Kilpatrick raided the area around Richmond in retaliation for the defeat of Dahlgren.

4. Probably Thomas Ferguson, a participant in the Richmond charades and major of the Sixth S.C. Cavalry Regiment.

5. Dahlgren was killed in the ambush of his troops on the night of March 2. The next day a boy found Dahlgren's body and discovered in his pockets the "horrid tablets": a memorandum book, orders to a subordinate, and the draft of an undelivered speech to his troops. The memorandum book revealed Dahlgren's intention to kill Davis and the Confederate cabinet; the speech called on the Union cavalry to "destroy and burn the hateful city" of Richmond. Then and later, there were claims that the Confederates had forged these papers.

Fitzhugh Lee was proud that the Ninth Virginia captured him.

Buck shook a roll of something at me—"30 pages from Sam."

What would the gossips say? People who said to me: "What does that soldier creature find to talk to all of you? They say all of you are about to translate a German play."

"No, merely a French one."

"Oh, but they say *all of you* could do either."

"Or neither."

Found Mrs. Semmes covering her lettuce and radishes as calmly as if Yankee raiders were a myth.

This last affair has left [us] sore and disheartened. We have shown our weakness and the imbecility of our arrangements.

Mr. and Mrs. Preston are glad all the honor of it fell on John McElhenny's command.[6] He was Alfred Preston protégé.[7] After a variety of adventures since first he followed Alfred from New Port years ago, it has ended in his being in command of a battalion of department clerks, who did gallant service in the fray.

And to think—here I sat reading *Romola* at my ease. And I might have been roused at any moment by fire and fury—rapine, murder—&c&c&c.

While Beast Butler holds Fortress Monroe he will make things lively for us. On the alert must we be now.

March 8, 1864.   Met an antique virgin of vinegar aspect, whose mind seemed occupied by the unmentionable horrors we had so narrowly escaped. No one else as far as I know had thought of *all that*. J. C., when I told him her apprehensions in figurative language, cited to me Lord Byron's "Siege of Ishmael" in *Don Juan,* where I would find the same kind of talk from the same kind of person.

Bragg does not supersede General Cooper, but is Mr. Davis's chief of staff.

Read "Jean Val Jean."[8] What a beastly little ingrate is Cosette. Genius can make a hero of a man who has dragged himself through all the sewers of Paris.

Reading *Adam Bede* again to measure the distance—up or down—to *Romola.*

Shopping:

30 dollars for a pair of gloves

50 for a pair of slippers

24 for six spools of thread

32 for five miserable, shabby, little pocket handkerchiefs—

---

6. Capt. John McAnerney of Ala., leader of Henley's battalion. Richmond newspapers mistakenly reported his name as "McElhenny" and M. B. C. repeated their error.

7. Alfred Hampton Preston, son of John S. and Caroline (Hampton) Preston, died in Italy in 1859.

8. The final part of *Les Misérables.*

When I came home, found Mrs. Webb. At her hospital there was a man who had been taken prisoner by Dahlgren's party. He saw the negro hung who had misled them—unintentionally, in all probability. He saw Dahlgren give a part of his bridle to hang him. Details are melancholy—as Emerson says. This Dahlgren had also lost a leg.[1]

In the afternoon came the cleverest woman in Richmond—and she does not know it. She is also very handsome. I mean Miss Nicholas.[2]

As I came home from escorting Miss Nicholas part of her way to Linden Row—met Maria Lewis. L. Q. Washington joined us. Told us of Muscoe Garnett's will and of Mary Stevens's ready acquiescence in it. His children he left to Mrs. Hunter's care, and they were to be educated at the South.

Mr. Washington described to us the fight of the department clerks. He is one of them. He saw no enemy. "It was pouring rain—cold and pitch-dark. Still, we were near enough to hear their words of command given distinctly. I fired my gun once." And he showed us a *Herald* which vaingloriously foretold all that Kilpatrick was going to do to Richmond. To sack it was the best word in their mouths, as the Irish say.

The man who sold the lion's skin that he was going to hunt &c&c&c.

Constance Cary, in words too fine for the occasion, described the homely scene at my house—how I prepared sandwiches for my husband and broke with trembling hand the last bottle of anything to drink in the house, a bottle I destined to go with the sandwiches. She called it a Hector and Andromache performance.

Telegram from Camden: "For God sake see if my son is ill." Son is a good soldier—father of the kind always in fits. Think of "for God sake" in a telegram. He is allied with the descendants of the pretender line of the Stuarts—ought to know better.

Mrs. Preston's story. As we walked home, she told me she had just been to see a lady she had known more than twenty years before. She met her in this wise—one of the chambermaids of the St. Charles Hotel, New Orleans, told Mrs. Preston's nurse—it was when Mary P was a baby—that up among the servants in the garret there was a sick lady and her children. She knew she was a lady, and she thought she was hiding from somebody. Mrs. P went up there, knew this lady, had her brought down into comfortable rooms, and nursed her until she recovered from her delirium and fever. She had, indeed, run away and was hiding herself and her children from a worthless husband. Now she has one son in a Yankee prison, one mortally wounded, and the last of them dying there, under her eyes, of consumption. This last had married here in Richmond—not wisely and too soon, for he is a mere boy, his pay as a private

1. Dahlgren had a leg amputated after Gettysburg in July 1863.
2. Elizabeth Byrd Nicholas, daughter of a former attorney general of Va., was prominent in the art and literary circles of Richmond.

eleven dollars a month. And his wife's family charged him three hundred dollars a month for her board. So he had to work double tides—odd jobs by night and by day—and so killed himself by exposure to cold in this bitter climate to which his constitution was unadapted.

They had been in Vicksburg during the siege and during the bombardment sought refuge in a cave. The roar of the cannon ceasing, they came out gladly for a breath of fresh air. At the moment they emerged, a bomb burst there—among them, so to speak—struck the son already wounded and smashed off the arm of a beautiful little grandchild not three years old. There was this poor little girl with her touchingly lovely face—and her arm gone. This mutilated little martyr, Mrs. P said, was really to her the crowning touch of the woman's affliction. Mrs. P put up her hand—"Her baby face haunts me."

March 11, 1864. Letters from home—one from J. C.'s father, now over ninety, written with his own hand and certainly his own mind still. I quote: "Bad times—worse coming. Starvation stares me in the face. Neither John nor James's[3] overseer will sell me any corn. I despise your Confederate government—it cheats."

Now what has the government to do with the fact that on all his plantations he made corn enough to last for the whole year, and by the end of January his negroes had stolen it all?

Poor old man, he has fallen on evil days after a long life of unbroken ease and prosperity. All other muscles are relaxed by age, but his grip on his gold is as firm as ever.

I do not believe Lamar. With *Adam Bede* fresh in my mind, I cannot believe the woman who wrote it "is a fallen woman"—"living in a happy state of high intellectual intercourse and happy, contented immorality." She could not be happy. Dinah and the retribution that overtook Hetty speak out that she knows good from evil.

Lamar heard all this of some other of those literary ladies.

Today read *Blithedale*.[4] *Blithedale* leaves such an unpleasant impression. I like pleasant, kindly stories now. We are so harrowed by real life.

Tragedy is for hours of ease.

J. C. wants me to read for him the case of a young man who was cashiered for writing a reconstruction article. This cashiered man favors return to the Union.

Enemy coming up James River.

3. Old Mr. Chesnut's nephews.
4. Nathaniel Hawthorne, *The Blithedale Romance* (1852).

Ransom sent them back howling from Suffolk.[5]

March 12, 1864.   Constance Cary went shopping with me. Prices worse than ever.

Found Buck in bed—Dr. Garnett there. She said, with a smile in her eye: "Write to Johnny. He was not here, and I have been percussed and auscultated, after all." Pointing to Dr. Garnett—"He would do it." Dr. Garnett—twirling himself lightly, with a decided look in the mirror as he turned our way:

"I pronounce her lungs all right. Nothing the matter with her." Twirling back again, with a second good look at himself in the glass. "Broad chest—noble specimen of physical woman—finest neck and shoulders I ever saw *in my life*, hand and arm to match, that is faultless. Nothing amiss with this girl. Mind worried, maybe, about something—or—or—or—*other*."

"Active campaign has begun everywhere," says M. P. in an aside to me. "She never talks. She is anxious. No doubt that is the matter with most of us. Kilpatrick still threatens us. Bragg has organized his fifteen hundred of cavalry to protect Richmond. Why can't J. C. be made colonel of that? It is a new regiment. No—he must be made a general."

"Now," says Mary P, "Dr. D is at the mercy of both Yankees and the rolling sea, and I am anxious enough—but instead of taking [to] my bed and worrying mama, I am taking stock of our worldly gear and trying to arrange for wedding paraphernalia for two girls."

Mr. and Mrs. Preston drive out together every afternoon of their lives. They have done so for thirty years or more. Yesterday they saw the antique spinster who dreaded Kilpatrick's and Dahlgren's ravishing raids. Mrs. Preston told him that I only answered "Fiddlesticks" to her tirade, and now they have put an oration in my mouth. He said: "Women who respect themselves will always be respected. Even those stories, those infernal tales of the treatment of their women in India which so maddened the Englishmen, have turned out mostly exaggerations. They were murdered in cold blood—*nothing worse*. 'Unbridled soldiery let loose' so far have found negro women to answer all their purposes. White women are safe. Even in New Orleans—so far."

There is lovemaking and loving making in this world. What a time the sweethearts of that wretch young Shakespeare must have had. What experiences of life's delights he must have had before he evolved the Romeo and Juliet business from his own internal consciousness—also that delicious Beatrice, Rosalind, &c&c&c. The poor creature that he left his second-best bedstead to came in second-best all the time, no doubt, and she hardly deserved more.

5. On March 9, at Suffolk, Va., Brig. Gen. Matthew Whitaker Ransom of N.C. fought a minor skirmish with a black Union cavalry unit on reconnaissance from Portsmouth, Va. A full-scale Federal expedition up the James was still two months away.

Fancy people wondering that Shakespeare and his kind leave no progeny like themselves. Shakespeare's children were half his only. The other half was only the second-best bedstead's. What could you expect of that commingling of materials? Goethe used his ladyloves as schoolbooks are used. He studied them from cover to cover—got all that could be gotten of self-culture and knowledge of human nature from the study of them—and then threw them aside as of no further account in his life. Byron never could forget Lord Byron, poet and peer—and mauvais sujet—and he must have been a trying lover—like talking to a man looking in the glass at himself. Lady Byron was as much taken up with herself, so they struck each other often and bounded apart.

My sister told me a story last night which would have annoyed my Lord more perhaps than Mrs. Stowe and Lady Byron's odious and disgusting imagination of his wickedness. For he posed a fiend in human shape—and after all was tender and kind-hearted. A solitary clerk in a country store asked my sister to lend him a book. He wanted something to read—the days were so long. "What style of book would you prefer?" "Poetry." "Any particular poet?" "*Brown* I hear much spoken of." "Brown*ing?*" "No, Brown—short—that is what they call him." "Byron, you mean." "No. I mean the poet Brown."

"Oh, you wish you had lived in the time of the Shakespeare creature."

"He knew all the forms and phases of true love. Straight to one's heart he goes. Tragedy or comedy—he never misses fire. He had been there (as the slang goes). No doubt the man's bare presence gave pleasure to the female world, and he saw them at their best. And he effaced himself. He told no tales of his own life. Compare old sad, solemn, sublime, sneering, snarling, faultfinding Milton. A man whose family doubtless found 'des absences délicieuses.' That phrase describes a type of man at a touch—took a Frenchwoman to do it."

"But there is an Italian picture of him, taken in his youth. And he was as beautiful as an angel."

"No doubt. But love flies before everlasting posing and preaching. The deadly requirement of a man, always to be looked up to. A domestic tyrant— guindé, formal, awfully learned. A mere man—for he could not do without women. When he tired out the first poor thing—who did not fall down and worship him, obey him, and see God *in him,* and she ran away—immediately he arranges his creed to take another wife. For wife he must have—à la Mohammedan creed. What the seer and prophet *wants* is the true morality."

The Deer Stealer never once thought of justifying theft because he loved venison and could not come by it lawfully.

Shakespeare was a better man—or may I say a purer soul—than self-upholding, Calvinistic, puritanic, king-killing Milton!

There is no muddling of right and wrong in Shakespeare—and no pharisaical stuff of any sort.

General Hood writes that he dines with General Joe Johnston very often and finds him cordial and kind.

"Oh, that's the game always," says Buck. "Then, when they find they cannot make an officer take sides against the president, they will abuse him as they do everybody who is a friend of Jeff Davis. You see, Hood will soon be sent to Coventry by the Joe Johnston clique."

Mrs. J writes she is glad to hear that the beautiful Miss Preston has accepted General Hood. She thinks it a capital match for both parties. Willie P showed us the letter.

"Oh," said B, "goodness gracious!" and then a long sigh. "Too smooth water. I see breakers ahead."

Went to see Mrs. E of the Treasury.[6] She related with an air of great amusement what she called the first truth ever told in Clarendon. A man said he would not go in the army for fear of being killed.

Then the lamentations of his mother-in-law: "To have him stay at home—an overseer of negroes—and to give as a reason that he is afraid!"

We admired this lady's delightful candor.

Hetty Cary dashed by us on horseback with her General Pegram. Generals galore. Franklin Street swarms with them. General Clingman stopped us. He was walking with a man. He waved his hand toward him—"*The* general, *you know*." We did not, however, but we did not say so.

Then George Deas joined us. Fresh from Mobile. There we left peace and plenty. Went to sixteen weddings—twenty-seven tea parties. For breakfast everything nice. There are acres there of those horrid beasts from which pork and sausages are made.

"Cows?" asked M. P. innocently. He scorned her sneer.

"Ah! Pigs—you know! Hogs."

"Is Mrs. _____ here?"

"Yes—faute de mieux. Faute de mieux. That is being interpreted, she cannot find a more convenient home just now."

Lily's fun is strong. She was describing a stuttering man's courtship. He would not care if his desired bride ma-ma-marred his joys in future, if only— but we laughed so much we did not hear the rest.

Then Lily told of what she had seen the day before at the Spotswood. She was in the small parlor, waiting for someone. In the large drawing room sat Hood—solitary, sad, with crutches by his chair. He could not see them. Mrs. Buckner came in, and her little girl spied Hood. And she bounded into the next room, sprang into his lap. He smoothed the little dress down and held her close. She clung round his neck for a while, then, seizing him by the beard, kissed him to an illimitable extent. The soldier and the child—evidently enraptured with each other. "Prettiest picture I ever saw," said Lily.

---

6. Probably Lily Elmore, who was the wife of the Confederate treasurer, Edward Carrington Elmore.

John Thompson sent me a New York *Herald* only three days old. Down on Kilpatrick for his miserable failure before Richmond. Also it acknowledges a defeat before Charleston and a victory for us in Florida.

General Grant is charmed with Sherman's successful movements—says he has destroyed millions upon millions of our property in Mississippi. Hope that may not be true. Hope Sherman may fail as Kilpatrick did.

Now, if we had still Stonewall or Albert Sidney Johnston where Joe Johnston and Polk are, I would not give a fig for Sherman's chances.

They say at last they have scared up a man who succeeds, and they expect him to remedy all that is gone. So they have made their brutal (*Suwarrow*) Grant lieutenant general.

Dr. Garnett at the Prestons' proposed to show me a man who was not F.F.V.

"Here he is in this house, and these people seem so fastidious, too—and they have such beautiful daughters, too. He is a low-born loafer, this fellow is."

When I told Buck of Dr. Garnett's annoyance at a black sheep having slipped into their fold (drawing room)—

"Between our folding doors, say. Well, well, until we came here we never heard of our social position. We do not know how to be rude to people who call. Dear Mrs. C, did you ever hear of your social position at home? No. I thought so. To talk of that sort of thing seems so vulgar. Down our way that sort of thing was settled beyond a peradventure, like—like the earth and the sky. We never gave it a thought. We talked to whom we pleased. And if they were not comme il faut, we were ever so much politer to the poor things. After all, what harm does he do? To save my life I cannot see a way to get rid of this man, without forgetting our manners. His manners are as good as anybody else's, and he talks ever so much better than most of these men who are F.F. to the core. And they say he is writing a book."

"Let him alone. He will soon fall out of place."

Dr. Garnett from that time desisted from further quixotic efforts to keep us clear of detrimentals or—so to speak—L.B.L.'s (low-born loafers).

Whenever Mr. Minnegerode falls short in his English—finds himself thinking in German, I daresay—he shouts his battle cry, "Oh, Lamb of God, I come!" He gave it to us so often today, I fear he knows we are in critical straits. So I told the president as we walked out of the pew. He had remarked how often and how excited that cry became. Finally Mr. Minnegerode had given us the whole hymn—not leaving out a word.

Somebody counted fourteen generals in church and suggested that less piety and more drilling of commands would suit the times better. There were Lee,

Longstreet, Morgan, Hoke,[7] Clingman, Whiting, Pegram, Elzey, Gordon,[8] Bragg.

Now that Dahlgren has failed to carry out his orders, the Yankees disown them. They disavow it all. He was not sent here to murder us all, hang the president, and burn the town. There is the notebook, however, at the executive office, with the orders to hang and burn.

Mr. Preston walked home with me, found J. C. had gone to see Melton[9] at the adjutant general's office. We sat on the marble steps to wait for him. Frank Parker[1] and Colonel Urquhart came, found us discussing the propriety of putting 20,000 negroes in the army.

"A heavy topic—for a 'meet me by moonlight alone' tête-à-tête—which you two seemed to be having out here."

"Respect our gray hairs," said J. C., as he came up, too.

March 15, 1864.   Mrs. Chesnut is dead.[2]

Gave 375 dollars for my mourning. Which consists of a black alpaca dress and a crape veil. Bonnet, gloves, and all, it came to ($500.00) five hundred. Before the blockade these things would not have been thought fit for a chambermaid.

Saw General Lee, Smith Lee, and Rooney go by. Met the general the other day. He spoke of Rooney.

"Poor boy, he is sadly cut up about the death of that sweet little wife of his."

"But we hope, " said Smith Lee more cheerfully, "that in a few days he will be brighter."

I said to Smith Lee, "I am afraid of the great general."

"How I wish broken glass could be as easily mended as widowers' hearts."

"Why?"

"Then I would not be left with only three glass tumblers."

Mrs. Grundy came in with a story of a negro woman who had killed her child.

---

7. Brig. Gen. Robert Frederick Hoke of N.C., who had compiled a distinguished record with the Army of Northern Va. before being wounded at Chancellorsville.

8. Either Brig. Gen. James Byron Gordon of N.C. or his cousin, Brig. Gen. John Brown Gordon of Ga.

9. Samuel Warren Melton, a S.C. College graduate who had served as an aide to Gens. G. W. Smith and P. G. T. Beauregard before becoming assistant adjutant general in Richmond.

1. Lt. Francis Simons Parker was an aide to Braxton Bragg and the son of a member of the S.C. secession convention. Like J. C., Parker and Urquhart were trying to resolve a dispute between Bragg and Beauregard over the transfer of troops from Charleston to Va.

2. Mary (Cox) Chesnut died on the fifteenth.

"You and the Prestons abhor slavery. I read my Bible, and I know it is sanctioned there."

"Look up there on the wall—Hagar and Ishmael—that is in the Bible!"

"No explicit denunciation of the patriarch in that case as there was of David and Bathsheba. But does not the Ten Commandments make *all* that impossible? And Christ's gospel of charity and love eliminates slavery—and a quantity of other sins which have lasted these 19 long years [i.e., centuries] in spite of his teaching and example."

Then we spoke of Mrs. Mason and Mrs. Child.[3]

"How could Mrs. Mason go and pit herself against that professional writer—apprenticed, hand-trained to the literary trade, &c&c?"

"Mrs. Mason is a Philadelphia woman. She was Miss Chew. For one thing, however, that fling of Mrs. Child: they aided mothers in their confinements but did not sell the babies when they were born. I daresay Mrs. Child had sold as many babies as Mrs. Mason. I know she had sold as many babies—or grown up, either—as we have ever done. But it is so easy, so cheap, that sort of railing."

"Mrs. Mason called her a hypocrite."

"That was in bad taste, *but* Mrs. Child's philanthropy paid in the sale of her books far better than Mrs. Mason's slave-owning."

"I like Thackeray's idea. You buy an elephant when you own slaves. It takes all you can do to find him—&c&c."

The negro had murdered the white child she was nursing—that is the story now.

Mrs. Davis took me to drive with her. We went to Laburnum to inquire of the Lyons's welfare since the fire.

It was really pitiful. Only a few days before, we had been there to see Mrs. Penn of Louisiana, Mrs. Lyons's sister, and found them all taking tea under those beautiful shade trees. And now—smoke and ashes—nothing more. There were crowds of friends there, so I did not get out of the carriage. They lost everything. Library filled with books and papers—&c&c. Even Mrs. Lyons's diamonds. Mr. Lyons, trying to save something, got a horrid fall and knocked out his front teeth.

It was the work of an incendiary. A few weeks before, they accused a negro of theft. He was put in jail and bailed out just in time to do this thing.

Everybody is in trouble, Mrs. Davis says. Money, paper money, has depreciated so in value, they cannot live within their income, so they are going to put down their carriage and horses.

3. In 1859, Mrs. James Murray Mason wrote a bitter letter to Lydia Maria Child, the abolitionist and novelist, to condemn her for supporting John Brown's raid on Harpers Ferry. Mrs. Child published the letter and her reply in *Correspondence Between L. M. Child and Gov. Wise and Mrs. Mason (of Virginia)* (1860).

When I got home General Hampton came with his troubles. Stuart had taken one of Hampton's brigades and given it to Fitz Lee. General H complained of this to General Lee—who told him curtly, "I would not care if you went back to South Carolina with your whole division."

Wade said his manner made this speech *immensely* mortifying.

While General Hampton was talking to me, the president sent for him. It seems General Lee has no patience with any personal complaints or grievances. He is all for the cause and cannot bear officers to come to him with any such matters as Wade Hampton came.

Have just read the much-talked-of Thompson Scott letter. That is, Pemberton's charges against Joe Johnston.[4]

> That here you maintain several factions,
> While a battle should be dispatched and fought,
> You are disputing of your generals.
> One would have lingering wars, with little cost,
> Another could fly swift with wings;
> A third man thinks without expense at all,
> By guileful words peace may be obtained.
>
> —Henry VI[5]

March 18, 1864.   Went to sell some of my colored dresses.

What a scene—such piles of rubbish—and mixed up with it all, such splendid Parisian silks and satins.

A mulatto woman kept the shop under the roof of an out-of-way old house. The ci-devant rich, the white ladies, sell to, and the negroes buy of, this woman.

Buck had a letter which she read as soon as it was handed to her. She blushed a good deal, laughed, twitched that beautiful little nose of hers, pinched the letter, and threw it in the fire. With a knowing nod: "This man is awfully in love with me." Then: "You know, R. L. heard, you know—" (Here her eyes opened wide.) "It happened oddly. He went to his tailor and chose a fine piece, Confederate gray, for a new uniform.

"'No, my dear sir. You can't have that. It is laid aside. General H asked us to keep that and our best stars for his wedding clothes.'"

After some whispering among us, she cried: "Don't waste your delicacy. Sally H is going to marry a man who has lost an arm—also a maimed soldier, you see—and she is proud of it. The cause glorifies such wounds."

4. While the facts of this letter are unknown, it apparently reflected John C. Pemberton's contention that Johnston, not he, was responsible for the surrender of Vicksburg and its Confederate garrison in 1863.

5. Slightly misquoted from *Henry VI, Part I*, act 1, scene 1.

Annie said meekly, "I fear it will be my fate to marry one who has lost his head."

"Tudy has her eye on one who has lost an eye. What a glorious assortment of noble martyrs and wrecks—heroes, I mean."

"The bitterness of this kind of talk is appalling."

"Better than Miss S, who is to marry a refugee Italian! Suppose we go wandering round the world, driven out by political persecution? You know we don't believe a word—exile Poles, exile anything, say. We, in our hearts, put them all down as imposters. Suppose we have to set out, some day, with a tale of wrongs. Nobody will credit us. And we will have to eat our 'bitter bread,' too."[6]

"We can hold our tongues."

"That is just what we can't do. We will be like Irish emigrants, but we can't write poetic laments. We will be base Poles and buy-a-broom girls, Hungarian brothers, and all that rubbish."

"Say what you will, people think all Italians organ grinders—or wonder where they hid the tray with little plaster casts of infant Samuels, Venuses, and Apollos."

"They are the best confectioners. Look at Pizzini! His nougat! Frenchmen are dancing masters &c."

General Lee had tears in his eyes when he spoke of his daughter-in-law just dead—that lovely little Charlotte Wickham, Mrs. Rooney Lee.

Mrs. Preston thinks Hampton had better ask to be sent to the Army of the West after General Lee's snub.

Johnny, Captain Chesnut, now that the summer is coming, has been ordered to the South Carolina coast (Sickly Swamp) to recruit.

Rooney Lee says Beast Butler was very kind to him while he was a prisoner. And the Beast has sent him back his war-horse. The Lees are men enough to speak the truth of friend or enemy, unfearing consequences.

March 19, 1864.   New experience. Molly and Laurence both gone home, and I am to be left, for the first time in my life, wholly at the mercy of hired servants.

Mr. Chesnut being in such deep mourning for his mother, we see no company.

I have a maid of all work.

Tudy came with an account of yesterday's trip to Petersburg. C. C.[7] raved of the golden ripples in Tudy's hair. Tudy vanished in a halo of glory, and C. C. gave me an account of the wedding as it was given to her by Major von Borcke.

"The bridesmaids were dressed in black, the bride in Confederate gray

---

6. The Preston family did become exiles in Paris after the war.
7. Constance Cary.

homespun. She had worn the dress all winter, but it had been washed and turned for the wedding. The female critics pronounced it 'flabby dabby.' They also said her collar was only 'net'—and she wore a cameo breastpin. Her bonnet was self-made." (By herself or itself?—which? Oh! only his German way of putting things.)

Whenever a foreigner marries here, the ill-natured begin at once to speculate on the probability of another wife left at home.

The bridegroom said: "My father-in-law *must* have money. After so many adventures he *must* cut up well." All this being interpreted, for his English is unintelligible.

C. C. also told of a new toy—Fitz Lee's new-found joy—a little negro boy. This toy, when wound up, danced Ethiopian minstrel fashion. Fitz Lee sings corn-shucking tunes and the toy boy dances. C. C. has already made the little black boy two suits of clothes. He is the delight of Richmond salons and is so much handled his dress soon grows shabby.

March 24, 1864.   Second account of the wedding. First, all hands were ready to answer muster roll in the lodger's parlor.

Seated there—and asserting her right to be there as a boarder and so having paid for her seat—sat a grim old Confederate dame engaged in some sort of intricate needlework. Her nose and chin well in the air and a disdainful sniff ever and anon, which meant:

"I am here in my own right. I dare you to try and turn me out, and I will see the wedding, will ye nill ye!"

Major von Borcke was asked to close the folding doors where an unpleasant crack was visible and behind which some giggling girls were seen and heard. He advanced his fine profile to obtain a glimpse of the enemy. The door was closed with a snap from behind. He hastily clapped his hand to his nose—it had barely escaped being snapped off.

The bride called for her opera cloak, and they brought her a red blanket shawl.

"Heavens! What a contretemps—but I will not keep you waiting." So she accepted the shawl and did not institute a further search for her opera cloak.

"One of the shifts of honest poverty."

"What do you mean?"

"That shawl scene."

The bishop looked pathetically at the bride—and then at the sleek foreigner in his shell jacket.

And then in plaintive accents (nasal, most of all):

"Till death do us part. Do you understand?" He would then take the bride-groom aside, as it were—and warn him. Nevermore in this world can you get rid of her. Nevermore. And then, in like manner, he would turn to the bride and try to hammer the same idea into her head. "For better, for worse," he will be on your hands—forevermore. The bride smiled enchantingly. She faced all these dangers gallantly—curls &c having given self-made bonnet a most defiant cock.

Apparently the bishop had succeeded in appalling the bridegroom, for he looked sulky and hung his head as he muttered. "I, Maria Joseph, Jesus, Lay-me-down-to-sleep (it sounded like that!), take thee, Virginia Melenda Carter Bird Page Nelson Harrison—&c&c." For the bride is an F.F. of the first water. And she stood her ground, with head erect and lips apart, and ran through the gamut of the two sets of names, responding joyously and with a light heart.

Bishop asked for the ring.

Bride, with a sweet smile: "Bishop, won't you bless it?"

"Put it on her finger," said the bishop emphatically.

Half-married lady: "Bishop, you do not understand him. He hesitates because he wants you to bless the ring." Said the bishop decidedly:

"Proceed with the ceremony. Maybe I will bless the ring another time."

General Morgan and his wife were there, and Colonel Alston, from whom I had these melancholy details.

Yesterday we went to the capitol grounds to see our returned prisoners. First Frank Huger[8] and Mr. Dobbin walked off with Tudy. Then Captain Roberts with Lily. Mary P said: "What shall we do, alone in this crowd?"

"Have faith!" and our faith was rewarded. The president joined us first, and then Mr. Mitchel, the Irish patriot.[9]

We walked slowly up and down until Jeff Davis was called upon to speak to the prisoners. Then I stood almost touching the bayonets, where he left me. I looked straight into the prisoners' faces. Poor fellows! They cheered with all their might—and I wept for sympathy, enthusiasm, and all that moved me deeply. Oh! these men were so forlorn, so dried up, shrunken, such a strange look in some of their eyes. Others so restless and wild looking—others again, placidly vacant, as if they had been dead to this world for years. A poor woman was too much for me. She was hunting her son. He had been expected back with this batch of prisoners. She said he was taken prisoner at Gettysburg. She kept going in and out among them, with a basket of provisions she had brought for him to eat. It was too pitiful. She was utterly unconscious of the crowd. The anxious dread—expectation—hurry and hope which led her on showed in her face.

The Lees were all there—stood in a group in full fig—Custis, Rooney, Robert, Chapman Leigh,[1] Mary, Agnes, Mildred.[2] Custis will be gazetted in a few days

8. A son of Benjamin Huger.

9. Transported by the English for sedition, Irish nationalist John Mitchel escaped from Van Diemen's Land in 1853 and came to the U.S. Mitchel became editor of the Richmond *Enquirer* in 1862, but his growing opposition to the Davis administration led him to resign from the paper at the end of 1863 and join the Richmond *Examiner*.

1. Probably Chapman Johnson Leigh, the son of the influential antebellum politician Benjamin Watkins Leigh.

2. Mildred Childe Lee, the general's eighteen-year-old daughter.

major general and put in command of Richmond. General Elzey has been made commander of the Marylanders—[*more than half a page cut out*].

"There's the bride!" cried an enfant terrible. "And she has the same net collar and camomile pill, mama says."

"What does it mean?"

"Cameo pin—breastpin, you know. Remember Colonel Alston's description of what the bride was dressed in?"

Johnny down here, on his way home.

Read Hood's letter to J. C.

"If a captain were to write such a letter, it would be called *flat;* but everything is permitted a lieutenant general."

Spiteful.

Buck got her daily letter—read it before his face, he said. She was all giggle, blush. Twitched her nose—stuffed the letter up her sleeve, as there was no fire.

"Oh, he is very angry. They should not have published his letter about 'old women in trousers.' "[3]

These Virginia haute volée names! Miss Page Waller married Captain Leigh Page the other day. Now she is Mrs. Page Page. Someone said she had turned over a new leaf—still, she was the same Page.

Paid one hundred and sixty dollars for having a shabby black alpaca made.

One day Mrs. Davis was there with us in the shop. The woman wanted to induce us to buy something very high priced.

"The officers' ladies buy them—always."

"Look here—see these things? She says our poor officers' wives buy them at any price she chooses to ask."

"No, I didn't. I said no such thing." (Tossing her head as she flounced away.) " 'Their wives,' indeed! I said 'their ladies'! *That's* a different thing."

C. C. came with a note she wanted J. C. to take to Burton Harrison, private secretary to his excellency the president. It snowed, and she stayed awhile. But the snow showed no signs of ever stopping, so she waltzed home with Johnny. He said they had to waltz to keep themselves from freezing.

He is here in deep mourning. Heard of the death of his grandmother.

Mr. Seddon offered J. C. a good place—Trans-Mississippi. I was fool enough to be miserable—thinking he would take it.

A sister of Mrs. Lincoln is here. She brings the freshest scandals from Yankee

3. In mid-March, Confederate newspapers printed excerpts from a private letter in which General Hood sought to reassure "some of the old women in trousers in our country" who had questioned whether he was healthy enough to command an army in the field.

land. She says she rode with Lovejoy. And a friend of hers commands a black regiment. Two Southern horrors, a black regiment—and Lovejoy.[4]

March 31, 1864.   My new English maid has come—Mrs. Bones. She says Lady I-forget-what called her Bones. Mrs. Joe Heyward, who brought her to this country, called her Charlotte. So I determined to call her so, too. She was too much of "a bag of bones" to adopt so suggestive a name as her patronymic.

———————

The foreigner's description of his vision, which he found verified in his bride, so often spoken of lately. He saw her first by dreams. As soon as he saw "dis lady mit de fair hair and mit de blue eye" he knew it was Miladi of his dreams. For her sake he became master of de fence. But no, never—Miladi would touch nothing short of a soldier. So to de army he must go. And all his laurels and his wreath of stars would be hers. He would "lie dem at her foot."

Met Preston Hampton. C. C. was with me. She showed her regard for him by taking his overcoat and leaving him in a drenching rain. What boyish nonsense he talked. Said he was in love with Miss Dabney[5] now, that his love was so hot within him that he was waterproof. The rain sizzed and smoked off. It did not so much as dampen his ardor or his clothes.

Preston Hampton's account of the picnic on the water.

It rained cats and dogs, and there was no intermission. A sharp March wind added its inclemencies. One girl fell down a ladder. (Companionway?) Several had their hoops blown over their heads—but were solaced by the fact of being sure of beautiful underclothes. Colonel Chestney[6] betook himself to a bunk and slept there. Afterward wondered why all of the others did not follow his example.

C. C. and Maggie pulled open a bureau drawer and sat there. Everybody was wet through and through, and in the stuffy, hot, close cabin they steamed as clothes do, hung out on a clothes line. And the men were like wet Newfoundland dogs—made to keep their distance. They danced round dances, however, their damp and draggled dresses flapping round their damper feet. Draggled and limp feathers, wet as the eyes they were forever falling over—&c&c. So vulgar it all was, so rowdy and so funny—I wish you could have seen!

———————

Custis Lee again has refused to jump over heads. The stride from a colonel to a major general he says is too much for him.

4. Mrs. Lincoln's half sister, Martha (Todd) White of Selma, Ala., passed through the lines in Dec. 1863 and visited Washington. She returned South without seeing Mrs. Lincoln but apparently did meet Owen Lovejoy, the abolitionist.

5. Probably Emmeline Dabney, daughter of Miss. planter Thomas Smith Dabney and sister of Virginius Dabney and Susan (Dabney) Smedes.

6. Col. Theodore Chestney, assistant adjutant general to Gen. Arnold Elzey.

John Taylor Wood has been given the steamer *Fredericksburg*.[7]

Read the life of Sir Samuel Romilly.[8]

April 1, 1864. Mrs. Davis utterly depressed. Said the [siege] of Richmond must come. She would send her children to me and to Mrs. Preston.

We begged her to come to us also.

J. C. as depressed as I ever knew him to be. He has felt the death of that angel mother of his keenly, and now he takes his country's woes to heart.

Dr. Garnett came in, and I blamed him for leaving that smallpox case in the president's yard.

"How light your attack is. How small your scolding. It falls feebly on my case-hardened ears. I have just seen a Mrs. Grant, who wished herself a man, that she might horsewhip me."

"Why?"

"Because I have sent her son back to the army—cured."

Bones went with me to the Prestons'. They had asked her to come "an' do their 'airs." We came back like monks of St. Bernard, wrapped in our waterproofs, with cowls over our heads, the wind whistling, snow blinding us as we struggled and slipped up on those Richmond hills of streets.

Poor Bones could not see the fun.

April 5, 1864. Record of the piety of the owners of my hired darky. They could not think of such a thing as letting her break the Sabbath by coming to me that holy day. She has three children, this black woman. Every day, that is, six days of the week, she gets the breakfast at home—for they are early birds—and then she comes to me and earns two dollars a day. Sundays Bones and I do our own work, or Bones works double tides. Fortunately, she does not mind.

Mrs. Preston wrote a note to J. C., asking him if he would take the place of general of reserve forces in South Carolina. He answered promptly, "Certainly—if it is offered to me."

Yesterday Mrs. Davis dined here. Bones did give us everything that was nice. Poor Bones. What would I give to take her home with me—but she holds up

---

7. Though the privateering exploits of John Taylor Wood had been much in the news, this was a false rumor.

8. The only biography of Sir Samuel Romilly, the English law reformer, was *Memoirs of the Life of Sir Samuel Romilly. . . . Edited by His Sons* (1840).

both hands. She has been in Clarendon, and her horror of South Carolina is great indeed.

April 11, 1864. Drive with Mrs. Davis and all her infant family. Wonderfully clever and precocious children—but unbroken wills. At one time there was a sudden uprising of the nursery contingent. They fought, screamed, laughed. It was Bedlam broke loose.

Mrs. Davis scolded, laughed, and cried.

She asked me if J. C. would speak to the president about that place in South Carolina, which everybody said suited him.

"No, Mrs. Davis."

"That is what I told Mr. Davis. Colonel C rides so high a horse—you and he will never come to an understanding. Now Browne is so much more practical; he goes to be general of conscripts in Georgia, and his wife will stay at the Cobbses'."

Mrs. Ould gave me a luncheon on Saturday. I feel this is my last sad farewell to Richmond and the people I love so well.

Mrs. Davis sent her carriage for me, and we went to the Oulds together. Such good things. Oranges, guava jelly, &c&c. The *Examiner* says Mr. Ould, when he goes to Fortress Monroe, replenishes his larder. Why not?

The *Examiner* took another fling at the president. Haughty and austere with his friends, affable, kind, subservient to his enemies (Yankees). I wonder if the Yankees would endorse that certificate. Both sides abuse him. He cannot please anybody, it seems.

No doubt he is right.

———————

John Thompson sent me a *Blackwood's*. With *Tony Butler*—and the *Perpetual Curate*.[9]

John Darby brought us from across the water *Rachel Ray*, *Eleanor's Victory*, and *Vincenzo*. Anything from Trollope is very welcome. And certainly anything from the author of *Dr. Antonio*.[1]

John Darby, who reads admirably, read aloud for us Orpheus C. Kerr's "New Year's Day." Mrs. Lincoln's ball and her half-mourning for Prince Albert.[2]

"The Captain, who looked like a bag of indigo which had gone out in a shower of rain without an umbrella. No—a shower of brass buttons. That is not half a bad idea, now, is it?" said John Darby, trying to adopt the English style.

9. This novel, published in book form in 1864, was one of the five volumes of Margaret Oliphant's *Chronicles of Carlingford*.

1. Anthony Trollope, *Rachel Ray* (1863), and Mary Elizabeth (Braddon) Maxwell, *Eleanor's Victory* (1863). Giovanni Ruffini was the anonymous author of *Doctor Antonio* (1855) and *Vincenzo; or, Sunken Rocks* (1863).

2. Robert Henry Newell, the author of *The Orpheus C. Kerr Papers* (1862–65), first published his humorous sketches of wartime Washington in the New York *Mercury*. M. B. C. probably heard letter 9, "Descriptive of the gorgeous fete at the White House, February 7, 1862." Kerr's invitation reads "Half-mourning for Prince Albert. No smoking aloud (*sic*)."

The garrison at Fort Pillow said to be put to the sword. Tell that to the marines![3]

Lincoln threatens to murder all of our prisoners by way of reprisal. If there are any marines more credulous than those you told the first story to, tell them this last.

Hoke has taken Fort Plymouth and has been made major general. Ransom is put in command of Richmond.[4] "Bully! for North Carolina!" they cry.

The female brigade of Memminger's Treasury Department has been moved to Columbia. That looks squally.

Willie Preston has not been promoted, he says, because he is with Johnston. Bragg says he is a junior major, and the senior majors must have the first showing.

J. C. is now brigadier general, and he is sent to South Carolina to organize and take command of the reserve troops.

C. C. Clay and L. Q. C. Lamar are both spoken of to fill the vacancy made among Mr. Davis's aides by J. C.'s promotion.

Willie Preston writes it is his war as well as Bragg's, and he will fight to the bitter end, promoted or not.

The *Examiner* cries, parodying the Mexican order of General Taylor, "A little more *brains*, Captain Bragg."[5]

Constance Cary sent me Madame Girardin's book.[6]

Went to Lucy Haxall's wedding.[7] Ours was a distinguished party as far as good looks are concerned, certainly. Captain Smith Lee was with me. He is handsome enough to bring up the average. Mary Preston and Major von Borcke, Tudy and Captain Frank Parker, Annie and Tom Ferguson, Maggie and Burton Harrison.

3. Of the 557 troops in the Fort Pillow garrison, 226 were black and only 58 were taken prisoner; but of the 295 whites, 168 were taken. The rest were either dead or in no condition to march. The shooting was clearly not "indiscriminate," and it was excessive. Some were shot attempting to surrender. Three days later Lincoln ordered an investigation. Grant wired Sherman: "If our men have been murdered after capture, retaliation must be resorted to promptly." Sherman investigated but did not recommend retaliation.

4. Brig. Gen. Robert Hoke captured Fort Plymouth, N.C., together with 2,800 Federal troops and a large quantity of supplies, on April 20; five days later, Maj. Gen. Robert Ransom of N.C. was assigned to command the Department of Richmond.

5. Facing a Mexican charge at the battle of Buena Vista in Feb. 1847, Zachary Taylor allegedly ordered Braxton Bragg, then a lieutenant of artillery, "Give them a little more grape, Mr. Bragg."

6. Any of several volumes of poems, short novels, and comedies written by Delphine Gay de Girardin (1804-59), a popular figure in European Romantic circles.

7. To Edward Coffey, thus the pun below.

Someone said they were to travel two months in the South before they sailed for Europe.

"So she will have her coffee parched, roasted, ground, before it settles."

Some people pushed and shoved us, so we gave way at once, thinking they had a better right to be there, probably were part of the affair. Suddenly Captain Smith Lee called my attention—a man with both elbows out, pushing and shoving, stopped to ask Captain Lee, "Whose wedding is it, anyhow?"

After that we held our ground. We were invited guests, at least.

The church windows were closed that it might be a candlelight wedding. A woman in the gallery had a cataleptic fit, and they were forced to open a window. Mixed daylight and gas was ghastly and greatly marred the effect below. The poor woman made a bleating noise like a goat. Buckets of water were handed over the heads of the people, as if it was a fire to be put out, and they dashed water over her as fast as the buckets came in reach. We watched the poor woman from below in agony, fearing she might die before our eyes. But no—far from it. The water cure answered. She came to herself, shook her dress, straightened up her wet feathers, and put her bonnet on quite composedly. Then watched the wedding with unabated interest—and I watched her. She fascinated me beyond any mere Captain Coffey and Lucy Haxall. For one thing, the poor woman could not have been gotten out of that jam, that crowd, unless, like the buckets of water, she had been handed out over the heads of the public.

April 27, 1864.   Today Captain Smith Lee spent the morning here. It was a review of the past—Washington gossip.

I am having such a busy, happy life—so many friends. And my friends are so clever, so charming.

And the change to that weary, dreary Camden! Mary P said: "I do think Mrs. C deserves to be canonized. She agrees to go back to Camden." Captain Chesnut gave me a snub.

"You, too—after all your jeers, you repeat things dull as ditch water because generals say them. And show letters flat as pancakes because lieutenant generals write them. I did not think it of you!"

Governor of North Carolina making a bolder bid for peace than even Joe Brown of Georgia has dared do yet.

The Prestons gave me a farewell dinner—my 24th wedding day.

The very pleasantest day I have spent in Richmond.

Maria Lewis was sitting with us on Mrs. Huger's steps, and Smith Lee was lauding Virginia people as usual. As he would say, "hove in sight," Frank Parker riding one of the finest of General Bragg's horses. By his side, Buck on Fairfax, the most beautiful horse in Richmond, his brown coat looking like satin, his proud neck arched, moving slowly, gracefully, calmly, no fidgets—aristocratic in his bearing to the tips of his bridle reins. There sat Buck, tall and fair, managing her horse with infinite ease, her English riding habit showing plainly the exquisite proportions of her figure.

"Supremely lovely," said Smith Lee.

"Look at them both," said I proudly. "Can you match those two in Virginia?"

"Three cheers for South Carolina!" was his answer. . . .[8]

《Custis Lee at our house. He hung his head in shame that he had never been out in a battle yet. As soon as J. C. came in, he stopped. They talk very much the same way, but J. C. has been in the hardest fought battles.》[9]

Examiner says today: "Grant at Chattanooga." Now, Joe Johnston, we say to you a word of warning such as James Fitz James received at the dreadful hug of Roderick Dhu.[1]

"Now, hold your own. *No maiden's* arm is round you thrown."

In South Carolina they received Wade Hampton with a grand ovation.

Today Hetty Cary greeted me with a kiss and congratulations on my husband's promotion as general of reserves.

8. Deleted is an obscure reference to an unidentified inscription in an unidentified book M. B. C. sent Buck.

9. Rough draft of the 1880s Version.

1. An allusion to Sir Walter Scott's *Lady of the Lake,* canto 5.

XXIV

"Blows Now Fall So Fast"

May 8, 1864. Mulberry. My friends crowded round me so those last days in Richmond, I forgot the affairs of my country utterly.

Though I showed my faith in my Confederate country by buying poor Bones's Confederate bonds. I gave her gold thimbles, bracelets, &c—whatever was gold galore and would sell in New York or London. . . .[1]

My friends in Richmond grieved so that I had to leave them—not half so much, however, as I did, that I must come away. Could not persuade my poor Bones, my best of ladies' maids, to come to Carolina. Clarendon experience had cured her once for all. "That black Carolina!" What a store she could carry to Mrs. Stowe! Her tales made my flesh creep. Faith stronger than money, for I bought her Memminger bond.

Bony and Monkey went together.[2] Betsey Monks, as she bade me goodbye, said: "I have always lived with tip-top people. These Prestons that I have lived with last are a tip-top family."

A bridegroom is reported to have fled with the bride's jewels. Camomile pin—and all.

Madame Coffey wrote from Petersburg—"Honeymoon. So nice, that long drive in the moonlight—married and still only lovers."

Grundy sniffed and pulled his moustache. "He is sixty—she a bride of forty."

"Antony and Cleopatra," said Miss Nicholas.

Those last weeks were so pleasant before the crash came. Poor little Joe.

No battle, no murder, no sudden death. All went merry as a marriage bell. Clever, cordial, kind, brave friends rallied around me.

But I must come to it.

Maggie and I went down the river to see an exchange of prisoners. Our party—Mrs. Buck Allen,[3] the Lees, Mallorys, Mrs. Ould.

One woman so pretty, I had seen her before at her home in the South. They say her husband beats her. Here we said, let us look at a creature who stays with a man after a beating.

---

1. Omitted are two letters from Constance Cary about Richmond social life.
2. Mrs. Bones and Betsey Monks.
3. Catherine (Jessup) Allen was the wife of William Allen, a Surry County, Va., planter. She was also known as Mrs. "Irish" Allen, to distinguish her from Louisa Allan—Mrs. "Scotch" Allan—whom M. B. C. had already met.

After listening to her for a while I went over to the husband's side. "Listen to the everlasting clack of that foolish tongue," moaned Dr. Covey.[4] "I don't blame the man. My God! No."

Another one said: "If I were a striking character, I might box her ears. On so slight an acquaintance—she irritates my nerves almost beyond endurance"....[5]

In all these years I have seen no Yankees. All the prisoners, well or wounded, have been Germans, Scotch regiments, Irish regiments—most German, however.

Now, on this Yankee vessel there was the genuine Yankee to be seen. Some little boys on board of her cried,

"Come here—come look at the cotton pickers."

And as our returned prisoners came on board, someone sung out, "We are so glad to see live rebels."

Amidst this crowd was a gentleman with whom I had exchanged letters, though I did not know him. A friend of mine whose fiancé was killed wanted her letters &c&c, and she was told this young officer had charge of them. I gave him her address. He said he would give them into her own hands.

One other showed me some wonderfully ingenious things he had made while a prisoner. He said they gave him rations for a week. He always devoured it in three days—he could not keep it—and then the gnawing agony of those inevitable four remaining days. I was listening with rapt attention when up stepped the beautiful one whose husband was said to have beaten her so soundly. She came smiling, chattering, overwhelming us with silly questions. She dispersed the crowd.

"Thrashed her? Certainly he did! Who would not?"

"On this side of the water, that is never done."

"Pshaw! You mean the free and independent American woman would not stand it. Such nonsensical drivel might drive a man mad."

Afterward some friends of Mrs. Mallory among the returned prisoners joined us. We sat on deck while the others went below to dinner, or supper—whatever the nondescript meal may be called. There was ice cream for all and to spare. They brought us up some.

These men told us that we could never understand the revulsion of feeling that simple change of vessels made—under one flag and then the other—on one side all enemies, now all friends. Most of them had been wounded. Some were maimed for life.

These were very cheerful. One man tapped another on the shoulder.

"Now old fellow, how *do* you feel?"

"Never was nearer crying in my life—for very weakness and comfort."

---

4. Edward N. Covey, a medical officer supervising the vaccination of troops in the Richmond area.

5. Unrelated anecdotes deleted.

The band was playing "Home Sweet Home."

Governor Cumming, a Georgian, late governor of Utah, was among the returned prisoners. He had been in prison two years.[6] His wife was with him.

He was a striking-looking person—huge and with snow-white hair, fat as a prize ox—no sign of Yankee barbarity or starvation about him.

And now the pleasant trip came to an end. As we walked up to Mrs. Davis's carriage—Dr. Garnett with Maggie, Major Hall with me—suddenly I heard her scream. And someone slipped back in the dark and said in a whisper, "Little Joe! He has killed himself!" I felt reeling—faint—bewildered.

The chattering woman clutched my arm.

"Mrs. Davis's son? Now, was he? Impossible? Who did you say? Was he an interesting child? How old was he?"

The shock was terrible, and enervated as I was, I cried,

"For God sake, take her away."

Then Maggie and I drove silently two long miles, broken only by Maggie's hysterical sobs. She was wild with terror, broken to her in that abrupt way at the carriage door. At first she thought it had all happened there and that poor little Joe was in the carriage.

Mr. Burton Harrison met us at the door of the house. Mrs. Semmes and Mrs. Barksdale[7] were there, too. Every window and door of the house seemed wide open—and the wind blowing the curtains. It was lit up, even in the third story.

We went in. As I sat in the drawing room, I could hear the tramp of Mr. Davis's step as he walked up and down the room above—not another sound. The whole house as silent as death.

It was then twelve o'clock, so I went home and waked Mr. Chesnut, who had gone to bed. We went immediately back to the president's. We found Mrs. Semmes still there. We saw no one but her, but we thought some friends of the family ought to be in the house.

Mrs. Semmes said when she got there, little Jeff was kneeling down by his brother. And he called out to her in great distress,

"Mrs. Semmes, I have said all the prayers I know how, but God will not wake Joe."

Poor little Joe, the good child of the family, so gentle and affectionate, he used to run in to say his prayers at his father's knee. Now he was laid out somewhere above us—crushed—killed. Mrs. Semmes said he fell from that high north piazza, upon a brick pavement.

Before I left the house I saw him lying there, white and beautiful as an angel—covered with flowers.

Catherine, his nurse, lying flat on the floor by his side, weeping and wailing as only an Irish woman can.

6. M. B. C. is confusing Alfred Cumming, territorial governor of Utah during the so-called Mormon War of 1857–58, with a nephew of the same name. The younger man held the rank of brigadier general, C.S.A., when he was captured at Vicksburg.

7. Elizabeth (Beirne) Barksdale was the wife of Randolph Barksdale, a Richmond physician who served on the staffs of Beauregard and Longstreet.

As I walked home met Mr. Reagan. He said he would go at once to the president's. I stopped to tell the Prestons. There I met Wade Hampton, who walked home with me. Even then! He told me again the story of his row with General Lee. I could see or hear nothing but little Joe and the brokenhearted mother and father. And Mr. Davis's step still sounded in my ear as he walked that floor the livelong night.

Immense crowd at the funeral. Sympathetic but shoving and pushing rudely, thousands of children. Each child had a green bough or a bunch of flowers to throw on little Joe's grave, which was already a mass of white flowers, crosses, &c&c.

The morning I came away from Mrs. Davis, early as it was, I met a little child with a handful of snowdrops. "Put these on little Joe," she said. "I knew him so well." And then she turned and fled without another word. I did not know who she was, then or now.

These people, the Davises, had enough to bear without calamity at home. And now it comes to the very quick.

We stayed one day longer then we expected, for the funeral. I was completely upset. Horror—grief—excitement—sympathy.

Capt. E. M. Boykin came one day before we left Richmond. Pleased at his promotion, glad that his company got to Virginia before Trenholm and Rutledge, who had their marching orders in advance of his, he said: "We Carolinians owe a great deal to Chesnut. He stays here, pushing our claims to promotion, watching out for us, seeing we are not overlooked."

"Yes, he is at it, night and day. And a thankless post it is, after all. You all believe that you rise by your own unaided merit, that you don't get half you deserve."

I ought to have said *Major* Boykin, for that was his step up the ladder. He is stout and jolly, radiant at being sent to the front, the very picture of a debonaire devil-may-care cavalier.

At home I found his wife the picture of love—pale, thin, sad, dispirited. Men must fight—and women weep.

"Separated so far—and he in such danger always."

General Lee was to have a grand review the very day we left Richmond, and quantities of people were to go up by rail to see it. Turner MacFarland writes, "They did go, but they came back faster than they went. They found the army drawn up in battle array."[8]

How many of the brave and gay spirits that we saw so lately have taken flight—the only flight they know—and their bodies left dead upon the battlefield.

---

8. At Gordonsville on April 29, General Lee reviewed the First Corps of the Confederate army, commanded by Longstreet. Three days later, Union troops under General Grant crossed the Rapidan River and, on May 5, the battle of the Wilderness began.

Poor old Edward Johnson—wounded again and a prisoner. Jones's brigade broke first; he was wounded the day before.[9]

At Wilmington we met General Whiting. He sent us to the station in his carriage and bestowed upon us a bottle of brandy which had run the blockade.

Now they say Beauregard has taken his sword from him! Never—I will not believe it. At the taking of Fort Sumter they said Whiting was the brains, Beauregard only the hand. Lucifer, Son of the Morning! How art thou fallen! That [they] should even say such a thing![1]

And we came home with Baron Münchausen, in the flesh.[2]

Ferdinand Mendes Pinto was but a type of thee—thou liar of the first magnitude![3]

And I thought, after four years of war, that I knew what men could do—swelling, repeating lying rumors, falsifying the half-time, exaggerating, depreciating, bragging!

They fight—but they crow. When it is all crow and no fight, it is more than one can bear. These are but the few, thank God!

There are the quiet gentlemen, the mob of gentlemen who went into the army because their country called. I believe one-half of them did not know or care why. The best and the bravest went first. They die—and make no sign.

At first we took Don Braggadocio[4] for an English gentleman we had seen somewhere. At least, J. C. thought he was Grenville. Was it?

The man spoke to him, and he introduced him to me. "No, you are mistaken. I am &c&c&c&c—not English at all—of French origin &c&c."

And it was not even amusing. Flat, lame lies, cruelly transparent. And I was not in the mood to have patience.

Dr. Covey was along. In the Judith and Holofernes scene just before we left Richmond, while the private theatrical mania was at its height, he had enacted the man with his head cut off. First he spoke of it as an oriental scene. Then it became fixed in his memory as a Turkish picture. "You see, she was in a Turkish dress and so was my head." Judith was holding his head, dripping with gore, just above a table through a hole in which it had emerged, but the deception was complete. At first a dead silence—then a feeble voice, as if remonstrating with her own terror:

9. Brig. Gen. John Marshall Jones, who served under General Johnson, was killed on May 5 at the Wilderness; Johnson himself was wounded and captured a week later, while defending the "Bloody Angle" at Spotsylvania.

1. An allusion to Isaiah 14:12. Maj. Gen. William Henry Chase Whiting, the Confederate commander at Wilmington, N.C., was transferred to the Petersburg, Va., area on May 13 and ordered to assist Beauregard's move against B. F. Butler. On the seventeenth, Whiting's failure to advance as ordered led to charges of drunkenness, denied by both Whiting and Beauregard. Soon after, Whiting returned to Wilmington at his own request.

2. Baron Karl von Münchausen, the eighteenth-century German cavalry officer who was considered the author of many well-known tall tales. A friend, Rudolph Erich Raspe, collected them in English as *Baron Münchausen's Narrative of His Marvellous Travels and Campaigns in Russia* (1785).

3. Fernão Mendes Pinto, the Portuguese traveler whose account of his experiences in Africa and Asia (published as *Peregrinação* in 1614), once dismissed as wholly fanciful, is now seen as simply exaggerated. The entire phrase is from William Congreve's play *Love for Love* (1695).

4. The vainglorious braggart who masquerades as a knight in *The Faerie Queene*, book 5, canto 3.

"Why! It's old Covey!"

On the train *I remonstrated* with him. "Doctor, Judith was not a houri, as you say. She was a Jewess."

"Nonsense! I ought to know. I acted with her, you know."

J. C. and the aforesaid Covey got out at Florence to procure for Mrs. General Miles a cup of coffee. They were slow about it, and they got left. I did not mind so very much, for I remembered we were to be all day at Kingsville and that J. C. would overtake me there by the next train. My maid belonged to the Prestons. She was only traveling home with me and would go straight on to Columbia. So without fear I stepped off at Kingsville. My old Confederate silk, like most Confederate dresses, had seen better days. And I noticed, like Oliver Wendell Holmes's famous shay, it had gone to pieces suddenly and all over.[5] It was literally in strips. I became painfully aware of my forlorn aspect when I asked the telegraph man the way to the hotel, and he was by no means respectful. I was a *lone* and not too respectable-looking old woman. It was my first appearance in the character, and I laughed aloud.

A very haughty and highly painted dame greeted me at the hotel.

"No room. Who are you?"

I gave my name.

"Try something else. Mrs. Chesnut don't travel round by herself, no servants, no nothing."

I looked down. There I was—dusty, tired, tattered, and torn.

"Where do you come from?"

"My home is in Camden."

"Come now, I know everybody in Camden."

I sat down meekly on a bench in the piazza that was free to all wayfarers.

"Which Mrs. Chesnut, I say?" (sharply) "I know both."

"I am now the only one. And now what is the matter with you? Do you take me for a spy? I know you perfectly well. I went to school with you at Miss Henrietta DeLeon's—and my name was Mary Miller."

"The Lord sakes alive—and to think you are her. Now I see—dear! dear me! Heaven sakes, woman, but you are broke!"

"And tore," I added, holding up my dress, "but I had no idea it was so difficult to effect an entry into a RR wayside hotel." And I picked up a long strip of my old black dress, torn off by a man's spur as I passed him getting off the train.

"Where are all your people?"

"My husband was accidentally left at Florence. He will be here in a few hours."

"Now, you know, you do look funny, that bright Balmoral petticoat grinning through all these tears, and you see we are 'bliged to be pertickler here—and respectable."

5. "The Deacon's Masterpiece; or, The Wonderful 'One-Hoss Shay'. A Logical Story," in *The Autocrat of the Breakfast-Table* (1858), tells of a carriage that fell to pieces all at once.

"You look like it," I *thought*, looking her straight in the face—and wiping my own.

"Molly and Laurence both went by a month ago. *They* said you'd an English lady for a maid. Where is she?"

"I never had a lady for a maid in my life."

"They said she was white as anybody. You know, lots come here, call themselves any name they think we know, and then slip away on a train and don't pay."

"Oh, that was it? I did not understand."

"Yes—we don't take in no imposters now. We mean to reform this house. No stray ladies with no servants and no protectors. But then, I made an awful mistake not to know you."

"It was not pleasant. At any rate, it is a new experience," said I coolly, but I was inwardly raging.

"Now, you just listen." She began a Sodom and Gomorrah story. I put both hands to my ears.

"Show me my room." Up stepped the valiant Captain DePass.

"Let me be of use to you. Let me look after your baggage." And he showed me how I could walk off at once to the Camden cars and stay in them till Mr. C came, as he would in time for the last Camden train.

"Thanks, thanks! Captain DePass to the rescue!" I cried, and all was well again.

J. C. did not join us until the trains met at Manchester. After hearing my adventures he was by no means proud of his performance—leaving me to contend with the "Specked Peach" alone. I said, "She told me she had not seen me for twenty years, but she met you constantly."

"God bless my soul, I never saw the woman in my life. She is the creature who caused the separation between old _____ and his wife."

"She says she means to reform the hotel at Kingsville."

"Reformatory, the very place for her."

"'Men are kittle cattle to shoe behind,' as the Scotch say. Remember that scene at the church door in Richmond?" The first Sunday after we went in last year—J. C. had been there without me all summer—as we turned a corner suddenly going to church, we met a very handsome woman—very handsomely dressed. She rushed up to J. C., both hands extended.

"So glad! Did not know you had come. When did you come? And you have not been to see me! &c&c."

I expected him to introduce me, but he said not a word—only continued to shake her hands.

"Who is it?" I asked as we walked.

"Don't know. Never saw the woman before in my life. She evidently took me for somebody else."

"Very odd!" The subject was renewed again and again until it became a screaming farce—but he stuck to his formula.

"Never saw the woman before in my life—took me for somebody else— explanations always a bore—so I let her have it all her own way."

"What a credulous fool you must take me to be." So on to the end of the chapter.

———————

Sad enough at Mulberry without Mrs. Chesnut, who was the good genius of the place. It is so lovely here in spring—the giants of the forest, the primeval oaks, water oaks, live oaks, willow oaks, such as I have not seen since I left here. Popinacs, violets, roses, yellow jasmine—the air is laden with perfume. Araby the blest was never sweeter.

Inside, creature comforts of all kinds—green peas, strawberries, asparagus, spring lamb, spring chickens, fresh eggs, rich yellow butter, clean white linen for one's beds, dazzling white damask for one's table. Such a contrast to Richmond—where I wish I was.

John Chesnut ill here. Rode at a tournament in Columbia—crowned Nathalie Heyward queen of love and beauty.[6] Came home and took [to] his bed.

And there sits J. C. by his bedside, and they talk from morn to dewy eve. Horse, horse, horse. Never have I heard either of them mention the war from which they came a few days back. John is one of the silent heroes. To be, to do, to suffer—he is prompt to take his place in front, and then has never a word to say about it.

There is a queer coalition here—Uncle Hamilton, John Manning, Judge Withers—joined in unnatural bonds by hatred of Jeff Davis.

Fighting going on. Hampton frantic, for his laggard new regiments fall in slowly. No fault of the soldiers. They are as disgusted as he is. Bragg—Bragg, the head of the War Office—cannot organize in time.

John Boykin died in a Yankee prison. He had on a heavy flannel shirt. They were lying on an open platform car, on their way to their cold prison on the lakes. A Federal soldier wanted this shirt. Prisoners have no right, so John had to strip it off and hand it to him. So that was his death. In two days he was dead of pneumonia. Maybe frozen to death.

One man said, "They are taking us there to freeze." But then their men will find our hot sun in August and July as deadly as their cold Decembers &c&c are to us. Their snow and ice finish our prisoners at a rapid rate, they say. Napoleon's soldiers found out all that in the Russian campaign.

Met our lovely relative, the woman who might have sat for Eva's mother in *Uncle Tom's Cabin*. Beautifully dressed, graceful, languid, making eyes at all comers. Softly and in dulcet accents regretting the necessity she labored under, to send out a sable Topsy who looked shining and happy—quand même—to

———

6. Nathalie was the daughter of Barny Heyward's brother Nathaniel, a Combahee River planter.

her sabler parent, to be switched for some misdemeanor—which I declined to hear as I fled in my haste.

Bring my houseless, homeless friends who are refugees here to luxuriate in Mulberry's plenty—strawberries, green peas, &c&c. I can but remember the lavish kindness of the Virginia people when I was there and in a similar condition. The Virginia people do the rarest acts of hospitality and never seem to know it is not the ordinary course of events.

The president's man Stephen came with the Arabian. He said: "Why, Missis, your niggers down here are well off. I call this Mulberry place heaven. Plenty to eat, little to do, warm house to sleep in, good church, good preacher—all here, right at hand."

———

The dreadful work of death is beginning again.
John L. Miller, my cousin, killed at the head of his regiment.[7]
The blows now fall so fast on our heads it is bewildering.

———

Rev. Stephen Elliott preached in our negro church Sunday afternoon. Thin congregation. "Takes a Methodist to fetch 'em."

A capital sermon. It made me cry, and I have no gift that way. Laughing is my forte.

———

Secretary of war authorizes General Chesnut to reorganize men who have been hitherto detailed for special duty and also those who have been exempt. He says General Chesnut originated the plan and organized the corps of clerks which saved Richmond in the Dalhgren raid.

John Witherspoon says [the] president did wrong once when he did not arrest Joe Johnston before Seven Pines. Our Xenophon was then in full retreat *through* Richmond. But Virginia would not have it. "If you cannot defend our Capitol, we will." General Lee then arrested the progress of retreating tactics. Now every newspaper (except some Georgia ones) in the Confederacy is busy as a bee, excusing Joe Johnston's retreats. He gives up one after another of those mountain passes where one must think he could fight and is hastening down to the plain.

"Yes," says John W, growing red with suppressed fury. "If the president had sent him then out of the Confederacy—sent him to Sherman and McClellan, who admire him so much—he would have saved us, in all probability. For Joe Johnston's disaffection has been the core round which all restless halfhearted disappointed people consolidated, and Joe Johnston's dissatisfaction with our

———

7. M. B. C.'s thirty-three-year-old first cousin John Lucas Miller of York District had left a promising career as a lawyer, editor, and state legislator to become colonel of the Twelfth S.C. Regiment.

president and our policy has acted like a dry rot in our armies. It has served as an excuse for all selfishness, stay-at-home-ativeness, all languid patriotism. A man who begins to snarl and sneer and quarrel at the very beginning because he is not put ahead of General Lee! Could conceit and folly go further?"

"Now," said John, after this, for him, long speech, "Did you ever see Joe Johnston and the president together?"

"No, and I rarely see anybody but Joe Johnston's friends. You see, I am a woman and not in the army. Stay-at-homers all for Joe Johnston. But I did see Mr. and Mrs. Davis with their "dear Lydia" at the Spotswood. And I firmly believe if he could have promoted Joe Johnston consistently with his duty to his country, he would have done so. They were so devoted to Mrs. Johnston and to her Joseph.

"I do not know how the split began. They were as intimate and as affectionate as people could be, when I left them."

"I'll tell you. He made Joe Johnston a dissatisfied general when he refused to make him *No. 1* in the Confederate army. To begin a row about himself and his promotion at such a time—such preposterous self-sufficiency!"

"You and Mr. Theo Stark are the hottest defenders of Mr. Davis I know."

"Jack Preston says his mother and myself are the warmest admirers of the president that he knows."

"This breach has been ruinous. They got Wigfall at last, though he fought manfully against the row at first."[8]

May 27, 1864. ⟪Had a letter from Buck. She hears from "mon général," and she writes him not so often. At first, she says, it was a letter of thirty pages. Now she rarely hears more than one a month. He is so busy.⟫[9]

Mrs. Phil Stockton has named her baby Lydia for Mrs. Johnston. She loves the fair Lydia, and this is the litany day and night that she chants—how clever Mrs. J is, how amusing, how kind. General J did not quarrel on a personal tiff. He has not turned all to malice and spite. He has so many noble qualities. Bravest of the brave (who denies that?). He has above all men the art to make friends. He has on his staff a noble band of men who can write. It is impossible but that offenses must come, and these men can turn everything against the president in the papers."

Says John, with a bitter chuckle: "Old hard-sense Lincoln, the essence of a cute[1] Yankee, says, don't swap horses crossing a stream. In battering down our administration, these people are destroying our last hope of success."

"Now, John, in all this beautiful sunshine, in the stillness and shade of these long hours in this piazza, all comes back to me—it haunts me. In Richmond it all seemed confusion madness! A bad dream!"

8. Wigfall's long private feud with President Davis had been public knowledge since Jan., when Wigfall began attacking the president on the floor of the Confederate Senate.

9. From the rough draft of the 1880s Version.

1. "Cute" was then closer in meaning to "acute."

Here I see that funeral procession as it wound among those tall white monuments up that hillside. The James River tumbling about below, over rocks and around islands.

The dominant figure, that poor old gray-haired man. Standing bareheaded, straight as an arrow, clear against the sky by the open grave of his son. She stood back in her heavy black wrappings, and her tall figure drooped. The flowers, the children, the procession as it moved, comes and goes. But these two dark, sorrow-stricken figures stand—they rise before me now.

That night, with no sound but the heavy tramp of his foot overhead, the curtains flapping in the wind, the gas flaring, I was numb—stupid—half-dead with grief and terror. Then Catherine's Irish howl. Cheap—that. Where was she, when it all happened? Her place was to have been with the child. Who saw him fall?

Who will they kill next, of that devoted household?

———————————

Read today the list of killed and wounded. One long column was not enough for South Carolina's dead.

I see Mr. Federal Secretary Stanton[2] says he can reinforce Suwarrow Grant at his leisure—whenever he calls for more. He has just sent him 25,000 veterans.

Old Lincoln says, in his quaint backwoods way, "Keep a-peggin'." Now we can only peg out. What have we left of men &c&c to meet these—"reinforce as often as reinforcements are called for."

Our fighting men have all gone to the front. Only old men and little boys at home now. And the Joe Johnston disaffection eating into the very vitals of our distracted country.

Mrs. Phil Stockton has it from the Canteys that the president's personal abuse of John Manning alienated him![3]

Why? Does Mr. Davis know John Manning? He is handsome beyond measure, clever, and all the rest of it moderately enough—politically and socially of consequence somewhat in South Carolina. I doubt if Mr. Davis thought of John Manning twice, except as part and parcel of Beauregard's useless and superb staff. But it was the regular thing at the Spotswood to tell people that Mr. and Mrs. Davis said dreadful things of them when Mr. and Mrs. Davis hardly knew of the persons so abused at all.

Judge Withers says, "Jeff Davis drinks!"

"No, he is an austere man, quiet, grave, devoted to his work, without a vice in the world."

"Oh! he don't drink then. I daresay he takes opium, for his brain is obfuscated!"

Words are wasted on them. They have made Jeff Davis their scapegoat.

———————————

2. Edwin McMasters Stanton, the secretary of war.

3. The family of Camilla (Richardson) Cantey of Camden was related to both the Stocktons and the Mannings.

For their sins he is tied to the altar. We made the altar or burning bush—whatever that goat has to come out of.

———————

It is impossible to sleep here because it is so solemn and still. The moonlight shines in my window, sad and white.

And the wind, the soft south wind, literally comes over a bank of violets, lilacs, roses, orange blossoms, and magnolia flowers thrown in.

———————

Mrs. Chesnut was only a year younger than her husband—he is ninety-two or three. She was deaf. He retains his senses wonderfully for his great age.

I have always been an early riser. Formerly I often saw him, sauntering slowly down the broad passage from his room to hers, in a flowing flannel dressing gown when it was winter. In the spring he was apt to be in shirtsleeves, with suspenders hanging down his back. He had always a large hairbrush in his hand.

He would take his stand on the rug before the fire in her room, brushing scant locks which were shining fleecy white. Her maid would be doing hers, which were dead-leaf brown—not a white hair in her head. He had the voice of a stentor. And there he stood, roaring his morning compliments. The people who occupied the rooms above said he fairly shook the window glasses. This pleasant morning greeting and ceremony was never omitted.

Her voice was "low and sweet" (the oft quoted). Philadelphia seems to have lost the art of sending forth such now. Mrs. Binney, Mrs. Chesnut's sister,[4] came among us with the same softly modulated, womanly, musical voice. Her clever and beautiful daughters were *criard.* Judge Hare said, "Philadelphia women scream like macaws."

This morning, as I passed Mrs. C's room, the door stood wide open. And I heard a pitiful sound. The old man was kneeling by her empty bedside, sobbing bitterly.

I fled down the middle walk—anywhere out of reach of what was never meant for me to hear.

———————

I was telling them today of a woman who came to Mrs. Davis in Richmond, hoping to get her help. She wanted her husband's pardon. She was shabbily dressed, chalk white and pinched in her face. She spoke very good English. And there was an attempt to be dressed up, apparent in all her forlorn clothes—knots of ribbon, rusty artificial flowers, and draggled feathers in her old hat. Her hands hung listlessly down by her side. She was strong, and her way of

———————

4. Elizabeth (Cox) Binney, wife of the Philadelphia lawyer, was old Mrs. Chesnut's youngest sister.

telling her story was hard and cold enough. She told it simply, but over and over again, with slight variations as to words—never as to facts.

She seemed afraid we would forget.

The army had to pass so near her. Poor little Susie had just died, and the boy was ailing. Food was so scarce and so bad. They all had chills. She was so miserable. The negroes had all gone to the Yankees. There was nobody to cut wood, and it was so cold. They were coming so near. "I wrote—and I wrote—if you want to see the baby alive, come. If they won't let you—come anyhow. *You see, I did it*—if he is a deserter.

"He said they would not let him come. Only colonels and generals can get furloughs now. He only intended to stay one day, but we coaxed and begged him, and then he stayed and stayed, and he was afraid afterward to go back. He did not mean to be a coward nor to desert. So he went on the gunboats on the river, to serve there. And then some of his old officers saw him. And they would not believe his story. I do not know if he told them anything. He does not talk much any time. They are going to shoot him. I would not let him alone. You see, I did it. *Don't you see?"*

Mrs. Davis was gone ever so long. And the stiff, cold woman, white as wall, sat there and told it to me many times. I wanted to go home, but she clutched me. "You stay—you are sorry for me."

"Yes, I am the friend of that hard-driven soldier."

Mrs. Davis came in, smiling.

"Here it is—all that you want."

The creature stood straight up—then fell down on the sofa pillow, sobbing as if soul and body would come asunder. So I fled—rather blind myself.

Now, this is a beautiful outlook from my window—calves and sheep peacefully browsing on the deep green grassy lawn. As if there was not a butcher or a Yankee in the world. Nor a slave—nor a slave-owner.

They asked for a description of the man I call Ferdinand Mendes Pinto—as a liar of the greatest magnitude that I have *met yet.* And for three years we have been familiar with the "reliable gentleman on horseback—just come in from the lines"—and the less reliable who came afoot and brought as astounding news by night and by day. You see, it began by J. C. taking him for an English baronet whom he had met somewhere at dinner only a few days before. When he began to tell lies too much for human credence, I appealed helplessly to J. C.

"He is a consummate braggart &c&c."

"It looks so, certainly," he answered dubiously, for he clung to his English theory, and they are expected to speak the truth.

Finally the true state of things came out. F. M. P. had no idea of concealing it. He was a baker or a barber in New Orleans. "A base mechanical," he called himself.

He was tall and stout and had a genuine John Bull complexion. His English was peculiar, but then *we* supposed that all right, as our English was only American. And he was a Louisiana Creole, after all. Now when Mrs. Davis sent J. C. to bring me to the president's, where the marquis of Hartington and his party were, and he would not—afterward accounting for his laziness by saying "running after English noblemen was so snobbish" and telling me Lincoln's savoir faire. When the aforesaid marquis of Hartington was presented at the Federal drawing room, Mr. President Abe said affably, "Any relation to Mrs. Partingdon?[5] Your names rhyme—&c&c. Such fun, eh?" Now he was inclined to make up his shortcomings to this suppositious baronet, who was so tall and straight, florid and with bright blue eyes, splendid eyes indeed, muttonchop whiskers.

"No. His whiskers were trimmed like a French marshal's."

He was no phlegmatic Britisher. That we saw from the first. For this splendid specimen of the physical man received our unexpected civility with exuberant rapture. And he soon made it manifest that he thought New Orleans, Louisiana, the center of the world.

How was he dressed? "Gaily—rich red and yellow cravat, blue broadcloth coat, brass buttons, trousers with the widest stripes. But then, the Englishmen we saw in Richmond were proverbially eccentric in dress. He clove to us as Ruth did to Naomi and would not be shaken off. Never in his life, he said, had he been met—when he made advances—with such friendly courtesy. (Shade of Sir Somebody Something, forgive us?) So he fell *down* and worshiped us. His romances, treated as pure fiction, were entertaining. Luncheon he had and to spare—edibles and wine beyond our wildest imagination.

So, as he was firm and resolute not to be separated from our party until a ruthless RR schedule did it, we made the best of our blunder.

June 1, 1864.   Back to Bloomsbury. William Kirkland wounded. A scene there—Mary weeping bitterly, Aunt B frantic as to Tanny's danger.

I proposed to make arrangements for Mary to go on at once. The Judge took me aside, frowning angrily.

"You are unwise to talk in that way. She can neither take her infant nor leave it. The cars are closed, by order of the government, to all but soldiers."

I told him of the woman who, when the conductor said she could not go, cried at the top of her voice,

"Soldiers, I want to go to Richmond to nurse my wounded husband."

In a moment twenty men made themselves her bodyguard, and she went on unmolested.

The Judge said I talked nonsense. I said I would go on in my carriage, if needs be. Besides there would be no difficulty in getting her a "permit."

---

5. A popular character, known for her sayings, created by Mass. journalist Benjamin Penhallow Shillaber (1814–90).

He answered hotly—in no case would he let her go and that I had better *not* go back into the house. We were in the piazza, and my carriage at the door. I took it and crossed over to see Mary Boykin.[6] She was weeping, too, so washed away with tears one would hardly know her. "So many killed—my son and my husband—I do not hear a word from them."

At Bloomsbury, found Armsted waiting for me, a most unpleasant scene. He refuses to go to Columbia.

"Very queer doings, Missis. When you let me learn to be a shoemaker, I thought I was done with being your house servant. Now you want to take me away from my shoeshop—&c&c&c."

Mr. C thought his impudence intolerable, and said he should go with me and resume his place as my butler when I went to housekeeping in Columbia.

"Never, never. Dissatisfied servants are not to my taste. I hope never to see Armsted's face again in this world."

Next day Armsted sent me a nice pair of shoes as a present.

Mr. C asked, "After all, what did you say to him yesterday?"

"I told him he was an ungrateful wretch and to keep to his trade. I had had enough of his disagreeable airs."

"And that pair of cloth shoes ends the chapter."

June 2, 1864.   At Miss McEwen's, met the telegraph operator John Wither-spoon,[7] grandson of the signer, president of Princeton College, and all that. The telegraph office exactly opposite Miss McEwen's, the milliner's. John Wither-spoon with the long pedigree is her brother-in-law. As soon as a carriage drives up, he dashes over with the news. Priscilla Perkins said John Witherspoon has fairly fattened on news. The latest is that William Kirkland is doing well. The MacFarlands have him at their house.

Mary is having dresses made and getting ready to go on to Virginia. Today she pitched into the president for his conduct to Joe Johnston. What has Mr. Davis done to Joe Johnston—given him command of army no. 2? He gave General Lee army no. 1. Who blames him for that? The quarrel between Joe Johnston and Mr. Davis is that General Lee outranks Joe Johnston. Hence these sulks.

Gone today for 2 lbs. of tea, 40 lbs. of coffee, and 60 lbs. of sugar—800 dollars.

Then came Mrs. Reynolds. Emma Bradley's quaint marriage. She is two years older than I am—not my idea of a bride—forty-two if she is a day. She was alone in that large old house. And married there all by herself Sebastian Sumter,[8]

6. Mrs. Edward Boykin.
7. John Knox Witherspoon, the brother of Susan Kollock (Witherspoon) McDowell and a distant relation of M. B. C.'s cousin John Witherspoon.
8. Sebastian d'Amblimont Sumter, a planter of Sumter District, was the brother of Paul Thomas DeLage and Francis Brasilimo Sumter.

who ran away from the army long enough for that. Her family is scattered everywhere.

Wonder where Ellen has wandered off into space. I saw her last, seated on a box at Kingsville, with a peacock fly brush in her hand, exactly in the attitude of the goddess of liberty on the silver quarters of dollars. She has been engaged off and on to Ransom Spann for thirty years. I mean twenty. She may sing:

> My life thou knowest but a span,
> A cipher seems past years—
> And every man, in best estate,
> To me, but Vanity appears.

June 4, 1864.   Mary Boykin's bitter weeping was prophetic. Major Edward Boykin wounded in the knee. They hope he can be brought home. She was trying to be satisfied that it was no worse. But then: "Why does he not mention my son Tom? He might say in the telegram Tom is safe—don't you think?"

Poor Aunt B so unreasonable.

"Why did you send Munro and not let us know?"

"Who is interested in Mr. K, out of this house?"

"Mary B thought it unneighborly in you. Her husband is wounded in Richmond, too."

Then she began arraigning Providence.

"What good was a victory? And we were all heartbroken." After all, nobody had trouble as her household had it. There was Doctor B—only a flesh wound in his knee. Besides, there were all those fat things in good, comfortable, *safe* offices, and her *all* before the enemies' guns."

"Well, nobody of mine is either fat or in a comfortable office. Anything more uncomfortable than my husband's positions since the war began one could hardly conceive—badgered by friend and foe."

> Did I propose to embark with thee
> On the smooth surface of a summer sea
> While gentle zephyrs play with prosperous gales.
> And fortune's favours fill the swelling sails—
> But would forsake the ship and make the shore,
> When the winds whistle and the tempests roar.

Poor old Confederacy of my heart—desert thee, never. See Micawber.[9]

One illustration in *Orpheus C. Kerr* was good. Mr. Davis, seated in the middle of a highway with a pile of stones which he was in the act of throwing at all comers and crying aloud at the same time, "All that I want is to be let alone."[1]

Now, it seems to me that is all that the Confederacy wants.

How soon would we cease to throw stones if they would let us alone?

---

9. At every new crisis, Emma Micawber, wife of the feckless Wilkins Micawber in Charles Dickens's *David Copperfield* (1850), repeats that she will never leave her husband.

1. A reference to Davis's inaugural address of 1861: "All we ask is to be let alone."

Now I like this:

A New York paper speaks of General Lee as *our representative man.*

What more could we ask? But then this wiseacre goes on to say General Lee is as base a liar as Beauregard.

Beauregard is a gentleman and was a genius as long as Whiting did his engineering. He, our Creole general, is not quite so clever as he thinks himself. Of late they say he has fallen into a green sickness—melancholia. He is overlooked, too, but does not rave and growl and roar as doth the great Joe.

Mary Ford[2] writes for schoolbooks for her boys. She is in great distress on that subject. When Longstreet's corps passed through Greenville, there was great enthusiasm—handkerchief waves, bouquets, and flowers were thrown regardless, and in their excitement her boys, having nothing else, threw the soldiers their schoolbooks. That is a mother's laughing complaint of her boys.

A wife's story. Mr. Bailey came into the Confederacy under a cloud—that Floyd business, you know—and so on—&c&c.

Mr. B told me today that Joe Kershaw made it a point with the president.

"Unless John Kennedy is made colonel in my place, I will not be made general."

There was a disinterested affection for you. When I saw him, however, in Richmond, he did not say John Kennedy once. He was pushing his own promotion, even to the point of being polite to me. And as the Christians say, it was his own soul he wanted to save. I heard of nobody else's.[3]

Two grandfathers:

Aunt B says Jane J wrote to her children's grandfather that she had taught her children to pray to God to punish him as he deserved to be. Says Aunt B, there is a depth of hatred in that beyond my wildest imaginings.

Then poor Mr. Murray was too candid by far and was frowned down. In spite of cowering faces he answered these questions.

"How do my grandsons look?"

"Oh, they look well enough. One has spent a fortune in substitutes. Two have been taken from him, and two he paid to change with him when he was even ordered to the front. He is at the end of his row now. All able-bodied men are ordered to the front. I hear he is going as some general's courier."

---

2. Mary Mazyck (Hume) Ford was the wife of Frederick Wentworth Ford, a wealthy rice planter of Georgetown District.

3. John Doby Kennedy followed Kershaw up the promotional ladder and assumed command of Kershaw's brigade in the spring of 1864. Six months later, at the age of twenty-four, Kennedy became one of the Confederacy's youngest brigadier generals.

XXV

"Is Anything Worth It?"

[**June 4, 1864, continued.**]   Columbia once more—and at the Prestons. Brewster here. He treats Buck as his queen, swears allegiance to her &c. Today at dinner, to J. C.:

"What are Miss Isabella's habits?"

"Very good, I believe," answered J. C. gravely.

"I mean, does she take her siesta before or after dinner? I want to call there this [*page torn*]. Most Southern girls take [*rest of page torn out*].

He said Joe Johnston was kept from fighting at Dalton by no plan—by no strategy.[1] It was his best stand, and he missed it. "What is the matter with him? Overcautious."

Hood and Polk wanted to fight. He resisted their council. It is said he is afraid to trust them because they do not hate Jeff Davis enough—maybe at all—and all this delay is breaking Hood's heart. Hood's is the reserved corps. So much retreating would demoralize General Lee's army.

"Hood's Texians?"

"Yes, even Texians. Retreating kills out all fire. Oh! for an hour of Stonewall! The reckless old Puritan. We want a hardened fellow who does not value men's lives—only wants to beat Suwarrow Grant and to shunt Sherman aside. Johnston is jealous of the favor shown Hood at Richmond. He hates everybody that Jeff Davis likes."

He also described Hood's baptism. Being a Catholic, he found it anything but solemn or touching—as the newspapers had represented it. "There stood the battered old hero (barely thirty years old). There the Warrior Bishop Polk. And there stood your humble servant, with a flaring tallow candle in one hand and a horse bucket of water in the other. You must always put me in the picture."

One night at Mrs. Preston's—it was a long heavy rain, a regular tropical downpour. It had rained for hours and showed no signs of ever stopping.

When I came down I found two strangers seated on one of those leather sofas near the front door, which was open wide, the broad piazza keeping the rain out. Nobody said who they were. One had on a surgeon's uniform. Also I noticed pools of water on the carpet which had dripped from their saturated

---

1. When Sherman's army flanked Johnston, the Confederates abandoned Dalton May 10 and moved to face the Yankees at Resaca to the south.

clothes. Strangers and all were in a religious controversy. I went back to Mrs. Preston's room—described the party of newcomers.

"Daresay it is Charles Darby. Do you know him?" "No." "He is a surgeon in the army."

I remained under this impression until Mary Darby[2] came in and asked if I knew who Mr. Chesnut's friends were. "But Mr. C asked me who your friends were."

"At any rate," said Mrs. B, "whoever they are, they are soaking wet. Let us send them some hot toddy, and General Chesnut had given them some cigars."

This was all promptly done. Indeed J. C. thought we were all neglecting some guests of Mr. Preston and so devoted himself to them assiduously.

They were evidently Morgan's men, for of him they talked and so betrayed their whereabouts in the army without so intending. One of them had just escaped from prison and had much to tell which was interesting. About eleven o'clock J. C. said coolly,

"After all the long talk, I did not catch your name as I came in."

Which was not surprising, as no one had called it—not knowing it. No names, it seemed, had been mentioned on either side.

Here they took up their parable anew. They were brothers. Their names were Long. Another brother of theirs was with General Lee. The very man who had married that handsome Miss Sumner, Mrs. McLean's sister. And then they bethought them that it would be satisfactory also to know the names of the kind people in whose house they were. They had run in out of the rain at the first open door and had met such a charming party and such unquestioning, frank hospitality.

June 28, 1864.   Bloomsbury—where Buck came over with me.

She told me her whole life's story. When she came to the last episode, she always spelled the name—H-O-O-D.

"To think, I told him all about my affair with Ransom Calhoun. And oh! if I had only known how intimate he was with Cousin Ransom—and that he had heard it from him, how differently I would have told it! When I said that to H-O-O-D, he laughed in my face."

These Prestons, from the oldest to the youngest, are straightforward, bluntly truthful people. I find them so curiously candid, so utterly without guile, and yet so kindly courteous. They never do or say an unpleasant thing. Utterly charming, I call this family, and clever—so wonderfully good-looking.

If Buck and I had been worth poisoning! It really looked like it—we were both so ill. "Saleratus biscuits—or the hot drive over," said the doctor coolly, to our miserable suspicions.

My friend Godard Bailey, who is an editor here, has just been distinguishing himself by fighting and brawling with a brother editor who lives here now.

2. An anachronism, since Mary Preston had not yet married John Darby.

They used sticks, knives, pistols, and from the bloody fray no serious damage ensued, after all—no death or disaster. At a man named Hocott's expense, we have two daily papers in Camden.

Fancy Miss Deenie's[3] triumph! Two newspapers and a telegraph wire—all the news fresh.

Mrs. Kirkland discomfits the natural village curiosity. She will see no one— literally—not even her father, they say. And so the sympathizing neighbors are disappointed. They like to go and see for themselves and examine everybody's grief and tell every peculiar symptom.

General Kemper[4] saw poor Kirkland. He was as quiet and composed in view of certain and immediate death as he had ever seen him before, discussed it coolly, knew the end had come, and was glad, as things had turned out, that his wife could not go on.

Kirkland died [the] 19th, and when people rush across the street to ask the Judge, "How is poor Kirkland's wife?" he answers, "What idle curiosity!" He says it is all nonsense, her refusing to come downstairs. He refuses to go up to her room, and so they have not met. He is devoted to her children, and his wife brings him full accounts of his daughter. She goes upstairs, dear old soul, and sees Mary and her children.

Memminger has succumbed to the storm of his own raising. He resigned and retreated under a cloud of hot shot poured in from every point of the compass. Yea—verily.

Weeping, wailing women are pitiful enough—but save me, good Lord, from such cold, hard, stony faces as Mary Boykin. She sits by her wounded husband, her eyes fixed, dead eyes, to all, seemingly. She is heartbroken but tearless. Tom, her splendid boy—there is her agony. The girls are near at hand, ready to fly at a sign of their father's hand for any possible want of his. If the utter self-abnegation of a family could give a man happiness, he ought to be so. Their very existence seems swallowed up in the thought of tending the wounded father.

I think he knows more than he tells of Tom's fate, because though cheerful enough otherwise, if Tom's name is casually mentioned, a queer spasm, and his whole expression is changed. Wounded and in prison—that is bad enough. He says Tom was slightly wounded, and he ordered him off the field, but he saw him afterward in his place in the ranks.

Converse Frierson is killed.[5] And his fiancée's face is harder, colder, and as tearless as miserable Mary B's.

July 6, 1864. Columbia. At the Prestons, Mary was laughing at Mrs. Lyons's complaint. The person from whom we rented rooms in Richmond. "She com-

---

3. Dinah McEwen.
4. Brig. Gen. James Lawson Kemper, commander of Va.'s reserve forces.
5. A son of John Napoleon Frierson.

plained of Molly and Laurence's deceitfulness. They went about the house, quiet as mice while we were at home. Laurence sat at the door and sprung to his feet if we passed. When we were out they sung, laughed, shouted, danced, and if any of the Lyonses passed him, Laurence kept his seat and his hat on, too. Mrs. Chesnut said 'Oh!' so meekly to the whole tirade, and, 'I will see about it.' "

And when Mrs. Lyons went upstairs, she cried: "I am so glad the poor things relieve their feelings while we are away. It must be an awful bore to be deaf, dumb, blind, and go about with yellow sphinxlike faces. I often pity the awful self-control servants must practice—and then they pay the Lyonses back. The Lyonses young people dance over our heads nearly every night—and that awful piano."

There was a chorus of girls after dinner. Colonel Urquhart and Edmund Rhett dined here.

Charming men both. No Bragg—no detraction. Talk is never pleasant where there is either.

And yet Colonel Urquhart is aide to Bragg, or was. He is so nice and formal and precise and tells of the glories of his New Orleans home, delightful.

"And I am sure Edmund Rhett is aide to General Detraction," said the pungent Isabella. "Chief of staff, I should say."

When I told him people said he sat for that picture of Gerald Grey in Mrs. King's book, he replied, with a change of his sad countenance.

"Do I laugh to show my perfect mouth and teeth? Do I laugh at anything? Is my face cameo-cut, &c&c? Oh, no. That book is a tribute of respect to Edward Barnwell."

"There is giggling for the exquisite mouth, and then there is rascality enough for two. She means both of you," sung the chorus, Edmund Rhett being no longer present.

"He said his time would come, and he shuddered when he thought of it."

"She will call that story Nemesis—or mauvaise langue. I hope he may catch it as he deserves."

"Now," said Mary P, "if I had never heard a word against Edmund Rhett and came across him on a desert isle—you know, a perfect stranger—I believe I should find him awfully agreeable. He is so clever, so witty, so audacious."

Our noble Georgian dined here today. He says Hampton was the hero of the Yankee rout at Stony Creek.[6] Says he has no use for Fitzhugh Lee. Rooney is all right, but lazy, inert—but then, a son or a nephew of General Lee can do no wrong. He claims that citizens' militia and lame soldiers kept the bridge at Staunton and gallantly repulsed Wilson's raiders.

---

6. One of several engagements during a Union cavalry expedition against railroads south of Petersburg, led by Brig. Gen. James Harrison Wilson from June 22 to July 2.

G. W. Smith, he told us, is now generalissimo in Georgia by Governor Joe Brown's appointment, Toombs and Vice President Stephens his A.D.C.'s.

"Oh," shouted the chorus. "Now send Joe Johnston and Wigfall there, too. All the discontented in one army corps, and Joe Brown to lead them—happy military family!"

"Under Joe Brown's fig tree and vine they lie down, and no man to molest them or make them afraid."

"I say, is not *your* lame lover out of place in Johnston's retreating army? A lame man can't reverse—as they call it waltzing."

"If they go and give up Atlanta, we are cut in two!"

"We will go and hunt like the foxes for holes to hide our heads in, then!"

At intervals, subject to what Mr. Venable calls *Gallic* invasion at all moments, I have read a jumble of things. *Fitz-Boodle,*[7] translations from Pindar, *Hudibras,* Sappho.

> The shades of night are falling fast
> As through a Secesh village past
> A youth who bore mid corn and rice
> A banner with this strange device—
> Skedaddle—
> Oh, stay, the culled pussons said,
> Upon this shuck bed rest thy head—
> A tear stood in his clear blue eye—
> But still he answered with a sigh—
> Skedaddle.

This was given to me by way of explanation. I asked what "Skedaddle" meant.

The other explanation, more mysterious if possible, a western captain's words of command, in place of boots and saddle, &c&c, by the trumpet: Git ready to git, git—and then you hear nothing but the thunder of retreating hooves.

The present rage among the young people is to call everything and everybody by an initial letter only.

"No, my dear Madame," said General P, in his softest cadences but with his grandest manner. "You will hear all over my house 'H and the D.' Do not be alarmed. They do not mean hell and the devil. They allude to my sons-in-law apparent—or expectant."

"Certainly not apparent, papa, for we have not seen them for a year. They are backing down into the Gulf of Mexico with Joe Johnston, for aught we know."

---

7. Probably Thackeray's *The Confessions of Fitz-Boodle; and, Some Passages in the Life of Major Gahagan* (1852).

Jack Preston has not his father's imposing presence, but he understands as well all the acts of a gracious hospitality. Jack is such a good fellow, so kind, so witty himself, and so ready to make the most of other people's wit and humor.

July 18, 1864.   At Mrs. Slocum's last night, the sensation of the evening, a frail young invalid who has had hemorrhages without number. The Confederacy is scant of clothes. We give that up. But this fair one was too thin. Peasant's waist[coat?] and next to nothing under that.

"Weak lungs! No wonder—so exposed!"

She tottered as she walked, so weak was she. Not tottered—rolled and pitched. I accept the correction. But when the round dancing began, she was there. And Deadly Smooth ⟨⟨Edmund Rhett⟩⟩[8] her partner. Now he makes no concealment of the fact that he is dying of consumption. He sat by Mary P and myself. When the weak one danced up toward us, holding her dress—"Cancan," whispered Mary P—asked the invalid:

"Why do you suppose I am so ill—why? I give it to you in a hundred guesses."

"We give up."

"Before I dressed to come here this evening, I ate twelve eggs."

"Dressed? Undressed you mean," in the same tone as "cancan," was whispered. Then: "Oh—ain't she common! At least she is unenclosed." How Edmund Rhett laughed—he who asserts that he never feels inclined to smile at aught this world can do.

Mrs. Slocum came up, saying, in New Orleans, four people never met together without dancing.

Ed Rhett turned to me. "You shall be pressed into the service."

"No, I belong to the reserve corps. Too old to volunteer—or be drafted as a conscript."

But I had to go—faute de mieux. And I was led, a resisting victim, to the floor.

"A woman over forty ought not to dance if she wears Armsted's clumsy homemade shoes."

My partner showed his English descent. He took his pleasure sadly.

"Oh, Mr. Rhett—at his pleasure—can be a most agreeable companion."

"I never happened to meet him when he pleased to be otherwise."

Still, with a hot draggled old alpaca dress and those clodhopping shoes, to stumble slowly and gracefully through the mazes of a July dance was too much for me.

"What depresses you so?" he anxiously inquired.

"That carnival of death." For our fevered one flew madly from right to left—holding the scanty skirts high.

"Poor thing! You can read her fate in her face. There is Gwin—worse—or at

---

8. The name is supplied in the rough draft of the 1880s Version.

best, nearer his end. What a blunder, to bring us all together here. A reunion of consumptives—to dance and sing until almost one can hear the death rattle."

Surely this was enlivening conversation.

Then came blindman's bluff. I *would not play*. My age and infirmities made me confirmed in that resolution.

So I retreated to a quiet seat in the lovely front piazza, there to consider myself.

I was making pleasant pictures, there in the beautiful moonlight—things to come off "when this cruel war is over."

Suddenly a black object sprang from a window beyond the piazza—and it fell fifteen feet or more to the ground. Somebody killed! My heart, as it has a way of doing, stood still. And, queer to say, in my agony, I muttered the first words that came to my lips—"A demned moist unpleasant body."[9] There were shrieks, and the crowd poured out of doors. Edmund Rhett had picked himself up and was walking coolly up the steps.

"What's the row?" he inquired.

Nothing disturbs the equanimity of that ineffable dandy—not even a fall of fifteen feet. He said, looking round: "This is a mere porch. I took it for a piazza extending the whole front of the house—so I stepped out of a window in the game and fell to the ground."

He walked home with us. Tudy and Teddy Calhoun were seated in the Preston piazza, likewise enjoying the moonlight. Teddy said hastily,

"Johnston has been relieved from the command of the western army."[1]

Tudy dramatically added, "Hood replaces him in that command."

Buck in her flowing white dressing gown met us at the head of the stairs, her blue eyes wide open and shining black with excitement.

"Things are so bad out there. They cannot be worse, you know. And so they have saved Johnston from the responsibility of his own blunders—and put Sam in. Poor Sam!"

"Why? Buck, I thought you would be proud of it," said Mary.

"No—I have prayed God as I have never prayed him before since I heard this. And I went to the convent and asked the nuns to pray for him, too."

She did not sleep one wink that night nor the next, she told us.

July 25, 1864.   So she was in a bad way when the killing blow came.

Here we are, in a cottage rented from Dr. Chisolm.[2]

Hood full general. Johnston removed, superseded.

9. Dickens, *Nicholas Nickleby*, chapter 34.

1. Johnston's Army of Tenn. had retreated across the Chattahoochee River on July 9, allowing Federal troops within ten miles of Atlanta; on July 17, he was relieved of command.

2. John Julian Chisolm, a professor of surgery at S.C. Medical College before the war, directed a laboratory producing medicine for the C.S.A. at Charleston.

Early threatening Washington City.[3] Semmes, of whom we have been so proud—he is a fool after all—risked the *Alabama* in a sort of duel of ships! He has lowered the flag of the famous *Alabama* to the *Kearsarge*.[4] Forgive who may! I cannot.

We moved into this house on the 20th of July. J. C. was telegraphed to go to Charleston. General Jones[5] sent for him—part of his command is on the coast.

Willie Preston killed—his heart literally shot away—as he was getting his battery in position.

The girls were at my house. Everything in the utmost confusion. We were lying in a pile of mattresses in one of the front rooms while the servants were reducing things to order somewhat in the rear.

All the papers were down on the president for this change of commanders—except the Georgia papers. Indeed, Governor Brown's constant complaints I dare[say] caused it—and the rage of the Georgia people as Johnston backed down on them.

We were the saddest three. The straits the country was in, the state of things in Atlanta then, was the burden of our talk.

Suddenly Buck sprang up.

"Mrs. C, your new house is very hot. I am suffocated. It is not so oppressively hot at home, with our thick brick walls, you know."

Isabella soon after came here. She said she saw the sisters pass her house, and as they turned the corner, there was a loud and bitter cry. It seemed to come from the Hampton house. And both of the girls began to run at full speed.

"What is the matter?" asked Mrs. Martin.

"Mother! listen—that sounded like the cry of a broken heart," said Isabella. "Something has gone terribly wrong at the Prestons."

Mrs. Martin is deaf, however, so she heard nothing and thought Isabella fanciful.

Isabella hurried over there. They had come to tell Mrs. Preston that Willie was killed. Willie! his mother's darling! No country ever had a braver soldier—a truer gentleman—to lay down his life in her cause.

Dick Manning came with the poor boy's body.

He talked Joe Johnstonism run mad. He coupled Lee and Davis and abused them with equal virulence. Lee was a solemn hypocrite. He used the garb of religion to mask his sins, but his iniquities were known.

Never were people too sad to talk called upon to hear a greater mass of horror and wicked nonsense.

Alex Haskell told of the arrangement by letter writing, to throw all the blame of the retreats on Jeff Davis.

---

3. Lt. Gen. Jubal Anderson Early's raid on suburban Washington, D.C., July 9–12.

4. The Confederate raider *Alabama* was sunk off the coast of France on June 19. Her commander, Raphael Semmes, known before the war as a career U.S. Navy officer, lawyer, and author, had captured eighty-two merchant ships valued at 6,000,000 dollars during his service with the C.S.N.

5. Maj. Gen. Samuel Jones, then commander of the Department of S.C., Ga., and Fla.

A misunderstanding between the president and one of his generals will serve the general to explain any disaster. A general who is known to disdain obedience to any order, who refuses to give the president any information, for fear the president will betray him to the enemy—if that is not the madness of self-conceit, what is!

Seward's little bell would have lodged Joe Johnston within triple walls in the twinkling of an eye many years ago.

We agreed that Jeff Davis believed in Joe Johnston's patriotism and loyalty or he would not have placed him, knowing him to be his fiercest enemy personally, in command of the army west.

Brewster says Joe Johnston is like the snakes, so blinded by his own venom. He thinks *to spite him*—Joe Johnston—his subordinate generals would disgrace themselves and destroy their country. Says he was afraid to risk a battle, for fear the Davis generals would betray him. That is the [height?] of idiotic conceit.

July 26, 1864.   Isabella went with me to the bulletin board. Mrs. D_____ (with the white linen as usual pasted on her chin) asked me to read aloud what was there written. As I slowly read on, I heard a suppressed giggle from Isabella. I knew her way of laughing at everything—and tried to enunciate more distinctly—read slower, louder, and with precision. As I finished and turned round, I found myself closely packed in by a crowd of Confederate soldiers eager to hear the news. They took off their caps, thanked me for reading out to them all that was on the board, and made way for me, cap in hand, as I hastily returned to the carriage which was waiting for us. Isabella proposed, "Call out to them to give three cheers for Jeff Davis and his generals."

"You forget, my child, that we are on our way to a funeral."

Found my new house already hospitably open to all comers.

J. C. had arrived. He was seated at a pine table on which someone had put a coarse red table cover. And by the light of one tallow candle he was affably entertaining Edward Barnwell, Isaac Hayne, and Uncle Hamilton.

He had given them no tea, however. After I had remedied that oversight, we adjourned to the moonlit piazza, [where] by tallow candlelight and by the light of the moon we made out that wonderful smile of Teddy's—which identifies him as Gerald Grey.

In Sydney Park, as I was driving alone, had an encounter at long range with Mrs. Singleton and Mrs. Ambler. The former shouted that she was a Joe Johnston man.

I stood my guns.

"All right, but who brought us into these dismal straits? Who pitched us on the horns of this dilemma? If he would not fight in the mountain passes, do you think he could stop Sherman in the plains?"

We have laughed so at broken hearts, the broken hearts of foolish love stories.

Now Buck is breaking her heart for brother Willie. Hearts do break—in silence—without a word or a sigh.

Mrs. Means, Mary Barnwell made no moan—turned their faces to wall and died. How many more that we know nothing of?

When I remember all the true-hearted, the lighthearted, the gay and gallant boys who have come laughing, singing, dancing in my way in the three years past, I have looked into their brave young eyes and helped them as I could every way and then seen them no more forever. They lie stark and cold, dead upon the battlefield or moldering away in hospitals or prisons—which is worse. I think, if I consider the long array of those bright youths and loyal men who have gone to their deaths almost before my very eyes, my heart might break, too.

Is anything worth it? This fearful sacrifice—this awful penalty we pay for war?

Willie Preston came to my house on Clay St., Richmond, just one year ago. He was worn out. He had had fever in the west. For once there was no laugh in his bonny blue eye, shaded like a girl's with the longest tangled black lashes.

"Mrs. C, what a beastly hole—as the English would say—no ice."

"Indeed? Laurence has discovered a mine of ice across the 'Noble Jeems' river."

Mrs. Davis says all true F.F.'s pronounce it the "raging Jeems." At any rate, across the river there is ice in exchange for gold. And I hastened away, to return in a moment with a julep. A mint julep, cold within, and the outside of the goblet frosted with ice.

"Dear Mrs. Chesnut—you have saved my life!" And the old laugh came back. And the blue eyes grew wide and deep in his delight. Heavens, what a handsome fellow he was!

Such queer letters.

John Kennedy only wants J. C. to help him on his upward path to a generalship. But that blessed Wade Hampton is writing in the maddest way. Says he will be forced to resign. Since his tiff with General Lee, that prince and potentate is so prejudiced against him! "Did you ever," J. C. says. "Let them alone—no answer. It will all come right. There is really nothing the matter."

Dick Manning called the western army General Lee's Botany Bay. General Lee never permitted any soldier who was of service to him to leave him. When a man was promoted for gallantry and sent west it simply meant—sent to Coventry.

Mrs. Bartow said, "After all, Hood is only expected to hold Atlanta until reinforcements can be got there."

"Where are the reinforcements to come from?" Echo answers, "Where?"

Hood tells his troops that it is safest always to be nearest the enemies' guns. Hood is a splendid proof to the contrary—shot to pieces as he is.

Joe Johnston is personally so brave, he dares to be overcautious, they say.

Marshal Ney did not better deserve the name—bravest of the brave—but taking care of his army will not do everything. Saving the army is not our object just now. It is risk all to save the country. Personal courage in a general goes without the saying. How could a coward rise to the rank of general? In our war, at any rate.

I was amazed that Mrs. Bartow answered me sharply when I said my feeble word with all my strength for our government.

"*You* are right—best always to side with those in power."

It was never so hard—never in all my life—to keep my temper. I thought of how Mrs. Davis stood by her when Bartow was killed.

Edmund Rhett has a heart somewhere about him—much as he keeps it hid. His note to Mary P when Willie was killed would draw tears from the stoniest, hardest eye.

From London *Punch:*

Who knows anything definite about things over here? Which side now is Federal? Which side Confederate—which side North, which side South?

We were on the piazza of that sad, still house. In rushed Toby G,[6] shouting, laughing, calling at the top of his voice for "Susan."

He had not heard of Willie's death. Fancy the revulsion of feeling.

At dinner, a soldier on crutches—from typhoid fever, however, no wound. He could not be hurt in his heart—he has none. He fancies himself a mimic and a humorist. His idea was to amuse the dinner table by the variety of fixed grins on the faces of the dead found on the battlefield. Can the hardening process of war go further than that? What next in the indurating process?

Specimen talk:

"Oh! but one expects women to be better than men!"

"Why?"

"Well, for one thing, they have less sense."

"But the authoress of *Gerald Grey* has as much sense as the average man. Why expect her to be better morally? Her father, now—he was acknowledged to be great and good. Is she not as good as he was?"

"No, the code is different between the sexes."

"Hood intrigued to be put over Joe Johnston's head!" said Sally H.

"He does not know what intrigue means. He is a bold, straightforward, honest, brave, simple-hearted soldier."

"You know, William Mazyck heard General Lovell say, on Main St., to a terrified audience, "No country can stand many such victories as Hood's on the 22nd."[7]

"Allen Green says Johnston was a failure. He gives that up. Now he will wait and [see] what Hood can do before he pronounces judgment on him. He liked

---

6. Toby Gibson.
7. The battle of Atlanta, marking the beginning of the Federal siege of the city.

his address to his army. It was grand and inspiring—but everybody knows a general has not time to write that kind of thing himself."

And Mr. Kelly from New Orleans says, "Dick Taylor and Kirby Smith have quarreled."[8]

"One would think we had a big enough quarrel on hand for one while. The Yankees are enough and to spare."

And General Lovell says, "Joe Brown, who importuned our government to remove Joe Johnston with his Georgians at his back, they are scared now and wish they had not."

How they smash the obloquy on Jeff Davis now—for no fault of his, but because the cause is falling. A ruined country—who can bear it? We are so unreasonable. One tried to remember. The English—with Sir Walter Scott to write it down—called Napoleon the Great a coward and a fool![9] And the Masons, his country neighbors, tell scandalous stories of Washington! The first, the last, the only one—the Cincinnatus of the West and all that!

In our democratic republic, if one rises to be its head, whoever he displeases takes a Turkish revenge—defiles the tombs of his father and mother. His father a horse thief and his mother no better than she should be, his sisters barmaids and worse, his brothers Yankee turncoats and traitors. It is all hurled at Lincoln or Jeff Davis indiscriminately.

"Chickamauga—the only battle we have gained of great importance since Stonewall was shot by Mahone's brigade."

"Jeff Davis is a tyrant, and Hood is his pet and his minion," answers Dick Manning.

"Who won Chickamauga?" shouts Isabella the Hoodite.

"The general[1] has a dangerous new acquaintance, and thereby hangs a tale," says small Isaac.

"What is her name?"

"Oh, it rhymes to rascal and fast gal." And then came rhymes upon rhymes. Maids and all forlorn, men all Earl Van Dorn, &c, cows with the crumpled horn, who tossed, &c. Bonham dashing down the back way because he would not receive one so beautiful and so notorious in his executive office. Our general will not go to his office at all while she hovers round. They must surprise her—these gallant Carolinians—with their wives in sight.

---

8. Maj. Gen. Richard Taylor, commander of the Department of Western La., had long believed that his superior, Lt. Gen. Kirby Smith, commander of the Trans-Miss. Department, was responsible for the failure to recapture New Orleans. In the summer of 1864, after seemingly defying Smith's orders by engaging and defeating Maj. Gen. N. P. Banks's Red River expedition, Taylor was promoted and transferred from Smith's command.

9. Sir Walter Scott, *The Life of Napoleon Buonaparte* (1827).

1. Identified as "Mr. C" in rough draft.

August 1, 1864.   Stoneman—artillery parked—line of battle formed before Atlanta.

When we asked Brewster what Sam meant to do at Atlanta,

"Oh, oh! Like the man who went, he says he means to stay there."

Hope he may—that's all.

Kit Hampton out on a warpath. "I abhor all doctors" (the poor D_____). Our rulers are fools. That we know by the generals they appoint. Our statesmen are fools. That we know by the generals' appointments that they confirm—such generals! faugh!" (Poor Sam.)

Read once more *Mill on the Floss.*[2] The hard way brothers show their love, brotherly love—say "brotherly hate." Old sisters' love turns so easily sour. See the aunts. I am so taken up with Tom. At first I revolted at the sacrifice. Why give up Stephen Guest to her cousin? Love pays its own way. Maggie had the right divine to him. But then—right and wrong, morality aside—death is better for Maggie than a life with a *thin* soul like Stephen Guest. He was too small for her. Death was less painful than life would have been with him.

Went in for the warlike—Scott's *Marmion* and the battle scene—Campbell's stirring odes.[3] Forget to weep my dead—feel exalted. Oh, my Confederate heroes fallen in the fight! You are not to be matched in song or story.

We talk so calmly of them.

"Remember, now, was he not a nice fellow? He was killed at Shiloh."

Day after day we read the death roll. Someone holds up her hands. "Oh, here is another of our friends killed. He was such a good fellow."

August 2, 1864.   Spent today with Mrs. McCord at her hospital. She is dedicating her grief for her son. Sanctifying it, one might say, by giving up her soul and body, her days and nights, to the wounded soldiers at her hospital.

Every moment of her time is given up to their needs and their wants—two very different things, she says she finds.

Today General Taliaferro[4] dined with us. He served with Hood at Second Manassas and at Fredericksburg, where Hood won his major general's spurs.

"On the battlefield Hood has military inspiration."

We were thankful for that word, for our all now depends on that army at Atlanta. If that fails us—the game is up.

General Taliaferro says his place on the river was burned.

"Why not? I am not less patriotic than my forefathers. Our house was burned by the British in the first revolution, again by the British in 1812. We are so easy to get at, so near the coast, and the Yankees have followed suit and burned me out once more."

"So you feel a worthy son of rebel ancestors."

J. C. likes Dr. Chisholm's book on surgery[5] but will not bring it home on

2. George Eliot's novel, published in 1860.
3. Thomas Campbell (1777-1844) was a Scottish poet best known for his war songs.
4. Brig. Gen. William Booth Taliaferro of Va., commander of the defenses on James Island.
5. John Julian Chisolm, *A Manual of Military Surgery* (1861) was widely used by Confederate field surgeons.

account of its painful illustrations, on my account. What foolishness. Alone in our new house, we are very friendly and very confidential. Tell stories to each other not to be repeated, sit out on the piazza in the bright moonlight and discuss high art, military strategy—last night until after twelve o'clock.

And yesterday was such a lucky day for my housekeeping in our hired house. Oh, ye kind Columbia folk! Mrs. Alex Taylor, née Hayne,[6] sent me a huge bowl of yellow butter and a basket to match, of every vegetable in season. Mrs. Preston's man came with mushrooms freshly cut. And Mrs. Tom Taylor's with fine melons.

August 3, 1864.   Now yesterday was a day of small worries. Sent Smith and Johnson (my house servant and a carpenter from home) to the commissary's, with our wagon for supplies. They made a mistake, they said, went to the depot and stayed there all day. I needed a servant sadly in many ways all day long, but I hope Smith and Johnson had a good time. I did not lose patience until Harriet Grant came in an omnibus because I had neither servants nor horse to send to the station for her. With her usual tact she repaid our hospitality at dinner by asking her uncle about the beautiful "rascal-fast gal" who said she had traveled from Columbia under his protection and he had promised her a recommendation to the department.

"It is very queer. He looks so staid and formal, and he is so outrageously proper and precise. And yet—that sort of cattle are forever turning up in his wake."

"Why such women ever came South I cannot imagine," he gravely replied.

"Because Southern men are such fools about women—so soft, so rash, so easily imposed on—*if* the woman is only pretty enough!"

Whereupon he declared himself "in a devil of a passion"—which fact there was no gainsaying. He was to dine that day with General Taliaferro somewhere and was walking up and down while we sat at table. Laurence drove up to the door—something was wrong about the harness. He stormed at Laurence, and I made myself further agreeable by saying: "It is not Laurence you are angry with but *me*. Besides, I can't run away, and if you abuse Laurence, he may." At which he laughed and drove off.

I had a business appointment with Mrs. Preston, but Laurence showed his resentment for the insult and did not come home. Smith straggled back and said Johnson was still at the depot. So I sent Smith to hunt up Laurence and my ponies. But daylight was over, and the ponies had to be sent for J. C. at his dinner.

And what how [*sic*] trifling all that seems.

---

6. Sarah Martha (Hayne) Taylor was the mother of William Hayne Taylor and the sister of S.C. Attorney General Isaac Hayne.

Stephen Elliott is wounded. His wife and his father have gone to him.

Six hundred of his men destroyed in a mine. Part of his brigade taken prisoners.[7] Stoneman and his raiders captured.[8]

This last fact gives a slightly different hue to our horizon. Yesterday it was unmitigated misery.

J. C. came home in fine spirits. So sorry he had lost his temper. But I said, "Why scold Laurence instead of the real offender?" He answered:

"It would have been a thousand times worse if I had spoken so angrily as that to you. Besides, I gave Laurence a half-dollar—and he grinned. He knew he was only a safety valve."

Teddy [Barnwell] the handsome and his beautiful wife and his beautiful sister-in-law came to tea. In spite of all our woes, we had the jolliest evening. They came in my general's ambulance. And so for the first time I recognized the fact that I was a general's wife, de facto.

General Lovell told us of the unpleasant scene at the president's last winter. He called there to see Mrs. McLean. Mrs. Davis was in the room, and he did not speak to her. He did not intend to be rude. It was an oversight. How he called again and tried to apologize—tried to remedy his blunder. *But* the president was inexorable and would not receive his overtures of peace and good will.

General Lovell is a New York man. Talk of the savagery of slavery—heavens! How perfect are our men's manners, how suave, how polished. Fancy one of them forgetting to speak to Mrs. Davis in her own drawing room.

A man's being a tyrant does not prevent his being well-bred.

Alas! that we know.

"The mildest mannered man that ever, &c&c"—Scott's description of Claverhouse.[9] Shoot the mad preacher—look after a place where the saddle rubbed his horse's back—&c&c.

Buck came today—read us a letter from Hood which has been some time on the way, apparently.

They had left all the good fighting ground behind them. An army, by constant retreating, loses confidence in itself. There was a talk of some new man to be put in command. He hoped not. God help the new commander, whoever he should be, for he had a rough road to travel.

August 5, 1864.   Made sandbags all day, to be sent to the coast.

---

7. This was the battle of the Crater at Petersburg, Va., July 30.

8. U.S. Gen. George Stoneman and most of his command were taken during an abortive cavalry raid on Macon, Ga., on July 31.

9. John Graham of Claverhouse, first viscount Dundee, the seventeenth-century Scottish Royalist, fictionally represented by Sir Walter Scott in *Old Mortality.*

Sally H: "Will she marry that man? He has no manners, no fortune. He is only a lucky soldier!"

"They say he has no education, even."

"That is a drop too much," screamed Isabella. "He is a graduate of West Point. As for his luck—he has lost a leg and has a disabled wrist. What was Bonaparte before he was a lucky soldier—or Bernadotte,[1] whose descendants sit on the throne of Sweden, &c&c&c."

Then I asked Toby Gibson to come with me. I was going to a tea party. He agreed, and strange to say, J. C. offered to go likewise. I was grateful and amazed. He eschews tea drinking.

It was at the Elmores. I warned Toby that five fascinating virgins awaited him.

Everything was cool and comfortable, spacious and handsome, a great point gained in August, and the thermometer among the nineties.

We heard as we entered a refugee audibly narrating to Captain Gwin the glory and pride and honor she had left behind her when by flight she sought safety from the ruthless Yankee invader.

J. C. was instantly captured by a mature beauty and, like Kathleen O'Moore's dun cow, from that moment "ne'er offered to stir," so sweet was his Kathleen—&c&c&c.

A flashy department girl tackled Toby, who surrendered without a murmur. And in a few minutes they were amicably engaged in a thorough flirtation. I do not see what more he could have done if he had known her for years, not seconds. This red red Rose from the department assaulted South Carolina men.

"They actually wear stays, the stiff things, and they are padded," an irate South Carolina girl screamed, with pointed finger, which was hardly needed.

"And Virginia women paint their faces!"

Supper was here announced. And it was all that could be desired of an August night. Ices—cake—melons.

"Ye gods!" cried Toby. "She is the queen of love and beauty. Hear how those spiteful women are tearing her to pieces."

"She is throwing herself away—to marry a maimed man."

"That's too much. If she have the heart of a woman, she will love and honor him fourfold for his honorable wounds. All women love a good soldier."

"Her family are mute as mice. They know he is unfit for this high command—and they are frightened."

"You are going too far. I daresay they know no mortal man can right Joe Johnston's unaccountable and silly vacillating. What else?"

"Blunders and overcaution."

"Hood will be rash enough for you."

"Never heard so many women at it before. It is awful."

---

1. Jean Baptiste Bernadotte (1763–1844), the French soldier who rose from the ranks of Napoleon's army to become Charles XIV, king of Sweden and Norway.

The music, however, was heavenly. One might put up with many discordant harsh words if they were sure of such singing afterward.

There is a call upon the citizens to furnish General Chesnut with horses to mount his men, in case we are threatened by raiders.

Two exchanged prisoners, General Archer and General Edward Johnson, are to be at my house today.

Captain Gwin and the women in controversy.

"I was brought up to think Joe Johnston and G. W. Smith the best soldiers in our army—the most accomplished and efficient officers of the U.S. Army, I mean."

"What have they done?"

"We are so sorry Joe Johnston was brevet lieutenant colonel. Quartermaster in the old army. He has been the most intolerable load the Confederacy has had to carry."

"Yes, I understand. If he had not been brevet something-or-other he would not have kicked over the traces when General Lee was put over his head."

August 6, 1864. Archer came. Edward Johnson did not stop. Archer was a classmate of my husband's at Princeton College. They called him Sally Archer then. He was so girlish and pretty. No trace of feminine beauty about this grim soldier now. He has a hard face, black-bearded, sallow, with the saddest black eyes. His hands are small, white, and well shaped. His manners are quiet. He is abstracted, weary-looking—mind and body—deadened by long imprisonment. He seems glad to be here, and J. C. is charmed. "Dear Sally Archer," he calls him cheerily, and the other responds in a far-off, faded kind of way.

Hood and Archer were given the two Texas regiments at the beginning of the war. They were colonels, and Wigfall was their general.

Archer's comments on Hood.

"He does not compare intellectually with General Johnston, who is decidedly a man of culture and literary attainments, with much experience in military matters. Hood, however, has the help of youth and energy to counterbalance. He has a simple-minded directness of purpose always. He is awfully shy. He has suffered terribly, but then he has had consolations. Such a rapid rise in his profession. And then his luck, to be engaged to the beautiful Miss P &c&c."

General Archer's mother and sisters were allowed to see him once during his fourteen months in Fort Delaware Prison. Literally to see him. They were allowed to stand thirty feet away from him, and there they might look at each other. No word was allowed, nor sign of recognition.

While they were transferring him from Fort Delaware to Fort Johnson, he wrote on a scrap of paper and handed it to a passenger, a total stranger, merely saying, "Will you have the kindness to put that in the telegraph office?" It was asking his mother to meet him where they had been ten years before, at the Marshall House in Philadelphia. He persuaded his guard to go by the Marshall House in Phila. There was none, however. It had been pulled down to make way for shops long ago. Afterward he heard that the kind Yankee had sent his telegram, and his mother had hastened to the Marshall House to meet with the same disappointment. There was no such hotel now. "Poor old mother!"

They tried Archer again and again on the heated controversy of the day, but he stuck to his text.

Joe Johnston a fine military critic, a capital writer, accomplished soldier, as brave as Caesar in his own person, cautious to a fault in manipulating an army.

Hood—all the dash and fire of a reckless young soldier, and his Texians would follow him to the death. Too much caution might be followed easily by too much headlong rush. There was where the swing back of the pendulum would ruin us—&c&c.

Joe Johnston in person, on his own hook, headed the party who went out from Macon to intercept raiders.

Today a Virginia gentleman dined here, a bluff Englishman to all seeming, a regular, red, big, strong John Bull—or the descendant of one. This Colonel Carter[2] is a cousin of General Lee. He has been on Joe Johnston's staff, and he actually considers him superior to his kinsman Lee.

"There is where Joe Johnston's power comes in," says J. C. "He has the qualities which attach men to him. You may depend [on it], that is a tremendous power in a republic. It is a gift of the gods."

Colonel Carter on the topic of the hour.

"Hood's a fine daredevil of a soldier. I give him all the credit due him. But that he is as smart a man as old Joe—I'm a fool. And if there is a braver man than Joe, I have to meet him yet."

General Archer, who is unmarried, said, "Surely no man ever asked the same woman *twice* to marry him?"

Colonel Carter simply roared. His glee was unutterable for a while.

"Look at that old bachelor. The forlorn fellow that he is! Twice, did he say? Aye—and twice over again! I courted my wife steadily for six years, and I asked her whenever I saw her—nearly. It took six persistent years' courting to get her to have me. Now I tell you, that is the way to do it."

"It is dogged as does it," says Isabella.

Later in the day, a beautiful Miss Waring from Baltimore—she is an exile, and her father is in Fort Warren Prison. She wants to go with General Archer as far as Richmond. She was sent out of Baltimore, Maryland, without a word of

2. Probably Col. Thomas Henry Carter, an artillery commander in the Army of Northern Va.

warning. Put in a wagon and sent across the lines, without bag or baggage, and has been working in one of the departments here to earn her daily bread. She wants to run the blockade and go home if she can, poor thing. No wonder.

Governor Bonham had taken Colonel[3] Archer away with him, so Dr. Lynch and this lady waited here for him two hours.

Colonel Carter said to Archer as he came in—so that the lady did not hear, however: "Now, my fine fellow, you are about to assume a dangerous position. Take care of your heart—that is all."

Sunday Colonel Archer went with me to church. He said it was many a long day since he had entered a church. The last time he went with his mother.

We had one of the cursing psalms of David. He was sure he had never heard it before and declared it altogether shocking.

"Why? He is only calling for swift destruction to fall upon the heads of his enemies. What are you soldiers doing?"

"There is all the difference in the world between fighting yourself—and *praying for vengeance.*"

August 10, 1864.   Today General Chesnut and his staff departed. His troops are ordered to look after the mountain passes beyond Greenville, on the North Carolina and Tennessee quarter.

Misery upon misery.

Mobile going as New Orleans went.[4] Those western men have not held their towns as we held and hold Charleston, or as the Virginians hold Richmond. And they call us frill-shirt, silk-stocking chivalry, a set of dandy Miss Nancys. They fight desperately in their bloody street brawls. We bear privation and discipline best. Brag is a good dog. Holdfast, a better.

Mary Boykin's son Tom is dead, after all. He died on the battlefield at Old Church the same day his father was wounded and borne from the fight. Tom was shot three times. The last shot in the side was fatal. Lynch Deas,[5] now in prison at the North, has written home all about it. It was on the 30th day of May, and now in August they hear for the first time that he is not a prisoner but dead. Pleasant doings from all quarters—Mobile ticklish, Atlanta bound to go up, a raid from Pensacola.

August 13, 1864.   Murdock Matheson,[6] another of that Princeton class, sent me today from Charleston a photograph of Colonel Archer, who had written to ask that favor of him.

3. Here and below, she meant to write "General."
4. Victories by U.S. Adm. David Farragut preceded the fall of both New Orleans and Mobile. At the battle of Mobile Bay on Aug. 5, Farragut steamed past Confederate shore batteries to enable Union troops to besiege forts protecting the city.
5. Lynch Horry Deas, Jr., the son of Dr. Lynch Horry Deas of Camden.
6. Murdock Pratt Matheson, an 1835 graduate of Princeton, was a Charleston broker.

August 14, 1864.   Conflicting testimony. Young Wade Hampton says Hood lost 12,000 men in the battles of the 22nd and 24th. Brewster says not *three* thousand at the uttermost.[7]

Now here are two people strictly truthful who tell things so differently. War? In this war people see the same thing so oddly—one does not know what to believe.

One respected parent—whose moral maxim, "a fool and his money soon parted," and his military maxim, "might will tell in the end," were equally disagreeable to his hearers—now says: "Wait till we see who can hold Atlanta. The proof of the pudding is chewing the bag."

Brewster says when he was in Richmond, Mr. Davis said Johnston would have to be removed and Sherman blocked. He could not make Hardee full general because when he had command of that army he was always importuning the War Department for a general in chief to be sent there—over him. Polk would not do, brave soldier and patriot as he was. He was a good soldier and would do his best for his country and do his duty under whoever was put over him by those in authority. But Mr. Davis did not once intimate to him who it was that he intended to promote to the head of the western army.

Brewster calls Joe Brown, governor of Georgia, a trump, and G. W. Smith, a great general.

(Again, what has he done in all these four years of war and trial?)

"Toombs is out there. What is he doing?"

"Talking."

"This blow at Joe Johnston, cutting off *his* head, ruins the schemes of the enemies of the government. Wigfall said to me, 'Go at once. Get Hood to decline to take this command. It will destroy him if he accepts it. He will have to fight under Jeff Davis's orders. That no one can do now and not lose caste in the western army.' Joe Johnston does not exactly say that Jeff Davis betrays them to the enemy, but he says he dares not let the president know his plans, as there is a spy in the war office who invariably warns the Yankees in time. Consulting the government in military movements is played out. That's Wigfall's way of talking. Now," added Brewster, "I blame the president for keeping a man at the head of his armies who treats the government with open scorn and contumely, no matter how the people at large rate this disrespectful general."

More Brewsterania.

The day Hood took command he and General Johnston talked all day. The new commander asked the old one for all his views and plans. And they were given freely—apparently.

If he had only stopped and fought where he could choose the ground, no

---

7. Between seven and ten thousand men of the Army of Tenn. were killed, wounded, or captured at Atlanta.

mortal would have thought he ought to be superseded, let the result have been what it might. But mortal flesh and blood could not stand so much senseless retreating. Mr. Davis's mistake was to keep Johnston too long. Things are well-nigh hopeless. Three weeks ago there would have been a chance for the country. These are the Delphic oracles of Brewster. Also, Halsey Wigfall has sense *a-plenty* and he is a brave soldier, but he lacks manners.

"Manners à la Brewster?" snaps Isabella.

Mobile stripped for the fight—noncombatants ordered out of the town. Horrid times ahead.

One of Clancy's[8] bits of fun. An Englishman said to Miss Brewster (no kin to ours, however), who dropped her glove:

> If from this glove you take the letter *g*,
> It makes it "love"—which now I make to thee.

And Clancy continued the rhymes:

> If from this Brewster you take the letter *b*,
> It makes "rooster"—and now I crow to thee.

8. Most likely William D. Clancy, a Charleston bank officer.

XXVI

A President Pays a Call

August 19, 1864. Began my regular attendance in the Wayside Hospital, which was gotten up and is carried on by that good woman Jane Coles Fisher.

Today we gave wounded men (as they stopped for an hour at the station) their breakfast. Those who are able to come to the table do so. The badly wounded remain in wards prepared for them, where their wounds are dressed by nurses and surgeons, and we take bread and butter, beef, ham, &c&c, hot coffee, to them there.

One man had hair as long as a woman's. A vow, he said. He has pledged himself not to cut his hair until war [was] declared [over] and our Southern country *free*.

Four of them had made this vow. All were dead but himself. One was killed in Missouri, one in Virginia, and he left one at Kennesaw Mountain. This poor creature had one arm taken off at the socket. When I remarked that he was utterly disabled and ought not to remain in the army, he answered quickly.

"I am First Texas. If old Hood can go with one foot, I can go with one arm. Eh?"

How they quarreled and wrangled among themselves! Alabama, Mississippi, all loud for Joe Johnston—save and except the long-haired one-armed hero, who cried at the top of his voice,

"Oh, you all want to be kept in trenches and to go on retrenching. Eh?"

"Oh, if we had had a leader such as Stonewall, this war would have been over long ago. What we want is a leader!" shouted a cripple.

They were awfully smashed up—objects of misery, wounded, maimed, diseased. I was really upset and came home ill. This kind of thing unnerves me quite.

As [soon as] I came into my room I stood on the bare floor and made Ellen undress me and take every thread I had on and throw them all into a washtub out of doors. She had a bath ready for me and a dressing gown.

Brave soldiers—but <you are not nice.>

Letters from the army. Grant's dogged stay about Richmond very disgusting and depressing to the spirits.

Perriman DePass's letter says they hope to stop Sherman.

Wade Hampton put in command of Southern cavalry.[1]

---

1. Hampton had only been given the cavalry corps of the Army of Northern Va.

"Now the Hamptons will be satisfied. And if General Hampton is ordered to supersede Lee, the row against Jeff Davis will subside in this latitude."

Read Dr. Doran's *Queens of the House of Hanover*.[2]

Pleasant ladies, truly.

August 22, 1864.   Hope I may never know a raid except from hearsay. Mr. Huger describes the one at Athens—the proudest and the most timid of women running madly in the streets, corsets in one hand, stockings in the other—déshabille as far as it will go.

Paid the Silcox [?] man a hundred dollars too much.

"Madame, you are absent-minded. Count your money. You gave me wrong change." And he handed me back the superfluous hundred.

"Who steals my purse steals trash—if it contains Confederate bills," I laughed in answer.

Mobile half-taken.

The RR between us and Richmond tapped.

Heavy fight in Florida. A company of South Carolinians surprised and taken prisoners. Captain Smart—alas, not a smart captain. No one has failed to make that too-evident comment.

So hardened are we to war and war's alarms.

"No mind. Nobody must praise anyone that we dislike, or the conversation will cease to be pleasant."

"How you are narrowing down. Yesterday it was 'No brag—no detraction.' Today it is 'no praise'—for we all hate somebody or other."

Extract from a letter written by a young lady who is riding a high horse. Her fiancé is abused.

> My dear,
> You say, with a sneer, "so you love that man." Yes, I do. And I thank God that I love better than all the world the man who is to be my husband. "Proud of him are you." Yes, I am, in exact proportion to my love. You say, "I am selfish." No doubt. Yes, I am selfish. He is my second self, so utterly absorbed am I in him. There is not a moment, day or night, that I do not think of him. In point of fact I do not think of anything else.

No reply was deemed necessary by the astounded recipient of this outburst of indignation. She showed me the letter and continued to say:

"Did you ever? And she seems so shy, so timid, *so cold.*"

Sunday Isabella took us to a chapel—Methodist, of course—and her father had a hand in building it.

It was not clean, but it was crowded, hot, and stuffy. An eloquent man preached. Delightful voice. No wonder he likes to hear it. And wonderful fluency. Nearly eloquent—and at times nearly ridiculous.

---

2. John Doran, *The Queens of the House of Hanover* (1855).

He described a scene during one of his sermons.

"Beautiful young faces turned up to me, radiant faces, though bathed in tears, moral rainbows of emotion playing over them, &c&c."

He described his own conversion—stripped himself naked morally. All that is very revolting to one's innate sense of decency. Then he tackled the patriarchs—Adam, Noah, on down to Joseph, "a man whose modesty and purity was so transcendent, it enabled him to resist the greatest temptation to which fallen man is exposed."

"Fiddlesticks! That is played out," my neighbor whispered. "Everybody gives up now. Old Mrs. Pharaoh was forty."

"Potiphar, you goose, and she was fifty. That solves the riddle."

"*Sh-sh-sh*"—from the devout Isabella. Then she forgot herself, too.

"That settles our debate. Does a man desire promotion that he may hurry up the war and marry his sweetheart—*or* only for his country's good?"

"That is all humbug. Every man wants promotion for his own dear self's sake."

"A soldier wants promotion first of all things!"

"No, never, but I allow he would be a fool if he did not take it when he can get it. Brides will await like love-lighted watch-fires for years at the gate. And promotion—*that's* like time and tide—waits for no man—then—"

"*Sh-sh-sh.*"

At home—met General Preston on the piazza. He was vastly entertaining. Gave us Darwin, Herodotus, Livy. We understood him and were delighted, but we did not know enough to be sure when it was his own wisdom or wise saws and cheering words from the authors of whom he spoke.

August 23, 1864.   All in muddle, and yet the news, confused as it is, seems good from all quarters.

Row in New Orleans—Memphis retaken[3]—2,000 prisoners captured at Petersburg—Yankee raid on Macon, come to grief.

John Taylor Wood, fine fellow, in his fine ship *Tallahassee*. He is all right.

At Mrs. Izard's—met there a clever Mrs. Calhoun who had sojourned once in Marshall, Texas, on the trail of the Fair Lucy[4]—Flower de Luce, as Dr. Gibbes calls her.

Mrs. Calhoun is a violent partisan of Dick Taylor. Says Dick Taylor does the work—Kirby Smith gets the credit of it.

That the *Mercury* should abuse Dick Taylor, *the president's brother-in-law,* she found shocking.

---

3. Nathan Forrest's Confederates seized Memphis on Aug. 21 but abandoned the city the same day.
4. Mrs. Pickens.

"Oh! It is a sin and a shame. He is a splendid soldier, a brave and true man, and a noble gentleman. What has he done that they dare slander him so?"

Allen Green has lost his place again—one more unfortunate Confederate, sadly importunate—for a good place. Mrs. Izard naturally took a gloomy view of a war in which Allen was left without a command.

Mrs. Calhoun described the behavior of some acquaintance of theirs at Shreveport, one of that kind whose faith removes mountains. Her love and confidence in the Confederate army were supreme. Why not? She knew so many of the men who composed that dauntless band. When her husband told her New Orleans had surrendered to the foe she despised, she did not believe a word of it. Then he told her [to] pack up his traps. It was time for him to leave Shreveport. She determined then to run down to the levee and see for herself. She saw the Yankee gunboats having it all their own way down there. It was too [much?]. She made a painful exhibition of herself. First she fell on her knees and prayed. Then she got up and danced with rage. Then she raved and dashed herself finally on the ground in a fit.

There was patriotism run mad for you. As I did not know the poor soul, Mrs. Calhoun's fine acting was somewhat lost on me, but the others enjoyed it— quand même!

The cross-grainedness of fate. Old Edward Johnson sent to Atlanta against his will. Archer made major general and, contrary to his earnest request, ordered not to his beloved Texians but to the Army of the Potomac.

Mr. C. F. Hampton deplores the untimely end of McPherson.[5] He was so kind to Mr. Hampton at Vicksburg last winter, and also General McPherson drank General Hampton's health then and there. Now Mr. Hampton has asked Brewster if it be a mistake and that General McPherson is a prisoner that every kindness and attention shall be shown to him. General McPherson said at his own table at Vicksburg that General Hampton was the ablest general on our side.

"How I wish General Lee had been sent west to stop Sherman."

Grant can hold his own as well as Sherman. Lee has a heavy handful in the new Suwarrow. He has worse odds than anyone else, for when Grant has ten thousand slain, he has only to order up another ten thousand and they are there—ready to step out to the front. They are like the leaves of Vallombrosa.[6]

Read an old *Blackwood*—Alcibiades—the very cleverest thing. How I wonder who wrote it.

5. Maj. Gen. James Birdseye McPherson, Federal commander of Vicksburg from July 1863 to March 1864, led the Army of the Tennessee during the Atlanta campaign until he was killed on July 22.
6. An allusion to *Paradise Lost,* book 1, lines 301–02: "Thick as autumnal leaves that strow the brooks / In Vallombrosa. . . ."

August 29, 1864.   I take my hospital duty in the morning. Most persons prefer afternoon, but I dislike to give up my pleasant evenings. So I get up at five o'clock and go down in my carriage all laden with provisions. Mrs. Fisher and Mr. Bryan generally go with me. The provisions are sent by people to Mrs. Fisher. I am so glad to be a hospital nurse once more. I had excuses enough, but at heart I felt a coward and a skulker. I think I know how men feel who hire a substitute and shirk the fight. There must be no dodging duty. It will not do now to send provisions and pay for nurses.

Something inside of me kept calling out, Go, you shabby creature. You can't bear to see what those fine fellows have to bear.

Mrs. Izard was staying with me last night, and as I slipped away I begged Molly to keep everything dead still and not let Mrs. Izard be disturbed until I got home. About ten I drove up, and there was a row to wake the dead. Molly's eldest daughter nurses her baby sister. She let the baby fall, and Molly, regardless of Mrs. Izard, *as I was away,* was giving the nurse a switching in the yard—accompanied by howls and yells worthy of a Comanche!

The small nurse welcomed my advent, no doubt, for in two seconds peace was restored. Mrs. Izard said she sympathized with the baby's mother so forgave the uproar.

I have excellent servants. No matter for shortcomings behind my back. They save me all thought as to household matters, and they are so kind and attentive and quiet.

They must know what is at hand if Sherman is not hindered from coming here. "Freedom! My masters!" But these sphinxes give no sign, unless it be increased diligence and absolute silence—as certain in their action and as noiseless as a law of nature when we *are in the house.*

Plowden Weston has left a great fortune to the Mazycks.[7] Nannie says she feels like Cinderella when the glass coach drove up with the four footmen &c&c. Sally Goodwyn made, as one might expect, her usual cheerful and charitable remarks upon the windfall in the family....[8]

Read *Indiana*[9]—altogether worse than I expected—jealousy between mistress and maid—rivals! My disgust was unspeakable for a time—and then I forgot all that when those eloquent letters from the Isle of Bourbon turned up.

Life was a nightmare without *Indiana.* Madame Sand.

That fearful hospital haunts me all day long—worse at night. So much suffering, loathsome wounds, distortion, stumps of limbs exhibited to all and not half cured.

7. Anne Wyche "Nannie" (Taylor) and William St. Julien Mazyck. Nannie was the daughter of Sally Webb (Coles) Taylor; William, a Charleston cotton factor, was the son of William Mazyck.

8. Nannie's widowed sister, Sally Coles (Taylor) Goodwyn. A description of an unidentified man is deleted.

9. George Sand's first novel, published in 1832.

Then when I was so tired yesterday: Molly, looking more like an enraged lioness than anything else, roaring that her baby's neck was broken. Howling cries of vengeance. And the poor little careless nurse's dark face had an ashen tinge of gray terror, and she was crouching near the ground, like an animal trying to hide, and her mother striking at her as she rolled away. All this was my welcome as I entered the gate. It takes these half-Africans but a moment to go back to their naked, savage animal nature. Mrs. Izard is a charming person. She tried so to make me forget it all and rest.

August 31, 1864.   J. C. at home—came down on the cars with Trescot, who is writing a book. Hero to be a representative statesman, to drink mean whiskey, to have no principles, to be very clever and very dirty.[1]

Today read *Christie Johnstone*.[2] *Hetty Cary*—Eh?

September 1, 1864.   The battle is raging at Atlanta—our fate hanging in the balance.

Atlanta gone. Well—that agony is over. Like David when the child was dead, I will get up from my knees, will wash my face and comb my hair. No hope. We will try to have no fear.

Isabella to the rescue.

"Be magnanimous. Now I daresay you never tried the affectionate dodge."

"Never to mortal man."

"Then try it now. If my fiancé had lost a battle, I would—"

"What would you—eh?"

"I'd make love to him—straight out!"

At the Prestons, found them drawn up in line of battle, every moment looking for the *D* on his way to Richmond.

Now to drown thought—for our day is done.

Read Dumas—*Maître d'armes*.[3] Russia ought to sympathize with us. We are not as barbarous as this, even if Mrs. Stowe's word be taken. Brutal men with unlimited power are the same all over the world. See Russell's *India*. Bull Run Russell!

---

1. Trescot never published such a novel.
2. The heroine of Charles Reade's *Christie Johnstone* (1853) is a strong fisherwoman careful in business but impulsive with men.
3. A novel by Dumas père, published in 1840–41.

Mr. John Rutledge dead, and the obituary notice says he was a son of the "Dictator" John Rutledge and father-in-law of General Capers.[4]

The D stopped to see his mother, and these girls are shocked that he did not rush by his mother to greet his lady love.

"A woman wants to be worshiped to the utter suppression or momentary forgetfulness of all other ties"—&c&c. And all this they come here and say with the utmost gravity.

They say General Morgan has been killed.[5] We are hard as stones. We sit unmoved and hear any bad news chance may bring. Are we stupefied?

Stephen Elliott is a very silent man, but when he speaks it is to the purpose. Today Teddy Barnwell told us this. When Colonel McMaster[6] heard Stephen Elliott was wounded, he rushed over to condole with him, sympathize and all that.

"Not a word from you! If you had obeyed orders this would never have happened."

《**September 8, 1864.**   Yesterday J. C. said, "It is not good manners to show what you feel. When you are bored by people you are absent-minded, sad and weary of aspect. Sometimes you groan and often frown and fidget. I wonder you can do so."》[7]

September 19, 1864.   Mr. Preston says Bragg is acting as lightning rod: drawing off some of the hatred of Jeff Davis to himself.

My pink silk dress I have sold for six hundred dollars, to be paid in installments, two hundred a month for three months. And I sell my eggs and butter from home for two hundred dollars a month. Does it not sound well—four hundred dollars a month, regularly? In what?

"In Confederate money." Hélas!

I am knitting a heavy woolen shirt for Tom Taylor at Mrs. Ben Taylor's request.

Mrs. Magill says if Bob Alston is a prisoner, the Yankees won't keep him long.

---

4. Charleston planter John Rutledge was not the son but the grandson of "Dictator" John Rutledge, the Revolutionary leader who headed the war government of S.C. Brig. Gen. Francis Withers Capers of Ga., the engineer who constructed the defenses for Johnston's army during the Atlanta campaign, married Susan Rose Rutledge in 1863.
5. Morgan was killed in a surprise raid by Union cavalry near Greenville, Tenn., on Sept. 4.
6. Fitz William McMaster, a Columbia lawyer and colonel of the Seventeenth S.C. Regiment.
7. From the rough draft of this version.

He has a pleasant way of making himself so intolerable they will long to get rid of him.

September 21, 1864.   The president has gone west.[8] Sent for J. C.

Went with Mrs. Rhett[9] to hear Dr. Palmer.[1] I did not know before how utterly hopeless was our situation. This man is so eloquent. It was hard to listen and not give way. Despair was his word—and martyrdom. He offered us nothing more in this world than the martyr's crown. He is not for slavery, he says. He is for freedom—and the freedom to govern our own country as we see fit. He is against foreign interference in our state matters. That is what Mr. Palmer went to war for, it appears. Every day shows that slavery is doomed the world over. For that he thanked God. He spoke of these times of our agony. And then came the cry:

"Help us, oh God. Vain is the help of man." And so we came away—shaken to the depths.

Johnny is here with his fine pair of carriage horses and finer riding horses.

Isabella went with us to the Wayside Hospital today. She said:

"Calline is out on a rampage—she is a hired nurse—because we expect her to attend to her duties on Sunday. And that man there abused Hood, so I would not put any sugar in his coffee. And in her rage Calline let a secret out of the bag—cat, I mean. She acknowledges that the hired nurses take the real coffee for themselves and give the poor soldiers the imitation articles—rye, &c&c&c.

"You see now, Isabella, why we must come—rain or shine—Sunday and every day. We feed them for love, not money. The hired nurses look out for number one only." While I was making this point for Isabella's benefit, a sulky officer sneered:

"Is this all you have to give us? Why, it is a regular farce. I say wayside ministrations are played out."

"Yes, we can do no better. Here is coffee, bread, and beef."

"Waysides are a humbug. After this I will always go to a hotel."

"Good heavens! Are you able to go to a hotel?" cried the irrepressible Isabella. "Then you have no right here. This is charity—for those who cannot pay. You had better go at once." But he did not—and ate his breakfast without another snarl.

We went to the station to meet Maggie Howell. She came with Mr. Preston. Her visit is to me and to the Prestons.

We went to a charity concert. Maggie wonders if our lean commissary Bacon[2] is a descendant of the [*illegible word*] Bacon.

8. Davis left Richmond on Sept. 20 to visit the army in Ga. and discuss strategy with Hood.

9. Probably Sarah Cantey (Taylor) Rhett.

1. Benjamin H. Palmer, a Presbyterian minister and professor at Columbia Theological Seminary.

2. John Edmund Bacon, a lawyer and quartermaster of the Seventh S.C. Volunteers, was the son-in-law of former governor Francis Pickens.

"After the McGillie pretender line from the Stuarts, one may claim anything."

"But," says Teddy, the brave and beautiful brother-in-law, "our Bacon is genuine. And pretends to nothing whatever."

He pointed out a scene which attracted many more eyes than the stage. A citizen's wife here took a handsome department girl to board with them. "So cheap," she said—but she proved dear in the end, as good bargains often are. The lord and master of the mansion fell into the toils of the siren, and madame ordered her out of her house. Here were the whole party in a few feet of one another. Monsieur le mari sat by his wife, devoted in manner, and Madame the lawful wife received his brandishments with scorn and contumely. "You old humbug"—that was the way we read her grim indifference to his advances.

L'autre sat near with her attendant cavalier, gotten up regardless, and she watched the married pair, too, and seemed to enjoy the spectacle of the man's discomfiture.

"But," said Maggie, "it is very odd the man's wife is ever so much better looking than the other!" [*Remainder of the page cut out.*]

"Oh, he is the Insatiate Archer—whom one will not suffice."[3]

"One rarely will—either Cupid, if he be the archer, or the Bony Bowman."

The end has come. No doubt of the fact. Our army has so moved as to uncover Macon and Augusta.[4]

We are going to be wiped off the face of the earth.

What is there to prevent Sherman taking General Lee in the rear? We have but two armies. And Sherman is between them now.

⟨⟨**September 22, 1864...**[5]   J. C. and I had a most uncalled-for row. I reminded him of how I laughed when years and years ago I saw his name among the list of distinguished citizens. He grew angry and said my levity had ruined him, had effectually prevented his being anything, &c&c, all before Harriet Grant. I grew absolutely hysterical with rage and mortification, and he sulked the rest of the evening and did not sleep the whole night. Very odd. Such an unexpected turn to a small joke. Poor me. The mirth must be innate and constitutional that Sandy Hill and Mulberry could not drown out long years ago, and constant snubbing I live under. Thank God it is *irrepressible* and I will laugh at the laughable while I breathe.

⟨⟨This morning at seven the president sent for J. C. to the [railroad] cars, and as he has not been at home since, I fancy he has gone to Kingsville.

3. Allusion to Edward Young, *Night Thoughts*, "Night I," line 212.

4. In his meeting with Hood, Jefferson Davis had approved the general's plan to pull out of Ga. into Tenn. in hope of cutting Sherman's supply line and forcing the Federals from Ga.

5. The following excerpts from the 1870s version, dated Sept. 22, 26, and 27, 1864, cover material omitted from the 1880s Version.

《The *Carolinian*[6] had a noble defense of Hood, and the *Guardian* quotes the *Mercury* that Beauregard would be certainly sent to command the western army.

《Harriet Grant left, saying she was sent away from her uncle's house because I wanted the room for John and Maggie Howell. I knit day and night for Tom Taylor. Harriet Grant had no right to be respected in *my house*.

《**September 26, 1864.**   I have not written since Thursday. Consequently have forgotten everything. . . .

《Mr. C came home to dinner. He went as far as Kingsville with the president. Said Custis Lee was urging the president to relieve Hood and put Beauregard in his place, but the president was undecided. . . .

《Brewster came to tea, and J. C. asked him to stay with us. He remained two nights. He had the articles from the *Examiner* in his pocket [*two illegible words*], said every word was a falsehood, but he could not write an answer, as he was General Hood's friend and Johnston's friends would say so. Mr. C offered to write the article in answer if Brewster would give him the facts. Brewster then said he had been four times ordered back to the army but would not go for a week yet and again put off his departure for Mary Preston's wedding. I said if Hood had any friends, now was the time for them to show themselves. It was hard if his enemies could abuse him and his friends give as an excuse that they did not answer because they were his friends. Brewster said he would give de Fontaine his facts. The next day I inquired, but he had not seen de Fontaine. The Lord deliver us from such friends as Brewster and John Darby!

《Buck came here. I tried to prepare her for Hood's removal. The first instant she took the idea, she turned as white as the wall but soon took a saner view. Said she would like to see him so much, and she knew he would do better in Lee's army, where his men would fight, than in that [*illegible word*] army which would never support him. And she left me as bright and as blooming as ever. . . .

《Saturday I remained home all day and arranged my house for the president's proposed visit. Drove Mary Preston out in the afternoon. She is as serene as the moonbeams. . . .

《Yesterday . . . I walked home [from church] and the deep blue sky without a cloud. No Italian sky could ever have been more glorious—its wonderful beauty and the air heavy and delicious with olea fragrans. All saddened, this world so beautiful, so sweet as nature shows it to us, and man so mean, so vile, so unworthy of his home. I said all this as I entered the piazza to J. C. And he meekly remarked, *women* are mean also. And then, with *dramatic* power of loathing and shame, he told that the day before he saw a poor negro woman in the last stages of pregnancy, sitting by the roadside in bitter wailing, her eyes smashed up, and frightfully punished in the face. He rode up and said: "Poor

---

6. The Columbia *Daily South Carolinian*, edited by one of the South's finest war correspondents, Felix Gregory de Fontaine.

soul what can I do for you? How have you hurt yourself so?" She answered: "Ride on, Massa. You can do no good. My Missis has been beating me." He asked the brute's name and was answered "Mrs. Fergusson," some woman we did not know, thank Heaven. . . .

《《**September 27, 1864.**   Yesterday I went shopping after a long discourse with John. Stopped at the Prestons. Found Buck in bed, with a diamond ring from Hood. She needs something, for her beloved's star is under a cloud. Beauregard now is the lord of the ascendant, and Hood cannot be sufficiently abused.

《《I find a letter in the *Mercury* which either Slocum or [*illegible*] wrote, for it is identically what Slocum said to me at his own house last Friday. Our defeats in the Valley are fearful. . . .⁷

《《The papers make the president pay an extravagant compliment to Hardee at the expense of Hood. Maggie was charming, handsome, and saucy. . . . How she gave it to poor Hood for not justifying her brother's choice in selecting him.⁸ She said Mr. Preston said he was a half-educated man and that she thought Buck would have trouble yet, Mr. Preston not liking the match. She gave it to Hood so roundly. I could not sleep for misery for my darling. I will hope. I dread what effect Maggie's talk will have on Mr. Preston. He evidently was vastly impressed. When Mr. Preston expressed his amazement at Buck's falling in love with Hood, Maggie expressed her cordial assent.

《《All this torments me so. I often wish Buck and Hood had never met, or that all was over in peace.》》

September 28, 1864.   The *Mercury* is almost too shocked to find words to express *its* feelings. It is really touching in its account of the president's speech at Macon. More in sorrow than in anger it declares there must be some hoax. It cannot believe he made such a speech. . . .⁹

Well, Maggie has gone to drive with Johnny. The colts went off on their hind legs, the forelegs straight up in the air, for the most part. He will bring them back tame enough, poor things.

Last night Maggie told Captain Bacon, before she knew his position on the staff: "I mean to marry a commissary. Their wives have plenty of horses. They have always sugar for their tea."

Then a pause which came suddenly, and a shrill voice was heard to say:

"One and one make two. In matrimony two are expected to make one. Two into one—you can't cipher away, do your sum, 'carry one,' &c&c."

---

7. Maj. Gen. Philip Sheridan's victories at Winchester on Sept. 19 and at Fisher's Hill on the twenty-second helped to drive Lt. Gen. Jubal A. Early's Confederates from the Shenandoah Valley.
8. That is, the choice of Jefferson Davis, her brother-in-law.
9. At Macon, Ga., on Sept. 22, Davis cautioned Southerners against despair, defended Hood's "honest and manly blow" in the struggle for Atlanta, and argued that Sherman would soon fall back to protect his lines of communication. Omitted is an unintelligible reference to a friend of the president.

《I wrote a long letter to Mrs. Davis today and showed it to Maggie, that nothing might go that she disapproved. We had a merry evening. More laughing and more talk on my part than for many a long day.》[1]

September 29, 1864.   These stories of our defeats in the Valley fall like blows upon a dead body. Since Atlanta I have felt as if all were dead within me, forever.

> All was ended now—the hope, the fear, and the sorrow.
> All the aching of heart, the restless unsatisfied longing;
> All of dull, deep pain, and the constant anguish of patience.[2]

Captain Ogden of General Chesnut's staff dined here today. Had ever brigadier with little or no brigade so magnificent a staff? The reserves are, as somebody said, but robbing the cradle and the grave—men too old, boys too young. Isaac Hayne, Edward Barnwell, Bacon (sugar-cured) and Ogden, Richardson Miles—they are the picked men of the agreeable world.

Ogden seemed so detached. I ranked him with Isaac Hayne, who is the bachelor of "ours." Ogden says he is from New Orleans—and a man less like New Orleans I never saw. I had heard him say he was barely 24. How was I to dream that he had a wife and children? Today when he had it made plain to him that I expected him to assist Isaac Hayne when there were girls about, he thought it right to explain that he had been married several years.

Today we left Mary Preston's wedding cards. Johnny acted as charioteer. Isabella went along to show us where the people lived. It was not a bad way to spend a day out-of-doors in charming weather. Isabella and Maggie are wittier than most young ladies and certainly as reckless talkers as one need want.

So we combined business and pleasure.

October 1st, 1864, was Mary Cantey Preston's wedding day. This event transpired (as newspaper letter-writers would say) last Wednesday night. Maggie dressed the bride's hair beautifully, they said, but it was all covered by her veil. Which was blond lace—and the dress tulle and blond lace—diamonds and pearls. The bride walked up the aisle on her father's arm. Mrs. Preston on the D's. I think it was the handsomest wedding party I ever saw, from the father to the youngest child. They certainly are magnificent specimens of humanity at its best. We—Colonel Chesnut and Maggie, Captain Chesnut and myself— marched up to where the Prestons and Hamptons were drawn up in battle array. The Darbys in solid mass on the opposite side of the church, sad of visage "at losing John."

Mary McDuffie (Mrs. Wade Hampton), made audible and not too complimentary remarks upon the enemy's forces. John Darby had brought his wedding uniform home with him from England. And they did all honor to his perfect figure. I forget the name of the London tailor, the best, of course.

---

1. From the 1870s Version.
2. These three lines are from the back of the previous page of the manuscript.

"Well," said Isabella, "it would be hard on any man to live up to those clothes."

We were not invited to the house—nor was anybody, so soon after Willie's death. So we came home to a nice little supper of our own.

And now to the amazement of us all, Captain Chesnut—Johnny, who knows everything—has rushed into a flirtation with Buck such as never was. He drives her every day—and those wild, runaway sorrel colts terrify my soul, rearing, pitching, darting from side to side of the street. And my lady enjoys it!

When he leaves her he kisses her hand, bowing so low, to do it unseen, that we see it all. They seem utterly content with one another. She says she does it to keep him out of mischief. And he answers, "You are engaged—even if you do say you are sorry it is so." *So* there is no deception on either part.

Mrs. Slocum sent an invitation to her party to Mrs. John Darby accompanied by one (to the president's sister-in-law) addressed to Miss Howell. She wrote a note to Mrs. Darby, saying she could send this invitation or not, as she pleased. Maggie Howell was staying with us. We were also all invited to Mrs. Slocum's, but we preferred to take tea at the Martins. Now, how can any one be so small as to think an impertinence aimed at Miss Howell could hurt the president?

At the Martins a stentor sung "Lorena" and then "Oh, cast that shadow from thy brow." There never was so loud a voice, and Miss Bryce's[3] faint tum-tum-tweedledum on that old piano came so modestly that it was scarcely heard at all.

October 7, 1864.   The president will be with us here in Columbia next Tuesday—so Colonel McLean brings us word.

I began at once to prepare to receive him in my small house. His apartments were decorated as well as Confederate stringency would permit.

There were mirrors of the first Wade Hampton—pre-Revolutionary relics. Some fine old carpets of ci-devant Governor Miller—curtains to match, &c&c.

The possibilities were not great, but I did all that could be done for our honored chief. Besides, I like the man. He has been so kind to me, and his wife is one of the few to whom I can never be grateful enough for her generous appreciation and attention.

Maggie laughed at high South Carolina. She said Captain C went off in the midst of all my bustle of preparation. He could not be induced to show one atom of interest in the mere matter of the president of this great Confederacy.

"Such people as presidents and all that," jeered Maggie.

I went out to the gate to meet the president—who met me most cordially, kissed me, in fact. Custis Lee and Governor Lubbock[4] were at his back.

At breakfast—for the party arrived a little after daylight—Governor Lubbock told a Texas story. A man drank a gallon of sizing for milk—and pulled a piece of cloth out of his mouth, thread by thread. Oh! appetizing table talk.

Immediately after breakfast General Chesnut drove off with the president's

---

3. Probably a daughter of Columbia merchant and planter Campbell Robert Bryce.

4. Francis Richard Lubbock, governor of Tex. from 1861 to 1863, then serving as special adviser to Davis on Trans-Mississippi affairs.

aides, and Mr. Davis sat out in our piazza. There was nobody there but myself, and some little boys strolling by called out: "Come here and look! There is a man in Mrs. Chesnut's porch who looks just like Jeff Davis on a postage stamp."

And people began to gather at once on the street. Mr. Davis then went in.

Mrs. McCord sent a magnificent bouquet. I thought: of course—for the president. But she gave me such a scolding afterward. She did not know he was here. And having made that mistake about the bouquet, of course I thought she knew and did not send her word.

What a comfort it is. In all this upsetting foolish talk, Mrs. Preston, one of the most sensible women I know, and Mrs. McCord, the very cleverest—both are Jeff Davis's supporters and friends, heart and soul. I must not forget good and staunch and fearless Miss Mary Stark. Men may be selfish—self-seeking. My noble female friends are purely patriotic.

The president was watching me prepare a mint julep for Custis Lee when Colonel McLean came in to inform us that a great crowd had gathered and that they were coming to ask the president to speak to them at one o'clock.

An immense crowd assembled—men, women, and children. About eleven I saw Mem Cohen ushering a party through my back door. After that—"Your [*illegible word*]," as Isabella flung at me, "was overflowed—upstairs, downstairs, and in my lady's chamber. There was not standing room anywhere." I tried to go up to Maggie's room to look at the crowd from the window, but an unknown strong-minded female stood her ground, parasol in hand, and called out, "*Who* is this rude woman trying to push her way through the crowd?" There was nobody that I knew there to identify me, and as I was not prepared to fight my war against a parasol leveled as a lance, I meekly went back. The president's room, which opened on the front piazza, was sacred.

Mr. Martin, the reverend, held his hands over Mr. Davis's head and blessed him with all his heart.

Mr. Theodore Stark came back to us for another glass of brandy and said, with the air of a connoisseur:

"Jeff Davis will do. I like that game look the fellow has."

When Mr. Davis went out into the piazza to make his speech, we slipped into his room and locked the door—the <Prestons, Maggie, and Isabella.>

"If he should come here and find us?"

"Goose! He cannot be in two places at once. And can't we see when he moves this way."

We were looking through the venetian blinds.

"Mrs. C is a regular Cassandra, but she can't stay miserable. She is happy as the day is long, now playing at loyalty to the head of the Southern Confederacy."

"Don't Southern men flatter? Listen how they are going on, through the cracks of the venetians, with this old soul."

"Excitement is good for you. You look ten years younger than you did yesterday."

"Why, how did you know me in here?"—from the piazza.

"You have the patent right to those eyes. They have never been duplicated, even."

"Her back is turned to me," said Governor Bonham gallantly. "But I would know her voice in heaven—among the angels."

That was the climax. And then we listened to the president.

John Wallace[5] got pushed up near our window. He was as good as a play. He was so utterly in sympathy with the president, who bore him along with his speech, that he wept, prayed, and cursed.

"Stop that," I whispered—for I could touch him, so near was he, though the blinds were between us. "Stop that. Fight—go to the front and fight—now is your time."

"That is you. Ten thousand pardons! Not for worlds would I use bad words before you."

"Mrs. Chesnut is flirting with these old graybeards as if she was fifteen," cried the girls.

Isabella began to tell how loyal a visit to Carlton House made Sir Walter Scott,[6] and added—"because Mrs. Chesnut has Jeff Davis here, she is in the seventh heaven"—&c&c.

Said Governor Bonham—for we frankly fraternized now—open the venetians, and outside and inside were as one party. "The crowd would have been far greater if all able-bodied fighting men skulking round had not been ashamed to show themselves." They gave us notice when the thing was drawing to an end, and we fled from Mr. Davis's private apartments. He was thoroughly exhausted, but we had a mint julep ready for him as he finished.

While Jeff Davis stood up for his general, my *A.D.C.*, Buck, said she would kiss him for that—and she did. He all the while smoothing her down on the back from the shoulders, as if she were a ruffled dove.

I left the crowd overflowing the house and the president's hand nearly shaken off. And my head was then intent on the dinner to be prepared for them—with only Confederate commissariat. So the patriotic public had come to the rescue. I had been gathering what I could of eatables for a month, and now I found everybody in Columbia, nearly, sent me whatever they had that they thought nice enough for the president's dinner. We had the sixty-year-old Madeira from Mulberry and the beautiful old china—&c&c. Mrs. Preston sent a boned turkey stuffed with truffles, stuffed tomatoes, and stuffed peppers. Each made a dish as pretty as it was appetizing.

But it would take too long to tell all that was sent here. For a week I was busy gathering up stray dishes and serviettes, &c&c.

---

5. A Richland District planter and former state legislator.
6. Despite his Jacobite sympathies, Scott attended a reception in his honor given by the Prince of Wales, later George IV, at the future king's London residence, Carlton House, in 1815.

A mob of boys exclusive came to pay their respects to the president. He seemed to know how to meet that queer crowd. At dinner Governor Bonham, who sat at my left hand, complimented my cook. I had to own that Mrs. Preston's man dominated the kitchen for the day, and Molly was too glad to have him lift from her shoulders the awful responsibility. Likewise William Walker volunteered to assist Laurence and Smith and was welcomed with joy by the dusky fraternity of waiters.

Mars Kit sent a dozen or two of the choicest wine from Millwood for the president to take along on the railway.

Then they had to go, and we bade them an affectionate farewell. Custis Lee and I had spent much time gossiping on the back porch. I was concocting dainties for the dessert, and he sat on the bannister with a cigar in his mouth. But he spoke very candidly and told me many a hard truth for the Confederacy and the bad time which was at hand. What he said was not so impressive as the unbroken silence he maintained as to that extraordinary move by which Hood expects to entice Sherman back from us. Mrs. Preston says they do things that our woman's common sense regards as madness—no less—and then they talk so well, and we listen until almost they fool us into believing they have some reason for the wild work. But say what you will (none of us had said anything), this movement of the western army is against common sense.

Well, we bade them an affectionate farewell. Mr. Martin gave our thoughts a voice and prayed God to bless the president—to save him! And then we were still once more, and I was so tired.

The reaction set in. And I am Cassandra worse than ever.

"Stop that miserable talk unless you want to set us howling!" . . .[7]

《Now I must write carefully what he [Davis] said of Hood and Hardee. He said Hood was a gallant soldier and noble gentleman, that he advised Beauregard's appointment because the Macon clique were undermining him and the public would be better satisfied with a name they knew.[8] Mr. Davis said unless requested by Hood, he would not have done so. He said Hood's strategy was good, excellent, and if he had been seconded, the defeat of Sherman in the [illegible word] would have been complete. General Govan, who was prisoner,[9] told him that the entrenchments before Hardee, after he had gotten in their rear, were deserted. Five minutes more, and Sherman would have either been in full retreat or have surrendered. Alas, Hardee had excellent reasons for not advancing. His men were tired, the sacrifice of life would be too great, &c&c. Mr. Davis said he did not mortify Hardee by telling what Govan said, but he hoped somebody would. He said his confidence in Hood was increased by these

7. There follows a cryptic anecdote about an unidentified couple.

8. This passage is from the 1870s Version. M. B. C. is apparently referring to the president's private remarks. In his public speech at Columbia, Davis did not mention the "Macon clique—Hardee and Joe Johnston—by name. Beauregard had been given a new department called the "Military Division of the West," which included the Army of Tenn.

9. Brig. Gen. Daniel Chevilette Govan, an Ark. planter who fought with Hood's army until his capture at the last of the battles for Atlanta.

later events. Sally Hampton said if Mr. Davis endorsed Hood, it was a pity. He did not do so publicly, as the putting Beauregard over him was considered by the public as practically condemning him. She furthermore stated that [*illegible name*], their overseer, was a cousin of Hood's. Which, being sifted, proved that some distant relation of Hood's had married a connection of some cousin of [*the same illegible name*]. But Sally felt it quibbling. She [Buck?] has not heard from J. B. [Hood] for a month and thinks there is foul play with his letters.⟩⟩

XXVII

"Cassandra Wails"

October 18, 1864. For ten days I have not touched pen or paper. I gave myself a holiday from sad forebodings. And now I know one of the pleasantest weeks of my life has just slipped away.

Madam Malapropos[1] called today. She said, "After all, everybody knows you talk too much." Dead silence—fatal fact. Then she asked Maggie Howell if the report was true that she had once ordered Mrs. Lee out of the president's pew.

Fancy Maggie's face. I said:

"I wish what you accused me of—talking too much—could as easily be proved a preposterous and stupid slander."

"Oh, but I can tell you a real scandal. Caroline B—they would not let her marry the man because he was beneath her socially. Now did you ever? Who are the B's, to be sure! Now they do say he is giving her things to make her miscarry."

"I think," cried the irrepressible Isabella, "he had better make her Mrs. Carry."

All this rubbish was today.

My pleasant ten days I owe to my Sister Kate, who descended upon me unexpectedly from the mountains of Flat Rock. We are true sisters. She understands me without words. And she is the cleverest, sweetest woman I know—so graceful and gracious in manner, so good and unselfish in character, but the best of all, she is so agreeable. Any time or place would be charming, with Kate for a companion. We had dinners, suppers, parties of pleasure. Clancy the clever was here and that pleasant fellow George Deas. We had elderly people for Kate and gay young ones for Maggie. "How happily the days of Thalaba passed by."[2]

Richard Miles stopped my ponies. "Beauregard Felix is put in command of this department."

Cassandra had an inward groan at the *Felix*.

"And so he is coming out at the same hole he went in at—Fort Sumter," she said.

---

1. Virginia Clay, who was staying at the home of former U.S. senator James Hammond. Jefferson Davis had sent her husband, Clement Clay, Jr., to Canada to foster anti-Union sentiment in British North America and to plan sabotage and subversion in the U.S.
2. Robert Southey, *Thalaba the Destroyer* (1801), volume 1, book 3.

Kate brought her little son with her, a bright and beautiful boy about five years old. She came under Mr. Urquhart's care. The carriage broke down in one of those mountain streams, Mr. Urquhart said. "Mrs. Williams, I can carry you out dry-shod if David will sit quietly on this log until I come back for him." Kate said, "But put me on the log and take David first." "No, the log would not bear your weight." "There, my child, sit here quietly. If you move, you may be drowned before we could get to you."

"Bully!" said little David. "I'm all right—catch me being such a fool as to move." "Maybe he will be frightened?" "You take mama—never mind me." And there he sat until he was brought safely to dry land.

One day at dinner someone mentioned a new member of *Les Misérables* had reached Columbia.

"Oh, buy it, mama. I am so interested in Cosette's fate."

"Are you reading the translation, or do you prefer the original?" asked Maggie gravely, but that he did not understand.

"Mama reads it aloud at night," he said. That we might lose nothing, Pink Starke[3] came and discussed scientifically (if possible) the difference between mind and soul—I should have said "transcendentally." And then he broke out into stories so comical that he left Clancy in the lurch.

General Chesnut was in Camden. But I could not wait. I gave the beautiful bride Mrs. Darby a dinner. Which was simply perfection. I was satisfied for once in my life with my own table, and I know pleasanter guests were never seated around any table whatsoever in the world.

"Thank God," cries Isabella. "Cassandra has forgotten to wail for one while."

My house is always crowded. After all, what a number of pleasant people we have, thrown by war's catastrophes in Columbia.

"I call such society glorious. It is the wind-up, Cassandra says. And the old life means to die royally."

General Chesnut came back disheartened. He growls that such a life as I lead gives him no time to think.

"Think! If you have to think still—God help you."

"What do you mean?"

"The [time] is past now for anything but *action*."

Sat today restrained by sacred laws of hospitality and heard a Connecticut Yankee—in my house—sneer at everything Southern—and abuse Jeff Davis!!!

J. C. came home in splendid spirits from a dinner at Governor Bonham's. There met the governor of North Carolina and Extra Billy Smith.[4] In some way picked up some crumbs of comfort as to our affairs.

Godard Bailey announced that these men had been sent for by Joe Brown,

3. William Pinkney Starke, a planter, lawyer, and man of letters from Clarendon District.
4. Governor William "Extra Billy" Smith of Va., a former U.S. congressman and Confederate brigadier general, received his nickname early in life because of his success in winning extra payments for private mail deliveries from the Post Office Department.

governor of Georgia, who wanted a peace conference. They mean to ignore Jeff Davis and Lincoln and settle our little differences themselves. "If there had been any treason hatching, General Chesnut would not have been asked to meet them," replied his wife quickly.

Letter from Mrs. Kershaw. She is in money difficulties, too—wants General Chesnut to buy her house—or, if he does not need one, to try and sell it for her to someone else.

Burton Harrison writes to General Preston that supreme anxiety reigns in Richmond.

October 28, 1864.   Large meeting. They want to instruct their representative man Boyce to resign. Boyce was heard in his own defense.[5] The *D* heard Boyce's speech—said it was a brave and plucky stand-up for his own opinions. "We have been fighting five years for life and liberty. Has he struck one blow?"

"Then let us off about his courage and pluck. Has he ever been under fire? And we have needed every man."

"Every single, solitary man," echoed the girls.

We have not for any cause missed one day's attendance at the Wayside Hospital.

Today a man (a Camden man) just from Point Lookout prison answered, when we asked him what he would have, that he was too weak to eat—then ate steadily through two breakfasts. When he called for a smaller spoon to stir his coffee, Calline refused indignantly, but I humored him about the spoon. Even gave him the milk and rice he demanded with a sigh of repletion.

October 30, 1864.   Some days must be dark and dreary.[6] At the mantua makers, however, saw an instance of faith in our future—a bride's paraphernalia. And the radiant bride herself—the bridegroom expectant and elect, now within twenty miles of Chattanooga and outward bound to face the foe.

Mrs. Preston continues to say midsummer madness has seized upon the men who guide this go-behind-Sherman action. It lacks common sense.

A fatuous friend of Alex Haskell said he had killed eleven men with his own hand.

"Were they in buckram?" inquired the irrepressible Isabella.[7] But she said aside, "A man who has gone one eye on his country ought not to be made ridiculous in the house of his friends."

Read *Small House at Allington*—Lady Dumbello. You I understand.[8]

---

5. In an open letter published in Sept., William Waters Boyce charged that the South had become a despotism and demanded that Jefferson Davis respond to Northern Democrats' call for a peace convention. Though the Columbia meeting described by M. B. C. did pass a resolution asking for his resignation, Boyce remained in Congress until the end of the war.

6. Last line of Longfellow's "The Rainy Day," *Ballads and Other Poems* (1841).

7. An allusion to *Henry IV, Part I*, act 2, scene 4, where Prince Henry, listening to Falstaff's tales of bravery, exclaims, "O monstrous! Eleven buckram men grown out of two."

8. Anthony Trollope, *The Small House at Allington* (1864). Lady Dumbello is much in demand at society gatherings, though one of her admirers is forced to admit, "I'll be hanged if I can understand how she does it. . . . She won't speak ten words a whole night through."

Gave twenty-two dollars for a copy of *Joseph II*—printed badly on thick dingy paper.[9]

Saw at the Laurenses' not only Lizzie Hamilton, a perfect little beauty, but the very table the first Declaration of American Independence was written upon.[1] These Laurenses are grandchildren of Henry Laurens of our first Revolution.

Alas, we have yet to make good our second declaration, of Southern independence from Yankee meddling and Yankee rule.

Hood has written to ask them to send General Chesnut out to command one of his brigades! In whose place?

"She lets the cool N^2 go everywhere. She can trust her, but she keeps an eye on her sister—no round dances—&c&c.

"Good heavens! Why?" asks Johnny.

"Oh, she says *that one* is a house afire!"

"Oh, you tell all this of Madame Fractious to scare the cool Captain. He is sweet on No. 1."

"You are so anxious concerning the cool Captain, why do you not marry him yourselves?"

"Surely you mean your*self*."

"Yes."

"But which of us?"

"Either would be too good for him."

"In his heart he would prefer me," said Buck plaintively.

"Oh, as to that, he has given every one of us to understand—one way or another—that he is ready to marry the one he is insinuating love to at the time. But he seems waiting for us to propose—and we do not mean to do it."

Macon paper says, "Hood's brilliant movement will free Georgia from Yankees."

No doubt. Send them on their way, lighthearted and rejoicing, into the Carolinas.

They say both Beauregard and General Lee counseled that strategic reverse waltz of Hood's, but his vis-à-vis would not dance to Hood's music.

The day Mr. Davis dined with us, there was a chair left vacant. And Mr. William F. DeSaussure called. Laurence brought him straight into the dining room. Soup was being served.

"Oh," said Mr. Chesnut, "you know we could not wait. The president takes the train at an early hour this evening."

Mr. DeS seated himself, saying polite things in the easiest, politest manner.

Mr. C said it was a triumph of good manners on Mr. DeSaussure's part.

9. A translation of Klara (Müller) Mundt's German historical novel, *Joseph II and His Court* (1856), published in Mobile in 1864.

1. The 1870s Version, Oct. 18, 1864, has it "signed on" instead of "written upon."

2. Probably Nathalie Heyward.

Nobody could imagine that he was surprised to find us at dinner, or that he was not looked for to fill that vacant chair.

"Old and dried up as he is, he made himself vastly agreeable to me," said Maggie.

"He is an ex–U.S. senator and famous as the father of three beautiful daughters."

"When he came in we were discussing the fast department girls, and to my surprise, instead of moral disapprobation, he made a grimace of disgust and said, with wonderful precision and distinctness, 'There is a vast amount of ugliness among them.' To think, he is still looking out for pretty women."

His wife was a famous beauty. He knows one when he sees one. Then about the wine—he tasted it, thought awhile, tasted it again, smacked his lips, and smiled.

"Laurence, this wine came from Camden—from your old master's cellar."

"Yes, sir."

"Leave the decanter here." "Then," said Maggie, "with awful solemnity he rolled up the whites of his eyes and informed me, 'This is some of Colonel Chesnut's old Madeira.'"

"He was wise in women and wine—and he did not look it."

"To think that Brewster had quarreled with and left the western army before Johnston was removed! To think of the bunches of papa's best cigars that I gave him—papa not at home. To think of the brandy that I coaxed mama to let me have and the toddies I made and took to him in the piazza when nobody knew! To think how I waved my hair in front—not as it was—how I wore all of my best dresses when the other girls went about in their cool calico gowns—all that he might make a lovely report of me to H-O-O-D. They say he has gone to Texas—that Brewster! And I feel actually swindled." Everybody laughed as in that sweet plaintive voice of hers she enumerated her wrongs.

⟨⟨Buck told me[3] how bitterly Mary had turned against J. B., and I attempted to tell what the New York *Herald* said of Hood's skillful movement and that he had out-generaled Sherman, and Mary Cantey in the midst of it began to talk of something else. . . . It is evident, the leaven of John Darby is working. He is shocked at Hood's lack of *refinement*. And Mrs. Preston was in a dreadful state of mind at Buck's having to associate with Brewster and the like of him. She thinks Brewster wants to break Buck's engagement, and she prays he may succeed. So do I. John D[arby] is much more bent upon it than anyone else. Poor J. B., after all he has suffered. And now that fool Creole goes to take his credit from him—if he can! or if there is any credit. God help the noble Christian soldier! and make him arrive safely through this labyrinth woven by his pretended friends. I see the speeches of all the generals. I hang my head for my country. . . . Only brave old J. B. spoke like a man and a soldier—decently!⟩⟩

Maggie then took up her parable. "That cool Captain! How he can hold his tongue. When he is in a tight place he winds up his watch—looks into it—says

3. From entry dated Nov. 2, 1864, in the 1870s Version.

something is wrong and puts it right. He will certainly miss that watch. But it tides him over his difficulty. Then, if you abuse anyone he likes—he can't bear to hear people abused—he makes the sorrels stand on end—how they rear and pitch and try to run away! It is all make-believe. Those sorrel colts are as gentle as dogs! He makes them do all that just when it suits him. They perform a series of circus tricks—that is all—wild as they look. Their antics are too apropos. I began today—while we were bowling along, as smooth as a rocking chair—to say something disagreeable—and very true—of his last love. In one second they were plunging like mad and he could hardly hold them. He was a picture, with his face set and his feet braced against the splashboard. How does he do it? This I do know—that white horse he has for Nathalie Heyward to ride will do anything, exactly as he tells it to do."

"What language does he use in his horse talk?"

"Oh, I do not know. He whispers in its ear—"

Today he was taking me to see Minnie Hayne's foot. Said it was the smallest, the most perfect, thing in America. Now, I will go anywhere to see anything which can move the cool Captain to the smallest ripple of enthusiasm. He is different from anything I ever knew before. He says Julia Rutledge knew his weakness and would not show her foot. His Uncle James had told of its arched instep and Spanish symmetrical beauty—lots of fine words. So he followed her trail like a wild Indian, and when she stepped in the mud took a paper pattern of her track—or a plaster cast—something that amazed Miss Rutledge at his sagacity.

You can get a rise if you only begin about Company A. 1. Cavalry—or Hampton or Butler or that first plunge into the Potomac—or you may get a sneer if you remind him that von Borcke wanted to teach him and his company to swim their horses.

Captain Boykin says when they went too far from their wagons, the cool Captain and some of his men, to whom a bath and clean clothes was more than life, used to strip, bathe, wash their clothes, and run about like picked chickens—mother-naked till their clothes dried.

Now England and France are never mentioned—and once we counted so strongly on them for a good stout backing. We thought this was to be a bloodless duel, and we would get out of the Union—because they hated us—and why, then, should they want to keep us? We are as sanguine as ever—desperate as our case seems.

Oh, for one single port! If the *Alabama* in the whole world had had a port to take her prizes—refit—&c&c, I believe she would have borne us through—one single point by which to get at the outside world and *refit* the whole Confederacy. If we could have hired regiments from Europe or even imported army ammunition and food for our soldiers.

"What did our monster ironclads do but blow themselves up?"

"We crippled ourselves—blew ourselves up by intestine strife. Can you deny that?"

Today General Chesnut mentioned casually, at dinner, "I dare [say] I have as large a stake in the country as any man. No man has ever doubted my patriotism. And yet so high does party feeling rage among us that when I was sent by the president to inspect and report—"

"A tour of inspection, they call it, eh?"

"Well, in Johnston's camp and Beauregard's, I was always treated more as a foreign spy than an aide-de-camp of the president of the Confederacy. At first at Johnston's headquarters I could see and hear nothing—so guarded were they. But in driving to the station I mentioned to one of the understaffers that Joe Johnston's father and mine had been great friends and that I knew his brother Sidney well in Columbia &c&c. And soon the ice thawed. There was a general unfreezing, and I was once more treated as a loyal gentleman from South Carolina."

"Old Stonewall, now—how he would have despised all that nonsense!"

"If Albert Sidney Johnston had lived. Poor old General Lee has no backing."

"Stonewall would have saved us from Antietam!"

"Sherman will catch General Lee by the rear—while Grant holds him by the head. And Hood and Thomas are performing an Indian war dance on the frontier."[4]

"Hood means to cut his way to Lee—see if he does not."

"The Yanks have had a squeak for it. More than once we seemed to have been too much for them."

"We have been so near success it aches one to think of it."

So runs the table talk.

Tonight Cassandra wails in the beautiful moonlight. The sky is blue and clear. And the scent of the sweet olive fills the air.

"What does Cassandra see, that she shudders so?" asked Maggie with a laugh.

"She sees swarms of black buzzards."

"Flocks," corrects General Chesnut.

"Well, flocks of buzzards swirling round—swooping down—flapping their nasty wings—crowding in a black cloud to pick the carcass of the dead Confederacy."

Somebody sent me *Denis Duval*[5] and it was borne in on me sadly. You have got all you are ever to get from Thackeray.

Captain Bacon has a keen sense of fun—camp fun—though he won his spurs as secretary of legation at St. Petersburg.

"You mean, won his wife."

Captain Bacon says when they spent their winter in the mud, the months

---

4. Sherman had sent Brig. Gen. George H. Thomas, commander of the Army of the Cumberland, to Nashville early in Oct. to keep Hood from attacking Tenn.

5. Thackeray's last novel, incomplete at the time of his death, was serialized in *Cornhill Magazine* in 1864.

before Seven Pines &c&c, and the army got tired of Johnston's tactics, they sung—I can't remember all of the words but this was the refrain:

> Ole Joe he kick up behind and befo'!
> And de yallar gal kick up behind Ole Joe!

McClellan was the yaller gal typified here.

Next to our house—which Isabella calls "Tillietudlem"[6] since Mr. Davis's déjeuner and dinner—is a common, green grass and very level—then there comes a belt of pine trees.

On this open space, within forty paces of us, a regiment of foreign deserters has camped. They have taken the oath of allegiance to our government and are now being drilled and disciplined into form before sending them to our army.

They are mostly German—some Irish, however. Their close proximity keeps me miserable—treacherous once, traitors forever.

Jordan has always been held responsible for all the foolish proclamations— and indeed, whatever Beauregard reported or proclaimed. Now he has left that mighty chief, and lo! here comes from Beauregard the silliest and most boastful of his military bulletins.

He brags of Shiloh. That was not the way the story was told to us. They said Sidney Johnston died in the very arms of victory—and Beauregard, away off on the outside edge of the battle, lying in his tent, consumed by a green sickness—melancholia—let the lucky moment go by and lost all that our dead hero had died to gain.

"Men will boast of anything!"

Tom Boykin, the brightest, bravest, best of Uncle William's boys, was killed at Rome.

I wrote that awkward uncomfortable thing, a letter of condolence today. When one really feels, it is a hard task to perform.

Such a letter to a bereaved father.

It rains in torrents. What cares Maggie? For her solace she has *My Novel.*

General Chesnut has *Joseph II. Romola* is in my hands. So without protest or fidgets we let it rain its worst.

Can this woman be a fallen woman—a creature Shakespeare would call a————, Carlyle, an unmentionable woman? Dress it up as you will, smother the Seventh Commandment with Genesis—here it stands. An unchaste woman must be immodest. We don't go into morals at all. You could as well imagine a

6. In Sir Walter Scott's *Old Mortality,* the royalist Lady Margaret Bellenden serves the king a royal dinner at her home, Tillietudlem Castle.

man who was thief, liar, or coward to be good and decent the while. No, no. It is all Lamar's wrong hearing of English scandal. She writes such beautiful things of love and duty, faith, charity, and purity. They even say she is an atheist, that she believes in God as little as she cares for his commandments.

Today's paper congratulates the country on its generals. Beauregard brings us the tact and skill lacking in Hood. Hood will lend Beauregard dash and boldness.

Yankee paper's description of Hood.
"A man whose want [of] beauty is furthermore embellished by a wooden leg and a wilted arm. Lackluster eyes. Sad, weary, baleful eyes. He can only smile by a facial revolution—a face that speaks of wakeful nights and nerves strung to their utmost tension by anxiety." Even his old gray cloak lined with red flannel comes in for a fling.

Every man is being hurried to the front. Today J. C. said he met a poor creature coming from the surgeon's with a radiant face and a certificate. "General, you see, I am exempt from service—one leg utterly useless, the other not warranted to last three months."

November 6, 1864.

> Desperate valor oft made good
> Even by its daring venture rude
> Where prudence might have failed—

《My nervous system has had some severe shocks. After my quarreling with the whole world for Mr. Davis—Miles, MacFarland, Randolph, Wigfall, &c&c—Harrison tells Mrs. Davis that all the anecdotes derogatory to that family have been traced to *me*. Which of course Mrs. D does not believe, as she sent Maggie Howell here. But the first time anything untoward (which I cannot prevent) occurs, she will recur to this and think there was some foundation for it.》[7]
A letter which was long coming and then misplaced—but I will copy it here—

October 8, 1864

My dear friend,
  I should have written to you long since but have been in such a state of anxiety, and so unsettled, that I could not summon my mind (never great)

---

7. From the 1870s Version.

to its duty. Finding it eminently useless to wait longer—behold a petty maze, without a plan—meandering on coarse paper with thick ink, a bad pen, and the animus only fit to offer you.

Thank you a thousand times, my dear friend, for your more than maternal kindness to my dear child. As to Mr. Davis, he thinks the best ham, the best Madeira, the best coffee, the best hostess in the world, rendered Columbia delightful to him when he passed through.

I do not think he realized how much he cared for the general until called upon to leave him in South Carolina. I really think it did his heart good to see your reserved general and you once more. Colonel Lubbock was funny about your breakfast—and your stuffed peppers. His eyes dilated, and he assured me that there never had been such. "Why really—why, I'll tell you what! Really it was delightful!"

We are in a sad, an anxious, state here now. The dead come in—the living do not go out so fast. However, we hope all things, and trust in God as the only one able to resolve the opposite states of feeling into a triumphant happy whole.

I cannot read—but I *sew* hard and look to household matters constantly. I have only been out of the house twice since Maggie left. Her being with you is a great relief to me—for in looking forward to contingencies, I feel *she* is safe and—what is better than safe in these times—happy. I am fearful she has not clothes enough with her. Tell me frankly if it is so? I cannot depend upon her in this, for she is afraid of being a great expense to me. I cannot afford unnecessary expenses but can give her such things as her position requires—and would feel only too glad to do so.

I had a surprise of an unusually gratifying nature a few days since. I found I could not keep my horses—so I sold them. The next day they were returned to me, with a handsome anonymous note to the effect that they had been bought by a few friends for me. But I fear I cannot feed them. So my attention is now turned upon the green satin as a source of revenue. Can you make a suggestion about it? I think it will spoil if laid up and also go out of fashion. I shall probably never go into colors again and therefore can never want it. Maggie is not imminent in the matrimonial line, or she might have it. And now, dear friend, I must blow a little about my baby. No, *I* will not, for Maggie has split the trumpet, and you are disgusted with the sound. *Only*—she is so soft, so good, and so very *ladylike*—and knows me very well. She is white as a lily and has such exquisite hands and feet and such bright blue eyes. She is Piecake still. Jeff is going to dancing school. He says with great triumph that twelve lessons are nothing to him and he can take a great many more without finishing. Which I can readily believe—for I think I see an awning and four elephantine legs, and the proboscis begins to grow, and I feel tempted to say, "Look here, gentlemen, see the sense of this here animal—how he knows music and will not tread upon me as I lie extended." He has precisely the nature of an elephant. He is doing finely at school—says he likes it better than home a great sight. Maggie is also learning to dance—at a fearful rate of shoe leather. Her grace is undeniable, but she comes out at the toes. If there are any good stockings in Columbia, please send her a dozen pair. I telegraphed Mrs. Preston for some merino and some calico. As I have heard nothing of it, I conclude she did not buy it. If not, I expect it would be better not. Please telegraph me if she did so.

Mrs. George Randolph left here just before the blockade became so stringent at Wilmington. And in consequence has been detained there, waiting for a passage out with her poor husband, who has been ordered to sea by his physicians. They are staying with that Cornucopia Ficklin. But poor thing she has the 'stalled ox,' without the peace she would gladly exchange it for. She showed the womanly, tender side of her character when she bade me farewell—and seemed utterly miserable.

Nothing has so impressed me as the account of poor Mrs. Greenhow's sudden summons to a higher court than those she strove to shine in.[8] And not an hour in the day is the vivid picture which exists in my mind obliterated of the men who rowed her in across "the cruel crawling, hungry foam" and her poor wasted beautiful face all divested of its meretricious ornaments and her scheming head hanging helplessly upon those who but an hour before she felt so able and willing to deceive. She was a great woman spoiled by education—or the want of it. She has left few less prudent women behind her—and many less devoted to our cause. "She loved much," and ought she not to be forgiven? May God have mercy upon her and upon her orphan child.

Strictly between us, *things look* very anxious *here*—verbum sap.

I do wish so I could have seen Mary Preston married. She must have looked magnificently. Few people love the dear child better than I, or wish her more happiness.

I am so constantly depressed that I dread writing—even four lines betray the feeling. So I do not write to her. Kiss her and Buck and Susan for me.

Do write as often as you can, for added to my very sincere love for you, I have an enjoyment in your letters quite independent of friendly feeling. They are so charming in style. I always did insist the women who write letters in books do not do so as well as those who have no books in which to put them and therefore give bent to thoughts which critics might deride as trivial but which are the more precious to those we love because it is our only means of conveying the inner life. So tell me of yourself, of your enjoyments, your cares—everything.

I cannot bear to think we shall grow further apart until you forget me.

As ever your devoted friend

V[arina] D[avis]

Love to Mr. Chesnut.

---

8. Rose Greenhow, released from prison in Washington, had gone to Europe in 1863. Returning to the South to report to Jefferson Davis, she drowned in a vain attempt to run the blockade off Wilmington on the night of Sept. 30, 1864.

Sally Hampton went to Richmond with Rev. Mr. Martin. She arrived there on Wednesday; on Thursday her father Wade Hampton fought a great battle—and just did not win it. A victory narrowly missed. Darkness supervened, and impenetrable woods prevented that longed-for consummation.[9]

Preston Hampton rode recklessly into the hottest fire. His father sent his brother Wade to bring him back. Wade saw him reel in the saddle and galloped up to him. General Hampton followed. As young Wade reached him, Preston fell from his horse. And as he stooped to raise him was himself shot down. Preston recognized his father but died without speaking a word. Young Wade, though wounded, held his brother's head up. Tom Taylor and others hurried up. The general took his dead son in his arms, kissed him, and handed his body to Tom Taylor and his friends—made them take care of Wade—and then rode back to his post. At head of his troops in the thickest of the fray he directed the fight for the rest of the day. Until night he did not know young Wade's fate. He might be dead, too.

Now he says no son of his must be in his command. When Wade recovers he must join some other division.

The agony of that day—and the anxiety and the duties of the battlefield—it is all more than a mere man can bear.

We went to our brave boy's funeral. I loved that splendid young soldier.

Buck ran away.

"I can't bear to think of Preston," she said. "Can't bear to hear any more moaning, and weeping and wailing—if I do, I shall die."

Dr. Gibbes, who had gone to Augusta in a powerful uniform, was back already reporting everything *blue*—blue.

General Hampton had ordered Preston's grave to be dug by that of his mother. But Dr. Gibbes interfered, saying there was no space there for it. So it was dug somewhere near. That night Mr. Motte Alston[1] heard of this and went up to make a personal inspection. He found there was room enough for the poor boy by his mother's side, so he had his grave made there. So as we stood, his yawning graves awaited us. It was sad enough, God knows, without that evil augury—or omen.

Preston was not twenty.

Isabella in her rage and grief grew lightheaded anent the omen. Bury Dr. Gibbes there, alive in the grave he would dig. He would be so proud to be in the Hampton graveyard—for aye.

---

9. On Oct. 27, Hampton's cavalry prevented Federal troops from flanking the Confederate defenses at Petersburg and severing Richmond's southern lines of communication.
1. Jacob Motte Alston, a wealthy planter of Richland District.

There is a Boyce party forming. Orr denies that he belongs to it, but they are "all tarred with the same stick."

Edward Boykin told us how it worked like a dry rot in the army, all this abuse of the government.

"If it is as the newspapers say—and as Mr. Boyce &c&c&c say—why waste our blood?" grumble the soldiers. "Why should we fight and die when it is no use?" And so they disappear. They quietly desert at night and slip away home.

Richmond, Va.
Nov. 6th, 1864

My dear friend,

I had intended that General Preston should be troubled with these letters but did not get an opportunity to write them before he left.

Maggie is engaged in a stupendous letter of thanks for the dainty and beautiful diamond ring you sent her. She was more than delighted. She assumed all the airs of a woman who wears her trousseau *a little* in the country so as to get the fit of it perfect before, or against, the grand occasion. She laid it by with a sigh, remarking that after all, it was too handsome to wear to school just yet. I assured her it would ruin the shape of her finger and quickly put it on my own. It fits—and looks very well, thank you.

Maggie and Jeffie are going to school, and Jeff is actually getting an interest in Baker, Cider, and such-like two-syllable commissary stores. He tells the children "to dry up" and such-like school phrases. And then gives vent to a good many schoolboy antics and astounding tricks with slings and bows and arrows. Altogether he seems in a fair way to graduate in down street dialect.

Piecake is not well. She has been teething for some weeks and is not herself at all. She seems conscious who I am, or rather that I am her supply store—that is all. She is an immense source of comfort to me.

I was dreadfully shocked at Preston Hampton's fate—his untimely fate. I know nothing in history more touching than Wade Hampton's situation at the supremest moment of his misery—when he sent one son to save the other and saw them both fall. And he did not know for some moments whether both were not killed.

I had no patience with old Torquil—ever—when he sees his son's fate and calls so cheerily, "Another for Hector."[2]

But to come back from my little trip to Scotland—I went to see Sally Hampton. She, poor thing, does her best to keep up, for Wade's sake. I

---

2. In Sir Walter Scott, *St. Valentine's Day; or, The Fair Maid of Perth*, chapter 34, Torquil, a warrior of Clan Quhele, cries out "Another for Hector!" as each of his eight sons dies defending the clan's cowardly chieftain, Eachin (Hector) MacIan, in battle. Then Torquil himself is killed while protecting his chief.

shall go to take her to drive out with me in a few days. You know, they are staying at Mrs. Huger's.

I did not see Ally or Mrs. Huger. I had but a moment to stay with Sally. I did not ask for them. I hear the baby is sweet. What a dear old gentleman Dr. Martin is. I delighted in the little I saw of him, but the baby sent for me, and I went out of the room to nurse her, and when I returned he was gone, and I did not have the pleasure of seeing him again. Do give my love to Isabella, and tell her how glad I am to know her papa.

Mrs. Pringle and daughter passed through here a day or two since—apropos of agreeable people—and Mrs. Stanard brought them to see me. I had undressed for bed—for I am still quite weak and sent her word so—but she insisted upon my seeing them, and I was forced to decline because there were gentlemen in the only room with a fire (the little sitting room), and no other parlor had a fire. It takes me at best an hour to do my hair and dress, and I could not ask them to wait. I felt really irritated that Mrs. Stanard should make me put on the air of repulsing their civility by her insisting so strongly on my performing an impossibility. If you see Mrs. Pringle, please explain. I have read nothing—seen nothing—*heard everything*. My head is so addled I shall not repeat it. One does not like to commit murder in cold blood.

Do write to me often, and I am not sure I should be able to define what I consider often—certainly not once a week.

Maggie so happy that I dread to speak of home to her, but I think *she* must think a little of returning soon.

I should like to see a little deeper into Mr. Grant's performances before risking her here.

Tell Maggie Mrs. O'Malla is in full fig here as housekeeper-in-ordinary to the house.

I write to her by this mail. Love to dear Mrs. Preston, Mary, and the girls. My respectful regards to General Chesnut.

For you dear, the sincerest affection and gratitude of your friend.

V[arina] D[avis]

––––––––––

Mrs. Alex Taylor told us of an ingenious exchange of prisoners—a most satisfactory arrangement. Mr. Taylor undertakes to look after the brother of an Ohian M.C. who is prisoner of war here, and in return the Ohio M.C. undertakes to make John Taylor on Johnson's Island as comfortable as Mr. Taylor does his brother down here.

––––––––––

Buck and Tudy went down to the hospital with me today. There were several wounded men to be given breakfast after their wounds were attended to by the surgeons and nurses. We are only in the feeding department. At one time I was on duty, detailed to see to the breakfast of four men who could not chew at all—so *cat lap* was the word. Hominy, rice with gravy, &c&c, milk and bread. One was shot in the eye, but his whole jaw was paralyzed. Another—and the worse case—had his tongue cut away by a shot, and his teeth with it. Fortunately the father of this one had him in charge.

The father told me that he was a Southern author—had written a songbook. Madame Pelletier[3] was there and harangued us in French.

We worked like galley slaves from five in the morning until half-past eight, when the train bore away the whole of them, and we waved our handkerchiefs to them joyfully and sat down—tired to death.

A handsome specimen from Young's cavalry brigade told stories of the war—called Hampton Mars Wade and General Lee Ole Mars Robert. There was a table where all the men with crutches were sent, and Tudy told Buck to go and wait on them, which she did— her blue eyes swimming in tears all the time. She was so shy, so lovely, so efficient. All the same, I cannot bear young girls to go to hospitals, wayside or otherwise. The comments those men made on Buck's angelic beauty!

Mrs. Fisher, the good genius of our Wayside Hospital—just as her house was hospitably thrown open to a host of Virginia refugees—had her fine cow stolen by one of her own servants and made into beef before the theft was discovered. "Virtue is not rewarded in this world," said Isabella solemnly, "or Jane Fisher would never have a trouble."

Madame Pelletier denounced Calline to us. Poor Calline's want of manners infuriates the French woman. She spoke fiercely and in a foreign language, but Calline eyed us askance, as if she suspected what it all was about. Calline is a sandhiller—and rough to the hungry, sick, and sore soldiers.

A thousand dollars has slipped through my fingers already this week. At the commissaries I spent five hundred today for sugar, candles, a lamp, &c. Tallow candles are bad enough, but of them there seems to be an end, too. Now we are restricted to smoky terebene lamps—terrabene is a preparation of turpentine. When the chimney of the lamp cracks, as crack it will, we plaster up the place with paper, thick letter paper, preferring the highly glazed kind. In that hunt queer old letters come to light.

No wonder Mr. Peterkin[4] said our provisions could be carried in a porte-monnaie, and our money to buy them required a market basket to hold it. If you could see the pitiful little bundles this five hundred dollars bought. . . . [5]

Our cool Captain writes from Wilmington: there are no gnats there—but they call his fine horses "critters."

A letter from the western army signed Western Man—out and out for peace—peace at any price. ⟨⟨I call this treason.⟩⟩[6]

---

3. A French milliner who was a refugee from Charleston.
4. Probably Rev. Joshua A. Peterkin, rector of St. James Episcopal Church in Richmond.
5. Omitted is a letter, "M. F. to Dear Cousin," dated Sullivans Island, Oct. 23, 1858.
6. From the 1870s Version.

Sherman in Atlanta has left Thomas to take care of Hood. Hood has 30,000 men—Thomas 40,000 now—and as many more as he wants—he has only to ring the bell and call for more. Grant can get all that he wants, both for himself and for Thomas. All the world open to them. We shut up in a Bastille.

We are at sea. Our boat has sprung a leak.

XXVIII

"Listen for Sherman's Bugles"

November 17, 1864. Maggie Howell went back to Richmond with the Prestons. Mrs. Davis wrote to her to stay if she wished it. She seemed reluctant to go. She told John Darby it had been one of the happiest times of her life. We tried to make it so. The last weeks were gay enough. The staff did duty nobly.

Wartimes—and it comes in everywhere. A party at the Martins—supper cut short. Mrs. McKenzie, the party cook and confectioner of Columbia par excellence—and a nice old Scotch dame she is—her son, poor soul, was killed the very day of the party—and instead of a tray of good things, came back that news to the Martins.

We must sup on death and carnage or go empty.

Clancy said we could understand the French prisoners in the Reign of Terror now. They danced and flirted until the tumbril came for them, too.

Buck came and looked in at the window. As we came out, she pinned me. "You were talking about me to Clancy. I saw you."

"How could you see it? You could not hear—that is certain."

"Don't deny it. Your face always tells on you. You don't take interest in anything but me now. When you begin anything that brings me up, you grow excited, and your soul comes close up behind your eyes."

"It was Clancy who raves about you, says you are the noblest specimen of womanhood. That a man might write himself happy if you loved him, should he lose name, fame, life, and limb—&c&c. Many men loved you, he said, laying his hand tragically on his heart, who knew you were out of their reach—as high above them as the skies and the stars shining up there."

The blessed child threw her arms around my neck and nearly smothered me with kisses. Mrs. Martin drew us into her chamber for our love scene, she said, but it was only an outburst, and we parted gaily.

《Thursday Mary Cantey and Buck dined here, the latter so sad, so utterly depressed. She does not hear from Hood. Every insanity enters her head, even that J. B. may be tired of his engagement.... Buck wept and told me all her woes, all her love and trust and hope for future peace with J. B.》[1]

1. Under Nov. 11, 1864, in the 1870s Version, a roundup covering more than a week.

At five o'clock next day I went with them to take the train for Richmond.

While the whistle was blowing I saw Mary Darby shake hands with a jeune soldat—and she found time to whisper to me: "He was in college here. Decca Singleton said to him, as a quadrille was forming, 'Have you a vis-à-vis?'

" 'No—I haven't any. I have just been walking in the garden—dare say they were handed round when I was out.' "

J. C. was angry with me that I let Maggie go. How could I keep her here? Sherman is at Atlanta, and he does not mean to stay there, be it heaven or hell. Fire and sword for us here. That is the word.

And now I must begin my Columbia life anew—and alone. It will be a short shrift.

Lizzie Hamilton, who is a perfect beauty and has an eye for fun, too, told today a story of a little three-year-old.

Lizzie had called to see some young people at a house where several families were staying.

"Don't go in there," cried the little girl, pulling her skirts.

"Why?"

"The devil is in there, and the devil's name is Mrs. Tom Taylor."

"Family jokes," I said, "but rough ones." "No, family jars." No less.

General Lovell called today. "If Lincoln is not reelected," he remarked, "with his untold millions at command, his patronage, and his army and his navy, he must be a great fool indeed."

Captain Ogden came to dinner on Sunday and in the afternoon asked me to go with him to the Presbyterian church and hear Mr. Palmer. We went—and I felt very youthful, as the country people say—like a girl and her beau. Ogden took me into a pew, and J. C. sat afar off.

What a sermon! The preacher stirred my blood. My very flesh crept and tingled. A red-hot glow of patriotism passed over me. Such a sermon must strengthen the hearts and the hands of any people. There was more exhortation to fight and die à la Joshua than meek Christianity, however.

Judge Magrath dined here. He is besetting J. C. to be a candidate for governor. I take it for granted he wants to be governor himself and to use J. C. in the canvass, as a sort of lightning rod to draw off the troublesome opposition of his friends—*at first*.

Then came Mrs. Bartow, bringing me some very good tea—blockade-running tea—but it was in a glass case, shaving-soap case. So powerful is the imagination and so unreasonable the human appetite, I could not drink tea taken from a thing where shaving soap was wont to be.

Went out to drive with Mrs. Izard.

November 25, 1874.   Came home and found my nieces, Serena and Mary Williams. Le roi est mort—vive le roi. Girls are gone, girls have come, girls are my fate.

Serena is a brunette with glorious brown eyes. She carries her head proudly. She is handsome enough, but more graceful and gracious even than pretty— her mouth and teeth are exquisitely beautiful. To be truthful in small matters, I must say her red lips and her white regular teeth, for her mouth is a trifle too broad. "A real Spanish beauty," said Teddy Barnwell, when he saw her.

Mary is a delicious contrast. She is lovely—I cannot say less. Mrs. St. Julien[2] says she is the beauty of a century. She is fair and feminine, blonde with blue eyes and the longest black lashes, golden hair, rosebud mouth, a regular cupid's bow, short upper lip, complexion the purest pink and white. Affectionate in temperament, rough and abrupt in manners, audaciously clever, left-handed, near-sighted, rather clumsy in movement, beautifully formed. Serena has too much tact to show her cleverness so eagerly. These charming children—for children they are, one sixteen, the other barely fourteen—will be an awful care.

I was to have a rest—but no, here are two premature belles on my hands again.

Met William Matthews.[3] "Where did you get your new beauties? Do you keep a reserve corps of them? Always with a bevy of beauties—picked girls—as we say in the army, 'picked men for forlorn hopes.'"

These children are pets of Sally Rutledge. Ordered out my ponies and drove with them to see her—come home to meet the cool Captain driving those aforesaid sorrels through our gate, with two led horses following him.

"An unexpected *pleasure*," smiled Serena. He began his flirtation with Serena as he took his hat off. He seems overwhelmingly in love with Mary and can show it without let or hindrance. Her fourteen years are still no bar to cousinly kisses.

Brief time has Conrad now to greet Gulnare.[4]

Sherman is thundering at Augusta's very doors.[5]

My general was on the wing—somber, full of care. The girls merry as grigs. The staff who fairly live here no better.

---

2. Harriott Horry (Rutledge) Ravenel, whose husband St. Julien Ravenel was in charge of the Confederate medical laboratory at Columbia.

3. The son of a Barnwell District planter.

4. Paraphrased from Lord Byron, *The Corsair* (1814), canto 2, stanza 6.

5. Although no one was sure whether Sherman's destination was Savannah or Augusta, M. B. C. had special reason for concern: J. C. had been sent to Augusta to help prepare for the possible attack.

Cassandra with a black shawl over her head, chased by the gay crew from sofa to sofa—for she avoids them, being full of miserable anxiety.

Nothing but distraction—confusion. All things tend to the preparation for the departure of the troops.

General Chesnut left us on Tuesday. The cool Captain—as Company A is at Wilmington, N.C., and no enemy near there—did not hurry himself. He left us on Thursday.

It rains all the time—such rains as I never saw before—incessant torrents. These men came in and out in the red mud and slush of Columbia streets. Things seemed dismal and wretched *to me* to the last degree—but the staff and the girls and the youngsters did not see it.

Yesterday found an enemy in my own camp. We received a most abusive and insulting letter from Harriet Grant. She sneered at everything Southern. Her unfeeling taunts directed toward Buck by name exceeded anything I ever imagined. She seemed to hold me responsible for Confederate disasters because I would never join the cabal to tie Mr. Davis's hands and ruin our own government. If I had done so—who am I to alter or effect things, anyway? Thank God I am loyal. I am for *our side*—come what may—for Jeff Davis! The head of the Southern Confederacy! These people 19 hundred years ago would have been all for Pontius Pilate. They only care for those who are successful. It was a brutal letter.

Then Mrs. Slocum (born in Connecticut)—she was radiant. She did not come to see me—but my nieces. She says exultingly: "Sherman will open a way out at last. I will go at once to Europe or go North to my relatives there." How she derided our misery and "mocked when our fear cometh."

I daresay she takes me for a fool. I sat there dumb. She was in my own house. I have heard of a woman so enraged that she struck someone over the head with a shovel. Today for the first time in my life I know how that madwoman felt. I could have given her the benefit of shovel and tongs both.

So it is too serious. I say nothing. Mrs. Joseph Johnston behaved so differently—for after all, it is the day of her triumph. She is quiet and polite and carefully avoided awkward topics. She said General Johnston took a gloomy view of affairs. Certainly he is not singular in that. In the small matter of good manners, Mrs. Johnston is a notable example to her understrappers and followers.

When Kate came here on an exploring expedition—sort of skirmishers thrown out to feel for the enemy—I told her plainly: "You see, my house is only a barrack—soldiers running in night and day. The place is open at all hours—they come and go. One scene, par exemple—seated in our front piazza, which is only a few steps from the street. Some men in uniform asked the way to Mr. Martin's depository of clothes for soldiers. They leaned on the gate. J. C. went down and pointed out the way. Then he said, 'Come in and have some supper.' 'No, thanks we have had dinner given us on the cars by some kind ladies.'"

"Who are they?" asked Sally Goodwyn, as he came back to us.

"I do not know—soldiers asking the way, it seemed."

"Do you mean to say you ask men in to supper you never saw before, whose very names you don't know? I call that hospitality run mad."

Besides, I was so tired, so brokenhearted, I could not count on myself. I could not take care of girls now—life had gone out of me. But they came. Their mother must bear the blame if harm comes of it. She knew the risk. And I did not know how beautiful they were—and how young and thoughtless and gay and lighthearted they would be, quand même.

I sit here and listen for Sherman's bugles. I know we have nothing to put in his way but a brigade or so of troopless dismantled *generals*.

That splendid fellow Preston Hampton—home they brought their warrior dead[6]—and wrapped in that very Legion flag he had borne so often in battle in his own hand, poor boy.

Richmond, Va.
November 20th, 1864

My dear friend,

Maggie arrived safely after a good many hours detention; and looking very much better than she was when she went to you. And it is a pleasure to see a girl who has had such a good time and enjoys so much, saying so, upon all occasions. You must know how much I thank you, my dear good friend, for all your kindness to her. She is my most assailable point.

I have suffered a good deal from a sense of isolation since you and the Prestons went away. Though I think grief produces that feeling when our friends are present. However, Maggie's and the Prestons' return has brightened me up considerably.

Affairs west are looking so critical now that before you receive this you and I will be in the depths or else triumphant.

I confess I do not snuff success "in every passing breeze," but I am so tired—hoping, fearing, and being disappointed—that I have made up my mind not to be disconsolate, even though thieves break through and steal. Some people expect another attack upon Richmond shortly, but I think the avalanche will not slide until the spring breaks up its winter quarters. I have blind kind of prognostics of victory for us, but somehow I am not cheered.

6. Allusion to the song "Home They Brought Her Warrior" in Tennyson, *The Princess* (1847), part 6.

The temper of Congress is less vicious but more concerted in its hostile action. Boyce has not lost caste. "State rights," and consequently state wrongs, are rampant. Perhaps the new wine will burst the old bottles.

People do not snub me any longer, for it was only while the Lion was dying that he was kicked—dead he was beneath contempt.

Not to say I am worthy to be called a lion—nor are the people here asses.

Only I mean that I am so forlorn that they do not tell me how forlorn they think I am but are kind, and some are even affectionate—for which I thank them.

Scandal is rife here. God forbid I should repeat such black reports as I was treated to a few days ago. Girls and women are the victims—and to tell you the truth, I think the most of it is told over campfires by idle men.

Mrs. Randolph has at last been able to run the blockade. The ship was fired into one hundred times. He is much better since they arrived in Bermuda.

They say S. S. is to be married very soon to Miss Giles—who I hear is at last going to have use for her trousseau.[7]

I generally let out my crazy bone to you—so I must tell you how exquisite my little baby is. In pink she looks like a little rosebud. It is the only point upon which I feel not very sane. I should laugh at an old stout woman who was so absurd a child. So justify my fate.

The children are quite well.

X is extremely well—for him—but very anxious. How is the general? Remember me affectionably to him and to John Chesnut. Believe me gratefully and devotedly your friend,

V[arina] D[avis]

A woman that my heart aches for—in the trouble ahead!!!
Note from Mrs. McCord.

Dear Mrs. Chesnut—

At the hospital today I spoke to a Frenchman who, indeed, seemed to have not much the matter with him.

He says he is in our service because martial law compels it—but that he cared nothing about the cause and would as soon fight for the North as the South. And only wants to get away.

His manner altogether struck me as fiercely discontented and—except that he can speak little or no English—calculated to do harm.

I do not know whether I am wrong in supposing that I ought to communicate his unlucky state of mind to somebody in authority. Should I

---

7. Elizabeth Giles did marry Samuel Shannon of Camden but soon after divorced him for nonsupport.

speak to Mr. Chesnut or anybody else? If this (perhaps) trifling thing is of sufficient importance to require Mr. Chesnut to be troubled with it, shall I step round to your lodgings at any time this evening to make my report?

Hoping that you may feel better

Yours very truly

Louisa S. McCord

Things in a muddle. Johnny's colonel here today, trying to find out where his regiment is. Things are growing hopelessly mixed up.

My journal—a quire of Confederate paper—lies wide open on my desk in the corner of my drawing room. Everybody reads it who chooses. Buck came regularly to see what I had written last and made faces when it did not suit her. Isabella still calls me Cassandra and puts her hands to her ears when I begin to wail. Well, Cassandra only records what she hears—she does not vouch for it. For really, one never nowadays feels certain of anything.

Becky Wallace[8] dilated upon the doctor's horror of our actual condition—wished she was dead and that his daughters had never been born.

Mrs. Waties dwelt proudly on what "Uncle Huger" (the venerable ci-devant postmaster) thought of our danger. As for herself, she was calm and serene. She would take refuge in the insane asylum of which her father is the head.[9] She knew no Yankees would venture there—and it was bombproof.

Mr. Petigru said all South Carolina was an insane asylum. That will not save us now from fire and sword.

Mrs. Cuthbert gave us this comfort for her contribution to the conversation. All of the troops from the mountainous parts of South Carolina, and from North Carolina's mountains, too, were disaffected. They wanted peace—said this was a rich man's war—they had no part nor lot in it, would gladly desert in a body. That our returned prisoners were broken-spirited and said they had had enough of it.

I sat down, dumb—and then came in Malley Howell, who said, not knowing anything of the preceding talk,

"Our returned prisoners come back, fired with patriotism, and will fight this thing through to the death."

He was in such excellent spirits—mine rose, too. Then he showed us maps and traced with his finger how and where Sherman was sure to be bagged.

Absolutely I found myself believing him.

The two Wigfall girls dined here today—and a daughter of Senator Hill.[1] Mr.

8. The wife of John Wallace.

9. Frances (Parker) Waties was the wife of Columbia attorney John Waties and the daughter of Dr. John W. Parker.

1. Louly and Fanny Wigfall were en route to rejoin their parents in Richmond. Henrietta Hill was going to her father's house in western Ga.

Hill wrote to ask me to take charge of her and keep her with me at my house. When we went for her at the convent, she had already left it and was staying at Nickersons'.

She likes the Nickersons so much—she refuses to leave them. They have a fine turnout, and she drives with them in their landau every evening.

Nickerson is the hotel keeper. I tried to persuade her to come with me, as her father wished it, but I had no power to coerce her. And maybe with them it is the new rule—parents, obey your children—and she will make it all right. She said, "Leave me to deal with my father—he trusts me implicitly."

My girls thought themselves well read in modern poetry. That is, standard and classic English. But little Hill had the floor. They were nowhere. She spread all sail—or took the wind out of their sails completely. She had Owen Meredith at her fingers' ends, and they did not know him at all.

"Don't you remember this—or that?"

"Alas, no—I have not read Owen Meredith."

"It is as well as it is," I said. "I am not sorry—better for you to find out while you are young how much more other people know than you do. Anything, my dears, better than the awful self-complacency of the modern American girl." I said not a word of how small was the shame of not knowing Owen Meredith. But I sent to Camden at once for my copy—that they might keep up with the world.

———————

At the Wayside Hospital a young man from Louisiana fell to my lot. He was clever and good-looking—and a Beauregard man down to the ground. "If you have Beauregard, you are all right. No Joe Johnston for me. He was backing straight into the Gulf of Mexico when they nipped him. I know what I am talking about. Haven't I retreated with Joe Johnston for four years—and was just about tired of it? I tell you, he was about to take water. Bully for Beauregard! He is the man for me!" &c&c.

November 28, 1864. We dined at Mrs. McCord's. She is as strong a cordial for broken spirits and failing heart as one could wish.

How her strength contrasts with our weakness! Like Dr. Palmer, she strings one up to bear bravely the worst. She has the intellect of a man and the perseverance and endurance of a woman.

Poor Cheves's beautiful young widow[2] was there—not yet twenty, and for more than two years in widow's caps. She has a touchingly pathetic smile. It enhances her beauty wonderfully.

———————

2. Charlotte (Reynolds) McCord.

Saw Boylston, my old friend, now Speaker of the House.[3] He is Mr. Preston's main reliance, his chief friend in the legislature. I hope he will make Mr. Preston governor.

Mrs. Singleton says, "Unfortunately Mr. Preston has paid him beforehand."

"That's bad."

"How?"

"Got him some office or place he coveted."

General Hampton's house has been robbed—all of his wife's jewelry taken, everything available stolen. Isabella: "It took her to leave it in an empty house."

The robbers left derisive notes behind them: "Hang Hampton," "Damn Hampton." All the compliments of the season—"Rebel," "Cattle Stealer," &c&c.

The foreign battalion gets the credit of this deed—composed as it is of renegades from every nation and Yankee deserters (with them, anything to get out of prison, I fancy).

And they are here, camped under my nose. Stark Means says squads of Yankee prisoners escape every night.

The impudence of this robbery strikes one—with its accompanying written defiance. It is trying.

Halcott Green, too, raises one's spirits. A male Mrs. Nickleby—he expected every minute to see a man on horseback gallop up—not to announce that Cheeryble Bros. have taken young Nicholas into copartnership but that by the help of, or in spite of, Old Nick, every Yankee in the land is killed. At least he says: "Take my word for it. Good news—wonderful news is coming."

That horseman had better hurry up, then—time is short now. We have lost nearly all of our men, and we have no money. And it looks as if we had taught them to fight since Manassas. Our best and bravest are under the sod. We have to wait for another—till another generation grows up. Here we stand—despair in our hearts ("Oh, Cassandra, don't!" shouts Isabella) and our houses burnt, or about to be, over our heads.

They have just got things shipshape. Splendid army—perfectly disciplined—new levies coming in day and night to them. We could bear that, but think of these women and children. What are a handful of officers? These gentry do not go into the ranks. They hardly know there is a war up there.

"Yes—they know of the shoddy fortunes they are piling up, cheating their government. They dwell in these comfortable cities—tranquil, in no personal fear. The war is only a pleasurable excitement."

"When are we to have peace?"

"When the wicked cease some trembling and the weary are at rest."[4]

"If we had *only* freed the negroes at first and put them in the army—that would have trumped their trick."

---

3. Robert Bentham Boylston, a wealthy lawyer from Fairfield District, had served in the general assembly throughout the war.

4. Slight misquotation of Job 3:17.

"No use now. Years ago when J. C. spoke to his negroes about it, his head-men, they were keen to go in the army—free, and bounty after the-war. Now they say coolly they don't want freedom if they have to fight for it."

"That means they are pretty sure of having it anyway."

November 30, 1864.   Cassandra watches the drill of the First Foreign Battalion from her windows.

"They are arming them—they are training them. Then the wretches will burn the town and march to meet Sherman!"

The girls went with Mrs. Singleton and Sally Rutledge. A legislator, soiled and wounded, joined them. He has lost an arm. Lost it at Seven Pines. How can he, poor helpless creature, keep neat and clean? Another came up in a carriage. He had lost a leg in the service of his country. He is likewise a member of the legislature. What a noble use to make of our wounded veterans. Put them, the disabled ones, in the halls of the legislature—and turn out the able-bodied and send them to the front.

Red-hot resolutions by Trescot and the Rhetts—the temper of the House roused, states rights rampant—we are about to secede again from the Confederacy.[5] No doubt the Devil raved of "Devil's rights" in Paradise. Luther protesting is sublime, but when the groundlings take to protesting against Luther, it is troublesome. The Yankees were right in one thing—how stay disintegration when it once begins?

"How—don't you like Dr. Gibbes's philosophy in the *Carolinian?*"

"I understand it. I cannot say I sympathize exactly with it."

"Here it is—condensed. Let those fight on who have fought for four years—they know how, they have caught the trick of it. And leave those in peace who have printed and published and farmed skillfully for number one and no other and have carefully skulked the fight with credit and comfort to themselves so far. How beastly, as the British Bierne[6] says, to interfere with them now!"

At Mrs. St. Julien's, met the exquisitely highbred, the fragile and beautiful, Miss Rutledge.[7] She was shocked, she said, "to hear this question mooted—putting negroes in the army. Alas! If you had left our dear Joe Johnston in command of the western army, things would never have come to this pass." Her sister Sally came home with us. She is not a regular beauty (as Miss Lize is). She is

5. Trescot and Robert Barnwell Rhett, Jr., were responding to the startling message with which Jefferson Davis opened the last session of the Confederate Congress on November 7, 1864. No longer unwilling to discuss arming the slaves, the president called for government purchase of 40,000 slaves who would be emancipated after "service faithfully rendered" in noncombatant military roles. Davis also suggested sending slaves into combat if white soldiers alone could no longer guarantee Southern independence. The president's proposal did not win congressional approval, and it prompted Trescot's and Rhett's resolutions in the S.C. general assembly that any emancipation law would be an unconstitutional interference with the states' control of slavery.

6. A captain of the foreign battalion.

7. Eliza Pinckney Rutledge, a cousin of Mrs. Ravenel.

good and clever as the cleverest. Looks like one of Stuart's Revolutionary high-born dames just stepping out of its frame.

December 1, 1864.   Through the deep waters we wade. General Chesnut writes from Allendale—wherever that is.[8] In my faraway youth I sung the "Rose of Allandale"—long since faded. Alas.

At Coosawhatchie, Yankees landing in great force.[9] Our troops down there are raw militia—old men and boys never under fire before. Some college cadets—in all, a mere handful. "The cradle and the grave" is robbed by us, they say.

Sherman goes to Savannah and not to Augusta.

————————

The girls went with the Martins to the State House. Senate deliberating how much cotton they would allow a man to plant next year.

The House put off until noon tomorrow a bill to raise men for home defense.

The enemy thundering at their gates—they can still fool themselves with *words*. Sounds signifying nothing.

And yet the men who would not join Noah in his Ark-building must have left no descendants.

————————

Isabella is the chaperon en titre of this young party. They do not count Sherman at all among the devastating forces of nature. I do believe they forget his existence. Youth is enough for happiness. These lighthearted creatures had also Tim Trezevant[1] to assist Isabella tonight. They have gone to a party.

December 2, 1864.   Isabella and I put on bonnets and shawls and went deliberately out for news. We determined to seek until we found some.

Met a man so ugly I could not forget him—or his sobriquet. He was awfully in love with me once. He did not know me—and blushed hotly when Isabella told him who I was. Forgotten me, I hope—or else I am changed by age and care past all recognition. He gave us the encouraging information that Grahamville was burned to the ground.[2]

Then we met Mr. Conrad, Confederate States senator from Louisiana. He was in high spirits. That sort of thing is catching—so we were under obligation to him for lifting up our hearts.

Met Nannie Mazyck, who said she was coming with her daughters to tea with

8. Allendale, S.C., was near the Savannah River, about midway between Augusta and Savannah.

9. Seeking to isolate Savannah, Federal forces from Beaufort moved against the Charleston and Savannah Railroad in late Nov. To meet this threat, J. C.'s command was ordered to Coosawhatchie and Grahamville, S.C., northeast of Savannah.

1. John Timothée Trezevant, a cousin of Dr. Daniel Trezevant, was a lieutenant of engineers in the foreign battalion.

2. A false report of the outcome of a fight at Honey Hill, a few miles from Grahamville, on Nov. 30.

us that night. Met Mrs. Cuthbert, who said she was coming—that is, if we were sure you would not meet a soul. She was too miserable, she said, to face any company whatever. "So do not ask anyone to meet me." We promised that we would not. Nannie, who was along, said after Mrs. Cuthbert left us that she counted for naught—besides, we had not invited her. Since Mrs. Cuthbert's expressed desire for solitude, she did not [think] Mrs. C would find it quiet enough.

Then we saw some soldiers with most militia backs, awkwardly arresting some skulkers or deserters. One man we saw turn as white as a sheet. He was the picture of abject terror. Another, of altogether another mettle, jeered.

"Don't you come near me with that gun. I am afraid of a gun."

"I wish I could sketch that scene," said Isabella. "It had its comic side."

"And for our cause, it is no laughing matter. Ten men—to drag in two."

When the call for horses was made, Mrs. McCord sent in her five bays. She comes now with a pair of mules—and looks *too* long at my ponies. If I were not so much afraid of her, I would hint: those mules would be of far more use in camp than my ponies. But they will seize the ponies, no doubt.

In all my life before, stables were far off from the house, and I had nothing to do with them. Now my ponies are kept under an open shed next the back piazza. Here I sit with my work or my desk or my book, basking in our Southern sun—and I watch Mat feed, curry, and rub down the horses and then clean their stalls as thoroughly as Smith does my drawing room. I see their beds of straw comfortably laid. Mat says, "Ow, Missis, ain't lady business to look so much in de stable." I care nothing for his grumbling—and I have never had horses in better condition. Poor ponies, you deserve every attention and enough to eat. Grass does not grow under your feet. Night and day you are on the trot. Mat has been on the coast at some fortification there. And as he rubs down a horse he tells war stories—not to me, but he knows I hear.

"You see Buckra hard run down there! I didn't mind helping them—but dere overseer so mean. When a bomb come—a whiz, a-whiz, a-whizzz—we all had to run for de dear life an' fall on top de overseer. He lay down flat soon as he hear bomb a-coming, and we pile on him, we niggers, till we mek pile on niggers, high as dish here shed Missis call her stable. Buckra down below, nigger heap on top—dat's de way he try to save he life."

"Mat, are we to believe such a foolish tale as that?"

"Clar to God, Missis, it's a fac'."

Mrs. McCord's mules I left at the door of this narrative. Hannah came and bore me off to question Richardson Miles. He has for us always the best of bad news. Today he was grandly patriotic. He fairly hung his head, so shocked and mortified was he that Sherman had marched unmolested through Georgia.

Today General Chesnut was in Charleston, on his way from Augusta to Savannah by rail. Telegraph still working between Charleston and Savannah. Grahamville certainly burnt. Fighting down there today. Came home with enough to think about, heaven knows.

And then all day long we compounded a pound cake in honor of Mrs. Cuthbert, who has things so nice at home. The cake was a success. Was it worth all that trouble? Molly was not grateful for our aid. Said we did not help—we *hindered* her—and threatened, if we did not keep out of her kitchen, to pin the dish rag to Serena.

Teddy Barnwell came with his wife. He said goodbye on his way to the coast. So far he could not impress the horses, as he was detailed to do, for the brigade. Promised to keep us better advised as to what was going on in the army. For the last ten days he knows how it is himself—this frantic anxiety to hear that we stay-at-homes feel. He left Dr. Gibbes in tears over his valuable paintings that damp walls were ruining (and the rain it raineth every day). Teddy comforted him. If fire could dry his walls, he thought Sherman would soon do it for him. Dr. Gibbes signified that he was then packing for a flight in time to save nine.

Mrs. Cuthbert came beautifully dressed for the solitude she had bespoken.

Nannie and her nice little daughters were on hand. As we were drinking our tea, Smith handed me a note.

"A soldier man brought this to Miss Serena."

The young Trezevant whom we met at Mrs. Slocum's—and who has haunted the house since these girls came—wrote this note to Serena, asking her to go with him to a concert. She was all in a flutter at being written to by a strange young man. I answered the note in the third person—bade him come to tea with us—and we could see about it. He must have been "the soldier" who brought the note, for he walked right in.

After a faint remonstrance Mrs. Cuthbert was induced to chaperone the girls. She would go as a victim to duty for she would not deprive the girls of such a pleasure. She would not be obstinate or selfish. Young Trezevant opened his eyes as I marshaled the clan he was to escort. He had come to take Serena—alone. That is his wild western fashion, he told me.

Nannie and I had enough to talk about. We scarcely missed them before they were back upon us—enchanted. Such a good time!

Mrs. Cuthbert was repaid for all her sacrifices. Stephen Elliott joined her at once—and with General Elliott at her side, she was the cynosure of all eyes. Then he told her what was known of Sherman and Savannah—&c.

And this was the end of her solemn declaration that she would only come if we promised not one human being but herself &c&c&c.

As my party were driving off to the concert, an omnibus rattled up. Enter Captain Leland of General Chesnut's staff, of as imposing a presence as a field marshal—handsome and gray-haired. He was here on some military errand and brought me a letter. He said the Yankees were repulsed, and down in those swamps we could soon give a good account of them—if they would only send us men enough. With a sufficient army to meet them down there, they would be annihilated.

"Where are the men to come from?" asked Nannie mildly. "General Hood has gone off to Tennessee. Even if he does defeat Thomas there, what difference would that make here? He could not overtake Sherman, you know."

"Sherman," wailed Cassandra, "will soon effect a juncture with Grant and leave us a howling wilderness. If General Hood could get to Lee's army, it would be *no use* now." And I fairly broke down. Mrs. McCord does not weep. She works like a Trojan.

Read *Mademoiselle de Seiglière.*[3] In its way, perfection.

Letter from the cool Captain. Why he has been kept in Wilmington till now a mystery to him. He is ordered to Virginia at last.

"He must make up to stand up to some—I ought to say 'one'—of his flirtations," quoth Isabella.

"No, the scamp says a saber cut or a shot from the Yankees may soon solve all of his difficulties in that matter."

⟨⟨Buck is happy. J. B. has written, and she says, fancy "my raptures"—two letters, and he is coming in January to be *married.*⟩⟩[4]

December 3, 1864.   Foreign legion now muster eleven hundred strong. The War Office has sent down a corps of youngsters from the military institute in Virginia, to drill and muster this battalion into service. And a finer set of young men I never saw. Was Kate mad, after all I made plain to her, that she sent these beautiful children here? After dress parade stood Serena, surrounded by them. These splendid six-feet boys with their clear white and red complexions, fresh from the mountains, bright and laughing faces—withal made irresistible by their uniforms. It was young Trezevant who presented the Virginia contingent. A formidable force, I should say, to anxious mothers of grown daughters.

We drank tea at Mrs. McCord's. She had her troubles, too. The night before, a country cousin claimed her hospitality—one who fain would take the train at five this morning. A little after midnight Mrs. McCord was startled out of her sleep by loud ringing of bells—an alarm at night may mean so much just now. In an instant she was on her feet. She found it was her guest, who thought it was daylight and wanted to go. Mrs. McCord forcibly demonstrated how foolish it was to get up five hours too soon.

Mrs. McCord, once more in her own warm bed, fell happily to sleep. She was waked by feeling two ice-cold hands pass cautiously over her face and person. It was pitch-dark. Even Mrs. McCord (the "Mother of the Gracchi") gave a scream in her fright. She found it was only the irrepressible guest up and at her. So though it was but three o'clock, to quiet this perturbed spirit she got up and at five drove her to the station—where she had to wait hours. But Mrs. McCord said, "Anything for peace at home."

3. Léonard Sylvain Jules Sandeau, *Mademoiselle de la Seiglière* (1847).
4. From the 1870s Version.

Met there a young person from Tennessee. She was an ardent partisan of Joe Johnston. And in this wise she stated her case—and backed them.

"So I was told—and my authority? Oh, high up as a major general. He said, says he, 'Miss,—.' And says I,

" 'Now, I do declare, general,' &c&c&c."

Grahamville
December 2, 1864

My dear Mary,

When I wrote you last, my destination was Savannah, but the attack on this place caused me to be here. We marched all night Tuesday and reached the battlefield in the morning and found the enemy had been repulsed with great slaughter in proportion to the numbers engaged. The enemy had about five thousand men. We had two thousand five hundred. I have not slept since I left Hamburg, being in command of the forces here. General Hardee informed me this morning that I am to be left here in command with only my four hundred and fifty reserves and two pieces of artillery to hold this place.

The force is in the main undisciplined, broken down, and by *itself* comparatively worthless—*entre nous.*

God bless you. Write to me here as soon as practicable. I may get your letter. As ever yours,

J. C., Jr.

We will do the best we can.

December 5, 1864.   General Lee has had seven hundred men surprised and taken prisoner—and we cannot spare a man![5]

Down here we are surprised at nothing.

Now they say G. W. Smith with the Georgia militia won the fight at Grahamville.

Half of the Yankee force was negroes. It was the bloodiest of fights—a carnage.

Before the dead were buried next day, the battlefield was awful to see.

Introduced to a legislator who is a Methodist parson and a colonel of infantry—a Cerberus, as Mrs. Malaprop would say, three persons in one.[6] He is vastly agreeable—specially as he is a friend of my husband. So with Captain Bierne and Lieutenant Brockenbrough, who were so devoted *to me* at dress parade, I asked him to tea. Sally Rutledge hints so much foreign battalion is a

---

5. Apparently a false rumor.
6. A line, slightly misquoted, from Sheridan, *The Rivals,* act 4, scene 2.

mistake on my part. I think so, too. They are at my doors, however. And I know of no way to keep them out.

These splendid young fellows have fine old Virginia names—Dinwiddie, Barton, Brockenbrough—absolutely historic.

Louly Wigfall came to say goodbye, for her father and mother's sake. I would like to see more of her and be kind to her, but her Johnston proclivities made her stand aloof very stiffly. Besides, my young ones fill my carriage now with their cronies. They never leave me a corner for mine.

They have elected Lizzie Hamilton and Maggie Martin[7] for their devoted and inseparable friends. Surely they are not afraid of beauteous rivals. Little Lizzie Hamilton is that rare thing—a perfect beauty. And a clever little witch, beside.

And the foreign battalion comes closer and closer. They fairly drill now at my front steps. We are sitting on the porch or at our windows, as a general rule, never enough to catch the eyes of the officers as they step about—inspired, no doubt, by that fact. We can see their white teeth as they smile in passing us. This is enlivening if it is a dangerous proximity for the *too* young ladies. Also they have a capital band of music, which every afternoon—another distraction. We need all that we can get of that.

Miss Olivia Middleton and Mr. Frederick Blake[8] are to be married tomorrow night. We Confederate have invented the sit-up-all-night—the wedding night. Isabella calls it the wake—not the wedding of the partners married.

The ceremony will be performed early in the evening. The whole company will then sit up until five o'clock, at which hour the bridal couple take the train for Combahee.

Hope Sherman will not be so inconsiderate as to cut short the honeymoon.

Arnoldus VanderHorst is a queer kind of old-fashioned gentleman. He can be grateful for a kindness and is not ashamed to show it. He asked J. C. to get him a place on General Whiting's staff. The War Office made no objection, and his appointment was sent by return mail. Governor Allston spoke to J. C. and thanked him for his prompt action in the matter. And now Arnoldus VanderHorst is very attentive and kind to John Chesnut at Wilmington and tells him also how much obliged he is to J. C. for a good place—in all this mad confusion.

Here comes in the oddness of Mr. VanderHorst. Of all the hundreds that J. C. has helped in this business of promotion, no one has even come back to thank him. Indeed, they seem to grow restive under a sense of ill-usage and attribute their rise to their unaided military merit. To themselves alone they ascribe all of the credit.

---

7. A sister of Isabella Martin.
8. Capt. Frederick Rutledge Blake, a surgeon of the Twenty-fifth N.C. Regiment, was a son of Walter Blake.

Our cool Captain—like Dick Swiveller and his debts—the Captain's too numerous flirtations are shutting up all streets or places to him. He does not know which to avoid most strenuously. Still, the comedy may turn to a tragedy—with the bullets flying as they are now.

Compliment to Richardson Miles. We drove as usual to his office in quest of news and got our invariable answer.

"Nothing new."

"Don't grumble. It is not waste time. I do not grudge it—he is so nice—so agreeable, &c&c."

December 6, 1864.   The fortunes of war! A fascinating [conversation]. At the door he left Serena. It was wide open, and I heard a sentimental murmur.

"Ah. It will be six long hours ere I see you again. Will you write to me?" And then her ringing laugh and her answer.

"A most modest request!"

So when he came tonight I asked him when he had last heard from *his wife*.

When he had gone—the cry of amazement.

"And the wretch is married!"

Chaperon Isabella boasted of her day's daring exploit.

At the door of the House of Representatives they met Nathalie Heyward—who begged they would send her cousin the Hon. Barnwell Rhett out to her. It was [not] comme il faut for ladies to go in alone. Selon les règles or not, said Isabella, we were going in without a man to make it respectable, and we resented Nathalie's insinuation and our destitute situation. So we sat, watching Barnwell Rhett's fine gray head, but we sent him no word. How we chuckled at the idea of Nathalie cooling her heels in the lobby—she who had so frankly reproved our way of doing things.

The First Foreign is too near. Three of their men have been taken up for an attempt at garotting. They were heavily manacled, poor wretches, as they marched them by, and they were driven with bayonets pointed at their backs—up and down the line. They had put on barrel shirts on some others—and they had to march to the tune of "Rogues' March." I could not bear to look. The man in the barrel shirt is an Irishman born in this country. He seems to feel his degradation cruelly. In Baltimore politics he had made his mark as a plug ugly. A man was bucked—and another riding the wooden horse. When the men refused to hoot at these poor things as they were driven along, an officer struck several of them with the flat of his sword. These are the dumb, driven cattle expected to be heroes in the strife after such treatment.

We have shut all the windows on the house on that side.

Captain Bierne, who is an Englishman, Lieutenant Trezevant—I may say a dozen or so of them—are here every day. They drink tea here every night and often come to breakfast. Molly thinks our hospitality overdone. "Name o'

God—'young ladies, give me some warning night before when they are coming to breakfast, so I may set more rolls and muffins to rise."

Governor Bonham has issued a proclamation. If we credit it, things are looking brighter for us. I do not see why. I could understand a brightening of our prospects, a rift in the cloud, if we had only some men to our generals. We could form a brigade of generals any day.

Read *Ruth*[9] today. Mrs. McCord sent me a life of Savonarola.

Romola drove me into looking up a life of Savonarola.

Uncle H came—calm and serene, self-poised, self-satisfied, cool and dignified, stiff with his company manners.

He was riding that animal commonly called a high horse. Now for his information.

Franklin Moses, Trescot, Whaley,[1] &c&c are openly for reconstruction.

Nobody there to answer them. These howl of personal grievances and private animosities all taking refuge behind the shield of partialism.

Stephen Elliott, who fights his country's battles so effectively, is dumb—can only vote against them. He said Magrath would be the next governor, then Perry, then Franklin Moses, for reaction had set in. They would not make Mr. Preston governor. When they found someone was needed to beat Magrath, they wanted to nominate Mr. Chesnut, but Uncle Hamilton for him firmly declined.

"My friend's name shall not be used this way at the last moment to lead a forlorn hope. So I have refused the office of governor for Chesnut. I hope I did not make a mistake. Candidly, I am sure I lost him the senator's election. That was when I refused to join forces with Mr. Barnwell's friends until after Chesnut's election was over. As he was the incumbent and there was no fault found with him, I thought it due him to elect him first of all."

The girls were furious. It would have been so nice to be governor—&c&c.

"There was no talk of anything more than candidate for governor, little goslings. And thank God, no one you care for will be in the governor of South Carolina's shoes *now*."

"Why, he will walk through the valley of the shadow of death."

"Oh, you screech owl!"

"But, Uncle Hamilton, are we going down to perdition? You talk of Franklin Moses!!" Then wailed Cassandra, who hopes they will not call her screech owl, too:

"Such is our fate! Down, down we go—in manners, morals, and common honesty."

Then Uncle Hamilton attacked our finances. Serena fell asleep, but Mary listened attentively. After he went away:

---

9. A novel by Elizabeth Cleghorn (Stevenson) Gaskell published in 1853.
1. William Whaley, a Charleston lawyer and state legislator.

"Auntie, did you understand what he was saying?"

"No. Neither did he—and there is where the confusion came in, and Serena dozed comfortably."

We were very tired, and it was late.

"Weariness of spirit has overtaken me. I am dead beat. To bed, to bed, said sleepyhead." A violent knocking.

"Wake up Smith. Tell him to find out who it is before he opens the door."

In tripped Brewster, with his hat on his head, both hands extended, and his words of greeting:

"Well, here we are!"

He was travel-stained, disheveled, grimy with dirt. The prophet would have to send him to bathe many times in Jordan before he pronounced him clean.

Hood will not turn and pursue Sherman. Thomas is at his heels with forty thousand men—and can have as many more as he wants for the asking. Between Sherman and Thomas, Hood would be crushed. So he was pushing—I do not remember where or what. I know there was no comfort in anything he said.

Serena's account of money spent.

paper and envelopes	$12.00
tickets to concert	10.00
toothbrush	10.00
	$32.00

December 10, 1864.   Sally Rutledge went with [me] to hunt for Mrs. Dick Anderson.[2] We met a squad of the Foreign Legion going to guard the Prestons' house. Is it not putting a cat to take care of the cream?

At a party at Isabella's last night, the Virginia contingent came out strong.

Captain James sings well. So does Lieutenant Trezevant. While they were playing "Consequences," another accomplishment developed itself. Another James, cleverer still, sketched all of them. When he ought to have written their names, he drew their heads—admirable likenesses &c&c—picture writing. Mary in some of the forfeits had to recite a German poem—and as she did so, James translated it into English verse. Sketching, rhyming, and all that— knowing German! They think he is a genius and an improvisatore. They came radiant. They found Cassandra moaning on the sofa, with her shawl over her head.

---

2. The wife of Gen. Richard Heron Anderson.

Allen Green and Joe Barnwell wounded.[3] That was Richardson Miles's news today. Mrs. McCord and I drove at once to the Greens. Sally Goodwyn met us at the door—her teeth chattering with excitement.

"Allen's wound only a flesh wound. It is in his cheek. May make an ugly scar, but he is in no danger of his life."

"Such a handsome boy. I hope he will not be disfigured."

"I am glad the brave boy has escaped anything more deadly. He would go. Just now he said none of his family were handling a musket for his country—and he could not stand it."

We then went to the Barnwells. Joe is as much too young as Allen.

Nancy Barnwell came out to the carriage. Joe is wounded in the knee, and she is miserably anxious. She has three other brothers under fire down on the coast.

The struggle was a fierce one. Militia do not often stand and they had elected their officers only the night before the Honey Hill fight.[4] General Chesnut sent Stephen Barnwell[5] to take command of them, but after they had elected their own officers, he returned to his own troops.

December 12, 1864. Such rumors all day long. Road cut at Pocataligo.

Isabella came, she said, "to raise a corner of the shroud of misery that wraps Cassandra in."

She took her fling at the mighty ones of the earth. . . . [6]

Everybody comes to tea at my house every evening, I think. Last night said Bierne, the Britisher,

"How did Mrs. Chesnut look when she called her husband P.D.? Precious darling, you know."

"Very much as she did a moment ago, when you kindly informed her that in England they called an Earl "my lord." When they begin to play cards Isabella leaves. She thinks that sinful.

"Now you confuse me. How can I play if you confuse me with that kind of talk of Miss Hamilton?"

Now, nobody had mentioned Lizzie Hamilton, but he was obliged to introduce that topic himself. Of the fullness of the heart the mouth speaketh.

3. Allen Green III was the son of Halcott Green and the nephew of Sally Goodwyn; Joseph Walker Barnwell was a brother of Teddy Barnwell. The two boys, members of the cadet corps of the S.C. Military Academy, were wounded in a minor fight a few miles from Coosawhatchie.

4. Although G. W. Smith's Ga. militia had withstood the Federal assault at Honey Hill on Nov. 30, Union forces remained encamped within sight of the Charleston and Savannah Railroad. As the Georgians withdrew, they were replaced by S.C. reserves, some of them under J. C.'s command, who had arrived too late for the battle itself.

5. Stephen Elliott Barnwell, a brother of Joe and Nancy Barnwell.

6. Unintelligible speech of Isabella's deleted.

At supper Lieutenant Trezevant raised his glass. "I drink confusion to Captain Bierne—the confusion he likes so well."

"Then, since he will have it—"

At twelve o'clock I turned them all out and announced my fixed determination to do so every night.

"No more words will be needed. I will say twelve o'clock, and you must go, hereafter."

———————

And now the young ones are in bed—and I am wide awake. It is an odd thing. In all my life how many persons have I seen *in love*? Not a half-dozen—and I am a tolerably close observer. A faithful watcher have I been from my youth upward—of men and manners. Society has been for me only an enlarged field for character study.

Flirtation is the business of society. That is, playing at lovemaking. It begins in vanity—it ends in vanity.[7] It is spurred on by idleness and a want of any other excitement. Flattery—battledore and shuttlecock—how in this game flattery is dashed backward and forward. It is so soothing to self-conceit. If it begins and ends in vanity, vexation of spirit supervenes sometimes. They do burn their fingers awfully sometimes—playing with fire—but there are no hearts broken.

Each party in a flirtation has secured a sympathetic listener to whom they can talk of themselves. Somebody who for the time admires them exclusively—and, as the French say, *incessamment.* It is a pleasant but very foolish game—and so to bed.

———————

William Evans[8] was here tonight. We asked him to vote for General Preston for governor.

"We came here to vote for General Chesnut, but as I find he will not have it, I will vote as you say. Why am I always looking up in the galleries? My future daughter-in-law may be there. I am speculating as to that. I have four sons—no daughters."

At any rate, that was an original way of accounting for attention to pretty girls.

Mrs. Bartow was here with her budget of news. The letter from Richmond urging Mr. Preston's election had defeated him.

"There never was any such letter."

"I have seen it."

"Oh—we did not believe in its existence."

And now old Arthur P. Hayne is denouncing Mr. Davis and Hood in his senile way, in the streets and to all who will stop and listen to him.

And old Boxplaits, too. He went to Richmond for an office for his son or

———————

7. Here and below, allusions to Ecclesiastes.
8. William Henry Evans, a wealthy planter and state legislator from Darlington District, was the brother-in-law of John and Mary Serena Chesnut (Williams) Witherspoon.

himself—maybe both. He did not get it. And he has joined the malignants. He breathes fire and sword.

"Pity he would not turn his breath against the Yankees."

Richardson Miles:

"Cleburne and Gist are killed." And (mournfully): "Can any victory pay for so much death?"[9]

General Hardee telegraphed for General Lovell—then to Richmond: "May be he employed once more in the service?"

Answer: "No." Fancy Mrs. Bartow's face as she told us of this snub to Berrien Lovell. Mrs. Bartow—née Berrien.

And Lovell brought us such good news. He came in such a sanguine mood—before the War Office would have none of him. He said Savannah was safe—we have men enough there. Dick Taylor was behind Sherman with another army.

"Where did he get it?" from the irrepressible Isabella. "How these people manufacture men in buckram! Do you wonder New Orleans fell, with this sanguine person in command of it?"

"As Miss Ann Hampton says, have you a ray of hope? I try to lay hold of one, but it is evanescent."

Note from Sue King. Went to Nickerson's to see her. Found her in scarlet facings, as Mr. Capers[1] said, having hauled down the flag of distress (widow's cap) and run up a Union Jack.

She was on the wing to hear McGowan[2] speak—another governor expectant.

And then I had to walk home this freezing day in slippers. Had to get out and send the carriage to the coach makers—something the matter with one wheel which made it unsafe.

Last night the usual amount of Bierne, Trezevant, Brockenbrough—when Sally Rutledge and I found Mrs. Dick Anderson at Nickerson's. And Linden saw another sight—&c&c. We had a glimpse of hotel life *in wartimes.* Saw little Hill, who ought to [be] staying with me—as indeed her father thinks she is. But I see now how life at my house would pall upon her, after this free and easy existence. It was an exciting scene, that hotel drawing room. I fancied some of the men, *whose wives I knew,* drew away an inch or two from the sirens by whom they were lolling on sofas. I do not wonder now that the department girls living at these hotels get themselves talked about. The degree of familiarity and

---

9. Patrick Cleburne and States Rights Gist were two of the five Confederate generals who died in John Bell Hood's futile assault on the command of U.S. Maj. Gen. John Schofield at the battle of Franklin, Tenn., on Nov. 30.

1. Possibly Samuel Capers, a Columbia bank officer.

2. Samuel McGowan, a member of the S.C. general assembly from Union District.

intimacy between our noted legislators and some of these women whose names are in everybody's mouth was unconsciously and frankly exhibited to us. And I took a queer way of showing my disapproval (according to Sally Rutledge). I walked across the room and took my seat by the one most maligned of all by the town. I wanted to show them, then and there, that I did not believe a word of their vile stories.

───────────

Hood and Thomas have had a fearful fight.[3] Carnage—loss of generals excessive in proportion to numbers. That means they were leading, urging their men up to the enemy. I know how Bartow and Barnard Bee were killed, bringing up their men. One of Mr. Chesnut's sins, thrown in his teeth by the legislature of South Carolina, was that he procured the promotion of Gist— States Rights Gist—by his influence in Richmond. What have these comfortable stay-at-home patriots to say of General Gist now!

> And how could man die better
> Than facing fearful odds
> For[4]—

───────────

Sue King dropped in. She found Mrs. Anderson was to stay to tea. She at once borrowed the carriage which drove up at the moment—*she said* to see Helen Singleton.[5] Afterward we thought: to rush home and array herself gorgeously for the fray. My mature matrons unbosomed themselves bravely. They are all as old as I am. Again, said Isabella, "Their style is the unenclothesed common." Mrs. Lovell is handsome and accomplished, too. These three clever women of the world must have been annoyed to meet each other in this quiet nook. A remarkable trio—for this dead-alive village. Youngsters were fenced off in another room.

We had an excellent salad and sandwiches, good wine—nay, the best of old sherry. Eggnog left nothing to be desired.

The young crew had cake and lemonade served out to them.

Mrs. King went for Captain James, straight as an arrow. There was a link between them, a mutual friend, now in jail as a convicted spy—once an ardent admirer of poor Sue.

General Lovell laughed, and rejoiced that we did not treat him as a spy but gave him a place among us as Berrien Lovell, ex–Confederate general. He is bitter at not being in active service—laid on the shelf, so to speak.

Plain talk between Sue and me. She spoke of a girl who was said to have refused an old lover. "No, never. She was shamelessly in love with him

───────────

3. The battle of Franklin.
4. Thomas Macaulay, "Horatius," *Lays of Ancient Rome,* stanza 27. The concluding lines are: "For the ashes of his fathers / And the temples of his gods?"
5. Helen Coles Singleton, the daughter of Martha Rutledge (Kinloch) Singleton.

openly—defiantly in love. *She* did [not?] break it off. She was *that* willing." She (Sue) then offered to give the last touch to my salad dressing—for which she has a light hand—and taste. As we came back to the drawing room:

"Oh, Sue, keep on that shawl."

"Why?"

"Such shoulders &c&c—bare &c&c—makes you look *that* willing—too willing, you know."

"Willing for what?" she said angrily.

"Another husband." And yet I am as afraid of her as death.

Wilmot DeSaussure came to see me, fresh from General Chesnut's camp. Says he is in the saddle from six in the morning until six at night.

"What is the use? They will not concentrate men enough to block Sherman's way. What is the use of a handful here, a handful there?"

"Oh, aunty, don't fret so. Port Royal has been in Yankee hands four years. They can't get up here."

I do not think these girls or the First Foreign contingent who haunt my house ever give Sherman a thought. They are lighthearted and happy as the days are long.

"Somebody came in the other night while I had the Lovell, Anderson, King coalition—"

"Aunty, did you mean 'cold collation'?"

"No. Somebody came in with a message from Captain Bacon. He could not come because he had a sick baby. Sue King found that a very amusing message. 'Women have babies—men only have children'—&c&c. Then she said: 'But it is natural. He wants to save his little Bacon.'"

So Fort Pulaski has fallen.[6] Goodbye, Savannah!

Our governor announces himself a follower of Joe Brown of Georgia. Another famous Joe!

6. Apparently an ironic reference to the inaugural address of Andrew Gordon Magrath, who had defeated John S. Preston and Samuel McGowan for the governorship. Taking a states' rights, anti-Davis stance, Magrath praised Ga. and its governor for seizing Fort Pulaski in 1861 but did not mention that the Union retook the fort the next year.

XXIX
"Thermopylae Business"

December 19, 1864. The deep waters closing over us. And we are—in this house—like the outsiders at the time of the Flood. We care for none of these things. We eat, drink, laugh, dance, in lightness of heart!!!

Savannah—a second Vicksburg business. Troops kept there that would be so useful in the outside swamps—kept there to capitulate.[1] When they found they could not hold the place, why did they not silently decamp and come up here?

They have no chance now to cry "treason" and "take away your Yankee general," as they did at poor Pemberton and at the fatuous Lord Lovell—who rode out on his milk-white steed &c&c.

Dr. Trezevant came to tell me the dismal news. How he piled on the agony! Desolation—mismanagement—despair. General Young with the flower of Hampton's cavalry in Columbia. Horses cannot be found to mount them. Neither the governor of Georgia nor the governor of South Carolina moving hand or foot. *They have given up.* Eight hundred such cavalry as Young's might make a change in this campaign, but the country is demoralized. Our legislature is debating states rights and the encroachments of the Confederate government—with an occasional fling backward at the governor and council—the much-abused council who wanted to train the militia, fortify Columbia, and *did* put negroes to work on fortifications. A set of tyrants, Marats, Robespierres, &c, these poor councilmen—at least, so Judge Withers called them—*and now.*

Where is Beauregard Felix? We would gladly have the Felix—prefix—a *fixed fact.*

And our governor, Isabella says, was most theatrically inaugurated yesterday.

All this is Trezevan*tiana.*

Yankees claim another victory for Thomas.[2] Hope it may prove like most of their victories—brag and bluster.

1. Savannah fell Dec. 21.
2. Maj. Gen. Thomas crushed Hood's army at the battle of Nashville on Dec. 15–16.

Can't say why—maybe I am benumbed—but I do not feel so intensely miserable. Heard the girls, as Smith opened the door for them, ask,

"Is she lying on the sofa with a shawl wrapped around her head?"

"Yes'm."

"Then let us run for it"—and they dashed upstairs.

Mrs. Feaster (the mother of the too-famous beauty Boozer),[3] according to Captain James, has left her husband. She has had husbands enough. She has been married three times. And yet by all showing did not begin to marry soon enough. Witness the existence of Boozer.

Boozer, who is always on exhibition—walking, riding, driving—wherever a woman's face can go, there is Boozer. She is a beauty—that none can deny. They say she is a good girl. Then why does she not marry some decent man, among the shoals who follow her, and be off, out of this tangle while she has a shred of reputation left?

"Listen, she is saying a good word for Boozer. Don't you know her engagement to Willie Capers is just broken off because she stole his watch and some money he had in his picket? And he found her out and made her give it back to him."

"I do not believe all that. The girl's beauty is as plain to be seen as the nose on your face. It is so stupid to deny it."

"Who does?"

"All of you. And now for business. Your fine foreigners gave the first half of the afternoon yesterday—as I saw from the window—to Boozer et cie demi-monde—en évidence. Then as Boozer's equipage drove off, they sauntered up to *my party*. Isabella! not a word. I saw it. No lady feels that sort of thing a compliment. It is an insult, rather—that way of dividing time."

"I felt in a fierce indignation—one of the youths disporting himself with Enie's[4] red ribbon in his buttonhole—"his colors nailed to the mast," as he pretends to say—&c&c.

"And this I said again to Captain James and his company. How dumbfounded they were. They only know the prudish American female who would die before she acknowledged that she saw—or that she knew of—the improper half of the world."

Today I relented and sent breakfast to one of the delinquents who I hear is ill in bed. [*Half a page cut out.*]

December 27, 1864.   Oh, why did we go to Camden! The very dismalest Christmas overtook us there. Foreign bats [battalion] in full fig saw us on the train. Miss Rhett went with us. A brilliant woman—and very agreeable. Which brilliant are not always. She said:

"The world, you know, is composed of men, women—and Rhetts. (See Lady

---

3. Amelia Feaster was the Northern-born wife of a Columbia shopkeeper and the mother of Marie Boozer. These two notorious women harbored an escaped Union prisoner during the war and ran off with Union forces after the burning of Columbia in 1865.

4. Serena Williams.

Mary Montagu.)[5] Now, we feel that if we are to lose our negroes, we would as soon see Sherman free them as the Confederate government. Freeing negroes seems the last Confederate government craze."

"They are a little too slow about it, that is all," moaned Cassandra.

Sold fifteen bales of cotton. Took a sad farewell look at Mulberry—that I have always hated. Now I think, perhaps I may have been mistaken. It is a magnificent old country seat. Old oaks, green lawns, and all.

Buck writes she would [give] ten years of her life for an hour with me. And then to Isabella she writes, "I wish I was in my quiet grave."

Beware of ambition—by that sin the angels fell—&c&c.[6]

The wedding.

The girls insisted upon their chaperon wearing velvet, point lace, and diamonds. There was another velvet there, so old that it was fashioned "burst bosom," a mode unknown now to the oldest inhabitant.

These people knew so little of the etiquette of society that they left Miss Rhett and myself alone as they surged into supper. The distinguished strangers!! We, however, walked humbly in at the tail of the procession—sustained by point lace and diamonds—to defiance and proper pride.

One of my married Marys was there. Oh, it was bitter cold. And all the folding doors thrown open—and doors leading out into the freezing open air. Mary was wrapped in a snowy swansdown sortie de bal. She looked like a small Alp and sat resignedly, with her hands clasped upon the highest peak. Her devoted husband gave her so much more than she cared for—she graciously asked him to look after the forlorn ones, Miss Rhett and me. For the first time in my life I was nobody.

The wedding guests were divided. We saw the ceremony &c and were of the first night. There was a second night. The second-best did not like it.

Said Milly C:

"Am I invited to eat up the scraps? Or do they expect me to put on an apron, roll up my sleeves, and help wash dishes?"

Darkest of all Decembers
Ever my life has known,
Sitting here by the embers
Stunned—helpless—alone—

5. "This world consists of men, women, and Herveys." Lady Mary Montagu, *Letters* (1763), volume 1.

6. *Henry VIII*, act 3, scene 2.

Dreaming of two graves lying
Out in the damp and chill—

x x x x

Theirs the heroic story
Died by land and by sea
Theirs the *peace* and the glory
Theirs the cross and the crown.

Mine to linger and languish
Here by the wintry sea
Ah!weak heart in thy anguish,
What is there left to thee?

Only the sea intoning
Only the wainscot mouse—
Only the wild wind moaning—
Over the lonely house—

Yes, thou may it sigh
And look once more all around
At stream and bank and sky and ground
Thy life its final course has found
And thou must die.

Yes, lay thee down,
And while thy struggling pulses flutter
Bid the grey monk his soul—must mutter
And the deep bell its death tone utter—
Thy life is gone.

Be not afraid.
'Tis but a pang, and then a thrill,
A fever fit—and then a chill,
And then an end of human ill,
For thou are dead.

Took a last fond farewell of Mulberry—once so hated, now so beloved.

At that wedding in Camden—with the utter scorn of the public eye so wonderful in the incipient honeymoon—the bride sat in a chair near the center of the room, which was but scantly filled (the room, I mean). After supper the rejoicing bridegroom knelt by her and put his arms around her—chair and all.

"Oh!" said Isabella, "if he took in the chair, that was not so trying to the feelings of the *enforced* sightseers."

Louis Wigfall is here. He is staunch in his faith. "Make Joe Johnston dictator, and all will be well." We thought this was a struggle for independence—Southern states against odds—in the U.S.A. Now it seems it is only a fight between Joe Johnston and Jeff Davis.

"Well, if the end has come, try Joseph the Xenophontic. He will retreat the last thousand with grace and dignity, down into the Gulf of Mexico (and misery)."

Wigfall disdained to notice that spiteful fling. He continued, "Hood is dead—smashed, gone up forever."[7] And then he praised him as he buried him.

And Wigfall himself, from whom we hoped so much, he has only been a destructive. Like the smith—Hal of the Wynd.[8] He can only "fight for his own hand."

A reception at my house last night. For. bat. in full force. These young Virginia F.F.'s refuse to bring their colonel to our house. They say he is not the sort of person for us to know.

January 7, 1865.   Trezevant looking a woodpecker in his red cap. Isabella with a resolute girl who captured Bierne. The Captain James came where I was and "talked so sociable," as Yankee Hill says.[9] Told his family history.

Yankees burned a flour mill for him, for which the C.S. government paid him 28,000 dollars. The Yanks ruined his plantation, but he ran off his negroes in time.

He was an assistant something to Colonel Blake, Mrs. ———'s friend. "What a friendship that was!" All right—Colonel ——— was a greater friend of Blake's than his wife. Colonel Blake had never been known to speak to a woman but his friend Mrs. ———."

Sherman at Hardeeville.[1] Hood in Tennessee. The last of his men not gone, as Louis Wigfall so cheerfully prophesied.[2]

Miss Mary Stark—as good as gold. Saw her today. A glorious old soul, loyal quand même. She said,

"I love and honor my president and I trust my generals!" Faith that removes mountains. A steadfast mind like that is something to thank God for.

---

7. Not literally, of course.

8. The quarrelsome armorer in Sir Walter Scott, *St. Valentine's Day; or, The Fair Maid of Perth.*

9. Probably a reference to George Handel Hill (1809–48), the actor and humorist famous for his performances as the stereotypical Yankee.

1. On Jan. 1, Sherman, regrouping his forces around Savannah in preparation for their drive through the Carolinas, sent troops across the Savannah River a few miles into S.C., where they skirmished with Confederates near Hardeeville.

2. By this time, Hood and the remnants of the Army of Tenn. had crossed into Miss. Wigfall's prophecy was not far wrong: the army, fifty-one thousand strong when Hood took command in July 1864, had dwindled to fifteen thousand ill-equipped, underfed men by Jan. 1865.

Mrs. McCord came next. She is as true and as devoted, but she gave way to a furious anger. Half of our legislature is, she said, reconstructionist.

Yesterday at dinner, just as Serena was about to carve a fat fowl, a message came from Sally Goodwyn to say she was going to bring our Virginia cousin Boykin here tonight.[3]

"Take your fork out of that fowl. We will keep it for salad tonight."

"Rescued from the jaws of famine," said Isabella, "just in time." And Smith removed it to a lock-up safe. We sent for Molly to order some cake. She came to the dining-room door with a fiery face, which she wiped with her apron.

"Name o' God! Why don't dey ax you dere? It is cook, cook in dis house, from daylight till dark. Yo' time is come to be axed somewhere." She spoke at the top of her voice.

"Molly, you forget yourself," I said in a low tone. Sally G's little maid standing open-mouthed, all eyeballs and white teeth.

"'Blige to talk dish here way. You'll soon have nothing left for yo'self to eat."

"Never mind. The Yankees are coming, and I am going to leave you to help a cheap boardinghouse here for them."

She laughed aloud.

"Missis is always running her rigs."

Not by one word or look do these slaves show that they know Sherman and freedom is at hand. They are more obedient and more considerate than ever—to me.

Molly's temper was always violent. And as Buck told her, she had no manners ever—but then she is the best cook, the best dairy maid, the best washerwoman, and the best chambermaid I know. And she will [be] all that and more—*for me*. She has an idea people impose on my good nature.

Sally Goodwyn came with nine females. Captain Bierne came with a message—and stared at this feminine flock with amazement. And in a few minutes he was back again. For. bat. to the rescue. I think they came en masse, from the look of the crowd in the piazza as they slowly defiled through the hall.

About twelve, Mr. Martin thundered at my door—an irate Methodist parson, indeed as fiercely angry as such a reverent person ever allows himself to be. As he walked off with his brood I could hear him scold—until his growls died away in the distance. It was not all on one side, however. He cannonaded in his deep tones. They shrilly fired back resolutely, shot for shot.

Enie was gone for half-hour today to the dentist. Her teeth are of the whitest and most regular, simply perfection. She fancied it was better to have a dentist look in her mouth before she went back to the mountains. For that look she paid three hundred and fifty Confederate money.

"Why, has this money any value at all?" she asked.

---

3. Probably M. B. C.'s fourth cousin once removed, Francis Marshall Boykin of Isle of Wight County, Va., who was colonel of the Thirty-first Va. Regiment.

Mars Kit stopped at our door. We were enjoying our piazza privileges.
"How do you like Hood's defeats?"

"They will hardly hurt us more than Johnston's victories. Johnston was tow-
ing them here. Hood has at least stopped Thomas's half of them for a while in
Tennessee."

He said he liked my pluck—and would send Annie to see me. A sort of
reward of merit he thinks that, no doubt.

Brewster was here and stayed till midnight. Said he must see General Chesnut. He had business with him. His "Me and Gen'l Hood" is no longer comic. He
described Sherman's march of destruction and desolation. "Sherman leaves a
track fifty miles wide, upon which there is no living thing to be seen," said
Brewster, before he departed.

General Chesnut being at Grahamville, with reserves and raw militia—of
course, Brewster could not see him.

Beauregard and Bragg have gone down to the coast. Now, I hope when those
two important personages get there they will not be satisfied with such scant
materials of defense but collect veteran troops from Charleston and elsewhere.

By special request of the town authorities for. bat. ordered away from Columbia. So Mr. Theodore Stark told me.

Miller[4] and the girls will go with me to the Wayside—though they have to be
there by five o'clock of a winter's morning.

Yesterday General Preston dined with us. In the afternoon I went with him to
the dress parade of the for. bat. Colonel had to be introduced to me—looks like
a little Spanish Jew. He and I walking immediately in front of General Preston.
I know how we looked—General P a huge seventy-four gun ship towed by two
very small steam tugs. Presented arms and all that—in our honor. Poor for.
bats. And you have to go tomorrow.

Allen Green said there was a report in the street that Hood was killed—and
there was great rejoicing. Sherman will soon disturb the skulkers hiding here.
To rejoice at the death of one of our own generals!

At the bazaar Gen. Joe Johnston came up to speak to me. We had a very
pleasant conversation. As he walked away Sally G fairly raved of "his noble
brow." Then we had a stump speech, if ever there was a stump speech. She (the
orator)[5] said the real sinner against our cause is the man who began the inside
fight. A row with our *government de facto* is more disastrous than a dozen lost
battles. General J was a great general. When he had backed before the enemy
until they reached Columbia—would he have stopped them any more than he
had stopped [them] in the Georgia mountains? They say he is a famous military

4. Stephen Miller Williams, ten-year-old eldest son of Kate Williams.
5. Apparently M. B. C. herself.

critic and sees all of General Lee's faults, mistakes, &c. He is a poor subordinate general because he is so fine a critic that he disdains to obey orders for a general campaign. He is always dissatisfied and grumbling at those above him. Unless he were in supreme command, his business was to conspire and manufacture public opinion with his staff of newspaper writers.

Lieutenant Governor McCaw—who had listened to all this, dumb with amazement—now said a change had come over the spirit of our dream.[6] Two-thirds of the South Carolina legislature openly avowed—other things being equal— [that] for any office in their gift they preferred a man who was not a soldier. They were awfully tired of soldiers. "The fever fit is over. The chill has set in."

"Has our country come to that?"

"Listen—and you will find out."

"The dirty dogs—the dastards," howled Isabella. "Never mind—our *men* are all in the army."

"Lying stark and stone, in bloody graves—and what for?" moaned a childless mother.

Sue King will have it she is engaged to Beauregard. She showed his letters and his photograph. Incredulous we were and openly pronounced the photograph proof worth nothing. Anybody can get that for a small pile of Confederate money. It is in every shop window. Then she took a letter from her pocket. This we read—written in the French language. He was kind and awfully civil, the very politest of letters, but there was no love or marriage in it that I could see. Said Miss Middleton, when she heard of this:

"Well, I did think better of Alexander Robert Chisolm[7]—he is an aide of Beauregard's. He might have saved his chief from that."

"What else is he good for?" piped up the irrepressible.

January 16, 1865.   You do Anabasis business when you want to get out of the enemy's country. And the Thermopylae business when they want to get into your country. But we retreated in our own country—and we gave up our mountain passes without a blow.

"Never mind the Greeks. If we had only our own Gamecock Sumter—our own Swamp Fox Marion."

Marion's men and Sumter's—or the equivalent of them—now lie under the sod in Virginia or Tennessee.

And as old Torquil says, "For what were they born? save to die" for their country. Nobody laments the loss of an arrow if it hits the mark.[8]

6. A play on Lord Byron, *The Dream* (1816), stanza 3.

7. Lt. Col. Alexander Robert Chisolm, a planter of Beaufort and Colleton districts, was Susan Matilda Middleton's distant cousin.

8. The words, slightly misquoted here, with which Torquil justifies the death of his sons in defense of their chieftain, in Sir Walter Scott, *St. Valentine's Day; or, The Fair Maid of Perth*, chapter 34.

There is the rub.

Of that group Mrs. McCord and Mrs. Goodwyn had lost each a son—Mrs. McCord her only one. Some had lost their husbands, brothers, sons. The thought that their lives had been given up in vain was very bitter to them. The besom of destruction had swept over every family there. Miss Middleton's only brother, the brave little Oliver, only a child, after all—but he would go.[9]

What a cohort would rise to view, if thoughts took shape. Splendid young life sacrificed—in vain.

At the station as we drove away the girls stood up in my wagon—and the for. bats. ran around like beggars, each determined to have the last touch of their fair hands. They ran along—and it was a mad scene—as much handshaking as at a presidential reception. They are gone—and not a day too soon, from what I saw this morning at the wayside. After all, the jewelry, silver, &c&c stolen from General Hampton's house was found in the tent of one of the soldiers of the foreign battalion.

But it was the splendid young officers, high born, high-spirited, handsome, agreeable, broad-shouldered, golden-haired, with a complexion as rosy as the dawn, that I feared—not the rogues and deserters who made up the rank and file of the foreign battalion.

I wrote to my sister that her daughters would not go back home with [*illegible name*] and that I could not make them do it. But I am afraid for them to stay here. And she must see to it.

Last night it was again—Le roi est mort, vive le roi.

For. bats. gone—but the room crowded with as indefatigable, if a new, set of admirers. These fine fellows have been wounded all—some are maimed. And they seem as utterly oblivious of the volcano we stand upon as our girls themselves. Many of them are officers passing through from one command to another. We tolerate nobody in this house but men who have done their duty. A man must wear Confederate uniform and must have done his due share of fighting to find favor with this bevy of high-spirited young beauties. Generally these poor fellows tangibly give evidence of where they have been lately—nearly all palpably wounded soldiers.

January—. Yesterday I broke down—gave way to abject terror. The news of Sherman's advance—and no news of my husband. Today—wrapped up on the sofa—too dismal for moaning, even. There was a loud knock. Shawls and all, I rushed to the door. Telegram from my husband.

"All well—be at home on Tuesday." It was dated from Adams Run.[1]

I felt as lighthearted as if the war were over.

9. Susan Matilda Middleton's brother Oliver Hering Middleton, Jr., was eighteen when killed while on duty with the Charleston Light Dragoons in Va. in May 1864.

1. A point on the Charleston and Savannah Railroad about fifty miles west of Charleston.

Then I looked at the date—Adams Run. It ends as it began. Bulls Run—from which their first sprightly running astounded the world. Now if we run—who are to run? They ran full-handed. We have fought until maimed soldiers and women and children are all that is left to run.

Today Kershaw's brigade, or what is left of it, passed through. The shouts that greeted it and the bold shouts of thanks it returned—it was all a very encouraging noise, absolutely comforting. Some true men left after all.

Today the *Mercury* republished the president's speech at Macon with bitter comments. We like every word of that speech—Georgia—Macon—no Moscow nor Muscovites now.

To think the downtrodden subjects of tyrant Russia could rise to that height of patriotism and self-devotion. After all, it was their emperor's country. *This is our very own.*

Soldiers are not demoralized. Their shouts as they go by gladden my heart. I sit at my window and watch them hastening from one train to the other.

Went to hear Mr. Palmer, to have my heart lifted up and my hands strengthened. But no—he was demonstrating *natural* history—family relations from a physical and biblical point of view. Just on the verge, always, of frightful moral and indecent precipices. One difficulty is that in church [when] such unpleasant topics are broached, one does not know where to look.

"Sit and stare blankly at the parson—even if he forgets he is a man. And you must try and forget it, too. Think of him only as a parson," cries the irrepressible.

Opened by mistake—a strange letter. As my beautiful niece—she who is called by the poet James "Her Serene Highness, the Princess Bright-Eyes"— went off, she said, "Any letters for me, open them." We are expecting their mother's final decision—go or stay.

When she came back—I had been struck dumb. It was in the P.D., precious darling, style—as easy and as affectionate as if this boy had been her betrothed lover for years. And we barely know him. It was directed to my care. She took the letter calmly and read it aloud—not omitting one expression of his fatuous and excessive lovesickness. What a cruel ordeal for her—but she is a proud soul and brave. And she wanted to clear her skirts of complicity. Smith ushered in Lieutenant Trezevant, with the princess's red ribbons still in his buttonhole. There was that in his eye—and a hardly repressed smile about his mouth that made me suspect he had heard my savage comments on this self-complacent love letter. The door was open—and some overcoats take time in pulling off, hanging up, &c&c. Mr. Trezevant opened the conversation by an anecdote. He had just caught Miss —— at the corner of a back street, reading to a group of friends a love letter the *Miss* had concocted for one of their members too shy to write for himself. Miss —— denied the charge that it was poor ——'s letter which she was reading to amuse her friends—but Trezevant knew it, as he had written it himself.

Here was food for thought. After he left us, the irrepressible:

"That wretch wrote them all. He is a good artillery officer and calculated when his bomb would explode. He ran up from Kingsville. His luck was wonderful. They actually burst—well, so to speak—in his face."

Farmer[2] came for Kate's children. They will not go. "Oh, auntie, we are having such a good time, we cannot go." If Kate could see that letter!

Farmer on the *Mercury:*

"Surely such abuse as the Rhetts are heaping in the *Mercury* on Jeff Davis ought to conciliate the Yankees. The *Mercury* is doing their work nobly for them."

"Yes, disintegration is all they need now to end the struggle. The Yankees are bound to think those who hate our government so are ready to join with its enemies."

My small drawing room crammed to its utmost limit—and I so weary, full of care—so utterly discomfited, so stupid, so dead. How can I bear it?

Mary sent Lieutenant T a pair of gloves. He came last night and said gaily: "I sent you no answer. I dared not risk the shortest note. Of late I have chanced to hear—or overhear—letters and so laughed at—I have fairly shuddered to think such a fate might be mine someday."

Today they say Sherman has recrossed into Georgia and that Hood is between Sherman and Thomas. So goes the upper, and the nethermost, millstone to work.

"No, auntie. Today they said the Hood balloon went up a skyrocket, fire rocket—was it? At any rate, they said it had come down a *stick*."

"Comments are cruel."

January 16, 1865.   My husband is at home once more—for how long, I do not know. And his aides fill the house, and a group of hopelessly wounded haunt the place. And the drilling and the marching goes on—and as far as I can see, for. bats. happily forgotten.

It rains a flood—freshet after freshet. The forces of nature are befriending us, for our enemies have to make their way through swamps.

A month ago my husband wrote me a letter which I promptly suppressed after showing it to Mrs. McCord. He warned us to make ready—for the end had come. Our resources were exhausted—and the means of resistance could not be found.

It was what we could not bring ourselves to believe. And now—he thinks, with the RR all blown up, the swamps impassable by freshets which have no time to subside, so constant is the rain. The negroes are utterly apathetic (would they be so, if they saw us triumphant!), and if we had but an army to seize the opportunity. No troops—that is the real trouble. Dr. Gibbes took it on himself to send a telegram. Some people are cool enough—and fools enough for anything.

"Does Jeff Davis so hate South Carolina that he means to abandon her to her fate?" I wonder if they showed Mr. Davis this.

---

2. Probably Henry T. Farmer, proprietor of a hotel in Flat Rock.

The answer has come.

"No. Jeff Davis loves South Carolina—only Yankees hate her. He will do all he can to save her."

Hardee—he of Hardee's *Tactics*[3]—he has a head for tactics, but it is not large enough to plan a campaign. He can only fight well when under orders.

We seem utterly without a head down here—utterly at sea. If some heaven-born genius would rush in and take command—

The pilot in calm weather lets any sea boy toy with his rudder—but when the winds howl and the waves rise, he seizes the helm himself.

And our pilot? Where is he?

"Napoleon had to go to St. Helena when he had exhausted his levies. No more soldiers until France could grow them."

"Suppose we try Stephen Elliott—everybody trusts him."

Today Mrs. McCord exchanged 16,000 dollars, Confederate bills, for gold—300 dollars. Sixteen thousand—for three hundred.

The bazaar will be a Belshazzar affair.[4] The handwriting is on the wall. Bad news everywhere.

Miss Garnett was in agony.

"I fear the very worst—before they find out, those stupid Yankees, that I am Irish."

The fears of old maids increase, apparently in proportion to their age and infirmities—and hideous ugliness.

Isabella fairly white and shining—resplendent in apparel—has gone down to Millwood.

She reproved the "weary heart" for dragging so in the road of life, or as she put it:

"What do you mean to do if your father dies—or anybody that you really care for dies? You leave yourself no margin for proper affliction—when the time comes."

January 17, 1865.   Bazaar opens today.

Sherman marches always—all RR's smashed.

And if I laugh at any mortal thing, it is that I may not weep.

Generals as plenty as blackberries, none in command. Beauregard with his Shiloh green sickness again. Bad time for a general seized by *melancholia*.

And this refrain is beating in my brain—

> March—March—Ettrick and Teviotdale—
> Why the de'il do ye not march all in order,
> March—March—Teviot and Clydesdale—
> *All* the blue bonnets are over the Border.[5]

3. William Joseph Hardee was the author of a standard textbook, *Rifle and Light Infantry Tactics* (1853–55).

4. Daniel 5.

5. The first lines, slightly misquoted, of a "ditty" sung to "the ancient air of 'Blue Bonnets over the Border,'" in Sir Walter Scott, *The Monastery. A Romance* (1820), volume 2, chapter 11.

"What a blessing that quire of dingy Confed paper is to auntie."

"Why?"

"She comes away from it quite relieved."

"Oh, it is a splendid opportunity to shower down fine words. It's a safety valve—a journal. You quit crying about what you write about. Mother goes off in poetry."

"That's better—the agony of finding a rhyme would divert any sorrow."

" 'Borrowing' rhymes to 'sorrowing'—'pluck' to 'luck'—'fibs' to 'Gibbs'— 'laugh' to 'quaff.' Gather your roses while you may! Old time will still be flying. That's my motto."

"Did you know Wilmington had fallen?"

"Oh, auntie—how can we help that?"

They want to inaugurate a "bower of fate" in a corner by our table.

[Thirteen pages torn out.]

Did he not lose us Missionary Ridge? Old Early now and his Valley campaign. Well—we will see if General Lee can hold his own against greater odds than crushed Napoleon."

And she picked up her last parcel—and as I followed her and stood at the gate, I cried:

"Stonewall—and Albert Sidney Johnston—death guards their fame. Thank God. They are safe in their graves."

In a republic a general ought to have a staff who can write him up—coûte que coûte. Newspapers lead public opinion, and their pets win fame when they lose a battle. It was always somebody's fault in the War Office.

Here is startling news. Politely but firmly the Virginia legislature requests Jeff Davis and all of his cabinet to resign. They make an honorable exception—Trenholm, secretary of the treasury. Seddon, being a Virginian, accepted the invitation to go out. And Northrop, the hated of all, did likewise (Mr. Chesnut is one of the few who sees any good in poor old Northrop). Breckinridge is to take Seddon's portfolio. He will be war minister. If we had had Breckinridge in Walker's place at the beginning, what a difference it might have made. Walker, who wandered wildly and blindly and ruined us almost before we were under way. Clay of Alabama is responsible for that Walker.

Manassas—and all that stupidity in not following up victory.

The Peace Commissioner Blair has come. They say he gave Mrs. Davis the kiss of peace.

And we have sent Stephens, Campbell—all who never believed in this thing—to negotiate for peace.[6]

6. With Lincoln's unofficial approval, Francis Preston Blair, Sr., of Md., traveled twice to Richmond in Jan. to discuss peace terms with Jefferson Davis but only secured arrangements for

No hope—no good. Who dares hope?

Isabella came. She says Mrs. Slocum told Mrs. Joe Johnston that I called her—the aforesaid Slocum—a Yankee. Jack Preston offered to go to Mrs. J. J. and deny for me.

"But Jack, she is—and I laugh at the dreadful charge, and so does Mrs. J. J., in her sleeve. She has a keen sense of fun, and by this time she has heard so much worse."

Said Isabella, "These infatuated people are talking of a dancing school—and they want our Cassandra to give a strawberry festival!"

"For what—oh, ye fatuous folk?"

Went to see Mrs. Prioleau Hamilton[7]—at Mrs. [*illegible*]. Was ushered into a wrong room. Mr. Motte Middleton[8] was lying on a sofa, reading a novel.

With languid urbanity he rose—and with greater politeness, decorum, and suavity, he invited us out again.

I did not know him—nor did he know me.

Gave thirty dollars for a bottle of cologne and fifty for a little French mustard pot.

The town swarming with troopless generals—Joe Johnston, Lovell, Governor Manning, &c&c. My husband dines out every day to meet this lordly party.

General Chesnut has gone again. He is rarely here for many days at a time.

Harriet engaged—at last. Oh, ye gods! And to the grandson[9] of a signer—the American patent of nobility.

And I am calm and serene as the moonbeams. Such terrible danger steadies me. I never moan or put a shawl over my head now. And I am never ill—no time for that.

---

the fruitless Hampton Roads Conference of Feb. 3. On Jan. 28, Davis designated Vice-President Alexander Stephens, former assistant secretary of war John Archibald Campbell, and Senator R. M. T. Hunter of Va. as commissioners to the conference.

7. Emma (Levy) Hamilton, younger sister of Eugenia (Levy) Phillips and Marthy Levy. Emma's husband, Maj. Samuel Prioleau Hamilton of Chester District, was the son of a former governor of S.C.

8. Jacob Motte Middleton, an Ogeechee, S.C., rice planter, was a distant cousin of Eweretta, Ellen, and Matilda Middleton.

9. Identified in the 1860s Journal as Richard Stockton.

At church today a great RR character was called out of church. He soon returned and whispered something to Joe Johnston, and they went out together.

Somehow the whisper moved around to us. "Sherman is at Branchville."

My husband gave Miller Williams, aged *ten* (who was sent down here for his sisters, who, he says, "are like the donkeys as wouldn't go"), a pony—a sort of reward of merit. He saw the little chap stick on so manfully when the pony tried so hard to throw him. So, in his pleasure at the boy's fine riding, he made him a present of the pony. And now there is one perfectly happy creature in the Southern Confederacy. Miller is to ride his horse up to Flat Rock in company with Mr. Blake and Mr. Lowndes. Miller tells us in confidence: but for himself and a negro named Scipio, he does not think they could ever drive all of those horses to Flat Rock.

Hood came yesterday. He is staying at the Prestons' with Jack. They sent for us.

What a heart-full greeting he gave us! He can stand well enough without his crutch, but he does very slow walking. How plainly he spoke out these dreadful words: "My defeat and discomfiture"—"My army is destroyed"—"My losses"—&c&c. He said he had nobody to blame but himself.

Isabella, who adores Hood, said, "May[be] you attempted the impossible?"

And then she began one of her funniest stories. "Sam" did not listen. Jack Preston touched me, and we slipped away unobserved into the piazza.

"He did not hear a word she was saying. He had forgotten us all. Did you notice how he stared in the fire. And the livid spots which came out on his face and the huge drops of perspiration that stood out on his forehead?"

"Yes, he is going over some bitter hour. He sees Willie Preston with his heart shot away. He feels the panic at Nashville and its shame."

"And the dead on the battlefield at Franklin, they say, was a dreadful fight," said tenderhearted Jack, with a shiver. "And that agony in his face comes again and again. I can't keep him out of those absent fits. It is pretty trying to anyone who has to look on. When he looks in the fire and forgets me and seems going through in his own mind the torture of the damned—I get up and come out, as I did just now."

Jimmy Dick Hill's carriage was put at the general's service, and he came for us to drive with him. And he gave us his reason for asking to be relieved. The Virginia legislature asked to have Joe Johnston put back in command. That was equivalent to a vote of censure, as far as he was concerned. He asked to be sent across the Mississippi to bring all the troops from there. They might have saved us—they might save us still. Then he wants to be in Richmond by the 8th of February. That was his lucky day, ⟨⟨the day he became engaged. He wants to be married and dreads opposition. . . . He has Mrs. P[reston] to overcome yet.⟩⟩[1]

---

1. This and the following from the original 1860s Journal, dated Feb. 5, 1865, an entry summarized under Jan. 17 in the 1880s Version.

He blushes like a girl. After all, he is a queer compound. ⟨⟨"Sam," the *simplest,* most transparent soul I have met yet in this great revolution. . . .⟩⟩

Toady Barker is here. Says he refuses to give his consent. He is in love with her himself—always was. The list of killed and wounded is long—in her [Buck's] army, the death roll has been awful. Still, enough are alive still to stop this thing. He says John Chesnut is among them but that I never found him out. We got into heroics. He said that slender pale-faced Johnny of ours is a quiet daredevil. On the battlefield he is as cool and quiet as in my drawing room. And then we decided a glorious death at the head of one's company was the fittest end of all this—specially for Carolinians.

———————

Brewster left the general's wedding clothes here in a trunk six months ago. Johnny said then: "Why don't he put them on his back and go and be married? Here in a trunk. He will not, when he may. When he will, he shall have nay—*no good.* There will be no wedding, you see. He lost his chance last winter. He made his siege too long. He grows tedious. And since—too much rawllicking," says the cool Captain, who sees more than most persons, with those stony blue eyes of his.

The last bazaar lags superfluous. Mrs. Singleton said to Clancy, "Who is that bride?" "A Miss Judea. Sore-pressed for a husband, she married Lazarus."

[Three pages torn out here]

⟨⟨**February 5, 1865 . . .**[2]   Isabella nagged Hood to get married—said if he let them put him off, he was not the man she took him to be. Fancy his face at such a taunt. Mr. Martin, only seeing his laughing *face* before the *dark* one dawned on him, said if he had brought us Louisville and Kentucky in his coat pocket, he could not look happier. Much he knows of the tortures of that stalwart frame maimed and lamed—or that ambitious heart. All gone now but "Buckie"—I think I hear him now. The Charlottesville leg is a far better looking one than the French one. . . .

⟨⟨**February 7, 1865.**   Sunday afternoon I was partly wild. I could only see Sam maimed and helpless—with his face of the tortured in Hades—and my heart was wrung for Buck, and I felt Isabella and I had been too free of our sympathy and love for him and had not looked poor Buck's future in the face. I was morbid and miserable. Isabella came, and Jack Preston, and I grew sane again. How we talked poor Sam over. Jack is a government man but no Davis man. He says it is curious Sam should have his greatest enemy's son, Halsey Wigfall, on his staff. After all, I see the aide of General Taylor says the Army of Tennessee is in splendid order—the army which until they had written Hood out of it they

2. Where the three pages are torn from the 1880s Version, the original 1860s Journal takes up immediately from the last line quoted above. M. B. C. in the 1880s Version is summarizing under one date entries under Feb. 5, 7, and 8, 1865, from the 1860s Journal.

called demoralized, scattered, ruined, lost. Louis Wigfall said Hood might by
good luck cut his way *alone* to Richmond—poor old soldier. However, unless he
is frozen to death *now,* he is "Monsieur l'Amant" and no longer the unhappy
general (I hope Buck's mother won't give in!). . . .

⟨⟨**February 8, 1865.**   I hope poor Sam got to Richmond by this day—the 8th is
his good luck day, the anniversary of his engagement. General Hampton was
here last night. Said Longstreet had behaved magnanimously. He recommended him for lieutenant general for winning the battle of Chickamauga.
Said he liked Hood, that he was a good soldier &c, but decried his *ability.* When
J. C. said either Hood or Johnston would do. . . . He said Hood had given him a
most interesting account of his western campaign—just when I was called out.
When I came back he was telling that Hood left 18,000 muskets in the western
army and had not lost more than 8,000, all told—dead, wounded, and prisoners! General Hampton is a Johnston-Wigfall man out and out. . . . He says
Sam was promoted too fast, he wanted experience, was not long enough major
general, not long enough lieutenant general. . . .⟩⟩

[*After the three missing pages:*] arch enemy Louis Wigfall.

Telegram from Beauregard today to my husband. He does not know if
Sherman means to advance on Branchville, Charleston, or Columbia. If
Beauregard can't stop Sherman down there, what have [we] got here to do it
with? Can we check or impede his march? Who can?

The telegram was in cipher. Edward Barnwell brought it here. They first
made their key to it. The first sentence, "Complete Victory" <was the date>.
That was for the late forlorn Georgia campaign. Now the words are "Come
retribution."

"Hardly worthwhile to call it," cried Isabella. "It is coming fast enough—with
Sherman."

General Lee [is] generalissimo of all our forces. Rather late—when we have
no forces. Breckinridge secretary of war.

"Splendid hand—quantity of trumps—no playing cards, however."

"Grant us patience, good Lord," was prayed aloud.

"Not Ulysses Grant—good Lord," laughed Teddy.

Our commissioners the Laodicean Stephens, Campbell, &c were received by
Lincoln with taunts and derision.[3] Why not? He has it all his own way now.

London *Times* ridicules us for being such fools as to suppose they would
recognize our independence if we abolished slavery. If we offered ourselves to
any foreign power, the offer would be declined with thanks.

Abolish slavery to propitiate England. What does she care? She is holding
both hands over the Turk's head to protect him from Russia—slaves to the
contrary notwithstanding.

---

3. At the Hampton Roads Conference on Feb. 3, Lincoln offered the Confederates some conces-
sions, but not the independence that Jefferson Davis demanded for the South. "Laodicean," from
Revelation 3:15-16, signifies one who is lukewarm in politics or religion.

"The U.S.A. is England's sole real rival on earth. Some day she will bitterly repent her lost opportunity. This was her chance to cripple her mortal foe."

Mr. Clay, who has been to Canada, says we have to thank Prince Albert for that. Without his opposition, the emperor[4] would have moved up to us. Mr. Clay sent a trunk here for his dear wife. And as I was so soon to be on the wing—I know not whither—I sent it to Mr. Martin, who promises to see that it is safe.

Mr. Clay said:

"We have the sympathy of Europe—nothing more. We will have to paddle our own canoe." But he did not discuss public affairs if he could help it. He preferred to narrate his shipwrecks and his hairbreadth escapes. By that token I know, in his mission abroad he had no luck whatever.

Last night General Hampton came in. I am sure he would do something to save us if he were put in supreme command here. As it is, he takes no interest—for he has no power. He says, "The people now, educated by the press of the country, will not stand Hood for anything."

Hampton says Joe Johnston is equal, if not superior, to Lee as a commanding officer. Caw me—caw thee!

He has not quite forgiven Lee yet—that cruel blow to his vanity.

Janney, the hotel man with the very fieriest looks that ever scorched the eye—he was excessively affable and kept exhorting General Chesnut to seize horses and mount his men. Which looked more like a preparation to run than a wish to stand and defend Columbia. Finally the true object of his visit came out. He wanted to know if the time had come to pack his valuables and move his females.

That work I have under way. My silver is in a box and delivered for safekeeping to Isaac McLaughlin, who is really my beau idéal of a grateful negro. I mean to trust him. My husband cares for none of these things now—he lets me do as I please.

Met Mem Cohen—in full flight—in company with literary folk. "He is the funny man (dreary fun?) for some newspaper. Describes his wife [in] print as 'the Confederate female who loves to bathe my head.'" Mem said, "I would like to punch it—the wretch."

A man came who had been detailed for some arduous duty. He wanted to get off from it and rattled off his ailments with the glib fluency of a vendor of quack medicines when he recommends his stuffs—rheumatism, dyspepsia, loss of the use of my limbs, &c&c. When he saw General Chesnut's unmoved air, he added, "My daughter is about to have typhoid fever." They made short work of him. And after he was gone they called him a pusillanimous, lying dog. J. C. was not rude to this man, and I kept from laughing at his catalogue of ills—but it was hard.

4. Napoleon III.

《Jack Preston announced his perfect satisfaction with his future brother-in-law—stick and all. . . . I wonder how that war-worn head will stand it in Virginia, with his Wigfalls.》[5]

February 10, 1865.   Yesterday General Lovell dined here—and then they went to poor old Winder's funeral. Well, Winder is safe from the wrath to come. General Lovell suggested that if the Yankees ever caught Winder, "it would go hard with him—the prisoners complain of him, you know."[6]

Such a nice dinner we had—but spoiled in the course of it—interruptions, delays. At a certain hour, as he was in command of the troops, General Chesnut had to be off to the funeral. So he sent Mat for his horse, and then he sent Smith off on an errand. Neither returned, and after General C departed I had to go and look up somebody—both menservants gone. Molly remained in the kitchen—took so long to make herself decent. General Lovell excused himself for not being able to wait any longer. I rushed out again, to hurry Molly with that nice pudding &c&c. When I came back the men were all putting on their hats and swords &c&c in the entry—and away they went. Who could stand all that upsetting work at a regular dinner?

Mary's letter. I did send them off—nolens volens—under Robert Rutledge's charge. He was a trusted friend of their mother. Nat Butler[7] was too sharp for me. I kept them quietly here until he came up on horseback and told [me] goodbye on his way to the army. He went only to the first station beyond Columbia and waited there for them. So did the others Mary mentions. Robert Rutledge must have had his hands full.

"Se plaindre est une lâcheté" (Silvio).

Flat Rock
February 13th, 1865

Mrs. Genl.—Command Corps,
Reserved Young Ladies.

Mrs. Gen.,

I have the honor to inform you of the safe arrival of the retreating column sent to this place by your order.

The right wing of my force being placed under command of General

---

5. 1860s Journal, Feb. 8, 1865.
6. Until his death on Feb. 7, Brig. Gen. John Henry Winder of Md. had been provost marshal of Richmond in charge of Union prisoners and Confederate deserters and commissary general of Confederate prisons east of the Mississippi.
7. Oliver Nathaniel Butler, younger brother of Matthew Calbraith Butler.

Conversation, the left under General Circumspection, the center being led by General Indifference. In this manner we passed safely through the enemy's lines.

The column under the command of Princess Bright-Eyes met with more varied fortune.

Soon after leaving Columbia, skirmishing commenced on the right and left, but with her usual tact she parried all attacks and reached Newberry without damage, where we halted and bivouacked for the night.

An effort was made there by Lieut. Genl. Breakheart (one of the enemy's most skillful commanders) to take her by surprise; the attack, however, was repulsed with skill.

In the morning of the next day the march was resumed in order. Through the day the princess was much harassed by Genl. Breakheart, light artillery—Company I (Eye). But being aided by General Recollection, First Foreign Bat., and Captain Handsome of the Reserves, she succeeded in reaching Greenville the second night, having sustained slight loss of ammunition and colors and commissary stores. The loss of the latter was very seriously felt before reaching our destination.

At that place the enemy asked for time to bury his dead.

The princess there held a council of war, and knowing her foe (worthy of her steel) to be determined, skillful, and with great experience in this kind of warfare, she decided with her usual prudence and foresight to evacuate that town before her plans were known.

At four o'clock in the morning the retreat commenced, and was so silently conducted that not a suspicion of it was entertained until hours afterward.

The enemy, finding that pursuit was vain, relinquished it.

The march across the mountains was dreary.

> Snow to the right of us,
> Snow to the left of us.
> Snow in the front of us.
> Down in the ditch we fell!
> Up rose two hungry ones!

Here the elements were our most formidable enemies. All attacks made by others during this portion of the march were conducted in such a bungling and unskillful manner that they gave us no trouble.

On the night of the third, we reached this almost inaccessible fortress. Where all behaved so well it would be invidious to make distinctions; but I cannot refrain from mentioning the services rendered by Lieutenants Castor and Pollux—who were brevetted on the field.

> Then, like a blast, away they passed,
> And no man saw them more.

Also of Private Rupert Longbeard, who for his vigilance and gallantry is highly recommended to His Excellency the commander in chief for promotion.

Since our arrival here, Gen. Breakheart has brought some heavy guns to bear on the fortress. The shelling being at long range, no serious damage has been inflicted so far.

These bullet(ings) occasionally have a slightly stunning effect upon Her Highness the Princess Bright-Eyes, but she soon rallies.

I would call your attention to the fact that these projectiles are of extreme length and are composed on the outer surface of paper and ink. Her Serene Highness has examined them through and through, but being extremely reticent on all such subjects, she has not made known the entire contents.

On the north side the enemy, led by that veteran Capt. Conflict of the Second Regiment, frequently makes a dash down the post office road; but so far her lines have not been broken.

We propose to establish here an army of observation to obtain information and study our tactics and will be ready at any time you may see fit to recall us into the field for active service, trusting that time is not far off, that kind of service being much more to our taste.

I have, Mrs. General, the honor to remain you obt. servant,

Mamie and Wretched Lt. Genl. Commanding Small Fry

Mrs. Genl. Chesnut. . . . [8]

---

8. The letter was, of course, addressed *to* M. B. C. There follow three pages of verse, other quotations, and jottings. Of the latter the most coherent is the following: "To think, Tom Archer died almost as soon as he got to Richmond. Prison takes the life out of them. He was only half-alive here. He had a strange, pallid look, and such a vacant stare until you roused him. Poor, pretty Sally Archer—that is the end of you." See p. 166 on "Sally" Archer.

XXX

Refugees in Lubberland

February 16, 1865. Lincolnton, North Carolina. A change came o'er the spirit of my dream—dear old quire of yellow, coarse, Confederate homemade paper! Here you are again—and an age of anxiety and suffering has passed over my head since I wrote and wept over your forlorn pages.

My ideas of those last days are confused.

The Martins left Columbia the Friday before I did. And their mammy, the negro woman who had nursed them, refused to go with them. That daunted me. Then Mrs. McCord, who was to send her girls with me, changed her mind. She sent them upstairs in her house—and actually took away the staircase—that was her plan.

Then I met Mr. Christopher Hampton arranging to take off his sisters. They were flitting—but only as far as Yorkville. He said it was time to move on, Sherman at Orangeburg was barely a day's journey from Columbia, and that he left a track as bare and blackened as a fire in the prairies.

So my time had come, too. My husband urged me to go home. He said Camden would be safe enough. They had no spite to that old town—as they have to Charleston and Columbia. Molly, weeping and wailing, came in while we were at table, wiping her red-hot face with her cook's grimy apron. She said I ought to go among our own black people on the plantation. They would take care of me better than anyone else. So I agreed to go to Mulberry or the Hermitage plantation and sent Laurence with a wagon load of my valuables.

Then a Miss Patterson called—a refugee from Tennessee. She had been in a country overrun by Yankee invaders—and she described so graphically all the horrors to be endured by those subjected to fire and sword and rapine and plunder that I was fairly scared and determined to come here. This is a thoroughly out-of-all-routes place. And yet I can go to Charlotte. I am halfway to Kate at Flat Rock. And there is no Federal army between me and Richmond.

As soon as my mind was finally made up, we telegraphed Laurence, who had barely got to Camden in the wagon when the telegram was handed to him. So he took the train and came back. Mr. Chesnut sent him with us to take care of the party.

We thought if the negroes were ever so loyal to us, they could not protect me from an army bent upon sweeping us from the face of the earth. And if they tried to do so—so much the worse for the poor things with their Yankee friends.

715

So I left them to shift for themselves, as they are accustomed to do—and I took the same liberty.

My husband does not care a fig for the property question. Never did. Perhaps if he had ever known poverty it would be different. He talked beautifully about it—as he always does about everything. I have told him often if at heaven's gates St. Peter will listen to him awhile—let him tell his own story—he will get in, and they may give him a crown extra.

Now he says he has only one care—that I should be safe and not so harassed with dread. And then there is his blind old father! "A man can always die like a patriot and a gentleman—no fuss—take it coolly. It is hard not to envy those who are out of all this, their difficulties ended." "Who?" "Those who have met death gloriously on the battlefield. Their doubts are all solved. One can but do their best and leave the result to a higher power."

After New Orleans, those vain passionate impatient little Creoles were forever committing suicide, driven to it by despair and Beast Butler. As he read these things, Mr. Davis said, "If they want to die, why not kill Beast Butler—rid the world of their foe and be saved the trouble of murdering themselves?" However, that practical way of ending their intolerable burden did not seem to occur to them.

I repeated this suggestive anecdote to our horde of generals without troops. This very distinguished party rode superb horses and rode to the lines every day. They congregated at our house—they laid their fingers on the maps spread out on the table (covering this "quire of paper") and pointed out where Sherman was going and where he could be stopped.

They argued over their plans eloquently. Every man jack of them had a safe plan to stop Sherman if—

Even Beauregard and Lee were expected. But Grant had double-teamed on Lee. He could not save his own. How can he come to save us? Only read the list of the dead in those last battles around Richmond and Petersburg if you want to break your heart.

I took French leave of Columbia, slipped away without a word to anybody. Isaac Hayne and Mr. Chesnut came down to the Charlotte depot with me. Ellen, my maid, left husband and only child—but she was willing to come—very cheerful in her way of looking at it.

"Who guine trouble my William—dey don't dares to. Claiborne" (her husband) "kin take good care of William. I never traveled 'round with Missis before—and I wants to go this time." As for Laurence, he turned the same unmoved face toward our trunks and luggage. Smith grinned farewell.

A woman fifty years old, at least—and uglier than she was old—sharply rebuked my husband for standing at the car window for a few last words to me.

She said rudely, "Stand aside, sir. *I* want air." With his hat off—and his grand air—he bowed politely.

"In one moment, Madame. I have something of importance to say to my wife."

She talked aloud and introduced herself to every man, claiming his protection. She had never traveled alone before in all her life. Old age and ugliness are protective—in some cases. She was ardently patriotic for a while. Then she was joined by her friend, a man as crazy as herself to get out of this. From their talk I gleaned she had been for years in the department. They were about to cross the lines. The whole idea was to get away from the trouble, to come here. They were Yankees. Were they spies?

S. H. was talking loudly and violently to a deep-toned officer. It was wonderful that his low modulated voice did not give her a hint to moderate hers. But the cars rumbled and banged—and she shrieked above all. ⟨⟨We were detained 12 hours on the road and so had to remain a day and night at Charlotte.⟩⟩[1]

Here I am brokenhearted—an exile.

Such a place. Bare floors. For a feather bed, a pine table, and two chairs I pay 30 dollars a day. Such sheets!—but I have some of my own.

At the door—before I was well out of the hack—the woman of the house packed Laurence back, neck and heels. She would not have him at any price. She treated him as Mr. F's aunt did Clennam in *Little Dorrit*.[2] She said his clothes were too fine for a nigger—"his airs indeed"—and poor Laurence was as humble—and silent. He said at last, "Miss Mary, send me back to Mars Jeems." I began to look for a pencil to write a note to my husband. In the flurry could not find it. "Here is one," said Laurence, producing a gold pencil case. "Go away," she shouted. "I wants no niggers here with pencils—and airs." So Laurence fled before the storm—not before he had begged me to go back. He thought, "If Mars Jeems knew how you was treated he'd never be willing for you to stay here."

The Martins had seen my well-known traveling case as the hack trotted up Main St.—and they arrived at this juncture out of breath.

We embraced and wept.

I kept my room. After dinner Ellen presented herself—blue-black with rage. She has lost the sight of one eye—so that is permanently *bluish*, opaque. The other flamed fire and fury. "Here's my dinner. A piece of meat—and a whole plateful of raw ingins. I never did eat raw ingins, and I won't begin now. Dese here niggers say dis ole lady gives 'em to 'em breakfast and dinner. It's a sin and a shame to do us so. She says I must come outen her kitchen—de niggers won't work for looking at me. I'se something to look at, surely." She [put] down her odorous plate—held her fork and made a curtsy.

1. 1860s Journal, Feb. 16, 1865.
2. In chapter 13 of Dickens, *Little Dorrit* (1857), Arthur Clennam dines with the family of his old love, Flora Finching. Mrs. Finching's eccentric aunt frightens Clennam by staring at him and making strange comments.

"Ellen—for pity sake!"

"Lord ha' mercy. She say you bring me and Laurence here to keep us from running away to de Yankees—and I say, 'Name o' God, ole Missis! If dat's it—what she bring Laurence and me for? She's got plenty more. Laurence and me's nothing—to our white people. De ole soul fair play insulted me."

Then came an invitation to tea at Mrs. Munro's. Ellen retired in contrition and confusion.

Isabella told Ellen what a shame it was to add to my trouble in this way.

We wanted to rent part of Mrs. Munro's house, but Mrs. Ben Rutledge[3] was before us. Then we tried a Miss McLean. She blew hot and cold. She would—and then she would not. I was left utterly uncertain.

Mrs. Munro's husband has been killed in battle. She has one child, a boy of seven. Her husband was a son of Judge Munro of South Carolina. Mrs. Munro is handsome, accomplished, and very clever. She is from Virginia. A noted thing about her in this small town is the fact that she is a Roman Catholic.

She comes from Abingdon, Va., the home of the Prestons, Floyds, Lewises, &c&c, and Joe Johnston. The latter is expected here daily—so I am in the regular line of strategic retreat. Mrs. Munro is a violent abolitionist ⟨⟨in the sense I am one.⟩⟩[4] Isabella says she never saw a true woman who was not, but Mrs. Munro is a Yankee sympathizer, and that is one too much for us.

She gave us pound cake at tea—and such nice tea it was, after a week of Mrs. ———'s horrid coffee. I forgot my beautiful tea caddy on the mantelpiece at my house in Columbia. Strange to say, a French one—on it was marked in gilt letters "Thé." Said Sam Shannon once: "Here is a box with only 'The' on it. 'The'—*what* does it mean?" Buck asked him, "Do you understand French?" "Certainly." "There is an accent on that *e*, but we won't translate for you, as you know the language."

And my caddy was filled with English breakfast tea! Gone forever.

The Fants are refugees here, too. They are Virginians, too, and have been in exile since Second Manassas. Poor things, they seem to have been everywhere and seen and suffered everything. They even tried to go back to their own house. Of that they found one chimney alone standing, which had also been taken possession of by a Yankee in this wise. His name was written on it—and his claim by that established, the writer said.

The day I left home, I had packed a box of flour, sugar, rice, coffee, &c&c, but my husband would not let me bring it. He said I was coming to a land of plenty. Unexplored North Carolina, where the foot of Yankee marauder was unknown—and in Columbia they would need food.

---

3. Susan Middleton's sister Eleanor Maria (Middleton) Rutledge was the wife of Benjamin Huger Rutledge, a Charleston lawyer, member of the secession convention, and colonel of the Fourth S.C. Cavalry Regiment.

4. 1860s Journal, Feb. 16, 1865.

Now I have written to send me that box and many other things by Laurence, or I will starve.

The Middletons have come. How joyously I sprang to my feet to greet them. Mrs. Ben Rutledge describes the hubbub in Columbia—everybody flying in every direction, like a flock of swallows. She heard the enemy's guns booming in the distance.

The train no longer runs from Charlotte to Columbia.

Miss Middleton possesses her soul in peace—cool, clever, rational, and entertaining as ever. We talked for hours.

Mrs. Read[5] was in a state of despair. I can well understand that sinking of mind and body in the first days—as the abject misery of it all closes upon you.

I remember my suicidal tendencies when I first came here.

We were off through mud and slush to the RR to hear the news when the train came in. At the station, saw a wounded soldier, a handsome fellow—and sympathetic. "Madame, I feel like seizing a musket and going to help South Carolina—*whether or no.*" He was a Virginian, of course—and I wept, of course.

It was at their house—so Miss Middleton told me—that Miller joined Mr. Blake's party—droves of horses, mules, wagons, &c&c—en route for Flat Rock.

She seemed somewhat of Miller's opinion as to his merits. "The boy—is he ten years old? Was so clean, so polite, so decided in his ways, so evidently [determined?] to ride that pony straight to his father's house. I whispered to mama, "That young man knows what he is about. He will take command. The others are all demoralized—not to say *subjugated.*"

Our landlady evinces great repugnance still to Ellen—but we begin to laugh at her tantrums. For we hope to get away.

February 18, 1865.   Here I am, thank God, settled at the McLeans—clean, comfortable room, airy and cozy. With a grateful heart I stir up my own bright wood fire.

"Lord, Missis, we can't move today. It is Friday—bad luck all round." But Ellen succumbed—swallowed her superstitions. She was too keen to get away from "dirt and raw ingins"—and the raking fire of the landlady's sharp tongue. The sight of Ellen acted upon her as a red rag to a mad bull.

My bill for four days at this splendid hotel was 240 dollars, 25 dollars additional for fire. I tried to propitiate the termagant. I was mild humility and patient politeness.

"Do not waste your time. They will never comprehend the height from which

---

5. Mary Julia (Middleton) Read, another of Susan Middleton's sisters, was the wife of Charleston planter and physician Benjamin Huger Read.

we have fallen," suggested Miss Middleton. She is reckless. They have their own hired house and can move at once.

My kind young landlady is a cousin of the Brevards—Haynes &c&c of South Carolina, also a near relative of Mrs. Stonewall Jackson and Mrs. D. H. Hill.

Once more my lines have fallen in pleasant places.

Miss McLean is one of the beauties, the belles, the heiresses of the place. Think of that. And sister-in-law to General Hoke—of this ilk ⟨⟨but she does not brush her teeth, the first evidence of civilization, and lives amidst *dirt* in a way that would shame the poorest overseer's wife. May we teach them godliness is only better than cleanliness. A lady evidently she is, in manners and taste! And *surroundings* worthy a *barbarian*. Such kindness they have shown me. I feel I shall love this N.C. flower in spite of her growing in this bed of dirt—like a pure white lily.⟩⟩ [6]

Can North Carolina haute volée go further!

She brought her guitar—and I renewed my youth by singing for her (guitar accompaniment) "Bergères délaissées"—"Tomorrow will be a market day—but hearts they say—are given away—And I can't be bought on market day." "Hearts fresh caught"—it is the old story. There is a splendid young soldier cousin here who sings, too. Her soldier cousins are as plentiful as blackberries. "Gardez-vous, Bergerette—Gardez-vous d'aimée," I sing, and then went off into:

> Had you ever a cousin, Love?
> Did your cousin happen to sing?
> Cousins we have by the dozen, Love—
> But a cousin's a different thing—

Well the cousin took the point of my song—"those sweet demi-sisterly" kisses, &c&c. But the young lady did not move an eyelash.

As we came up on the train from Charlotte a soldier took out of his pocket a filthy rag. If it had lain in the gutter for months, it could have been no worse. He unwrapped this cloth carefully and took out two biscuits of the species known as "hardtack." Then he gallantly handed me one and, with an ingratiating smile, asked me "to take some." Then he explained, "Please take these two—swap with me—give me something softer that I can eat—I am very weak still." Immediately, for his benefit my basket of luncheon was emptied—but as for his biscuits, "I would not choose any."

Dirt—dirt—the Scripture states it plainly—cleanliness next to godliness.

---

6. 1860s Journal, Feb. 18, 1865.

Isabella: "But what did you say to him when he poked them under your nose?"

"I held up both hands. 'I would not take from you anything that is yours—far from it! I would not touch them for worlds.'"

Today dirt has given me a black eye. I have fought a hard battle with that dread antagonist, and it is rather a drawn battle. Ellen has my washing to do, as well as my cooking. So I have elected to do some housework. I must needs make my own tea. And Isabella's account of my woeful state at the door of that hotel—landlady out on a rampage. I sat by and listened to her as she told the story to Mrs. Munro and Miss Middleton.

"The old fury eyed Ellen and Laurence with disgust. 'Did you bring these niggers to keep 'em from the Yankees?'

"Here Ellen flew out of the hack. 'Name o' God! What is de matter wid dis 'oman? You think Missis ain't got no niggers but we two? Don't you know? Molly didn't come cause her baby is only six month old. Now, my William is ten years old. Claiborne take care of him. Lige couldn't take care Molly's baby. I never been traveling with Missis before. I am here in Molly's place.'

"'That woman is saucy. The airy hussy shall not put her foot in my door.'

"'I always did de washing and ironing. I ain't a regular maid—but I knows how to behave myself,' shouted Ellen. 'You no need to 'buse me so.'

"Mrs. Chesnut gets out of the hack—white as a sheet. 'Hold your tongue, Ellen! Do you want us to be left out in the street here?'

"Ellen dropped behind her Missis, mute as a mouse. That was nothing to her amazement when she saw Laurence had a pencil of his own. Laurence, in sorrow more than in anger:

"'Send me back to Mars Jeems. I can't do you any good here. I'll tell him how they are doing you.'"

Tremendous day's work—and I helped with a will. Such window glass—all to be washed. Then the brass and irons—green and grimy. After we rubbed them bright, how pretty they were. Much scrubbing wanted still. Miss Middleton thinks they have played tobacco juice around the sides of the wall with a *hose.* No mortal expectoration could have accomplished such a feat.

Ellen tied up her clothes and with bare feet and legs scrubbed the floor.

"He! Missis, this is harder than hoeing corn!" First I sat on the bedside and watched. Then she would none of me—after I was too tired to work.

"You go—dat's a good Missis. Put on your bonnet and stay to Miss Isabella's till de flo' dry." I am very docile now. And I obeyed orders.

On the way I met a cousin—male, elderly, a ci-devant fire-eater, nullifier, secessionist—extreme in everything.[7] In Columbia refused to be seen with his son-in-law who was not in the army, did not wear the Confederate gray. A

---

7. Identified in 1860s Journal as J. C.'s first cousin William Jesse Taylor, a Richland District planter. The son-in-law referred to here is Johnny Chesnut's brother Tom.

disciple of Judge Withers—who denounced Mr. Chesnut and the council when they tried to put the state on a war footing in 1862—i.e., interfering with states rights, citizens rights, &c&c, by sending negroes away from their owners' plantations to work on fortifications.

Here he is, this violent hero—bag and baggage—fleeing before the face of Yankees. Wife, children, negroes, all banked up in one room. One poor negro woman was taken ill, so the family had to go and camp in the hotel drawing room, leaving the poor soul to herself and her sister, who nurses her in the sole chamber the landlady would let them have for love or money.

At this day, trying to save property! Any man who is not in the army—who stays at home to save property—may hang his head. Shame on you, Carolinians, if such there be among you.

The handsome young cousin sings, "We will never give it up—no, never" in a way that thrills me through. I am almost roused to the Joan of Arc pitch. Confederate songs have failed to touch me as a general rule. I could but laugh at "Lorena."

"Dixie"—"I'll take my stand by Dixie land" was mere prosaic truth. It never moved me a jot. In Montgomery, when the band played "Massa is in the cold, cold ground," it sent a cold chill to the marrow of my bones. Nothing could they contrive to play but that—when Miss Tyler first ran up the Confederate flag.

And yet I am not superstitious.

Young Brevard is to send me the song "We will never give it up—no, never." I hope it will not recall Mr. Benjamin's funereal eloquence in the Senate—"You will never conquer us. Never. Never."

Conquer—that is not the word. They fall on us as Mat describes the negroes, en masse falling on and smothering the overseer when a bomb fell.

February 19, 1865. Sunday.

Text—"Set thy mark upon our house and give order to the destroyer not to hurt us."[8] Tolerably pitiful, that.

Yesterday Mrs. Munro routed me—horse, foot, and dragoons—in a religious controversy. She is clever and cultivated and an enthusiastic Catholic. Taking up my books of devotion—

"St. Augustine, Thomas à Kempis both belong to us," she cried with a radiant face. "And look—she has Fénelon[9] and Pascal—Catholics, quand même!" She

---

8. She is paraphrasing from Exodus 12.

9. François de Salignac de La Mothe-Fénelon (1651–1715), French bishop and leader of the Quietist heresy, whose works were available in French and English.

thought fit to ask the old question, and I gave the old answer—knowing better and having no wit to a new one.

"Where was the Protestant Church in all those years before Luther?"

"Where was your face before you washed it?"

"Why did your church stop growing so suddenly? Now we gain on you."

"Because the Reformation reformed you, too—and that was all you needed. Maybe the enlightenment of the world—art of printing, &c&c, did it. I find one church as good as another. Example of Christ is the leaven to save us."

She called me a worldling with crude and undigested ideas. She threatened me with the dread account I would have to give of neglected opportunities— "You who were privileged to hear Bishop England's sermons in the days of your youth."[1]

Mrs. Ben Rutledge came to my rescue. She is lovely. The beauty of exquisite refinement. Her eyes are large and brown, sad and soft, her mouth simply perfect. And yet Mrs. Middleton, the mother, must have been more beautiful than any of them. She is my ideal of beautiful old age. Mrs. Rutledge has a wistful way of saying things, though her manner is quiet and composed—and certainly these are the times to try it.

"Butler cannot be killed. I would have heard it. My husband is with him, you know!" Then household difficulties were the topic. "If I had been taught to make bread!" Here Mrs. Middleton came in.

"You are not looking—dear, anything the matter?"

"But mama, I have not eaten one mouthful today! The children can eat mush—I can't. I drank my tea, however."

She does not understand taking favors and, blushing violently, refused to let Ellen make her some biscuits. I went home and sent her the biscuits, all the same. And they were nice ones. A few minutes later, a negro woman came in who absolutely bakes bread. She brought not half a bad loaf in her basket. When she found out how delighted I was, she went for more, and I sent her with three good fresh well-baked loaves of bread to Mrs. Rutledge. I almost felt we had saved her life. That look of disgust she gave the mush haunted me. She sent me word she had learned to make waffles, and her nurse cooked them.

The Fants say all of [the] troubles at the hotel came from our servants bragging. They represented us as millionaires. The Middleton menservants smoked cigars. Mrs. Read's averred he had never done anything in his life but stand behind his master at table with a silver waiter in his hand. So they charged us accordingly. But perhaps she did not get the best of us, after all—for we paid her in Confederate money. And Ellen's onions, albeit raw, really were onions.

Now they won't take Confederate money in the shops here—how are we to live? Miss Middleton says quartermaster's families are all clad in good gray

1. John England (1786–1842), the Irish-born Roman Catholic bishop of Charleston. In school, Mary dined with the bishop every Wednesday at Madame Talvande's table.

cloth, but the soldiers are naked. Well, we are like the families of whom the novels always say "poor but honest." Poor—well-nigh beggars. For I do not know where my next meal is to come from. To think of fulfilling Scriptures. Now we know "bread is the staff of life."

Our joy at the sight of that loaf!

Read Madame de Genlis.[2] An exile's story is curiously interesting now. Contrast our fate and hers.

Some more violent contrasts. In the Revolution—when the English called us rebels—John Rutledge was dictator. Now Magrath rules in South Carolina. Our Lee would be a cool, staunch Wellington—but the weight of troops is on the other side. General Lee has done wonders—and no words wasted. His troops were as good as the bulldog British article. But then, Wellington was never left in the lurch, for want of an army to back him.

Mrs. Martin says: "Only genius can create something out of nothing. Lee or Wellington could not work without material. Genius, like love, pays its own expenses. Stonewall was our genius. He was inspired—some say, a little mad. We wanted a Napoleon to create an army and enthuse it. We had the best fighting material in the world—but it was not properly handled, and our men could only die in their tracks."

"Don't you feel better now? You have railed and scolded so."

"No—not quite. We have ceased to look for gentlemen, when we elect rulers. We fairly rake them up from the ashes, the cinders, the gutters."

"Stop, Ellen! No more 'Massa in the Cold, Cold Ground.' Sing something else."

"Well, so they are, most of them," says Isabella.

Time's revenges—

Leitner has lost a leg—he is a hero. A few years ago it was almost sacrilege, the thought that he dared challenge William Shannon, who has now for three years been safely housed in a bombproof—a bank president paying himself three thousand dollars a year in gold while all the rest of Confederate mankind are starving and before the enemy's guns. Edward Boykin wounded—and a lieutenant colonel in active service. Mr. Shannon might as well have let him accept the captaincy of the Kirkwood Rangers in peace. But his hard hit is that brave young son, Tom Boykin—dead upon the battlefield.

February 23, 1865.   Isabella has been reading my diaries. How we laugh. My sage ratiocinations—all come to naught. My famous insight into character—utter folly. They were lying on the hearth, ready to be burned, but she told me to hold on—think of it awhile. *Don't be rash.*" ⟨⟨. . . the *10* volumes of memoirs of the times I have written . . . still I write on, for if I have to burn—and here lie my treasures, ready for the blazing hearth—still they have served already to while away four days of agony.⟩⟩[3]

2. Stéphanie Félicité du Crest de Saint-Aubin, comtesse de Genlis, recounted her flight from France during the French Revolution in *Mémoires* (1825).
3. 1860s Journal, Feb. 23, 1865.

Afterward Isabella and I were taking a walk. General Joseph E. Johnston joined us. He explained to us all of Lee and Stonewall Jackson's mistakes. He was radiant and joyful. We had nothing to say. How could we? He always impresses me with the feeling that all of his sympathies are on the other side. Still, he was neither gruff nor rude today—as he can be when he chooses. He said he was very angry to be ordered to take command again. He might well be in a genuine rage. This on-and-offing is enough to bewilder the coolest head.

Mrs. Johnston knows how to be a partisan of Joe Johnston—and still not make his enemies uncomfortable. She can be pleasant and agreeable, quand même, as she was to my face.

Letter from my husband—he is at Charlotte. He came near being taken prisoner in Columbia, for he was asleep the morning of the 17th, when the Yankees blew up the RR depot. That woke him, of course. He found everybody had left Columbia and the town surrendered by the mayor, Colonel Goodwyn. Hampton and his command had been gone several hours. Isaac Hayne came away with General Chesnut. There was no fire in the town when they came away. They overtook Hampton's command at Meeks Mill. That night, from the hills where they encamped they saw the fire and knew the Yankees were burning the town—as we had every right to expect they would. ⟨⟨Such a letter. Says our retreat was disgraceful and unnecessary and that he nearly was taken prisoner.⟩⟩

Molly was left in charge of everything—Mrs. Preston's cow, which I was milking, and Sally Goodwyn's furniture ⟨⟨I hope not to keep boardinghouse for the Yankees.⟩⟩

Charleston and Wilmington—surrendered. I have no further use for a newspaper. I never want to see another one as long as I live.

Wade Hampton lieutenant general—too late. If he had been lieutenant general and given the command in South Carolina six months ago, I believe he would have saved us. Achilles was sulking in his tent—at such a time!

Shame, disgrace, beggary—all at once. Hard to bear.

Grand smash—

Rain—rain outside—inside naught but drowning floods of tears.

I could not bear it, so I rushed down in that rainstorm to the Martins. He met me at the door.

"Madame, Columbia is burned to the ground."

I bowed my head and sobbed aloud.

"Stop that," he said, trying to speak cheerfully. "Come here, wife. This woman cries with her whole heart—just as she laughs." But in spite of his words, his voice broke down—he was hardly calmer than myself.

Will try now and go to Greenville. I hear Kate and her children are there.

Enie—sitting on an addled egg forever—as if there was not a fresh egg in the world.

Shame – disgrace –
misery – Hampton
sent for – Much
good it may do
him. The grand
smash day comes –
poor Jeff – how little
he is – what would
I not have given to
be with him yesterday.
Today I am burning
papers all day –
expecting a Yankee
raid – gave some
silver to Mr Lane –
& two books of J –
Shall try & get
them if I go to

Greenville – how I have
wept this day! My
poor heart is weary – &
then how it poured –
rain rain rain –
& in it all I walked
down to Mrs Martin.
I wanted her to get
away – I want now
to get to Kate –
I am so utterly heart
broken – I hope John &
Mr C will get together
at least in the same
army – Miss Mattilda
Middleton spent the
morning here. She is
so clever – to analyse

the town when they came away — The
Overtook Hampton's command at
Meeks Mill — That night from the Hills
where they encamped they saw the
fire — and knew the Yankees were
burning the town — as we had every
right to expect they would.

Molly was left in charge of every thing.
Mrs Preston's Cow — which I was milking — and
all of Goodwyn's furniture.

Charleston and Wilmington — surrendered.
I have no further use for a newspaper
I never want to see another one as long
as I live.

Wade Hampton Lieut General —
too late — If he had been made Lieut
General and given the command in South
Carolina six months ago — I believe he
would have saved us — Achilles was
sulking in his tent — stupid to time!

Shame — disgrace — beggary — all at once —
Hard to bear.

Grand Smash —

Rain — Rain outside — inside naught
but drowning flood of tears —
I could not bear it — So I worked

"Grand Smash." The Fall of Columbia, from the 1880s Version, February 23, 1865

I want to get to Kate. I am so utterly heartbroken. I hope John Chesnut and General Chesnut may at least get into the same army. We seem scattered over the face of the earth.

Isabella sits there calmly reading.

I have quieted down after the days of rampage.

May our heavenly father look down on us and have pity.

Mrs. Johnston told me that somebody at the North—sister, aunt, cousin—had sent Mrs. Wigfall one of those dollars ⟨⟨one thousand dollars in gold⟩⟩, which she at once exchanged for twenty-eight thousand Confederate dollars. And that the Wigfalls were now living like fighting cocks.

"By this time they wish they had not changed that gold," Isabella thought. . . . [4]

They say I was the last refugee who came from Columbia—allowed to enter by the door of the cars. Government took possession then. And women could only be smuggled in by the windows. Stout ones stuck and had to be pushed, pulled, and hauled in by main force.

Dear Mrs. Izard, with all her dignity, was subjected to this rough treatment. She was found almost too much for the size of car windows. Mrs. Izard! Haute volée.

February 25, 1865.   The Phifers who live opposite are descendants of those Phifers who came South with Mr. Chesnut's ancestors after the Fort Duquesne disaster.[5] They have been driven out of the Eden, the Valley of Virginia, once before. They may have to go again. This Phifer is the great man, rich man par excellence, of Lincolnton. They say with something very near unto tears in his eyes he heard of our latest defeats.

"It is only a question of time with us now. The raiders will come, you know."

---

4. Omitted are several quotations attributed to "Jean Paul"—the pseudonym of German novelist Johann Paul Friedrich Richter (1763–1825).

5. On July 9, 1755, a force of French and Indians defeated Gen. Edward Braddock's English regulars and Lt. Col. George Washington's colonials several miles from Fort Duquesne at the junction of the Monongahela and Allegheny rivers in Penn. According to M. B. C., J. C.'s great-grandfather, who had migrated from Ireland to Va., died in this fight, one of the major battles of the French and Indian War (see p. xxxvi). The defeat opened the way to Indian raids in Va. and forced the Chesnut family, including J. C.'s grandfather John Chesnut I, to move first to N.C. and then to the Kershaw District of S.C.

General and Mrs. Johnston stay at the Phifers.

Mrs. Johnston said she would never own slaves.

"I might say the same thing. I never would. Mr. Chesnut does, but he hates all slavery, especially African slavery."

"What do you mean by African?"

"To distinguish that form from the inevitable slavery of the world. All married women, all children, and girls who live on in their father's houses are slaves."

"Oh! Oh!"

"General Johnston went off in the very devil of a bad humor. He was only put back to be the one to surrender."

She was bitter against Columbia but said, "A wise woman uses her foes as well as her friends for her own purposes."

Which I did not gainsay. I knew she detested me. I am a philosopher, and I found her vastly agreeable and entertaining. In Washington—before I knew any of them except by sight—Mrs. Davis, Mrs. Emory, and Mrs. Johnston were always together, inseparable friends, and the trio were pointed out to me as the cleverest women in the U.S. Now that I do know them all well, I think the world was right in its estimate of them.

My friend Mrs. Mason said, "Lydia Johnston will laugh at you, no matter how friendly you may find her."

"Is she singular in that? I laugh at everybody, friend or foe."

Today I was telling Mrs. Johnston [about] the first time I ever heard the word "nigger" used by people comme il faut.

A magnificent creature in London—attaché or something of Mr. McLane's—Gansevoort Melville—at table said, "Oh, Miss McLane, look, there is a genuine nigger."[6]

Now it is in everybody's mouth, but I have never become accustomed to it.

Mrs. Munro came in, evidently burdened with a mystery. It came out at last. Mrs. Phifer, kind soul, had written Mrs. Munro a note. She thought Mrs. Munro ought to warn me to be on my guard. Mrs. Johnston did not like me, sneered at me, particularly at my prejudices against slavery. Said, "I wonder when she took to that dodge"—&c&c. Mrs. Munro could not understand my lack of indignation.

I handed her what I had written.

"You see, I knew all about it. See what I have written of the fair Lydia." But now I can not go there again. She must be awfully dismal, left to Phifers, true. Flutes—and soft recorders.

In burning papers, as I have done steadily for a week, I came across an old letter written by me to my husband more than twenty years ago—here it is—

6. In 1845–46, Gansevoort Melville, elder brother of Herman Melville, was secretary of the American legation in England headed by Ambassador Louis McLane.

[*one page missing; letter lost or omitted, but from the rough draft of the 1880s Version, the following:*]

《I wrote a passionate antislavery letter to my husband a few years after I was married. He was then in Mississippi. . . . I kept it, for I anticipated Mrs. Stowe not in imagining facts but in abhorrence and loathing.》

My days are past—my purposes broken off—even the thoughts of my heart (Job).[7]

Be fair, or foul—or rain, or shine,
The joys I have possessed *in spite of fate* are mine,
Not Jove himself upon the past has power,
What has been—has been—and I have had my hour.[8]

"Time and the hour run through the roughest day."[9]

Mrs. Glover gave us Dr. Palmer's last sermon. "We are on a lone rock—Atlantic and Pacific Ocean surging around—every point of land submerged—we alone—the waters closing over us—slowly but surely."

Met a Mr. Ancrum of a serenely cheerful aspect—happy and hopeful.

"All right now. Sherman sure to be thrashed now. Joe Johnston is in command now." John Darby said when the oft-mentioned Joseph the Malcontent gave up his command to Hood, he said with a smile: "I hope you will be able to stop Sherman. It was more than I could do." General Johnston is not of Mr. Ancrum's way of thinking as to his own powers, for he stayed here several days after he was ordered to the front. He must have known he could do no good, and I am of his opinion.

Not in this, however—General Joe thinks himself so prominent a fact in the country's history as Mr. Davis's enemy, he actually feels Mr. Davis would sacrifice wife, children, country, God, to gratify his hate of Joe Johnston. Now I am sure that Mr. Davis's dislike to General Johnston assumes no such colossal proportions. And even though I am sure of the tenfold power of Joe Johnston's hatred to Mr. Davis—and I think I understand his intense rancor—we all know old Sid Johnston in Columbia, with his prejudices and impracticable cranks. Joseph is his own brother.

Mr. Sidney J was a gentleman and a patriot. So is General J. J., and I do not think he would ruin his country to spite Mr. Davis. He acts according to his nature. He is a born retreater—bravest of the brave—and I think it awfully conceited of him to feel himself worthy of so much presidential consequence, importance, hate.

---

7. Job 17:11.
8. From Horace, *Odes*, book 3, ode 29.
9. Shakespeare, *Macbeth*, act 1, scene 3.

Heaven is helping us weep. Rain, rain, rain—in sympathy with our calamities. It has rained for six months. Yesterday the wagon in which I was to go to Flat Rock drove up to the door, covered with a tentlike white cloth. Ellen flew up to me.

"Oh, Missis! For the love of the Lord. Don't go off in that there thing. Make a blue homespun bonnet with oak splits, poke your head out of the *ee*nd of that wagon, and you'll be po' buckra for true. I don't min' rain—no, not an ole cent, a brass cent—but you gwine lef' boxes and trunks here—you lef' boxes and trunks in Richmond full o' good clothes—and you lef' ever so much in Columbia. All done burn up. For lord sake, Missis, go home and stay dere. Keep running round—'stributing your things everywhere."

"Ellen, this distributing of ourselves and our things is pretty bad. But they say we have no home."

Here she threw her apron over her head and howled.

The man who owned the wagon was standing in the door. I asked him to walk in and told Ellen to walk out. I asked the man his name—in my embarrassment—for an opening of the conversation. He showed great hesitation in giving it. At last:

"My name is Sherman—and now I see by your face that you won't go with me. My name is against me these times." Here he grinned: "But you leave *Lincoln*ton."

The name was the last drop in my cup, but I gave him Mrs. Glover's reason for staying here. General Johnston told her, "This might be the safest place of all—after all." For he thinks the Yankees are making straight for Richmond and General Lee's rear, and they will go by Camden and Lancaster, leaving Lincolnton on their west flank.

The McLeans are kind people. They ask no rent for their rooms, only 20 dollars a week for firewood—twenty dollars! and such dollars—mere wastepaper.

How our generals (poor things) are abused—and the variety of abuse they indulge in. Hood was drunk at Franklin. Then he was scared into joining the church! Beauregard is a Frenchman, too gay and frivolous. Beauregard is in a green melancholy. Sickness and sadness unutterable devour his energies.

Then there is a report which comes as regular as clockwork—Hampton has cut off Kilpatrick.

Mrs. Munro took up my photograph book. I have one of all the Yankee generals.

"I want to see the men who are to be our masters."

"Not mine, thank God—come what may. This was a *free fight*. We had as much right to fight to get out as they had a right to fight to keep us in. If they try to play the masters—anywhere upon the habitable globe I will go, never to see a Yankee. And if I die on the way, so much the better."

Then I sat down and wrote to my husband—so much worse than anything I can put in this book—and as I wrote I was blinded by tears of rage. Indeed, I nearly wept myself away.

In vain, years of death, depopulation, bondage, fears have all been borne.

Governor Vance took a fling at us in his speech. He saw daily the South Carolinians who would do this thing. The devil could not stop them. They were ready to shed the last drop of their blood, to die in the last ditch—&c&c—and *now* their line of march through *N.C.* was pretty lively. Shame! shame!

Mrs. Glover endorsed the sentiments of Vance. She said she told everyone she was a North Carolinian. Her father really is one.

She will not have to make believe. She looks the thing perfectly. The old man is rather the nicest fellow of the two.

XXXI

"Job Is My Comforter"

February 26, 1865. Mrs. Munro offered me religious books which I declined, being already provided with the Lamentations of Jeremiah, the Penitential Psalms of David, the denunciations of Isaiah, and above all the patient wail of Job. Job is my comforter now.

And yet I would be so thankful to know it never would be any worse with me. My husband is well and ordered to join the Great Retreater. I am bodily comfortable, if somewhat dingily lodged, and I daily part with my raiment for food. We find no one who will exchange eatables for Confederate money. So we are devouring our clothes. Ellen is a maid—comme il y en a peu—and if I do a little work it is quite enough to show me how dreadful it would be without her *if I should have to do it all.*

Appliances for social enjoyment are not wanting. Miss Middleton and Isabella often drink a cup of tea with me. One might search the whole world and not find two cleverer or more agreeable women. Miss M is brilliant and accomplished. She must have been a hard student all of her life. She knows everybody worth knowing, and she has been everywhere. Then she is so highbred, highhearted, pure and true. She is so clean-minded she could not harbor a wrong thought. She is utterly unselfish, a devoted daughter and sister. She is one among the many larger brained women a kind Providence has thrown in my way—such as Mrs. McCord, daughter of Judge Cheves, Mary Preston Darby, Mrs. Emory, granddaughter of old Franklin the American wise man, and Mrs. Jefferson Davis. How I love to praise my friends. The fair Lydia over the way, though no friend of mine, she says, is a charming person, clever as any. Just now, as I look out of my dim glass window, I wonder how life goes on with her—with only a Phifer accompaniment to all her music.

Of course, if this rain continues we must have a deluge.

As a ray of artificial sunshine, Mrs. Munro sent me an *Examiner.* Daniel thinks we are at the last gasp, and now England and France are bound to step in. England must know if the U.S.A. are triumphant they will tackle her next, and France must know she will have to give up Mexico—en cas.

My faith fails me. It is too late. No help for us now—in God or man.

Also—that Thomas was now to ravage Georgia. Never. Sherman from all accounts has done that work once for all. There will be no aftermath.

They say no living thing is found in Sherman's track—only *chimneys,* like telegraph poles, to carry the news of Sherman's army backward.

In all that tropical downpour Mrs. Munro sent me overshoes and an umbrella with the message "Come over"—and I went. As well drown in the streets as hang myself at home to my own bedpost. Oh, this dismal, lonely hole!

At Mrs. Munro's I met a Miss McDaniel. Her father for seven years was the Methodist preacher at our negro church. The negro church is in a grove just opposite Mulberry House. She says her father has so often described that fine old establishment and its beautiful lawn, live oaks, &c&c&c.

"Now, I daresay, there stands only Sherman's sentinels—stacks of chimney. We have made up our minds to the worst. Mulberry House is no doubt razed to the ground."

She was inclined to praise us, she said. As a general rule the Episcopal minister went to the family mansion, and the Methodist missionary preached to the negroes and dined with the overseer at his house. But at Mulberry her father always stayed at the "House," and the family were so kind and attentive to him. Rather pleasant to hear one's family so spoken of among strangers.

So well equipped to brave the weather, armed cap-à-pied, so to speak, I continued my prowl further afield and brought up at the Middletons. I may have surprised them—"at such an inclement season." They hardly expected a visitor. Never, however, did lonely old woman receive such a warm and hearty welcome.

Wheeler's[1] men had found a Yankee hid in a barn, an escaped prisoner. He reported that Hampton had cut off Kilpatrick again somewhere near Greenville.

They congratulated me that I had not ventured in Sherman's white-covered wagon.

"Into the jaws of the Yankees"—"Into the jaws of death rode the six hundred."

"After all, they would not eat you."

Some people report that Sherman left a negro garrison in Columbia. Another story is there is no Columbia to garrison. Sherman marched off in solid column, leaving not so much as a blade of grass behind. A howling wilderness—land laid waste—dust and ashes.

Another: Wheeler's cavalry sacked the old Hampton house before Sherman's bummers got a chance at it.

"On, Stanley! on!" Last words of Jeff Goodwyn. Stanley and Radcliffe were the heroes who with a white flag bore the keys of Columbia to the conquerors of women and children.[2]

Mrs. Blake and Mr. Rutledge[3] (who is wounded) are in Columbia still—*or*

---

1. Maj. Gen. Joseph Wheeler of Ga., who had been replaced by Wade Hampton as chief of cavalry of the Army of Tenn.
2. Mayor Goodwyn surrendered the city on Feb. 17. William B. Stanley and Thomas W. Radcliffe were local merchants.
3. Probably Col. Benjamin Huger Rutledge.

where? They were in Columbia the night it was fired. The Middleton household are anxious and sad enough.

———————

Tea at the Munros. Village gossip the same everywhere. And women's chatter.

"So we whimper and whine, do we? Always we speak in a deprecating voice, do we? And sigh gently at the end of every sentence—why? Plain enough. Does a man ever speak to his wife and children except to find fault? Does a woman ever address any remark to her husband that does not begin with an excuse? When a man does wrong, does not his wife have to excuse herself if he finds out she knows it? Now, if a man drinks too much and his wife shows that she sees it, what a storm she brings about her ears. She is disrespectful, unwifelike. Does she set up for strong-minded? So unwomanly—*so unlike his mother.* So different from the women of his family, the women he was accustomed to at home. Do you wonder that we are afraid to raise our voices above a mendicant's moan?"

"And yet, they say our voices are the softest, sweetest, in the world."

"No wonder. The base submission of our tone must be music in our masters' ears."

"Female rebellion she is preaching."

A perfect shriek of rage, overcoming our small talk.

"Oh! That was Mars Kit. He said the man was such a fool[4] he did not know his campaign in Tennessee was a failure. No doubt Mars Kit thought him a fool—up there fighting to the best of his poor ability, risking his life and limb. So much more sensible hobnobbing with McPherson at Vicksburg—praising Hampton in a whole skin—saving one's cotton, with Mrs. Henry Duncan to help."

"I like fools who are Confederate martyrs. Maybe I am a fool, too—but I like that sort best!"

———————

"Oh, Miss Improper was too smart for them. Have you seen her leading her child? She was to be married—the man was killed in battle. Horrible! That child was born. The sister would not come home—the married sister—saying this poor thing must be put out. She disgraced the family. Married sister's husband killed, too."

Miss Improper is a brave lassie. She answers her sister. "My child is the child of your husband—there." She answers: "I will behave myself if you let me stay here. If you turn me out—look out for—for—from bad to worse, you understand." She shames them all into passive submission—and you saw her and little Toosoona in the bosom of her family."

"I do not even know their names, poor things, but this tale is told to everybody whenever they are seen abroad or at church."

———————

4. Hood.

They tell strangers this strange story. Sometimes poor married sister revolts. Nobody believes the scandal against her dead husband, but if she grows restive, Miss Improper raises her finger. "Hoity-toity—you beginning again. *Your* crape and bombazine becomes you, truly." The dead man cannot rise to give the lie to her vile accusations.

"Women can be so bad."

"I think they are right to be good to the poor little child."

"Did you see that beautiful woman on the train? A major—by his stars we knew him. Two stars—a colonel has three. He was so soft-spoken—and he pulled his long yellow moustache so. We guessed they were a runaway couple in the honeymoon. Someone else said they were an old married couple who had had a tiff, and we were witnessing the reconciliation. Don't you see how they are making it up? No, no—they are only engaged, and he is to leave her the next station to join his regiment."

"As our friends the enemy up North say, 'They are having a puffickly splendid time,'" said an envious man.

"The whistle drowned all conjecture, and we stopped at Charlotte. A gray-haired old man walked in. Up jumps the lady. 'Oh, uncle. Is that you? So glad—&c&c. Take my things. Here is my traveling bag. This gentleman, major—I did not catch your name, sir, when I was introduced to you this morning on the train.' (She smiled sweetly at the major.)

"'Oh,' said the grave and dignified uncle, 'I know the major. By the way, major I bring you good news of your wife and children. I saw them two days ago in Richmond.'

"Oh, what a look she gave him then. It was so full of rage. Off went niece and uncle. The major lolled back on his seat, with a smile of perfect self-satisfaction.

"'I would like to kill him,' said one of our party who had grown so restive under all that kissing.

"Never mind. Let us hope the Yankees will save you that trouble. He is on his way to Lee's army."

"For one thing—when this cruel war is over, those department girls must go home. Oh, the pity of it! Nice girls learning to misbehave that way."

"Everybody speak for herself. Mrs. C stands up for the president—Mrs. R[5] for Joe Johnston—Isabella adores Hood. We all pitch into Beauregard. He has no friends here."

"Comfort to have one safe spot. Abuse Beauregard, and you won't bring a wasp's nest about your ears."

Next came the story of the kleptomaniac. "But she is the richest girl of all." "So much the better. Her father pays and hushes it up. They make him pay for more than she takes. He dares not investigate charges—&c&c."

---

5. Eleanor (Middleton) Rutledge.

Surely that was scandal enough for one long rainy evening.

Now we know the worst. Are we growing hardened? We avoid all allusion to
Columbia. We never say "home." We begin to deride the sure poverty ahead.

"I say, when Ellen is a lady and driving about in your carriage, won't you miss
that tray of nice breakfast she brings to your bedside every morning?" Ellen
does make such nice coffee. At any rate we [are] not of the crybaby kind.

Mrs. Rutledge, that plate of biscuits still rankling, has sent me a tumbler of
milk, the very first milk I have tasted since I deserted our Alderney cow in Plain
St., Columbia. Mrs. Preston's cow it was.

How it pours! Could I live many days in solitary confinement? Things are
beginning to be unbearable. Sit down—be satisfied. Your husband is safe—so
far. Be thankful it is no worse with you.

But there is the gnawing pain all the same. What is the good of being here at
all? Our world has gone to destruction.

And across the way the fair Lydia languishes. She has not even my resources
against ennui. She has no Isabella, no Miss Middleton—two as brilliant women
as any in Christendom. Oh, how does she stand it?

I mean to go to church, if it rains cats and dogs. My feet are wet two or three
times a day. We never take cold. Our hearts are too hot within us for that.

Then a carriage drove up to the door. I began to tie on my bonnet, and I said
to myself in the glass, "Oh, you lucky woman!" I was all in a tremble, so great was
my haste to be out of this.

Mrs. Glover has a carriage, it seems. She came for me to go and hear Rev. Mr.
Martin preach.

Text: "Why are ye so fearful, oh, ye of little faith." We are all women, so fear
is no disgrace. I do think we possess our souls in wonderful patience. But I must
say Brother Martin has a wonderful gift in prayer. He lifts our spirits from this
dull earth. He takes us up to heaven. That I will not deny. Still, he cannot keep
my attention. My heart wanders, and my mind strays back to South Carolina.
Oh, vandal Sherman, what are you at there now? Hardhearted wretch that you
are!

That sphinx Serena, the Princess Bright-Eyes, suddenly wakes up from her
dreams to write and ask of what Butlers is Nat. Who was his grandfather on the
spindle side? Oh, Serena Highness—no less than Oliver Perry of the Lakes,
Butlers, Dukes of Ormond—but never mind all that. Pierce Butler, Pickens
Butler before him, and now General Butler—his brother in our army—and
ever so many more brothers.[6] Then, too—all Butlers are accredited to the

6. Oliver Perry was Nat Butler's uncle, as were former S.C. governor Pierce Mason Butler and
former U.S. senator Andrew Pickens Butler of S.C.

Dukes of Ormond and the dead son Ossory, of whom he was so proud in his grief.

Pretty good record—commodores, judges, senators, colonels of crack regiments, Palmettos in Mexico, par exemple, generals of Confederate armies, et cie.

And so I answered our beautiful flirt with this—question for question: "What is Nat Butler to you?" Brockenbrough is with Hardee. So is General Chesnut. And we would fain hope Brockenbrough will reconsider his somewhat rash determination to make a confidant of General Chesnut.

The shrinking and the daring—both ways we missed it. Sherman and Johnston, Hood and Thomas. So easy to write pretty sentences if you are born a poet.

The wise conquer difficulties—by daring to attempt them.

Sloth and folly shiver and shrink at sight of toil and hazard—and make the impossibility *they fear*.

I laugh aloud. All comes to grief with the unlucky, the shrinking, or the daring.

—Bet my money on the bobtail horse
Let who will—bet on the gray.

comes up from the street. Inside: "We will never give it up—no never."

I think that young man down there with the guitar—his attentions are what you would call "particular."

Letter from General Chesnut.

In camp near Charlotte
February 28, 1865

My dear Mary,

I thank you a thousand, thousand times for your kind letters. They are now my only earthly comfort—except the hope that all is not yet lost. We have been driven like a wild herd from our country—not [so much] from a want of spirit in the people or the soldiers as from want of energy and competency in our commanders. Hampton and Butler are the only ones who have done anything. The restoration of Joe Johnston, it is hoped, will redound to the advantage of our cause and the reestablishment of our fortunes! I am still in not very agreeable circumstances. For the last four days completely waterbound. As soon as a wagon can move, will go in search of General Hardee's corps, the whereabouts of which is still in doubt. He has, I suppose, the remnant of my command. All, or nearly all, who were here with the prisoners left the night before I arrived—*without leave*. They were left unwisely without officers, in the hands of the commandant of the post. I have not seen Beauregard. Have had a very pleasant interview with General Johnston.

I am informed that a detachment of Yankees were sent from Liberty Hill to Camden with a view to destroy all the houses, mills, provisions &c about that place. No particulars have reached me. You know I expected the worst that could be done and am fully prepared for any report which may be made.

If you desire it I will endeavor to convey a message to Laurence or Isaac to come up to you. Though perhaps it would not be safe to attempt to bring anything with them yet. I had intended to run up to Lincolnton to see you two days ago, when I received your letter saying you would leave there today. It is better, however, that I should not now place myself out of the line of movement of the army, which may take place at any moment.

It would be a happiness beyond expression to see you—even for an hour. I have heard nothing from my poor old father. I fear I shall never see him again. Such is the fate of war.

I do not complain. I have deliberately chosen my lot and am prepared for any fate that awaits me. My care is for you. And I trust still in the good cause of my country and the justice and mercy of God.

When you write, please do not omit to date your letters. It is satisfactory to know the day they are written. In this horrible spell of weather I am as wet and uncomfortable as a drenched dog. N'importe!

We are informed that General Lee has beaten Grant and Hampton and Butler, the enemy about Lancaster. God bless and protect you dear wife—

J. C.

On est gentilhomme avant tout.

It was a lively, rushing, young set South Carolina put to the fore. They knew it was a time of eminent danger—the fight would be ten to one. They expected to win by activity, energy, enthusiasm. Then came the wet blankets—Pickens old, Orr halfhearted in the cause, Mr. Barnwell octogenarian and low-church Episcopalian in his first *sympathies*.

Memminger—et cie.

Now they are posing, wrapping Caesar's mantle about their heads—to fall with dignity. Those gallant youths who dashed so gaily to the front lie mostly in bloody graves. Well for them, maybe. There are worse things than honorable graves.

Wearisome thoughts—late in life we are to begin anew—laborious, difficult days ahead.

I wonder if a note went from here to tell Mrs. Phifer all I said of Joe Johnston. At any rate, Mrs. Johnston was not so insincere, after all. She did not return my call. No doubt she was *notified*. I saw her go off. The Phifers say she was lovely to them to the last.

Contradictory testimony. Governor Aiken passed through, saying Sherman left Columbia as he found it and was last heard of at Cheraw. Dr. Chisolm walked home with me. He says that is the last story. Now my husband wrote that he saw the fires which burned up Columbia—himself—the first night. His camp was near enough to the town for that.

Then there came in someone who said the road was open to Columbia—and then Mrs. Munro's cousin, who said the enemy were in full force in Chester, halfway to Columbia—thereby blocking the way most effectually.

Miss Middleton and Isabella here, looking over this. "Why do you write such contradictory statements? It is all contradiction and counterstatements. It is absolutely laughable."

"I write what I hear, not what I know. I think what I say—*at the time*. But I am reckless—almost shameless about changing my mind."

St. Julien Ravenel here—left his wife, and she was not in traveling trim—obliged to stay. He has not heard a word—says sometimes in his madness he hopes it may be no worse than that a bomb has destroyed them all.

They say he has burned Lancaster—*that* Sherman nightmare, ghoul, hyena. That I do not believe. He takes his time. There is none to molest him. He does things leisurely and deliberately. Why stop to do so needless a thing as burn Lancaster courthouse, the jail, and the tavern? As I remember it, that constitutes Lancaster.

A raiding party, they say, did for Camden.

Mrs. Munro admires Sherman. She likes to get up a shindy. Such a speech leads to a row worthy of Donnybrook Fair.

They showed me a note from Gen. Joseph E. Johnston. He communicates to us the fact that the political horizon is black.

Maybe he is like the doctors who represent their patients as lying at death's door—so they may have all the more credit for saving their lives. If Joe saves us, I will throw up my cap for him, in spite of all past and gone. Magnanimous me!

Gave today 50 dollars for a small wooden bucket—in better days, or in metallic currency, worth twenty-five cents.

Columbia hospital tales. An Irish nurse smothering a man booked to die. She wanted his bed for a man whose life could be saved.

Then came the English cavalier history of our proud blue-blooded Huguenots. Huguenots pur sang were often converted Jews, oftener thrifty citizens, artisans, French puritans. We ought to blow our clarion as boldly and as excessively and as exhaustively as the Plymouth Rock gentry tout over their crew.

Story from Columbia, day before Sherman—Mrs. D with her chin cloth, both arms covered with plunder, kicking a flour barrel—in that way utilizing her feet as rollers.

Millions of soldiers' clothes were left in Columbia. Could have been brought here in lieu of the old chairs and tables we see piled here every day. The last people who came away say the streets were lined with commissary stores— candles, coffee, &c&c&c, ready to be removed. *If* Sherman had waited a day or two longer.

Young Brevard at it. It is now "Billikins and his Dinah." Guitaring fellow. Recollections that still will leap—from out their fountains—ten years deep.

February 27, 1865.   Ash Wednesday. No train from Charlotte yesterday— rumor Sherman in Charlotte. The natives quite cool on the subject. Content to bide their time. They are Union people, they say—they always were. Sherman will take what he wants, but he will hold out to them the right hand of fellow- ship. The same people who are so proud of Hoke, Ramseur, et cie, who went forth to do or die for their country—so many who came back no more, dead upon the field of battle! They think now they can eat their cake and have it, too.[7]

Sat by Mrs. Hoke[8] at church—was told she is the great lady of the town. Hoke père held up as an example. He was a cabinetmaker—worked in his shop, made his fortune. Told his customers, "Buy it or leave it—can't waste time on your chatter. Cut it short—I must back to my work."

La carrière ouverte aux talents—here it is. Napoleonic. No mudsills in America. Every living piece of timber can be a top rail, if properly handled young.

Two very fine looking officers sat behind us at church. Said to be spies— Yankees—have been seen talking to negroes on the sly. Their papers examined—in pencil, badly spelled, every word beginning with a capital letter.

"Papers very suspicious, but then all Yankees go to free schools and know how to spell."

So we all thought until we began to pick up their letters on the battlefield, and that delusion was dispelled.

"Where is Isabella?" "Teaching her cousin to play on the piano." "Somebody ought to teach Isabella."

7. Like Brig. Gen. Robert F. Hoke, Confederate Maj. Gen. Stephen Dodson Ramseur was a native of Lincolnton. He died of wounds received at the battle of Cedar Creek, Va., in Oct. 1864.
8. Probably Frances (Burton) Hoke, the mother of General Hoke.

Oh, how Mrs. Munro harried my soul with her tales of the way the Yankee prisoners are suffering at Salisbury.[9]

February 29 [*sic*] 1865.   Trying to brave it out. They froze John Boykin and Mr. Venable's brother to death in cold blood. Would you be willing to be as wicked as they are? A thousand times no.

We must feed our army first. They need not have starved, if Lincoln would consent to exchange prisoners, *but* men are nothing to them—a thing to throw away. If they send our men back, they strengthen our army—and then their policy is to keep everything here to help starve us out. That is what Sherman's destruction means.

"Stop it, Mrs. Munro. This thing cannot be willfully done."

So away I ran from blood-curdling tales. It goes to my heart like a stab. Oh, how can people be cruel to the helpless? Came home.

Young Brevard asked me to play accompaniments for him. The guitar is my instrument (or was). So [he] sung and I played, to my own great delight. It was a distraction. Then I made eggnog for the soldier boys below and came here, having spent a very pleasant evening. Be gone, dull care—you and I can never agree.

Ellen and I are shut up here. Rain, rain—everlasting rain. And as our money is worthless, are we to starve? Heavens! how grateful I was today when Miss McLean sent me a piece of chicken!

Ellen: "Missis, ain't you 'shame—crying for joy like a beggar 'oman. You dat had turkey and everything home. If you only would*en* gone home."

I think [news of] my empty larder has leaked out. Today Mrs. Munro sent me hotcakes and eggs for my breakfast.

Miss McLean said triumphantly: "Sherman will be cut off. Joe Johnston, Cheatham,[1] Hoke, Beauregard, surround him."

"Dear, these are not the days of Jericho. Names won't do it—blowing horns does not come to much. Mere waste of breath, indeed."

"He is sure to be cut off," she said doggedly.

Sent the Fants some good old brandy for their wounded soldier.

They say he is a Catholic accidentally fallen into Mrs. Munro's and the Fants' hands—good Catholics all—and they say he must die.

Met another Mrs. Johnston.

"Where are the Carolina chivalry?" she said with a sneer.

"With Lee or Johnston. Where did you suppose they were?"

9. Between Oct. 1864 and Feb. 1865, more than thirty-four hundred died in the overcrowded Confederate prison at Salisbury, N.C.

1. Maj. Gen. Benjamin Franklin Cheatham of Tenn., commander of a corps of the Army of Tenn.

"Oh, I meant Rhetts and all that."

"It strikes me that a good many Rhetts have fallen in battle. Of those who are alive I know nothing."

"Oh! We will not hear much more of that sort of thing. It is played out."

The Fants interfered, piously wishing they had some sacred ashes to put on their foreheads—Ash Wednesday, as it is. No, not even ashes. I have no wood to burn, cannot afford even sackcloth to wail in. We are below the luxury of woe—sackcloth and ashes. Only Jews and blockaders can do the thing in that style.

These people are proud of their heroic dead and living soldiers—but are prepared to say with truth that [they] always preferred to remain in the Union and are ready to assure the first comers of Yankees that they have always hated South Carolina seceders and nullifiers as much as the Yankees do.

"You say Miss Giles is as clever as she is beautiful. Nonsense. Clever! She was out of the Confederacy and then came rushing in. Fool or mad, that was."

"Conduct of a fool. Most women atone for their sins when they marry."

"Spinsters and vestal virgins—how do you know? You have not tried it."

"We have ears to hear, eyes to see, and a heart to understand, all the same. Lookers-on see more of the game than players—&c&c."

F.F.'s have a dialect. Her cousin said "mighty little" for *very small*. She called a ball or a tea party "only a little company"—and another form of the simple word "very" was "right much." And she lived in the house where Mrs. Mat Singleton used English as pure as that of Victoria Regina.

"How I like to hear Mrs. John Singleton's clean-cut sentences, every word distinctly enunciated."

"I should say she was the delight of her friends, the terror of her foes. I am afraid of those words dropped one by one with such infinite precision—drops of vitriol, sometimes.

Remember that night as the train stopped—a ponderous bank president filled the door of the car.[2]

"What was the use of bank presidents? We have no money."

"He says he paid himself his salary in gold, so there is money somewhere for the stay-at-homes. He is a descendant-in-law of the pretender branch of the Stuarts.

"And he is as loud as a centaur."

"You mean *stentor*. He said, 'Miss_____, yes, yes—I come for yer—Huddy, come 'long.' Now, this was only a slovenly habit of speech. He writes admirably."

What a look she gave me then.

"Worse, that 'right much'—eh?"

"What did you do?" "Nothing." Terebene lamps do not disclose blushes.

We had been bragging of South Carolina's purity of accent—Mrs. Mat's well

2. William M. Shannon.

of English undefiled, Mrs. Richardson Miles's sweetest and softest of voices, Miss Middleton's sweet low voice *and* wit *and* wisdom.

"Galore."

"Then came the rough boatswain's hoarse bawl."

March 5, 1865.   Is the sea drying up? Is it going up into mist and coming down on us in this waterspout? The rain—it raineth every day, and the weather represents our tearful despair on a large scale.

It is also Lent—quite convenient, for we have nothing to eat. So we fast and pray. And go draggling to church like drowned rats, to be preached at.

To think, there are men who dare so defile a church, a sacred sanctuary dedicated to God the Father, and we have to hold up our skirts and walk tiptoe, so covered is the floor, aisle, and pews with the dark shower of tobacco juice. "How do Americans expectorate?" I know where Dante would place these—animals.

My letter from my husband was so—well, what in a woman you would call "heartbroken." So I began to get ready for a run up to Charlotte. My hat was on my head. My traveling bag in my hand.

Ellen was saying, "Which umbrella, ma'am?"

"Stop, Ellen, someone is speaking out there." A tap at the door. Miss McLean threw the door wide open, and in a triumphant voice:

"Permit me to announce General Chesnut!"

She goes off singing, "ah, does not a meeting like this make amends!"

We went after luncheon to see Mrs. Munro. J. C. wanted to thank her for all her kindness to me. We had been seeing the rough side of life so long, the seamy side. I was awfully proud of him. I had ceased to think everybody had the air and manners of a gentleman. I know now, it is a thing to thank God for.

Mr. Chesnut knew Mr. Munro in our legislature long ago. So it was all very nice. Father O'Connell was there, fresh from Columbia.[3] News at last. Sherman's men had burned the convent. Mrs. Munro had pinned her faith to Sherman because he was a Catholic—and now![4] Father O'Connell was there—he saw it. The nuns and girls marched to old Hampton house (Mrs. Preston's now) and so saved it. They walked between files of soldiers. Men were rolling tar barrels and lighting torches to fling over the house when the nuns came. Columbia is but dust and ashes—burned to the ground. Men, women, and children left there, houseless, homeless, without one particle of food—picking up the corn left by Sherman's horses in their picket ground and parching it to stay their hunger.

---

3. Jeremiah Joseph O'Connell, Roman Catholic priest and president of St. Mary's College, which had been destroyed in the burning of Columbia.

4. Although his wife was a Roman Catholic, Sherman himself was not.

General Chesnut said he had sent Isaac Hayne with a party of scouts. They would go to Columbia and come back by Camden. So we will hear something definite from home through Isaac Hayne.

How kind my friends were—on this my fête. Mrs. Rutledge sent me a plate of biscuits, Mrs. Munro nearly enough for an entire dinner. Miss McLean sent in a cake for dessert. And Ellen cooked and served up the materials so happily at hand, very nicely indeed. There never was a more successful dinner. My heart was too full to eat, but I was quiet and calm and at least spared my husband the trial of a broken voice or tears.

As he stood at the window with his back to the room, he said:

"Where are they now, my old blind father and my sister? Day and night I see her leading him out from under his own rooftree. That picture pursues me persistently. But come, let us talk of pleasanter things."

"Where will you find them?"

He took off his heavy cavalry boots, and Ellen carried them off to dry and wash the mud off. She brought them back as Miss Middleton walked in. In his agony, struggling with those huge boots to get them on, he spoke to her *volubly* in French. She turned away from him instantly, as she saw his shoeless plight, and said, "I had not heard of your happiness. I did not know the general was here."

Not until next day did we have time to remember and laugh at that outbreak of French. Miss Middleton answered him in the same language. He told her how charmed he was with my surroundings and that he would go away with a much lighter heart since he had seen the kind people with whom he would leave me.

I asked J. C. what that correspondence of Sherman and Hampton meant.[5] That was while I was preparing something for our dinner and his back was still turned as he gazed out of the window. He spoke in the low and steady monotone that characterized our conversation the whole day—and yet there was something in his voice that thrilled me.

"The second day after our march from Columbia we passed the M's. He was a bonded man—and not at home. His wife said at first that she could not find forage for our horses—afterward she succeeded in procuring some for us. I noticed a very handsome girl who stood beside her as she spoke to me, and I suggested to her mother the propriety of sending her daughter out of the track of both armies. Things were no longer as heretofore—so much straggling, so many camp followers, no discipline on the outskirts of an army. The girl answered quickly, 'I will stay with my mother.'

"That very night a part of Wheeler's men came to our camp. Such a tale they

5. Angered by the death of Union foragers in incidents such as the one J. C. describes below, Sherman wrote Wade Hampton on Feb. 24 threatening to execute a Confederate prisoner for each Federal killed. Hampton responded the next day in a letter promising the execution of two Union prisoners for each Southern prisoner killed, condemning the foragers as "thieves" justifiably murdered, and accusing Sherman of ordering the burning of Columbia. Sherman did not reply, and no executions took place.

told! They had passed the horror and destruction—the mother raving of what had been done. This outrage was done before her very face—she being secured first. This straggling party of the enemy—after their crime—moved on. They were seven of them only, and the women said had been gone but a short time. Wheeler's men went off in pursuit full speed, overtook them, cut their throats—and marked upon their breasts, "These were the Seven."

"But the girl!"

"Oh—she was dead." "Now I suppose the 24th February was a case of a similar kind."

"Are they as violent as ever against the president?"

"Sometimes I think I am the only friend he has in the world. At these dinners, which they give us everywhere, I spoil sport, for I will not sit there and hear Jeff Davis abused. Abused for things he is no more responsible for than any man at table. I lost my temper. I told them it sounded arrant nonsense to me—putting Lee second to Joe Johnston—and that Jeff Davis was a gentleman and a patriot with more brains than the assembled company."

"You lost your temper, truly."

"And I did not know it. I thought I was as cool as I am now. In Washington when we left it Jeff Davis ranked second to none in intellect—maybe first from the South—and Mrs. Davis the friend of Mrs. Emory, Mrs. Joe Johnston, Mrs. Montgomery Blair, &c&c. Now they rave he is nobody—never was."

"And she?"

"Oh, you would think, to hear them, that he found her yesterday in a Mississippi swamp."

"Well, in the French Revolution it was worse. When a man failed he was guillotined. Mirabeau did not die a day too soon. Even Mirabeau!"

Well, he has gone. With despair in my heart I left that RR station. Allen Green walked home with me. I met his wife and his four ragged little boys a day or so ago. She is the neatest, the primmest, the softest of women. Her voice is like the gentle cooing of a dove. In her dulcet accents she murmured—without the slightest excitement of manner:

"You see me. I am going around like a raging lion, seeking what I may devour." A man she had introduced as a faraway cousin of her stepfather interposed.

"She talks that way because they would not take Cousin Sarah's money. But one of the storekeepers said to pa—you know he calls pa Rafe—'Now, Rafe, none of your kin shall suffer.' So he paid for Cousin Sarah's something-to-eat—in yarn."

Abuse Mr. and Mrs. Davis! What horrors did they devise and lay at the door of Marie Antoinette! In revolutions men seem to go mad.

Colonel Childs walked down to the train with us. He is an ardent Joe Johnston man, and his mission seemed to instruct that general in some particular. He said, "I mean to put him straight. I'm for him, up to the hub."

J. C. gave me his last cent. It was a sad parting—though his words were cheerful enough.

That lowering black future hangs there—all the same. The end of the war brings no hope of peace or security to us.

Mrs. Green, in a meek aside: "And I have to bear that, too." This I told to Allen. You see I have gone back to my Greens. Yarn is our circulating medium. It is the current coin of the realm. At a factory here, Mrs. Glover traded off a negro woman for yarn. The woman wanted to go there as a factory hand, so it suited all round. I held up my hands! Mrs. Munro said:

"Mrs. Glover knows she will be free in a few days. Besides, that's nothing. Yesterday a negro man was sold for a keg of nails."

"God's will be done," escaped from Mr. Martin's lips, in utter amazement.

"This shows slavery is in its death throes."

"General C said we were lighthearted at the ruin of the great slave-owners. An unholy joy."

They will have no negroes now to lord it over. They can swell and peacock about and tyrannize now over only a small parcel of women and children—those only who are their very own family.

Letter from Quentin Washington:

"I have given up," he writes. "The bitterness is over." But then he adds, "I will write to you no more—I have not the heart."

General Manigault told Miss Middleton that Sherman burnt out all families whose heads had signed the secession ordinance. Members of legislature's houses were burned.

"And if he had thrown in the members of the legislature themselves, nobody would mind."

"They are in bad odor, but that would have created a worse—burning members, you know."

Ellen said I had a little piece of bread and a little molasses today for my dinner—and then Mrs. M sent to ask me to dine with her today. Providential! Jack Middleton[6] writes from Richmond: "The wolf is at the door here. We dread starvation far more than we do Grant or Sherman. Famine—that is the word now."

6. Maj. John Izard Middleton, Jr., a staff officer with the Army of Northern Va., was the son of John Izard Middleton, Sr., and the first cousin of Susan Middleton.

Saw a sister of Captain Corrie:

"Captain Corrie is the anachronism who tried in the 19th century to reopen the African slave trade." The captain of the *Wanderer*—⟨⟨Governor Adams assisting . . . [7]

⟨⟨One day that I dined at the White House, Mr. Buchanan asked me some questions about it all. I knew J. C. had some difficulty with the president, connected with this mad scheme of Adams &c. So I answered gravely, the whole thing must be a myth. There could not be such demented benighted people in the world. I did not believe in the *Wanderer* any more than I did in the Flying Dutchman or the Red Rover or the water witch. Rip Van Winkle was a wide-awake who kept abreast of the times, in comparison with a man who in the 19th century attempted to bring African slaves to America.

⟨⟨The president listened with unmoved composure.

⟨⟨"What I like is the childlike candor of your face. You will do in Washington. You would do for a member of the diplomatic corps."⟩⟩

March 6, 1865.   Today—a godsend. For even the small piece of bread and the molasses were things of the past. My larder was empty.

A tall mulatto woman walked in with a tray. This tray was covered by a huge white serviette. Ellen ushered her in with a flourish.

"Mrs. McDonald's maid." She set down the tray she bore upon my bare table and uncovered it—with conscious pride.

Fowls ready for roasting, sausages, butter, bread, eggs, preserves.

"What a windfall!" cried Ellen.

I was dumb with delight. After silent thanks to heaven, my powers of speech returned, and I exhausted myself in messages of gratitude to Mrs. McDonald.

"Missis, you oughtn't to let her see how glad you was—it was a letting of yourself down." (Ellen has high notions of what is due to our position at home.) "F'all that—it's well enough—for we was at our last mouthful."

Mrs. Glover gave me some yarn, and I bought five dozen eggs with it from a wagon.

Eggs for Lent. And to show that I have faith yet in humanity, I paid her in advance—in yarn for something to eat, which she promises to bring tomorrow.

Two weeks have passed, and the rumors from Columbia are still of the vaguest. No letter has come from there—no direct message or messenger.

"My God," cried Dr. Frank Miles, "but it is strange. Can it be anything so dreadful they dare not tell us?"

---

7. Rough draft of the 1880s Version. In 1858, William C. Corrie, captain of the schooner *Wanderer*, landed a cargo of several hundred Africans on an island off Savannah. Local authorities allowed the Africans to be sold as slaves in violation of Federal law and court cases against three crew members of the *Wanderer* and the slave auctioneer were dismissed. Two years earlier, Governor James H. Adams of S.C. called in vain for the reopening of the slave trade in his annual message to the legislature.

Dr. St. Julien Ravenel has grown pale and haggard with care. His wife and children were left there.

Dr. Brumby[8] has been at last coaxed into selling me some leather to make me a pair of shoes—else I should have had to give up walking.

He knew my father well. He intimated that in some way my father helped him through college. Dr. Brumby's money did not suffice. Mr. William C. Preston and my father advanced funds sufficient to let him be graduated. And then my uncle Charles Miller married his aunt—and I listened in rapture. All this tended to leniency in the leather business—and I bore off the leather gladly.

March 7, 1865. We go to church every day. The air was clear and bracing—a sniff of snow from the mountains—and such a blue, unclouded sky. After so much rain—how refreshing, and yet—

It is "bonny doon weather." The birds singing, flowers blooming, sun shining—and "we so weary, full of care."

Maggie pointed out a shop and its sign, over it still.

"Anywhere else than in North Carolina, when a man rises to be a congressman &c, he pulls down his name from off a little shop door. And he would begin to get up a pedigree from Adam or William the Conqueror."

Here a Lincolnton lady halted us.

"Miss M, did your mother *really* give ten dollars a dozen for eggs, *as it is said*—and all the town believes it?"

"No, the woman asked us five—and we were not such fools as to give even that." Miss M spoke in the quiet and humble spirit we have determined to exhibit on all occasions here. I was the delinquent, with my yarn—but I did not criminate myself. She asked me 20 dollars for five dozen eggs and then said she would take it in "Confederick." Then I would have given her 100 dollars as easily. But if she had taken my offer of yarn! I haggle in yarn for the millionth part of a thread! And I bought a tub from the same wagon. When they ask Confederate money, I never stop to chaffer. I give them 20 or 50 dollars cheerfully for anything.

March 8, 1865. Colonel Childs gave me a letter from my husband and a newspaper containing a full account of Sherman's cold-blooded brutality in Columbia.

Then we walked three miles to return the call of my benefactress—McDaniel is her name, not McDonald. They were kind and hospitable, but my heart was like lead. My head ached, and my legs were worse than my head—and then I had a nervous chill. So I went to bed and stayed there until the Fants brought me a letter saying my husband would be here today.

8. Richard Trapier Brumby, former professor of chemistry, mineralogy, and geology at S.C. College, read law with M. B. C.'s father, Stephen Decatur Miller.

Then I got up and made ready to give him a cheerful reception.

Soon a man came, Troy[9] by name, the same who kept the little corner shop so near my house in Columbia and of whom we bought things so often. We fraternized—he shook hands with me, looked in my face pitifully. We seemed to have been friends all our lives.

He says they stopped the fire at the Methodist college—perhaps to save old Mr. McCrady's house. Our house still stands, being next to the McCradys'. Mr. Sheriff Dent, being burnt out, has taken refuge in our house. He contrived to find favor in Yankee eyes.

Troy heard Molly hotly disputing the possession of my house with the Dents. "Lord," said Troy, "what a row she did make." She had saved our Alderney cow and loved it as a brand snatched from the burning. She was loath to part with it to the Dents. He says a Yankee general, Logan[1] by name, snatched a watch from Mrs. McCord's bosom.

"Mrs. Munro is miserably disappointed in Sherman. He is a Roman Catholic."

"And there is where her faith in him came in."

The soldiers tore the bundles of clothes &c&c that the poor wretches tried to save from their burning houses and dashed them back into the flames. They meant to make a clean sweep. They were howling round the fires like demons, these Yankees, in their joy and triumph at our destruction. Well, we have given them [a] big scare and kept them miserable for five years—the little handful of us.

They overhauled the Halcott Greens at Lancaster, stripped them bare, and threatened to shoot Allen before her very eyes. Some Yankee soldier to whom he had been kind in Charleston recognized him and saved his life.

Virginia has a gift of eloquence. Poor darling! No doubt she tried it then.

Mrs. Childs and the Hokes ride a high horse. It seems they have been living in Columbia, and I did not call on them—did not so much as know they were there. So they say to the Lincolnton folk they have no reason to come and see me here.

Colonel Childs is magnanimous, bears no malice for my neglect of his womenkind. He comes every day and patronizes me.

Colonel Fant has turned up. He is a handsome, big Virginian. He is his *own* man, hangs onto nobody, and he knows the laws and his rights—and knowing, dares maintain them.

The landlady at the hotel got into one of her trantrums because they [the Fants] wanted eggs in Lent. He calmly says he won't go. He has a right to stay.

9. James Troy, a carpenter.
1. Maj. Gen. John A. Logan of Ill., commander of the Fifteenth Corps of the Army of the Tennessee.

They are three in family. They pay 80 dollars a day, fires extra. *In Confederate* currency.

They told me a fearful thing. That family who came like the patriarch—man, servants, maidservants, wife, and children—and were huddled into one room by the greedy landlady. Then a negro woman was taken sick, and they all had to camp out in the drawing room. Now the poor woman is dead and laid out in their *one* room, and they still camp in the drawing room. She says they nursed her with faithful kindness.

"I do not think a room can be used as a sleeping apartment by more than one person—if that person wishes to be comfortable."

"There were dozens in that black hole. And old Mrs. Graspall will not have the best of it at last. They pay their 100 dollars a day in Confederate brown paper."

A woman we met on the street stopped to tell us a painful "coincidence."

"The general was married, but he could not stay at home very long after the wedding. When his baby was born, they telegraphed him. He sent back a rejoicing answer, 'Is it a boy or a girl?' Then he was killed before he got the reply. 'Was it not sad,' his poor young wife says, 'he did not live to hear that *his son* lived.'"

The kind woman added sorrowfully, "Died and did not know the *sect* of his child."

"Let us hope it will be a Methodist," said Isabella the irrepressible.

Isabella is of the Methodist persuasion. She was asked to supper last night at the Michals.[2] They had venison steak, chicken salad. Isabella confessed that when she viewed the spread she had some difficulty in controlling her feelings.

Mrs. Glover, to prove to us the plenty that reigned here in peaceful times, described an "infair" which she attended here in the early years of the war.

An "infair" means a table standing for days, against all comers. At this one they began to dine at two o'clock in the day and dined on continuously. As soon as one relay were glutted (forgive the vulgar phrase), another came, table—or tables—constantly replenished. There were two tables in separate rooms—one for beef, bacon, turkeys, fowls, all meats, and vegetables, the other for sweets. Everybody fared alike—all fared sumptuously. Without haste, without rest, on flowed the crowd of eaters. Mrs. Glover heard ravenous soldiers aver with delight that they had dined three times that day. And the last dinner was as good as the first. I record this because I have never known of an infair before. Perhaps you may be as ignorant.

At the venison feast Isabella heard a good word for me—and one for General Chesnut's air of distinction, a thing people cannot give themselves, try as ever they may. Lord Byron says everybody knows a gentleman. He knows the

2. Probably the home of Col. William H. Michal, a merchant and Presbyterian churchman.

thing—he can't describe it. Now, there are some French words cannot be translated, and we all know the thing—*gracieuse* and *svelte,* applied to a woman. Not that anything was said of me like that—far from it. I am fair, fat, forty, jolly—and in my unbroken jollity, as far *as they know,* they found my charm.

"You see, she don't howl, she don't cry, she never never tells anybody what she was used to at home and what she has lost—&c&c." High praise—and I mean to try and deserve it ever after.

"Isabella, my loss is an Irish bull. Comprenez-vous? We have lost what we never had. We have never had any money, only unlimited credit—for J. C.'s richest kind of a father ensured us all manner of credit. It was all only a mirage at last. It has gone—just as we drew nigh to it."

Old Mr. Chesnut never gave. Sherman took away. Blessed be the name of the only son of his father—the *nonagenarian* chief of Mulberry.

———

Mrs. Middleton has heard from her daughter Mrs. Blake, who is at Flat Rock. "Thank God—I have one child who has enough to eat," said Mrs. Middleton, with deep feeling.

XXXII

Keeping Ahead of Sherman

March 10, 1865. Went to church, crying to Ellen "It is Lent—we must fast and pray." When I came home my good fairy Colonel Childs had been here, bringing rice and potatoes and promising flour. He is a trump. He pulled out his pocketbook and offered to be my banker. He stood there on the street—Isabella and Miss Middleton witnessing the generous action—and straight out offered me money.

"No, put up that. I am not a beggar, and I never will be. To die is so much easier."

Alas, after that flourish of trumpets—when he came with the sack of flour, I accepted it gratefully. I receive things I cannot pay for. Money is different. There I draw a line—imaginary, perhaps. Once before the same thing happened. Our letters of credit came slowly in 1845, when we left unexpectedly for Europe and our letters were to follow us. I was a poor little inoffensive bride. And a British officer who guessed our embarrassment, for we did not tell him (he came over with us on the ship), asked J. C. to draw on his banker until J. C.'s letters came. We did not do it, and our letters came, but it was a nice thing for a stranger to do.

Colonel Childs says the mob runs after Joe Johnston and curses Jeff Davis.

"We were never of the mob," was all I had to say.

"When you give the mob its choice, it selects Barabas and crucifies our Savior."

"Of course, a mob murders those who fail—or appear to do so. They do not wait to find out the truth."

"Napoleon died at St. Helena. Is success a test of genius—or good generalship? Caesar, now—stabbed in the house or capitol of his friends. He was really a successful character—if they had waited to know it. Eh? Marshal Ney—shot by Frenchmen. Surely that was a cruel fate for the bravest of the brave—shot down in cold blood, he who had fought a thousand battles for France, never one against her. If I could but express the scorn I feel for popular resentment against the unfortunate!"

Colonel Childs diverted the tide.

"Boozer went off with flying colors. She sat in state in Mrs. Singleton's landau. And she has married a Philadelphia officer."

"No doubt. And by this time she has married one from Boston—from New York—indiscriminately. Will she marry the Yankee army?"

"Your defense of Boozer in Columbia was a mistake, you see."

The Boozer talk was sotto voce. Colonel Childs caught "mistake."

"Oh, 'mistake'—yes, there was the mistake, trying to hold Charleston and Columbia both. Beauregard lost both. You must prefer, in your hearts, Joe Johnston to Beauregard?"

"We do. Johnston is a quarrelsome, aggravating man—and a retreater. Beauregard is a chicken sick of the pip," said the irrepressible.

Colonel Childs saw a Confederate female who had walked forty miles. He saw her at Blackstock followed by her maid, carrying her traveling bag! Then he jumped to a new subject. "Eight of our senators are for reconstruction." And that a ray of light had penetrated inward from Lincoln, who told Judge Campbell that Southern land would not be confiscated.[1]

Well, after all, my husband did not come. So I gave up, went to bed, and had it out with the fever which had been devouring me for two days without stint.

All the time as I tossed and tumbled, our young soldier below sung, and it came up in snatches: "We will never give it up—no, never."

Hetty Cary married General Pegram. In two weeks after the marriage, he was killed in the trenches around Petersburg.

This, they say, was written by Constance Cary—I do not know. It sounds as if I had been hearing its dirgelike wail all my life. . . . [2]

Poor Pegram! "Truer, nobler, trustier heart, more loving, and more loyal, never beat within a human breast."

Again fever without stint. The highest fever going.

March 12, 1865. Better today—a long, long weary day in grief has passed away. I suppose General Chesnut is *somewhere*. Where? That is the question. Only once has he visited this sad spot—which holds, he says, all that he cares for on earth. Unless he comes or writes soon—I believe he can come if he will—I will cease, or try for it, this wearisome looking, looking, looking for him.

And Mrs. Michal thinks—or *says* (which is after all somewhat different)—that I am like sunshine in a house. What a compliment in this cold, damp, dismal, cloudy, rain-forever place.

The last day I was out, Colonel Childs stopped me to present a Mr. Stowe— "Who keeps a sto'," he whispered in an aside. "Now do be pleasant with him." To please Colonel Childs I did my best—went in for "the frisky-old-girl style." Colonel Childs said Mr. Stowe, if he did keep a sto', was a millionaire, and he was trying to induce him to let me have a bag of flour.

The flour came and a tray of butcher's meat—provisions for more than a week.

Very kind of Mr. Stowe, as I had no money. Only smiles, which are cheap.

---

1. A reference to the Hampton Roads Conference.
2. A long poem entitled "Dead" follows.

"No, no," yells Isabella. "Money is ever so much cheaper than forced smiles."

In Columbia, the munificent Childs tells me, our friends are following horses to pick up grains of corn to parch.

Then Isabella pulled out a letter from a young person who will not let even this state of things stop her wedding. To be sure, she begins in hysterics—her brother's grave, her home in ashes, &c&c—dwindling her hysterics off slowly to a giggle, as she has only the rent garments of mourning for her bridal array. And then the true business of the letter comes in. She asks that we will hunt up purple and fine linen in Lincolnton—*for the event,* as she fatuously calls it.

"Society men are here. Look out of the window. There is the handsomest of men—Thomas by name, and a Marylander. He married a girl from New Orleans who died here. They boarded at the Hokes' or Phifers'—paradisiacal altitude of boarding. The poor young thing died without the consolation of her religion, but they were devotedly, tenderly kind to her in all things but that."

"What?"

"Do you think the severe Calvinistic dame would let a touch of holy water or sacred oil—which she calls the mark of the beast—come into her house—or a priest either? So she died unsprinkled."

"The baby is here still, and they so good to the little angel."

"How lovely Thomas would look in Confederate gray! That fascinating mouth, that divine complexion of his, begins to madden the female world again. He is sublimely handsome. If only he were in uniform!"

"And that you will not see. He has had enough of it. He is on his way across the Mississippi to avoid the draft. It might tow him in."

"Conscript him in—may he escape."

My husband did come, for two hours—brought Laurence, who had been in Camden, was there, indeed, during the raid.

Serena's brief note by Mr. Farmer:

> They have brought us a letter from Aunt Sally. They give terrible accounts of the behavior of Yankees below. After their tales we are (almost?) quite reconciled to staying up here, where we are only robbed generally. Love to Miss Isabella and Maggie.
>
> Yours affectionately,
>
> *Enie*

Do you know where Johnny is? Dear auntie, *do come.* It is safe here now—as Mr. Farmer will tell you.

> *Enie*

My husband is ordered to Chester, South Carolina.

We are surprised to see by the papers that we had behaved heroically in leaving everything we had to be destroyed—without one thought of surrender. We had not thought of ourselves from the heroic point of view.

————————

Isaac McLaughlin hid and saved everything we trusted him with.
A grateful negro is Isaac.
A patriot in a passion[3]—

Richmond, Va.
February 21, 1865

My dear Madam,

I wrote to [you] last summer, and I received no answer to my letter. So I stood on my dignity—or rather, what is left of it. For I am snubbed so often and in so many ways by people of highest respectability and fashion whom I had regarded as my friends that I have not much dignity left. The various slights and cuts I receive, especially here, are more humiliating than a Yankee yoke can possibly be.

After this war is over, I want to live in some country where etiquette is understood and practiced. To attain to it I am indifferent to all forms of government. I really care more for my personal honor and self-respect than all beside. About most of these cases there is no mistake. In your case I am willing to solace myself with the idea that you did write—though you don't say so. Therefore I reply to your letter at once on its receipt. Indeed, if I were to delay I am not sure this would reach you, for the great Beauregard has telegraphed that he cannot concentrate at Charlotte—and that place will I suppose have to be abandoned. I know the village where you are; and though it is a pleasant place, still it is hardly safe.

The factories would naturally attract a raiding party. The place to which you ought to go is the pretty village of Shelby, about thirty or forty miles west of where you are and not very hard to be reached by *you*, while it is well out of the way of military operations. It is a beautiful country—cheap, though for the matter of that, I do not know how long the currency will be available to purchase with.

Richmond has been quite pleasant this winter; we have had a few parties which I have enjoyed very much. Of late the gaiety has all stopped.

My rule is to be happy while I can—and at all events not to blame others for innocent happiness.

Our friends the Prestons are well. General Hood is here and, rumor says, ere long to be married. Report, apparently well-founded, says my friend Miss S. H. is to marry John Haskell.

I see the Prestons quite often.

I have seen little of the ladies at the president's lately. Mr. Hunter is in fine health. Mr. Seddon has been forced out of the cabinet by the general

3. Evidently L. Q. Washington.

spirit of calumny and detraction which obtains nowadays. The new secretary [of war] (Breckinridge) is very popular now. How long will it last? I see no inducement for men to be in public trust.

I have turned to the society of young ladies, and to books, more than ever, as a refuge from my own thoughts and the talk of men about the war. Plague take the war.

I have just read *Adela Cathcart,* a charming English novel by Mac-Donald.[4] And I have also read more of *Tony Butler;* it is very clever. Tony is to marry Alice, as I always thought he ought to do.

I have read *Salem Chapel* and *The Doctor's Family*[5] [and] *The Story of Elizabeth.*[6]

I had also *Enoch Arden,*[7] which I have lent to my friends without reading. Such is the title given to Tennyson's last volume of poems.

I hardly form a plan or indulge a hope for the future. But the *bitterness* I went through last fall!

As to negroes, I have always been in favor of the experiment of freeing them, but prejudice has stood in the way. It is evident that opinion here is changing rapidly on this subject.

I have thought frequently and especially of late about you and General Chesnut. And as this may be the last time we ever exchange letters for many long months, be assured you will always have my sincerest wishes for your happiness.

I need not put my name—

Yours truly—

"I call that lively," said Isabella, for once with a grave face. "Quentin Washington is at headquarters. He knows everything, and this reads like a 'last fond farewell to thee,' friends and country."

Laurence says Miss Chesnut is very proud of her presence of mind and her cool self-possession in the presence of the enemy. She lost, after all, but two bottles of champagne, two of her brother's gold-headed canes, and her brother's horses—Claudia, the brood mare that he valued beyond price, and her *own* carriage—a fly-brush boy called Battis. His occupation in life was to stand behind the table and with his peacock feather brush flies. He was the sole member of his dusky race at Mulberry who deserted "old Marster" to follow the Yankees. Now for *our* losses at the Hermitage. Added to the gold-headed canes and Claudia, we lost every mule and horse. John's were there, too. My light dragoon and heavy swell is stripped light enough for the fight now. Jonathan that we trusted betrayed us, and the plantation and mills, Mulberry house, &c&c, [were] saved by Claiborne, that black rascal, suspected by all the world.

4. Scots author and clergyman George MacDonald published this novel in 1863.
5. Two more of the novels in Margaret Oliphant's *Chronicles of Carlingford.*
6. A novel published in 1863 by William Thackeray's daughter, Lady Ann (Thackeray) Ritchie.
7. Published in 1864.

Claiborne boldly affirmed that Mr. Chesnut would not hurt by destroying his place. They would only hurt the negroes. Mars Jeems hardly ever came there and only took a little "sompen nurren to eat" when he came.

***

Ill again. Was trying to discuss our dinner to the generals' wives in Columbia. The girls said Clancy wanted to be out of it and away with them. Said "fat old women's big bare arms always looked like legs—to him."

Poor old unenclosed commons!

***

Fever continuing, sent for St. Julien Ravenel.

" 'Ravenel'—that means 'little raven.' He justifies his name—how he does croak. 'Pickens,' now—that means 'little Pickens.' In our first revolution there was a Great Pick."[8]

"He is not ravenous, however. Always Ellen has something nice to offer him (thanks to the ever bountiful Childs), but he is too angry, too anxious, too miserable to eat. He croaks—croaks."

Today he gave us an antislavery tirade. He was very violent at first. But from the high pillows of my very high bed I launched my bolts. I out-heroded Herod. Mine were barbet guns on the summit of the fortress. Then he began to cool down, meeting no opposition as he expected. He contrasted the condition of African slaves now in this country and what they are in their native jungles—negroes in Africa.

"Those pious persons, Governor Hammond and Governor Adams, wanted them brought here, to make Christians of them, you know. They are Bible Christians—literal interpreters of the words of the Christian Scriptures," I said.

"No, no. Whatever a separated text may be made to connive at, the teachings of Christ, the New Testament, eliminates slavery. Do unto others as you would they should do to you. Love, goodwill to men, charity."

His blue eyes were blazing. He was transformed.

"The New Testament is evolved from the Old. The world could then bear it."

"The Mormons are evolved from what?"

"Oh, they marry their slaves—acquire slaves that way. If they want a cook, they marry one. If they need a sempstress, they steal another. They had to make a new Bible, and New England with its free love will not keep our Bible long. They will construct a self-worshiping, Boston, Plymouth-Rock Brahminical high-caste embodiment of themselves in book form. At least we will do the North this justice—they do their own thinking. We let one man do ours—Mr. Calhoun. And if fate left us good wine, good dinners, fine horses, and money enough to go abroad every summer, we asked no more of gods or men. We let things drift, and now we are in this snarl."

"Jeff Davis is a disciple of John C. Calhoun," I said.

8. Brig. Gen. Andrew Pickens.

This was the oft-mentioned red rag shaken before the mad bull. He fairly plunged at it.

"I never had any faith in this frantic movement. From the first I knew it was worse than folly. *Now* I look back and see we had every chance to free ourselves forever from any connection with New England. And we have thrown them away. This man's heavy-headed stupidity, his abiding self-conceit, his everlasting wrongheadedness! Puts the money of the Confederacy in the hands of a man who would not be left alone with a five-dollar bill by those who know him at home. Northrop, Mallory, Benjamin, Moore—I would not waste words on them."

Then the ill person—with the wisdom of the serpent—began to wail over the injustice which had been done the patriot Wigfall and the daring Joe Johnston.

Instantly he fell foul of the faults of those two and, almost before he knew it, lauded Mr. Davis, who would have none of them. He told me that Wigfall took great credit to himself for having proposed in secret session a resolution asking Jeff Davis to resign. What he wanted was a vote of "want of confidence."

Then he pitched into Ellen, who stood glaring at him from the fireplace, her blue eye nearly white and her other eye blazing as a comet. On Sunday he gave her some Dover's Powder for me—directions written on the paper in which it was wrapped. He told her to show this to me and then put what I gave her in a wineglass and let me drink it. Ellen put it all in the wineglass—and gave it to me at one dose.

"It was enough to last you your lifetime. It was murder" (to me). Turning then to Ellen: "What did you do with the directions?"

"I never see no directions. You never give me none."

"I told you to show that paper to your Missis."

"Well, I fling dat ole brown paper in de fire. What you making all dis fuss for? Soon as I give Missis de physic, she stop fretting and flinging about wid fever. She go to sleep sweet as a suckling baby, and she sleep two days an' nights, and now she heap better." And Ellen withdrew from the controversy.

"Well, all is well that ends well. You took opiate enough to kill an army. Well! you were worried and worn-out and you wanted rest. You came near getting it—thoroughly. Fortunately I have been too busy to call since Sunday. Well! Well! Ellen came near giving you your rest with a vengeance. You were in no danger from your disease, but your doctor and your nurse combined were deadly."

The comic side of my being able to stand that horse's dose has since given us both some hearty laughs. He says I will die hard, that it is not easy to kill me, and that I have a sturdy constitution.

Maybe I was saved by the adulteration so often complained of in all Confederate medicine.

One crumb of comfort—Mary C with her dearest D, safe in York.[9]

Sally Green[1] came. Her father, Mr. Clarke, best known for forty years as the best giver of good dinners in Columbia.

Mrs. Green—meek, gentle, refined, low-voiced as ever—began at once to declare her good fortune. She had been again asked to a Lincolnton dinner. She held up one hand and counted her fingers.

"I took the goods the Gods provided," she said unctuously. "My dear, turkey—roasted, stuffed! plenty of gravy. Rice as white as snow—every grain standing out, separated. *No* gummy stuff without salt—as if the washerwoman had dropped her bag of bluing in it. Sweet potatoes browned with butter and sugar—and a pound cake pudding—wine sauce!" She grew more excited at every item and raised her voice at pudding sauce.

"Look at her eyes—Sally Green's eyes, gloating over a feast."

"And oh! to see my boys have enough to eat once more!" she murmured softly.

———————

Miss Middleton and Isabella stayed to tea.

"Ellen, you make delightful cakes." Ellen glowed with pride at the compliment. She is very useful now—she has learned to save me from thinking. I have nothing on my mind. All things come in their season. She even knows when to let me alone. A good servant knows what we want, what we need, and what she can do under the circumstances. Wants and needs are synonymous exactly with frail humanity.

"I have got to know nearly as well as Molly what Missis ought to have."

"She caught the tail end of that idea."

Last night she gave me a fright. Lying there asleep before the fire, she screamed again and again.

"Nightmare?"

"Yes," and I sat up in bed, scared to death. "What is it?"

"Nothing, only I was dreaming somebody was troubling my William. I don't mind. Claiborne can take care of William. You see, it was a bad dream." As neither of us could go to sleep anymore—she fell into discourse.

"Missis, nex' time you is bound for de Yallerbam [Alabama], take me in place of Molly. I want to see my old mother—she is ole 'oman now. I wonder if she ever care for me as I care for my William."

If these people are freed, won't somebody get good servants—those we have been training in all these years!

The young gentleman private, now—and the plantation negro who can make cotton. The man who can hoe cotton has an avocation. He is trained for the business in hand. A good hand hires for one hundred dollars, papa says—his

———

9. Mary (Preston) and John Darby.
1. Mrs. Allen J. Green, Jr.

clothes and food. Do you know a young planter who can earn one hundred by the labor of his own hands?

"So they can earn their living at once if they are freed."

"The old ones—and the too young ones?"

"That is as heaven pleases. Rory Cameron, a Scotch overseer, a rugged old covenanter, used to say as he passed old Cunningham's[2] plantation, 'That man owes his negroes sixty thousand dollars for food and clothes.'"

Well, the general says, *his* negroes owe him thirty thousand he has furnished to the plantation and drawing nothing from it. Joe Cunningham is a born fortune maker. His father was a rope maker. This millionaire makes shoes. They say neither his family nor his negroes have ever worn a shoe unless he made it for them. And he eats out of a wooden bowl—and they have no light but firelight.

"Go to bed with the chickens, I daresay. All the same, he knows how to grow rich."

This Rory Cameron made a shrewd answer to Mr. Tom Lang. Mr. Lang was freshly converted and zealous, so he exhorted Rory to be a Christian. "So I am. Besides, if I am ever converted it won't be to the kind of Christianity that goes about, Bible in one hand, *whip* in the other."

"That's as bad as Mohammed—Koran in one hand, sword in the other. Mr. Lang was a good man. Rory took his fling at all pious slave-owners. How rich Presbyterians always grow. The unearned increment comes to them, foreordained by Calvin's foreknowledge absolute."

"There are no poor Presbyterians but H's parents—but that was because he could not manage to articulate a *p*. It cost him moments of agony to say 'My parents were poor but pious Presbyterians.'"

Then they overhauled my library, which was on the floor because the only table in the room they had used for a tea table.

Shakespeare—Molière—Sir Thomas Browne—*Arabian Nights* in French—Pascal's letters—folk songs.

"*Lear* I read last. The tragedy of the world—it entered into my heart to understand it first—now."

"Spare us Regan and Goneril and the storm and eyeballs rolling round."

"And an old king, and I am every inch a king."

That is not it. It is the laying bare the seamy side—going behind the pretty curtain of propriety we hold up. Poor humanity morally stripped makes us shiver. Look at that judge—look at that thief. Presto—change sides—which is the judge, which is the thief? And more unmentionable horrors. He preceded Thackeray in that tearing off of shams. [Old] Mrs. Chesnut set her face resolutely to see only the pleasant things of life and shut her eyes to wrong and said

2. Joseph Cunningham of Camden, the grandfather of John Doby Kennedy.

it was not there. The most devoted, unremitting reader of fiction I ever knew—everything French or English that came to hand—would not tolerate Thackeray. "He is a very uncomfortable, disagreeable creature."

We have seen Mrs. Chesnut. She sat like a canary bird in her nest, with no care or thought of tomorrow. She lived in a physical paradise and made her atmosphere a roseate-hued mist for her own private delusion. Thackeray pulls all ostrich heads out of the sand and will make them see—will they nill they.

———————————

Chester Court House
March 15, 1865

My dear Mary—

In the morning I send Lieutenant Ogden with Laurence to Lincolnton to bring you down. I have three vacant rooms—one with bedsteads, chairs, washstand, basins, and pitchers—the other two bare. You can have half of a kitchen for your cooking.

I have also at Dr. Da Vega's a room furnished to which you are invited (board also). You can take your choice.

If you can get your friends in Lincolnton to take charge of your valuables, only bring such as you will need here. Perhaps it will be better to bring bed and bedding and other indispensables.

I have not sent Laurence again to Camden because it has rained constantly since I came here and the roads are horrible.

In all of your arrangements I think your judgment is better than mine, and therefore what you bring and what you leave must be left to your own judgment.

God bless and protect you.

As ever yours,

J. C.

P.S. I wish you would ask Colonel Childs if he would like to buy cotton or can sell it for me.

———————————

Isabella made a list of the things sent me in my time of need—1 bag of flour, bacon, beef, sausages, cranberries, bunches of flowers, blue pills, sole leather and calfskin, morphine, Dover's Powders, camphor, biscuits, bread, milk, plates of dinner, backbones, spareribs. Ellen supplemented in haste:

"Oh, Miss Isbel, don't forget the two picked chickens fat as pigs Miss McDaniel just this minute send."

"'Heavenly chicking,' as the small morsel of a child in the hospital sighed— you know, in *Little Dorrit*. Don't let us forget moonshine and stickies."

Moonshine is a sort of paste—light and fairylike, white as snow, twisted and twining, shining, intangible, mystic, wonderful—crumbles under one's fingers when touched—a sort of magical "marvelles," and yet delicious. Stickies are, as their names denote, cakes which are sticky with sugar—maybe molasses.

———————

Met Dr. Garnett, who said he had just seen Mary C and Dr. Darby. Did not know they were married until he saw them. Talked with them only five minutes. That she was married was a surprise to him.

"How did you see she was married?" asked Isabella anxiously, "if you had never heard it and she did not tell you?"

"Oh, anybody sees that sort of thing at a glance."

Dr. Miles then told us that Mrs. St. Julien made good her old John Rutledge blood. She actually awed the Yankees into civil behavior. She was so cool, so dignified, so brave!

"Jeff Davis had better make her a general, if she can awe the Yankees into good behavior," suggested Isabella.

Mrs. Raven Lewis, née VanderHorst,[3] died of fright during the fire. And another lady, a born lady who shall be nameless here for very shame, went off with the Yankees. That was the worst tragedy of all. Mrs. Guignard—I knew her years ago as Anna Coffin—when her house was burned, she ran out with her family and stood shivering with cold in the woods. Some Yankee soldiers saw them and in rude horseplay derided them.

"Are you cold? Go in there and warm. There seems fire enough there to warm you all. We have made it hot for you."

I see Colonel Young has captured many horses, I hope Mr. Davis's Arabian among them and that Johnny's beautiful creatures are once more between Confederate knees, under the bonny blue flag.

More of St. Julien's raving—and we listen breathless: he is usually so quiet.

"From the strong-minded, the young, the stout-hearted, the able-bodied, the active, the energetic, the wide-awake, the ardent spirits ready to give all for the cause—such men as Napoleon's marshals, people to lead, to excite enthusiasm, and to do heroic deeds—did they choose any to put in command? *No. No.* Every old loggerhead that did not so much as believe in the thing stepped to the front. *As soon as they came over* from the other side, they were put over the heads of the live leaders, to stamp out the very hearts of the gallant spirits."

"Who are you after now? Mr. Davis did not select or elect Orr, Pickens, or—low be it spoken—Mr. Barnwell," asked Isabella. "The truth is, the young men did seem horribly held back."

"We had a cabinet, too—who tried the 'how not to do it.'"

"Nothing would have made any difference [to] the young men, if they had been given the lead. Well! They would have rushed the thing through sooner, got themselves killed the first year."

"Never mind," said our solemn oracle, to St. Julien. "The weight of metal was

———

3. Anna Raven (VanderHorst) Lewis, wife of planter John Williams Lewis of Colleton District.

on the other side—the odds too great. But our *mettle* did not have a fair showing."

"Listen at him. Their *metal*—our *mettle*."

March 21, 1865. Chester, South Carolina. Another flitting.

> Beyond the smiling and the weeping we shall be soon.
> Beyond the sowing and the reaping—
> The waking and the sleeping—we shall be soon—
> Love—Rest—Home. Sweet Hope![4]

"Lord, tarry not, but come," they sing. If they believe all that—that the Lord is coming, and *coming for them*—they are in heaven already.

Without faith—no *salvation* in *this* world or the next.

Well, Captain Ogden came for me. The splendid Childs was true as steel to the last. Surely he is the kindest of men—that Childs. I saw Captain O was slightly incredulous when I depicted the wonders of Colonel Childs's kindness. So I skillfully led out the good gentleman, who walked to the train with us. He offered me Confederate money, silver, gold. Finally he agreed to buy our cotton and pay now in gold. Of course I laughed at his overflowing bounty and accepted nothing but begged him to come down to Chester or Camden and buy our cotton of General Chesnut there.

On the train after leaving Lincolnton: as Captain Ogden is a refugee (has had no means of communicating with his home since New Orleans fell—he is sure to know how refugees contrive to live), I beguiled the time acquiring information. "When people are without a cent, how do they live? I am about to enter the noble band of homeless houseless refugees. Confederate pay does not buy one shoestrings."

"Sponge. Sponge. Why did you not let Colonel Childs pay your bills?"

"I have no bills. We never make bills anywhere. Even at home, where they would trust us. Certainly nobody would trust me in Lincolnton."

"Why did you not borrow his money? General Chesnut could pay him at his leisure."

"I am by no means sure General Chesnut will ever again have any money."

As the train rattled and banged along and I waved my handkershief to Miss Middleton, Isabella, and my other devoted friends, I could but wonder—will fate throw me again (can it?) with such kind, clever, agreeable, congenial friends?

4. From a hymn by Horatius Bonar appearing in *Hymns of Faith and Hope,* 1st series (1857).

The McLeans refused to be paid for their rooms. No plummet can sound the depths of the hospitality and kindness of the North Carolina people.

Misfortune dogged us from the outset. Everything went wrong with the train. We broke down in two miles of Charlotte and had to walk that distance. Pretty rough on an invalid barely out of a fever, and my spirit was further broken by losing an invaluable lace veil, worn because I was too poor to buy a cheaper one. That is, if there had been any veils at all for sale in Lincolnton.

J. C. had ordered me to a house kept by some great friends of his. They put me in the drawing room—a really handsome apartment—and they made up a bed there and put in a wash handstand—plenty of water, everything refreshingly clean and nice. But it continued to be a public drawing room, open to all—and I was half-dead and wanted to go to bed. The piano was there, and the company played it.

The hostess told me she was keeping supper back till "Paw and Sis" came home.

Paw came, politer and more affable still. He walked up to the mirror and took a long look at himself. Then washed his face and hands in what I thought was my basin and water, and he brushed his hair before the glass and told us all his adventures. I sat as one in a dream.

The landlady announced proudly that for supper there were nine kinds of custard. Custard sounded nice and light, so I sent for some. Found it a heavy potatoe pie. I said,

"Ellen, this may kill me—though Dover's Powder did not."

"Don't you believe it—try." We barricaded ourselves in the drawing room and left next day at dawn. Arrived at the station—another disappointment—train behind time. There we sat on our boxes nine long hours. The cars might come at any moment; we dared not move one inch from the spot.

Then came the train, overloaded with paroled prisoners. Heaven helped us—a kind mail agent took us, with two other forlorn women, into his comfortable clean mail car. Ogden, true to his theory, did not stay at the boardinghouse as we did, but some Christian acquaintances took him in for the night. This he explained with a grin.

J. C. at the Chester station with a carriage. We drove at once to Mrs. Da Vega's.

I have been ill. What could you expect? My lines again have fallen in pleasant places. Mrs. Da Vega is young, handsome, agreeable, a kind, a perfect, hostess. And the house—my room is all that I have seen—leaves nothing to be desired. So very fresh, clean, warm, comfortable. Again, it is the drawing room, suddenly made into a bedroom for me. *But* it is my very own. We are among the civilized of the earth once more.

Mrs. Pride[5] lent me *Mrs. Halliburton's Troubles.*[6] They made me forget my own for a while. Then I was ill, and they gave me an overdose of morphine. I

5. The wife of a Chester physician.
6. A novel by Ellen (Price) Wood, published in London in 1862 and in Richmond in 1865.

seem fated to die of opium in some shape, and life seems a senseless repetition of the same blunders.

March 27, 1865. Moved again. Now I am looking from my window high—with something more to see than the sky. We have the third story of Dr. Da Vega's rooms, and it opens on the straight street that leads to the RR about a mile off.

This is another Dr. Da Vega who has a drugstore on Main Street. There his own family occupy the floor below us.

Mrs. Bedon is the loveliest of young widows. Today at church Isaac Hayne nestled so close to her cap strings, I had to touch him and say "Sit up." Mrs. Bedon—wife of Josiah Bedon that we knew so well. He was killed in that famous fight of the Charleston Light Dragoons. They stood still, to be shot down in their tracks. Having no orders to retire, they were forgotten, doubtless, and scorned to take care of themselves.

Mrs. Phoenix, Sissy Legare, Sissy Blake, Sissy Phoenix—and her Phoenix still in the ashes: no rise in him.

In this high and airy retreat—as in Richmond, then in Columbia, then in Lincolnton—my cry is still: if they would only leave me here in peace. If I were sure things never would be worse with me.

"Miss Middleton says Mrs. Chesnut will laugh when the time to laugh comes, with no respect whatever to fatal consequences. Witness—when the irate landlady took fright at Laurence's gold pencil case."

"Look again," said Mrs. C. "It is only a pencil—not a rifled cannon."

Then at the McLeans—when Mrs. C was ill. Miss McLean by the bedside, claiming Brevards and Haynes as "my father's kin"—proud of the fact, as she had a right to be. "Did you ever know any of the Shankses?" said Miss McLean. "My Mother was a Shanks."

For a moment Mrs. C tossed on her pillows. Then: "Yes, all the world knows Shanks' mare."

Sensible and kind Miss McLean laughed as merrily as any of us.

Again am I surrounded by old friends. People seem to vie with each other how good they can be to me.

Today Smith opened the trenches. He appeared laden with a tray covered by a snow-white napkin. My first step toward housekeeping. Mrs. Pride has a boiled ham, a loaf of bread, a huge pound cake, coffee already parched and ground, a loaf of sugar already cracked, candles, pickles, and all the things one must trust to love for now. Such money as we have avails us nothing. Even if there was anything left in the shops to buy.

Teddy Barnwell owned that he scented the bottle from afar. That is, he saw that heavily laden messenger with his white flag over all bearing down our way, and he followed until it was all uncovered on my dinner table. He said: "Why, the man asked me where you lived. What could I do but show him?" We had a jolly luncheon. Then James Lowndes came, the best of good company. He said of Buck: "She is a queen. She ought to reign in a palace. No prince charming yet. No man has ever approached her that *I* think half good enough for her."

Then Mrs. Prioleau Hamilton, née Levy. Some awkwardness was spoken of—trying to get a man's name when the man seemed to know you so well. She said her father tried this:

"Well, after all, how do you spell your name?

"S-M-I-T-H."

"Some Smiths have a lordly crest, a bird's head." An Englishman at tea, examining his spoon in an absent manner: "Little Tom Noddy—all head, nobody."

She answered to a remark on the beauty of her name, "Emma Hamilton."

"Never. Lord Nelson had made it too famous." And now her story of their progress—not a royal one—from Columbia here.

"Before we left home Major Hamilton spread a map of the United States on the table. And he showed me with his finger where Sherman was likely to go. Womanlike, I demurred, 'But suppose he does not choose to go that way?' 'Pooh—pooh, what do you know of war?'

"So we set out. My husband, myself, and two children, all in one small buggy. The 14th of February we took up our line of march. And straight before Sherman's men, *five* weeks we fled together. By incessant hurrying, scurrying from pillar to post, we succeeded in being a sort of avant-courier of the Yankee army.

"Without rest and with much haste we got here last Wednesday. And here we mean to stay and defy Sherman and his legions.

"Much the worse for wear were we," she sighed. The first night their beauty sleep was rudely broken into at Alston. "Move on, the Yanks are on us." So they hurried on, half-awake, to Winnsboro. No better luck. Then they had to lighten the ship—leave trunks &c&c and put on all sail. For this time the Yankees were only five miles behind. "Whip and spur—ride for your life, was the cry. Sherman's objective point was our buggy. For you know that when we got to Lancaster, Sherman was expected there—and he keeps his appointments. That is, he kept that one. Two small children were in our chariot, and I began to think of the Red Sea expedition. But we lost no time, and soon we were in Cheraw, clearly out of the track now. We thanked God for all his mercies and hugging to our bosoms the fond hope of beds and a bath, so much needed for all, but above all for the children.

"At twelve o'clock General Hardee himself knocked us up. 'March, march. Ettrick and Teviotdale—all the blue bonnets are over the border.'

"In mad haste we made for Fayetteville. There they said, 'God bless your soul, this is the seat of the war now, the battleground where Johnston and Sherman are to try conclusions.' So we tried back, as the hunters say, and cut across the country, aiming for this place.

"Clean clothes, my dear, never a one except as we took off garment by garment and washed it and dried it by our campfire, with our loins girded and in haste."

I was snug and comfortable all that time in Lincolnton.

Today Stephen D. Lee's corps marched through—only to surrender, sighed Cassandra. The camp songs of these men were a heartbreak—so sad, yet so stirring. They would have warmed the blood of an Icelander. The leading voice was powerful, mellow, clear, distinct, pathetic, sweet—so I sat down as women have done before when they hung up their harps by strange streams, and I wept.[7] The bitterness of such weeping! Music: "Away—away. Thou speakest to me of things which in all my long life I have not found—and I shall not find" (Jean Paul). You have told us how music brings on that agony. Then I wiped mine eyes as I heard squads of cavalry dashing by. How different is the sound now from what it was two years ago in Richmond.

> And from my window high—
> I look out on the sky—

There they go, the gay and gallant few—doomed, the last gathering of the flower of Southern youth, to be killed—to death or worse. Prison.

They continue to prance by—lightly and jauntily the caracole. Maybe there are younger eyes than mine looking out, and they know it. They march with as airy a tread as if they still believed the world was all on their side—and that there were no Yankee bullets for the unwary. What will Joe Johnston do with them now?

A woman here, high and mighty with money and a large house, she entertained the generals. She also said:

"Society is too mixed here. A line should be drawn *some*where."

"But then," said my informant, "on which side of the line would she go? She was a nursery governess—he is an *ex*-policeman." So it is not all as sweet as the garden of Eden here, after all. Devil of hate has crept in—&c&c&c.

---

7. Allusion to Psalm 137.

I can defy fate now. My darling Preston girls flew in. Mrs. Lawson Clay was with them. Unknowingly, with her facts she let me into one thing, [as] she talked on and told little anecdotes—&c&c. The Hood melodrama is over, though the curtain has not fallen on the last scene.

Cassandra croaks and makes many mistakes—but today she believes that Hood stock [is] going down. When that style of enthusiasm is on the wane, the rapidity of its extinction is miraculous. Like the snuffing out of a candle—one moment here, then gone forever. No, that is not right. It is the snow wreath on the river. I am getting things as mixed as the fine lady's society.

Lee and Johnston have each fought a drawn battle.[8] Only a few more dead bodies stiff and stark on an unknown battlefield. For we do not so much as know where these drawn battles took place.

One can never exaggerate the horrors of war on one's own soil. You understate the agony, strive as you will to speak, the agony of heart—mind—body.

"A few more men killed." A few more women weeping their eyes out, and nothing whatever decided by it *more* than we knew before the battle.

Teddy Barnwell, after sharing with me my first luncheon, failed me cruelly. He was to come for me to go down to the train and see Isabella pass by. One word with Isabella worth a thousand ordinary ones. So she has gone.

Mrs. Pride was driving with me today. We met him, and he called out.

"I will not disappoint you next time. I promise never to keep you waiting again."

No, you never will, for I will never again give you a chance.

Went with Mrs. Pride to a Columbia milliner. She was in Columbia with Sherman—I mean, at the same time. She says all day, indeed until the fires began. Colonel Goodwyn, the mayor of the town, fraternized with the Yankee generals freely. *Then,* when they burnt his house over his head, a change came o'er the spirit of his dream.

He assured the Yankee generals as he greeted them, come what might, they would not be as destructive as Wheeler's men had been. He made a slight miscalculation, apparently. He thanked them in *advance* for their kindness and consideration.

> But Linden saw another sight—
> When the fire began at dead of night—

And hot as the town was, Mayor Goodwyn's gratitude and good feeling went down many degrees below zero. Old Colonel Chesnut refuses to say grace but,

8. On March 25, Lee's troops suffered heavy losses in storming and then abandoning Fort Stedman, east of Petersburg. A few days earlier, Joe Johnston also sustained many losses when he unsuccessfully attacked one of Sherman's columns at Bentonville, N.C.

as he leaves the table, audibly declares, "I thank God for a good dinner." When asked why he did this odd thing, he said, "My way is to be sure of a thing before I return thanks for it." So Mayor Goodwyn said grace and had nothing to return thanks for.

Our milliner was handsome. From her own showing she had been a heroine in the strife. She made eyes so shamelessly at my generals that I failed to credit a word she said.

She said generals did not come in her way every day. Here she giggled and said she was bound to improve the occasion.

I am afraid of pride now. It comes before a fall. So I am humble, umble, stumble, and tumble—rhyme it down to its end.

So I received the wife of a post-office robber. The poor thing had done no wrong. I felt so sorry for her.

Who would be a woman? Who that fool—a weeping, pining, faithful woman? She hath hard measures still when she hopes kindest, and all her bounty only makes *ingrates*.

March 29, 1865.   Wakened by a bunch of violets from Mrs. Pride. Always remind me of Kate, of the sweet south wind that blew in that garden-of-paradise part of my life. And then it all came back—the dread unspeakable that lies behind every thought now.

Dear old Boxpleats came. After I had given him cake with his tea he would go, because I forbade all cursing of Jeff Davis under my hired roof. One thing he said, with that laugh of his which seems to open his countenance to the back hinge, like a pair of nut crackers, "Oh—as I wandered in front of Sherman's vandals there was three weeks that I did not see my own face." And how shocked he was at his own appearance when he once more beheld himself! And then he pleated up his lips to the size of an ordinary human mouth once more. He quoted Scripture: "He had gone away and straightway forgotten what manner of man he was."[9]

No wonder the sudden reminder of a look in the glass was a blow. I composed my face as best I might, bending over my teacups.

---

9. From Mark 4:41.

XXXIII

"The Game Is Up"

March 29, 1865. I find I have not spoken of the boxcar which held the Preston party that day on their way to York from Richmond—Mr. and Mrs. Lawson Clay, General and Mrs. Preston and their three daughters, Captain Rodgers, Mr. Portman,[1] whose father is an English earl and connected financially and happily with Portman Square. In my American ignorance I may not state the case plainly. He is of course a younger son. Then there was Cellie and her baby and her wet-nurse—no end of servants male and female. In this ark they slept, ate, and drank. Such are the fortunes of war. We were there but a short time, but Mr. Portman in that brief visit of ours was said to have eaten three luncheons, and the number of his drinks were counted, too, toddies, so-called. Mr. Portman's contribution to the larder had been three small pigs. They were, however, run over by the train and made sausage meat of unduly and before their time.

General Lee says to the men who shirk duty: "This is the people's war. When they tire, I stop."

Wigfall says: "It is all over. The game is up." He is on his way to Texas. When the hanging begins, he will step over to Mexico.

I am plucking up heart. Such troops as I see go by every day—they must turn the time [tide?]. Surely they are going for something more than—than surrender.

It is very late. The wind flaps my curtain. It seems to moan "too late."

All this will end by making a nervous lunatic.

Yesterday while I was driving with Mrs. Pride, [Lieutenant] Governor McCaw passed us. He called out, "I hope you are in comfortable quarters?"

"Very comfortable," I replied.

"Oh, Mrs. Chesnut," cried Mrs. Pride, "how can you say that!"

Perfectly comfortable, and hope it may never be worse with me. I have a clean

---

1. A. P. Portman of Dorsetshire, a friend and hunting companion of Wade Hampton III.

little parlor 16 by 18, with its bare floor well scrubbed, a dinner table, six chairs and—well, that is all. But I have a charming lookout—from my window high.

My world is now divided—where Yankees are and where Yankees are *not*.

Read *Dr. Thorne* today once more.

General Chesnut has established a hospital here. The night he came, on the floor of the barroom was one soldier dead, another dying, and men stepped in and out regardless. Against the wall were [those] so fortunate as to find a bench or a chair to die decently upon. There was no need for orders from Richmond or aid from there. People here were prompt to aid, and the hospital was instantly set going.

Isaac Hayne says Harriet [Grant] at Bloomsbury is loud in her wail—"And they have not hanged Jeff Davis yet." She had better wait awhile. The man she means to marry—will he nill he—though born in New Jersey took our side of his own free will. What is the use of being a grandson of a signer if one is not a loyal gentleman and true to the colors he enlisted and fought under? No doubt he will be disgusted with all base sentiments—and a disposition to kick the dead or dying lion.

My husband has gone with a wagon train to Columbia.

March 30, 1865.

> Through storm and darkness
> Yawns the rending ground
> The gulf is full of phantoms—

As I sat disconsolate looking out, ready for any new tramp of men and arms, the magnificent figure of General Preston hove in sight. He was mounted on a mighty steed worthy of its rider, followed by his trusty squire William Walker, who bore before him the general's portmanteau. When I had time to realize the situation, I perceived at General Preston's right hand Mr. Christopher Hampton and Mr. Portman. They passed by. Soon Mrs. Pride in some occult way divined or heard that they were coming here, and she sent me at once no end of good things for my tea table. General Preston did come very soon after, and with him, Mr. Clement Clay of Alabama—the latter in pursuit of his wife's trunk. I left it with the Rev. Mr. Martin and have no doubt it is perfectly safe—but where? We have written to Mr. M to inquire. Then Wilmot DeSaussure came in. "I am here," he said, "to consult with General Chesnut. He and I always think alike."

Then he added emphatically, "Slavery is stronger than ever."

"If you think so, you will soon find that for once, you and General Chesnut do not think alike. He has held that slavery was a thing of the past this many a year."

Then he told us how dreadfully the Yankees had treated Mazyck Porcher.

Afterward the ill-used man proved to be Mr. Porcher's eldest son. Then, said Mr. DeSaussure, "As we know there is no eldest son in that cast, Mazyck being the least married of men, the most bachelor, as the Frenchman said, we suppose the whole tragic story falls to the ground with the shooting of Allen Green, who was not with his mother at all."

Tables are turned. Today they say it is Kilpatrick who has the best of the fight with Hampton and that Joe Johnston is hard pressed by Sherman.

I said to General Preston, "I pass my days and nights partly at this window. I am sure our army is silently dispersing. Men are passing the *wrong way*—all the time they slip by. No songs nor shouts now. They have given the thing up. See for yourself—look there!" For a while the streets were thronged with soldiers, and then they were empty again. The marching now is without tap of drum. I told him of the woman in the cracker bonnet at the depot at Charlotte who signaled to her husband as they dragged him off. "Take it easy, Jake—you desert agin, quick as you kin—come back to your wife and children." And she continued to yell, "Desert, Jake! desert agin, Jake!"

General Chesnut told a story of Wheeler's men in Columbia. Either they did not know Hampton or were *drunk* and angry at his being put over Wheeler's head. Hampton was sitting on his horse alone and beset by about twenty of Wheeler's men. He called out, "Chesnut, these fellows have drawn their pistols on me." He is a cool hand, our Wade. General Chesnut galloped up—"Fall in there, fall in"—and by instinct the half-drunken creatures obeyed. Then Chesnut saw a squad of infantry and brought them up swiftly. The drunken cavalry rode off. Wade was quite tranquil about it all. He insisted that they did not know him, and besides they were too much intoxicated to know anything. He did not order any arrests or any notice whatever to be taken of this insubordination.

Letter from Mary Williams says the Princess Bright-Eyes is kept busy writing explanatory letters. She can't say yes and she will not say no. Hence this waste of paper and penmanship. Her B's are buzzing around her in a swarm. It is becoming troublesome. One B (the giant of the Brocken) is getting angry—my sting. She is all serene, however.

"This incessant buzzing of Bees, even if through the P.O., is puzzling to Her Serene Highness."

If they were but going to Johnston camp! All of these fine-looking men on fine horses! This crowd of soldiers in Confederate uniform seem slowly moving west by twos and threes. If they were going the right way, I would have hope yet. They might give a good account of themselves yet.

Hon. C. C. Clay spent the day here. I have had to talk sensibly and to listen to sense until I am exhausted.

Hardee is his scapegoat. He does not like Hardee at all. Says Hood would have won the battle of Atlanta but for Hardee. Mr. Clay is a great friend of Joe Johnston's. He left with my spirit prostrate. A Yankee raid to Lincolnton to cut the road between Lee and Joe Johnston.

March 31, 1865. My birthday—aged 42 ⟨⟨a hundred, in thought and feeling⟩⟩.[2]

Was on my way to dine at Mrs. Bedon's. Governor Bonham halted me at the head of a troop of men. "I will not be interviewed in this manner. There is General Chesnut's headquarters." And I left them planté.

I was joined there by Mr. Prioleau Hamilton and his wife. He told us of a queer adventure. Mrs. Preston was put under his care in the train. He soon found the only other women along were strictly "unfortunate females," as Carlyle calls them—beautiful and aggressive. He had to communicate the unpleasant fact to Mrs. Preston on account of their propinquity. He was lost in admiration of her silent dignity, her quiet self-possession, her calmness, her deafness, blindness, her thoroughbred ignoring of all that she did not care to see. "You know, some women, no matter how ladylike, would have made a fuss, fidgeted, &c&c. But Mrs. Preston dominated the situation and possessed her soul in innocence and peace."

Mrs. Hamilton reproved him vehemently for the impropriety of his anecdote. He was always bringing up risky subjects.

Then she told me infinitely worse, which I omit. Also she said there were a certain class here who were everlastingly asking you to set—or lay. They think we are fowls, that we must needs set or lay.

"The hens lay before they set. Men lie and sit down on that."

I am afraid I have made some mistakes in recording their wit.

In the evening Mr. Clay came again. He said the Senate were inclined to pity Hood after his failure—that is, until his report came out. Then Wigfall fell foul

2. Rough draft of the 1880s Version.

of him savagely.[3] "Hood did not write that report," said Mr. Clay, "and that is the disgrace of it."

"Why? I know Beauregard did not write his reports. Jordan and others wrote for him. I have no doubt some of those very clever aides of General Lee write his—Marshall, Venable, et cie. So little do I know about military matters, I thought it was the aides' business to do it."

April 1, 1865.   Read *Jacques*—(George Sand).[4]

Teddy Barnwell dined with me. Said he found comfort in my white tablecloth, my white rice, mealy potatoes. He said they gave him nice bread and meat here but seemed not to know that vegetables were a desirable adjunct to a good dinner.

Met Robert Johnson from Camden. He has been a prisoner, was taken prisoner at Camden. They—the Yankees—robbed Jack Cantey[5] of his forks and spoons. When Jack did not seem to like it, they laughed at him. When he did not seem to see any fun in it, they pretended to weep and wiped their eyes with their coattails.

All of this maddening derision, Jack said, was as hard to bear as to see them ride off with Albine. They stole all of Mrs. Zack's jewelry, silver, &c&c. When General Hazen[6] heard of it, he wrote her a very polite note saying how sorry he was that she had been annoyed and returned to her a bundle of Zack's love letters written to her before they were married!

Mrs. Reynolds lost nothing—in this wise. A Lieutenant McQueen,[7] Yankee army, had befriended the William Reynoldses in Columbia. So they gave him a note to Mrs. George Reynolds, Camden. Lieutenant McQueen made his headquarters at Mrs. Reynolds', and she saved everything of hers. The young ladies were infatuated with Lieutenant McQueen. He even lent his horse to bury Mrs. Sam Capers. In the same cause we lost Claudia. She was safely hidden from the

---

3. In his report, Hood blamed everyone but himself for the plight of the Army of Tenn. Johnston's retreats, he argued, had left the army demoralized and undermanned. His subordinates, Hardee and Cheatham, had failed to follow orders. In spite of these obstacles and defeats at Atlanta, Franklin, and Nashville, Hood estimated, his command had cost the Confederacy only ten thousand men. The general concluded that he "left the Army in better spirits and with more confidence in itself, than it had at the opening of the campaign." Wigfall's speech, delivered at the last session of the Confederate Senate, was confined to a defense of Johnston's command of the defeated army.

4. Published in 1834.

5. John M. Cantey, a planter and Confederate veteran, was a cousin of James Chesnut, Jr.

6. Maj. Gen. William B. Hazen, commander of a division in John A. Logan's Fifteenth Corps.

7. Lt. John A. McQueen, a Union scout wounded near Camden late in Feb. and left behind when his unit moved on.

Yankees. Miss Chesnut sent for her to be put into the hearse, and she was stolen at sight. She was a beauty, poor Claudia!

Robert Johnson said Miss Chesnut was a brave and determined spirit. One Yankee officer came in while they were at breakfast. He sat down to warm himself at the fire. Rebels have no rights. Miss Chesnut said to him politely: "I suppose you have come to rob us. Please do so and go. Your presence agitates my blind old father."

The man jumped up in a rage: "What do you take me for? A robber? No, indeed!" And for very shame he marched out empty-handed.

The ups and downs. Robert Johnson married a granddaughter of old Adam McWillie, or McGillie, as they claim to be now. The Adam of that ilk is said to ride around Camden still, a veritable ghost. He was in the flesh a slave-owner—comme il y en a peu. A savage, he put negroes in hogsheads with nails driven in all around it and rolled the poor things downhill. The negroes say they know the devil would not have him in hell, he was too bad. So his spirit is roaming about where he made a little hell of his own while he was alive. All that, however, was long, long, ago. My nurse told me. The son, William McWillie, was an amiable person.

April 3, 1865. Saw Mr. Preston ride off. He came to tell me goodbye. Told him he looked like a crusader on his great white horse and William his squire at his heels.

How different these men look on horseback—they are all consummate riders, with their servants as well mounted behind them, carrying cloaks and traps—from the same men packed like sardines in dirty RR cars. Which cars are usually floating inch deep in liquid tobacco juice.

At this late day, the eleventh hour, General Bonham has been given his long-coveted cavalry brigade. They are moving the departments to Coventry—I mean Cokesbury. Oh, ye of great faith!

Every now and then I see Miss Chesnut, with an air of great politeness, soliciting the Yankee officer to steal what he wanted and leave them as soon as possible.

General P has not gone. Mrs. Bedon dropped in to say he was to dine here and then sent me, as soon as she could get home, a custard and a cake for dessert. Then came ice cream. At a later hour Richardson Miles and Wm. St. Julien Mazyck. There was but one tumbler of ice cream left that I gave to Richie Miles. Surely that was showing favor and affection. But he is the oldest of General C's aides—and has been so kind and attentive always.

"Could you not have divided it?"

I remember now, with remorse, that I divided it.

Today Governor Bonham came to dinner, quite pleased that he has a cavalry brigade.

Said Lovell was coming with him, but he heard Lovell say he did not know the way to my house. So he dodged him, as he (B) meant to stay to dinner.

Ellen did her best. She has her hands full. Yesterday it was a tête-à-tête dinner with General Preston—today Governor Bonham. The latter, as we sat at that window which overlooks two thoroughfares:

"All this marching and countermarching, changing of generals and all that—it is but Caesar's death scene—drawing his mantle around him to die decently."

"See how the stream westward never ceases. Lee's army must be melting like a Scotch mist."

"Mist—mist," he answered. "Yes, these men will be missed if there is another battle soon."

Without any concert of action, everybody in Columbia seems to have suppressed the first letters written by them after Sherman's fire, arson, burglary, called "a raid." Miss Middleton sent me a letter from Sally Rutledge, hardly alluding to Sherman. She said she had written a folio in the first red-hot wrath which consumed her—indignation, disgust, despair—but upon sober second thoughts she had thrown it in the fire.

Mrs. McCord's first letter reached me. It was like herself—cool and businesslike. In a postscript she said she had written a letter in her first futile rage at the senseless destruction &c&c, but that letter she thought it wisest to destroy.

Mrs. St. Julien Ravenel's first letter which was received alluded to the burning of Columbia by saying the letter telling of it she did not send for reasons she would give someday.

William Mazyck was present, he says, at the scene between the dismal Jimmy, who wept and wiped his eyes with his coattails as he stole Jack Cantey's silver and hoped nobody would ever serve his mother and sisters so.

For the kitchen and Ellen's comfort I wanted a pine table and a kitchen chair. A woman sold me one today for three thousand Confederate dollars.

Robert Johnson told me that Mr. A. H. Boykin camped out all the time the Yankees were in Camden. Said he liked the life—was always happiest in the woods or hunting.

Mrs. Hamilton disappointed again. Prioleau Hamilton says he to whose house they expected to move today came to say he could not take boarders for three reasons—first they had smallpox in the house.

"And the other two?"

"Oh—I did not ask for the other two reasons."

April 5, 1865.   Miss Middleton's letter in answer to mine telling how generously my friends divided with me here—what little was left to them still.

My dear Mrs. Chesnut,

I fear you will think you have been entrapped into a dull correspondence, but I want to ask you to ask somebody else to forward the accompanying letter for me if the mail communication with Columbia is not yet reestablished. No one here knows.

At a certain point in your letter (it was the page about the baked ham and the bureau, the lard and the looking glass, the cake and the candles) as I read it aloud to Mrs. Munro she exclaimed: "Surely she writes from dreamland. It must be a romance." And I could not contradict her, for there was neither date nor signature to sustain me. I confess my own faith had been somewhat staggered by that wonderful narration; it sounded as if you had landed on one of the "Happy Islands" rather than on part of this Confederate world of ours—and we finally agreed it would be wise to pack up at once, and like the gentleman that rode by Travers, "ask the way to Chester."

A more moving argument still was Stoneman, with his six thousand only twenty miles off! We have been in a quiet commotion here for days. Be sure Lincolnton keeps quiet in its moments of wildest excitement. At first it was Kirk[8] coming down from the mountains. I kept that report from mama. She was ill that day and papa had just left us. The next morning it was only some escaped prisoners unarmed going to, not coming from, East Tennessee. We slept more soundly that night. Yesterday it was Stoneman bearing down in this devoted place, burning all in his way. Today they say he has turned his face toward Salisbury and Greensboro, Danville being his point. There is an Italian proverb which I have forgotten, but I remember my own translation of it—" 'They say' is a liar." Nowadays, alas, no one will dispute this assertion.

The A. Greens went off, I heard, in a fright. The Taylors followed, and there was a ceaseless sending away of boxes, bundles, and bags. We refugees, having no valuables to dispose of, stood fire and feel very heroic, now that the danger seems over, past.

But we feel, too, that [it] is not so safe after all, and if papa does not see too much of the nakedness of the land, we are ready to go back to Columbia *at once*. We long for our own small sufficiency of wood, corn, and vegetables, for life here it is a struggle unto death. Altho' the neighbors continue to feed us, as you said, "with a spoon." We have fallen, too, upon a new device. We keep a cookery book on the mantelpiece, and when our dinner is deficient we just read a pudding or a crême. It does not entirely satisfy the appetite, this dessert in imagination, but perhaps it is as good for the digestion.

I hope Mr. Rutledge will have the pleasure of meeting you as he passes through on his return. And if fortune is ever so kind as to throw me again in the same place with you, *shan't* I make amends to myself for oppor-

8. Capt. George W. Kirk of N.C., a Union commander in western N.C.

tunities wasted in Columbia. With kind regards from mama and my sisters, I am always yours truly—

S. M. Middleton

Mrs. Prioleau Hamilton was in my parlor on high when Richardson Miles came to say General Hood had sent an orderly to find out where my house was.

He said he could make an excuse for me if I did not want to receive General Hood.

"Ask him up" was my answer—and then we sat on pins for two mortal hours, expecting Hood. And also Mrs. Bedon we looked for every moment; she was coming for me to go down to the station to meet Mrs. Davis. At this late day and as things stand now, not for worlds would I fail in any outward show of my deep reverence and respect for the president and Mrs. Davis. In the days of their power they were so kind to me.

As I was ready to go, though still upstairs, they came to say General Hood was there. Mrs. Hamilton cried, "Send word you are not at home." "Never." "Why make him climb all these stairs when you must go in five minutes?"

"If he had come here, with Sherman dragging, a captive at his chariot wheels, I might say 'not at home'—*but now*—" And I ran down and greeted him on the sidewalk—in the face of all. And I walked slowly up with him as he toiled up those weary three stories—limping gallantly.

He was so well dressed, so cordial, not depressed in the slightest. He was so glad to see me. He calls his report self-defense, says Joe Johnston attacked him, so he was obliged to state things from his point of view.

Lawley, the Englishman, defends his campaign. Humphrey Marshall will answer Wigfall's attack upon him in the Senate. The author of *Cause and Contrast*[9] is to say something in his favor, in his interest, "a word for me," he put it, in some paper—I forget what—and a New Orleans editor whose name likewise escapes me is writing on the Hood side of things.

And now follows statements where one may read between the lines what one chooses. He has been offered a command in western Virginia, but General Lee thought, as he and Joe Johnston were not on cordial terms—and that as the fatigue of a mountain campaign would be too great for him—he jumped at the chance of going across the Mississippi. Texas was true to him, would be his home, had voted him a ranch somewhere out there. Troops of the Trans-Mississippi he would bring over &c. Then his comic fear of York, to which he was wending his way, and the Hampton and Preston ladies drawn up in battle array!

Mrs. Davis did not come. Hood stayed to dinner. We had a good glass of wine for him General Chesnut brought from Camden when he went there the other

9. T. W. MacMahon was well known for his proslavery polemic, *Cause and Contrast: An Essay on the American Crisis* (1862).

day, some of the best wine the Mulberry cellars contain. The raids have broken up that establishment and the wine scattered everywhere.

The general thinks it is all winding up. He tried to persuade me to go to York with him.

Will I have the usual six weeks' housekeeping here and then have to strike my tent, leave everything behind—"Go on 'stibuting my things over the whole world," as Ellen says—pack up, break up, move on? Well, I won't make the worst of everything. I'll go in for making the best.

Lincolnton
April 4, 1865

My dear Mrs. Chesnut,

Your letter reached me yesterday. I was prevented by several causes from writing before, and then I knew Miss Middleton had written, and I felt that her graphic pen had done more than justice to any subject of interest which this place afforded at the time.

The description you give of your present style of living—the wonderful donations you receive—have so astonished us here we fear that your fever has returned and that it [is] all the ravings of delirium.

And these feasts are visions, merely wild phantasmagoria—bowls of white sugar, hams baked in biscuit dough, trays of innumerable delicacies! I can't bear to think of it! The other parts of your letter showing no trace of a 'mind diseased'—I must relinquish my theory. Pray do not tempt the struggling refugees of this place too far. We may in our frenzy rise in our might (puny as that might may be from long fasting) and precipitate ourselves en masse on Chester—hoping, hapless creatures that we are, to be allowed to share your spoils.

x x x x

Did you hear of our threatened raid? The inevitable Yankees seemed coming at last. Such burning, burying, parking away in inconceivable places—to a rational mind, the very places the Yankees would go to look for them. Women hurried from house to house, repeating every absurd rumor, screaming children followed at the heels of their mothers; infuriated nurses rushed after and captured the straying children. Men gathered in ominous groups in the streets, with elongated, nay, blanched faces. In a word, *Lincolnton was aroused.* And after all—the Yankees would not come. They have not made their appearance yet!

x x x x

I suppose Mr. Middleton will return with his family to Columbia. At this time Mrs. Middleton is very ill. Yesterday she was stricken with paralysis. They telegraphed their father instantly. She may be in no immediate danger. The doctor cannot decide as yet how it may terminate. I hope not fatally.

I suppose you enjoy the preeminent satisfaction of having the general, your husband, constantly with you. Such quiet dignity, and withal so winning a manner, is not often found—for of all qualities, *dignity* is, or has been, my great admiration. Really, now I am so perfectly *dead* to anything earthly.

x x x x

What does your friend Mrs. Pride do on days of "humiliation, fasting, and prayer"? You must enjoy her carriage and her trays of delicacies. In charity your friends may be permitted to pray that such "Pride may not go before destruction."

I read Mrs. Johnston's letters to the Phifers. She still looks *backward* with regret to *Lincolnton*. And fondly hopes some day to return to its charming society and surroundings!

This morning I have spent in tears. No heart could be more desolate than mine.

Pray sometimes for me among the stricken ones of earth. Paul sends his love to you.

Very truly,

Mary C. Munro

In Lincolnton they had a way of tolling the bell whenever any news came, by way of calling the men of the town to the town hall. Before I left this happened so often! And during the expected raids, that horrid bell tolled like a nightmare.

One day Isabella and I met Mr. Clarke from Columbia, and from him I derived my first real idea of the ruin this war had brought—or Sherman, rather. Mr. Clarke all unshaven and shorn was brandishing a chair, holding it aloft, like a banner, by its one remaining rung. "This is all I have left of my Columbia house and all my earthly possessions!" Mr. Clarke was one of the rich men of Columbia.

Late yesterday evening, when I was tired to death—my small parlor had been crammed all day—just as Judge Upshur was handing Hood his crutches, I found a new man turning an immense ear trumpet in my face. I needed a trumpet, too, for a woman with a voice to raise the dead was singing to the guitar on the landing below, and it came up louder than life. As the sound rose, my deaf friend did not hear this reverberating din from below. He talked affably, but the only sound I heard was—"In the wild chamois track at the breaking of day." Then, "He never said he loved" came up, in stentorian tones. Then "Merry Swiss boy" was warbled. The deaf man for a while was like Tennyson's. He "flowed on forever."[1] Suddenly he stopped, said good night, and

---

1. Perhaps an allusion to "The Two Voices" (1833).

departed. He realized the fact that I was growing distracted under his very eyes, I suppose, and if he asked me what was the matter with me I could not hear him.

They say General Lee is utterly despondent and has no plan if Richmond goes—as go it must. Somebody remarked it was the everlasting "no plan" and trusting to the chapter of accidents which had ruined us.

April 7, 1865. Richmond has fallen—and I have no heart to write about it. Grant broke through our lines. Sherman cut through them. Stoneman is this side of Danville.

They are too many for us.

Everything lost in Richmond, even our archives.

Blue-black is our horizon.

Buck writes to me peremptorily, "Keep Sam in Chester." To him she writes, "I leave it to your discretion." The discretion of a man madly in love. He will go. What can I say that will keep him away?

Bonham took tea here. His beautiful command of three regiments of cavalry not visible yet to the naked eye.

Madame F, the milliner, wants to go west. "Westward the star of empire takes its course,"[2] she whimpered.

General Hood said, "You will all be obliged to go west, Texas, I mean. Your own country will be overrun."

"Yes, a solitude and a wild waste—but as to that we can 'rough it in the bush' at home."

In an unexpected pause of the conversation we heard:

"Is his engagement broken?"

He understood in an instant and very significantly answered,

"Is my neck broken, did you ask?"

Poor Mrs. Middleton—paralysis. Has she not had trouble enough? How much she has had to bear. Their plantation and home on Edisto destroyed. Their house in Charleston burned. Her children scattered, starvation, almost, in Lincolnton, and all as nothing to the one dreadful blow—her only son killed in Virginia.

The western army sneer and swear Mr. Davis has added this to all of his evil deeds, *so-called.* He says, "General Lee with the finest army in the Confederacy."

With this storm of woe impending, we snatched a moment of reckless gaiety—Major and Mrs. Hamilton, Captain Barnwell, and Ogden—patriots

2. Allusion to George Berkeley, "On the Prospect of Planting Art and Learning in America" (1752), stanza 6.

supposed to be sunk in gloomy despondency. We played cards. Then the stories told were so amusing I confess I laughed to the point of tears.

I knew the trouble was all out there, but we put it off, kept it out one evening—let it bang at the door as it would.

William Matthews, who married Miss Perroneau—he walked home with me. Says his wife was in her confinement—baby only two weeks old when Columbia was burned. But she had to get out [of] bed or be burned in it. She sat with her baby all night in the woods. And yet they are alive! She is ill, has never left her bed since. She was carried back to some of the houses left standing.

A kind Yankee officer begged her to stay in her house. He would protect it. But she found he could not do it, even if he tried. He said de Fontaine in his newspaper was on the old cry—"Now Richmond is given up (it was too heavy a load to carry), we are stronger than ever."

"Stronger than ever! Nine-tenths of our army are underground. Where is another to come from? Will they wait until we grow one?"

A forlorn Confed came by, with his head coming out of a hole in the middle of a blanket, Indian fashion, and his hair in such a state. This man had been a high functionary.

"He looks as if the very crows had picked him." Out stepped his wife in deep mourning, with her high roman nose, fierce black eyes.

"There is the crow that did it."

Major Hamilton laughed. "That is a joke I can understand."

April 15, 1865.   Hood brought Mary Darby and Buck with him from York. He sent Judge Upshur here to herald their advent. Hood was awfully proud of that feat. He had never dreamed they would come back with him.

What a week it has been—madness, sadness, anxiety, turmoil, ceaseless excitement. The Wigfalls passed through on their way to Texas. We did not see them. Louly told Hood they were bound for the Rio Grande and intended to shake hands with Maximilian, emperor of Mexico. Yankees were expected here every minute.

There was a money train—so many boxes of specie. Teddy Barnwell said adventurous spirits tapped it here. It seemed folly to send it on to the Yankees, who were bound to get it if it went much further. These patriots were disappointed. It had been saved from the Yankees before it got here. There was no specie in those boxes.

Mrs. Davis came. We went down to the cars at daylight to receive her. She dined with me. Lovely little Piecake, the baby, came, too. Buck and Hood were here, and that queen of women Mary Darby. Clay behaved like a trump. He was as devoted to Mrs. Davis in her adversity as if they had never quarreled in her prosperity.

in those boxes.

Mrs Davis came. We went
down to the cars at day light to recieve her
She dined with me — Lovely little Pie cake
— the baby — came too — Buck and Hood
were here — and that queen of women Mary
Darby — Clay behaved like a trump — he
was as devoted to Mrs Davis in her adversity as
if they had never quarrelled in her prosperity
Reople sent me things for Mrs Davis — as
they did in Columbia — for Mr Davis —
& Mrs. Shame on them — there were people here
so base as to be afraid to befriend Mrs Davis
thinking when the Yankees came they would
take vengeance on them for it.

In fact — it was a luncheon or breakfast
She stayed for here — Mrs Brown prepared
a dinner for her at the Station — I went
down with her — She left here at five oclock
My heart was like lead — but we did
not give way — She was as calm and smiling

Varina Davis as Fugitive, from the 1880s Version, April 15, 1865

People sent me things for Mrs. Davis, as they did in Columbia for Mr. Davis. *But* shame on them. There were people here so base as to be afraid to befriend Mrs. Davis, thinking when the Yankees came they would take vengeance on them for it.

In fact it was a luncheon or breakfast she stayed for here. Mrs. Brown prepared a dinner for her at the station. I went down with her. She left here at five o'clock.

My heart was like lead, but we did not give way. She was as calm and smiling as ever. It was but a brief glimpse of my dear Mrs. Davis—and under *altered skies*. One of the staff did not rise from his chair when she entered the room. Could ill manners go further!

Dr. Cheves said he knew the thing was up when he saw how anxious the Charlotte people were for the Yankees to come.

I hope they will get enough of them and take our share, too.

General Butler offered to assist in defending Chester, but there was no army. Plenty of officers—no men.

We laugh—that is our way—at our losses. Teddy Barnwell mimicked Porcher Miles's distinct enunciation.

"Bettie and her babies are safe at her father's." There were tears in his eyes as he recounted his losses, but it was for Bettie, not himself, that he felt.

Today somebody sent me a New York *Herald* in which there was something not unpleasant.

Our negroes told the Yankees they could not hurt General Chesnut without hurting them. "If you destroy these provisions, you only starve us. He does not come here—hardly ever—and never takes anything from us."

"The lazy rascals," cried J. C. "No wonder they owe me fifty thousand dollars for bread and meat furnished them since the war began." Only one person left our place to go with the Yankees, and that was the little black wretch who betrayed the hiding place, in the swamp, of our horses—Mr. Davis's Arabian among them.

Hood has gone. He held his hat off while he was in sight of the house.

"Why did he remain uncovered so long?"

"In honor of my being here," said B quietly.

And said Mary D: "Atra cura can sit behind a man in an open carriage as well as behind a horseman. Black care was Hood's outrider this morning."

How queerly trouble comes sometimes. It lies in wait and suddenly stabs you to the heart when you are least thinking.

A few days before the First Foreign Battalion was carried off from Columbia, and while the parading was at its height I was lying on the sofa, with a shawl around my head one afternoon, quiet as a lamb. Without any warning the band crashed out in a thunder of military music. I sprang into the floor as if I was shot and gave a howl of agony worthy of an Irish wake.

"What is the matter, auntie? You are crying as if your heart would break."

"Let her alone," said the wise Isabella. "Let her have her cry out. She has hardly been in her right mind since Sherman left Atlanta behind him." [*Remainder of page cut out.*]

April 19, 1865.   Keitt on Vice President Stephens.

"Stephens of Georgia is a smart man. Who denies it? I like old Howell Cobb best of them all. Stephens will sit like a spider in his web, silent and quiet, but he does not miss a word spoken in the House of Representatives. He makes a note of the wisdom which falls from the lips of friend or foe. At the end of the session Stephens makes an elaborate speech—a great speech. He has condensed and arranged and made use of every good thing. His speech is the concentrated sense of that whole house—the brains of Congress double-distilled. Something of the same sort was said of Mirabeau. At least, a man named Dumont[3] supposed he furnished Mirabeau with all of his ideas." Keitt said this in the year 1864, at my house in Richmond at breakfast.

April 7th, 1865

My very dear Friend,

After life's fitful fever is o'er, I sleep well.[4] Out of the depths of wretchedness and uncertainty, the *worst* has raised and buoyed me a little. I, at least, expect nothing more just now of a public nature. Like Shanks Evans's legs, "the conformation of the recruit won't admit of any more."

So I am sitting down, taking account of my dead hopes. There is one effect of this stifling pressure upon us which is not altogether undesirable—we are benumbed.

I am putting down carpets—hanging little pastel drawings—reading Scott's *Border Minstrelsy,*[5] getting new recipes, mixing them up, hopeful of success in the culinary art from one half an hour to the next, with more of housekeeping fervor than I have felt for years. I seem fixed, like Hood's man, "for a sentry" in this rural felicity.

Now let me address myself to the argument of my letter. Do come to me, and see how we get one [on?]. I shall have a spare room by the time you get here, indifferently furnished but oh, so affectionately placed at your service. You will receive such a loving welcome.

One perfect bliss have I. The baby—who grows fat and is smiling always—is christened and not old enough to develop the world's vices or to be snubbed by it. The name so long delayed is Varina Anne. My name is a heritage of woe, but as no one is exempt now, the chances are greater for her than in the days when some were happy.

Mr. Clay and Mr. Hudson called today to see me. The former so affectionate that I really wonder why a man who can be so pleasant ever fails to make his powers manifest.

---

3. Pierre Etienne Louis Dumont (1759–1829), the Swiss scholar who wrote many of Comte de Mirabeau's speeches.
4. Mrs. Davis was in Charlotte, N.C.
5. Sir Walter Scott, *Minstrelsy of the Scottish Border* (1802–3).

Lydia Johnston is here. I infer disapprobative. She possesses the town. She lives with a Mrs. Dewy (a very handsome woman) and a Mrs. McPhail, whose husband was once on J's staff. *They* called to see me and were polite and pleasant. There is an old fable of the tortoise and hare. Perhaps my luck may be that of the tortoise. If not, I have my shell to go into. If that does not do, the Yankees may apply fire, probably, and set me running.

Are you delighted with your husband? I am, with him as well as my own. It is well to lose an Arabian horse if it elicits such a tender and at the same time knightly letter as Mr. Chesnut wrote to my poor old Prometheus. I do not think that for a time he felt the vultures after the reception of the general's letter.

I hear horrid reports about Richmond. It is said that all below 9th Street to the Rocketts has been burned by the beggars who mobbed the town. The Yankee performances have not been chronicled.

May God take our cause into His own hands—and save by few, as by many.

With love to your dear husband from Maggie and myself.

Believe me very affectionately and sincerely your friend.

[*Varina Davis*]

Sorting old letters and burning many—not Mrs. McCord's, however. To begin with—

Columbia
Dec. 8th, 1862

Dear Mrs. Chesnut,

I think your sister should by all means "try for blankets and shoes, &c&c," rather than go on making hospital boxes. From the little I have seen and all I have heard, I think we have a hard task before us to keep our soldiers from freezing to death this winter. My son, who is improving, thanks you for your kind inquiries and agrees with me. Heaven only knows what is to become of our ragged, shoeless troops in Virginia this winter. It seems a Herculean task for us to be thinking of such an undertaking; but even little helps, and every *one* relieved is a fraction of the great whole.

Carolina troops are now proverbially the raggedest of the ragged. We must work. I am about trying here to buy up old carpets, old blankets, anything which if I can get we will line with cotton dyed some sober color and cut into blanket size. I do not know if we can do anything, but it is to be tried at least.

Affectionately yours,

Louisa McCord

After Cheves's death—

Forgive me, my dear friend, if only in a few words I can answer your kind letter.

The light of my life is gone, my hope fled, and my pride laid low. God pity my poor girls. I can scarcely rouse myself to take care of them. My helpless daughters! And his poor young wife, who daily expects her confinement.

I cannot write more, but only to thank yourself and Colonel Chesnut for your efforts to help my darling.

It is all over now, and it is right perhaps that the country will never know how much it has lost in my glorious boy.

Affectionately your friend

Louisa S. McCord

Mrs. M. B. Chesnut

John Darby tells of a most culpable negligence of Longstreet. General Lee sent him written orders for the next day's fight at Gettysburg. Longstreet left them on his table. When he struck tent, they were swept off and fell on the ground. The Yankees found them the same day and with that key to his place of battle were able to forestall every movement that he made. Old Peter was always too slow, though a bulldog to fight.

Miss Middleton writes.

You remember I dared not give you a cup of tea before our Lincolnton visitor. If they saw us with tea they could not send us bread. They feed us, but they will not tolerate luxuries in pauper exiles. Our menservants, sauntering around the yard with cigars in their mouths, cost us our lives nearly. We were near starvation. We are utterly dependent on these "kind folk" for our daily bread.

x x x x

Shopkeepers are so different from what we thought them, in our insolent prosperity. This man is well educated, well mannered, well dressed, and positively agreeable in conversation. And yet a small shopkeeper, pur sang.

I remember how Joe Heyward astonished people in Washington, when he said he had never known anybody but planters.

Just now Mr. Clay dashed upstairs, pale as a sheet.

"General Lee has capitulated."[6]

I saw it reflected in Mary Darby's face before I heard him. She staggered to the table, sat down, and wept aloud. Clay's eyes were not dry.

6. At Appomattox Court House on April 9.

Quite beside herself, Mary shrieked, "Now we belong to negroes and Yankees!" Buck said, "I do not believe it."

Edward Barnwell has sent his wife home. He was here last night, said it was all over. He was hilarious. The special subject of his mirth was my attention—devotion—to the royal family in exile. Showed how I ran after little Maggie, little Jeff, and darling little Billy and tried to make them happy. Billy is Mr. Chesnut's special pet.

I faced the fun gallantly. Standing up, I cried:

"Know all men by these presents—whatever that means—that from the bottom of my heart I am true to them in their adversity. I would do tenfold more for them now than I would have done in the days of their prosperity and power. They were then so kind to me. And *then* you were all glad enough to be their friends."

General Preston is very bitter. He says General Lee fought first well enough to make the Yankees more conceited and self-sufficient than ever, that they were too much for him. They pay us a compliment we would never pay them. We fought to get rid of Yankees and Yankee rule. We had no use for Yankees down here and no pleasure in their company. We wanted to separate from them for aye.

How different is their estimate of us. To keep the despised and iniquitous South within their borders, as part of their country, they are willing to enlist millions of men at home and abroad and to spend billions. And we know they do not love fighting per se—nor spending their money. They are perfectly willing to have three killed for our one. We hear they have all grown rich—shoddy—whatever that is. Genuine Yankees can make a fortune trading jackknives.

"Somehow it is borne in on me that we will have to pay the piper."

"No. Blood can not be squeezed from a turnip. You cannot pour anything out of an empty cup. We have no money, even for taxes or for their confiscation."

"All gone up the spout," cry the flippant. The sentimental sigh.

"We hang out harps by the rivers of Babylon and make our lament."

While the Preston girls are here my dining room is given up to them, and we camp on the landing, with our one table and six chairs.

Beds are made on the dining room floor. Otherwise there is no furniture but buckets of water and bathtubs in their improvised chamber.

Night and day this landing and these steps are crowded with the elite of the Confederacy, going and coming. And when night comes, or rather bedtime, more beds are made on the floor of the landing place, for the war-worn soldiers to rest upon. The whole house is a bivouac—as Pickens said of South Carolina in 1861, "an armed camp."

My husband is rarely at home. I sleep with the girls, and my room is given up to soldiers, too. General Lee's few but undismayed, his remnant of an army, or the part from the South and West—sad and crestfallen they pass through Chester. Many of the discomfited heroes find their way up these stairs.

They say Johnston will not be caught as Lee was. He can retreat. That is his trade. If he would not fight Sherman in the hill country, Georgia, what will he do but retreat in the plains of North Carolina—with Grant, Sherman, and Thomas all to the fore?

Ogden slyly quoted Davy Crockett to Buck.

"As all men's thoughts turn to Texas. You remember Crockett's farewell to the Democratic party: 'You are going to the devil. I am going to *Texas.*'"[7]

We are going to stay. Running is useless now. So we mean to bide a Yankee raid, which they say is imminent. Why fly? They are everywhere, these Yankees—like red ants—like the locusts and frogs which were the plagues of Egypt.

The plucky way our men bear up is beyond praise. No howling—our poverty is made a matter of laughing. We deride our own penury. Of the country we try not to speak at all.

"And those gallivanting heroes—Menelaus now must needs go back to Helen. I wonder if in the privacy of home he called her his darling, his little *Hel.*"

"I think this goose fancies that Menelaus ran away from Helen. No. It was Ulysses who, when the time came to go home to his Penny, left Calypso—qui ne pouvait se consoler du départ d'Ulysse—&c&c&c."

"Every schoolboy knows that and 'Sont celles-là les pensées qui doivent occuper le fils d'Ulysse.' And it is not Grant we are quoting, either. Some of you know no other Ulysses."

"Some of those chaps did console themselves a little, and now they go back, rampantly faithful to their foolish wives who were so faithful and so anxious about them from *first to last.*"

"Well, Menelaus has got to go back to Hel," said the incorrigible *Greek scholar*—or did he say?

"They are bringing Hel back to my deserted, desolated hearth."

"Oh, please say Helen. It all sounds so profane."

"The Trojans cry, Paris brought us Hel, and we gave it back to the Greeks."

"Oh, we just did not win our freedom from Yankees, and we were so near it. They have had a narrow squeak for it."

Penny Mason[8] said, when there was any mourning for the killed in battle: "Well, what did they come here for? Was it not to kill or be killed? They got the [*page cut out*].

---

7. This probably apocryphal description of Crockett's reaction to his defeat for a second term as a Whig congressman from Tenn. appears in Richard Penn Smith, *Col. Crockett's Exploits and Adventures in Texas* (1836), chapter 2.

8. Arthur Pendleton Mason.

XXXIV
The Smoking Ruins

April 22, 1865.   This yellow Confederate quire of paper blotted by my journal has been buried three days with the silver sugar dish, teapot, milk jug, and a few spoons and forks that follow my fortunes as I wander. With these valuables was Hood's silver cup, which was partly crushed when he was wounded at Chickamauga.

It has been a wild three days. Aides galloping around with messages. Yankees hanging over us like the sword of Damocles. We have been in queer straits. We sat up at Mrs. Bedon's, dressed, without once going to bed for forty-eight hours. And we were aweary. Mariana in the grange[1] does not know anything about it. No Yankees to spright her or fright her there.

Colonel Cad Jones came with a dispatch, a sealed secret dispatch. It was for General Chesnut. I opened it.

Lincoln—old Abe Lincoln—killed—murdered—Seward wounded![2]

Why? By whom? It is simply maddening, all this.

I sent off messenger after messenger for General Chesnut. I have not the faintest idea where he is, but I know this foul murder will bring down worse miseries on us.

Mary Darby says: "But they murdered him themselves. No Confederates in Washington."

"But if they see fit to accuse us of instigating it?"

"Who murdered him?"

"Who knows!"

"See if they don't take vengeance on us, now that we are ruined and cannot repel them any longer."

Met Mr. Heyward. He said: "Plebiscitum it is. See, our army are deserting Joe Johnston. That is the people's vote against a continuance of the war. And the death of Lincoln—I call that a warning to tyrants. He will not be the last president put to death in the capital, though he is the first."

"Joe Johnston's army that he has risked his reputation to save from the very first year of the war—*deserting*. Saving his army by retreats, and now they are deserting *him*."

"Yes, Stonewall's tactics were the best—hard knocks, blow after blow in rapid succession, quick marches, surprises, victories quand même. That would have

1. Tennyson, "Mariana," *Poems, Chiefly Lyrical* (1830).
2. The president was shot on April 14.

791

saved us. Watch, wait, retreat, ruined us. Now look out for bands of marauders, black and white, lawless disbanded soldiery from both armies."

An armistice, they say, is agreed on.

Taking stock, as the shopkeepers say. Heavy debts for the support of negroes during the war—and before, as far as we are concerned. No home—our husbands shot or made prisoners.

"Stop, Mrs. C. At best, Camden for life—that is worse than the galleys for you."

At Mrs. Bedon's, Buck never submits to be bored. They (the bores) came to tea and then sat and talked. So prosy, so wearisome was the discourse, so endless it seemed. We envied Buck, mooning in the piazza. She rarely speaks now. Serene she seems, but in deep reveries ever.

Softly she came in from the piazza. With face unmoved and eyes devoid of all expression, she said quietly:

"Guns in the distance. Don't you hear?" Our guests were off at a bound, hardly taking time to say good night.

"Buck, did you hear anything?"

"No."

"All the same, that was a crack shot of yours. It saved our lives. I was nearly dead." She smiled in the same listless unconcerned way and went back to her post in the piazza.

Things people say. We sit in silent wonder.

"Now, if Jeff Davis had been in earnest, if he had been truly a secessionist, no halfhearted Union man, as we all know he is and was—things would have gone so differently with us."

Again, when Col. Cad Jones brought the dispatch.

"That man is a Yankee spy. Don't tell me! If he were not a spy, would he not ride for his life and give that dispatch himself to General Chesnut? He stopped here to spy out for the Yankees."

"Man alive! This was Cad Jones, Cadwalader Jones, twice promoted for gallantry in action. This is almost his home. He was born in twenty miles of this place."

"I do not believe it is Colonel Jones. I am sure he should be taken up as a spy."

Are we all going mad with misery and suspicion?

April 23, 1865.   My silver wedding day—and, I am sure, the unhappiest day of my life.

Mr. Portman came with Kit Hampton. The latter spoke sneeringly of the Confederacy, said, "Jeff Davis has sold us." "Who paid him for it?" was asked. Portman told of Kate Hampton, who is perhaps the most thoroughly ladylike person in the world. When Mr. Portman rushed in—"Lee has surrendered"— she started up from her seat. "That is a lie." "Well, Miss Hampton, I tell the tale as it was told to me. I can do no more."

When they spoke of John Darby, they quoted Isabella.

"Dr. Darby is not himself. No wonder. It is hard for any man to live up to those clothes." "What clothes?"

"Oh, the last suit Poole sent him from England."

> And from our window high
> Which looks out on the sky—
> John Chesnut I do spy.
>
> —sung Buck.

He looked up from the pavement below. We saw the gleam of his white teeth as he caught our eyes and shouted joyfully:

"Oh, you live up there. I am coming." He stopped to kiss his hand to her frantically and then dashed up half a dozen steps at a time.

"That is the cool Captain?" asked Mary Darby. And he answered,

"Yes, but then, I do love you girls so!" "Both?" "Certainly."

"We are not conquered. We are on our way to Maximilian in Mexico."

With his philosophical foot foremost, General C reasoned in the most aggravating manner. Yankees would be after Mexico next—and the emperor of the French.[3] We might be sure they would leave no Austrian prince down there—&c&c. The French and English by leaving us in the lurch had solidified and glorified the Yankees, and now their turn would come. We gave them a chance, and they threw it away forever.

"Slavery! You know."

"That is all rubbish. Virtue in a nation is a matter of latitude and longitude. Look at the English in India—or even Ireland—the French in Algiers—both in Turkey. And the Yankees hug the Mormons to their Puritan bosoms yet awhile."

Polygamy flourishes under the Stars and Stripes. Yankees recoil in horror at the passion negroes have for marrying or doing without it. It must be polyandry they dislike. As they tolerate Mormons.

No wonder he is bitter. Mulberry has been destroyed by a corps commanded by General Logan.[4]

We began with Ripley—with Ripley we end. He is here in command.

"Bragg is our evil genius. We had the best of it at Kingston.[5] Bragg came and spoiled it all."

Buck wrote the epitaph of the Southern Confederacy. I forget all but the rhymes.

---

3. Ferdinand Maximilian, the Austrian archduke established as emperor of Mexico by Napoleon III in 1864.

4. Mulberry had been damaged on one side and pillaged, not destroyed.

5. A point along the Army of Tenn.'s line of retreat from Dalton, Ga., to Atlanta in 1864.

Lee's tears—outsider's sneers—Yankees' jeers. Did we lose by imbecility or because one man cannot fight ten for more than four years? We waited and hoped. They organized and worked like moles, with the riches of all the world at their backs. They have made their private fortunes by their country's war. We talked of negro recruits.[6] The Yankees used them—18 million against six. The odds too great.

Johnston and Sherman hobnobbing. Hampton and Kilpatrick amicably disagreeing. Jeff Davis offering bounties in gold to all who will cross the Mississippi. Edward Barnwell says gold train robbed before it got here, even—much less caught up with Jeff Davis.[7]

Poor Nat Butler here—right arm gone.

John C basking at Buck's feet—yet jealous of Nat Butler.

Someone asked coolly, "Will General Chesnut be shot as a soldier—or hung as a senator?"

"I am not of sufficient consequence," answered he. "They will stop short of brigadiers—and then, I resigned my seat in the Senate months before there was any secession."

"But after all, it is only a choice between drumhead court-martial, short shrift, and a lingering death at home from starvation—&c&c."

And these negroes—unchanged. The shining black mask they wear does not show a ripple of change—sphinxes. Ellen has had my diamonds to keep for a week or so. When the danger was over she handed them back to me, with as little apparent interest in the matter as if they were garden peas.

Saw a mob of soldiers break open a commissary store. *Millions* were lost in that robbery, it was said. Why not? Why leave it here for the Yankees?

Mrs. Huger was in church in Richmond when the news of the surrender came. They were in the midst of the communion service. Mr. MacFarland was called out to send off the gold of his bank. Mr. Minnegerode's English grew frantic. Then the president was summoned, and distress of mind showed itself in every face.

The night before, one of General Lee's A.D.C.'s, Walter Taylor, was married. He left immediately after the ceremony—and was killed.[8] The bride of an hour saw him no more forever.

6. The Confederate Congress had belatedly approved the use of slaves in combat on March 13.

7. Johnston and Sherman met to negotiate an armistice at the Bennett House, near Durham's Station, N.C., on April 17. As the two generals talked, their cavalry commanders, Wade Hampton and Hugh Judson Kilpatrick, traded insults outside in the courtyard. Hampton vowed never to surrender and, two days later, wrote Davis offering a cavalry escort for an escape to Tex., where the war could be carried on. The rumor of gold bounties was as unfounded as Teddy Barnwell's tale of specie plundered from Richmond banks by the president in his flight from the city on April 2.

8. A false rumor.

"In Danville, Smith Lee mingled his tears with mine," said Mrs. Huger, half-laughing, half-crying as she told her stories.

Joe Johnston has made his last retreat—as Stonewall and Lee have gained their last victory.

While the cool Captain was here, riding in the opposite direction with Buck, Dukes sent to John's camp for horses. When John went out to the camp, his servants told him that Confederate soldiers had just impressed or taken his horses and gone off with them.

Every horse was missing but the one he rode. So without a word he galloped after the horse thieves. He saw a man on one of his horses and shot at him. "Halt there!" cried the man. "Do you shoot before you hail a fellow?" "Yes, if he is riding off on one my horses."

"You are brave enough—firing at an unarmed man," called out an officer.

"Well," said the cool Captain, "I see you have all your pistols. If any of you doubt my willingness to shoot at an armed man, let him try to stop me from taking back my horses." Some of John's men came galloping up in hot haste, and they led their horses back without let or hindrance.

"You see," said Buck, "we all know he loves his horses better than his life."

Quarreling over the generals. "Hood won Chickamauga. What victories have Hardee and Johnston won?" screamed Mary.

Portman told of what happened at the house of a man the night before. Two travelers stopped and asked to stay all night. They were such unnatural fire-eaters at this stage of the game that the man grew suspicious. While they slept he overhauled their papers—found they were Yankees sent to spy out the land. He cut their throats and buried them. Seeing that Mr. Portman did not believe a word that he said, the man offered to go and show him the spies half-buried in the bushes.

"No, no—the smells about this house are odious enough without that."

And they took care not to trust themselves to the tender mercies of such a landlord.

Mr. Davis has gone, they say—not this way, but by Abbeville. Gone where?

"Oh!" said Mary Darby vengefully one night, as Burton Harrison had left us after telling all manner of wrongs done Mr. Davis. "Oh! One thing is so respectable in those awful Yankees. If they did choose a baboon to reign over them, they were true to him, they stuck to him through weal and through woe. Oh! they were sharp Yankees and saw in his ugly hide the stuff to carry them through, and he saved them—if he could not save himself."

"That mad man that killed him! Now he will be Saint Abe for all time, saint and martyr."

"When they print his life I wonder if they put in all of the dirty stories his soul delighted in."

"Faugh!" said Mary Darby, whose darling D had enlightened her in many ways. "Now most of the anecdotes, funny as they were told me as coming [from] Lincoln, were so eminently calculated to raise a blush upon a young person's cheek that I had never been able to repeat them."

"Faugh! We chose a proud soldier, and what did we do?"

"Hamstrung him instantly."

"We quarreled like the Jews did among themselves when Titus was before Jerusalem."

"We were poor sticks."

"You mean the fable about the sticks that ought to stay in a bundle."

"From the word go. Joe Johnston put this insult upon the president of the Confederate State—he refused to obey his orders, and he refused even to communicate his plans to him. He said there was a spy in Mr. Davis's office."

"Some say it was Ives."

"How dare you say such a thing? If Joe Johnston set Mr. Davis at defiance, why was he not cashiered? A house divided against itself, you know. If he would not report to the War Office, why was he put in command?"

"Vox populi is vox dei in a republic."

The men sit silent and the women rave in this wise. Mr. Chesnut roused himself to say he hoped to see England and France democratic republics. He would like them to know how that sort of thing worked.

"You are spiteful."

"Well," said Mary Darby, "the worst has come—and after so many left dead on battlefields, so many dead in hospitals and prisons."

"Or worse—left alive with hideous wounds and diseases."

"Some frozen to death—starved to death."

"And the brokenhearted women we have seen die."

"Yesterday these poor fellows were heroes. Today they are only rebels to be hung or shot, at the Yankees' pleasure."

"One year ago we left Richmond. The Confederacy has double-quicked downhill since then. One year since I stood in that beautiful Hollywood by little Joe Davis's grave."

"Burned towns, deserted plantations, sacked villages."

"You seem resolute to look the worst in the face," said General Chesnut wearily.

"Yes, poverty—no future, no hope."

"But no slaves—thank God," cried Buck.

"We would be the scorn of the world if the world thought of us at all. You see, we are exiles and paupers."

"Pile on the agony."

"How does our famous captain, the Great Lee, bear the Yankee's galling chain?" I asked.

"He knows how to possess his soul in patience," answered my husband shortly. "If there was no such word as subjugation, no debts, no poverty, no negro mobs backed by Yankees, if all things were well—you would shiver and feel benumbed." He went on pointing at me in an oratorical attitude. "Your sentence is pronounced—*Camden for life.*"

May 1, 1865. In Chester still. I climb these steep steps alone. They have all gone—all passed by. Buck went with Mars Kit to York. Mary, Mrs. Huger, and Pinckney took flight together.

One day just before they began to dissolve in air, Captain Gay was seated at the table halfway between me, on the top step, and John, in the window with his legs outside. This small landing (which is now our dining room—reception room—drawing room—and where men sleep at night) is only about twelve feet by fourteen. So we are all very much drawn together—so sociable in such close quarters, as Yankee Hill said.

Buck said in her plaintive way: "You can't turn round without running against people. If I try to slip into your room for a sly glass of Madeira or sherry for Mr. Portman—"

"Poor Portman, his British thirst is never quenched."

"But just as I open the door, out rushes somebody."

"Somebody, doubtless, who has found out what is hid behind the fire screen in the chimney in Mrs. C's room. Tell Portman where it is, and you will not have to forage for him. Tell him there is wine and brandy there, and he will trouble you to go for it no more forever." Buck went into her room to prepare for the afternoon ride.

Captain Gay, nodding toward her door: "They are engaged—Captain C and herself."

"No," from the window—emphatically—and the captain then brought his legs inside. "I have been barking up that tree a long time, but—"

"I saw you put a diamond ring on her hand."

"When?" I asked.

"He held her hand under the breakfast table and put on that ring. She had it on at dinner."

"She showed me her engagement ring and I put it back on her hand. She is engaged, but not to me."

"By the heavens, that is above us all! I saw you kiss her hand."

"That I deny."

Captain Gay glared in angry surprise. *He had seen it.*

"Sit down, Gay," said the cool Captain in his most mournful way. "You see my father died when I was a baby, and my grandfather took me in hand. To him I owe this moral maxim. He is ninety years old, a wise old man. Now remember my grandfather's teaching forever more. 'A gentleman must not kiss and tell.'"

"Well, well, I have seen many a man do far less courting and get married on it—get killed and leave a widow and orphans—since this war began. I will say that for the lovemaking in wartime," said John Rhett. "It is short, sharp, incisive, effective, no fooling, no waste time."

"You see—if a woman has a human heart in her bosom, how can she snub a fellow who may be killed in an hour or so?"

"Which of those girls are you really in love with?" asked John Rhett.

"I thought it was Tudy."

"I am in love with all three," in low but distinct tones.

"Well," said Captain Gay, "that beats me. I give it up."

Then Vizetelly, whom I had not seen since our theatricals in Richmond. He was in full force then. Vizetelly came charging up those many stairs and handed Mary Darby a roll of Confederate bills as big as his head.

"These I give you for your hospital, &c&c—any charitable object."

"How kind—how generous!" said Mary, profuse in thanks.

"But after all, he might as well keep them to light his pipe—for all they are worth," murmured the sensible Buck.

Yesterday a fiery parson who has always preached blood and thunder from his pulpit—drum ecclesiastic beat with fist instead of a stick—was as peaceful as a dove. He advised his congregation "to cultivate a submissive spirit and to betake themselves quietly to agricultural pursuits."

And does he think, after four years fighting as men never fought before, after killing more of their men than we ever had in the field—Burton Harrison said the Yankee dead were over three hundred thousand—does he think they will let us quietly slide back into the old grooves as we were before?

A fling at Bragg—

"We were crushed by West Point," said the high functionary. "Today Bragg, who disbanded our cavalry in the face of the enemy, orders Lipscomb[9] to reorganize it. Why did he not order them to report to Bonham long ago?"

Mrs. Huger says, "In Richmond a too grateful and affectionate, fat, greasy negro barber threw his arms around a Yankee general and hugged him in a close embrace. The Yankee freed himself and shot him dead."

"It was time to stop that damned nonsense," he said.

General Preston came to say goodbye. He will take his family abroad at once. Burnside in New Orleans owes him some money and will pay it.

"There will be no more confiscation, my dear Madam. They must see that we have been punished enough."

"They do not think so, my dear general. This very day a party of Federals passed in hot pursuit of our president."

"Specie train they are after," said an A.D.C. "There were so many boxes—they must have been filled with Confederate bills."

"Sand—sand. It was bored into here, and there was nothing in it."

9. Col. Thomas J. Lipscomb of the Second S.C. Cavalry.

Like Sir Charles Coldstream's craters.[1]

History reveals men's deeds—their outward characters but not themselves. There is a secret self that hath its own life "rounded by a dream"— unpenetrated, unguessed.

A terrible fire-eater—one of the few men left in the world who believes we have a right divine, being white, to hold Africans who are black in bonds forever—he is six feet two, an athlete, a splendid specimen of the animal man. But he has never been under fire; his place in the service was a bombproof office—so-called. With a face red-hot in its rage, he denounced Jeff Davis and Hood. Now Teddy Barnwell is always ready for a shindy and does not care very much who he attacks or defends.

"Come now," said Edward the handsome. "Men who could fight and did not—they are the people who ruined us. We wanted soldiers. If the men who are cursing Jeff Davis now had fought with Hood—fought as Hood fought— we'd be all right now."

And then he told of my trouble one day while Hood was here.

"Just such a fellow as you came up on this little platform and before Mrs. Chesnut could warn him began to heap insults 'on Jeff Davis and his satrap Hood.' Mrs. Chesnut held up her hand. 'Stop—not another word. You shall [not] abuse my friends here—not Jeff Davis behind his back, not Hood to his face—for he is in that room and hears you.' Fancy how dumbfounded the creature was."

And I took up my parable. A few days after, I met the discomfited one on the sidewalk.

"Now there is no chance of his hearing me. Why was Hood promoted?"

"Oh! that is easy to answer. Ask me something harder. He was promoted for gallantry in action, recommended for promotion first by Stonewall, then, after Chickamauga, by Longstreet."

Mrs. Huger described graphically Joe Johnston's glow of satisfaction whenever he heard of a disaster in Lee's army. "Whenever General Lee could be found fault with, Johnston's joy was so exuberant he could not hide it."

"What with all his well-known tact and policy!"

"My dear, he discusses General Lee's blunders with a free hand. He is a keen military critic and a hard one to satisfy. And this you may depend on—he shows no favor to Stonewall or Uncle Robert."

---

1. Sir Charles Coldstream, the languid hero of Charles James Matthews, *Used Up: A Petite Comedy in Two Acts* (1845), recounts his trip to Mount Vesuvius: "A horrid bore . . . saw the crater—looked down, but there was nothing in it."

And then she told a story of Joe Johnston before he was famous, in his callow days. After an illness the Johnston hair all fell out. Not a hair was left on his head, and it shone like a fiery cannonball. One of [the] gentlemen from Africa who waited at table sniggered, so he was ordered out—the grave and decorous black butler. General Huger, feeling for the agonies of young Africa as he strove to stifle his mirth, suggested that Joe J should cover his head with his handkerchief. A red silk one was produced and, turban-shaped on his head, it finished the gravity of the butler, who fled, and his guffaw on the outside of the door was painfully audible. Huger then suggested, as they must have the waiters back or dinner could not go on, that Joe should eat in his hat, which he did.

Again will I recount another of Mrs. Huger's anecdotes.

At West Point the year before the war began, Mrs. Davis said to Mrs. Huger sadly: "The South will secede if Lincoln is made president. They will make Mr. Davis president of the Southern side. And the whole thing is bound to be a failure." So her worst enemies must allow her the gift of prophecy.

May 2, 1865.   Camden. From the roadside below Blackstock.

Since we left Chester—solitude. Nothing but tall blackened chimneys to show that any man has ever trod this road before us.

This is Sherman's track. It is hard not to curse him.

I wept incessantly at first. "The roses of these gardens are already hiding the ruins," said Mr. C. "Nature is a wonderful renovator." He tried to say something.

Then I shut my eyes and made a vow. If we are a crushed people, crushed by aught, I have vowed never to be a whimpering pining slave.

We heard loud explosions of gunpowder in the direction of Chester. Destroyers at it there.

Met William Walker. Mr. Preston left him in charge of a carload of his valuables. Mr. Preston was hardly out of sight before poor helpless William had to stand by and see the car plundered.

"My dear Missis, they have cleared me out—nothing left," moaned William the faithful.

We have nine armed couriers with us. Can they protect us?

Bade adieu to the staff at Chester. No general ever had so remarkable a staff—so accomplished, so agreeable, so well-bred and, I must say, so handsome—and I can add, so brave and efficient.

May 4, 1865.   Bloomsbury. Home again.

From Chester to Winnsboro we did not see one living thing—man, woman, or animal—except poor William trudging home after his sad disaster.

The blooming of the gardens had a funereal effect. Nature is so luxuriant here. She soon covers the ravages—of savages. Then the last frost occurred the seventh of March. So that accounts for the wonderful advance of vegetation. It seems providential to these starving people. In this climate, so much that is edible has been grown in two months.

At Winnsboro we stayed at Mr. Robinson's. There we left the wagon train. Only Mr. Brisbane, one of the general's couriers, came with us on escort duty. The Robinsons were very kind and hospitable, brimful of Yankee anecdotes. To my amazement the young people of Winnsboro had a May Day—amidst the smoking ruins. Irrepressible youth!

Fidelity of the negroes the principal topic. There seems not a single case of a negro who betrayed his master. And yet they showed a natural and exultant joy at being free.

After we left Winnsboro, in the fields negroes were plowing and hoeing corn. In status quo antebellum. The fields in that respect looked quite cheerful. And we did not pass in the line of Sherman's savages, so we saw some houses standing.

The Robinsons told us that it was a Confederate explosion yesterday at Chester. They are very cheerful and hopeful—take Mr. Boyce's sanguine view of Yankees.

Mrs. Robinson said: "My son was killed in the Charleston Light Dragoons. If I can forgive that—and I do—why should not they forgive anything? Indeed they ought."

"Ought counts for nothing in this calculating world," answered Cassandra.

⟨⟨**May 7, 1865.**   Camden. . . . Colonel C in a deplorable state, blind, feeble, fretful, miserable. Harriet Grant awaiting her dear Dick to be married. J. C. quiet, yet soon to be restless. These idiots (Camden gentry) because they are cut off from railroads and telegrams think they are to go back into the Union better off than we were before the war.⟩⟩[2]

Two houses left standing as we passed Longtown—Mrs. Peay's and Mr. Abraham Jones's—the owners of each standing at their gates.

Mr. Jones asked, "When may we look for our Yankee overseers?"

Tom Davis gave us a meek submission sermon.

Anne Bailey said Godard had gone North. "Where he ought to have stayed," she added venomously, "for we are behaving down here like beaten curs."

"How?"

The cool Captain wants to go across the Mississippi with Hampton.

"I do not think Hampton will go," said Dr. Boykin. "They may fight in the Trans-Mississippi *now*. I must say, they have done very little of it over there so far."

"Oh, they were principally what the man called Jake Thompson—'a partesian gorilla.'"

"What does he mean?"

"Partisan corps guerillas."

"Oh! oh!"

2. 1860s Journal.

Mary Kirkland's experience of Yankees. She has been pronounced the most beautiful woman on this side of the Atlantic and has been spoiled accordingly in all society.

Monroe, their negro manservant, told her to stand up and keep her children in her arms. She stood against the wall, with her baby in her arms and the other two as closely pressed against her knees as they could get. Mammy Selina and Lizzie stood grimly on each side of their young Missis and her children. For four mortal hours the soldiers surged through this room. Sometimes they were roughly jostled against the wall. Mammy and Lizzie were staunch supporters, and the Yankee soldiers reviled the negro women for their foolishness in standing by their cruel slave-owners. And they taunted Mary with being glad of the protection of her poor, ill-used slaves. Monroe had one leg bandaged and pretended to be lame so that he might not be enlisted as a soldier.

He kept making pathetic appeals to Mary.

"Don't answer 'em back, Miss Mary. Let them say what they want to. Don't answer them back. Don't give 'em any chance to say you are impident to 'em."

One man said to her: "Why do you shrink from us and avoid us so? We did not come here to fight for negroes. We hate them. At Port Royal I saw a beautiful white woman driving in a buggy with a coal black nigger man. If she had been anything to me, I would have shot her through the heart."

"Oh! oh!" said Lizzie. "That's the way you talk in here. I'll remember that when you begin outside to beg me to run away with you."

Finally poor Aunt Betsey fainted from pure fright and exhaustion. Mary put down her baby and sprung to her mother, lying limp on a chair. And she finally called to them: "Leave this room, you wretches. Do you mean to kill my mother? She is ill. I must put her to bed." And without a word they all slunk out, ashamed.

She said, "If I had only tried that hours ago."

Outside they said, "She was an insolent rebel hussy who thought herself too good to speak to a soldier of the United States." Some of them said, "Let us go in and break her mouth." But the others held the most outrageous back.

Monroe slipped in.

"Missy, for God sake, when they come in, be sociable with them. They will kill you."

"Then let me die."

The negro soldiers were far worse than the white ones.

Mrs. Bartow drove with me to our house at Mulberry. On one side of the house every window was broken, every bell torn down, every piece of furniture destroyed, every door smashed in. The other side intact.

Maria Whitaker and her mother, who had been left in charge, explained this odd state of things.

"They were busy as beavers. They were working like regular carpenters, destroying everything, when the general came in. He said it was shame, and he stopped them. Said it was a sin to destroy a fine old house like that whose owner was over ninety years old. He would not have had it done for the world. It was wanton mischief." He told Maria soldiers at such times were so excited, so wild and unruly.

They carried off sacks of our books. Unfortunately there were a pile of empty sacks lying in the garret. Our books, our papers, our letters, were strewed along the Charleston road. Somebody said they found some of them as far away as Vance's Ferry.

This was Potter's raid.[3] Sherman only took our horses. Potter's raid, which was after Johnston's surrender, ruined us finally, burning our mills and gins and a hundred bales of cotton. Indeed nothing is left now but the bare land and *debts* made for the support of these hundreds of negroes during the war.

A. H. Boykin was wiser in his generation. The troops who were sent to defend Camden—he without any authority crossed at a ferry opposite his plantation and Mr. John DeSaussure's. If these troops had been sent direct to Camden, as their marching orders declared, Stephen Elliott, who was in command here, would have saved the town.

As it was, Potter, by evading the troops (crossed so far below the town), came up by the Black River Road and destroyed the town, and our fortunes with it, a few hours before a courier came to declare peace.

So by being at home to look after his own interests, he with Mr. John DeSaussure have saved their cotton and their estates—with mules, farming utensils, and plenty of cotton as a capital to begin on. The negroes would be a good riddance. A hired man is far cheaper than a man whose father and mother, his wife and his twelve children have to be fed, clothed, housed, nursed, taxes paid, and doctors' bills—all for his half-done, slovenly, lazy work. So for years we have thought—negroes a nuisance that did not pay.

They pretend exuberant loyalty to us now. Only one man of Mr. C's left his plantation with the Yankees, and he was the boy who stole Mr. Davis's Arabian for them.

Well, when the Yankees found the western troops not at Camden but down below Swift Creek, like sensible folk they came up the other way. And while we waited at Chester for marching orders we were quickly ruined after the surrender!

Cotton at a dollar a pound—that cotton saved, and we would be comparatively in easy circumstances. Now it is the devil to pay—and no pitch hot.

Well—it was to be.

---

3. A Federal expeditionary force under Brig. Gen. Edward E. Potter spent three weeks in April destroying Confederate supplies and railroad lines around Camden.

Godard Bailey, whose prejudices are all against us, described the raids to me in this wise.

They were regularly organized. First squads demanded arms and whiskey. Then came the rascals who hunted for silver and ransacked the ladies' wardrobes and scared the women and children into fits. At least, those who can be scared. Some of these women cannot be. Then came some smiling, suave, well-dressed officers who regretted it all so much. And then, outside of the gate, officers, men, bummers, divided even—share and share alike—the piles of plunder.

"Women love—love."

"Write under any story you tell about me in your journal. This is translated from Balzac." She[4] rambled on, not knowing the meaning of half she said. The music and the moonlight and that restful feeling, her head on my knee, set her tongue in motion. She accounted for her unwonted fit of confidence that way, because she is as silent as the grave about her own affairs.

"I think it began with those beautiful, beautiful silk stockings that fit so nicely. I have been afraid to warm my feet on the fender ever since. You ought to hear him rave about my foot and ankle. Before that he was so respectful. He kissed my hand, to be sure, but that is nothing. Sometimes when he kissed my hand he said I was his queen and what a grateful fellow he was that I liked him, and I was proud of that very respectful style he adopted.

"But as I stood by the fender, warming my feet, he seized me round the waist and kissed my throat—to my horror—and when he saw how shocked I was, he was frightened in a minute and so humble and so full of apologies. Said it was so soft and white, that throat of mine, he could not help it. It was all so sudden. I drew back and told him I would go away, that I was offended. In a moment I felt a strong arm so tight around my waist I could not move. He said I should stay until I forgave his rash presumption, and he held me fast.

"I pretended to be in a rage. He said, after all, I had promised to marry him—and that made all the difference in the world. But I did not see it. So I wear boots, and I never warm my feet, and I wear a stiff handkerchief close up around my throat."

"Lead us not into temptation," I thought, but when people are opening their hearts, I never say a word. In one thing I heartily agree with the late lamented Lincoln. "I hate a fellow who is interruptious."

"You see, I never meant to be so outrageously treated again," she continued. "It was a shame. Now, would you believe it, a sickening, almost an insane, longing comes over [me], just to see him once more, and I know I never will. He is gone forever. If he had been persistent, if he had not given way under Mamie's violent refusal to listen to us, if he had asked *me*. When you refused to let anybody be married in your house—well, I would have gone down on the

4. Buck.

sidewalk. I would have married him on the pavement, if the parson could be found to do it. I was ready to leave all the world for him, to tie my clothes in a bundle and, like a soldier's wife, trudge after him to the ends of the earth. Does that sound like me? It was true that day."

"And now, how you flirt! Nothing but the love of you keeps _____ and _____ here. _____ is not flirting. He is badly hurt. He is in bitter earnest."

"Now let us talk of something else. Fancy we have been translating from the French."

Dr. Boykin and John Witherspoon were talking of a nation in mourning. They were deploring the glorious young blood poured out like rain on the battlefields. For what?

"Never let me hear that brave blood has been shed in vain. No. It sends a roaring voice down through all time," Scott says somewhere when he talks of his gallant Scots stiff and stark on so many bloody and hard-fought battle scenes.

When we crossed the river, coming home, the ferryman at Chesnut's Ferry asked for his fee. Among us all, we could not muster the small silver coin he demanded. There was poverty for you.

Nor did a stiver appear among us until Molly was hauled home from Columbia, where she was waging war with Sheriff Dent's family. And as soon as her foot touched her native heath, she sent to hunt up the cattle. Our cows were found in the swamp, many of them. Like Marion's men—non combatabus in swampo for the Yankees—and she sells butter for us now on shares.

Old Cuffee, head gardener at Mulberry, and Yaller Abram, his assistant, have gone on in the even tenor of their way. Men may come and men may go, but they dig on forever, "and they mean to as long as old Marster is alive." So we have green peas, asparagus, lettuce, spinach, new potatoes, and strawberries in abundance. Enough for ourselves and plenty to give to the refugees.

Early in May—and yet two months since frost. Surely the wind was tempered to the shorn lamb in our case.

My husband and Captain John laugh at my peddling, but I notice all of my silver that General Chesnut fails to borrow on Saturday is begged or borrowed by Captain Chesnut by Monday.

Old Mr. Chesnut had a summer resort for his invalid negroes and especially for the women with ailing babies. Myrtilla, an African, was head nurse then. She was very good, very sensible, very efficient, and her language a puzzle to me always. She went off with the Yankees. "Old Aunt Myrtilla run away," said Smith, with a guffaw. Ellen [said],

"She was a black angel—she was so good."

"Yes," said Smith, "her arms hung back of her jis' like wings. She was always more like flying than walking—the way she got over ground."

"And Marster did treat her like a lady. She had a woman to wash and cook for

her. You think the Yankees gwine do that for her? And then, she is that old—
she is so old—I thought she only wanted in this world a little good religion to die
with."

And now from Orangeburg comes the most pathetic letters. Old Myrtilla
begs to be sent for. She wants to come home. Miss C, who feels terribly any
charitable distress which can be relieved by other people, urges us to send for
"poor old Myrtilla."

"Very well," says her brother. "You pay for the horses and the wagon and the
driver, and I will send."

And that ended the Myrtilla tragedy as far as we were concerned, but poor
old Myrtilla, after the first natural frenzy of freedom subsided, knew too well
on which side her bread was buttered—and knew too, or found out, where her
real friends were. So in a short time old Myrtilla was on our hands to support
once more. How she got back we did not inquire.

Mrs. Burwell Boykin's coachman had always seen such devoted attention and
care bestowed upon negro children that he made an undue estimate of their
worth per se.

Quantities of negro mothers running after the Yankee army left their babies
by the wayside—left them—did not not spring from block of ice to block—as
Mrs. Stowe fondly imagines they do. ⟨⟨Surely the poor black mothers were
forced to leave them.⟩⟩[5] So Adam came in exultant: "Oh, Missis, I have saved a
wagon load of babies for you. Dem niggers run away an' lef' dem chillun all
'long de road—" ⟨⟨"Missus, I only took three. Nine were in the wagon."⟩⟩ I
fancy how sorely tried even Aunt Sally's Christian charity must be by such an
ill-timed gift.

"Expect us to support niggers," raves Bill Arp. "What have we to support our
own selves *on*?"[6]

When we parted with _____, the warlike captain, he took me aside. "Shall I
go west with the army or go to my wife? She is alone, without funds, and expects
her confinement every day."

"Go to your wife. The war is virtually [over]."

How thankful he looked for that advice. Going west was not in the back of his
head, but he wanted moral aid and comfort when he did what he pleased.

"*She* cannot travel, you know."

Johnny went over to see Hampton. His cavalry are ordered to reassemble on
the 20th. A little farce to let themselves down easily. They know it is all over.

Johnny smiling serenely, "The thing is up and *forever*."

Isabella writes—really seems to believe it!!—that Sherman at once offered
Hampton a command in the United States cavalry, and that Kilpatrick said to
Hampton,

5. This and other excerpts in the paragraph are from the 1860s Journal.
6. From Charles Henry Smith, "Bill Arp Addresses Artemus Ward," in *Bill Arp, So Called. A Side
Show of the Southern Side of the War* (1866).

"Well! we meet at last."

"If you wanted to see me so much, you could have waited for me to come up all this time."

Had a message from Buck. After a long ride with Rawlins Lowndes she was too tired to write. Le roi est mort—vive le roi.

Had our present position defined. General Lovell sent General Chesnut an order, showing that he considered him a paroled prisoner.[7]

Godard Bailey's presence of mind. Anne Sass left a gold card case—a terrible oversight—among the cards on the drawing room table. When Yankee raiders saw it their eyes glistened. Godard whispered to her. "Let them have that gilt thing. Slip away, hide the silver."

"No," shouted the man. "You don't fool me that way. Here's your old brass thing. Don't you stir. Fork over that silver."

And so they left a gold card case in Godard's hands and stole plated spoons and forks—left out because they were plated.

Mrs. Beach says two officers slept at her house. Each had a pillowcase crammed with silver and jewelry. "Spoils of war," they called it.

Floride Cantey[8] heard an old negro say to his master: "When you-all had de power, you was good to me, and I'll protect you now. No niggers nor Yankees shall touch you. If you want anything, call for Sambo. I mean, call for Mr. Samuel—that's my name now."

Sunday thoughts:

> I lift my soul to God
>   My trust is in his name
> Let not my foes that seek my blood
>   Still triumph in my shame.[9]

⟨⟨**May 9, 1865 . . .**   J. C. was so bitter last night. Said if he had come home a year ago and saved his property as *some* did—I said he did right to lose it. He replied, [that] I would go and dine with the ones who did it. "Yes, because Uncle H is the only one I know who did so, but I think still, as you aided in bringing on this war, you were bound to sacrifice all and stick to it, no matter where you were placed, no matter how unpleasant your position, for the poor conscripts had to stay in a worse place." He then said he had stayed, and from his own

---

7. Joe Johnston had given Mansfield Lovell command of S.C. in April.
8. Camilla (Richardson) Cantey's daughter, a cousin of J. C.
9. Quoted from Bogatzky, *A Golden Treasury.*

He was so bitter last night —
said if he had come home
a year ago & saved his
property as some did — I said.
he did right to lose it —
he replied — "I would go & dine
with the ones who did it" —
"Yes, because Uncle H is
the only one I know who
did so" — but I think still
as you aided in bringing
on this war — you were
bound to sacrifice all
& stick to it no matter
where you were placed
no matter how unpleas-
-ant your position — for
the poor conscripts had
to stay in a worse place" —
he then said — "he had
stayed — & from his own
conviction of duty — & not
from my persuasion" —

which is the honest truth —
but he cannot forbear the
gratification of taunting
me with his ruin — for
which I am no more responsible than the man in
the moon — but it is a
habit of all men to fancy
that in some inscrutable
way their wives are the
cause of all the evil
in their lives —
I read Gerald Gray — How
Teddy Barnwell can
bear that description of himself.
Cameo face & all — so
perfect in the physical
delineation — I found
Captain Edward Barnwell
charming — let the world
say what it will —

conviction of duty and not from my persuasion. Which is the honest truth, but he cannot forbear the gratification of taunting me with his *ruin,* for which I am no more responsible than the man in the moon. But it is the habit of all men to fancy that in some inscrutable way their wives are the cause of all evil in their lives.⟩⟩[1]

May 10, 1865.   A letter from a Pharisee[2] who thanks the Lord she is not as other women are. She need not pray as the Scotch parson did, for a good conceit of herself. She writes: "I feel that I will not be ruined, come what may. God will provide for me." But her husband has strengthened the Lord's hands, and for the glory of God, doubtless, invested a hundred thousand dollars in New York, where Confederate moth did not corrupt nor Yankee bummers break through and steal. She goes on to tell us: "I have had the good things of this world and I have enjoyed them—in their season. But I always held them as steward only for God. My bread has been cast upon the waters and will return to me."

E. M. B[oykin]: "We had a right to strike for our independence—and we did strike a bitter blow. They must be proud to have overcome such a foe. I dare look any man in the face. There is no humiliation in our position after such a struggle as we made for freedom from Yankees."

He is awfully sanguine. His main idea is joy that he has no negroes to support and can hire only those that he really wants. "I have read of no magnanimous conquerors of fallen states," whimpers Cassandra, at her old trade, prophesying evil.

"But they are cute[3] Yankees. They will not destroy a country which is now virtually their own."

"I look for the worst. Schofield has put Governor Vance aside in North Carolina. He says they need no civil government there."

Stephen Elliott told us that Sherman said to Joe Johnston: "Look out for yourself. This agreement only binds the military—not the *civil authorities.*"[4]

Is our distraction to begin anew? For a few weeks we have had peace.

Minnie Frierson tells a story as of an eyewitness—a pendant of Adam's present of the negro babies to his mistress by the wagon load. Minnie says: "Eigh-

---

1. 1860s Journal.

2. Identified in the 1860s Journal as Sarah Cantey (Witherspoon) Williams, the widow of John Nicholas Williams.

3. In usage then closer to "acute."

4. President Andrew Johnson had rejected the Johnston-Sherman armistice of April 18, which guaranteed "rights of person and property" to Southerners and promised Federal recognition of existing Southern state governments whose officials took loyalty oaths. On the twenty-sixth, Sherman negotiated a second agreement pertaining only to the surrender of Johnston's troops and then left Maj. Gen. John M. Schofield to assume power in N.C.

teen negro women have been found along the road—stabbed by the retreating army. The Yankee soldiers could not rid themselves of these pests any other way. Poor animals."[5]

Andy Johnson says now it will be easy with his shears to snip off the heads of the rebellion. Poor tailor. See *Herald* of the 19th. Civil heads, military heads are paroled.

General Chesnut is busy carrying out General Lovell's orders. Lovell wrote to Joe Johnston to inquire, "if the consent of our government had been given to this convention of his with Sherman." The great Joe answers, "I was not aware that we had any government."

Nor has he ever been practically aware of it. Ignoring his own government has been Joe Johnston's chronic disorder. He did not seem to know that he owed any allegiance to our president, because he hated him—and there Joe Johnston's treason to his country came in, and our ruin—at the same break in the wall.

Sutherland [is] a carpenter from Philadelphia who has lived here twenty years. Today he sniggered and said:

"I'll have to go away from here, as I had to go away from Pennsylvania. I cannot make money where Northern people are. Only with lazy easygoing Southerners can I make a fortune."

He tried to compliment me.

"I see you could be sharp as a Yankee if you had a chance—not shiftless and helpless, as you were born."

Stanton has telegraphed to Georgia—"Let no rebel legislature stand." Take care of yourself, shifty old Joe Brown.

William M. Shannon says he would like to save the money he made in the bank during the war.

Harriet and Mattie.[6] When I was at home last, Harriet had made a vow over the padre's dead body to befriend Mattie—come weal, come woe! It was a case of Damon and Pythias—Jonathan and David run mad. Strange! I cannot remember any female precedents for such until-death friendships. I mean, *woman to woman*. Now these faith friends are barely bowing acquaintances.

Many causes of this direful result [are] given. I will write down the one which made the strongest impression on my mind.

Harriet fancied herself haunted by the ghost of old Mr. S. Hard on any sentimental girl—with her eyes turned up to heaven, where her sainted father

---

5. An unfounded rumor.
6. Sam Shannon's twin sister, Martha Allison English Shannon.

is—to have a creature come rushing in, wildly shrieking, "Old Mr. S's ghost is in there, I saw *it!*" with horrible details. As if any respectable ghost would come down out of heaven to haunt Harriet. It became unbearable, and the scenes of deepest grief soon grew into scenes of the most commonplace quarreling, mixed up with "your father's ghost did," "and my father's ghost never would"—with queenly dignity and drawing up heads and necks.

And Johnny! His country in mourning, with as much to mourn for as country ever had! That cold, calm, unmoved air of his is only good form. Under all he is as volatile, as inconsequent, as easily made happy, as any lighthearted son of the South. To my amazement he wants me to give a picnic at Mulberry. Just now I would as soon dance on my father's grave.

Harriet is more maddening *just now.* She daily wishes her dear Richard had fought on the other side. Being from New Jersey, he could (so well) have done so. New York and South Carolina being equally Yankee land now, how much nicer to live in New York.

Molly tells me all of the men on our plantation have Enfield rifles. The whites are disarmed—*supposed to be,* ordered to be. Now will come (if we were disarmed in fact and the negroes knew it) the long hoped-for rising against former masters—and murdering them. Missing which—our enemies have been so unhappy.

Mr. C says quickly: "There is 'such a divinity doth hedge a king.'[7] I could take twenty men and clear this country of armed negroes to the Sumter line." Which is a comforting, quieting faith.

"I wish [I] was in New York," cried Harriet.

"If this should prove a second St. Domingo, I prefer to be here."

"Dick, the captive of her bow and spear, the fiancé of this Hawkeye, is an arrant Southerner. When he comes she will change her tune, you see"—is whispered around.

Sitting in the moonlight, given o'er to sad memories, my mother's sad forebodings in '61 were repeated.

"May we all be twenty feet underground—rather than subjugated."

Harriet, with a sneer: "Are you like Aunt Mary? Would you be happier if all the men of the family were killed?"

To our amazement, quiet Miss C took up the cudgels—nobly.

"Yes, if their life disgraced them. There are worse things than death."

---

7. *Hamlet,* act 4, scene 5.

Upon [upward?] of a thousand Confederate soldiers have come here. A man named Latta took it upon himself to invite them here to divide Confederate stores. He is a commissary agent.

And hear how they talk—this handful. Daredevils still, gentlemen privates—rash, reckless, Southerners to the last. These thousands who came to divide the commissary stores alarmed us. Our handful of gentlemen privates reassured us.

"There will be no disorder. Half a dozen of us could clear away this crowd. They see us lounging about here, idle but ready. There will be no trouble."

"Rascality," says Carlyle, "has always outnumbered gentility a hundred to one—and yet."

Johnny calls him the captive of her long bow—which she draws so well. Today at breakfast he talked more than I have ever known him to do. From some dark corner he had unearthed Miss Burney's *Cecilia*. And he persisted in giving us the story. The incredible part, according to him, was the scene at the altar.[8] "Any just cause or impediment &c&c—" One old woman cries, "Stop this marriage," and hobbles off before she can be seized to know what she means by her ill-timed interruption. Bride faints. Bridegroom curses and swears. Ceremony stopped unceremoniously. Miss Burney did not know women. If that girl had landed her fish after playing him so beautifully, do you believe *one* old woman could head her? No—not all Sherman's army. They do not faint now.

"They curse a little still," said H spitefully.

"I am sure, after that girl had her man in hand at last, wild horses could not have dragged them from the altar until his chains were riveted."

"That fool Dick Taylor will not disband and let this nasty Confederacy smash and be done with it."[9]

"Excuse me—I will go. I cannot sit at table with anybody abusing my country."

So I went out on the piazza. But from the windows the loud screams came of vituperation and insult.

"Jeff Davis's stupidity—Joe Johnston's magnanimity—Bragg's insanity."

So I fled. Next day she flew at me again and raved until I was led out [in] hysterics. And then I was very ill. They thought I was dying. And I wish I had died.

At it again. This is worse than fighting the Yankees.

"Is there any power?" cried H, "any power to force my dear across the Mississippi to join Dick Taylor?"

"No," said the cool Captain mournfully, "nor was there even any power strong enough to make him join our army on this side of the Mississippi."

Sally Reynolds told a story of a little negro pet of Mrs. Kershaw's. The little

8. Frances Burney, *Cecilia; or, Memoirs of an Heiress* (1782), book 7, chapter 7.
9. Actually, Taylor had surrendered his army north of Mobile, Ala., on May 4.

negro clung to Mrs. K and begged her to save him. The negro mother, stronger than Mrs. K, tore him away from her. Mrs. K wept bitterly. Sally said she saw the mother chasing the child before her as she ran after the Yankees, whipping him at every step. The child yelled like mad, a small rebel blackamoor. The mother soon came back, but Mrs. K would not allow any of them to enter her yard again.

Carlyle glorified Yankee doodle-doo and Boston harbor black with tea—1876.[1]

Now in 1861 he said, "Let them alone—only the foulest chimney in the world, burning itself out."

No longer "rifled-wing Democracy in death volleys, enveloping the world."

《**May 15, 1865 . . .** I have a long letter from Isabella. Tudy flirting with Portman. Buck rides with Rawly Lowndes. . . . Buck always flirts, but miserable, utterly miserable. Says she has consumption. Buck, my poor darling, as far as I see, they did you cruel wrong when they did not let you marry and share the fate of your poor wounded hero and patriot, the only true man I have seen in your train yet.》

1. M. B. C. meant "1776," of course.

XXXV
Survivors

May 16, 1865. We are scattered—stunned—the remnant of heart left alive with us, filled with brotherly hate.

We sit and wait until the drunken tailor who rules the U.S.A. issues a proclamation and defines our anomalous position.

Such a hue and cry—whose fault? Everybody blamed by somebody else. Only the dead heroes left stiff and stark on the battlefield escape.

"Blame every man who stayed at home and did not fight. I will not stop to hear excuses. Not one word against those who stood out until the bitter end and stacked muskets at Appomattox."

Yesterday John Whitaker and Dr. Charles Shannon said they would be found ready enough to take up arms when the time came![1]

Rip Van Winkle was a light sleeper to these two—their nap has lasted four years.

"He cometh not—and I am aweary," she said. And truly it is an awkward predicament. The bride[2] shall wait like a love-lighted watch-fire all night at the gate for a bridegroom who seems backward, as the Irishman says, in coming forward.

The "reporters in the gallery" give me a most amusing account while I was out. I quite envy the parties the fun.

May 18, 1865. This poor *old* blind man. They had his property—and they hoped his only son would be killed.

A feeling of sadness hovers over me now, day and night, that no words of mine can express.

Plenty of character study in this house—if one had the heart.

Colonel Chesnut ninety-three—blind, deaf—apparently as strong as ever,

---

1. John Whitaker was a cousin of M. B. C.; Charles John Shannon, Jr., was a younger brother of William M. Shannon.
2. Harriet Grant.

certainly as resolute of will. African Scipio walks at his side. He is six feet two, a black Hercules, and as gentle as a dove in all his dealing with the blind old master who boldly strides forward, striking with his stick to feel where he is going. The Yankees left Scipio unmolested. He told them he was absolutely essential to his old master, and they said, "If you want to stay so bad, he must have been good to you always." Scip was silent, he says. It made them mad if you praised your master.

Partly patriarch, partly grand seigneur, this old man is of a species that we will see no more. The last of the lordly planters who ruled this Southern world. He is a splendid wreck. His manners are unequaled still, and underneath this smooth exterior—the grip of a tyrant whose will has never been crossed. I will not attempt what Lord Byron says he could not do—"Everybody knows a gentleman when he sees one. I have never met a man who could describe one." We have three very distinct specimens in this house—three generations of gentlemen, each utterly different from the other—father, son, grandson.

Sometimes this old man will stop himself just as he is going off in a fury because they try to prevent his attempting some impossible feat. In his condition of lost faculties he will stop and ask gently:

"I hope that I never say or do anything unseemly. Sometimes I think I am subject to mental aberrations."

At every footfall he calls out, "Who goes there?" If a lady's name is given, he uncovers and stands, hat off, until she passes. He has the old world art of bowing low and gracefully still.

《His peculiarities, to me, have always been great shrewdness and wonderful quickness to perceive the minutest harm his earthly possessions (his god) could receive from others, perfect blindness to their harm from his own neglect or want of power to take care of them. But an open preference for the utter destruction of "the property he is trying to keep together for his children" in his own hands—to deliver up ten dollars of it to be saved by one of those children. He would not leave me alone in his wine cellar but left the wine at Mulberry for the negroes and Yankees. He don't believe anybody; he don't trust anybody; he has a horror of extravagance; he has a firm and abiding faith in the greatness and power of the North, caught from his wife. Great hospitality and beautiful courtly manners when he was in a good humor; brusque, sneering, snarling, utterly unbearable when angry. Consistent in one thing—I have never heard him use a noble or a high or fine sentiment; strictly practical and always with a view to save his property for his own benefit are all the ideas I have ever heard from him. "A fool and his money soon parted," "Never be in a hurry"—his wisdom and wit, over and over and over. He will take the oath now and leave the remnant of his wasted estate to his mean grandchildren in Florida, the only ones who ever thoroughly pleased him.》

He came of a race that would brook no interference with their own sweet will by man, woman, or devil. But then, such manners would clear any man's character—*if it needed it.*

Mrs. Chesnut used to tell us that when she met him at Princeton in the nineties of the 18th century, they called him there the Young Prince. He and Mr. John Taylor of Columbia[3] were the first up-country youths whose parents were wealthy enough to send them off to college.

When a college was established in South Carolina, Colonel John Chesnut, the father of the aforesaid Young Prince, was among the first batch of its trustees. Indeed, I may say, since the Revolution of 1776 there has been no convocation of the notables of South Carolina—in times of peace and prosperity or war and adversity—that the representative man of this family has not appeared. The estate has been kept together until now. There has always been an only son.

Mrs. Chesnut said she drove down from Philadelphia in her bridal trip—chariot and four, cream-colored chariot, and outriders.

They have a saying here. On account of the large families with which people are usually blessed in these parts and the subdivision of property consequent upon that fact—besides the tendency of one generation to make and to save and the next to idle and to squander—that there is rarely more than three generations between shirtsleeves and shirtsleeves. These people have secured four—from the John Chesnut who was driven out from his father's farm in Virginia by French and Indians when that father was killed at Fort Duquesne, to the John Chesnut who saunters along here now, the very perfection of a lazy gentleman who cares not to move unless it be for a fight, a dance, or a fox hunt.

The first comer of that name to this state was but ten when he got here. Leaving his land in Virginia, being penniless otherwise, he went into Mr. Joseph Kershaw's grocery shop as a clerk. And the Kershaws, I think, have that fact on their coat of arms. Our Johnny, as he was driving me down to Mulberry yesterday, declared himself delighted with the fact that the present Joseph Kershaw had so distinguished himself in our war that they would let the shop of a hundred years ago rest for a while. "Upon my soul," cried the cool Captain, "I have a desire to go in there and look at the Kershaw tombstones. I am sure they have put it on their marble tablets that we had an ancestor one day a hundred years ago who was a clerk in their shop."

In the second generation the shop was so far sunk that the John Chesnut of that day refused to let his daughter[4] marry a handsome dissipated Kershaw. And she, a spoiled beauty who could not endure to obey orders when they were disagreeable to her, went up in her room—and there stayed, never once coming out of it for forty years. Her father let her have her own way in that, provided servants to wait upon her and every conceivable luxury that she desired—but neither party would give.

Among my father's papers—he was the lawyer at the time of Joe Kershaw's father (our present Joe) and filed a bill in equity for him against Col. John Chesnut's estate—there is a letter from my father, advising the Kershaws not to go to law. And then there is a letter from Joe Kershaw's father asking Col. James Chesnut not to go to law with them—as by so doing he would beggar Miss Mary

3. J. C.'s uncle, governor of S.C. from 1826 to 1828.
4. Old Colonel Chesnut's elder sister, Harriet Chesnut.

Kershaw, the only daughter left alive of the original Joseph. She still owned a few negroes and some land and was highly respected by all the Camden world.

Col. James Chesnut dropped the suit. And it must be remembered to his credit, for he did not part with money easily. How could he? His own moral maxim was "A fool and his money soon parted."

Col. John Chesnut had been kindly treated by the representative Kershaw of the shop before the revolution of '76, and he would never allow anything to be done when the family lost their prosperity which could in any way annoy them.

"Barring marrying them!" cried Johnny, as he finished reading this.

"Johnny, did you know what all this fuss was about when you went off as a private with Gregg four years ago?"

"I had no need to know. It was the sort of thing for a gentleman to do," said he, bristling up.

"Well, well, you stuck it out—you fought it out."

"The mud and the dirt and the cold and the snow—now, mind you, I say it, and I know—the battlefield is but play to the hard stuffs of a life in camp. I thought it was the cold and rain and freezing &c in Virginia—but you see, on our coast in summer, heat and dust and dirt and mosquitoes and snakes and gnats were worse.

"I did not ask for promotion. Uncle James was at headquarters, and he would never try to promote me because I was his nephew. Now you'll see, I am going to make no faces at poverty. I can face one fortune as, as—"

"Well, as gallantly as another. You boggled at the word which came to your lips."

"Oh, there are thousands like me."

"I wish we had had millions. I would have sent every man of them to Uncle Robert Lee.

"I am too thankful that I am an old woman, forty-two my last birthday. There is so little life left in me now to be embittered by this agony."

"Nonsense! I am a pauper, and I am as smiling and as comfortable as ever—you see."

"When you have to give up your horses, how then?"

May 21, 1865.   Harriet is radiant. She had heard that Jeff Davis has been captured.[5] And that Columbia has been garrisoned at last.

Lieutenant Fairly, A.D.C. of Whiting. He denounces Bragg for sacrificing General Whiting at Fort Fisher. He knew what was coming. He sent Hoke off. He remained in gunshot with ten thousand men, when one thousand would have saved Fort Fisher. Whiting was nearly well, so the surgeon said. He alone was not paroled. They left him there. He died of a broken heart.

And then he went on to tell us of that lovely little Mrs. Jasper Whiting, as she flew down the streets of Columbia with her baby in her arms. Every now and

5. At Irwinville, Ga., on May 10.

then she would have to stop and shake off the flakes of fire and the shower of ashes and cinders. Like all the rest of us, the Ingrahams have lost everything.

Lieutenant Fairly showed himself a man of lively faith. He sold my husband a horse on credit. Now no one knows from day to day where he will be—or *what*.

We were threatened with a mob. And those conservatives, the law-and-order men, General and Captain Chesnut, Colonels Haskell and Boykin buckled on their armor and sallied forth to protect commissary stores. Who for? It will be the private property soon of the commissary—whose else?

They say Governor Magrath has absconded.[6] And the Yankees said, "If you have no visible governor, we will send you one."

(And if we had one—and they found him, they would clap him in prison—instanter.)

How the negroes flocked to the Yankee squad which has come. They were snubbed, the rampant freemen. "Stay where you are," say the Yanks. "We have nothing for you." And they sadly "peruse" the way. Now they have picked up that word, they use it in season and out. When we met Mrs. Preston's William— "Where are you going?" "Perusing my way to Columbia." When they said (the Yanks) that they had no rations for idle negroes, John Walker answered mildly, "This is not at all what we expected."

The women dressed in their gaudiest array carried bouquets to the Yankees. It was a jubilee. Now in this house there is not the slightest change. Everyone has known he or she was free for months, and I do not see one particle of alteration. They are more circumspect, politic, quieter, that's all. All goes on—in status quo antebellum. Every day I expect to miss some familiar face. So far, I have been disappointed.

Mrs. Huger we found at the hotel here and brought her to Bloomsbury. She told us that Jeff Davis was traveling leisurely, with his wife, twelve miles a day, utterly careless whether he were taken prisoner or not.

Also that General Hampton is paroled. ⟨⟨Mrs. Huger says Buck has lost twenty pounds since I saw her and is a perfect wreck. Mrs. Preston ought either to have broken her engagement or to have permitted the marriage.⟩⟩

Harriet said: "And now why don't they hang Jeff Davis and clear the decks for peace. I want this row over."

"And clear the way," murmured the Captain, "for the laggard in love. It will take more than a rope to drag him here."

"Johnny, how long can you stand such things as that said of President Davis?"

"I can't stand it at all—not one second."

Dr. Lord was here. Mr. Davis attended his church in Mississippi, and he knew him well at home on his own plantation. Dr. Lord is a Princeton man, married a

---

6. A false rumor. Magrath was arrested by the Union on May 28.

Miss Stockton.[7] Here are his words describing the much abused martyr, Jeff Davis.

"I have never had a parishioner that I liked better. He is one of the purest and best of men, one of the kindest-hearted."

"And yet," said H, "you think he ruined the South when he removed Joe Johnston."

"Yes—more by keeping Pemberton in command, however, than even by superseding Johnston."

Dr. Lord was a fighting parson—discussed our military matters ably. General C began to give his far-from-orthodox views of theology. Miss C wished to stop that in presence of a clergyman.

"No. Let him go on. The parson seems an oracle on war and its ways. Let the general enlighten him as to creed and dogma and church affairs."

"Let him put me straight on religion—what does she mean? Oh, I see. She means let the shoemaker stick to his last, &c."

Fighting Dick Anderson and Stephen Elliott of Fort Sumter memory are quite ready to pray for Andy Johnson and to submit to the powers that be. Not so our belligerent clergy. "Pray for people when I wish they were dead?" cries Mr. Trapier. "No—never. I will pray for President Davis till I die. I will do it to my last gasp. My chief is a prisoner, but I am proud of him still. He is a spectacle to gods and men. He will bear himself as a soldier, a patriot, a statesman, a Christian gentleman. He is the martyr of our cause."

And I replied by my tears.

"Look here—taken [in] woman's clothes," added Mr. Trapier, "rubbish—stuff and nonsense.[8] If Jeff Davis has not the pluck of a true man, then there is no courage left on this earth. If he does not die game—I give it up. Something, you see, was due to the manner of Lincoln and the Scotch cap that he hid his ugly face with in that express car when he rushed through Baltimore in the night. It is that escapade of their man Lincoln that set them on making up the waterproof cloak story of Jeff Davis."

John Witherspoon was in agony. What might the Yankees not do to him?

"Not hang him—not they—too cute for that. They won't have his blood crying to heaven against them and make him a martyr on the scaffold, like Charles I, for us to worship down here forever."

Look at Lincoln now. How we used to hate him—abuse him, anyway. And now who is so base as to utter a word against the murdered president? No. The Yankees will fling him back among us—our beloved Jeff Davis—and in the house of his friends—*Mercury*—Rhett—Joe Johnston et cie—he will be mangled con amore."

Said Harriet with a sneer: "Does she want the man killed? Does she fancy

---

7. William Wilberforce Lord, a Northern-born poet and Episcopal priest, served as rector of Christ Church in Vicksburg, Miss., in the 1850s and became a close friend of Jefferson Davis. His wife was Margaret Stockton.

8. It had been falsely reported that Davis was captured dressed as a woman.

every man put into a soldier's grave—that his soul marches straight up to heaven? If she does, she is an idiot."

After which amenities—I left the room.

Dr. Lord was literary. In spite of those hawk eyes—and nose to match—in dulcet accents imitating Buck's low coo with its dying fall, the lady said—with an undercatching of her breath (I must premise that Dr. Lord's prône had been of Milton the sublime, and *Comus*[9] was used as his text)—

"Byron was the hero of my youth," she whispered low.

"A poor stick," said Dr. Lord in surprise. "A poor stick of a hero—whatever he was as a poet."

"But those lines of his on Marceau—the sweetest thing in *Childe Harold.*"[1]

"Oh!" said the Lordly Parson, in tones more insulting than a blow. "Oh, oh!"

We asked Mrs. Kershaw if she had heard from her husband.

"From the general, do you mean?"

I was near laughing. I was near saying, "*The general,* your husband." What I did say was, "General Kershaw, of course. I know letters now are received from prisoners."

"Aunt Mary," said Johnny, "I will drive you in one of the back streets, that you may have your laugh out. To you—who moaned that generals were so cheap and privates so dear. I mean, generals so many—privates so rare in Richmond drawing rooms."

"Yes, I have been for four years snowed up with generals, but I honored the gentleman privates when I saw them. But I tittered. It is a pitiful thing—I have lost due regard for the dignity of a general."

Poor Camden—

"She made it a condition when she accepted him that he would never bring her back to Camden after her marriage."

"No, there was no parley," cried the captain. "The surrender was prompt and unconditional. Garrison with a white flag went out to meet the enemy."

Dr. Mark Reynolds[2] today said: "I admire the Yankees so, as a nation I find it difficult to quarrel with them individually, even when they come to rob me. Our girls will soon be marrying Yankees, and then the thing will blow over. And yet I was born a rebel—being an Irishman. Ireland was never conquered. We were conquered."

"I hope you will not teach us to keep up the fight—firing behind a hedge."

9. John Milton, *Comus, A Masque* (1634).

1. Byron, *Childe Harold's Pilgrimage,* canto 3, stanzas 56–57, pays tribute to Francois Séverin Marceau, the French general whose death in battle in 1796 was mourned by the opposing Austrian army as well as by his own troops.

2. The brother-in-law of Mary Cox (Chesnut) Reynolds.

The arrows of scorn these people shoot at our country in her day of humiliation and sorrow.

He went back to his nieces and called me a fiery Southerner—said I folded my hands behind me when he tried to help me in the carriage, that I would not let him touch me.

June 1, 1865.   If we had a royal Bengal tiger among us, a man-eater, we could not live in greater terror of our lives. She is here, with her trunks packed, ready for flight and matrimony at a moment's warning—and "he cometh not." Fast and furious the telegraph wires tingle.

Edward Stockton says he may have some glimmering of reason left. He has gone by Nassau to New York. Maybe in a stage fright he may run for his life. Who could blame him?

Edward Stockton went out on a British vessel. The captain passed him off as his steward. He met in New York men who had served with him in the old navy, but he kept out of their way. He went to hear a clairvoyant in New York who in his trance cried, "Why hang Booth and let the generals, the rebels who killed thousands of as good men as Lincoln, go scot-free?"

He met his father, who greeted him kindly on the street but said, "Do not go to my house—there they are bitter against the South."

Mrs. W[3] drives up. She too is off for New York to sell four hundred bales of cotton and a square or something which pays tremendously in the Central Park—and to capture and bring home her belle fille, who remained North during the war.

She knocked at my door—I was in bed—and as I sprung up discovered that my old Confederate nightgown had to be managed—it was so full of rents. I am afraid I gave underattention to the sad condition of my gown—and could nowhere see a shawl to drape my figure.

She was very kind. In case my husband was arrested and needed funds, she offered me some "British securities"—bonds &c&c. We were very grateful—the day was barely dawning—but we did not accept the loan (almost the same as a gift—so slim was our chance of repaying it) of money. It was a generous thought on her part—own that.

Went to the Hermitage yesterday (our plantation). Saw no change—not a soul absent from his or her post. I said, "Good colored folks, when are you going to kick off the traces and be free?"

In their furious emotional way they swore devotion to us to their dying day.

All the same, the minute they see an opening to better themselves they will move on.

William, my husband's foster brother, came up.

"Well, William, what do you want?"

"Only to look at you, Marster—it does me good." No doubt it paid. Both parties, white and black, talked beautifully.

3. Sarah Cantey (Witherspoon) Williams, widow of John N. Williams. The "belle fille" is her daughter-in-law, Augusta Rebecca (Howell) Williams.

Edward Adamson,[4] without money, has set out for Florida, bag and baggage. He has as circulating medium a barrel of whiskey to pay his way on the journey.

"I do not believe it—this parched and patriotic Camden would never let that barrel of whiskey go out of its limits."

"Well—we are all thirsty in our trouble."

Uncle H to the fore—

"When we were in Richmond, I warned Memminger and Jeff Davis—&c&c&c."

Johnny sat with his eyes glued to the floor.

"Why did you not respond to your captain?"

"When I was along, Company A did not see much of Memminger and Jeff Davis."

"But we all know Uncle Hamilton attributes Confederate ruin to the Treasury smash—and to putting negroes to work on fortifications."

Mrs. Huger says a fat and furious woman showed her 30,000 dollars in Confederate bills that vile government owed her for things she furnished them. "What sort of things?" "Provisions." "Then do not make such an outcry. A few dollars in gold would pay for those provisions."

Mrs. Huger told us of her brother-in-law, Alfred Ravenel,[5] and his adventures in Charleston with the Yankee officers. He was glad to be unnoticed and unmolested and went quietly to his own house. He found his house occupied by negroes. Next day he went to the place where people take the oath of allegiance to the United States once more. He found it surrounded by applicants for that honor several squares deep.

The individual there installed to listen to all that "swearing in" for the good of his country is a New York butcher and is no ornament to the butchers as a class. Being brutal, however, in one's manners is no bar to being a good butcher. His manner to Mr. Ravenel was insulting in the extreme.

"Hey, you! Sir! You are a spy!" And when Mr. Ravenel denied the soft impeachment:

"You lie! You rascal. If you are not a spy, why have you changed your dress? You are not in the clothes you had on yesterday. I had you watched."

"The clothes I had on yesterday were of white linen and easily soiled. I changed them because they were no longer clean. And I came to Charleston because I was sent for by your officer in command."

They passed him on to the commanding general, and again he was bullied and abused and then remanded to the butcher, who coolly remarked, when he read the paper Mr. Ravenel handed him, "What a pile of lies you must have told to get an order like this."

---

4. A Kershaw District planter and private in the Kirkwood Rangers.

5. Alfred Ford Ravenel, president of the Northeastern Railroad Company, was the brother of Frank and St. Julien Ravenel.

Frank Ravenel in his quiet grave on Malvern Hill has the best of it.

New York *Herald* today quotes General Sherman, who says, "Columbia was burnt by Hampton's sheer stupidity." But then, who burnt everything before they got to Columbia and after the Sherman army left it? We came down, for three days' travel, on a road laid bare by Sherman's torches. There were nothing but smoking ruins left in Sherman's track. That I saw with my own eyes—no living thing left, no house for man or beast. They who burnt the countryside for a belt of forty miles—did they not burn the town? Hampton's stupidity is an afterthought. This *Herald* announces that Jeff Davis will be hung at once—not so much for treason as for his assassination of Lincoln. "Stanton," the *Herald* says, "has all the papers in his hands to convict him."

The Yankees here say: "The black man must go—as the red man has gone. This is a white man's country."

The negroes want to run with the hare but hunt with the hounds. They are charming in their professions to us but declare that they are to be paid in lands and mules for having been slaves—by those blessed Yankees.

"They were so faithful to us—why should the Yankees reward them?"

"It would be by way of punishing the rebels only."

June 4, 1865.   The cool Captain surprised us by his piety today. He told us of his conduct today in church. He astonished himself by praying fervently, the first private prayer he ever offered up in church.

"What did you pray for?"

"That the bridegroom should come! But there is not such a fool in the world," said he, lapsing from his pious attitude. "He ain't coming—I'll bet you anything." ⟨⟨She rides down to the ferry to meet him every evening.⟩⟩

John Kershaw[6] came with astounding news. "The very latest," he said. "Jeff Davis has taken the oath, and the negroes are not to be emancipated!" Also, another story to match, Mrs. Adger saw a Yankee soldier strike a woman, and she prayed God to take him in hand, according to his deed. The soldier laughed in her face, swaggered off, stumbled down the steps. His revolver went off by the concussion and shot him dead.

The black ball is in motion. Mrs. DeSaussure's cook shook the dust off her feet and departed from her kitchen today, free, she said. The washerwoman packing to go.

Scipio Africanus, the colonel's body servant, is a soldierly looking black creature to delight the eyes of old Frederick William, who liked them giants. We asked him how the Yankees came to leave him.

"Oh, I told them Marster couldn't do without me nohow, and then I carried them some nice hams that they never could have found, they were hid so good."

Eben dressed himself in his best and went at a run to meet his Yankee deliverers, so he said. At the gate he met a squad coming in. He had adorned

6. The son of Joseph Brevard Kershaw.

himself with his watch and a chain, like the cordage of a ship, with a handful of gaudy seals. He knew the Yankees came to rob white people, but he thought they came to save niggers.

"Hand over that watch!" Minus his fine watch and chain, Eben returned a sadder and a wiser man. He was soon in his shirtsleeves, whistling at his knife board.

"Why? You here? Why did you come back so soon?"

"Well, I thought maybe better stay with ole Marster that give me the watch and not go with them that stole it."

The watch was the pride of his life. The iron had entered his soul.

Ropers here today.

"Oh, Camden is not false, but fickle people are taken up here—then dropped—and never a reason given why."

Went up to my old house, "Kamchatka." The Trapiers live there now. And in those drawing rooms, where the children played "Puss-in-Boots," where we have so often danced and sung but never prayed before, Mr. Trapier held his prayer meeting. I do not think I ever did as much weeping—or as bitter—in the same space of time. I let myself go. It did me good. I cried with a will.

He prayed that we might have strength to stand up and bear our bitter disappointment, to look on our ruined homes and our desolated country and be strong. And he prayed for the man "we elected to be our ruler and guide—that he might be given power from on high to bear all that a base and cowardly tyranny might heap upon him—that strength may be his to be true to himself, true to us, true to his own fame, true to his country, true to his God."

We knew that they had put him in a dungeon and in chains. Men watch him, day and night. By orders of Andy, the bloody-minded tailor.

Nobody above the rank of colonel can take the benefit of the amnesty oath. Nobody who owns over twenty thousand dollars or who has assisted the Confederates.[7]

And now the rich men howl, for your misery has come upon you. You are beyond the outlaw—camping outside.

Howell Cobb and R. M. T. Hunter arrested—our turn next, maybe.

Ben Perkins,[8] in view of all this, says he fought the best he knew how for four years, and he only begins to know why he did it. "How they hate us is plain enough now. He who runs may read."

Damocles' sword hanging over a house does not conduce to a pleasant life.

---

7. Andrew Johnson's amnesty proclamation of May 29 pardoned all who had participated in "the existing rebellion"—with certain exceptions. Southerners with taxable property worth more than 20,000 dollars, high-ranking Confederate military officers and government officials, and men who had resigned from the U.S. military or government had to apply individually to the president for clemency.

8. Benjamin Elias Perkins, a private in the Kirkwood Rangers, was the son of Priscilla (Jumelle) Perkins.

Minnie Frierson told of her negroes' figurative way of elucidating the freedom problem.

"Look a da—da jay bird. He free. You see 'em hop round. He gwine die sho' if he don't hop round an' pick up worrum. I no better nor jay bird. I got to pick up my worrum or die. So I might as well stay home—pick up my worrum here wid you'll at home."

"Not there does fear dwell, nor uncertainty nor anxiety.[9] It dwells here, haunting us, tracking us, running like an accursed sound, discord through all the music tones of our existence.

"Why smite the fallen?" asks magnanimity, out of danger now. He is fallen so low, that once high man. No criminal nor traitor—how far from it—but the unhappiest of human solecisms, whom if abstract justice had to pronounce upon she might well become concrete pity and pronounce only sobs and dismissal—

"So argues retrospective magnanimity. But pusillanimity present—prospective?

"Knights-errant themselves, when they conquered giants, slew the giants. Quarter was only for other knights-errant who knew courtesy and the laws of battle.

"Giant lies prostrate, bound with peg and pack thread. They cannot believe that he will not rise again, man-devouring, and that the victory is not palpable a dream. Terror has its skepticism, miraculous victory its rage of vengeance. Vae victis! Who loses pays! Pays all scores run up by whomsoever; on him must all breakage and charges fall."

Which, being interpreted, means Jeff Davis must pay for the awful scare we have given them.

June 12, 1865.   Andy, made Lord of all by the madman Booth, says: "Destruction only to the wealthy classes." Better teach the negroes to stand alone before they break up all they leaned on. After all, the number who own over 20,000 dollars is comparatively few.

And the dark horse will not come—I mean, will not run—and mum is the word in that quarter.

Andy has shattered fond hopes. He denounces Northern men who came South to espouse our cause. They may not take the life-giving bath. Instantly the bride-elect ceases to pour a stream of glory over all Northerners. She was planning to pay a bridal visit to her in-laws North.

《《I hear from Columbia that Buck's engagement with J. B. is broken. I daresay she told Rawlins Lowndes so. Won't he catch it! She will marry R. L.? Her innocent flirtations will be a dead fall for him. . . . I look for J. C.'s arrest daily.》》

My husband will remain quietly at home. He has done nothing that he has not

---

9. This and the following lines are quoted and paraphrased from Carlyle, *The French Revolution,* chapters 3 and 4, "Discrowned" and "The Loser Pays."

a right to do nor anything that he is ashamed of. He will not fly his country nor hide anywhere in it. These are his words.

He has a huge volume of Macaulay which seems to absorb him. Slyly I slipped *Silvio Pellico*[1] in his way. He looked at the title and moved it aside. "Oh, I only wanted you to refresh your memory as to a prisoner's life and what a despotism can do to make its captives happy."

General Manigault was here—and Dr. Deas last night. The Gabriel Manigault who wrote that clever and unanswerable pamphlet making Beauregard's inefficiency plain. Showing up the useless expenditure of life due to Beauregard's blunders or dense stupidity. He could have forestalled the enemy so easily. He could have seized and fortified those islands from which the enemy has for years battered us, day and night. Such a bombardment was never known. It ceased not—there was no interval—and our brave fellows stood there to the last.

These men talked, and I listened. It was the mere audacity of despair.

Two weddings last night. In Camden, Ellen Douglas Ancrum[2] to Mr. Lee— engineer, architect, &c&c, clever man, which is the best investment now.[3] In Columbia, Sally Hampton and John Cheves Haskell, the bridegroom a brave, one-armed soldier.

"If you rave in that way, you will be taken for a Yankee spy," said her aunt, Mrs. Reynolds, to Harriet.

"No," said the cool Captain. "If she were a spy, she would conceal her sentiments."

"Yes—I prefer any government to the tyranny which has marked the Confederate government for years. Sherman was right. What we suffered at his hands is only the fortunes of war. I would take the oath tomorrow—for a piece of cake."

"Wedding cake—yes?" sung the Captain, as he walked off. "Sherman's her darling, her young chevalier."

I have been ill since I wrote last. Serena's letter. They have been visited by bushwhackers, the roughs that always follow in the wake of an army.

My sister Kate they forced back against the wall. She had Katie, the baby, in her arms, and Miller, the brave boy, clung to his mother, though he could do no more. They tried to force brandy down her throat. They knocked Mary down with the butt end of a pistol, and Serena they struck with open hand, leaving the mark on her cheek for weeks. When they struck Mary, Serena seized the cap-

---

1. A translation of Silvio Pellico's popular account of political imprisonment, *Le Mie Prigioni* (1832).

2. The daughter of J. C.'s neighbor and friend, William A. Ancrum.

3. Maj. Francis Dickinson Lee of Charleston, the inventor of a Confederate torpedo boat, was the brother-in-law of Mrs. Benjamin Lee.

tain's arm. "Do you let your men do that?" And she showed Mary's bleeding head. "No, no," he said, "that's too bad. You keep all together, and I will get them away for tonight, and then you go off at once." Which they did that night to the Kings—the next day to Greenville. It was too much. It made me ill. Next day, while Mary had her head bound up, some Confederate prisoners passed. "What is the matter with your head?" "A soldier struck me." All the blood in the man rushed up into his face. "You!" Fancy Mamie's beautiful face—and Her Serene Highness, the Princess Bright-Eyes. That there could be men found on this earth so brutal as to strike either of these!

How this war has brought bad passions to the surface.

"H wished her uncle dead—whenever she came within my hearing," said the Captain calmly. "And now she has her sin in vain, for if the land is confiscated, he will not have the lion's share she was always grumbling about."

"But Colonel Chesnut is not dead yet."

"No, and his son is in rude health. He has come home and means to stay. Hence this rage. That is the reason of her howl—'When will those blessed Yankees come?' You see the old man's bank stock, his bonds, his railroad stocks, his hundreds of negroes—all given up. Nothing but land remains—and debts. The negroes say Aunt Sally has barrels of money hid away in the cellar—gold and silver money. If it is Confed, it will be funny. She is just the woman to do it. 'En cas.' To have waited so long—and now it has all turned to dust and ashes in their hands—this old man's money."

"There are horrid people in the world besides Yankees, eh?"

Captain Barnwell came to see us. We had a dinner for them at Mulberry—out of the Bloomsbury air. Stephen Elliott was there. He said when people began at him with Sherman or Potter raids, &c&c, he clapped his hands to his ears. He was so tired of it. And the commoner sort—"How well the niggers done, after all." Then he fled amain. General Elliott is a modest man, but he has been made to sup on flattery ad nauseam.

"They make me ashamed to show my face, these noncombatants. They cannot be made to understand why I did not die for my country."

"At Petersburg now, they say, you did your best toward that end."

"In sober earnest, these men who failed to find their way to the front in the row—now it is over—call up pusillanimous and subjugated. They are ready to begin the thing over again."

He gave us an account of his father's plantation at Beaufort, from which he has just returned.

"Our negroes are living in great comfort. They were delighted to see me and treated me with overflowing affection. They waited on me as before, gave me beautiful breakfasts, splendid dinners, &c&c. But they firmly and respectfully informed me: 'We own this land now. Put it out of your head that it will ever be yours again.'"

Edward Barnwell said all the Rhetts of that ilk had taken the oath. Burnett Rhett expressed anxiety about his father's fate, Robert Barnwell Rhett, the greatest of seceders.

"You need not be."

"Why?"

"The Yanks are too grateful to the *Mercury*. The *Mercury* did them yeoman service during the war—disintegrating the Confederacy. They will never allow a hair of the head of anybody connected with the Charleston *Mercury* to be singed."

Then he met Edmund Rhett, who as usual opened the conversation by a volley of oaths against Jeff Davis.

"I dare not listen to you."

"Good heavens—why?"

"Read this general order. All Confederates are forbidden to discuss their affairs with loyal citizens."

"I do not understand."

"*You* have taken the oath of allegiance to the U.S.A. You are a truly loyal citizen. I am a poor disabled Confederate still."

For once the ready-witted Edmund was silenced.

A Yankee general, one Hartwell,[4] he means well and ends well.

"This proclamation is to the negroes." He urges them to respect henceforth the marriage tie &c&c.

"I like his impudence. He thinks he can do by a proclamation what the Christian religion and civilization has failed to do this eighteen hundred years ⟨⟨for the white race⟩⟩.

"'Respect the marriage tie.' Well, if he gets the nigs to do it, I hope he will proclaim awhile toward Utah. And then turn the big end of his speaking trumpet toward New England, Illinois, &c&c, where there is no marriage tie at all—only a loose knot, a slipknot that any judge or jury can divorce at pleasure."

"Well, well—where millions of parsons have preached in vain, a Yankee proclamation may reform the brute nature of African blackamoors."

Now says Molly, to whom I read the proclamation, "one garrison in a town will demoralize us more &c&c."

"That will do, Molly. I do not want details."

"But Missis, Mr. Whittemore's[5] marrying all the old niggers over again, tho' they was married by a regular preacher in church, and he makes everyone pay him two dollars fifty cents, and them that he divorces, he ask them three dollars."

"Oh, divorce is the luxury and costs half a dollar more."

Met Mr. John M. DeSaussure. He said: "I will take the oath gladly, joyfully. I have never willingly aided or abetted the rebellion."

On Mr. A. H. Boykin's plantation they read the Lincoln proclamation declar-

---

4. Bvt. Brig. Gen. Alfred S. Hartwell, commander of a black regiment in S.C.

5. Benjamin Franklin Whittemore, a Methodist minister serving as a U.S. Army chaplain. Whittemore settled in Darlington District after the war and represented Kershaw District in Congress.

ing all negroes free. An old white-headed darky listened with his whole soul. When it ended he remarked,

"They have taken the bridle out of our mouths, but the halter is round our necks still". . . . [6]

Newspaper says in Columbia the garrison are treated as enemies—in Camden as friends. In Columbia Miss Preston drew her veil closer and tossed her head. And the soldier cried,

"Don't be scared. We have no orders to bayonet you."

"The truth is," they write to me, "we have never been on the street at all. And we have not seen a bluecoat, not even from a distance."

To hear Harriet talk—and such as Mr. John DeSaussure—these Yankees have poured out all this blood and money to put us just where we were before!

"They are coming," she cries, "these blessed Yankees, to build up our RR and telegraphs &c&c. What good does your sulking do?"

"And what will your crawling to their feet do? You are asking them to wipe their shoes on you as you sit in the gutter. And they will kick you in the face."

Kit Hampton says in New York they were simply intoxicated with the fumes of their own glory. Military prowess was a new wrinkle of delight to them. Mad with pride that, ten to one, they could after five years hard fighting prevail over us—and we handicapped with a majority of aliens and quasi-foes—slaves, negroes shut up with us in our [*the sentence is incomplete*]

They pay us the kind of respectful fear the British meted out to Napoleon when they sent him off, with his Sir Hudson Lowe,[7] to St. Helena, the lone rock by the sea, to eat his heart out where he could not alarm them more. Of course the Yankees know—and say—they were too many for us. And yet they would, all the same, prefer not to try it again.

Would Wellington be willing to take the chances of Waterloo once more—grouchy Blücher and all that left to haphazard? Wigfall said to old Cameron in 1861, "Then you will a sutler be—and profit shall accrue." Kit Hampton says, in some inscrutable way [in] the world North, "everybody has contrived to amass fabulous wealth by this war."

We are richer by some new readings. Molly when she goes out to walk calls it "perusing the street." And she is "blockaded by such a cold in the head."

Jealousy as rough as the Moor of Venice's. Adam Team saw Molly heat a red-hot poker and go for a negro woman her husband Lige had given *one of Molly's calico frocks.* She knocked the woman down the first blow and proceeded to burn the frock off her back with the red-hot poker, when help came and the victim was "put out."

And then it was she came to me to swear allegiance anew. "Never lef' Missis for no husband an' childen in this world."

6. There follows an unintelligible story by Teddy Barnwell.

7. The tactless and pedantic British general whose main duty as governor of St. Helena Island was to guard Napoleon.

Ellen went off then for a day or two. Her only child fell down and hurt himself badly, fell from a tree. While she was gone her husband Claiborne came to bargain for her hire. He asked enormous wages for her. "Cause white people want a heap of waiting on—you know, ma'am."

"I do not mean to give her one cent—for the best of all reasons. I have none to give her. You and your child are living in one of our houses, free of rent. Ellen can go or stay as she pleases."

When Ellen came back I said, "I have no money, Ellen."

"Claiborne is an old fool—always meddling and making _____. I don't care for money. I gits money's worth."

There are two classes of vociferous sufferers in this community: (1) those who say, "If people would only pay me what they owe me!" (2) "If people would only let me alone. I cannot pay them. I could stand it if I had anything to pay debts."

Now we belong to both classes. Heavens! What people owe us and will not or cannot pay would settle all our debts ten times over and leave us in easy circumstances for life. But they will not pay. How can they?

We are shut in here—turned with our faces to a dead wall. No mails. A letter is sometimes brought by a man on horseback, traveling through the wilderness made by Sherman. All RR's destroyed—bridges gone. We are cut off from the world—to eat out our own hearts.

And yet from my window I look out on many a gallant youth and maiden fair. The street is crowded, and it is a gay sight. Camden is thronged with refugees from the low country, and here they disport themselves. They call the walk in front of Bloomsbury "The Boulevard."

Today H. Lang[8] [was] told poor sandhill Milly Trimlin was dead, that as a *witch* she had been denied Christian burial. Three times she was buried in consecrated ground at different churchyards and three times dug up by a superstitious horde and put out of their holy ground. Where her poor old ill-used bones are lying now I do not know. I hope her soul is faring better than her body. She was a good, kindly creature. Why supposed to be a witch? That H. Lang cannot elucidate.

About this time last year Mrs. McCord was doing all she could to soothe her maternal bosom, wrung by anxieties in regard to a wounded son.

Everybody gave Milly a helping hand. She was a perfect specimen of the sandhill tackey race, sometimes called country crackers. Her skin was yellow and leathery; even the whites of her eyes were bilious in color. She was stumpy and strong and lean, hard-featured, horny-fisted. Never were people so aided

8. Thomas Lang's daughter, Harriet McRae Lang, was a second cousin of J. C.

in every way. Why do they remain sandhillers from generation to generation? Why should she never have bettered her condition?

My grandmother lent a helping hand to her grandmother. My mother did her best for her mother. And I am sure the so-called witch could never complain of me. As long as I can remember, gangs of these sandhill women traipsed in, with baskets to be filled by charity, ready to carry away anything they could get. And all made on the same pattern—more or less alike. They were treated as friends and neighbors, not as beggars. They were asked in, asked to take seats by the fire—and there they sat hours, stony-eyed, silent, wearing out human endurance and politeness. Their husbands and sons, whom we never saw, were citizens and voters! When patience was at its last ebb, they would open their mouths and loudly demand whatever they had come to seek.

One, called Judy Bradly, a one-eyed virago who also played the fiddle at all of the sandhill dances and fandangos, made a deep impression on my youthful mind. Her list was rather long, and my grandmother grew restive—actually hesitated.

"Woman, do [you] mean to let me starve?" she cried furiously. My grandmother then attempted a meek lecture as to the duty of earning one's bread. Judy squared her arms and, akimbo, answered.

"And pray, who made you a judge and the criterion of the world? Lord, Lord, if I had 'er knowed I had ter stand all this jaw, I wouldn't 'a took your old things." But she did take them—and came again—and again.

There are sandhillers born and sandhillers fallen to that estate. Old Mrs. Simons, now—Mr. C says she was a lady once—now they are very good to her. She pays no rent for her house and the fields around it. She knits gloves which are always bought for her sake. She has many children—all grown and gone— only one son left, and he is a cripple. Once a year he has a drive in his carriage. Some uneasy candidate is sure to drive by there and haul the lame man to the polls. Everybody remembers Mrs. Simons has seen better days. In coming from Society Hill once, Sally had Mrs. Simons's house pointed out to her. She stopped the carriage, got out, and knocked at the door. All was silent as death. The old creature was locked in and barricaded. After a parley she undid her door. When she saw it was Sally, she fell upon her neck and wept aloud.

"Why, honey—to think you've come to see me."

We asked Sally, "How did it all look there?" "Sad and sorrowful—empty, clean, faded, worn-out—just as poverty-stricken and old as Mrs. Simons looks in that old shawl and bonnet of hers." They're a hopeless tribe.

My mother had a protégé who had also fallen from a higher station. She was once a handsome young girl of good family. A dashing young doctor in a gig fascinated her. He was to marry her and did not. She was ruined, and her severe parents turned her out-of-doors. Then began her sandhill life. She lived alone with her child for a while, and then she lived with a sandhill man. She always spoke of him as "he."

She came always with a half-dozen daughters, all alike gaunt, pale, freckled, white hair or sandy, as near white as sandy could get. And they sat in their oak-split bonnets, in a row. They all clutched bags—and glared at us. But never a word spake they. The eldest girl was named for my mother. The others, we thought, had no fixed names but were called Betsey, Sally, Charlotte, Amelia, as the people happened to be present whose namesakes she claimed them to be.

The mother of this strange brood was exactly my idea of Meg Merrilies.[9] One day she drew my mother to the window. We saw her clutch my mother's arm and say something. Then they shook hands, and tears were in the eyes of both of them. Afterwards, my mother:

"Did you hear her? She gripped me and said, 'Woman! he has married me.' Neither of us said another word, but Fanny knew I felt for her."

At another time these old friends met at church. "A big meeting." More politics than religion in the wind, and my mother was a keen hand at electioneering. Sue proposes to take Fanny home in her carriage.

"No, no—never mind me. I'm done in this world—take your namesake. Let 'em all see my girl setting by you in your carriage."

Black 4th of July—1865. Saturday I was in bed with one of my worst headaches. Occasionally there would come a sob as I thought of my sister— insulted—and my little sweet Williamses! Another of my beautiful Columbia quartet had rough experiences.

Lizzie Hamilton. They asked the plucky little girl for a ring which she wore.

"You shall not have it." The man put a pistol to her head. "Take it off. Hand it to me, or I will blow your brains out."

"Blow away." The man laughed and put down his pistol.

"You knew I would not shoot you."

"Of course I knew you dared not shoot me. Even Sherman would not stand that."

But my little sweet Williamses had only Captain Kirk. Even he stopped it when he saw a bushwhacker strike Mary.

Then given up to headaches and tears. Suddenly downstairs I heard a rush of many footsteps, hurryings to and fro. H giving orders in a shrill voice, at the top of the stairs—mad tearings in and out of the room next to mine.

"After all, are not raids a thing of the past? This sounds like one."

"Dick has come!" said the Captain, putting his head in the door. "I have brought a note from him. He is at the hotel in Camden—will be here in a few minutes. *I* am the harbinger of great joy."

Bedlam generally outside. Maids chattering, racing about, slamming doors, giggling—shh—shh. "Miss Mary's nerves, remember." They were trampling my nerves underfoot. Then a long rolling sound. They were shutting those hard creaking folding doors whose rollers make as much noise as an ammunition wagon.

---

9. The gypsy woman in Sir Walter Scott, *Guy Mannering* (1815).

The lovers were penned up in that smoking hot night. The cool Captain and the Reynoldses, enjoying the breezes in the piazza, the Captain for their benefit performing a pantomime—solus—of what he imagined was going on behind the venetians.

Next day bride-elect arrayed herself like a May queen—crown of natural flowers on her head and wreaths of flowers and evergreen looped up her dress on every side.

Her uncle like a Goth took his knife and cut off the body garlands—left the wreaths of green flowing over the skirt of her gown.

"You are not young enough for such nonsense. You will disgust the man. Dress like a Christian woman—not in masquerade."

"A Christian woman—I would like to see her in that character."

The redoubtable Dick is fair, with light hair and blue eyes. He lisps. His trousers were blue, and he wore a shell jacket of yellow nankin. In his shirt front dully gleamed a diamond breastpin.

They say he is clever. He told that Adèle Auzé was arrested by the Federals for clapping her hands when she heard that Lincoln was murdered. They seized her instantly, did not give her time to get bonnet or shawl. The general only reprimanded her sharply, and she went home wholly undisturbed by this adventure. Also, Lucy Gwin introduced General Sherman to a party of ladies, among them Mrs. Thomas Anderson, who is a niece of President Davis. The ladies shook hands with him. Sherman noticed that Mrs. Anderson held back and did not give him her hand as did the others.

"Madame, *you* do not seem glad to see me."

"No, I am not glad to see you."

Wedding to be next Tuesday, then they go for a week to Mary W's[1] and from thence to New Jersey.

Mrs. Henry Cantey[2] informed him of the senseless prejudices of Carolinians. One lady here called Mrs. Davis a western woman. Even Emma Warren[3] said some girl was too western to be nice.

"And we know such aristocratic ladies, on the Mississippi—and on the Alabama."

And then Mrs. Cantey told of Harry's prejudices and his strict ideas of propriety where women were concerned.

They talked of the negroes wherever the Yankees had been, who flocked to them and showed them where the silver and valuables were hid by the white people. Ladies' maids dressing themselves in their mistresses' gowns before their faces and walking off. Two sides to stories. Now, before this, everyone told me how kind and faithful and considerate the negroes had been. I am sure, after hearing these tales, the fidelity of my own servants shines out brilliantly. I had taken it too much as a matter of course.

1. Mary Serena Chesnut (Williams) Witherspoon.
2. A sister-in-law of Sarah (Cantey) and Phil Augustus Stockton, Sr.
3. Emma (Maxwell) Warren was the wife of Thomas Warren, editor of the Camden *Journal*.

Yesterday there was a mass meeting of negroes, thousands of them were in town, eating, drinking, dancing, speechifying. Preaching and prayer was also a popular amusement. They have no greater idea of amusement than wild prayers—unless it be getting married or going to a funeral.

In the afternoon I had some business on our place, the Hermitage. John drove me down. Our people were all at home—quiet, orderly, respectful, and at their usual work. In point of fact things looked unchanged. There was nothing to show that anyone of them had even seen a Yankee or knew that there was one in existence.

"We are in for a new St. Domingo all the same. The Yankees have raised the devil, and now they cannot guide him."

A Jacquerie—not a French Revolution, say the soldiers. They mean this to be a white man's country. . . . [4]

July 26, 1865.   I do not write often now—not for want of something to say, but from a loathing of all I see and hear. Why dwell upon it?

I even feel a repugnance toward making mention of the wedding.

Colonel C, poor old man, was worse. More restless. He seems to be wild with "homesickness." He wants to be at Mulberry. He cannot see the mighty giants of the forest, the huge old wide-spreading oaks. He says he feels that he is there as soon as he hears the carriage rattling across the bridge at the beaver dam.

After many consultations as to this old gentleman's condition, in family conclave it was decided to consign the Lords to Mrs. Reynolds' hospitable cares. So with their menservants and their maidservants, the cattle and the stranger were shoved in that gate. Much to the bride's disgust, who scented offense and want of consideration for her august brideship in every one of our movements.

Nankin Jacket was on hand, in due time. How Minnie and I baked and brewed for the wedding. And the bride denounced us with her usual furious temper, unmollified by honeymoon, within grasp at last.

It was a quiet midday celebration. The fête was at the Reynoldses'. The bride was gotten up regardless. Dr. Lord showed most unhallowed joy when for the first time for many days a sherry cobbler was offered to his sacred lips. "And such sherry!" he murmured, as he sipped. Champagne frappés *I* did not disdain, with a heart grateful for heaven's good gifts. The happy couple went to Society Hill, a wagon at ten dollars a day hired to haul their big trunks. But they came back, saying the North was inaccessible by that opening. So they are to be hauled to Winnsboro.

I am reading French with Johnny. Anything to keep him quiet. We gave a dinner to his company, the small remnant of them, at Mulberry House. About twenty idle negroes, trained servants, came without leave or license and as-

4. There follows in two pages the words to a song by a young friend of M. B. C.

sisted. So there was no expense. They gave their time and labor for a good day's feeding. And I think they love to be at the old place.

Yesterday John saw Dr. Charles Shannon lying drunk on the Yankees' bed. All of the men-about-town go in and drink with them.

Johnny took the Yankee captain with him to Knights Hill. That ceremony is necessary when making a contract with plantation hands now. Johnny called, "Joe"—"William"—"Milly"—

"But is that a lady?"

"What? She was a woman servant." The lieutenant said, pointing carelessly toward the group of negroes.

"I did not fight for these. I fought for the Union."

"And I fought to be out of your Union."

Then said Johnny to me, "Aunt Mary, after all, the Yankee was not half a bad fellow."

Wrote Lina that I am hopeless—penniless. She must look out for a governess place.

Then I went up to nurse Kate Withers. That lovely girl, barely 18—she is dead, died of typhoid fever. Tanny wanted his sweet little sister to have a dress for Mary Boykin's wedding.[5] Kate was to be one of the bridesmaids. So Tanny took his horses, rode one, led one thirty miles, in this broiling sun to Columbia—sold the led horse—came back with a roll of Swiss muslin. As he entered the door he saw her lying there, dying.

She died praying that she might die. She was weary of earth. She wanted to be at peace. I saw her die. I saw her put in her coffin. No words of mine can tell how unhappy I am.

Six young soldiers, her friends, were her pallbearers. As they marched out with that burden, sad were their faces.

And yet, that night all save one danced at a ball given by Mrs. Courtney from Charleston!

"Time's dull deadening;
   The world's tiring;
Life's settled cloudy *afternoon*"—evening—
   Night—

---

5. Mary Boykin, daughter of M. B. C.'s uncle Burwell, married to E. B. Cureton.

Forgiveness is indifference. Forgiveness is impossible while *love lasts*.

> Make no deep scrutiny
> Into our mutiny[6]—

Eliza Lee, while some Yankees were robbing her house, tumbling out her children's clothes out of their presses &c&c, answered one who ordered her about in this wise. He said, "Ho! you rebel woman, bring us some water." "Rebel!" she said, "and rebel against whom? *Such as you?*" That is the point that hurts.

General Manigault said a good thing. Joe Johnston and McClellan—a pair of them—several times saved their armies—their countries, *never*.

Eliza Lee describes various manners of bows. James Chesnut takes off his hat grandly, like a prince of the blood. Edward Boykin bows and smiles so cordially—you feel he is your friend. Sam S touches his hat like a footman.

Once more, as Rabelais says, we are in that "Paradis de salubrité, aménité, sérénité, commodité, et tous honnêtes plaisirs d'agriculture et vie rustique."

And—and the weight that hangs upon our eyelids—is of lead.

---

6. From Thomas Hood, "The Bridge of Sighs" (1844), stanza 5.

Index

Prepared by Michael McGerr

*Names mentioned in the journals have been included here
even when full identification proved impossible.*